Travel Discount Coupon

This coupon entitles you to special discounts
when you book your trip through the

TRAVEL NETWORK ®
RESERVATION SERVICE

Hotels ♦ Airlines ♦ Car Rentals ♦ Cruises
All Your Travel Needs

Here's what you get: *

♦ A discount of $50 USD on a booking of $1,000** or
more for two or more people!

♦ A discount of $25 USD on a booking of $500** or more
for one person!

♦ Free membership for three years, and 1,000 free miles
on enrollment in the unique Miles-to-Go™ frequent-
traveler program. Earn one mile for every dollar spent
through the program. Earn free hotel stays starting at
5,000 miles. Earn free roundtrip airline tickets starting
at 25,000 miles.

♦ Personal help in planning your own, customized trip.

♦ Fast, confirmed reservations at any property
recommended in this guide, subject to availability.***

♦ Special discounts on bookings in the U.S. and around
the world.

♦ Low-cost visa and passport service.

♦ Reduced-rate cruise packages.

Visit our website at http://www.travnet.com/Frommer or
call us globally 201–567–8500, ext. 55. In the U.S., call toll-
free at 1-888-940-5000, or fax 201-567-1838. In Canada,
call toll-free at 1-800-883-9959, or fax 416-922-6053. In
Asia, call 60-3-7191044, or fax 60-3-7185

FLF123

Frommer's

1st Edition

FRUGAL TRAVELER'S GUIDES

Florida
FROM $50 A DAY

by Bill Goodwin, Rena Bulkin, Victoria Pesce
Elliot, & Cindy Dupre

with Special Sports Coverage
by Karen T. Bartlett

Macmillan • USA

MACMILLAN TRAVEL

A Simon & Schuster Macmillan Company
1633 Broadway
New York, NY 10019

Find us online at **http://www.mcp.com/mgr./travel**
or on America Online at **Keyword: Frommer's.**

ISBN 0-02861136-5
ISSN 1090-2317

Executive Editor: Alice Fellows
Production Editor: Lori Cates
Map Editor: Douglas Stallings
Design by Michele Laseau

Maps © by Simon & Schuster, Inc.

SPECIAL SALES

Bulk purchases (10+ copies) of Frommer's and selected Macmillan travel guides are available to
corporations, organizations, mail-order catalogs, institutions, and charities at special discounts,
and can be customized to suit individual needs. For more information write to Special Sales,
Macmillan General Reference, 1633 Broadway, New York, NY 10019.

Manufactured in the United States of America

Contents

5 Settling into Miami 55

by Victoria Pesce Elliott

6 What to See & Do in Miami 98

by Victoria Pesce Elliott

List of Maps

ABOUT THE AUTHORS

Karen Bartlett is the Travel Editor of *Gulfshore Life* magazine. She is based in Naples, Florida, and her travel articles appear in many regional and national publications.

Rena Bulkin, who began her travel-writing career writing about hotels and restaurants for the *New York Times* International Edition, has since authored dozens of magazine articles (including a roundup of the nation's best theme parks) and travel guides to far-flung destinations. She is the author of *Frommer's Walt Disney World & Orlando,* and has been covering the Sunshine State for years.

Cindy Dupre lives in Largo, Florida, and has been writing feature articles about the Tampa Bay area for the last 10 years. Her work has appeared in a variety of national publications, including *Travel & Leisure, Bridal Guide, Family Circle, W,* and the *St. Petersburg Times.* She is a graduate of the University of South Florida. She is assisted by researcher and writer Joan Horden, who lives in Clearwater, Florida, and has covered the Sarasota area for the last 10 years.

Victoria Pesce Elliott is a freelance journalist who contributes to many local and national newspapers and magazines, including the *New York Times.* A native of Miami, she returned there after nearly a decade in New York City, where she graduated from the Columbia Graduate School of Journalism. She is also the author of *Frommer's Miami & the Keys.*

Bill Goodwin began his career as an award-winning newspaper reporter before becoming legal counsel and speechwriter for two U.S. senators. Now a lawyer and freelance writer, he is based in Washington, D.C. He is also the author of *Frommer's South Pacific* and *Frommer's Virginia.*

AN INVITATION TO THE READER

In researching this book, we discovered many wonderful places—resorts, inns, restaurants, shops, and more. We're sure you'll find others. Please tell us about them, so we can share the information with your fellow travelers in upcoming editions. If you were disappointed with a recommendation, we'd love to know that, too. Please write to:

Frommer's Florida from $50 a Day, 1st Edition
Macmillan Travel
1633 Broadway
New York, NY 10019

AN ADDITIONAL NOTE

Please be advised that travel information is subject to change at any time—and this is especially true of prices. We therefore suggest that you write or call ahead for confirmation when making your travel plans. The authors, editors, and publisher cannot be held responsible for the experiences of readers while traveling. Your safety is important to us, however, so we encourage you to stay alert and be aware of your surroundings. Keep a close eye on cameras, purses, and wallets, all favorite targets of thieves and pickpockets.

WHAT THE SYMBOLS MEAN

✪ **Frommer's Favorites**

Hotels, restaurants, attractions, and entertainment you should not miss.

⑨ **Super-Special Values**

Hotels and restaurants that offer great value for your money.

The following abbreviations are used for credit cards:

AE	American Express	EU	Eurocard
CB	Carte Blanche	JCB	Japan Credit Bank
DC	Diners Club	MC	MasterCard
DISC	Discover	OPT	Optima Card
ER	enRoute	V	Visa

Getting to Know Florida

by Rena Bulkin & Bill Goodwin

Every year millions of visitors escape the bleak northern winters to bask in Florida's warmth, lured here by the promise of sunny skies and 800 miles of sandy beaches.

But there's a lot more than sun and sand here. You'll find a host of kid-pleasers—Walt Disney World, water parks such as Wet 'n Wild, alligator and crocodile parks, Universal Studios, Busch Gardens, Sea World and Marineland, and Lion Country Safari. They make Florida America's most popular year-round vacation destination for families.

Florida will keep active vacationers very busy: Golfing, tennis, hiking, fishing, boating, canoeing, kayaking, sailing, hunting—you name it, the Sunshine State has it. Fans can also cheer their favorite major-league baseball teams as they head into each season with spring training here. If you're lucky enough to get tickets, you can see the mighty University of Florida, Florida State University, and University of Miami football teams dominate their gridirons. There are major golf and tennis tournaments here, plus local favorites like jai alai and greyhound racing. And, of course, there's Daytona Beach, mecca for auto-racing enthusiasts.

While the great outdoors is its prime draw, Florida also is steeped in history, beginning with the Spanish conquistadors who came searching for gold and the mysterious "fountain of youth" in the 16th century. Visitors today can walk the charming streets of St. Augustine, founded 55 years before the Pilgrims landed at Plymouth Rock in 1620. Rivaling St. Augustine as America's oldest city, Pensacola displays a fascinating blend of Spanish, French, British, and American cultures. Elsewhere, you'll discover many remnants of "old Florida," when there were more cattle here than tourists.

Indeed, you can do as much or as little in Florida as your heart desires, for there literally is something for everyone in this sunny land.

1 The Natural Environment

Although the presence of beach resorts and theme parks means that many parts of the state are intensely developed, Floridians have managed to maintain thousands of acres of wilderness and to protect many miles of their beautiful beaches in national seashores and state parks.

Florida

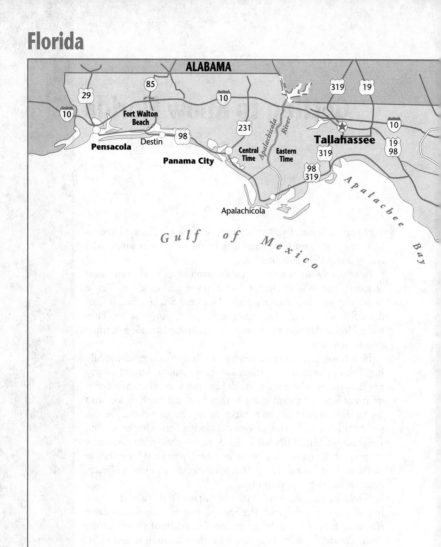

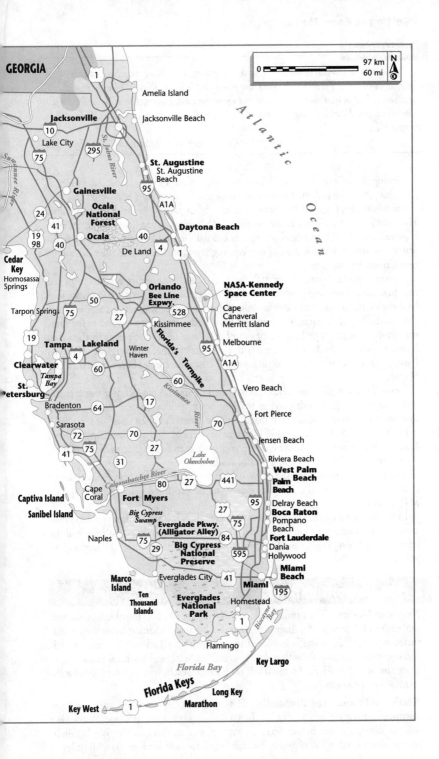

GEORGIA

Amelia Island

Jacksonville
1
10
Lake City
Jacksonville Beach
75
295
St. Johns River
St. Augustine
St. Augustine
Beach
Gainesville
95
Suwannee River
Ocala
National
Forest
24
A1A
41
19
Daytona Beach
98
40
Ocala
40
De Land
1
4
Cedar
Key
Homosassa
Springs
Orlando
NASA-Kennedy
Bee Line
Space Center
50
Expwy.
Cape
27
528
Canaveral
Tarpon Springs
75
Kissimmee
Merritt Island

19
Florida's Turnpike
Tampa
Lakeland
Winter
95
Melbourne
Haven
Clearwater
60
4
A1A
St.
Tampa
Petersburg
Bay
Vero Beach
60
Bradenton
64
17
Kissimmee River
Sarasota
70
Fort Pierce
72
70
75
Jensen Beach
41
27
31
Lake
Riviera Beach
Okeechobee
West Palm
Beach
Caloosahatchee River
80
27
441
Palm
Captiva Island
Beach
Cape
95
Sanibel Island
Coral
Delray Beach
Fort Myers
27
Boca Raton
Big Cypress
75
Pompano
Swamp
Everglade Pkwy.
84
Beach
(Alligator Alley)
Fort Lauderdale
Naples
75
595
Dania
29
Big Cypress
Hollywood
National
Preserve
Miami
Marco
Everglades City
41
Beach
Island
Miami
195
Ten
Everglades
Thousand
National
Homestead
Islands
Park
1
Biscayne Bay
Flamingo

Florida Bay
Key Largo

Florida Keys
Long Key
Key West
1
Marathon

Atlantic

Ocean

0 ⊏▭▭▭▭ 97 km
60 mi

N

3

Geologists believe that the Florida peninsula wasn't even connected to North America when the present-day continents began forming eons ago—that this flat, limestone-coated finger of land may once have been part of the Bahamas and Cuba. However it formed, Florida today has some 1,350 miles of shoreline. Inland, the state is dotted with 30,000 lakes and springs stocked with some 115 species of native freshwater fish. Another 175 species of marine, migratory, and exotic creatures inhabit its many rivers and streams.

Indeed, Florida abounds in wildlife that will thrill the naturalist in you. Unspoiled marshes, mangroves, and mudflats provide habitats for great egrets, wood storks, ibis, bald eagles, flamingos, roseate spoonbills, pelicans, hawks, and herons, among other shorebirds; dolphins, otters, and manatees frolic in diverse waterways; and in the summer months huge loggerhead turtles lumber ashore to lay their eggs in the sand. Nowhere is the natural environment better experienced than in Everglades National Park, a vast primeval prairie sweeping some 2,100 square miles between Miami and Naples.

Dense forests of pine, oak, and cypress draped in Spanish moss contrast with gracefully swaying palms and displays of brilliant bougainvillea, azaleas, hibiscus, crape myrtles, and fragrant jasmine and magnolias. The world's largest stand of sand pines is in Ocala National Forest, a 366,000-acre wilderness. And the huge Apalachicola National Forest near Tallahassee encompasses more than 600,000 acres of woodlands, rivers, streams, lakes, caves, and a host of wildlife.

The Keys, a string of coral reef islets, offer topography ranging from upland jungle and mangrove swamp to a 21-mile underwater garden filled with over 600 species of tropical fish.

In Northwest Florida, the gorgeous Gulf Islands National Seashore protects mile after mile of America's whitest-sand beaches. And in the southwestern corner of the state the beaches of Sanibel and Captiva islands are considered one of the world's best places for seashells.

2 The Regions in Brief

Northeast Florida   The northeast section of the state contains the oldest permanent settlement in America—St. Augustine, founded by Spanish settlers more than 4 centuries ago. St. Augustine is bordered on the north by Jacksonville, an up-and-coming sunbelt metropolis with miles of oceanfront beach and beautiful marine views along the St. Johns River. To the south is Daytona Beach, home of the Daytona International Speedway.

Northwest Florida: The Panhandle   Historical roots run deep in Florida's narrow northwest extremity, which is called the Panhandle because of its shape. Pensacola's historic district, which blends Spanish, French, and British cultures, is a highlight of any visit to today's Panhandle. But the big draw here is more than 80 miles of powdery, dazzlingly white beaches stretching past the low-key resorts of Pensacola Beach, Fort Walton Beach, Destin, and Panama City Beach. The Gulf Islands National Seashore has preserved much of this beach and its wildlife, and inland are state parks that offer some of the state's best canoeing adventures. All this makes the area a favorite summertime vacation destination for middle- and working-class singles, couples, and families from the neighboring states of Georgia and Alabama. Prices of rooms and meals here are among the lowest in Florida. The proximity of Georgia and Alabama also lends this area the traditions and regional cuisine of the Deep South. With a southern charm all its own, the moss-draped, football-mad state capital of Tallahassee sits in a pine and oak forest just 30 miles from the Georgia line.

Central Florida Once a flat expanse of farmland, citrus groves, and scrub-pine forests, Central Florida was transformed forever when Walt Disney World came to town in 1971. Today it's the state's theme-park hub, and Orlando is its fastest-growing city. Another brand of excitement is offered by the Kennedy Space Center, launch site for all manned U.S. space missions since 1968.

The Tampa Bay Area Halfway down the west coast of Florida lies Tampa Bay, lined with miles of sandy beaches. Beside the bay flourishes one of the fastest-growing metropolitan areas in the country, Tampa and St. Petersburg. Just south is Bradenton, and Sarasota, a shopping and performing-arts mecca.

Southwest Florida Ever since inventor Thomas Alva Edison built a home there in 1885, some of America's wealthiest families have spent their winters along Florida's southwest coast. They still do, which makes this one of the more expensive parts of Florida to visit from mid-December to March. Now as then, the well-off are attracted by the area's subtropical climate, shell-strewn beaches, and intricate waterways winding among 10,000-plus islands. Many charming remnants of Old Florida coexist with modern resorts in the sophisticated riverfront towns of Fort Myers and Naples and on islands like Gasparilla, Useppa, Sanibel, Captiva, and Marco. And thanks to some timely preservation, the area has many wildlife refuges, including the "backdoor" entrance to Everglades National Park.

The Treasure Coast Just north of glittering Palm Beach, this coastal region resembles an older Florida. It extends roughly from Hobe Sound in the south to the Sebastian Inlet in the north, encompassing some of Martin, St. Lucie, and Indian

---

Dr. Beach

No one knows beaches like Dr. Steven Leatherman, a coastal geographer at the University of Maryland. He has studied so much sand and surf around the world that he's known as "Dr. Beach."

Using a list two legal-size pages long, he goes around looking at such factors as sand color and softness, presence of pests such as "no-see-um" sand flies, vegetation, noise, litter, and development, then comes up with lists of top-rated beaches.

Florida scored very well in his most recent rating of the 20 best beaches in the United States. In fact, he ranked St. Andrews State Recreation Area in Panama City Beach as first in the nation.

Also on Dr. Beach's top-20 list were St. George Island State Park and St. Joseph Peninsula State Park, both near Apalachicola; Bill Baggs Cape Florida State Recreation Area, on Key Biscayne in Miami; Delnor-Wiggins State Recreation Area, in Naples; and Perdido Key, near Pensacola.

River counties. Although it's one of the fastest-growing areas in the state, the locals are trying to keep the slow pace and small-town feel that distinguishes such towns as Port St. Lucie and Vero Beach. The region is rich in natural resources and has a vast array of wildlife—and there really is actual hidden treasure beneath its shores.

The Gold Coast   The palm-dotted sands of Florida's southeast coast are lined with beachfront hotels and posh resorts. Just north of Miami, the coast extends through Fort Lauderdale, Boca Raton, and Palm Beach, which has been famous for many years as a playground for the rich and famous.

Miami & Miami Beach   Sometimes it's hard to know which language to use when you introduce yourself in this polyglot mini-nation. You'll hear Spanish, French, Créole, and Portuguese. It's a major population center for Caribbean and Latin American immigrants, especially a thriving Cuban community. Long a resort haven, Miami is a sophisticated, cosmopolitan city with striking architecture, gorgeous beaches, and glittering nightlife that attracts tourists from all over the world.

The Keys   From the southern tip of Florida, U.S. 1 travels through a 100-mile string of islands, with the Atlantic on one side and the Gulf of Mexico on the other. While the Upper Keys have suffered from overdevelopment because of their proximity to Miami, environmental activism and government protection have contained development in the Lower Keys. The Keys don't offer spectacular beaches but there are other visitor attractions—excellent deep-sea fishing, snorkeling, many wildlife refuges, and the relaxed, bohemian atmosphere of Key West.

The Everglades   Encompassing more than 2,000 square miles and 1.5 million acres, Everglades National Park covers the southern tip of Florida. The park, along with Big Cypress National Preserve, protects a unique and fragile ecosystem teeming with wildlife, best explored by canoe, boat, or hiking. To the east of the Everglades is Biscayne National Park, preserving the northernmost living coral reefs in the United States.

3 Florida Today

Who are the Floridians who wait to greet you? Most Florida residents today hail from "somewhere else"—even Mickey came from California. But before these newcomers there were the Seminole peoples, whose descendants today are actively seeking to control their native lands (if not get all of Florida back). There were the "Florida Crackers," whites whose great-great-grandchildren still are more Southern than Yankee in speech, demeanor, and outlook. There were African-Americans who escaped from cotton plantations to set up camp in Florida's wilderness areas and whose progeny still experience slavery's legacy of racism.

Today, however, the majority of Florida's population is a mix of immigrants from both home and abroad. Among the wide variety of ethnic groups here are Cubans and Haitians in Miami, Greeks in Tarpon Springs, and Vietnamese near the large military bases in Northwest Florida.

At the forefront of this influx, however, is a steady stream of retirees. Of the 13 million-plus people who live in Florida, about one in five is over 65 years of age, and the percentage of seniors approaches a third in 15 of the state's 67 counties. They live everywhere in the state, although the best known contingents are northeasterners who have settled in the Miami area and midwesterners who have made the lower Gulf Coast their home. Silver-haired politicians have organized their peers into a force to be reckoned with in state politics and have won seniors a level of social services rarely found elsewhere. Elderly newcomers have plunged into Florida retirement with youthful enthusiasm, returning to school, taking up sports again (as in the Kids and Kubs Senior Baseball League), and enjoying Florida's balmy air and sunshine.

Politics in the state goes beyond ethnic interests and age, however, for Floridians have taken steps to preserve their state's natural beauty and resources, including major initiatives to protect the Everglades and control the spread of tacky commercial districts. There is every reason for optimism as they deal with challenges to Florida's continuing vitality—challenges both man-made and natural (such as Hurricane Andrew in 1992 and Hurricane Opal in 1995, which severely damaged parts of South Florida and the Panhandle, respectively).

4 A Look at the Past

Some archeologists believe the first Floridians were Native Americans who came from the north to the Panhandle some 10,000 years ago. Others think the first settlers arrived instead from the Caribbean and Central America. Whatever their origin, Native Americans had tamed the peninsula by 5000 B.C., and they created America's first red-clay pottery about 1200 B.C. In the north you can visit ancient burial mounds, while in the south you can stay on islands built entirely of shells discarded by a fierce and now-extinct tribe known as the Calusa.

THE FOUNTAIN OF YOUTH An event occured on April 2, 1513, that would change Native American life forever. On that day, Juan Ponce de León, conqueror and colonial governor of Puerto Rico in search of the fabled fountain of youth, laid anchor just south of present-day Cape Canaveral, rowed ashore, and confidently claimed the place for the Spanish Crown. Observing that the land was "very pretty to behold with many refreshing trees," he named it La Florida, or "the Flowery Land."

Eight years later, with a fighting force of 200 conquistadors, missionary priests, and a writ from the Spanish king promising him de facto ownership of any profits his endeavor might produce, Juan Ponce de León returned to conquer and colonize Florida. His party landed at Charlotte's Bay, north of present-day Fort Myers, but the fledgling settlement was ferociously attacked with arrows and stones by hostile indigenous tribes. Ponce de León was wounded by an arrow. He and the other survivors retreated to Cuba, where he died; his body was buried in Puerto Rico.

Ponce de León's fate proved a harbinger of the difficulties the Spanish would encounter in Florida. Over the next 50 years, five expeditions pursuing rumors of golden cities attempted and failed to establish a colonial foothold on the peninsula.

Dateline

- 1513 Ponce de León makes landfall near Cape Canaveral, becoming the first European to step on Florida soil.
- 1565 Pedro Menéndez de Avilés establishes St. Augustine.
- 1566–1703 Scores of Franciscan missions dot interior Florida.
- 1586 Sir Francis Drake sacks St. Augustine.
- 1695 St. Augustine's Castillo de San Marcos completed.
- 1763 Under the terms of the Treaty of Paris, Spain relinquishes Florida to the British.
- 1784 Florida reverts to Spanish control after the American Revolution.
- 1813 Gen. Andrew Jackson drives the British from Pensacola in the War of 1812.
- 1818 During First Seminole War, Jackson leads U.S. troops into Florida on punitive raids against the native peoples.
- 1821 Florida becomes a U.S. territory.
- 1823 Tallahassee selected as territorial capital.
- 1835–42 Second Seminole War, bloodiest and costliest of all U.S.–Native American conflicts.

continues

continues

It wasn't until 1565 that Pedro Menéndez de Avilés, 1,000 settlers, and a priest established St. Augustine, the first permanent European settlement in North America. In the years that followed, Franciscan friars created a chain of missions throughout Florida. Though the missions' ostensible aim was converting the tribes and instructing them in European trades and agricultural methods, they only succeeded in wreaking havoc among them. Many tribesmen died taking up primitive arms against Spanish steel and firepower, and many more were drafted into slavery. But the greatest toll was taken by European infectious diseases, against which Native Americans had no immunity. By the middle of the 16th century, three-quarters of Florida's original inhabitants had been wiped out.

THE BRITISH ARE COMING   Though their colony survived, life was difficult for the Spanish settlers, beset by the harsh climate (those Florida hurricanes), hostile natives, famine, fire, and disease. St. Augustine was attacked time and again by pirates and by the armies of the rival French and British empires. Florida was important to the defense of Spain's commercial coastal route, but it never produced such wealth as did Mexico, the Caribbean, and South America. When the British captured the important Spanish port of Havana in Cuba during the French and Indian War (1754–63), they offered to exchange it for the rights to Florida. Forced to choose, the Spanish reluctantly agreed.

During two decades as stewards of Florida (1763–84), the British brought zeal and resources to the territory's development that far exceeded Spanish efforts. They began establishing Florida as a major agricultural center. Stately plantations, producing indigo, rice, and oranges, rose up along the Atlantic coast and the St. Johns River. St. Augustine bustled with activity.

Bolstered by stipends from the British Parliament, Florida remained loyal to George III during the American Revolution and, in fact, became a haven for Tories from the northern colonies (whose descendants are known even today as "Conchs"). But when the newborn United States prevailed over England in 1783, the Treaty of Paris acknowledged Spain's wartime assistance by returning Florida to Spanish control.

SETTLEMENT, WARS & STATEHOOD   Florida remained in Spanish hands until 1821. To attract settlers, Spain offered land grants to anyone willing to immigrate to the colony. So many English-speaking homesteaders from the United States accepted the offer that Florida's Spanish character quickly changed. Soon the U.S. government began maneuvering to take over the colony. Those efforts reached the boiling point during the War of 1812 and the First Seminole War of 1818. Gen. Andrew Jackson's unopposed marches through Florida during these two conflicts convinced Spain that it had no choice but to negotiate a graceful departure, so in 1821 it ceded all of Florida to the United States.

The new American territorial government aggressively set about encouraging growth. Tallahassee, once a thriving Apalachee settlement, was chosen as the capital. Streets were laid in Cowford, a cattle crossing on the St. Johns River, and the village was renamed Jacksonville in honor of Old Hickory. Florida's population, numbering 8,000 in 1821, quadrupled by the 1830s. But one major obstacle to settlement yet remained—the Seminole.

- **1971** Walt Disney World opens.
- **1974** Big Cypress Swamp National Preserve created, a harbinger of Florida's growing environmental awareness.
- **1982** Epcot (Experimental Prototype Community of Tomorrow) opens at Walt Disney World.
- **1990** Universal Studios, a theme park and working film studio, opens its doors.
- **1992** Hurricane Andrew slams into the Gold Coast, causing $1 billion in damage.
- **1995** Hurricane Opal does extensive damage all along the Northwest Florida coast.

The Seminole had migrated into the peninsula from Georgia toward the end of the 18th century and by the 1820s much of Florida's richest farmland—which the territorial government was eager to open to white homesteaders—lay in their hands. After a series of compromise treaties that left both sides dissatisfied, the federal government threw down the final gauntlet with the Indian Removal Act of 1830, stipulating that all eastern tribes be removed to reservations west of the Mississippi. The spark that ignited the Second Seminole War of 1835–42 was provided by a young warrior named Osceola. At a treaty conference at Payne's Landing in 1832, he strode up to the bargaining table, slammed his knife into the papers on it, and pointing to the quivering blade, proclaimed, "The only treaty I will ever make is this!" Guerrilla warfare thwarted the U.S. Army's attempts to remove the Seminole for almost 8 years. But finally the Seminole population in Florida dwindled to fewer than 100 survivors who took refuge deep in the impenetrable swamps of the Everglades, where some of their descendants still live today. With the Seminole out of the way, the Territorial General Legislature met at Port St. Joe and petitioned Congress for statehood. On March 3, 1845, President John Tyler signed a bill making Florida the 27th state.

Florida grew rapidly over the next 15 years. Cotton, cattle ranching, and forest industries thrived; railroads began to appear; and visitors from the North arrived to enjoy the state's sunny winters. By 1860 Florida's population had jumped to 140,000, 40% of whom were slaves. Then came the Civil War.

REBELS & RECONSTRUCTION   In 1861 Florida became the third state to secede from the Union, and the modest progress it had achieved as a state came to a standstill. The stars and bars flew from every flagpole. Only one major battle of the Civil War was fought on Florida soil, however, when Confederate forces met federal troops seeking to destroy Florida farms at Olustee, on February 20, 1864. The Rebels routed the Yanks, and, in the months that followed, successfully continued to defend interior Florida against Union attack. When Robert E. Lee surrendered at Appomattox, Tallahassee was the only southern capital still in Confederate hands, but this was little consolation to Floridians, who had lost some 5,000 of their own during the strife.

Florida's fledgling cities and industries emerged from the Civil War relatively unscathed, but residents did not escape the social and political turmoil of Reconstruction. The Emancipation Proclamation released nearly half of Florida's population from slavery, and intense wrangling ensued between Northern reformers and white Floridians over the role the former slaves would play in postwar society. Blacks enjoyed some initial gains. Local elections of 1868 saw 19 blacks ride the Union victory to seats in the Florida legislature, and schools for black children were founded. But as elsewhere in the South, the traditional political power base of white Democrats soon regained the upper hand.

THE GILDED AGE   Florida emerged from the rigors of Reconstruction to rebuild the state's economy and usher in an era of rapid growth and development. North-central Florida enjoyed the benefits of a booming citrus industry. Cigar factories sprang up in Tampa. Large tracts of swamp in the peninsula's interior were drained for agricultural use, and this newly arable land was sold to eager immigrants. Many of those arriving were recently freed African-Americans, who by the 1890s accounted for 47% of the state's population (it's now about 14%).

State planners recognized that the expansion of the railroads was the requisite catalyst for economic growth. Industrialists Henry Plant and William Chipley built railroads that connected Tampa and Pensacola to the developed regions in Florida's northeast. To ensure the profitability of their new railroads, both men invested heavily in the isolated cities at the end of the line. Plant's posh Tampa Bay Hotel still graces the city's skyline as the home of the University of Tampa.

But the man who revolutionized Florida tourism was the flamboyant Henry Morrison Flagler, a partner in John D. Rockefeller's Standard Oil Company. Visiting Florida in the early 1880s, he envisioned the sunny Atlantic coast state as a winter playground for millionaires—a southern version of posh Newport, Rhode Island. He bought up and knit together the short rail lines that extended south from Jacksonville and laid track as far as West Palm Beach, incorporating it all under the Florida East Coast Railway Company. In 1896 Flagler's trains chugged into the infant hamlet of Miami, and by 1912 the rail line extended south to Key West. In Palm Beach, Flagler built his own mansion, Whitehall, as well as two palatial hotels, the Poinciana and the Breakers. And in St. Augustine, his fabulous Ponce de León Hotel (today Flagler College), complemented by two other deluxe hostelries, the Alcazar and the Cordova, also drew moneyed visitors.

BOOM ...   Florida entered the 20th century with a diversified economy centered on ranching, citrus, timber, and tourism. Prosperity was everywhere. The expanded rail system vastly improved mail service around the state, telephones and electricity reached most of rural Florida, a crude passenger airline—the first such outfit in the world—began operating flights between St. Petersburg and Tampa, and an extensive road system accommodated the rapid growth of the automobile.

Congress passed the Eighteenth Amendment in 1919 and the Florida legislature, reflecting the staid attitudes of the rural population, quickly made Prohibition Florida law. But no such attitude ruled the increasingly cosmopolitan and sophisticated Gold Coast. People arrived in droves for holidays in Palm Beach and Miami, and illegal speakeasies rose up to serve them. Wild chases between lawmen and "rum runners" became commonplace. Florida quickly became one of the loosest environments of the Roaring Twenties.

As Henry Flagler had envisioned decades earlier, real estate was going through the roof. Millions of immigrants, speculators, and builders descended on the state, and new communities sprang up seemingly overnight. Miami Beach, for example, in a decade went from a barren strip of sand to a sprawling resort city with over 50 hotels. Land that had been available free to anyone who wanted it after the city's incorporation in 1915 was going for tens of thousands of dollars in 1925. The mayors of Miami, Miami Beach, Hialeah, and Coral Gables proclaimed Dade County to be "The most Richly Blessed Community of the most Bountifully Endowed State of the most Highly Enterprising People of the Universe."

. . . & BUST Quite suddenly everything that could go wrong did go wrong. First the land boom went bust. As *The Nation* commented in July 1926, "The world's greatest poker game, played with building lots instead of chips, is over. And the players are now . . . paying up." Construction stopped dead, and many newcomers went back home to the North. Two hurricanes, the first to hit the state in over a decade, catastrophically damaged the Gold Coast resort areas and the interior farmlands in 1926 and 1928. A fruit-fly infestation crippled the citrus industry. The 1929 stock-market crash seemed almost an afterthought to Florida's ruined economy. Within a few years the announcers at Tampa's radio station WDAE were giving wry notice of the state's suffering by changing the station's slogan from "Wonderful Days and Evenings" to "We Don't Always Eat."

President Franklin D. Roosevelt's New Deal programs helped the state begin to climb back on its feet. The Works Progress Administration (WPA) put 40,000 unemployed Floridians back to work building public projects, including the automobile causeway from the mainland to Key West. By 1936 the tourist trade had revived somewhat, and the state began attracting a broader range of visitors than ever before.

But the event that finally lifted Florida—and the nation—out of the Depression was World War II, when scores of army bases and training facilities were expanded or opened all over Florida. Thousands of U.S. servicemen did part of their hitch in the state, and hotels were filled to capacity with military personnel. The war came right to Florida's shores—German subs sank more than two dozen Allied ships in plain sight of Florida's beaches. When the war ended, many soldiers returned to settle in the Sunshine State, and in the 1940s, Florida's population nearly doubled.

BLASTING OFF Florida shared the bullish economy of the 1950s with the rest of the nation. Its population grew a whopping 78.7% during the decade, making it America's 10th most populous state, and tourists came in droves, nearly 4.5 million in 1950 alone. One reason for the influx was the advent of the air-conditioner, which made life in Florida infinitely more pleasant.

A brand-new industry came into being at Cape Canaveral in 1950—the government-run space program. Cape Canaveral became NASA's headquarters for the Apollo rocket program that eventually blasted Neil Armstrong and Buzz Aldrin to the moon in 1969. The Space Shuttles now blast off from "the Cape."

Beginning in 1959, great numbers of middle- and upper-class Cuban immigrants fleeing Fidel Castro's socialist revolution began arriving on Florida's shores, and collectively they created a remarkable American success story, planting an indelible stamp on the business and cultural life of the state. Other immigrants, most notably Haitians, have been arriving in Florida's cities in recent years and are jostling for a piece of the economic pie.

THE MOUSE THAT ROARED But the state's most important new arrival since Flagler was a cute rodent. In the 1960s Walt Disney began secretly buying up Central Florida farmland and laying plans for the world's most spectacular theme park. Opening in 1971, Walt Disney World soon turned the sleepy citrus-growing town of Orlando into the fastest-growing city in the state and attracted so many visitors that they easily outnumbered the town's residents. "WDW" has continued to grow and expand, adding Epcot, Disney–MGM Studios, and other adjuncts. Today, not just Orlando but the entire state abounds in theme parks.

5 Florida's Bill of Fare

A BOUNTY OF SEAFOOD   With 1,350 miles of coastline, it's no surprise that Florida seafood is a major culinary draw all across the state. Some waterfront restaurants even operate their own fishing boats, so you're guaranteed super-fresh offerings. You'll dine on snapper, swordfish, amberjack, triggerfish, pompano, grouper, clams, gulf shrimp, blue crab, and sweet deep-sea scallops.

Some of the state's seafood specialties may be new to your palate. The local clawless **lobsters** are smaller and sweeter than the Maine variety, with most of their meat concentrated in the tail. You should also try **conch,** a chewy shellfish that's often served in deep-fried fritters, in chowder, or in a spicy salad marinated in lime juice. You're sure to fall in love with the taste of Florida's succulent **stone crabs,** and you won't soon forget the slightly briny taste of **Apalachicola oysters** (which reputedly have aphrodisiac properties).

If you have the chance to eat in a **fish camp,** don't pass it up. These rustic, informal eateries are usually located right on a river or creek and serve the very freshest of fish at low prices. Any long-term resident can tell you where to find the local camp.

CITRUS FRUITS & OTHER PRODUCE   Florida's farms and citrus groves produce billions of dollars' worth of oranges, grapefruit, and tangerines each year. Bags of grapefruit and fresh, sweet oranges are sold at roadside stands throughout the state. And that's not all. Tomatoes, coconuts, kumquats, and tangy lemons and limes grow

---

Grilled Gator Tail

The wetlands of Florida provide a perfect habitat for a unique creature, the American alligator. Early wildlife attractions like the St. Augustine Alligator Farm, founded in 1893, discovered that the alligator would successfully breed and thrive in captivity. Their expertise has been shared among other pioneering farmers and today over 30 Florida farms raise alligators from egg to adult. They sell the meat already cleaned—good news to anyone who has ever tried to skin a gator.

By the way, you should never order "alligator" tail. It's "gator" tail. And if anyone tells you that it tastes like chicken, hit them with your alligator purse or kick them with your alligator boots.

Serves 6

2 pounds young gator tail sliced thin	2 tablespoons lemon juice
	2 tablespoons olive oil
1 cup dry white wine	1 teaspoon salt
1 teaspoon black pepper	2 cloves garlic, minced

Mix the ingredients in a glass container and marinate the gator tail 2 to 3 hours. Grill the gator tail over hot coals and serve immediately with lemon slices.

—From the *Seasonal Florida Cookbook* by Jo Manning

here, along with more exotic fruits like mangoes and papaya. Florida chefs are adept at using local produce in creative sauces and garnishes. A favorite regional dish is graham cracker–crusted **key lime pie,** made with the tiny yellowish limes that grow only in Florida.

OTHER CUISINES Southern and Cajun culinary influences have found their way into Florida's kitchens, so you may find traditional favorites like catfish, hush puppies, frogs' legs, Créole-style blackened fish, gumbo, cheese grits, turnip greens, and southern fried chicken on many menus. As Florida's Asian population has increased, so has the number of restaurants across the state offering authentic Chinese, Thai, Japanese, Indian, and Vietnamese dishes. And Caribbean specialties—from Bahamian conch fritters to fruity cocktails made with rum from the islands—have become so popular here that the name "Floribbean" cuisine has been coined.

But Latin American and South American cuisines have had the most profound effect on Florida. Especially if you're visiting Miami, you should try one of the Cuban restaurants in Little Havana, which serve specialties like *pan cubano* (crusty white Cuban bread), *arroz con pollo* (succulent roast chicken served with yellow rice), roast suckling pig, plantains, and *café cubano,* rich (and very strong) black coffee. Find a place that serves *tapas,* Spanish-style appetizers served in small portions, and try several dishes at once.

2 Planning a Trip to Florida

by Rena Bulkin & Bill Goodwin

After you've chosen the Sunshine State as your destination, you'll find that doing a little homework before you go can save a lot of time, trouble, and money later on. For example, you can save significantly on hotel rooms by picking one season over another for your visit. This chapter pulls together visitor information sources, the best times of year to go, how to get there, and other advance-planning details that can help you enjoy a smooth, successful trip.

If you pick the right place at the right time of year to visit, you can have your own Florida vacation without being forced into bankruptcy. We'll show you how in these pages.

1 The $-a-Day Premise

With careful planning, two people can travel in Florida from $50 a day, combining their money for a room and at least two meals a day. We say "from" because it can be difficult for a couple to visit some parts of Florida on a combined $100 a day in high season, particularly during winter at beach-resort areas in the southern half of the state. For example, the least expensive double room on Sanibel Island costs $82 a night, including tax, from mid-December to April, leaving the two of you just $8 for meals. On the other hand, that same room drops to $45 during spring, summer, and fall. Also, you can survive on $50 a day even during the high summer season in Northwest Florida. From a cost standpoint, therefore, your most important decisions will be where to go and especially *when* to visit Florida (see "When to Go," later in this chapter).

MONEY-SAVING TIPS

Don't ignore "Florida on the Go" and those other colorful give-away booklets in racks at the Florida Welcome Centers, local tourist information offices, and elsewhere. They may look like junk mail, but they're loaded with discount coupons you can use at hotels, motels, restaurants, and attractions throughout the state.

The *Florida Traveler Discount Guide* is a good source for discounts on accommodations, restaurants, and attractions throughout the state. You can get it for $3 for postage and handling by calling 904/371-3948.

Choose a hotel or motel a block or more from the beach, since these usually are less expensive than those directly facing the sand.

Mainland hotels and motels usually cost less than their island brethren, and are more likely to offer discounted weekday or weekend rates. Remember that rooms are often priced according to the view; those overlooking a garden or a backwater bay usually cost less than units with a view of the Atlantic Ocean or Gulf of Mexico. For stays of a week or more, consider a cottage or an apartment in one of Florida's multitudinous condominium developments. Most have weekly rates that are less than paying by the night.

And take advantage of "early-bird specials," offered all over Florida if you dine between 4:30 and 6:30pm. The early-bird selections may be limited, but they're a less expensive way to sample the fine fare at otherwise expensive eateries. Many Florida restaurants also offer an all-you-can-eat happy hour.

2 Visitor Information

For information about the state in general, contact the **Florida Department of Commerce, Division of Tourism, Visitor Inquiry,** 126 W. Van Buren St., Tallahassee, FL 32399-2000 (☎ **904/487-1462**). The helpful staff will gladly answer your questions. Be sure to ask for their *Florida Vacation Guide,* a free rundown of all the state's attractions.

Once you've chosen a specific destination within Florida, get in touch with the local visitor information office or chamber of commerce. We've listed each of these in the following chapters. For information about Walt Disney World, call or write the **Walt Disney World Company,** P.O. Box 10000, Lake Buena Vista, FL 32830-1000 (☎ **407/824-4321**).

3 When to Go

To a large extent, the time of year you visit the Sunshine State will determine how much you'll spend—and how much company you'll have—once you get there. That's because room rates can more than double during the high season, when countless visitors migrate to Florida.

High season in the southern half of the state is from mid-December to mid-April, when millions of vacationers head south from the snowbound north. On the other hand, you'll be rewarded with incredible bargains if you're willing to brave the heat and humidity of a South Florida summer between July and early September. In northern Florida, the reverse is true: Tourists flock here during the summer, from Memorial Day to Labor Day.

Both north and south share the same "shoulder seasons" during April and May and from September to November. The weather is pleasant throughout Florida during these months, and hotel rates are considerably less than during the high season. If price is a consideration, then these months are the best times to visit.

If you want to time your visit to Walt Disney World to avoid crowds, keep in mind that Orlando area attractions are packed during any holiday (especially Christmas) and when school's not in session during the summer. See Chapter 11 on Walt Disney World and Orlando for details.

See the "Where to Stay" sections in the following chapters for specifics about the local high-, shoulder-, and off-seasons.

CLIMATE   Odds are, whenever you visit Florida you're going to find sunny skies and warm temperatures. The climate here is subtropical and not tropical, however, so the state has more extremes of temperature than, say, the Caribbean islands.

The Boys of Spring

Throngs of fans head to Florida in late February and all of March to watch their favorite major-league baseball teams tune up for the regular season with "Grape-fruit League" exhibition games.

Most of the Florida stadiums are relatively small, so fans can see their favorite players up close—maybe even get a handshake or an autograph. Also, tickets are priced at $5 to $12, a bargain when compared to the regular-season games back home. Most games sell out by early March, so don't wait until you're in Florida to buy tickets.

Although the teams used to return year after year to the same towns, some clubs recently have changed sites. You can contact the **Florida Sports Foundation,** 107 W. Gaines St., Tallahassee, FL 32399 (☎ **904/488-8347**), or the main office of **Major League Baseball,** 350 Park Ave., New York, NY 10022 (☎ **212/339-7800**), to find out the schedules and to make sure of where your favorite teams will be playing.

Here's where the teams played in 1996, with their ticket office phone numbers. See "Spectator Sports" in the following chapters for specifics.

Atlanta Braves, West Palm Beach (☎ 407/683-6100); **Baltimore Orioles,** Fort Lauderdale (☎ 954/776-1921 or 800/236-8908); **Boston Red Sox,** Fort Myers (☎ 941/334-4700); **Chicago White Sox,** Sarasota (☎ 941/287-8844, ext. 232); **Cincinnati Reds,** Plant City (☎ 813/752-7337); **Cleveland Indians,** Winter Haven (☎ 941/293-3900); **Detroit Tigers,** Lakeland (☎ 941/499-8229); **Florida Marlins,** Melbourne (☎ 407/633-9200); **Houston Astros,** Kissimmee (☎ 407/839-3900); **Kansas City Royals,** Davenport (☎ 941/424-2500); **Los Angeles Dodgers,** Vero Beach (☎ 407/569-6858); **Minnesota Twins,** Fort Myers (☎ 941/768-4200 or 800/338-9467); **Montréal Expos,** West Palm Beach (☎ 407/684-6801); **New York Mets,** Port St. Lucie (☎ 407/871-2115); **New York Yankees,** Tampa (☎ 813/879-2244 or 813/287-8844); **Philadelphia Phillies,** Clearwater (☎ 813/442-8496); **Pittsburgh Pirates,** Bradenton (☎ 941/748-4610); **St. Louis Cardinals,** St. Petersburg (☎ 314/421-3060 or 813/894-4773); **Texas Rangers,** Port Charlotte (☎ 813/625-9500); **Toronto Blue Jays,** Dunedin (☎ 813/733-0429).

Spring sees warm temperatures throughout Florida, but it also brings tropical showers, and May contributes the first waves of humidity.

Summer is hot and *very* humid throughout the state, so if you're in an inland city you may not want to schedule anything too taxing when the sun is at its peak. Coastal areas, however, reap the benefits of ocean breezes.

Fall is a great time to visit—the hottest days are behind you and the crowds have thinned out a bit. August to November, however, is the tropical storm season—you may remember Hurricanes Andrew and Opal in 1992 and 1995, respectively, which caused billions of dollars' worth of damage to South Florida and to the Panhandle. Fortunately, the National Weather Service closely tracks hurricanes and gives ample warning if there's any need to evacuate coastal areas.

Winter can get a bit nippy throughout the state, and sometimes downright cold in northern Florida. Although snow is pretty rare, a flake or two has been known to fall as far south as Miami. The "cold snaps" usually last only a few days in the southern half of the state, however, and warm temperatures quickly return. Indeed, when the rest of the country is bracing itself for icy winter winds, "snowbirds" are heading for Southwest Florida, Miami, Palm Beach, and the Keys to bask in the sun.

Average Temperatures (°F) in Selected Florida Cities

	Jan	Feb	Mar	Apr	May	Jun	July	Aug	Sept	Oct	Nov	Dec
Key West	69	72	74	77	80	82	85	85	84	80	74	72
Miami	69	70	71	74	78	81	82	84	81	78	73	70
Tampa	60	61	66	72	77	81	82	82	81	75	67	62
Orlando	60	63	66	71	78	82	82	82	81	75	67	61
Tallahassee	53	56	63	68	72	78	81	81	77	74	66	59

4   Health & Insurance

STAYING HEALTHY   Florida doesn't present any unusual health hazards for most people. Folks with certain medical conditions such as liver disease, diabetes, and stomach ailments, however, should avoid eating raw oysters. The bivalves harvested in the Gulf of Mexico between April and October can carry a natural bacteria known as *vibro vulnificus,* which can cause severe diarrhea, vomiting, and even fatal blood poisoning. Cooking kills the bacteria, so if in doubt, order yours steamed, broiled, or fried.

Florida has millions of mosquitos, especially in the coastal and marshy areas, and nearly invisible biting sand flies (known as "no-see-ums") plague many South Florida tidal flats at dawn and dusk. Fortunately, neither of these insects carries malaria or other diseases.

It's especially important to protect yourself against sunburn. Don't underestimate the strength of the sun's rays down here, even in the middle of winter or on cloudy days. Limit the amount of time you spend in the sun, and avoid the sun from 11am to 2pm, when the sun's rays are most intense.

If you have a serious condition or allergy, consider wearing a Medic Alert identification bracelet; contact the **Medic Alert Foundation,** P.O. Box 1009, Turlock, CA 95381-1009 (☎ **800/432-5378**).

INSURANCE   Many travelers buy insurance policies providing health and accident, trip cancellation and interruption, and lost luggage protection. If you're going by plane, train, or bus, some credit- and charge-card companies insure their customers against travel accidents if you buy tickets with their cards. Before purchasing additional insurance, read your policies and agreements over carefully.

Many health insurance companies and health maintenance organizations (HMOs) provide coverage for illness or accidents while their members are traveling, but you may have to pay the local provider up front and file for a reimbursement when you get home. Collect adequate receipts and other documentation at the time of treatment. Some traveler's health insurance policies will pay the local provider directly, saving you this hassle; ask your provider about requirements before you leave home. Canadians should check with their provincial health plans or call HealthCanada (☎ **613/957-3025**).

Trip-cancellation insurance covers your loss if you've made nonrefundable deposits, bought airline tickets that provide no or partial refunds, or if you've paid for a charter flight or package tour and for some good reason you can't travel. Trip-interruption insurance, on the other hand, gives refunds when an airline or tour operator goes bankrupt or out of business.

Lost luggage insurance covers your loss over and above the limited amounts for which the airlines are responsible, and some policies provide instant payment so you can replace your missing items on the spot.

Here are some American firms:

Travel Assistance International (TAI) (☎ **202/347-2025,** or 800/821-2828). TAI is the American agent for Europ Assistance Worldwide Services, Inc., so holders of this company's policies can contact TAI for assistance while in the United States.

Travel Guard International (☎ **715/345-0505,** or 800/782-5151).

Access America (☎ **804/285-3300,** or 800/284-8300).

Health Care Abroad (Wallach & Co., Inc.) (☎ **703/687-3166** or 800/237-6615).

Mutual of Omaha (☎ **800/228-9792**).

Divers Alert Network (DAN) (☎ **919/684-2948** or 800/446-2671) insures scuba divers.

5 Tips for Special Travelers

FOR PEOPLE WITH DISABILITIES   Although it was out of print at press time, the Florida Department of Commerce, Division of Tourism, Visitor Inquiry (see "Visitor Information," earlier in this chapter) usually distributes a free *Florida Planning Companion for Travelers with Disabilities.* When available, it offers valuable information about services and accessibility at tourist facilities throughout the state.

Walt Disney World does everything possible to facilitate guests with disabilities. Its many services are detailed in the "Guidebook for Guests with Disabilities." To obtain a free copy, contact Guest Letters, P.O. Box 10040, Lake Buena Vista, FL 32830-0040 (☎ **407/824-4321**).

Mobility International USA (☎ **503/343-1284**) offers its members travel accessibility information and has many interesting travel programs. Annual membership dues are $25. It also publishes a quarterly newsletter called *Over the Rainbow,* which is sent to its members (nonmembers can subscribe for $15 per year). Help is also available from the **Travel Information Service** (☎ **215/456-9600**).

The **Society for the Advancement of Travel for the Handicapped** (☎ **212/447-7284**) sends out information sheets on specific subjects for a small charge.

Twin Peaks Press, P.O. Box 129, Vancouver, WA 98666 (☎ **360/694-2462**), specializes in travel-related books for people with disabilities. Write for their *Disability Bookshop Catalog,* enclosing a check or money order for $4 (the price is $5 if using MasterCard or Visa).

Companies offering tours for those with physical or mental disabilities include **Accessible Journeys** (☎ **610/521-0339** or 800/TINGLES); **Flying Wheels Travel** (☎ **507/451-5005** or **800/535-6790**); **The Guided Tour, Inc.** (☎ **215/782-1370**); and **Wilderness Inquiry** (☎ **612/379-3858** or 800/728-0719).

In addition, both **Amtrak** (☎ **800/USA-RAIL**) and **Greyhound** (☎ **800/752-4841**) offer special fares and services. Call at least a week in advance of your trip for details.

FOR SENIORS   With one of the largest retired populations of any state, Florida offers a wide array of activities and benefits for senior citizens. Don't be shy about asking for discounts, but always carry some kind of identification, such as a driver's license, that shows your date of birth.

Also, mention the fact that you're a senior citizen when you first make your travel reservations. For example, both **Amtrak** (☎ **800/USA-RAIL**) and **Greyhound** (☎ **800/231-2222**) offer discounted senior fares. And don't forget that many hotels and motels offer discounts to seniors. For example, in 1996 the Econo Lodge chain instituted a 30% break for anyone 50 or older.

Members of the **American Association of Retired Persons (AARP)**, 601 E St. NW, Washington, DC 22049 (☎ **202/434-2277**, or 800/424-3410), get discounts not only on hotels but on airfares and car rentals, too.

Elderhostel, headquartered at 75 Federal St., Boston, MA 02110-1941 (☎ **617/ 426-7788**), is a national organization that offers low-priced educational travel programs for people over 55 (nonspouse companions must be at least 50). For information on programs in Florida, call or write Elderhostel headquarters and ask for a free U.S. catalog.

Grand Circle Travel, 347 Congress St., Suite 3A, Boston, MA 02210 (☎ **617/ 350-7500**, or 800/221-2610), is a tour operator offering extended vacations, escorted programs, and cruises that feature unique learning experiences for seniors at competitive prices. Contact them for a free copy of "101 Tips for the Mature Traveler."

SAGA International Holidays, 222 Berkeley St., Boston, MA 02115 (☎ **800/ 343-0273**), is known for its all-inclusive tours and cruises for seniors 50 years of age or older. Both medical and trip-cancellation insurance is included in the net price of any of its tours, except cruises.

Information is also available from the **National Council of Senior Citizens**, 1331 F St. NW, Washington, DC 20004 (☎ **202/347-8800**). A nonprofit organization, the council charges $12 per person/couple, for which you receive a regular magazine, part of which is devoted to travel tips. Benefits of membership include discounts on hotel and auto rentals and also include supplemental medical insurance for members.

Mature Outlook, 6001 N. Clark St., Chicago, IL 60660 (☎ **800/336-6330**), is a travel organization for people over 50 years of age. Members are offered discounts at ITC-member hotels and will receive a bimonthly magazine. Annual membership is $9.95, which entitles its members to discounts and in some cases free coupons for discounted merchandise from Sears Roebuck Co. Savings are also offered on selected auto rentals and restaurants.

Golden Companions, P.O. Box 5249, Reno, NV 89513 (☎ **702/324-2227**), helps travelers 45-plus find compatible companions. It's the only travel companion network to offer personal voicebox mail service enabling members to connect instantly 24 hours a day. Membership services also include free mail exchange, a bimonthly newsletter (*Golden Gateways*), get-togethers, and tours. Write for a free brochure or send $2 for a sample newsletter.

FOR SINGLES   Singles are often at a disadvantage when it comes to travel since most package tours are based on double occupancy, and regular rates for most single rooms in Florida are only a few dollars less than those charged for doubles. One way to find someone to share the expenses is through **Travel Companion**, P.O. Box P-833, Amityville, NY 11701-0833 (☎ **516/454-0880**), which matches single travelers with compatible partners. For a fee, you'll be listed in the organization's records, and you'll receive a list of potential companions (you can request companions of the same sex or the opposite sex).

FOR FAMILIES   Florida is a great family destination, with most of its hotels and restaurants willing and eager to cater to families traveling with children. Many hotels and motels let children 17 and under stay free in their parents' room. At the beaches, it's unusual for a resort not to have a children's activities program (some will even mind the youngsters while the parents enjoy a night off!). Even if resorts don't have their own children's program, most will arrange baby-sitting services. If you call ahead before dining out, you'll see that most restaurants have some facilities for children, such as booster chairs and low-priced kids' menus.

Contact **Travel with Your Children,** 40 5th Ave., New York, NY 10011 (☎ 212/477-5524), to subscribe to *Family Travel Times,* a newsletter about traveling with children. It's packed with useful information, and subscribers can call in for advice on Wednesday between 10am and 1pm.

FOR STUDENTS It's worth your while to bring along your valid high school or college identification. Presenting it can open the door to discounted admission to museums and other attractions. And remember, alcoholic beverages cannot be sold in Florida to anyone who is under 21, so bring your driver's license or another valid identification showing both your date of birth and your picture if you intend to imbibe.

Hostelling International / American Youth Hostels, 733 15th St. NW, Suite 840, Washington, DC 20005 (☎ 202/783-6161, or 800/444-6111), offers low-cost accommodations in Miami Beach, Key West, Fort Lauderdale, and Orlando (see their respective chapters, below). Rates can be as little as $15 per person per night for members, slightly more for nonmembers. Annual HI/AYH memberships cost $25 for adults, $10 for those 17 and under, $15 for those over 54, and $35 for families with children 15 and under. Lifetime memberships are $250 per person.

FOR GAY & LESBIAN TRAVELERS Men can order *Spartacus,* the international gay guide ($29.95), or *Odysseus 1996, The International Gay Travel Planner,* a guide to international gay accommodations ($25). Both lesbians and gay men might want to pick up a copy of *Ferrari Travel Planner* ($16), which specializes in general information, as well as listings of bars, hotels, restaurants, and places of interest for gay travelers throughout the world. These books and others are available from **Giovanni's Room,** 1145 Pine St., Philadelphia, PA 19107 (☎ 215/923-2960).

Our World, 1104 N. Nova Rd., Suite 251, Daytona Beach, FL 32117 (☎ **904/ 441-5367**), is a magazine devoted to options and bargains for gay and lesbian travel worldwide. It costs $35 for 10 issues. *Out and About,* 8 W. 19th St., Suite 401, New York, NY 10011 (☎ **800/929-2268**), has been hailed for its "straight" reporting about gay travel. It profiles the best gay or gay-friendly hotels, gyms, clubs, and other places, with coverage of destinations throughout the world. It costs $49 a year for 10 information-packed issues. It aims for the more upscale gay male traveler, and has been praised by everybody from *Travel & Leisure* to the *New York Times.*

The **International Gay Travel Association (IGTA)**, P.O. Box 4974, Key West, FL 33041 (☎ **305/292-0217**, or 800/448-8550 voicemail), has around 1,200 member agencies worldwide and specializes in networking, providing information to individual travelers on linking up with the appropriate gay-friendly service organization or tour specialist. It offers quarterly newsletters, marketing mailings, and a membership directory that's updated four times a year. If they are IGTA members, travel agents will be tied into this organization's information resources.

6 Getting to Florida

BY PLANE
THE AIRLINES Domestic airlines with the most flights to and from Florida are **American** (☎ 800/433-7300), **Continental** (☎ 800/525-0280), **Delta** (☎ 800/

221-1212), **Northwest** (☎ 800/225-2525), **TWA** (☎ 800/221-2000), **United** (☎ 800/241-6522), and **USAir** (☎ 800/428-4322).

Many so-called no-frills airlines, which offer low fares without such amenities as in-flight meals, have been increasing their flights to Florida in recent years. Airlines worth calling are **Air South** (☎ 800/247-7688), **Kiwi** (☎ 800/538-5494), **Carnival** (☎ 800/824-7386), **Midway** (☎ 800/44-MIDWAY), **Midwest Express** (☎ 800/452-2022), **Southwest Airlines** (☎ 800/435-9792), **SunJet** (☎ 800/4SUNJET), and **Tower Air** (☎ 800/348-6937).

The airlines increase both the frequency of their flights and the number of cities they serve during South Florida's winter high season.

SAVING ON AIRFARES   Because Florida is such a popular destination, there's usually no shortage of discounted fares, even in the high seasons and even by the no-frills carriers mentioned above. For example, **Southwest Airlines** (☎ 800/435-9792) recently began flying round-trip between Baltimore and Tampa for $318, less than half the regular fare on that route. That immediately set off a "fare war" among the other carriers on this route. November, December, and January often see such fare wars between carriers, which can result in savings of 50% or more off the regular fares (the tickets usually are nonrefundable, however, and must be purchased immediately or as much as 30 days in advance). Watch for advertisements in your local newspaper and on TV or call the airlines.

On the other hand, you're not likely to see fares discounted during peak holidays such as Thanksgiving, Christmas, and the Presidents' Day weekend in mid-February.

Your best bet for securing a low fare is to book your flight well before your departure—you can often find good deals if you buy your ticket 14 or 30 days in advance. Ask the airline for the *lowest* fare, and find out if you can get an even better deal by booking farther in advance, flying in midweek, or staying over a Saturday night. Remember, too, that many of the best deals are nonrefundable, so you may have to stick with the travel dates you've chosen.

CHARTER FLIGHTS   Many charter flights go to Florida, especially during the winter season. They cost less than regularly scheduled flights, but there are some drawbacks that you need to consider. Advance booking, for example, of up to 45 days or more may be required, there are hefty cancellation penalties, and you must depart and return on your scheduled dates or else lose your money. If you don't have proper insurance (see "Health & Insurance," earlier in this chapter), it won't do any good to call the airline and tell them you've had a ski accident in Aspen—if you're not on the plane, kiss your money good-bye.

Since charter flights are very complicated, it's best to go to a good travel agent to find out the problems and advantages.

CONSOLIDATORS, REBATORS & TRAVEL CLUBS   **Consolidators** (sometimes called "bucket shops") act as clearinghouses for blocks of unsold tickets that airlines discount and consign to them during normally slow periods of air travel. Tickets are sometimes—but not always—discounted as much as 20% to 35%. Terms of payment can vary, from 45 days prior to departure to the last minute. Some consolidators require you to buy their discounted tickets through a regular travel agent, who usually marks up the ticket 8% to 10% or more, reducing your discount. If you go through an agent, ask him or her to comparison-shop for you, since prices can vary from consolidator to consolidator.

There are two possible hitches here: The tickets often don't allow advance seat assignments, so you could be assigned a "poor seat" at the last minute. Also, the airlines will sometimes match the price of the consolidator ticket by announcing a promotional fare, thus eliminating your savings. Because the situation is a bit tricky, you need to investigate carefully just how much you can expect to save. Always ask about any and all restrictions, and always pay by credit or charge card.

Bucket shops abound from coast to coast. Look for their usually small ads in your local newspaper's Sunday travel section. One is **TFI Tours International,** 34 W. 32nd St., 12th Floor, New York, NY 10001 (☎ **212/736-1140,** or 800/745-8000 in the U.S. outside New York State).

Rebators are organizations that pass along to the passenger part of their commission, although many of them assess a fee for their services. Although they're not the same as travel agents, some offer roughly similar services. Sometimes a rebator will sell you a discounted travel ticket and also discounted land arrangements, including hotels and car rentals. Most rebators offer discounts averaging anywhere from 10% to 25%.

Rebators include **Travel Avenue,** 10 S. Riverside Plaza, Suite 1404, Chicago, IL 60606 (☎ **312/876-1116,** or 800/333-3335); and **The Smart Traveller,** 3111 SW 27th Ave. (P.O. Box 330106), Miami, FL 33133 (☎ **305/448-3338,** or 800/448-3338 in the U.S.). Travel Avenue also discounts hotel or condo packages and cruises. The Smart Traveller also rebates 6% on package tours.

Another possibility for low airfares are **travel clubs,** which supply an unsold inventory of tickets with discounts in the range of 20% to 60%. After you pay the club's annual fee, you're given a "hotline" number to call to find out what discounts are available. Many of these become available several days before the departure, some as long as a week, and some as much as a month beforehand. Of course, you're limited to what's available, so you have to be fairly flexible.

Moment's Notice, 7301 New Utrecht Ave., Brooklyn, NY 11228 (☎ **718/234-6295**), has a members' 24-hour hotline (regular phone toll charges) and a yearly fee of $25 per year for membership. The **Sears Discount Travel Club,** 3033 S. Parker Rd., Suite 900, Aurora, CO 80014 (☎ **800/433-9383,** or 800/255-1487 to join), offers members, for $49, a catalog, maps, discounts at select hotels, and a limited guarantee that equivalent packages will not be undersold by any other travel organization. It also offers a 5% rebate on the value of all airline tickets, tours, hotel accommodations, and car rentals that are purchased through them.

PACKAGE TOURS   Given the size of tourism in Florida, it's little wonder that travel agents offer hundreds of package tour options to the Sunshine State. These vary a great deal from year to year, so consult your travel agent to find out the best deals at the time you want to travel.

Quite often a package tour will result in savings, not just on airfares but on hotels and other activities as well. You pay one price for a package that varies from one tour operator to the next. Airfare, transfers, and accommodations are always covered, and sometimes meals and specific activities are thrown in.

There are some drawbacks: The least expensive tours may put you up at a bottom-end hotel. And since the lower costs depend on volume, some more expensive tours could send you to a large, impersonal property. Also, because the tour prices are based on double occupancy, the solo traveler is almost invariably penalized. You could end up traveling with strangers who become friends for life; they also could be loud-mouthed bores.

Most tour companies require that payment be made well in advance of travel. If possible, pay by credit or charge card, which will give you some protection in case the company doesn't come through with the tour. Also consider buying both trip cancellation and trip interruption insurance (see "Health & Insurance," earlier in this chapter). If you decide to go, read the fine print carefully.

Many of the major airlines have subsidiaries which offer package tours to Florida. Check with **American Airlines Flyaway Vacations** (☎ 800/433-7300), **Continental Airlines Grand Destinations** (☎ 800/634-5555), **Delta Air Lines Dream Vacations** (☎ 800/872-7786), **TWA Getaway Vacations** (☎ 800/ GET-AWAY), and **United Airlines** (☎ 800/328-6877). **American Express** (☎ 800/241-1700) also has several tours available. In Orlando, the **Walt Disney World Central Reservations Office** (☎ 407/W-DISNEY) has numerous packages.

Premier Cruise Lines (☎ 800/726-5678), known as the "Big Red Boat," offers 3- and 4-night luxury ocean cruises to The Bahamas in conjunction with 3- or 4-day Orlando theme-park package vacations. Cruises depart from and return to Port Canaveral, 45 minutes from Walt Disney World. Looney Tunes characters (Bugs Bunny, among others) are your on-board hosts. Cruises can be booked only through a travel agent.

In addition to these all-inclusive tours, many Florida hotels and resorts, and even some motels, offer **golf and/or tennis packages,** which bundle the cost of room, greens- and/or court fees, and sometimes equipment into one price. These deals usually don't include airfare, but they do represent savings over paying for the room and golf or tennis separately. See "Where to Stay" in the following chapters for properties offering special packages to their guests.

BY TRAIN

Amtrak (☎ 800/USA-RAIL) offers train service to Florida from both the East and West Coasts. The train takes 26 hours from New York to Miami, 68 hours from Los Angeles to Miami, and Amtrak's fares aren't much less than many promotional deals offered by the airlines. Nevertheless, rail is a viable option for many travelers, especially for those who don't like to fly.

Along the East Coast, Amtrak's *Silver Meteor* and *Silver Star* both run twice daily between New York and Miami or Tampa. Intermediate stops include Philadelphia; Wilmington and Baltimore, Del.; Washington, D.C.; Richmond, Va.; Charleston, S.C.; and Savannah, Ga. In addition to Miami and Tampa, one or the other of these trains stops in Florida at Jacksonville, Palatka, DeLand (Daytona Beach), Sanford, Winter Park, Orlando, Kissimmee, Lakeland, Waldo (Gainesville), Ocala (Silver Springs), Wildwood, Dade City, Winter Haven (Cypress Gardens), Sebring, Okeechobee, West Palm Beach, Delray Beach, Deerfield Beach, Fort Lauderdale, and Hollywood. Amtrak's Thruway Bus Connections are available from Tampa to St. Petersburg, Treasure Island, Clearwater, Bradenton, Sarasota, and Fort Myers.

Depending on date of travel, round-trip fare between New York and Miami for midweek travel ranges from about $146 to $326. The highest fares are between mid-June and mid-August.

From the West Coast, the *Sunset Limited* runs three times weekly between Los Angeles and Miami. It goes through Arizona, New Mexico, Texas, Louisiana, Mississippi, and Alabama before crossing Northwest Florida and then turning south down the state. There are 52 stops along the way, including many of the Florida towns mentioned above plus Pensacola, Crestview (Fort Walton Beach and Destin), Chipley (Panama City Beach), and Tallahassee in the Panhandle. Round-trip coach fares between Los Angeles and Miami start at $286 in low season. Sleeping accommodations are available for an extra charge.

If you intend to stop off along the way, you can save money with Amtrak's **All Aboard America** fares, which are based on three regions of the country. In 1996, for example, you could stop three times in the eastern states for $318 in summer, $198 off-season.

If you want to take the train to Florida *and* bring your own car, Amtrak's **Auto Train** runs daily from Lorton, Va. (12 miles south of Washington, D.C.), to Sanford, Fla. (just northeast of Orlando). You'll travel in comfort while your car is secured in an enclosed car carrier. At press time, round-trip fares ranged from $121 to $205 for passengers, $261 to $420 for cars, depending on the season.

Call Amtrak or contact a travel agent for detailed information on schedules and fares. It's a very good idea to make your train reservations as far in advance as possible.

BY BUS

If you have the time for a leisurely trip, **Greyhound** (☎ 800/231-2222) offers low fares to a number of destinations in Florida. Service is available from almost anywhere in the country, and fares vary according to the point of origin. Discounted fares may be available if you can purchase your ticket in advance or if you travel in midweek.

BY CAR

Local public transportation is lacking in most Florida locales, so having a car makes good sense if you want to see the sights or just get to and from the beach. Countless visitors drive to Florida each year, and the state is reached by three major Interstate highways: **I-95** along the East Coast, **I-75** from the central states, and **I-10** from the West. If you enter Florida on these major highways, you'll soon come across a state Welcome Center.

If you're a member, call your local branch of the **American Automobile Association (AAA)** and ask about the AAA's travel insurance, towing services, and free trip-routing plans. AAA's nationwide telephone number for emergency road service is 800/AAA-HELP.

7 Getting Around Florida

BY PLANE Most major Florida cities are connected by both the major commuter airlines and smaller intrastate airlines such as **Gulf Stream International** (☎ 800/992-8532), which has an extensive in-state network, and **Cape Air** (☎ 800/352-0714), which flies among Key West, Fort Myers, and Naples. Fares for these short hops tend to be reasonable. For example, Gulf Stream International recently introduced a $19 one-way fare between Tallahassee and Gainesville. Call the toll-free numbers listed in "Getting to Florida," earlier in this chapter, for the major airlines to book flights within Florida on their connecting carriers.

BY TRAIN You'll find that train travel from destination to destination isn't really feasible in Florida, and it's not a great deal less expensive than flying. See "Getting to Florida," earlier in this chapter, for Florida towns served by **Amtrak** (☎ 800/USA-RAIL).

BY BUS Taking the bus, however, is fairly easy, as **Greyhound** (☎ 800/231-2222) offers extensive service, even to the smaller cities and towns. Fares are reasonable, and short trips on buses are more comfortable than you might expect. Ask for a regional timetable at any local Greyhound office or call the number above.

BY RENTAL CAR Most visitors opt for the freedom and flexibility of driving. If you're flying into Florida and want to rent a car, you'll have to sort out the maze of rental offers available.

Almost every rental firm pads its profits by selling Loss-Damage Waiver (LDW) insurance that usually costs an extra $8 to $15 per day. Check with your insurance carrier and credit- or charge-card companies before succumbing to the rental company's hard-sell. Many people don't realize that they're already covered by either one or both. If you're not, the LDW may be a wise investment. Also, don't fall for the rental companies' pitch about selling you gasoline at "competitive" prices; fuel invariably will be less expensive at a service station in town.

A minimum age, ranging from 19 to 25, is usually required of renters. Some rental agencies also set maximum ages, and others deny cars to those with bad driving records. If you're concerned that these restrictions may affect you, ask about rental requirements when you book to avoid problems later.

Many packages are available that include airfare, accommodations, and a rental car with unlimited mileage. If you compare these prices with the cost of booking an airline ticket and renting a car yourself, you may find these offers to be a good deal.

If you opt to rent a car on your own, call several rental companies to compare prices, and if you're a member of any organization (the AARP or AAA, for example), check to see if you're entitled to discounts. Every major rental company is represented in Florida, including **Alamo** (☎ 800/327-9633), **Avis** (☎ 800/331-1212), **Budget** (☎ 800/527-0700), **Dollar** (☎ 800/800-4000), **Hertz** (☎ 800/654-3131), **National** (☎ 800/227-7368), **Thrifty** (☎ 800/367-2277), and **Value** (☎ 800/GO-VALUE).

8 Short Cruises from Florida Ports

The Port of Miami, Fort Lauderdale's Port Everglades, and Port Canaveral are the major jumping-off points for a variety of cruises to The Bahamas, the Caribbean islands, and Mexico. To most people a cruise means lots of advance planning, thousands of dollars, and a week or more on the water. That's not altogether true, for many ships based in Florida go on shorter excursions geared to smaller pocketbooks.

The shortest cruises go "nowhere." In other words, they spend a few hours or a day on the Atlantic Ocean or the Gulf of Mexico, basically to gamble, and then return to the same port. Most of these vessels make a beeline for a point 9 miles offshore, where Florida law no longer applies and they can open their casinos with fanfare. Eating is the second most popular activity on board (meals often are included in the fare, which makes the price of these trips fairly reasonable). On-board games, movies, and live entertainment are also common. The chapters that follow give the details on gambling ships such as the *ExtaSea* in Destin (see Chapter 13), and the *SeaKruz* in Fort Myers Beach and the *Royal Princess* on Marco Island (see Chapter 15).

Better known for their one- and two-week voyages from Florida to the Caribbean islands and Mexico, the big cruise companies offer a few one-day to three-night cruises.

Usually all-inclusive, these short cruises can be an exceptional value. For example, **Discovery Cruises** (☎ **305/525-7800**, or 800/937-4477) recently charged as little as $29 for a 1-day voyage to nowhere on the *Discovery Sun* from Miami or on the *Discover I* from Fort Lauderdale. One-night cruises on these ships to Freeport in The Bahamas cost as little as $99 per passenger, a steal since it includes accommodation and all meals.

Most big cruise companies sell tickets only through travel agents. If yours is not familiar with the business (not all agents are), ask for a recommendation to one who specializes in cruises.

You can get information and brochures by contacting the major companies: **Carnival Cruise Lines** (☎ 305/599-2600 or 800/327-9501), **Dolphin Cruise Line** (☎ 305/358-5122 or 800/992-4299), **Majesty Cruise Line** (☎ 305/358-2111 or 800/532-7788), **Norwegian Cruise Line** (☎ 305/460-4808 or 800/262-4NCL), **Royal Caribbean Cruise Line** (☎ 305/539-6000 or 800/432-6559), and **SeaEscape Cruises** (☎ 305/379-0000, or 800/327-7400 or 800/327-2005).

For a full list of options out of Miami, the busiest cruise port, contact the **Metro-Dade Seaport Department**, 1015 North America Way, Miami, FL 33132 (☎ **305/371-7678**). Also see the individual chapters that follow for information on other short cruises, and "Package Tours" under "Getting to Florida," earlier in this chapter, for information on Premier Cruise Lines' "Big Red Boat" from the Orlando area.

If your cruise goes to nowhere, you don't need identification for reentry into the United States, but if you disembark in The Bahamas, you must carry a passport or proof of citizenship.

FAST FACTS: Florida

American Express   Call Cardmember Services (☎ **800/528-4800**) for the most convenient location.

Area Codes   At last count Florida had six telephone area codes. It's **305** for the Miami area and the Florida Keys; **954** for Fort Lauderdale, Hollywood, and Pompano Beach; **407** for east-central Florida, including the Gold Coast and the Orlando area; **813** for most of the Tampa/St. Petersburg area, including Clearwater and Tarpon Springs; **941** in Southwest Florida, including Bradenton, Sarasota, Boca Grande, Fort Myers, Naples, and Sanibel, Captiva, and Marco islands; and **904** across northern Florida, including Pensacola, Tallahassee, Jacksonville, St. Augustine, and Daytona Beach.

Banks   Banks are usually open Mon–Fri 9am–4pm, with ATMs for 24-hour banking. First Union Bank and NationsBank have offices throughout Florida. Barnett and Sun are the largest in-state banks.

Business Hours   Most offices throughout the state are open Mon–Fri 9am–5pm. Shopping malls are generally open until 8 or 9pm Mon–Sat, and until 5pm on Sun.

Car Rentals   See "Getting Around," earlier in this chapter.

Drugstores   Eckerd Drugs and Walgreens are two major chains; you'll see branches all over the state.

Emergencies   Call **911** anywhere in the state to summon the police, the fire department, or an ambulance.

Liquor Laws   You must be 21 to purchase or consume alcohol in Florida. This law is strictly enforced, so if you look young, carry some photo identification that gives your date of birth. Minors can usually enter bars where food is served.

Newspapers & Magazines   Most cities of any size have a local daily paper, but the well-respected *Miami Herald* is generally available all over the state, with regional editions available in many areas. *USA Today* is sold in coin boxes throughout the state.

Safety   Whenever you're traveling in an unfamiliar city, state, or country, stay alert. Be particularly careful with cameras, purses, and wallets, all favorite targets of thieves and pickpockets. Always lock your car doors and the trunk when your vehicle is unattended, and don't leave any valuables in sight. See also the "Safety" section in Chapter 4 for specific information on car and driving safety.

Taxes   The Florida state sales tax is 6%. In addition, most municipalities levy a special tax on hotel and restaurant bills, and some add 1% to the general sales tax. See the individual chapters that follow for details.

Time   Most of Florida is in the eastern time zone, but most of the section west of the Apalachicola River is on central time, 1 hour behind the rest of the state.

Tipping   Tipping is expected in Florida. For how much, see "Fast Facts: For the Foreign Traveler," in Chapter 4.

Tourist Information   See "Visitor Information," earlier in this chapter, for the tourist office serving the entire state. Florida also maintains Welcome Centers on the major highways entering the state.

3

For Foreign Travelers

Although American fads and fashions have spread across Europe and other parts of the world so that the United States may seem like familiar territory before your arrival, there are still many peculiarities and uniquely American situations that any foreign visitor will encounter.

In this chapter we will point out to you some of the perhaps-unexpected differences from what you're used to at home, and explain some of the more confusing aspects of daily life in the United States.

1 Preparing for Your Trip

ENTRY REQUIREMENTS

DOCUMENT REGULATIONS   Immigration laws are a hot political issue in the United States these days, and the following requirements may have changed by the time you plan your trip. Check at any U.S. embassy or consulate for current information and requirements.

Canadian citizens may enter the United States without passports or visas; they need only proof of residence.

The U.S. State Department has a **Visa Waiver Pilot Program** allowing citizens of certain countries to enter the United States without a visa for stays of up to 90 days. At press time these included Andorra, Austria, Belgium, Brunei, Denmark, Finland, France, Germany, Iceland, Ireland, Italy, Japan, Liechtenstein, Luxembourg, Monaco, the Netherlands, New Zealand, Norway, San Marino, Spain, Sweden, Switzerland, and the United Kingdom. Citizens of these countries need only a valid passport and a round-trip air or cruise ticket in their possession upon arrival. If they first enter the United States, they may then visit Mexico, Canada, Bermuda, and/or the Caribbean islands and return to the United States without needing a visa. Further information is available from any U.S. embassy or consulate.

Citizens of all other countries, including Australia, must have (1) a valid **passport** with an expiration date at least 6 months later than the scheduled end of their visit to the United States; and (2) a **tourist visa,** which may be obtained without charge from the nearest U.S. consulate.

To obtain a visa, you must submit a completed application form with a 1 1/2-inch-square photo and demonstrate binding ties to your residence abroad. Usually you can obtain a visa at once or within 24 hours, but it may take longer during the summer rush from June to August. If you cannot go in person, contact the nearest U.S. embassy or consulate for directions on applying by mail. Your travel agent or airline office may also be able to provide you with visa applications and instructions. The U.S. embassy or consulate that issues your visa will determine whether you receive a multiple- or single-entry visa and if there are any restrictions regarding the length of your stay.

Foreign **driver's licenses** are recognized in Florida, although you may want to get an international driver's license written in English.

MEDICAL REQUIREMENTS No inoculations are needed to enter the United States unless you are coming from, or have stopped over in, areas known to be suffering from epidemics, particularly cholera or yellow fever.

CUSTOMS REQUIREMENTS Every adult visitor may bring in free of duty: 1 liter of wine or hard liquor; 200 cigarettes *or* 100 cigars (but no cigars from Cuba) *or* 3 pounds of smoking tobacco; and $100 worth of gifts. These exemptions are offered to travelers who spend at least 72 hours in the United States and who have not claimed them within the preceding 6 months. It is altogether forbidden to bring into the country certain foodstuffs (particularly fruit, cooked meats, and canned goods) and plants. Foreign tourists may bring in or take out up to $10,000 in U.S. or foreign currency with no formalities; larger sums must be declared to Customs on entering or leaving.

Penalties are severe for smuggling illegal narcotics into the United States, so if you require medications containing narcotics (especially those administered with a syringe), carry a valid signed prescription from your physician.

HEALTH & INSURANCE

Unlike Canada and elsewhere, there is no national health-care system in the United States, and the cost of medical care here is extremely high. For this reason, we strongly advise every traveler to secure health insurance coverage before setting out. You may want to take out a comprehensive travel policy that covers costs of sickness, injury, accident, repatriation or death; loss or theft of baggage; trip-cancellation costs; and guarantee of bail in case you're arrested. Packages such as Europ Assistance Worldwide Services in Europe are sold by automobile clubs and travel agencies at attractive rates. **Travel Assistance International (TAI)** (☎ **202/347-2025,** or 800/821-2828) is the agent for Europ Assistance Worldwide Services, Inc., so holders of this company's policies can contact TAI for assistance while in the United States.

Canadians should check with their provincial health scheme offices or call **HealthCanada** (☎ **613/957-3025**) to find out the extent of their coverage and what documentation and receipts they must take home in case they're treated in the United States.

MONEY

CURRENCY The U.S. monetary system has a decimal base: one American **dollar ($1)** = 100 **cents** (100¢).

Notes come in $1 ("a buck"), $5, $10, $20, $50, and $100 denominations (the last two are not welcome when paying for small purchases and are not accepted in taxis). There are also $2 bills and silver dollars, but you're unlikely to come across them.

There are six denominations of coins: 1¢ (one cent, known here as a "penny"), 5¢ (five cents or "a nickel"), 10¢ (ten cents or "a dime"), 25¢ (twenty-five cents or "a quarter"), and the rare 50¢ (fifty cents or "a half dollar") piece.

CURRENCY EXCHANGE   The "foreign-exchange bureaus" so common in Europe are rare in the United States. You'll find currency-exchange desks in the Orlando, Tampa, and Fort Myers airports, and one in Concourse E of the Miami International Airport. Elsewhere they're almost nonexistent, even in the major cities. A few big-city banks exchange foreign currency, but try to avoid having to change even traveler's checks denominated other than in U.S. dollars at small-town banks, and leave your own currency at home.

An exception is **Thomas Cook Foreign Exchange** (☎ 800/287-7362), which changes foreign currency and sells commission-free foreign and U.S. traveler's checks, drafts, and wire transfers. It also does check collections (including Eurochecks). Thomas Cook maintains offices in Miami, Fort Lauderdale, and Orlando. The Miami branch is at 155 SE 3rd Ave., downtown (☎ 305/381-9252). It's open Monday to Friday from 9am to 5pm.

TRAVELER'S CHECKS   Traveler's checks denominated in U.S. dollars are readily accepted at most hotels, motels, restaurants, and large stores.

CREDIT & CHARGE CARDS   The method of payment most widely used in the United States is credit and charge cards: Visa (Barclaycard in Britain), MasterCard (EuroCard in Europe, Access in Britain, Chargex in Canada), American Express, Diners Club, Discover, and Carte Blanche. You can save yourself trouble by using "plastic money" rather than cash or traveler's checks in most hotels, motels, restaurants, and retail stores (many food and liquor stores now accept credit/charge cards). You must have a credit or charge card to rent a car. Many Automatic Teller Machines (ATMs) will allow you to draw U.S. currency against your MasterCard or Visa card; just remember that you'll need your Personal Identification (PIN) to do so.

SAFETY

GENERAL   While tourist areas are generally safe, crime is on the increase everywhere, and U.S. urban areas tend to be less safe than those in Europe or Japan. Visitors should always stay alert. This is particularly true of large U.S. cities. It's wise to ask your hotel front-desk staff or the city's or area's tourist office if you're in doubt about which neighborhoods are safe. Avoid deserted areas, especially at night. Don't go into any city park at night unless there's an event that attracts crowds. Generally speaking, you can feel safe in areas where there are many people and many open establishments.

Avoid carrying valuables with you on the street, and don't display expensive cameras or electronic equipment. Hold on to your pocketbook, and place your billfold in an inside pocket. In theaters, restaurants, and other public places, keep your possessions in sight.

HOTELS   Remember that hotels are open to the public, and in a large hotel, security may not be able to screen everyone entering. Always lock your room door—don't assume that once inside your hotel you're automatically safe and no longer need be aware of your surroundings. Request the front desk or concierge to call you before allowing visitors upstairs.

If possible, get a room that's *not* on the ground floor or facing an outside corridor. Don't leave the PLEASE CLEAN MY ROOM sign on the doorknob; it alerts potential thieves that your room is empty. Don't display your room key to strangers. Don't leave valuables lying around, and lock your suitcases when you leave your room. Ask the front-desk staff for an escort if you're unsure about the security of the hotel's parking area.

DRIVING   Safety while driving is particularly important. Question your rental agency about personal safety, or ask for a brochure of traveler safety tips when you pick up your car. Obtain written directions or a map with the route clearly marked from the agency showing how to get to your destination. And, if possible, arrive and depart during daylight hours.

Recently more and more crime has involved cars and drivers. If you drive off a highway into a doubtful neighborhood, leave the area as quickly as possible. If you have an accident, even on the highway, stay in your car with the doors locked until you assess the situation or until the police arrive. If your car is bumped from behind on the street or you're involved in a minor accident with no injuries and the situation appears to be suspicious, motion to the other driver to follow you and go directly to the nearest police precinct, well-lighted service station, or all-night store. *Never* get out of your car into the street or road in such situations.

If you see someone on the road who indicates a need for help, do *not* stop. Take note of the location, drive on to a well-lighted area, and telephone the police by dialing 911.

Park in well-lighted, well-traveled areas if possible. Always keep your car doors locked, whether attended or unattended, and look around you before you get out of your car. If someone attempts to rob you or steal your car, do *not* try to resist the thief/carjacker—report the incident to the police department immediately.

Also, make sure that you have enough gasoline in your tank to reach your intended destination, so that you're not forced to look for a service station in an unfamiliar and possibly unsafe neighborhood—especially at night.

You may wish to contact the local tourist information bureau in your destination before you arrive, as they may be able to provide you with a safety brochure. (See "Visitor Information," in Chapter 3, and the individual city units for specific tourist organization names and addresses.)

2 Getting To & Around the U.S.

GETTING TO THE U.S.

Many of the major international airlines, such as **British Airways** and **KLM Royal Dutch Airlines,** have direct flights from Europe to various Florida cities, either in their own planes or in conjunction with an American "partner" airline. Call the airlines' local offices or contact your travel agent.

Attractive values are offered by **Virgin Atlantic Airways** (☎ 800/662-8621 in the U.S., or 01/293-74-77-47 in the U.K.), which has cut-rate fares on its flights from London to Miami and Orlando.

Travelers from overseas also can take advantage of the **APEX (Advance Purchase Excursion) fares** offered by all the major international carriers. Most require tickets to be bought 21 days prior to departure, but British Airways has a 90-day purchase plan with London–Miami round-trip fares $100 less than its normal 21-day advance fare ($796 in 1996).

Canadians should check with **Air Canada** (☎ 800/776-3000), which offers service from Toronto and Montréal to Miami, Tampa, West Palm Beach, Fort Lauderdale, and Fort Myers.

No matter what the port of entry, visitors arriving by air should cultivate patience and resignation before setting foot on U.S. soil. Getting through Immigration

Control may take as long as 2 hours on some days, especially summer weekends. Add the time it takes to clear Customs and you'll see that you should make very generous allowance for delay in planning connections between international and domestic flights.

In contrast, travelers arriving by car or by rail from Canada will find border-crossing formalities streamlined to the vanishing point. And air travelers from Canada, Bermuda, and some places in the Caribbean can sometimes go through Customs and Immigration at the point of departure.

For further information, see "Getting There," in Chapter 3.

GETTING AROUND THE U.S.

BY PLANE   The United States is one of the world's largest countries, with vast distances separating many of its key sights. From New York to Miami, for example, is more than 1,350 miles (2,173km) by road or train. Accordingly, flying is the quickest and most comfortable way to get around the country.

The least expensive way for foreigners to see the United States is with a **Visit USA** discount ticket sold by some large American airlines (for example, American, Delta, Northwest, TWA, and United) to travelers on their transatlantic or transpacific flights. It allows travel between many U.S. destinations at minimum rates. The Visit USA tickets are not on sale in the United States and must be purchased before you leave your foreign point of departure. You should obtain information well in advance from your travel agent or the local office of the airline concerned, since the conditions attached to these discount tickets can be changed without warning.

BY TRAIN   Long-distance trains in the United States are operated by **Amtrak** (☎ 800/USA-RAIL), the national rail passenger corporation. Visitors should be aware, however, that with a few notable exceptions (for instance, the Northeast Corridor line between Boston and Washington, D.C.), intercity service is not up to European standards. Delays are common, routes are limited and often infrequently served, and fares are seldom significantly lower than discount airfares. Thus, cross-country train travel should be approached with caution.

International visitors can buy a **USA Railpass,** good for 15 or 30 days of unlimited travel on Amtrak. The pass is available through many foreign travel agents and, with a foreign passport, you can also buy them at some Amtrak offices in the United States, including Boston, Chicago, Los Angeles, Miami, New York, San Francisco, and Washington, D.C. The prices are based on a zone system: eastern, central, and western United States. In 1996 a 15-day pass good in the eastern third of the country cost $185 off-peak, $205 peak; a 30-day pass cost $240 off-peak, $265 peak. The peak seasons are from mid-June to mid-August and around major holidays such as Thanksgiving and Christmas. Reservations are generally required and should be made for each part of your trip as early as possible.

See "Getting There," in Chapter 2, for more information about Amtrak's services to and within Florida.

BY BUS   Long-distance bus travel in the United States can be both slow and uncomfortable, so this option is not for everyone. Nevertheless, it is a way to get around the country rather inexpensively. The only national bus company is **Greyhound** (☎ 800/231-2222 in the U.S.), which offers a **New Ameripass** for unlimited travel anywhere on its system. In 1996, prices for a 7-day pass started at $179; 15 days, at $289; 30 days, at $399; and 60 days, at $599. Senior citizens got a discount ranging from $20 to $60.

BY CAR   Travel by car gives visitors the freedom to make—and alter—their itineraries to suit their own needs and interests. And it offers the possibility of visiting some of the off-the-beaten-path locations, places that cannot be reached easily by public transportation. For information on renting cars in the United States, see "Getting Around Florida," in Chapter 2, and "Automobile Organizations," in "Fast Facts: For the Foreign Traveler," later in this chapter.

Note that in the United States we drive on the **right side of the road** as in Europe, not on the left side as in the United Kingdom, Australia, and New Zealand.

LOCAL TRANSPORTATION   Except for a few large cities such as New York, Washington, Chicago, or San Francisco, local public transportation is either sketchy in smaller cities, or nonexistent in small towns.

FAST FACTS: For the Foreign Traveler

Automobile Organizations   Auto clubs will supply maps, suggested routes, guidebooks, accident and bail-bond insurance, and emergency road service. With almost 1,000 offices nationwide, the **American Automobile Association (AAA)** (☎ **800/222-4357**) is the major auto club in the United States. Members of some foreign auto clubs have reciprocal arrangements with the AAA and enjoy its services at no charge. If you belong to an auto club in your home country, inquire about AAA reciprocity before you leave. You may be able to join the AAA even if you're not a member of a reciprocal club; call the AAA to inquire. The AAA is actually an organization of regional auto clubs; in Florida, look under "AAA Automobile Club South" in the White Pages of the telephone directory.

In addition, some automobile-rental agencies now provide many of these same services. Inquire about their availability when you rent your car (see "Getting Around Florida," in Chapter 2.

Business Hours   See "Fast Facts: Florida" in Chapter 2.

Climate   See "When to Go," in Chapter 2.

Currency & Currency Exchange   See "Preparing for Your Trip," earlier in this chapter.

Drinking Laws   See "Liquor Laws" in "Fast Facts: Florida," in Chapter 2.

Electricity   The United States uses 110–120 volts A.C., 60 cycles, compared to the 220–240 volts A.C., 50 cycles, found in most of Europe, Australia, and New Zealand. In addition to a 100-volt transformer, small appliances of non-American manufacture, such as hair dryers and shavers, will require a plug adapter, with two flat, parallel pins. Downward or reverse transformers—those that change 110–120 volts to 220–240 volts—are difficult to find in the United States, so bring one with you.

Embassies & Consulates   All embassies are located in the national capital, Washington, D.C. Some consulates are located in major U.S. cities, and most nations have a mission to the United Nations in New York City.

The embassy of **Australia** is at 1601 Massachusetts Ave. NW, Washington, DC 20036 (☎ **202/797-3000**). There are consulates in New York, Honolulu, Houston, Los Angeles, and San Francisco.

The embassy of **Canada** is at 501 Pennsylvania Ave. NW, Washington, DC 20001 (☎ **202/682-1740**). There's a Canadian consulate in Florida at 200 S. Biscayne Blvd., Suite 1600, Miami, FL 33131 (☎ **305/579-1600**). Other

Canadian consulates are in Atlanta, Buffalo (N.Y.), Chicago, Cleveland, Dallas, Detroit, Los Angeles, Minneapolis, New York, and Seattle.

The embassy of the **Republic of Ireland** is at 2234 Massachusetts Ave. NW, Washington, DC 20008 (☎ **202/462-3939**). Irish consulates are in Boston, Chicago, New York, and San Francisco.

The embassy of **New Zealand** is at 37 Observatory Circle NW, Washington, DC 20008 (☎ **202/328-4800**). New Zealand consulates are in Los Angeles, Salt Lake City, San Francisco, and Seattle.

The embassy of the **United Kingdom** is at 3100 Massachusetts Ave. NW, Washington, DC 20008 (☎ **202/462-1340**). In Florida, there's a British consulate for emergency situations in Orlando at the Sun Bank Tower, Suite 2110, 200 S. Orange Ave. (☎ **407/426-7855**). Other British consulates are in Atlanta, Boston, Chicago, Cleveland, Dallas, Houston, Los Angeles, and New York.

Emergencies Call **911** to call the police, get an ambulance, or report a fire. This is a toll-free call (no coins are required at public telephones).

If you encounter traveler's problems, check the local telephone directory to find an office of the **Traveler's Aid Society,** a nationwide, nonprofit, social-service organization geared to helping travelers in difficult straits. Their services might include reuniting families separated while traveling, providing food and/or shelter to people stranded without cash, or even emotional counseling.

Gasoline (Petrol) Petrol is known as gasoline (or simply "gas") in the United States, and petrol stations are known as both gas stations and service stations. Gasoline costs about half as much here as it does in Europe. One U.S. gallon equals 3.8 liters or .85 Imperial gallons. There are three grades (and price levels) available at most stations, based on octane ratings of 87, 90, and 93. Most rental cars take the least expensive 87 octane ("regular") gas. Some stations charge less if you pay in cash instead of by credit or charge card. A majority of gas stations in Florida are now actually convenience grocery stores with gas pumps outside; they don't service automobiles. All but a very few stations have self-service gas pumps.

Holidays Banks, government offices, post offices, and many stores, restaurants, and museums are closed on the following legal national holidays: January 1 (New Year's Day), the third Monday in January (Martin Luther King Day), the third Monday in February (Presidents Day), the last Monday in May (Memorial Day), July 4 (Independence Day), the first Monday in September (Labor Day), the second Monday in October (Columbus Day), November 11 (Veterans' Day), the last Thursday in November (Thanksgiving Day), and December 25 (Christmas). Also, the Tuesday following the first Monday in November is Election Day, and is a federal government holiday in presidential-election years (1996 was the most recent, 2000 is the next).

Legal Aid The foreign tourist will probably never become involved with the American legal system. If you're "pulled over" for a minor infraction on the street or highway (such as speeding), never attempt to pay the fine directly to a police officer; you may wind up arrested on the much more serious charge of attempted bribery. Pay fines by mail, or directly into the hands of the clerk of the court. If you're accused of a more serious offense, it's wise to say and do nothing before consulting a lawyer, since here the burden is on the state to prove a person's guilt beyond a reasonable doubt (remember O. J. Simpson?), and everyone has the right to remain silent, whether he or she is suspected of a crime or actually arrested. Once arrested, a person can make one telephone call to a party of his or her choice. Call your embassy or consulate.

Mail If you want your mail to follow you on your vacation and you aren't sure of your address, it can be sent to you, in your name, **c/o General Delivery** at the main post office of the city or region where you expect to be. The addressee must pick it up in person and must produce proof of identity (driver's license, credit or charge card, passport, etc.).

Generally found at intersections, **mailboxes** are blue with a red-and-white stripe and carry the inscription U.S. MAIL. If your mail is addressed to a U.S. destination, don't forget to add the five-digit postal code, or ZIP Code, after the two-letter abbreviation of the state to which the mail is addressed (FL for Florida).

Domestic **postage rates** are 20¢ for a postcard and 32¢ for a letter. Airmail postcards and letters to Canada both cost 46¢ for the first half ounce; those to other countries cost 60¢ for the first half ounce.

Newspapers/Magazines National newspapers include the *New York Times, USA Today,* and the *Wall Street Journal.* National news weeklies include *Newsweek, Time,* and *U.S. News & World Report.* All over Florida, you'll be able to purchase the *Miami Herald,* one of the most highly respected dailies in the country.

Radio and Television Television plays a major part in American life, with five nationwide broadcast networks—ABC, CBS, NBC, Fox, and the Public Broadcasting System (PBS)—and scores of cable channels from which to choose. Many hotels and motels also have pay-per-view channels carrying recent movies. All options are usually indicated on your hotel TV set or in your guest services directory. You'll also find a wide choice of local radio stations, each broadcasting particular kinds of talk shows and/or music punctuated by news broadcasts and frequent commercials. Some Florida radio stations even carry news reports from Canada. While most broadcasts are in English, many radio stations in Florida use Spanish.

Safety See "Safety" in "Preparing for Your Trip," earlier in this chapter, and in "Fast Facts: Florida," in Chapter 3.

Taxes In the United States there is no Value-Added Tax (VAT) or other indirect tax at the national level. Every state, county, and city has the right to levy its own local tax on all purchases, including hotel and restaurant checks, airline tickets, and so on. For Florida's taxes, see "Fast Facts: Florida," in Chapter 3.

Telephone, Telegraph, Telex, and Fax The telephone system in the United States is run by private corporations, so rates, especially for long-distance service and operator-assisted calls, can vary widely. Generally, hotel surcharges on long-distance and local calls are astronomical.

You're usually better off using a **public pay telephone,** which you'll find clearly marked in most public buildings and private establishments as well as on the street. They are less numerous outside the metropolitan areas but are still widespread. Convenience grocery stores and gas stations always have them. Many convenience groceries and packaging services sell prepaid calling cards in denominations up to $50; these can be the least expensive way to call home. Many public phones at airports now accept American Express, MasterCard, and Visa credit/charge cards. Local calls made from public pay phones in Florida cost 25¢.

Most **long-distance and international calls** can be dialed directly from any phone. For calls within the United States and to Canada and most of the Caribbean, dial 1 followed by the area code and the seven-digit number. For other international calls, dial 011 followed by the country code, city code, and the telephone number of the person you're calling.

Note that all calls to area codes 800 and 888 are toll free. However, calls to numbers in area codes 700 and 900 (chat lines, bulletin boards, "dating" services, etc.) can be very expensive—usually a charge of 95¢ to $3 or more per minute, and they sometimes have minimum charges that can run as high as $15 or more.

For **reversed-charge or collect calls,** and for **person-to-person calls,** dial 0 (zero, *not* the letter O) followed by the area code and number you want; an operator will then come on the line, and you should specify that you are calling collect, or person-to-person, or both. If your operator-assisted call is international, ask for the overseas operator.

For local **directory assistance** ("information"), dial 411; for **long-distance information,** dial 1, then the appropriate area code and 555-1212.

Like the telephone system, **telegraph** and **telex** services are provided by private corporations like ITT, MCI, and above all, Western Union. You can bring your telegram in to the nearest Western Union office (there are hundreds across the country), or dictate it over the phone (☎ **800/325-6000**). You can also telegraph money, or have it telegraphed to you, very quickly over the Western Union system, but this service can cost as much as 15% to 25% of the amount sent.

Many travelers consider running out of funds to be one of their worst travel experiences. Assuming you have friends or relatives who will advance you the money, a new service sponsored by American Express might be of help to you. **MONEYGRAM,** 6200 S. Quebec St. (P.O. Box 5118), Englewood, CO 80155-5118 (☎ **800/926-9400**), is the fastest-growing money-wiring service in the world. Funds can be transferred from one individual to another in less than 10 minutes from any of thousands of locations. An American Express phone representative will give you the names of four of five offices nearby. (You don't have to go to an American Express office for this: In the United States, locations are as diverse as a local pharmacy or convenience store in many small communities.) Requirements include filling out a form. Acceptable forms of payment include cash, MasterCard, Visa, or Discover, and—in some rare instances, if proper ID is presented—personal check. The service charge is $10 for the first $300 sent, with a sliding scale after that.

Most hotels have **fax** machines available for guest use (for a charge), and many hotel rooms are even wired for guests' fax machines. A less expensive way to send and receive faxes may be at stores such as **Mail Boxes Etc.,** a national chain of packing-service shops (look in the *Yellow Pages* directory under "Packing Services").

Telephone Directory   There are two kinds of telephone directories in the United States. The general directory is the so-called **White Pages,** in which private and business subscribers are listed in alphabetical order. The inside front cover lists the emergency number for police, fire, and ambulance, and other vital numbers (like the Coast Guard, poison-control center, crime-victims hotline, and so on). The first few pages are devoted to community-service numbers, including a guide to long-distance and international calling, complete with country codes and area codes. Government numbers usually are on pages printed on blue paper.

The second directory, printed on yellow paper (hence its name, *Yellow Pages*), lists all local services, businesses, industries, churches and synagogues by type of activity, with an index at the front or back. The *Yellow Pages* also include city plans or detailed area maps, often showing postal ZIP Codes and public transportation routes.

Time   The continental United States is divided into four **time zones.** From east to west, these are: eastern standard time (EST), central standard time (CST), mountain standard time (MST), and Pacific standard time (PST). Alaska and Hawaii have their own zones. For example, noon in Miami (EST) is 11am in Chicago (CST), 10am in Denver (MST), 9am in Los Angeles (PST), 8am in Anchorage (AST), and 7am in Honolulu (HST).

Most of Florida is in the eastern time zone, though the Panhandle west of the Apalachicola River is in the central time zone (1 hour earlier than Tallahassee, Orlando, and Miami).

In most of the United States—including Florida—**daylight saving time** is in effect from 2am on the first Sunday in April through 2am on the last Sunday in October. Daylight saving time moves the clock 1 hour ahead of standard time.

Tipping   This is part of the American way of life, on the principle that you must expect to pay for any service you get. Many service personnel receive little direct salary and must depend on tips for their livelihood (the annual income tax of tip-earners is based on how much they should have received in light of their employers' gross revenues; therefore, they may have to pay tax on a tip you didn't actually give them). Here are some rules of thumb:

In **hotels,** tip bellhops $1 per piece and tip the chamber staff $1 per day. Tip the doorman or concierge only if he or she has provided you with some specific service such as calling a cab for you or obtaining difficult-to-get theater tickets.

In **restaurants, bars, and nightclubs,** tip the service staff 15% of the check (excluding the sales tax), tip bartenders 10% to 15%, tip checkroom attendants $1 per garment, and tip valet-parking attendants $1 per vehicle. Tip the doorman only if he has provided you with some specific service (such as calling a cab for you). Tipping is not expected in cafeterias and fast-food restaurants.

Tip **cab drivers** 15% of the fare.

As for **other service personnel,** tip redcaps at airports or railroad stations $1 per piece and tip hairdressers and barbers 15% to 20%. **Do not tip** gas-station attendants and ushers in cinemas, movies, and theaters.

Toilets   You won't find public toilets (euphemistically referred to here as "rest rooms") on the streets in most U.S. cities, but they can be found in hotel lobbies, bars, restaurants, museums, department stores, railway and bus stations, or service stations. Note, however, that restaurants and bars in resort or heavily visited areas may display a notice that REST ROOMS ARE FOR THE USE OF PATRONS ONLY. You can ignore this sign or, better yet, avoid arguments by paying for a cup of coffee or soft drink, which will qualify you as a patron. Some public places are equipped with pay toilets that require you to insert one or two dimes (10¢) or a quarter (25¢) into a slot on the door before it will open. In rest rooms with attendants, a tip of at least 25¢ is customary.

THE AMERICAN SYSTEM OF MEASUREMENTS

Length

1 inch (in.)			=	2.54cm			
1 foot (ft.)	=	12 in.	=	30.48cm	=	.305m	
1 yard (yd.)	=	3 ft.			=	.915m	
1 mile	=	5,280 ft.				=	1.609km

To convert miles to kilometers, multiply the number of miles by 1.61 (for example, 50 mi. × 1.61 = 80.5km). Note that this conversion can be used to convert speeds from miles per hour (m.p.h.) to kilometers per hour (kmph).

To convert kilometers to miles, multiply the number of kilometers by .62 (example, 25 km × .62 = 15.5 mi.). Note that this same conversion can be used to convert speeds from kilometers per hour to miles per hour.

Capacity

1 fluid ounce (fl. oz.)			=	.03 liter		
1 pint (pt.)	=	16 fl. oz.	=	.47 liter		
1 quart (qt.)	=	2 pints	=	.94 liter		
1 gallon (gal.)	=	4 quarts	=	3.79 liters	=	.83 Imperial gal.

To convert U.S. gallons to liters, multiply the number of gallons by 3.79 (example, 12 gal. × 3.79 = 45.48 liters).
To convert liters to U.S. gallons, multiply the number of liters by .26 (example, 50 liters × .26 = 13 U.S. gal.).
To convert U.S. gallons to Imperial gallons, multiply the number of U.S. gallons by .83 (example, 12 U.S. gal. × .83 = 9.96 Imperial gal.).
To convert Imperial gallons to U.S. gallons, multiply the number of Imperial gallons by 1.2 (example, 8 Imperial gal. × 1.2 = 9.6 U.S. gal.).

Weight

1 ounce (oz.)			=	28.35g		
1 pound (lb.)	=	16 oz.	=	453.6g	=	.45 kg
1 ton	=	2,000 lb.	=	907kg	=	.91 metric ton

To convert pounds to kilograms, multiply the number of pounds by .45 (example, 90 lb. × .45 = 40.5kg).
To convert kilograms to pounds, multiply the number of kilos by 2.2 (example, 75kg × 2.2 = 165 lb.).

Area

1 acre			=	.41ha	
1 square mile	=	640 acres	=	2.59ha	= 2.6 sq. km

To convert acres to hectares, multiply the number of acres by .41 (example, 40 acres × .41 = 16.4ha).
To convert hectares to acres, multiply the number of hectares by 2.47 (example, 20ha × 2.47 = 49.4 acres).
To convert square miles to square kilometers, multiply the number of square miles by 2.6 (example, 80 sq. mi × 2.6 = 208 sq. km).
To convert square kilometers to square miles, multiply the number of square kilometers by .39 (example, 150 sq. km × .39 = 58.5 sq. mi.).

Temperature

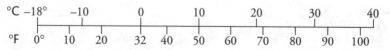

To convert degrees Fahrenheit to degrees Celsius, subtract 32 from °F, multiply by 5, then divide by 9 (example, 85°F − 32 × $^5/_9$ = 29.4°C).
To convert degrees Celsius to degrees Fahrenheit, multiply °C by 9, divide by 5, and add 32 (example, 20°C × $^9/_5$ + 32 = 68°F).

Outdoor & Sports Vacations

4

by Karen T. Bartlett

Florida offers something for everyone, from resort vacations to on-your-own adventures. You can have a vacation full of free or almost-free activities, or you can splurge on your dream activity. The pages that follow will point you toward the best sports options and outdoor experiences in the state's most striking natural areas.

SAVING MONEY ON YOUR OUTDOOR VACATION If you know how to go about it, you can take advantage of free or practically free sports and outdoor programs, and even splurge on high-budget items at a fraction of their value.

Long days of sunshine let you enjoy your sport more hours than ever. And while in Florida, why not try a new sport or two? For some tempting ideas, read on.

If backcountry adventures excite you, get ready for a rich and diverse ecosystem unlike anyplace else in North America, where ever-increasing acreage is being acquired by state, federal, and private preservation organizations. Many parks and preserves are free for visitors to enjoy.

Some of the finest golf courses in Florida are low-cost municipal courses, and some of the most famous courses, although they're part of expensive resorts, are available for public play. The world tennis headquarters is in Florida, and if you know who to call, you can lounge in the club and play on the same Grand Slam surface courts as the top pros in the business.

A FEW SAFETY TIPS Do bring your hiking shoes, your binoculars and camera. Don't forget the sunscreen (yes, even in winter and on overcast days), a hat, and the insect repellent—a must during the rainy season.

The most common injuries are due to inadequate safety precautions when swimming, boating, biking, or exploring the wilderness.

Never swim alone. Know the water depth before diving, and swim in designated areas only.

Never try to feed a wild animal. You risk getting bitten, of course, but you're also upsetting the balance of nature. Animals fed by humans lose their ability to find their own food. Some creatures, such as alligators, can't tell the difference between the food and the feeder's hand. Most Florida snakes are harmless but a few have deadly bites, so it's best not to handle any snakes.

Central Florida is said to be the lightning capital of the United States, so during thunderstorms get out of the water, off the beach, and off the golf course. Avoid high ground, tall trees, and open fields.

1 Beach Sports, Snorkeling & Scuba Diving

Wherever there are beachfront hotels and resorts, there are independent outfitters who run beach sports concessions. Favorite rentals are Waverunners and jet skis, windsurfers and paddleboats, which are available by the half hour, hour, or day, starting at about $35. Private lessons, group classes, and special excursions are often available also. The best windsurfing spots are generally the same places where wind and tide conditions make sailing spectacular: the Keys, the Panhandle, and along the Atlantic coast.

Snorkeling gear is inexpensive (you just need a mask, a snorkel, and fins) and can be purchased at most beachside variety stores, or can be rented from resort concessions. Snorkeling requires a free 2-minute lesson and no certification. Scuba diving requires certification, which is earned after intensive lessons, plus written tests and an open-water dive test. A number of beach hotels offer "resort courses" in diving: abbreviated classes that allow guests to take supervised shallow-water dives during their stay. The cost is usually between $125 and $200, including the equipment, classes, and dive. More information is available through local dive shops.

Let's face it, scuba diving is not a "frugal" sport, but if you're hooked these pages will give you tips on the most rewarding and least expensive places to enjoy it! Definitely easier on your wallet is a popular new alternative to scuba called "snuba," combining aspects of scuba and snorkeling. Your snuba tank stays on the surface of the water, attached to a raft that follows you around. A 20- to 30-foot regulator hose, clipped to a harness on your shoulder, allows you to go where the scuba divers go. Unlike scuba diving, certification is not required, just a 1-hour pool class. A snuba class and first dive run by **Caribbean Watersports** at the Sheraton Key Largo Resort (☎ **800/223-6728**) is typically priced at about $100 (half the cost of a scuba class). Subsequent dives, minus the lesson, cost less.

Snorkelers and divers should observe certain safety rules. Don't dive beyond your certification level. And *never* dive alone.

BEST REEF-DIVING SPOTS   You can contact the **Florida Association of Dive Operators,** 335 Beard St., Tallahassee, FL 32303 (☎ **904/222-6000**), for information about the best places to dive.

More than 4,000 sunken ships along Florida's entire coast are waiting to be explored. The clearest water to view them in will be found in the Middle Keys and the waters between Key West and the Dry Tortugas.

The Keys are a vast underwater extension of the continental shelf, housing one of the world's largest living coral reef systems. Magnificent formations of tree-size elkhorn coral and giant brain coral, as well as colorful sea fans, and dozens of other varieties, share space with 300 or more species of rainbow-hued fish.

Remember that coral is a living organism. Don't stand on it. Don't touch it (some of it can deliver a serious, long-lasting sting), and don't break it. The tiny piece a souvenir seeker takes home takes thousands of years to regrow. Don't kick up sand as you move along—sand smothers coral.

Snorkeling in the Keys is particularly fine between Islamorada and Marathon. Reef diving is good all the way from Key Largo to Key West, and there are plenty of tour operators, outfitters, and dive shops along the way. Following are some highlights in the area:

Looe Key National Marine Sanctuary, off Big Pine Key, was voted the no. 1 dive spot in North America by *Skin Diver* magazine. Local dive outfitters can take you there.

John Pennekamp Coral Reef State Park, Key Largo, is a large, impressive park about an hour south of Miami that was established to protect the only living coral reef in the United States. Better late than never—but, sadly, much of the reef close to shore has been trampled by the heavy traffic. The best viewings are in the more remote regions where the big boats don't go. A popular attraction is *Christ of the Deep,* a statue submerged in 25 feet of water at Largo Dry Rocks. The facilities at the park are "touristy" but excellent.

Divers interested in an underwater wedding should check out the Caribbean plantation–style **Amoray Dive Resort,** 104250 Overseas Hwy., Key Largo, FL 33037 (☎ **305/451-3595,** or 800/426-6729). Romantic yet affordable (rooms in summer start at $50), this is a popular spot for Florida scuba students to stay for their final checkout and open-water dive. The 15 units range from single rooms to two-bedroom, full-kitchen apartments. Visitors are urged to call in advance: Repeat business keeps the place full during the peak summer season. Eighteen-year dive and guide veteran Amy Slate and her staff can certify divers under PADI, NAUI, and ESAC (British) programs. Bring your own gear or they'll provide it.

More crystal-clear waters are the **gulf waters of the Panhandle** in the Destin area, and the freshwater springs of North-Central Florida. The 100-fathom curve draws closer to the white, sandy Panhandle beaches than at any other spot on the Gulf of Mexico. This means you don't need a boat to see to the bottom. You can observe Timber Hole, an undersea "petrified forest" of all kinds of wrecks: planes, ships, even a railroad car. There are plenty of dive shops to outfit, tour, and certify visitors.

CAVE DIVING IN NORTHERN FLORIDA   The "cave diving capital of the world" is located between High Springs and Branford about 30 minutes northeast of Gainesville in northern Florida. Write to the **National Speleological Society,** Cave Diving Section, P.O. Box 950, Branford, FL 32008, for information.

The two most renowned spots for diving are Ginnie Springs on the Santa Fe River and Ichetucknee Springs State Park, a few miles farther north. Several modestly priced inns and motels are nearby.

At **Ginnie Springs** there are nine crystal-clear springs within this 200-acre forest-land for scuba and snorkeling. NSS/CDS-certified divers can explore the world-famous caves and caverns. Others can take a 2-day course which lets you dive in the caverns ("daylight zone") or the extended course to certify you for the caves ("total-darkness zone").

While much of the same scuba equipment is used as in reef diving, the skill requirements vary. The **Ginnie Springs Resort,** 7300 NE Ginnie Springs Rd., High Springs, FL 32643 (☎ **904/454-2202,** or 800/874-8571), is a 200-acre campsite park along the Santa Fe River with camp/dive packages, canoe rentals, and other recreation.

Ichetucknee Springs State Park in Branford is named for the Native American words "pond of the beaver." This superb diving spot also claims nine springs. Underwater explorers have found artifacts from the native tribes that once inhabited the region, and topside explorers often sight limpkin, wood duck, otter, and beaver. The 2,241-acre state park offers camping, nature trails, canoeing, and—a popular lazy-day sport of the nearby college crowd—tubing. You float on giant inner tubes or rafts down the icy Ichetucknee River under a canopy of lovely hardwood trees. The price is right—admission is $3.50; tubes cost $1, and rafts, $5—and it's a great way to spend a day seeing nature without getting tired or too wet.

The **Steamboat Dive Inn,** U.S. 27 at U.S. 129, Branford, FL 32008 (☎ **904/ 935-DIVE**), on the Suwannee River, has modestly priced accommodations and its own on-site, full-service diving center with certified instructors for every level. The **Branford Dive Center**, U.S. 27 and the Suwannee River, Branford, FL 32008 (☎ **904/935-1141**), also offers guides, air, rentals, accessories, and instruction.

SUGGESTED READING   *Coral Reefs of Florida,* by Gilbert L. Voss (Sarasota, Fla.: Pineapple Press); *Diver's Guide to Florida and the Florida Keys,* by Jim Stachowicz (Miami: Windward Publishing, Inc.).

2 Fishing

Anglers age 16 and older need fishing licenses for any kind of saltwater or freshwater fishing, including lobstering and spearfishing. There are some exemptions (such as for totally disabled fishermen), but they apply to Florida residents only. You don't need a license to fish from a licensed party boat or with a licensed charter captain. Saltwater fishing licenses for non–Florida residents range from $6.50 for a 3-day license to $31.50 for an annual license. Freshwater licenses cost $15 for 7 days or $30 for a year. (Florida residents pay $13.50 annually for saltwater and $12 for freshwater licenses.)

Licenses are sold at bait and tackle shops or through the local county tax office. For more information, call the **Office of Fisheries & Management** (☎ **904/ 488-7910** for saltwater licenses) or the **Florida Game & Freshwater Fish Commission** (☎ **904/488-3641**).

The **Florida Department of Environmental Protection,** 3900 Commonwealth Blvd., Tallahassee, FL 32399 (☎ **904/488-7326**), publishes an annual *Fishing Lines,* a free magazine with a wealth of information about fishing in Florida, including regulations and licensing requirements. It also distributes free brochures with annual freshwater and saltwater limits.

Florida's state parks offer a variety of fishing opportunities, including piers, jetties, and shoreline. Some of the best fishing is from bridges over fast-running passes between Florida's barrier islands. The bridge in Matlacha on Pine Island calls itself the "Fishingest Bridge in the World."

You'll see local anglers fishing in the canals along highways—a "hot spot" is the Tamiami Trail between Naples and Miami. Be careful if you try it—the canals and banks are loaded with alligators, and they tend to blend right in with their habitat!

If you want to go deep-sea fishing, it's more affordable to go on a group "party boat" than to charter a single boat and skipper.

According to Florida's most serious anglers, the following are some of the best fishing spots in the state:

The deep, shadowy holes in **Boca Pass,** located between Gasparilla and Cayo Costa islands in Southwest Florida, are where the mighty tarpon, the "silver kings of the seas," run. Each July, fishing enthusiasts converge from the world over to pay the $3,500 entry fee for the annual Boca Grande Tarpon Tournament. The prize catch (which is released) wins $100,000. Gasparilla and its surrounding islands also harbor redfish, snook, grouper, pompano, and a dozen more species. Local guides know their stuff.

Cedar Key, tucked into the Gulf Coast's "big bend," is a haven for Spanish mackerel, redfish, and sea trout, and paradise for those looking for some Old Florida ambience. You won't have trouble finding a guide—fishing is the main livelihood for most folks here. You'll pay about $43 per person for a half day of fishing based on a party of four, all-inclusive (bring your own bag lunch). The most popular lodging is the historic (about 1859) **Island Hotel,** Main Street, Cedar Key, FL 32625 (☎ **904/543-1111**), loaded with rustic charm and budget priced.

Destin, in the Florida Panhandle, calls itself the "World's Luckiest Fishing Village," and lots of people have great luck around these waters between Panama City and Fort Walton Beach. Nearly 150 party boats stay busy all the time, and their rates are low. About 27 miles offshore is the "Billfish Capital of the Gulf"—and that's not all. Between April and October the prospects are excellent for sailfish, white and blue marlin, dolphin fish, and wahoo. Rates are at their lowest then, and the Panhandle is popular for its already-modest accommodations and restaurant prices.

Lake Okeechobee, Florida's "Big O," the second-largest freshwater lake in the country, covers nearly half a million acres. Claiming the title "Speckled Perch Capital of the World," it's also famous for its largemouth bass and bream. Fishing tournaments are always happening, year round. There are plenty of budget accommodations and campgrounds in the area; in fact, there are no fancy resorts at all. The country's largest and fanciest KOA campground is here, featuring eco-tours, family and adults-only swimming pools, a lively country and western bar, Bingo, and even an executive golf course. Call the **Lake Okeechobee Resort KOA Kampground** (☎ **800/ 845-6846**).

The local chamber of commerce has an exhaustive list of bait and tackle shops, fishing guides, RV parks, outfitters, and marinas where you can rent your own boat. Okeechobee Boat Rentals has a special night-fishing deal. Rent a fully equipped boat (including bait) between 5 and 11pm for $27 per person based on four people. The pros say they're jumpin' at that time of night! You must have a fishing license. Boats can be rented at **Okeechobee Boat Rentals** (☎ **813/763-2700**). Contact the **Okeechobee County Chamber of Commerce,** 55 S. Parrott Ave., Okeechobee, FL 34974 (☎ **800/871-4403**), for information.

The title "Sailfish Capital of the World" is claimed by the town of **Stuart,** about halfway between Miami and Melbourne on the Atlantic coast. You can fish all year, but the peak months are December to March plus June and July. If you have a choice of times, your best accommodations deals will be available in summer. Sailfishing is an art of its own, and beginners need to learn that delicate moment to release the reel drag and let the fish run with the lure. Learning is fun, and bringing one in is a thrilling experience. Stuart is big on catch-and-release.

3 Golf

Not surprisingly, Florida has more golf courses (close to 1,100) than any other state in the country. Designed by some of the world's greatest golfers and course designers, Florida's courses range from Scottish-style links to hardwood hammocks featuring moss-draped oaks to the lushest of subtropical settings. In this land of instant landscaping, golf courses mature quickly and are replete with fragrant tropical fruits and colorful flowers. It's an unusual course that doesn't feature majestic water views of the Atlantic Ocean, the Gulf of Mexico, or one of Florida's thousands of rivers and lakes.

You can play golf in Florida 365 days a year. Even in the "rainy season," the rains come predictably in early afternoon and disappear as instantly as they came. The best summer tee times to avoid the hottest sun are early morning and late afternoon. With daylight savings time, late sunsets let you play well into the dinner hour.

Best news: After 2 or 3pm in summer you can take advantage of twilight rates, which are usually less than half the regular greens fee. For example, you can play one of the renowned Disney courses for as little as $35 per round.

You can contact the **Professional Golfers' Association (PGA),** 100 Ave. of the Champions, Palm Beach Gardens, FL 33418 (☎ **407/624-8400**), or the **Ladies Professional Golf Association (LPGA),** 2570 Volusia Ave., Suite B, Daytona Beach, FL 32114 (☎ **904/254-8800**). Golfers should also request a pamphlet called "Fairways in the Sunshine" from the **Florida Sports Foundation,** 107 W. Gaines St., Tallahassee, FL 32399 (☎ **904/488-8347**), that describes all the state's golf courses.

A few healthy precautions: Summer storms bring lightning, and an open golf course with that lightning rod you call a club is not the place to be. If you see lightning, postpone the game. If you get caught without warning, don't take refuge under a tree. And remember that the Florida sun is powerful: Drink plenty of water, and wear a cap and at least a 15-spf sunscreen. Most golf courses have excellent insect-control programs, but with all that water and all those trees, be smart and take the insect repellent!

It's a rare town in Florida that doesn't have an affordable municipal golf course—even Key West has 18 great holes. The highest concentration of excellent courses is found in the Naples/Fort Myers area (1,000 holes!), Orlando (Disney alone has 99 holes open to the public), and the Panhandle areas around Destin and Panama City. Some of the best of the best are listed here:

Everyone seems to love the perfectly maintained Rees Jones course at **Falcon's Fire Golf Club,** 3200 Seralago Blvd., Kissimmee, FL 34746 (☎ **407/239-5445**). Major-league baseball players take a break from spring training here, and insiders at Orlando-based *Golfweek* magazine say that it's the best public course close to home, tucked away behind the touristy hubbub of U.S. 192. With 136 bunkers and water on 10 holes, it has its challenges.

The Links at Key Biscayne, 6700 Crandon Blvd., Key Biscayne, FL 33149 (☎ **305/361-9139**), is a stop on the men's Senior PGA Tour. Many people are surprised that this delightful course is a county-managed public course. Located on a posh residential island, it's one of the few courses remaining in South Florida not surrounded by development. Golfers enjoy pristine nature views and the Miami skyline to the north.

The Registry Resort, 475 Seagate Dr., Naples, FL 33940 (☎ **941/597-3232** or 800/247-9810), is on the pricey side, but the benefits may be worth it. Elegant, pristine Naples is smack in the center of the Gulf Coast—the region claiming to have the most golf holes in the world, topping 1,000 in 1996. Though many of the best courses are private, the Registry—which has no course on site—has all the inside contacts. Its Caddymaster Program can get resort guests onto almost any course in the region, including Fazio's Pelican's Nest, Arthur Hills's Quail West, and Robert Trent Jones, Jr.'s Kensington courses.

Are 99 holes enough? You needn't be a Disney resort guest to play at the **Walt Disney World Resorts,** P.O. Box 10100, Lake Buena Vista, FL 32830-0100 (☎ **407/824-2270** or 407/W-DISNEY). Day visitors can reserve tee times on any of the five 18-hole courses or the 9-hole walking course up to 7 days in advance, and resort guests can reserve 30 days ahead. Check out the area's most famous hazard, on the Magnolia Course's sixth hole: a sand trap in the shape of Mickey's head. Best deal: If you plan to be in the area for 2 days or more, buy a season golf badge. Twilight play (which can start as early as 1pm) can cost as little as $35 per round between May and December. Save the hassle of their ever-busy phone lines and call your travel agent.

The **World Woods Golf Club,** 17590 Ponce de Leon Blvd., Brooksville, FL 34614 (☎ **904/796-5500**), is a "best-kept secret." This club has some of the best courses open to the public in Florida, ranking right up there with with the TPC Club, the Bay Hill Club, and the Doral's Blue Monster. It has two superb Fazio-designed 18-hole courses and a 9-hole short course (also by Fazio) in an Old Florida setting. The club claims to have the most extensive practice park in the world, sprawling over 20 acres. Last year *Golf Digest* magazine named its Pine Barrens course the no. 1 new course in America. Reservations are taken up to 3 days in advance, but you can just hop over from I-75 on U.S. 98 and your chances are good for getting a tee time.

SUGGESTED GOLF GUIDES   *Florida Golf Guide,* by Jimmy Shacky (Open Road Publishing); *The Miami Herald's Florida's Best Golf Courses; A Guide to the Best-Ranked Courses You Can Play,* by Ronnie Ramos (Andrews & McMeel); "Fairways in the Sunshine," available free from the Florida Sports Foundation (see above).

4 Tennis

Sunshine and year-round playing make Florida a tennis paradise. The courts (some 7,700 of them, according to state tourism calculations) open early for cool morning play and many public and hotel courts offer lighted evening play. More and more budget lodgings are adding tennis courts for the complimentary use of their guests. So bring your racquet to Florida—and don't forget the sunscreen!

For information, contact the **Florida Tennis Association,** 801 NE 167 St., Suite 301, North Miami Beach, FL 33162 (☎ **305/652-2866**).

If you're ultra-serious about your tennis and want to splurge a little, I've also highlighted some of Florida's best academies.

No tennis guide to Florida would be complete without mention of the **ATP Tour International Headquarters,** 200 ATP Tour Blvd., Ponte Vedra Beach, FL 32082 (☎ **904/285-8000** or 800/963-2444). Though it's pricey, there are ways to get on the courts of the champions without breaking the bank (read on). As the home of the pros, the ATP Tour Headquarters showcases the best professional tennis in the world. Besides being a superior training center for players on the ATP Tour and management headquarters for tournaments on six continents, it's an academy where amateurs can hobnob with the superstars. The 21 courts encompass all Grand Slam surfaces: Wimbledon grass, French Open red European clay, and U.S. Open hard courts. Director of Tennis Brian Gottfried has been a Wimbledon and Davis Cup contender. The brochures say that you must stay either next door at the ATP's official hotel, the Marriott at Sawgrass Resort, or at the equally luxurious Lodge and Bath Club at Ponte Vedra Beach in order to get ATP privileges. The cheapest package deals, which include daily instruction, unlimited court time, club amenities, and some ATP goodies to take home, start at $98 per person per night (a real deal, considering what you'll be getting!). It's worth the splurge, but insiders also know that even more economical arrangements can be made by calling Jenny Wooten at ATP headquarters.

Nick spends more of his time at his world headquarters, the **Bollettieri Sports Academy,** 5500 34th St. West, Bradenton, FL 34210 (☎ **941/755-1000,** or 800/ 872-6425), than at any other of his Bollettieri tennis camps. If you're bringing junior tennis enthusiasts to Florida, this is their kind of place. Juniors have their own all-inclusive campus: dorms, recreation, cafeterias—the works. While the kids have their own evening recreational programs, the adult guests socialize with the tennis pros at the "in" spots around sophisticated Sarasota. Day, week, and mini-week packages are offered.

The **Innisbrook Hilton Resort,** 36750 U.S. 19 North, Palm Harbor, FL 34684 (☎ **813/942-2000,** or 800/456-2000), is one of Nick Bollettieri's 20 or so tennis academies worldwide. The Innisbrook's $5-million, 15-court tennis center is great for recreational and instructional programs. Another family-friendly resort, the Innisbrook offers attractive junior and family packages, especially May to October.

The **Saddlebrook Resort,** 5700 Saddlebrook Way, Wesley Chapel, FL 33543 (☎ 813/973-1111 or 800/729-8383), is the home of the Harry Hopman/ Saddlebrook International Tennis Academy. Saddlebrook has 45 courts and serious instruction programs for all levels. A separate juniors' campus with extensive amenities is a popular feature.

The **World Tennis Center Resort & Club,** 4800 Airport-Pulling Rd., Naples, FL 33942 (☎ 941/263-1900, or 800/292-6663 in the U.S., 800/621-6665 in Canada), is an 82-acre condominium resort. The WTC features a 2,500-seat stadium and 16 courts. The new World Tennis Academy, headed by renowned tennis psychologist and coach Roland Carlstedt, offers instruction at all levels. Exceptional value deals are available, especially off-season, from May to mid-December—some condos less than $50 per night. Full resort amenities are also offered.

The **Grenelefe Golf & Tennis Resort,** 3200 Fla. 546, Haines City, FL 33844 (☎ 941/422-7511, or 800/237-9549), has 20 courts with clay, grass, and hard surfaces. Instruction is available. The resort hosts many adult and junior USTA tournaments.

The **Sanibel Harbour Resort & Spa,** 17260 Harbour Pointe Rd., Fort Myers, FL 33908 (☎ 941/466-4000, or 800/767-7777), is a luxury resort hotel, but its rates compare very favorably with others of this quality. Twice the site of Davis Cup matches, the Sanibel Harbour has a 5,500-seat stadium and 13 courts. Under the stadium is a 40,000-square-foot full-service spa for serious workouts and after-the-match pampering. Private and group lessons, with video analysis, are available.

5 Boating & Sailing

There's hardly a waterfront resort or beach town in Florida that doesn't offer sailing courses and rentals. Since the trend is for independent outfitters to run the concessions, you no longer have to be a hotel guest to participate. The sheltered Gulf of Mexico, the wilder Atlantic, the exciting (and unpredictable) Keys, and the inland lakes offer different experiences for novices and experienced sailors alike.

If you're staying in an expensive area, rent your boat in a less costly area nearby— for example, boat rentals cost considerably less in Fort Myers and Naples than on Sanibel and Captiva islands, although they share the same waters.

Send for "Boat Registration and Regulations," free from the **Department of Environmental Protection,** 3900 Commonwealth Blvd., Mail Station 660, Tallahassee, FL 32399 (☎ 904/488-1195). At the same address, the **Florida Marine Patrol** (☎ 904/488-5600) publishes a free *Florida Boater's Guide* with tips about safe boating in the state.

Key West keeps gaining prominence as a world sailing capital. *Yachting* magazine sponsors the largest winter regatta in America there each January, and smaller events take place regularly. It takes tremendous skill to navigate offshore around the Keys—even lifelong sailors know when to postpone an outing because of rough conditions.

Steve and Doris Colgate's **Offshore Sailing School** is headquartered at the South Seas Plantation, Captiva Island, 16731 McGregor Blvd., Ft. Myers, FL 33908 (☎ 941/221-4326). Steve, an Americas Cup and Olympic sailor, started his schools 30 years ago and has been conducting classes at South Seas for more than 20 years. Some 75,000 people hold Offshore Sailing School diplomas. Whether you've never been on a sailboat before or you're an old hand ready to move into racing, there's a class for you. There's a four-to-one student/teacher ratio, and the team offers weekend, week-long, and longer programs, including a live-aboard cruise that takes you to the British Virgin Islands for your "final exam." Classes are held all year; best prices are off-season, June to October.

The prestigious **Annapolis Sailing School** has two locations in Florida: one at the Days Inn Resort in Clearwater, and the other at Faro Blanco Oceanside, Marathon, in the Keys. The 14 course plans range from basic to the most advanced, including live-aboard programs. A weekend introductory course costs $225, and depending on your progress and general conditions, you could be sailing a 24-foot day sailer on your own at the end of the second day. For a brochure package call the school's head-quarters in Annapolis (☎ **800/638-9192**).

You can charter your own sailing or yachting vessel at marinas up and down both coasts. The largest charter company in the world has a location on Tampa Bay. You can charter bareboat, skippered, or full-crewed (captain and cook) 31- to 51-foot sail-boats, and fly-sail packages are available. The cruising area ranges from the Tampa Bay area to the Barrier Islands and, for experienced sailors, to the Keys. Contact **The Moorings,** 19345 U.S. 19 North, Clearwater, FL 34624 (☎ **813/530-5424** or 800/ 535-7289).

Houseboating is a popular Florida adventure. Two particularly nice spots are along the St. Johns River in the northeastern part of the state and at the Flamingo Lodge in the southernmost part of the Everglades. Rates in the Everglades range from $860 to $1,550 per week, fully equipped except for food. (Rates for the fancier craft on the river start at $1,095 for a week.) Shorter rentals, including one company's "mini-weekend" (from 10am Saturday to 4pm Sunday) are available at $499 and up. No special licensing is required, but expect preboarding briefings, hefty deposits, and strict cancellation policies. During the winter season, bookings are often needed 6 months or more in advance, so it pays to call well ahead of your Florida vacation. It's always possible, though, to walk up and take your chances, especially during the summer months. Contact **Houseboat Vacations of the Florida Keys,** Mile Marker 85.9, Islamorada, FL 33036 (☎ **305/664-4009**), or **Hontoon Landing Marina,** 2317 River Ridge Rd., Deland, FL 32720 (☎ **904/734-2474**).

SUGGESTED READING   The annual *Florida Cruising Directory* ($9.95) is a trea-sure trove of charts and tables; Coast Guard customs and regulations; locations of marinas, hotels, and resorts; sources of marine products and services; and more in magazine format. Pick it up at a bookstore or marina.

6 Canoeing & Kayaking

The picturesque rivers and sandy coastlines that grace the Florida map, its magnifi-cent Lake Okeechobee (the Big "O"), the winding canoe trails through the marshes of northern and Central Florida, and the mangroves of Southwest Florida give almost unlimited options to the canoer and kayaker. Many parks and preserves, particularly the Ten Thousand Islands, the Everglades, and J. N. (Ding) Darling Wildlife Ref-uge have exceptional canoe and kayak trails. Another favorite among locals is Myakka River State Park near Sarasota, with some 28,000 acres of pure Southwest Florida backcountry, and the aptly named Peace River near Arcadia.

Want white water? There are only three white-water rivers in the state, all served by **Canoe Outpost Suwannee River,** Rte. 1, Box 98A, Live Oak, FL 32060 (☎ **904/364-4991,** or 800/428-4147), which offers 7- and 13-mile day trips.

North American Canoe Tours, Inc., P.O. Box 5038, Everglades City, FL 33929 (☎ **941/695-4666** November to April, 203/739-0791 May to October), offers 4-day and week-long guided expeditions via canoe through the Everglades as well as 1-day excursions (see also Chapter 9).

Most major parks and preserves offer canoe and/or kayak rentals. Costs start at under $15 for a 2-hour rental, often with reduced rates for additional hours. Basic equipment included are paddles, life jackets, and sometimes maps and charts. Overnight to week-long rentals are often available, and some are quite comprehensive. In Everglades National Park, for instance, you can rent a canoe outfitted with basic camping gear for about $50 a day.

Some 36 creek and river trails, covering about 950 miles altogether, are itemized in the excellent free "Canoe Trails" booklet published by the **Florida Department of Natural Resources, Office of Communications,** 3900 Commonwealth Blvd., Tallahassee, FL 32399 (☎ **904/488-6327**). Included in the booklet are valuable tips, from common sense (don't canoe flooded rivers) to legal advice (Florida law requires a Coast Guard–approved personal flotation device for each occupant) to practical (allow a minimum of 2 miles per hour of canoeing time under normal river conditions; add an extra hour to a 3-hour trip if you're traveling against the wind and tide).

Many conservation groups throughout the state offer half-day, full-day, and overnight canoe trips (see "Field Trips & Eco-Tours," later in this chapter). Others offer short guided tours, some free and some at a small fee. Even privately owned recreation companies offer "introductory" tours and excursions at no charge periodically during the month, and particularly during festival weeks. Value Rent-a-Car and American Express sponsor the annual "Florida Value Activities Guide," which lists free and low-cost nature tours. It's available from the **Florida Department of Commerce, Division of Tourism,** 107 W. Gaines St., Suite 543, Tallahassee, FL 32399. City and county chambers of commerce in the areas you plan to visit are also rich resources for low-cost eco-touring. For addresses, see the appropriate sections of this book.

7 Camping in Florida's State Parks

About half of Florida's 110 state parks have camping facilities. Options range from full-facilities camping with most of the conveniences of home to primitive island and beach camping with essentially no facilities. A free reference book is published by the **Florida Park Service,** 3900 Commonwealth Blvd., MS 535, Tallahassee, FL 32399 (☎ **904/488-9872**), categorizing all the state parks by region and special interest. The book highlights the scenic, cultural, and offbeat activities available in the various state parks.

For a comprehensive listing of privately owned campgrounds and RV parks, send for the official *Florida Camping Directory,* available from the **Florida Association of RV Parks and Campgrounds,** 1340 Vickers Rd., Tallahassee, FL 32303 (☎ **904/562-7151**). Another resource is the **Florida Campground Association,** 1638 N. Plaza Dr., Tallahassee, FL 32308.

For excellent color maps of Florida's state parks, canoe trails, aquatic preserves, caverns, and more, contact the **Florida Department of Natural Resources, Office of Communications,** Marjory Stoneman Douglas Building, 3900 Commonwealth Blvd., Tallahassee, FL 32399 (☎ **904/488-6327**). It also publishes a guide to tent and RV sites in Florida's state parks.

Camping is allowed on 4 out of the top 10 beaches: St. Andrews State Recreation Area, Caladesi Island State Park, St. Joseph Peninsula State Park, and Bill Baggs Cape Florida Recreation Area. St. Andrews State Recreation Area in Panama City Beach, with its magnificent dunes, was named the nation's best beach last year.

Primitive camping in St. Joseph Peninsula State Park in Port St. Joe is a bird-watcher's dream. Boat camping is available in several parks, such as Caladesi Island State Park, one of the few remaining undeveloped barrier islands on Florida's Gulf Coast. The banks of Stephen Foster's Suwannee River, which runs 245 miles from the town of Suwannee into Georgia's portion of the Okefenokee Swamp, are loaded with great places to camp or lodge at budget prices.

One of the most exciting backcountry camping experiences is a chickee hut on stilts in Everglades National Park. They're accessible only by canoe and the facilities include no hookups and cold showers only. Reservations are required. Contact **Everglades National Park Headquarters,** 40001 Fla. 9336, Homestead, FL 33034 (☎ **305/242-7700**).

Pets are not permitted in state park camping areas or on the bathing beaches.

STATE PARK RATES & HOURS   Out-of-state visitors pay the same fee as Florida residents year round to use state park camping and other facilities. Reservations for camping spaces can be made by telephone up to 60 days in advance. Cabins are the hottest commodity; reservations are taken up to a year in advance and a deposit equal to a 2-night stay is required. Personal checks, MasterCard, and Visa are accepted. Cabins sometimes become available on short notice, so it doesn't hurt to call. The rates vary according to season, site, number of people, use of electricity, and extra vehicles—and are subject to change. About half the parks charge $8 to $10 per night; others range from $14 to $19 per night. Cabins range from $20 to $110, depending on the facility and location. The parks are open from 8am to sunset 365 days a year.

Note: National park fees are often lower than state park fees, and in many cases national parks are free. You may want to purchase a good guide to national parks. An excellent one is the *Complete Guide to America's National Parks,* National Park Foundation, 1101 17th St. NW, Washington, DC 20036.

8 Field Trips & Eco-Tours

The Florida chapter of the Nature Conservancy has protected 578,000 acres of natural lands in Florida and presently owns and manages 36 preserves. For a small fee, you can join one of its field trips or work parties that take place periodically throughout the year. Participants get a chance to learn about and even participate in the preservation of the ecosystem. The cost of an average half-day excursion, involving a hike, four-wheel-drive excursion, walk, and/or boat tour, is $8. Some of the longer or more elaborate trips can cost up to $40. Two of the Nature Conservancy's most fascinating preserves are Blowing Rocks Preserve and the newly opened, 11,500-acre Disney Wilderness Preserve, each briefly described here. For details of all the preserves and adventures, contact **The Nature Conservancy, Florida Chapter,** 222 S. Westmonte Dr., Suite 300, Altamonte Springs, FL 32714 (☎ **407/682-3664**).

The **Sierra Club,** Dept. J-319, P.O. Box 7959, San Francisco, CA 94120 (☎ **415/923-5653**), America's oldest and largest grassroots environmental organization, offers exceptional eco-adventures through its Florida chapters. You can canoe or kayak through the Everglades, hike the Florida Trail in America's southernmost national forest, camp on a barrier island, or explore the sinkhole phenomenon in north central Florida.

Several local chapters throughout Florida conduct day trips or weekend outings with some prices as low as $2—and you don't have to be a member. Some recent programs included a wild pig, armadillo, and vegetarian roast; a 15-mile night hike to listen for owls; and a 4-day birding trip to the Dry Tortugas. For a truly hands-on experience, you can participate in a "service program," helping to restore marine wetlands, clean up beaches and mangrove swamps, etc. Prices start around $50. You do have to be a Sierra Club member to participate in these programs, and you can join at the time of the trip. Membership is $15 for students and seniors, $35 for adults, $43 for joint memberships. Advance signup is essential; if possible, contact the **Florida outings leader** before you leave home (☎ 813/746-6563). Write or phone the national office in San Francisco for a current outings magazine and local chapter contacts.

All Florida Adventure Tours, 8263B SW 107th Ave., Miami, FL 33173 (☎ 305/270-0219, or 800/338-6873), offers recreational and educational tours that emphasize local and environmental education.

"Soft" eco-adventure experiences are available, too. **Silver Springs,** P.O. Box 370, Silver Springs, FL 34489 (☎ 904/236-2121, or 800/234-7458), a 350-acre nature theme park, has been conducting eco-tours since before the term was invented. You can take a sunrise breakfast cruise to photograph great blue herons, white-tail deer, and other wildlife, or take a "Jungle Cruise" or "Jeep Safari" to get a feeling of the ecosystem without getting your feet dirty.

In **Blowing Rocks Preserve,** on Jupiter Island, an amazing outcropping of Anastazia limestone stands in dramatic contrast to the typical sandy coastline along Florida's Atlantic coast. Created by a gradual cementation of marine sediments and the force of wind and tides, the result is dramatic, especially when high seas breaking against the rocks force tons of water skyward in spectacular saltwater plumes. The preserve protects an important habitat for West Indian manatees and loggerhead turtles. Hiking, fishing, snorkeling, diving, and swimming are allowed in the park. Contact **Preserve Manager,** Blowing Rocks Preserve, P.O. Box 3795, Tequesta, FL 33469 (☎ 407/575-2297).

The **Disney Wilderness Preserve,** 6075 Scrub Jay Trail, Kissimmee, FL 34759 (☎ 407/935-0005), is located along the Osceola/Polk County line in the Upper Kissimmee Chain of Lakes. Headwaters of the Florida Everglades system, this mosaic of native communities ranging from freshwater marshes to dry prairies harbors some 160 animal species. Litigation orchestrated by the Nature Conservancy saved the land from the double impact of Disney development and the enlargement of Orlando International Airport.

Uninhabited **Cayo Costa State Island Preserve,** in Boca Grande, is a great place to base yourself for backcountry canoeing. A huge variety of sea and shore birds congregate at the tip of the Ten Thousand Islands, which begin around Sanibel/Captiva and their neighbors Useppa, Cabbage Key, Gasparilla, and Cayo Costa and continue deep into the Everglades. Camping and a few very rustic cabins are available. Guides are easy to find through the Boca Grande (Gasparilla) and Sanibel chambers of commerce; highly recommended are Capts. Duke Sells and Mike Fuery, based at the 'Tween Waters Inn on Captiva. The Tropic Star at the Four Winds Marina on Pine Island runs eco-tours through the islands and ferries campers back and forth to Cayo Costa.

A huge cluster of wildlife refuges, millions of acres of them on federally protected lands, draw eco-tourists from around the world to **Everglades National Park**. Naples and Everglades City are the northern gateway to the Everglades. To the north are the Big Cypress National Preserve and the Big Cypress Swamp, the National Audubon Society Corkscrew Swamp Sanctuary (see "Bird & Wildlife Watching," later in this chapter), and the Collier Seminole State Park near Marco Island.

The Upper Keys embrace the southern boundary of **Everglades National Park,** where visitors will see manatees, dolphin, occasionally an endangered Key deer and smaller animals, and hundreds of species of birds. Canoes, some rustic accommodations, and tent camping are available, and there are plenty of budget lodgings just outside the park. Enter the park about 10 miles south of Homestead.

Note: Avoid taking the airboat tours of this area—they damage and pollute the fragile ecosystem and some of them defy the rules by throwing out marshmallows to lure alligators, a dangerous practice. Better options are the outfitters that use Waverunners, Zodiac inflatable craft, catamarans, canoes, kayaks, or pontoons.

Nearly anywhere you leave the clutter of the Overseas Highway (U.S. 1) you'll be richly rewarded by the subtropical ambience, birds, and wildlife of the **Florida Keys,** free for the looking. The entire lower half of the Keys on the gulf side is designated the Great White Heron National Refuge, and numerous other preserves here offer good opportunities to view these magnificent birds and other wildlife.

MORE INFORMATION   The **Florida Conservation Foundation, Inc.,** 1191 Orange Ave., Winter Park, FL 32789 (☎ **407/644-5377**), publishes information about the state's ecology, including "Common Florida Natural Areas," an illustrated brochure explaining what you'll find in each ecosystem.

9 Hiking on Your Own

There are thousands of beautiful hiking trails in Florida. The ideal hiking months are October to April, when the weather is cool and dry and the mosquitoes are less evident. Some trails are gentle and short; others are challenging—some trails in the Everglades require you to wade waist-deep in water! It's important to know what's ahead before you venture out. The **Florida Trail Association,** P.O. Box 13708, Gainesville, FL 32604 (☎ **904/378-8823** or 800/343-1882), maintains a large percentage of the public trails in the state, and it puts out an excellent book packed with maps, details, and color photos. For a copy of "Florida Trails," contact the **Florida Department of Commerce, Division of Tourism,** Direct Mail, 126 W. Van Buren St., Tallahassee, FL 32399 (☎ **904/488-5607** or 800/785-4465).

The Florida Trail Association offers the following trail etiquette:

- Pack in / pack out.
- Don't feed wild animals.
- Native plants and animals are protected in state and federal parks. Don't take anything out of the park.
- If you're building a campfire (where allowed), use only dead-and-down wood. Camp stoves are preferred.

For a copy of *A Guide to Your National Scenic Trail,* write to **Office of Greenways and Trails, Dept. of Environmental Protection,** Mail Station 795, 3900 Commonwealth Blvd., Tallahassee, FL 32399 (☎ **904/487-4784**). Another information source is **National Forests in Florida,** Woodcrest Office Park, 325 John Knox Rd., Suite F-100, Tallahassee, FL 32303 (☎ **904/942-9300**).

10 Birding & Wildlife Watching

In their book the *Florida Wildlife Viewing Guide,* Susan Cerulean and Ann Morrow profile 96 great parks, refuges, and preserves throughout the state. The authors give detailed descriptions of the facilities and specifics on the birds, animals, and marine life you're likely to encounter. They also offer tips on planning your trip. For instance, to observe sea turtle nests, come in summer; if you're interested in hawks, September and October are good migration months. They also cover the proper methods of tracking, stalking, and calling animals. The book is available through the **Madalyn Baldwin Center for Birds of Prey,** located behind the Audubon House just off East Avenue in Maitland (☎ **407/260-8300,** or 800/874-BIRD). This emergency room, hospital, and rehabilitation center for raptors is open to the public free of charge Tuesday to Saturday. Guided tours and off-site programs are available.

A wealth of Florida birding tips is available free from the **Florida Audubon Society,** 460 Fla. 436, Suite 200, Casselberry, FL 32707 (☎ **407/260-8300**).

The National Audubon Society's Florida chapter manages four exceptional sites worth visiting: Besides the Madalyn Baldwin Center in Maitland, there are the Turkey Creek Wildlife Sanctuary in Palm Bay, Corkscrew Swamp Sanctuary near Naples, and Sabal Point Wildlife Sanctuary on the Wekiva River in Central Florida.

The following are a few of the top-rated birding spots around the state:

The **Apalachicola National Forest,** a 193,000-acre forest south of Tallahassee, is the largest national estuarine sanctuary in the United States. Some 250 species of birds and 900 species of fish thrive here, including several endangered species. The wildlife-rich seashore to the south is a nature lover's paradise. Canoeing and birding are superb on the four adjacent barrier islands, especially Dog Island, accessible only by boat. Birders also get close sightings at St. Marks, about 15 miles south of Tallahassee.

The **Cedar Keys National Wildlife Refuge** on Cedar Key is accessible only by boat. This collection of islands shelters some 200,000 nesting birds in winter. Because public access is limited, the shelling is also excellent on these island beaches.

The **J. N. (Ding) Darling National Wildlife Refuge** on Sanibel Island is renowned as the shelling paradise of North America. A lesser-known fact is that 40% of the island is a wildlife preserve. The nearly 5,000-acre refuge is rich in barrier-island wildlife such as roseate spoonbill, osprey, shore birds, white pelicans, ducks, loons, and mangrove cuckoos. Visitors can hike, bike, or canoe through the park (rentals are available), and there are several boardwalk trails winding through mangrove swamp.

A huge variety of sea and shore birds congregate on **Cayo Costa Island,** a state preserve encompassing one of the northernmost of the Ten Thousand Islands. This uninhabited island is accessible only via boat. Primitive camping is available. See "Field Trips & Eco-tours," earlier in this chapter, for more details.

The **Canaveral National Seashore / Merritt Island,** in Titusville, is located midway between Jacksonville and Palm Beach. Canaveral National Seashore, with Merritt Island to the south—together running about 30 miles along the coast—are said to be a haven for more federally protected endangered species than any other refuge in the United States. The park has beautiful backcountry camping spots and hiking trails. Expect to see western Indian manatees, southern bald eagles, and Atlantic loggerhead turtles.

The **Corkscrew Swamp Sanctuary** is a wood stork nesting ground. In fact, it's the largest colony of endangered birds in North America. Only a small part of the 11,000-acre sanctuary is open to the public via self-guided walks.

The northern entrance to **Everglades National Park** is in Everglades City. The **Big Cypress Swamp** area offers close-up views of manatees and dolphins, great blue heron, snowy egret, white pelicans, and hundreds of other species. More than 350 species of birds live in the Everglades, and there are a dozen ways to see them. The park hands out free checklists to keep track of them.

Fort Jefferson / The Dry Tortugas, 70 miles west of Key West, offers extraordinary views of migratory birds of all types. Spring and fall are the best times for viewing. For serious birders, live-aboard boat trips cruising the islands depart Key West regularly. Campers used to roughing it can stay over at Fort Jefferson at no charge; be aware, however, that there are no facilities here except rest rooms and grills.

11 Offbeat Vacations & Other Options

BICYCLING TRIPS **Vermont Bicycle Touring,** P.O. Box 711, Bristol, VT 05443 (☎ 802/453-4811, or 800/537-3850), offers deluxe Florida bike tours for cyclists at all fitness levels.

HORSEBACK RIDING & DUDE RANCHES Some 15 state parks have equestrian trails, and several have staging areas/corrals and overnight camping. To bring a horse into a state park, you must have proof of a recent negative Coggins (sleeping sickness) test.

The **Circle F Dude Ranch,** P.O. Box 54784, Orlando, FL 32854 (☎ 407/299-2136), is laid-back and simple, with bunkhouse accommodations. You get a lot for your money at the Circle F. Besides riding, there's tennis, lake sailing, and campfire programs for adults. It also offers summer camps for kids. One weekend getaway deal is $175 per person, covering 2 nights' accommodations, five meals, entertainment, and all amenities.

For a taste of Old Florida, "Back in the Saddle . . . in Florida" is a dream adventure, worth the splurge. From horseback rides along the beach to dinner on a Seminole reservation, from rope and six-shooter shows to dairy farm tours and bass fishing, this 100-mile-plus week-long trek covers the backroads of Florida where real cowboys still live. By day you're on the trail; at night, a comfortable hotel room awaits. There were six safaris (groups of about 14 each) in 1996, three going coast to coast in 8 days and three going from Lake Okeechobee to the gulf in 6 days. The gateway is Fort Myers. Prices start at $1,570 all-inclusive. Itineraries and suggested reading lists are available from **Royal Palm Tours,** P.O. Box 60079, Ft. Myers, FL 33906 (☎ 941/368-0760).

SWIMMING WITH DOLPHINS The **Dolphin Research Center,** Mile Marker 59, Overseas Highway, Grassy Key, FL 33050 (☎ 305/289-1121), an educational/research facility, offers guided walking tours of its premises five times a day Wednesday to Sunday; the cost is $9.50 for adults, $7.50 for seniors over 55, $6 for children 4 to 12, free for children 3 and under. The organization's Dolphin Insight Program, held three times a week, allows visitors to touch and interact with the dolphins—but not to get into the water with them. The cost is $75 per person, advance reservations are required, and it's recommended that children be at least 12 to participate. Especially popular is the Dolphin Encounter, a program that allows visitors to actually swim with dolphins. Advance reservations are required, and the center starts taking them the first day of the month for dates available the following month (for example, call March 1 to make April reservations). The cost is $90 per person; children must be at least 5 years old, and those 11 or under must be accompanied by a paying adult.

Even the sportiest beach outfitters are now offering "ecologically responsible" tours. For instance, **FUN Rentals** (☎ 941/463-4441), which has concessions on several beaches around the state, offers a dolphin-watch excursion from Fort Myers Beach into the back bays, where a friendly pod of dolphins responds to the sound of the Waverunners and swims over to show off for the visitors. The guide gives a dolphin lesson and explains their habitat while pointing out specific dolphins and describing their personalities. It's particularly popular with families, school groups, and seniors.

A DAY AT THE SPA Florida has more top-rated spas than any other state. Most are attached to luxurious hotels or resorts and are expensive, but the good news is that you don't necessarily have to be a resident spa guest to be pampered with an herbal wrap, massage, or other mind-body therapy. The following are some of my favorite spas that offer day rates and special packages that might just appeal to the bone-weary diver, golfer, or camper. Half-day rates, which typically include a massage and one other treatment, an exercise class, and use of the steam, sauna, and fitness equipment, average about $75 to $100.

Tip: If you schedule an à la carte service only, you often get to use the facilities, too. Safety Harbor, for instance, has a $23 deal which includes an exercise class, sauna, and use of the Jacuzzi and pool. In some cases, if you know a member you can go as a guest for a small fee, about $25 to $30. Package prices are lowest off-season, April to December.

The **Bonaventure Spa & Fitness Resort,** 250 Racquet Club Rd., Fort Lauderdale, FL 33326 (☎ **954/389-3300,** or 800/327-8090), a 500-room luxury resort on 1,250 acres, is renowned as one of the best spas in North America. Day packages include the "Mini-Perfect Day," "Perfect Day," "Golf Perfect Day," and "Tennis Perfect Day," each including spa treatments, lunch, and use of sauna, steam, plunge pools, Siesta Room, exercise equipment, and spa clothing.

The **Palm-Aire Spa,** 2601 Palm-Aire Dr. North, Pompano Beach, FL 33069 (☎ **954/977-7763,** or 800/2-PALM-AIR), is an east coast spa favored by the rich and famous. The Palm-Aire offers all imaginable spa services, including massages, facial masks, herbal wraps, scrubs, essential-oil hydrotherapy baths, and Swiss needle showers.

The **Safety Harbor Resort and Spa,** 105 N. Bayshore Dr., Safety Harbor, FL 34695 (☎ **813/726-1161,** or 800/237-0155), is tucked away off the beaten track amid moss-draped oaks and cobblestone streets. Safety Harbor was built around natural healing springs that date back to Hernando de Soto.

When world-class spas are rated internationally, **The Spa at Doral,** 8755 NW 36th St., Miami, FL 33178 (☎ **305/592-2000,** or 800/331-7768), consistently lands on top. The ambience is pure luxury—marble, crystal, formal gardens, soft-spoken white-clad therapists, and a color-coordinated spa wardrobe for you. The healing muds and minerals used are imported from the ancient volcanic pools of Saturnia, home of the Doral Spa's sibling spa, the Terme di Saturnia, in Tuscany. You can get a taste of the supreme pampering with day programs starting at $99.

ADVENTURE TOUR OPERATORS **Florida Outback Safaris,** 6440 SW 42nd St., Davie, FL 33314 (☎ **305/792-7393,** or 800/423-9944), offers camping, canoeing, tubing, snorkeling, marine biology programs, paleontology trips, and excursions in Florida's Everglades and Keys as well as throughout the state.

Rock Rest Adventures, Rte. 2, Box 424, Pittsboro, NC 27312 (☎ **919/542-5502**), offers 5- to 7-day canoeing, kayaking, and camping adventures in Florida's Everglades and Keys.

Camping, snorkeling, and other adventure trips—including Everglades hiking, canoeing, and kayaking—can be arranged through **Wilderness Southeast,** 711 Sandtown Rd., Savannah, GA 31410 (☎ **912/897-5108**).

Passport Travel & Tours (☎ **800/549-8687**) operates a 1-week Florida Wildlife Tour each February. It originates in Miami and visits Everglades National Park, the J. N. (Ding) Darling National Wildlife Refuge on Sanibel Island, Corkscrew Swamp Sanctuary near Naples, Merritt Island National Wildlife Refuge near Titusville, and Blue Springs State Park near Daytona Beach.

Settling into Miami

by Victoria Pesce Elliot

Sometimes it's hard to know which language to use to introduce yourself in this polyglot mini-nation. Here you'll find a curious mix of retirees seeking easier winters, models, movie actors and executives, artists, wealthy real-estate moguls, Caribbean immigrants, and Hispanics, all layered on top of an already-diverse crowd of Florida "crackers"—pioneer settlers who were so named because they were said to carry crackers with them as they traveled Florida's swampy terrain—Native Americans, and the descendents of Bahamian railroad workers and African-Americans who came here fleeing slavery. You'll hear Spanish, French, Portuguese, and Créole. The city is a virtual mosaic of colors, sounds, and scents.

And although there are some who lament "It's just not like it used to be," the truth is that ever since the Spanish first colonized the area in the 16th century, Miami has been a magnet for a diverse population of runaways, castaways, and dreamers. Through its many incarnations, two things have remained constant—its predictable year-round warmth and its location on a peninsula that points emphatically toward the nations southward.

"The Capital of the Americas," as it's known, Miami now serves as Latin American and international headquarters for hundreds of multinational corporations, and it's the second-largest banking center in the United States. Encompassing both the mainland and the barrier islands of Miami Beach, Greater Miami now boasts about two million residents and hosts nearly nine million visitors annually. Since 1980 Dade County's population, with Miami as its largest municipality, has grown nearly 33%.

In recent years Miami has had a spate of publicity—some good and some bad. In the 1980s the news of a rash of tourist murders resulted in a sharp drop in the number of international visitors coming to the city, and to the state overall.

More recently Miami has made the news for more positive reasons. The Summit of the Americas in 1994 brought together more than 30 heads of state from throughout the Western Hemisphere, the city hosted tens of thousands of sports fans for the Superbowl in 1995, and in 1996 extravagant celebrations, including an 850-pound cake, helped mark the city's Centennial. On the sports front, a new celebrity-coach, Pat Riley, has joined the Miami basketball team, the Heat, along with a new star player, center

Alonzo Mourning. And Jimmy Johnson has taken over the Dolphins. Also, in 1996 Miami Beach was chosen as the site for MTV's *The Real World*.

As a result of all this attention, thousands of visitors have seen for the first time the splendor of South Florida and many are returning for more.

Since the television hit *Miami Vice* spotlighted the quirky and colorful city as a haven for drug dealers and killers, filmmakers have found it hard to resist the rich texture and year-round accessibility of Miami as a backdrop. The Miami Office of Film, Television and Print issued a total of about 350 permits in 1985. Ten years later, in 1995, it issued nearly 5,000 permits for everything from movies to television programs and magazine shoots. Now many celebrities like Sylvester Stallone, Madonna, Cher, and Whitney Houston, who passed through during a film shoot, call Miami their home.

1 Budget Bests & Discounts

Long a haven for retirees, Miami offers discounts on almost everything from dinners to attractions for senior citizens. In addition to the numerous early-bird dinner specials, most places honor AARP membership as well.

Students, too, can get a break at most attractions and some restaurants, especially near the local colleges, in downtown Miami and Coral Gables.

Check the *Miami Herald* and *New Times* for coupons and specials at restaurants, nightclubs, and attractions.

Airlines fight perpetual price wars to woo tourists to the Sunshine State. In fact, airfares are so competitive that, unless you're visiting from an adjacent state, flying to Miami will almost always be your most economical option. However, take a look at your alternatives, too. An overland journey to Florida's Gold Coast is both a more scenic and a more flexible way to travel. Greyhound/Trailways offers several types of bus passes, and Amtrak offers a host of rail services to Miami.

2 Orientation

ARRIVING

BY PLANE Carved out of scrubland in 1928 by Pan American Airlines, **Miami International Airport (MIA)** has emerged as one of the busiest airports in the world. Unfortunately, as it undergoes major reconstruction to expand its facilities, the airport can feel like a maze, with inadequate signage and surly employees. The airport is located about 6 miles west of downtown and about 12 miles from the beaches, so it's likely that you can get from the plane to your hotel room in less than an hour. If you're arriving from an international destination, you'll have to go through Customs and Immigration, a process that can double your time in the airport.

Tourist information booths are located on the lower levels of Concourses B, D, E, and G. You can use your Honor or Plus System ATM card, and international travelers can change money at Barnett Bank of South Florida, located near the exit.

Lockers are located at the end of each of the airport's concourses and are available for use to passengers with a valid ticket to or from Miami. For $1 you can stow carry-on size bags or parcels for up to 24 hours. If you need to store bigger items for a longer time, find one of the three attended baggage storage areas. The round-the-clock storage area is on the first level of concourse G. Two others, on the lower level of concourse H or the second level at concourse B, are open from 8am until 9pm. Passengers can store suitcases, boxes and bags for up to 90 days in any of the three newly expanded luggage storage spaces. Prices for storage start at $2 a day for items between one and 18 inches long. Larger items cost up to $16 a day. Although there is no specified limit to the size of items that can be left, one attendant warned, "You can't leave, like, a house." Call for more information, since security concerns may require an alteration of current standards (☎ **305/876-7360**).

Virtually every major **car-rental company** has a desk at Miami airport. If you're renting a car, take one of the free shuttles to the rental site. Buses and vans, clearly marked with rental-car logos, circle the airport regularly and stop at the wave of a hand. Make sure you get a free map and clear directions to your destination before you leave the car-rental desk; bright-orange sunbursts at the exit point the way to tourist-friendly zones of the city, but they can still be confusing.

Multipassenger vans circle the arrivals area looking for fares. Destinations are posted on the front of each van, and a flat rate is charged for door-to-door service to the area marked. **SuperShuttle** (☎ **305/871-2000**) is one of the largest operators, charging between $10 and $20 per person for a ride within Dade County. Its vans operate 24 hours a day and accept American Express, MasterCard, and Visa.

Public transportation, though not very efficient, is available. Buses heading downtown leave from the arrivals level. **Bus no. 7** to downtown leaves the airport every 40 minutes Monday to Friday from 5:30am to 8:30pm and on Saturday and Sunday from 7am to 7pm. **Bus J** heads south to Coral Gables every 30 minutes from about 6am to midnight, and east to Miami Beach every 30 minutes from about 5:30am to 11:30pm. **Bus no. 42** goes to Coconut Grove hourly from 5:30am to 6:30pm. All city buses cost $1.25 and exact change is required.

Taxis line up in front of a dispatcher's desk outside the airport's arrivals terminals. Cabs are metered and will cost about $14 to Coral Gables, $22 to downtown, $24 to South Miami Beach, and $30 to Key Biscayne. Tip 10% to 15%.

Safety   Board buses and taxis at the airport only at authorized pickup points. Avoid anyone who solicits you with low-cost transportation services. When arriving in Miami late in the evening, consider shuttling to your hotel by taxi, then renting a car the next day when you have the time to read a map and familiarize yourself with the city. Many rental agencies will deliver a vehicle directly to your hotel.

BY TRAIN   If you're traveling to Miami by train (see "Getting to Florida," in Chapter 3), you'll pull into the **Amtrak Miami terminal** at 8303 NW 37th Ave. (☎ **305/835-1205**). Unfortunately, none of the major car-rental companies has an office at the train station; you'll have to go to the airport to rent a car. **Hertz** (☎ **800/654-3131**) will reimburse part of your cab fare (up to $10) from the train station if you rent from them.

Taxis meet each Amtrak arrival. The fare to downtown will cost about $22; the ride takes less than 20 minutes.

BY BUS   Greyhound (☎ **800/231-2222**) buses pull into a number of stations around the city, including 4111 NW 27 Ave. (airport), 700 Biscayne Blvd. (downtown), and 16560 NE 6th Ave. (North Miami Beach).

BY CAR   No matter where you start your journey, chances are you'll reach Miami by way of **I-95.** This north-south Interstate is the city's lifeline and an integral part of the region. The highway connects all of Miami's neighborhoods, the airport, and the beach; and it connects all of South Florida to the rest of America. Unfortunately, many of Miami's road signs are completely confusing and notably absent when you need them. Take time out to study I-95's route on the map because you'll use it as a reference point time and again.

BY BOAT   If you enter the country on a craft weighing less than 5 tons, the craft must proceed to designated marinas and report to U.S. Customs. The **Haulover Marine Center,** 15000 Collins Ave., Miami Beach (☎ **305/945-3934**), and the **Watson Island Marina,** 1050 MacArthur Causeway, Miami (☎ **305/579-6955**), are the two sanctioned marinas in Greater Miami.

VISITOR INFORMATION

The **Greater Miami Convention and Visitors Bureau,** 701 Brickell Ave., Miami, FL 33131 (☎ **305/539-3063,** or 800/283-2707; e-mail: miami&beaches.com), is the best source of information about the city. Even if you don't have a specific question, you may want to phone ahead for the free magazine *Destination Miami,* which includes several good, clear maps. The office is open Monday to Friday from 9am to 5pm.

For information on traveling in the state as a whole, contact the **Florida Division of Tourism (FDT),** 126 W. Van Buren St., Tallahassee, FL 32399 (☎ **904/ 487-1462**), open Monday to Friday from 8am to 5pm. Europeans should note that the FDT maintains an office in Great Britain at 18/24 Westbourne Grove, 4th Floor, London W2 5RH (☎ **0171/727-1661**).

The **Miami Design Preservation League,** 1001 Ocean Dr. (P.O. Bin L), Miami Beach, FL 33119 (☎ **305/672-2014**), offers an informative guide to the art deco district for $10, as well as several books on the subject. It's open Monday to Saturday from 10am to 7pm.

Greater Miami's various chambers of commerce also send maps and information about their particular parcels. These include the **Coconut Grove Chamber of Commerce,** 2820 McFarlane Rd., Miami, FL 33133 (☎ **305/444-7270**); the **Coral Gables Chamber of Commerce,** 50 Aragon Ave., Coral Gables, FL 33134 (☎ **305/ 446-1657**); the **Florida Gold Coast Chamber of Commerce,** 1100 Kane Concourse (Bay Harbor Islands), Miami, FL 33154 (☎ **305/866-6020**), which represents Bal Harbour, Sunny Isles, Surfside, and other North Dade waterfront communities; the **Greater Miami Chamber of Commerce,** Omni International, 1601 Biscayne Blvd., Miami, FL 33132 (☎ **305/539-3063,** or 800/283-2707); and the **Miami Beach Chamber of Commerce,** 1920 Meridian Ave., Miami Beach, FL 33139 (☎ **305/ 672-1270**).

CITY LAYOUT

It's not difficult to get lost in Miami. If it weren't for the abundance of landmarks— like the ocean and the tall city center—you might easily drive for an hour without noticing that you're traveling in the wrong direction. The city is divided into two parts: a mainland and a barrier island. These two parts are connected by a series of causeways that hopscotch their way across the many artificial islands that dot Biscayne Bay. Miami's international airport and towering city center are located on the mainland. Coconut Grove and Coral Gables, two of the city's most popular neighborhoods, sit more or less adjacent to one another a short drive south of the center. The working-class streets of Little Havana are immediately west of the center, and Little Haiti is immediately north.

The barrier island is divided crosswise into the communities of Miami Beach, Surfside, Bal Harbour, and Sunny Isles—areas that, collectively, are simply called Miami Beach.

FINDING AN ADDRESS   Here's how the city's numbering system works on the mainland: The City of Miami is divided into quadrants—NE, NW, SE, and SW— by the intersection of **Flagler Street and North Miami Avenue.** These two

Miami at a Glance

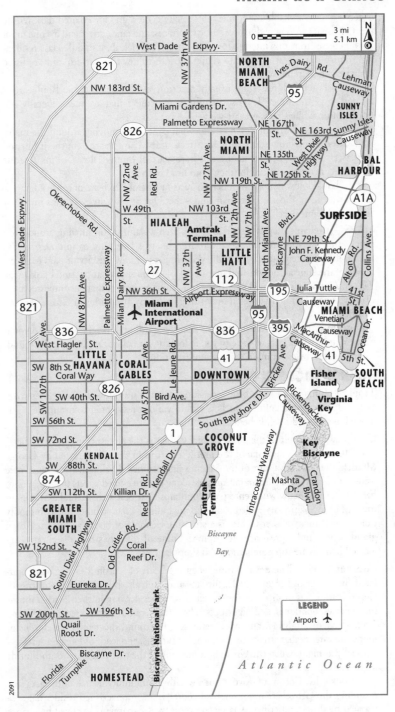

otherwise unremarkable roads meet in the city center, and are colored dark red on most city maps. Along with places, courts, terraces, and lanes, street and avenue numbers increase from this intersection. The streets of Hialeah, a middle-class residential suburb northwest of the city center, do not follow this pattern and are listed separately in map indexes.

Establishment addresses are usually descriptive—12301 Biscayne Boulevard is located at 123rd Street. It's also helpful to remember that avenues generally run north-south, while streets go east-west.

Getting around Miami Beach is somewhat easier than moving around the mainland. Street numbering starts with 1st Street, near Miami Beach's southern tip, and increases to 192nd Street, in the northern part of Sunny Isles. Collins Avenue (Fla. A1A) makes the entire journey from head to toe.

You should know that the numbered streets in Miami Beach are not the geographical equivalents of those on the mainland—the 79th Street Causeway runs into 71st Street on Miami Beach.

MAPS   A reliable map is essential. If you aren't planning on moving around too much, the maps located inside the tourist board's free publication *Destination Miami* may be adequate. If you really want to get to know the city, it pays to invest in one of the large accordion-fold maps available at most gas stations and bookstores. *The Trakker Map of Miami* ($2.50) is a four-color accordion that encompasses all of Dade County, handy if you plan on visiting the many attractions in Greater Miami South.

Some map indexes organize Miami's streets according to neighborhood, so you'll have to know which part of the city you're looking for before the street can be found. All the listings below contain this area information.

NEIGHBORHOODS IN BRIEF

Tropical climate and long beaches aside, Miami's unique identity comes from extremely interesting cultural pockets within various residential communities. The following are listed in alphebetical order.

Coral Gables   Built in the 1920s, Coral Gables is the closest thing to "historical" that Miami has. It's also one of the prettiest parcels in the city. Created by George Merrick, the Gables was one of the Miami's first planned developments. Houses here were built in a unified Mediterranean style along lush tree-lined streets that open onto beautiful plazas, many with centerpiece fountains. The best architectural examples in the area have Spanish-style tiled roofs and are built of a native limestone commonly called "coral rock." Coral Gables is a stunning example of boom architecture on a grand scale—and a great area to explore. Some of the city's best restaurants are located here, as are top hotels and good shopping.

Coconut Grove   There was a time when the heart of Coconut Grove was populated by artists and intellectuals, hippies and radicals. But times have changed. Gentrification has pushed out most alternative types, leaving in their place a multitude of cafés, boutiques, and nightspots. The Grove's hub is the intersection of Grand Avenue, Main Highway, and McFarlane Road. Around this center are dozens of shops and eateries that attract businesspeople, students, and loads of foreign tourists—especially at night, when the Grove becomes one of the best places in South Florida to people-watch.

Paradoxically, Coconut Grove is not a wealthy community. Much of the area surrounding the Grove's rich commercial center is an impoverished residential area plagued by drugs and crime. A large community of Bahamians has lived here since the turn of the century, and today they make up the largest ethnic group living in the Grove. Some wooden Bahamian-style homes, built by early settlers, still stand on Charles Street. Goombay, a lively annual Bahamian festival, celebrates the Grove's Caribbean link and has become one of the largest black-heritage street festivals in America.

Miami Beach The barrier island called Miami Beach is made up of a number of small areas named to attract winter-weary northerners. If you look at a map, you'll see that the island east of the Miami mainland is long and narrow with no real boundaries dividing one city from the next. To tourists in the 1950s, Miami Beach *was* Miami. Its huge, self-contained resort hotels were worlds unto themselves, providing a full day's worth of meals, activities, and entertainment. In the 1960s and 1970s people who fell in love with Miami began to buy apartments rather than rent hotel rooms, and many area hotels converted into condominiums. In the late 1980s Miami Beach began a massive revitalization. Huge beach hotels found international tourist markets, conventions returned, and a new generation of Americans and foreigners discovered the special qualities that made Miami Beach so popular to begin with.

Surfside, Bal Harbour & Sunny Isles These areas lie in the northern part of Miami Beach. Collins Avenue, Miami Beach's most active thoroughfare, crosses town lines without formality, while a long row of similar motels, restaurants, and beaches blur the area's geographical distinctions.

Surfside, packed with moderately priced "resort" motels, is very popular with elderly Canadian and Scandinavian tourists who return to the same rooms year after year. Bal Harbour, the wealthiest community on the beach, is a shopping mecca and the highest net-worth ZIP Code in South Florida. Elegant bayfront homes are clustered on small islands that are part of the city. Sunny Isles, at the far-north end of the beach, is for budgeteers. With some outstanding exceptions, the farther north you go on Miami Beach, the cheaper lodging and eating becomes.

North Dade A suburban area north and west of Miami, it has a number of excellent restaurants and good shopping but very few accommodations, except for the Turnberry resort. Areas include Aventura, North Miami, and North Miami Beach (a residential area on the mainland near the Dade-Broward county line).

South Beach The art deco district has been the most celebrated area in Miami for the last several years. This 15-block area at the southern tip of Miami Beach contains the largest concentration of art deco architecture in the world and was the first 20th-century neighborhood to be put on the Historic Register. South Miami Beach, or South Beach, as the locals call it, is an exciting renaissance community, populated by young investors, artists, and the usual Miami smattering of Cubans, African-Americans, and Caribbeans. Although some public relations person came up with the abbreviation "SoBe," locals wouldn't be caught dead using the term. Hip clubs and cafés are filled with vacationing Europeans, working models, photographers, musicians, and writers who enjoy the exciting and sophisticated atmosphere.

Key Biscayne Located south of Miami Beach, off the shores of Coconut Grove, Key Biscayne is protected from the troubles of the mainland by the long Rickenbacker Causeway and a $1 toll—which the city is considering raising to make the island less accesible. For the most part, the island is an exclusive residential community with million-dollar homes enjoying priceless views. For tourists, this key offers great beaches, a top resort hotel, and a couple of good restaurants. Hobie Beach, adjacent to the causeway, is the city's premier spot for sailboarding and jet skiing. On the island's southern tip is Bill Baggs State Park, a large, wooded preserve with a long beach and quiet bike paths.

Downtown From afar, Miami's downtown coalesces into one of America's most beautiful cityscapes. Inspired high-tech architectural designs make the city almost as beautiful close-up, but Miami's downtown is far from tourist-friendly. Downtown streets are almost always devoid of pedestrian traffic, a fact that's somewhat unsettling. The attractions here are both self-contained and security conscious, and city strollers are not encouraged. Seemingly abandoned on weekends as well as after office hours during the week, most of the area's shops and restaurants cater to the nine-to-five crowd.

Little Haiti Once called Lemon City for all the lemon trees flourishing there, Little Haiti is an economically depressed neighborhood of over 70,000 residents, most of whom are of Haitian origin. During a brief period in the late 1970s and early 1980s as many as 60,000 Haitians resettled in Miami, a large number in this 200-square-block area north of downtown, extending from 41st to 83rd streets, and bordered by I-95 and Biscayne Boulevard.

You can see the remnants of Little Haiti's Iron Market, or Marché au Fer, a colorful tin-roofed shopping bazaar and copy of one of the same name in Port-au-Prince, built in 1990 on NE 2nd Avenue, the region's main thoroughfare. Opened with the promise of becoming the soul of the Haitian community in Miami, the market has been an economic failure and, in a way, a symbol of the difficulties of the community as a whole.

Little Havana Miami's original Cuban center is still the city's most important ethnic enclave. Referred to locally as "Calle Ocho," SW 8th Street, which radiates west from downtown, is the region's main thoroughfare. Car-repair shops, tailors, electronics stores, and inexpensive restaurants all hang signs in Spanish, salsa rhythms thump from radios, and old men in guayaberas chain-smoke cigars over their daily games of dominoes. The area is extremely safe and has some of the best eating spots in town.

Greater Miami South To locals, South Miami is both a specific area, southwest of Coral Gables, and a general region that encompasses all of southern Dade County and includes Kendall, Perrine, Cutler Ridge, and Homestead. For purposes of clarity, this book has grouped all these southern suburbs under the rubric "Greater Miami South." Similar attributes unite the communities: They're heavily residential, and all are packed with condominiums and shopping malls as well as rapidly diminishing acres of farmland. Few tourists stay in these parts, as there is no beach and few cultural offerings. But Greater Miami South does contain many attractions, making it likely that you'll spend some time here during your stay.

3 Getting Around

Unfortunately, the public transportation system in Miami is not very efficient. The biggest and newest system, the Metrorail and Metromover, doesn't go to the beach areas or to the airport. But if you want to maneuver around downtown, you can take advantage of these Disney-like, high-flying rails. It's a great way to see the city.

BY PUBLIC TRANSPORTATION Greater Miami's mass transit system is operated by the **Metro-Dade Transit Agency,** 360 NE 185th St., Miami, FL 33179 (☎ **305/654-6586,** or 305/638-6700 for route information). Free schedules, maps, and a "First-Time Rider's Kit" are available at Government Center Station, 111 NW 1st St., or by mail from the address above. Discounts are offered to senior citizens, students, and those with disabilites; call for information.

BY RAIL   The two rail lines, operated by the **Metro-Dade Transit Agency** (☎ **800/872-7245** for information), run in concert with each other.

Metrorail, the city's modern high-speed commuter train, is a 21-mile elevated line that connects Miami's northern and southern suburbs to downtown and each other. If you're staying in Coral Gables or Coconut Grove, you can park your car at a nearby station and ride the rail downtown. Unfortunately for visitors, the line's usefulness is limited. There are plans to extend the system to service Miami International Airport, but until those tracks are laid, these trains don't go most places that tourists go. Metrorail operates daily from 6am to midnight; trains run every 7½ minutes during rush hours and every 15 minutes at other times. The fare is $1.25.

Metromover, a 4½-mile elevated line, circles the city center in two big loops, and connects with Metrorail at Government Center and Brickell Station. Riding on rubber tires, the single-train car winds past 21 stations and through some of the city's most important business and retail locations, including the Omni International Mall and the Brickell Financial District. At 25¢ a ride, the Disneyesque Metromover is one of Miami's best sightseeing bargains. Service runs daily from 6am to midnight about every 2 minutes. Transfers to Metrorail are $1.

BY BUS   Miami's suburban layout is not conducive to getting around by bus. **Metrobus** provides service with widely varying frequency. Stops are marked by green-and-blue signs that are usually accompanied by route information. Standard bus fare is $1.25, though some express routes charge $2.75, and exact change is required. Transfers cost 25¢. Most buses are wheelchair accessible. Passengers with disabilities, students, and those over 65 pay only 60¢ (10¢ per transfer).

BY CAR   If you want to stay in South Beach, you should dump the car for a few days and save the rental money. Parking is nearly impossible on South Beach, and always expensive. You can get around easily with cabs and bikes. Otherwise, a car is a necessity since Miami is so spread out and its attractions scattered in every region.

Rentals   Every major car-rental company has at least one office in Miami. Consequently, the competition has made the city one of the cheapest places in the world to rent a car. Many firms regularly advertise prices in the neighborhood of $180 per week for their bottom-of-the-line tin can, and it can often be had even cheaper. Rates vary seasonally. See "Getting Around Florida," in Chapter 3, for a list of national car-rental companies. A ubiquitous company is **Enterprise** (☎ **305/534-9037,** or 800/325-8007), which rents cars from dozens of well-placed locations throughout the city and offers extremely competitive rates. During the season you can rent a car for a week for about $180.

Special Driving Rules   In Miami, you can make right turns at red lights, so long as you come to a complete stop first. Anyone sitting in the front seat of a moving car must be buckled up. Children under the age of four must be in a car seat, whether they are seated in the front or back seat.

Safety   When driving around Miami, always have a good map and know where you're going. Be extra-wary when driving through Little Haiti and areas just north or west of downtown. Also see the section on driving safety under "Preparing for Your Trip," in Chapter 3.

Parking   Parking in Miami Beach is a hassle. The space chase gets more frenzied the farther south you go, climaxing day and night on Ocean Drive. On beach-perfect weekends parking is close to impossible. It's good to know about the parking lot on 13th Street, between Collins Avenue and Ocean Drive; it charges $3 on weekdays and $6 on weekends. Metered Miami Beach public parking lots are located along Collins Avenue at 1st, 7th, 21st, 35th, 46th, 53rd, 64th, 73rd, 93rd, 96th, 108th, and 167th streets.

If you do find parking, remember to bring plenty of quarters for the hungry meters. Depending on the block, Miami Beach metered parking is enforced daily, including Sunday and holidays, from 9am to 9pm, and sometimes until midnight.

Valet services at restaurants and nightclubs are commonplace. Expect to pay $5 to $15 for parking in Coconut Grove and on South Miami Beach's Ocean Drive on busy weekend nights.

BY TAXI   If you're not planning on traveling much, an occasional taxi is a good alternative to renting a car. If you plan on spending most of your holiday in South Miami Beach's art deco district, you'd be especially wise to avoid the parking hassles and expense that come with having a car. You may want to rent a car only for the days you choose to venture onto the mainland.

The meter starts at $1.10 for the first one-seventh of a mile, and increases at the rate of $1.75 for each additional mile. Major cab companies include **Metro** (☎ 305/888-8888) and **Yellow** (☎ 305/444-4444). On South Miami Beach, the reigning cab company is **Central** (☎ 305/532-5555).

BY BICYCLE   The sprawling nature of Miami makes distance bicycling both difficult and dangerous, but if you're staying in South Miami Beach or Coral Gables, cycling as a form of local transportation makes good sense. See "Water Sports & Other Activities Indoors & Outdoors," in Chapter 6, for complete information.

ON FOOT   With the exception of isolated pockets in Coconut Grove and South Miami Beach, Miami is not a walker's city. Most attractions are too far apart to make walking feasible. Like the citizens of Los Angeles, most Miamians get into their cars even when going just a few blocks.

FAST FACTS: Miami

American Express   For travel arrangements, traveler's checks, currency exchange, and other member services, Miami offices include 330 Biscayne Blvd., downtown (☎ 305/358-7350); 9700 Collins Ave., Bal Harbour (☎ 305/865-5959); and 32 Miracle Mile, Coral Gables (☎ 305/446-3381). Offices are open Mon–Fri 9am–5pm and Sat 10am–4pm. Bal Harbour also keeps hours Sun noon–6pm.

To report lost or stolen traveler's checks, call 800/221-7282.

Baby-Sitters   Hotels can often recommend a baby-sitter or child-care service. If yours can't, try Central Sitting Agency, 1764 SW 24th St. (☎ 305/856-0550).

Business Hours   Banking hours vary, but most **banks** are open Mon–Fri 9am–3pm. Several stay open until 5pm or so at least one day during the week, and most banks have ATMs for 24-hour banking.

Most **stores** are open daily 10am–6pm; however, there are many exceptions. Shops in the Bayside Marketplace are usually open until 9 or 10pm, as are the boutiques in Coconut Grove. Stores in Bal Harbour and other malls are usually open an extra hour 1 night during the week (usually Thursday).

As far as **business offices** are concerned, Miami is generally a Mon–Fri 9am–5pm town.

Camera Repair   Because of the large fashion industry in South Florida, camera shops abound. The following are known for reliable repair work: Dan's Camera Clinic, at 5142 Biscayne Blvd., downtown (☎ 305/759-2541); World Wide Photo, with various locations, including 219 7th St., South Beach (☎ 305/672-5188); and Aberbach's of Miami Beach, 441 41st St., Miami Beach (☎ 305/532-5446).

Car Rentals See "Getting Around," above.

Convention Center The 1988 reopening of the Miami Beach Convention Center, 1901 Convention Center Dr., Miami Beach, FL 33139 (☎ 305/673-7311), marked the rebirth of South Florida conventioneering. A high-tech "new-deco" facade fronts over a million square feet of exhibition space.

Dentists The East Coast District Dental Society staffs an Emergency Dental Referral Service (☎ 304/285-5470). A&E Dental, 11400 N. Kendall Dr., in the Mega Bank Building (☎ 305/271-7777), also offers round-the-clock care and accepts MasterCard and Visa.

Doctors In an emergency, call an ambulance by dialing **911** from any phone. No coins are required.

The Dade County Medical Association sponsors a Physician Referral Service (☎ 305/324-8717) Mon–Fri 9am–5pm. Health South Doctors' Hospital, 5000 University Dr., Coral Gables (☎ 305/666-2111), is a 285-bed acute-care hospital with a 24-hour physician-staffed emergency department.

Drugstores see "Pharmacies," below.

Embassies & Consulates See "Fast Facts: For the Foreign Traveler," in Chapter 4.

Emergencies To reach the police, ambulance, or fire department, dial **911** from any phone. No coins are needed. Emergency hotlines include Crisis Intervention (☎ 305/358-4357 or 305/358-HELP), Poison Information Center (☎ 800/282-3171), and the Rape Hotline (☎ 305/585-6949).

Eyeglasses Pearle Vision Center, 7901 Biscayne Blvd. (☎ 305/754-5144) and many other locations in Miami, can usually fill prescriptions in about an hour.

Information Always check local newspapers for special things to do during your visit. The city's only daily, the *Miami Herald*, is an especially good source for current events listings, particularly the "Weekend" section in Friday's edition. Also, *New Times*, a well-written alternative weekly, is distributed free in big, red vending boxes throughout the city. For a complete list of tourist boards and other information sources, see "Visitor Information" under "Orientation," earlier in this chapter.

Laundry/Dry Cleaning All Laundry Service, 5701 NW 7th St., west of downtown (☎ 305/261-8175), does dry cleaning and offers a wash-and-fold service by the pound in addition to self-service machines; it's open daily from 7am to 10pm. Clean Machine Laundry, 226 12th St., South Miami Beach (☎ 305/534-9429), is convenient to South Beach's art deco hotels; it's open 24 hours. Coral Gables Laundry & Dry Cleaning, 250 Minorca Ave., Coral Gables (☎ 305/446-6458), has been dry cleaning, altering, and laundering since 1930. It offers a lifesaving same-day service and is open Mon–Fri 7am–7pm and Sat 8am–3pm.

Libraries The Main Library in the Dade County system is located downtown at 101 W. Flagler St. (☎ 305/375-2665). It's open Mon–Wed and Fri–Sat 9am–6pm, Thurs 9am–9pm, and Sun 1–5pm during the school year.

Liquor Laws Only adults 21 or older may legally purchase or consume alcohol in the state of Florida. Minors are usually permitted in bars that serve food. Liquor laws are strictly enforced. Beer and wine are also sold in most supermarkets and convenience stores. Liquor stores in the City of Miami Beach and most of Miami are open all week.

Lost Property   If you lost it at the airport, call the Airport Lost and Found office (☎ 305/876-7377). If you lost it on the bus, Metrorail, or Metromover, call Metro-Dade Transit Agency (☎ 305/638-6700). If you lost it somewhere else, phone the Dade County Police Lost and Found (☎ 305/375-3366). You may also wish to fill out a police report for insurance purposes.

Luggage Storage/Lockers   In addition to the baggage check at Miami International Airport (see "Arriving" under "Orientation," earlier in this chapter), most hotels offer luggage-storage facilities. If you're taking a cruise from the Port of Miami, bags can be stored in your ship's departure terminal.

Mail   The Main Post Office, 2200 Milam Dairy Rd., Miami, FL 33152 (☎ 305/599-0166), is located west of Miami International Airport. Letters addressed to you and marked "c/o General Delivery" can be picked up at 500 NW 2nd Ave. Conveniently located post offices include 1300 Washington Ave. in South Miami Beach (☎ 305/531-7306) and 3191 Grand Ave. in Coconut Grove (☎ 305/443-0030).

Maps   See "City Layout" under "Orientation," earlier in this chapter.

Newspapers & Magazines   The well-respected *Miami Herald* is the city's only English-language daily. It's especially known for its Latin American coverage and its excellent Friday "Weekend" entertainment guide. There are literally dozens of specialized Miami magazines geared toward tourists and natives alike. Many are free and can be picked up at hotels, at restaurants, and in vending machines all around town. The most useful alternative weekly is the well-respected tabloid *New Times*. Incredibly, *Ocean Drive*, a gorgeous oversize glossy magazine, is given away at most South Miami Beach establishments. *South Florida*, on sale at newsstands, is the area's trendy glossy with articles and listings to keep local readers up on events. *TWN* is a big gay publication distributed free in Miami in purple boxes.

Pharmacies   Walgreens Pharmacies are all over town, including 8550 Coral Way in Coral Gables (☎ 305/221-9271), 1845 Alton Rd. in South Miami Beach (☎ 305/531-8868), and 6700 Collins Ave. in Miami Beach (☎ 305/861-6742). The branch at 5731 Bird Rd., at SW 40th Street (☎ 305/666-0757), is open 24 hours, as is Eckerd Drugs, 1825 Miami Gardens Dr. NE (185th Street), North Miami Beach (☎ 305/932-5740).

Photographic Needs   Drugstores and supermarkets are probably the cheapest places to purchase film and have it developed (see "Pharmacies," above). You'll pay loads more for the same product at specialized kiosks near tourist attractions. Walgreens or Eckerd's will develop film for the next day for about $6 or $7.

Police   For emergencies, dial 911 from any phone; no coins are needed. For other matters, call 305/595-6263.

Radio   About five dozen radio stations can be heard in the Greater Miami area. On the AM dial, 610 (WIOD), 790 (WNWS), 1230 (WJNO), and 1340 (WPBR) are all-talk. The only all-news station in town is 940 (WINZ). WDNA (88.9 FM) has the best Latin jazz and multi-ethnic sounds. WDBF (1420 AM) is a good Big Band station and WPBG (1290 AM) features golden oldies. The best rock stations on the FM dial include WZTA (94.9), WGTR (97.3), and the progressive-rock station WVUM (90.5). WKIS (99.9) is the top country station, and public radio (PBS) can be heard on WLRN (91.3).

Rest Rooms   Stores rarely let customers use the rest rooms, and many restaurants offer their facilities for customers only. Most malls have bathrooms, as do many of the ubiquitous fast-food restaurants. Many public beaches and large parks provide toilets; in some places you have to pay or tip an attendant. Most large hotels have clean rest rooms in their lobbies.

Safety   Florida has one of the highest crime rates in the nation. The good news is that, following the trend in the rest of the country, the crime rate in 1995 dropped 9% from the previous year. Miami has been plagued by a spate of bad press and for good reason. In general, visitors are safe in the beach areas and in the daylight hours. Don't walk alone after dark, and, after dark, avoid downtown Miami, Little Haiti, and residential areas off I-95. Also see "Safety" under "Preparing for Your Trip," in Chapter 3.

Taxes   A 6% state sales tax (plus .5% local tax, for a total of 6.5% in Miami) is added on at the register for all goods and services purchased in Florida. In addition, most municipalities levy special taxes on restaurants and hotels. In Surfside, the sales and hotel taxes total 10.5%; in Bal Harbour, 9.5%; in Miami Beach (including South Miami Beach), 11.5%; and in the rest of Dade County, 12.5%.

In Miami Beach, Surfside, and Bal Harbour, the resort (hotel) tax also applies to hotel restaurants and restaurants with liquor licenses.

Television   In addition to cable television stations, available in most hotels, all the major networks and a couple of independent stations are represented. They include Channel 4, WCIX (CBS); Channel 6, WTVJ (NBC); Channel 7, WSVN (Fox); Channel 10, WPLG (ABC); Channel 17, WLRN (PBS); Channel 23, WLTV (independent); and Channel 33, WBFS (independent).

Time   Miami, like New York, is in the eastern time zone. Between April and October, eastern daylight saving time is adopted, and clocks are set 1 hour ahead. America's eastern seaboard is 5 hours ahead of Greenwich mean time. To find out what time it is, call 305/324-8811.

Transit Information   For Metrorail or Metromover schedule information, phone 305/638-6700. See "Getting Around," earlier in this chapter, for more information.

Weather   For an up-to-date recording of current weather conditions and forecast reports, dial 305/229-4522.

4 Where to Stay

There's no shortage of places to stay in Miami; however, the prices and quality of the city's hotels vary dramatically. During the winter months, after Thanksgiving until March or April, the beach hotels fill up with travelers seeking refuge from the cold, the international jet-set crowd on their way to the Caribbean, and even locals from inland who want a weekend getaway. Since so much of the beach action is geared toward tourists, you'll find deals if you're flexible and willing to come midweek and especially off-season.

You'll also find low rates in hotels that haven't been renovated recently. While many of the old hotels from the 1930s, 1940s, and 1950s (when the bulk of Miami resorts were constructed) have been totally overhauled from the ground up, others have survived with occasional coats of paint and new carpeting (which some owners like to call renovation). Be sure to ask what work has been done, since sea air and years of tourist-wear can result in musty, paint-peeled rooms. Also, be sure to find out if the hotel you're booking will be undergoing reconstruction while you're there. There's nothing worse than the sounds of jack-hammers over breakfast. I've ignored the more worn hotels and tried to list only those that have been fully upgraded in the past few years. Exceptions are noted.

You may already know that South Florida's tourist season is well defined, beginning in mid-November and lasting until Easter. From the season's commencement, hotel prices escalate until about February, after which they again begin to decline. During the off-season, hotel rates are typically 30% to 50% lower than their winter highs. Oceanfront rooms are also more accessible between Easter and November, as are shops, roads, and restaurants.

But timing isn't everything. In many cases, rates will also depend on your hotel's proximity to the beach and how much ocean you can see from your window. Small motels a block or two from the water can be up to 40% cheaper than similar properties right on the sand. When a hotel *is* right on the beach, it's probable that its oceanfront rooms will be significantly more expensive than similar accommodations in the rear.

In addition to hotels, there are some great guesthouses in Miami Beach. They may not offer all the amenities of the high-priced resorts, but they're generally intimate, clean, and well run by hospitable hosts.

If, after inquiring about room availability at the hotels listed in this guide, you still come up empty-handed (an extremely unlikely prospect), look for an availability along Miami Beach's Collins Avenue. There are dozens of hotels and motels on this strip—in all price categories—so a room is bound to be available.

Also note that the prices listed below are based on 1996 rates and do *not* include state and city taxes, which, in some parts of Miami are as high as 12.5% (see "Fast Facts: Miami," earlier in this chapter). Be aware that many hotels make additional charges for parking and levy heavy surcharges for telephone use. Some, especially those in South Beach, also tack on an additional service charge. Inquire about these extras before committing. Room rates include breakfast where noted.

RESERVATION SERVICES   A centralized reservation service, **Central Reservations** (☎ **305/274-6832,** or 800/950-0232; on the Internet: http:www.//reservation-services.com; e-mail: rooms@america.com) work with many of Miami's hotels and can often secure discounts of up to 40% off for otherwise unyielding hotels and offer advice on the specific locales, especially in Miami Beach and downtown; the **South Florida Hotel Network** lists more than 300 hotels throughout Palm Beach to Miami and the Keys (☎ **305/538-3616** or 800/538-3616).

SOUTH MIAMI BEACH

In South Miami Beach, or South Beach as it's more commonly called, the hotels were mostly built in the 1930s, just after the Great Depression. Since the area was originally built as an affordable destination for the middle class from the Northeast, none of these hotels was really luxurious—they just happened to be situated on one of the most beautiful strips of beach in the country.

But after many years of transition, South Beach gained national recognition for its unique architecture, now known as art deco. What the hotels lacked in real luxury they made up for in innovative details. Now the area is the no. 1 tourist destination in South Florida, and where the bulk of the city's best restaurants and nightclubs are located.

The most expensive rooms are on Ocean Drive, just across the street from the beach. Thankfully, for at least most of South Beach, buildings cannot be built directly on the sand and cannot exceed three stories.

South Beach Accommodations

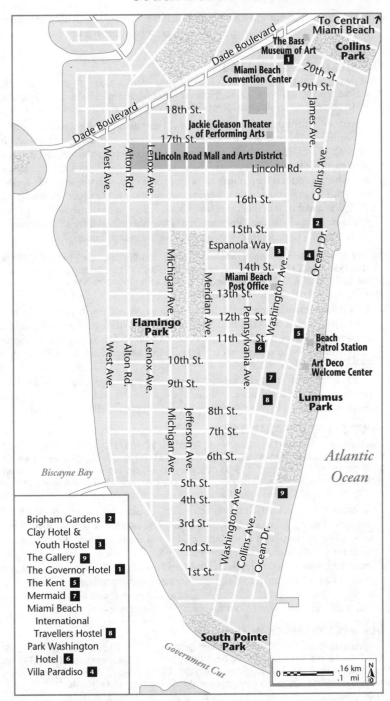

To Central Miami Beach

The Bass Museum of Art **1**

Collins Park

Miami Beach Convention Center

20th St.
19th St.
18th St.

Dade Boulevard

Jackie Gleason Theater of Performing Arts
17th St.

Lincoln Road Mall and Arts District
Lincoln Rd.

James Ave.
Collins Ave.

West Ave.
Alton Rd.
Lenox Ave.

16th St.

15th St.
Espanola Way
14th St.

2
3
4
Ocean Dr.

Miami Beach Post Office
13th St.
12th St.
11th St.

Michigan Ave.
Meridian Ave.
Pennsylvania Ave.
Washington Ave.

Flamingo Park

5
6
Beach Patrol Station

10th St.
9th St.

West Ave.
Alton Rd.
Lenox Ave.

7
Art Deco Welcome Center

8
Lummus Park

8th St.
7th St.
6th St.

Jefferson Ave.
Michigan Ave.

Atlantic Ocean

5th St.
4th St.
3rd St.
2nd St.
1st St.

Biscayne Bay

9

Washington Ave.
Collins Ave.
Ocean Dr.

Brigham Gardens **2**
Clay Hotel & Youth Hostel **3**
The Gallery **9**
The Governor Hotel **1**
The Kent **5**
Mermaid **7**
Miami Beach International Travellers Hostel **8**
Park Washington Hotel **6**
Villa Paradiso **4**

South Pointe Park

Government Cut

0   .16 km
0   .1 mi

N

Collins Avenue, just 1 block west, runs parallel to Ocean Drive. This pretty stretch of the street is not on the water, but staying here usually means lower room rates and a quieter night's sleep.

DOUBLES FOR LESS THAN $40

Clay Hotel & Youth Hostel. 438 Washington Ave., Miami Beach, FL 33139. ☎ **305/534-2988.** Fax 305/673-0346. 200 beds in singles, doubles, and multishares. $29–$35 double; $10–$14 per person in a multishare. Sheets $2 extra. Weekly rates available. JCB, MC, V.

A member of the International Youth Hostel Federation (IYHF), the Clay occupies a beautiful 1920s-style Spanish Mediterranean building at the corner of historic Espanola Way. Like other IYHF members, this hostel is open to all ages and is a great place to meet like-minded travelers. The usual smattering of Australians, Europeans, and other budget travelers make this place Miami's best clearinghouse of "inside" travel tips. Even if you don't stay here, you might want to check out the ride board.

Understandably, rooms here are bare-bones. Reservations are essential for private rooms year round and recommended from December to April for all accommodations. Ask for a room with air-conditioning in the summer months.

Miami Beach International Travellers Hostel. 236 9th St., Miami Beach, FL 33139. ☎ **305/534-0268,** or 800/978-6787. Fax 305/534-5862. 12 rms, 16 hostel rms (with three or four bed bunks). A/C. $36.80 double; $12 hostel bed for members, $14 for nonmembers. MC, V.

This family-run addition to the hostel scene on Miami Beach couldn't be in a better spot. Only 2 blocks from the beach, the old building has been tidied up for the droves of young backpackers and explorers who find their way here to stay in simple rooms, some with wooden-planked bunk beds and others with plain but adequate single beds.

The helpful staff are always available to help plan trips and give tips on what's happening in town. For the price, you can't beat this warm and friendly little South Beach crash pad. As in other hostels, be particularly careful with your valuables.

DOUBLES FOR LESS THAN $60

The Gallery. 436 Ocean Dr., Miami Beach, FL 33139. ☎ **305/532-7093** or 800/987-9867. Fax 305/532-2620. 62 studios. A/C TV TEL. Winter, $44–$67 double ($275–$295 per weekly, $540 per month). Off-season, $35–$51 double ($195–$215 per week, $535 per month). Additional person $6 extra; additional bed $12 extra. Parking $5 ($20 per week, $40 per month). AE, MC, V.

As if frozen in time, the Gallery still houses some families and retirees who live amid the South Beach renaissance in happy oblivion. The rates at this somewhat-rundown hotel reflect the condition of the building, but not the area. Across the street is one of South Beach's most exclusive accommodations, La Voile Rouge, and all around the neighborhood has made the transition to fabulous. Still, the rooms are decent enough and services are plentiful, including kitchenettes and laundry facilities. On a budget, you can consider this rambling old apartment house as a place to call home and spend your time at the beautiful beach across the street—while it lasts.

DOUBLES FOR LESS THAN $80

Brigham Gardens. 1411 Collins Ave., Miami Beach, FL 33139. ☎ **305/531-1331.** Fax 305/538-9898. 18 rms and suites. A/C TV TEL. Winter, $75–$125 double or suite ($375–$775 per week). Off-season, $50–$95 double or suite ($295–$575 per week). Additional person $5 extra; young children stay free in parents' room. Pets $6 per night extra. AE, MC, V.

You'll feel as though you're in a rain forest or a zoo at this guesthouse—and I mean that in the nicest of all possible ways. The lush grounds are framed by pleasant, quaint

Mediterranean buildings that are in need of some sprucing up. Ask for a listing of the exotic plants that grace the gardens—literally hundreds of indigenous plants on display make the property seem even more secluded and special. Thanks to the fact that many of the rooms have kitchens, you'll find many people staying for longer than a weekend. So may you, once you've settled in to this happy spot, run by a mother and daughter who go out of their way to see that you, too, are thriving. Laundry facilities are available.

✪ **Park Washington Hotel.** 1020 Washington Ave., Miami Beach, FL 33139. ☎ **305/532-1930.** Fax 305/672-6706. 35 rms, 15 suites. A/C TV TEL. Winter (including continental breakfast), $69–$99 double; $119 suite. Off-season (including breakfast), $49–$69 double; $99 suite. Additional person $10 extra; children stay free in parents' room. AE, MC, V.

A large, refurbished hotel only 2 blocks from the ocean, the Park Washington has made a name for itself by offering good-quality accommodations at incredible prices. It was designed in the 1930s by Henry Hohauser, one of the beach's most famous architects. The hotel reopened in 1989, and most of the rooms have original furnishings and well-kept-up interiors.

The Park Washington also runs the adjacent art deco Taft House and Kenmore hotels, which attract a large gay clintele. The three properties are connected by a geometric wall for privacy, lush landscaping, consistent quality, and a value-oriented philosophy. The property has an outdoor heated pool and 16 rooms have fully equipped kitchenettes for cheap dining.

DOUBLES FOR LESS THAN $100

Governor Hotel. 35 21st St., Miami Beach, FL 33139. ☎ **305/532-2100** or 800/542-0444. Fax 305/532-9139. 125 rms. A/C TV TEL. Winter, $85–$125 double. Off-season, $55–$85 double. Children 17 and under stay free in parents' room. AE, DC, DISC, MC, V. Free parking.

This inexpensive hotel on the northernmost border of South Beach is frequented by conventioneers who up until recently had no real hotel to serve them. It's nothing special, but the rooms are decent enough and it's pretty cheap. No-smoking rooms are available. A recent revamping improved the slightly tacky decor and introduced some more service-oriented staff to the place. You'll want to drive to the beach since it's a few long blocks through a pretty seedy neighborhood of unrenovated hotels. A medium-size outdoor pool is here for getting a little sun without the hastle of a trip to the beach.

As an example of art deco architecture, this hotel is one of the most stylish in the area. It has streamlined details, from the checkerboard floor tiles to the steel marquee and looming flagstaffs.

✪ **The Kent.** 1131 Collins Ave., Miami Beach, FL 33139. ☎ **305/531-6771** or 800/OUTPOST. Fax 305/531-0720. 52 rms, 2 suites. A/C MINIBAR TV TEL. Winter (including continental breakfast), $95–$135 double; $175 suite. Off-season (without breakfast), $65–$95 double; $125 suite. Additional person $15 extra; children 11 and under stay free in parents' room. Valet parking $14, self-parking $6. AE, DC, DISC, MC, V.

One of the larger buildings on South Beach, this moderately priced hotel is one of the most recent additions to the superbly maintained Island-Outpost group's art deco hotels. The staff includes a young, hip bunch of Caribbeans who cater primarily to the fashion industry. Frequent shoots are coordinated in the lobby and conference room, where full office services are available. In addition, each room has a VCR made available upon request; video rental costs $7, and videos can be delivered to the room.

Thanks to a vacant lot in the backyard, some rooms in the rear offer nice views of the ocean. The decor is modest but tasteful, and no-smoking rooms are available. For the price, this is an excellent value right in South Beach's active center.

The Mermaid. 9309 Collins Ave., Miami Beach, FL 33140. ☎ and fax **305/538-5324.** 9 rms, 1 suite. A/C MINIBAR TEL. Winter (including continental breakfast), $85–$95 double; $200 suite. Off-season, $65–$85; $175 suite. Additional person $10 extra; small children stay free in parents' room. AE, MC, V.

There's something magical about this little hideaway tucked behind tropical gardens in the very heart of South Beach. You won't find the amenities of the larger hotels, but this one-story guesthouse offers charm and hospitality that keeps people coming back. In 1996 the new owners did a thorough clean-up, adding new brightly colored fretwork around the doors and windows and installing phones in each room. Also, the wood floors have been stripped or covered in straw matting, one of the many Caribbean touches that make this place so cheery. Unfortunately, a nearby club makes a few of the rooms noisy. Ask for a room in the main building for a good night's sleep. You'll frequently find a young set of travelers from Europe and Uruguay (the owners' original home) hanging out in the garden in the evenings. The owners host a free impromptu dinner on the patio at least once a month.

Villa Paradiso. 1415 Collins Ave., Miami Beach, FL 33139. ☎ **305/532-0616.** Fax 305/667-0074. 17 apts. A/C TV TEL. Winter, $85–$135 apt for two ($495–$750 per week). Off-season, $55–$95 apt for two ($350–$550 per week). Additional person $10 extra. AE, DC, MC, V.

This guesthouse, like the Mermaid and Brigham Gardens, is more like a cozy apartment house than a hotel. There's no elegant lobby or restaurant, but rather a well-intentioned host who is happy to give you a room key and advice on what to do. The apartments are simple, but the style is fine for the beach, since you'll be spending most of your time outside anyway, and they're quiet considering their location, smack in the middle of the bustling area, a few blocks from Lincoln Road and all of Miami Beach's best clubs. Most have Murphy beds or foldout couches for extra friends. One big advantage here is that most units have a full kitchen, which will save you lots of money when it comes to eating out. There are also laundry facilities on the premises.

MIAMI BEACH, SURFSIDE, BAL HARBOR & SUNNY ISLES

The area just above South Beach is known as "Condo Canyon." Unrestricted by zoning codes throughout the 1950s, 1960s, and especially the 1970s, the area went nuts building bigger and more brazen structures, effectively blocking out the ocean views for passersby but maximizing oceanfront space for those who could afford to buy in. The result is now a glut in the market of medium-quality condos and a few scattered holdouts of older hotels and motels that front the ocean.

Most of the high-end beach resorts are designed to be a destination unto themselves. And while it's possible to spend your entire stay on the premises of a single hotel, you're just a few minutes from the art deco district and the entire mainland, just across the bay.

The area of Miami Beach described here runs from 21st Street to 192nd Street, and varies from end to end, with Bal and Bay Harbour, the part most retaining its exclusivity and character, at its center. The neighborhoods north and south, Surfside and Sunny Isles, have nice beaches and some shops, but are severely in need of rehabilitation. Those I've recommended below are the best of the budget hotels.

DOUBLES FOR LESS THAN $60

Compestela Motel. 9040 Collins Ave., Miami Beach, FL 33154. ☎ **305/861-3083.** Fax 305/865-2845. 20 suites, efficiencies, and apts. A/C TV TEL. Winter, $55–$75 one-bedroom suites; $55 efficiency; $75 apt. Off-season, $50–$55 one bedroom suite; $40 efficiency or apt. Additional person $5 extra; children 17 and under stay free in parents' room. AE, MC, V. Free parking.

Miami Beach Accommodations & Dining

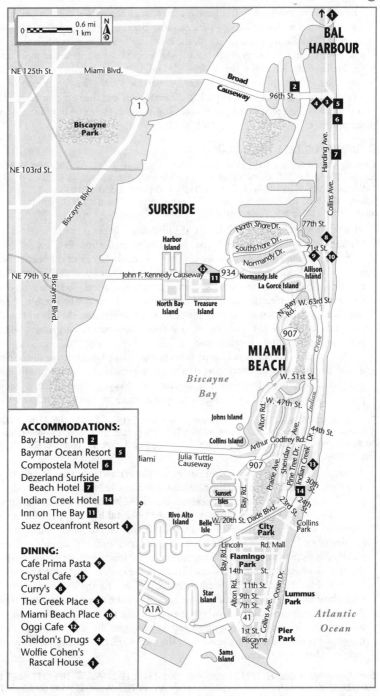

0.6 mi
1 km

N

BAL HARBOUR

NE 125th St.   Miami Blvd.

Broad Causeway   96th St.

Biscayne Park

NE 103rd St.

Biscayne Blvd.

Harding Ave.

Collins Ave.

SURFSIDE

North Shore Dr.
South Shore Dr.
Normandy Dr.

77th St.

71st St.

Harbor Island

NE 79th St.   John F. Kennedy Causeway   934   Normandy Isle   Allison Island
La Gorce Island

North Bay Island   Treasure Island

N. Bay Rd.   W. 63rd St.

907

MIAMI BEACH   W. 51st St.

Biscayne Bay   W. 47th St.

Johns Island   44th St.

Collins Island   Arthur Godfrey Rd.

Miami   Julia Tuttle Causeway   907   Indian Creek

Sunset Isles   30th St.

Rivo Alto Island   Belle Isle   W. 20th St. Dade Blvd.   24th St.   23rd St.   Collins Park   City Park

Lincoln   Rd. Mall

Flamingo Park   14th St.

Star Island   11th St.   9th St.   7th St.   Lummus Park

A1A   41   1st St.   Pier Park   Atlantic Ocean

Biscayne St.   Sams Island

ACCOMMODATIONS:
Bay Harbor Inn **2**
Baymar Ocean Resort **5**
Compostela Motel **6**
Dezerland Surfside Beach Hotel **7**
Indian Creek Hotel **14**
Inn on The Bay **11**
Suez Oceanfront Resort **1**

DINING:
Cafe Prima Pasta **9**
Crystal Cafe **13**
Curry's **8**
The Greek Place **3**
Miami Beach Place **10**
Oggi Cafe **12**
Sheldon's Drugs **4**
Wolfie Cohen's Rascal House **1**

The owners of the Compestela have recently set to renovating their three buildings, all within walking distance of the exclusive Bal Harbour shops and many good shopping and dining areas. Although the buildings were rundown efficiencies for many years, the new interiors are really quite nice. All are carpeted and most have full kitchenettes, a bonus when you're on a budget in a town full of expensive eateries. You get a lot of space and a great location for a low price. There's no fancy lobby and no amenities to speak of, but the area is safe and the staff courteous, plus you're across the street from a great beach. If you prefer, there's an outdoor pool on the property.

DOUBLES FOR LESS THAN $80

Baymar Ocean Resort. 9401 Collins Ave., Miami Beach, FL 33154. ☎ **305/866-5446** or 800/8-BAYMAR. Fax 305/866-8053. 38 rms, 35 efficiencies, 20 suites. A/C TV TEL. Winter, $75–$95 double; $85–$105 efficiency; $115–$185 suite. Off-season, $60–$80 double; $70–$90 efficiency; $95–$185 suite. Additional person $10 extra; children 11 and under stay free in parents' room. AE, DC, DISC, MC, V. Free parking.

This year's renovation did wonders for the little hotel on the strip just south of Bal Harbour, owned by first-time hoteliers, the Martayan family from Belgium and New York. Depending on what you're looking for, this could be one of the beach's best buys if prices hold. The hotel is right on the ocean and has a pool and all the modern conveniences; some units have kitchenettes and large closets. You won't flip over the decor, but it's pleasant enough and all brand-new. It may not be worth it to pay more for the oceanfront rooms since they tend to be smaller than the others. You do get a nice shared balcony space on the first-floor ocean-view rooms, behind which you'll be happy to find a low-key beach with few other tourists.

Many families and conservative religious groups seemed comfortable in the new digs as construction was concluding on the lobby bar and restaurant. A really outgoing staff seem eager to please. The Baymar has an olympic-size heated outdoor pool, laundry facilities, and even fully equipped kitchens in their efficiencies.

The Inn on the Bay. 1819 79th St. Causeway, Miami, FL 33141. ☎ **305/865-7100** or 800/624-3961. Fax 305/868-3483. 122 rms. Winter, $65–$95 double. Off-season, $54–$84 double. Additional person $5 extra; children 13 and under stay free in parents' room. AE, DC, MC, V. Free parking.

Although it's not actually on Miami Beach, this just-renovated hotel is literally steps over the bridge that connects to the mainland. The comfortably large rooms are decorated in a tropical motif and are pleasant, if a little like the interior of a dentist's office. The rooms with views look out over the beautiful bay and marina. For the price, you can't beat this new addition to the Miami hotel scene. Although there's nothing much in the neighborhood (except a good Italian restaurant across the street), it's relatively safe and quiet. You'll have to drive to the beaches (about 5 minutes over the bridge), or you can choose to sun and swim in the spacious pool on the premises.

You'll share the hotel with a boating crowd, who stay for the large and relatively cheap boat slips (which explains why the rates at this otherwise-budget hotel triple during February, when the boat show is in town). In the well-known bar on the adjacent premises, you may run into local anchors from the blood-and-gore news station, Channel 7, just down the street. In the back you'll find a volleyball court and a pleasant breeze year round.

Suez Oceanfront Resort. 18215 Collins Ave., Sunny Isles, FL 33160. ☎ **305/932-0661** or 800/327-5278 . Fax 305/937-0058. 150 rms, suites. A/C TV TEL. Winter, $65–$88 double; $175 suite. Off-season, $39–$67 double; $125 suite. Kitchenettes $10–$15 extra. Additional person $15 extra. AE, DC, MC, V. Free parking.

Guarded by an undersize replica of Egypt's famed Sphinx, this motel, with its orange-and-yellow motif, is more reminiscent of a fast-food restaurant than anything in ancient Egypt. It offers decent rooms on the beach, where most of the other hotels have gone condo. The thatch umbrellas over beach lounges and the Spanish Mediterranean–style fountains in the courtyard add to the confused decor.

But it's on the ocean and technically in Miami Beach, though its location in Sunny Isles is closer to Hallandale in Broward County than to South Beach. There's an outdoor heated pool and a free launderette—perfect for long stays. A kitschy but pleasant lounge offers good prices and a palm-lined area reminds you that you're indeed in a tropical paradise.

DOUBLES FOR LESS THAN $100

✪ **Bay Harbor Inn.** 9660 E. Bay Harbor Dr., Bay Harbor Island, FL 33154. ☎ **305/868-4141.** Fax 305/868-4141, ext. 602. 38 suites, 10 penthouse suites. A/C TV TEL. Winter, $85–$120 suite; $150–$235 penthouse suite. Off-season, $70–$80 suite; $90–$150 penthouse suite. Rates include continental breakfast. Additional person $25 extra; children 15 and under stay free in parents' room. AE, CB, DC, MC, V. Free parking.

This quaint little inn looks as though it ought to be in Vermont or somewhere woodsy and remote, but it's moments from the beach, some fine restaraunts, and some of the city's best shopping. Actually the inn comes in two parts. The more modern section sits squarely on a little river, or "the creek" as it's called, and overlooks a kidney-shaped pool and a boat called the *Celeste* where patrons eat breakfast. On the other side of the street is the cozier, antique-filled portion where glass-covered bookshelves hold good beach reading. You'll also find an eclectic array of Victorian desks and chairs scattered among modern oak side tables.

The rooms, too, have a hodgepodge of wood furnishings: oak-framed mirrors, canopied beds, Victorian chairs, and modern vanities—all comfortably arranged on a commercial brown carpeting. Some of the rooms are slightly larger (try no. 301, 305, 308, or 311) and boast an extra half-bath at no extra cost. Call to request Room 302 with a corner view of a quaint street. You'll want to invite your friends up for drinks in your suite. At times you smell the aroma of cooking from the restaurant below, but it only adds to the charm of this homey inn. Be warned that this little find is a favorite among those in the know. Some guests book the same room season after season, so you may have a hard time getting anything here unless you call months in advance.

Dezerland Surfside Beach Hotel. 8701 Collins Ave., Miami Beach, FL 33154. ☎ **305/865-6661** or 800/331-9346 in the U.S., 800/331-9347 in Canada. Fax 305/866-2630. Telex 4973649. 225 rms. A/C TV TEL. Winter, $85–$115 double. Off-season, $60–$75 double. Additional person $8 extra; children 18 and under stay free in parents' room. Special packages and group rates available. AE, CB, DISC, MC, V. Free parking.

Designed by car enthusiast Michael Dezer, Dezerland is a unique place—part hotel and part 1950s automobile wonderland. Visitors, who include many German tourists, are welcomed by a 1959 Cadillac stationed by the front door, and a 1955 Thunderbird hardtop sits in the lobby. A dozen other mint-condition classics are scattered about the floors, while the walls are decorated with related 1950s and 1960s memorabilia.

Billed as "America's largest 1950s extravaganza," this Quality Inn member features rooms that are named after some of Detroit's most famous models, like the "Dodge Deluxe" or the "The Belvedere." While it isn't pristine, the place is clean and constant renovations improve it every year. Dezerland is located directly on the beach and features a mosaic of a pink Cadillac at the bottom of its surfside pool. If you get hungry, look no farther than the lobby lounge which serves an all-you-can-eat buffet. For even more savings, some rooms have fully equipped kitchenettes, and a launderette is on the premises. No-smoking rooms are available.

DOWNTOWN

As you'd expect, most downtown hotels cater primarily to business travelers, but this doesn't mean that tourists should overlook these well-located, good-quality accommodations. Miami's downtown is small, so getting around is relatively easy. Locating here means staying between the beaches and the Grove, within minutes of the Bayside Marketplace and the Port of Miami.

Although business-hotel prices are often high and less prone to seasonal mark-downs, quality and service are also of a high standard. Look for weekend discounts, when offices are closed and rooms often go empty. After dark there's virtually nothing outside the hotels since the streets tend to be deserted and crime can be a problem.

DOUBLES FOR LESS THAN $100

Everglades Hotel. 244 Biscayne Blvd., Miami, FL 33136. ☎ **305/379-5461,** or 800/327-5700. Fax 305/577-8445. 311 rms, 60 suites. A/C TV TEL. Year round, $80 double; $115 suite. Additional person $10 extra; children 4 and under stay free in parents' room. AE, DC, DISC, MC, V. Parking $7.

This hotel has been around about forever on downtown's most active street, Biscayne Boulevard. Though the lobby and rooms are in sore need of renovation, you're in a great location and have access to a multitude of services (including a bank) in the building. Many traveling business types and Latin American families stay here because of its convenient location, low rates, and many services. Also, it's one of the only downtown hostelries with a pool. The location is quite safe and near to the highways, Metrorail, and great shopping across the street at Bayside Marketplace.

✪ Miami River Inn. 118 SW South River Dr., Miami, FL 33130. ☎ **305/325-0045.** Fax 305/325-9227. A/C TV TEL. 40 rms, 38 with bath. Winter, $89–$109 double. Off-season, $69–$89 double. Rates include continental breakfast. Additional person $15 extra; children 11 and under stay free in parents' room. AE, CB, DC, DISC, MC, V. Free parking.

Five buildings make up this compound of historic Florida on the trade-laden Miami River. Some of the buildings date from as early as 1910 and have since been well restored by careful and loving hands. The rooms are nicely furnished with a mix of antiques from all eras and gentle wallpaper prints. In the common area is a collection of books about old Miami, with histories of this land's former owners, Julia Tuttle, William Brickell, and Henry Flagler.

You can walk to many downtown eateries and museums, but you'll want to drive or take the nearby Metrorail to stops like the Bayside Marketplace. Some consider the area dicey, but the immediate vicinity is just filled with working people and tradesmen. Don't venture too far out of the enclave, though, unless you want to see the ugly underside of Miami. The low year-round rates make this an attractive option for those who appreciate old things. There's a small outdoor pool on the premises and a Jacuzzi. No-smoking rooms are available.

Riande Continental Bayside. 146 Biscayne Blvd., Miami, FL 33132. ☎ **305/358-4555** or 800/RIANDE-1. Fax 305/371-5253. 250 rms. A/C MINIBAR TV TEL. Winter, $105–$115 double. Off-season, $85–$95 double. Children stay free in parents' room. AE, DC, MC, V. Parking (limited to 35 spaces) $7.

Like its sibling hotel in South Beach, this Riande caters to a Latin American crowd who descend on downtown in droves to load up on cheap electronics and clothes. The location is ideal, since it's steps away from Bayside, a multitude of great ethnic

Accommodations in Downtown Miami

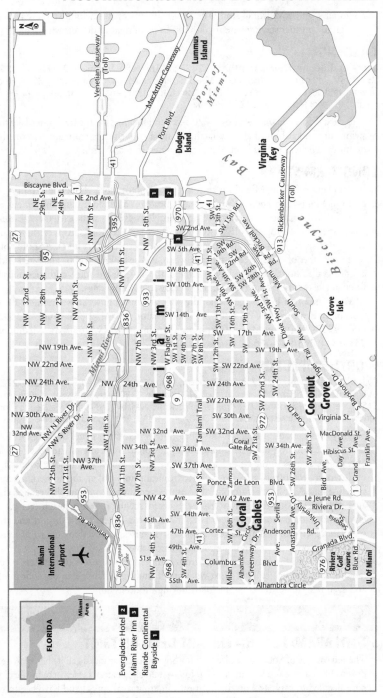

FLORIDA

Everglades Hotel **2**
Miami River Inn **3**
Riande Continental
Bayside **1**

restaurants, and a Metrorail stop. The reasonable prices and helpful staff are reason enough to consider staying here if you want to be in right in downtown Miami.

CAMPING

Larry and Penny Thompson Park. 12451 SW 184th St., Miami, FL 33177. ☎ **305/ 232-1049.** 240 campsites. Year round, $14–$20 campsite for up to four people. MC, V. From downtown, take U.S. 1 south to SW 184th Street, turn right, and follow the signs for about 4 miles; the park entrance is at 125th Avenue.

This inland park encompasses over 270 acres and includes a large freshwater lake for swimming and fishing. Laundry facilities and a convenience store are also on the premises. The tent area is huge and not separated into tiny sites.

LONG-TERM STAYS

If you plan on visiting Miami for a month, a season, or more, think about renting a room in a long-term hotel in South Miami Beach or a condominium apartment in Miami Beach, Surfside, Bal Harbour, or Sunny Isles. Rents can be extremely reasonable, especially during the off season. And there's no comparison in terms of the amount of space you get for the same money you'd spend on a hotel. A short note to the chamber of commerce in the area where you're looking will be answered with a list of availabilities. Also check with some of the inexpensive hotels and guesthouses listed above that often offer discounted weekly or monthly rates.

Many area real-estate agents handle short-term rentals. These include **Keys Company Realtors,** 100 N. Biscayne Blvd., Miami, FL 33152 (☎ **305/371-3592,** or 800/327-7934); and **Marco Corporate Housing,** 490 NW 165th St., Miami, FL 33169 (☎ **305/947-5668**).

WORTH A SPLURGE

✪ **Indian Creek Hotel.** 2727 Indian Creek Dr., Miami Beach, FL 33140. ☎ **305/531-2727** or 800/207-2727. 55 rms, 6 suites. Winter, $110 double; $190 suite. Off-season, $90 double; $150 suite. Additonal person $10 extra. Group packages available. 18% gratuity added to room service, 15% added to restaurant checks. DISC, DC, MC, V. Limited parking available on street.

Slightly north of South Beach is this small hotel where every detail of the 1936 Pan Coast–style building has been meticulously restored, from one of the beach's first operating elevators to the period steamer trunk in the lobby. The modest rooms are outfitted in deco furnishings, with pretty tropical prints and all the modern amenities. Just one short block from one of Miami Beach's most comfortable beaches, the area is perfectly situated—away from the hectic scene on South Beach, yet close enough to walk to most activities there, and with easy access to the airport and the mainland. New this year are large bungalow-style suites that overlook the palm-lined landscaped pool, and no-smoking rooms are available.

Guests in this little treasure range from international travelers to business types looking for good value. That's just what you'll find here. There's an outdoor pool, and even free coffee service in the lobby during the afternoon.

5 Where to Eat

SOUTH MIAMI BEACH—THE ART DECO DISTRICT

The renaissance of South Miami Beach (or South Beach, as locals call it) has spawned dozens of first-rate restaurants. In fact, long-established eateries elsewhere in the city have decided to capitalize on the location's international appeal and have begun to open branches in South Beach with great success. A few old standbys remain from the old *Miami Vice* days, but a flock of newcomers dominate the scene, with places

South Beach Dining

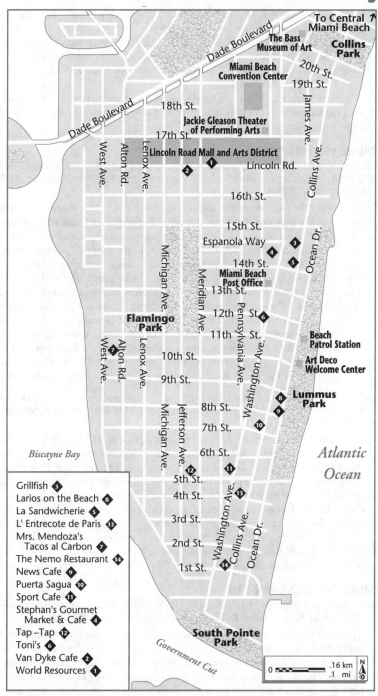

Grillfish ❸
Larios on the Beach ❽
La Sandwicherie ❺
L' Entrecote de Paris ⓭
Mrs. Mendoza's
  Tacos al Carbon ❼
The Nemo Restaurant ⓮
News Cafe ❾
Puerta Sagua ❿
Sport Cafe ⓫
Stephan's Gourmet
  Market & Cafe ❹
Tap –Tap ⓬
Toni's ❻
Van Dyke Cafe ❷
World Resources ❶

going in and out of style as quickly as the tides. This listing represents those that have quickly gained national attention—or should.

In addition, there are a few areas like Lincoln Road where many places provide good food and great atmosphere. Since it's impossible to list all of them, I recommend that you go and browse. Most post a copy of the menu and staffs are happy to chat with curious passersby.

With very few exceptions, the eateries on Ocean Drive are crowded with tourists and priced accordingly. Venture into the pedestrian-friendly streets just west of Ocean Drive and enjoy.

MEALS FOR LESS THAN $7

La Sandwicherie. 229 14th St. (behind the Amoco Station), South Miami Beach. ☎ **305/ 532-8934.** Sandwiches and salads $4.50–$7. No credit cards. Sun–Thurs 10am–4am, Fri–Sat 10am–5am. FRENCH SNACKS.

If you want the most incredible gourmet sandwich you've ever tasted, stop by the green-and-white awning that hides this fabulous French lunch and snack counter. Choose pâté, saussison, salami, prosciutto, turkey, tuna, ham, or roast beef or any of the perfect cheeses (Swiss, mozzarella, Cheddar, or provolone). You could make a meal of the optional sandwich toppings—black olives, cornichons, cucumbers, lettuce, onions, green or hot peppers, tomatoes—many people do and they call it a Vegetarian. The fresh French bread has a slightly golden crust and is just thick enough to hold all you'll want to have stuffed in it. You can choose to have your sandwich made on a croissant, though I've found flakier croissants elsewhere on the beach. If the six or so wooden stools are all taken, don't despair. You can stand up and watch the tattoo artist do his work through the glass wall next door, or douse your creation with the light and tangy vinaigrette and bring lunch to the beach. In addition to the cans and bottles of teas, sodas, juices, and waters, you can get a killer cappuccino here.

Mrs. Mendoza's Tacos al Carbon. 1040 Alton Rd., South Miami Beach. ☎ **305/535-0808.** Main courses $3–$5; side dishes 80¢–$3. No credit cards. Mon–Sat 11am–10pm, Sun noon– 9pm. FAST FOOD/MEXICAN.

This hard-to-spot storefront Mexican place is a godsend. It's the city's only fresh California-style Mexican restaurant—the steak and chicken are grilled as you wait and then stuffed into homemade flour or corn wrappings. You order at the tile counter and pick up your dish on a plastic tray in minutes. The vegetarian offerings are huge and hearty. One of my favorites is the veggie burrito, which includes rice, black beans, cheese, lettuce, and guacamole doused in one of the three tomato salsas, from mild to super-hot. You can see the fresh-cut cilantro and taste the super-hot chilis. The chips are hand-cut and flavorful, but a bit too coarse; skip them and enjoy your order of rich and chunky guacamole with a fork. A popular spot for locals and those who work in the area. Another branch is at Doral Plaza, 9739 NW 41st St.

MEALS FOR LESS THAN $10

News Café. 800 Ocean Dr., South Miami Beach. ☎ **305/538-6397.** Continental breakfast $2.75; salads $4–$8; sandwiches $5–$7. AE, MC, V. Daily 24 hours. AMERICAN.

The News Café has been around the longest of any of the chic spots around trendy South Beach. Inexpensive breakfasts and café fare are served at about 20 perpetually congested tables. Most of the seating is outdoors, and the terrace tables are the most coveted. This is the regular meeting place for Ocean Drive's multitude of fashion photography crews and their models, and where they can get all the international newspapers and magazines. Delicious and often health-oriented dishes include yogurt with fruit salad, various green salads, imported cheese and meat sandwiches, and a choice of quiches. The food isn't remarkable but the people-watching is.

Puerta Sagua. 700 Collins Ave., South Miami Beach. ☎ **305/673-1115.** Main courses $7–$17; sandwiches and salads $3–$9. AE, DC, MC, V. Daily 7:30am–2am. SPANISH/CUBAN.

This bar and restaurant has a steady stream of regulars who range from *abuelitos* (little old grandfathers) to hipsters who stop in after clubbing. The dingy, brown-walled diner is one of the few real old holdouts on South Beach. It has endured because the food is good, though the cooking style tends to be greasy. The faded plastic sign on the corner boasts: FAMOSO POR SUS MARISCOS ("famous for its seafood"). Some of the less heavy dishes are a super-chunky fish soup with pieces of whole flaky grouper, chicken and seafood paella, and marinated kingfish. Also good are most of the shrimp dishes, especially the shrimp in garlic sauce served with white rice and salad. This is one of the most reasonably priced places left on the beach for simple and hearty fare. Don't be intimidated by the waiters who speak little English— the extensive menu is translated into English. Hurry, before another boutique goes up in its place.

✪ **Sport Cafe.** 538 Washington Ave., South Miami Beach. ☎ **305/674-9700.** Reservations accepted only for parties of four or more. Main courses $6.95–$9.95; sandwiches and pizzas $4.50–$7. MC, V. Daily noon–1am (sometimes earlier for coffee). ITALIAN.

Inside the decor is dark and smoky, with a beautiful wooden bar and a large-screen TV that dominate the small dining room. But don't expect to see the latest football or baseball here; it's more likely to be soccer and bicycle races—this is a European crowd. Owned by brothers Tonino and Paolo Doino from Rome, the food is authentic. The simple menu lists only three entrees and a few pizzas. Ask for the day's specials and go for one of them. Always good is the penne with salmon served with a pink sauce. The noodles are perfectly *al dente* and the chunks of fish add a slightly salty and warm flavor. Even though the portions are large, the sauce is so delicious and light you can finish a whole bowl. Rosa, the Doinos' mother, also makes the very best eggplant parmigiana in the county (though not on the menu, it's available almost every day)—there's no heavy breading, oily residue, or excessive cheese that mar so many versions of this dish elsewhere.

Ordering from the newly arrived Italian waiters can be a challenge, but try to ask for a plate of fresh crushed garlic when they bring your bread and oil. The crusty dense loaf benefits from the dose of oil, pepper, and the pungent bulb. For a great tiramisù, try Sport's, which is served *semifreddo* (partially frozen). The prices are so low that on some nights you may have to wait for a seat. The brothers have opened a second and similar restaraunt, Al Vicolo Caffè, on Lincoln Road.

Van Dyke Cafe. 846 Lincoln Rd., South Miami Beach. ☎ **305/534-3600.** Reservations recommended for evenings. Main courses $6–$11. AE, DC, MC, V. Sun–Thurs 8am–midnight, Fri–Sat 8am–2am. AMERICAN.

The group that owns the successful News Café has used the same formula to guarantee Van Dyke's longevity on Lincoln Road. The smart, upscale decor inside and the European sidewalk café outside are always crowded. There's nothing too ambitious on the menu, which offers basic sandwiches and salads and—best of all— breakfast all day long. The pastas are decent, though not too exciting. House specialties include an excellent smoked salmon on a rustic and thick black bread, and a smooth and lemony hummus with pita chips. Service is fast and friendly. In the evenings you can enjoy the sounds of a talented jazz band that waft down from the elegant club upstairs.

World Resources. 719 Lincoln Rd., South Main Beach. ☎ **305/534-9095.** Main courses $6–8; sushi hand-rolls $3–$4. AE, DC, MC, V. Daily noon–midnight. INTERNATIONAL/SUSHI.

World Resources is an excellent little cafe and sushi bar masquerading as an Indonesian furniture and bric-a-brac store. Local hippy types and hipsters frequent this down-right cheap hangout. Offerings include many Thai specialties. The portions are generous and the cooking simple. The basil chicken, for example, is a tasty combination of white meat sautéed in a coconut sauce with subtle hints of basil and garlic. The Thai salad is heaped with fresh vegetables. Although you can get better pad Thai at a number of spots on the beach, you can't beat the atmosphere, which includes dozens of outside tables surrounding a tiny pond and stage where World Beat musicians perform nightly. From African drumming to Indian sitar playing, there's always some action at this stand-out on the road.

MEALS FOR LESS THAN $15

Grillfish. 1444 Collins Ave. (at Espanola Way), South Miami Beach. ☎ **305/538-9908.** Reservations recommended on weekends. Main courses $8–$13. AE, DC, MC, V. Winter, daily 6pm–midnight; off-season, daily 6–11pm. SEAFOOD.

From the beautiful Byzantine-style mural and the gleaming oak bar that runs the length of the corner storefront on stylish Espanola Way, you'd think you were eating in a much more expensive restaurant. No doubt they manage to pay the exorbitant South Beach rent because they have a loyal following of locals who come for the fresh and simple Italian-inspired rustic seafood in a relaxed but upscale atmosphere. The waiters are friendly and know the limited menu well. The barroom seafood chowder is full of chunks of shellfish as well as some fresh white fish filets in a tomato broth. The small ear of corn, included with each main dish, is about as close as you'll get to any type of vegetable offering besides the pedestrian salad. Still, at these prices it's worth a visit to try some local fare such as mako shark, marlin, and wahoo. They'll grill it or sauté it.

Larios on the Beach. 820 Ocean Dr., South Miami Beach. ☎ **305/532-9577.** Reservations recommended. Main courses $8–$15; lunch $4–$7. AE, MC, V. Sun–Thurs 11:30am–midnight, Fri–Sat 11:30am–1:30am. CUBAN.

Gloria and Emilio Estefan brought their favorite Cuban chef from the mainland to create this ultra-stylish restaurant in the heart of the South Beach hustle. Enjoy a few appetizers at the handsome chrome-and-wood bar while you wait for a seat amid the sea of Spanish-speaking regulars. The menu runs the gamut, from diner-style medianoches (Cuban sandwiches with pork and cheese) to a tangy and tender serrucho en escabeche (pickled kingfish) with just enough citrus to mellow the fishiness and still not cause a pucker. You could get away with ordering three or four *apertivos* and *ensaladas* (appetizers and salads) for a couple. Portions are large and prices are reasonable. Cuban food is not light, and this place is no exception. Try the camarones al ajillo (shrimp in garlic sauce), fabada asturiana (hearty soup of black beans and sausage), or palomilla (thinly sliced beef served with onions and parsley). Save room for the rich custard desserts, which include a few stunning variations on the standard flan. A spoonful of pumpkin- or coffee-accented custard with a cup of cortadito (espresso-style coffee with milk and sugar) will get you prepped for a full night of dancing.

Tap Tap. 819 5th St. (between Jefferson and Meridian aves., behind the Shell Station). ☎ **305/ 672-2898.** Reservations recommended in season and for special events. Main courses $8–$15; all-you-can-eat Sun buffet brunch $12. AE, DC, MC, V. Sun–Thurs 11:30am–11pm, Fri–Sat 11:30am–midnight. HAITIAN.

The whole place looks like an overgrown *tap tap,* a brightly painted jitney common in Haiti. Every bit of space of wall and floor and furniture and everything in between is painted neon blue or pink or purple. The atmosphere is always fun. It's where the Haiti-philes and Haitians hang out, from journalists to politicians. Even Manno Charlemagne, the mayor of Port-au-Prince, shows up to play his old brand of protest music and drink lots of Rhum Barbancourt. You don't really come here for the food, though it's not bad when you can get it (on crowded nights the service is impossible). The young and handsome service staff tend to disappear entirely or show up flustered with someone else's order. I recommend going for appetizers and drinks. The lanbi nan citron, a tart marinated conch salad, is perfect with a tall tropical drink and maybe some lightly grilled goat tidbits served in a savory brown sauce (they're less stringy than a typical goat dish). The pumpkin soup is a satisfying, rich, brick-colored purée of subtly seasoned pumpkin with a dash of pepper. An excellent salad of avocado, mango, and watercress is a great finish. Even if you don't stay for a full meal, try the pumpkin flan with coconut-caramel sauce, an ultra-Caribbean sweet treat.

Toni's. 1208 Washington Ave., South Miam Beach. ☎ **305/673-9368.** Reservations recommended. Main courses $9–$25; sushi hand-rolls $3.50–$8.50. AE, MC, V. Sun–Thurs 6pm–midnight, Fri–Sat 6pm–1am. SUSHI/JAPANESE.

One of Washington Avenue's first tenants, Toni has withstood the test of time on fickle South Beach. By serving fish caught locally daily, together with some imports from the Pacific and beyond, Toni has created a vast menu from teriyaki to hand-rolls. Consider the seaweed salad, a crunchy and salty green plant that's dressed with a light sesame sauce. The miso soup is hearty and a bit sweet. Some fun appetizers from the sushi bar include Miami Heat, which contains slabs of tuna with bits of scallion in a peppery sesame oil. Literally hundreds of appetizers and rolls makes this a fun place to go with a group and share. The atmosphere is comfortable and even allows for quiet conversation—a rarity on the beach.

MIAMI BEACH, SURFSIDE, BAL HARBOUR & SUNNY ISLES

The area north of the art deco district, from 21st Street to 163rd Street, had its heyday in the 1950s with the huge hotels and gambling halls blocking the view of the ocean. Now many of those hotels have been converted into condos and the bayfront mansions have been renovated by and for wealthy entrepreneurs, families, and speculators, leaving the area with many more residents, albeit seasonal, than tourists. On the culinary front, the result is a handful of super-expensive restaurants and a number of value-oriented spots that cater to regulars.

MEALS FOR LESS THAN $7

✪ **The Greek Place.** 235 95th St., Surfside. ☎ **305/866-9628.** Main courses $5–$6. No credit cards. Mon–Fri 10am–6pm. GREEK.

The only drawback of this tiny hole in the wall is that it's open only on weekdays. It's a little diner with sparkling white walls and about 10 wooden stools that's worth checking out. Daily specials like pastitsio, chicken alcyone, and roast turkey with all the fixings are the big draws for the locals working in the area who crowd the place at lunchtime. Every variety of salad and typical Greek dishes like shish kebab, souvlakis, and gyros are cooked to perfection as you wait.

Sheldon's Drugs. 9501 Harding Ave., Surfside. ☎ **305/866-6251.** Main courses $4.50–$5; soup and sandwiches $2–$5. AE, DISC, MC, V. Daily 7am–8pm. AMERICAN/DRUGSTORE.

This typical old-fashioned drugstore counter serves eggs and oatmeal, a good tuna melt, and a blue-plate special. The food's not bad and you can't beat the prices. More important, this was a favorite breakfast spot of Isaac Bashevis Singer, and where he was eating a bagel and eggs when his wife got the call that he had won the Nobel Prize for Literature in 1978. The menu hasn't changed much since then. Consider stepping into this historic site for a good piece of pie and a side of history.

Wolfie Cohen's Rascal House. 17190 Collins Ave., Sunny Isles. ☎ **305/947-4581.** Omelets and sandwiches $4–$6; other dishes $5–$14. MC, V. Daily 7am–12:45am. JEWISH/ DELICATESSEN.

Opened in 1954 and still going strong, this nostalgic culinary extravaganza is one of Miami Beach's greatest traditions. Simple tables and booths as well as plenty of patrons fill the airy 425-seat dining room. The menu is as huge as the portions— try the corned beef, schmaltz herring, brisket, kreplach, chicken soup, or other authentic Jewish staples. Take-out service is available.

MEALS FOR LESS THAN $10

✪ **Cafe Prima Pasta.** 414 71st St. (half a block east of the Byron movie theater), Miami Beach. ☎ **305/867-0106.** Main courses $12–$14; pastas $7–$9. No credit cards. Sun–Thurs 6–11pm, Fri–Sat 6pm–midnight. ITALIAN.

Another tiny pasta joint that serves phenomenal homemade noodles with good old Italian sauces like carbonara, diavolof, putanesca, and pomodoro. With only 30 seats it can feel a bit cramped, but the crowd, a young laid-back set, is generally easy to sit near. The stuffed agnolotti with either pesto, spinach and ricotta, or tomato are so delicate and flavorful, you'll think you're eating dessert; speaking of which, you'll want to try the apple tart with a pale golden caramel sauce. Ask for it à la mode and plan to come back again for more. It's closer to Collins and even more popular than Oggi (see below), which means an even longer wait to get in. In fact, I found this place after unsuccessfully searching for Oggi.

Curry's. 7433 Collins Ave., Miami Beach. ☎ **305/866-1571.** Reservations not accepted. Meals (including appetizer, main course, dessert, and coffee) $8–$11. AE, MC, V. Mon–Sat 4:30– 9:30pm, Sun 4–9:30pm. AMERICAN.

Established in 1937, this large dining room on the ocean side of Collins Avenue is one of Miami Beach's oldest restaurants. Neither the restaurant's name nor the Polynesian wall decorations are indicative of the menu's offerings, which are straight-forwardly American and reminiscent of the area's heyday. Broiled and fried fish dishes are available, but the best selections, including steak, chicken, and ribs, come off the open charcoal grill perched by the front window. The reasonable prices include appetizer, soup or salad, potato or vegetable, dessert, and coffee.

Miami Beach Place. 6954 Collins Ave., Miami Beach. ☎ **305/866-8661.** Main courses $10– $13; pizzas and pastas $7–$16. Mon–Fri 5pm–midnight, Sat 1pm–1am, Sun 2pm–1am. MC, V. ITALIAN/PIZZA.

This Brazilian-owned pizza parlor is packed most weekends, not only because of its good, inexpensive pastas and pizzas but also because of the fun Brazilian bands that play most weekends after 9pm. By midnight the place is full of Portuguese-speaking dancers who enjoy a late-night buffet and lots of wine and beer. The light and garlicky garlic rolls wrapped in golden twists are addictive. The pizza tends to be too cheesy for my taste, but has fresh toppings. If you've never tasted the ubiquitous Brazilian soda Guaraná, do. It's like a rich ginger ale with not as much zing.

MEALS FOR LESS THAN $15

Oggi Caffe. 1740 79th St Causeway (in the White Star shopping center next to the Bagel Cafe), North Bay Village. ☎ **305/866-1238.** Reservations accepted. Main courses $12–$20; pastas $8–$10. Mon–Thurs 11:30am–2:30pm and 6–10:30pm, Fri 11:30am–2:30pm and 6–11:30pm, Sat 6–11:30pm, Sun 5:30–10:30pm. ITALIAN.

Tucked away in a tiny strip mall on the 79th Street Causeway, this neighborhood favorite makes fresh pastas daily. Every one, from the agnolotti stuffed with fresh spinach and ricotta to the wire-thin spaghettini, is tender and tasty. A hearty soup, pasta e fagiola, is filled with beans and vegetables, and could almost be a meal. Though you could fill up on the starters, the main courses, especially the grilled dishes, are superb. The place is tiny and service is a bit rushed, but it's well worth the slight discomfort for this authentic and inexpensive food.

KEY BISCAYNE

Key Biscayne has some of the world's nicest beaches, hotels, and parks, but it's not known for great food. Most tourists eat at the largest hotel on the island, where the food is always reliable, if not outstanding. Locals, or "Key rats" as they're known, tend to go off-island for meals. There are a few exceptions.

MEALS FOR LESS THAN $7

✪ **La Boulangerie.** 328 Crandon Blvd. (in Eckerd's shopping mall), Key Biscayne. ☎ **305/361-0281.** Sandwiches and salads $5–$7. MC, V. Mon–Sat 7:30am–8pm, Sun 7:30am–6pm. FRENCH BAKERY.

Beware. You'll stop in this inconspicuous French bakery for a loaf of bread and find yourself walking out with your arms full of the freshest sandwiches, salads, groceries, and pastries anywhere. You can also sit down inside at one of the 15 or so tables to enjoy a great breakfast, lunch, or early dinner with the jet-set in their designer swimsuits. The prosciutto and goat cheese sandwich on crusty French bread is unbeatable. The friendly proprietors will no doubt talk you into a heavenly fruit tart, like the pointy-tipped apricot tart with plump fruit halves painted with a thin layer of sweet glaze. Try any of the cakes or rustic breads, too. Another Boulangerie is located at 3425 Main Hwy., in Coconut Grove.

MEALS FOR LESS THAN $10

The Oasis. 19 Harbor Dr. (at Crandon Blvd.). ☎ **305/361-5709.** Main courses $4–12; sandwiches $3–$4. No credit cards. Daily 6am–9pm. CUBAN.

Even Hurricane Andrew couldn't blow down this rugged little shack where everyone, from the city's mayor to the local handymen, meets for delicious paella or a good Cuban sandwich. In fact, after the storm the place expanded and now provides seating for those who used to gather around the little window for super-powerful cafesitos and rich croquetas. It's a little dingy—but the food is good.

MEALS FOR LESS THAN $15

✪ **Bayside Seafood Restaurant and Hidden Cove Bar.** 3501 Rickenbacker Causeway, Key Biscayne. ☎ **305/361-0808.** Reservations accepted only for groups larger than 15. Raw clams or oysters $7 per dozen; appetizers, salads, and sandwiches $4.50–$6; platters $7–$13. AE, MC, V. Sun–Thurs noon–10:30pm, Fri–Sat noon–midnight. SEAFOOD.

Known by locals as "the Hut," this ramshackle restaurant and bar is a laid-back outdoor tiki hut and terrace that serves pretty good sandwiches and fish platters on paper plates. A chalkboard lists the latest catches, which can be prepared blackened, fried, broiled, or in a garlic sauce. I prefer blackened, which is super-crusty, spicy, and dark. The fish dip is wonderfully smoky and moist, if a little heavy on the mayonnaise.

Bring bug spray or ask the waitresses for some (they usually keep packets behind the bar)—for some reason this place is plagued by mosquitoes even when the rest of town isn't. Local fishermen and yacht owners share this rustic outpost with equal enthusiasm and loyalty. On weekends the Hut features its house band playing live reggae and calypso.

DOWNTOWN

Downtown Miami is divided into two distinct areas: Brickell Avenue and the bayfront area near Biscayne Boulevard. Although they're not far from each other, you wouldn't walk from one to the other. Some shopkeepers in the area have tried to revitalize the nighttime scene, but in general, if your hotel is not downtown and you aren't going to a show at the Gusman, the Knight Center, or Bayside, put your visit off until the afternoon when you'll join hoards of Latin American shoppers, college students, and lots of professionals in suits. The area shuts down after dark, though a few of the better restaurants, especially in the hotels, stay open late.

MEALS FOR LESS THAN $7

Caribbean Delite. 236 NE 1st Ave. (across from Miami-Dade Community College), downtown. ☎ **305/381-9254.** Menu items $5.50–$9; lunch platters $4–$7. AE, MC, V. Daily 8:30am–7pm. Closed some Suns. JAMAICAN.

You'd never see this tiny storefront diner from the one-way street it's on, though the smell of succulent jerk chicken or pork might beckon you. Try Jamaican specialties like curried goat—tender and tasty pieces of meat on the bone in a spicy yellow sauce—or oxtail stew. The kitchen can be stingy with the spectacular sauces, leaving the dishes a bit dry, so ask for an extra helping on the side—they're happy to oblige. Also, if you come early in the day, you can get a taste of the national dish of Jamaica, salt fish and ackee (usually served for breakfast), outlawed in this country. Ackee, or akee, is the fruit of a tree native to Jamaica and is sometimes called "brain fruit" because of its curved compartmentalized shape. Importation of ackees is prohibited because certain parts of the fruit, including the seeds, are toxic, and because if harvested before it ripens the fruit can cause illness. Ask Carol Whyte, the chef and owner, to tell you the story of this interesting dish made with "brain fruit" or quiz one of the many Jamaicans who stop in while they're in port off the cruise ships a few blocks away.

The Crepe Maker. 200 S. Biscayne Blvd. (in front of the First Union Bank) and SE 3rd Ave. at 1st St. (in front of the Republic National bank), downtown. ☎ **305/274-2265** (for catering questions only). Crêpes $2–$6. Winter, Mon–Fri 11am–4pm; Off-season Tues–Fri 11am–4pm. No credit cards. CREPES.

Inspired by the wooden crêpe carts in Paris, Christopher Hoffman and his wife, Maria, decided that Miamians would appreciate cheap, healthful fresh meats and vegetables quick sautéed in sidewalk carts. The couple operate two carts where lawyers and students and tourists wait in line to watch the little pancakes turn golden brown on the edges in time for a cheerful chef in a flouncy white hat to throw a dash of olive oil and a handful of spinach leaves in the center. Specials change daily, but include classics as well as Havana chicken with sweet red peppers, black beans, and sweet pesto. You can also design your own. Of course, for dessert there are fruit- and jam-filled specialties. If you don't mind standing, this is one of the tastiest choices downtown.

Dining in Coral Gables & Coconut Grove

The Pizza Loft. 6917 W. Flagler St., Miami (west of downtown). ☎ **305/266-5111.** Main courses $5–$12; pizzas $9–$15. MC, V. Sun–Thurs 11am–11pm, Fri–Sat 11am–midnight. PIZZA/ITALIAN.

This Jewish-owned pizza restaurant packs 'em in for the delicious garlicky-sauced thin-crusted pizzas. You'll have to wait a bit to get one of the few seats here, but it's definitely worth it. I'd steer away from most of the other entrees, but the calzones and garlic bread are superb. Lunchtime finds the place almost too jammed.

✪ **Raja's.** 243 E. Flagler St. (in the Galeria International mall). ☎ **305/539-9551.** Menu items $3–$6; specials (including salad, rice, and vegetable side dish) $5–$7. No credit cards. Mon–Tues and Thurs–Sat 9am–6:30pm, Sun 9am–4:30pm. SOUTH INDIAN/FAST FOOD.

Not easy to find, this tiny counter in the bustling downtown food court serves some of the feistiest chicken stews and vegetarian dishes in Miami. It's surrounded by mostly Brazilian fast-food places that are packed with tour groups on shopping sprees. If you like it spicy, try the rich masala spicy chili chicken. For vegetarians, the heaping platters of dal (lentils), cauliflower, eggplant, broccoli, and chick-peas are a valuable find in otherwise meat-laden downtown. The masala dosa (rice crêpes stuffed with vegetable mash) is made fresh when ordered and is a filling lunch or dinner. Also, the side salad with fresh onions, cucumbers, and lettuce is free with the specials—but only if you ask for it. Try a mango lassi to finish—and to cool your tongue if you sampled one of the signature hot dishes.

Meals for Less than $10

S&S Restaurant. 1757 NE 2nd Ave., downtown. ☎ **305/373-4291.** Main courses $5–$11. No credit cards. Mon–Fri 6am–7pm, Sat 6am–2:30pm (later on Heat game nights).

This tiny chrome-and-Linoleum counter restaurant looks like a truck stop in some other town. But here in the middle of downtown since 1938, only locals keep coming back. The neighborhood has changed to a pretty undesirable one, but the basic diner fare, with some excellent stews and soups, hasn't changed in years. A slice of pie and a slice of Miami history at the same time are what you'll find at S&S. In addition to super-cheap breakfasts, the diner serves up some of the best comfort food in Miami—it's one of the only places I know that still serves creamed chicken on toast. Expect a wait at lunchtime with the mostly male clientele, from lawyers to linemen.

Meals for Less than $15

East Coast Fisheries. 360 W. Flagler St., downtown (south) ☎ **305/372-1300.** Reservations recommended. Main courses $9–$15 (most under $14); lunch from $7. AE, DC, MC, V. Daily 11am–10pm. Take I-95 south to exit 5A (NW 8th St/Orange Bowl). Proceed down the ramp (south) until NW 3rd Ave. Turn right (west) until you see River Drive. Turn left. The restaurant is in the large building on the right at the intersection of W. Flagler and River Drive. SEAFOOD.

This is a no-nonsense retail market and restaurant, offering a terrific variety of the freshest fish available. The dozen or so plain wood tables are surrounded by refrigerated glass cases filled with snapper, salmon, mahi mahi, trout, tuna, crabs, oysters, lobsters, and the like. The absolutely huge menu features every fish imaginable, cooked the way you want it—grilled, fried, stuffed, Cajun style, Florentine, hollandaise, or blackened. The smell of frying grease detracts from the otherwise quaint Old Miami feel. Service is fast, but good prices and excellent food still mean long lines on weekends. Highly recommended.

✪ **Fishbone Grille.** 650 S. Miami Ave. (SW 7th Ave., next to Tobacco Rd.). ☎ **305/530-1915.** Reservations recommended on weekends. Main courses $9–$16. AE, DC, MC, V. Mon–Thurs 11:30am–10pm, Fri 11:30am–11pm, Sat 5:30–11pm. SEAFOOD.

Located in a small strip center it shares with Tobacco Road, this sensational fish shop prepares dozens of outstanding specials daily. The atmosphere is nothing to speak of, though there is a cool table where you can stare into a fish tank. This is by far Miami's best and most reasonably priced seafood restaurant. Try the excellent ceviche, which has just enough spice to give it a zing, yet doesn't overwhelm the fresh fish flavor. If you like a nice Caribbean flavor, try the jerk covina (the biblical fish) or one of the excellent dolphin (fish) specialties.

Las Tapas. In the Bayside Marketplace, 401 Biscayne Blvd., downtown. ☎ **305/372-2737.** Reservations accepted. Tapas $4–$7; main courses $12–$19; lunch about half price. AE, CB, DC, DISC, MC, V. Sun–Thurs 11am–midnight, Fri–Sat 11am–1am. SPANISH.

Occupying a large corner of downtown's Bayside Marketplace, glass-wrapped Las Tapas is a fun place to dine in a laid-back, easy atmosphere. Tapas, small servings of Spanish delicacies, are the featured fare here. Good main dishes are on the menu, but it's more fun to taste a variety of the tapas. Try shrimp in garlic, smoked port shank with Spanish sausage, baby eel in garlic and oil, and chicken sauté with garlic and mushrooms. The open kitchen in front of the entrance greets diners with succulent smells. The long dining room is outlined in red Spanish stone and decorated with hanging hams. Bayside Marketplace is on Biscayne Bay in the middle of downtown.

LITTLE HAVANA

The main artery of Little Havana is a busy commercial strip called Southwest 8th Street, or *Calle Ocho*. Here there are auto body shops, cigar factories, furniture stores, and, on every corner, a pass-through window serving strong Cuban coffee and snacks. In addition, many of the Cubans, Dominicans, Nicaraguans, Peruvians, and others have opened eateries ranging from intimate candlelit full-scale restaurants to bustling stand-up lunch counters. Many list menu items in English for the benefit of *norteamericano* diners.

MEALS FOR LESS THAN $7

La Carreta. 3632 SW 8th St., Little Havana. ☎ **305/446-4915.** Main courses $3–$9. DC, MC, V. Open daily 24 hours. CUBAN.

At this cavernous family-style restaurant the waitresses are brusque but efficient, and will help anyone along who may not know all the lingo. The menu is vast and very authentic. Try the sopa de pollo, a rich golden stock loaded with chunks of chicken and fresh vegetables, or the ropa vieja, a shredded beef stew in a thick brown sauce.

Because of its immense popularity and low prices, La Carreta has opened several branches througout Miami. Check the White Pages for others.

✪ **Versailles.** 3555 SW 8th St., Little Havana. ☎ **305/444-0240.** Soup and salad $2–$5; main courses $5–$8. DC, MC, V. Mon–Thurs 8am–2am, Fri 8am–3:30am, Sat 8am–4:30am, Sun 9am–2am. CUBAN.

Versailles is the meeting place of Miami's Cuban power brokers who meet daily over café con leche to discuss the future of the exiles' fate. A glorified diner, the place sparkles with glass, chandeliers, murals, and mirrors meant to evoke the French city. There's nothing fancy here, and nothing French either—just straightforward food from the home country. The menu includes specialties like Moors and Christians (flavorful black beans with white rice), ropa vieja, and fried whole fish.

MEALS FOR LESS THAN $10

Hy-Vong. 3458 SW 8th St. (between 34th and 35th aves.), Little Havana. ☎ **305/446-3674.** Reservations not accepted. Main courses $8–$12. No credit cards. Tues–Sun 6–11pm. Closed 2 weeks in Aug. VIETNAMESE.

Expect to wait for hours for a table at this tiny storefront restaurant. And don't even think of mumbling a complaint—the owner/chef/waitress will be sure to forget to stop by your small wooden table to refill your glasses or take an order if you do. Enjoy the wait with a traditional Vietnamese beer and the company of interesting musicians and foodies who come for the large and delicious portions, not for the plain wood-paneled room or painfully slow service. But it's worth it. The food at Hy-Vong is elegantly simple and super-spicy. Star offerings include pastry-enclosed chicken with watercress/cream-cheese sauce and fish in tangy mango sauce.

MEALS FOR LESS THAN $15

✪ **Casa Juancho.** 2436 SW 8th St., Little Havana. ☎ **305/642-2452.** Reservations recommended; not accepted Fri–Sat after 8pm. Tapas $6–$8; main courses $11–$20; lunch $6–$12. AE, CB, DC, MC, V. Sun–Thurs noon–midnight, Fri–Sat noon–1am. SPANISH/CUBAN.

Perhaps one of Miami's finest Hispanic restaurants, Casa Juancho offers an ambitious menu of excellently prepared main dishes and tapas. A few dishes stand out, like roast suckling pig, baby eels in garlic and olive oil, and Iberian-style snapper. The several dining rooms are enlivened nightly by strolling Spanish musicians. Try not to be frustrated with the older staff who don't speak English or respond quickly to your subtle glance—they're used to an aggresive clientele.

NORTH DADE

The population explodes in this area in the winter months, when the seasonal residents come down from the Northeast to enjoy the fair weather and calm of this suburban area on the mainland. A demanding clientele, many of them dine out nightly. That's good news for visitors, who can find superior service and cuisine at value prices.

MEALS FOR LESS THAN $7

The Juice Bar. 18315 W. Dixie Hwy. (1 block west of Biscayne Blvd.), North Miami Beach. ☎ **305/935-9544.** Sandwiches and salads $4–$6. No credit cards. Daily 8:30am–6pm. HEALTH FOOD.

This brightly painted stand in the middle of a busy road attracts a varied crowd from young ponytailed Europeans to bikers who stop in for a fresh smoothie or vegetable juice made on the spot. If you don't mind a bit of car exhaust with your snapper sandwich, consider this landmark, where the food includes one of the most unusual tuna salads I've ever run across. The smooth paste, with no trace of fishiness, is served in a pita with tons of crisp vegetables including alfalfa sprouts, tomato, and lettuce. The hummus is superb, though garlic lovers might want a hint more spark.

Laurenzo's Cafe. 16385 W. Dixie Hwy. (at 163rd St.), North Miami Beach. ☎ **305/945-6381.** Main courses $4–$5; salads $2–$5. AE, MC, V. Mon–Sat 8am–7pm, Sun 8am–4pm. SOUTHERN ITALIAN CAFETERIA.

This little lunch counter in the middle of a chaotic grocery store has been serving delicious buffet lunches to the *paesanos* for years. A meeting place for the minuscule Italian population in Miami, the store has been open for more than 40 years. Daily specials usually include a lasagne or eggplant parmigiana and two or three salad options. Choose a wine from the vast selection and take your meal to the trellis-covered seating area amid busy shoppers buying their evening's groceries. You'll get to eavesdrop on some great conversations over your plastic tray of real southern-style Italian cooking. A good Italian fixed-price dinner, with slightly more atmosphere and service, is offered just down the street at 2255 NE 164th St. (☎ 305/948-8008).

MEALS FOR LESS THAN $10

Here Comes the Sun. 2188 NE 123rd St. (west of the Broad Causeway), North Miami.
☎ **305/893-5711.** Reservations recommended in season. Main courses $10–$14; early-bird special $7.95; sandwiches and salads $5–$7.50. AE, DISC, DC, MC, V. Mon–Sat 11am–8:30pm (early-bird special served 4–6:30pm). AMERICAN/HEALTH FOOD.

One of Miami's early health-food spots, this bustling grocery-store-turned-diner serves hundreds of plates a night. It's noisy and hectic but worth it. In season, all types pack the place for a $7.95 early-bird special, which includes a choice of more than 20 main dishes, soup or salad, coffee or tea, and a small frozen yogurt. The miso burgers with "sun sauce" are a vegetarian's dream.

MEALS FOR LESS THAN $15

The Gourmet Diner. 13951 Biscayne Blvd. (between NE 139th and 140th sts.), North Miami Beach. ☎ **305/947-2255.** Reservations not accepted. Main courses $10–$17. No credit cards. Mon–Fri 11am–11pm, Sat 8am–11:30pm, Sun 8am–10:30pm. BELGIAN/FRENCH.

This retro 1950s-style diner serves plain old French fare without pretentions. The atmosphere is a bit brash and the lines are often out the door. You'll want to get there early anyway to taste some of the house specialties like beef burgundy, trout almondine, and frogs' legs provençal, which sell out quickly. Check the chalk-board for the salads and soups, all prepared to order. Even a simple hearts of palm becomes a gourmet treat under the tangy vinaigrette. A well-rounded wine list with reasonable prices makes this place a stand-out. The homemade daily pastries are also delicious.

CORAL GABLES

This historic area is home to some of Miami's wealthiest families and best dining spots. A profusion of high-priced Italian restaurants epitomize the area's offerings, though there a number of lower-priced options as well.

MEALS FOR LESS THAN $7

Biscayne Miracle Mile Cafeteria. 147 Miracle Mile, Coral Gables. ☎ **305/444-9005.** Main courses $3–$4. No credit cards. Mon–Sat 11am–2:15pm and 4–8pm, Sun 11am–8pm. SOUTHERN AMERICAN.

Here you'll find no bar, no music, and no flowers on the tables—just great Southern-style cooking at unbelievably low prices. The menu changes, but roast beef, baked fish, and barbecued ribs are typical offerings, few of which exceed $4. The kitschy 1950s decor is an asset in this last of the old-fashioned cafeterias, where the gold-clad waiters are proud and attentive. Enjoy it while it lasts.

MEALS FOR LESS THAN $10

Sergio's. 3252 Coral Way, Coral Gables. ☎ **305/529-0047.** Reservations not accepted. Main courses $5–$7; lunch $2–$5. AE, DC, MC, V. Sun–Thurs 6am–midnight, Fri–Sat 24 hours. CUBAN/AMERICAN.

Located across from the Miracle Center Mall, Sergio's stands out like a Latin-inspired International House of Pancakes, with red-clothed tables, neon signs in the windows, and video games along the back wall. Serving everything from ham-and-eggs breakfasts to grilled-steak-sandwich lunches and dinners, Sergio's is not a place for vegetarians. The family-style restaurant also specializes in native Cuban-style dishes. Low prices and late-night dining keep it popular with locals.

MEALS FOR LESS THAN $15

House of India. 22 Merrick Way (1 block north of Miracle Mile, near Douglas and Coral Way), Coral Gables. ☎ **305/444-2348.** Reservations accepted. Main courses $7–$10; lunch buffet (served Mon–Fri 11:30am–3pm and Sat noon–3pm) $6.95. AE, MC, V. Mon–Thurs 11:30am–10pm, Fri–Sat 11:30am–11pm, Sun 5–10pm. INDIAN.

House of India's curries, kormas, and kebabs are some of the city's best, but the restaurant's well-priced all-you-can-eat lunch buffet is unsurpassed. All the favorites are on display, including tandoori chicken, naan bread, various curries, as well as rice and dal (lentils). If you've never had Indian food before, this is an excellent place to experiment since you can see the food before you choose it. Veterans will know this high-quality cooking from the subcontinent. The restaurant's not fancy (in fact, I've heard it described as a greasy spoon), but it is nicely decorated, with hanging batik prints. The place could use a good scrub-down.

Uva Wine Bar & Eatery. 3850 SW 8th St., Coral Gables. ☎ **305/529-2264.** Reservations recommended Fri–Sun for dinner. Main courses $11–$19; lunch $7–$12. AE, DC, MC, V. Mon–Fri 11am–3pm and 5–11pm, Sat–Sun 5–11pm. CUBAN/ITALIAN.

The pairing of Cuban and Italian flavors results in outrageously delicious specialties at this dark and cozy restaurant way down Calle Ocho. Good starters are ceviche modo nostrum and the crostini with mushrooms and mozzarella. The truth is, I go only for the incredible seafood risotto—it's so buttery I've been known to get a take-out order and eat it in the car. They have a decent selection of wines and a pleasant staff who speak some English. The place is mostly populated with well-dressed Latinos who come for the live music and woodsy bar scene. There's also a rather elegant little cigar room upstairs.

COCONUT GROVE

Like one big shopping mall, "the Grove" offers a variety of good eating options at every price. From white-glove excess to stand-in-line counter shops, the Grove is a place to find lots of deals interspersed with a number of tourist traps.

MEALS FOR LESS THAN $7

Cafe Tu Tu Tango. 3015 Grand Ave. (on the second floor of Cocowalk), Coconut Grove. ☎ **305/529-2222.** Reservations not accepted. Main courses $4–$8. AE, DC, DISC, MC, V. Sun–Wed 11:30am–midnight, Thurs 11:30am–1am, Fri–Sat 11:30am–2am. SPANISH/INTERNATIONAL.

In the bustling microcosm of Cocowalk, this second-floor restaurant is designed to look something like a disheveled artist's loft. Dozens of original paintings—some only half finished—are placed with seeming thoughtlessness on the walls and studio easels. Seating at sturdy wooden tables and chairs is either inside among the clutter or outdoors overlooking the Grove's main drag. Flamenco and other Latin-inspired tunes complement a menu with a decidedly Spanish flare. Main dishes include roast duck with dried cranberries, toasted pinenuts, and goat cheese, plus Cajun chicken eggrolls filled with corn, Cheddar cheese, and tomato salsa. Pastas, ribs, fish, and pizzas round out the eclectic offerings, and several visits have proved each consistently good. Especially when the rest of the Grove has shut down, Tu Tu Tango is an oasis—try the sweet and potent sangría and enjoy the warm and lively atmosphere from a seat with a view.

MEALS FOR LESS THAN $10

Fuddrucker's. 3444 Main Hwy., Coconut Grove. ☎ **305/442-8164.** Burgers and sandwiches $4–$5; salads $4–$6. AE, DISC, DC, MC, V. Mon 11am–11pm, Tues–Thurs and Sun 11am–midnight, Fri–Sat 11am–2am. AMERICAN/FAST FOOD.

The best part of this burger chain is that you can load up on as many fixings as you want at a well-stocked salad bar with tons of sauces. It's a chain, but probably the best place for a burger and beer. The lively atmosphere attracts locals and visitors who come for the Bennigan's-type setting and the reasonably priced sandwiches. There's a pretty outdoor area covered with a canopy where you can enjoy Florida's comfortable atmosphere and do a bit of people-watching as well.

Green Street Cafe. 3110 Commodore Plaza, Coconut Grove. ☎ **305/567-0662.** Reservations not accepted. Main courses $6–$12; breakfast $3–$6. AE, MC, V. Sun–Thurs 6:45am–11:30pm, Fri–Sat 6:45am–1am. CONTINENTAL.

Green Street is located at the "100% corner," the Coconut Grove intersection of Main Highway and Commodore Plaza that 100% of all tourists visit. This enviable location—with loads of outdoor seating that's great for people-watching—relieves the pressure on Green Street to turn out great meals, but the food is well above average. Offerings are continental-style or heartier American-style breakfasts and soup, salad, and sandwich lunches. Dinners are more elaborate, with several decent pasta dishes as well as fresh fish, chicken, and burgers, including one made of lamb.

The Last Carrot. 3133 Grand Ave., Coconut Grove. ☎ **305/445-0805.** Main courses $4–$8. No credit cards. Daily 10am–7pm. HEALTH/NATURAL.

The last outpost for healthy food in an area that was once defined by its granola and Birkenstock roots, the Last Carrot serves hot spinach turnovers with cheese and tomato, and pita sandwiches with the freshest tuna, chicken, and salads with ample lettuce, sprouts, and of course, carrots. When offered a choice of herb dressings, choose the pink tomato-based dressing—it's the best. It's crowded throughout the day with a young and diverse group.

MEALS FOR LESS THAN $15

✪ Kaleidoscope. 3112 Commodore Plaza, Coconut Grove. ☎ **305/446-5010.** Reservations recommended. Main courses $12–$15 for pasta, $14–$20 for meat and fish; lunch $8–$13. AE, CB, DC, DISC, MC, V. Mon–Fri 11:30am–3pm and 6–11pm, Sat 6–11pm, Sun 5:30–10:30pm. NEW AMERICAN.

Kaleidoscope is one of the few restaurants in the heart of Coconut Grove that would still be recommended even if it were located somewhere less exciting. The atmosphere is elegantly relaxed, with low-key, attentive service, comfortable seating, and a well-designed terrace overlooking the busy sidewalks below. Well-prepared pastas, topped with sauces like seafood and fresh basil, or pesto with grilled yellowfin tuna, are especially tasty. The linguine with salmon and fresh dill is perfection. Although there's no special pretheater dinner, many locals stop into this reliable second-floor spot for dinner before a show down the street at the Coconut Grove Playhouse.

Señor Frog's. 3008 Grand Ave., Coconut Grove. ☎ **305/448-0999.** Reservations recommended on weekends. Main courses $9–$12. AE, CB, DC, MC, V. Mon–Sat 11:30am–2am, Sun 11:30am–1am. MEXICAN.

You know you're getting close to Señor Frog's when you hear laughing and singing spilling out of the restaurant's courtyard. Filled with the college-student crowd, this rocking cantina is known for a raucous good time, its mariachi band, and its powerful margaritas. The food is as good as its atmosphere, featuring traditional Mexican/American favorites. The mole enchiladas, with 14 different kinds of mild chiles mixed with chocolate, are as flavorful as any I've tasted. Almost everything is served with rice and beans in quantities so large that few diners are able to finish.

SOUTH MIAMI

This mostly residential area has some very good dining spots to stop at on your way to area attractions. Most are scattered along U.S. 1. Since the hurricane, many have rebuilt and are better than ever.

MEALS FOR LESS THAN $7

✪ **Shorty's.** 9200 S. Dixie Hwy. (between U.S. 1 and Dadeland Blvd.), South Miami. ☎ **305/670-7732.** Main courses $5–$9. MC, V. Daily 11am–11pm. BARBECUE.

A tradition in Miami since 1951, this hokey log cabin is still serving some of the best ribs and chicken in South Florida. People line up for the smoky-flavored slow-cooked meat that's so tender it wants to jump off the bone into your mouth. The secret, however, is to ask for your order with sweet sauce—the regular stuff tastes bland and bottled. All the side dishes, including cole slaw, corn on the cob, and baked beans, look commercial but are necessary to complete the experience. This is B-B-Q, with a neon B.

A second Shorty's is located in Davie at 5989 S. University Dr. (☎ 305/944-0348).

MEALS FOR LESS THAN $10

✪ **Pollo Tropical.** 18710 S. Dixie Hwy. (at 186th St.), South Miami. ☎ **305/225-7858.** Main courses $3–$6. No credit cards. Sun–Thurs 11am–10pm, Fri–Sat 11am–11pm. CUBAN/FAST FOOD.

This Miami-based chain is putting up new terra-cotta arched fast-food places so fast you can hardly finish an order of garlic-drenched yuca before another one has taken root. Lucky for Miamians and the Southeast, the dozens of these restaurants provide hot and tender chicken with a variety of healthful side dishes. A recent addition is fresh chunks of carrots, onions, zucchini, and squash on wooden skewers, and a variety of salads.

MEALS FOR LESS THAN $15

Anacapri. 12669 S. Dixie Hwy. (in the South Park Center at 128th St. and U.S. 1). ☎ **305/232-8001.** Main courses $8–$16. AE, DC, DISC, MC, V. Sun–Mon and Wed–Thurs 5–10:30pm, Fri–Sat 5–11:30pm. ITALIAN.

Neighborhood fans wait in line happily with a glass of wine and pleasant company for this somewhat heavy but flavorful Italian cuisine. An antipasto with thinly cut meats and cheeses and green peppers is a great start to a hearty meal. Stick with the basics here, like the pastas with red sauce, which are flavorful though a bit heavy on the garlic and oil. The chicken is marinated in a seriously secret sauce and served with well-seasoned black beans and rice. The menu, though Latin inspired, is clearly spelled out in English as well. Everyone is treated like a member of the family. It's a good place to get an education in Latin *sabor,* or taste.

Two other locations are at 1454 Alton Rd., Miami Beach (☎ 305/672-8888), and 11806 Biscayne Blvd., North Miami (☎ 305/895-0274). Check the phone book for still others.

Cafe Hammock. 500 SW 177 Ave. (in the Miccosukee Indian Gaming Site, at Krome Ave. and Tamiami Trail). ☎ **305/222-4600.** Reservations accepted. Main courses $10–$22; dinner specials $5–$6. MC, V. Daily 11am–1am. CONTINENTAL.

In the clanging environs of the Miccosukee gaming village way down south, you can dine on stone crab claws and decent steak for a few bucks while overlooking hundreds of fanatical Bingo players. If you can keep away from the dealers and slots and don't mind a bit of smoke, you'll be amazed at the excellent service and phenomenal specials they run to entice gamblers to this bizarre outpost.

Call in advance to see if there are any worthwhile specials. Otherwise, the regular menu, with intriguing-sounding offerings like Cajun-style cod nuggets and Bahamian conch fritters, is disappointing. Some of the entrees are delicious but no bargain. The alligator, too, is tasty, though a bit dry. Don't expect Native Americans in native dress; you'll find servers from New Jersey and California before you see a Miccosukee serving burgers here.

WORTH A SPLURGE

❖ **Crystal Cafe.** 726 41st St., Miami Beach ☎ **305/673-8266.** Reservations recommended on weekends. Main courses $13–22. AE, MC, V. Tues–Sun 5–11pm. CONTINENTAL/NOUVELLE.

The place is sparse, the decor black and white, with Lucite salt and pepper grinders and a bottle of wine as an only centerpiece on each of the 15 or so tables. I promise that you won't need the sesoning—chef Klime (pronounced *Klee*-me) has done it all with the help of a superb service staff and his affable wife. They have created a neighborhood bistro that attracts stars like Julio Iglesias. The attentive staff never seems obtrusive yet is always there to refill a water glass, inquire about your needs, or tempt you with yet more delicious food. With something like 30 entrees listed on the unpretentious and ever-changing menu, it's amazing the way each comes out perfectly prepared, often with some unexpected addition. The shrimp cake appetizer is the size of a bread plate and rests on top of small mound of lightly sautéed watercress and mushrooms. Surrounding the delicately breaded disc are concentric circles of beautiful sauces—tomato and a basil-mayonnaise. The veal marsala is served in a luscious brown sauce that's thickened not with heavy cream or flour but with delicate vegetable broth and a hearty mix of mushrooms. The osso bucco is gaining renown among Miami foodies with good reason: It's a masterpiece—the tender, almost-buttery meat is steeped in chicken broth and is piled high with an assortment of vegetables. The desserts are tempting but hard to manage after such generous portions. If you can, consider the crêpe stuffed with warm berry compote with a nutty topping.

The Lagoon. 488 Sunny Isles Blvd. (163rd St.), North Miami Beach. ☎ **305/947-6661.** Reservations accepted. Main courses $12–$22; lobster special $19.95; early special $8.95–$17.95. AE, CB, MC, V. Daily 4:30–11pm (early-bird specials 4:30–6pm). SEAFOOD/CONTINENTAL.

This old bayfront fish house has been around since 1936. Major road construction that makes it nearly impossible to get to should have guaranteed its doom years ago. But the excellent view and incredible specials have kept it going. Yes, it's true! Lobster lovers, you can get two 1¼-pounders for $19.95. Broiled is best, with a light buttery seasoned coating. Side dishes include fresh vegetables like broccoli or asparagus as well as a huge baked potato, stuffed or plain. The bathrooms could use a good cleaning, as could the whole cavernous restaurant. Disregard that and the nonchalant service and you'll find the best-priced juicy Maine lobsters around.

L'Entrecote de Paris. 413 Washington Ave., South Miami Beach. ☎ **305/538-0021.** Reservations suggested on weekends. Prix-fixe meal (including potatoes and salad) $16. MC, V. Daily 6pm–1am. FRENCH BRASSERIE.

Everything in this classy little bistro is simple. For example, for dinner your choice is salmon or steak. Yes, that's it. Meat or fish and maybe a few salads. They're all great. The salmon, served with a pile of bald steamed potatoes and a salad with pedestrian greens and a nice vinaigrette, looks like spa cuisine. But the steak, on the on the other hand, even for a non–meat enthusiast, is the stuff cravings are made of. Its salty and sharp sauce is rich but not thick, and full of the beef's natural flavor. The slices are served on top of your own little habachi, which also keeps the skinny pommes frites warm. The half-dozen tables and booths are so cramped that you may be tempted to take a stab at your neighbor's plate while you wait for your own. The waiters are super-quick and professional, almost friendly, in a French kind of way. A short and very Franco-oriented wine list includes several well-priced bottles for under $20. Even if you're on a diet or have forsaken chocolate, try the profiteroles au chocolat, a perfect puff pastry filled with vanilla ice cream and topped with a dark bittersweet-chocolate sauce. The crème brûlée and tarte aux pommes are also excellent.

Mark's Place. 2286 NE 123rd St., North Miami. ☎ **305/893-6888.** Reservations recommended. Main courses $10–$15 for pasta and pizza, $16–$20 for meat and fish; lunch about half price. AE, MC, V. Mon–Thurs noon–2:30pm and 6–10:30pm, Fri noon–2:30pm and 6–11pm, Sat 6–11pm, Sun 6–10pm. MIAMI REGIONAL.

This restaurant attracts an upscale but leisurely crowd, and its claim to fame is owner/chef Mark Militello, an extraordinarily gifted artist who works primarily with fresh, natural, local ingredients. A smart, modern bistro, Mark's Place shines with off-white walls, an aquamarine ceiling, contemporary glass sculptures, and a friendly, open kitchen. Each table has its own pepper mill and fresh home-baked bread.

Mark's food is inspired, often unusual, and it rarely misses the mark. Appetizers include oak-grilled mozzarella and prosciutto, curry-breaded fried oysters, and an unusual petite pizza topped with smoked chicken and Monterey Jack cheese. The best main dishes are braised black grouper, Florida conch stew, and flank steak in sesame marinade. Try one of Mark's suggestions. Desserts like Icky Sticky Coconut Pudding are equally unusual and created with the same originality as the rest of the menu.

Monty's Bayshore Restaurant. 2560 S. Bayshore Dr., Coconut Grove. ☎ **305/858-1431.** Reservations recommended upstairs on weekends. Sandwiches $6–$8; platters $7–$12; main courses $19–$35. AE, CB, DC, MC, V. Daily 11am–3am. SEAFOOD.

This place comes in three parts: a lounge, a raw bar, and a restaurant. Among them, Monty's serves everything from steak and seafood to munchies like nachos, potato skins, and buffalo chicken wings. This is a fun place. There are usually more revelers and drinkers than diners at the downstairs bar. At the outdoor dockside bar there's live music nightly, as well as all day on weekends. Upstairs is an upscale dining room that serves one of the city's best Caesar salads and an all-you-can-eat stone crab claws special in season for $36.95. Be sure, however, not to order the claws from May to October since you'll be served an imported version that simply doesn't compare.

Nemo Restaurant. 100 Collins Ave., South Miami Beach. ☎ **305/532-4550.** Reservations recommended. Main courses $17–$20; lunch $8–$12; sandwiches and platters $4–$12; brunch $16. Mon–Fri noon–3pm and 7pm–midnight, Sat 6pm–midnight, Sun noon–4pm and 6–11pm. MULTICULTURAL.

This super-stylish and dark hotspot is an oasis in a newly hip area of South Beach below 5th Street. Here models and celebrities literally rub elbows since the tables are so close together, lighted by only a pinpoint of light that dangles over each terra-cotta table top. Ask to be seated in the back, which for some reason is considered less desirable but to me is the only way to hear your dining companions or your waiter (in the main dining room the din is unbearable). In the back, you look out onto a pleasant garden and, with only six tables, feel as if you have a private dining room. Somehow, the management has found the only really professional and flawless service staff on the beach—personable, intelligent, efficient, and full of helpful suggestions. Amazing! Try the all-you-can eat-brunch with fresh fruits, omelets and hash browns, and lots of fresh juices. For the price, you get to experience one of South Beach's best new hotspots.

Stephan's Gourmet Market & Cafe. 1430 Washington Ave. (at Espanola Way). ☎ **305/674-1760.** Main courses $6–$12; dinner special for two (with salad and a bottle of wine) $24.95. AE, MC, V. Sun–Thurs 10am–midnight, Fri–Sat 10am–2am (dinner special, daily 5:30–11pm). DELI/ITALIAN.

This deli, which could be in New York's Little Italy, sells a huge assortment of fresh pastas, breads, and salads as well as cold cuts, cheeses and grocery items. But upstairs, in a tiny loft used to store wine bottles, is a cozy dining room that few people know about with space for about 10 couples. A chalkboard displays the chef's special, usually a pasta dish with some kind of chicken or fish. One of my favorites is the linguine Alfredo, with tender pieces of chicken breast mixed into the light and cheesy sauce. While you wait, you'll want to eat baskets and baskets full of the super-garlicky bread and get started on the bottle of wine that comes with the daily special. The red is an excellent full-bodied Italian merlot. The pinot grigio, on the other hand, I find undrinkable. If the special doesn't strike you, consider any of the other moderately priced dishes. You can choose whatever looks good to you from the glass case downstairs and see what else the chef is dishing out. Dinner is also available out on the sidewalk or delivered to your hotel.

6

What to See & Do in Miami

by Victoria Pesce Elliott

Unlike the theme-park landscape of Central Florida, Miami is a real working city that just happens to call tourism its no. 1 industry. As a popular local bumper sticker reads: SOME OF US ARE *NOT* ON VACATION. The bustle of tourism just blends into the life of the city.

The best things to do in Miami don't revolve around the man-made attractions. Head for the treasures that nature put here, like the sea and sand, or check out the places that locals built for their own enjoyment, like Villa Vizcaya or Coral Castle. But don't discount the man-made attractions altogether. The city was, and is still, built to court visitors (and their dollars) from around the world, and many of these efforts to lure them in make for fantastic entertainment. Some of the city's older attractions, such as Monkey Jungle, Parrot Jungle, and the Seaquarium, attract visitors as well as a steady stream of locals.

Add to all the resources here a new wave of world-class exhibitions, like the Wolfsonian, and a plethora of sports- and water-related activities. There's a lot of do, so check out the suggested itineraries for a good guide to how to spend your time.

SUGGESTED ITINERARIES

IF YOU HAVE 1 DAY   If you arrive early, take the morning to explore Key Biscayne and Virginia Key, where you'll find a beautiful island ringed with beaches and sporting a fantastic state park at its tip. Take a swim off the sandy tip of Bill Baggs State Park or tour the area on foot, looking at the lush native landscape, birds, and wildlife. Have a bite at the snack shop, El Farito, as you gear up to make the short trip—really just an exaggerated U-turn—to South Beach. Make your way to the art deco district to see the whimsical architecture along Ocean Drive. Park at Lincoln Road to walk the strip, and choose any of the excellent restaurants to have a late-afternoon snack or dinner.

IF YOU HAVE 2 DAYS   You can spend a little more time on Key Biscayne on your first day (as described above). You can also include a trip to the Miami Seaquarium, especially if you have children along—kids love the Killer Whales and performing dolphins. Tour South Beach in the evening when the lively café scene and nightlife will keep you up late.

On your second day, drive down to Greater Miami South to visit one or more of the attractions described in this chapter, such as

Parrot Jungle, Monkey Jungle, or the Miami Metrozoo. On your way, consider a quick tour of Coral Gables and see the spectacular Biltmore Hotel. Or if shopping is your thing, head downtown where you can browse galleries in the design district and stroll in Bayside Marketplace, where, if you're feeling ambitious, you can enjoy an evening boat cruise.

IF YOU HAVE 3 DAYS Spend your first 2 days as described above and plan to really delve into South Beach on your third day when you can visit the Wolfsonian, the Bass Museum, the Holocaust Memorial, and the Jewish Museum. Punctuate the afternoon with some in-line skating or biking on the boardwalk, and stops into one or more of the many cafés lining Ocean Drive. In the evening, drive down Calle Ocho for dinner and a show, or head to Coconut Grove for your meal. Afterward, enjoy a Latin nightclub or a bar in Cocowalk, or some live music.

IF YOU HAVE 4 OR MORE DAYS You've only just begun to get a flavor of this multifaceted region. With a few extra days, take advantage of the many outdoor activities. Spend a day at the beach, collecting shells, working on your tan, or being a little more active. You can rent a charter boat to catch your own dinner, sail from the Coconut Grove Marina, or kayak through the mangroves. You can take a tour of Villa Vizcaya, a historic tour of the city, or a funky art deco walking tour. With an extra day, you can drive down to the Keys (see Chapter 7) or across to the Everglades (see Chapter 8).

1 Beaches

There are more than 35 miles of pristine beaches in Dade County. The character of each of Miami's many beaches is as varied as the city's population. Some are shaded by towering palm trees, while others are darkened by huge condominiums. Some attract families or old-timers; others, a chi-chi singles scene. In short, there are two distinct beach alternatives: Miami Beach and Key Biscayne. It's all explained below.

MIAMI BEACH Collins Avenue fronts 10 miles of white-sand beach and blue-green waters from 1st to 192nd streets. Although most of this stretch is lined with a solid wall of hotels, beach access is plentiful and you're free to frolic along the entire strip. There are lots of public beaches here, complete with lifeguards, toilet facilities, concession stands, and metered parking (bring lots of quarters). Miami Beach's beaches are both wide and well maintained. Except for a thin strip close to the water, most of the sand here is hard-packed—the result of a $10-million Army Corps of Engineers Beach Rebuilding Project meant to protect buildings from the effects of eroding sand.

In general, the beaches on this barrier island become less crowded the farther north you go. A wooden boardwalk runs along the hotel side of the beach from 21st to 46th streets—about 1 1/2 miles—offering a terrific sun and surf experience without getting sand in your shoes. Aside from the "Best Beaches" listed below, Miami Beach's lifeguard-protected public beaches include **21st Street,** at the beginning of the boardwalk; **35th Street,** popular with an older crowd; **46th Street,** next to the Fontainebleau Hilton; **53rd Street,** a narrower, more sedate beach; **64th Street,** one of the quietest strips around; and **72nd Street,** a local old-timers spot.

KEY BISCAYNE If Miami Beach isn't private enough for you, Key Biscayne might be more what you have in mind. Crossing Rickenbacker Causeway ($1 toll) is almost like crossing into The Bahamas. The 5 miles of public beach here are blessed with softer sand and are less developed and more laid-back than the hotel-laden strips to the north.

THE BEST BEACHES

Here are my picks for the best beaches for the following activities and audiences:

Best Picnic Beach: I happened upon this incredible gem only because a local invited me to his apartment, which happened to overlook this gorgeous little island. When I asked what it was, he couldn't tell me, even though he had lived in the apartment for years. Well, after a bit of digging, I discovered that it was **Pelican Island** (☎ 305/754-9330), a 10-acre picnickers' paradise that's owned by the county. It's accessible by a 35-seat pontoon boat that departs on weekends from the marina on the 79th Street Causeway. You can use any of the 18 barbecue grills, 200 picnic tables, horseshoe pits, and volleyball courts. And while it isn't technically a beach, it's Miami's best spot anywhere for a picnic. You'll also find great picnic facilities at **Crandon Park** on Key Biscayne (see below).

Best Surfing Beach: Just north of Miami Beach, **Haulover Beach / Harbor House** seems to get Miami's biggest swells. Go early and avoid the rush of young locals who wish they were on Maui.

Best Party Beach: In Key Biscayne, the **Crandon Park Beach**, on Crandon Boulevard, has 3 miles of oceanfront beach, 493 acres of park, 75 grills, three parking lots, several soccer and softball fields, and a public 18-hole championship golf course. The beach is particularly wide and the water is usually so clear you can see to the bottom. Admission is $2 per vehicle. It's open daily from 8am to sunset.

Best People-Watching: The ultra-chic **Lummus Park Beach,** which runs along Ocean Drive from about 6th to 14th streets in South Beach, is the best place to go if you're seeking entertainment as well as a great tan. On any day of the week you might spy models primping for a photo shoot or topless sunbathers avoiding tan lines.

Best Swimming Beach: The **85th Street Beach,** along Collins Avenue, is the best place to swim away from the madding crowds. It's one of Miami's only stretches of sand with no condos or hotels looming over the sunbathers. Lifeguards patrol the area throughout the day.

Best Windsurfing Beach: On the right side of the causeway leading to Key Biscayne, **Hobie Beach** is a secluded inlet with predictable winds and a number of places where you can rent windsurfers.

Best Shell-Hunting Beach: You'll find plenty of colorful shells at **Bal Harbour Beach,** Collins Avenue at 96th Street, just a few yards north of Surfside Beach. There's also an exercise course and good shade—but no lifeguards.

Best All-Around Tanning Beach: Although the state has been trying to pass ordinances to outlaw nudity, several nude beaches are thriving in the region. In Dade County, **Haulover Beach**, just north of the Bal Harbour border, attracts nudists from around the world and has created something of a boom for area businesses that cater to them.

2 The Art Deco District

Miami's best sight is not a museum or an amusement park but a part of the city itself. Located in South Beach, the art deco district is a whole community made up of outrageous and fanciful 1920s and 1930s architecture. After years of neglect and calls for the wholesale demolition of its buildings, South Beach got a new lease on life in 1979 when, under the leadership of the Miami Design Preservation League, approximately 1 square mile of South Beach was granted a listing on the National Register of Historic Places—and the art deco district was born.

A Deco District Glossary

You don't have to be an architect to enjoy the fanciful styles that are so prevalent in these parts; the intrinsic beauty of these buildings is easy to see. Still, it always helps knowing what to look for.

Eyebrows   Colorfully painted cantilevered window shades are a common ornament on Streamline Moderne buildings.

Etched glass   Flamingos, fish, palm trees, and other tropical motifs are found in many area lobbies.

Finial, spire, or trylon   These futuristic-looking vertical ornaments are located atop a building's highest point.

Neon light   This seems to be an area trademark.

Porthole windows   Nautical imagery is one of South Beach's most important motifs.

Rounded corners   These most obviously reflect the influence of airplanes, automobiles, trains, and ships on Streamline Moderne architecture. Fast, sleek, aerodynamic designs looked futuristic in the 1930s and 1940s.

Terrazzo   This mosaic flooring is frequently arranged in geometric patterns.

Ziggurat or stepped pediment   Seen on roofs and incorporated into other areas, this Egyptian style is common in art deco design.

The art deco district is roughly bounded by the Atlantic Ocean on the east, Alton Road on the west, 6th Street on the south, and Dade Boulevard (along the Collins Canal) to the north. Most of the best buildings are concentrated along three parallel streets—Ocean Drive, Collins Avenue, and Washington Avenue—from about 6th Street to 17th Street.

Leonard Horowitz, a gifted young designer, began to cover the buildings' peeling beige paint with his now-famous flamboyant colors. Long-lost architectural details were highlighted with soft sherbets, and the colors of peach, periwinkle, turquoise, and purple received worldwide attention. Developers soon moved in, and the full-scale refurbishment of the area's hotels was under way.

Today, new hotels, restaurants, and nightclubs continue to open, and South Beach is on the cutting edge of Miami's cultural and nightlife scene.

If you're exploring on your own, start at the **Art Deco Welcome Center,** at 1001 Ocean Dr., which has several informative giveaways, includings maps and art deco architecture information. Art deco books, T-shirts, postcards, mugs, and other similarly styled items are sold. It's open Monday to Saturday from 9am to 6pm, sometimes later.

Among the highlights to seek out are the **Essex House,** 1001 Collins Ave., at 10th Street, an excellent example of Nautical Moderne, complete with porthole windows and sleek "racing stripes" along its sides. And along Ocean Drive, between 6th Street and the beach, there's the **Park Central,** and the **Imperial, Majestic,** and **Colony Hotels.** At 1020 Ocean Dr., the **Clevelander Hotel** is one of the few in the area with an original swimming pool and a deco-style sundeck area. The huge outdoor stage, located behind the pool, hosts live rock and reggae bands almost every night and turns the Clevelander into one of the liveliest locales on the beach.

Other particularly memorable areas for strolling include **Lincoln Road** (the pedestrians-only section, starting at Washington Street and heading west), which is lined with galleries, cafés, and funky art and antiques stores. And **Espanola Way,** around 14th and 15th streets, is a lovely Mediterranean-style section with interesting shops and restaurants.

On Thursday evening and Saturday morning, the **Miami Design Preservation League** (☎ 305/672-2014) sponsors walking tours that offer a fascinating inside look at the city's historic art deco district. Tourgoers meet at the Art Deco Welcome Center, 1001 Ocean Dr., for a 1½-hour walk through some of America's most exuberantly "architectured" buildings. The Design Preservation League led the fight to designate this area a National Historic District and is proud to share the splendid results with visitors. Walking tours cost $6 per person and depart on Thursday at 6:30pm and on Saturday at 10:30am; call for schedules.

If you'd rather bike or in-line skate around the area, catch the Sunday morning **Art Deco Cycling Tour**. Since the bicycle seems to be the most efficient mode of transportation through the streets of South Beach, what better way to view the historic art deco district than perched on the seat of a bike. Tours depart on Sunday at 10:30am and 12:30pm from the Miami Beach Bicycle Center, 601 5th St. (☎ 305/672-2014 or 305/674-0430). The tour costs $5 per person, plus another $5 if you rent a bike. Call the Art Deco Welcome Center to reserve a spot.

"See Miami like a native" is the motto of **Deco Tours Miami Beach,** 420 Lincoln Rd., Suite 412, Miami Beach (☎ 305/531-4465). Not only will you get the history of Miami Beach's deco buildings, you'll also learn which big stars are in town shooting a flick, which new restaurants and clubs are hot, and where to get your hair done. Who said learning wasn't fun? Tours cost $10, and leave Monday to Friday at 10:30am and 4pm (none offered in July and August). Meet at the Miami Beach Chamber of Commerce at Meridian Avenue and Dade Boulevard.

Lummus Park Beach, which runs along Ocean Drive from about 6th to 14th streets in South Beach, is quite chi chi. If you put your towel down here, you'll get in some great people-watching and maybe even see a fashion shoot.

3 Animal Parks

Kids of all ages will enjoy Miami's animal parks, which feature everything from dolphins to lions to parrots.

Miami Metrozoo. SW 152nd St. and SW 124th Ave., south of Coral Gables. ☎ 305/251-0403. Admission $6 adults, $3 children 3–12. Daily 9:30am–5:30pm (ticket booth closes at 4pm). From U.S. 1, take the SW 152nd Street exit west 3 blocks to the Metrozoo entrance.

Rarely does a zoo warrant mention as a city's top attraction, but the Miami Metrozoo is different. This huge 290-acre complex is completely cageless—animals are kept at bay by cleverly designed moats. The original Mufasa and Simba of Disney fame were modeled on Metrozoo's lions, still in residence. Star attractions include two rare white Bengal tigers, a Komodo dragon, rare koala bears, and a monorail "safari." Especially appealing for both adults and children is PAWS, a unique petting zoo. You can even ride an elephant.

Miami Seaquarium. 4400 Rickenbacker Causeway (south side), Key Biscayne. ☎ 305/361-5705. Admission $18.45 adults, $14.45 seniors over 65, $13.95 children 3–9. Daily

Greater Miami South Attractions

Coral Castle ⑥
Fairchild Tropical Gardens ②
Miami Metrozoo ③
Monkey Jungle ④
Parrot Jungle ①
Preston B. Bird and Mary Heinlein
    Fruit and Spice Park ⑤

9:30am–6pm (ticket booth closes at 4:30pm). From downtown Miami, take I-95 South to the Rickenbacker Causeway.

It takes about 4 hours of your time to tour the 35-acre oceanarium if you want to see all four daily shows starring the world's most impressive ocean mammals. Trained dolphins, killer whales, and frolicking sea lions take your breath away. If you're inclined, you can even volunteer for one of their big wet fishy kisses! If you remember the TV show *Flipper* (she was really named Bebe), come see one of the original dolphins that played the title role. She just celebrated her 30th birthday.

Monkey Jungle. 14805 SW 216th St., Greater Miami South. ☎ **305/235-1611.** Admission $10.50 adults, $9.50 seniors and active-duty military, $5.35 children 4–12. Daily 9:30am–5pm (last tickets sold at 4pm). Take U.S. 1 South to 216th Street; it's about 20 minutes from downtown.

See rare Brazilian golden lion tamarins. Watch the "skin diving" Asian macaques. Yes, folks, it's primate paradise! Visitors are protected, but there are no cages to restrain the antics of the monkeys as they swing, chatter, and play their way into your heart. Where else but in Florida would an attraction like this still be popular after 60 years? Screened-in trails wind through acres of "jungle," and daily shows feature the talents of the park's most progressive pupils. You've got to love primates to get over the heavy smell of the jungle.

Parrot Jungle and Gardens. 11000 SW 57th Ave., Greater Miami South. ☎ **305/666-7834.** Admission $10.95 adults, $7.95 children 3–12. Daily 9:30am–6pm. Take U.S. 1 South, turn left at SW 57th Avenue, and continue straight for 2¹/₂ miles.

Not just parrots, but hundreds of magnificent macaws, prancing peacocks, and fabulous flamingos occupy this park, now more than 50 years old. Alligators, tortoises, and iguanas are also on exhibit. But it's the parrots you came for and it's parrots you get. With brilliant splashes of color, these birds appear in every shape and size. Continuous shows in the Parrot Bowl Theater star roller-skating cockatoos, card-playing macaws, and more stunt-happy parrots than you ever thought possible. Other attractions include a wildlife show focusing on indigenous Florida animals, a children's playground, and a petting zoo.

Parrot Jungle is planning to move to its own island closer to downtown Miami; the move is scheduled to be completed by 1998.

4 Miami's Museum & Art Scene

Miami's museum scene has always been quirky, interesting, and inconsistent at best. Though several exhibition spaces have made forays into collecting nationally acclaimed work, limited support and political infighting have made it a difficult proposition. Recently, with the opening of the Wolfsonian in 1995 and MOCA in 1996, the scene has improved dramatically. It's now safe to say that world-class exhibitions start here. Listed below is an excellent cross section of the valuable treasures that have become a part of the city's cultural heritage, and as such, are as diverse as the city itself.

IN SOUTH BEACH

Bass Museum of Art. 2121 Park Ave. (at 21st St.), South Beach. ☎ **305/673-7530.** Admission $5 adults, $3 students with ID and senior citizens, free for children 5 and under; Wed by donation. Tues–Sat 10am–5pm, Sun 1–5pm (every second and fourth Wed 1–9pm). Closed holidays. Go north on Collins Avenue and turn right on 21st Street; the museum is directly behind the public library on the right.

The Bass, with its small permanent collection of European art, is the most important visual-arts museum in Miami Beach. Temporary exhibitions alternate between traveling shows and rotations of the Bass's stock, with themes ranging from 17th-century Dutch art to contemporary architecture.

Built from coral rock in 1930, the Bass sits in the middle of 6 tree-topped, landscaped acres. Wander the grounds to enjoy the changing outdoor sculpture exhibits.

✪ **The Wolfsonian.** 1001 Washington Ave., South Beach. ☎ **305/531-1001.** Admission $6 adults, $4 senior citizens, students, and children 11 and under; $7 tour groups. Tues–Thurs and Sat 10am–6pm, Fri 10am–9pm, Sun noon–5pm.

Micky Wolfson, Jr., an eccentric collector of late 19th- and 20th-century art and other paraphernalia, was spending so much money storing his booty that he decided to buy the warehouse. Now his incredibly diverse and controversial collection is housed in the former storage company. And the warehouse has been retrofitted with such painstaking detail that it's the envy of curators around the world.

They won't call it a museum or a gallery, but the works on display are definitely worth a look. For example, the inaugural exhibition, "The Arts of Reform and Persuasion," depicted works from the machine age from 1855 to World War I. Also on display are Nazi propaganda posters, deco mailboxes, board games celebrating capitalism, and WPA iconography. One can only wait to see what this great tinkerer has in store for the next go-round.

IN MIAMI BEACH

Holocaust Memorial. 1933 Meridian Ave., Miami Beach. ☎ **305/538-1663.** Free admission. Daily 9am–9pm. From Alton Road, turn left on Dade Boulevard and right on Meridian Avenue; the memorial is half a block down on the left.

This heart-wrenching memorial of the genocide that took place in 1940s Europe is hard to miss and would be a shame to overlook. The powerful centerpiece is a bronze statue by Kenneth Treister that depicts millions of people crawling into an open hand to freedom. You can walk through an open hallway lined with photographs and the names of concentration camps and their victims. From the street, you'll see the out-stretched arm, but do stop and tour the sculpture at ground level. What's hidden behind the beautiful stone facade is quite moving.

Sanford L. Ziff Jewish Museum of Florida. 301 Washington Ave. (at 3rd St.), Miami Beach. ☎ **305/672-5044.** Admission $4 adults, $3 senior citizens and students, free for children 5 and under; free for everyone on Sat; $9 family; $2.50 adults in a group of 20 or more with reservations. Tues–Sun 10am–5pm. Closed New Year's, Thanksgiving, and Jewish High Holidays.

Built on the site of a decaying synagogue, this spectacular museum is a time capsule of old Miami Beach. You'll find unbelievable old photos and documents as well as a number of traveling exhibitions from around the world detailing Jewish life. Call to find out the schedule, since the museum is closed on many Jewish holidays and in between shows.

IN & NEAR DOWNTOWN

Florida Museum of Hispanic and Latin American Art. 1 NE 40th St. (at N. Miami Ave.), Miami. ☎ **305/576-5171.** Admission $2 adults, $1 children 6–12. Tues–Fri 11am–5pm, Sat 11am–4pm. Closed Aug and major holidays.

In addition to the permanent collection of contemporary artists from Spain and Latin America, this museum, with more than 3,500 square feet, hosts monthly exhibitions of works from Latin America and the Caribbean Basin. Usually the group shows focus on a theme, such as international women or surrealism.

Metro-Dade Cultural Center. 101 W. Flagler St., Miami. ☎ **305/375-1700.** Center for the Fine Arts, $5 adults, $2.50 senior citizens and students with ID, free for children 11 and under; free for everyone Thurs 5–9pm. Historical Museum, $4 adults, $2 children 6–12, free for children 5 and under; discounts for groups of 20 or more with advance reservations. Center for the Fine Arts, Tues–Wed and Fri 10am–5pm, Thurs 10am–9pm, Sat–Sun noon–5pm. Historical Museum, Mon–Wed and Fri–Sat 10am–5pm, Thurs 10am–9pm, Sun noon–5pm. Both closed on major holidays. From I-96 North, take the NW 2nd Street exit and turn right, continue east to NW 2nd Avenue, turn right, and park at the Metro-Dade Garage at 50 NW 2nd Ave. From I-95 South, exit at Orange Bowl–NW 8th Street and continue south to NW 2nd Street; turn left at NW 2nd Street and go 1¹/₂ blocks to NW 2nd Avenue, turn right, and park at the Metro-Dade Garage. Bring the parking ticket to the lobby for validation.

The Metro-Dade Cultural Center is an oasis for those seeking cultural enrichment during their trip to Miami. The center houses the main branch of the **Metro-Dade Public Library** and sometimes features art and cultural exhibits. In addition to the library, the center houses the Historical Museum of Southern Florida and the Center for the Fine Arts.

The **Center for the Fine Arts** (☎ 305/375-3000) features an eclectic mix of modern and contemporary works by such artists as Eric Fischl, Max Beckman, Jim Dine, and Stuart Davis. Rotating exhibitions span the ages and styles. Call for updated schedules.

The primary exhibit at the **Historical Museum of Southern Florida** (☎ 305/375-1492) is "Tropical Dreams," a state-of-the-art chronological history of the last

Miami Area Attractions & Beaches

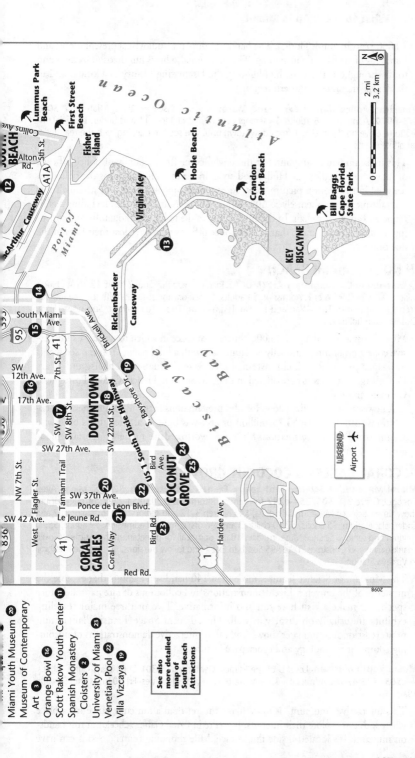

Miami Youth Museum 🄷
Museum of Contemporary
Art 🄷
Orange Bowl 🄷
Scott Rakow Youth Center 🄷
Spanish Monastery
Cloisters 🄷
University of Miami 🄷
Venetian Pool 🄷
Villa Vizcaya 🄷

See also
more detailed
map of
South Beach
Attractions

107

10,000 years in South Florida. The hands-on displays, audiovisual presentations, and hundreds of artifacts are intriguing. The museum also hosts hundreds of lectures and tours throughout the year, highlighting the fascinating history of Florida, and in particular, the state's southern region.

American Police Hall of Fame and Museum. 3801 Biscayne Blvd., Miami. ☎ **305/ 573-0070.** Admission $6 adults, $4 seniors over 61, $3 children 11 and under. Daily 10am– 5:30pm. Drive north on U.S. 1 from downtown until you see the building with the real police car affixed to its side.

This museum will mainly interest those who come from a family of police officers, or kids who will enjoy the Hollywood-style drama of such displays as the police car featured in the motion picture *Blade Runner* and a mock prison cell, where visitors can take pictures of themselves. Also displayed are execution devices, including a guillotine and an electric chair. In the entry, more to the point, is a thoughtful and touching memorial to the more than 3,000 police officers who have lost their lives in the line of duty.

IN NORTH MIAMI BEACH

✪ **Museum of Contemporary Art (MOCA).** Joan Lehman Building, 770 NE 125th St., North Miami. ☎ **305/893-6211.** Admission $4 adults, $2 seniors and students with ID, free for children 11 and under. Tues–Wed and Fri–Sat 10am–5pm, Thurs 10am–9pm, Sun noon–5pm. Closed major holidays.

MOCA just acquired a new 23,000-square-foot space in which to display its impressive collection of internationally acclaimed art with a local flavor. You can see works by Jasper Johns, Roy Lichtenstein, Larry Rivers, Duane Michaels, and Claes Oldenberg. Guided tours are offered in English, Spanish, French, Créole, Portuguese, German, and Italian.

A new screening facility allows for film presentations that will complement the exhibitions. Although the $3.75-million project was built in an area that's otherwise an uncharted tourist destination, MOCA is worth a drive to view important modern art in South Florida.

IN CORAL GABLES & COCONUT GROVE

Miami Museum of Science and Space Transit Planetarium. 3280 S. Miami Ave., Coconut Grove. ☎ **305/854-4247** for general information, 305/854-2222 for planetarium show times. Science Museum, $6 adults, $4 children 3–12 and seniors, free for children 2 and under; planetarium, $5 adults, $2.50 children and seniors; combined admission, $9 adults, $5.50 children and seniors. Science Museum, daily 10am–6pm; call for planetarium show times. Closed Thanksgiving and Christmas. Take I-95 South to Exit 1 and follow the signs. Or take the Metrorail to Vizcaya Station.

The Museum of Science features more than 140 hands-on exhibits that explore the mysteries of the universe. Live demonstrations and collections of rare natural-history specimens make a visit here fun and informative. Two or three major traveling exhibits are usually on display as well. The adjacent Space Transit Planetarium projects astronomy and laser shows, and offers interactive demonstrations of upcoming computer technology and cyberspace features.

Miami Youth Museum. Level U of the Miracle Center Mall, 3301 Coral Way, Coral Gables. ☎ **305/446-4FUN.** Admission $3 anyone over 1 year old. Tues–Fri 10am–4pm, Sat–Sun 10am–5pm.

This interactive "museum" is more like a theater than a museum, since it's a place where kids can explore their interests. If you're in Coral Gables, check out this hands-on museum. It's located inside the Miracle Mile shopping center, so kids can have a fun time after shopping. The museum has a mini–grocery store complete with cashier and stockboy assignments for role playing. Maybe the kids want to pretend to be Dr. Smiles, the dentist, or publish their own newspaper from the Hot off the Press exhibit.

5 More Attractions

✪ **Villa Vizcaya.** 3251 S. Miami Ave. (just south of Rickenbacker Causeway), North Coconut Grove. ☎ **305/250-9133.** Admission $10 adults, $5 children 6–12, free for children 5 and under. Villa, daily 9:30am–5pm (ticket booth closes at 4:30pm); gardens, daily 9:30am–5:30pm. Closed Christmas. Take I-95 South to Exit 1 and follow the signs to Vizcaya.

Sometimes referred to as the "Hearst Castle of the East," this magnificent villa was built in 1916 as a winter retreat for James Deering, co-founder and former vice president of International Harvester. The industrialist was fascinated by 16th-century art and architecture, and his ornate mansion—which took 1,000 artisans 5 years to build—became a celebration of these designs. Most of the original furnishings, including dishes and paintings, are still intact. Pink marble columns, topped with intricately designed capitals, reach up toward hand-carved ceilings. The spectacularly opulent villa wraps itself around a central courtyard, and outside, lush formal gardens front an enormous swath of Biscayne Bay, neighboring on the present-day homes of Sylvester Stallone and Madonna.

The Barnacle. 3485 Main Hwy. (1 block south of Commodore Plaza), Coconut Grove. ☎ **305/448-9445.** Admission $1. Tours Mon–Thurs at 10am, 11:30am, 1pm, and 2:30pm on the main house porch. From downtown Miami, take U.S. 1 South to South Bayshore Drive, continue to the end, turn right onto McFarlane Avenue and then left at the traffic light onto Main Highway; the museum is 5 blocks ahead on the left.

The former home of naval architect and early settler Ralph Middleton Munroe is now a museum in the heart of Coconut Grove. The house's quiet surroundings, wide porches, and period furnishings illustrate how Miami's privileged class lived in the days before skyscrapers and luxury hotels. Enthusiastic and knowledgeable state park employees offer a wealth of historical information.

Coral Castle. 28655 S. Dixie Hwy., Homestead. ☎ **305/248-6344.** Admission $7.75 adults, $6.50 seniors, $5 children 7–12. Daily 9am–6pm (closes at 3pm Thanksgiving and Christmas Eve). Closed Christmas. Take U.S. 1 South to SW 286th Street in Homestead.

There's plenty of competition, but the Coral Castle is probably the zaniest attraction in Florida. In 1923, the story goes, a man crazed by suffering from unrequited love, immigrated to South Florida and spent the next 25 years of his life carving massive amounts of stone into a prehistoric-looking, roofless "castle." It seems impossible that one person could have done all this, but there are scores of affidavits from neighbors swearing that it happened. Apparently experts have used this South Florida phenomenon to help figure out how the Great Pyramids and Stonehenge were built.

Listen to the audio tour to learn about this bizarre spot, now on the National Register of Historic Places. The commentary lasts about 25 minutes and is available in four languages. Although the Coral Castle is a bit overpriced and undermaintained, you might visit this monument to one man's madness, especially if you're in the area with kids in tow.

Spanish Monastery Cloisters. 16711 W. Dixie Hwy. (at 167th St.), North Miami Beach. ☎ **305/945-1462.** Admission $4.50 adults, $2.50 seniors, $1 children 11 and under. Mon–Sat 10am–4pm, Sun noon–4pm. From downtown, take U.S. 1 North, turn left onto 163rd Street, and make the first right onto West Dixie Highway; the Cloisters are 3 blocks ahead on the right.

Did you know that the oldest building in the Western Hemisphere dates from A.D. 1141 and is located in Miami? Well, it is. The Spanish Monastery Cloisters were first erected in Segovia, Spain. Centuries later, newspaper magnate William Randolph Hearst brought the Cloisters to America in pieces. The carefully numbered stones were quarantined for years until they were finally reassembled on the present site in 1954.

Venetian Pool. 2701 DeSoto Blvd. (at Toledo St.), Coral Gables. ☎ **305/460-5356.** Admission $4 adults, $3.50 children 13–17, $1.60 children 12 and under (children under 36 months not allowed in the water). June–Aug, Mon–Fri 11am–7:30pm, Sat–Sun 10am–4:30pm; Apr–May and Sept–Oct, Tues–Fri 11am–5:30pm, Sat–Sun 10am–4:30pm; Nov–Mar, Tues–Fri 11am–4:30pm, Sat–Sun 10am–4:30pm.

Miami's most unusual swimming pool, dating from 1924, is hidden behind pastel stucco walls and is honored with a listing in the National Register of Historic Places. Underground artesian wells feed the free-form lagoon, which is shaded by three-story Spanish porticos and features both fountains and waterfalls. During summer the pool's 800,000 gallons of water are drained and refilled nightly, ensuring a cool, clean swim. Visitors are free to swim and sunbathe here year round, just as Esther Williams and Johnny Weissmuller did decades ago. For a modest fee, you or your children can learn to swim during special summer programs.

6 Nature Preserves, Parks & Gardens

The Miami area is a great place for outdoors-minded visitors, with beaches, parks, and gardens galore. Plus, South Florida is the country's only area with two national parks; see Chapter 8 for coverage of the Everglades and Biscayne National Park.

BOTANICAL GARDENS & A SPICE PARK

In Miami, **Fairchild Tropical Gardens,** 10901 Old Cutler Rd. (☎ **305/667-1651**), feature a veritable rain forest of both rare and exotic plants on 83 acres. Palmettos, vine pergola, palm glades, and other unique species create a scenic, lush environment. It's well worth taking the free hourly tram on a 30-minute narrated tour to learn what you always wanted to know about the various flowers and trees.

Although there are picnic facilities sprinkled throughout the park, the new Chachi House is a must for that feeling of breaking bread in an authentic rain forest. Built by the Chachi peoples of northern Ecuador, this large hut has a thatched roof and no walls for an open-air lunch. It's situated near one of Fairchild's many lakes.

Admission is $8 for adults, free for children 12 and under accompanied by an adult. Open daily from 9:30am to 4:30pm. Take I-95 South to U.S. 1, turn left on LeJeune Road, and drive straight ahead to the traffic circle; there, take Old Cutler Road 2 miles to the park.

A testament to Miami's unusual climate, the **Preston B. Bird and Mary Heinlein Fruit and Spice Park,** 24801 SW 187th Ave., Homestead (☎ **305/247-5727**), harbors rare fruit trees that cannot survive elsewhere in the country. You'll see Jamaicans getting weepy-eyed at the abundance of the plants from their native country, including ackee, mango, ugly fruit, carambola, and breadfruit.

Definitely ask for a guide. If a volunteer is available, you'll be told some fascinating things about this 20-acre living plant museum where the most exotic varieties of fruits and spices grow on strange-looking trees with unpronounceable names. One daily tour is offered at 10am by group reservation.

The best part? You're free to sample anything that falls to the ground. You'll also find dishes of interesting fruits, muffins, and jellies made from the park's bounty in

Seasonal Pleasures

There's a singular pleasure in getting your fingers stained red with berries while friends up north shovel snow. As South Florida's farm region quickly gets gobbled up by tract homes and shopping malls, the self-pick farms are disappearing, too. Some of the remaining berry fields offer the ambitious a chance to find their own treasures beneath the trailing vines of strawberry rows for about $2.25 a pound.

If you don't feel like waking up early to pick the juicy red jewels, at least stop by to buy a few boxes of South Florida's winter's bounty. Nothing tastes like just-picked berries. They bloom between January and April, but be sure to call to see if there are any in the fields. At other times of year you may find pick-your-own vegetables and herbs, including carrano, cayenne, jalapeño, and orange peppers, as well as eggplant, zucchini, lettuce, cabbage, and broccoli.

Burr's Berry Farms, 12741 SW 216th St., Goulds (☎ **305/235-0513**), also makes outrageous fruit milkshakes and ice creams. Open daily from 9am to 5:30pm.

At **Knaus Berry Farm,** 15980 SW 248th St., Redland (☎ **305/247-0668**), you'll also find flowers, herbs, and other seasonal vegetables. Go early to snatch up some of the fast-selling pastries, tartes, and jams. At all hours a line of anxious ice-cream lovers wait for fresh-made fruit treats from a little white window. Open Monday to Saturday from 8am to 5:30pm.

Bring your sunglasses and a big appetite to **Strawberries of Kendall,** SW 137th Avenue at 94th Street, SW 117th Avenue at 160th Street, and SW 144th Street west of the turnpike. Straight up strawberry picking is available at **Rainbow Farms,** 18001, 20800, and 22601 Krome Ave. (☎ **305/342-9340**). Get there before the sun does.

---

the gift store. Cooks who like to experiment must visit the park store, which carries hard-to-find ingredients like callalou, burnt-orange maramalades, and Indian and Caribbean spices, plus cookbooks, posters, and explanatory pamphlets on hundreds of topics.

Admission to the spice park is $1.50 for adults, 50¢ for children. Open daily from 10am to 5pm (closed New Year's, Thanksgiving, and Christmas). Take U.S. 1 South, turn right on SW 248th Street, and go straight for 5 miles to SW 187th Avenue.

MORE MIAMI PARKS

The **Amelia Earhart Park,** at 401 E. 65th St., Hialeah (☎ **305/685-8389**), has five lakes stocked with bass, brim, and mullet for fishing; a private island for kids to swing to and tunnel around; playgrounds; picnic facilities; and a big red barn that houses cows, geese, and goats for petting and ponies for riding. There's also a country store and dozens of old-time farm activities like horseshoeing, sugarcane processing, and more. Parking costs $3.50 per car, $6 per bus. Beach admission is $4 for adults, $1.50 for youths, and $1.25 for senior citizens. Open daily from 9am to sunset. To drive here, take I-95 North to the NW 103rd Street exit, go west to East 4th Avenue, and turn right; parking is 1 1/2 miles down the street.

In Key Biscayne, the historic **Bill Baggs Cape Florida State Park,** 1200 Crandon Blvd. (☎ **305/361-5811**), features a recently reopened lighthouse. You can explore the unfettered wilds and enjoy some of the most secluded beaches in Miami. A rental shack rents bikes, hydro-bikes, sailboats, kayaks, jet skis, and many more water toys. It's a great place to picnic, and a newly constructed restaurant serves homemade

Cuban food, including great fish soups and sandwiches. Just be careful the raccoons don't get your lunch, because the furry black-eyed beasts are everywhere. Admission is $3.25 per car with up to eight people. Open daily from 8am to sunset.

In Miami, the **Larry and Penny Thompson Park,** at 11451 SW 184th St. (☎ **305/232-1049**), with four lakes for fishing and swimming, is popular with campers, fishers, and day-trippers. Many fishing contests are held at the freshwater lake, which is filled with bass, bluegill, and catfish. You can stroll through the park's more than 270 acres of South Florida woodlands, hiking paths, and bridle trails. For campers, this place is a paradise, with laundry facilities and hot showers. Open daily from sunrise to sunset.

Tropical Park, at 7900 SW 40th St. (☎ **305/226-0796**), has it all. Enjoy a game of tennis and racquetball for a minimal fee or swim and sun yourself on the secluded little lake. You can use the fishing pond for free, and they'll even supply you with the rods and bait. If you catch anything, however, you're on your own. Open daily from sunrise to sunset.

7 Especially for Kids

The **Scott Rakow Youth Center,** at 2700 Sheridan Ave. (☎ **305/673-7767**), is a hidden treasure on Miami Beach. This three-story facility boasts an ice-skating rink, bowling alleys, a basketball court, gymnasium equipment, and full-time supervision for kids. Call for a complete schedule of organized events. The only drag is that it's not open to adults (except on Sunday). Admission is $6 per day for children 9 to 17 ($3 for Florida residents). Open daily from 2:30 to 9pm.

Following is a roundup of other attractions kids will especially enjoy. Details on each one can be found earlier in the chapter.

Amelia Earhart Park   This is the best park in Miami for kids. They'll like the petting zoos, pony rides, and a private island with hidden tunnels.

The Miami Metrozoo   This completely cageless zoo offers such star attractions as a monorail "safari" and a petting zoo. Kids love the elephant rides.

Miami Museum of Science and Space Transit Planetarium   At the planetarium, kids can learn about space and science by watching entertaining films and cosmic shows. The space museum also offers child-friendly explanations for natural occurrences.

Miami Seaquarium   Kids can volunteer to be kissed by a dolphin and watch performances by Flipper, the original dolphin from the TV series.

Miami Youth Museum   Here children can dabble in fantasy land, playing at what they're interested in. It's one huge game of "What do you want to be when you grow up?".

8 Sightseeing Cruises & Organized Tours

Always call ahead to check prices and times. Reservations are usually suggested.

BOAT & CRUISE SHIP TOURS

Gondola Adventures. Docked at the Bayside Marina, at the Biscayne Marketplace, 401 Biscayne Blvd., downtown. ☎ **305/573-1818.** Rates $5 and up.

A real gondola in Miami? Well, it may not be the canals of Venice, but with a little imagination the Bayside Marina will do. You can go on a simple ride around Bayside for $5, or splurge on your own private and cozy sunrise cruise to an island.

Heritage *Miami II* Topsail Schooner. Docked at the Bayside Marketplace Marina, 401 Biscayne Blvd., downtown. ☎ **305/442-9697.** Tickets $12 adults, $7 children 11 and under. Sept–May only. The 2-hour tours leave daily at 1:30, 4, and 6pm, and on weekends also at 9, 10, and 11pm.

More adventure than tour, this relaxing ride aboard Miami's only tall ship is a fun way to see the city. The 2-hour cruises pass by Villa Vizcaya, Coconut Grove, and Key Biscayne and put you in sight of Miami's spectacular skyline. Call to make sure the ship is running on schedule.

Lady Lucille. 4441 Collins Ave. (docked across from the Fontainebleau Hotel), Miami Beach. ☎ **305/534-7000.** Tickets $12.50 adults, $6 children 11 and under. The 3-hour cruise leaves daily at 11am, 1:30pm, and 4pm.

Set your sights and sails on Miami's man-made beauty: Millionaire's Row. You can cruise along Biscayne Bay and check out Cher's or Fitipaldi's mansion all in the comfort of an air-conditioned 150-passenger boat, complete with snacks and two full bars.

Sea Kruz. 1280 5th St., Miami Beach. ☎ **305/538-8300** or 800/688-PLAY. Tickets $19.95 Sun–Thurs, $24.95 Fri–Sat. Sun–Thurs at 1:30, 5:30, and 7:30pm, and 12:30am; Fri–Sat at 1:30, 5:30, and 7:30pm, and 1am.

If you don't have time to hit the Caribbean on this trip and you like to gamble, consider one of the many mini-cruises to nowhere. The *Sea Kruz* takes you 3 miles off the coast into international waters so you can indulge in a little hedonistic pleasure on your visit to Miami.

For $5 more on the lunch cruise, there's an all-you-can-eat soup-and-salad bar, and for an additional $9 on the dinner cruise there's an all-you-can-eat dinner with a carving station. Throw in a little dancing to a live band and the evening's complete. Ask for free chips or coupons, usually offered for the asking.

Water Taxi. 651 Seabreeze Blvd., Ft. Lauderdale. ☎ **305/467-6677.** $15 all-day pass, $7.50 trip downtown only. Daily 10am–1am.

Here's a novel way to get around Miami—on a boat. You can work on your tan while the old port boats or canal boats ferry you all over downtown Miami, Bayside, and Miami Beach. The water taxis run every 25 minutes, but if you buy an all-day pass, you'll be picked up when you call. Visit the Seaquarium, Viscaya, the Hard Rock Cafe, and even exclusive Fisher Island. While it's not the most effective mode of transportation, the Water Taxi can guarantee that you'll never get stuck in traffic.

WALKING TOURS

I recommend taking ✪ **Dr. Paul George's Tours** (☎ 305/375-1492). Dr. Paul George is Mr. Miami, who happens to be a history teacher at Miami-Dade Community College and a historian at the Historical Museum of Southern Florida. Tours focus on themes or neighborhoods, from a tour of Little Havana, Brickell Avenue, or Key Biscayne to the City of Miami Cemetery Tour. Call ahead for the agenda. Tours cost $15 to $25; reservations are needed. Tours leave from the Historical Museum of Southern Florida, at the Metro-Dade Cultural Center, 101 W. Flagler St.

If you've never been to the **Biltmore Hotel Coral Gables,** 1200 Anastasia Ave., Coral Gables (☎ 305/445-1926), take advantage of the free walking tours offered on Sunday at 1:30, 2:30, and 3:30pm to enjoy the hotel's beautiful grounds. The Biltmore is chock-full of history and mystery, so go out there and uncover it. Call for more information.

If you're in Coral Gables the first Friday of the month from 7 to 10pm, you can join the **Coral Gables Art and Gallery Tour.** Vans shuttle art lovers to more than 20 galleries that participate in Gables Night in the gallery section of Coral Gables. Viewers can sip wine as they view American folk art; African, Native American, and Latin art; and photography. Most galleries are on Ponce De Leon Boulevard between SW 40th Street and SW 24th Street. The vans run every 15 minutes from 7 to 10pm. For more information, call Richard Arregui (☎ **305/447-3973**).

9 Special Events & Festivals

JANUARY January brings national attention to Miami when the ✪ **Orange Bowl** kicks off on New Year's Day, featuring two of the year's toughest college teams doing battle at Joe Robbie Stadium. Tickets are available, starting March 1 of the previous year, through the Orange Bowl Committee, P.O. Box 350748, Miami, FL 33135 (☎ **305/371-4600**).

During the first week of January, there's the **Three Kings Parade** (☎ **305/447-1140**). Since Fidel Castro outlawed this religious celebration more than 25 years ago, the Cuban-Americans in Little Havana have put on a bacchanalian parade winding through Calle Ocho from 4th Avenue to 27th Avenue with horse-drawn carriages, native costumes, and marching bands. Call for the exact date during the first week of January.

Art Miami (☎ **407/220-2690**) is an annual art fair that's especially known for attracting an impressive collection of Latin American works. Thousands of visitors and buyers flock to the Miami Beach Convention Center in early January. Call for information and ticket prices.

Mid-January brings ✪ **Art Deco Weekend** (☎ **305/672-2014**). Held along the beach between 5th and 15th streets, this festival—with bands, food stands, antiques vendors, tours, and other festivities—celebrates the whimsical architecture that has made South Beach one of America's most unique neighborhoods.

Around the same time, you might also check out the **Taste of the Grove Food and Music Festival** (☎ **305/444-7270**). This fundraiser in the Grove's Peacock Park is an excellent chance for visitors to sample menu items from some of the city's top restaurants.

January also brings the **Royal Caribbean Classic** (☎ **305/365-0365**). World-renowned golfers compete for more than $1 million in prize money at the Links golf course on Key Biscayne. Lee Trevino is a two-time winner of this championship tournament.

FEBRUARY The ✪ **Miami Film Festival** has made an impact as an important screening opportunity for Latin American cinema and American independents. Held for 10 days in mid-February, it's relatively small, well priced, and easily accessible to the general public. Contact the Film Society of Miami, 7600 Red Rd., Miami, FL 33157 (☎ **305/377-FILM**).

In mid-month, the **Coconut Grove Art Festival** (☎ **305/447-0401**) is the state's largest art festival and the favorite annual event of many locals. More than 300 artists are selected from thousands of entries to show their works at this prestigious and bacchanalian fare. Almost every medium is represented, including the culinary arts.

February's annual **Miami International Boat Show** (☎ **305/531-8410**) draws almost a quarter of a million boat enthusiasts to the Miami Beach Convention Center to see the mega-yachts, sailboats, dinghies, and accessories. It's the biggest anywhere. Call for more information and ticket prices.

In mid-February, the **Lipton Championships** (☎ 305/446-2200), one of the world's largest tennis events, are hosted at the lush International Tennis Center of Key Biscayne.

The **Doral Ryder Golf Open** (☎ 305/477-GOLF), held from late February to early March, is one of the county's most prestigious annual tournaments.

MARCH   March brings the **Grand Prix of Miami,** an auto race that rivals the big ones in Daytona. This high-purse, high-profile event attracts the top Indy car drivers and large crowds. For information and tickets, contact the Homestead Motorsports Complex, 1 Speedway Blvd., Homestead (☎ 305/230-5200).

One of the world's biggest block parties, the **Calle Ocho Festival** (☎ 305/644-8888) in March is a salsa-filled blowout that marks the end of a 10-day extravaganza called Carnival Miami. It's held along 23 blocks of Little Havana's SW 8th Street between 4th and 27th avenues.

JUNE   Early June's ♥ **Coconut Grove Goombay Festival** (☎ 305/372-9966) is Bahamian bacchanalia with dancing in the streets of Coconut Grove and music from the Royal Bahamian Police marching band. This bash is one of the country's largest black-heritage festivals. The food and music draw thousands to an all-day celebration of Miami's Caribbean connection. It's lots of fun if the weather isn't scorching.

JULY   July brings the **Miccosukee Everglades Music and Crafts Festival** (☎ 305/223-8380). Native American rock, razz (reservation jazz), and folk bands perform down south while visitors gorge themselves on exotic treats like pumpkin bread and fritters. Watch the hulking old gators wrestle with Native Americans. Call for prices and details.

AUGUST   Jamaica's best dancehall and reggae artists turn out for the 2-day **Miami Reggae Festival** in early August. Some of the participants in previous years have included Burning Spear, Steel Pulse, Spragga Benz, and Jigsy King. Call Jamaica Awareness, which has been hosting the event since 1984 (☎ **305/891-2944**).

SEPTEMBER   Beginning in September, **Festival Miami** is a 3-week program of performing and visual arts centered in and around Coral Gables. For a schedule of events, contact the University of Miami's School of Music, 6200 San Amaro Dr., Coral Gables, FL 33146 (☎ **305/284-4940**).

Find anything that can float from an inner tube to a 100-foot yacht and you'll fit right in at the ♥ **Columbus Day Regatta**. Yes, there's actually a race, but who can keep track when you're partying with a bunch of semi-naked psychos in the middle of Biscayne Bay? It's free and it's wild. You may want to consider renting a boat, jet ski, or sailboard to check out this event up close. Be sure to book early though; everyone wants to be there.

OCTOBER   They close the streets for **Oktoberfest,** a German beer and food festival thrown by the Mozart Stub Restaurant in Coral Gables. You'll find loads of great music and dancing at this wild party. Call Harald Neuweg (☎ **305/446-1600**) to find out where and when (it's held some weekend other than Columbus Day).

NOVEMBER   November's **Miami Book Fair International** (☎ 305/754-4931) draws hundreds of thousands of visitors, including foreign and domestic publishers and authors from around the world, with great lectures and readings by world-renowned authors.

DECEMBER   December ushers in the **Fair of Seville** (☎ 305/442-1586). Eat from a giant pot of paella, watch hundreds of flamenco performers, see the Andalusian horse show, and dance the macarena at this nonstop weekend fair. Call for the specifics.

On December 30, the **King Mango Strut** runs from Commodore Plaza to Peacock Park in Coconut Grove. This fun-filled march encourages everyone to wear wacky costumes and join the floats in a spoof on the King Orange Jamboree Parade, held the following night. Comedians and musical entertainment follow in the park.

And the year ends with the ✪ **King Orange Jamboree Parade.** This special New Year's Eve event may be the world's largest nighttime parade and is followed by a long night of festivities. It runs along Biscayne Boulevard. For information and tickets (which cost $7.50 to $13), contact the Greater Miami Convention and Visitors Bureau.

10 Water Sports & Other Activities, Indoors & Outdoors

WATER SPORTS

BOATING & SAILING   Boating and sailing is expensive, no matter how you try to cut corners.

Key Biscayne Boat Rental, 3301 Rickenbacker Causeway, Key Biscayne (☎ **305/ 361-RENT**), is next to the Rusty Pelican. If you want to cruise Key Biscayne's lovely waters, a 21-footer costs $175 for a half day to $250 for a full day. If you're looking for just a few hours of thrills, a 2-hour minimum for $100 is available. Key Biscayne Boat Rental is open daily from 9am to 5pm, and will open earlier for special fishing requests.

If speedboats are not your style, **Sailboats of Key Biscayne Rentals and Sailing School,** in the Crandon Marina next to Sundays on the Bay, 4000 Crandon Blvd., Key Biscayne (☎ **305/361-0328** days, 305/279-7424 evenings), offers a slightly more subdued ride. A 22-foot sailboat can be rented for $27 an hour, or $81 for a half day. A 23-foot Hunter or Catalina is available for $35 an hour, or $110 for a half day. If you've always had a dream to win the America's Cup but can't sail, Sailboats will get you started. It offers a 10-hour course over 5 days for $250 for one person or $300 for you and a buddy.

Shake a Leg, 2600 Bayshore Dr., Coconut Grove (☎ **305/858-5550**), is a unique sailing program for disabled and able-bodied people alike. The program pairs up sailors for day and evening cruises and offers sailing lessons as well. Consider a moonlight cruise (offered monthly) or a race clinic. The group is a lot of fun and can teach you a lot. Shake-a-Leg members welcome able-bodied volunteers for activities on and off the water. It costs $50 for nonmembers to rent a boat for 3 hours; free for volunteers. Open on Saturday from 9am to 1pm.

JET SKIING   If you must jet ski, the cheapest place is **Fun Watersports Waterski & Jet-Ski Rentals,** 5101 Blue Lagoon Dr., West Miami (☎ **305/261-7687**). The lake you ride on is small and in an odd location (right next to Miami International Airport), but if you've never jet skied, it's somewhat safer than braving the sometimes-heavy chop of the ocean. For $25 a half hour and $45 an hour, you can rent a jet ski and learn how to operate it. For $35 a half hour and $60 an hour, a Waverunner is available if you prefer to sit rather than balance on a moving jet ski. Fun Watersports is open daily from 9am to 5pm.

KAYAKS & CANOES   I think that every visitor should rent a canoe and paddle through the clear blue water and mangroves of Biscayne National Park. You can rent canoes from **Biscayne National Park Boat Tours**, at the east end of SW 328th

Street, Homestead (☎ 305/230-1100), for $7 an hour, or $20 for a half day. Open daily from 10am to 4pm.

The laid-back **Urban Trails Kayak Company** rents boats from two nearby locations in North Dade: 10800 Collins Ave., Miami Beach (☎ 305/947-1302), and 17530 W. Dixie Hwy. (☎ 305/919-7689). Both offer scenic routes through rivers with mangroves and islands as your destination. Most of the kayaks are sit-on-tops, which is what it sounds like. Most boats are plastic, though there are some fiberglass ones available, too. Rates are $8 an hour, $20 for up to 4 hours, $25 for more than four people. Tandems are $15 an hour, $35 for up to 4 hours, $40 for the day. Open daily from 9am to 5pm.

The outfitters give interested explorers a map to take with them and quick instructions on how to work the paddles and boats. If you want a guided tour, you'll need at least four people and will pay $35 per person for a half day. This is a fun way to experience some of Miami's unspoiled wildlife (but it's a lot harder than it looks!).

SCUBA DIVING   In 1981 the government began a wide-scale project designed to increase the number of habitats available to marine organisms. One of the program's major accomplishments has been the creation of nearby artificial reefs, which have attracted all kinds of tropical plants, fish, and animals. In addition, Biscayne National Park (see Chapter 8) offers a protected marine environment just south of downtown.

Scuba diving isn't cheap. However, if you want to splurge, here are two options:

Divers Paradise of Key Biscayne, 4000 Crandon Blvd. (☎ 305/361-3483), offers two dive expeditions daily to the more than 30 wrecks and artificial reefs off the coast of Miami Beach and Key Biscayne. A 2-week certification course costs $159, and a dive trip costs about $90 for those with no equipment, only $35 if you show up prepared. It's open Monday to Friday from 10am to 6pm and on Saturday and Sunday from 9am to 6pm. Call ahead for times and locations of dive trips.

Team Divers, on South Beach, at 300 Alton Rd. (☎ 305/673-3483), can certify those who have always wanted to explore the ocean floor. A 2-week course costs $150; those in a hurry can take an abbreviated 3-day course for $300. It offers dive trips off Key Biscayne and Miami Beach, including some breathtaking reef and wreck dives for more experienced divers. The dives cost $57, including equipment, or $45 if you bring your own mask, snorkel, and fins. Call ahead for dive and course information.

WINDSURFING   **Sailboards Miami,** Rickenbacker Causeway, Key Biscayne (☎ 305/361-SAIL), operates out of big yellow trucks on Hobie Beach, the most popular windsurfing spot in the city. For those who've never windsurfed but want to try their hand at it, for $39 Sailboards Miami offers a 2-hour lesson that's guaranteed to turn you into a wave warrior or you get your money back. After that, you can rent a windsurf board for $20 an hour or $37 for 2 hours. If you want to make a day of it, a 10-hour card costs $130. Open daily from 10am to 6pm.

OTHER ACTIVITIES, INDOORS & OUTDOORS

BIKING & SCOOTERS   The hard-packed sand that runs the length of Miami Beach is one of the best places in the world to ride a bike. Biking up the beach is great for surf, sun, sand, exercise, and people-watching. You may not want to subject your bicycle to the salt and sand, but there are plenty of oceanfront rental places here. Try the **Miami Beach Bicycle Center**, 601 5th St. (☎ 305/674-0150). Located in South Beach, the shop rents bicycles for $3 per hour or $14 a day. It's open Monday to Saturday from 10am to 7pm and on Sunday from 10am to 5pm.

Bikers can also enjoy more than 130 miles of paved paths throughout Miami. The beautiful and quiet streets of Coral Gables and Coconut Grove beg for the attention of bicyclists. Old trees form canopies over wide, flat roads lined with grand homes and quaint street markers. Several bicycle trails are spread throughout these neighborhoods, including one that begins at the doorstep of **Dade Cycle**, 3216 Grand Ave., Coconut Grove (☎ **305/444-5997**); it's open Monday to Saturday from 9:30am to 5:30pm and on Sunday from 10:30am to 5:30pm. MasterCard, Visa, and Discover are accepted.

Although the shopkeeper and his employees tend to be a little disorganized, **Gary's Megacycles,** 1260 Washington Ave., Miami Beach (☎ **305/534-3306**), rents the best bikes on the beach. Aluminum-frame bikes, helmets, and locks rent for $5 an hour or $15 for the day. Consider junking the rental car and cruising South Beach on one of these hot wide-rimmed combination bikes. There are a lot of styles to choose from—just be sure to lock up. It's open Monday to Saturday from 10am to 7 pm and on Sunday from 10am to 4pm.

If the park isn't flooded from excess rain, **Shark Valley** in Everglades National Park is South Florida's most scenic bicycle trail. Many locals haul their bikes out to the Glades for a relaxing day of wilderness trail riding. You can ride the 17-mile loop with no other traffic in sight. Instead, you'll share the paved flat road only with other bikers and a menagerie of wildlife. Don't be surprised to see a gator lounging in the sun, a deer munching on some grass, or a picnicker eating a sandwich along the mangrove shore. The **Shark Valley Tram Tour Company** (☎ **305/221-8455**) rents old-fashioned coaster-brake bikes on the premises for $3.25 an hour and accept MasterCard and Visa.

Or if you'd like an audio guided tour, call Follow the Yellow Brick Road, a bike tour company run by **Gary's Megacycles,** at 1260 Washington Ave., Miami Beach (☎ **305/534-3306**). For $25, a representative will pick you up from anywhere from Miami Beach to Hollywood. Along with a high-tech Coloi bike, you'll get an audiotape guide in any of four languages, a map, a helmet, and all the accoutrements. They're open daily from 10am to 7pm and accept reservations 24 hours a day. Pay with a MasterCard or Visa.

Intra Mark, 350 Ocean Dr., Key Biscayne (☎ **305/365-9762**), rents scooters for $15 an hour or $45 for a half day, and bicycles for $5 hour or $10 for 4 hours. The eco-minded staff directs bikers to the best paths for nature watching. You'll find them off the Rickenbacker bridge across from the Rusty Pelican every day between 10am and 5pm.

Key Cycling, 61 Harbor Dr., Key Biscayne (☎ **305/361-0061**), rents mountain bikes and beach cruisers for $3 hour. It's open daily from 10am to 5pm.

BINGO You can play Bingo at **Miccosukee Indian Gaming**, 500 SW 177th Ave., west of Miami (☎ **305/222-4600**, or 800/741-9600). This huge glitzy casino isn't Vegas, but you can play slot machines, all kinds of Bingo, and even poker (with a $10 maximum pot).

North Collins Bingo, 18288 Collins Ave., Sunny Isles (☎ **305/932-7185**), features games every day from noon to midnight (with a break from 4 to 7pm). It costs $5 to $20 a night. There are no-smoking areas, door prizes nightly, and "the largest cash prizes allowed by law."

FISHING **Bridge fishing** is popular in Miami; you'll see people with poles over almost every waterway.

Some of the best **surf casting** in the city can be had at Haulover Beach Park, at Collins Avenue and 105th Street, where there's a bait and tackle shop right on the pier. South Pointe Park, at the southern tip of Miami Beach, is another popular fishing spot and features a long pier, comfortable benches, and a great view of the ships passing through Government Cut.

You can also choose to do some **deep-sea fishing**, although the cost is pretty steep. The **Kelley Fishing Fleet,** at the Haulover Marina, 10800 Collins Ave. (at 108th Street), Miami Beach (☎ **305/945-3801**), has half-day, full-day, and night fishing aboard diesel-powered "party boats." The fleet's emphasis on drifting is geared toward trolling and bottom fishing for snapper, sailfish, and mackerel; but it also schedules 2-, 3-, and 4-day trips to The Bahamas. Half-day and night fishing trips are $19.75 for adults and $12.75 for children; full-day trips are $29.75 for adults and $18.75 for children; rod and reel rental is $4.25. Daily departures are scheduled at 9am, 1:45pm, and 8pm; reservations are recommended.

GOLF   There are dozens of golf courses in the Greater Miami area, many of which are open to the public. Contact the **Greater Miami Convention and Visitors Bureau** (☎ **305/539-3063,** or 800/283-2707) for a complete list of courses and costs. Take advantage of "twilight" rates, available at almost any golf course in Miami. These rates start anywhere between 1 and 4pm, and sometimes reduce greens fees by as much as 50%. Call ahead to inquire about these before heading out to play.

Good for both beginners and pros, the 9-hole, par-36 course at **Greynolds Park,** 17530 W. Dixie Hwy., North Miami Beach (☎ **305/949-1741**), offers bargain-basement golf games. Greens fees are $10 per person during the winter and $8 per person during the summer. Cart fees are $10 for two people. Special twilight rates are also available. Mark Mahanna designed the 3,100-yard course in 1964. The course is open from 7am to 5pm daily during the winter, until 7pm in summer.

Golfers on a budget looking for some cheap practice time will appreciate **Haulover Park,** 10800 Collins Ave., Miami Beach (☎ **305/940-6719**). The longest hole on this par-27 course is 125 yards in a pretty, bayside location. Greens fees are $5 per person during the winter, $4 per person during the summer. Hand carts cost $1.40. The course is open daily from 7:30am to 5:30pm during the winter, until 7:30pm during the summer.

Another recommended public course is the **Bayshore Par Three Golf Course,** 2795 Prairie Ave., Miami Beach (☎ **305/674-0305**). Greens fees are $7 to $10 per person during the winter and $5 to $7 during the summer. Special twilight rates are available. You'll have fun trying to avoid all the water traps at this inexpensive and gorgeous course just north of the Miami Beach Convention Center. The course is open daily from 6:30am to sunset.

✪ **The Links at Key Biscayne,** 6700 Crandon Blvd., Key Biscayne (☎ **305/361-9129**), is the number-one-ranked municipal course in the state and one of the top five in the country. Greens fees (including cart) are $68 per person during the winter and $37.50 per person during the summer, but special twilight rates are available. The park is situated on 200 bayfront acres and offers a pro shop, rentals, lessons, carts, and a lighted driving range. The course is open daily from dawn to dusk.

One of the most popular courses among real enthusiasts is the **Doral Park Golf and Country Club,** 5001 NW 104th Ave., West Miami (☎ **305/591-8800**); it's not related to the Doral Hotel or Spa. Call to book in advance since this challenging 18-holer is so popular with locals. The course is open daily from 6:30am to 6pm during the winter and until 7pm during the summer. Cart and greens fees vary, so call 305/594-0954 for information.

Known as the best in Miami, the **Golf Club of Miami**, 6801 Miami Gardens Dr., at NW 68th Avenue (☎ **305/829-8456**), has three 18-hole courses of varying degrees of difficulty. Cart and greens fees are $45 to $75 per person during the winter, $20 to $34 per person during the summer. Special twilight rates are available, when the rates go down by as much as half. Designed in 1961 by Robert Trent Jones and updated in the 1990s by the PGA, this was where Jack Nicklaus played his first professional tournament and Lee Trevino won his first professional championship. The course is open daily from 6:30am to sunset.

HEALTH CLUBS   Several health clubs around the city will take nonmembers in on a daily basis.

In Coral Gables, try the **Body and Soul Fitness Club**, 355 Greco Ave. (☎ **305/443-8688**). This club has top-of-the-line Body Master machines, aerobic machines, and free weights. You'll be charged $9.50 per aerobics class or workout. Special packages are available at a reduced cost: 4 visits for $36 and 10 visits for $85, including aerobics and weights. Open Monday to Friday from 5:30am to 9:30pm, on Saturday from 8am to 6pm, and on Sunday from 8am to 4pm.

In Miami Beach, **The Gridiron Club**, 1676 Alton Rd. (☎ 305/531-4743), is a muscle gym for sure. Come on in and sweat with the *big* boys on South Beach. Aerobics classes are offered for those watching their girlish figures. A daily workout will run you $9; talk to the manager about extended rates. Open Monday to Friday 5:30am to 11pm, on Saturday from 8am to 8pm, and on Sunday from 8am to 6pm.

The **Olympia Gym**, 20335 Biscayne Blvd., in North Miami Beach (☎ **305/932-3500**), is a huge, top-of-the-line gym where the elite of North Miami Beach meet. If you don't mind working out to the sounds of beepers and cellular phones, the Olympia Gym has much to offer, including a juice bar on the premises and an extra-large aerobics room. Workouts cost $10 per day, $30 per week, and $75 per month. Open Monday to Friday from 5am to 10pm, on Saturday from 8am to 7pm, and on Sunday from 8am to 5pm.

On the second floor of the Clevelander Hotel is the **South Beach Gym**, 1020 Ocean Dr., Miami Beach (☎ 305/672-7499). Although there are no aerobics classes, this gym offers a workout with an ocean view. Model-watch on the Stairclimbers with Ocean Drive at your feet. It costs $15 daily, $35 weekly, and $60 monthly. Open Monday to Friday from 7am to 11pm, on Saturday from 9am to 9pm, and on Sunday from 10am to 6pm.

IN-LINE SKATING   The consistently flat terrain makes in-line skating an easy endeavor. Remember to keep a pair of sandals or sneakers with you since many area shops won't allow you inside with skates on. The following rental outfits can help chart an interesting course for you and provide you with all the necessary gear.

In Coral Gables, **Extreme Skate & Sport**, 7876 SW 40th St. (☎ 305/261-6699), is one of South Florida's largest in-line skate dealers. Even if you know nothing about this trendy sport, a knowledgeable sales staff and a large selection to choose from ensures that you can't go wrong.

In Miami Beach, **Fritz's Skate Shop,** 726 Lincoln Rd. Mall (☎ 305/532-1954), rents skates for $8 an hour and $24 a day. If you're an in-line skate virgin, an instructor will hold your hand for $25 an hour.

Also in Miami Beach, **Skate 2000,** 1200 Ocean Dr. (☎ 305/538-8282), will help you keep up with the beach crowd by renting in-line skates and the associated safety accessories. Rates are $8 per hour or $24 per day. Skate 2000 also offers free lessons by a certified instructor on South Beach's boardwalk every Sunday at 10am. You can either rent or bring your own skates.

JOGGING   Throughout Dade County you'll find a number of safe and well-planned jogging courses. The following are only a sampling of some of the best. For more good routes in your area or for running buddies, call the **Miami Runners Club** (☎ **305/227-1500**).

In Key Biscayne, **Crandon Park,** at 4000 Crandon Blvd., has a 15-station Fitness Course as well as great secluded trails that run along the island's east side, past the old zoo and over the causeway. In **Coconut Grove,** jog along South Bayshore Drive on a clearly marked path along the bay.

In North Miami Beach, **Greynolds Park,** 17530 W. Dixie Hwy., has many trails winding past lakes and hills as well as a 15-station Vita-Course. At **Haulover Beach Park,** 10801 Collins Ave. in Miami Beach, you can run along the sandy paths with the ocean at your side through a rigorous 20-station Fitness Course. The **Miami Beach Boardwalk,** a wood-decked course, runs along the ocean from 21st to 46th streets. Though you share the well-lighted path with strollers and walkers, it's a beautiful route in a safe area.

The **Larry and Penny Thompson Park**, 12451 SW 184 St., in Homestead, has more than 250 acres of parkland with trails running through varied terrain. They also have a 20-station Fitness Course if you're feeling ambitious.

TENNIS   Hundreds of tennis courts in South Florida are open to the public for a minimal fee. Most courts operate on a first-come, first-served basis, and most are open from sunrise to sunset. For information and directions to the one nearest where you're staying, call one of these government offices: the **City of Miami Beach Recreation, Culture, and Parks Department** (☎ 305/673-7730); the **City of Miami Parks and Recreation Department** (☎ 305/575-5240); or the **Metro-Dade Park and Recreation Department** (☎ 305/533-2000).

The three hard courts and seven clay courts at the **Key Biscayne Tennis Association,** at the Links, located at 6702 Crandon Blvd. (☎ **305/361-5263**), get crowded on weekends since they're some of Miami's nicest courts. There's a pleasant, if limited, pro shop, plus many good pros. Only four courts are lit at night, but if you reserve at least 48 hours in advance you can usually take your pick. The lush foliage surrounding the courts makes you feel as though you're on an exclusive island somewhere—which you are, in Key Biscayne. It costs $4 to $5 per person per hour. The courts are open daily from 8am to 9pm.

In Coral Gables, **Salvadore Park,** 1120 Andalusia Ave. (☎ **305/460-5333**), is a favorite local spot with eight clay courts (the most popular) and five hard courts— all lighted at night. Though plans are in the works to get a real pro shop, the current facilities can string racquets, sell balls, and offer snack vending machines. It costs $4 to $5 per person per hour. The courts are open Monday to Friday from 8am to 10pm and on Saturday and Sunday from 8am to 7pm.

11 Spectator Sports

Check the *Miami Herald's* sports section for a daily listing of local events and the paper's Friday "Weekend" section for comprehensive coverage and in-depth reports. For last-minute tickets, call the stadium directly since many season ticket holders sell singles and return unused tickets. Some tickets may be available through **Ticketmaster** (☎ **305/358-5885**).

BASEBALL   The National League **Florida Marlins,** one of baseball's newest expansion teams, played their first (and quite successful) season in 1993. Home games are at the Joe Robbie Stadium, 2269 NW 199th St., Greater Miami North (☎ **305/ 626-7417**). The team currently holds spring training in Melbourne, Florida; tickets are $4 to $30. Box office hours are Monday to Friday from 8:30am to 6pm and on Saturday and Sunday from 8:30am to 4pm, and prior to games; tickets are also available through Ticketmaster.

BASKETBALL   The **Miami Heat,** now coached by celebrity coach Pat Riley, made its NBA debut in 1988. Predictably, it's also one of Miami's hottest tickets. The season of approximately 41 home games lasts from November to April, with most games beginning at 7:30pm at the Miami Arena, 1 SE 3rd Ave. (☎ **305/ 577-HEAT**). Tickets are $14 to $41. The box office is open Monday to Friday from 10am to 4pm (until 8pm on game nights); tickets are also available through Ticketmaster.

DOG RACING   Greyhound racing is generally held from April 27 to the end of November. The fun, high-stakes **Flagler Greyhound Track,** 401 NW 38th Court (☎ **305/649-3000**), features some of America's top dogs, with racing 7 days a week. The track hosts the $110,000 International Classic, one of the richest races on the circuit. General admission is $1, and $3 to the clubhouse; parking costs 50¢. Post times are Monday to Sunday at 7:30pm, with matinees on Tuesday, Thursday, and Saturday at 12:30pm.

An average crowd of 10,000 fans wager a collective $1 million nightly at the **Hollywood Greyhound Track,** 831 N. Federal Hwy. (at Pembroke Road), Hallandale (☎ **800/959-9404**), considered by experts to be one of the best in the country. If you've never been to the dog track before, arrive half an hour early for a quick introduction to greyhound racing, shown on the track's TV monitors. General admission is $1, $2 to the clubhouse, and parking is free. Racing is from late December to late April. Post times are Monday to Sunday at 7:30pm, with matinees on Tuesday, Thursday, and Saturday at 12:30pm.

FOOTBALL   Miami's golden boys are the **Miami Dolphins,** the city's most recognizable team, followed by thousands of "dolfans." With Don Shula's retirement, it will be interesting to see what the new coach, Jimmy Johnson, can do with this once-unstoppable team, led by the great Dan Marino. The team plays at least eight home games during the season, between September and December, at 7500 SW 30th St., Davie (☎ **305/452-7000**). Tickets cost about $30, and are predictably tough to come by. The box office is open Monday to Friday from 10am to 6pm; tickets are also available through Ticketmaster.

The **University of Miami Hurricanes** play at the famous Orange Bowl from September to November. The stadium, at 1501 NW 3rd St., is seldom full, and games here are really exciting. If you sit high up, you'll have an excellent view over Miami. Call for the schedule (☎ **305/284-CANE,** or 800/GO-CANES in Florida). Tickets start at $13. The box office is open Monday to Friday from 8am to 6pm and prior to all games.

HORSE RACING   Wrapped around an artificial lake, **Gulfstream Park,** at U.S. 1 and Hallandale Beach Boulevard, Hallandale (☎ **305/931-7223**), is both pretty and popular. Large purses and important races are commonplace at this suburban course, and the track is often crowded. Call for schedules. Admission is $2 to the grandstand, $4.50 to the clubhouse. Parking begins at $1. Post times from January 4 to March 16 are Tuesday to Sunday at 1pm.

You've seen the pink flamingos at **Hialeah Park,** 2200 E. 4th Ave., Hialeah (☎ **305/885-8000**), on *Miami Vice,* and indeed, this famous colony is the largest of its kind. This track, listed on the National Register of Historic Places, is one of the most beautiful in the world, featuring old-fashioned stands and acres of immaculately manicured grounds. Admission is $2 to the grandstand, $4 to the clubhouse; children 17 and under are admitted free with an adult. Parking begins at $1.50. Races are held mid-November to mid-May, but the course is open year round for sightseeing Monday to Saturday from 10am to 4pm. Call for post times.

JAI ALAI   Jai alai, sort of a Spanish-style indoor lacrosse, was introduced to Miami in 1924 and is regularly played in two Miami-area frontons. Although the sport has roots stemming from ancient Egypt, the game as it is now played was invented by Basque peasants in the Pyrenees Mountains during the 17th century. Players use woven baskets, called *cestas,* to hurl balls, *pelotas,* at speeds that sometimes exceed 170 m.p.h. Spectators, who are protected behind a wall of glass, place bets on the evening's players.

The **Miami Jai Alai Fronton,** 3500 NW 37th Ave., at NW 35th Street (☎ **305/ 633-6400**), is America's oldest fronton, dating from 1926. It schedules 13 games per night. Admission is $1 to the grandstand, $5 to the clubhouse. It's open year round, except for a 4-week recess in the fall. The first game starts Monday and Wednesday to Saturday at 7pm, with matinees on Monday, Wednesday, and Saturday at noon.

12 Shopping

A mecca for hard-core shoppers from Latin America, the Caribbean, and the rest of the state, Miami has everything you could ever want and things you never dreamed of. This shopping capital has strip malls, boutiques, and enclosed malls in every conceivable nook and cranny of the city, which makes for lots of competition among retailers and good bargains for those who like to hunt.

BEST BETS

Locally produced and widely distributed goods are easily Miami's best buys. Not surprisingly, local seafood and citrus products are among the city's most important exports.

There was a time when it seemed as though almost every other store was shipping fruit home for tourists. Today such stores are a dying breed, although a few high-quality operations still send out the freshest oranges and grapefruit. **Todd's Fruit Shippers,** 260 Minorca Ave. (☎ **305/448-5215**), can take your order over the phone and charge it to American Express, MasterCard, or Visa. Boxes are sold by the bushel or fractions thereof and start at about $20.

East Coast Fisheries, 330 W. Flagler St., downtown (☎ **305/577-3000**), a retail market and restaurant, has shipped millions of pounds of seafood worldwide from its own fishing fleet. It's equipped to wrap and send 5- or 10-pound packages of stone crab claws, Florida lobsters, Florida Bay pompano, fresh Key West shrimp, and a variety of other local delicacies to your door via overnight mail.

THE SHOPPING SCENE
THE MALLS

The **Aventura Mall,** at 19501 Biscayne Blvd. (☎ **305/935-4222**), is an enclosed mall with more than 200 generic shops and a Macy's. The **Bayside Marketplace,** 401 Biscayne Blvd., downtown (☎ **305/577-3344**), consists of 16 beautiful waterfront acres along Biscayne Bay with lively and exciting shops and carts selling everything from plastic fruit to high-tech electronics. The **Dadeland Mall,** 7535 N. Kendall Dr., Kendall (☎ **305/665-6226**), is the granddaddy of Miami's suburban mall scene, featuring more than 175 specialty shops, anchored by five large department stores. **The Falls,** 8888 Howard Dr., in the Kendall area (☎ **305/255-4570**), is an outdoor shopping center set among tropical waterfalls, with dozens of moderately priced, slightly upscale shops, including Miami's only Bloomingdales. **Sawgrass Mills,** 12801 W. Sunrise Blvd., Sunrise (☎ **305/846-2300**), which is actually located in Broward County, west of Ft. Lauderdale, is a phenomenon worth mentioning—it's a behemoth with more than 300 shops and kiosks in nearly 2.5 million square feet covering 50 acres. Vans shuttle eager shoppers from Miami daily.

GREAT SHOPPING AREAS

DOWNTOWN MIAMI   The place for discounts on all types of goods—from watches and jewelry to luggage and leather. But watch out for a handful of un-scrupulous businesses trying to rip you off. Look around Flagler Street and Miami Avenue for all kinds of cluttered bargain stores. Most of the signs around here are printed in both English and Spanish, for the benefit of locals and tourists alike.

COCONUT GROVE   Downtown Coconut Grove is one of Miami's few pedestrian-friendly zones. Centered around Main Highway and Grand Avenue and branching onto the adjoining streets, the Grove's wide, café- and boutique-lined side-walks provide hours of browsing pleasure. Look for dozens of avant-garde clothing stores, funky import shops, and excellent sidewalk cafés.

CORAL GABLES / MIRACLE MILE   Actually only half a mile, this central shopping street was an integral part of George Merrick's original city plan. Today the strip still enjoys popularity for its old-fashioned ladies' shops, haberdashers, bridal stores, and gift shops. Lined primarily with small 1970s storefronts, the Miracle Mile, which terminates at the Mediterranean-style City Hall rotunda, also features several good and unusual restaurants and is worth a stop on your tour of Coral Gables.

SOUTH BEACH / LINCOLN ROAD   This luxurious pedestrian mall recently underwent a multi-million-dollar renovation that includes new lighting, over 500 palm trees, and necessary repairs of the infrastructure. Here shoppers can find an array of clothing and art and a collection of Miami Beach's finest restaurants. Enjoy an afternoon of gallery hopping, and be sure to look into the open studios of the Miami City Ballet. Monthly gallery tours, periodic jazz concerts, and a weekly Farmer's Market are just a few of the offerings on "The Road."

HOURS & TAXES

For most stores around the city, **shopping hours** are Monday to Saturday from 10am to 6pm and on Sunday from noon to 5pm. Many stay open late (usually until 9pm) one night of the week (usually Thursday). Shops in trendy Coconut Grove are open until 9pm Sunday to Thursday and even later on Friday and Saturday nights. Department stores and shopping malls keep longer hours, staying open from 10am to 9 or 10pm Monday to Saturday and noon to 6pm on Sunday.

The 6.5% state and local **sales tax** is added to the price of all nonfood purchases.

SHOPPING A TO Z
ART & ANTIQUES

Though you may not be in the market for costly antiques, it's fun to browse antiques stores and art galleries. The best hunting grounds are scattered in small pockets around Miami. Some of these areas are located in North Miami Beach, along West Dixie Highway and some on Miami Gardens Drive. The bulk of the antiques district is in Coral Gables, mostly along Ponce de Leon Boulevard, extending from

U.S. 1 to Bird Road. Many antiques shops and art galleries line this street, conveniently within walking distance of each other.

Ambrosino Fine Arts, Inc. 3155 Ponce de Leon Blvd., Coral Gables. ☎ **305/445-2211.**

This well-respected gallery shows works by contemporary Latin American artists. Stop by anytime to get an education from the knowledgeable staff.

Elite Fine Art. 3140 Ponce de Leon Blvd., Coral Gables. ☎ **305/448-3800.**

Touted as one of the finest galleries in Miami, Elite features modern and contemporary Latin American painters and sculptors.

Evelyn S. Poole Ltd. 3925 N. Miami Ave., Miami. ☎ **305/573-7463.**

Known as the top fine antiques dealer, the Poole collection of European 17th-, 18th-, and 19th-century decorative furniture and accessories is housed in 5,000 square feet of space in the newly revived Decorator's Row. It's interesting to view these vast museumlike galleries.

Gallery Antigua. In the Boulevard Plaza Building, 5103 Biscayne Blvd. ☎ **305/759-5355.**

Gallery Antigua, dedicated to African-American and Caribbean artists, boasts a vast collection of prints and reproductions, as well as masks and sculptures. They will frame on the premises and ship for you.

Miami Twice. 6562 SW 40th St., Coral Gables. ☎ **305/666-0127.**

Here you'll find the Old Florida furniture and decorations, like lamps and ash trays that define South Florida's unique style. In addition to deco memorabilia, you'll find some fun old clothes, shoes, and jewelry, too—but prices can be a bit steep.

BEACHWEAR

As you'd expect, there's a plethora of beachwear stores in Miami. However, if you want to get away from the cookie-cutter styles available at any local mall, here are a few notable stores that will surely make you stand out while you're basking on the beach or out giving the waves a workout.

Alice's Day Off. 5900 SW 72nd St., South Miami. ☎ **305/284-0301.**

Alice's may have a corner on the neon trend, but it also comes out season after season with pretty and flattering floral patterns. If an itsy-bitsy bikini is not your style, Alice's has a range of more modest cuts.

Bird's Surf Shop. 250 Sunny Isles Blvd., North Miami Beach. ☎ **305/940-0929.**

If you're a hardcore surfer, head to Bird's Surf Shop. Although Miami doesn't regularly get huge swells, if you're here during the winter and one should happen to hit, you'll be ready. The shop carries over 150 boards.

Call their **surf line** before going out to find the best waves from South Beach to Cape Hatteras, and even The Bahamas and Florida's west coast. Dial 305/947-7170.

Island Trading. 1332 Ocean Dr., Miami Beach. ☎ **305/673-6300.**

One more part of music mogul Chris Blackwell's empire, Island Trading sells everything you'll need to wear in the tropical resort town, like batik sarongs, sandals, sundresses, bathing suits, cropped tops, and more. Many of the styles are created on the premises by a team of young and innovative designers.

Island Water Sports. 237 NE 167th St., North Miami Beach. ☎ **305/652-2573.**

You'll find everything from booties to gloves to baggies. Check in here before you rent that Waverunner or windsurfer.

BOOKS

Books & Books. 933 Lincoln Rd., Miami Beach. ☎ **305/532-3222.**

Need a good beach book? An obscure biography? The history of the deco district? Stop in at the Lincoln Road location for a wide selection of trash or culture and rub elbows with tanned and buffed South Beach bookworms sipping cappuccino at the Russian Bear Cafe located inside the store. Check your in-line skates at the door, please. Dial 305/444-POEM hear a new poem every day.

There's another location at 296 Aragon Ave., Coral Gables (☎ 305/442-4408).

Coco Grove Antiquarian. 3318 Virginia St., Coconut Grove. ☎ **305/444-5362.**

One of very few out-of-print bookstores in Miami, Coco Grove Antiquarian specializes in Florida and the Caribbean, but also boasts a large selection of out-of-print cookbooks, sci-fi, and first editions.

Cuba Art and Books. 2317 LeJeune Rd., Coral Gables. ☎ **305/567-1640.**

This place specializes in old Cuban books about that island nation and some prints and paintings by Cuban artists. Most titles are in Spanish and focus on art and politics.

CIGARS

Although it's illegal to bring Cuban cigars into this country, somehow Cohibas show up at every dinner party and nightclub in town. Not that I condone it, but if you hang around the cigar smokers in town, no doubt one will be able to tell you where you can get some of the highly prized contraband. Be careful, however, of counterfeits.

Some of the following stores sell excellent hand-rolled cigars made with domestic and foreign-grown tobacco, as well. Many of the *viejos* (old men) got their training in Cuba working for the government-owned factories in the heyday of Cuban cigars.

Ba-balú. 432 Espanola Way, Miami Beach. ☎ **305/538-0679.**

Including an extensive collection of Cuban memorobilia from pre-1959 Cuba, Ba-balú offers a taste of Cuba, selling not only hand-rolled cigars (it produces about 1,000 a week) but also T-shirts, baseball caps, Cuban coins, bills, postcards, stamps, and coffee. Enjoy live bongo music nightly and ask Herbie Sosa, the owner, for a free shot of Cuban coffee.

La Gloria Cubana. 1106 SW 8th St., Little Havana. ☎ **305/858-4162.**

This tiny storefront employs about 45 veteran Cuban rollers who sit all day rolling the very popular torpedoes and other critically acclaimed blends. They've got back orders until next Christmas, but it's worth stopping in. They *will* sell you a box and show you around.

Mike's Cigars. 1030 Kane Concourse (at 96th St.), Bay Harbor Island. ☎ **305/866-2277.**

Recently moved to this location, Mike's is perhaps one of the oldest cigar stores in Miami. Since 1950 Mike's has been selling the best of Honduras, the Dominican Republic, and Jamaica, as well as the very hot local brand, La Gloria Cubana. Most say it's got the best prices, too.

South Beach News and Tobacco. 1701 Washington Ave., Miami Beach. ☎ **305/673-3002.**

A walk-in humidor stocks cigars from the Dominican Republic, Honduras, and Jamaica, and a hand-roller comes in as he pleases to roll for the tourists. You'll also find a large selection of wines, coffees, and cigar paraphernalia in this pleasant little shop.

ELECTRONICS

Many people travel to Miami from South America and other parts of the world to buy playthings and gadgets. Although there are many electronics stores around, a trip to downtown Miami is both amazing and overwhelming when shopping around for a good Walkman or television. The streets of downtown are littered with bargain electronics stores. But beware—make sure any equipment you buy comes with a warranty. It would be wise to charge instead of paying cash. Here are a few reputable stores with several chain locations where you can safely shop:

Incredible Universe. 7800 NW 25th St., Miami. ☎ **305/716-5800.**

It's Incredible! It's scary! This is essentially an electronics department store. Once you get over the size and all the promotional gimmicks that masquerade as entertainment, you can find some really great deals, especially in the "Black Hole," a section where items that have been bruised are sold at deeply discounted prices. Bring the kids. The Universe has intelligent life and has even thought of a supervised computer play room to keep kids occupied while mom and dad spend.

Sound Advice. 1220 SW 85th St., Kendall. ☎ **305/594-4434.**

An audio junkie's candy store, Sound Advice features the latest in high-end stereo equipment, as well as TVs, VCRs, and telephone equipment. Techno-minded, but sometimes pushy, salesmen are on hand to educate.

Other locations in Miami include 1595 NE 163rd St., North Miami Beach (☎ 305/944-4434), and 1222 S. Dixie Hwy., Coral Gables (☎ 305/665-4434).

ETHNIC FOOD

Bombay Bazaar. 2008 NE 164th St., North Miami Beach. ☎ **305/948-7258.**

This little storefront is filled with bags and boxes of exotic spices, rice, and beans. Also, a small section of saris, jewelry, scarves, magazines, and videos sell well to the little Indian community that has formed around North Miami Beach.

Kingston Miami Trading Company. 280 NE 2nd St., downtown. ☎ **305/372-9547.**

With a disorganized array of canned goods, spices, and bottles, this little grocery store in downtown Miami has some great Jamaican specialties, including salt codfish, scotch bonnet sauces, hard-do bread, jerk seasoning, and lots of delicious drinks like Irish moss, Ting, and young coconut juice.

Gardner's Market. 7301 Red Rd., South Miami. ☎ **305/271-3211.**

This place is a tradition in South Miami, with anything a gourmet or novice cook could desire—the freshest and best from fish to cheese.

Laurenzo's Italian Supermarket and Farmer's Market. 16385 and 16445 W. Dixie Hwy. ☎ **305/945-6381** and 305/944-5052.

These landmarks in North Miami Beach (or NMB, as it's known to old-timers) are the meeting place for those in the know. Anything you want from homemade ravioli to hand-cut imported Romano cheese to smoked salmon to fresh fish and ground pork, you'll find it here. Be sure to see the neighboring store full of just-picked herbs, salad greens, and every type of vegetable from around the world. Incredible daily specials, like 10 Indian River pink grapefruits for 99¢, lure the thrifty from all over the city.

Sedano's. 13794 SW 152nd St., South Miami. ☎ **305/255-3386.**

Sedano's caters to the large Hispanic community with an assortment of ethnic fare, including fresh produce such as yuca, platanos, mamey, avocado, boniato, and guanabanas.

Vinham Oriental Market. 372 NE 167th St., North Miami Beach. ☎ **305/948-8860.**

Blue crabs, rice cookers, and cookbooks—this store is a one-stop shop for anything you might need for Chinese cooking. A helpful owner will instruct.

GOLF

Alf's Golf Shop. 524 Arthur Godfrey Rd., Miami Beach. ☎ **305/673-6568.**

The best pro shop on the beach, Alf's can sell you balls, clubs, gloves, and instructional videos—plus, the neighboring golf course offers discounts to Alf's clients.
Another Miami location is at 15369 S. Dixie Hwy., Miami (☎ 305/378-6068).

Edwin Watts Golf Shops. 15100 N. Biscayne Blvd., North Miami Beach. ☎ **305/944-2925.**

This full-service golf retail shop has it all, including clothing, pro-line equipment, gloves, bags, balls, videos, and books. Ask the pros for advice, and ask for coupons for discounted greens fees for various courses.

Nevada Bob's. 36th St. and NW 79th Ave., Miami (near the airport). ☎ **305/593-2999.**

Discounted Greg Norman and Antigua clothing, pro-line equipment, steel-shafted conventional clubs to the high-tech Yonex clubs; with more than 6,000 square feet of store this place has everything for golfers. Practice your swing at an indoor driving range with radar gun. No commission salesmen here—they're a laid-back crew and very up on the latest soft and hard equipment.

JAMES BOND GADGETS

Spy Shops International, Inc. 350 Biscayne Blvd., downtown. ☎ **305/374-4779.**

Where else could you find electronic surveillance equipment, day and night optical devices, stun guns, mini safes, doorknob alarms, and other anticrime gadgets?
A second branch is located at 2900 Biscayne Blvd. (☎ 305/573-4779).

JEWELRY

International Jeweler's Exchange. 18861 Biscayne Blvd. (in the Fashion Island), North Miami Beach. ☎ **305/931-7032.**

At least 50 jewelers hustle their wares from individual counters at one of the city's most active jewelry centers. Haggle your brains out for excellent prices on everything from timeless antiques from Tiffany's, Cartier, or Bulgari to unique designs you can create yourself. Closed Sunday.

MUSIC

Blue Note Records. 16401 NE 15th Ave., North Miami Beach. ☎ **305/940-3394.**

New and used and discounted CDs and old vinyl, too—this place has hard-to-find progressive and underground music and a good bunch of music afficionados who can tell you a thing or two.

Casino Records, Inc. 1208 SW 8th St., Little Havana. ☎ **305/856-6888.**

Here you'll find the largest selection of Latin music in Miami, including pop icons like Willy Chirino, Gloria Estefan, Albita, and local boy Nil Lara. Their slogan translates, "If we don't have it, forget it." Believe me, they've got it.

CD Solution. 13150 Biscayne Blvd., North Miami. ☎ **305/892-1048.**

Buy, sell, or trade your old CDs at this eclectic music hut.

Revolution Records and CDs. 1620 Alton Rd., Miami Beach. ☎ **305/673-6404.**

A quaint and fairly well organized collection of CDs, from hard-to-find jazz to origi-nal recordings of Buddy Rich. They'll search for anything and let you hear whatever you like.

SEAFOOD

Miami's most famous restaurant is **Joe's Stone Crab,** 227 Biscayne St., South Miami Beach (☎ **305/673-0365** or 800/780-CRAB). Joe's makes overnight air ship-ments of stone crabs to anywhere in the country. Joe's is open only during crab season (from October through May).

East Coast Fisheries. 330 W. Flagler St., Downtown. ☎ **305/577-3000.**

This retail market and restaurant has shipped millions of pounds of seafood world-wide from its own fishing fleet. It is equipped to wrap and send 5- or 10-pound pack-ages of stone crab claws, Florida lobsters, Florida Bay pompano, fresh Key West shrimp, and a variety of other local delicacies to your door via overnight mail.

WINE & SPIRITS

Crown Liquors. 6751 Red Rd., Coral Gables. ☎ **305/669-0225.**

One of the most diverse selections in Miami, the ever-rotating stock here comes from estate sales around the country and worldwide distributors. And since there are sev-eral stores in the chain, the owners get to buy in bulk, resulting in lower prices for oenophiles. If you want one of the tastiest and most affordable champagnes ever, try their exclusive import, Billecarte Salmon.

Other locations in Miami include 1296 NE 163rd St. (☎ 305/949-2871).

Sunny Isles Liquor. 18180 Collins Ave., North Miami Beach. ☎ **305/932-5782.**

This well-located store has hundreds of brands of imported beer and hard-to-find liquor. The staff will search and find decanters and minis for your collection.

13 Miami After Dark

Miami's nightlife is as varied as its population. On any given night you'll find world-class opera or dance as well as grinding rock and seductive salsa. Restaurants and bars are open late and many clubs, especially on South Beach, stay open past dawn. It's no secret that Cuban and Caribbean rhythms are extremely popular, and the sound of the conga, inextricably incorporated into Miami's club culture, makes dancing irresistible.

For up-to-date entertainment listings, check the *Miami Herald's* "Weekend" section, which runs on Friday, or the more comprehensive *New Times,* Miami's free alternative weekly. Available each Wednesday, this award-winning paper prints articles, previews, and advertisements on upcoming local events.

Several telephone hotlines—many operated by local radio stations—give free re-corded information on current events in the city. These include the **Love 94 Con-cert Hotline** (☎ **800/237-0939**) and the **UM Concert Hotline** (☎ **305/ 284-6477**). Other information-oriented telephone numbers are listed under the ap-propriate headings below.

Tickets for most performances can be purchased by phone through **Ticketmaster** (☎ 305/358-5885). The company accepts all major credit/charge cards and has phone lines open 24 hours. If you want to pick up your tickets from a Ticketmaster outlet, call for the location nearest you. Outlets are open Monday to Saturday from 10am to 9pm and on Sunday from noon to 5pm. There's a small service charge.

For sold-out events, you're at the mercy of ticket brokers who charge a premium, especially for big-name concerts. One well-known broker in Coral Gables is **Ultimate Travel & Entertainment,** at 3001 Salzedo in Coral Gables (☎ **305/444-8499**). It's open Monday to Friday from 9am to 6pm and on Saturday from 10am to 4pm.

THE PERFORMING ARTS
CLASSICAL MUSIC & OPERA

Although it looked as though classical music was in trouble for a while in Miami, the influx of international music lovers to the area has revitalized Miami's classical scene. Most companies still suffer from economic problems, but there are many offerings, especially in winter.

In addition to a number of local orchestras and operas, each year brings a slew of special events and touring artists. One of the most important and longest-running series is produced by the **Concert Association of Florida (CAF),** 555 17th St., South Miami Beach (☎ **305/532-3491**). Known for almost a quarter of a century for its high-caliber, star-packed schedules, CAF regularly arranges the best classical concerts for the city. Season after season the schedules are punctuated by world-renowned dance companies and seasoned virtuosi like Itzhak Perlman, Andre Watts, and Van Cliburn. CAF does not have its own space. Performances are usually scheduled in either the Dade County Auditorium or the Jackie Gleason Theater of the Performing Arts. The performance season lasts from October to April, and ticket prices range from $20 to $60.

The **Florida Grand Opera**, Coral Way in Coral Gables (☎ **305/854-1643**), has been featuring singers from America's and Europe's top houses for nearly 60 years. All productions are sung in their original language and staged with projected English supertitles. Tickets become scarce when Plácido Domingo or Luciano Pavarotti (who made his American debut here in 1965) comes to town. The opera's season runs roughly from November to April, with performances 5 days per week.

The **New World Symphony,** at Lincoln Road in South Beach (☎ **305/ 673-3331**), is a stepping-stone for gifted young musicians seeking professional careers. Accepting artists on the basis of a 3-year fellowship and led by artistic adviser Michael Tilson Thomas, the orchestra specializes in ambitious, innovative, energetic performances and often features guest soloists and renowned conductors. The symphony's season lasts from October to May. Tickets cost $10 to $40; student and senior discounts are available.

The **Florida Philharmonic Orchestra,** 169 E. Flagler St., Miami (☎ **305/ 930-1812,** or 800/226-1812), is South Florida's premier symphony orchestra, under the direction of James Judd. It presents a full season of classical and pops programs interspersed with several children's and contemporary popular music dates. The Philharmonic performs downtown in the Gusman Center for the Performing Arts and the Jackie Gleason Theater of the Performing Arts, and puts on children's concerts at the Dade County Auditorium.

An inexpensive alternative to the high-priced classical venues is the **Miami Chamber Symphony,** at 5690 N. Kendall Dr., Kendall (☎ **305/858-3500**). Renowned international soloists regularly perform with this professional orchestra. The symphony performs October to May, and most concerts are held in the Gusman Concert Hall, on the University of Miami campus. Tickets are $12 to $30.

DANCE

Several local dance companies train and perform in the Greater Miami area. In addition, top traveling troupes regularly pass through the city, stopping at the venues listed above. Keep your eyes open for special events and guest artists.

Ballet Flamenco La Rosa at the Performing Arts Network. 555 17th St., Miami Beach. ☎ **305/672-0552.**

For a taste of local Latin flavor, see this lively troupe perform impressive flamenco and other styles of dance. In addition to frequent performances on Miami stages, you'll find a host of classes offered by Miami's best Latin dancers. Call for schedules.

Miami City Ballet. Lincoln Rd. Mall at 9th St., Miami Beach. ☎ **305/532-4880.** Tickets $17–$49.

Headquartered in a storefront in the middle of the art deco district's popular pedestrian mall, this Miami company has quickly emerged as the area's top troupe. The artistically acclaimed and innovative company is directed by Edward Villella, whose performing career was spent with George Balanchine's New York City Ballet. The company has a repertoire of more than 60 ballets, many by Balanchine, and has presented more than 20 world premières of new works. Stop by most afternoons to watch rehearsals through the large storefront window. The City Ballet season runs from September to April, with performances at the Dade County Auditorium.

THEATER

Miami has an active and varied selection of dramas and musicals throughout the year. Thanks to the support of many loyal theater aficionados, especially the crowd of New York transplants, season subscriptions allow the theaters to survive. Some traveling Broadway shows make it to town, as do revivals.

The two well-known acting companies in Miami have suffered from poor financing and real-estate woes. At press time, neither knew where it was going to be housed for the upcoming season. Luckily, both have use of the beautiful Colony Theater on Lincoln Road and the support of a loyal crew of theater aficionados. Call for schedules and locales.

The **Acme Acting Company** (☎ 305/576-7500) usually puts on offbeat contemporary plays. Tickets are $15 to $25, depending on the venue (students and seniors pay $10 to $20). The **Area Stage Company** (☎ 305/538-2187) lived on Lincoln road for nearly 7 years until rents drove it searching for a new space. This award-winning company has won respect from local and national audiences for its dramatic work in all manner of contemporary theater.

Most theaters are dark in the summer or show a limited schedule. Call the following venues to see what's coming up.

The **Actors' Playhouse,** at the newly restored Miracle Mile Theater in Coral Gables (☎ 305/444-9293), is a grand 1948 art deco movie palace with a 600-seat main theater as well as a smaller theater/rehearsal hall where a number of excellent musicals for children are put on throughout the year.

The **Coconut Grove Playhouse,** 35th Street and Main Highway in Coconut Grove (☎ 305/442-4000), was also a former movie house, built in 1927 in an ornate Spanish rococo style. Today this respected venue is known for its original and innovative staging. The more intimate Encore Room is well suited to alternative and experimental productions.

The **Florida Shakespeare Theatre,** at the Biltmore Hotel, Anastasia Avenue in Coral Gables (☎ 305/446-1116), stages at least one Shakespeare play, one classic, and one contemporary piece a year. In addition, this well-regarded theater usually tries to produce a national or local première as well. Tickets cost $20 and $22; $12 and $17 for students and seniors.

The recently renamed **Jerry Herman Ring Theatre** is on the main campus of the University of Miami in Coral Gables (☎ **305/284-3355**). The University's Department of Theater Arts uses this stage for advanced student productions of comedies, dramas, and musicals. Faculty and guest actors are regularly featured, as are contemporary works by local playwrights. Performances are usually scheduled Tuesday to Saturday during the academic year only.

The **New Theater,** 65 Almeira Ave., in Coral Gables (☎ **305/443-5909**), recently celebrated its 10th birthday. This theater prides itself on presenting world-renowned pieces from America and Europe. As the name implies, you'll find mostly contemporary plays, with a few classics thrown in for variety. Performances are staged year round Thursday to Sunday. Tickets sell for $18 to $20, half price for students. They don't widely advertise it, but on Thursday you can get a second ticket for half price.

THE CLUB & MUSIC SCENE
LIVE MUSIC/JAZZ

Despite the spotty success of local music, South Florida's jazz scene is very much alive with traditional and contemporary performers. Keep an eye out for guitarist Randy Bernsen, vibraphonist Tom Toyama, and flutist Nestor Torres, young performers who lead local ensembles.

The **University of Miami** has a well-respected jazz studies program in its School of Music (☎ **305/284-6477**) and often schedules low- and no-cost recitals. Frequent music shows also are scheduled at the **Miami Metrozoo.** The lineup changes frequently, and it's not always jazz, but the quality is good, and the concerts are included with zoo admission.

Additionally, many area hotels feature live music of every assortment. Schedules are listed in the newspaper entertainment sections. Try calling the **Blues Hotline** (☎ **305/666-MOJO**) and the **Jazz Hotline** (☎ **305/382-3938**) for the most up-to-date bookings in Miami.

The Hungry Sailor. 3064 Grand Ave., Coconut Grove. ☎ **305/444-9359.** No cover Wed–Thurs, $5–$10 Fri–Sat.

This small wood-paneled pub has Watney's, Bass, and Guinness on draft and reggae regularly on tap. The club attracts an extremely mixed crowd. A short British menu and high-quality live music are featured Wednesday to Saturday.

MoJazz Cafe. 928 71st St., Miami Beach. ☎ **305/867-0950,** or 305/865-2636 for the 24-hour information line. Cover none–$10.

A good smoky jazz club with lots of great acts from all over. Ask for the big-spender option—if you spend $22 per person on food, drinks, or T-shirts, you skip the cover. There's also great Vietnamese food starting at 5:30pm. Open Tuesday to Sunday.

Tobacco Road. 626 S. Miami Ave., downtown. ☎ **305/374-1198.** Cover none–$6.

Blues, zydeco, brass, jazz, and more—this place has been around since 1912 doing more in the back room than just dancing. These days you'll find a good bar menu along with the best live music anywhere. Some regulars include the Dirty Dozen Brass Band from New Orleans, who play a mean mix of zydeco and blues with an actual dozen brass players; Bill Warton and the Ingredients, who make a pot of gumbo while up on stage; Monkey Meet; Ico Ico; Chubby Carrier and his band; and many others. Friday and Saturday the music is upstairs, where people dance like crazy though it's packed and there's no real dance floor. Cool off in the backyard patio. The down-right-cheap dinner specials, like a $9 lobster dinner, are quite good. This is a Miami institution and a must see. Open daily until 5am.

Van Dyke Cafe. 846 Lincoln Rd., Miami Beach. ☎ **305/534-3600.** No cover.

Live jazz 7 nights a week until midnight and it's free! In an elegant little upstairs lounge, the likes of Eddie Higgins, Mike Renzi, and some locals like Don Wilner, play strictly jazz for a well-dressed crowd. You can have a drink or two at the pristine oak bar or enjoy some snacks from the bustling restaurant downstairs.

DANCE CLUBS

A new trend in Miami's club scene is the popularity of "one-off" nights—events organized by a promoter and held in established venues on irregular schedules. Word of mouth, local advertising, and listings in the free weekly *New Times* are the best way to find out about these hot events.

Alcazaba. In the Hyatt Regency Hotel, 50 Alhambra Plaza, Coral Gables. ☎ **305/441-1234.**

The Hyatt's Top 40 lounge plays an eclectic mix of music but exudes a decidedly Mediterranean atmosphere that mixes fantasy with reality. Cool out with some tropical drinks and authentic tapas in between songs. Happy hour—Wednesday and Friday from 5 to 7pm and Saturday from 9 to 11pm—offers half-price beer, wine, and drinks, plus a free buffet.

Bermuda Bar and Grill. 3509 NE 163rd St., North Miami Beach. ☎ **305/945-0196.** Cover $5 for women Fri and Sun, $10 for men Wed–Sun.

This huge North Miami Beach danceteria specializes in Ladies' Nights as well as occasional contests awarding cash prizes to the woman with the skimpiest outfit. If you like to dance, however, it does have high-energy dance music that will get anyone but a dead person up on the floor. Thursday night is salsa night for those craving a Latin beat. Wednesday, Thursday, and Saturday are Ladies' Nights, with no cover. Open Wednesday to Sunday from 5pm to 6am.

Cafe Nostalgia. 2212 SW 8th St. (Calle Ocho), Little Havana. ☎ **305/541-2631.** Cover $10.

As the name implies, Cafe Nostalgia is dedicated to reminiscing about Old Cuba. After watching a film with Celia Cruz, you can dance to the hot sounds of Afro-Cuban jazz. With pictures of old and young Cuban stars smiling down on you and a live band celebrating Cuban heritage, it's hard not to get excited about the island. Be prepared—it's packed after midnight and dance space is mostly between the tables. Films are shown from 10pm to midnight Wednesday to Sunday, followed by live music till 4am.

Cameo Theater. 1445 Washington Ave., Miami Beach. ☎ **305/532-0922.** Cover varies according to theme night.

This is a South Beach institution. The old converted theater enjoyed a renaissance of sorts when it became a regular concert spot and nightclub a few years ago. Theme nights come and go, but the one that seems as though it's here to stay is Sunday's Disco Inferno night, when the huge nightclub goes retro and Gloria Gaynor proves that she did survive. Open Friday to Sunday until 5am.

Casa Panza. 1620 SW 8th St. (Calle Ocho), Little Havana. ☎ **305/643-5343.** No cover.

Clap your hands or your castanets if you have them. Every Tuesday and Thursday night Casa Panza, in the heart of Little Havana, becomes the House of Flamenco. Patrons of the restaurant can enjoy a flamenco show (at 8 and 11pm) or don their own dancing shoes and participate in the celebration. Enjoy a fantastic dinner before the show or have a few drinks before you do some stomping.

Glam Slam. 1235 Washington Ave., Miami Beach. ☎ **305/672-4858.** Cover varies.

Opened by "the artist formerly known as Prince," this most happening club on South Beach has had its share of closings. With a large gay clientele, it also has great dance music and a fun, huge bar scene. In the back alley on Thursday nights is a private club, the Fat Black Pussy Cat. If you can get the weekly password (which is usually obtainable by asking a hip-looking waiter at any South beach restaurant), you'll get in. Open Wednesday to Sunday, with various theme nights.

✪ **Groove Jet.** 323 23rd St. (next to the Fina gas station), Miami Beach. ☎ **305/532-2002.** Cover usually $5 before midnight and $7 after.

This fantastic hidden spot north of the South Beach scene has been through many incarnations. Its most recent, Groove Jet, has three distinct areas playing totally different music. Whatever name it's going by, do drive by this spot to see what's happening—usually out back it's acid jazz and in the other two rooms inside you'll hear house and alternative or trance. A very hip young crowd hangs in this out-of-the-way scene, which gets going late, Thursday to Sunday.

Mango's. 900 Ocean Dr., Miami Beach. ☎ **305/673-4422.** Cover $6–$15 depending on performer.

If you want to dance to a funky, loud Brazilian beat till you drop, check out Mango's on the beach. It features nightly live Brazilian and some Latin music on a little patio bar. When you need refreshment, you can choose from a schizophrenic menu of Caribbean, Mexican, vegetarian, and Cuban specialties. Open daily from 11am to 5:30am.

Swiss Chateau Club. 2471 SW 32nd Ave., Miami ☎ **305/445-3633.** No cover Fri and Sun, $5 for men Sat (couples and women free).

If you're looking to sample some authentic Cuban nightlife, look no further. Although the name sounds anything but Hispanic, the Chateau offers authentic salsa and merengue music every weekend to a mostly older crowd of *exilios*. When you've worked up an appetite, try a snack from the tapas menu, which includes steak, shrimp, and chicken croquettas. Open Friday to Sunday from 7pm to 4am.

THE GAY & LESBIAN SCENE

See also Glam Slam, under "Dance Clubs," above.

821. 821 Lincoln Rd., Miami Beach. ☎ **305/534-0887.** No cover.

821 is something between a neighborhood bar and a nightclub with a live DJ every night. Thursday and Saturday are for ladies, though they're welcome the other nights too. Offering good music and limited attitude in a basic black box, this hotspot is a staple on Lincoln Road. Open daily until 3am or 5am.

Warsaw Ballroom. 1450 Collins Ave., Miami Beach. ☎ **305/531-4555.** Cover $12.

One of Miami's oldest and most fun nightclubs, Warsaw hosts various theme nights and some of the best dance music in town. After all these years, regulars still line up down the sidewalk waiting to get in. Open daily until 5am.

West End. 942 Lincoln Rd., Miami Beach. ☎ **305/538-9378.** No cover.

A mellow bar and pool hall, this Lincoln road standby is a favorite hangout for women and men. Enjoy a relaxed atmosphere and a good place to meet people. Open daily from midnight to 5am.

LATE-NIGHT BITES

Although many dining spots in Miami stop serving at 10pm, South Beach eateries stay open very late, especially on weekends.

If you want a quick bite after clubbing and you find that it's 4am, don't fret! There are a vast number of pizza places lining Washington Avenue in Miami Beach that are open past 6am. **La Sandwicherie,** 229 14th St., behind the Amoco Station (☎ **305/ 532-8934),** serves up a great late-night sandwich until 4 or 5am. Another place of note for night owls is the **News Café,** 800 Ocean Dr. (☎ **305/538-6397),** a trendy sidewalk café with a menu ranging from a Middle Eastern platter to a fruit bowl or steak and potatoes.

If you've just left a Latin club, stop in at **Versailles,** 3555 SW 8th St. (☎ **305/ 444-0240).** What else but a cuban *medianoche* (midnight sandwich) will do? It may not be open all night, but the hours extend well past midnight, catering to gangs of revelers young and old.

FILMS

In addition to the annual Miami Film Festival, the Italian Film Festival, and the Jewish Film Festival, Miami is lucky to have three wonderful art cinemas showing a range of films from *Fresas y Chocolate* to *Crumb.*

The **Alliance Cinema,** tucked behind a tropical little walkway just next to Books & Books at 927 Lincoln Rd., Suite 119, in Miami Beach (☎ **305/531-8504),** shows art films and many Latin American independent features. It features the Anti-Film Festival in February, a showing of underground movies, and the Queen Flickering Light Gay Film Festival in June. You may want to bring a pillow—the seats are old and rickety. Tickets cost $6. The **Astor Art Cinema,** at 4120 Laguna St. in Coral Gables (☎ **305/443-6777),** is an oasis in the midst of a sea of Cineplex Odeons and AMCs. The quaint double theater hosts foreign, classic, independent, and art films, and serves decent popcorn, too. The charge is $5, $3 for seniors. The **Bill Cosford Cinema** at the University of Miami, on the second floor of the Memorial Building off Campo Sano Avenue (☎ **305/284-4861),** is named after the deceased *Herald* film critic. This well-endowed little theater was recently revamped and boasts high-tech projectors, new air-conditioning, and new decor. It sponsors independent films as well as lectures by visiting filmmakers and movie stars. Andy Garcia and Antonio Banderas are a few of the big names that this "little theater that could" attracts. It hosts the many annual film festivals, including the Italian, the African-American, and Student Film Festivals. Admission is $5.

14 Quick Trips to The Bahamas

Most people think that taking a cruise means spending thousands of dollars and booking a ship far in advance. But most of the Caribbean-bound ships sailing weekly out of the Port of Miami are relatively inexpensive, can be booked without advance notice, and make for an excellent excursion.

Home to 22 cruise ships from all around the world, the Port of Miami is the world's busiest, with a passenger load of close to three million annually. All the shorter cruises are well equipped for gambling, and casinos open as soon as the ship clears U.S. waters—typically 45 minutes after leaving port. Usually, four full-size meals are served daily, with portions so huge they're impossible to finish. Games, movies, and other on-board activities ensure that you're always busy. Passengers can board up to 2 hours prior to departure for meals, games, and cocktails.

There are dozens of cruise options—from a 1-day excursion to a trip around the world. A full list can be obtained from the **Metro-Dade Seaport Department,** 1015 North America Way, in Miami (☎ **305/371-7678**), open Monday to Friday from 8am to 5pm.

Most of the ships listed below offer 2- and 3-day excursions to The Bahamas. Cruise ships usually depart Miami on Friday night and return Monday morning. If you want more information, contact **The Bahamas Tourist Office,** at 19495 Biscayne Blvd., Suite 809, in Aventura (☎ **305/932-0051**). All passengers must travel with a passport or proof of citizenship for reentry into the United States.

Carnival Cruise Lines, 35201 Blue Lagoon Dr., Miami (☎ **305/599-2200** or 800/327-9501), sails the *Fantasy* and *Ecstasy* on 3- to 4-night cruises to Nassau, usually departing Friday at 4pm and returning Monday at 7am. The cost starts at $360. One of the largest cruise ships in the world, the *Fantasy* made its debut in 1990 with lots of publicity. Several swimming pools, games rooms, and lounges surround a spectacular multistory foyer that has quickly made the *Fantasy* the centerpiece of Carnival's fast-growing fleet. The 70,000-ton ship can accommodate up to 3,000 passengers.

Norwegian Cruise Line, 95 Merrick Way, Coral Gables (☎ **305/445-0866** or 800/327-7030), offers the *Leeward.* Departures are on Friday at 6pm, returning Monday at 7am. Bookings start at $430. A more intimate ship, the 950-passenger *Leeward* spends a full day in Nassau or Key West (they alternate weekly). As on other Caribbean-bound ships, you can choose to disembark at any destination or you can stay on board for food, drinks, and games.

If you want a quick getaway to the Caribbean without the experience of cruising, many airlines and hotels team up to offer extremely affordable weekend packages. Competitively priced packages are available from **American Flyaway Vacations,** operated by American Airlines (☎ 800/321-2121); **Bahamas Air** (☎ 800/222-4262); **Pan Am Bridge** (☎ 305/359-7980); the slightly rundown **Princesss Casino** in Freeport (☎ 305/359-9898); and **USAir** (☎ 800/842-5374). Call for rates, since they vary dramatically throughout the year and depend on the type of accommodations you choose.

The Florida Keys 7

by Victoria Pesce Elliott

Juan Ponce de León, the 16th-century Spanish explorer who was searching for the Fountain of Youth, found the Florida Keys instead—islands he called Los Martieres (The Martyrs), because they looked to him like men in distress. *Cayo* is the Spanish word for "small island." To those of us with less active imaginations, the Keys appear more like little tropical islands strung out in a chain that reaches from Miami halfway to Cuba.

Although there are about 400 islands in the Keys, the best known are the 34 that are connected to the mainland by the Overseas Highway (U.S. 1). The hundreds of small, undeveloped islands that surround these "mainland" keys are known locally as the "backcountry." Most backcountry islands are wildlife refuges protected by either the federal government or the Nature Conservancy, a private environmental organization.

The Keys are surrounded by the world's third-largest barrier reef system, a variety of living corals that supports a complex and delicate ecosystem of plants and animals including sponges, anemones, jellyfish, crabs, rays, sharks, turtles, snails, lobsters, and thousands of types of fish.

The Keys are divided into three regions—Upper Keys, Lower Keys, and Key West—each with its own distinctive character. The Upper Keys are commercial and overdeveloped—the result of their close proximity to Miami, and the merciless dredging and filling that occurred in the 1940s. Under a mandate by President Franklin Roosevelt, chemical-based mosquito-abatement programs were instituted, coral reefs were slashed, trees were chopped, and towns were built. There are few unspoiled spots left between the strip malls and condominium complexes, but several resort hotels and plenty of parks take advantage of the area's intrinsic beauty.

Fishing and diving also fuel the economic engine that drives the Lower Keys, but because of environmental activism and governmental protection, development here has been contained. As you head south, the discount stores give way to seashell shops and sandy beaches. A rich variety of indigenous plants and animals live here, including many endangered species. Eagles, egrets, and Key deer are some of the most visible, as are gumbo-limbo trees, mangroves, royal poincianas, banyans, and aloe.

Key West sits literally at the end of the road. It operates on "island time"—you'd think there was an ordinance against wearing

What's Special About the Florida Keys

Annual Events
- Offbeat events, such as Fantasy Fest, Ernest Hemingway weekend, the Looe Key underwater music festival, fishing tournaments in Islamorada, Old Island Days, and more.

The Pace
- A land of perennial vacation, where time is of little importance—take off your watch or you'll be immediately identified as a tourist.

Natural Wonders
- John Pennekamp Coral Reef State Park, the U.S. mainland's only living coral reef and underwater state park, with a dazzling vista of fish, plants, coral, and water for divers and snorkelers.
- Indian Key and Lignumvitae Key, two small islands, now state botanical sites, that sustain a complex and diverse ecosystem as fragile as it is unusual, allowing visitors a glimpse of the natural Keys.

Wildlife
- A birdwatcher's paradise where, depending on the season, you can see more than 300 species, including frigate birds, ospreys, spoonbills, wood storks, pelicans, sea gulls, and falcons.

watches in this land of perennial vacation. (Take yours off or you'll be immediately identified as a tourist.) Its residents, a bohemian lot of individualists, characters, and misfits, jealously guard their island's identity. In 1982, when a federal Customs roadblock was thrown up across U.S. 1 to help reduce drug smuggling, locals responded with a mock secession from the United States and the declaration of an independent "Conch Republic."

EXPLORING THE KEYS BY CAR

With just one main road running through the entire chain of the Keys, you'd think that there wouldn't be much to explore. But there is! You'll find plenty of hidden treasures off the beaten path. And I've included lots of out-of-the-way spots and backwater adventures in this chapter.

One of the best things about Key West is getting there, so unless you're really pressed for time, don't even think of flying in—driving is the way to go. Motoring across the Keys on U.S. 1 (the Overseas Highway), over 42 bridges and across 34 islands, is one of the greatest road trips anywhere. For much of the drive, expansive skies and sweeping water vistas surround you with innumerable shades of blue. The clear water appears to "blossom" with little mangrove islands that compete for your attention with families of ospreys nesting on the telephone lines that follow you all the way to Key West. At other points along the way the road is clogged with shopping centers and billboards advertising restaurants, rest stops, and attractions.

Most of U.S. 1 is a narrow, two-lane highway, though in the Upper Keys it opens up to four lanes. The legal speed limit is 55 m.p.h. (45 m.p.h. on Big Pine Key and in commercial areas), and passing is restricted for most of the way. Still, on a good day you can make the trip from Miami to Key West in less than 4 hours. But don't rush. There are plenty of worthwhile places to stop along the way.

Gasoline prices rise rapidly the farther south you go, but then descend slightly when you arrive on Key West. Fill up in Miami.

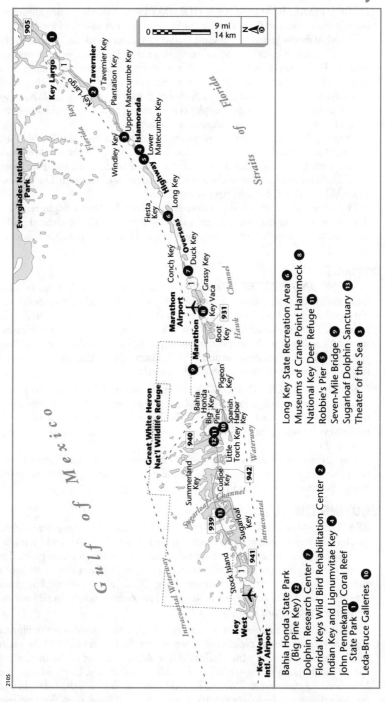

Bahia Honda State Park (Big Pine Key) 12
Dolphin Research Center 7
Florida Keys Wild Bird Rehabilitation Center 2
Indian Key and Lignumvitae Key 4
John Pennekamp Coral Reef State Park 1
Leda-Bruce Galleries 10

Long Key State Recreation Area 6
Museums of Crane Point Hammock 8
National Key Deer Refuge 5
Robbie's Pier 11
Seven-Mile Bridge 9
Sugarloaf Dolphin Sanctuary 13
Theater of the Sea 3

EN ROUTE: ALABAMA JACKS & HOLIDAY ISLE   Two stops are required on any trip to or from the Keys. The first, in Florida City, just south of Homestead, is known as **Alabama Jacks.** It's on Card Sound Road, also called the old road to the Keys. This landmark was built on a floating barge in 1953 and today is the meeting point for Harley owners, weekend cyclists, midwestern tourists, and hip couples from Miami. All these folks get together to drink beer and listen to a hokey cowboy band that plays on weekends from 2pm until closing (which is 7pm). Other days, enjoy the decent bar food, including some spicy crab cakes, and great waterfront atmosphere from 11am to 7pm. It's a great introduction to the Keys.

To get to Alabama Jacks, when you get off the Turnpike at its end in Florida City, turn right at the stoplight onto U.S. 1. You'll see the Mutineer restaurant on your left and signs for the toll plaza. Make a left onto Card Sound Road and drive about 11 miles. You can't miss the trucks parked on both sides of the road. The bar is at about Mile Marker 125 on the right before the toll.

The other place to stop is the renowned **Holiday Isle**. After a bright-red Rum Runner or two you may want to enter the limbo contest and be cheered on by an assortment of yuppie business types and kids in Hawaiian shirts. (See below for specifics.)

DRIVING TRIP TIPS

FINDING AN ADDRESS   Most addresses in the Keys are delineated by Mile Markers (MM), small green signs on the right side of the road that announce the distance from Key West. The markers end with no. 126, just south of the Florida mainland. The zero marker is in Key West, at the corner of Whitehead and Fleming streets. All addresses in this chapter are accompanied by a MM designation to help you determine its location on (or near) U.S. 1. Listings in this chapter are organized first by price, then by location, from north to south.

FINDING A PLACE TO STAY   Accommodations in the Keys run the gamut from simple fishing lodges to top-of-the-line hideaway resorts. The best rooms face the water and are set back far away from the Overseas Highway. In general, hotels in the Keys are pricier then those of similar quality elsewhere, and winter weekends command top dollar.

You can often drive down the Keys without a reservation and find a room at any hotel that pleases you, but beware. There are many festivals and special events in the Keys, when rooms sell out far in advance.

ENJOYING THE OUTDOORS

BEACHES   Most people don't realize that the Keys really don't have any beaches. You'll find a few small man-made beaches at the hotels on Key West and a few others. Instead, most of the ocean activity takes place on boats or in grassy parks. But if you want to go to the beach, here are your options: Smathers Beach, off South Roosevelt Boulevard west of the airport; Higgs Beach, along Atlantic Boulevard between White Street and Reynolds Road; or Fort Zachary Beach, located off the western end of Southard Boulevard.

BICYCLING   The almost-flat 126 miles of U.S. 1 that run down the Florida Keys are tailor-made for cyclists—if it weren't for the cars. There are bike paths paralleling the road from Mile Markers 106 to 86, but the rest of the route is on narrow shoulders, so biking the Keys is for serious cyclists only. Larger islands, like Marathon, Big Pine, and Key West, offer good family cycling on dedicated paths and smaller side streets. In Marathon, try Sombrero Beach Road from the Overseas

The Truth About Keys Cuisine

There are few world-class chefs in the Florida Keys. But that isn't to say that the food isn't great. You'll find restaurants that are bursting with atmosphere serving very fresh fish and a few local specialties.

Even the humblest of restaurants can be counted on to take full advantage of the gastronomic treasures in its own backyard. The Keys have everything a cook could want: the Atlantic and the Gulf of Mexico for impeccably fresh fish; a tropical climate for year-round farm-stand produce, with great tomatoes, beans, berries, and citrus fruit; and a freshwater swamp for rustic delicacies like alligator, frogs' legs, and hearts of palm.

Keep a few things in mind: The fish you order in the Keys may very well have been caught elsewhere—don't be shy about asking where it's from. Conch fritters and chowder are mainstays on most tourist-oriented menus. But since the queen conch was listed as an endangered species by the U.S. government in 1985, the conch in your dish was most likely shipped fresh-frozen from The Bahamas or the Caribbean.

Key lime pie, *the* dessert in the Keys, is one of the easiest things to make. There are only about three ingredients, with condensed milk a staple in most authentic versions. The real pain is squeezing all those tiny key limes; they're small, not-very-juicy little yellow fruits. That's why some chefs cheat and use regular limes, or worse, bottled juice. Experts debate whether key lime pie should have a whipped cream or a merengue topping, but all agree that it should never be green.

You don't need a great chef to make great stone crabs or lobster. You just need to be around at the right time of year—generally, October to March for stone crabs and August to late March for lobster. Stone crabs are my all-time favorites. They've been written about and talked about by kings, presidents, and poets. Most restaurants crack the claws for you since the effort puts many people off—believe it or not, there have been lawsuits filed after some people cut themselves on the tough, sharp shells. I like to buy a few pounds of claws at a fish shop, plus a jar of creamy mustard, and then take them to the beach to eat while sitting in the sand. In a bathing suit, you tend to be less concerned about a slight mess.

Florida lobster is a different species from the more common Maine crustacean and has a slightly sweeter meat. You'll only see the tails on the menu—the Florida lobster has no claws. And it's that very lack of claws that makes the Florida lobster vulnerable to its one and only real predator, people.

Highway (at Mile Marker 50) to the public beach. On Big Pine, cruise along Key Deer Boulevard (at Mile Marker 30)—those with fat tires can ride into the National Key Deer Refuge. And on Key West, just about any street will do.

BIRDWATCHING A stopping point for migratory birds on the Eastern Flyway, the Keys are populated with many West Indian bird species, especially during spring and fall. The small vegetated islands of the Keys are the only nesting sites in the United States for the great white heron and the white-crowned pigeon. It's also one of a very few breeding places for the reddish egret, the roseate spoonbill, the mangrove cuckoo, and the black-whiskered vireo.

Many factors threaten the health of these bird populations, but paramount among them is loss of habitat. Some 40% of the shallow-water mangrove pools on the

Upper Keys were lost to human development between 1955 and 1985, and transitional wetlands, shallow-water mangrove sites, freshwater ponds, and hardwood hammocks continue to be filled and developed.

The Dry Tortugas, a chain of seven coral islands 70 miles west of Key West, is one of the best birding spots in the world. Accessible only by boat or plane, these islands are a mecca for the most serious birders. See "The Dry Tortugas," later in this chapter, for complete information.

DIVING & SNORKELING   While scuba diving isn't cheap, this may be the place where you want to splurge. According to 22,000 votes cast by readers of *Scuba Diving* magazine, the Florida Keys are the best place to dive in America, topping even California and Hawaii. The Keys are surrounded by one of the world's largest barrier reef systems in relatively shallow water, which attracts a plethora of sealife. John Pennekamp Coral Reef State Park (at Mile Marker 102.3) is an especially popular place to dive and snorkel (see the section on the Upper Keys), offering regular excursions to its protected reefs.

If you aren't a certified diver, you can take a quick course that will allow you to go out with an instructor. Or you might want to try snuba, a relatively new, and less expensive, version of diving offered in Key Largo; swimmers go down attached to a communal air supply rather than with cumbersome tanks.

FISHING   You can probably find more boats, rods, and reels in South Florida and the Florida Keys than any place else on earth. Almost two dozen local fish species—including amberjack, barracuda, snapper, king mackerel, sailfish, tarpon, swordfish, and white marlin—attain a weight of 50 pounds or more, the respectable minimum for seasoned trophy hunters.

There are three different kinds of fishing in the Keys: deep-sea fishing for big-game fish like marlin, sailfish, and tuna; reef fishing for "eating fish" like snapper and grouper; and backcountry fishing for bonefish, tarpon, and other "stalking" fish.

Unless you're fishing from land, a pier, or a sanctioned bridge, a saltwater-fishing permit is mandatory, and costs $7 for 3 days and $17 for 7 days. Permits can be purchased from almost any bait or boat shop, many of which are listed geographically below.

If your catch will not be eaten or mounted, release your fish to preserve the area's severely depleted fish population. Always pay close attention to your baited hooks—they will tempt hungry birds. Over 80% of bird injuries are caused by fishing hooks and monofilament. Never discard fishing line in the water, and if you accidently hook a bird, never allow it to fly off without first removing any attached fish line.

HIKING   You can hike throughout the Keys, on both marked trails and meandering coastlines. The best places to trek through nature are Bahia Honda State Park (at Mile Marker 29.5), the National Key Deer Refuge (at Mile Marker 30), Crane Point Hammock (at Mile Marker 50.5), Long Key State Recreation Area (at Mile Marker 68), and John Pennekamp Coral Reef State Park (at Mile Marker 102.3). See below for complete information.

KAYAKING & CANOEING   The Overseas Highway (U.S. 1) only touches on a few dozen of the many hundreds of islands that make up the Florida Keys. I can think of no better way to explore the uninhabited shallow backcountry than by kayak or canoe. You can reach places big boats just can't get to because of their large draft. Sometimes manatees will cuddle up to the boats thinking they're another friendly species.

For a more enjoyable time, ask for a sit-inside boat—you'll stay dryer. A fiberglass boat (as opposed to plastic) with a rudder is generally more stable and easier to maneuver. Many area hotels rent kayaks and canoes to guests, as do a multitude of outfitters, listed geographically below.

1 The Upper Keys: Key Largo to Marathon

48–105 miles SW of Miami

Although it hardly looks like it from the busy main road, the Upper Keys is all about water and wilderness. This is the fishing and diving capital of America, and a profusion of outfitters and billboards never lets you forget it.

In Islamorada, the unofficial capital of the Upper Keys, both commercial and private fishing fleets are docked at almost every inlet. Marathon, the Upper Keys' other main population center, is a curious mixture of a modern tract-home community, tourist resort, and old fishing village. This island's highly developed infrastructure includes resort hotels, a commercial airport, and a highway that expands to four lanes. In between Islamorada and Marathon are about 35 miles of highway, alternating between wetlands, strip malls, nesting grounds, resort hotels, and blue waters.

ESSENTIALS

GETTING THERE   By Car   From Miami, take the Florida Turnpike south along the east coast to Exit 4, Homestead/Key West. This is the Turnpike Extension that meets U.S. 1 in Florida City. Islamorada is about an hour south. If you're coming from Florida's west coast, take Alligator Alley to the Miami exit, then turn south onto the Turnpike Extension.

By Plane   American Eagle (☎ 800/433-7300) flies nonstop from Miami to Marathon, and charges $128 to $234 round-trip.

By Bus   Greyhound (☎ 800/231-2222) operates three buses daily in each direction between Miami and Key West, and stops in both Key Largo and Marathon. The fare is $11 each way.

VISITOR INFORMATION   The **Key Largo Chamber of Commerce,** 105950 Overseas Hwy., Key Largo, FL 33037 (☎ 305/451-1414), is open daily from 9am to 6pm. The **Islamorada Chamber of Commerce,** in the Little Red Caboose, Mile Marker 82.5 (P.O. Box 915), Islamorada, FL 33036 (☎ **305/664-4503** or 800/322-5397), also offers maps and literature on the Upper Keys. The **Greater Marathon Chamber of Commerce,** 12222 Overseas Hwy., Marathon, FL 33050 (☎ **800/842-9580**), has a big blue visitor center at Mile Marker 53.5.

INDIAN KEY & LIGNUMVITAE KEY

Most of the Florida Keys that are not connected by the Overseas Highway are protected as wildlife preserves and are off-limits to casual visitors. Two unusual exceptions are Indian Key and Lignumvitae Key, backcountry islands that offer visitors a glimpse of the "real" keys, before modern development. Both are preserved and managed by the Florida Department of Natural Resources.

Named for the lignum vitae ("wood of life") trees found there, 280-acre **Lignumvitae Key** supports a virgin tropical forest, the kind that once thrived on most of the Upper Keys. Over the years human settlers, importing "exotic" plants and animals to the Keys, have changed the botanical makeup of many backcountry islands. Sometimes the damage is incredibly devastating. When the Department of Natural Resources adopted Lignumvitae Key in 1971, it embarked on an aggressive campaign to remove all exotic vegetation and restore the key to its original state.

Indian Key, located on the Atlantic side of Islamorada, is a 10-acre historic site that was occupied by Native Americans for thousands of years. It was also the original seat of Dade County before the Civil War. An 1840 rebellion by Native Americans almost wiped out the island's once-growing population, leaving the ruins for posterity.

There are two options for exploring Indian Key and Lignumvitae Key. You can **rent your own boat** at Indian Key Fill (Mile Marker 79). Rates range from $60 for a 14-foot boat for half a day to $155 for an 18-foot boat for a full day. It's then a $1 admission fee to each island. You could also take a **ferry service** for $15, which includes the $1 park admission. Ferries depart Thursday to Monday at 9am and 1pm for Indian Key, and at 10am and 2pm for Lignumvitae Key. Reservations are required 48 hours in advance during the high season. Call 305/664-4815 for information from the park service, or 305/664-9814 for Robbie's ferry service.

MORE THINGS TO SEE & DO

✪ Dolphin Research Center. U.S. 1 at Mile Marker 59, on the bay side. ☎ **305/289-1121.** Educational walking tours five times per day starting at 10am (at 12:30pm on Tues). Admission $9.50 adults, $7.50 seniors, $6 children 4–12, free for children 3 and under. MC, V. Daily 9:30am–4pm.

This is one of only three such centers in the United States (all in the Keys) where you can touch, swim, or play with dolphins. The group's main goal is to protect the mammals and educate the public about these unusually smart beasts. Although some people argue that training dolphins is cruel and selfish, the knowledgeable trainers at the Dolphin Research Center will tell you that the dolphins need stimulation and enjoy human contact. The center has received positive reviews from a federal inspection of the program. The "family" of 15 dolphins swim in a 90,000-square-foot coral natural saltwater pool carved out of the shoreline. You can take a walking tour or a half-day class in how to do hand signals and feed the dolphins from docks. Yes, you can pet them.

You can also swim with the dolphins, but the cost is a pricy $90. If you want to do this, the procedure for making reservations is quite rigid: On the first of every month starting at 9am, the phone lines open for dolphin lovers to call to be put in a lottery and hope to be chosen to swim. Kids should be at least 12 years old.

✪ Florida Keys Wild Bird Rehabilitation Center. 93600 Overseas Hwy., Mile Marker 94, Tavernier. ☎ **305/852-4486.** Free admission. Daily 8:30am–5pm. Look for wooden bird sculptures by the westbound lane of the highway.

Almost anytime you visit the rehabilitation center, you're likely to see naturalist Laura Quinn in her "operating room," removing a fish hook from a bird's throat or untangling fishing line from a broken wing. The ultimate goal of this center is to return wildlife to the wild, but when a bird arrives with a permanent injury, these protective wetlands become the animal's home for life. As a result, this is the best place in the Keys to get close to a large variety of native birds, including broad-wing hawks, great white heron, brown pelicans, and even osprey.

This is not a zoo built for gawkers; the birds are exhibited reluctantly, and Laura Quinn's greatest wish is that the zoo could be closed for a lack of exhibits.

Museum of Crane Point Hammock. 5550 Overseas Hwy., Mile Marker 50, Marathon, FL 33050. ☎ **305/743-9100.** Admission $7.50 adults, $6 seniors 65 and older, $4 students, free for children 6 and under. Mon–Sat 9am–5pm, Sun noon–5pm.

Most of the land surrounding Crane Point Hammock is highly developed; there's even a shopping mall across the street. This 64-acre nature area didn't escape the builders accidentally. It was purchased in 1949 by the Crane family, ardent conservationists who recognized the significance of this special parcel. Now managed by the Florida Keys Land and Sea Trust, Crane Point Hammock contains what is probably the last virgin thatch palm hammock in North America.

The hammock's small nature museum teaches visitors about Keys flora and fauna, both on land and underwater. A walk-through replica of a coral reef cave unravels the complexities of the tropical reef ecosystem, while life-size wildlife dioramas teach about birds and Key deer. Other exhibits contain finds that illustrate over 5,000 years of human history in the Keys. A walkway leads to a single-room children's museum with interactive displays that include a miniature railway station and a small saltwater touch tank.

Outside, visitors are encouraged to wander through the museum's quarter-mile nature trail, a self-guided loop that circles the palm hammock.

Robbie's Pier. Overseas Hwy., Mile Marker 77.5 (just southwest of Lignum Vitae Channel), Lower Matecumbe Key. No phone. Admission $1. Daily 8am–5pm. Look for the HUNGRY TARPON sign on the right.

The steely tarpon is a fierce fighting fish and a prized catch for backcountry anglers who stalk them on the Florida Bay side of the Keys. You'll probably see these prehistoric-looking giants—which grow up to 200 pounds—stuffed and mounted on many local restaurant walls. To see them live, you either have to have a rod and reel and lots of patience, or head to Robbie's Pier, where tens, and sometimes hundreds, of these behemoths mill about waiting for free food. For $1 the proprietor will let you walk out onto Robbie's rickety wooden wharf and create a tumultuous feeding frenzy with a bag of food pellets.

✪ Seven Mile Bridge. Overseas Hwy., Mile Markers 40–47.

Oil magnate Henry Flagler first visited Florida in 1878. Realizing the state's potential for growth, he built the Florida East Coast Railroad from Jacksonville to Miami. After years of planning, the decision was made to extend the line to Key West, a project that pundits labeled "Flagler's Folly." Construction began in 1904, and thousands of workers battled insects, hurricanes, intense heat, and water shortages, but on January 21, 1912, the Overseas Extension was completed. The railroad operated until 1935, when a Labor Day hurricane damaged the rails beyond repair. A large portion of the Overseas Highway (U.S. 1) was built on Flagler's abandoned rail bed. Many remnants of the rail line can still be seen along the highway; most notable is a large portion of the original Seven Mile Bridge that runs alongside the newer roadway. The islands' most celebrated span rests on 546 concrete piers, and rises to a 72-foot crest, the highest point in the Keys.

Heading south on the Overseas Highway, slow down just before the bridge and turn right, off the road, into the unpaved parking lot at the foot of the bridge. From here you can walk or bicycle along the old bridge that goes for almost 4 miles before abruptly dropping off into the sea. The first half mile of this "ghost bridge" is popular with area fishermen, who use shrimp as bait to catch barracuda, yellowtail, and a host of other fish. At the far end of the bridge is the University of Miami's Institute of Marine Science, a research facility not open to the public.

Theater of the Sea. Overseas Hwy., Mile Marker 84.5 (P.O. Box 407), Islamorada, FL 33036. ☎ **305/664-2431.** Admission $14.25 adults, $7.95 children. Daily 9:30am–4pm.

Established in 1946, the Theater of the Sea is one of the world's oldest marine zoos. Although the facilities seem a bit tired, and sea mammal acts have fallen from political correctness, the theater's dolphin and sea lion shows can be both entertaining and informative, especially for children. Sharks, sea turtles, and other local creatures are also on display. The park also offers a "Dolphin Adventure" for $80, in which visitors have the opportunity to swim with the dolphins in their supervised ocean-water lagoon. Reservations must be made in advance.

STATE PARKS

Although the Keys don't have all that much in the way of beaches, the beaches that do exist are by and large located in the state parks. These are among the nicest and cleanest:

One of the best-known parks is **John Pennekamp Coral Reef State Park,** located at Overseas Highway Mile Marker 102.5, in Key Largo (☎ **305/451-1202**). Named for a former *Miami Herald* editor and conservationist, the 188-square-mile park is the nation's first undersea preserve. It's a sanctuary for part of the only living coral reef in the continental United States. The original plans for Everglades National Park included this part of the reef within its boundaries, but opposition from local homeowners made its inclusion politically impossible.

Because the water is extremely shallow in many places, the 40 species of corals and more than 650 species of fish are particularly accessible to divers, snorkelers, and glass-bottom-boat passengers. Unfortunately the reef is a little *too* accessible, and the ecosystem is showing signs of stress from careless divers and boaters.

You can't see the reef from shore. To experience this park, visitors must take to the water. Your first stop should be the excellent visitor center, which is full of demonstrative fish tanks and a mammoth 30,000-gallon saltwater aquarium that re-creates a reef ecosystem. At the adjacent dive shop, visitors can rent snorkeling and diving equipment and join one of the boat trips that depart for the reef through-out the day. It also rents motorboats, sailboats, windsurfers, and canoes. Two-hour glass-bottom-boat tours take riders over coral reefs.

Canoeing around the park's narrow mangrove channels and tidal creeks is also popular. Canoes can be rented here, and during winter, naturalists lead canoe tours. Hikers have two short trails to choose from: a boardwalk through the mangroves, and a dirt trail through a tropical hardwood hammock. Ranger-led walks are usually scheduled daily from the end of November to April. Phone for schedule information and reservations.

Park admission is $3.75 per vehicle, plus 50¢ per passenger; $1.50 per pedestrian or bicyclist. Call 305/451-1621 for information. Glass-bottom-boat tours cost $13 for adults, $8.50 children 11 and under. Sailing and snorkeling tours are $28.95 for adults, $23.95 for children 17 and under, including equipment but not tax. Scuba dives cost $37.50 per person, not including equipment. Canoes rent for $8 per hour, or $24 for 4 hours. Reef boats (powerboats) rent for $25 to $45 per hour; call 305/ 451-6325. Open daily from 8am to 5pm; phone for tour and dive times.

Another state park in the Upper Keys is the **Long Key State Recreation Area,** on the Overseas Highway at Mile Marker 68, Long Key (☎ **305/664-4815**), with the second-nicest beach (the best is Bahia Honda in the Lower Keys). Situated atop the remains of ancient coral reef, this 965-acre park is one of the best places in the Upper Keys for hiking and canoeing.

Railroad builder Henry Flagler created the Long Key Fishing Club here in 1906, and the waters surrounding the park are still popular with game fishers. Sand beaches are rare in the Keys, and the ones here are accessible only by boat. In summer, giant sea turtles lumber onto the protected beach to lay their eggs.

You can hike along two nature trails. The Golden Orb Trail is a 1-mile loop around a lagoon that attracts a large variety of birds. Rich in West Indian vegetation, the trail leads to an observation tower that offers good views of the pond and beach.

The Layton Trail, the only part of the park that doesn't require an admission fee, is a quarter-mile shaded loop that goes through tropical hammock before opening up onto Florida Bay. The trail is well marked with interpretive signs; you can easily walk it in about 20 minutes.

The park's excellent 1½-mile canoe trail is also short and sweet, allowing visitors to loop around the mangroves in about an hour. It couldn't be easier. Canoes are rented at the trailhead, and cost $4 per hour. Long Key is also a wonderful picnic spot if you get hungry on your way to Key West.

Admission is $3.25 per car, plus 50¢ for each person (except for the Layton Trail, which is free). Open daily from 8am to sunset.

SPORTS & OUTDOOR ACTIVITIES

BOATING   Captain Pip's, Overseas Highway, Mile Marker 47.5, Marathon (☎ 305/743-4403), rents 20-foot motorboats with 88-, 120-, and 150-horsepower engines for $110 to $130 per day.

Robbie's Rent-a-Boat, Overseas Highway, Mile Marker 77.5, Islamorada (☎ **305/ 664-9814**), rents 14- to 27-foot motorboats with engines ranging from 15 to 200 horsepower. Boats cost $60 to $205 for a half day and $80 to $295 for a whole day.

CANOEING & KAYAKING   The **Coral Reef Park Co.,** Overseas Highway, Mile Marker 102.5, Key Largo (☎ **305/451-1621**), is another rental outlet at John Pennekamp Coral Reef State Park. Canoes can be rented for $8 per hour, $28 for a half day.

FISHING   Robbie's Partyboats & Charters, Overseas Highway, Mile Marker 84.5, Islamorada (☎ **305/664-8070** or 305/664-4196), located at the south end of the Holiday Isle Docks (see "Where to Stay," below), offers day and night deep-sea and reef-fishing trips on 47- and 65-foot party boats. Big-game-fishing charters are also available, and "splits" are arranged for solo fishers. Party-boat fishing costs $25 for a half day, $40 for a full day, and $30 at night. Charters run $375 for a half day, $550 for a full day; splits begin at $65 per person. Phone for information and reservations.

SNORKELING   Snorkling tours cost an arm and a leg and it's nearly impossible to find a budget one—especially in the Keys, where everything is even costlier than in Miami. My suggestion is that you bring your own snorkel and fins and get out there yourself! Maybe a few could split the cost of a boat rental and snorkle offshore yourselves.

WHERE TO STAY

It's surprisingly hard to find good budget accommodations in the Keys. Some of the bigger hotel chains that operate in the Upper Keys are **Best Western** (☎ 800/ 462-6079) and **Holiday Inn** (☎ 800/843-5379).

DOUBLES FOR LESS THAN $40

Sea Cove Motel. 12685 Overseas Hwy., Mile Marker 54, Marathon, FL 33050. ☎ **305/ 289-0800**, or 800/653-0800. 29 units. A/C TV TEL. Winter, $34–$49 double without bath, $49–$69 double with bath; $79–$99 efficiency. Off-season, $24–$39 double without bath, $39–$69 double with bath; $59–$89 efficiency. Year round, $69–$125 double on the house-boat. Additional person or pet $5 extra; children 15 and under stay free in parents' room. AE, DISC, MC, V.

Sea Cove's large, economical motel rooms aren't the Ritz, but they are the very best available for the money. They have Oriental rug–covered concrete floors, plastic tables and chairs, small tiled bathrooms, overhead fans, and little porches in front. Some have kitchens. Before committing, check out the motel's unusual "Floating Castle," a large, multi-unit houseboat that's anchored in the back of the property. Thin walls could make sleeping hard if your neighbor snores, but otherwise this unusual floating home just might be one of the best deals in the Keys. The wood-paneled rooms are small and charming. Some rooms share a common bathroom. Snorkeling and diving trips leave from the harbor next door.

DOUBLES FOR LESS THAN $60

Bay Harbor Lodge. 97702 Overseas Hwy., Mile Marker 97.7 (off the southbound lane of U.S. 1), Key Largo, FL 33037. ☎ **305/852-5695.** 16 rms, efficiencies, and cottages. A/C, TV TEL. Year round, $55 double; $70 efficiency; $80 cottage. MC, V. Additional person $8 extra.

A small simple retreat that's big on charm, the Bay Harbor Lodge is a welcoming place, made especially friendly by owners Laszlo and Sandra Simoga. The lodge is far from fancy, and the wide range of accommodations are not all created equal. The motel rooms are small in size and ordinary in decor, but even the least expensive is recommendable. The efficiencies are larger motel rooms with fully stocked kitchenettes. The underpriced oceanfront cottages are larger still, have full kitchens, and represent one of the best values in the Keys. None of the accommodations' vinyl-covered furnishings and old-fashioned wallpapers will win a design award, but elegance isn't what the "real" keys are about. The 1 1/2 lush acres of grounds are planted with banana trees. Guests can use the pool, outdoor hot tub, and rowboats, paddleboats, canoes, and kayaks. Bring your own beach towels.

DOUBLES FOR LESS THAN $80

Breezy Palms Resort. Overseas Hwy., Mile Marker 80 (P.O. Box 767), Islamorada, FL 33036. ☎ **305/664-2361.** Fax 305/664-2572. 39 rms, 23 one-bedroom apts. A/C TV TEL. Winter, $75–$90 double; $105–$180 one-bedroom apt. Off-season, $65–$80 double; $100–$165 one-bedroom apt. AE, DISC, MC, V.

The appellation "resort" is used euphemistically at Breezy Palms, a simple, palm-studded pink-and-blue hotel in two parts. One side of this very well maintained mom-and-pop property is a two-story motel with spacious bedrooms, soft beds, big closets, and bathrooms with separate vanity areas. They have refrigerators, VCRs, and screened-in porches overlooking a large swimming pool. Rooms on the second floor enjoy ocean views. The one-bedroom apartments, located across a large U-shaped driveway, have separate living areas with rattan furnishings and VCRs. Each also has a separate small kitchen stocked with plenty of plates and utensils and enough cookware for a simple meal. The good-size bathrooms have low-pressure water-saving shower heads and plenty of counter space. Breezy Palms is located oceanfront and has a sheltered harbor with lots of dock space. There are volleyball and shuffleboard courts, and barbecue pits on the beach. Complimentary coffee is served each morning. All in all, this hotel is a very good value.

Faro Blanco Marine Resort. 1996 Overseas Hwy., Mile Marker 48.5, Marathon, FL 33050. ☎ **305/743-9018** or 800/759-3276. 100 rms, 23 condos. A/C TV TEL. Winter, $65–$119 cottage for two; $99–$198 houseboat for two; $185 lighthouse for two; $233 condo for two. Off-season, $55–$99 cottage for two; $79–$145 houseboat for two; $145 lighthouse for two; $206 condo for two. Additional person $10 extra. AE, DISC, MC, V.

Spanning both sides of the Overseas Highway, and all on waterfront property, this huge, two-shore marina and hotel complex offers something for every taste. Free-standing, camp-style cottages with a small bedroom are the resort's least expensive accommodations. Built on concrete slabs, the cottages are very basic, most with two single beds and slightly fading interiors. They surround a small wooded park with a children's slide and swing. On the other end of the spectrum are extremely large, first-class condominium apartments contained in a cluster of modern circular four-story "towers." Each has three bedrooms, two baths, a living room, and a contemporary kitchen.

The houseboats are the happiest choice. Tethered in a relatively tranquil marina, these rectangular white boats look like buoyant mobile homes and are uniformly clean, fresh, and recommendable. They have colonial American-style furnishings, front and back porches, and water, water everywhere. The boats rock ever so slightly.

Finally, there are two unusual rental units in a lighthouse on the pier; circular staircases, unusually shaped rooms and showers, and nautical decor make this a unique place to stay, but some guests might find that it literally cramps their style. Most cottages and houseboats are equipped with full kitchens or kitchenettes. Be sure to request cooking facilities if you want them.

DOUBLES FOR LESS THAN $100

Banana Bay Resort & Marina. 4590 Overseas Hwy., Mile Marker 49.5, Marathon, FL 33050. ☎ **305/743-3500** or 800/BANANA-1. Fax 305/743-2670. 60 rms. A/C TV TEL. Winter, $95–$175 double. Off-season, $75–$125 double. Rates include breakfast. Additional person $15 extra; children 4 and under stay free in parents' room. Weekend and other packages available. AE, DC, DISC, MC, V.

It doesn't look like much more than a motel from the sign-cluttered Overseas Highway. But turn into the arched entranceway and you're suddenly in a bucolic property that's one of the best run in the Upper Keys. Built in the early 1950s as a fishing camp, the resort is a puzzle of pink-and-white two-story buildings hidden among banyans and palms. The Banana Bay's 10 acres accommodate just 60 rooms. This means peace and quiet and little competition for use of the resort's facilities. The accommodations and grounds of Banana Bay are particularly well maintained, a function of hands-on management by the owners who live on site. All the fresh-looking guest rooms are similar; their primary difference is view and price. They're of moderate size and are fitted with either one king-size bed or two doubles. Many have private balconies.

The Cabana Restaurant serves lunch and dinner both poolside and inside its 1950s-style dining room. There's also a waterfront tiki bar that enjoys great sunset views. Charter fishing, sailing, and diving are offered from the resort's 50-slip marina.

Conch Key Cottages. Near the Overseas Hwy., Mile Marker 62.3 (RR 1, Box 424), Marathon, FL 33050. ☎ **305/289-1377** or 800/330-1577. 10 efficiencies, apts, and cottages. A/C TV. Winter, $96 efficiency ($605 per week); $114 one-bedroom apt ($720 per week); $134 one-bedroom cottage ($845 per week); $183 two-bedroom cottage ($1,147 per week). Off-season, $70 efficiency ($441 per week); $87 one-bedroom apt ($550 per week); $96 one-bedroom cottage ($605 per week); $150 two-bedroom cottage ($945 per week). During festivals, $70–$96 efficiency ($441–$605 per week); $87–$114 one-bedroom apt ($550–$720 per week); $96–$134 one-bedroom cottage ($605–$845 per week); $150–$183 two-bedroom cottage ($945–$1,147 per week). DISC, MC, V.

Occupying its own private micro-island just off the Overseas Highway, Conch Key Cottages is a midscale hideaway run by live-in owners Ron Wilson and Wayne Byrnes. The best accommodations here—by far—are the one- and two-bedroom waterside cottages. The all-wood cabins overlook their own private stretch of natural, private beach and have screened-in porches and cozy bedrooms and baths. Each has a hammock and barbecue grill.

You could walk around the entire island in about 4 minutes, if it weren't so full of mangroves. On the other side of the pool are a handful of efficiency apartments, outfitted similarly to the cottages, but without beach frontage. Tailor-made for couples or families, Conch Key Cottages is the perfect place to get away from it all.

Holiday Isle Resort. 84001 Overseas Hwy., Mile Marker 84, Islamorada, FL 33036. ☎ **305/664-2321,** or 800/327-7070. Fax 305/664-2703. 180 rms, 19 suites. Winter, $80–$190 double; $200–$395 suite. Off-season, $50–$150 double; $135–$350 suite. AE, DC, DISC, MC, V.

A huge resort complex encompassing five restaurants, lounges, and shops, and four distinct (if not distinctive) hotels, Holiday Isle is one of the biggest in the Keys. The company's marketing strategy is decidedly downscale, attracting a spring break–style crowd year round. Their Tiki Bar claims the invention of the Rum Runner drink (151-proof rum, blackberry brandy, banana liquor, grenadine, and lime juice), and there's no reason to doubt it. Hordes are attracted to the resort's almost-nonstop merrymaking, live music, and beachfront bars. As a result, some of the accommodations here can be noisy.

El Captain and Harbor Lights, two of the least expensive hotels on the property, are both austere and basic. Like the other hotels here, frills are few and "deferred" maintenance is in abundance, including broken hangers and door locks. Howard Johnson's, Holiday Isle's fourth hotel, is a little farther from the action and a shred more civilized.

CAMPING

John Pennekamp Coral Reef State Park. Overseas Hwy., Mile Marker 102.3 (P.O. Box 487), Key Largo, FL 33037. ☎ **305/451-1202.** 47 campsites. $24–$26 per site. MC, V.

One of Florida's most celebrated parks (see "State Parks," above), Pennekamp offers 47 well-separated campsites, half available by advance reservation, the rest distributed on a first-come, first-served basis. The car-camping sites are small, but well facilitated with bathrooms and showers. A little lagoon nearby attracts many large wading birds. Reservations are held until 5pm and the park must be notified of late arrival by phone on the check-in date. Pennekamp opens at 8am and closes around sundown, and pets are not allowed.

Long Key State Recreation Area. Overseas Hwy., Mile Marker 67.5 (P.O. Box 776), Long Key, FL 33001. ☎ **305/664-4815.** 60 campsites. $24–$26 per site for one to four people. Additional person $2 extra. MC, V.

The Upper Keys' other main state park is more secluded than its northern neighbor and somewhat more popular. All sites are located oceanside, and are as nice as paid legal camping can be. If possible, make reservations 60 days in advance.

WHERE TO DINE

Realistically speaking, the better restaurants in the Upper Keys are housed in the big resorts and are costly. Most of the inexpensive eateries are small seafood/casual-dining–style places to accommodate those seeking a quick bite on their way to Key West. Here are a few recommendations:

MEALS FOR LESS THAN $10

Mrs. Mac's Kitchen. 99336 Overseas Hwy., Mile Marker 99.4, Key Largo. ☎ **305/451-3722.** Reservations not accepted. Breakfast $3–$5; lunch $3–$7; dinner $6–$13. No credit cards. Daily 7am–9:30pm. AMERICAN.

Bypass Key Largo's swell of fast-food outlets and head for the "real Keys McCoy" of Mrs. Mac's, a roadside diner that from the outside looks suspiciously like an oversize aluminum mobile home. The restaurant has wood-paneled walls decorated with the traditional license-plate and beer-can clutter, and vinyl booths surround a circular bar that's crammed with stools. Breakfast, served until 11am, includes eggs, waffles, and crêpes. Lunch and dinner mean meat- and cheese-stuffed pita sandwiches, cheese steak, burgers, and fresh fish specials. The Syrian sub—a meaty sandwich with ham, salami, bologna, cheese, onions, lettuce, and tomato—is particularly recommended.

MEALS FOR LESS THAN $15

Barracuda Bistro. Overseas Hwy., Mile Marker 49.5, Marathon. ☎ **305/743-3314.** Main courses $11–$23. AE, DISC, MC, V. Mon–Sat 6–10pm. BISTRO/SEAFOOD.

This relative newcomer to the Upper Keys dining world is a welcome addition. It's owned by Lance Hill and his wife, Jan, who used to be Little Palm Island's daytime sous-chef. This casual but starched-clean bistro serves excellent seafood and traditional bistro fare. Some of the best are an old-fashioned meatloaf, classic beef Stroganoff, rack of lamb, and a seafood stew. In addition, this small barracuda-themed restaurant features a well-priced exclusively American wine list with a vast selection of California vintages.

✪ **Lazy Days Oceanfront Bar and Seafood Grill.** Overseas Hwy., Mile Marker 79.9, Islamorada. ☎ **305/664-5256.** Main courses $11–$20; lunch $5–$9. AE, DISC, MC, V. Tues–Sun 11:30am–10pm. AMERICAN/SEAFOOD.

Opened in 1992, Lazy Days quickly became one of the most popular restaurants around. A glass-enclosed rectangle on story-high stilts, the restaurant is unique in its modernity. Climb the stairs to a single, large, and refreshingly bright dining room that's surrounded by an outdoor terrace. The 6-foot picture windows overlook the ocean. The meals are pricier than the dining room would suggest, but the food is very good and the portions are large. Some of the more tempting appetizers include steamed clams with garlic and bell peppers; and nachos with seasoned beef, beans, cheese, and jalepeños. Lunch selections include meaty chowders, salads, and a large selection of sandwiches, including charcoal-grilled fish and spicy Caribbean jerk chicken. Dinners rely heavily on seafood—and they really know how to cook fish here. Caribbean- and Italian-style foods are also served. Most main courses come with baked potatoes, vegetables, a tossed salad, and French bread.

Lazy Days is set slightly back from the road behind willowy palms. It's located on your left, when heading toward Key West.

Makoto Japanese Restaurant. At the Marina del Mar Resort, 99470 Overseas Hwy., Mile Marker 101.5, Key Largo. ☎ **305/451-7083.** Reservations suggested on weekends in season. Main courses $8–$19. DC, DISC, MC, V. Mon–Thurs 11:30am–2:30pm and 5–9:30pm, Fri 11:30am–2:30pm and 5–10pm, Sat 5–10pm, Sun 5–9:30pm. JAPANESE.

This Japanese restaurant run by a Laotian family is worth a stop for the unusual raw fish selections that are sometimes available. In addition to ample slices of standard Pacific Ocean fish like salmon and yellowtail, the restaurant serves local cuts that may include Florida snapper, tuna, black grouper, and wahoo. Cooked dinners include fish teriyaki, chicken curry, vegetable tempura, and sukiyaki. The dining room is not particularly cozy; its mounted-fish collection includes shark and swordfish, two varieties that seldom appear on the menu. The restaurant is located on the bay side of the Overseas Highway.

✪ **Manny & Isa's Kitchen.** Overseas Hwy., Mile Marker 81.6, Islamorada. ☎ **305/664-5019.** Reservations not accepted. Main courses $9–$18; lunch $4–$9. AE, MC, V. Wed–Mon 11am–9pm. SPANISH-AMERICAN.

Opened over a dozen years ago as a small shop selling key lime pie and conch chowder exclusively, this pint-size café-style restaurant has expanded its menu and become a very popular local hangout. It's a great little place. There are fewer than 10 tables here, and a moderate-length menu is packed with Florida-influenced Spanish-American specialties like pork chops with black beans and rice, lobster enchiladas, and sandwiches. And it's still one of the best places around for conch chowder and key lime pie.

Papa Joe's. Overseas Hwy., Mile Marker 79.7, Islamorada. ☎ **305/664-8109.** Main courses $10–$14; lunch $5–$8. AE, MC, V. Wed–Mon 11am–10pm. AMERICAN.

Opened in 1937, Papa Joe's is a veritable living museum of early Keys life. From the road, this two-story wooden landmark—under a big palm tree and a yellow-and-white tiki-style sign—looks like the ultimate island eatery. It's well-weathered and right on the water but, like so many eateries from this era, there are no outdoor tables and only mediocre views. Inside it's so dark that it feels like night even on the brightest days. Whatever the fresh catch is, order it sautéed, on a platter, or on a bun and you won't be disappointed. The usual variety of burgers, salads, sandwiches, steaks, and chicken are also available. If you're arriving in the late afternoon, take advantage of the second-story tiki bar that's raised just high enough to see the sun set over the nearby mangrove islands. The raw bar is particularly appealing, and a full range of drinks is served.

The restaurant is located across from Bud and Mary's Marina, at the foot of Tea Table Bridge.

Seven Mile Grill. 1240 Overseas Hwy., Mile Marker 47, Marathon. ☎ **305/743-4481.** Reservations not accepted. Dinner $8–$9; lunch $2–$5. No credit cards. Thurs–Tues 7am–8:30pm. Closed Thurs off-season. AMERICAN.

Everybody knows the Seven Mile Grill. You'd have to be blind to miss its enormous red, white, and blue sign that's a masterpiece of 1950s roadside art. Of all the "authentic" downscale fry shacks that line the Overseas Highway, this home-style cookery is the best. The restaurant is little more than a long J-shaped linoleum counter with 20 bar chairs. The entire dining counter is exposed to the highway by a "wall" made of garage doors that stay open during business hours, no matter the weather. The Seven Mile Grill opened in 1954, but has changed with the times. The beer-can decor is augmented by a wall of aphoristic signs and bumper stickers that include WE DON'T CARE HOW YOU DO IT UP NORTH and UNARMED TOURIST ON BOARD.

Very good food, friendly waitresses, and three domestic beers on tap keep locals loyal. Appetizers include good chili, better shrimp bisque, and the best conch chowder. Straightforward fry-house fare includes thickly battered fish, clam strips, sea scallops, shrimp, and oysters. Burgers, salads, and sandwiches are also served. Note that this is one of the few places where you can get authentic key lime pie. The restaurant is located at the foot of Seven Mile Bridge.

Sid & Roxie's Green Turtle Inn. Overseas Hwy., Mile Marker 81.5, Islamorada. ☎ **305/664-9031.** Main courses $12–$18; lunch $6–$12. AE, DC, DISC, MC, V. Tues–Sun noon–10pm. SEAFOOD/AMERICAN.

An Islamorada landmark since 1947, the Green Turtle comes from an age when dark interiors were equated with elegance. It's a family kind of place, where broiled American surf-and-turf dinners come with soup, potatoes, and a salad. Soups, breads, and pies are all made on the premises and served by career waitresses who've been here for years. In addition to prime beef and fresh-caught fish, the restaurant offers alligator steak, shrimp, and chicken dishes. When driving south on the Overseas Highway, look for the giant turtle.

THE UPPER KEYS AFTER DARK

Nightlife in the Upper Keys tends to happen in the afternoon, because many fishermen and sports-minded folks go to bed early. It's not that they're a puritanical lot—it's just that many have been drinking all day and crash before midnight in order to be able to get up and do it all over again. Here are a few good choices, particularly if you want to catch a spectacular sunset:

No trip is complete without a stop at the **Tiki Bar** at Holiday Isle, 84001 Overseas Hwy., Mile Marker 84, Islamorada (☎ **800/327-7070** or 305/664-2321). Hundreds of partying types stop here for drinks and dancing any time of day, but in the evening live rock music starts at 8:30pm.

The most fun spot in the afternoons and early evenings (when everyone is either sunburned, drunk, or just happy to be alive and dancing to reggae) is **Kokomos's**, just next door to the thatched-roof tiki bar. Kokomos's closes up at 7:30pm on weekends, so get there early and then head over to the restaurant or tiki bar for more fun and food and music that lasts past midnight every night.

The **Whale Harbor Inn**, Overseas Highway, Mile Marker 83.5, Islamorada (☎ **305/664-4959**), isn't exactly a nightspot, but it's a good place for a sunset drink and snack. Bypass the building with the imposing lighthouse exterior and cross the small marina to the second-story wood-beamed bungalow that's decked out with football pennants, photos of lucky fishermen, and a profusion of mounted monster fish. It's popular with locals (they're the ones who bring their own foam beer-can coolers to the old wooden bar). Good, greasy appetizers here include conch fritters, chicken wings, smoked fish, and fried mozzarella. The inn closes at 9 or 10pm.

The hottest local bar in the Upper Keys, **Woody's Saloon and Restaurant,** Overseas Highway, Mile Marker 82, Islamorada (☎ **305/664-4335**), is a lively, raunchy place serving up mediocre pizzas and live bands almost every night. The house band, Big Dick and the Extenders, features a 300-pound Indian who does a lude, rude, and crude routine of jokes and songs. Don't think you're lucky if you walk in and are offered the front table, because it's the target seat for Big Dick's haranguing. He has been playing here for years to the joy of the locals and visitors who can take it. You can get up and tell jokes on stage, but they'd better be good or you'll really get it. You can also play pool or video games.

2 The Lower Keys: Big Pine Key to Coppitt Key

110–140 miles SW of Miami

Big Pine, Sugarloaf, Summerland, and the other Lower Keys are less developed and more tranquil than their Upper Keys neighbors. If you're looking for haute cuisine and a happening nightlife, look elsewhere. If you're looking to commune with nature or for adventure in solitude, you've come to the right place. Unlike their neighbors to the north and south, the Lower Keys are devoid of rowdy spring break–style crowds and have few T-shirt and trinket shops, and almost no late-night bars. What they do offer are opportunities to hike, boat, bicycle, and camp. Stay overnight in the Lower Keys, rent a boat, and explore the reefs—it might be the most memorable part of your trip.

ESSENTIALS

The **Lower Keys Chamber of Commerce,** Overseas Highway, Mile Marker 31 (P.O. Box 430511), Big Pine Key, FL 33043 (☎ **305/872-2411,** or 800/872-3722), offers information on area sights, restaurants, and hotels.

SEEING THE SIGHTS

✪ **Leda-Bruce Galleries.** Overseas Hwy., Mile Marker 30.2, Big Pine Key. ☎ **305/872-0212.** Free admission. Tues–Sat 10am–6pm.

Owners Leda and Bruce Seigal are longtime residents of the Keys and famous in these parts for both their art and their eccentricities. In this concrete building, just past the island's only traffic light (when heading toward Key West), the couple displays works from the Keys' most important artists. In short, this is the finest gallery between Miami and Key West. Antiques and curios and top-quality antique clothes are also sold here. Plays and classical-music concerts are sometimes staged in the attic theater. It's a great place to browse, and the friendly owners are usually on hand to chat.

✪ **National Key Deer Refuge.** Key Deer Blvd., near Mile Marker 30.5, Big Pine Key. ☎ **305/872-2239** for information Mon–Fri 8am–5pm. Free admission. Refuge lands open daily from a half hour before sunrise to a half hour after sunset. When heading toward Key West, turn right at Big Pine Key's only traffic light onto Key Deer Boulevard (take the left fork immediately after the turn), and continue 1¹/₂ miles to the observation site parking lot, on your left.

You know you've reached Big Pine Key when the speed limit drops to 45 m.p.h. (35 m.p.h. at night) and road signs trumpet warnings to drivers to stay alert. Strict enforcement of driving rules is designed to protect the Key deer, 28-inch miniatures that are closely related to the common full-size Virginia white-tailed deer. Scientists believe that the diminutive deer are descendants of full-size animals that wandered south from the Florida mainland thousands of years ago. The reduced land, food, and fresh water available to the deer created environmental pressures that led to a prolonged "downsizing." They exist almost exclusively on Big Pine Key because this is the only key with fresh water year round.

Once prized by trophy hunters, the dwindling population was protected in 1957 with the establishment of this 8,000-acre refuge. The deer's rehabilitation is a qualified success in environmentalism. There are about 300 Key deer left and, given current conditions and resources, this is the maximum number of deer that can be expected to survive. However, in the last 25 years growth in the island's population, from about 700 to almost 5,000 residents, has been causing some distress. Restrictions on development have hampered the construction of an elementary school, prompting a graffito on Key Deer Boulevard that reads KIDS BEFORE DEER. A visit to the refuge is your best chance of seeing a Key deer. The best place for observation is called the Blue Hole, a former rock quarry that's now filled with fresh water. The half-mile Watson Hammock Trail, located about a third of a mile past the Blue Hole, is the refuge's only marked footpath. Deer can often be seen here during early morning and late evening.

Sugarloaf Bat Tower. Next to Sugarloaf Airport by Mile Marker 17. Turn right at the Sugarloaf Airport sign, then right again, onto the dirt road that begins just before the airport gate; the tower is about 100 yards ahead.

It's really a peculiar sight—especially if you don't know what it is. Standing silently alone, surrounded by nothing but weeds, the large and stocky Sugarloaf Bat Tower was constructed in 1929 in an effort to attract bats that would eat the ever-present mosquitoes that plague most of the Keys. Unfortunately, the bats have yet to come—the failed "bat motel" attracts only curious tourists.

BAHIA HONDA STATE PARK

The Lower Keys has only one state park, but ✪ **Bahia Honda State Park,** 36850 Overseas Hwy. (Mile Marker 37.5), Big Pine Key (☎ **305/872-2353**), has one of the most beautiful beaches in South Florida, and certainly the most beautiful beach in the Keys. Meaning "deep bay" in Spanish, Bahia Honda is a great place for hiking, birdwatching, swimming, snorkeling, and fishing.

The 635-acre park encompasses a wide variety of ecosystems, including coastal mangroves, beach dunes, and tropical hammocks. There are also large stretches of white-sand beach and miles of trails packed with unusual plants and animals. Shaded beachside picnic areas are fitted with tables and grills. Bahia Honda is also a popular place to camp.

The park is true to its name, with deep waters close to shore that are perfect for snorkeling and diving. Daily **snorkel trips** (☎ **305/872-3210**) are operated to the nearby Looe Key coral reef. These depart daily March to September and cost $22 for adults, $18 for children 6 to 16, and free for children 5 and under. Call for hours of departures and rentals.

Admission to the park is $3.75 per vehicle, $1.50 per pedestrian or bicyclist, and free for children 5 and under. There's a $2 boat-ramp fee. The park is open daily from 8am to sunset.

Bahia Honda is as loaded with facilities and activities as it is with campers. For information about camping, see "Where to Stay," below.

SPORTS & OUTDOOR ACTIVITIES

BOATING   Several shops rent powerboats for fishing and reef exploring. Most also rent tackle, sell bait, and have charter captains available. Rental shops include **Bud Boats,** at the Old Wooden Bridge Fishing Camp & Marina, Overseas Highway, Mile Marker 59, Big Pine Key (☎ **305/743-6316**); **Jaybird's Powerboats,** Overseas Highway, Mile Marker 33, Big Pine Key (☎ **305/872-8500**); and **T.J.'s Sugarshack,** at the Sugarloaf Lodge Marina, Overseas Highway, Mile Marker 17, Sugarloaf Key (☎ **305/745-3135**).

FISHING   Fishing is outrageously expensive if you charter a boat to fish off the reefs. Bridge fishing, however, is completely free if you bring your own rod and reel. Many anglers can be spied fishing off the ruins of the old Seven Mile Bridge in the Lower Keys. If you forgot your fishing equipment, there are several small establishments next to Holiday Isle that can supply a rod and reel for a minimal cost.

SNORKELING & DIVING   In addition to snorkeling or diving at Bahia Honda State Park, the **Looe Key Dive Center,** Overseas Highway, Mile Marker 27.5, Ramrod Key (☎ **305/872-2215**), transports snorkelers and divers to the reefs of the Looe Key National Marine Sanctuary.

WHERE TO STAY

The best part of staying in the Lower Keys is that although there are a lot of big pricey resorts like those in the Upper Keys, they're not always the best choice if you really want to experience the pristine and nature-oriented Lower Keys. Staying indoors or by a hotel pool would almost be a crime! So after an invigorating day outdoors, go ahead and stay at a smaller motel; there are plenty of charming ones to choose from.

DOUBLES FOR LESS THAN $40

Bonefish Resort. Overseas Hwy., Mile Marker 58, Grassy Key, FL 33050. ☎ **305/743-7107.** 12 rms. A/C. Winter, $39–$77 double. Off-season, $29–$60 double. MC, V.

This is a bare-bones accommodation with charm. Paula and Jackie have been running the "resort" for the past 5 years and simply refuse to raise their rates. All the rooms are different; some have futons and a potpourri of art on the wall, sent from around the world by loyal return guests. There's a gas grill on the property, as well as a friendly pot-bellied pig named Willie.

DOUBLES FOR LESS THAN $80

Parmer's Place Cottages. Barry Ave., near Mile Marker 28.5 (P.O. Box 445), Little Torch Key, FL 33043. ☎ **305/872-2157.** 19 rms, 22 efficiencies. Winter and during festivals, $70–$85 double; $85 efficiency. Off-season, $60–$65 double; $75 efficiency. Additional person $12.50 extra; children 11 and under stay free in parents' room. AE, DISC, MC, V.

One of my favorite places in the Lower Keys, this downscale resort offers modest but comfortable cottages in a variety of configurations. Every unit is different: Some face the water, while others are a few steps away. Some have small kitchenettes and others hold just a bedroom. Unit 26, a one-bedroom efficiency, is especially nice, and contains a small sitting area that directly faces the water. Unit 6, a small efficiency, has a little kitchenette and an especially large bathroom. The rooms have Linoleum floors, dated 1970s-style painted rattan furnishings, fake flowers, and thrift-store art. They're very clean, and many can be combined to accommodate large families. There's a horseshoe pit, a boat ramp, and a heated swimming pool. Parmer's has been a fixture here for almost 20 years, and is well known for its charming hospitality and helpful staff.

DOUBLES FOR LESS THAN $100

Sugarloaf Lodge. Overseas Hwy., Mile Marker 17 (P.O. Box 148), Sugarloaf Key, FL 33044. ☎ **305/745-3211** or 800/553-6097. Fax 305/745-3389. 55 rms, 10 efficiencies. A/C TV TEL. Winter, $85–$95 double; $100 efficiency. Off-season, $65–$80 double; $85 efficiency. Additional person or pet $10 extra; children 11 and under stay free in parents' room. AE, CB, DC, DISC, MC, V.

On the one hand, this is just a two-story motel: plain rooms, good parking, swimming pool—you get the idea. But its ideal location, on the water in the heart of the Lower Keys, and its immediate proximity to the backcountry reefs make the Sugarloaf Lodge special. There are two wings to this sprawling property, which surrounds a lagoon where the motel's mascot dolphin lives. Efficiency rooms outfitted with small, fully equipped kitchenettes are also available. The motel is close to tennis courts and a miniature golf course, and adjacent to T.J.'s Sugarshack, an excellent marina from which you can fish or sightsee on the reef. There's a restaurant and lounge serving meals and drinks all day.

WORTH A SPLURGE

The Barnacle. 1557 Long Beach Dr., Big Pine Key, FL 33043. ☎ **305/872-3298.** 4 rms. A/C TV TEL. Winter, $100–$110 double. Off-season, $75–$85 double. Rates include breakfast. MC, V.

Joan Cornell, the Barnacle's owner, was once an innkeeper in Vermont, so she knows what amenities travelers are looking for and goes out of her way to fulfill special requests. Her Big Pine Key home has only four bedrooms, each with its own character. Two are located upstairs, in the main house—their doors open into the living room, which contains a small Jacuzzi-style tub. For privacy, the two downstairs rooms are best; each has its own entrance and is out of earshot of the common areas. The Cottage Room, a free-standing, peak-topped bedroom, is outfitted with a beautiful kitchenette. The accommodations are standard, and all rooms have queen-size beds, small refrigerators, and bathrooms. The rooms are not luxurious and don't have fancy amenities, but the house has its own private sandy beach where you can float all day on the inn's rafts, rubber boat, or kayak. Beach towels, chairs, and coolers are provided for guests' use.

Deer Run Bed and Breakfast. Long Beach Dr. (P.O. Box 431), Big Pine Key, FL 33043. ☎ **305/872-2015.** 3 rms. Winter, $85–$110 double. Off-season, $75–$95 double. Rates include breakfast. No credit cards.

Located directly on the beach, Sue Abbott's small, homey, smoke-free B&B is a real find. One upstairs and two downstairs guest rooms are comfortably furnished with queen-size beds, good closets, and touch-sensitive lamps. Rattan and 1970s-style chairs and couches furnish the living room, along with 13 birds and three cats. Breakfast, served on a pretty, fenced-in porch, is cooked to order by Sue herself. The wooded area around the property is full of deer, often spotted on the beach as well.

CAMPING

✪ **Bahia Honda State Park.** 36550 Overseas Hwy., Mile Marker 37, Big Pine Key, FL 33043. ☎ **305/872-2353.** 80 campsites, 6 cabins. Dec 15–Sept 14, $125 cabin for one to four. Sept 15–Dec 14, $97 cabin for one to four. Year round, $25.85 campsite for one to four with electricity, $21.70 without electricity. Additional person $5.60 extra in cabins, $2.25 extra in campsites. MC, V.

One of the best parks in the whole state of Florida, Bahia Honda is as loaded with facilities and activities as it is with campers. Don't be discouraged by its popularity—this park encompasses over 500 acres of land, and some very private beaches (see "Bahia Honda State Park," above, for complete information). If you're lucky enough to get one, the park's cabins represent a very good value. Each holds up to eight guests, and comes complete with linens, kitchenettes, and utensils.

WHERE TO DINE

As you progress south to Key West, you'll notice the prices getting higher. Although you may still find the occasional roadside joint, they become more and more sparse. Here are a few of the best of the cheapest eateries:

MEALS FOR LESS THAN $10

Sugarloaf Lodge. Overseas Hwy., Mile Marker 17, Sugarloaf Key. ☎ **305/745-3741.** Reservations not accepted. Breakfast $2–$5; lunch $5–$8; dinner $7–$20. AE, DC, DISC, MC, V. Sun–Thurs 7:30am–2:30pm and 5–9pm, Fri–Sat 7:30am–2:30pm and 5–10pm. AMERICAN.

It's just a simple, small-town restaurant that could be anywhere if it weren't for the mounted marlin and view of the dolphin pool. It's hard to believe that this huge dining room ever fills to capacity, though the adjacent wood-paneled bar is often hopping with local fishermen. Breakfasts here include the usual variety of egg dishes, served with corned-beef hash, sausage, ham, or steak. At lunch and dinner, you can get a variety of hot and cold sandwiches, including chicken and steak, fish, burgers, and other traditional American foods. This is a good place for the whole family since it serves a variety of choices and the staff is happy to accommodate children. In deference to its dolphin, which you can feed at appointed hours throughout the day, the diner never serves tuna. But for a small fee it will happily cook anything you catch and serve it with a salad, vegetables, and bread.

MEALS FOR LESS THAN $15

✪ **Island Reef Restaurant.** Overseas Hwy., Mile Marker 31.3, Big Pine Key. ☎ **305/872-2170.** Reservations not accepted. Lunch $3.95–$7.95; dinner $9–$14. MC, V. Mon–Sat 11am–9:30pm. AMERICAN.

This colorful ramshackle restaurant seems almost as old as the Keys themselves. It's extremely popular with locals, and you'll overhear conversations about today's catch and tomorrow's weather. There are only about a dozen tables, as well as six stools at a small diner-style bar.

Breakfasts tend toward fresh-fruit platters and French toast, while lunches mean simple sandwiches and tasty island chowders. Dinner specials change nightly; sometimes it's roast chicken with stuffing or leg of lamb, and other times it's prime rib or baked dolphin fish. The specials are served with so many fixings (soup of the day or salad, potatoes, vegetables, and dessert) that appetizers would be overkill even if they were offered. Permanent menu items, served with soup or salad, vegetable, and potato, are English-style fish and chips with malt vinegar, veal sweetbreads, vegetarian stir-fry, and frogs' legs.

Monte's. Overseas Hwy., Mile Marker 25, Summerland Key. ☎ **305/745-3731.** Reservations not accepted. Main courses $10–$14; lunch $3–$8. No credit cards. Tues–Sat 9:30am–10pm, Sun 11am–9pm. SEAFOOD.

Nobody goes to this restaurant/fish market for its atmosphere: plastic place settings on plastic-covered picnic-style tables in a screen-enclosed dining patio. Monte's has been open for almost 20 years because the food is very good and incredibly fresh. The day's catch may include shark, tuna, lobster, stone crabs, and a variety of shrimp. In addition, the restaurant prepares clam chowder, spiced crayfish pie, and even barbecued spareribs.

3 Key West

158 miles SW of Miami

Accessible only by boat until 1912, when Henry Flagler's railroad reached it, Key West's relative isolation from the North American mainland has everything to do with its charm. Cuban, Caribbean, and American wanderers, plus a smattering of writers, outlaws, musicians, and misfits have found a home here. Few islanders are actually *from* Key West. The majority of Key West's residents have been drifters who headed south down the states until they could drift no farther. The island has long attracted luminaries, among them Ernest Hemingway, John James Audubon, and Tennessee Williams, and was once one of the wealthiest towns in America. Hit hard by the double whammy of hurricane and recession, the city declared bankruptcy in 1934, then recovered by catering to mass tourism.

Key West's very tolerant live-and-let-live atmosphere was born of its residents' fierce devotion to personal independence and individual freedom. This liberal philosophy has made Key West especially welcoming to gays. It has also given rise to a government that is widely believed to be corrupt and that fostered unchecked growth. Only recently has concern about the environment been building among Key West's residents. AIDS has claimed the lives of many of the island's most creative characters, and increasing tourism and gentrification have sapped the once-funky fishing village of much of its charm. T-shirt shops are edging out smart boutiques and old gin-joints, and strollers are less likely to be longtime locals than cruise-ship passengers on a few hours' leave. But Key West is still a fun place, and hedonism still outpaces consumerism.

The best thing to do on this island is to loosen your shirt, pocket your watch, and take a long stroll down Duval Street, the island's famously fun thoroughfare. Although Duval was tamed long ago by gourmet ice-cream parlors and tacky T-shirt shops, pubbing along the street remains one of the world's best crawls. Stop in at some of the open-air bars, have a few drinks, meet some locals, and end up at Mallory Docks by sunset.

Key West

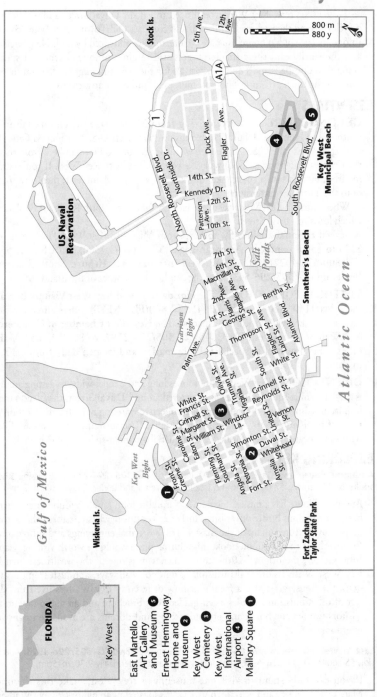

0 800 m
   880 y

Stock Is.
5th Ave.
12th Ave.
A1A
1
Duck Ave.
Flagler Ave.
North Roosevelt Blvd.
Northside Dr.
14th St.
Kennedy Dr.
12th St.
Patterson Ave.
10th St.
7th St.
6th St.
Macmillan St.
2nd Ave.
Harris Ave.
1st Ave.
George St.
Staples St.
Bertha St.
Thompson St.
Flagler St.
Laird St.
Atlantic Blvd.
South St.
White St.
Palm Ave.
White St.
Francis St.
Olivia St.
Truman Ave.
Virginia St.
Windsor La.
Grinnell St.
Reynolds St.
Caroline St.
Margaret St.
Eaton St.
William St.
Fleming St.
Southard St.
Simonton St.
United St.
Vernon St.
Front St.
Greene St.
Angela St.
Petronia St.
Fort St.
Duval St.
Whitehead St.
Amelia St.
South Roosevelt Blvd.
Key West Municipal Beach
Smathers's Beach

US Naval Reservation

Garrison Bight
Key West Bight
Salt Ponds

Gulf of Mexico
Atlantic Ocean

Wiskeria Is.
Fort Zachary Taylor State Park

FLORIDA
Key West

East Martello Art Gallery and Museum **5**
Ernest Hemingway Home and Museum **2**
Key West Cemetery **3**
Key West International Airport **4**
Mallory Square **1**

To see the "real" Key West, you'll need to get off Duval Street and wander (or bicycle) around the backroads of the island's compact Old Town. Lined with "conch" (pronounced "conk") houses that are architecturally influenced by both New England and the Caribbean, these smaller streets still retain a unique charm that speaks volumes about the island's quixotic past. Along the way, you might even want to visit some of the town's historical houses, museums, and other attractions.

ESSENTIALS

GETTING THERE   If you're **driving from Miami,** take the Florida Turnpike south to the Homestead Turnpike Extension that meets U.S. 1 in Florida City. Alternatively, just take U.S. 1 the entire way from Miami to Florida City. From there, the Overseas Highway (U.S. 1) will take you all the way to Key West. If you're driving from Florida's west coast, take Alligator Alley to the Miami exit, then turn south onto the Turnpike Extension.

When entering Key West, stay in the far-right lane onto North Roosevelt Boulevard, which leads to Duval Street.

Several **regional airlines** fly nonstop from Miami to Key West; fares are about $120 to $300 round-trip. American Eagle (☎ 800/443-7300) and USAir Express (☎ 800/428-4322) land at **Key West International Airport,** South Roosevelt Boulevard (☎ 305/296-5439), on the southeastern corner of the island.

VISITOR INFORMATION   The **Florida Keys and Key West Visitors Bureau,** P.O. Box 1147, Key West, FL 33041 (☎ **800/FLA-KEYS**), offers a free vacation kit that's packed with visitor information. The **Key West Chamber of Commerce,** 402 Wall St., Key West, FL 33040 (☎ **305/294-2587,** or 800/527-8539), also offers general as well as specialized information and is open daily from 8:30am to 5pm.

ORIENTATION   Key West is just 4 miles long and 2 miles wide, so getting around is easy. The mile-square Old Town is centered around **Duval Street,** the island's most important commercial thoroughfare and collective watering hole. It's the location of most of the island's bars, restaurants, and sights. The surrounding streets are filled with some beautifully refurbished Victorian/Bahamanian-style "conch" homes.

EXPLORING KEY WEST

Audubon House and Gardens. 205 Whitehead St. ☎ **305/294-2116.** Admission $7.50 adults, $6.50 seniors, $2 children 6–12, free for children 5 and under. Daily 9:30am–5pm.

Audubon House has a misleading name. Naturalist John James Audubon never lived here—the famous birder only visited in 1832. Yet this flawlessly restored three-story house now features many of the master artist's original engravings and lithographs. Even without the Audubon hook, this alluring place would be worth visiting. Capt. John Geiger, the original 19th-century owner, was one of the wealthiest men in Key West. With its original furnishings, outdoor walkways, and lush tropical gardens, the house gives you a feeling of how differently Key Westers live from the rest of us. Admission includes a self-guided-tour brochure and an audio-tape tour. Visitors wander the house and grounds freely, and docents are available to answer questions.

East Martello Museum and Gallery. 3501 S. Roosevelt Blvd. ☎ **305/296-3913.** Admission $5 adults, $1 children 7–12, free for children 6 and under. Daily 9:30am–5pm.

If you can only stand to visit one museum in Key West, make this the one. Man-ageable in size and eclectic in variety, it's located in an old brick Civil War–era fort that itself is worth a visit. The museum contains a bizarre variety of exhibits

The Ten Keymandments

The Keys have always attracted independent spirits, from Ernest Hemingway and Tennessee Williams to Jimmy Buffett, Mel Fisher, and Zane Grey. Writers, artists, and free-thinkers have come here to get away from society's rigid demands.

When drug enforcement agents blocked off the main highway leading into Key West in 1982, the residents did what they do best—they threw a party. The festivities were to mark the "independence" of the newly formed "Conch Republic." You'll see the distinctive flag with its conch insignia throughout the "Republic." But despite its very laid-back and tolerant code of behavior, there are *some* rules in the Keys. Be sure to respect the Ten Keymanments while you're there or suffer the consequences:

- Don't anchor on a reef. (Reefs are alive.)
- Don't feed the animals. (They'll want to follow you home and you can't keep them.)
- Don't trash our place. (Or we'll send Bubba to trash yours.)
- Don't touch the coral. (After all, you don't even know them.)
- Don't speed. (Especially on Big Pine Key where deer reside and tar-and-feathering is still practiced.)
- Don't catch more fish than you can eat. (Better yet, let them all go. Some of them support schools.)
- Don't collect conch. (This species is protected. By Bubba.)
- Don't disturb the birds' nests. (They find it very annoying.)
- Don't damage the sea grass. (And don't even think about making a skirt out of it.)
- Don't drink and drive on land or sea. (There's absolutely nothing funny about it.)

that collectively do a fairly thorough job of interpreting the city's intriguing past. Historical artifacts include ship models, a deep-sea diver's wooden air pump, a crude raft from a Cuban "boatlift," and a horse-drawn hearse. Exhibits depict America's wars and illustrate the Keys' history of wrecking, sponging, and cigar making. And if all that's not enough, the museum also exhibits modern works by local artists. After seeing the galleries, you can climb a steep spiral staircase to the top of a lookout tower for good views over the island and ocean. The museum is located on the "far" side of the island, away from the Duval Street crowds.

✪ **Ernest Hemingway Home and Museum.** 907 Whitehead St. ☎ **305/294-1575.** Admission $6.50 adults, $4 children. Daily 9am–5pm.

Key West's commercialization of Ernest Hemingway has turned this former local resident into a touristic icon, both figuratively and literally. The novelist's gruff image is emblazoned on T-shirts and mugs, and used to sell everything from beer to suntan lotion. Hemingway's particularly handsome stone Spanish Colonial house was built in 1851, and was one of the first on the island to be fitted with indoor plumbing and a built-in fireplace. The author lived here from 1928 until 1940 along with about 50 six-toed cats. During that time, the author produced some of his most famous works, including *For Whom the Bell Tolls, A Farewell to Arms,* and *The Snows of*

Kilimanjaro. Hemingway habitually awoke early and crossed the elevated walkway he built from his bedroom to his writing studio. He often wrote all day, but "If the words are coming hard," he admitted, "I often quit before noon."

The Hemingway House Museum was opened to the public 2 years after the novelist's death. Visitors are guided around the property by knowledgeable docents, after which they're free to browse through displays of Hemingway's personal possessions and admire furnishings acquired on his many travels to Africa and Cuba. You can also pet dozens of six-toed cats, descendants of Hemingway's own pets.

Key West Cemetery. Margaret and Angela sts. Free admission. Daily dawn–dusk.

Key West's quirky image is coveted by its residents and capitalized on by its tourist board. But no place on the island is wackier than this old and picturesque cemetery, a 21-acre graveyard that's as irreverent as it is original. Key West's rocky geological makeup forced early residents to "bury" their dead above ground, in stone-encased caskets that are sometimes stacked several high, condominium style. And pets are often buried beside their owners. You'll notice that many of the memorials are emblazoned with nicknames—a common Key West informality that's literally taken to the grave. Look for headstones labeled "The Tailor," "Bean," "Shorty," and "Bunny." Other headstones also reflect residents' lighthearted attitudes toward life and death. "I Told You I Was Sick" is one of the more famous epitaphs, as is a tongue-in-cheek widow's inscription "At Least I Know Where He's Sleeping Tonight."

✪ **Mallory Square Sunset Celebration.** Mallory Square Dock.

Every evening just before sunset, locals and visitors gather at the dock behind Mallory Square to celebrate the day gone by. It sounds like a quaint Caribbean tradition, and it once was, but sunsets have become big business in Key West. Don't miss this carnival of food vendors, portrait artists, acrobats, and dog acts. On the water, boatloads of drunken sunset cruisers glide by in private and party yachts, while single-engine tour planes buzz overhead.

Key West Aquarium. 1 Whitehead St. ☎ **305/296-2051.** Admission (2-day pass) $6.50 adults, $3.50 children 8–15. Daily 10am–6pm.

Built by the WPA as an open-air aquarium, this 1930s-era "fish zoo" has since been topped by a roof, but its interior is as antiquated as ever. The Key West Aquarium can't hold a candle to newer, glitzier ones, but it's not supposed to. Small and user-friendly, this aquarium is basically a single large room with fish tanks embedded in every wall and huge open touch tanks in the center. If you show up in time for one of the frequent show-and-tell tours, you'll learn specifics about horseshoe and hermit crabs, starfish, sea rays, and queen conchs; feedings also coincide with the lectures. Three large outdoor pens in back of the aquarium house animals of the Atlantic shore, but are a snore.

Key West Lighthouse Museum. 938 Whitehead St. ☎ **305/294-0012.** Admission $5 adults, $1 children 7–12, free for children 6 and under. Daily 9:30am–5pm (last admission at 4:30pm).

When the Key West Lighthouse was opened in 1848, many locals mourned. Its bright warning to ships also signaled the end of a profitable era for wreckers, pirate salvagers who looted reef-stricken ships. When radar and sonar made the lighthouse obsolete, it was opened to visitors as a tourist attraction. There's a small museum in the former keeper's quarters that tells the story of the wreckers and the Keys lighthouses. It's worth mustering the energy to climb the 88 claustrophobic stairs to the top, where you're rewarded with magnificent panoramic views of Key West and the ocean.

Mel Fisher's Treasure Museum. 200 Greene St. ☎ **305/294-2633.** Admission $6 adults, $2 children 6–12, free for children 5 and under. Open daily 9:30am–5pm.

Mel Fisher found a multi-million-dollar treasure trove when he discovered the wreck of the Spanish galleon *Nuestra Señora de Atocha* in 1985. Fisher is one lucky guy. And at this small museum, full of doubloons, emeralds, and solid-gold bars, they never let you forget it. Some of the $400 million in gold and silver artifacts are displayed along with many copies. Cannons, ship parts, and other items of purely historical value are also exhibited. An aging, 20-minute video tells the story.

ORGANIZED TOURS

TROLLEY-BUS TOURS   The city's whole story is packed into a neat, 90-minute package on the **Conch Train** tour, which comprehensively covers the island. The "train's" engine is a propane-powered truck disguised as a locomotive. Sitting in one of the little cars is more than a bit hokey, but worth the embarrassment. Tours depart from both Mallory Square and the Welcome Center, near the intersection of U.S. 1 and North Roosevelt Boulevard, on the other side of the island. For more information, contact the Conch Train at 1 Key Lime Sq., Key West (☎ **305/ 294-5161**). The tour costs $14 for adults, $6 for children 4 to 12, and free for children 3 and under. Departures are daily, every half hour from 9am to 4:30pm.

It's remarkable that there are enough tourists in Key West to keep two competing trolley tours afloat. The **Old Town Trolley**'s open-air tram drivers maintain a running commentary as they loop around the island's streets past all the major (and many minor) sights. The main advantage of this 90-minute tour is that it allows riders to disembark at any of 14 stops on the tour route, explore a museum or visit a restaurant, then reboard at will. Trolleys depart from Mallory Square and other points around the island. For details contact them at 1910 N. Roosevelt Blvd. (☎ **305/296-6688**). Tours are $15 for adults, $6 for children 4 to 12, and free for children 3 and under. Tours depart daily from 9am to 4pm.

BOAT TOURS   The *Pride of Key West / Fireball*, docked at the Ocean Key House, 0 (zero) Duval St. (☎ **305/296-6293**), is a 58-foot glass-bottom catamaran that goes on coral-reef tours by day and sunset cruises by evening. Reef trips cost $18 per person; sunset cruises are $23 per person and include snacks, sodas, and a glass of champagne.

The *Wolf*, docked at Schooner Wharf, Key West Seaport (☎ **305/296-9653**), is a 44-passenger topsail schooner that sets sail daily for daytime and sunset cruises around the Keys. Key West Seaport is located at the end of Greene Street. Day tours cost $20 per person; sunset sails cost $29 per person and include champagne, wine, beer, or soda.

SPECIAL EVENTS & FESTIVALS

Anything goes in the Keys—just walk through downtown and you'll be convinced. And in that spirit, the annual festivals that take place in Key West are wacky, to say the least. Plus, fishing tournaments are so common in the Keys that there seems to be one every month.

In early May, the **Texaco / Hemingway Key West Classic** (☎ **305/294-4440**), hailed as the top fishing tournament in Florida, is held. This catch-and-release competiton offers a $50,000 purse to the best angler for sailfish, marlin, and light tackle. The **Coconuts Dolphin Tournament** (☎ **305/451-4107**) in mid-May is the largest fishing tournament in the Keys, offering $5,000 and a Dodge Ram pickup truck to the person who breaks the record for the largest fish caught. The competition is fierce! November brings the **Mercury Outboards Cheeca/Redbone**

Celebrity Tournament to Islamorada (☎ **305/664-2002**). Curt Gowdy from *American Sportsman* hosts this tournament, whose proceeds go to finding a cure for cystic fibrosis. The likes of Wade Boggs and actor James B. Sikking compete almost yearly.

If you happen to be in the Keys during the summer, mark your calender for late May and join the locals for the **Super Boat Racing Series** in downtown Key West (☎ **305/296-8963**). It's a day of food, fun, and powerboat racing.

In July, the **Lower Keys Underwater Music Fest** (☎ **305/872-2411**) comes to town. At this outrageous celebration, boaters go out to the underwater reef off Little Torch Key, drop speakers into the water, and pipe in music. It's entertainment for the fish and swimmers alike! The snorkeling Elvises have sometimes been the main act for this celebration.

In late July, Key West puts on a massive shindig celebrating its most noteworthy resident with the **Hemingway Days Festival** (☎ **305/294-4440**). For a week, the "conchs" and their visitors pay homage to the tortured novelist by putting on Ernest Hemingway look-alike contests, attracting participants from all over the United States and sometimes other countries. You'd be surprised to find out how many men actually look like him! Writer's workshops and conferences are offered for more serious-minded visitors.

In town for Halloween? It might feel as though the rest of the world is joining you if you're in Key West for the world-famous **Fantasy Fest** (☎ **305/296-1817**). This insane gathering of thousands of people is Florida's version of Mardi Gras. Crazy costumes, wild parades, and even more colorful revelers gather for an opportunity to do things Mom said not to do. Check out the **Goombay Festival**—it coincides with Fantasy Fest—if you want to sample Caribbean dishes and purchase art and ethnic clothing in this celebration with a Jamaican flair.

SPORTS & OUTDOOR ACTIVITIES

BICYCLING & MOPEDING   The best way to get around Key West is by bicycle. The island is relatively small and as flat as a board, and the streets are safe.

Several shops rent one-speed cruisers for about $10 per day and ugly pink mopeds for about $30 per day. They include **The Bike Shop,** 1110 Truman Ave. (☎ **305/ 294-1073**); the **Moped Hospital,** 601 Truman Ave. (☎ **305/296-3344**); and **Tropical Bicycles & Scooter Rentals,** 1300 Duval St. (☎ **305/294-8136**).

DIVING   One of the area's largest scuba schools, the **Key West Pro Dive Shop,** 3128 N. Roosevelt Blvd. (☎ **305/296-3823,** or 800/426-0707), offers instruction on all levels. Dive boats take participants to scuba and snorkel sites on nearby reefs.

FISHING   Several charter-fishing boats operate from Key West marinas. They include Capt. Jim Brienza's 27-foot *Sea Breeze,* docked at 25 Arbutus Dr. (☎ **305/ 294-6027**); and Capt. Henry Otto's 44-foot *Sunday,* docked at the Hyatt in Key West (☎ **305/294-7052**). A host of deep-sea vessels are docked at the **Municipal Marina,** 1801 N. Roosevelt Blvd. (1st Street and Palm Avenue; ☎ **305/292-8167**) and at the **Garrison Bight Marina,** Eaton Street and Roosevelt Boulevard (☎ **305/ 296-9969**).

GOLF   The **Key West Resort** (☎ **305/294-5232**), an 18-hole course, is located just before the island of Key West at Mile Marker 4.5 (turn onto College Road to the course entrance). Designed by Rees Jones, the course features plenty of mangroves and water hazards on its 6,526 yards. It's open to the public. There's a driving range open from 7am to sunset every day, and a pro shop. Tee-time reservations are required.

SHOPPING

Key West is hardly a shopper's paradise. If you're looking for souvenir T-shirts or jewelry or art, you'll find Key West rewarding. Here you'll find an eclectic selection of boutiques; there's even a kiosk specializing in leather shoes with vivid impressions of the sunset or anything you might choose to have painted on them! Bring your walking shoes to cruise Duval Street for Key West goods.

Fast Buck Freddie's, 500 Duval St. (☎ **305/294-2007**), is downtown's oldest department store, but for the same merchandise at much reduced prices, try **Half Buck Freddie's**, 726 Caroline St. (☎ **305/294-6799**). Here you can shop for out-of-season bargains and "rejects" from Fast Buck Freddie's that are anything but secondhand. Half Buck is open only on Friday and Saturday from 11am to 5pm.

Key West has a good number of **art galleries** and stores selling beautiful native art and even antiques for collectors. Many galleries are clustered on Whitehead Street, which runs parallel to Duval Street. You'll also find shops scattered along the side streets off Duval. One of particular note is the **Haitian Art Company**, 600 Frances St. (☎ **305/296-8932**), where you can browse through room upon room of original paintings from well-known and obscure Haitian artists.

WHERE TO STAY

Downtown Key West is extremely expensive, so finding a hotel at a reasonable price is a difficult task. Below are a few recommendations, although I suggest that you stay in the Lower Keys and merely visit Key West for the day. If you *must* stay in Key West, try some of the big hotel chains that operate out of the Keys for more reasonable prices: **Best Western** (☎ 800/432-4315), **Comfort Inn** (☎ 800/695-5150), **Econo Lodge** (☎ 800/533-9378), **Holiday Inn** (☎ 800/465-4329), and **Ramada Inn** (☎ 800/330-5541).

DOUBLES FOR LESS THAN $60

Caribbean House. 226 Petronia House, Key West, FL 33040. ☎ **305/296-1600**, or 800/543-4518. Fax 305/296-9840. 1 rms, 3 cottages, 1 penthouse. Winter and special holidays, $69 double, $79–$89 cottage or penthouse; Off-season, $49 double, $59 cottage or penthouse. Rates include continental breakfast. Additional person free. 1-night deposit required in advance by cashier's check. MC, V.

For the really budget-conscious, Key West offers a funky inn with 11 modest but brightly decorated rooms and two separate cottages. The walls behind the beds in the tiny but clean rooms have been painted with likenesses of elaborately styled headboards, and the rich turquoise and shocking pinks are reminiscent of a quaint Bahamian fish-shack—appropriate to this gingerbread home's location in the largely untouristed Bahama Village. Here you'll run into European backpackers, descendants of Bahamian immigrants, and local bohemians who share the streets with roosters and stray dogs. The hospitable Jamaican hosts are happy to welcome a third guest to any room, and will even provide an extra futon. Across the street is Blue Heaven, a hip gallery and restaurant (see "Where to Eat," below).

DOUBLES FOR LESS THAN $80

Southernmost Point Guest House. 1327 Duval St., Key West, FL 33040. ☎ **305/294-0715.** Fax 305/296-0641. 3 rms, 3 suites. A/C TV TEL. Winter, $80–$120 double; $130 suite. Off-season, $55–$80 double; $95 suite. Rates include continental breakfast. Additional person $5–$10 extra. AE, MC, V.

Built in 1885, this well-kept and architecturally stunning home pays tribute to the romantic charm of Old Key West. The B&B's antiseptically clean rooms are not as fancy as the house's ornate exterior. Each has basic beds and couches and a hodgepodge of furnishings, including futon couches, highback wicker chairs, and plenty of mismatched throw rugs. Each room is different and Room 5 is best. Situated upstairs, it has a private porch and an ocean view, and windows that gulp in large quantities of light. Every room has a refrigerator and comes with a complimentary decanter of sherry. Mona Santiago, the hotel's kind and laid-back owner, provides chairs and towels that can be brought to the beach, located just 1 block away.

Wicker Guesthouse. 913 Duval St., Key West, FL 33040. ☎ **305/296-4275** or 800/880-4275. Fax 305/294-7240. 11 doubles with bath, 3 doubles without bath, 5 efficiencies, 2 suites. Winter, $85 double without bath, $155 doubles with bath or suite, $165 efficiency. Off-season, $63 double without bath, $79–$89 double with bath or suite, $95 efficiency. Rates include continental breakfast. Additional person $15 extra in winter, $10 extra off-season. AE, DC, DISC, MC, V.

Occupying six separate buildings, one overlooking busy Duval Street, the Wicker offers some of the best-value accommodations in Key West. The cheapest rooms are in the front of the complex. These have shared baths and are predictably sparse, with no telephones, TVs, or even closets. The guest rooms get nicer, quieter, and more expensive the farther back on the property you go. Way back, beyond a kidney-shaped, heated swimming pool, are the guesthouse's top accommodations, each furnished with two double beds, cable TVs, and the ubiquitous wicker furnishings that give this house its name. Some have small kitchenettes. Three connected units share a living room and stoveless kitchen, and are particularly recommended for families and small parties. There's a communal kitchen for guests' use and a payphone by the pool.

DOUBLES FOR LESS THAN $100

South Beach Oceanfront Motel. 508 South St., Key West, FL 33040. ☎ **305/296-5611** or 800/354-4455. Fax 305/294-8272. 47 rms. Winter, $99–$197 double. Off-season, $67–$138 double. Additional person $10–$15 extra; children 17 and under stay free in parents' room. AE, MC, V.

This standard two-story motel is located directly on the ocean, within walking distance of Duval Street. Because it was built perpendicular to the water, however, most of the rooms overlook a particularly pretty Olympic-size swimming pool rather then a wide swath of beach. The best—and most expensive, by far—rooms are those lucky two on the end (nos. 115 and 215) that are beachfront. All rooms share similar aging decor and standard furnishings. The smallish bathrooms, with showers but no tubs, could also use a makeover. There's a private pier, an on-site water-sports concession, and a laundry room available for guests' use. When booking, ask for a room that's as close to the beach (and as far from the road) as possible.

WORTH A SPLURGE

Chelsea House. 707 Truman Ave., Key West, FL 33040. ☎ **305/296-2211** or 800/845-8859. Fax 305/296-4822. 18 rms, 2 apts. A/C TV TEL. Winter, $115–$165 double; $270 apt. Off-season, $75–$125 double; $165–$190 apt. Rates include breakfast. Additional person $20 extra in winter, $15 extra off-season. Pets $5 extra. AE, DISC, MC, V.

This lovely gray-and-white Queen Anne house, surrounded by a white picket fence and flying the U.S. flag, seems straight out of a Norman Rockwell painting. Despite its decidedly English name, Chelsea House *is* "all-American," a term that in Key West isn't code for "conservative." Chelsea House caters to a mixed gay/straight clientele with a liberal philosophy that exhibits itself most demonstratively on the clothing-optional sundeck.

The amply sized bedrooms are augmented by beautiful wood floors, firm beds, and TVs that are connected to VCRs. The apartments come with full kitchens and a separate living area, as well as a palm-shaded balcony in back. The baths and closets could be bigger, but both are adequate and serviceable. Like the floors and ceilings of the house, the pastel-colored wood walls are built from Dade County pine, a particularly fine termite-resistant tree that has been logged to extinction. When weather permits, which is almost always, breakfast is served outside by the pool. There is private parking. Note that children under 15 are not accepted.

La Pensione. 809 Truman Ave., Key West, FL 33040. ☎ **305/292-9923.** Fax 305/296-6509. 7 rms. A/C. Winter, $148–$158 double. Off-season, $68–$88 double. Rates include breakfast. Additional person $25 extra. AE, DISC, MC, V.

Opened on Valentine's Day in 1991, the yellow-and-white two-story La Pensione is a lovely restoration of an 1891 Victorian home that, like so many on the island, is on the National Register of Historic Places. Guests enter the house via front steps that lead to a porch and a hallway with red floral carpeting. The rooms are colorful and airy, painted in solid colors and uncluttered with wall art. Firm king-size beds are topped with bright, flowery spreads that match the prints of the well-chosen Ethan Allen furnishings. The bathrooms are serviceable. All in all, the new owners have done a bang-up job creating a modestly priced, charming inn that's thoroughly recommendable. Breakfast, which includes Belgian waffles and fresh fruit, is served in a pleasing downstairs dining room. Note that no children are accepted.

WHERE TO DINE
MEALS FOR LESS THAN $7

✪ **The Bangalore.** 504 Petronia St. (half a block east of Duval St.). ☎ **305/292-2209.** Reservations not accepted. Main courses $3–$6. No credit cards. Tues–Sat 6pm–midnight. INDIAN.

Quite literally a hole-in-the-wall, the Bangalore is an all-vegetarian Indian-inspired dining counter accommodating just four outdoor stools situated beneath a leaky awning. Both dead-cheap and delicious, the restaurant is run by owner/waiter/chef/busboy Philip Simons, a well-traveled American who's always up for some interesting chat. Start with a baked phyllo samosa, containing curried potatoes, peas, ginger, and cilantro. Main courses include tofu and peas in a coriander-based tomato sauce, cauliflower and potato sautéed with cumin and fennel, okra with roasted red peppers and onions, and mushrooms sautéed with garlic, onion, ginger, and spices. The Bangalore is open late.

MEALS FOR LESS THAN $10

Blue Heaven. 729 Thomas St. (in the heart of Bahama Village). ☎ **305/296-8666.** Main courses $7–$19. DICS, MC, V. Mon–Sat 8am–3pm and 6–10:30pm, Sun 8am–1pm and 6–10:30pm. AMERICAN/NATURAL.

You'll wait in line forever at this little hippy-run gallery and restaurant that has become the place to be in Key West—and with good reason: The ramshackle Mediterranean Revival house serves up some of the best food anywhere in town, especially for breakfast. In this former bordello, where Hemingway was said to hang out watching cockfights, you can enjoy homemade granolas, fruit, huge tropical fruit pancakes, and seafood Benedict (but skip the store-bought doughnuts). Dinners are just as good and run the gamut from just-caught fish dishes, Jamaican-style jerk chicken, curried soups, and vegetarian stews. While you wait, go up to the galleries to see local work ranging from the absurd to the incredible. Be sure to call to see if they're open, especially in the summer when they sometimes close for weeks at a time.

Jimmy Buffett's Margaritaville Cafe. 500 Duval St. ☎ **305/292-1435.** Reservations not accepted. Sandwiches $5–$6; fresh fish platter $10; margarita $4. AE, MC, V. Sun–Thurs 11am–2am, Fri–Sat 11am–4am. AMERICAN.

This easygoing restaurant/bar is heavy on soups, salads, sandwiches, and local catches. A long bar runs the length of the place. Most people come to drink, but the food's not bad. Don't get too ambitious, though. You and the rest of the tourists just come for the myth. So have a margarita, enjoy the view, and have fun.

MEALS FOR LESS THAN $15

✪ **Mangia, Mangia.** 900 Southard St. (at Margaret St.). ☎ **305/294-2469.** Reservations recommended. Main courses $9–$13. MC, V. Daily 5:30–10pm. ITALIAN/AMERICAN.

A low-key Italian trattoria, Mangia, Mangia is one of Key West's best values and a favorite among locals who appreciate the inexpensive and good food in this town of tourist traps. Off the beaten track, in a little corner storefront, this great Chicago-style pasta place serves some of the best Italian food in the Keys. The family-run restaurant offers superb homemade pastas of every description, including one of the tastiest marinaras around. A tasty, simple grilled chicken breast is brushed with olive oil and sprinkled with pepper. You wouldn't know it from the glossy glass front room, but there's also a great little outdoor patio dotted with twinkling pepper lights and lots of plants. There's often a wait for one of the tables outside when the weather's nice, so relax out back with a glass of one of their excellent wines or homemade beer while you wait.

Turtle Kraals Wildlife Grill. 213 Margaret St. (at Caroline). ☎ **305/294-2640.** Main courses $12–$18. DISC, MC, V. Mon–Thurs 11am–1am, Fri–Sat 11am–2am. SOUTHWESTERN/ SEAFOOD.

You'll join lots of locals in this out-of-the-way converted warehouse that serves innovative seafood at great prices. Try the twin lobster tails stuffed with mango and crabmeat or any of the big quesadillas or fajitas. Kids will like the wildlife exhibits and the very cheesy menu. Blues bands play most nights. There's never a cover.

WORTH A SPLURGE

Bagatelle. 115 Duval St. ☎ **305/296-6609.** Reservations recommended. Main courses $16– $24; lunch $5–$12. AE, CB, DC, DISC, MC, V. Daily 11:30am–3pm and 5:30–10pm. SEAFOOD/ TROPICAL.

Tables on the second-floor veranda of Bagatelle's historical gray-and-pink Queen Anne house are some of Florida's most coveted. Dining up here is intimate while offering a bird's-eye view of the Duval madness below. It's even more fanciful when a keyboardist is at the grand piano. A nod away is a contemporary interior dining room in which an entire wall has been removed for unrestricted access to the balcony. A massive mounted marlin and wooden schoolhouse chairs at white-clothed tables keep formality at bay. There's also a lively ground-floor bar in what was once the house's living room.

A large lunch selection includes a blackened-chicken-breast sandwich with crumbled bleu cheese and a variety of grilled fish. Your dinner should begin with the herb- and garlic-stuffed whole artichoke or the sashimilike seared tuna rolled in black peppercorns. The best entrees are the local Florida fish selections like shrimp-stuffed grouper crowned with shrimp- and lobster-cream sauce, and garlic-herb pasta topped with gulf shrimp, Florida lobster, local fish, and mushrooms. The best chicken and beef dishes are given a tropical treatment: grilled with papaya, ginger, and soy.

KEY WEST AFTER DARK
THE CLUB, MUSIC & BAR SCENE

Duval Street is the Bourbon Street of Florida. Between the T-shirt shops and clothing boutiques there's bar after bar, serving stiff drinks to revelers who usually bounce from one to another. Here's a rundown of the best:

Captain Tony's Saloon. 428 Greene St. ☎ **305/294-1838.**

Just around the corner from Duval's beaten path, Captain Tony's jealously retains its seasoned and quixotic pretourist ambience, complete with old-time regulars who remember the island before cruise ships docked here; they say that Hemingway drank, caroused, and even wrote here. Smoky, small, and cozy, the bar is owned by Capt. Tony Tarracino, a former Key West mayor who is known in these parts for his acerbic wit and unorthodox ways.

Durty Harry's. 208 Duval St. ☎ **305/296-4890.**

One of Duval's largest entertainment complexes, Durty Harry's features live rock bands almost every night (and most afternoons, too) and several outdoor bars. **Upstairs at Rick's** is an indoor/outdoor dance club that's very popular almost every night. **The Red Garter,** yet another related business on this property, is a pocket-size strip club popular with local bachelor parties and the few visitors who know about it.

Fat Tuesdays. 305 Duval St. ☎ **305/296-9373.**

Over 20 colorful, slushy, slightly chemical-tasting alcoholic concoctions swirl in special see-through dispensers behind this lively outdoor bar. Located on an elevated deck near the busiest end of Duval, the bar attracts a rowdy college-age crowd as well as rowdy any-age locals.

Hog's Breath Saloon. 400 Front St. ☎ **305/296-4222.**

Except for the fact that it sells lots of T-shirts, there's no relationship between this bar and its namesake corporate chain with locations in California and around the country. It's an inviting, fun place to hang out, with several outdoor bars, good live music, a raw bar, and decent food, all earning it a top recommendation from this guide. There are daily happy-hour specials from 5 to 7pm.

Jimmy Buffett's Margaritaville Cafe. 500 Duval St. ☎ **305/292-1435.**

This large, friendly, and easygoing restaurant/bar/gift shop features live bands most nights, and Mr. Buffett himself has even been known to take the stage. The touristy café is furnished with plenty of Buffett memorabilia, including gold records, photos, and drawings. The margaritas are standard in both quality and strength.

Sloppy Joe's. 201 Duval St. ☎ **305/294-5717.**

Scholars and drunks debate whether this is the same Sloppy Joe's that Hemingway wrote about, but there's no argument that this classic bar's turn-of-the-century wooden ceiling and cracked-tile floors are Key West originals. The popular and raucous bar is crowded with tourists almost 24 hours a day, and there's almost always live music.

Sunset Pier Bar. At Ocean Key House, 0 (zero) Duval St. ☎ **305/296-7040.**

Located behind Ocean Key House at the end of Duval Street, the bar offers a limited menu and a full range of tropical coolers. Live music begins as the sun goes down.

THE GAY SCENE

A 1995 fire on Duval Street destroyed the famous Copa nightclub, and at press time the gay scene had dispersed to various small, intimate bars around the town. Below are a few of the more popular watering holes. The parties may not be as large as those the Copa once hosted, but they're lively nonetheless.

Atlantic Shores Motel. 510 South St. ☎ **305/296-2491.**

Every Sunday night is "Tea by the Sea" on the pier at the Atlantic Shores Motel. Disco is the music of choice, and whoever's in town usually comes to this well-known gathering place. Show up at dusk.

The Copa. 623 Duval St. ☎ **305/296-8521.**

At press time the Copa was in the midst of being rebuilt after its August 1995 fire, but there's no set opening date as of yet. Once the busiest and biggest nightclub in Key West, the Copa's main attraction was a large dance floor featuring disco music and nine rooms able to accommodate up to 1,200 patrons. Call—or just ask around—to find out about the reopening; they're shooting for Labor Day 1996.

La Terraza. 1125 Duval St. ☎ **305/296-6706.**

Better known around town as La-Te-Da, La Terraza puts on themed poolside parties every Sunday that vary weekly at the discretion of the owners. The nightspot is open daily from 10am to 4am, although the hours have also been known to change.

One Saloon. 524 Duval St. ☎ **305/296-8118.**

This popular gay dance bar features a male dancer strutting across the top of the bar nightly. A mostly male clientele frequents this spot with nondescript decor. There's an outdoor garden bar for those who want to get away from yet more disco music.

THEATER

The **Red Barn Theater,** 319 Duval St. (☎ **305/296-9911**), was originally a carriage house connected to one of the island's oldest homes and now houses one of Key West's best stages. The 88-seat theater has gone through many changes since it was reborn in the 1940s as the home to the Key West Community Players. Local and visiting productions vary in quality, but are sometimes very good. Phone for current performance information.

The **Waterfront Playhouse,** Mallory Dock (☎ **305/294-5015**), is larger and prettier than the Red Barn and attracts a variety of theatrical performances, most often drama or musicals. Performances are usually held from December to May. Call for information and show times.

4 The Dry Tortugas

70 miles W of Key West

Because the Dry Tortugas are only accessible by boat or seaplane, few visitors realize that Florida's Keys don't end at Key West. Ponce de León discovered this far-flung cluster of coral keys in 1513, and named them Las Tortugas (The Turtles) for their abundance of nesting sea turtles. Oceanic charts later carried the preface "dry" to warn mariners that fresh water was unavailable here. The seven keys that make up the Tortugas—Garden, Loggerhead, Bush, East, Middle, Hospital, and Long—are all very small; Loggerhead Key, the largest, is only 25 acres. The primary reason to visit the Dry Tortugas is for birdwatching—the islands are nesting grounds and roosting sites for thousands of tropical and subtropical oceanic birds. There's also a historical fort, good fishing, and terrific snorkeling around shallow reefs.

GETTING THERE

The **Yankee Fleet,** based in Key West (☎ **305/294-7009,** or 800/634-0939), offers day trips from Key West for sightseeing, snorkeling, or both. Cruises leave from the Land's End Marina at Margaret Street on Monday, Wednesday, and Saturday at 7:30am, and breakfast is served on board. The journey takes 3 hours. Once on the island, you can join a guided tour or explore Garden Key on your own. Boats return to Key West by 7pm. Including breakfast, tours cost $75 for adults, $65 for seniors, students, and military personnel, and $45 for children 16 and under. Snorkeling equipment is available for rent and costs $5. Phone for reservations.

EXPLORING THE DRY TORTUGAS

Fort Jefferson, a huge six-sided 19th-century fortress, occupies the entire island of Garden Key and is the primary destination for most visitors. Begun in 1846, the stone fort was built with 8-foot-thick walls and parapets accommodating 450 guns. The invention of the rifled cannon during the 30 years of the fort's construction made masonry fortifications obsolete, so the building was never completed. For 10 years, from 1863 to 1873, Fort Jefferson served as a prison, a kind of "Alcatraz East." Among its prisoners were four of the "Lincoln Conspirators," including Samuel A. Mudd, the doctor who set the broken leg of fugitive assassin John Wilkes Booth. In 1935 Fort Jefferson became a National Monument administered by the National Park Service.

BIRDWATCHING   Birding is the Dry Tortugas' main attraction—more than 100 species can be spotted here. The islands are located in the middle of the migration flyway between North and South America, and serve as an important rest stop. The birding season peaks from mid-March to mid-April, when thousands of birds, including thrushes, orioles, and swallows, show up. In season, a continuous procession of migrant birds fly over or rest at the islands. About 10,000 terns nest here each spring, and many other species from the West Indies can be found here year round.

FISHING   Snapper, tarpon, grouper, and other fish are common, and fishing is popular. A saltwater-fishing permit is mandatory, and costs $7 for 3 days and $17 for 7 days. No bait or boating services are available in the Tortugas, but there are day docks on Garden Key as well as a cleaning table. The waters are roughest during the winter, but the fishing is excellent year round.

SNORKELING & DIVING   The warm, clear, and shallow waters of the Dry Tortugas combine to produce optimum conditions for snorkeling and scuba diving. Four endangered species of sea turtles—the green, leatherback, Atlantic ridley, and hawksbill—can be found here, along with myriad marine life. The region just outside the sea wall of Garden Key's Fort Jefferson is excellent for underwater touring; an abundant variety of fish, corals, and more live in just 3 or 4 feet of water.

CAMPING

A more isolated spot can't be found anywhere else in Florida. The abundance of birds doesn't make it quiet, but camping here—literally a stone's throw from the water—is as picturesque as it gets. Campers are allowed to pitch tents only on **Garden Key.** Picnic tables, cooking grills, and toilets are provided, but all supplies must be packed in and out. Sites are free, and are available on a first-come, first-served basis.

8 The National Parks of South Florida

by Victoria Pesce Elliott

This year, 1997, marks the 50th birthday of the Everglades' official park status. As is fitting for this quiet, undercelebrated region, there hasn't been much fanfare or celebration—just tacit acknowledgement by the state's more environmentally minded residents of the wonders of this huge expanse that contributes to the ecological balance of the entire state. President Bill Clinton and Vice President Al Gore have pushed for a major cleanup initiative, to be financed by a tax on local sugar farmers and manufacturers.

Described poetically as the "river of grass" by conservationist Marjory Stoneman Douglas, the Everglades is actually a shallow, 40-mile-wide, slow-moving river. Most folks viewed it as a worthless swamp until Ms. Douglas called attention to it with her moving and insightful book, *The Everglades: River of Grass*, published in 1947. Rarely more than knee-deep, the water is the life-blood of this wilderness. Variations in land elevation of just a few feet make the difference between a sawgrass marsh and a hardwood key, and subtle shifts in water level dictate the life cycle of plants and animals.

In 1947, when 1.5 million acres—less than 20% of Everglades wilderness—were established as Everglades National Park, few lawmakers understood how neighboring ecosystems relate to each other: You can't just chop off a chunk of a much larger wilderness and expect to preserve it—the land is vitally intertwined with its surroundings. With the additions of the adjacent 181,000-acre Biscayne National Park and 716,000-acre Big Cypress National Preserve, some of those past wrongs have been righted, but this exotic and uniquely beautiful area has suffered from human shortsightedness.

The Everglades lies on a delta, at the butt-end of every environmental insult that occurs upstream. Yet it remains one of the few places left where you can see dozens of endangered species in their natural habitat, including the swallowtail butterfly, American crocodile, leatherback turtle, southern bald eagle, West Indian manatee, and Florida panther. The farther south or west you venture, the closer you'll come to the original, untouched wetlands. For now, visitors can still drive into Everglades and Biscayne national parks and Big Cypress National Preserve and easily see alligators, egrets, herons, deer, and a dozen varieties of orchids.

At first glance, the Everglades seems like a flat, unmoving expanse of water covered by tall stalks of sawgrass, but this fragile ecosystem has hidden wonders to be discovered. It takes a gallon of water 1 month to move through the park. A similar pace is recommended to visitors who want to fully experience its grandeur. Take your time on the trails and the hypnotic beauty begins to unfold. Follow the rustling of a bush and you might see a small green tree frog or a tiny brown anole lizard with its bright-red, spotted throat. Crane your head around a bend and discover a delicate, brightly painted mule-ear orchid.

1 Everglades National Park

35 miles SW of Miami

In the 1800s, before the southern Everglades was designated a national park, the only inhabited piece of this wilderness was a quiet fishing village called Flamingo. Accessible only by boat and leveled every few years by hurricanes, the mosquito-infested town never grew very popular. When the 38-mile road from Florida City was completed in 1922, many of those who lived here fled to someplace either more or less remote. Today Flamingo is the center of park activities and the park's primary jumping-off point for backcountry camping and exploration. The town is now home to Park Service and concession employees and their families.

Everglades National Park's northern Shark Valley entrance offers a scenic, though more superficial, survey of the wetlands. An excellent tram tour takes visitors deep into the park along a trail that's also terrific for biking. Approaching from this angle is recommended if you're crossing the state on a tight time schedule, or are just looking for a brief and easy introduction to the Everglades.

There are few hiking trails from Everglades City, the "backdoor" to Everglades National Park. This entrance provides access to a maze of islands and swamps that can be reached only by boat and is home to a number of recommendable boat tours of the area.

ESSENTIALS

GETTING THERE & ACCESS POINTS   The Everglades National Park has three entrances.

The park's **main entrance,** on the park's east side, is located 10 miles southwest of Florida City. From Miami, take U.S. 1 south about 35 miles, and turn right (west) onto Fla. 9336 to the park. This entrance is most popular and for good reason. From here, a single 38-mile road winds its way southwest, allowing visitors greatest access to the park.

The **Shark Valley entrance,** on the park's north side, is located on Tamiami Trail (U.S. 41), about 35 miles west of downtown Miami. It's known for its 15-mile trail loop that's used for an excellent interpretive tram tour, bicycling, and walking. The trail leads to a tall observation tower (see "Exploring the Park," below, for complete information).

The **Everglades City entrance,** on the northwest side of the park, is located 80 miles west of downtown Miami, or 36 miles southeast of Naples. To reach Everglades City from Naples, take I-75 or U.S. 41 east to Fla. 29 south to the park entrance. The entrance area is riddled with canoe trails and is the best approach for those wishing to explore the park by boat.

VISITOR INFORMATION   General inquiries and specific questions should be directed to **Everglades National Park Headquarters,** 40001 Fla. 9336, Homestead, FL 33034 (☎ **305/242-7700**). Ask for a copy of *Parks and Preserves,* a free newspaper that's filled with up-to-date information on goings-on in the Everglades.

The **Flamingo Lodge, Marina and Outpost Resort,** in Flamingo (☎ **941/695-3101,** or 800/600-3813), is the one-stop clearinghouse for in-park accommodations, equipment rentals, and tours.

The **Main Visitor Center,** located at the park's main entrance, has educational displays, free brochures outlining trails and activities, and information on tours and boat rentals. A small shop here sells postcards, film, insect repellent, unusual gift items, and the best selection of books about the Everglades.

The **Royal Palm Visitor Center,** a small nature museum located 3 miles past the park's main entrance, is a smaller information center located at the head of popular Anhinga and Gumbo-Limbo trails.

The **Shark Valley Information Center,** at the park's northern entrance, and the **Everglades City Gulf Coast Ranger Station,** at the park's western entrance, are also staffed by knowledgeable rangers who provide brochures and personal insight into the goings-on in the park.

The **Everglades City Area Chamber of Commerce,** P.O. Box 130, Everglades City, FL 33929 (☎ **941/695-3941**), provides information on tours and outfitters operating near the park's northwestern entrance. The chamber staffs an office at the intersection of U.S. 41 and Fla. 29.

The Shark Valley and Everglades City entrances are staffed daily from 8am to 5pm and the main entrance's park headquarters building is open 24 hours.

ENTRANCE FEES, PERMITS & REGULATIONS   Permits and passes are sold at each of the park's entrances and visitor centers.

A 7-day permit for Everglades National Park costs $5 per vehicle at the main entrance and Everglades City entrance, and $3 per vehicle at the Shark Valley entrance. Pedestrians and cyclists are charged $3 per person at the main entrance and Everglades City entrance, and $2 per person at the Shark Valley entrance.

An **Everglades Park Pass,** valid for a year's worth of unlimited entrances, is available for $15. U.S. citizens may purchase a 12-month **Golden Eagle Passport** for $25, which is valid for entrance into any U.S. national park. U.S. citizens aged 62 and older pay only $10 for a **National Park Passport** that's valid for life. A **Golden Access Passport** is available free to U.S. citizens with disabilities.

Campers can pick up free permits, which are required, at either the Flamingo or Everglades City ranger station. Backcountry campers must register at the ranger station in either Flamingo or Everglades City, and are allowed to use only designated campsites, which are plentiful and well marked on visitor maps.

Those who want to fish must obtain a standard State of Florida fishing license. These are not available in the park, but can be obtained at any tackle shop or sporting-goods store nearby. A 7-day freshwater license costs $16. Those expecting to cast their lines in Florida Bay, the Gulf of Mexico, or other surrounding waters must purchase a separate saltwater license: 3-day licenses cost $7; 7-day licenses, $17.

Firearms are not allowed anywhere in the park, and open fires are prohibited.

SEASONS   There are two distinct seasons in the Everglades: high season and mosquito season. High season is also dry season, and lasts approximately from December to May. This is the best time to visit, as low water levels attract the largest variety of wading birds and their predators. As the dry season wanes, wildlife follows the receding water, and by the end of May most of the big animals are clustered in the southernmost end of the Glades.

During wet season, which lasts from June to November, migratory birds are absent, wildlife is harder to spot, and mosquitoes will deter even the most determined visitor. Even in the wet season, however, the river of grass rarely gets very deep, most

Everglades National Park

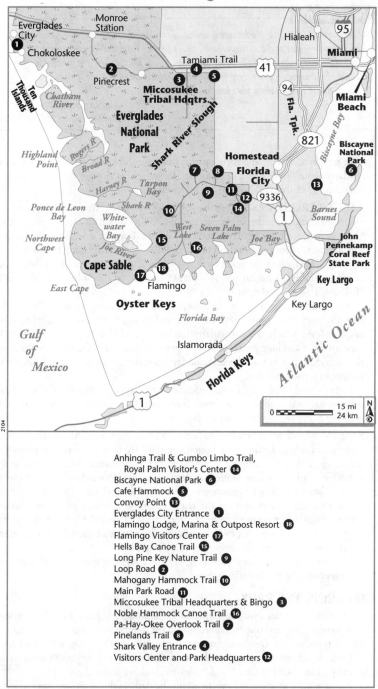

Anhinga Trail & Gumbo Limbo Trail,
 Royal Palm Visitor's Center ⑭
Biscayne National Park ⑥
Cafe Hammock ⑤
Convoy Point ⑬
Everglades City Entrance ①
Flamingo Lodge, Marina & Outpost Resort ⑱
Flamingo Visitors Center ⑰
Hells Bay Canoe Trail ⑮
Long Pine Key Nature Trail ⑨
Loop Road ②
Mahogany Hammock Trail ⑩
Main Park Road ⑪
Miccosukee Tribal Headquarters & Bingo ③
Noble Hammock Canoe Trail ⑯
Pa-Hay-Okee Overlook Trail ⑦
Pinelands Trail ⑧
Shark Valley Entrance ④
Visitors Center and Park Headquarters ⑫

Impressions

There are no other Everglades in the world. They are, they have always been, one of the unique regions of the earth, remote, never wholly known. Nothing anywhere else is like them: their vast glittering openness, wider than the enormous visible round of the horizon, the racing free saltness and sweetness of their massive winds, under the dazzling blue heights of space.

—Marjory Stoneman Douglas,
The Everglades: River of Grass, 1947

trails remain accessible, and there's plenty to see for those who avail themselves of it.

Many establishments and operators in the area either close or curtail offerings in the summer, so always call ahead to check schedules.

RANGER PROGRAMS   More than 50 ranger programs, free with admission, are offered each month and give visitors an opportunity to gain an expert's perspective. Some programs occur regularly, such as **Glade Glimpses,** a walking tour during which rangers point out flora and fauna and discuss issues affecting the Everglades' survival. These tours are scheduled at 10:15am, noon, and 3:30pm daily. The **Anhinga Ambles,** a similar program that takes place on the Anhinga Trail, start at 10:30am, 1:30pm, and 4pm.

A more interesting program, the **Slough Slog,** is offered only occasionally. On this journey, participants wade into the park and through the muck, stopping at an alligator hole, which is a particularly interesting and vital ecosystem unto itself. Lace-up shoes and long pants (preferably ones you don't care about) are required on this walking trip. On Saturday and Sunday, rangers can choose programs they wish to offer in some time slots.

Rangers tend to be helpful, well informed, and happy to answer questions. Since times, programs, and locations vary from month to month, check a schedule, available at any of the visitor centers (see above).

SAFETY   Accidents are more common to the area than theft. Always let someone know your itinerary before you set out on an extended hike. It's mandatory that you file an itinerary when camping overnight in the backcountry. When on the water, watch for weather changes; severe thunderstorms and high winds often develop very rapidly. Swimming is not recommended because of the presence of alligators, sharks, and barracudas. Watch out for the region's four indigenous poisonous snakes: diamondback and pygmy rattlesnakes; coral snakes (identifiable by their colorful rings); and water moccasins (which swim on the surface of the water). And bring insect repellent to ward off mosquitoes and biting flies.

First-aid is available from park rangers. The nearest hospital is in Homestead, 10 miles from the park's main entrance.

EXPLORING THE PARK

Shark Valley provides a fine introduction to the wonder of the Everglades, but visitors shouldn't expect to spend more than a few hours there. Bicycling or taking a guided tram tour can be a satisfying experience, but don't fully capture the wonders of the park. Likewise, boaters who choose to explore via the Everglades City entrance to the park are likely to see a lot of mangroves and not much else.

If you want a more varied experience in the park, seeing a greater array of plant and animal life, make sure you venture into the park through the main entrance, and dedicate at least a day to exploring from here.

Stop first along the **Anhinga and Gumbo-Limbo trails,** which start right next to one another 3 miles from the park's main entrance. These trails provide a thorough introduction to the flora and fauna that inhabit the Everglades, and are highly recommended to first-time visitors. Arrive early to spot the widest selection of exotic birds; many of them travel deeper into the park during daylight hours. And take your time: At least an hour is recommended. If you treat the trails as pathways to get through quickly, rather than destinations to experience and savor slowly, you'll miss out on the still beauty and hidden treasures that await you. (See below for details.)

Those who love to mountain-bike, and who prefer solitude, might check out the infrequently traveled Old Ingraham Highway. This dirt road delves deeper into the Glades and isn't used by most visitors. Since this pathway is sometimes closed, check at the visitor center when you arrive.

If you want to get close to nature, a few hours in a canoe along any of the trails allows paddlers the chance to sense the park's fluid motion, and to become a part of the ecosphere. Visitors who choose this option end up feeling more like explorers than merely observers. (See "Sports & Activities," below.)

The **Coastal Prairie Trail** runs 15 miles beyond the end of the 38-mile-long Main Park Road. Hiking boots and a reasonable degree of fitness are required. The payoff? A land teeming with wildlife, one that hasn't been disturbed by ecological purges that afflicted other parts of the Everglades, and a sense that you're traveling back in time to discover unexplored and unsullied lands.

No matter which option you choose (and there are many), I strongly recommend staying for the 7pm evening program at the Long Pine Key Amphitheatre. This talk by one of the park's rangers, along with the accompanying slide show, gives a detailed overview of the park's history, natural resources, wildlife, and threats to its survival.

HIKING TRAILS ALONG THE MAIN PARK ROAD

Most of the Everglades' hiking trails are located along a single main road that winds its way for about 38 miles from the Main Visitor Center at the park's main entrance to Flamingo, in the southwest corner of the state. They're listed geographically below:

ANHINGA TRAIL (3 miles from the main entrance): The half-mile-long Anhinga Trail is named for a large black fishing bird that's a permanent resident in these parts. The birds are so used to humans that they often nest within plain view of the trail.

The first short stretch of the Anhinga Trail is paved, as it was once part of the Ingraham Highway, the first Homestead-to-Flamingo road, built in 1922. The rest of the trail is an elevated wooden boardwalk that courses through sawgrass marsh and follows a canal built along the edge of the freshwater Taylor Slough (pronounced "slew"). Because the slough and adjacent canal are slightly deeper than the surrounding marshlands, there's more water and wildlife here than in most parts of the Everglades, especially during dry season. Alligators, turtles, river otters, herons, egrets, and other animals abound, making this one of the best trails for spotting wildlife. Many of the fish you see here are not native to Florida, but were introduced— usually accidentally—over the last century. The most common of these "exotic" species include oscar (from South America), poke killifish (from Central America), and blue tilapin (from Africa). The white flowers popping up from the sawgrass are called swamp lilies. You can reach out and touch them, but beware: True to its name, the tall sawgrass blades can cut like a knife.

Because the trail is largely unprotected by tall trees, mosquitoes are less a problem here than in many other parts of the Glades. The trailhead begins just behind the Royal Palm Visitor Center.

GUMBO-LIMBO TRAIL (3 miles from the main entrance): The Gumbo-Limbo Trail, which begins right next to the Anhinga Trail, is named for the gumbo-limbo tree, a subtropical hardwood that's sometimes called the "tourist tree" because it continuously sheds its bronze bark—much like a tourist who peels after a few days in the hot Florida sun. Contrary to its monotonously flat appearance, the Everglades actually contains subtle topographic changes—elevations of just a few feet create entirely different environments. The Gumbo-Limbo Trail is on one of these elevated "hammocks," drier ground that provides firmer footing for an abundant variety of trees, including the gumbo limbo, poison wood, and the strangler fig. Sumac, red maple, and live oak—varieties that are more closely associated with temperate climates—can also be found here. Under the shade of the trees' dense canopy is a lushly vegetated protected environment that has a distinctive jungle feel.

The cool Gumbo-Limbo Trail is dense with insects (including mosquitos) and small animals like lizards, tree snails, frogs, and songbirds. Orchids, ferns, and bromeliads abound. Look up and you'll see many species of "air plants" that use host trees for support. Most air plants are not parasitic, but obtain moisture and nourishment from the air. Their lofty positions are more favorable to growth than the shady forest floor.

LONG PINE KEY (5 miles from the main entrance): Twisting through a variety of habitats, Long Pine Key's 7-mile nature trail is one of the Everglades' longest. The wide, unpaved, hard-packed dirt road runs west, roughly parallel to the main park road. The majority of the route is characterized by a large stand of slash pines, a habitat of tall, skinny trees that's maintained by periodic burns managed by the National Park Service. The pines intermingle with satinleaf, smaller trees distinguishable by leaves that are dark green on top and satiny bronze underneath; when the wind blows, the trees appear to shimmer in the sun. A few times the trees thin out to reveal open marshes. Pine Glades Lake, at the trail's end, is a popular fishing spot, despite posted warnings about mercury contamination.

PINELANDS TRAIL (6 miles from the main entrance): Pineland's three-quarter-mile loop through slash pine is good for hikers who want a quick look at this typical Everglades habitat without committing to a long trek. This trail also reveals plenty of oolitic limestone, the bedrock that underlies most of South Florida. Deposited over five million years ago, when Florida was covered by shallow sea, the rock is characterized by jagged outcroppings, as well as smooth hollows, called "solution holes." Varying in size from almost microscopic to several feet across, these solution holes are created by rainwater mixed with acidic plant matter. During the dry season some of the larger holes become important water reservoirs, attracting quail, panther, deer, and other large animals.

The low, shrub-size palms growing under the pines are saw palmettos. These lush trees, along with wild tamarind, beauty berry, tetrazygia, and others, are marked along the trail with interpretive signs.

PA-HAY-OKEE TRAIL (11 miles from the main entrance): Short and sweet, this extremely accessible trail is perfect for day-trippers. Only a quarter of a mile long, the entire trail is actually a wooden boardwalk built over a sawgrass prairie that the Seminoles called *pa-ha-okee,* or grassy waters. Along the boardwalk, stop to read the interpretive signs embedded in the railings, and look into the surrounding water for small white apple snails, the exclusive food of the endangered snail kite bird. Don't miss the opportunity to climb the **observation tower** at the end of the boardwalk. The panoramic view of undulating grass and seemingly endless vistas gives the impression of a semi-aquatic Serengeti. Flocks of tropical and semitropical birds traverse the landscape, alligators and fish stir the surface of the water, small grottos of trees thrust up from the sea of grass marking higher ground, and the vastness of the hidden world you've entered seems unparalleled.

The Pa-hay-okee Trail is located about 1 1/2 miles past Rock Reef Pass, a 3-foot-high limestone ridge that forms the highest elevation in the park. More hospitable to vegetation than lower-lying areas, Rock Reef Pass is identifiable from the air by its thin line of large trees and shrubs.

MAHOGANY HAMMOCK TRAIL (18 miles from the main entrance): Another short, elevated boardwalk, the half-mile Mahogany Hammock Trail winds its way through a subtropical hardwood forest that includes the largest living mahogany tree in the United States. Almost logged to extinction, mahogany trees were once common throughout the Everglades. The lanky, fan-shaped palms to your right, at the head of this trail, are threatened paurotis palms. Native to South Florida, these trees thrive in brackish marshes exclusively.

The entire trail is incredibly lush and junglelike, and the dense vegetation supports an enormous variety of wildlife. Take your time searching out frogs, insects, snails, and small birds. Patience might also reward you with a sighting (or hearing) of the barred owl, a normally nocturnal predator that makes this hammock its home. The pine trees across the park's Main Road from Mahogany Hammock are a roost for bald eagles. They're most likely to be spotted here during winter evenings.

WEST LAKE TRAIL (29 miles from the main entrance): West Lake's quarter-mile-long elevated boardwalk cuts through a dense mangrove swamp before jutting out into large, brackish West Lake. The mangroves' complex, branchlike root system, often visible above the waterline, is the nursery ground for a majority of the Glades' marine animals. In late winter hundreds of ducks can be seen here, along with alligators and several species of wading birds. There are plenty of interpretive signs along the route explaining important aspects of the mangrove ecosystem.

SPORTS & ACTIVITIES

BIKING   The relatively flat 38-mile paved **Main Park Road** is excellent for bicycling, as are many park trails, including **Long Pine Key.** Cyclers should expect to spend 2 to 3 hours along the path.

If the park isn't flooded from excess rain (which it has been for several months in recent years), **Shark Valley** in Everglades National Park is South Florida's most scenic bicycle trail. Many locals haul their bikes out to the Glades for a relaxing day of wilderness trail riding. You can ride the 17-mile loop with no other traffic in sight. Instead, you'll share the paved flat road only with other bikers and a menagerie of wildlife. Don't be surprised to see a gator lounging in the sun, a deer munching on some grass, or a picnicker eating a sandwich along the mangrove shore. Otters, turtles, alligators, and snakes are common companions in the Shark Valley area—although I don't think a single shark has been sighted lately.

You can rent bikes from the **Flamingo Lodge, Marina and Outpost Resort** (see "Where to Stay," below) for $16 per 24 hours, $13 per full day, $7.75 per half day (any 4-hour period), and $2.75 per hour. Bicycles are also available from **Shark Valley Tram Tours,** at the park's Shark Valley entrance (☎ 305/221-8455), for $3.25 per hour; rentals can be picked up beginning at 8:30am and must be returned by 4pm. In Everglades City, the **Ivey House Bed & Breakfast,** 107 Camellia St., a block behind the Circle K store (☎ 941/695-3299), rents bikes from November to May for $3 per hour or $15 per day; it's open daily from 8:30am to 4:30pm.

If you'd like to try an audio guided tour, call **Follow the Yellow Brick Road,** a bike-tour company run by Gary's Megacycles, at 1260 Washington Ave., Miami Beach (☎ **305/534-3306**). For $25, a representative will transport you and a rental bike from anywhere from Miami Beach to Hollywood. Along with a high-tech Coloi bike, you'll get an audiotaped guide in any of four languages, a map, a helmet, and all the accoutrements. It's open from 10am to 7pm and accepts reservations 24 hours a day; you can pay with MasterCard or Visa.

BIRDING   More than 350 species of birds make their homes in the Everglades. Tropical birds from the Caribbean and temperate species from North America can be found here, along with exotics that have blown in from more distant regions. **Eco Pond and Mrazek Pond,** located near Flamingo, are two of the best places for birding, especially in early morning or late afternoon in the dry winter months. Pick up a free birding checklist from a visitor center (see "Essentials," above), and ask a park ranger what's been spotted in recent days.

BOATING   Motorboating around the Everglades seems like a great way to see plants and animals in remote habitats. However, environmentalists are taking stock of the damage motorboats inflict on the delicate ecosystem. If you choose to motor, remember that most of the areas near land are "no wake" zones, and for the protection of nesting birds, landing is prohibited on most of the little mangrove islands. There's a long list of restrictions and restricted areas, so get a copy of the park's boating rules from National Park Headquarters before setting out (see "Essentials," above).

Several boat ramps are located throughout the park, but the Everglades' only marina—accommodating about 50 boats with electricity and water hookups—is the **Flamingo Lodge, Marina and Outpost Resort,** located in Flamingo. The well-marked channel to Flamingo is accessible to boats with a maximum 4-foot draft and is open year round. Reservations can be made through park headquarters (see "Essentials," above). Skiffs with 15-horsepower motors are available for rent. These low-power boats cost $65 per day, $47 per half day (any 5-hour period), and $15 per hour. A $50 deposit is required.

Motorboats are also available for rent on the west side of the Everglades at **Chokoloskee Island Park,** on Chokoloskee Island, 3 miles south of Everglades City (☎ **941/695-2414**). The cost is $40 for a half day and $60 for a full day. Rentals are available Monday to Friday from 7am to 5pm and on Saturday and Sunday from 6am to 5pm.

CANOEING   The most intimate view of the Everglades comes from the humble perspective of a simple low boat. From a canoe, you'll get a closer look into the park's shallow estuaries where water birds, sea turtles, and endangered manatees make their homes.

Everglades National Park's longest "trails" are designed for boat and canoe travel, and many are marked as clearly as walking trails. The **Noble Hammock Trail,** a 2-mile loop, takes 1 to 2 hours, and is recommended for beginning canoers. The **Hell's Bay Trail,** a 3- to 6-mile course for hardier paddlers, takes 2 to 6 hours, depending on how far you choose to go. Park rangers can recommend other trails that best suit your abilities, time limitations, and interests.

Canoes can be rented at the **Flamingo Lodge, Marina and Outpost Resort** (see "Where to Stay," below) for $25 per day, $20 per half day (any 4-hour period), and $7 per hour. A deposit is required. Skiffs, kayaks, and tandem kayaks are also available. The concessionaire will shuttle your party to the trailhead of your choice and pick you up afterward. Rental facilities are open daily from 6am to 8pm.

Canoes are also available at Everglades City, near the Park Ranger Station at the Everglades' western entrance, from **North American Canoe Tours,** 107 Camelia St., Everglades City (☎ **941/695-4666** Nov–Apr or 860/739-0791 May–Oct; fax 941/ 695-4155 Nov–Apr). The 17-foot aluminum canoes can be rented with or without camping equipment, a personal guide, or fully outfitted tour. Canoes cost $20 per day. Canoes with camping supplies cost $50 per person per day.

FISHING   Open water comprises about one-third of Everglades National Park. Freshwater fishing is popular in brackish Nine-Mile Pond (25 miles from the main entrance) and other spots along the Main Park Road, but because of the high mercury levels found in the Everglades, freshwater anglers are warned not to eat their catches. Before casting, check in at a visitor center, as many of the park's lakes are preserved for observation only. Freshwater fishing licenses are required and cost $16 for 7 days. They're not sold in the park, but you can purchase one from a tackle shop or sporting-goods store.

Separate saltwater licenses are sold at the Flamingo Lodge, Marina and Outpost Resort (see "Where to Stay," below), and are required for fishing in Florida Bay, the Gulf of Mexico, and the sounds that surround the park. Licenses for nonresidents cost $7 for 3 days and $17 for 7 days. Snapper and sea trout are plentiful and charter boats and guides are available for hire at Flamingo. Phone for information and reservations.

ORGANIZED TOURS

AIRBOAT TOURS   Although airboats are not allowed in the park proper, a number of operators on the western edge of the Everglades offer rides through the surrounding waterways. See Section 2 of this chapter, on Everglades City, for more information.

MOTORBOAT TOURS   Both Florida Bay and backcountry tours are offered at the **Flamingo Lodge, Marina and Outpost Resort** (see "Where to Stay," below). Both are available in 2- and 4-hour versions that cost $12 and $32 per person, respectively. Florida Bay tours cruise nearby estuaries and sandbars, while six-passenger backcountry boats visit smaller sloughs. Tours depart throughout the day, and reservations are recommended.

Boat tours from Everglades City are offered by **Everglades National Park Boat Tours** (☎ **941/695-2591,** or 800/445-7724 in Florida). The Mangrove Wilderness Tour explores the Glades' inland rivers and creeks at high tide. White ibis, cuckoos, egrets, herons, and other animals can often be seen through the thick mangroves. The Ten Thousand Islands Cruise navigates through the mangrove estuaries of the Gulf Coast. The endangered manatee can often be spotted, along with dozens of species of birds, including the southern bald eagle. Tours depart daily, every half hour from 9am to 5pm (less frequently off-season), last about 90 minutes, and cost $11 for adults, $5.50 for children. Reservations are not accepted. Tours depart from the Park Docks, on Chokoloskee Causeway (Fla. 29), half a mile south of the traffic circle by the ranger station.

CANOE TOURS   David Harraden and sons Jason and Jeremy of **North American Canoe Tours** (☎ **941/695-4666** Nov–Apr or 860/739-0791 May–Oct; fax 941/695-4155 Nov–Apr) have been leading canoe expeditions into the Everglades every winter since 1978, offering trips ranging from a day to a week. The 1-day trips cost $40 per person. They operate out of Everglades City, but also provide van shuttle service to and from Flamingo. The Harradens operate from November to April.

TRAM TOURS   At the park's Shark Valley entrance, open-air tram buses take visitors on 2-hour naturalist-led tours that delve 7½ miles into the wilderness. At the trail's midsection, passengers can disembark and climb a 65-foot observation tower that offers good views of the Glades. The tour offers visitors considerable views that include plenty of wildlife and endless acres of sawgrass. Tours run from November to April only, daily from 9am to 4pm, and are sometimes stalled by flooding or particularly heavy mosquito infestation. Reservations are recommended from December to March. The cost is $7.75 for adults, $7 for seniors, and $4 for children. For further information, contact the Flamingo Lodge, Marina and Outpost Resort (see "Where to Stay," below).

WHERE TO STAY

In addition to the choices below, the town of Everglades City at the western edge of the park has several lodging options. See Section 2 of this chapter for more information.

IN FLAMINGO & ENVIRONS

Doubles for Less than $80

Flamingo Lodge, Marina and Outpost Resort. 1 Flamingo Lodge Hwy., Flamingo, FL 33034. ☎ **941/695-3101** or 800/600-3813. Fax 941/695-3921. 103 rms, 24 cottages. A/C TV TEL. Apr and Nov–Dec 14, $74 double; $99 cottage; $110 suite. Dec 15–Mar, $87 double; $125 cottage; $130 suite. May–Oct, $65 double; $79 cottage; $85 suite. Rates for cottages and suites are for up to four people. Additional person $10 extra; children 11 and under stay free in parents' room. AE, DC, DISC, MC, V.

The Flamingo Lodge is the only option actually located within the boundaries of Everglades National Park. An attractive and spacious motel, the air-conditioned lodge is situated right in the center of the action. Nothing's fancy, but there's a "fishing camp" feel and a very friendly atmosphere. The rooms are relatively simple and clean and overlook Florida Bay; each has two double beds and a private bathroom. The cottages, which come with small kitchens equipped with dishes and flatware, are larger, more private, and somewhat romantic.

Facilities include a restaurant and bar, freshwater swimming pool, gift shop, and coin-op laundry (available from 8am to 10pm). Binoculars can be rented at the front desk, which is open daily from 6am to 11pm, and fishing poles and ice chests are available at the marina. The hotel is open year round and reservations are accepted daily from 8am to 5pm.

IN HOMESTEAD & FLORIDA CITY

Homestead and Florida City, two adjacent towns that were almost blown off the map by Hurricane Andrew, are located about 10 miles from the park's main entrance, along U.S. 1, 35 miles south of Miami.

Doubles for Less than $80

Best Western Gateway to the Keys. 1 Strano Blvd. (U.S. 1), Florida City, FL 33034. ☎ **305/246-5100** or 800/528-1234. Fax 305/242-0056. 90 rms, 24 suites. A/C TV TEL. Dec–Apr, $79 double; from $99 suite. May–Nov, $65 double; from $85 suite. AE, DC, DISC, MC, V.

Opened in late 1994, this two-story, pink-and-white Best Western offers contemporary style and comfort. Each identical room has new beds with bright, tropical bedspreads and oversize picture windows. The business-oriented hotel is well priced and well maintained, and is the best choice in the area. There's a swimming pool and a spa.

SHARK VALLEY

Doubles for Less than $60

Everglades Tower Inn. SR Box E 4910, Ochopee, FL 33943. ☎ **305/559-7779.** Fax 305/220-5814. 20 rms. A/C TV. Dec 20–Jan 15, $55 double. Jan 16–Apr and Oct–Dec 19, $44 double. May–Sept, $34 double. MC, V.

Run by the indigenous Miccosukee tribe, this inn is a simple and basic motel located about 1 mile west of the Everglades' Shark Valley entrance. All rooms have two double beds and private baths, but there are no telephones, no pool, no frills.

CAMPING

You can camp overnight almost anywhere you want in the Everglades backcountry, but permits are required (they're free) and you must register with your itinerary. The paperwork must be done in person at either the Flamingo or the Everglades City ranger station. If you're heading into the backcountry, you may use only designated campsites, which are plentiful and well marked on visitor maps. Open fires are prohibited.

Many backcountry sites are chickees—covered wooden platforms on stilts that are accessible only by canoe. Ground sites are located along interior bays and rivers, and beach camping is also popular. In summer, especially, mosquito repellent is required gear.

Car camping is available at the Flamingo and Long Pine Key campgrounds, where there are more than 300 campsites designed for tents and RVs. They have level parking pads, tables, and charcoal grills. There are no electrical hook-ups, and showers are cold water. Permits cost $4 to $8 per site from September to May, and are free the rest of the year. Private ground fires are not permitted, but supervised campfire programs are conducted during the winter months.

RENTING A HOUSEBOAT

Houseboat rentals are one of the park's best-kept secrets. Available through the **Flamingo Lodge, Marina and Outpost Resort** (☎ **941/695-3101** or 800/ 600-3813), motorized houseboats make it possible to explore some of the park's more remote regions without having to worry about being back by nightfall. You can choose from two different types of houseboats. The first, a 40-foot pontoon boat, sleeps six to eight people in a single large room that's separated by a central head (bathroom) and shower. There's a small galley (kitchen) that contains a stove, oven, and charcoal grill. It rents for $254 per night, with a 2-night minimum.

The newer, sleeker Gibson fiberglass boats sleep six and have a head and shower, air-conditioning, and an electric stove. There's also a full rooftop sundeck. These rent for $280 per night, also with a 2-night minimum.

Boating experience is helpful, but not mandatory, as the boats cruise up to only 6 m.p.h. and are surprisingly easy to use. Reservations should be made very far in advance; call the Flamingo Lodge.

WHERE TO EAT

For dining options at the western edge of the park, see Section 2 of this chapter.

HOMESTEAD & FLORIDA CITY

Meals for Less than $10

Potlikker's. 591 Washington Ave. (at NE 6th St., between Krome Ave. and U.S. 1), Homestead. ☎ **305/248-0835.** Reservations accepted. Main courses $6–$12; sandwiches $5–$6. AE, MC, V. Daily 7am–9pm. SOUTHERN AMERICAN.

This is one of the best restaurants in Homestead, but that's not much of a boast. Inside the restaurant's single A-frame dining room are wooden booths with paper placemats, loud light-rock radio, and large windows that are always darkened with closed blinds. The menu, presented on a large board at one end of the room, features hamburgers, fried fish and shrimp baskets, along with barbecued chicken and ribs, chicken pot pie, and lots of local veggies. It's a good feed at popular prices.

Meals for Less than $15

Capri Restaurant. 935 N. Krome Ave., Florida City. ☎ **305/247-1542.** Reservations accepted. Main courses $9–$13. AE, MC, V. Mon–Thurs 11am–10pm, Fri–Sat 11am–11pm. ITALIAN/AMERICAN.

Although the Capri was right in the path of Hurricane Andrew, it survived practically unscathed. It's no wonder—the restaurant occupies a squat, one-story, windowless stone building that looks something like a medieval fort. Inside the dark restaurant is a 1950s-style dining room and cocktail bar that has been an area landmark and meeting place since it opened in 1958.

Richard Accursio, the restaurant's original owner, still oversees the daily preparations of Italian-American standards that include fried calamari, baked stuffed mushrooms, and a variety of pastas. Meat main courses have veal or chicken bases, prepared marsala, scaloppine, cacciatore, or parmigiana style. There's live entertainment during the season.

2 Everglades City

35 miles SW of Miami   *by Bill Goodwin*

Everglades City was the brainchild of advertising magnate Barron Collier, who by 1923 owned Useppa Island and a million other acres of Southwest Florida. Collier promised the state that if Lee County were split into two, he would put up the money to complete the Tamiami Trail (U.S. 41) across the Everglades from Miami to Naples. The state accepted, and the southern half of Lee County became—you guessed it—Collier County.

Collier dredged a channel through the Ten Thousand Islands and created a new island with the spoil, upon which he laid out Everglades City. It was the base from which he built the Tamiami Trail and for a while the seat of his new county. Although it became a popular hunting and fishing destination for the rich and famous, Everglades City never became the metropolis he hoped. In 1947 Everglades National Park took in most of the land and bays around the town.

Everglades City lies in the Ten Thousand Islands area, and the Wilderness Waterway twists and turns 99 miles from here all the way to Flamingo at the southwestern edge of the Everglades. This makes the town a perfect starting point for canoe or boat explorations of the area.

ESSENTIALS

GETTING THERE   Take I-75 or U.S. 41 east to Fla. 29 and turn south to Everglades City. Fla. 29 runs through town and then over a causeway along beautiful Chokoloskee Bay to Chokoloskee Island, an old Calusa shell mound that's the highest point in the Everglades.

GETTING AROUND   Everglades City is small enough to be seen on foot, and a 4-mile paved **bike path** runs from town across a picturesque causeway to Chokoloskee Island. The **Ivey House Bed & Breakfast,** 107 Camellia St. (☎ **941/695-3299**), rents bikes during the winter months for $3 per hour.

VISITOR INFORMATION   The **Everglades City Area Chamber of Commerce,** P.O. Box 130, Everglades City, FL 33929 (☎ **941/695-3941;** fax 941/695-3919), has a visitors information center at the intersection of U.S. 41 and Fla. 29. See Section 1 on Everglades National Park for information sources in the park.

WHAT TO SEE & DO

The national park's **Gulf Coast Visitor Center,** on Fla. 29 at the south end of Everglades City (☎ **941/695-3311**), has an interpretive center and is the jumping-off point for **National Park Boat Tours.** Sunset cruises offer the best chance to observe the park's multitude of birds, which return to their rookeries at dusk. There also are mangrove tours, depending on the tides.

North American Canoe Tours, based in Everglades City, offers canoe expeditions into the Everglades from November to April. See Section 1 on Everglades National Park for details, and for other boating, fishing, and outdoor activities in the area.

The **E. J. Hamilton Observation Tower,** opposite the visitor center, is not part of the national park, but you can climb it for $1 and see for miles across the islands and sawgrass plains.

Looking exactly as it did in pioneering days, ✪ **Ted Smallwood's Store,** at the south end of Mamie Street on Chokoloskee Island, was established as a trading post in 1906 and operated continuously as a store, post office, and voting place until 1982. Some 90% of the stock still on its shelves was there when it closed. One-hour boat tours leave from the store's dock, where Ed Watson, reputed murderer of the notorious female outlaw Belle Star, was gunned down. The museum is open daily from 10am to 5pm during winter, Friday to Tuesday from 10am to 4pm the rest of the year. Admission is $2.50 for adults, $2 for seniors, and free for children 11 and under. Boat tours cost $15 per person.

Flat-bottom, airplane propeller-driven airboats can take from two people to large groups speeding across the waterways. They operate on privately owned property, since they're not allowed in the national park or other nearby federal preserves.

The most advertised—and touristy—operator is **Wooten's Everglades Adventure,** on U.S. 41 2 miles east of Fla. 29 (☎ **941/695-2781** or 800/282-2781). This large operation has airboat and swamp-buggy rides, an alligator farm, a gift shop, and a snack bar. Buggy and boat rides cost $12.50 each. Admission to the alligator farm is $5 (free for children 6 and under). Combined tickets for both rides and a visit to the farm are $26. Wooten's is open daily from 8:30am to 5pm, including Christmas Day.

In town on Fla. 29, **Jungle Erv's Airboat World** (☎ **941/695-2805** or 800/432-3367) has a large airboat tour charging $12 for adults and $8 for children. Private rides in small boats cost $30 per person. A jungle tour by pontoon boat costs $12. **Eden's Jungle Boat Tours** (☎ **941/695-2800** or 800/543-3367) has a nature tour by large pontoon boat as well as private airboat rides for the same prices.

WHERE TO STAY

Captain's Table Lodge & Villas. 102 E. Broadway (P.O. Box 530), Everglades City, FL 33929. ☎ **941/695-4211** or 800/741-6430. Fax 941/695-2633. 26 rms, 6 suites, 24 villas. A/C TV TEL. Winter, $70–$90 double; $5 for each additional person. Off-season, $55–$70 double. AE, DC, DISC, MC, V.

Located in the heart of town on Fla. 29, this collection of rooms, suites, and villas actually is a condo development, so the units are furnished and decorated in each owner's tastes. The rooms and suites are in a main building, while the villas are built on stilts and have a cottagelike feel to them. A swimming pool sits by canal-like Lake Placid along the property's eastern flank.

Ivey House Bed & Breakfast. 107 Camellia St. (P.O. Box 5038), Everglades City, FL 33929. ☎ **941/695-3299.** Fax 941/695-4155. 10 rms, none with bath; 1 cottage. A/C. $40–$50 double without bath ($60 during the Seafood Festival, with a 2-night minimum); $90 double with bath in the cottage. Rates include continental breakfast. MC, V. Closed May–Oct.

This wooden structure was operated by a Mrs. Ivey as a boarding house for men working on the Tamiami Trail in the 1920s. Today it's run during the winter by canoe specialist David Harraden and clan. A center hallway separates the simple rooms. Guests share separate men's and women's bathrooms. There are two decks and a large living room for relaxation. A cottage next door has two bedrooms with baths, a screen porch, and antiques. Breakfasts and dinners are served in a spacious kitchen at the rear of the main house (dinners cost $10 per person, and outsiders are welcome by reservation). Guests have free use of bicycles, but have to pay to use the coin laundry. They can smoke and drink on the decks, but not in the house.

Rod & Gun Lodge. Riverside Dr., at Broadway (P.O. Box 190), Everglades City, FL 33929. ☎ **941/695-2101.** 17 rms. A/C TV. Winter, $65–$80 double. Off-season, $50 double. No credit cards.

This white clapboard house on the banks of the sleepy Barron River was built as a private residence in 1830, but Barron Collier turned it into a cozy hunting lodge during his Tamiami Trail days in the 1920s. President Herbert Hoover vacationed here after his 1928 election victory, and President Harry S Truman flew in to sign the Everglades National Park into existence in 1947. Other guests have included Richard Nixon, Burt Reynolds, and Mick Jagger. The public rooms are beautifully paneled and hung with tarpon, wild boar, deer antlers, and other trophies. Out by the swimming pool and riverbank, a screened veranda with ceiling fans offers a pleasant place for a libation. If you can do without modern conveniences, the rooms (all with bath) do have 1920s charm. The dining room serves breakfast, lunch, and dinner.

WHERE TO EAT

Everglades City has no gourmet restaurants, but you can get your fill of fresh seafood at several local eateries. Since the town produces about two-thirds of Florida's stone crab catch, all have fresh-off-the-boat claws from October to April.

Despite being in the old Spanish-style railroad depot at Collier Avenue and Broadway, the **Captain's Table Restaurant** (☎ **941/695-2727**) looks like the lower deck of a 16th-century galleon. It offers a wide selection of seafood, with main courses ranging from $11 to $27. It's Everglades City's swankiest eatery, and its bar is one of the town's favorite watering holes. Open daily from 11am to 10pm.

The **Oyster House,** on Fla. 29 opposite the national park visitor center (☎ **941/ 695-2073**), also specializes in seafood. Main courses range from $12 to $17; sandwiches are $4.50 to $9.50. Open daily from 11am to 9pm. A narrow, screened front porch here is a fine place to sip a drink while watching the sunset over the Everglades.

The down-home **Oar House Restaurant,** 305 Collier Ave. (Fla. 29), in town (☎ **941/695-3535**), offers "cooters, legs, and tails" (turtles, frogs' legs, and alligator tails) as specialties. Main courses range from $8 to $16, and sandwiches and seafood baskets run $2 to $8. Open daily from 6am to 9pm.

3 Big Cypress National Preserve

50 miles W of Miami, 22 miles E of Naples

In Big Cypress, northwest of the Florida Everglades, "big" refers not to the size of the trees but to the vastness of the stands. More than half a million acres of parkland were acquired by the National Park Service in 1974, and the Big Cypress National Preserve Addition Act of 1988 is gradually adding 146,000 additional acres. A national preserve has fewer restrictions than a national park, and this preserve was founded only after making the necessary concessions to area landowners.

Localized mining and oil drilling are permitted, along with limited hunting and off-road driving.

The main reason Big Cypress won protected status was to help defend the ecology of Everglades National Park to its south. The preserve is intentionally lean on visitor facilities and contains few marked trails of any kind. As a result, Big Cypress feels plenty big—and remote. A visit here is a true wilderness experience. Have a full tank of gas before entering—there are no gasoline stations or food services in the preserve.

Camping is available throughout the park. It's free, but there are no facilities: no fresh water, no toilets, no picnic tables, no grills.

ESSENTIALS

VISITOR CENTERS & INFORMATION   Contact **Big Cypress National Preserve Headquarters,** P.O. Box 110, Ochopee, FL 33943 (☎ **813/695-4111** or 813/695-2000), for a map and specialized information on the preserve.

On-site information is dispensed at the **Oasis Visitor Center,** at the park's main entrance, on the Tamiami Trail (U.S. 41) in Ochopee, 37 miles west of Florida City and 22 miles east of Naples. Information is also available at the **preserve headquarters,** on Tamiami Trail, about 18 miles west of Oasis. The visitor centers are staffed daily from about 8:30am to 5pm.

Entrance is free to Big Cypress National Preserve.

EXPLORING THE PRESERVE

You're probably better off visiting nearby Everglades National Park (see Section 1 of this chapter), as most of what's available here can be more fully experienced in the

---

Catting Around

The eight green-eyed beauties didn't come from Texas to Florida on vacation. They came here to find a few good men—Florida panther men, to be exact.

I'm talking here about real Florida panthers, which aren't black as in the movies but tan like their close relatives, the southern cougars—or mountain lions, as they're sometimes called up in the Appalachians.

These big cats once roamed throughout the southeastern United States, but reduced habitat and a fear that they preyed on people and livestock pushed the Florida version into the remote swamps of the Everglades. Less than 50 of them remained by the 1980s, and their dwindling numbers were debilitated by sterility and other genetic flaws resulting from inbreeding.

In order to save them from extinction, biologists figured that the Florida felines needed some new blood. If Florida panthers and southern cougars came from the same genetic stock, they argued, the remaining Sunshine State males would find their cougar cousins from Texas to be irresistible come mating season. Bingo, the problem would be solved.

Their proposal was controversial, but the scientists recently got permission to release eight Texas cougars into Big Cypress Swamp. As it worked out, they were right.

When a local boy they dubbed No. 45 met a Texas lass scientifically named TX 101, the attraction was anything but fatal. At last report, the biologists were tracking the smitten couple's pair of rambunctious kittens.

Everglades. The preserve is a sprawling expanse that was designated as a national preserve primarily to help protect the ecosystem of the Everglades. Therefore, there's little to attract tourists.

However, if you want to get a firsthand look, **Turner River Road and Birdon Road,** which are located about 18 miles east of Oasis on U.S. 41, form a U-shaped, 17-mile drive through mostly open grass prairie dotted with slash pine and bald cypress. This graded-dirt drive is ideal for viewing wildflowers in the prairies and along canals. An hour or two is all you'll need.

Cars and off-road vehicles are permitted on many of the preserve's trails. The best is the **Loop Road Scenic Drive,** a 26-mile stretch of narrow road that winds through several different habitats. Along the way, you can often spot deer, otter, wild turkeys, snakes, wading birds, and maybe even a panther. The first part of this single-lane road is paved, but the majority is packed dirt. It's messy, but accessible to two-wheel-drive vehicles. The road loops around the Tamiami Trail (U.S. 41) from Forty Mile Bend (about 15 miles east of Oasis) to Monroe Station (about 5 miles west of Oasis).

The **Florida Trail** is the preserve's main hiking trail, a long trail that stretches northwest (with significant gaps) all the way into the Florida Panhandle. The part of the trail that's inside Big Cypress is about 30 miles long, and runs north from the Oasis Visitor Center. Hikers should be prepared for wet areas ankle- to waist-deep in the rainy season. There are two primitive campsites, but no potable water on the trail.

Heading south, the trail is known as the **Loop Road,** a 7-mile hike that's not a circuit, but leads to unpaved Loop Road. Pick up a free trail map from the visitor center before heading out.

Shallow-draft, fan-powered airboats were invented in the Everglades by frog hunters who were tired of polling through the rushes. The federal government has recently ordered part of Big Cypress National Preserve closed to airboats and is considering extending the ban to the entire preserve. But airboating is big business, especially for the Native American Miccosukees, who operate regularly scheduled **airboat rides** from their Indian Village (☎ **305/223-8380**) on Tamiami Trail (U.S. 41), about 20 miles east of the Oasis Visitor Center. Here you can take a half-hour, high-speed tour through the reservation's rushes. Rides are offered daily from 9am to 5pm, and cost just $7.

4 Biscayne National Park

35 miles S of Miami

Many people who arrive at Biscayne National Park's main entrance at Convoy Point take one look around and exclaim "Are we there?" You see, the park is very large—181,500 acres to be exact—but some visitors don't realize that 95% of it is underwater. In 1968 President Lyndon Johnson signed a bill to conserve the barrier islands off South Florida's east coast as a national monument, a protected status that's a rung below national park. After being twice enlarged, once in 1974 and again in 1980, the waters surrounding the northernmost coral reef in North America became a full-fledged national park.

There's not much for landlubbers here. The park's small mainland mangrove shoreline and 44 islands are best explored by boat. Its extensive reef system is extremely popular with divers and snorklers. The concessionaire at Convoy Point rents canoes, runs dive trips, and offers popular glass-bottom-boat tours.

Elliott Key, one of the park's 44 little mangrove-fringed islands, contains a visitor center, hiking trails, and a campground. Located about 9 miles from Convoy Point, Elliott Key is accessible only by boat.

ESSENTIALS

GETTING THERE & ACCESS POINTS   The park's mainland entrance is **Convoy Point,** located 9 miles east of Homestead. To reach the park from Miami, take the Florida Turnpike to the Tallahassee Road (SW 137th Avenue) exit. Turn left, then left again at North Canal Drive (SW 328th Street) and follow the signs to the park. If you're coming from U.S. 1, whether you're heading north or south, turn east at North Canal Drive (SW 328th Street). The entrance is approximately 9 miles away.

Biscayne National Park is especially accessible to boaters. Mooring buoys abound, since it's illegal to anchor on coral. When no buoys are available, boaters must anchor on sand. Even the most experienced boaters should carry NOAA nautical chart no. 11451, which is available at Convoy Point. The water is often murky, making the abundant reefs and sandbars difficult to detect—and there are few less interesting ways to spend a day than waiting for the tide to rise. There's a boat launch at adjacent Homestead Bayfront Park. There are 66 slips on Elliott Key, available free on a first-come, first-served basis.

VISITOR CENTERS & INFORMATION   For information on park activities and tours, contact **Biscayne National Park Underwater Tours,** P.O. Box 1270, Homestead, FL 33030 (☎ **305/230-1100**).

The **Convoy Point Visitor Center,** 9700 SW 328th St., at the park's main entrance (☎ **305/230-7275**), is the natural starting point for any venture into the park. In addition to providing comprehensive information on the park, rangers will show you a 10-minute slide show and a short video about Hurricane Andrew, both on request. Open Monday to Friday from 8:30am to 4pm and on Saturday and Sunday from 8:30am to 5pm.

ENTRANCE FEES & PERMITS   Entrance is free to Biscayne National Park. Backcountry permits are also free, and available at the visitor center.

EXPLORING THE PARK

Since Biscayne National Park is primarily underwater, the only way to truly experience it is with snorkel or scuba gear. And you'll need a boat. Beneath the surface, the aquatic universe pulses with multicolored life: Bright parrot and angelfish, gently rocking sea fans, and coral labyrinths abound. Before entering the water, be sure to apply waterproof sunblock or wear a T-shirt. Once you begin to explore, it's easy to lose track of time, and the Florida sun is brutal, even during winter.

Afterward, take a picnic out to Elliot Key and taste the crisp salt air blowing off the Atlantic. Since the island is accessible only by boat, the beach is usually less crowded than those farther north.

Biscayne National Park is more a preserve than a destination, a place that's meant to be experienced, not an event. I suggest using your time here to explore—but most of all, to relax.

SPORTS & ACTIVITIES

CANOEING   Biscayne National Park offers excellent canoeing, either along the coast or across open water to nearby mangrove islands. Since tides can be strong, only experienced canoeists should attempt to paddle far from shore. If you plan to go far, first obtain a tide table from the visitor center (see "Essentials," above) and paddle with the current. Free ranger-led canoe tours are scheduled for most weekend mornings; phone for information. You can rent a canoe at the park; rates are $7 an hour or $20 for a half day.

FISHING   Ocean fishing is excellent year round; many people cast their lines right from the breakwater jetty at Convoy Point. A fishing license is required (see "Fishing" under "Sports & Activities" in "Everglades National Park," earlier in this chapter, for complete information). Bait is not available in Biscayne, but is sold in adjacent Homestead Bayfront Park. Stone crabs and Florida lobsters can be found here, but you're only allowed to catch these on the ocean side when they're in season. There are strict limitations on size, season, number, and method of take (including spearfishing) for both freshwater and saltwater fishing. The latest regulations are available at most marinas, bait and tackle shops, and at the park's visitor centers. Or you can contact the **Florida Game and Fresh Water Fish Commission,** Bryant Building, 620 S. Meridian St., Tallahassee, FL 32399-1600 (☎ **904/488-1960**).

HIKING   Since the majority of this park is underwater, hiking is not great, but there are some short trails. At Convoy Point you can walk along the 370-foot board-walk, and along the half-mile jetty that serves as a breakwater for the park's harbor. Even from here you can usually see brown pelicans, little blue herons, snowy egrets, and a few exotic fish.

Elliott Key is only accessible by boat, but once you're there, you have two good trail options. True to its name, the **Loop Trail** makes a 1¹/₂-mile circle from the bayside visitor center, through a hardwood hammock and mangroves, to an elevated oceanside boardwalk. It's likely that you'll see purple and orange land crabs scurrying around the mangrove's roots.

The **Old Road** is a 7-mile tropical hammock trail that runs the length of Elliott Key. Because the visitor center is located about a third of the way along the trail, you can walk (or bike) only about 2¹/₂ miles north, or 4¹/₂ miles south, before turning around. This trail is one of the few places left in the world to see the highly endangered Schaus' swallowtail butterfly, recognizable by its black wings with diagonal yellow bands. They're usually out from late April to July.

SNORKELING & SCUBA DIVING   The clear, warm waters of Biscayne National Park are packed with colorful tropical fish that swim in the offshore reefs. Snorkeling and scuba gear is rented and sold at Convoy Point. Or you can bring your own.

Biscayne National Park Underwater Tours, P.O. Box 1270, Homestead, FL 33090 (☎ **305/230-1100**), operates daily snorkel trips that last about 4 hours and cost $27.95 per person. It also runs two-tank dives for certified divers, and instruction for beginners. Prices are $34.50 per person. It's open daily from 8am to 5:30pm.

SWIMMING   You can swim at the protected beaches of Elliott Key and adjacent Homestead Bayfront Park, but neither of these beaches matches other South Florida beaches for width, softness, or surf.

ORGANIZED TOURS

Biscayne National Underwater Park Tours, P.O. Box 1270, Homestead, FL 33030 (☎ **305/230-1100**), offers regularly scheduled glass-bottom-boat trips. These tours offer a fish's-eye view of some of the country's most accessible coral reefs. Boats depart from Convoy Point year round, daily every half hour from 10am to 1pm. Tours cost $16.50 for adults and $8.50 for children 12 and under. Reservations are required.

The company also offers guided scuba and snorkeling reef trips led by underwater naturalists. Snorkeling tours and one-tank scuba dives depart daily at 1:30pm, and cost $27.95 and $35 per person, respectively, including equipment rental. Two-tank dive trips are offered on Wednesday, Saturday, and Sunday at 8:30am. Reservations are essential.

CAMPING

There are no hotels or lodges in Biscayne National Park, but camping is plentiful—for those with water transportation. Campsites are on Elliott Key, and are accessible only by boat. They're equipped with showers, rest rooms, and drinking fountains. With a backcountry permit, available from the ranger station, you can pitch your tent somewhere even more private. Camping is free.

9 | The Gold Coast

by Victoria Pesce Elliot

Public relations people have long been attaching alluring names to various spots throughout Florida to attract visitors, but in this instance, the name "Gold Coast" couldn't be more appropriate. On the one hand it evokes the palatial residences and evident wealth of Palm Beach and Boca Raton, and on the other it reminds us that beneath the ocean's surface still lies the gold of the Spanish galleons wrecked here in the 15th and 16th centuries. But this doesn't mean that you can't enjoy the incredibly lush area on just a few dollars. There's plenty to do here even if you aren't a millionaire.

The area's recorded history dates back to 1835, when the U.S. Army cleared trails while battling the Seminole peoples. Even as late as 1870 the keeper of the Jupiter lighthouse was the region's only known settler of European origin.

As elsewhere in Florida, the arrival of Henry Flagler's railroad in 1893 precipitated tremendous growth. Along with architect Addison Mizner, who built one of the region's first hotels, Flagler parcelled out much of the Gold Coast's land in the developments that would become Hollywood, Fort Lauderdale, Pompano, Lighthouse Point, Deerfield Beach, Boca Raton, Delray, the Palm Beaches, and Jupiter.

The Gold Coast has beautiful beaches, but very few are unspoiled. Developers in the area were allowed to build huge condominiums directly on the sand, and these now tower over sunbathers and block the sun by afternoon. In Palm Beach the problem is not tall buildings—there aren't any—but the fact that wealthy citizens own much of the beachfront real estate, leaving little accessibility to mere mortals. There are some exceptions, of course. Blowing Rocks Preserve, on Jupiter Island, made picturesque by a cluster of large rock formations, is one of my favorite spots.

Beyond the sands, the Gold Coast offers warm, clear waters year round, making northern Palm Beach County great for both diving and snorkeling. The closest coral reef is located a quarter mile from shore and can easily be reached by boat. Several companies offer regularly scheduled tours to the area's reefs and wrecks. This is also a major destination for golf. And it's no accident that the Gold Coast has produced some of the leading names in tennis. Chris Evert hails from Fort Lauderdale, Nick Bollitieri and Brenda Schultz live in Delray Beach, and Ivan Lendl and Steffi Graf live in Boca Raton. There are some leading tennis schools and countless public and private courts.

The Gold Coast's major towns hug the ocean, making navigation easy. The closer you get to the water, the narrower and more picturesque the roads become Interstate 95, which runs north-south, is the area's main highway, filled with commuters during rush hours. U.S. 1, which generally runs parallel to I-95 on the mainland side of the Intracoastal Waterway, is a narrower thoroughfare, plagued with badly timed traffic lights and lined with seemingly unending strip malls and fast-food restaurants.

I recommend taking Fla. A1A, on the coast. Its slow speed makes it best for touring and gets you into the ultra-relaxed atmosphere of the resort towns.

This chapter is arranged geographically from south to north, so that if you're driving from Miami you can follow it geographically as you go.

SPECIAL EVENTS & FESTIVALS ALONG THE GOLD COAST

FEBRUARY   February and March bring major-league baseball to West Palm Beach and Fort Lauderdale, with **spring training** and a full schedule of exhibition games.

If you're near Hollywood, stop in at C.B. Smith Park for some down-home cooking and entertainment at the annual **Chili Cook-Off** (☎ **954/431-6200**), held the first weekend in February. You may not be allowed to taste the spicy creations of the more than 50 competing chili teams, but the festival atmosphere and the country music concerts will more than likely make up for it.

Join your neighbors from the north at **Canadafest** (☎ **954/921-3404**), held in early February at the Hollywood Beach Broadwalk, for a dose of Canadian culture and music.

Stop by the **Palm Beach Seafood Festival** in mid-February at Currie Park in West Palm Beach (☎ **561/832-6397**). This festival features arts and crafts, kiddie rides, and of course, stone crabs, lobster, and more. Call for the word on the day's catch.

If you happen to be in Boca Raton, the **Annual Tour of Homes** (☎ **561/395-6766**), held in early February, opens doors to the exclusive mansions in Palm Beach County. Space is limited, so be sure to reserve early.

The **Boca Museum's Annual Artfest** (☎ **561/392-2500**), held later in February at the Crocker Center in Boca Raton, features the work of 200 artists. Live music and gourmet foods round out this exhibition of the top talent in the area.

The **Hatsume Fair**, held in late February at the Morikami Museum and Japanese Gardens in Delray Beach (☎ **561/495-0233**), is a celebration of spring Japanese style, with demonstrations, exhibits, and an arts-and-crafts fair in the tranquil Morikami Gardens.

APRIL   Be sure to mark your calendar for the **PGA Seniors Golf Championship** (☎ **561/624-8400**) in mid-April; it's held at the PGA National Resort & Spa in Palm Beach Gardens. It's the oldest and most prestigious of the senior tournaments. Call for the line-up.

What is Palm Beach without polo? Join royalty at the Palm Beach Polo and Country Club in mid-April for the **World Cup Polo Tournament** (☎ **561/793-1440**). See the best in international polo circles.

MAY   One of the biggest festivals in West Palm Beach is the **Sunfest** (☎ **561/659-5992**), on Flagler Drive in the downtown area. A huge party is put on in May with five stages of continuous music, a craft marketplace, a juried art show, a youth park, and fireworks.

Check out the **Cajun/Zydeco Crayfish Festival,** held at Mills Pond Park in Fort Lauderdale in mid-May. Spend 3 days dancing to Cajun music—if you don't know how, you'll want to sign on for lessons, offered free. Can you peel? If so, enter the crayfish eating contest. Call the Crazee Crawfish 24-hour hotline (☎ **954/761-5934**).

What's Special About the Gold Coast

Palatial Homes
- The estates of Palm Beach and Boca Raton, some of the swankiest in the world—enough to make your jaw drop.

Historic Hotels
- The Breakers, the grand dame of South Florida hotels and a tourist attraction in its own right.
- The Spanish Mediterranean–style main house of the Boca Raton Resort and Club, just the tip of a 350-acre complex that straddles both sides of the Intracoastal Waterway.

Top Shops
- A short stretch of Palm Beach's Worth Avenue, lined by some of the world's most exclusive shops, galleries, and restaurants.
- The Gardens Mall in Palm Beach Gardens, a 1.2-million-square-foot shopping complex boasting five major department stores and more than 200 other shops.

Best Beaches
- Blowing Rocks Preserve, on Jupiter Island, just one of many wonderfully picturesque beaches here, made beautiful by a cluster of large rock formations.
- Dozens of swimming beaches, from deserted to lively, guaranteeing plenty of sun and surf—and most have no admission charge.

The **Shell Air and Sea Show,** held on Fort Lauderdale Beach in mid-May, is a spectacular display of aeronautics featuring the Blue Angels and aquatic demonstrations by the navy guaranteed to give you goosebumps and leave you with a definite patriotic feeling.

If you find yourself in the Juno Beach area in early May, swing by the Marine Center and help the locals celebrate the beginning of sea turtle nesting season at the **Sea Turtle Awareness Day** (☎ 561/627-8280). The kids can learn about the marine environment with arts and crafts and children's activities.

JUNE   June brings **Soulfest** in West Palm Beach, celebrating African-American culture with cuisine, arts and crafts, and entertainment and as well as children's activities. Call the Suncoast Chamber of Commerce (☎ 561/842-7146).

JULY   The **Wine and All That Jazz** festival (☎ 561/395-4433) in July is a great way to quench your thirst on a sweltering Boca Raton summer day. It's one of the largest wine-tasting parties in the state; sample your choice from more than 100 wines and vintages while listening to a little live jazz.

At the **July 4th Festivities** on Atlantic Avenue and Fla. A1A in Delray Beach (☎ 561/278-0424), you can attend a celebration featuring art and jazz on the avenue, and enter a sand-sculpting contest, fly a kite, and sample fare from Delray's neighborhood restaurants.

OCTOBER   Snowbirds are in luck when visiting the Gold Coast. The area puts on so many festivals during the winter that it's difficult to keep track of them all. Among the best is the **SunBank Sunday Jazz Brunch at Riverwalk** (☎ 954/761-5363). Held the first Sunday of every month from October to March on the banks of the historic New River, this festival allows a leisurely Sunday of great live jazz and tasty food in the company of fellow music lovers.

The **Fort Lauderdale International Boat Show** (☎ 954/764-7642 or 800/940-7642) in late October is your chance to meet fellow boating enthusiasts and look over more than 1,400 boats.

NOVEMBER   The annual **Fort Lauderdale International Film Festival** (☎ 954/563-0500) in mid-November showcases a week's worth of independent films and national student film competition winners. Don't forget about the star-studded parties hosted by the festival.

DECEMBER   During the **Winterfest Celebration's Continental Airlines Boat Parade** (☎ 954/767-0686) in early December, 100 boats decorated with lights cruise up the Intracoastal Waterway from Port Everglades to Lake Santa Barbara. There's no better way to get in the Christmas spirit.

For serious music lovers, the **X/S Music Fest** (☎ 954/356-4943), put on the first Friday in December, is the largest 1-night music fest in the state of Florida. More than 100 local bands play jazz, blues, and rock at different nightclubs throughout Fort Lauderdale.

1 Fort Lauderdale & Broward County

23 miles N of Miami

Fort Lauderdale Beach, a 2-mile strip along Fla. A1A, gained notoriety in the 1950s as a spring-break playground. The partying college kids brought the city more mayhem than money, so they were made unwelcome in the 1980s when Fort Lauderdale made a conscious effort to attract a more mainstream and affluent crowd. The city has been surprisingly successful at transforming itself into "The Venice of the Americas." Home to wealthy industrialists from the Northeast, this region had the infrastructure to support the change of image and the canals to support the analogy.

In addition to miles of beautiful wide beaches, the city has more than 300 miles of navigable waterways, and is riddled with artificial canals that permit thousands of residents to anchor boats in their backyards. Boating is not just a hobby here, it's a lifestyle—and the reason many choose to live in an area known, along with a string of other evocative names, as the "yachting capital of the world." Visitors can easily get on the water too, by renting a boat, or simply by hailing a private, moderately priced water taxi.

Like many other South Florida communities, Hollywood, a small town south of Fort Lauderdale, was built in the 1920s by an entrepreneurial land developer. Today the town's paved beach Broadwalk is one of the "happeningest" strips in Broward County. The 3-mile hotel- and shop-lined path bustles with budget-conscious young locals who come for the cheap bars, and Canadians who fill the area's abundant inexpensive efficiencies for long holidays.

ESSENTIALS

GETTING THERE   By Plane   The **Fort Lauderdale / Hollywood International Airport** (☎ 954/357-6100) is small, extremely user-friendly, and located just 15 minutes from downtown. Major domestic carriers servicing the airport include **American** (☎ 800/433-7300), **Continental** (☎ 407/832-5200 or 800/525-0280), **Delta** (☎ 407/655-5300, or 800/221-1212), **Northwest** (☎ 800/225-2525), and **United** (☎ 800/241-6522).

By Train   **Amtrak** (☎ 800/USA-RAIL) trains departing from New York stop in Fort Lauderdale on their way to Miami. The local station is at 200 SW 21st Terrace, Fort Lauderdale (☎ 305/587-6692).

By Bus　Greyhound (☎ 800/221-2222) can get you to Fort Lauderdale from almost anywhere in the country.

By Car　If you're driving up or down the Florida coast, you'll probably reach Fort Lauderdale via I-95, a highway that runs all the way from Maine to Miami. Visitors on their way to or from Orlando should take the Florida Turnpike, a toll road that runs from just north of Fort Lauderdale to Walt Disney World.

VISITOR INFORMATION　The **Greater Fort Lauderdale Convention & Visitors Bureau,** 200 E. Las Olas Blvd., Suite 1500, Fort Lauderdale, FL 33301 (☎ 954/765-4466), is an excellent resource for visitors, not only before the trip but also while they're in town. It distributes a free comprehensive guide with everything you could want to know about events and sightseeing in Broward County.

In addition, by calling an **information line** (☎ 954/527-5600) from any telephone, visitors can immediately obtain easy-to-follow travel directions, travel advice, and assistance from operators who staff a round-the-clock line in English, Spanish, German, French, Italian, Portuguese, and up to 135 other languages.

BEACHES & OUTDOOR ACTIVITIES

BEACHES　Here's a rundown on the county's best beaches from south to north:

The Beach at Hallandale Beach Boulevard, near the Hallandale water tower, attracts a small crowd of young couples and families. Just north of the firehouse, a regular set of retirees who live in nearby condominiums and Hispanic families gather for picnics and games. On the south side, which is separated by a low sea wall, a younger crowd drinks beer and tosses Frisbees. The few metered parking spots fill up quickly on clear days, but you can usually grab a spot a couple of blocks south. Be sure to keep the meters fed, since the city is vigilant about ticketing.

Hollywood Beach, from Sheridan Street to Georgia Street, is sometimes described as "Venice Beach without the weirdos." The 3-mile-long Hollywood Beach Broadwalk is packed with a potpourri of young hipsters, middle-aged strollers, and French-Canadian vacationers who take daily ritualistic strolls past the path's gift shops, cafes, and restaurants. A visit here will also give you a quick feel of what South Florida means to millions of retirement-age "snowbirds" who attend senior-citizen dances and shows at the beach's Theater Under the Stars. Part of the pavement is dedicated to bicyclers, who loudly proclaim their rights to wayward walkers. Take special notice of the police who skate along the Broadwalk on in-line "blades" that are specially designed with a quick-release mechanism so that they can shed them in an instant. The beach itelf is wide and clean.

The **Fort Lauderdale Beach Promenade** just underwent a $20-million renovation—and it looks marvelous. Once popular with spring-break revelers, this beach is still backed by an endless row of hotels, and is popular with tourists and locals alike. On weekends, parking along the oceanside meters is difficult to find. Try biking or blading there instead. It's located along Atlantic Boulevard (Fla. A1A), between SE 17th Street and Sunrise Boulevard.

Fort Lauderdale Beach at the Howard Johnson is a perennial favorite among locals and the tourists who stay at this oceanfront hotel. Many high school and college students share the beach with an older crowd who party in this rather private area. The water here gets a little choppy, but is clean and blue. The beach is located at 4660 N. Ocean Dr. in Lauderdale-by-the-Sea.

Pompano Beach, which has an authentic fishermen's charm, is very family oriented. This 3½-mile-long stretch of sand is dotted with barbecue grills, playgrounds, and mini-picnic pavilions. The Pompano Fishing Pier, the beach's most prominent

Fort Lauderdale Area Attractions

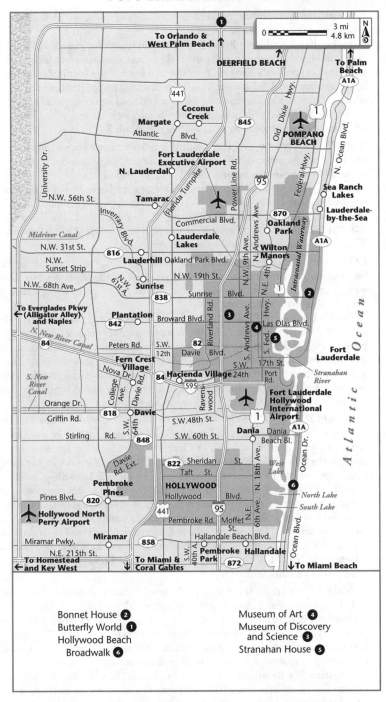

Bonnet House ❷
Butterfly World ❶
Hollywood Beach
Broadwalk ❻

Museum of Art ❹
Museum of Discovery
and Science ❸
Stranahan House ❺

landmark, can make anyone feel like hanging a line and drinking a beer. Parking is usually plentiful on the street.

Jupiter Beach, at Jupiter Beach Road, has a great path for joggers who want to cruise through the beachside state park to the Jupiter inlet while watching families and young couples walk along the narrow stip of beach. It's a favorite because early in the morning you'll feel as though you've discovered it for the first time despite the occasional large hotels. The sand is hard-packed and good for running, and leads right into a park fully equipped with barbecue grills and picnic tables. Parking is never a problem in this quiet town. Enter at 1375 Jupiter Beach Rd.

BOATING   A boating city, Fort Lauderdale provides ample opportunity for visitors to get on the water, either along the Intracoastal Waterway or out on the open ocean. **Bill's Sunrise Watersports,** 2025 E. Sunrise Blvd., Fort Lauderdale (☎ **954/462-8962**), rents jet skis, Waverunners, 13-foot cigarette boats, 18-foot powerboats, and 24-foot party boats year round. It's open daily from 9am to 5:30pm. Phone for rates and information. **Trish's Watersports,** 425 Seabreeze Blvd., Fort Lauderdale (☎ **954/522-7572**), also rents Waverunners and boats, and offers captained Intracoastal Waterway tours and open-water excursions.

GOLF   Several excellent courses are open to the public. Ask your hotel for top recommendations in your area and advice on how to get a tee time at the big ones. Most semiprivate clubs set prohibitive greens fees, but most offer special twilight rates on weekend afternoons and early evening.

The Club at Emerald Hills, 4100 N. Hills Dr., Hollywood (☎ **954/961-4000,** or 954/962-PUTT), is an incredibly posh spot for golf. They charge $80 to $95 per person during peak hours on weekends, but call for huge discounts at off-hours, and they offer many twilight specials even on busy weekends. This is the site of the Doral qualifer in February and the Joe DiMaggio celebrity tournament. This 18-holer sports elevated greens, rolling fairways, bulkheads, and great ladies' tees. A semiprivate club, reservations are required at least 5 days in advance for the public.

SNORKELING & DIVING   Though boat dives are generally pricey, you can often rent full gear packages and just walk off the sand to explore the coastal reefs. One good spot is just north of Commercial Boulevard at Fla. A1A, where about 200 yards offshore you can find one of the region's most scenic spots, with bright coral and a variety of saltwater fish. The **Force E Dive Shop,** nearby at 2160 W. Oakland Park Blvd. (☎ **561/735-6227**), is a great source for information as well as equipment. For $24 you can rent a complete dive package with a BC, regulator, and two tanks. While you're there, you might want to purchase (or at least browse through) Ned De Loach's *Guide to Underwater Florida* for $17. It describes the region's best and most accessible dive spots. Or call **Lauderdale Undersea Adventures,** 2150 SE 17th St., Fort Lauderdale (☎ **954/527-0187**), which can outfit you and arrange for boat trips.

TENNIS   There are dozens of good public tennis facilities in the Fort Lauderdale area. The phone book or chamber of commerce can tell you where the nearest is.

Holiday Park, 701 NE 12th Ave., Fort Lauderdale (☎ **954/761-5378**), has 18 clay and 3 hard courts (15 lighted). Non–Florida residents pay $3 to $4 per hour. Reservations are accepted on weeknights, but cost an extra $3.25. Skip the reservations and just be sure to show up before 5pm, when all the working folk leave the office.

At **Marina Bay Resort,** 2175 Fla. 84, west of I-95, (☎ **954/791-7600**), visitors can play free on any one of nine hard courts on a first-come, first-served basis. Three are lighted at night. It's least crowded at midday when the sun is high and weekday afternoons.

WHAT TO SEE & DO

✪ **Museum of Discovery & Science.** 401 SW 2nd St., Fort Lauderdale. ☎ **954/467-6637.** Museum, $6 adults, $5 children 3–12 and seniors 65 and older, free for children 2 and under; IMAX theater, $5 adults, $4 children 3–12 and seniors 65 and older, free for children 2 and under; combination ticket, $8.50 adults, $7.50 children 3–12 and seniors 65 and older, free for children 2 and under. Mon–Sat 10am–5pm, Sun noon–5pm.

This excellent interactive science museum on two floors is a model of high-tech "infotainment" that's especially suitable for children. However, most weekend nights you'll find a diverse crowd of hip high school to 30-somethings enjoying a rock film in the IMAX theater, which also shows short science-related super-size films daily. Out front, see the 52-foot tall *Great Gravity Clock,* the largest kinetic-energy sculpture in the state of Florida. Although the price of admission may seem steep, there's so much entertainment to be had here that you can easily make a day out of it. The kids will never get bored.

ORGANIZED TOURS

The *Jungle Queen,* Bahia Mar Yacht Center, Fla. A1A, Fort Lauderdale (☎ **954/462-5596**), is a Mississippi River–style steamer, one of Fort Lauderdale's best-known attractions. This paddleboat is a popular sight as it cruises up the New River. All-you-can-eat dinner cruises and 3-hour sightseeing tours take visitors past Millionaires Row, Old Fort Lauderdale, the new downtown, and the Port Everglades cruise-ship port. Dinner cruises depart nightly at 7pm and cost $23 for adults, $11 for children 10 and under. Sightseeing tours are scheduled daily at 10am and 2pm, and cost $10 for adults and $7 for children. Let's face it—dinner and entertainment cost big in Fort Lauderdale, and here, for $23, you get all the food you can eat and an evening out on the water, a great value!

The ✪ **Water Taxi of Fort Lauderdale,** 651 Seabreeze Blvd. (☎ **954/565-5507**), is one of the greatest innovations for tourists since room service. This fleet of old port boats serves the dual purpose of transportation and entertainment in this city of canals. The taxi operates on demand and carries up to 48 passengers. Stay at a hotel on the canals to take best advantage of this great system—you can be picked up at your hotel, usually within 15 minutes of calling, and then shuttled to any of the dozens of restaurants and bars on the route for the rest of the night, without having to worry about parking or drinking and driving. The personable captains are happy to point out historic and fun spots along the way. The service operates daily from 10am to midnight or 2am. The cost is $7 per person per trip, $12 round-trip, $15 for a full day. Opt for the all-day pass—it's worth it, and you can do without a car for a day or two.

SPECTATOR SPORTS

Greyhound racing is always a great way to catch a little gambling fever at bargain-basement prices. There's dog racing from December to April at the **Hollywood Greyhound Track,** 831 N. Federal Hwy. in Hallandale (☎ **954/454-9400**). Post times will vary, but races generally begin every evening at 7:30pm with matinees at 12:30pm on Tuesday, Thursday, and Saturday. Be sure to call for specials. Ladies' night is usually Thursday, and student night is Wednesday, when admission is free. Otherwise, admission is $1 for the grandstand and $2 for the clubhouse. Bets start at $2.

The **Pompano Harness Track,** 1800 SW 3rd St., Pompano Beach (☎ **954/972-2000**), Florida's only harness track, features racing and betting from October to early June (varies from year to year). Admission is $1 for grandstand seating and $2 for the clubhouse.

Gulfstream Park, at 901 S. Federal Hwy. in Hallandale (☎ **954/454-7000**), just recieved a revamping that has made it one of the state's biggest and best-known tracks. It gets the best race days and has a popular, well-stocked clubhouse. Admission is $3. Call for specials throughout the week; they're also advertised in the local paper.

Jai alai, sort of a Spanish-style indoor lacrosse, was introduced to Miami in 1924 and is regularly played in two Miami-area frontons. Although the sport has roots stemming from ancient Egypt, the game as it's now played was invented by Basque peasants in the Pyrenees Mountains during the 17th century. Players use woven baskets, called *cestas,* to hurl balls, *pelotas,* at speeds that sometimes exceed 170 m.p.h. Spectators, who are protected behind a wall of glass, place bets on the evening's players. **Dania Jai-Alai,** 301 E. Dania Beach Blvd. in Dania (☎ **954/920-1511** or 954/426-4330), is one of the nicest frontons in the United States. If you've never been, you should check out this fun, fast-action sport. Don't expect to win big, but have fun. Thursday is 99¢ night. Call for current schedules and many weekly specials. Admission is $1 to $4 and includes parking (better parking is $1 to $3). Seniors are admitted free before games start and ladies are often given discounts on appointed nights.

SHOPPING

Everyone on the Gold Coast knows about "Schmatta Row," a row of wholesale stores on **Hallandale Beach Boulevard** that's the best place to go for cheap handbags, shoes, and some clothing. Depending on your taste and patience, you'll either love it or hate it. Most shops offer up to half off moderately price goods. To get there, take I-95 to Hallandale Beach Boulevard East, go over the railroad tracks to NE 1st Street, and turn left; you'll see all the shops lining both sides of the street.

Another great discount area is **Antique Row,** a strip of U.S. 1 around North Dania Beach Boulevard in Dania (about a mile south of Fort Lauderdale/Hollywood International Airport) that holds about 200 antiques shops. Some are a bit overpriced, but if you're persistent there are some good finds. Most are closed Sunday.

Do also stop by the huge **Fort Lauderdale Swap Shop** at 3291 W. Sunrise Blvd. (☎ **954/791-SWAP**), one of the world's largest flea markets. In addition to endless acres of vendors, there's a mini-amusement park, a 12-screen drive-in movie theater, weekend concerts, and even a free circus complete with elephants, horses, high-wire acts, and clowns. It's open daily and admission is free.

Sawgrass Mills, 12801 W. Sunrise Blvd. in Sunrise (☎ **954/846-2300**), recently expanded, adding more than 30 new designer-outlet stores. This behemoth, shaped like a Florida alligator, now holds over 300 discount shops and kiosks in nearly 2.5 million square feet covering 50 acres. Wear your Nikes to trek around the shops that include Donna Karan, Saks Fifth Avenue, Levi's, Sunglass Hut, Ann Taylor, Barney's New York, Cache, Waterford crystal, and hundreds more, selling at 30% to 80% below retail. If you're driving, take I-95 North to I-595 West to the Flamingo Road exit and turn right; then drive 2 miles until you reach Sunrise Boulevard—you can't miss this monster on the left. Parking is free. Don't forget where you parked your car.

WHERE TO STAY

Fort Lauderdale beach has a hotel or motel on nearly every block, ranging from rundown to luxury. A number of chains are represented here, including **Days Inn** (☎ 800/329-7466), **Hampton Inn** (☎ 800/776-7677), and **Travelodge** (☎ 800/ 578-7878).

In general, this southern end of the Gold Coast has, by far, the most afford-able accommodations in the region. The strip in Hollywood Beach also has rows and rows of little family-run hotels. Most put out VACANCY signs when they have space.

Besides the accommodations listed below, there are two bare-bones hostels, rare enough in this area. The **International House Hostel**, 3811 N. Ocean Blvd., Fort Lauderdale (☎ **954/568-1615**), has 84 bunk beds and costs $15 per person in six-bed rooms. There's beach access and a large swimming pool. **Sol-y-Mar,** 2839 Vistamar St. (☎ **954/565-1419**), charges $12 per person in winter and $11 off-season; the hostel also has four private rooms, at $35 per night. This place attracts a very young crowd from all over the world.

Of course, ocean views are always priced much higher. In the winter there's virtually nothing on the beach that's less than $100 a night, but travel a few blocks inland and you'll find a few options, all of which are subject to the local tax of 9%.

Summer rates are much lower, when all of South Florida is humid and buggy and the rest of the country has gone back home to bearable climates. In any event, be sure to ask what kind of cooling system your accommodation has. Air-conditioning is great in the really mean months, but a fan works wonders, too. The winter season generally runs from November to April, though different establishments use differ-ent scales.

DOUBLES FOR LESS THAN $60

Bermudian Waterfront Motel and Apartments. 315 N. Birch Rd., Fort Lauderdale, FL 33304. ☎ **954/467-0467.** Fax 954/467-0467. 24 rms, efficiencies, suites, and two-bedroom apts. A/C TV TEL. Winter, $30–$56 double; $62–$80 efficiency; $82–$105 suite; $95–$150 apt. Off-season, $21–$30 double; $30–$42 efficiency; $43–$54 suite; $65–$75 apt. MC, V. Additional person $10 extra. 10% discount for AARP members.

This formerly elegant little Spanish-style building sits right on a gorgeous waterfront spot that's on the route of the incredibly efficient and fun water taxi. Besides that, what it has going for it is price, quiet, and decent-sized rooms. The hodgepodge of secondhand furniture is comfortable and functional. All rooms have new carpeting and small tiled baths, and some overlook a small tropical courtyard or the bay. The two-story 1950s-era building could use some repairs, but it couldn't be more private. All rooms are quiet and well laid out. You probably won't see your fellow travelers since there isn't any kind of lobby or common area, but they tend to be a mix of vacationing Americans and Europeans. The managers, when they're around, seem a bit harried. Still, for the money this is one of the best deals on the block, which is only 2 blocks from the ocean.

Ronny Dee Resort Motel. 717 S. Ocean Blvd., Pompano Beach, FL 33062. ☎ **954/943-3020.** 35 rms. A/C TV. Winter, $58–$70 double; from $78 apt. Off-season,$31–$35 double; from $41 apt. MC, V. Additional person $6 extra.

The bad news is that this family-owned motel is located on busy Fla. A1A. The good news is that it's just 100 yards from the beach, and amazingly inexpensive. Popular with European guests, this two-story yellow motel, wrapped around a central swim-ming pool, contains almost three dozen suburban-style wood-paneled guest rooms filled with an eclectic mix of furniture. All contain small refrigerators, but none has a telephone; pay phones are located in a public area, near a large room that contains a pool table, VCR, books, and assorted games. Ping-Pong and shuffleboard are also available. Complimentary coffee and doughnuts are served each morning in the lobby of this rundown but decent motel.

۞ The Sea Downs. 2900 N. Surf Rd., Hollywood, FL 33019. ☎ **954/923-4968.** Fax 954/923-8747. 6 efficiencies, 8 one-bedroom apts. A/C TV TEL. Winter, $42–$77 efficiency; $59–$103 apt. Off-season, $40–$52 efficiency; $52–$69 apt. Weekly and monthly rates available. No credit cards.

Claudia and Karl Herzog have been coming to Hollywood Beach since they were children. Now they own a piece of it, right on the Hollywood Broadwalk. Nearly 10 years ago they purchased this charming two-story 1950s-era building and another, the Bougainvillea, nearby, and have set to restoring the two modest inns with style and charm. The Sea Downs has a lovely landscaped courtyard, heated pool, and barbecue with a pleasant Mexican-tiled patio. The rooms are simply furnished but have the money-saving advantage of fully equipped kitchens. Plus, an outdoor barbecue area makes eating in that much more attractive. The two well-situated properties are extremely popular with German and other European tourists, who often stay for weeks at a time. Book early in season, since these are two of the best-kept secrets in an area of otherwise pretty weathered options.

DOUBLES FOR LESS THAN $80

✪ Banyan Marina Apartments. 111 Isle of Venice, Fort Lauderdale, FL 33301. ☎ **954/524-4430.** Fax 954/764-4870. 10 one- and two-bedroom apts. A/C TV TEL. Winter, $80–$175 apt. Off-season, $50–$120 apt. Weekly and monthly rates available. MC, V.

You'll feel as if your best friends left you their keys to their well-kept waterfront apartment at Peter and Dagmar Neufeldt's Banyan Marina. One of the best accommodation values in South Florida, this hidden treasure is built around a dramatic 75-year-old banyan tree and is located directly on an active waterway, halfway between Fort Lauderdale's downtown and the beach. The accommodations— one- and two-bedroom apartments—are all decorated differently, some with art deco accents, others with more contemporary ivory laminates and brass highlights. There are leather sofas, potted plants, and full kitchens and living rooms in every apartment. A small pool is just off the center courtyard, and there is boat dockage for eight yachts.

DOUBLES FOR LESS THAN $100

Lauderdale Colonial. 3049 Harbor Dr., Fort Lauderdale, FL 33316. ☎ **954/525-3676.** Fax 954/463-3787. 13 rms. A/C TV TEL. Winter, $99–$105 double; from $190 suite. Off-season, $55–$69 double; from $110 suite. Additional person $15 extra. MC, V.

It's not on the ocean, but the Lauderdale Colonial is situated on the waterfront, right at the point where the New River empties into the Intracoastal Waterway, only a 2-minute walk from the beach. Listed here for its excellent location and above average quality, this affordable 1950s-style motel is relatively straightforward, offering basic rooms, suites, and efficiencies in two adjacent two-story buildings. Every room in the compact black-and-white motel is different, but all are simply furnished with light tropical rattan pieces, refrigerators, and tea/coffee-making facilities. The suites include an additional sitting area and are substantially larger than the standard motel rooms. Every room has a water view, and the top accommodations enjoy unobstructed sunsets over the Intracoastal Waterway. There's a heated swimming pool, barbecue area, and laundry facilities for guests' use. This popular hotel books up months in advance, so don't just drop in unexpectedly.

✪ Riverside Hotel. 620 E. Las Olas Blvd., Fort Lauderdale, FL 33301. ☎ **954/467-0671** or 800/325-3280. Fax 954/462-2148. 110 rms, 7 suites. A/C TV TEL. Winter, $109–$189 double; from $199 suite. Off-season, $74–$129 double; from $139 suite. Additional person $10–$15 extra. AE, CB, DC, MC, V. From I-95, exit onto Broward Boulevard, turn right onto Federal Highway (U.S. 1), then left onto Las Olas Boulevard.

Fort Lauderdale Area Accommodations

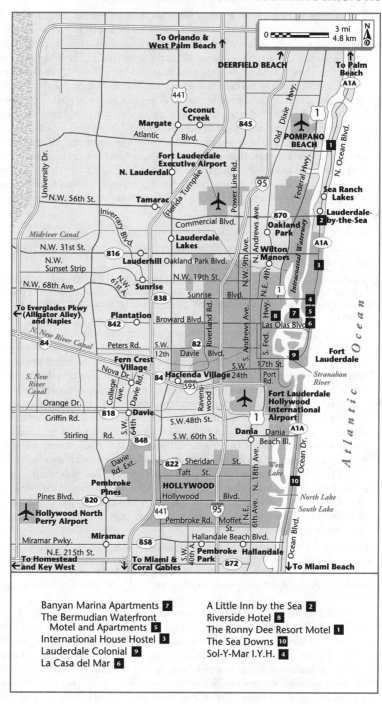

Banyan Marina Apartments **7**
The Bermudian Waterfront
    Motel and Apartments **5**
International House Hostel **3**
Lauderdale Colonial **9**
La Casa del Mar **6**

A Little Inn by the Sea **2**
Riverside Hotel **8**
The Ronny Dee Resort Motel **1**
The Sea Downs **10**
Sol-Y-Mar I.Y.H. **4**

The six-story Riverside Hotel is one of the oldest in South Florida. Built in 1936 in the middle of what is now Fort Lauderdale's most fashionable commercial thoroughfare, the Riverside looks like a Wild West movie set, complete with a second-floor wooden terrace and an enormous mural on the front facade. The lobby contains wicker furnishings, paddle fans, terra-cotta floors, and a fireplace that crackles even on the hottest days. On weekends it's often packed with wedding guests attending ceremonies that are held outside by the small heated swimming pool. The rooms upstairs are a bit nicer than the public areas, and contain oak furnishings and intricately tiled baths. The best rooms face the New River, but it's hard to see the water past the parking lot and trees. Standard rooms come with a writing desk and a small refrigerator. Most are priced over $100, but there are usually eight or nine less desirable rooms for about $89. Most of these are near the elevator, so if you can get used to the constant drone of the motor, you'll be all right; or if you plan to be out late enjoying the many offerings on Las Olas, you're set. It usually lets up by midnight.

WORTH A SPLURGE

These B&Bs may seem a bit high-priced, but the location and personal services you get, plus free breakfast and complimentary evening extras, mean saving money at restaurants and bars.

✪ **La Casa del Mar.** 3003 Granada St., Fort Lauderdale, FL 33304. ☎ **954/467-2037.** Fax 954/467-7439. 10 rms. A/C TV TEL. Winter, $90–$140 double. Off-season, $65–$95 double. Rates include breakfast and evening wine and cheese. Additional person $25 extra. AE, MC, V. Free parking.

Opened in 1994 by a pair of hospitable Chicagoans, Larry Ataniso and Lee Prellowitz, this charming two-story Spanish Mediterranean–style B&B is the area's quaintest and most private. In fact, while I'm not an overwhelming fan of B&Bs, even I love to stay here. The set-up is more like a motel in which each of the 10 rooms in the two-story curved building is separate and has its own bathroom. An outdoor pool serves as the setting for wine and cheese, nachos, focaccia, or other treats served most nights.

The 1940s building offers spacious guest rooms, which have remained intact over the years and have benefited from an extensive redecorating and enough refurbishing to make them clean, if not pristine. Choose the Stolen Kiss Room, based on Fragonard's painting, or a modest rendition of a Victorian room, decorated with period reproductions and warm colors. All rooms are equipped with limited kitchenettes (you get a microwave but no range) and VCRs. You can choose any video you like from the hosts' library. There isn't much of a view, though you're less than a block from the ocean. This unique inn attracts an eclectic mix of budget-conscious European and American vacationers.

A Little Inn by the Sea. 4546 El Mar Dr., Lauderdale-by-the-Sea, FL 33308. ☎ **954/ 772-2450.** Fax 954/938-9354. 30 rms, 7 suites. A/C TV TEL. Winter, $99–$139 double; $159–169 suite. Off-season, $69–$89 double; $105–$120 suite. Rates include continental breakfast. Additional person $10 extra; children 11 and under stay free in parents' room. AE, MC, V.

This little bed-and-breakfast by the sea is one of the most imaginatively designed inns on the Gold Coast and is recommendable for those who can do without all the services and facilities of a resort hotel. Meticulously fashioned both inside and out, the B&B is actually a pair of former motels connected by a fountain courtyard with small cafe tables. The rooms are themed with boats or birds or shells, and many come with balconies and small kitchenettes. Some rooms include a romantic mesh canopy over the bed and sofas in a tasteful sitting area. Breakfast is served in the courtyard, and guests are welcome to bring the pool furniture onto the adjacent beach.

WHERE TO EAT

The Fort Lauderdale and Broward dining scene is rapidly learning from Miami, its famous southern neighbor, that diversity is the key to success. A number of ethnic and "New World" options are joining the ranks of the expensive steakhouses and four-star French restaurants that have been the standard here for so long. This is good news for the budget-conscious, who can usually rely on finding a number of lower-priced menus amid the fancy names.

MEALS FOR LESS THAN $7

East Coast Burrito Factory. 261 E. Commercial Blvd., Fort Lauderdale ☎ **954/772-8007.** Tacos and burritos $3–$6; salads $4–$5. No credit cards. Mon–Sat 11am–10pm, Sun 10am–8pm. FLORIDA/MEXICAN.

A dozen wooden benches line the counter at this super Mexican diner that serves made-to-order soft tacos, burritos, hot dogs, and salads. For a healthier spin on a burrito, try the Florito, made with black beans instead of refried beans—a uniquely Florida invention. My favorite is the the "Super Veggie," stuffed with corn, salsa, mushrooms, black olives, carrots, peppers, and hearts of palm doused with their own super-hot chile-pepper sauce. The guacamole and various huge salads are also fantastic, especially on a sunny day on the back patio. To finish off your meal, try a Latin dessert of flan, a sweet caramel-topped custard, or an honest slice of key lime pie. There's talk of trying to franchise this little shack. Good idea!

Max's International Restaurant. 109 NE 20th Ave., Hollywood. ☎ **954/920-0935.** Breakfast $1.75–$5.25; lunch $3–$6.45. No credit cards. Daily 7am–4pm. HUNGARIAN.

Max's is a little joint that serves up homemade Hungarian food at bargain-basement prices. The family-run restaurant is an eclectic blend of diner and sit-down restaurant. Don't expect anything fancy, though—it's just a small pleasant place that even features an occasional singer and band. Check out the chalkboards with daily specials that might be anything from chicken cutlet platters to baked pork or lamb for only $6.45! Oh yes, lest I forget, there's also goulasch.

MEALS FOR LESS THAN $10

Mama Mia Italian Ristorante. 1818 S. Young Circle, Hollywood. ☎ **954/923-0555.** Reservations accepted. Lunch $4.95–$8.95; dinner $4.75–$12.95. AE, MC, V. Sun–Thurs 11:30am–11pm, Fri–Sat 11:30am–midnight. ITALIAN.

Mama Mia is a good, old-fashioned Italian joint that serves up authentic food at a great price. They make a fine calzone, if that's your weakness, and a great pizza with a crust so thin you can feel the cheese through the bottom. As for the toppings themselves, they're eclectic to say the least. You can choose your own or order one of the "theme pizzas" named after different regions of Italy. Be warned or be prepared for lunch tomorrow—the portions are huge, especially the steaming plate of sausages and peppers.

Tark's. 1317 S. Federal Hwy. (at SE 13th Terrace), Dania. ☎ **954/925-TARK.** Main courses $5–$9. MC, V. Mon–Fri 11am–10pm, Sat 1pm–midnight, Sun 1–10pm. SEAFOOD.

This popular clam shack is little more than a big U-shaped counter with a harried waitress and a busy short-order chef who cranks out fried, steamed, and baked fish-oriented dishes. Small in size and big on atmosphere, the chowder room's business-card and neon-sign decor sets the mood for hearty eating. Appetizers include calamari rings, conch fritters, shrimp cocktail, and chicken wings. Fried, charcoal-broiled, and blackened fish are main-course staples, but burgers, frogs' legs, and fried alligator are also available, as are raw and steamed oysters and clams.

MEALS FOR LESS THAN $15

Aruba Café. 1 Commercial Blvd., Lauderdale-by-the-Sea. ☎ 954/776-0001. Reservations accepted only for parties of six or more. Main courses $9–$16; lunch $6–$9. AE, DC, DISC, MC, V. Daily 11am–11pm. (Bar stays open later.) SEAFOOD/AMERICAN.

Brightly colored wicker chairs, a lively bar, indoor/outdoor seating, and large windows overlooking a particularly beautiful stretch of beach combine to make this contemporary restaurant one of Fort Lauderdale's most atmospheric. The ambience is as easy as the menu, which is replete with salads, sandwiches, and the requisite local seafood offerings. Two of the best lunchtime choices are pasta with clams and broccoli, and herb-roasted chicken with new potatoes. The Aruba clambake includes Maine lobster, clams, shrimp, mussels, crab legs, and corn. Any time of day you'd be well advised to start with conch fritters (the area's best), smoked fish dip served with seasoned flat bread, or a selection from the raw bar. There's a complimentary happy hour buffet Monday to Friday from 4 to 7pm, and the bar stays busy till late on most nights.

B's Bistro. 609 E. Las Olas Blvd., Fort Lauderdale. ☎ 954/728-9282. Reservations accepted only for parties of six or more. Main courses $11–$20. AE, DC, DISC, MC, V. Sun–Thurs 11:30am–10pm, Fri–Sat 11:30am–midnight. AMERICAN/BISTRO.

This Las Olas newcomer is a hit. The casual elegant decor and open design give diners a chance to people-watch and enjoy a great meal from a vast and varied menu. Lots of starters—like roasted peppers, smoked salmon terrine, calamari in tomato sauce, and a spicy ceviche—make it tempting to order half a dozen to share and skip the rest. Don't! The grilled yellowfin tuna is excellent and served with an Asian-style salad of mixed vegetables with wasabi. The Cajun-dusted frogs' legs are tender, though perhaps a bit too heavy on the spice for some. You can also get a good old-fashioned meatloaf and a variety of other excellent beef choices. Because of its success, expect to wait, especially on weekends when the competent but stressed staff are running like mad.

✪ The Good Planet. 214 SW 2nd St., Fort Lauderdale. ☎ 954/527-GOOD. Main courses $9–$13. AE, DISC, MC, V. Daily 11:30am–11pm. SOUTHWESTERN/ECLECTIC.

This little hangout is one of the best additions to the newly refurbished area just east of the lavish Center for the Performing Arts. The young staff and cool decor make it a perfect place for the young hipsters and intellectuals who frequent it. Like a California coffee shop by day, the place turns into more of a cosmic scene at night, when the waiters are happy to expound on the virtues of vegetarianism or serve you an incredibly tender chicken fajita. The Indian vegetable bake is superbly flavored with a hint of cumin and lots of curry. Many good seafood and Mediterranean specialties and pastas make it hard to choose what to eat next. Every single dish that comes out of the kitchen is competent, if not excellent. Add to that a full list of imported beers and wines and you've got the Good Planet, which, from a seat in a recycled chair near the bar, looks very good indeed.

My Thai. 2003 Harrison St., Hollywood. ☎ 954/926-5585. Reservations accepted. Main courses $6.95–$8.50 for noodle and vegetarian dishes, $8.50–$19.95 for meat and fish dishes; lunch $5.50–$7.95. AE, DISC, MC, V. Mon–Fri 11:30am–2:30pm and 5–10:30pm, Sat 5–10:30pm, Sun 5–10pm. THAI.

There's good Thai . . . and then there's bad Thai. My Thai is good Thai! Dishes run the gamut from vegetarian to carnivorous, but no matter which category you choose from, at least one dish is likely to have a silly name. Order the "Evil Jungle Princess," thinly sliced meats on finely sliced cabbage; or "A Fish Called Wanda," a whole deep-fried snapper served in a Thai garlic-and-wine sauce. If you're feeling adventurous, sample some "Kiss Me Squid," served with a generous portion of garlic, or even "Foster Care Alligator," served in chili paste, broccoli, and scallions. When you order take-out, ask for a little rice for tomorrow's meal.

Old Florida Seafood House. 1414 NE 26th St., Wilton Manors. ☎ **954/566-1044.** Reservations accepted. Main courses $12–$19. AE, MC, V. Mon–Sat 5–10pm, Sun 4–9pm. SEAFOOD.

The Old Florida Seafood House is packed even when other restaurants are slow, and for three simple reasons: top quality, generous portions, and friendly prices. More attention is paid to food than mood, which is plain and dinerlike. Dedicated locals have consistently rated this place one of the top seafood restaurants in South Florida—and that's saying a lot. A huge selection of reliably fresh fish is skillfully handled with simple, traditional preparations. More complex meals include lobster chunks tempura and shrimp au gratin, but just order today's catch broiled with butter and you won't be disappointed. All main dishes include salad, potato, and vegetables. Chicken, veal, and beef are also available, and a children's menu is offered.

WORTH A SPLURGE

East City Grill. 505 N. Atlantic Blvd., Fort Lauderdale. ☎ **954/565-5569.** Reservations recommended. Main courses $13–$27; lunch $7–$16. AE, DC, DISC, MC, V. Mon–Fri 8am–3pm and 5:30–11pm, Sat 9am–3pm (brunch) and 5:30pm–midnight, Sun 9am–3pm (brunch) and 5:30–10pm. NOUVELLE CUISINE.

This happening new scene on the beach combines the best of oceanside location with a killer nouvelle-style menu to create yet another hit by the mega-Maxx group. At lunch you'll see Lauderdale's power brokers dining on grilled sandwiches of snapper, salmon, portobello mushrooms, and lobster in an ultra-contemporary setting. The dinner menu features many Asian and Caribbean-inspired dishes such as steamed crab and goat-cheese dumplings for starters, or Jamaican beer-steamed prawns. A steamer bar allows diners to create their own dinners, with a choice of steaming broths, sauces, and sides.

FORT LAUDERDALE & BROWARD COUNTY AFTER DARK

THE PERFORMING ARTS

With the completion of the **Broward Center for the Performing Arts,** 201 SW 5th Ave., Fort Lauderdale (☎ **954/462-0222**), in 1991, Fort Lauderdale finally got a venue worthy of the kind of talent the community was craving. This stunning $55-million complex contains both a 2,700-seat auditorium and a smaller 590-seat theater. The center attracts top concerts, and opera, dance, and Broadway productions, as well as more modest-size shows. The **Opera Guild** (☎ **954/462-0222**) has sponsored a wide-ranging series of shows featuring top names for more than 40 years. For concerts by the **Florida Philharmonic** (☎ **954/561-2997**) and the **Symphony of the Americas** (☎ **954/561-5882**), look for listings in the *Sun-Sentinel* or the *Miami Herald.*

This region has some good theater groups whose seasons run roughly from October to May, to coincide with the heavy influx of winter visitors to the area. A landmark in the Fort Lauderdale theater community is the **Parker Playhouse,** 707 NE 8th St. (☎ **954/763-2444**), which offers a popular series of Broadway touring shows with nationally known actors and pre-Broadway specials. This is a really good, "insider" kind of place, well supported by the community. The **Hollywood Boulevard Theatre,** 1938 Hollywood Blvd., Hollywood (☎ **954/929-5400**), is the newest addition to the area's performing-arts world, with a successful first season under its belt. Although it employs local actors in its performances, it features seasoned performers whenever it can. **Off Broadway,** on East 26th Street, Fort Lauderdale (☎ **954/566-0554**), specializes in smaller, independent, and sometimes offbeat productions of contemporary plays. The stage operates year round with professional actors from around the country.

THE BAR, CLUB & MUSIC SCENE

Many of the bars around Fort Lauderdale have no cover unless there's a special event going on, and many places don't have a drink minimum either, so no one will frown if you sit nursing a beer.

Bars

Bermuda Triangle. 219 S. Atlantic Blvd., Fort Lauderdale. ☎ **954/779-2544.**

Although you might not want to come to this huge place for lunch or dinner, it's terrifically raucous at night when all four bars are in full swing. On weekday evenings you'll find lots of suits and lots of pickups. There's often live music and a bunch of locals playing volleyball out back. Open daily from 11am to 4am.

Elbo Room. 241 S. Atlantic Blvd., Fort Lauderdale. ☎ **954/463-4615.**

A beachfront dive that was once almost synonymous with spring break, the Elbo Room nourishes its rowdy reputation with frequent drink specials and occasional live music. The lively upstairs bar is usually crammed with tourists and college kids enjoying panoramic views and the occasional wet T-shirt contest. A downstairs cafe stays open late. Open daily from 10am to 2am.

Parrot Lounge. 911 Sunrise Lane, Fort Lauderdale. ☎ **954/563-1493.**

A cluttered sports bar, the Parrot Lounge is the kind of place where most of the customers are known to the staff by name, and if you're new here, you'll soon be asked yours. Hit music from the 1960s, 1970s, and 1980s plays from an active jukebox, which is loud, but not so loud as to overpower the pumped-up football commentary blaring from the many TVs.

Sunrise Lane is located just off Sunrise Boulevard on the ocean side of the Intracoastal Waterway in a little area called "The Village." The bar is open daily from 11am to 2am.

Country-Music Clubs

Desperado. 2520 S. Miami Rd., Fort Lauderdale. ☎ **954/463-2855.** Cover none–$5.

Contemporary country tunes, both live and on disc, play to huge crowds that come for line dancing and food in an upscale Santa Fe environment. Desperado features live music from touring regional bands. You might want to ride the mechanical bull, but only desperados eat here. Open Wednesday to Sunday from 8pm to 4am.

Rock, Blues & Jazz Clubs

Club M. 2037 Hollywood Blvd., Hollywood. ☎ **954/925-8396.** Cover none Sun–Thurs, $5 Fri–Sat.

On weekends it's hard to get in the door of Club M, one of the area's busiest music bars. Although the small club is primarily a local blues showcase, electric and traditional jazz bands also perform. On Friday and Saturday nights arrive early or you'll be the one singing the blues. Open daily from noon to 4am.

✪ **Musician's Exchange.** 729 W. Sunrise Blvd. (east of I-95). ☎ **954/944-2627.** Cover none–$15.

Come hear the area's best in live music in a seedy upstairs bar with a range of greats like Koko Taylor, Buddy Rich, Maynard Ferguson, Jefferson Starship, and many lesser-known talents. If it's here, it's probably good. Rumors abound that the place is going to close, but it has been around a long time and has managed to survive with a solid lineup of the area's best. Shows are Thursday to Saturday at 8:30 and 11pm; call the **concert line** (☎ 954/764-1912) for the current schedule. The cover depends on who's performing.

O'Hara's Pub and Sidewalk Cafe. 722 E. Las Olas Blvd., Fort Lauderdale. ☎ **954/ 524-1764.** Two-drink minimum per set at tables.

O'Hara's packs 'em in at this smoky little club right on Las Olas. It's known especially for presenting original jazz performers, but also has blues, rock, and big band groups. Call the **jazz hotline** (☎ 954/524-2801) to hear the lineup. They serve a great selection of pizzas and sandwiches which will do when it gets late. There's a two-drink minimum at the tables per set. Open daily until at least 2am.

Dance Clubs

Cafe Casablanca. 100 Ansin Blvd., Hallandale. ☎ **954/454-8400.** Cover none–$20.

There's a real mix of Latin, American, and disco here in a club that has changed names so many times it's hard to keep track. Now there are lots of fun theme nights, drink specials, and a very diverse crowd, mostly in their 30s and 40s, who love to drink and dance. Maybe this time? Open Sunday to Thursday from 8pm to 4am and on Friday and Saturday from 8pm to 8am.

The Copa. 624 SE 28th St., Fort Lauderdale. ☎ **954/463-1507.** Cover none–$15.

Fort Lauderdale's best-known gay club maintains the same good reputation as its more famous sibling club on Key West's Duval Street. The Copa sports several stages surrounding a large and loud dance floor, and an adjacent pool room and bar open onto a patio outfitted with numerous video monitors. The Copa has been the cornerstone of Fort Lauderdale's gay community for over 20 years, and it's still going strong. Open daily from 10pm to 4am.

The Edge. 200 W. Broward Blvd., Fort Lauderdale. ☎ **954/525-9333.** Cover varies.

Rockers, ravers, new wavers, and everyone in between gather at this cavernous space which includes an outdoor bar and pool. A mostly young crowd (18 and up) in black turns out for the super-lively dance scene. The bar is open nightly until 4am, unusually late for Fort Lauderdale.

2 Boca Raton & Delray Beach

26 miles S of Palm Beach, 40 miles N of Miami

Wealthy Boca Raton was named "Mouth of the Rat" in Spanish by conquistadors who landed here with Ponce de León. The sailor's "rats," it's believed, were actually the large and dangerous rocks that protrude from the water in Boca's protected harbor. Boca boomed in the 1960s when IBM set up a manufacturing plant and attracted other high-tech industries. Strict building codes and a profusion of low-density developments have made the area attractive to rich retirees.

Many of Boca's toney residents would shudder if you mentioned Delray Beach in the same breath. Delray, named after a suburb of Detroit, grew up completely separately. It was founded in 1894 by a midwestern postmaster who sold off 5-acre lots through Michigan newspaper ads. Because of their close proximity, Boca and Delray can easily be explored interdependently. Budget-conscious travelers would do well to eat and sleep in Delray and dip into Boca only for sightseeing purposes.

ESSENTIALS

GETTING THERE   See "Essentials" in Section 3, "The Palm Beaches," later in this chapter.

VISITOR INFORMATION   The **Palm Beach Convention and Visitor's Bureau,** 1555 Palm Beach Lakes Blvd., Suite 204, West Palm Beach, FL 33401 (☎ 407/471-3995, or 800/554-PALM), distributes an informative brochure and will answer questions about visiting the Palm Beaches. Ask for a map, as well as a copy of their "Arts and Boca Raton and Delray Beach" brochure.

BEACHES & OUTDOOR ACTIVITIES

BEACHES   Before South Florida was completely overrun with development, the state set aside many beaches for protection and preservation. Some are left alone and remain in a relatively natural state; others are groomed and lifeguarded.

The **Delray Beach Public Beach,** on Ocean Boulevard at the east end of Atlantic Avenue, is regularly cleaned and cared for. It's a good swimming beach. There's limited parking along Ocean Boulevard.

Spanish River Park, on North Ocean Boulevard (Fla. A1A) 2 miles north of Palmetto Park Road in Boca Raton, is a huge oceanfront park with a large grassy area, making it one of the best for picnicking. Facilities include picnic tables, grills, rest rooms, and a bi-level, 40-foot observation tower. You can walk through tunnels under the highway to nature trails that wind through fertile grasslands.

South Inlet Park, on Ocean Boulevard (Fla. A1A) between Ponce de León and DeSoto roads, is a good family beach at Boca Inlet. There's a protected swimming area, a beach boardwalk, picnic tables and barbecue grills, rest rooms, and outdoor showers. The plentiful parking costs $2.

DIVING & SNORKELING   **Red Reef Park,** 1400 N. Fla. A1A (☎ 561/393-7974), a fully developed 67-acre oceanfront park in Boca Raton, has year-round lifeguard protection and good snorkeling for beginners around the rocks and reefs that lie just off the beach in 2 to 6 feet of water. There's also good swimming, and a small picnic area with grills, tables, and rest rooms. The park, located a half mile north of Palmetto Park Road, is open daily from 8am to 10pm.

Moray Bend, a 58-foot dive spot located about three-quarters of a mile off Boca Inlet, is the area's best. It's home to three moray eels that are used to being fed sardines and ballyhooed by scuba divers. The reef is accessible by boat from the **Force E Dive Center,** 877 E. Palmetto Park Rd. in Boca Raton (☎ 561/368-0555). Phone for dive times. Dives cost a pricy $38 to $45 per person.

GOLF   From May to October or November, close to a dozen private golf courses open their greens to visitors staying in a Palm Beach County hotel. This "Golf-A-Round" program is free (carts are additional), and reservations can be made through most major hotels. Ask at your hotel, or contact the **Palm Beach Convention and Visitors Bureau** (☎ 561/471-3995) for information on which clubs are available for play.

The **Boca Raton Municipal Golf Course,** 8111 Golf Course Rd. (☎ 561/483-6100), is located just north of Glades Road, a half–mile west of the Florida Turnpike. This public 18-hole, par-72 course covers approximately 6,200 yards. There's a snack bar and a pro shop where clubs can be rented. Greens fees are $11 to $14 for 9 holes and $19 to $25 for 18 holes.

TENNIS   The snazzy **Delray Beach Tennis Center,** 201 W. Atlantic Ave. (☎ 561/243-7360), has 19 lighted clay courts available by the hour. Phone for rates and reservations.

WHAT TO SEE & DO
MUSEUMS

Boca Raton Museum of Art. 801 W. Palmetto Park Rd. (a mile east of I-95), Boca Raton.
☎ **561/392-2500.** Admission $3 per person (donation requested). Mon–Fri 10am–4pm, Sat–Sun noon–4pm.

In addition to showing its relatively small but well-chosen permanent collection, strongest in 19th-century European painting, the museum stages a wide variety of temporary exhibitions by local and international artists. Lectures and films are offered on a fairly regular basis; phone for details.

Children's Science Explorium. In the Royal Palm Plaza, 131 Mizner Blvd., Boca Raton.
☎ **561/395-8401.** Admission $2, free for children 2 and under. Tues–Sat 10am–5pm, Sun noon–5pm.

Here, 30 interactive exhibits teach children—and adults—about how things work. There are displays on electrical fields, gravitational forces, recycling, and computer technology. Even if you're not in a museum mood, you might want to visit the Explorium's unusual gift shop for freeze-dried astronaut food, hologram cards, and other unique presents you just can't get at home.

✪ **International Museum of Cartoon Art.** 201 Plaza Real at Mizner Park, Boca Raton.
☎ **561/391-2200.** Call for admission charges and open schedule.

Reborn after nearly 20 years of life in New York City, this extensive collection of cartoon art spans the decades and styles. In a gorgeous 52,000-square-foot gallery space, due to be completed in late 1997, works by some of the world's greatest cartoonists will be exhibited along with educational programs, a library, and a research center. Already the works of the museum's founder, Mort Walker, of Beatle Bailey fame, and others have received national recognition in the museum's limited opening in 1996. I can't wait for the remainder of this $15-million project to be completed.

GARDENS & NATURE PRESERVES

✪ **Gumbo-Limbo Environmental Complex.** 1801 N. Ocean Blvd., Boca Raton. ☎ **561/338-1473.** Free admission. Mon–Sat 9am–4pm, Sun noon–4pm.

Much of Boca is highly developed residential and commercial property that seems to have little to do with its unique physical surroundings. Environmental enlightenment is a recent phenomenon in South Florida, evidenced by the 1984 opening of this outdoor nature preserve and indoor learning center. Named for an indigenous hardwood tree with continuously shedding bronze bark, the 20-acre complex protects one of the few surviving coastal hammocks, or forest islands, in South Florida. Visitors can walk through the hammock on a one-third-mile-long elevated boardwalk that ends at a 40-foot observation tower from which you can see the Atlantic Ocean, the Intracoastal Waterway, and much of Boca Raton. A second trail leads through mangrove wetlands to a coastal dune. From mid-April to September, sea turtles come ashore here to lay their eggs. During this time the center conducts turtle-watching tours and sea turtle lectures. The complex's museum building displays local flora and fauna, including live snakes, fish, crabs, sea turtles, and scorpions. Sea-shell collections, mounted fish and birds, and stuffed armadillos, bobcats, raccoons, and owls round out the collection.

Morikami Museum and Japanese Gardens. 4000 Morikami Park Rd., Delray Beach.
☎ **561/495-0233.** Museum, $4.25 adults, $3.75 seniors, $2 children 6–18, free for children 5 and under, free for everyone Sun 10am–noon; gardens, free. Museum, Tues–Sun 10am–5pm; gardens, Tues–Sat 10am–5pm. Closed major holidays.

Slip off your shoes and into a serene Japanese garden community that dates to 1905, when an entrepreneurial farmer, Jo Sakai, came to Boca Raton to build a tropical agricultural community. The Yamato Colony, as it was known, was short-lived; by the 1920s only one tenacious colonist remained—George Sukeji Morikami. But Morikami was quite successful, eventually holding one of the largest pineapple plantations in the area. The 200-acre Morikami Museum and Japanese Gardens, which opened to the public in 1977, was Morikami's gift to Palm Beach County and the State of Florida. The park, dedicated to the preservation of Japanese culture, is constructed to appeal to all the senses. An artificial waterfall that cascades into a koi- and carp-filled moat, a small rock garden for meditation, and a large bonsai collection that includes miniature maple, buttonwood, juniper, and Australian pine trees are all worth contemplation—and it's free.

SHOPPING

Even if you don't want to buy anything in pricey Boca Raton, the city has some great malls available for people-watching and window-shopping.

Mizner Park, on Federal Highway in Boca Raton (☎ **561/362-0606**), is the area's most celebrated shopping arcade. It's a small mall, with a handful of specialty shops, a couple of good restaurants, and a multiscreen movie house. Each shop front faces a grassy island with blue and green gazebos, potted plants, and garden benches. It's extremely popular with strollers who come here just to stroll, often until late in the evening. The park entrance is between Palmetto Park Road and Glades Road.

Royal Palm Plaza, on Federal Highway (U.S. 1) between Palmetto Park Road and Camino Real (☎ **561/395-1222**), is an equally quaint, though sleepier, outdoor shopping center. Called the "Pink Plaza" for its distinctive architecture, the Royal Palm features two-story buildings with terra-cotta roofs, courtyard fountains, white stone benches, and large banyan trees. Specialty stores, boutiques, restaurants, and the Royal Palm Dinner Theater make this a popular place to shop.

A large number of antiques shops are clustered along **Atlantic Avenue** in downtown Delray Beach. Most of these stores are open Monday to Wednesday and Friday and Saturday from 10am to 5pm, plus Thursday from 10am to 9pm. Pick up the "Delray Beach Antique Shop Guide" at almost any of the stores on this strip.

WHERE TO STAY

Because of a lack of inexpensive accommodations in Boca Raton, those in the know gravitate toward Deerfield Beach and Delray to find decent hotels and motels. Follow their lead and seek out these sparse pockets of inns.

DOUBLES FOR LESS THAN $60

Riviera Palms Motel. 3960 N. Ocean Blvd., Delray Beach, FL 33483. ☎ **561/276-3032.** 21 rms, 13 efficiencies. A/C TV. Winter, $50–$60 double; from $65 efficiency. Off-season, $40 double; from $45 efficiency. Additional person $6 extra. Weekly rates available. No credit cards.

The Riviera Palms offers plain, simple, and relatively inexpensive accommodations. Behind the motel's two-story, cream-colored exterior are large rooms filled with a mixed bag of 1950s-era furnishings. The efficiencies come with full kitchens complete with dishes and flatware. There are no phones in the rooms. A large swimming pool is surrounded by a nice courtyard with sunning lounges, patio tables, barbecue grills, and shuffleboard courts.

DOUBLES FOR LESS THAN $80

Ocean Lodge. 531 N. Ocean Blvd., Boca Raton, FL 33432. ☎ **561/395-7772.** Fax 561/395-0554. 7 rms, 11 efficiencies. A/C TV TEL. Winter, $75–$90 double; $90–$95 efficiency. Off-season, $75–$80 double; $90 efficiency. AE, MC, V.

Recently bought by a New York decorator, this modest lodging couldn't be in a better spot. It's within walking distance of Mizner Park and across the street from the beach. Many New Yorkers end up here for the season. The rooms are done in Formica and in beige and sand tones. The large pool is lighted for nighttime swimming and a barbecue is accessible at all times.

The Sea Breeze. 820 N. Ocean Blvd., Delray Beach, FL 33483. ☎ **561/276-7496.** 2 rms, 7 studios, 5 one-bedroom apts, 5 two-bedroom apts. A/C TV TEL. Dec 15–Jan, $55 double; $65–$73 studio; $87–$99 one-bedroom apt; $107–$160 two-bedroom apt. Feb–Mar, $69 double; $74–$90 studio; $109–$119 one-bedroom apt; $136–$194 two-bedroom apt. Apr, $63 double; $66–$79 studio; $94–$102 one-bedroom apt; $116–$169 two-bedroom apt. May–Oct, $49 double; $52–$59 studio; $69–$79 one-bedroom apt; $85–$127 two-bedroom apt. Nov–Dec 14, $51 double; $53–$64 studio; $74–$85 one-bedroom apt; $92–$135 two-bedroom apt. Additional person $15 extra. MC, V.

The Sea Breeze has been around for a long time, but didn't deserve an endorsement until recently, when it was purchased by hard-working, friendly young hoteliers. The motel still isn't perfect, but its updated rooms are thoroughly recommendable. New carpeting and window treatments have been installed in every room, and many also have new furnishings that include plush comfortable chairs and sofas, glass breakfast tables, and whitewashed armoires. The studios and apartments have either a kitchenette or a full kitchen, and both have larger bathrooms than are normally found in comparable motels. There's a swimming pool on the property, as well as gas barbecue grills and laundry facilities available for guest use.

Shore Edge Motel. 425 N. Ocean Blvd. (Fla. A1A), Boca Raton, FL 33432. ☎ **561/395-4491.** 16 rms. A/C TV TEL. Winter, $75–$95 double. Off-season, $45–$75 double. AE, MC, V. From I-95, exit onto Palmetto Park Road east, turn left onto Ocean Boulevard (Fla. A1A), and continue four blocks to the motel.

Despite its name, the Shore Edge Motel is not located on the sand but across the street from a public beach, just north of downtown Boca Raton. It's the quintessential South Florida motel: a small, pink, single-story structure surrounding a modest swimming pool and courtyard. Although the rooms are a bit on the small side, they're very neat and clean. The higher-priced accommodations are larger, and come with full kitchens. The motel's owners, Lauren and Don Manuel, are terrific hosts, and are more than willing to share their knowledge of the surrounding area with you.

WHERE TO EAT

There are not a lot of inexpensive dining options in this small, conservative enclave of wealthy northerners. But the few good options are listed below.

MEALS FOR LESS THAN $10

Cafe Olé. In the Arvida Parkway Center, 7860 Glades Rd., Boca Raton. ☎ **561/852-8063.** Main courses $9–12; tacos and salads $6–$9. AE, DC, DISC, MC, V. Mon–Thurs 5:30–9:30pm, Fri–Sun 5–11pm. MEXICAN.

Offering upscale Mexican at down-home prices, the Olé has won the hearts of Boca-ites and travelers who are hard-pressed to find down-and-dirty Mexican anywhere in this chi-chi town. This spot is a bit polished, with a heavy dose of southwestern paraphernalia around the shopping-center storefront, but the food is good. Especially good is the Montezuma pie, a casserole of tortillas, chicken, mushrooms, and a thick red-chili sauce. Be sure to insist on spicy if you like it that way, since most dishes are rather toned down.

L & N Seafood. In the Town Center Mall, 6000 Glades Rd., Boca Raton. ☎ **561/368-5888.** Reservations accepted only for large parties. Lunch $5–$13; dinner $7–$25. AE, DC, DISC, MC, V. Sun–Thurs 11am–10pm, Fri–Sat 11am–11pm. SEAFOOD.

After a hard day of shopping (window or otherwise), it's great to find a restaurant in a mall that serves decent food. L & N caters to seafood lovers with all kinds of seafood platters and specials. It has great pasta dishes with a wide variety of sauces. The early bird gets the worm at L & N—usually from 4 to 5:30pm in winter and 4 to 6pm off-season. For anywhere from $6 to $14, gorge yourself on soup, salad, a main dish, and even dessert and a beverage.

Max's Coffee Shop. 402 Plaza Real in Mizner Park, Boca Raton. ☎ **561/392-0454.** Breakfast $3.95–$7.95; lunch $6.95–$12.95; dinner $6.95–$12.95. AE, DC, DISC, MC, V. Mon–Thurs 11am–11pm, Fri 11am–1am, Sat 8am–1am, Sun 8am–11pm. AMERICAN BISTRO.

A less pricy offshoot of trendy Max's Grill, this coffee shop, with a much smaller menu to choose from, is still a great value if you want a decent meal in a pleasant setting. For Boca Raton, the prices here are great. Max's has a slew of salads to choose from for lunch, as well as the old stand-by favorite, meatloaf, which will always do in a culinary pinch. A children's menu is available.

✪ **Tom's Place.** 7251 N. Federal Hwy., Boca Raton. ☎ **561/997-0920.** Reservations not accepted. Main courses $8–$12; sandwiches $4–$6. MC, V. Tues–Fri 11:30am–10pm, Sat noon–10pm. BARBECUE.

There are two important factors in a successful barbecue—the cooking and the sauce. Tom and Helen Wright's no-nonsense cook shack wins on both counts, offering flawlessly grilled meats paired with well-spiced sauces. Beef, chicken, pork, and fish are served soul-food style, with your choice of two side dishes, like rice with gravy, collard greens, black-eyed peas, cole slaw, or mashed potatoes. The restaurant itself is a simple, over-air-conditioned family eatery with peaked ceilings, brick walls, and lots of windows. Decoration is limited to signed celebrity photographs and plastic tablecloths. Pay at the counter on your way out.

MEALS FOR LESS THAN $15

Banana Boat. 739 E. Ocean Ave. (between Fla. A1A and Federal Hwy.), Boynton Beach. ☎ **561/732-9400.** Main courses $10–$15; sandwiches and salads $3–$8. AE, MC, V. Mon–Sat 11am–midnight, Sun 9am–midnight. AMERICAN.

Though it's more a bar than a restaurant, this Boynton Beach hotspot is crowded most nights with an eclectic crowd. Bikers hang out at the dark woodsy bar with office workers and fishermen. The varied menu has lots of fried fish choices, though the best bet is a burger or sandwich, served with lots of fixings by a waitress clad in tight athletic shorts. Though more mayonnaise than fish, the fish dip is tasty and served with crackers, lettuce, carrots, celery, and super-hot bottled jalapeños. You can't beat the waterfront setting and the Sunday reggae parties. Call for seasonal schedules.

Splendid Blended. 432 E. Atlantic Ave., Delray. ☎ **561/265-1035.** Reservations recommended. Main courses $11–$17; lunch $7–$10; sandwiches and salads $3–$8. AE, MC, V. Mon–Fri 11:30am–2pm and 5:30–10pm, Sat 5:30–10pm. ECLECTIC.

This storefront bistro is a secret favorite not to be let out. Otherwise the lines of loyal regulars will get even longer on weekends. They come for the fresh, uncomplicated seafood and pastas that are interesting without being overly ambitious.

The southwestern-inspired chicken Santa Cruz is tender and juicy and served with a black-bean sauce and tangy pico del gallo. Many seafood specialties, like tuna, snapper, and shrimp dishes, represent slight departures from the classics and seem to work most of the time. The drawback to this simple, narrow spot is the well-meaning but clueless staff who manage to botch simple requests.

BOCA RATON & DELRAY BEACH AFTER DARK
THE PERFORMING ARTS

There are limited offerings in this resort area for world-class entertainment, though several exceptions are worth mentioning. Most Boca-ites travel to Miami Beach or Fort Lauderdale for performances. The **Boca Raton Symphonic Pops** (☎ 561/393-7677) performs jazz, swing, pops, and classical music, sometimes with well-known guest stars. Call for a schedule. A full winter schedule keeps the local thespians busy at the **Delray Beach Playhouse,** 950 NW 9th St., Delray Beach (☎ 561/272-1281); call to see what's on. For kids, the **Little Palm Theater** (☎ 561/394-0206) is a popular venue for story-telling and plays. This long-running favorite puts on its Saturday morning performances at different venues throughout the season; call for details. The **Pope Theatre Company,** 262 S. Ocean Blvd. in exclusive Malapan (☎ 561/585-3404), is the nearest theater for Boca theater lovers; call for the performance schedule.

THE CLUB & MUSIC SCENE

✪ **The Back Room.** 16 E. Atlantic Ave. (near Swinton Ave.), Delray Beach. ☎ **561/243-9110.** Cover $2–$6.

A funky decor, eclectic crowd, and excellent booking policy make the Back Room the area's top live-music venue. Great music almost every night runs the gamut from jazz to big band, to classic rock 'n' roll. The room is comfortable and unpretentious, with sofas lining the walls and little tables nuzzling the dance floor. Unfortunately, only beer and wine are served—and worse, in plastic glasses. Open Tuesday to Saturday from 9pm to 3am.

Boston's on the Beach. 40 S. Fla. A1A, Delray Beach. ☎ **561/278-3364.** Cover none–$3.

One of the first places in the area to give reggae bands a stage, Boston's is still one of the best, especially on Monday night when it gets quite crowded. It's not always Caribbean music, however, and the club's popularity depends on who's playing. Boston's is always a good choice for happy hour, Monday to Friday from 4 to 7pm. It's open daily from 6:30am to 2am.

Club Boca. 7000 W. Palmetto Rd., Boca Raton. ☎ **561/368-3333.** Cover none–$5.

Because it's a little far from the beach, Club Boca is relatively devoid of tourists, but extremely popular with those in the know. The club is a huge danceteria with a club menu. Open Tuesday and Thursday to Sunday from 9pm to 5am.

Pete Rose Ballpark Cafe. 8144 W. Glades Rd., Boca Raton. ☎ **561/488-PETE.** No cover.

Naturally, there's plenty of Cincinnati Reds memorabilia at Pete Rose's place, and the requisite TV and games room with videos, air hockey, and skeetball. The bar is a frenzy Monday to Friday from 7 to 9pm when a live radio sports show is broadcast from a glass booth. There's a large gift shop selling a plethora of items emblazoned with the slugger's signature. Happy hour is daily from 4 to 7pm and 10pm until closing. Open Monday to Thursday from 11:30am to 1am and Friday to Sunday from 11:30am to 2am.

Polly-Esther's. 99 E. 1st Ave., Boca Raton. (☎ **561/447-8955.** Cover none–$5.

True to her word, Gloria Gaynor has survived. She and other disco divas can be heard blasting from the enormous sound system as the mixed young and 30-something crowd dances as though it's Saturday night and they have the fever. Bring your bell bottoms and scarves and enjoy. Open Wednesday to Saturday from 8pm to 2am.

6 South. 6 Ocean Blvd. (at Atlantic Blvd.), Delray Beach. ☎ **561/278-7878.** No cover.

This ultramodern restaurant with an industrial interior is especially recommended for its lively bar scene. The crowd, in their late 20s and 30s, is more VH1 than MTV. A huge stone bar is set on a concrete floor with funky tiled inlays, and slanted skylights top high ceilings that are tall enough to accommodate a full-size palm tree. 6 South is open daily from 11am to 2am, and is best after 10pm when the live music starts.

3 The Palm Beaches

65 miles N of Miami, 193 miles E of Tampa

Located across the Intracoastal Waterway from modest West Palm Beach, Palm Beach is an island densely packed with some of the most expensive mansions and estates in the entire world. For almost a century Palm Beach has been the traditional winter home of America's super-rich—the Kennedys, the Rockefellers, the Trumps, and plenty of CEOs. Gawking at these palatial homes is the no. 1 tourist activity, and a stroll along Palm Beach's toney store-lined Worth Avenue is a must, even for visitors with no interest in shopping.

By contrast, West Palm Beach is a work-a-day city, with office towers and strip malls, much like any other South Florida city. Palm Beach County is home to many golfing communities, unique nature areas, and a world-class art museum.

ESSENTIALS

GETTING THERE **By Plane** The **Palm Beach International Airport** (☎ **407/471-7420**) is easy to negotiate and a pleasure to use. Volunteer "Airport Ambassadors," recognizable by their distinctive teal-green shirts and jackets, are usually on hand to help visitors with free information. Major domestic carriers landing here include **American** (☎ 800/433-7300), **Continental** (☎ 407/832-5200 or 800/525-0280), **Delta** (☎ 407/655-5300 or 800/221-1212), **Northwest** (☎ 800/225-2525), **TWA** (☎ 407/655-3776 or 800/221-2000), and **United** (☎ 800/241-6522).

By Train Amtrak (☎ **800/USA-RAIL**) trains from all major cities in the United States stop in West Palm Beach on their way to Miami. The local station is at 201 S. Tamarind Ave., West Palm Beach (☎ **561/832-6169**).

By Bus Greyhound (☎ **800/231-2222**) can get you to the Palm Beaches from almost anywhere. Phone for reservations and information.

By Car If you're driving up or down the Florida coast, you'll probably reach the Palm Beach area on I-95, a highway that extends all the way from Maine to Miami. Visitors on their way to or from Orlando should take the Florida Turnpike, a toll road that runs almost directly from this county's beaches to Walt Disney World. Finally, if you're coming from Florida's west coast, you can take either Fla. 70, which runs north of Lake Okeechobee to Fort Pierce, or Fla. 80, which runs south of the lake to Palm Beach.

Palm Beach & Boca Raton

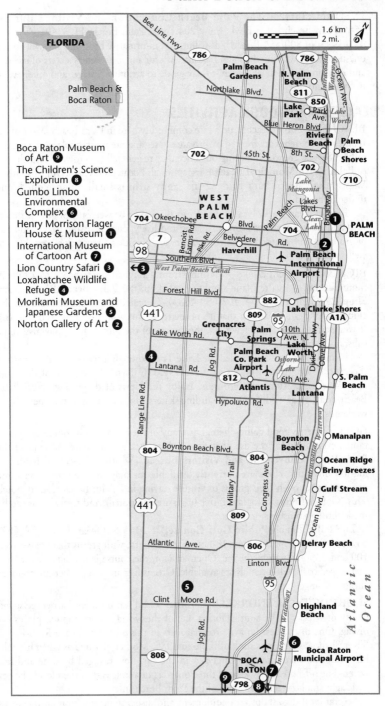

Boca Raton Museum of Art **9**
The Children's Science Explorium **8**
Gumbo Limbo Environmental Complex **6**
Henry Morrison Flager House & Museum **1**
International Museum of Cartoon Art **7**
Lion Country Safari **3**
Loxahatchee Wildlife Refuge **4**
Morikami Museum and Japanese Gardens **5**
Norton Gallery of Art **2**

FLORIDA

Palm Beach & Boca Raton

INFORMATION   The **Palm Beach Convention and Visitor's Bureau,** 1555 Palm Beach Lakes Blvd., Suite 204, West Palm Beach, FL 33401 (☎ **407/ 471-3995,** or 800/554-PALM), distributes an informative brochure and will answer questions about visiting the Palm Beaches. Ask for a map as well as a copy of its "Arts and Attractions Calendar," a day-to-day guide to art, music, stage, and other events in the county.

BEACHES & OUTDOOR ACTIVITIES

BEACHES   Public beaches are a rare commodity here in Palm Beach. Most of the island's best beaches are fronted by private estates and are inaccessible to the general public. Several are worth seeking out since they're generally uncrowded and clean.

Palm Beach Municipal Beach is exceptional. Located on Fla. A1A just south of West Palm's Royal Park Bridge, this sandy strip is small, undeveloped, and undercelebrated.

Phipps Ocean Park, located on Ocean Boulevard between the Southern Boulevard and Lake Avenue causeways, is large and lively, encompassing over 1,300 feet of groomed and guarded oceanfront. There are picnic and recreation areas here, as well as plenty of parking.

BICYCLING   Rent a bike—anything from a English single-speed to a full-tilt mountain bike—at the island's only rental shop, the **Palm Beach Bicycle Trail Shop,** 223 Sunrise Ave. (☎ 407/659-4583). The rate, $7 an hour or $18 a day, includes a basket and lock (not that it's necessary in this walled-off fortress of a town). If you want the bike for a few days, the owners of the shop will happily give you a substantial discount.

The most scenic route is called the **Lake Trail,** though it really runs the length of the island along the Intracoastal Waterway. On it you'll see some of the most magnificent mansions and grounds. Enjoy the views of downtown West Palm Beach, some great wildlife, and the in-line skaters who are out in force, especially on weekends.

GOLF   There's good golfing here, but many of the private club courses are maintained exclusively for the use of their members. Ask at your hotel, or contact the **Palm Beach Convention and Visitors Bureau** (☎ 407/471-3995) for information on which clubs are currently available for play. In the off-season some private courses open their greens to visitors staying in a Palm Beach County hotel. This "Golf-A-Round" program is free (carts are additional), and reservations can be made through most major hotels.

The **Palm Beach Public Golf Course,** at 2345 S. Ocean Blvd. (☎ **407/ 547-0598**), is a popular public 18-hole, par-54 course with greens that are between 100 and 235 yards from the tee. Open at 8am, the course is run on a first-come, first-served basis. Club rentals are available. Greens fees are $18 per person, about as cheap as you get here.

SCUBA DIVING & SNORKELING   Year-round warm waters, barrier reefs, and plenty of wrecks make South Florida one of the world's most popular places for diving. One of the best-known artificial reefs in this area is a vintage Rolls-Royce Silver Shadow which was sunk offshore in 1985. Mother Nature has taken her toll, however, and divers can no longer sit in the car, now ravaged by time and salt water. The offshore reef is located three quarters of a mile east of the Florida Power and Light smokestacks, just south of the Palm Beach Inlet.

Several local dive shops rent equipment and dispense information on the area's reefs. They include: **The Aqua Shop,** at 505 Northlake Blvd. in North Palm

Beach (☎ 407/848-9042); and **Atlantic Underwater,** at 901 Cracker St. (☎ 561/686-7066), **Dixie Divers,** at 1401 S. Military Trail (☎ 561/969-6688), and the **Ocean Sports Scuba Center,** at 1736 S. Congress Ave. (☎ 561/641-1144), all in West Palm Beach.

TENNIS   In addition to hotel tennis courts (see "Where to Stay," below), you can play at **Currie Park,** 2400 N. Flagler Dr., in West Palm Beach (☎ 561/835-7025). This public park has three lighted hard courts available free on a first-come, first-served basis.

The nine hard courts in the **South Olive Tennis Center,** 345 Summa St. in West Palm Beach (☎ 561/833-7100), are all lighted and open to the public. The center is located close to Dixie Highway, just south of Forest Hill Boulevard. Courts cost just $3 per person per day.

WHAT TO SEE & DO
MUSEUMS & THE ARTS

Norton Gallery of Art. 451 S. Olive Ave., West Palm Beach. ☎ 561/832-5196 or 561/832-5194 for a recording. Free admission, but a $5 donation suggested. Tues–Sat 10am–5pm, Sun 1–5pm. From I-95, take Belvedere Road (Exit 51) east to the end, then turn left (north) onto South Olive Avenue to the museum.

One of the best small museums in America, the Norton is world-famous for its prestigious permanent collection and top temporary exhibitions. The museum's major collections are divided geographically. The American galleries contain major works by Edward Hopper, Georgia O'Keeffe, and Jackson Pollack. The French collection features major impressionist and post-impressionist paintings. And the Chinese collection contains more than 200 bronzes, jades, and ceramics, as well as a group of monumental Buddhist sculptures. Recent top temporary exhibits have included a Man Ray retrospective and an exhibit on precision in art. Phone for information on current events and shows.

✪ **Society for the Four Arts.** 2 Four Arts Plaza, Palm Beach. ☎ 407/655-7226. Gardens, library, Sun-afternoon films, and gallery talks, free; movies, concerts, and lectures, $3–$25. Call for a schedule.

This multifaceted treasure is an institution in Palm Beach. It dates back more than 60 years, when it was founded with the purpose of encouraging the appreciation of art, music, drama, and literature. The institution does a stellar job with at least three of the four (there hasn't been much drama lately), with frequent concerts, year-round art exhibitions, and weekly lectures by such people as John Updike, Gregory Hines, Sir David Frost, and Gen. Colin Powell. You can explore the well-manicured and labeled gardens, once used by the prestigious garden society for demonstrations and lectures, and the expansive library facilities, which contain a meticulously catalogued collection of books on the arts as well as an impressive children's collection. Add to that the awesome galleries, sculpture gardens, and avant-garde films offered at minimal cost in an architecturally splendid property, and you'll be culturally sated for weeks.

NATURE PRESERVES & GARDENS

Loxahatchee National Wildlife Refuge. U.S. 441 and Lee Rd., West Palm Beach. ☎ 561/734-8303. Admission $4 per vehicle or $1 per pedestrian. Daily 6am–6pm.

Palm Beach County has its own slice of protected Everglades habitat: a federally preserved 220-square-mile refuge for a wide variety of reptiles, mammals, and waterfowl. Created in 1951, the Loxahatchee Refuge has several excellent hiking trails, but few facilities. From the visitor center, located at the main park entrance, there's a half-mile elevated boardwalk through a cypress swamp. The Marsh Trail, just beyond the boardwalk, is actually a series of loops that allows visitors to choose a walk from 1 to 10 miles long. The marsh is an intensively managed area that's considered to be one of the top birdwatching spots in Florida. Species regularly spotted here include egrets, hawks, herons, ibises, and the occasional Everglade snail kite. Birders can pick up a free checklist from the visitors center.

The main park entrance is located a mile west of U.S. 441, between Fla. 804 (Boynton Beach Boulevard) and Fla. 806 (Atlantic Beach Boulevard).

Mounts Horticultural Learning Center. 531 N. Military Trail, West Palm Beach. ☎ **561/ 233-1749.** Free admission, but donations accepted. Mon–Sat 8:30am–4:30pm, Sun and holidays 1–5pm.

The more than 500 varieties of native and exotic tropical and subtropical plants displayed here are a virtual catalog of Floridian flora. Almost everything that grows in the state is represented on Mounts' 14 acres, and every plant, tree, and bush is labeled to tell you what it is.

ORGANIZED TOURS

The *Star of Palm Beach,* 900 E. Blue Heron Blvd., Singer Island (☎ **407/ 848-7827**), runs regularly scheduled tours along the Intracoastal Waterway offering visitors unobstructed views of the area's grand mansions. Daily sightseeing as well as lunch, dinner, and theme cruises are offered, some with live entertainment. Opt for the dinner cruise, since the portions are large and satisfying and are included in the price of the comprehensive tour. Tours cost $9.95 to $30. Phone for more information and reservations.

SPECTATOR SPORTS

Greyhounds have been racing at the **Palm Beach Kennel Club,** 119 N. Congress Ave. (at Belvedere Rd.), West Palm Beach (☎ **561/683-2222**), since 1932. There is racing throughout the season; phone for post times. Admission is 50¢ to $2, free on Sunday.

Games are scheduled from September to July at the **Palm Beach Jai Alai Fronton,** 1415 45th St., West Palm Beach (☎ **561/844-2444**). Matches begin Tuesday at 6:30pm, Wednesday to Saturday at 1 and 6:30pm, and on Sunday at noon. Admission is 50¢ to $5. Call to see what specials are being offered.

The **Palm Beach Polo and Country Club,** 11809 Polo Club Rd., West Palm Beach (☎ **561/798-7000**), is one of the world's premier polo grounds. This posh West Palm Beach club attracts some of the sport's best players. Matches are open to the public and celebrities are often in attendance. Star-watchers will want to spend the price of admission to see the likes of Prince Charles, the Duchess of York, Sylvester Stallone, and Ivana Trump, among others. General admission is $8; box seats cost $18 to $26. Matches are held on Sunday at 3pm, January to April.

SHOPPING

Don't miss the experience of **Worth Avenue,** and don't be put off. These days shopkeepers have learned that sometimes the most affluent shoppers wear ripped jeans and cowboy hats. Go, pretend. The 4 blocks between South Ocean Boulevard and Coconut Row are home to the stores of Armani, Louis Vuitton, Cartier, Polo Ralph Lauren, and Chanel, among like company. Victoria's Secret, Limited Express, and several other less-impressive chains have snuck in here, too. Stop into **Paper Treasures,** an autograph gallery at 217 Worth Ave., with an inestimable collection of John Hancocks like those of Joe DiMaggio, Mickey Mantle, Andrew Jackson, Abe

Lincoln, Howard Hughes, and hundreds more, displayed in beautiful frames. At **Myer's Luggage,** at 313 Worth Ave., the proprietor, Richard Myers, is happy to demonstrate his impressive assortment of toys and gifts, including a vast collection of amusing alarm clocks, spy equipment, gorilla masks, and English picnic baskets. Most of the street's stores are open Monday to Saturday from 10am to 5pm, and for window-shopping around the clock.

One man's junk . . . There are plenty of treasures to be found among the cast-aways of the rich and famous. A number of excellent thrift-shopping opportunities abound in this region. Check out **The Church Mouse,** 231 S. County Rd. (☎ 407/655-0520); the **American Cancer Society,** 2419 10th Ave. North in Lake Worth (☎ 561/439-8490); the **Junior League Boutique,** 2884 S. Military Trail (☎ 561/433-4089); and the **Jewish Community Center of the Greater Palm Beaches,** 729 N. Military Trail (☎ 561/471-1077). Much of the china, silver, and paintings is high-priced, but lots of clothing, shoes, and accessories end up selling for a few bucks. Some stores close in the quiet summer months.

WHERE TO STAY

Staying in the Palm Beaches on a budget is a bit of a trick, since the rates are high even in the summer. Below are a few options in and around town that aren't exactly cheap, but do the trick, considering that this is the region where hotel rooms rent for what some people pay for a down-payment on a house.

DOUBLES FOR LESS THAN $40

Mt. Vernon Motor Lodge. 310 Belvedere Rd., West Palm Beach, FL 33405. ☎ **561/832-0094.** Fax 561/627-3218. 46 rms. A/C TV TEL. Winter, $35–$49 double. Off-season, $29–$39 double. Additional person $10 extra in winter, $5 extra off-season. AE, DISC, MC, V.

It isn't the presidential palace, but it's well located and just minutes to Palm Beach. The rooms are nearly hostel style and an old smell of food and perfume permeates the air. But it's safe and inexpensive.

DOUBLES FOR LESS THAN $80

Beachcomber Apartment Motel. 3024 S. Ocean Blvd., Palm Beach, FL 33480. ☎ **407/585-4646,** or 800/833-7122. Fax 407/547-9438. 46 rms, 4 suites. A/C TV TEL. Nov 1–Jan 14, $55–$100 double; from $85 suite. Jan 15–Easter, $80–$150 double; from $100 suite. Day after Easter–Oct, $42–$80 double; from $55 suite. Additional person $10 extra; children 14 and under stay free in parents' room. From I-95, exit onto Lake Worth Road east, stay to the right and take Lake Avenue over the Intracoastal Waterway, then turn left onto South Ocean Boulevard; the hotel is just ahead on your left. AE, DISC, MC, V.

It's not only because this squat, two-story motel is bright pink that it stands out among its neighbors. For more than 35 years the Beachcomber has been bringing sanity to pricey Palm Beach by offering a good standard of accommodation at reasonable prices. Squeezed between beachfront high-rises, the motel is located oceanfront, adjacent to Lake Worth Beach and a short drive from Worth Avenue shops and local attractions. Every room has two double beds, large closets, and distinctive green-and-white tropical-style furnishings. The most expensive rooms have kitchenettes and balconies overlooking the ocean. The bathrooms are basic, though not spotless, and amenities are limited to towels and soap. Of course, you're on the ocean and have a big outdoor pool with a nearby shuffleboard court and the convenience of coin-operated laundry facilities.

The Gulfstream. 1 Lake Ave., Lake Worth, FL 33460. ☎ **561/586-9250.** Fax 561/586-9256. 115 rms, 5 suites, 5 apts. Winter, $79–$89 double; $129 suite; $69 apt. Off-season, from $39 double; $79 suite; from $30 apt. Rates include breakfast. AE, DC, DISC, MC, V.

You may want to check out this hotel, which has changed hands so often that it sometimes has special promotions—for example, in the 1995–96 season it was offering introductory rates of $79 a night with super-discounts in summer. The hotel is a few steps off the Palm Beach bridge. A little bar and restaurant attracts lots of foreign travelers who drink beer and sing along with the live band. The rooms are very sparsely furnished with Formica and wood-veneer furniture. A recent coat of paint on top of the dozens that have been splashed on over the years has done some good to spruce the place up, though it's a far cry from being a renovated property. Still, it's a real bargain if it lasts. There's a romantic story that the hotel is haunted by a little girl on the fifth floor who slams doors and walks the halls at night. If the ghost keeps the rates this low, let's hope she keeps walking.

✪ **ParkView Motor Lodge.** 4710 S. Dixie Hwy., West Palm Beach, FL 33405. ☎ **561/833-4644.** Fax 561/833-4644. 28 rms. A/C TV TEL. Winter, $69–$84 double. Off-season, $44–$55 double. AE, DC, DISC, MC, V. Additional person $8 extra in winter, $5 extra off-season.

This clean, well-maintained spot is a real find in the Palm Beaches. There may not be a pool, but there are charming touches, like the colored sheets and towels in the rooms, and the bougainvillea that grows here and there. The rooms have refrigerators and the location is ideal, only 3 miles from downtown.

West Palm Beach Bed & Breakfast. 419 32nd St., West Palm Beach, FL 33407. ☎ **561/848-4064** or 800/736-4064. Fax 407/842-1688. On the Internet: wpbbb@aol.com. 4 rms. A/C TV TEL. Nov–Apr, $65–$115 double. May–Oct, $55–$85 double. Rates include expanded continental breakfast. Weekly rates available. AE, DC, MC, V. From I-95, take Exit 54 east (45th Street) and turn right on Dixie Highway; turn right again onto 32nd Street and the inn is the third house on your right.

A quaint little B&B with a mixed clientele, the West Palm Beach B&B is a compact and cozy home with just four individually styled, smallish guest rooms. The tropically inspired interior is decorated with plenty of knickknacks and it's a bright and clean place with lots of windows. Two of the bedrooms are located in the main house. The front room has a queen-size bed, white wicker furnishings, and a large carpet on hardwood floors. The room's semiprivate bathroom is down the hall, and a bathrobe is provided. The Amethyst Room, also in the main house, is painted pink and has a tiny private bathroom with a shower and sink—no tub, and no counter space for toiletries. Because they offer more privacy than the rooms in the main house, the two cottage rooms located out back are more recommendable. One has a queen-size bed and a kitchenette; the other has a double bed, a refrigerator, and a microwave. A full kitchen is available for guests' use in the main house, as is a common room and patio. A continental breakfast is served each morning from 8:30 to 9:30am and a glass of wine is offered each evening. The inn has complimentary bicycles for guest use and is entirely no-smoking.

DOUBLES FOR LESS THAN $100

Hibiscus House. 501 30th St., West Palm Beach, FL 33407. ☎ **561/863-5633** or 800/203-4927. 6 rms, 2 suites. A/C TV TEL. Winter, $85 double; $125 suite. Off-season, $65 double; $80 suite. Rates include breakfast. AE, MC, V. From I-95, exit onto Palm Beach Lakes Boulevard east and drive 4 miles; turn left onto Flagler Drive, continue for about 20 blocks, then turn left onto 30th Street; the inn is 2 blocks ahead on your right.

Located a few miles from the coast in a quiet residential neighborhood, this 1920s-era B&B-style hotel is not fancy, but very comfortable and highly recommended. The Hibiscus House has a very mixed clientele of both straight and gay and lesbian patrons. Each room is named for its predominant color scheme. Hence, the Red Room has cardinal walls and matching floral-print bedspreads and curtains; and the Peach Room has a charming four-poster bed, 19th-century-style furniture, and polished pine floors. Every accommodation features its own private terrace or balcony. There are plenty of pretty public areas as well, many of which are filled with antiques; one little sitting room is wrapped in glass and is stocked with playing cards and board games for guests' use. The backyard has been transformed into a planted courtyard with a swimming pool and lounge chairs. A substantial breakfast is served, either in the inside dining room or in the gazebo.

Palm Beach Historic Inn. 365 S. County Rd., Palm Beach, FL 33480. ☎ **407/832-4009.** Fax 407/832-6255. 9 rms, 4 suites. A/C TV TEL. Winter, $80–$150 double; from $225 suite. Off-season, $60–$75 double; from $95 suite. Rates include continental breakfast. AE, DC, DISC, MC, V.

Rates for the Christmas season double, but good buys can still be found September to November and after Easter at this quaint inn. Built in 1923, the inn is a Palm Beach landmark, located within walking distance of Worth Avenue and several good restaurants. The small lobby is filled with antiques, books, magazines, and an old-fashioned umbrella stand, all of which add to the homey sensation of this intimate bed-and-breakfast. All the rooms are on the second floor, and each is uniquely decorated and full of frills. Floral prints, sheer curtains, and the plethora of lace can sometimes be overwhelming, masking rather than complementing beautiful antique writing desks and dressers. Happily, there are also fluffy bathrobes, an abundance of towels, and plenty of good-smelling toiletries. The friendly innkeepers, Barbara and Harry Kehr, offer a complimentary afternoon drink, and extra-large continental breakfasts that include fruit, yogurt, muffins, juice, and coffee or tea—delivered to your room with the morning paper.

WORTH A SPLURGE

✪ Heron Cay. 15106 Palmwood Rd., Palm Beach Gardens, FL 33410. ☎ **561/744-6315** or 561/744-2188. 4 rms, 1 three-bedroom cottage. A/C. Winter, $95–$189 double; $250 cottage. Off-season, $85–$150 double; $200 cottage. Additional person $10 extra. Cash or checks preferred. MC, V. Take I-95 north to Donald Ross Road. Pass Alt A1A. Turn left on Palmwood Road. The resort is on the right.

This charming little bed-and-breakfast is minutes away from the hustle and bustle of Palm Beach but is located on its own private island. All rooms open onto a wraparound second-loor balcony. For the adventurous, there's a slide from the second floor to the 10-foot tiled mosaic pool! There's a dock for those who want to arrive by boat. Note that children are discouraged. For a little peace and quiet in an Old Florida–style home, this is the place to be.

Sea Lord Hotel. 2315 S. Ocean Blvd., Palm Beach, FL 33480. ☎ **407/582-1461.** 23 rms, 17 one-bedroom apts. A/C TV TEL. Jan 15–Apr 14, $126–$162 double; $192 apt. Apr 15–30 and Nov 15–Jan 14, $104–$136 double; $158 apt. May–Nov 14, $58–$75 double; $90 apt. Additional person $10 extra. DISC, MC, V.

The Sea Lord represents very good value for those who just *have* to stay on Florida's priciest beach. From the outside, the aged oceanfront hotel looks as if it has been around for a while, and the dated furnishings inside concur. The rooms are very clean and pleasant enough, fitted with old wood beds and bureaus, small refrigerators, and ordinary no-frills tiled bathrooms. The renovated rooms are more desirable than their nonrefurbished counterparts. The best of these are located in the five-story main building, and have a patio or balcony accessible via a sliding glass door. The apartments are larger and have fully stocked kitchens, along with the same homely furnishings and petite bathrooms that are found elsewhere on the property. Many are sandfront. The least desirable rooms are in the smaller south wing and have no views. The Sea Lord's exceptionally friendly employees staff the front desk 24 hours. Beach towels and lounge chairs are always available for use on the sand or at the well-maintained heated swimming pool. A small poolside cafe serves three American-style meals daily.

WHERE TO EAT
MEALS FOR LESS THAN $7

Green's Pharmacy. 151 N. County Rd., Palm Beach. ☎ **407/832-0304.** Breakfast $2–$5; burgers and sandwiches $3–$6. AE. Mon–Sat 7:30am–4:30pm, Sun 7am–1pm. AMERICAN.

This neighborhood corner pharmacy offers one of the best meal deals in Palm Beach. Both breakfast and lunch are served coffee-shop style at either a Formica bar or at plain tables above a black-and-white checkerboard floor. Breakfast specials include eggs and omelets, served with home-fries and bacon, sausage, or corned-beef hash. At lunch the grill serves burgers and sandwiches, as well as ice-cream sodas and milkshakes to a loyal crowd of pastel-clad Palm Beachers.

John G's. 10 S. Ocean Blvd., Lake Worth. ☎ **407/585-9860.** Reservations not accepted. Breakfast $3–$8.50; lunch $5–$14. No credit cards. Daily 7am–3pm. AMERICAN.

John Girago's coffee shop is the most popular diner in the county. For 25 years John G's has been attracting huge breakfast crowds, who often wait in a line that runs out the door, and on weekends, all the way down the block. It's not the simple nautical decor that attracts the faithful, but the good, greasy spoon–style food served in heaping portions right on the beachfront. It's known for its fresh and tasty fish and chips and the big breakfasts of various creative omelets and grill specials.

MEALS FOR LESS THAN $10

Hamburger Heaven. 314 S. County Rd., Palm Beach. ☎ **407/655-5277.** Reservations not accepted. Salads and sandwiches $3–$6; burgers and dinners $5–$15; breakfast $3–$5. No credit cards. Mon–Sat 7:30am–8pm. AMERICAN.

Hamburger Heaven hasn't changed much since it began flipping burgers in 1945. A central U-shaped bar, surrounded by low stools, is encircled by old-fashioned Formica booths which line the walls. The decor is limited to a large ocean mural that covers an entire wall. As you might have guessed, burgers are the main fare here, though daily dinner specials widen the variety: Tuesday means chicken and dumplings, Friday is pasta with tomato-basil sauce, and Saturday is homemade meatloaf day. Rice pudding and cakes and pies are always available. A full egg menu is offered at breakfast.

MEALS FOR LESS THAN $15

Toojay's. 313 Royal Poinciana Plaza, Palm Beach. ☎ **407/659-7232.** Reservations not accepted. Main courses $8–$11; lunch $5–$8. CB, DC, MC, V. Daily 8am–9pm. DELICATESSEN.

What John G's is to the breakfast crowd, Toojay's is to lunchers. This packed local favorite is a simple restaurant and take-out deli with vinyl chairs and booths surrounded by a jungle of potted plants. The food is excellent, and could hardly be fresher. The most popular lunch selections are overstuffed sandwiches filled with hot pastrami, roast beef, turkey, chicken, chopped liver, egg salad, and more. Burgers, fish platters, and a wide variety of salads are also available. At dinner the menu expands to include huge portions of stuffed cabbage, chicken pot pie, beef brisket, and sautéed onions and chicken livers.

THE PALM BEACHES AFTER DARK
THE PERFORMING ARTS

The stunning, $55-million **Raymond F. Kravis Center for the Performing Arts,** 701 Okeechobee Blvd., West Palm Beach (☎ **561/832-7469**), opened to rave reviews in late 1992. It's quite an architectural achievement, featuring a large, curved glass facade and several performance spaces. The elegant 2,200-seat main concert theater and adjacent 300-seat "black box" theater between them hold over 300 performances a year. The **Florida Philharmonic Orchestra,** under the direction of James Judd, presents a season here from September to May. During the winter season there's a performance of music, theater, or dance almost every night of the week. Phone for a current schedule. Go at show time just to see the latest in Palm Beach chic. (I'll bet you didn't think to bring a fur in September.)

The **Greater Palm Beach Symphony,** 139 N. County Rd., Palm Beach (☎ **407/655-2703**), gives 12 to 14 concerts from November to April throughout Palm Beach County in several area halls, including the Kravis Center.

Many concerts, sporting events, and festivals are held at the **West Palm Beach Auditorium and Municipal Stadium,** 610 Palm Beach Lakes Blvd., at Congress Avenue (☎ **561/683-6012**), half a mile east of Exit 53 off I-95. Musical guests include popular music stars and country greats.

The **Quest Theater Institute, Inc.,** 444 24th St., at Spruce Street, West Palm Beach (☎ **561/832-9328**), is Palm Beach's only African-American–oriented theater, and is also one of the city's most active, offering a wide range of professional, multicultural works. Past performances have included *Ain't Misbehavin'* and *A Raisin in the Sun.* The theater operates year round. The **Royal Poinciana Playhouse,** 70 Royal Poinciana Plaza, Palm Beach (☎ **407/659-3310**), stages Broadway and off-Broadway plays and musicals throughout the year. The playhouse promotes itself as "the most glamorous theater in the country," and this may be so. It's pretty, all right, and top names regularly perform. Music concerts are produced here as well.

THE CLUB & MUSIC SCENE

✪ **E. R. Bradley's Saloon.** 111 Bradley Place, Palm Beach. ☎ **407/833-3520.**

Casual restaurant by day, busy bar by night, Bradley's is the kind of place where singles literally dance on the bar—ducking to avoid the ceiling fans. (A sign notes that such behavior is no longer allowed, but I've seen it happen.) Go to happy hour hungry—for the price of two drinks you can fill up on a huge selection of chicken wings, pizzas, fresh vegetables, and more. The buffet is open Monday to Friday from 4:30 to 6:30pm and on Saturday and Sunday from 4 to 5pm. Bradley's is open Monday to Friday from 11am to 3am and on Saturday and Sunday from 10am to 3am.

✪ **Respectable Street Café.** 518 Clematis St., West Palm Beach. ☎ **561/832-9999.** Cover $2–$7.

This happening alternative-music spot in downtown West Palm Beach is a perennial favorite. The cafe's plain storefront exterior belies its funky high-ceilinged interior, decorated with large black booths, psychedelic wall murals, and a large checkerboard-tile dance floor. The young, alternative crowd dances to both live and recorded music. Theme nights vary; call for the latest. Open Tuesday to Saturday from 9pm to 4am.

Underground Coffeeworks. 105 Narcissus Ave., West Palm Beach. ☎ **561/835-4792.**

The latest word in hip cafe culture, Underground Coffeeworks is a subterranean java dungeon serving good strong brew to Palm Beach's most alternative crowd. Flashy art on even louder walls is a real eye-opener. Several rooms are outfitted with an eclectic mix of furnishings that include petite cafe tables and overstuffed sofas, and live music and poetry is performed most nights on a small stage. Open on Tuesday and Wednesday from 8pm to midnight, on Thursday to 1am, and on Friday and Saturday to 2am.

4 Jupiter & Northern Palm Beach County

20 miles N of Palm Beach, 81 miles N of Miami

Compared to the ritzy, developed southern part of the county, northern Palm Beach County and its major town, Jupiter, seem like a sleepy backwater. North county residents wouldn't have it any other way, and feel lucky to have been spared the concrete and congestion. This is a peaceful place, distinguished by slate-blue waters that are warmed in winter and cooled in summer by the powerful Atlantic Gulf Stream. In general, sights and attractions are outdoor affairs, beaches are clean, and recreational activities are plentiful. A few good hotels and restaurants make Jupiter and the surrounding area an excellent place to explore between the more barren lands to the north and the populous areas to the south.

ESSENTIALS

GETTING THERE   See "Essentials" in Section 3, "The Palm Beaches," earlier in this chapter.

VISITOR INFORMATION   For free maps, an arts-and-attractions calendar, and other information, contact the **Palm Beach Convention and Visitors Bureau,** 1555 Palm Beach Lakes Blvd., Suite 204, West Palm Beach, FL 33401 (☎ **561/471-3995,** or 800/554-PALM).

BEACHES & OTHER OUTDOOR ACTIVITIES

BEACHES   The farther north you head from populated Palm Beach the more peaceful and quiet it becomes. Just a few miles away from the bustle, castles and condominiums give way to open space and public parkland.

John D. MacArthur Beach, a state park, dominates a large portion of Singer Island, the barrier island just north of Palm Beach. Straddling the island from shore to shore, the park has lengthy frontage on both the Atlantic Ocean and Lake Worth Cove. The beach is great for hiking, swimming, and sunning. To reach the park from the mainland, cross the Intracoastal Waterway on Blue Heron Boulevard and turn north on Ocean Boulevard.

Dubois Park is located where Jupiter Inlet meets the ocean. An excellent family beach, it offers something for everyone. The shallow waters and sandy shore are perfect for kids, while adults play in the rougher swells of the lifeguarded inlet. A footbridge leads to Ocean Beach, an area popular with windsurfers and surfers. There's a short fishing pier, and plenty of trees shading the barbecue grills and picnic tables. Visitors can also explore the Dubois Pioneer Home, a small house situated atop a shell mound, or "midden," built by the Jaega peoples. The park entrance is on Dubois Road, about a mile south of the junction of U.S. 1 and Fla. A1A.

CANOEING   The 8-mile stretch of Intracoastal Waterway between Riverbend Park (located immediately off I-95 at Exit 59B) and **Jonathan Dickinson State Park,**

16450 S. Federal Hwy., Hobe Sound (☎ 407/746-1466), is the area's most popular for canoeing. Along the route, rowers pass a variety of botanical habitats and can spot a plethora of sea life, including the occasional manatee. Canoes are also available for rent for $6 per hour. Rentals are possible Monday to Friday from 9am to 5pm and on Saturday and Sunday from 8am to 5pm.

Canoe Outfitters, 16346 106th Terrace, North Jupiter (☎ 561/746-7053), drops canoers off at Riverbend Park and picks them up at Jonathan Dickinson about 5 or 6 hours later. Eric Bailey, a local who runs the concession, will sell the environmentally minded a pamphlet for $1 that describes local flora and fauna. It's open Wednesday to Sunday and charges $25 per couple, including park admission fees.

GOLF   The **Indian Creek Golf Club,** 1800 Central Blvd., Jupiter (☎ 561/747-6262), has a well-respected 18-hole, par-70/71 course over 6,038 yards. Greens fees include a mandatory cart and are seasonal. The course borders I-95.

The **Jupiter Dunes Golf Club,** 401 N. Fla. A1A, Jupiter (☎ 561/746-6654), enjoys some water views, just south of Dubois Park. The 18-hole, par-54 course is on a compact 1,850 yards. Fees are just $16.50 per person before 2pm and $11 per person afterward.

HIKING   ✪ **Jonathan Dickinson State Park** is a huge wilderness area that runs north from the Palm Beach and Martin county lines to Fla. 708. Several easily accessible park trails are particularly recommended. The quarter-mile **Hobe Mountain Trail** winds through sand pine scrub and up to an observation tower at the top of the squat 200-foot Hobe Mountain. From the tower you can see the entire park, as well as the Intracoastal Waterway and Jupiter Island beyond.

The **Kitching Creek Trail** is a 13-mile loop that takes hikers past a rich diversity of habitats including saw palmettos, slash pines, and of course, Kitching Creek. You can often find ground orchids here and there are always plenty of ferns. A numbered tour map, available at the trailhead kiosk, details sights along the way.

The 5-mile **Wilson Creek Trail** is also a nice walk, though it lacks the diversity of the Kitching Creek Trail. Both creek trails begin at the large picnic area just past the park's main entrance at 16450 S. Federal Hwy. (U.S. 1), just south of the town of Hobe Sound. A park ranger who staffs a kiosk here can direct you to the trailheads.

SNORKELING & SCUBA DIVING   Year round, warm, clear waters make northern Palm Beach County great for both diving and snorkeling. The closest coral reef is located a quarter mile from shore, and can easily be reached by boat. Several companies offer regularly scheduled tours to the area's reefs, including **Gulf Stream Diver II,** 1030 U.S. 1, Suite 105, North Palm Beach (☎ 561/627-8966 or 800/771-DIVE); the **Seafari Sport and Dive Shop,** 304 N. Old Dixie Hwy., Jupiter (☎ 561/747-6115); and **Subsea Aquatics,** 1870 U.S. 1, Jupiter (☎ 561/744-6674). These outfitters also rent diving equipment and dispense information on the area's reefs.

TENNIS   In addition to hotel tennis courts (see "Where to Stay," below), you can swing a racquet at a number of local clubs. The **Jupiter Bay Tennis Club,** 353 U.S. 1, Jupiter (☎ 561/744-9424), has seven clay courts (three lighted), and charges $12 per person per day. Reservations are highly recommended.

North Palm Beach Tennis, 951 U.S. 1, north of North Lakes Boulevard, North Palm Beach (☎ 561/626-6515), has 10 lighted clay courts, available for $8 per person per day. Reservations are recommended.

Carlin County Park is on State Road (Fla. A1A) in Jupiter (☎ 561/966-6600), just north of Indiantown Road. The six hard tennis courts are free, available on a first-come, first-served basis.

Blowing Rocks Preserve

In an area that's not particularly known for extraordinary natural diversity, Blowing Rocks Preserve wows with a terrific hiking trail along a dramatic limestone outcropping. The well-marked mile-long trail passes oceanfront dunes, coastal strands, mangrove wetlands, and a tropical coastal hammock. The preserve, owned and managed by the Nature Conservancy, also protects an important habitat for West Indian manatees and loggerhead turtles.

The cliff itself was formed over millions of years by an accumulation of marine sediments. You can see fissures and holes created by the repeated pounding of waves; when the tide is high, seawater crashes through the holes and sends spectacular plumes high into the air. There are no beach facilities and swimming is a bit dangerous, but I've often seen people dive and snorkel here. Fishing is also popular. Food, beverages, and pets are not permitted, and visitors must remain on designated trails. The preserve is located along South Beach Drive (Fla. A1A), north of the Jupiter Inlet, about a 10-minute drive from Jupiter. From U.S. 1, turn east on County Road 707 and cross the Intracoastal Waterway to the park. Admission is free, but a $3-per-person donation is requested. For more information, contact the Preserve Manager, Blowing Rocks Preserve, P.O. Box 3795, Tequesta, FL 33469 (☎ 407/575-2297).

EXPLORING THE WORLD OF NATURE

North Palm is well known for the **giant sea turtles** that lay their eggs on the county's beaches from May to August. These endangered marine animals return here annually, from as far away as South America, to lay their clutch of about 115 eggs each. Nurtured by the warm sand, but preyed upon by birds and other predators, only about one or two hatchlings from each nest survive to maturity.

Hobe Sound Wildlife Refuge, on Beach Road off County Road 707, at the north end of Jupiter Island, about 2 miles north of Hobe Sound Public Beach (☎ 561/546-6141), is one of the best places to see these lumbering giants. Because it's home to a large variety of other plant and animal species, the park is worth visiting at other times of year as well. Encompassing over 950 acres of mangrove swamps, pine forests, and sandy beaches, the multifaceted refuge is populated by many large birds, including bald eagles, osprey, and brown pelicans. Manatees can also sometimes be spotted here. Well-marked hiking trails begin at the parking area. Admission is $4 per car, and the preserve is open daily from sunrise to sunset.

Many environmentalists recommend that visitors take part in an organized turtle-watching program—rather than going on their own—to minimize disturbance to the turtles. The **Jupiter Beach Resort** (☎ 561/746-2511) and the **Marinelife Center of Juno Beach** (see below) both sponsor free guided expeditions to the egg-laying sites from May to August. Phone for times and reservations.

One of the most scenic areas on this stretch of the coast is nearby: **Jonathan Dickinson State Park** (☎ 561/546-2771), which is intentionally low-managed so that it will resemble the habitat of hundreds of years ago, before Europeans started chopping, dredging, and "improving" the area. On more than 11,500 acres live dozens of species of Florida's unique wildlife, including manatees and alligators. You'll find comfortable campgrounds with well-equipped cabins (see "Camping" under "Where to Stay," below). There are concession areas for daytime snacks and four different scenic nature and bike trails through the scrublands. You can also rent canoes from the concession stand to explore the Loxahatchee River on your own. Admission is $3.25 per car for eight adults. The area is open to day hikers, bikers, and walkers, weekdays from 8am until sundown and later on weekends. Call for a brochure or other information.

Just south of Jupiter is the **Marinelife Center of Juno Beach,** in Loggerhead Park, 1200 U.S. 1, Juno Beach (☎ **407/627-8280**). A small combination science museum and nature trail, the Marinelife Center is dedicated to the coastal ecology of northern Palm Beach County. Hands-on exhibits teach visitors about wetlands and beach areas, as well as offshore coral reefs and the local sea life. Visitors are encouraged to walk the center's sand dune nature trails, all of which are marked with interpretive signs. This is one place where you're guaranteed to see live sea turtles year round, and during breeding season (May to August) the center conducts narrative walks along a nearby beach. Admission to the center is free, although donations are accepted. Open Tuesday to Saturday from 10am to 4pm and on Sunday from noon to 3pm.

SEEING THE SIGHTS

Burt Reynolds' Ranch and Studio Tour. Jupiter Farms Rd., Jupiter. ☎ **561/746-0393.** Tours $10 adults, $5 children. Daily 10am–5pm (phone for tour times).

An old-time Florida boy, actor Burt Reynolds is northern Palm Beach's favorite celebrity. His expansive ranch property is the backdrop for many of his and other's movies, television shows, and videos, including *B. L. Stryker* and *Smokey and the Bandit.* On the 160-acre ranch there are a number of interesting houses, production facilities, and even a chapel where many weddings are held. This is a great place for kids or Burt lovers. Included in the price of admission for the informative tour is the wonderfully unstructured petting zoo where you can touch some of Burt's exotic pets, such as a 6-foot-tall blue emu, iguanas, llamas, sheep, goats, and miniature horses. There's enough here to keep you busy all day.

Jupiter Inlet Lighthouse. U.S. 1 and Alternate Fla. A1A, Jupiter. ☎ **561/747-6639.** Admission $5. Sun–Wed 10am–4pm (last tour departs at 3:15pm).

Completed in 1860, this red-brick structure is the oldest extant building in Palm Beach County. Still owned and maintained by the U.S. Coast Guard, the lighthouse is now home to a small historical museum. The Florida History Museum sponsors tours of the lighthouse, enabling visitors to explore the cramped interior, which is filled with artifacts and photographs illustrating the rich history of the area. Helpful volunteers are eager to tell colorful stories to highlight the tour.

Florida History Center & Museum. 805 N. U.S. 1, in Burt Reynolds Park, Jupiter. ☎ **561/747-6639.** Admission $5 adults, $3 seniors, $2 children. Tues–Fri 10am–5pm, Sat–Sun 1–5pm.

Surrounded by the Intracoastal Waterway, rocky Burt Reynolds Park is popular with local boaters and water-sports enthusiasts. The small museum is the park's centerpiece. Housed in a re-created Florida cracker–style building, the one-room hall is filled with exhibits relating to the history of northern Palm Beach County from 10,000 years ago to the present day. Artifacts are displayed chronologically, from Seminole utensils to Burt Reynolds's boots. The museum also sponsors regular guided tours of nearby historical sights—phone for current happenings.

ORGANIZED TOURS & SCENIC TOURS

The *Manatee Queen,* docked at the Blowing Rocks Marina, 18487 U.S. 1, Jupiter (☎ **561/744-2191**), a 40-foot catamaran with bench seating for up to 49 people, offers 2-hour tours of Jupiter Island that pass Burt Reynolds's and Perry Como's mansions, among other sites. Additional 2-hour nature-oriented excursions ply the Loxahatchee River to Jonathan Dickinson State Park. Tours cost $10 for adults and $8 for children. Jupiter Island tours depart daily at 2:30 and between 5 and 6:30pm; Loxahatchee River tours depart on Wednesday and Saturday at noon.

Loxahatchee River Adventures, Jonathan Dickinson State Park, 16450 S. Federal Hwy., Hobe Sound (☎ **561/746-1466**), offers daily narrated boat tours on a covered 35-foot pontoon boat holding up to 44 people. Cruises up the Loxahatchee River stop at Trapper Nelson's Site, a former zoo and home to "The Wildman of the Loxahatchee," an outdoorsman who moved here in 1930. Tours cost $10 for adults and $5 for children over 6 years old, and last approximately 2 hours. They depart daily at 9am, 11am, 1pm, and 3pm. Full-moon tours are scheduled monthly at 7pm.

The **Jupiter Beach Resort** and the **Marinelife Center of Juno Beach** both sponsor free guided expeditions to turtle egg-laying sites from May to August. See "Exploring the World of Nature," above, for details, times, and reservations.

WHERE TO STAY

There are virtually no budget accommodations in Jupiter Beach. The **Holiday Inn,** 4431 PGA Blvd. in Palm Beach Gardens (☎ 561/622-2260), may not technically be in Jupiter Beach, but it's close enough and is 8 miles from the beach. The seasonal rates range from $104 to $119 for a double, and although this may not quite fit our budget category, it will do in a pinch if the cheaper accommodations listed below are booked.

DOUBLES FOR LESS THAN $60

Cologne Motel. 220 U.S. 1, Tequesta/Jupiter, FL 33477. ☎ **407/746-0616.** 9 rms. A/C TV. Winter, $50–$60 double. Off-season, $45 double. Weekly and monthly rates available. MC, V.

The pleasant Hungarian couple who run this modest roadside hotel have big plans. After they finish the landscaping and pool, they hope to add to the nine-room one-story little gem. Here the pretty, newly retiled bathrooms are bright and clean. The rooms have just been updated with modest but attractive bright bedspreads and curtains. The area is clean and safe, and your hosts couldn't be more helpful. Though the motel is quite a few blocks from the ocean, it's within walking distance.

DOUBLES FOR LESS THAN $80

Baron's Landing Hotel. 18125 Ocean Blvd. (Fla. A1A), Jupiter, FL 33477. ☎ **407/746-8757.** 8 rms. A/C TV. Winter, from $75 double. Off-season, from $45 double. No credit cards. From U.S. 1, exit onto Ocean Boulevard (Fla. A1A) east; the hotel is on the right, at the corner of Love Street.

This charming family-run inn is a perfect little beach getaway. It's not elegant, but it's beachy and cozy. There are only 8 rooms. The single-story motel fronts the Intracoastal Waterway, and during winter many of the rooms are rented to "snowbirds," who dock their boats at the hotel's marina for weeks or months at a time. Nearly all the rooms, which are situated around a small pool, have kitchenettes and a hodgepodge of used furniture.

WHERE TO EAT
MEALS FOR LESS THAN $7

Athenian Cafe. Suite 7 in the Chasewood Shopping Center, 6350 Indiantown Rd., Jupiter. ☎ **561/744-8327.** Main courses $5–$12; lunch $5–$9; sandwiches and salads $3–$6. AE, MC, V. Mon–Sat 11am–9pm. GREEK.

Peter Papadelis and his family have been running this pleasant storefront cafe since this shopping plaza first opened nearly 10 years ago. Tucked in the corner of a strip mall, this place is a favorite among businesspeople who stop in for a heaping portion of rich and meaty moussaka or a flaky spinach pie made fresh by Peter himself. You could make a meal of the thick and lemony Greek soup and the large fresh antipasto. In a town replete with tourist-priced fish joints, this is a welcome alternative. Early-bird specials, before 7 pm, include many Greek favorites, and broiled local fish with soup or salad, rice, vegetables, and dessert starts at $7.95. Don't miss the homemade chocolate-chip cookies and the baklava.

Dune Dog. 775 N. Alternate Fla. A1A, Jupiter. ☎ **561/744-6667.** Main courses $2.50–$12.95. MC, V. Sun–Thurs 10am–10pm, Fri–Sat 10am–11pm.

This little outdoor hot-dog bar is a popular gathering spot in Jupiter for some of the best fish and chips and burgers anywhere. Outdoor picnic tables are set up in this roadside spot, where fresh cooked food is served all day long for a fast and thrifty meal.

MEALS FOR LESS THAN $10

Lanna Thai. In the Bluff's Square Shopping Center, 4300 S. U.S. 1, Jupiter. ☎ **561/694-1443.** Main courses $8; chef's specials $9–$16. MC, V. Mon–Fri 11am–3pm and 5–10pm, Sat–Sun 5–10pm. THAI.

There are dozens of great choices at Lanna Thai, including all the old reliables like pad Thai, panang, pad king, and pad puck to pair with meat, chicken, or fish. This inauspicious storefront has a quaint, whitewashed dining room where only a dozen tables sit beneath latticework bedecked with fake plants. Come for the $5 lunch specials that include spring rolls, slightly watery soup, and fried rice. The earnest service staff are always checking to be sure everything is all right—and it usually is.

MEALS FOR LESS THAN $15

✪ **Capt. Charlie's Reef Grill.** 126 U.S. 1 (behind O'Brian's and the French Connection), Juno Beach. ☎ **561/624-9924.** Reservations suggested on weekends. Main courses $9–$16. DISC, MC, V. Sun–Thurs 5–9:30pm, later Fri–Sat. SEAFOOD/CARIBBEAN.

For seafood with more integrity and taste than at anyplace else in the county, come to Capt. Charlie's, where you'll find more than a dozen daily local-catch specials, prepared any way you say, with side dishes that include black beans and rice, pasta, or fries. But the real trick is to arrive early, before the crowd of local "foodies" in the know. Sample the imaginative appetizers that include Caribbean chili or tuna spring rolls, crispy and spicy tubes big enough for two. The enormous Cuban crab cake is moist and perfectly browned, and is served with homemade mango chutney and black beans and rice. Sit at the bar to watch the hectic kitchen turn out perfect dishes on a 14-burner stove. Somehow the pleasant waitresses keep their cool even when the place is packed. Service is not white glove, and the ambience is early 1970s nautical. Concentrate instead on the extensive and affordable wine and beer selections—more than 30 of each, from around the world.

Nick's Tomato Pie. 1697 W. Indiantown Rd., Jupiter. ☎ **561/744-8935.** Reservations accepted only for parties of six or more. Main courses $11–$19; pastas $9–$14. AE, CB, DC, DISC, MC, V. Sun–Thurs 4:30–10pm, Fri–Sat 4:30–11pm. SOUTHERN ITALIAN.

A Bennigan's-style family restaurant, Nick's is a popular attraction in otherwise food-poor Jupiter. With a huge menu of pastas, pizzas, fish, chicken, and beef, this cheery spot has something for everyone. On Saturday night you'll see lots of couples and families walking out with doggie bags of leftovers from the impossible portions. The homemade sausage is a delicious treat, served with sautéed onions and peppers, reminiscent of a little Italy roadside stand. The pollo marsala is good and authentic.

I can't complain about anything here, except maybe the noise level, which makes conversation difficult.

JUPITER & NORTHERN PALM BEACH COUNTY AFTER DARK
THE PERFORMING ARTS

The **Burt Reynolds Institute for Theater Training,** 305 Tequesta Dr., Tequesta (☎ 561/746-8887), has been training promising young actors from across the country since 1979. The students stage a variety of well-known dramas and musicals as well as children-oriented productions. Call for the schedule of matinee and evening performances and ticket prices, which usually range from $17 to $25.

Another community theater group, **The Coastal Players,** perform in the Coastal Playhouse at 183 Tequesta Dr., Tequesta (☎ 561/746-6303). Tickets cost between $10 and $30.

THE CLUB & MUSIC SCENE

Brio Beach Club. 200 N. U.S. 1, Jupiter. ☎ **561/744-6600.** No cover.

This is *the* place in Jupiter—the only real place to dance and catch the local crowd late at night. The scene is activity-oriented—patrons are encouraged to participate in shooting hoops or playing pool, and to dance to the DJ music, which varies but is always upbeat. Several fully stocked bars and a particularly friendly atmosphere make it a fun night out. It's open on Tuesday and Thursday from 8pm to 2am and on Friday and Saturday from 8pm to 3am.

✪ **Waterway Cafe.** 2300 PGA Blvd., Palm Beach Gardens. ☎ **407/694-1700.** No cover.

Two large bars inside, and one floating on the water in back, make the Waterway a great place for an afternoon or evening drink. The bar is open Monday to Thursday from 11:30am to midnight, on Friday and Saturday from 11:30am to 1am, and on Sunday from 4pm to midnight, with music usually on Wednesday and Friday to Sunday, and live reggae most Sunday afternoons and Wednesday evenings.

The Treasure Coast 10

by Victoria Pesce Elliot

The Treasure Coast resembles an older Florida, before all the growth and development, crime and pollution, traffic and noise set in. And that's the way the visitors and residents like it. Though the area is one of the fastest growing in the state, the locals are trying to manage the rapid expansion in order to keep the small-town feel that distinguishes this area.

The Treasure Coast, for the purposes of this chapter, runs roughly from Hobe Sound in the south to the Sebastian Inlet in the north, encompassing parts of Martin, St. Lucie, and Indian River counties. It's true that the pace is slow here, and there isn't much to do at night, but this coastal region is rich in natural resources. A vast array of wildlife lives happily amid the small population here. And along its shore, actual hidden treasure still lies.

For hundreds of years the east coast of Florida was a popular route for European explorers, many of whom sailed from Spain to fill their coffers with gold and silver from the New World. Occasional ships were lost along the way because of rough weather and poor navigation. In 1715 came the worst loss of all. A violent hurricane swept over the northeast coast, sinking an entire fleet of Spanish ships laden with gold.

Though the Spanish salvagers worked for years to collect their lost treasure, much of it remained buried beneath the shifting sands. When builders began to excavate the area in the 1950s and 1960s, they found so many ancient coins that the area was christened "The Treasure Coast." To this day you'll see persistent scavengers with metal detectors walking along the beach after a heavy storm to see what new treasures might have turned up.

On these same beaches you'll find strollers and swimmers, surfers and tanners, who come to enjoy the uncluttered swaths of sand that stretch as far as you can see. These beaches have remained relatively free of hotel development, although building is on the rise as more people discover the Treasure Coast and its attractions—quaint towns, unspoiled beaches, flocks of migratory birds, winding rivers, and lakes filled with fish just waiting to be caught.

As appealing as it is as a tourist destination, the Treasure Coast has few well-priced options when it comes to places to stay. Towns like Vero Beach are built up with unsightly high-rises and condominiums, while areas like Hobe Sound have little in the way of tourist amenities. Some towns, like Jensen Beach, have a few modest

---

What's Special About the Treasure Coast

Fishing

- Edible and game fish, with world-class bottom fishing and inshore trolling.
- Big-game ocean fishing in towns like Stuart, which bills itself as the "Sailfish Capital of the World."

Water Sports

- Boating and sailing, surfing and windsurfing at Sebastian Inlet State Park.
- Good snorkeling and diving at several offshore sites where a number of wrecks make for particularly fulfilling dive experiences.
- Canoeing on the scenic Loxahatchee River, where alligators lurk and elegant blue herons take flight.

Beaches

- More than 26 miles of Atlantic coastline and an average year-round temperature of 73°.

Golf

- More than 60 courses designed by the world's most renowned designers like Fazio, Palmer, Nicklaus, Dye, and Van Hagge, with something for players of every level—from duffers to pros.

Marine Marvels

- "Turtle watches" led by local environmental groups to observe the endangered loggerhead turtles that crawl onto the sand from May to August to lay their eggs.

---

hotels built in the 1950s, but not much has been done to keep them up over the years. It's important to reserve in advance if you want a pleasant and affordable lodging.

SPECIAL EVENTS & FESTIVALS ALONG THE TREASURE COAST

January brings one of the region's silliest festivals: The **Fellsmere Frogs' Legs Festival,** in the town of Fellsmere (☎ 561/571-1221), just west of Sebastian, sponsors 4 days of amusement rides, arts and crafts, food, music, and of course, frogs' legs dinners. On the last Saturday of January, the Center for the Arts in Vero Beach puts on an outdoor party at Riverside Park called the **Art Exhibition** (☎ 561/231-0707). You can sample some home-cooked goulash and watch Hungarian dancers in their national costumes.

February and March bring serious baseball to Port St. Lucie and Vero Beach, when **spring training** comes around.

At the end of the February, the much-awaited **St. Lucie County Fair** rolls into Fort Pierce, with top country stars like Loretta Lynn, Brenda Lee, Mark Chestnut, and Johnny and June Carter Cash.

Sample some local seafood, enjoy music, and check out the arts-and-crafts exhibition at the **Grant Seafood Festival** (☎ 561/723-8687), held in Vero Beach's Grant Park in February.

To really get the local flavor of the Treasure Coast in mid-March, spend a day at the **Indian River County's Firefighter's Fair** in Vero Beach (☎ 561/562-2974) to watch the cattle judging and steer auction. The fair also features down-home cooking and carnival rides.

The Treasure Coast

Coastal
  Science Center **8**
Dodgertown **3**
Eco Center **2**
Elliot Museum **6**
Gilbert's House of
  Refuge Museum **7**
Harbor Branch
  Oceanographic
  Institution **4**
Indian River
  Citrus Museum **3**
Mel Fisher's
  Treasure Museum **1**
St. Lucie
  Historical Museum **5**
Stuart Heritage
  Museum
  at the Stuart
  Feed Store **9**
UDT-SEAL Museum **4**

0   8 mi
     12.7 km

N

Merritt
Island
Cocoa Beach
A1A
95
Satellite Beach
Indian Harbour Beach
Lake
Washington
W.
Melbourne
192
Melbourne
Sawgrass Lake
Lake Hell
Indialantic
Melbourne Beach
Palm Bay
1
Malabr
Grant
Sebastian Inlet
State Park
BREVARD
Barefoot Bay
Sebastian **1**
White
City
95
Fellsmere
Wabasso **2**
Winter Beach
Indian River Shores
INDIAN
RIVER
Gifford
Blue Cypress
Lake
60
Vero Beach **3**
Fort Pierce Inlet
State Rec. Area
Ft. Pierce
Inlet
Fort Pierce **4** **5**
Hutchinson Island
68
609
Eldred
Ankona
Walton
OKEECHOBEE
68
70
95
1
Port St. Lucie
441
Stuart **6**
ST. LUCIE
709
Jensen Beach **7** **8** **9**
70
Okeechobee
609
714
Palm City
St. Lucie Inlet
Port Salerno
Jupiter
Island
710
MARTIN
95
Lake
Okeechobee
Indiantown
76
Jonathan Dickinson
State Park
Hobe Sound
Hobe Sound
Nat. Wildlife Ref.
Tequesta
Port Mayaca
706
Jupiter
INTRACOASTAL
WATERWAY
St. Lucie Canal
Florida's Tpk.
PALM BEACH

Atlantic   Ocean

March also brings **Artsfest** (☎ 561/545-3990) to Stuart; arts and crafts share the spotlight with real blues and food from the best local restaurants. Call to find out who's coming to this 2-day event; Leon Redbone and Avery Summers have been featured in the past. Also in March, Vero Beach hosts the **Under the Oaks Art Show** (☎ 561/562-7687), a juried exhibition of fine art by Florida artists displayed in beautiful Riverside Park.

Celebrate the **Fourth of July** at the Dodger Home Stadium Fireworks Display in Vero Beach (☎ 561/569-4900) for a day of all-American fun with a barbecue and fireworks.

Head to the Stuart Area Airfield in November to see period aircraft, Navy and Coast Guard ships, and aerobatics in the annual **Veteran's Day** celebration (☎ 561/287-8500). On the St. Lucie River, later in the month, you can watch pirates battle to the death (with fake blood, of course) when the St. Lucie River Council holds its annual fundraiser, the **River Festival** (☎ 561/287-8500). Children can join in the many educational games and environmental demonstrations.

DRIVING ALONG THE TREASURE COAST

All the major roads in this region run north-south, making sightseeing easy. The best drive, either to or from Miami, is along Fla. A1A (also called the Dixie Highway), which hugs the ocean along most of the coast. U.S. 1 (also called the Federal Highway) doesn't cross the Intracoastal Waterway to the barrier islands, so it's a slightly faster (but less interesting) way to see Florida's east coast.

You can't get too lost while wandering around the Treasure Coast; you might be lulled by long stretches of lush hammocks, but soon you'll return to the coast and are suddenly faced with strips of (sometimes) delapidated beachfront hotels.

One of the nicest places to go exploring is out west of I-95, where you'll find yourself miles from the sea and heading into the backwater country; a whole world of birdlife and other swamp dwellers will show themselves to patient observers.

1 Stuart & Port St. Lucie/Fort Pierce

130 miles SE of Orlando, 100 miles N of Miami

It's hard not to wax nostalgic about Old Florida when you drive along this area's relatively quiet two-lane streets in an area that's even less built-up than its neighbors to the north.

Port St. Lucie and Fort Pierce thrive on sport fishing. A seemingly endless row of piers jut out along the Intracoastal Waterway and the Fort Pierce Inlet for both river and ocean runs. Here visitors can also enjoy adventures like diving and snorkeling, as well as more passive pastimes as beachcombing and sunbathing.

The towns in this area are centered around beach life, and though Stuart and Port St. Lucie have a relatively large mainland residential population, visitors tend to stay at the beach.

ESSENTIALS

GETTING THERE   By Plane   The closest gateway to the Treasure Coast region is the **Palm Beach International Airport** (☎ 561/471-7420), located about 25 miles to the south (see "Essentials" in Section 3, "The Palm Beaches," in Chapter 9 for more information).

By Train   Amtrak (☎ 800/USA-RAIL) trains departing from New York stop in West Palm Beach, about 19 miles to the south, and in Okeechobee, about 23 miles to the west. The West Palm station is located at 201 S. Tamarind Ave., West Palm

Beach (☎ **561/832-6169**). The Okeechobee station is located at 801 N. Parrot Ave., off U.S. 441 North (☎ **813/763-1114**).

By Bus Greyhound (☎ **800/231-2222**) can get you to and around the Treasure Coast area from almost anywhere. Several stops along U.S. 1 include 1995 U.S. 1 in Vero Beach.

By Car If you're driving up or down the Florida coast, you'll probably reach the Treasure Coast area on I-95, a highway that runs all the way from Maine to Miami. Visitors on their way to or from Orlando should take the Florida Turnpike, a toll road that runs almost directly from this region's beaches to Walt Disney World. Finally, if you're coming directly from the state's west coast, you'll probably take Fla. 70, which runs north of Lake Okeechobee to Fort Pierce, located just up the road from Stuart.

VISITOR INFORMATION The **Stuart/Martin County Chamber of Commerce**, 1650 S. Kanner Hwy., Stuart, FL 34994 (☎ **561/287-1088,** or 800/ 524-9704 in Florida), is the region's main source of information. The **Jensen Beach Chamber of Commerce,** 1910 NE Jensen Beach Blvd., Jensen Beach, FL 34957 (☎ **561/334-3444**), can provide good advice and suggestions on its stretch of sand.

GETTING AROUND Because the Treasure Coast is so large, the best way to get around is **by car.** You'll find almost no traffic, even in the winter season. On the smaller coastal routes, expect to travel at a slow pace like the rest of the drivers. Parking is plentiful in most areas and inexpensive.

Many towns along the coast offer many great trails for bikers, though I don't recommend travel **by bike** as your only means of transportation. The many bridges and wetlands make it hard to get to everywhere you'll want to go.

There are several local taxi companies in each town. One reliable local service is **Island Yellow Cab** (☎ **561/335-7510**). Rates are $1.90 per mile. You won't want to go far at those prices, but a run to the beach and back won't break you.

BEACHES & OUTDOOR ACTIVITIES

BEACHES Beaches are easily accessible throughout Hutchinson Island, the long, thin barrier island that stretches north from Stuart. Look for COASTAL ACCESS signs pointing the way to public beach areas. Parking is limited at many of these access points, and many locations are rather secluded.

Bathtub Beach, on Hutchinson Island, is one of the best oceanside parks in the county. Calm waters are protected by coral reefs, and visitors can explore the region on dune and river trails. Facilities include showers and toilets, open in the daylight hours. To reach the park, cross the Intracoastal Waterway on Ocean Boulevard and turn right, onto MacArthur Boulevard. The beach is located about a mile ahead, on your left, just past Gilbert's House and north of the Indian River Plantation (see below).

The **Fort Pierce Inlet State Recreation Area,** 905 Shorewinds Dr. (☎ **561/ 468-3985** for information), a half-mile-long beach, was once the training ground for Navy frogmen. A short nature trail leads through a hammock of live oaks, cabbage palms, sea grapes, and strangler figs. The western side of the area has swamps of red mangroves that are home to fiddler crabs, osprey, and a multitude of wading birds. The beach is north of Fort Pierce Inlet on North Hutchinson Island. Admission is $3.25 per vehicle. It's open from sunrise to sunset.

Jaycee Park, on SE Ocean Boulevard between Hutchinson Island and the mainland, is a waterfront park that's popular with picnickers and water-sports enthusiasts.

The park is divided into two sections: When you cross the Intracoastal Waterway on Ocean Boulevard, the first island you reach is the picnic area, and the second is best known for fishing and windsurfing.

Jensen/Sea Turtle Beach, on Ocean Boulevard at NE Causeway Boulevard, on Hutchinson Island, is a large developed beach with volleyball courts, a water-sports concession, outdoor showers, a picnic area, and plenty of parking.

BIKING   One of the best deals in bike rentals in the area is at **A-1 Bike Repair**, 1890 NE Jensen Beach Blvd. (☎ **561/334-5003**), where there are dozens of old beach bikes and a few high-tech versions for rent from the crowded little shop at the train tracks. Either is perfect for riding over the causeway to explore the beachfront area along Fla. A1A to the Indian River Plantation and north to Bathtub Beach, where there are many fun trails and roads to negotiate. Rates start at $5 a day for a really raggedy bike, or $20 a day for a better bike with all the necessities—lock, helmet, and car rack. The shop is usually open daily until at least 5pm.

FISHING   In addition to the many high-priced fishing opportunities along the Treasure Coast, the Stuart and Fort Pierce areas offer plenty of land fishing from the numerous bridges that dot the bays. If you didn't bring your own rod and reel, call Big Bob's or Rosemeyer's (see "Water Sports," below). Two especially good spots include the Stuart Causeway bridge and the Jensen Beach causeway. With a little luck and patience, you can have grilled snook, trout, or red fish for dinner.

At the **Fort Pierce Yachting Center,** 1 Ave. A, Fort Pierce (☎ **561/464-1245**), more than a dozen charter captains keep their motors running for anxious anglers who want to try to catch a few. The price can be as much as $150 per person in the busy season, but if you can get a group of four or more interested, you can usually rent a boat without a captain and save a bunch. Plus, if you catch a lot of fish, you have your dinner. Call or stop by the docks to see if it's slow. If you want to do some bottom fishing, try *The Fish Stalker* (☎ **561/464-4754**), one of the best-priced boats around. It sails every day at different times. Rates are $25 to $35 for 3- to 4-hour excursions. (For more rental bargains, see "Water Sports," below.)

WATER SPORTS   Big Bob's Waverunners and Boat Rentals, 3545 NE Indian River Dr., Jensen Beach (☎ **561/225-2266**), rents everything to do with the water. And while nothing is inexpensive, the rates are some of the lowest on the island. Waverunners go for $60 an hour, $35 for a half-hour ride. If you know how to sail, you may opt for lower-priced sailboats, for between $25 and $35 an hour. One great budget option is the 27-foot pontoon boat, which can hold up to 18 people; it costs $150 for 4 hours or $200 for the whole day. An 18-foot angler costs $75 for a half day and $140 for a full day. If you're planning to cast a rod, you'll need a fishing license too, for $16.

Rosemeyer's Boat Rentals, 3281 NE Indian River Dr., at Indian River Road and Jensen Beach (☎ **561/334-1000**), rents 16- to 22-foot boats. Rosemeyer's has the corner on budget Waverunners—rent one for $19.95 for a half-hour ride, or bring a buddy along for only $29.95! If you're having so much fun that a half hour is too short, an hour for the both of you will cost only $45. A half-day rental costs $99 to $175, and $149 to $275 for a full day. Parasailing trips are relatively cheap—a 10-minute ride at a height of 250 feet is $20 per person, and group package rates are available—bring 10 of your friends along and they'll take 10% off the whole thing. If you compare these boating rates with the $600 it would cost for a day's fishing in Miami, this is a real bargain! For diehard fishers there's a 3-day package for $405 in an 18-footer that could hold up to six people, and you don't need to use the 3 days consecutively. Plus, with all rentals, Rosemeyer's throws in rods and reels.

PARKS & NATURE PRESERVES

Jack Island State Preserve, north of the Fort Pierce Inlet on Fla. A1A, North Hutchinson Island (☎ 561/468-3985), offers hiking and nature trails on scenic Hutchinson Island. Jutting out into the Indian River, the mangrove-covered peninsula contains several marked trails, varying in distance from half a mile to over 4 miles. The trails go through mangrove forests and lead to a short observation tower. Admission is free. The park is open daily from 8am to sunset.

One of the Treasure Coast's most scenic areas is just south of Vero Beach in the **Jonathon Dickinson State Park** (☎ 561/546-2771). This intentionally low-managed park is meant to resemble the habitat of hundreds of years ago, before Europeans started chopping, dredging, and "improving" the area. On the more than 11,500 acres of land and river are dozens of species of Florida's unique wildlife. There are also comfortable campgrounds with well-equipped cabins (see "Camping" under "Where to Stay," below). There are four different scenic nature and bike trails through the scrublands, and you can also rent canoes from the concession stand to explore this intoxicating region yourself. Admission is $3.25 per car for up to eight adults. The area is open to day hikers, bikers, and walkers daily from 8am until sundown, later on weekends. Call for a brochure or other information.

WHAT TO SEE & DO
ECO-CENTERS

✪ **Coastal Science Center.** NE Ocean Blvd., Hutchinson Island, Stuart. ☎ **561/225-0505.** Admission $3 adults, $1.50 children, free for children 5 and under. Mon–Sat 10am–5pm.

Opened by the South Florida Oceanographic Society in late 1994, this 44-acre site, surrounded by coastal hammock and mangroves is its own little ecosystem, which serves as an outdoor classroom to teach visitors about the region's flora and fauna, both on land and underwater. The modest building houses saltwater tanks and wet and dry "discovery tables" with small indigenous animals. The incredibly eager staff of volunteers encourage visitors to wander the lush, well-marked nature trails.

Harbor Branch Oceanographic Institution. 5600 U.S. 1 North, Fort Pierce. ☎ **561/465-2400** or 561/567-7196. Admission $5 adults, $3 children 6–18, free for children 5 and under. Mon–Sat 10am–4pm (tours given at 10am, noon, and 2pm).

Harbor Branch is a working nonprofit scientific institute that studies ways in which humans can best use oceanic resources. Visitors are welcome to visit the 500-acre site on regularly scheduled guided tours. The first stop is the J. Seward Johnson Marine Education Center, which houses institute-built submersibles that are used to conduct marine research at depths of up to 3,000 feet. A video details the different research projects, and several large aquariums simulate the environments of the Indian River Lagoon and a saltwater reef. Tour-goers are then shuttled by minibus to the Aqua-Culture Farming Center, a research facility containing shallow tanks growing seaweed and other oceanic plants.

MUSEUMS

✪ **Elliott Museum.** 825 NE Ocean Blvd., Hutchinson Island, Stuart. ☎ **561/225-1961.** Admission $4 adults, 50¢ children 6–13, free for children 5 and under. Daily 11am–4pm.

Inventor and avid collector Harmon Parker Elliott built this museum in 1961. Elliott, along with his father, Sterling Elliott, claimed 222 patents between them. The museum is a treasure trove of early Americana. The exhibitions include local life from the Civil War through the 1920s, with life-size dioramas; half a million dollars' worth of baseball memorabilia, featuring an autographed item from every player elected to the Baseball Hall of Fame; and an impressive collection of antique luxury cars. Tinkerers will love this place.

Gilbert's House of Refuge Museum. 301 SE MacArthur Blvd., Hutchinson Island, Stuart. ☎ **561/225-1875.** Admission $2 adults, 50¢ children 6–13, free for children 5 and under. Tues–Sun 11am–4pm.

Gilbert's, the oldest structure in Martin County, dates from 1875 when it functioned as a rescue center for shipwrecked sailors. Restored to its original condition, the house now displays an intriguing collection of marine artifacts, turn-of-the-century lifesaving equipment, and photographs.

Stuart Heritage Museum at the Stuart Feed Store. 161 SW Flagler Ave., Stuart. ☎ **561/220-4600.** Free admission. Tues–Sat 11am–3pm.

In 1900, when the Stuart Feed Store was the territory's most important general store, the region's inhabitants, including the Seminole, would come here from miles around to buy feed and supplies. Today the former shop makes an interesting stop to view a piece of history.

St. Lucie Historical Museum. 414 Seaway Dr., Fort Pierce. ☎ **561/462-1795.** Admission $2 adults, $1 children 6–11, free for children 5 and under. Tues–Sat 10am–4pm, Sun noon–4pm.

Fort Pierce's little historical museum displays treasures from a 1715 shipwreck, uniforms and other objects from the 1838 Seminole War, and a re-creation of Old Fort Pierce, the garrison that gave this area its name. There's also a 1919 fire engine pumper, and an excellent collection of area photographs shot between 1880 and 1920. The 1907 Gardner House, next door, has been fully restored to give visitors a peek at local life at the turn of the century.

UDT-SEAL Museum. 3300 N. Fla. A1A, Fort Pierce. ☎ **561/462-3597.** Admission $2 adults, $1 children, free for children 4 and under. Mon–Sat 10am–4pm, Sun noon–4pm. Closed Mon off-season.

Florida is full of unusual museums, but none is more curious than the UDT-SEAL Museum, a most peculiar tribute to the secret forces of the U.S. Navy—frogmen and their successors, the SEAL teams. Chronological displays trace the history of these clandestine divers and detail their most important achievements. The best exhibits are those of equipment used by the navy's elite members.

ORGANIZED TOURS

The **Indian River Plantation,** at 555 NE Ocean Blvd., on Hutchinson Island in Stuart (☎ **561/334-1002**), sponsors many walking, biking, and eco-tours, especially in the summer months when the turtles are nesting. Many of the activities are open to nonguests when there's space, for a fee. One eco-tour starts at 9am and takes visitors on a 21-foot pontoon boat through the Indian River, past uninhabited islands, secluded beaches, and mangrove forests full of wildlife. Eco-boat tours start at $20 for adults and $15 for children 11 and under. Many of the walking tours cost only a few dollars and are especially tailored to kids. Call to find out the schedule of events, which changes with the seasons.

A tour boat, the *Loxahatchee Queen* (☎ 561/334-1002) takes daily tours of the area's otherwise inaccessible backwaters where curious alligators, manatees, and tortoises often peek out to see who's in their yard. Try to catch the 2-hour tour, offered Wednesday to Saturday, that includes a stop at Trapper Nelson's home. Known as the "Wildman of Loxahatchee," Nelson lived in the most primitive conditions, now preserved for visitors to see. Tours leave four times daily and cost $10 for adults, $5 for children 6 to 12, and free for children 5 and under.

The Spirit of St. Joseph **Cruise Line,** 424 Seaway Dr., Fort Pierce (☎ **561/ 467-BOAT**), takes up to 200 passengers on guided tours of the Indian River. Most of the regularly scheduled cruises include a meal and/or entertainment, a pretty good deal; the Sunday brunch cruise at 10:30am is one of the best. Phone for fluctuating schedules and prices, which range from $16 to $24. You can eat all you want and enjoy the live band and a 3-hour tour of the Indian River backcountry for only $18. Reserve in advance, since this tour fills up fast in season.

SHOPPING

You may have already realized that the Hutchinson Island area is no Paris or Milan, but that doesn't mean that there's nothing to buy. This area's specialty is food that, with surprisingly little effort, can be exported home.

Davis Groves, in Bruner Plaza, 642 SE Monterey Rd., Stuart (☎ **561/287-1588**), sells all types of locally grown produce, including the famous Indian River grapefruit and oranges. It will ship anywhere in North America starting at $30 for a half bushel, which includes the cost of shipping.

Mrs. Peter's, 1500 County Rd. 707, Rio/Jensen Beach (☎ **561/334-2184**), sells some of the most succulent smoked foods you've ever eaten. Their motto is "We Smoke Everything but Mermaids," and they've been doing so since 1931. Old-fashioned hand-smoked kingfish, amberjack, turkey breast, and other meats are sold and shipped from here; order forms are available for other smoked specialties. To get there, head north on the Roosevelt Bridge and turn right on County Road 707. You'll smell the smoke shack on the right.

WHERE TO STAY

Although the area boasts some beautiful beaches, the majority of the hotels here are pricey. There are a few more affordable options downtown, conveniently located next to quaint shops and restaurants. In general, however, you'll find that this area is monopolized by time-shares, condos, and private residences.

DOUBLES FOR LESS THAN $60

Edgewater Motel and Apartments. 1156 Seaway Dr., Fort Pierce, Hutchinson Island, FL 34949. ☎ **561/468-3555,** or 800/433-0004. 4 rms, 5 efficiencies, 5 apts. A/C TV TEL. Dec 20–Apr, $47 double; from $60 efficiency; from $80 apt. May–Dec 19, $37 double; from $45 efficiency; from $70 apt. Additional person $10 extra. Weekly rates available. AE, DISC, MC, V.

This budget alternative to the Harbor Light Inn, next door, offers modestly decorated rooms in a 50-year-old building filled with an eclectic mix of furniture. There's a private swimming pool, and guests have access to the adjacent fishing pier and boat docks. The efficiencies contain small kitchens and are available on a daily or weekly basis.

DOUBLES FOR LESS THAN $80

Harbor Light Inn. 1160 Seaway Dr., Fort Pierce, Hutchinson Island, FL 34949. ☎ **561/ 468-3555,** or 800/433-0004. 21 rms. A/C MINIBAR TV TEL. Dec 20–Apr, $78–$120 double. May–Dec 19, $58–$95 double. Additional person $10 extra. AE, CB, DC, DISC, MC, V.

Fronting the Intracoastal Waterway, the Harbor Light is a good choice for boating and fishing enthusiasts, offering 15 boat slips and two private fishing piers. The hotel itself carries on this nautical theme with pierlike wooden stairs and rope railings. While not exactly captain's quarters, the simply decorated rooms are adequate.

Higher-priced rooms either have waterfront balconies or small kitchenettes that contain a coffeemaker, refrigerator, oven, and toaster. There's a swimming pool with a large deck for sunbathing.

Harborfront Inn Bed & Breakfast. 310 Atlanta Ave., Stuart, FL 34994. ☎ **561/288-7289,** or 800/294-1703. Fax 561/221-0474. 3 rms, 3 suites. A/C TV. $65–$105 double; from $95 suite. Rates include breakfast. AE, MC, V.

The Harborfront Inn consists of a series of little blue-trimmed shingled cottages located riverfront and within walking distance of restaurants in downtown Stuart. Each room in this highly recommended B&B has its own exclusive entrance, making it more private than most. Every accommodation has a sitting area, clock radio, and private bathroom. The two best rooms are the bright Garden Suite, which has a queen-size bed, rattan furnishings, and a deck with river and garden views; and the Guest House, which has an extra-large bathroom with two sinks, and can be rented with an adjoining full kitchen. The inn's cozy public areas are surrounded by an enclosed porch where breakfast is served. The morning meal usually includes fresh fruit from trees that grow on the property. Children are not accepted, and there's a no-smoking rule.

Doubles for Less than $100

✪ **Hutchinson Inn.** 9750 S. Ocean Dr. (Fla. A1A), Jensen Beach, FL 34957. ☎ **561/ 229-2000.** 21 units. A/C TV TEL. Winter, $90 double; $140–$160 efficiency or apt. Off-season, $60 double; from $95 efficiency or apt. Rates include continental breakfast. Additional person $10–$20 extra. MC, V. From I-95, take the Stuart exit east to County Road 76 and continue to Fla. A1A north; the hotel is about 4 miles ahead on your right.

It may not look like much from the road, but you're soon greeted by striking white gazebos dotting thick green lawns and regal brick walkways leading to a two-story retreat. Located directly on the beach, this quiet hideaway is a 15-minute drive from anywhere. Unfortunately, so many people know about it that during the busy season, February to April, it gets booked up a year in advance. From its tiny lobby with its green canopy to the little love birds that live below the stairs leading to your room, it's hard to top it for charm. The well-proportioned rooms have rattan furniture, sofas convert into pull-out beds, and several rooms can be joined to accommodate large families. Facilities and services are few, but there's good swimming at the beach and a large outdoor pool, and freshly baked cookies each evening before bedtime. On Saturday afternoon guests are invited to join in a complimentary barbecue.

Worth a Splurge

✪ **The Home Place.** 501 Akron Ave., Stuart, FL 34994. ☎ **561/220-9148.** 4 rms, all with bath (1 with private bath down a hall). Year round, $75–$95 double Sun–Thurs, $95 double Fri–Sat. Rates include full breakfast. MC, V.

The gracious owners of this historic home, Suzanne and Michael Pescetello, are just the kind of innkeepers you want in a cozy little bed-and-breakfast. They offer taste, style, good conversation, superb homemade sweets in an always-open fridge, wine, and a perfectly maintained inn. The best part is that they live in the adjacent building, just a few steps from the 1913 guesthouse and beautifully landscaped pool and Jacuzzi area. You'll be comfortable in any of the Victorian rooms, chock full of lace curtains, old steamer trunks, and crystal decanters. The large captain's room is a favorite for its size and big fluffy bed. The couple host many weddings in this romantic inn. While you're a few miles inland from the beach, you're only a few blocks from the quaint and rejuvenated downtown area.

Mellon Patch Inn. 3601 N. Fla. A1A, North Hutchinson Island, FL 34949. ☎ **561/461-5231.** Fax 561/464-9841. 4 rms. A/C TV. $100–$110 double. Rates include breakfast. Additional person $20 extra. AE, MC, V.

Opened in mid-1994, the Mellon Patch Inn was built specifically as a bed-and-breakfast by innkeepers Andrea and Arthur Mellon. They offer just four bright rooms, each with a large bathroom and sturdy soundproofed walls. The Patchwork Quilt Room has a queen-size bed and a table and chairs, but like the others, lacks a comfortable sitting area. The Tropical Paradise Room is designed with hand-painted walls featuring palm trees and birds. Seaside Serenity has aqua-blue accents and seashell and fishnet decor. The Santa Fe Room is dressed in muted browns and yellows, and has an ocean view—from the bathroom. The public living room is nicer than any of the guest rooms. It has a two-story vaulted ceiling, a fireplace, and lots of windows that overlook the Indian River. A gourmet breakfast that might include waffles topped with strawberries and pecans, chocolate-chip pancakes, or spinach soufflé is served here each morning. There's a public beach and free tennis courts across the street. Smoking, children, and pets are not allowed.

CAMPING

Jonathon Dickinson State Park has a comfortable campsite where you can overnight in rustic cabins or in your tent in two different parts of the park. The River Camp area is near the Loxahatchee River, and the Pine Grove site is in a grove of beautiful shade trees. There are concession areas for daytime snacks, and more than 135 campsites with showers, clean rest rooms, water, optional electricity, and an open fire pit for cooking. Overnight rates in the winter are $18 without electricity, $20 with. In the summer rates are about $14 per person. Call the park manager (☎ **561/546-2771**) for information.

For a cushier camping experience, you can reserve a wood-sided cabin with a furnished kitchen, a bathroom with shower, heat and air-conditioning, and an outside grill. You'll have to bring your own linens. Cabins are part of the concession and are in the park, near the River Camp. They rent from $65 a night and sleep four people comfortably, or six if you're very friendly. In the winter it books up to 6 weeks in advance. Don't forget to bring a required $50 key deposit. Call 800/746-1466 Monday to Friday from 9am to 5pm.

WHERE TO EAT

Although this quiet area is not a gourmet's paradise, there are some reasonably priced spots interspersed among the tourist traps and overpriced seafood shacks. The residents tend to eat at home, which means that most restaurants cater to the seasonal crowd. Expect some waits in winter.

For picnic supplies, go to the **Plantation Pantry,** 650 NE Ocean Blvd., in Stuart (☎ **561/225-1100**), across the road from the Indian River Plantation and just behind a gas station. It offers a full deli, making both hot and cold sandwiches, as well as a large selection of gourmet treats. Try a piece of the locally produced fudge, which comes in an incredibly wide variety of flavors.

MEALS FOR LESS THAN $7

✪ **Harry and the Natives.** 1190 S. Federal Hwy., Hobe Sound. ☎ **561/546-3061.** Reservations not accepted. Breakfast $3.25–$7.25; lunch $3.25–$4.95. Tues–Sun 6am–2:30pm. No credit cards.

This afternoon bar scene is straight out of Key West—the Old Florida memorabilia hanging from the ceiling couldn't have been better placed by a film crew. Harry's mom, a slip of a silver-haired women behind the cashier stand, sings to the patrons and keeps the place pretty lively. Burgers and beer are staples, though the chili and dolphin fish sandwiches are also a great deal. Breakfasts here are huge and hearty. Disregard the silly menu selections like marinated beef lips and possum. This is "white trash" heaven and proud of it. Try a potato chip and mayonnaise sandwich on Wonder Bread or a Kiss-me-not (onions and mayo). Hang out in the outdoor patio for a more relaxed but less interesting experience.

Nature's Way Cafe. In the Post Office Arcade, 25 SW Osceola St., Stuart. ☎ **561/220-7306.** Reservations not accepted. Sandwiches and salads $3–$6; juices and shakes $1–$3. No credit cards. Mon–Fri 10am–4pm, Sat 11am–3pm. VEGETARIAN.

One large room with little tables and a few strategically placed bar stools overlooking the sidewalk—that's all there is to this pleasantly decorated, white-tiled eatery. A sort of health-food deli, Nature's Way offers an assortment of prepared salads, make-your-own vegetarian sandwiches, and frozen yogurt. There's also a healthy assortment of shakes, fresh juices, and homemade muffins. If it's a particularly nice day, you might ask them to pack your lunch so you can picnic in a park or on the beach.

Osceola St. Juice Bar and Take Out Cafe. 26 Osceola St., Stuart. ☎ **561/221-1679.** Reservations not accepted. Sandwiches and salads $3.50–$4.25; juices and shakes $2–$4. DISC, MC, V. Mon–Sat 10am–5pm, Sun (brunch) 9am–1pm. NATURAL FOOD.

This little natural-food store takes sprouts seriously. It's got wheat grass and carrot juice and smoothies to soothe the hearts of the most hard-core vegans. Tasty sandwiches and salads in an old general-store atmosphere should make the spot successful, though the young new-agey service staff need to wake up and smell the herbal tea. You can also buy lots of great bath and body products here.

MEALS FOR LESS THAN $10

Jan's Place. 1897 Jensen Beach Blvd., Old Jensen Beach Village. ☎ **561/334-9598.** Breakfast $3–$8; lunch $5–$9. MC, V. Sun–Fri 7am–11:30pm, Sat 7am–midnight. AMERICAN.

The wooden rafters are loaded with the weight of thousands of old photographs, blinking Christmas lights, fans, hanging lanterns, fish nets, and a 10-foot mural of swaying palms. The food isn't gourmet, but it's got a few decent selections. Especially for breakfast, you'll find some fresh and delicious dishes, like the Neptune Benedict, which has large chunks of shrimp, scallops, crab, and a very garlicky hollandaise. The seafood's from a can but tastes great. The large lunch menu is mostly dressed-up diner fare, but specials like blackened dolphin can be spectacular.

MEALS FOR LESS THAN $15

The Black Marlin. 53 W. Osceola St., Stuart. ☎ **561/266-3126.** Reservations not accepted. Salads and sandwiches $4–$10; main courses $9–$22. AE, MC, V. Mon–Thurs 5–10pm, Fri–Sat 5–11pm (bar open later). FLORIDA REGIONAL.

Although it sports the look and feel of an English pub, the Black Marlin happily stays away from English cuisine, opting instead for a medley of regional flavors. The "salmon BLT" is typical of the dishes here—grilled salmon on a toasted bun with bacon, lettuce, tomato, and cole slaw. Designer pizzas are topped with shrimp, roasted red peppers, and the like, and the main dishes, all served with vegetables and potatoes, include lobster tail with a honey-mustard sauce and a charcoal-grilled chicken breast served on radicchio with caramelized onions.

Captain's Galley. 827 N. Indian River Dr., Fort Pierce. ☎ **561/466-8495.** Reservations not accepted. Main courses $9; breakfast/lunch $2–$5. MC, V. Mon–Sat 7am–9pm, Sun 7am–noon. SEAFOOD/AMERICAN.

Anywhere else this might be just another coffee shop. But here, just over the Intracoastal Waterway at the north end of Hutchinson Island, it's a local institution. Dressed up with printed window valances and hanging plants, the Captain's Galley is busiest at breakfast, when locals catch up over eggs, toast, and home-fries. Lunch specials usually include a variety of burgers and a small selection of salads and sandwiches. And dinner is for seafood, when the Galley serves up shrimp scampi, the day's fish, or land specialties like strip steak and chicken français.

✪ **Conchy Joe's Seafood.** 3945 NE Indian River Dr., Jensen Beach. ☎ **561/334-1130.** Main courses $12–$20; lunch $5–$8. DISC, MC, V. Daily 11:30am–2:30pm and 5–10pm. (Happy hour Mon–Fri 3–6pm.) SEAFOOD.

Known for fresh foods and Old Florida hospitality, Conchy Joe's enjoys an excellent reputation that's far bigger than the restaurant itself. Dining is either indoors, at red-and-white cloth-covered tables, or on a covered patio overlooking the St. Lucie River. The restaurant features a wide variety of freshly shucked shellfish and daily-catch selections that are baked, broiled, or fried. Beer is the drink of choice here, though other beverages and a full bar are available. Conchy Joe's has been the most active place in Jensen Beach since it opened here in 1983. The large bar area is especially popular at night and during weekday happy hours.

Guytano's Grille. 2220 E. Ocean Blvd., Stuart. ☎ **561/286-7550.** Reservations suggested. Main courses $9–$17; lunch $5–$12. AE, DC, DISC, MC, V. Mon–Thurs 11:30am–10pm, Fri–Sat 11:30am–11pm, Sun 4–10pm. AMERICAN.

Located on the mainland just across from Hutchinson Island, Guytano's two large dining rooms are among the finest in town. The high ceilings and white stucco walls are made lively with ceiling fans, plants, and ultra-contemporary lighting. The food is both beautifully presented and delicious. Chef/owner Guy Ciccone presides over a skilled kitchen that creates such mouth-watering appetizers as spicy sautéed eggplant and escarole soup with tiny meatballs and ricotta ravioli. Dishes are slightly jazzed up but not overly fussy. You can get a serious meal here, with jazz background music and relatively young crowd. A second Guytano's is located at 2001 U.S. 1 in Vero Beach (☎ 561/778-4088).

Theo Thudpucker's Raw Bar and Seafood Restaurant. 2025 Seaway Dr., Fort Pierce. ☎ **561/465-1078.** Reservations not accepted. Main courses $8–$14; lunch $4–$7. No credit cards. Mon–Thurs 11:30am–9:30pm, Fri–Sat 11:30am–11pm, Sun 1–9:30pm. SEAFOOD.

Nobody comes here seeking luxurious ambience. Located in a little building by the beach, wallpapered with maps and newspapers, Thudpucker's only pretends to be what it is: a straightforward chowder bar. There's not much more to the dining room than one long bar and a few simple tables. Prominently placed signs attest to the food's purity: BOTH CLAMS AND OYSTERS ARE PACKED WITH ICE AND ARE NOT OPENED UNTIL YOU PLACE YOUR ORDER. PLEASE BE PATIENT. Chowder and stews, often made with sherry and half-and-half, make excellent starters or light meals. The most recommendable (and filling) dinner dishes are sautéed scallops, deviled crabs, and deep-fried Okeechobee catfish.

WORTH A SPLURGE

✪ **Scalawags Restaurant.** At the Indian River Plantation, 555 NE Ocean Blvd., Hutchinson Island. ☎ **561/225-6818.** Reservations recommended. Main courses $15–$21; Wed seafood buffet $25 (including tax and tip); Sun brunch $19. AE, DISC, MC, V. Mon–Tues and Thurs–Sat 6–10pm, Wed 5–10pm, Sun 11am–2pm (buffet brunch) and 6–10pm. SEAFOOD/STEAKS.

Scalawags' Wednesday-night seafood buffet is legendary in these parts. It's also the best deal in town. Table upon table filled with the area's freshest assortment of seafood and landfood is presented at this weekly all-you-can-eat feast. Here's what $25 will get you: any fish or shellfish you can name, salads, prime rib, fettuccine Alfredo, and an assortment of desserts. The restaurant's Sunday brunch buffet offers a similarly gluttonous abundance of food. Create-your-own omelet, and then fill your plate again and again with assorted salads, smoked salmon, pâtés, stuffed flounder, eggs Benedict, and more. There's also a large table filled with desserts, and champagne and mimosas flow freely. An excellent selection of seafood, steaks, and pasta is served the rest of the week.

STUART, FORT PIERCE & ST. LUCIE AFTER DARK

Though no one would claim this area as a cultural hotspot, there are some fun bars and nightclubs worth checking out, plus an occasional performance in downtown Stuart. Phone the following listings to find out what's happening.

THE PERFORMING ARTS

The centerpiece to Stuart's slowly expanding cultural offerings is the newly restored **Lyric Theater,** 59 SW Flagler Ave., Stuart (☎ **561/220-1942**). This beautiful 1920s-era, 600-seat theater hosts a variety of shows and films throughout the year, from amateur plays to top-name theatrical shows, poetry readings, and concerts, sometimes from the rock-music world. The Lyric is also home to the **Atlantic Classical Orchestra,** a young and serious music group that's larger than a chamber orchestra but not quite up to symphony size. The **McAlpin Fine Arts Center** at Indian River Community College is a popular venue for a varied series of plays, lectures, and concerts. The **Treasure Coast Opera Society** (☎ **561/462-4750**) performs January to March at the Civic Center in Fort Pierce; call for schedules.

THE BAR SCENE

Local restaurants serve double duty as the nightlife centers of these otherwise sleepy towns. The bar at the **Black Marlin** (see "Where to Eat," above) is popular with local professionals and tourists alike. The long wooden bar occupies about half the restaurant, and on Tuesday, Thursday, Friday, and Saturday nights it's packed three deep.

Younger revelers go to **Shuckers,** in the Island Beach Resort, 9800 S. Ocean Dr., Jensen Beach (☎ **561/229-1224**), a bustling place that's just about as wild as Jensen gets. The beer-sign-and-sports-banner decor is augmented by a couple of pool tables and video games, and a small dance floor that really thumps on weekends. Shuckers is open Monday to Saturday from 10am to 2am and on Sunday from 10am to midnight.

The lounge at **Scalawags Restaurant** (see "Where to Eat," above), at the Indian River Plantation, is the fanciest in town. There's low-key live musical entertainment almost every night.

No list of Jensen nightlife would be complete without mention of **Conchy Joe's Seafood** (see "Where to Eat," above), one of the region's most active spots. Inside, locals chug beer and watch a large-screen TV, while outside on the waterfront patio, live bands perform a few nights a week for a raucous crowd of dancers. Happy hours, weekdays from 3 to 6pm, draw large crowds with low-priced drinks and snacks.

2 Vero Beach & Sebastian

85 miles SE of Orlando, 129 miles N of Miami

Vero Beach is located at the northern tip of the Treasure Coast region in Indian River County. These two beach towns are populated with people who knew Miami and Fort Lauderdale in the days before massive high-rises and overcrowding. They appreciate the area's small-town feel, which also appeals to visitors—a laid-back, relaxed atmosphere, friendly people, and friendlier prices.

A crowd of well-tanned surfers from all over the state descend on the region to catch some of the state's biggest waves at Sebastian Inlet. Water-sports enthusiasts will enjoy the area's fine diving, surfing, and windsurfing. And in spring, baseball buffs can catch some action from the Los Angeles Dodgers as they train in exhibition games in Vero Beach.

ESSENTIALS

GETTING THERE & GETTING AROUND   See "Essentials" in Section 1, "Stuart & Port St. Lucie/Fort Pierce," earlier in this chapter.

VISITOR INFORMATION   The **Indian River County Tourist Council,** 1216 21st St., Vero Beach, FL 32961 (☎ **561/567-3491**), will send visitors an incredibly detailed information packet on the entire county, which includes Vero Beach and Sebastian, and Fellsmere. You'll find a detailed full-color map of the area, a comprehensive listing of upcoming events, a hotel guide, and more.

BEACHES & OUTDOOR ACTIVITIES

BEACHES   Most of Vero's beachfront is open to the public and parking is generally plentiful. The beach at the end of Beachland Boulevard is one of the most convenient, hence popular.

Jaycee Beach Park, on Ocean Drive and Mango Road in Vero Beach, is a small beach with good sand, picnic facilities, public rest rooms, and showers. The active boardwalk has a number of concession stands with snacks and sandwiches.

Riverside Park, located east of Barber Bridge at the end of Memorial Island Drive, is located directly on the Indian River. There are tennis and racquetball courts here, as well as a jogging course, boat ramps, and picnic pavilions.

At **Sebastian Inlet,** on either side of the bridge are flat sandy beaches with lots of facilities, including kayak, paddleboat, and canoe rentals, a well-stocked surf shop, and a beach snack shop. The winds seem to stir up the surf here, to the delight of surfers and boarders who get here early to catch the occasionally big waves.

South Beach Park, on South Ocean Drive, at the end of Marigold Lane, is a busy, lifeguarded beach with picnic tables, rest rooms, and showers. It's known as one of the best swimming beaches. It attracts a young crowd, who use the volleyball nets. A well laid out nature walk takes you into beautiful secluded trails.

GOLF   There are two courses at **Dodgertown,** on the corner of 43rd Avenue and 26th Street (☎ **561/569-4800**): an 18-hole championship course at the Dodger Pines Country Club, and a challenging 9-hole run located adjacent to the complex's baseball stadium. Club rentals are available and lessons are offered by PGA professionals. Greens fees are $12 to $21. Carts are an additional $8.

The **Whisper Lakes Golf Course,** a public course at U.S. 1 and 53rd Street (☎ **561/567-3321**), represents the best driving deal in town. Here you can play 9 or 18 holes of golf at this par-3 course, or just hit a practice bucket on the driving range. Clubs rent for $3; greens fees are $5 for 9 holes, $10 for 18 holes. Carts are an additional $2.

TENNIS   **Riverside Park,** 350 Dahlia Lane, on Royal Palm Boulevard at the east end of Barber Bridge in Vero Beach (☎ **561/231-4787**), has 10 hard courts (6 lighted) that can be rented for $3 per person per hour. Reservations are accepted up to 24 hours in advance. The club also has two racquetball courts at reasonable rates in a lush park setting that has nature trails and many other facilities.

The **Twin Oaks Tennis Club,** 1295 6th Ave. in Vero Beach (☎ **561/770-1149**), has seven championship clay courts (two are lighted), a fully equipped pro shop, and a well-respected tennis academy for children. The setting is inland beneath towering old oaks. After a game, you can relax in a cozy lounge and clubhouse that overlooks the courts. Rates are extremely reasonable, from $7 for the whole day. Open Monday to Thursday from 8:30am to 8pm, on Friday from 8:30am to 6pm, and on Saturday, Sunday, and holidays from 8:30am to 4pm. To get there, take the 17th Street Bridge west to 6th Avenue and turn left; you'll see the club on the right after you pass 13th Street (less than a mile).

WHAT TO SEE & DO
BASEBALL AT DODGERTOWN

Dodgertown, at 3901 26th St. in Vero Beach (☎ **561/569-4900**), is the winter home of baseball's Los Angeles Dodgers. Vero hosts the team in grand style. This 450-acre compound encompasses two golf courses, a conference center, country club, movie theater, and recreation room. You can watch afternoon exhibition games during winter months (usually from mid-February to the end of March) in the comfortable 6,474-seat outdoor stadium. Even if the game sells out, you can catch the action from a seat on the grassy field with a $5 standing-room ticket—the stadium has never turned away an eager fan. If you want something more filling than a "Dodger Dog," visit the Country Club Restaurant, where fans often report sightings of their favorite players. Even when spring training is over, you can still catch a game; the Dodgers' farm team has a full season of minor-league baseball in summer.

Admission to the complex is free and it's open daily from 8am to 11pm. Admission to the stadium is $5 to $8, and games begin at 1pm. To get there from I-95, follow Fla. 60 east for 5 miles to 43rd Avenue, turn left, continue to 26th Street, and turn right; the entrance is straight ahead.

NATURE PRESERVES

✪ **Environmental Learning Center.** 255 Live Oak Dr., Wabasso Island. ☎ **561/589-5050.** Free admission. Mon–Fri 9am–5pm; Sat–Sun the center is closed, nature walks only.

The Indian River is not really a river at all, but a large brackish lagoon that's home to a greater variety of species than any other estuary in North America. The privately funded Environmental Learning Center was created to protect the local habitat and educate visitors about their environment. Situated on 51 island acres, the center features dozens of hands-on exhibits that are geared to both children and adults. There are live touch tanks, bird exhibits, and microscopes for viewing the smallest sea life close-up. The best thing to do here is join one of the center's interpretive canoe trips, offered by reservation only. These cost $10 for adults and $5 for children. Phone for information.

MUSEUMS

Indian River Citrus Museum. 2140 14th Ave., Vero Beach. ☎ **561/770-2263.** Admission $1 donation. Tues–Sat 10am–4pm, Sun 1–4pm.

Prized as some of the best in the world, oranges and grapefruit from this region are valued for their outstanding flavor and juiciness. The tiny Indian River Citrus Museum and gift shop exhibits artifacts relating to the history of the citrus industry, from its initial boom in the late 1800s to the present. Displays include old photographs, antiquated farm tools, antique citrus labels, and original harvesting equipment. Unique citrus-themed gift items are sold, along with, of course, ready-to-ship bushels of fruit.

Mel Fisher's Treasure Museum. 1322 U.S. 1, Sebastian. ☎ **561/589-9874.** Admission $5 adults, $4 seniors, $1.50 children 7–12, free for children 6 and under. Mon–Sat 10am–5pm, Sun noon–5pm.

Here is where you can see the treasures from the fateful fleet that went down in 1715 as well as others, excavated since Mel Fisher and his crew perfected the art of treasure diving. They worked for years to improve their hunting skills, and here we see the fruits of his labor. Though not as extensive as the museum in Key West, this exhibit is worth a look. On display are gold coins, bars, and many Spanish artifacts. The preservation laboratory shows how the goods are extracted, cleaned, and preserved. The admission price is very steep, but if you're really interested in the process of gold excavation, you should check it out—otherwise, it's a wash.

SHOPPING

There are a hundred high-priced tourist shops selling everything from suntan oil to resortwear at high prices, but if you want to get some great bargains, drive out west a bit to the real find. The **Horizon Outlet Center**, at Fla. 60 and I-95, Vero Beach (☎ 561/770-6171, or 800/866-5900), contains over 50 discount stores selling shoes, kitchenware, books, clothing, and other items. Stores include Corning/Revere, Stone Mountain Handbags, Jones New York, Levi's Outlet by Design, Ann Taylor, and Rocky Mountain Chocolate. The center is open Monday to Saturday from 10am to 9pm and on Sunday from 11am to 6pm.

WHERE TO STAY

Compared to Stuart and Port St. Lucie, Vero Beach and Sebastian are much larger and much more tourist-oriented. It's easier to find accommodations in all price ranges than farther south. Here are the pick of the budget litter:

DOUBLES FOR LESS THAN $60

The Davis House. 607 Davis St., Sebastian, FL 32958. ☎ 561/589-4114. 12 rms. Dec–Apr, $59–$79 double. May–Nov, $49–$69 double. Rates include continental breakfast. Weekly and monthly rates available. DISC, MC, V.

Each of the dozen rooms in this contemporary three-story blue-and-white bed-and-breakfast has a private entrance and doorfront parking. Each of the somewhat-plain accommodations also has a small kitchenette, a king-size bed, and a pull-out sofa. The rooms are large and clean, and often house long-term guests. The bathrooms are equally ample, and have plenty of counter space. There's a large wooden deck for sunbathing, and a sunny second-floor breakfast room where cereal, muffins, juice, and coffee or tea are served.

DOUBLES FOR LESS THAN $80

Aquarius Resort Hotel/Motel. 3544 Ocean Dr., Vero Beach, FL 32963. ☎ **561/231-1133.** 28 efficiencies. Winter, $65–$115 efficiency for two. Off-season, $50–$85 efficiency for two. Additional person $5 extra; children 11 and under stay free in parents' unit. AE, DC, DISC, MC, V.

Hotels are a rare enough commodity in this condo-canyon, where seeing the sky is enough of a trick. Finding an inexpensive one should precipitate applause. Here it is! Just near Dodgertown in Vero Beach are two surprising facilities, the Aquarius Hotel and its sister, the Aquarius Motel. The motel is on the south end of the beach and has a swimming pool, shuffleboard courts, and a barbecue. And the best part is, there are kitchenettes in each of the 28 units. The decor is nothing spectacular— modern mica and dime-store prints—but the rooms are clean and well maintained. Just a few yards away is one of Vero's prettiest uncrowded beaches.

✪ **The Islander Motel.** 3101 Ocean Dr., Vero Beach, FL 32963. ☎ **561/231-4431** or 800/
952-5886. 16 rms. A/C TV TEL. Jan 21–Apr 20, $90–$99 double. Winter, $60–$75 double.
Off-season, $50–$65 double. Efficiencies cost $10 additional. Additional person $7 extra.
AE, MC, V.

Resident owners Robert and Winifred Carter run one of the most comfortable and
welcoming inns in the area. Well located in downtown Vero Beach, this motel is just
a short walk from the beach, restaurants, and shops. Every guest room has a small
refrigerator and either a king-size bed or two double beds. The accommodations are
designed in a Caribbean motif with brightly printed curtains and white rattan
furniture. There's a heated pool and a barbecue area in the handsomely landscaped
central courtyard, along with a small walk-up café.

DOUBLES FOR LESS THAN $100

Driftwood Resort. 3150 Ocean Dr., Vero Beach, FL 32963. ☎ **561/231-0550.** 86 rms,
10 two-bedroom suites. A/C TV TEL. Feb–Apr, $80–$190 double; from $190 two-bedroom
suite. Off-season, $55–$140 double; from $130 two-bedroom suite. AE, MC, V.

In 1930, world traveler and vacation visionary Waldo Sexton began construction on
a coastal hideaway built from local cypress logs. Originally planned as a private estate, the Driftwood was opened to the public after several travelers stopped to inquire
about renting a room. Today the hotel's rooms and public areas are filled with
nautical knickknacks collected by Waldo Sexton from throughout the world, with
hundreds of huge iron bells scattered about the grounds.
    Every guest room is different. Some feature terra-cotta–tiled floors and lighter
furniture, while others have a rustic feel, with hardwoods and antiques. Each accommodation has its own bath and few frills, but this is the place to stay in Vero, on the
beach and on a budget. You get tons of space and a lot of character.

CAMPING

Sunshine Travel Park. 9455 108th Ave.(County Rd. 512 and I-95, at the Sebastian/Vero
border), Sebastian, FL 32978. ☎ **561/589-7828.** 300 sites. $30–$35 per site. 10% discounts
for Good SAM and FMCA members. MC, V.

This very popular RV resort has all paved, all-even sites with all the hookups, and is
just 15 minutes from the beach. While it's hardly in a gorgeous area, it features a
heated pool, horseshoe pit, inside games room, shuffleboard, miniature golf, and a
full schedule of activities. Many regulars rebook year after year, so if you want a spot
here, call in advance.

Vero Beach KOA RV Park. 8850 U.S. 1, Wabasso, FL 32970. ☎ **561/589-5665.** 110 sites.
$20–$22 per site ($19 for tents). AE, DC, DISC, MC, V. From I-95, take County Road 512 east,
then turn south on U.S. 1 to the campground.

This campground is 2 miles from the ocean and the Intracoastal Waterway and a
quarter mile from the Indian River, the big draw for the fishing fanatics who come
regularly for the bluefish, kingfish, whitefish, shrimp, and snook. There's running
water and electricity, showers, a shop, and hookups for RVs. More than 80 regular
"snowbirds" come back year after, especially in February.
    At an adjacent campground, tenters can enjoy primitive camping on a 2-acre site
that has great open areas as well as woody regions shaded by old pines and oaks. So
far, the fire marshall hasn't given permission for ground fires.

WHERE TO EAT

Okay, so Vero Beach isn't a mecca for culinary excellence, but it's charming and Old
Florida, so food snobs grin and bear it; the seafood joints are actually quite good.

MEALS FOR LESS THAN $10

Crusty's. Humiston Park, 1050 Easterlily Lane, Vero Beach. ☎ **561/231-4728.** Main courses $5–$12. AE, DISC, MC, V. Mon–Thurs 11am–10pm, Fri–Sat 11am–11pm. SNACKS/SEAFOOD.

This place is true to its name. Jutting out on its own seafront spot, it looks as if it's about to fall into the ocean. You won't find many tourists or many niceties here—it's straight-up paper and plastic—but the place serves quality seafood and beach snacks at reasonable prices. Lots of choices, like subs, pizzas, hot dogs, and salads are carnival-priced but good. But where else can you a "clamwich" of fried clam strips, served between halves of a cornmeal bun? Everything is fresh, and the setting Old Florida. If you want to really go for it, do the stone crab dinner for $12 (prices vary seasonally) with all the fixings. You can't beat that.

Pearl's Bistro. Royal Palm Blvd., Vero Beach. ☎ **561/778-2950.** Reservations suggested. Main courses $5–$8. AE, DISC, MC, V. Mon–Fri 11:30am–2:30pm and 6–10pm, Sat 6–10pm. CARIBBEAN.

Unfortunately, Pearl's Bistro doesn't have a bar area, but braving the Florida heat waiting outside for your table isn't too much of a burden when you're anticipating one of the tastiest and best-value meals in town. A smaller, more casual version of Vero's well-known Black Pearl (see below), this bistro has a single narrow dining room brightened with a colorful tropical mural and soothing lime walls. White chicken chili and the grilled swordfish club sandwich are two top lunch recommendations. The unusual (for this area) dinner menu includes an excellent open-face grilled-chicken burrito, steak fajita salad, and shrimp enchilada with rice and beans.

MEALS FOR LESS THAN $15

✪ **The Black Pearl.** 1409 Fla. A1A, Vero Beach. ☎ **561/234-4426.** Reservations recommended. Main courses $12–$17. AE, MC, V. Mon–Fri 11:30am–2:30pm and 6–10pm, Sat–Sun 6–10pm. CONTINENTAL.

It's unusual that such a small, moderately priced, and unassuming restaurant should make absolutely everything served. But that's exactly what they do here, and you'll be wooed by seductive smells even before you walk through the front door. There's just a single, romantic dining room featuring bright prints on clean pastel walls. Full wine racks and black art deco accents round out the decor. The restaurant's small list of appetizers may include feta cheese and spinach fritters, chilled leek-and-watercress soup, or oysters baked with crabmeat and butter. Equally creative main courses recently included Cajun pasta (topped with shrimp, scallops, and sausage), sautéed crabmeat-stuffed veal covered with hollandaise sauce, and blackened rib-eye steak. There's a good wine list, and a better dessert selection, baked daily in the restaurant's kitchen.

Ocean Grill. 1050 Sexton Plaza, Vero Beach. ☎ **561-231-5409.** Reservations accepted only for large parties. Main courses $11–$18; lunch $6–$11. AE, CB, DC, DISC, MC, V. Mon–Fri 11:30am–2:30pm and 5:45–10pm, Sat–Sun 5:45–10pm. AMERICAN.

Something of a historical landmark, the Ocean Grill was founded in 1941 by some of the area's earliest developers. The restaurant's dark-wood interior and distinct musty aroma attest to its patriarchal authenticity. The room is warmest in winter, when a fire roars in an imposing stone fireplace. Summers are nice too, especially if you snare a table by the great glass windows that open onto the ocean. It almost doesn't matter what main course you choose as long as you accompany it with an order of onion rings. At lunch it might be a deviled-crab sandwich, hot thinly sliced roast beef on a toasted French roll, or spinach salad with hot bacon dressing. Dinners mean fresh fish, which is available broiled, fried, or Cajun style; grilled pork chops with homemade jalapeño apple sauce; and roast duckling that's deserving of the restaurant's self-congratulatory "gold seal."

Waldo's. In the Driftwood Resort, 3150 Ocean Dr., Vero Beach. ☎ **561/231-7091.** Main courses $10–$13; sandwiches and salads $5–$7. AE, MC, V. Mon–Sat 7am–10pm, Sun 8am–10pm. SEAFOOD/AMERICAN.

Everyone who hears that you went to Vero Beach will ask if you went to Waldo's. The restaurant isn't famous for its food, which is good but not great. Waldo's is known for its unusual setting: Outdoor picnic tables are set as close to the ocean as you can get without getting wet. Sandwiches are the best lunch bet; dinners are just slightly more elaborate, and include Danish-style barbecued ribs and Cajun seafood kebabs.

VERO BEACH & SEBASTIAN AFTER DARK

There isn't much of a night scene in Vero or Sebastian. Most locals and tourists congregate at the restaurant bars for happy hours and music. There is usually no cover charge and rarely a drink minimum. One popular spot is the **Riverside Cafe,** 1 Beachland Blvd., beneath the east end of the Barber Bridge (☎ **561/234-5550**), which hosts live music four or five nights each week. Find other tourists and many locals enjoying one of the area's best sunsets there. Also, check out **Waldo's** (see "Where to Eat"). Most weekends you will find live music and an active bar crowd.

The only legitimate dance club in the area from Stuart to Melbourne, at the corner of Rte. 60 and 15th Ave., has changed names so many times, it is impossible to guess what might be there by the time this book goes to press. In its current incarnation, **Moscow** opens on Fridays offering an eclectic mix of DJ music and a big dance area. The $10 cover includes free drinks all night. Women are allowed in free before 10pm. Look for flyers for discounted admission. Call **561/770-6044** for the details. In the same space, on Wednesdays, you'll find techno-funk music and a slightly more laid back scene. Both sponsors welcome an over-18 crowd.

Just a block away, at 1306 20th St., is the **Vampire Cafe,** a Bohemian coffee shop that hosts a variety of live blues, jazz and punk bands. Open Mon–Sat from 4pm until 1am, the spot is a gathering place for the area's "alternative" crowd. Call **561/770-6044** for a schedule of upcoming bands.

Vero Beach's boosters are justifiably proud of their **Center for the Arts,** 3001 Riverside Park Dr. (☎ **561/231-0707**). The beautifully designed and landscaped cultural center attracts important events to its lecture hall, museum, and 250-seat Leohardt Auditorium. Volunteer docents give free tours of the galleries Wednesday to Sunday from 1:30 to 3:30pm. Call for scheduled exhibitions and performances. The center is open October to April, Friday to Wednesday from 10am to 4:30pm and on Thursday from 10am to 8pm; May to September, on Tuesday, Wednesday, Friday, and Saturday from 10am to 4:30pm, on Thursday from 10am to 8pm, and on Sunday from 1 to 4:30pm.

Plays, musicals, children's shows, summer workshops, and celebrity events are scheduled at the **Riverside Theater,** on Riverside Park Drive, just past the drawbridge (☎ **561/231-6990**), from October to May. During the summer months there's usually only one major performance. Call for schedules.

3 A Fishing Excursion to Lake Okeechobee

Many visitors to the Treasure Coast come to fish and certainly can get their fill in the miles of Atlantic shores and inland rivers. But if you want to fish in fresh water and nothing else, the place to go is "The Lake"—Okeechobee, of course. It's the state's largest, and brim-full of good eating fish. It's only about an hour drive from the coast by car and makes a great day or weekend excursion.

Two things happen in the area surrounding Lake Okeechobee—sugar production and fishing. The area, which actually encompasses parts of five counties, is known as the bass fishing and winter vegetable capital of the state. The lake is a burgeoning mecca for sportfishermen who come from all over for warm winters and big fishing tournaments.

Okeechobee comes from the Seminole word for "Big Water"—and big it is. The lake covers more than 467,000 acres and 730 square miles. At one time the lake supported an enormous commercial fishing industry, but because of a ban on commercial net-fishing, much of that industry has died off, leaving to the sportsfishermen all the rich bounty of the freshwater lake.

As you approach the lake area, you'll notice a large levy surrounding it. This was built after two major hurricanes, including one in 1947 that killed hundreds of area residents and cattle. Soon afterward the U.S. Army Corps of Engineers, which had already built a cross-state waterway, set to building a series of locks and dams to control potential flooding. The region is now safe from the threat of floods, but the ecological results have not been as positive. Birds and wildlife suffered greatly, as did the northern portion of the Everglades, which relies on the water overflow from the lake to replenish and clean its source.

A threat to the region is also posed by the area's largest employer, U.S. Sugar. Most of the area around Belle Glade and Clewiston, "America's Sweetest Town," is owned by the country's largest sugar grower. Many small towns around the lake are home to the cane workers, mostly Caribbean immigrants, and those who cater to their needs.

However, ecologists and conservationists are in constant battle with the sugar producers, whose factories pollute the precious ecosystem whose heart is the Everglades. Many state legislators have long been pushing for a bill that would place a tax on sugar that would be used to clean up the waste, a measure backed by President Clinton in 1996. Meanwhile, as the conflict between development and nature continues, the area retains a primitive charm, and offers lots of opportunities for sporting on the waterways.

CLEWISTON—"AMERICA'S SWEETEST TOWN"

A number of other towns make their living chartering fishing boats on the lake, but Clewiston is one of the best outfitted and most accessible areas for fishermen. The town is on the southwestern side of the 730-square-mile lake, which is linked to the west and east coasts of the state by a series of rivers, locks, and dams.

ESSENTIALS

GETTING THERE   From West Palm Beach, follow Southern Boulevard (U.S. 98) west past I-95. This merges with Fla. 80 and U.S. 441. Follow the signs for Fla. 80 West through Belle Glade to South Bay. In South Bay, turn right onto U.S. 27 North and take U.S. 27 to Clewiston.

From Fort Lauderdale, take I-595 west to I-75 North. Take Exit 13 from I-75 (right turn) onto U.S. 27 North and follow U.S. 27 through South Bay to Clewiston.

VISITOR INFORMATION   Contact the **Clewiston Chamber of Commerce,** 544 W. Sugarland Hwy., Clewiston, FL 33440 (☎ **941/983-7979**), for maps, business directories, and the names of numerous fishing guides throughout the area. In addition, you might want to write or call the **Pahokee Chamber of Commerce,**

115 E. Main St., Pahokee, FL 33476 (☎ **561/924-5579;** fax 561/924-8116), which will send a complete package of magazines, guides, and accommodations listings.

For an excellent map and brief history of the area, contact the **Natural Resources Office,** 525 Ridgelawn Rd., Clewiston, FL 33440 (☎ **941/983-3335**), open to visitors Monday to Friday from 8am to 4:30pm.

CATCHING THE BIG ONE

Fishing on the lake is a year-round affair, though the fish tend to bite a little better in the winter for benefit of the many "snowbirds" who flock here, especially in February and March when the RV camps are mobbed with fish-frenzied anglers who come down for weeks at a time to catch the big one.

You'll need a fishing license to go out with a rod and reel. It's a simple matter to acquire one—the chamber of commerce and most fishing shops can sign you up on the spot. The cost for non–Florida residents is $16.50 for a 7-day license, $31.50 for the year.

You can rent, charter, or bring your own boat to Clewiston. Just be sure to schedule your trip in advance. You don't want to show up during one of the frequent fishing tournaments and find that you can't get a room, campsite, or fishing boat because hundreds of the country's most intense bass fishers are vying for the $100,000 prizes in the Redman Competition, which happens four times a year in the winter and spring.

There are, of course, more than a few marinas where you can rent or charter boats. If it's your first time on the lake, I suggest chartering a boat with a guide who can show you the lake's most fertile spots and handle your tackle while you drink a beer and get some sun. **Roland Martin's,** 920 E. Del Monte in Clewiston (☎ **941/ 983-3151**), the region's largest fishing outfitter, is the one-stop spot where you can find a guide, boat, tackle, rods, bait, coolers, picnic supplies, and a choice of boats. Rates start at $165 for a half day with the full set-up. However, if you want to save money, rent a boat and stock up on supplies yourself. The rates for a "john" boat, which can comfortably fit two or three, with a small outboard (10-horsepower) motor are about $60 a day, or $40 for half a day, and the first tank of gas is free.

Another reputable boat-rental spot is the **Angler's Marina,** 910 Okeechobee Blvd. (☎ **941/983-BASS,** or 800/741-3141). Full-day rentals for a 14-footer start at $40 for a half day, with a maximum of four people. I'd opt for the 22-foot "open fisherman," which comes with a 50-horsepower engine and more space for supplies and fish. If you want a guide, rates start at $150 (for two people)—though in the summer, when it's slow, you can usually get out on the water for something like $120.

BOAT TOURS

Captain JP's Boat Charters (☎ **561/924-2100**, or 800/845-7411) go out every day on a number of tour and dinner cruises on his 350-passenger *Viking Starliner* throughout the southern region of Lake Okeechobee. Most cruises leave from Pahokee or the Moore Haven Marina, though schedules change daily. Most cruises depart at 10am during the season and include breakfast and an all-you-can-eat buffet of salads, cheeses, and hot dishes. Prices start at $30. Call for seasonal schedules.

WHERE TO STAY

If you aren't camping, you'll want to book a room at the **Clewiston Inn,** 108 Royal Palm Ave., Clewiston, FL 33440 (☎ **941/983-8151**, or 800/749-4466). Built in 1938 by U.S. Sugar to house its executives and visitors, this Southern plantation–inspired hotel is the oldest in the Lake Okeechobee region. It still hosts many sugar executives and visiting sportfishers in its 52 simply decorated nondescript Holiday Inn–style rooms. The lobby and lounge area, where you can see a 1945 mural depicting the animals of the region, retain some of their original charm. Double rooms rent for $79 a night and bungalows go for $99. All have air-conditioning, TVs, and telephones.

Another choice, especially if you're here for the fish, is **Roland Martin's, 941/983-3151,** 920 E. Del Monte, Clewiston, FL 33440, the Disney of Clewiston, whose theme park includes a choice of modest hotel rooms, efficiencies, condominiums, apartments, or campsites, with two heated pools, gift and marina shops, and a restaurant. The modern complex, dotted with prefab buildings painted in sparse white and gray, is clean and well manicured. Rooms rent for $45 to $55; efficiencies, for $65 to $80.

Camping

In the winter, campers own the Clewiston area. Campsites are jammed with regulars who come year after year for the simple pleasures of the lake and, of course, the warm weather. Every manner of RV, from simple pop-top Volkswagens to Winnebagos to fully decked-out mobile homes, find their way to campsites along the lake. Several recommendable sites for mobile campers and tenters are situated off U.S. 27.

The **KOA Clewiston,** Rte. 2, Box 242, Clewiston, FL 33440 (☎ **941/983-7078,** or 800/KOA-2174), offers large, even sites from $24 a night with full hookups, including sewer. Campers are billed separately for electricity used. Rustic log cabins are available for $32 a night. Tenters are also welcome.

Okeechobee Landings, Inc., U.S. 27 East, Clewiston, FL 33440 (☎ **941/983-4144**), has every conceivable amenity included in the price of a site. More than 250 sites are situated around a small lake, clubhouse, snack bar, pool, Jacuzzi, horseshoe pit, shuffleboard court, and tennis court. Full hookup includes sewer, which is not the case throughout the county. RV spots are rented to regulars, but there are usually some spots available for rental to one-time visitors. Rates are $23 per day or $350 per month, including hookup. Year-round rates for trailer rentals, which sleep two people, are $32 for weeknights and $37 weekends.

WHERE TO EAT

If you aren't frying up your own catch for dinner, you can find a number of good eating spots in town. At the **Clewiston Inn** (see "Where to Stay," above) you can get catfish, beef Stroganoff, ham hocks, fried chicken, and liver and onions in a setting as Southern as the food. The dining room opens at 6am daily, serving breakfast, then lunch until 2pm. Dinner is served from 5 to 9pm and entrees cost $9 to $18.

At **Donnelly's,** 842 E. Sugarland Hwy. (☎ **941/933-8119**), in addition to the full menu of steaks and super-fresh seafood, you can order alligator tail, quail, or a choice of barbecued specialties. Don't miss the soft and greasy garlic bread. Dinners range from $10 to $18 and include salad and vegetables. You can bring your own catch—they'll cook it however you like it and serve it with hush puppies, french fries, and cole slaw for just $5.95. Breakfast starts early so the birds can get out by 5am to catch some worms. They close when "the fishers are done drinking," usually by 11pm.

Not to be missed is the **Old South Barbecue Ranch,** 602 E. Sugarland Hwy. (☎ **941/983-7756**). You'll see signs for miles around imploring you to turn around and come on back to this Lake Okeechobee landmark where the smoking sauce is renowned, in this haven of barbecued pork, meat, and chicken—and the catfish isn't bad either. Of course you can also opt for a "prairie delight" like the fine Florida gator tail fried in a golden batter and served with a secret sweet dipping sauce. The place looks like a movie set from an old western with just a facade of an old main street covering the entranceway. It's open Monday to Saturday from 11am to 10pm and on Sunday from 11am to 9pm.

The spot for a real Old Florida breakfast is **Robbie's,** 711 E. Sugarland Hwy. (☎ **941/983-7001**). The biscuits and sausage gravy are enough to keep you happy until the fish start biting. Full dinners, including a choice of fried pork chops, fried chicken or catfish, and hush puppies start at $5. Open daily, this greasy spoon has a week's worth of trucks parked out front, from opening until closing, usually from 6am past 10pm, which is late night for this town of early risers.

Walt Disney World & Orlando

11

by Rena Bulkin

Orlando was a sleepy Southern town ringed with sparkling lakes, pine forests, and citrus groves until Walt Disney turned 43 square miles of swampland into a Magic Kingdom. He sparked an unprecedented building boom, as hotels, restaurants, and scores of additional attractions arose to take advantage of the tourist traffic he had generated. The world's most famous mouse changed Central Florida forever.

Though the citrus industry still exists here, orange groves have largely given way to high-rise apartment complexes, vast hotels and resorts, and shopping malls. Many national firms have relocated their headquarters to this thriving sunbelt region, and it has also become one of the fastest-growing high-tech centers in the country.

There are so many tourist attractions that you can't possibly see everything in one trip. The original Magic Kingdom has been augmented by half a dozen additional Disney attraction areas and over 20 Disney resorts and "official" hotels. Throughout 1997, Walt Disney World will be celebrating its 25th anniversary, with special shows, parades, and attractions.

Scores of non-Disney attractions—most notably Sea World, Universal Studios Florida, Cypress Gardens, and the Kennedy Space Center—also compete for your dollar.

Advance planning is a must. But never fear. I've checked out every square inch of all the parks, ridden every ride, and inspected every hotel and restaurant. In the pages that follow, I'll share my discoveries and tips with you and help you plan your own itinerary—one that helps you get the most out of your trip and minimizes the time you spend standing in line.

Orlando's busiest seasons are whenever kids are out of school—summer (early June to about August 20), holiday weekends, Christmas season (mid-December to mid-January), and Easter. Obviously, the whole experience is more enjoyable when the crowds are thinnest and the weather most temperate. Best times are the week after Labor Day until Thanksgiving, the week after Thanksgiving until mid-December, and the 6 weeks before and after school spring vacations. The worst time is summer, when the crowds are large and the weather is hot and humid.

PACKAGE TOURS

Frankly, the number and diversity of package tours to Orlando is staggering. But significant savings are available for those willing to do the research. Best bet: Stop at a sizable travel agency and pick up brochures from all of the below-listed (and others). Pore over them at home, comparing offerings to find the optimum package for your trip. Also obtain the *Walt Disney World Vacations* guide (☎ 407/934-7639), which lists the company's own packages. Try to find a package that meets rather than exceeds your needs; there's no sense in paying for elements you won't use. Also, read over the advantages accruing to Disney resort guests in Section 2; some packages list as selling points services that are automatically available to every Walt Disney World guest.

When you call to reserve your flight, inquire about money-saving packages. **Delta's Dream Vacations** (☎ 800/872-7786) offer accommodations in different price ranges at your choice of all WDW resorts. Their packages also include round-trip airfare, car rental or airport transfer, accommodations, and more, including unlimited admission to all parks.

American Express Vacations (☎ 800/241-1700) is also officially authorized to use Disney resorts in its packages. Additional airline package sources include **American Airlines' Fly Away Vacations** (☎ 800/321-2121), **Continental Vacations** (☎ 800/634-5555), and **USAir Vacations** (☎ 800/455-0123). Most **hotels** listed below also offer packages; inquire when you call. Also check with your **travel agent.**

SPECIAL EVENTS & FESTIVALS IN THE ORLANDO AREA

JANUARY January kicks off with the **Comp USA Florida Citrus Bowl** (☎ 407/423-2476 for information, 407/839-3900 for tickets), featuring two of the year's top college teams. Tickets go on sale in late October or early November.

Also in January, the **Walt Disney World Marathon** (☎ 407/824-4321) is open to all, including the physically challenged, but preregistration is required.

FEBRUARY February brings the **Silver Spurs Rodeo** (☎ 407/847-5000 for details, 407/67-RODEO for tickets), one of the top 20 PRCA rodeos in the nation, held at the Silver Spurs Arena, 1875 E. Irlo Bronson Memorial Hwy. (U.S. 192) in Kissimmee the third weekend in February. Tickets are $15.

The 6-day **Kissimmee Valley Livestock Show and Osceola County Fair** (☎ 407/846-6046) takes place the third week of February at the Kissimmee Valley Agricultural Center, 1901 E. Irlo Bronson Memorial Hwy. (U.S. 192). Admission is $3 for adults, $1 for children 4 to 12, free for children 3 and under.

The **Mardi Gras Celebration at Pleasure Island** (☎ 407/824-4321) is a rollicking street party with food, drink, costumes, parades, and entertainment.

Spring training begins in February for the Houston Astros; there are games through March or early April at Osceola County Stadium, 1000 Bill Beck Blvd., in Kissimmee (☎ 407/933-5400). Tickets are $5 to $6. Call for details and tickets.

MARCH Major bluegrass and gospel entertainers from all over the country perform at the 4-day **Kissimmee Bluegrass Festival** (☎ 800/473-7773), beginning the first weekend of March, at the Silver Spurs Arena. Tickets are $10 to $17; multiday packages are available.

During 11 days in early March (some years beginning late February), the **Central Florida Fair,** at the Central Florida Fairgrounds, 4603 W. Colonial Dr. (☎ 407/295-3247), features rides, entertainers, 4H and livestock exhibits, a petting zoo, and food booths. Adults pay $6, children 6 to 10 are charged $3, and children 5 and under enter free.

Arnold Palmer hosts the **Nestlé Invitational,** a PGA Tour event, in mid-March at the Bay Hill Club, 9000 Bay Hill Blvd. (☎ 407/876-2888). Daily admission is $28; week-long admission, $50.

The **Sidewalk Art Festival** (☎ 407/623-3234 or 407/644-8281) in Winter Park's Central Park draws artists and artisans from all over North America during the third weekend in March.

The **Spring Flower Festival** (☎ 941/324-2111) goes from March to May at Cypress Gardens.

MAY   In May, the **Epcot International Flower and Garden Festival** is a month-long event that includes speakers and seminars.

JUNE   June brings the **Walt Disney World Wine Festival** (☎ 407/827-7200 or 407/824-4321); more than 60 wineries from all over the United States participate. Events include wine tastings, seminars, and celebrity-chef cooking demonstrations at Disney's Yacht and Beach Club Convention Center.

The **Walt Disney World All-American College Orchestra and College Band** perform at Epcot and the Magic Kingdom throughout the summer (☎ 407/824-4321).

JULY   **Independence Day** is celebrated with **Walt Disney World's Star-Spangled Spectacular** (☎ 407/824-4321), including unbelievable fireworks displays at all the Disney parks, which stay open late. **Sea World** (☎ 407/351-3600) also features a laser/fireworks spectacular.

The **Silver Spurs Rodeo** returns to Kissimmee in late June or July (see "February," above).

SEPTEMBER   Over several weekends in September, the Magic Kingdom hosts **Nights of Joy** (☎ 407/824-4321), a festival of contemporary Christian music featuring top artists. This is a very popular event; obtain tickets early. Admission is about $25 to $30 per night.

OCTOBER   Universal Studios Florida transforms its studios and attractions for **Halloween Horror Nights** (☎ 407/363-8000) during several long weekends prior to Halloween. Special admission is charged. Sea World hosts **Shamu's Halloween Spooktacular** (☎ 407/351-3600).

Top PGA tour players compete for a total purse of $1 million at WDW golf courses in October's **Walt Disney World Oldsmobile Golf Classic** (☎ 407/824-4321). Daily ticket prices range from $8 to $15. The event is preceded by the world's largest golf tournament, the admission-free Oldsmobile Scramble.

NOVEMBER   November's month-long **Mum Festival** (☎ 941/324-2111) at Cypress Gardens features millions of mums.

One of the South's largest arts-and-crafts shows takes place at Disney's Village Marketplace for 3 days, including the second weekend of November. The **Walt Disney World Festival of the Masters** (☎ 407/824-4321) features winners of juried shows throughout the country. Free admission.

Top doll and teddy bear designers from around the world travel to WDW for November's **Walt Disney World Doll and Teddy Bear Convention** (☎ 407/824-4321 or 407/560-7232).

Late November to mid-December, all-you-can-eat **Walt Disney World Jolly Holidays Dinner Shows** are offered at the Contemporary Resort's Fantasia Ballroom (☎ 407/W-DISNEY). A cast of more than 100 Disney characters, singers, and dancers performs in an old-fashioned Christmas extravaganza. Call for details and ticket prices.

A spectacular showcase of more than 50,000 poinsettia blooms highlight the **Poinsettia Festival** (☎ 941/324-2111), from late November to mid-January at Cypress Gardens.

DECEMBER   During the **Walt Disney World Christmas Festivities,** Main Street is lavishly decked out, and Epcot, MGM Studios, and all Disney resorts offer special entertainments throughout the holiday season. Highlights include: **Mickey's Very Merry Christmas Party,** an after-dark ticketed event weekends at the Magic Kingdom, and the **Candlelight Procession** at Epcot featuring hundreds of carolers, a celebrity narrator telling the Christmas story, and a 450-voice choir. Call 407/824-4321 for details about all of the above, 407/W-DISNEY to inquire about hotel/events packages.

   Sea World features a special Shamu show and a luau show called *Christmas in Hawaii* (☎ **407/351-3600**). The 400-foot sky tower is lit like a Christmas tree nightly.

   During the **Walt Disney World New Year's Eve Celebration** (☎ **407/824-4321**), the Magic Kingdom is open until 2am for a massive fireworks exhibition. Other New Year's festivities in the WDW parks include: a big bash at Pleasure Island featuring music headliners, a special *Hoop-Dee-Doo Musical Revue* show, and guest performances by well-known musical groups at Disney–MGM Studios and Epcot.

   The **Citrus Bowl Parade** (☎ **407/423-2476**) takes place on an annually selected date in late December. Reserved seats in the bleachers are $12. The official **New Year's Eve** celebration of the COMP USA Florida Citrus Bowl takes place at Sea World (☎ **407/423-2476**). Events include headliner concerts and a laser and fireworks spectacular. Admission is charged.

1 Orientation

ARRIVING

BY PLANE   **Delta** (☎ 800/221-1212) has the most flights into Orlando International Airport. It offers service from 200 cities and has a Fantastic Flyer program for kids.

   Other carriers include **Air Jamaica** (☎ 800/523-5585), **America West** (☎ 800/235-9292), **American** (☎ 800/433-7300), **American Trans Air** (☎ 718/917-6710), **British Airways** (☎ 800/247-9297), **Continental** (☎ 800/231-0856), **Kiwi** (☎ 800/538-5494), **Midway** (☎ 800/446-4392), **Northwest** (☎ 800/225-2525), **SunJet** (☎ 800/4-SUNJET), **Transbrasil** (☎ 800/872-3153), **TWA** (☎ 800/221-2000), **United** (☎ 800/241-6522), **USAir** (☎ 800/428-4322), and **Virgin Atlantic** (☎ 800/862-8621).

   Orlando International Airport is thoroughly user-friendly, with centrally located information kiosks (see "Visitor Information," below). All major car-rental companies are located at or near the airport.

   The airport is 25 miles from Walt Disney World. **Mears Transportation Group** (☎ **407/423-5566**) shuttle vans ply the route from the airport (board outside baggage claim) to all Disney resorts and "official" hotels as well as most other area hostelries. Their comfortable, air-conditioned vehicles operate around the clock, departing every 15 to 25 minutes in either direction. Rates vary with your destination. The round-trip cost for adults is $21 between the airport and downtown Orlando or International Drive, $25 for Walt Disney World/Lake Buena Vista or Kissimmee/U.S. 192. Children 4 to 11 are charged $14 for the Orlando route and $17 for the Walt Disney World route; children 3 and under ride free.

BY CAR   Orlando is 436 miles from Atlanta, 1,312 miles from Boston, 1,120 miles from Chicago, 1,170 miles from Dallas, 1,105 miles from New York City, and 230 miles from Miami.

From northern points, take I-75 south to the Florida Turnpike to I-4, which runs right through the city. If you're taking I-95 south, you'll intersect with I-4 near Daytona Beach.

American Automobile Association (AAA) (☎ **800/336-4357**) and some other automobile club members can call local offices for maps and optimum driving directions.

BY TRAIN Amtrak trains (☎ **800/USA-RAIL**) pull into stations at 1400 Sligh Blvd. in downtown Orlando (about 23 miles from Walt Disney World) and 111 Dakin Ave. in Kissimmee (about 15 miles from Walt Disney World).

To inquire about Amtrak's money-saving packages—including hotel accommodations (some at WDW resorts), car rentals, tours, etc., with your train fare—call 800/321-8684.

Amtrak's **Auto Train** offers the convenience of having a car in Florida without driving it there. The Auto Train begins in Lorton, Va., in the afternoon and ends up at Sanford, Fla. (about 23 miles northeast of Orlando) the next morning. Reserve early for the lowest fares. Call 800/USA-RAIL for details.

BY BUS Greyhound buses (☎ **800/231-2222**) connect the entire country with Orlando. They pull into terminals at 555 N. Magruder Blvd., a few miles west of downtown Orlando (☎ **407/292-3422**), and 16 N. Orlando Ave. in Kissimmee, about 14 miles from Walt Disney World (☎ **407/847-3911**). There is van transport from the Kissimmee terminal to most area hotels and motels. From Orlando, you can call a **Mears shuttle van** (☎ **407/423-5566**), which will cost $12 to $13 one-way to a Disney-area hotel, $8 for children 4 to 11, free for children 3 and under (round-trip fares are less). For the return trip, call from your hotel 24 hours in advance. A **taxi** to Disney-area hotels will cost about $40. Greyhound's fare structure tends to be complex, but the good news is that when you call to make a reservation, the agent will always give you the lowest-fare options. Once again, advance-purchase fares booked 3 to 21 days prior to travel represent vast savings.

VISITOR INFORMATION

Contact the **Orlando/Orange County Convention & Visitors Bureau,** 8445 International Dr. (in the Mercado Shopping Village), Orlando, FL 32819 (☎ **407/ 363-5871**). The staff can answer all your questions and will be happy to send you maps, publications (including the informative *Official Visitors Guide,* the *Official Attractions Guide*, the *Official Accommodations Guide*), and the Magicard™ (good for discounts of 10% to 50% on accommodations, attractions, car rentals, and more). Discount tickets to attractions other than Disney parks are sold on the premises, and the multilingual staff can also make dining reservations and hotel referrals. The bureau is open daily except Christmas from 8am to 8pm.

For general information about Walt Disney World, and a copy of the informative *Walt Disney World Vacations* guide, write or call the **Walt Disney World Co.,** P.O. Box 10000, Lake Buena Vista, FL 32830-1000 (☎ **407/934-7639**).

If you're driving, you can stop at the **Disney/AAA Travel Center** in Ocala, Fla., near the intersection of I-75 (Exit 68) and Fla. 200, about 90 miles north of Orlando (☎ **904/854-0770**). Here you can purchase tickets, get help planning your park itinerary, and make hotel reservations. It's open daily from 9am to 6pm (to 7pm June to August).

At the Orlando International Airport, arriving passengers can stroll over to **Greetings from Walt Disney World Resort** (☎ **407/825-2301**), a shop and information center on the third floor in the main lobby just behind the Northwest counter. This facility sells WDW park tickets, makes dinner show and hotel reservations at Disney hostelries, and provides brochures and assistance. It's open daily from 6am to 9pm.

Also contact the **Kissimmee–St. Cloud Convention & Visitors Bureau,** 1925 E. Irlo Bronson Memorial Hwy. (P.O. Box 422007), Kissimmee, FL 34742-2007 (☎ **407/847-5000** or 800/327-9159). It will send maps, brochures, discount coupon books, and the *Kissimmee–St. Cloud Vacation Guide,* which details the area's accommodations and attractions.

CITY LAYOUT

Orlando's major artery is **I-4,** which runs diagonally across the state from Tampa to Daytona Beach. Exits from I-4 take you to Walt Disney World, Sea World, International Drive, U.S. 192, Kissimmee, Lake Buena Vista, Church Street Station, downtown Orlando, and Winter Park. The **Florida Turnpike** crosses I-4 and links up with I-75 to the north. **U.S. 192,** a major east-west artery, stretches from Kissimmee (along a major motel strip) to **U.S. 27,** crossing I-4 near the Walt Disney World entrance road. Farther north, a toll road called the **Beeline Expressway (Fla. 528)** goes east from I-4 past Orlando International Airport to Cape Canaveral.

Walt Disney World property is bounded roughly by I-4 and Fla. 535 to the east (the latter also north), World Drive (the entrance road) to the west, and U.S. 192 to the south. Epcot Center Drive (Fla. 536, the south end of International Drive) and Buena Vista Drive cut across the complex in a more-or-less east-west direction; the two roads cross at Bonnet Creek Parkway. Excellent highways and explicit signs make it very easy to find your way around.

Note: The Disney parks are actually much closer to Kissimmee than to downtown Orlando.

NEIGHBORHOODS IN BRIEF

Walt Disney World   A city unto itself, WDW sprawls over more than 26,000 acres containing theme parks, resorts, hotels, shops, restaurants, and recreational facilities galore.

Lake Buena Vista   On the eastern end of Disney property, Lake Buena Vista is a hotel village/marketplace owned and operated by Walt Disney World. Though Disney owns all the real estate, many of the hotels and some shops and restaurants in this area are independently owned. Lake Buena Vista is a charming area of manicured lawns and verdant thoroughfares shaded by towering oak trees.

International Drive (Fla. 536)   This attractive area extends 7 to 10 miles north of the Disney parks between Fla. 535 and the Florida Turnpike. It contains numerous hotels, restaurants, shopping centers, and the Orange County Convention Center, and offers easy access to Sea World and Universal Studios. (*Note:* Locally, this road is always referred to as I-Drive.)

Kissimmee   South of the Disney Parks, Kissimmee centers on U.S. 192/Irlo Bronson Memorial Highway, an archetypically American strip lined with budget motels, lesser attractions, and every fast-food restaurant you can name.

Downtown Orlando   Reached via I-4 east, this burgeoning sunbelt metropolis is 17 miles northeast of Walt Disney World. Though many tourists never venture downtown, it does have a number of attractions.

Orlando Area/Walt Disney World Orientation

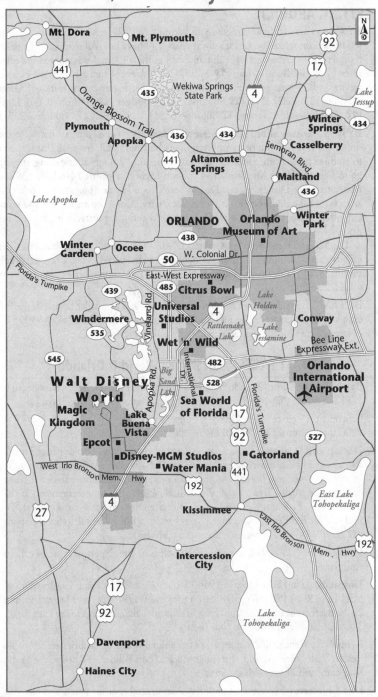

GETTING AROUND

BY CAR Though you can get to and around Walt Disney World and other major attractions without a car, it's always handy to have one. All major companies are represented in Orlando and maintain desks at the airport. I was quoted the lowest rates by **Value Rent-A-Car** (☎ 800/GO-VALUE), which also offered excellent service and 24-hour pickup and return. Some other handy phone numbers: **Alamo** (☎ 800/327-9633), **Avis** (☎ 800/331-1212), **Budget** (☎ 800/527-0700), **Dollar** (☎ 800/800-4000), **Hertz** (☎ 800/654-3131), and **Thrifty** (☎ 800/367-2277).

BY BUS **Disney shuttle buses** serve all Disney resorts and "official" hotels, offering unlimited complimentary transportation via bus, monorail, ferry, and/or water taxi to all three parks from 2 hours prior to opening until 2 hours after closing; they also go to Disney Village Marketplace, Typhoon Lagoon, Pleasure Island, Fort Wilderness, and other Disney resorts. Disney hostelries offer transportation to other area attractions as well, though it's not complimentary. Almost all area hotels and motels also offer transportation to Walt Disney World and other attractions, but it can be pricey.

   The **Mears Transportation Group** (☎ **407/423-5566**) operates buses to all major attractions, including Cypress Gardens, Kennedy Space Center, Universal Studios Florida, Sea World, Busch Gardens (in Tampa), and Church Street Station, among others. Call for details.

BY TAXI Taxis line up in front of major hotels, and at smaller hostelries the front desk will be happy to call you a cab. Or call **Yellow Cab** (☎ **407/699-9999**). The charge is $2.75 for the first mile, $1.50 per mile thereafter.

FAST FACTS: Walt Disney World & Orlando

Baby-Sitters Most Orlando hotels offer baby-sitting services. If yours doesn't, call KinderCare (☎ 407/827-5444); 24-hour advance notice is required.

Convention Center The Orange County Convention/Civic Center is located at 9800 International Dr. (☎ 407/345-9800).

Doctors and Dentists Disney has first-aid centers in all three major parks. There's also a local 24-hour service called HouseMed (☎ 407/396-1195); its doctors make "house calls" to local hotels, and they can dispense medication. HouseMed also operates the Medi-Clinic, a walk-in medical facility (not for emergencies) at the intersection of I-4 and U.S. 192, open daily from 8am to 9pm (same phone). To find the nearest dentist who meets your needs, call the Dental Referral Service (☎ 800/917-6453) between 5:30am and 6pm daily.

Emergencies Dial **911** to contact the police or fire department or to call an ambulance.

Hospitals Sand Lake Hospital, 9400 Turkey Lake Rd., is about 2 miles south of Sand Lake Road (☎ 407/351-8550). From the WDW area, take I-4 east to Exit 29, turn left at the exit onto Sand Lake Road, and make a left on Turkey Lake Road. The hospital is 2 miles up on your right.

Kennels All the major theme parks offer animal-boarding facilities at reasonable fees. At Walt Disney World, there are kennels at Fort Wilderness, Epcot, the Magic Kingdom, and Disney–MGM Studios.

Lost Children Every theme park has a designated spot for parents to meet up with lost children. Find out where it is when you enter any park and instruct your children to ask park personnel to take them there if they get lost. Young children should have name tags.

Pharmacies (Late-Night)   Walgreens Drug Store, 1003 W. Vine St. (U.S. 192), just east of Bermuda Avenue (☎ 407/847-5252), operates a 24-hour pharmacy. It can deliver to hotels for a charge ($10 from 7am to 5pm, $15 at all other times).

Photography   Two-hour film processing is available at all three major Disney parks—look for the PHOTO EXPRESS sign. You can also buy film and rent or buy 35mm, disc, and video cameras in all three parks.

Taxes   The hotel tax in both Orlando and Kissimmee is 11%, which includes the 6% state sales tax that's charged on all goods except most grocery store items and medicines.

Tourist Information   See "Visitor Information" under "Orientation," earlier in this chapter.

Weather   Call 407/851-7510 for a recorded weather forecast.

2 Where to Stay

Reserve as far in advance as possible—the minute you've decided on the dates of your trip.

Remember to factor in the 11% hotel tax.

HOW TO SAVE MONEY BY STAYING WITH MICKEY   Many people assume that motels outside the Disney parks will cost you less than staying on WDW premises, but that isn't always the case. Don't forget that if you don't have a car, you'll need to add the cost (as high as $12 per person per day) of hotel shuttle buses to and from Walt Disney World parks to your expenses, while the Disney-owned hostelries and "official" hotels offer complimentary transportation to and from WDW parks.

In or out of Walt Disney World, if you book your hotel as part of a package (details below) you'll likely enjoy big savings. Ask about special discounts for students, government employees, senior citizens, military, AAA, and/or corporate clients.

There are 15 Disney-owned properties (hotels, resorts, villas, wilderness homes, and campsites) and 9 privately owned "official" hotels. All of those within our price range are described below. In addition to their proximity to the parks, there are a number of advantages to staying at a Disney property or "official" hotel. Even the budget choices offer extensive resort facilities, not to mention accommodations and landscaping more typically found at luxury properties. At all Disney resorts and official hotels, benefits include:

- Unlimited complimentary transportation via bus, monorail, ferry, and/or water taxi to/from all three parks from 2 hours before opening until 2 hours after closing. Unlimited complimentary transport is also provided to/from Disney Village Marketplace, Typhoon Lagoon, Pleasure Island, Fort Wilderness, and other Disney resorts. This free transport can not only save money, but also means you're guaranteed admission to all parks, even during peak times when the parking lots sometimes fill up.
- Free parking at WDW parking lots (other visitors pay $5 a day).
- Reduced-price children's menus in almost all restaurants, and character breakfasts and/or dinners at most resorts.
- A guest services desk where you can purchase tickets to all WDW theme parks and attractions and obtain general information.

- Use of—and in some cases, complimentary transport to—the five Disney-owned golf courses and preferred tee times at them (these can be booked up to 30 days in advance).
- Access to most recreational facilities at other Disney resorts.
- Service by the Mears airport shuttle.

Additional perks at Disney-owned hotels, resorts, villas, and campgrounds (but not at "official" hotels): charge privileges throughout Walt Disney World; early admission to Epcot and Disney–MGM Studios on specific days; dining and show reservations (including Epcot restaurants) can be made through the hotel.

WALT DISNEY WORLD CENTRAL RESERVATIONS OFFICE   To reserve a room at Disney hotels, resorts, and villas, "official" hotels, and Fort Wilderness homes and campsites, contact **Central Reservations Operations (CRO),** P.O. Box 10100, Lake Buena Vista, FL 32830-0100 (☎ **407/W-DISNEY**), open Monday to Friday from 8am to 10pm and on Saturday and Sunday from 9am to 6pm. Have your dates and credit or charge card ready when you call.

The CRO can recommend accommodations that will suit your specific needs as to price, location, and facilities. It can also give you information about various park ticket options and make dinner-show reservations for you at the *Hoop-Dee-Doo Musical Revue* and the Polynesian Luau Dinner Show when you book your room.

When you call the CRO, be sure to inquire about the numerous package plans, which include meals, tickets, recreation, and other features. The right package can save you both money and time, and is helpful in computing the cost of your vacation in advance. Be sure to ask if any special discounts are being offered at the time of your trip.

DISNEY RESORTS
Doubles for Less than $80

Disney's All-Star Music Resort. 1801 W. Buena Vista Dr. (at World Dr. and Osceola Pkwy.; P.O. Box 10100), Lake Buena Vista, FL 32830-0100. ☎ **407/W-DISNEY** or 407/939-6000. Fax 407/354-1866. 1,920 rms. A/C TV TEL. $69–$79 double. Additional person $8 extra; children17 and under stay free in parents' room. AE, MC, V. Free parking.

Though the unbeatable combination of rock-bottom rates and extensive facilities at Disney's All Start Music and Sports resorts (see below) is very attractive to families, there is one caveat: The rooms are small (a mere 260 square feet). They're ideal for single adults or couples traveling with one child; larger families had best be into togetherness. Nestled among pristine pine forests, this Disney property is part of a 246-acre complex that also includes the adjacent All-Star Sports Resort (see below). Its 10 buildings are musically themed around country, jazz, rock, calypso, or Broadway show tunes. The calypso building, for instance, has a palm-fringed roof frieze and balconies adorned with tropical birds and musical notes, while a convoy of 18-wheelers travels around the country building, which is adorned with fiddles and banjos. The attractive rooms are also musically themed. In-room safes are a plus.

There's a cheerful food court with an adjoining bar. Room service (pizza only) is available, as are baby-sitting and a guest-services desk. Facilities include two vast swimming pools, a kiddie pool, a playground, coin-op washers/dryers, a large retail shop, a car-rental desk, and a video-game arcade.

Disney's All-Star Sports Resort. 1701 W. Buena Vista Dr. (at World Dr. and Osceola Pkwy.; P.O. Box 10100), Lake Buena Vista, FL 32830-0100. ☎ **407/W-DISNEY** or 407/939-5000. Fax 407/354-1866. 1,920 rms. A/C TV TEL. $69–$79 double. Additional person $8 extra; children 17 and under stay free in parents' room. AE, MC, V. Free parking.

Walt Disney World Accommodations

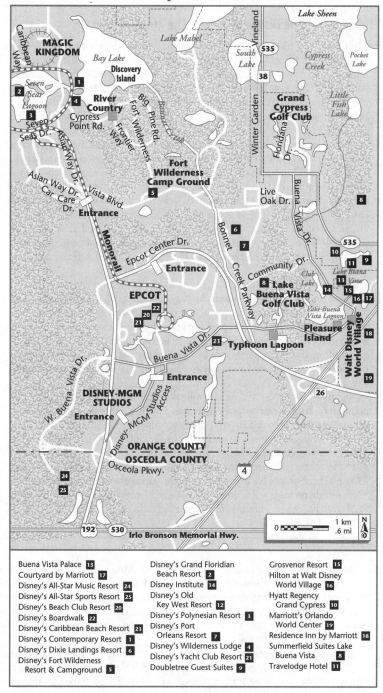

Buena Vista Palace **13**
Courtyard by Marriott **17**
Disney's All-Star Music Resort **24**
Disney's All-Star Sports Resort **25**
Disney's Beach Club Resort **20**
Disney's Boardwalk **22**
Disney's Caribbean Beach Resort **23**
Disney's Contemporary Resort **1**
Disney's Dixie Landings Resort **6**
Disney's Fort Wilderness
    Resort & Campground **5**

Disney's Grand Floridian
    Beach Resort **2**
Disney Institute **14**
Disney's Old
    Key West Resort **12**
Disney's Polynesian Resort **3**
Disney's Port
    Orleans Resort **7**
Disney's Wilderness Lodge **4**
Disney's Yacht Club Resort **21**
Doubletree Guest Suites **9**

Grosvenor Resort **15**
Hilton at Walt Disney
    World Village **16**
Hyatt Regency
    Grand Cypress **10**
Marriott's Orlando
    World Center **19**
Residence Inn by Marriott **18**
Summerfield Suites Lake
    Buena Vista **8**
Travelodge Hotel **11**

The Disney Institute: The Mouse Grows Up

The Disney Institute, opening shortly after press time, is an exciting new concept designed for adults and older children (10 and up). Designed to resemble a small town with a village green and architecture evocative of barns, mills, and country houses, it sprawls over 265 acres of lakes, streams, and woodlands.

The institute will enable guests to custom-design Walt Disney World vacations that focus on interactive programs in dozens of diverse areas. Anxiety-free learning experiences (no grades) will be enhanced by noted guest artists and speakers—for instance, Marshall Brickman, Chris Columbus, Siskel and Ebert, Randy Newman, and Morton Gould are among the dozens of well-known directors, critics, singers, and composers Disney has tapped to participate in its Entertainment Arts programs. Other areas of study will include Sports and Fitness, Lifestyles, Story Arts, Culinary Arts, Design, the Environment, and Architecture—options are almost limitless. You might opt for golf or tennis clinics, study animation, indulge in an array of luxurious spa treatments, learn topiary gardening, canoe on local waterways, trace your family roots, create puppets, go out on birdwatching expeditions, or try rock climbing. Guests are encouraged to participate in a variety of different programs during their stay.

Its resort-style public areas and accommodations (bungalows and one- and two-bedroom town houses) are gorgeous. An elegant on-premises restaurant called Seasons features nightly changing menus and cuisines. Sports and outdoor facilities include an 18-hole/par-72 championship golf course, four tennis courts, six swimming pools, five whirlpools, a kiddie pool, bike trails, three sand volleyball courts, a softball/multipurpose sports field, a rock-climbing wall, a state-of-the-art sports and fitness center and spa facilities, two playgrounds, a 3.4-mile jogging course, and more.

Nightly performances and recitals will take place in a 1,150-seat open-air amphitheater and a 250-seat performance center, and films will be screened weeknights in a state-of-the-art movie theater. A counselor-supervised youth center will offer a full roster of daytime programs and activities for children 10 to 13 and teens as well as evening activities for teens.

The institute is adjacent to the Disney Village Marketplace at 1960 N. Magnolia Way. Based on double occupancy, 3-night packages will range from $582 to $916, 4-night packages will be $690 to $1,135, and 7-night packages will run $1,208 to $1,986. For further information on programs and rates, call 407/827-4800 or 800/4-WONDER.

Adjacent to, and sharing facilities with the All-Star Music Resort (see above), this 82-acre property is elaborately sports themed. For instance, the turquoise surf buildings have waves along their rooflines, surfboards mounted on exterior walls, and pink fish swimming along balcony railings. The cheerful rooms feature a decor of sports-action motifs; in-room safes are among your amenities. As noted above, however, the rooms here are small.

There's a brightly decorated food court with an adjoining bar. Room service (pizza only), babysitting, and a guest-services desk are available. The facilities include two vast swimming pools (one surfing themed with two 38-foot shark fins, the other shaped like a baseball diamond with an "outfield" sundeck), a kiddie pool, a playground, coin-op washers/dryers, a shop, a car-rental desk, and a video-game arcade.

DOUBLES FOR MORE THAN $80

Disney's Caribbean Beach Resort. 900 Cayman Way (off Buena Vista Dr.; P.O. Box 10100), Lake Buena Vista, FL 32830-0100. ☎ **407/W-DISNEY** or 407/934-3400. Fax 407/354-1866. 2,112 rms. A/C MINIBAR TV TEL. $94–$124 double. Additional person $12 extra; children 16 and under stay free in parents' room. AE, MC, V. Free parking.

Though the facilities here aren't as extensive as those at some other Disney resorts, the Caribbean Beach offers especially good value for families. It occupies 200 lush, palm-fringed tropical acres, with accommodations in five distinct Caribbean "villages" grouped around a large, duck-filled lake. The main swimming pool here replicates a Spanish-style Caribbean fort, complete with water slide, kiddie pool, and whirlpool. There are other pools as well as lakefront white-sand beaches in each village. A 1.4-mile promenade—popular for jogging—circles the lake. An arched wooden bridge leads to Parrot Cay Island where there's a short nature trail, an aviary of tropical birds, and a picnic area. The rooms are charming, with pineapple-motif oak furnishings and floral-print chintz bedspreads. Amenities include coffeemakers and ceiling fans; refrigerators are available at $5 per night. All rooms have verandas, many of them overlooking the lake.

There's a festive food court, the nautically themed Captain's Tavern for American fare, and a pool bar. Room service (pizza only), a guest-services desk, and baby-sitting are available, and there's a complimentary shuttle around the grounds. Facilities include a video-game arcade, shops, boat rentals, bicycle rental, coin-op washers/dryers, and playgrounds.

Disney's Dixie Landings Resort. 1251 Dixie Dr. (off Bonnet Creek Pkwy.; P.O. Box 10100), Lake Buena Vista, FL 32830-0100. ☎ **407/W-DISNEY** or 407/934-6000. Fax 407/934-5777. 2,048 rms. A/C TV TEL. $95–$129 room for up to four. AE, MC, V. Free parking.

Low rates, extensive child-oriented facilities, and a food court make Dixie Landings popular with families, though adults traveling alone might prefer a more sedate setting. Nestled on the banks of the "mighty Sassagoula River" and dotted with bayous, it shares its 325-acre site with the Port Orleans Resort (described below). It includes Ol'-Man Island, a woodsy $3^{1}/_{2}$-acre recreation area containing an immense rustically themed swimming pool with waterfalls cascading from a broken bridge and a water slide, a playground, a children's wading pool, a whirlpool, and a fishin' hole (rent bait and poles and angle for catfish and bass). The accommodations areas, themed after the Louisiana countryside, are divided into "parishes." Rooms housed in stately colonnaded plantation homes are fronted by brick courtyards and manicured lawns, and elegantly decorated in Federalist blue and gold. Rural Cajun-style rooms are set amid bayous and stands of towering pine; they feature bed frames made of bent branches, patchwork quilts, and calico-print drapes.

Boatwright's Dining Hall, housed in a replica of an 1800s boatbuilding factory, serves American/Cajun fare at breakfast and dinner. The Cotton Co-op lounge airs Monday-night football games and offers entertainment (singers and comedians) Tuesday to Saturday night. A food court and pool bar round out the drinking and dining facilities. Room service (pizza only), a guest-services desk, and baby-sitting are available, as well as boat transport to Port Orleans, the Village Marketplace, and Pleasure Island. The facilities include six large swimming pools, coin-op washers/dryers, a video-game arcade, bicycle rental, car rental, boat rental, a 1.7-mile riverfront jogging/biking path, and Fulton's General Store.

Disney's Port Orleans Resort. 2201 Orleans Dr. (off Bonnet Creek Pkwy.; P.O. Box 10100), Lake Buena Vista, FL 32830-0100. ☎ **407/W-DISNEY** or 407/934-5000. Fax 407/934-5353. 1,008 rms. A/C TV TEL. $95–$129 room for up to four. AE, MC, V. Free parking.

This beautiful resort, themed after turn-of-the-century New Orleans, shares a site on the banks of the Sassagoula with Dixie Landings, described above. Its identical room rates and comparable facilities make it, too, a good bet for families. The rooms are housed in pastel-hued buildings with shuttered windows and lacy wrought-iron balconies; they're fronted by lovely flower gardens opening onto fountained courtyards. Cherrywood furnishings, swagged draperies, and walls hung with botanical prints make for pretty room interiors. The landscaping throughout the property is especially nice, with stately oaks, formal boxwood hedges, azaleas, and fragrant jasmine.

Bonfamille's Café is open for breakfast and dinner, the latter featuring Créole specialties. Scat Cat's Club, a cocktail lounge off the lobby, airs Monday-night football and features family-oriented live entertainment. A food court and pool bar round out the dining/drinking facilities. Room service (pizza only), a guest-services desk, babysitting are available, and boat transport is offered to Dixie Landings, the Village Marketplace, and Pleasure Island. The larger-than-Olympic-size Doubloon Lagoon swimming pool is surmounted by an enormous water slide. There is also a whirlpool, a kiddie pool, coin-op washers/dryers, a video-game arcade, bicycle rental, car rental, boat rental, a 1.7-mile riverfront jogging path, and shops.

A DISNEY CAMPGROUND / WILDERNESS HOMES

Disney's Fort Wilderness Resort and Campground. 3520 N. Fort Wilderness Trail (P.O. Box 10100), Lake Buena Vista, FL 32830-0100. ☎ **407/W-DISNEY** or 407/824-2900. Fax 407/354-1866. 784 campsites, 408 wilderness homes. A/C TV TEL (homes only). $35–$54 campsite, depending on season, location, number of people, size, and extent of hookup; $180–$215 wilderness home. AE, MC, V. Free self-parking.

This woodsy 780-acre camping resort—shaded by towering pines and cypress trees and crossed by fish-filled streams, lakes, and canals—is ideal for family vacations. Though it's a tad less central than other Disney properties, its abundance of on-premises facilities more than compensates. The secluded campsites offer 110/220-volt outlets, barbecue grills, picnic tables, and children's play areas. There's a comfort station in each campground area, with rest rooms, private showers, ice machines, phones, and laundry rooms. There are also wilderness homes—rustic one-bedroom cabins with piney interiors that accommodate up to six people. These have cozy living rooms with Murphy beds, fully equipped eat-in kitchens, picnic tables, and barbecue grills.

The rustic log-beamed Trails End offers buffet meals, and the cozy Crockett's Tavern features Texas fare. During summer, guests enjoy a dazzling electrical water pageant from the beach, nightly at 9:45pm. And the rambunctious *Hoop-Dee-Doo Musical Revue* takes place in Pioneer Hall nightly (details below in Section 13).

Guests here enjoy extensive recreational facilities ranging from a riding stable to a nightly campfire program hosted by Chip 'n' Dale. These include two large swimming pools, a white-sand beach, horseback riding (trail rides), a petting farm, pony rides, fishing, three sand volleyball courts, ball fields, tetherball, shuffleboard, bike rentals, boat rentals, a 1½-mile nature trail, a 2.3-mile jogging path, two tennis courts, two 18-hole championship golf courses, and two video-game arcades.

Baby-sitting is available, and there's a guest-services desk, shops, a kennel, and a car-rental desk. Boat transport is offered to Discovery Island, the Magic Kingdom, and the Contemporary Resort.

LAKE BUENA VISTA—AN "OFFICIAL" HOTEL

Properties designated "official" Walt Disney World hotels are located on and around Hotel Plaza Boulevard. Guests at these hotels enjoy many privileges (see above). The location is a big advantage—close to the Disney parks and within walking distance of the Disney Village Marketplace and Crossroads shops and restaurants, as well as Pleasure Island nightlife.

One difference between "official" hotels and actual Disney resorts is that the former (with the exception of the Swan and Dolphin) generally have less relentless themes; decide for yourself if that's a plus or a minus. *Note:* Only one "official" hotel meets our budget, and you can make reservations there through **Central Reservations Operations** (☎ 407/W-DISNEY); see details above.

DOUBLES FOR MORE THAN $80

Courtyard by Marriott. 1805 Hotel Plaza Blvd. (between Lake Buena Vista Dr. and Apopka-Vineland Rd./Fla. 535), Lake Buena Vista, FL 32830. ☎ **407/828-8888** or 800/223-9930. Fax 407/827-4623. 321 rms, 1 suite. A/C TV TEL. $89–$149 double, depending on view and season. AE, CB, DC, DISC, JCB, MC, V. Free parking.

Though it's a little on the pricey side for this book, Courtyard offers quite a bit. Guests enjoy many of the privileges described above. Courtyard is a moderately priced link in the Marriott chain, with lower prices achieved via limited services. But don't envision a spartan, no-frills atmosphere. This property was recently renovated to the tune of $4.5 million, and it's looking great. The attractive rooms—most with balconies—have in-room safes, coffeemakers, pay-movie options, and Nintendo; refrigerators are available on request. A full-service restaurant serves American fare at all meals and provides room service. There's also a lobby cocktail lounge, a poolside bar (in season), and an on-premises deli featuring pizza and frozen yogurt. The guest services desk sells tickets and arranges transport to all nearby attractions. Other facilities include two swimming pools, a whirlpool, a kiddie pool, boat rental at nearby Disney Village Marina, a playground, car rental, an exercise room, shops, coin-op washers/dryers, and a video-game arcade.

OTHER LAKE BUENA VISTA AREA HOTELS

All the hotels below are within a few minutes' drive of WDW parks.

DOUBLES FOR LESS THAN $60

Comfort Inn. 8442 Palm Pkwy. (between Fla. 535 and I-4), Lake Buena Vista, FL 32830. ☎ **407/239-7300** or 800/999-7300. Fax 407/239-7740. 640 rms. A/C TV TEL. $39–$69 room for up to four, depending on season. AE, CB, DC, DISC, MC, V. Free parking.

This is an ideally located, large, and attractively landscaped property with two small man-made lakes amid expanses of manicured lawn and lush greenery. It offers free transport to WDW parks, which are just 2 miles away. In-room safes are among the amenities in the immaculate guest rooms. The Boardwalk Buffet serves reasonably priced buffet meals at breakfast and dinner; kids 11 and under eat free. A bar/lounge adjoins, and complimentary tea and coffee are served in the lobby every afternoon. The guest-services desk sells tickets (most of them discounted) and provides transport to all nearby theme parks, dinner shows, and the airport. On-premises facilities include two swimming pools, coin-op washers/dryers, a gift shop, and a video-game arcade. Pets are permitted.

DOUBLES FOR MORE THAN $80

Holiday Inn Sunspree Resort Lake Buena Vista. 13351 Fla. 535 (between Fla. 536 and I-4), Lake Buena Vista, FL 32821. ☎ **407/239-4500** or 800/FON-MAXX. Fax 407/239-7713. 507 rms. A/C TV TEL. $89–$129 room for up to four, depending on season. AE, CB, DC, DISC, JCB, MC, V. Free parking.

About a mile from the Disney parks, this Holiday Inn offers the chain's "no surprises" dependability while catering to children in a big way. Kids "check in" at their own pint-size desk; receive a free fun bag containing a video-game token coupon, a lolli-pop, and a small gift; and get a personal welcome from animated raccoon mascots Max and Maxine. Camp Holiday activities—magic shows, clowns, sing-alongs, arts and crafts, and much more—are available at a minimal charge for kids 2 to 12. And parents can arrange (by reservation) for Max to come tuck a child into bed. The pretty rooms have kitchenettes with refrigerators, microwave ovens, and coffeemakers. And if you're renting a second room for the children, "kidsuites" here sleep up to three. Amenities include VCRs (tapes can be rented), hair dryers, and safes.

Maxine's serves all meals, including steak and seafood dinners. Max's Funtime Parlor offers nightly Bingo and karaoke; it also airs sporting events on a large-screen TV. Kids 12 and under eat all meals free, either in a hotel restaurant with their parents or in the Kid's Kottage, a cheerful facility where movies and cartoons are shown and dinner includes a make-your-own-sundae bar.

Room service and baby-sitting are available, and there's a guest-services desk that sells tickets to all nearby attractions (including WDW parks) and arranges for the free scheduled transport to WDW parks (there's a charge for transport to other nearby attractions), telephone grocery shopping, and the Mears airport shuttle.

Facilities include a large swimming pool, two whirlpools, a kiddie pool, poolside Ping-Pong and billiards, a playground, a fitness center, coin-op washers/dryers, shops, car rental, and a video-game arcade. And Camp Holiday, a counselor-supervised child-care/activity center for ages 2 to 12, will give mom and dad a breather.

Note: Under the same auspices and offering similar rates and facilities is the **Holiday Inn Hotel & Suites,** 5678 Irlo Bronson Memorial Hwy., Kissimmee, FL 34746 (☎ **407/396-4488** or 800/FON-KIDS).

Wyndham Garden Hotel. 8688 Palm Pkwy. (between Fla. 535 and I-4), Lake Buena Vista, FL 32830. ☎ **407/239-8500** or 800/WYNDHAM. Fax 407/239-8591. 164 rms, 3 suites. A/C TV TEL. $74–$104 double, depending on season; $125–$150 suite. Additional person $10 extra; children 17 and under stay free in parents' room. AE, CB, DC, DISC, OPT, MC, V. Free self-parking.

This property's location—on a pleasant tree-lined street and overlooking a lake out back—is a big plus. The Crossroads Shopping Center and Walt Disney World Village put dozens of shops, services, and restaurants within easy walking distance. And to compete with nearby "official" hotels, the Wyndham Garden offers free shuttle transport to/from Disney parks. A recent massive renovation gave the public areas a fresh new look, and the guest rooms have been redecorated with bleached pine furnishings and cheerful resort-themed prints. They're equipped with cable TVs (with pay movies, a tourism-information station, and Nintendo), hair dryers, irons and ironing boards, and coffeemakers; some have convertible sofas.

The Garden Café, serving American fare at breakfast and dinner, has an outdoor poolside seating area and an adjoining bar/lounge. Room service, baby-sitting, and a complimentary daily newspaper are available, and the guest-services desk sells tickets (many of them discounted) and arranges transport to all nearby attractions. On premises are a nice-size swimming pool and whirlpool, coin-op washers/dryers, an exercise room, a business center, and a small video-game arcade.

ON U.S. 192/KISSIMMEE

This very American stretch of highway dotted with fast-food eateries isn't what you'd call scenic, but it does contain many inexpensive accommodations within 1 to 8 miles of WDW parks. All the hostelries listed below are clean, safe, and well run. There are also two branches of the rock-bottom budget **Motel 6** (☎ **800/4-MOTEL6**) in

Kissimmee on U.S. 192; the one at 7455 W. Irlo Bronson Memorial Hwy. (☎ 407/396-6422) is a tad nicer because it has been recently renovated. The other branch is at 5731 W. Irlo Bronson Memorial Hwy. (☎ 407/396-6333).

DOUBLES FOR LESS THAN $40

Colonial Motor Lodge. 1815 W. Vine St. (U.S. 192, between Bermuda and Thacker aves.), Kissimmee, FL 34741. ☎ **407/847-6121** or 800/325-4348. Fax 407/847-0728. 83 rms, 40 apts. A/C TV TEL. $22.95–$50 room for up to four; $49.95–$89.95 two-bedroom apt for up to six. Rates range reflects season. Rates include continental breakfast. AE, DC, DISC, MC, V. Free parking.

This well-run motor lodge has a pleasantly furnished lobby—the setting for breakfast each morning. The standard motel rooms offer cable TV with HBO, and the two-bedroom apartments, with living rooms and fully equipped eat-in kitchens, represent a good choice for families. On-premises facilities include two junior Olympic-size swimming pools and a kiddie pool. Adjacent to the Colonial are an IHOP and a shopping center. Guest services sells tickets to all Disney parks and nearby attractions (some of them discounted) and offers paid transportation to/from them and the airport. Round-trip transport to WDW parks is $12.

Comfort Inn Maingate. 7571 W. Irlo Bronson Memorial Hwy. (U.S. 192, between Reedy Creek Blvd. and Sherbeth Rd.), Kissimmee, FL 34747. ☎ **407/396-7500** or 800/221-2222. Fax 407/396-7497. 281 rms. A/C TV TEL. $33–$65 double, depending on season; garden rooms $6–$10 additional. AE, CB, DC, DISC, JCB, MC, V. Free parking.

Just 1 mile from the Disney parks, this Comfort Inn houses clean, spiffy-looking standard motel accommodations. Most upscale are the garden rooms, facing a lawn with a gazebo; they're equipped with small refrigerators, coffeemakers, and hair dryers. A restaurant on the premises serves low-priced meals, and a comfortable bar/lounge adjoins. There's also a Waffle House right across the street. The guest-services desk sells tickets to Disney and other parks (most of them discounted) and provides transport to all nearby attractions and the airport; a round-trip to WDW parks costs $7. Facilities include a swimming pool, a playground, coin-op washers/dryers, and a video-game arcade.

Days Inn. 4104 and 4125 W. Irlo Bronson Memorial Hwy. (U.S. 192, at Hoagland Blvd. North), Kissimmee, FL 34741. ☎ **407/846-4714** or 800/647-0010 or 800/DAYS-INN. Fax 407/932-2699. 194 rms, 32 efficiencies. A/C TV TEL. $29–$59 room for up to four, depending on season; $37–$63 efficiency; $55–$75 double with Jacuzzi. Rates include continental breakfast. Rates may be higher during major events. AE, CB, DC, DISC, MC, V. Free parking.

Offering good value for your hotel dollar, these two Days Inn properties—on either side of U.S. 192—share facilities, including two swimming pools, coin-op washers and dryers, and a video-game arcade. Several restaurants (which deliver), a large shopping mall with a 12-theater movie house, and a supermarket are within close walking distance. The rooms at both locations are clean and attractive standard motel units. Best bet are the efficiencies with fully equipped kitchenettes at no. 4104. On the other hand, at no. 4125 you can ask for a room with a large Jacuzzi, a refrigerator, and a microwave oven. All accommodations offer pay-movie options and in-room safes. Guest services at no. 4104 sells tickets (many of them discounted) and arranges transport to all nearby attractions, including WDW parks. A big plus: Round-trip fare to WDW parks is free. Airport transfers can be arranged.

Econo Lodge Maingate East. 4311 W. Irlo Bronson Memorial Hwy. (U.S. 192, between Hoagland Blvd. and Fla. 535), Kissimmee, FL 34746. ☎ **407/396-7100** or 800/ENJOY-FL. Fax 407/239-2636. 173 rms. A/C TV TEL. $29–$79 room for up to four, depending on season. AE, CB, DC, DISC, JCB, MC, V. Free parking.

Ever spent a sleepless night at a motel (the word does derive from "motorist" and "hotel") because of traffic noise? It won't happen here. At this attractively landscaped Econo Lodge, the accommodations are set well back from the highway in rustic two- and three-story buildings with cedar balconies and roofing. The well-maintained rooms are equipped with safes, and small refrigerators can be rented. A pool bar serves light fare, including full breakfasts and lunches at umbrella tables under towering live oaks. The guest-services desk sells tickets (most of them discounted) and provides transport to all nearby attractions and the airport. Scheduled round-trip transport to/from WDW parks is free. On-premises facilities include a large swimming pool, a kiddie pool, volleyball, shuffleboard, horseshoes, coin-op washers/dryers, picnic tables, barbecue grills, and a video-game arcade. This is one of six area hotels under the same ownership, all of which can be booked via the above toll-free number.

Ramada Inn. 4559 W. Irlo Bronson Memorial Hwy. (U.S. 192, between Siesta Lago Dr. and Bass Rd./Old Vineland Rd.), Kissimmee, FL 34746. ☎ **407/396-1212** or 800/544-5712. Fax 407/396-7926. 114 rms. A/C TV TEL. $23.95–$44.95 room for up to four; $29.95–$50.95 efficiency. Rates range reflects season. AE, DC, DISC, MC, V. Free self-parking.

This Ramada offers standard motel rooms with cable TV and safes; refrigerators are available on request for $6 a night. The efficiencies offer two-burner stoves, extra sinks, and small refrigerators (no eating or cooking utensils are provided). Facilities include coin-op washers/dryers, a swimming pool, a children's playground, and picnic tables. The 1950s-style Hollywood Diner—which has an adjoining bar/lounge—serves American fare at all meals. Shuttle service to WDW parks is available for $10 per person, round-trip. Pets are accepted ($6 per night).

Ramada Ltd. 5055 W. Irlo Bronson Memorial Hwy. (U.S. 192, between Poinciana Blvd. and Fla. 535), Kissimmee, FL 34746. ☎ **407/396-2212** or 800/446-5669. Fax 407/396-0253. 107 rms. A/C TV TEL. $27.95–$45 room for up to four, depending on season. Rates include continental breakfast. AE, DC, DISC, MC, V. Free self-parking.

Less than 4 miles from the Walt Disney World parks, this Ramada houses its rooms in a three-story stucco building. The accommodations are equipped with cable TV (with Disney Channel and HBO movies), and safes; refrigerators are available on request for $6 a night. Facilities include a swimming pool and coin-op washers/dryers. Continental breakfast is served in the lobby each morning. Shuttle service to WDW parks is available for $9 per person, round-trip. Pets are accepted ($6 per night).

Rodeway Inn Eastgate. 5245 W. Irlo Bronson Memorial Hwy. (U.S. 192, between Poinciana and Polynesian Isle blvds.), Kissimmee, FL 34746. ☎ **407/396-7700** or 800/423-3864. Fax 407/396-0293. 200 rms. A/C TV TEL. $31–$55 room for up to four people, depending on view and season. Rates may be higher during major events. AE, CB, DC, DISC, JCB, MC, V. Free parking.

The Rodeway's U-shaped configuration of two-story pink stucco buildings forms an attractively landscaped courtyard around a large swimming pool. Families will appreciate the picnic tables and a children's play area on the lawn. The rooms are nicely decorated. Lucille's Cafe serves buffet breakfasts, and the comfy Half Time Lounge, where sporting events are aired on a large-screen TV, has a pool table and dart boards. Other facilities include a video-game room, coin-op washers/dryers, and a gift shop. Guest services sells tickets to all WDW parks and nearby attractions (many of them discounted) and offers transportation to/from them and the airport. Round-trip transport to WDW parks is $7.

Viking Motel. 4539 W. Irlo Bronson Memorial Hwy. (U.S. 192, between Fla. 535 and Hoagland Blvd. North), Kissimmee, FL 34746. ☎ **407/396-8860** or 800/396-8860. Fax 407/396-2088.

49 rms. A/C TV TEL. $25–$60 double; $35–$70 double with kitchenette. Rates range reflects season. Additional person $5 extra. AE, DISC, MC, V. Free self-parking.

Kids love this family-owned property housed in a fantasy castle, with towers topped by little Viking ships. Owners Bert and Christine Langenstroer are from Germany, and they've prettified their motel's alpine-style balconies with neat flower boxes. The immaculate rooms are equipped with cable TV, safes, and Magic Fingers bed massagers. Some units have refrigerators, and a few offer fully equipped kitchenettes and cozy breakfast nooks. On-premises facilities include coin-op washers/dryers, a shuffleboard court, a Viking-themed playground and sandbox, and a small free-form swimming pool with outdoor tables under thatched umbrellas and barbecue grills on the sundeck. A Waffle House restaurant and a miniature golf course are next door. The guest-services desk sells tickets (many of them discounted) to nearby attractions, though it does not carry WDW park tickets. Transportation is, however, available to WDW parks (round-trip fare is $8 per person), other area attractions, and the airport. The Viking is 6 miles from the Magic Kingdom.

DOUBLES FOR LESS THAN $60

○ **Larson's Lodge Main Gate.** 6075 W. Irlo Bronson Memorial Hwy. (U.S. 192, just east of I-4), Kissimmee, FL 34747. ☎ **407/396-6100** or 800/327-9074. Fax 407/396-6965. 128 rms. A/C TV TEL. $39–$79 double; $54–$94 efficiency. Rates range reflect season. Additional person $8 extra; children 18 and under stay free in parents' room. Inquire about packages. AE, CB, DC, DISC, MC, V. Free parking.

With its large, on-premises water park (Watermania), playground, poolside picnic tables, barbecue grills, and cheerful on-site Shoney's restaurant, Larson's Lodge is a good choice for families. The accommodations are equipped with cable TV (with HBO; VCRs and movie tapes can be rented), small refrigerators, microwave ovens, and safes. There are also efficiency units with fully equipped kitchenettes. A supermarket is just a few minutes away by car.

The guest-services desk sells tickets to all nearby theme parks (many of them discounted), and can arrange transport to other nearby attractions and the airport. Round-trip fare to WDW parks is $8. On-premises facilities include a large swimming pool and whirlpool, shops, coin-op washers/dryers, and a video-game arcade. Guests enjoy a free newspaper and coffee in the lobby each morning and free tennis at the Holiday Inn Kissimmee Downtown (see below). Pets are permitted.

DOUBLES FOR LESS THAN $80

Hojo Inn Main Gate. 6051 W. Irlo Bronson Memorial Hwy. (U.S. 192, just east of I-4), Kissimmee, FL 34747. ☎ **407/396-1748** or 800/288-4678. Fax 407/649-8642. 358 rms, 9 family suites. A/C TV TEL. $60–$75 room for up to four; $70–$85 efficiency; $80–$95 family suite. Rates range reflect season. Children 18 and under stay free in parents' room. Inquire about packages. AE, CB, DC, DISC, JCB, MC, V. Free self-parking.

Several factors make this Howard Johnson's property a worthwhile choice. Just 2 miles from the Magic Kingdom—and offering free transport to and from the Disney parks—it maintains a special guest-services phone number (☎ 800/TOUR-FLA) which you can call in advance of your trip to arrange attractions tickets, paid transportation, car rental, and other vacation needs. The accommodations here are nicely decorated; amenities include cable TV (with pay-movie options and Nintendo) and safes. The efficiency units have fully equipped kitchenettes with small refrigerators, two-burner stoves, and sinks. And the family suites have both full kitchens and living rooms with convertible sofas.

Among the facilities are a medium-size swimming pool, a whirlpool, a kiddie pool, a children's playground, coin-op washers/dryers, a video-game arcade, a car-rental desk, and a pool table. Adjoining the property is the large water park, Watermania (see Larson's Lodge Main Gate, above), and an IHOP where kids 11 and under with an adult eat free. On premises, a pool bar serves light fare and drinks, and coffee and tea are served each morning in the lobby. Guest services sells tickets to all Disney parks and nearby attractions (some discounted), and offers transportation to/from them and the airport.

✪ **Holiday Inn Hotel & Suites.** 5678 Irlo Bronson Hwy. (U.S. 192, between 1-4 and Poinciana Blvd.), Kissimmee, FL 34746. ☎ **407/396-4488** or 800/FON-KIDS. Fax 407/396-8915. 559 rms, 55 suites. A/C TV TEL. $75–$105 room for up to four; $99–$I95 one-bedroom suite with kitchenette. Rates range reflects season. Inquire about packages. AE, CB, DC, DISC, JCB, MC, V. Free parking.

Just 3 miles from the entrance to the Magic Kingdom, this attractively landscaped 23-acre property offers identical facilities to the Holiday Inn Sunspree Resort Lake Buena Vista (described above), including its own Camp Holiday and all the kid-pleaser features. There's even a small merry-go-round in the lobby. The accommodations are in two-story motel-style buildings enclosing courtyard swimming pools. Pets are permitted.

The Vineyard Cafe serves breakfast and dinner, the latter featuring steak and seafood. There's also a food court and a pool bar proferring frozen tropical drinks. Kids 12 and under eat all meals free, either in a hotel restaurant with their parents or in the Gingerbread House, a cheerful facility where movies and cartoons are shown on a large-screen TV and dinner includes a make-your-own-sundae bar.

Room service and baby-sitting are available, and the guest-services desk sells tickets to all nearby attractions (including WDW parks) and arranges the free scheduled transport to WDW parks (there's a charge for transport to other nearby attractions), telephone grocery shopping, and the Mears airport shuttle. Facilities include two Olympic-size swimming pools, two whirlpools, a kiddie pool, a playground, two tennis courts, sand volleyball, a basketball court, coin-op washers/dryers, shops, car rental, two video-game arcades, and Camp Holiday, a counselor-supervised child-care/activity center for children ages 3 to 12.

Holiday Inn Kissimmee Downtown. 2009 W. Vine St. (U.S. 192, at Thacker Ave.), Kissimmee, FL 34741. ☎ **407/846-2713** or 800/624-5905. Fax 407/846-8695. 200 rms. A/C TV TEL. $38–$89 room for up to four; $53–$104 efficiency with a kitchenette. Rates range reflects season. Children 18 and under stay free in parents' room. AE, CB, DC, DISC, MC, V. Free parking.

Just 8 miles from Walt Disney World, this Holiday Inn gives you a few more facilities—including a tennis court—than you might expect in this price range. Families should consider the efficiencies here, with living room areas and fully equipped kitchens. A steakhouse serves all meals and provides room service, and its adjoining bar/lounge features karaoke nights. The guest-services desk sells tickets (many of them discounted) to all nearby theme parks and can arrange transportation to/from other nearby attractions and the airport. Round-trip to WDW parks is $10. Facilities include two swimming pools (one very large), a kiddie pool, a whirlpool, a playground, a gift shop, coin-op washers/dryers, and a video-game arcade. Pets are permitted.

DOUBLES FOR MORE THAN $80

✪ **Residence Inn by Marriott on Lake Cecile.** 4786 W. Irlo Bronson Memorial Hwy. (between Fla. 535 and Siesta Lago Dr.), Kissimmee, FL 34746. ☎ **407/396-2056** or 800/468-3027. Fax 407/396-2909. 159 studios and suites. A/C TV TEL. $119–$129 studio for up to four; $189 bilevel penthouse suite for up to six. Rates include extended continental breakfast. AE, CB, DC, DISC, JCB, MC, OPT, V. Free parking.

Sylvan landscaping on the banks of beautiful 223-acre Lake Cecile—and home-away-from-home accommodations—set this Residence Inn apart from the neighboring properties. The tastefully decorated suites offer fully equipped eat-in kitchens and comfortable living room areas. All but the studio doubles have wood-burning fireplaces (logs are available), and the cathedral-ceilinged penthouses contain full baths upstairs and down. Many suites have balconies overlooking the lake. Amenities include cable TV (VCRs are available on request) and safes.

The lovely gatehouse lounge off the lobby, with comfy sofas facing a working fireplace, is the breakfast setting each morning. An alfresco bar serves light fare and drinks poolside on a canopied wooden deck, and a number of local restaurants deliver (there are menus in each room). Guest services sells tickets (most of them discounted) and provides transport to all nearby theme parks and attractions; round-trip to WDW parks is $7. There's a complimentary daily newspaper and free food-shopping service. Facilities include a small swimming pool, a whirlpool, a sports court (basketball, volleyball, badminton, paddle tennis), a playground, coin-op washers/dryers, a 24-hour food shop, picnic tables, and barbecue grills. Lake activities include fishing, jet skiing, bumper rides, and waterskiing.

INTERNATIONAL DRIVE

Hotels and resorts listed here are 7 to 10 miles north of the Walt Disney World parks (a quick freeway trip) and close to Universal Studios Florida and Sea World. International Drive hostelries tend to be somewhat less kid-oriented than hotels in other areas.

DOUBLES FOR LESS THAN $60

Fairfield Inn by Marriott. 8342 Jamaican Court (off International Dr. between the Beeline Expy. and Sand Lake Rd.), Orlando, FL 32819. ☎ **407/363-1944** or 800/228-2800. Fax 407/363-1944. 134 rms. A/C TV TEL. $35–$70 room for up to four. Range reflects season. Rates include continental breakfast. AE, CB, DC, DISC, JCB, MC, V. Free parking.

I love this inn's quiet and safe location in a secluded area off International Drive. It nestles in Jamaican Court, a neatly landscaped complex of hotels and restaurants (that means a number of eateries are within walking distance). The spiffy-looking rooms offer cable TV with HBO, and the phones are equipped with 25-foot cords and modem jacks. Daily newspapers and local calls are free, as is the continental breakfast served in the lobby each morning.

The guest-services desk sells tickets (most of them discounted) and can arrange transport to all nearby theme parks and attractions and the airport; round-trip to WDW parks is $10. A small swimming pool and video-game room are on the premises, and the lobby has a microwave oven for guest use.

DOUBLES FOR LESS THAN $80

Country Hearth Inn. 9861 International Dr. (between the Beeline Expy. and Sand Lake Rd.), Orlando, FL 32819. ☎ **407/352-0008** or 800/447-1890. Fax 407/352-5449. 150 rms. A/C TV TEL. $59–$139 double, depending on view and season. Additional person $10 extra; children 17 and under stay free in parents' room. Rates include continental breakfast. AE, CB, DC, DISC, MC, V. Free self-parking.

Though it doesn't offer much in the way of resort facilities, the Country Hearth Inn's low rates, great location, and very pretty rooms and restaurant—not to mention wine and cheese receptions for guests several times a week—make this an appealing choice. Centered on a white-trimmed octagonal building crowned by a windowed cupola, the inn evokes 19th-century Florida—the leisurely era of riverboat travel and gracious plantations. Ceiling fans whir slowly over verandas and balconies furnished with wicker rocking chairs, and a charmingly landscaped courtyard with neat lawns and flower beds encompasses a large free-form swimming pool backed by verdant woodlands and a wide canal. The charming guest rooms are furnished in handsome maple or mahogany pieces; French doors open onto patios, balconies, or courtyards; and the baths have art nouveau lighting fixtures. In-room amenities include cable TV (with HBO and Spectravision movie options), coffeemakers, phones with modem jacks, wood-bladed chandelier ceiling fans, safes, and small refrigerators. The larger deluxe rooms offer sleeper sofas, microwave ovens, and hair dryers.

The elegant Country Parlor, in the balustraded Victorian lobby, serves moderately priced American fare at all meals; a pianist entertains at Sunday champagne brunches. The Front Porch Lounge, a popular gathering spot for locals, features happy hour buffets Monday to Friday from 5:30 to 7pm. Room service is available. The guest-services desk sells tickets (many of them discounted) and arranges transport to all nearby attractions (including WDW parks), babysitting, and the Mears airport shuttle. Round-trip fare to WDW parks is $9.

DOUBLES FOR MORE THAN $80

Orlando Marriott. 8001 International Dr. (at Sand Lake Rd.), Orlando, FL 32819. ☎ **407/ 351-2420** or 800/421-8001. Fax 407/351-5016. 1,062 rms, 16 suites. A/C TV TEL. $79–$120 double, depending on view and season; $110–$300 suite. Additional person $10 extra; children 17 and under stay free in parents' room. AE, DC, DISC, MC, V. Free self-parking.

The grounds at this verdant 48-acre property make you feel that you're in a secluded, plush resort, but you're actually in the heart of a busy area, with proximity to many great restaurants. The rates are very reasonable in light of the facilities you'll enjoy here. The accommodations are housed in pale-pink stucco bilevel villas; half have balconies or patios, and some contain full kitchens. All offer pay-movie stations and safes; many are also equipped with hair dryers, electric shoeshine machines, and irons and ironing boards.

The tropical Grove specializes in steaks, prime rib, and seafood. The Chelsea Cafe serves American fare at all meals. A club, Illusions, features a DJ spinning Top 40 tunes, as well as blackjack, a pool table, and darts. Fast food is available, plus a cozy lobby bar and several poolside bars. Room service is offered.

The guest-services desk sells tickets (many discounted) and arranges transportation to/from WDW parks and all other nearby attractions (the round-trip fare to WDW parks is $8), and arranges for baby-sitting and the Mears airport shuttle. There's a 24-hour free tram service around the property. The facilities include three swimming pools (one quite large), two kiddie pools, a whirlpool, four tennis courts, a sand volleyball court, a playground, a business center, an exercise room, a 1.4-mile jogging trail, coin-op washers/dryers, car rental, a unisex hair salon, shops, and two video-game arcades.

Residence Inn by Marriott. 7975 Canada Ave. (just off Sand Lake Rd. a block east of International Dr.), Orlando, FL 32819. ☎ **407/345-0117** or 800/227-3978. Fax 407/352-2689. 176 studios and suites. A/C TV TEL. $105–$115 studio for up to four; $165 bilevel penthouse suite for up to eight. Rates include extended continental breakfast. AE, DC, DISC, MC, V. Free parking.

Marriott's Residence Inns were designed to offer home-away-from-home comfort for traveling businesspeople, but the concept also works well for families. These handsomely decorated suites offer full eat-in kitchens and comfortable living room areas. All but studio doubles have wood-burning fireplaces, and the two-bedroom penthouses (great for families) have full baths upstairs and down. Amenities include irons and ironing boards and safes.

The comfortably furnished gatehouse is the breakfast setting, and complimentary beer, wine, and hors d'oeuvres are offered Monday to Thursday from 5:30 to 7pm. Local restaurants deliver (there are menus in each room).

The guest-services desk sells tickets (most of them discounted), provides transport to all nearby theme parks and attractions (the round-trip fare to WDW parks is $10), and arranges for the Mears airport shuttle. There's a complimentary daily newspaper and a free food-shopping service (microwave dinners are sold in the lobby). On the property are a large swimming pool, a whirlpool, a basketball court, a sand volleyball court, coin-op washers/dryers, a food/sundries shop, picnic tables, and barbecue grills. Guests also have free use of a nearby health club.

3 Where to Eat

IN WALT DISNEY WORLD

Since most Orlando visitors spend most of their time in the Walt Disney World area, I've focused on the best—and most reasonably priced—choices throughout that vast enchanted empire. Also listed are some worthwhile budget establishments beyond the realm. Throughout Walt Disney World, look for **Mickey's Value Meals** (which are complete prix-fixe meals that are quite reasonable) and, even better value, attractively priced **Family Meals** that serve four.

Note that all Walt Disney World restaurants have no-smoking interiors (you can smoke on patios and terraces); that Magic Kingdom restaurants serve no alcoholic beverages, but liquor is available at Epcot and Disney–MGM eateries and elsewhere in the WDW complex; and all sit-down restaurants in Walt Disney World take American Express, MasterCard, Visa, and the Disney Card.

Parents will be pleased to see that just about every restaurant in town offers a low-priced children's menu and usually provides some kind of kid's activity as well. The down side of restaurants that cater to kids is that they're noisy; if you're looking for a quiet meal, head for restaurants in the International Drive area, which are farther from the Disney parks.

See also the listings for dinner shows in "Walt Disney World & Orlando After Dark," later in this chapter.

EPCOT

Though an ethnic meal at one of the World Showcase pavilions is a traditional part of the Epcot experience, most of the major restaurants here are not only expensive, but overpriced for the value received. Below you'll find the best strategies for getting the most out of Epcot's fancier restaurants, along with many lower-priced walk-in eateries throughout the park.

World Showcase

These restaurants are arranged geographically, beginning at the Canada pavilion and proceeding counterclockwise around the World Showcase Lagoon.

CANADA **Le Cellier** here is a good choice for families. Located in the Victorian Hôtel du Canada, it has a castlelike ambience with seating in tapestried chairs under vaulted stone arches. It's a self-service buffeteria, for which no reservations are required. Regional dishes include Cheddar-cheese soup, carved pemeal bacon (a pork loin with a light cornmeal crust), a French-Canadian pork- and potato-filled pie called a tourtière, maple syrup pie, and Canadian beers. Entrees cost $7.50 to $9.95 at lunch, $9.95 to $15.95 at dinner. *Note:* The $4 children's meal here isn't a bad bet for adults either. No one has to know you're not getting it for the kids.

How to Arrange Priority Seating at Walt Disney World Restaurants

Priority seating is similar to a reservation. It means that you get the next table available when you arrive at a restaurant, but a table is not kept empty pending your arrival. You can arrange priority seating up to 60 days in advance at almost all full-service Magic Kingdom, Epcot, Disney–MGM Studios, resort, and Disney Village restaurants—as well as character meals and shows throughout the complex—by calling **407/WDW-DINE.** Nighttime shows can actually be booked as far in advance as you wish. Exceptions to this format are noted in the listings below.

Since this priority-seating phone number was instituted in 1994, it has become much more difficult to obtain a table by just showing up. So I strongly advise you to avoid disappointment by calling ahead. Remember that guests at Disney resorts and "official" hotels can make restaurant reservations through guest-services or concierge desks.

However, if you don't reserve in advance, you can take your chances reserving in the parks themselves:

At Epcot: Make reservations at the WorldKey interactive terminals at Guest Relations in Innoventions East, at Worldkey Information Service Satellites located on the main concourse to World Showcase and at Germany in World Showcase, or at the restaurants themselves.

At the Magic Kingdom: Reserve at the restaurants themselves.

At Disney–MGM Studios: Make reservations at the Hollywood Junction Station on Sunset Boulevard or at the restaurants themselves.

UNITED KINGDOM The Tudor-beamed **Rose & Crown,** entered via a cozy pub with a pungent aroma of ale, has an interior evocative of Victorian England. The restaurant itself is expensive, but you can order low-priced light fare at the bar (sausage rolls, Cornish pasties, a Stilton cheese and fruit plate—all items under $4.50). Wash it all down with a pint of Irish lager beer, Bass ale, or Guinness stout.

FRANCE **Au Petit Café,** a sidewalk bistro overlooking the lagoon, serves traditional café fare: quiche Lorraine, salade niçoise, soupe à l'oignon gratinée, and the like. No reservations are required. Desserts range from French cakes and pastries to crêpes Melba (filled with peaches and vanilla ice cream and topped with raspberry sauce). French wines are available. Entrees range from $7.75 to $15.50.

And the **Pâtisserie/Boulangerie,** its interior redolent of croissants and pastries baking in the oven, offers tempting desserts plus French coffees and wines.

MOROCCO The palatial ✪ **Restaurant Marrakesh**—with its hand-set mosaic tilework, latticed teak shutters, and beamed ceiling painted with Moorish motifs—represents 12 centuries of Arabic design. Belly dancers perform in the central dining area to *oud, kanoun,* and *daburka* music while you dine. Dinner's out of our price range. Best bet for budgeteers is the lunchtime Moroccan diffa, a traditional feast that lets you sample a variety of dishes. Priced at $29.95 for two, it includes a salad, brochette of chicken, roast lamb, rice studded with almonds and raisins, and fruit salad. Combination appetizer plates ($12.95 for two at lunch or dinner) are another inexpensive way to experience culinary diversity. French and Moroccan wines are available to complement your meal. Call ahead for priority seating.

JAPAN Housed in a replica of the 16th-century Katsura Imperial Villa in Kyoto is **Yakitori House,** a bamboo-roofed cafeteria serving shrimp tempura over noodles, chicken yakitori, and other Japanese snack-fare items—all of them under $7; a full children's meal is $2.70. Umbrella tables on a terrace overlooking a rock waterfall are a plus.

But for me, the gem of this complex is the peaceful plant-filled **cocktail lounge** with large windows overlooking the lagoon—a very pleasant setting for appetizers and warm sake. Japanese music plays softly in the background. Menu items are $3.95 to $8.25, and no reservations are required. A window seat here is a great venue for viewing IlluminNations.

AMERICAN ADVENTURE The **Liberty Inn** is an immense cafeteria where the staff is attired in 18th-century costume. It has a pleasant interior with exposed-brick walls and seating around a central fountain under a skylight. However, weather permitting, I prefer an umbrella table on the plaza overlooking the lagoon. The fare is all-American: burgers and the like. Best bet is the Family Meal: a whole rotisserie chicken, a pound of cole slaw, a pound of baked beans, four corn muffins, and four 16-ounce sodas for $18.50. Other menu items are all under $7.25.

ITALY Patterned after Alfredo De Lelio's celebrated establishment in Rome, **L'Originale Alfredo di Roma Ristorante** suggests a seaside Roman palazzo with beautiful *trompe l'oeil* frescoes of 16th-century patrician villas inspired by Veronese. The theatricality of an exhibition kitchen and exuberant strolling musicians create a festive ambience. If you want a quieter setting, ask for a seat on the veranda. Though Alfredo's is expensive during regular hours, a $15.75 three-course early-bird dinner is served nightly from 4:30 to 6pm. It includes soup or salad, an entree such as fettuccine Alfredo (the restaurant's signature dish, invented by De Lelio) or chicken parmigiana, and homemade gelati. Call ahead for priority seating.

GERMANY Lit by streetlamps, the **Biergarten** simulates a Bavarian village courtyard at Oktoberfest. Musical shows take place five to seven times a day (depending on the season). Guests are encouraged to dance as the band strikes up and to sing along with yodelers and folksingers. All-you-can-eat buffet meals featuring traditional fare are offered at lunch and dinner. Beverages and desserts are extra. Lunch buffets cost $9.95; dinner buffets, $14.50. Call ahead for priority seating.

At **Sommerfest,** a cafeteria with indoor seating and courtyard tables, you can purchase bratwurst sandwiches with sauerkraut, goulash soup, desserts such as apple strudel, and beverages ranging from Beck's beer to Liebfraumilch. All items are under $5.

CHINA At the open-air **Lotus Blossom Café,** a pleasant self-service eatery, you can order archetypical Cantonese fare: eggrolls, pork fried rice, sweet-and-sour chicken, stir-fried chicken and vegetables served over noodles, and the like. Chinese beer and wine are options. Nothing is more than $6.25.

NORWAY **Akershus** re-creates a 14th-century castle fortress that stands in Oslo's harbor. Its pristine white stone interior, with Gothic stone archways and soft lighting, creates intimate dining niches. The meal is an immense smörgåsbord of traditional *småvarmt* (hot) and *koldtbord* (cold) dishes—smoked pork with honey mustard, strips of venison in cream sauce, gravlax in mustard sauce, an array of Norwegian breads and cheeses, and much more. Norwegian beer and aquavit complement a list of French and California wines. Desserts, such as a "veiled maiden"—an applesauce and whipped cream concoction—are à la carte. The lunch buffet costs $11.95 for adults, $4.50 for children 4 to 9, free for children 3 and under; the dinner buffet is $17.95 for adults, $7.50 for children. There are also non-smörgåsbord children's meals for $4. Call ahead for priority seating.

Another facility in this pavilion, the **Kringla Bakeri og Kafe,** offers covered outdoor seating and inexpensive light fare such as open-face sandwiches, cheese and fruit platters, and fresh-baked Norwegian pastries.

MEXICO　　The setting for the ✪ **San Angel Inn** is a hacienda courtyard amid dense jungle foliage in the shadow of a crumbling Yucatán pyramid. It's nighttime: Tables are candlelit (even at lunch). The Popocatepetl volcano erupts in the distance, spewing molten lava, and you can hear the sounds of faraway birds. Thunder, lightning, and swiftly moving clouds add a dramatic note, but the overall ambience is soothing. The fare is authentic and prepared from scratch. And though most of the menu (especially at dinner) is too expensive for this book, you might visit at lunch when many items—ranging from grilled chicken burritos to quesadillas stuffed with cheese and chorizo sausage—are under $12. Or at either meal, ask for the vegetarian menu, which offers more than half a dozen dishes priced from $7.25 to $11.75. There's chocolate Kahlúa mousse pie for dessert, and drink options include Dos Equis beer and margaritas. Call ahead for priority seating.

The **Cantina de San Angel,** a cafeteria on a terrace overlooking the lagoon, offers affordable tacos, burritos, and combination plates, along with frozen margaritas; a complete children's meal is $2.70.

Future World

These restaurants are arranged geographically, with listings beginning at Innoventions (the section to the right as you enter the park) and proceeding counterclockwise.

INNOVENTIONS　　If you haven't had breakfast, a good first stop in Epcot is the **Fountain View Espresso & Bakery,** a circular facility (to the right of the Spaceship Earth globe) with indoor and outdoor seating overlooking a beautiful splashing fountain. It offers sophisticated European *pâtisserie* fare, plus fresh-baked bagels and muffins. Later in the day, come by for gourmet coffees (spiked with liqueurs if you wish) and wines.

Adjoining the Fountain View is **Pizza Piazza,** a vast cheerful cafeteria with an exhibition pasta kitchen (all the pasta here is homemade). Its breakfasts (served to 11am; all items under $4.50) are more in the traditional American mode than those at Fountain Views, including muffins, French toast, and cheese omelets with Canadian bacon and fried potatoes. At lunch and dinner there are pizzas and Italian dishes such as eggplant parmigiana, lasagne, and meatball subs. A Mickey's Value Meal of chicken parmesan served over spinach pasta with salad and a soft drink is $8.40. Fresh-baked desserts run the gamut from a cannoli to Heath Bar cheesecake. Wine and beer are available.

The other Innoventions building (to the left of the Spaceship Earth globe) houses the **Electric Umbrella,** another spacious cafeteria with seating under colorful electric umbrellas lit by twinkling lights; there's also outdoor seating. Light American fare is featured: chili, fries, burgers, sandwiches, and salads (all under $7), which you can enhance from an extensive toppings bar. Wine and beer are available, and fresh-baked desserts include chocolate cream or peanut butter pie. Mickey's Value Meal here is a chicken fajita sandwich with fries and a beverage for $6.60.

THE LAND　　This pavilion's Garden Grill is the setting for the character meals descibed below. It also houses a lower-level food court (a good choice for family dining) called the **Sunshine Season Food Fair,** where vendors proffer an array of low-priced items—barbecued chicken and ribs, immense cinnamon rolls, stuffed baked potatoes, sandwiches, oven-fresh cakes and pastries, ice cream, and more.

WONDERS OF LIFE   This health- and fitness-oriented pavilion houses a cafeteria called **Pure and Simple,** where you might purchase fruit smoothies, fresh fruit, nonfat-yogurt shakes, a bran-and-grain waffle topped with fruit sauce, or even a sub on multigrain bread stuffed with turkey pastrami, turkey ham, sliced turkey breast, and low-fat mozzarella. Everything on the menu is under $5.50.

THE MAGIC KINGDOM

The full-service restaurants in the Magic Kingdom are almost ridiculously expensive, charging $8 to $10 even for burgers and sandwiches. Fortunately, there are dozens of fast-food eateries, almost all of them with pleasant outdoor tables. The listings below are arranged geographically, proceeding counterclockwise from Cinderella Castle. Remember: No alcoholic beverages are served in Magic Kingdom restaurants.

TOMORROWLAND   The major facility here is **Cosmic Ray's Starlight Cafe,** an enormous facility. If you sit indoors, you'll be entertained by Sonny Eclipse, an "alien" who sings, plays music, and cracks jokes while you dine. Or you can opt for the quieter terrace with alfresco seating at umbrella tables. Best deal here is the Family Meal: a whole rotisserie chicken, 16 ounces of rice and beans, 16 ounces of potato salad, and four corn muffins for $16. An individual serving of the above is $5 to $7, depending on what part of the chicken you choose. Other choices here (most of them $6 or less) include burgers, soups, sandwiches, subs, and salads. There's ice cream and fresh fruit for dessert.

Another possibility is the equally vast **Plaza Pavilion,** which, in addition to indoor seating, has a covered outdoor terrace overlooking the lagoon. Its menu is similar to the above. Mickey's Value Meal here is a 6-inch pepperoni pizza with salad and a soft drink for $6.05.

For a quick meal, pick up a smoked turkey leg—a WDW specialty which you can gnaw on like a barbarian—at the **Lunching Pad** for $3.75. Top it off with a sundae or soft ice creams from the nearby **Aunt Gravity's Galactic Goodies**.

FANTASYLAND   The **Pinocchio Village Haus,** a large cafeteria, has a charming alpine-castle/storybook-themed interior and outdoor seating at umbrella tables, some of them overlooking the fountained waters of It's a Small World. Items such as chicken with pasta salad, burgers and fries, and smoked turkey subs are under $6. Finish up with soft ice cream or a sundae from **Mrs. Potts' Cupboard** nearby.

LIBERTY SQUARE   The **Columbia Harbor House,** a pleasant cafeteria, has a New England interior with a nautical decor, and the food is more or less of the same genre. Items such as New England clam chowder, fried fish, seafood-pasta salad, and a smoked-turkey sandwich are all under $5, and there's apple pie for dessert.

Sleepy Hollow, with outdoor tables only, may be the park's best venue for vegetarian fare. You can order sandwiches on pita or Norwegian potato bread here stuffed with avocado, sprouts, Harvati cheese, jalapeños, sesame seeds, cucumber, tomato, and spinach. Other choices include a feta-cheese salad with tahini dressing, tabouleh salad, vegetarian chili, and peanut butter roll-ups with fresh fruit. All items are under $4.50.

In the mood for a light but satisfying meal? I'm partial to the **baked- and sweet-potato cart** in Liberty Square and the adjacent fresh fruit and juice stand.

FRONTIERLAND   Best choice here is the **Diamond Horseshoe Saloon Revue** (details below in Section 5). The food's not much, but you can enjoy it while watching a show in air-conditioned comfort.

The **Pecos Bill Cafe,** a large cafeteria adjacent to Adventureland, has a rustic interior with a vast stone fireplace. The fare (all items are under $6) consists of burgers, hot dogs, salads, sandwiches, and chili, which you can enhance at an extensive top-pings bar. Mickey's Value Meal here is a barbecued chicken sandwich served with fries or grapes and a soft drink for $6.60. There are brownies for dessert.

I also like **Aunt Polly's Landing** on Tom Sawyer's Island, reached via a short raft trip across the Rivers of America. With its outdoor tables on a porch overlooking the water, it provides a tranquil respite from park hyperactivity. The inexpensive light fare includes sandwiches and soft drinks. And you can relax over refreshing lemonade while the kids explore the island's dark caves and abandoned mines. It's open for lunch only.

ADVENTURELAND   The major facility here is **El Pirata y El Perico,** a cafeteria with covered seating on a Mexican-style Saltillo-tile patio. The fare—nachos, tacos, chili, salads, and hot dogs—is served up in hearty portions. Everything is under $5.

Juices, frozen yogurt, and iced cappuccino are available from the **Sunshine Tree Terrace,** a thatch-roofed structure topped by tiki gods holding flaming torches; it offers outdoor seating at umbrella tables.

DISNEY–MGM STUDIOS

There are over a dozen eateries in this Hollywood-themed park with names like the Studio Commissary and Starring Rolls Bakery. The best food is at:

The **Hollywood Brown Derby,** modeled after the now-defunct Los Angeles celebrity haunt where Louella Parsons and Hedda Hopper once held court—it evokes its West Coast counterpart with interior palm trees, derby-shaded sconces, and wainscoted walls hung with more than 1,500 caricatures (every major star from Barbara Stanwyck to Rin Tin Tin). Generally, the Derby is too pricey for this book. But budget travelers can take advantage of its three-course early-bird dinner served from 4 to 5:30pm for $15.75. It includes soup or salad, a choice of three main dishes (pan-seared salmon, roast chicken, or pasta tossed with feta cheese and tomatoes in garlic-basil sauce), and dessert. California wines are featured. Call ahead for priority seating.

A less expensive choice is the **Soundstage Restaurant,** a vast cafeteria designed to suggest a Hollywood warehouse filled with movie props and facades, most notably from recent Disney animated features like *Pocahontas* and *Aladdin.* Menu items ($3.35 to $4.25) include spaghetti and meatballs, a pasta salad, or a barbecued beef sandwich, with toffee cheesecake for dessert. Mickey's Value Meal here is a cheese pizza with salad and beverage for $5.50, and kids can order baked macaroni, character-shaped cookies, and a beverage for $2.70. Adults can find refuge in the Soundstage's upstairs **Catwalk Bar,** a secluded venue for a quiet drink and snack fare amid hundreds of movie and TV props—everything from a phonebooth from *Casablanca* to the *Happy Days* jukebox.

Also check out the **Backlot Express,** a gardenlike restaurant with open-air seating under a magnolia arbor. The menu features items such as chicken Caesar salad, burgers, hot dogs, and chili (everything's under $6), and there's a very extensive relish bar.

AT DISNEY RESORTS
MEALS FOR LESS THAN $10

The Colonel's Cotton Mill. At Disney's Dixie Landings Resort, 1251 Dixie Dr. (off Bonnet Creek Pkwy.). ☎ **407/934-6000.** Reservations not accepted. All items under $10. AE, MC, V. Daily 7am–11pm (bakery opens at 6am; pizza served to midnight). AMERICAN.

This rustic food court centers on a working cotton press powered by a rotating 30-foot water wheel. An array of food-court stations sell fresh-baked goods (including some New Orleans specialties), pizza, calzones, fresh fruit, tacos and nachos, sandwiches, burgers, and more. Entrees such as spit-roasted chicken or barbecued ribs served with red beans and rice, a vegetable, and a corn muffin are in the $8 range. Best bet: a three-piece fried-chicken dinner with red beans and rice and a biscuit for $4.50.

Dixie Landings' sibling property, **Disney's Port Orleans Resort,** at 2201 Orleans Dr. (☎ **407/934-5000),** has a similar food court, the festive Mardi Gras–themed **Sassagoula Floatworks and Food Factory.** New Orleans specialties here include beignets at breakfast, baked potatoes stuffed with andouille sausage, and blackened chicken in Créole sauce. Other fare is American.

Intermission Food Court. At Disney's All-Star Music Resort, 180l W. Buena Vista Dr. (at World Dr. and Osceola Pkwy.). ☎ **407/939-6000.** Reservations not accepted. All items under $10. AE, MC, V. Daily 7am–11pm (bakery opens at 6am; pizza served to midnight). AMERICAN.

This cheerful food court, adorned with music paraphernalia and memorabilia, has stations ranging from fresh-baked goods and pizza to chicken pot pie and meatball subs. A good deal here is the all-you-can-eat $10 buffet ($5 for children 9 and under), served from 5 to 11pm and including barbecued beef, chicken, and pork, along with corn muffins, mashed potatoes, macaroni and cheese, potato salad, cole slaw, corn on the cob, baked beans, and fruit cobbler. Or for the same price you can have a prime rib dinner with baked potato and vegetable. Wine and beer are available, and kids can adjourn to a vast video-game arcade while mom and dad linger over coffee. All-you-can-eat buffet breakfasts are another option here: $6 for adults, $3.20 for kids.

There's a similar food court operation at the adjoining All-Star Sports resort.

Old Port Royale. At Disney's Caribbean Beach Resort, 900 Cayman Way (off Buena Vista Dr.). ☎ **407/934-3400.** Reservations not accepted. All items under $10. AE, MC, V. Daily 7am–11pm (bakery opens at 6am; pizza served to midnight). AMERICAN.

Though it's a bit of a drag getting here (non–resort guests have to stop at the Custom House at the entrance for a visitor pass), it's worth the trouble. This festive Caribbean food court, entered via a Jamaican-style straw market, has all the usual food-court offerings, supplemented by such items as jerk chicken and Jamaican beef patties. Wine and beer are available. From 7 to 11:30am daily, an extensive breakfast—scrambled eggs, French toast, potatoes, bacon and sausage, grits, fresh fruit, and biscuits—is $5.75 for adults, $3.50 for children 10 and under. Kids will enjoy a large video-game arcade on the premises and a room where Disney movies and cartoons are aired.

MEALS FOR LESS THAN $15

Boatwright's Dining Hall. In Disney's Dixie Landings Resort, 1251 Dixie Dr. (off Bonnet Creek Pkwy.). ☎ **407/WDW-DINE** for priority seating. Breakfast items $4.25–$6.95; main courses $8.25–$14.95; sandwiches $6.95. AE, MC, V. Daily 7–11:30am and 5–10pm. AMERICAN/CAJUN.

Boatwright's is themed to look like an 1800s boatbuilding factory, complete with the wooden hull of a Louisiana fishing boat suspended from its lofty beamed ceiling. Kids will enjoy the wooden toolboxes on every table; each contains a salt shaker that doubles as a level, a wood-clamp sugar dispenser, a pepper-grinder-cum-ruler, shop rags (to be used as napkins), and a little metal pail of crayons.

The Cajun breakfasts offer intriguing possibilities. French toast here is made with sourdough/sweet-potato baguette tossed in rich egg custard, deep-fried, and coated with cinnamon sugar. Another option: a pan of sautéed crayfish, mushrooms, green onions, and tomatoes in mustard-cream sauce. Dinner here might consist of an appetizer of deep-fried bacon-wrapped oysters and scallops, followed by an entree of rich bouillabaisse redolent of oaken cognac or a medley of blackened seafood served over brown-buttered pasta in creamy garlic sauce. For dessert, there's homemade fruit cobbler topped with vanilla ice cream and smothered in whipped cream.

Bonfamille's Cafe. In Disney's Port Orleans Resort, 2201 Orleans Dr. (off Bonnet Creek Pkwy.). ☎ **407/WDW-DINE** for priority seating. Breakfast items $4.25–$6.95; main courses mostly $8.25–$14.95; salads and po-boy sandwiches $6.95. AE, MC, V. Daily 7–11:30am and 5–10pm. AMERICAN/CREOLE.

Named for a character in *The Aristocats*, the charming Bonfamille's is patterned after a French Quarter courtyard, and Dixieland jazz plays softly in the background. During breakfast it's light and sunny; evenings, candle lamps provide soft lighting.

The Louisiana-style breakfasts range from fresh hot beignets and café au lait to a skillet of crayfish and andouille sausage topped with zesty Créole sauce and melted sharp Cheddar. A typical dinner here: an appetizer of chicken wings tossed in spicy Louisiana hot sauce, followed by grilled Atlantic salmon with spicy pecan butter, and a dessert of Bourbon Street pudding with strawberry and caramel-bourbon sauces. After dinner, families can head over to the hotel's Scat Cats Lounge where entertainment—sing-alongs and live music with lots of audience participation—is featured most nights.

Crockett's Tavern. At Disney's Fort Wilderness Resort and Campground, 3520 N. Fort Wilderness Trail. ☎ **407/WDW-DINE** for priority seating. Main courses $10–$16. AE, MC, V. Sun–Thurs 5–10pm, Fri–Sat 5–10:30pm. Park near the Fort Wilderness Reception Center and take the internal bus to the restaurant; you can also get bus transport from other parts of WDW. STEAK/CHICKEN/RIBS.

A good choice for family dining is this charming tavern themed around the Wild West era of Davy Crockett. Rough-hewn wood-paneled walls are hung with hunting trophies, and artifacts on display range from Native American knives and tomahawks (a scalp, too!) to Fess Parker's coonskin cap.

Best budget bet is a $10 entree of half a roast chicken; it comes with a baked apple, salad, and two side dishes. All-American desserts include homemade fruit cobbler à la mode and strawberry shortcake. There's a full bar and an inexpensive children's menu.

Trail's End. At Disney's Fort Wilderness Resort and Campground, 3520 N. Fort Wilderness Trail. Buffet breakfast $6.95 adults, $4 children 3–11; buffet lunch $7.95 adults, $4.50 children 3–11; buffet dinner $12.95 adults, $7.50 children 3–11; pizza buffet $9.25 adults, $4.50 children 3–11; children 2 and under eat free at all meals. AE, MC, V. Daily 7:30–11am, 11:30am–3:30pm, 4–9pm, and 9:30–11pm (pizza buffet). Park near the Fort Wilderness Reception Center and take the internal bus to the restaurant; you can also get bus transport from other parts of WDW. BUFFETS.

Adjacent to Crockett's Tavern (described above), this rustic dining room (also popular with families) has a log-beamed interior, with wagon-wheel chandeliers overhead and rusty farm implements among its western-pioneer-days decorative elements. A piano player provides honky-tonk saloon music at dinner. The morning meal features "pizzas" topped with scrambled eggs, cheeses, and sausage, along with a buffet of breads, pancakes, breakfast meats, and grits. Both lunch and dinner buffets include dessert and beverage. At lunchtime, the table is laden with platters of fried chicken, bowls of spaghetti and meatballs, a fresh catch of the day, and an extensive soup-and-salad bar. At dinner, there's a roast beef carving station, along with a selection of main dishes, a soup-and-salad bar, and more. Beer and sangría are available by the glass or pitcherful.

WORTH A SPLURGE

✪ **Cape May Café.** At Disney's Beach Club Resort, 1800 EPCOT Resorts Blvd. ☎ **407/ WDW-DINE** for priority seating. Buffet $18.95 adults, $9.50 children 7–11, $4.50 children 3–6, free for children 2 and under; lobster is additional. AE, MC, V. Daily 5:30–9:30pm. CLAMBAKE BUFFET.

At less than $20 for a delicious all-you-can-eat meal, this hearty 19th-century-style New England clambake represents good value for your money. It takes place nightly in a charming restaurant with an upscale seaside resort ambience. Aromatic New England chowder, steamed clams and mussels, corn on the cob, chicken, and redskin potatoes are cooked up in a crackling rockweed steamer pit that serves as the restaurant's centerpiece. And these traditional clambake offerings are supplemented by barbecued pork ribs, smoked sausage, pastas, and a wide array of oven-fresh breads and desserts. Lobster is a available for an extra charge. There's a full bar.

'Ohana. At Disney's Polynesian Resort, 1600 Seven Seas Dr. ☎ **407/WDW-DINE** for priority seating. Buffet $19.75 adults, $13 children 12–16, $8 children 3–11, free for children 2 and under. AE, MC, V. Daily 5–10pm. PACIFIC RIM.

Like the above-described clambake, 'Ohana turns dinner into a special occasion, and its prix-fixe buffet for less than $20 is well worth the money. You'll be welcomed here with warm island hospitality by a server who addresses you as "cousin." *'Ohana* means "family" in Hawaiian, and you're about to enjoy a convivial meal with the extended clan in a South Seas exotic setting with an open kitchen centering on a wood-burning 18-foot fire-pit grill. There's lots going on at all times. The blowing of a conch shell summons a storyteller, coconut races take place down the central aisle, and people celebrating birthdays participate in hula-hoop contests as everyone sings "Happy Birthday" in Hawaiian. Kids especially love all the hoopla, but if you're looking for an intimate venue, this isn't it.

Soon after you're seated, a lazy susan arrives laden with steamed dumplings in soy/ sesame oil, Napa cabbage, black bean and corn relish, and several tangy sauces. And course succeeds course in rapid succession (ask your waiter to slow the pace if it's too fast). The feast includes salad; grilled chicken, smoky pork sausage, mesquite-seasoned beef, stir-fry noodles and vegetables, and more. Passionfruit crème brûlée is extra, but worth it. A full bar offers tropical drinks, including nonalcoholic ones for kids.

WALT DISNEY WORLD VILLAGE MARKETPLACE / PLEASURE ISLAND

Located about 2½ miles from Epcot, off Buena Vista Drive, the Marketplace is a very pleasant complex of cedar-shingled shops and restaurants overlooking a scenic lagoon. Pleasure Island, a complex of nightclubs and shops, adjoins.

With many waterside umbrella tables, the Marketplace is a lovely spot for a picnic. You can pick up reasonably priced fixings—including fresh-baked breads and pastries and wines—at the **Gourmet Pantry.** It's open daily from 8:30am to 11pm.

MEALS FOR LESS THAN $10

Planet Hollywood. 1506 E. Buena Vista Dr., Pleasure Island. ☎ **407/827-7827.** Reservations not accepted. Main courses $7.50–$18.95 (most under $13). AE, DC, MC, V. Daily 11am–2am. AMERICAN WITH INTERNATIONAL INFLUENCES.

Planet Hollywood crashed meteorlike into the Pleasure Island solar system in 1994 with a lavish opening-night party hosted by Schwarzenegger, Stallone, Willis, and Dudley Moore and attended by a galaxy of stars—everyone from Charlie Sheen to Cindy Crawford. The excitement they generated hasn't dimmed yet; crowds still patiently wait several hours to enter the Planet's precincts, where three levels of seating overlook a lagoon, a fiber-optic ceiling creates a planetarium effect, and a veritable show-business museum displays more than 300 items ranging from Peter O'Toole's *Lawrence of Arabia* costume to the front end of the bus from the movie *Speed* suspended from the ceiling! Previews of soon-to-be-released movies and video montages from films and TV are aired while you dine.

The big surprise amid all the special effects is that the food is pretty good, and, if you select carefully, pretty inexpensive. You can opt to nosh on a selection of appetizers; easily affordable are burgers and sandwiches served with fries, immense salads, pizzas, and pastas. Beverages run the gamut from chocolate malts to exotic specialty drinks. Try Arnold's mother's apple strudel topped with nutmeg ice cream for dessert.

MEALS WITH DISNEY CHARACTERS

Especially for the 10-and-under set, it's a thrill to dine in a restaurant where costumed Disney characters show up to interact with little kids, sign autographs, and pose for photos. It may be an area where you're willing to splurge a bit. Though I've included just about all the character meals in Walt Disney World, be sure to note that character dinners are a lot better value than character breakfasts. At Chef Mickey's, for instance (see below), wouldn't you rather pay $16.95 for a prime rib buffet than $13.95 for a buffet breakfast? Similarly, at the Garden Grill, you can enjoy an immense lunch or dinner for only $2 more than a buffet breakfast. Make reservations as far in advance as possible for these very popular meals. *Note:* On selected days, Disney resort guests can arrive earlier at some of the below-listed character breakfasts.

Artist Point. At Disney's Wilderness Lodge, 901 Timberline Dr. ☎ **407/WDW-DINE.** Character buffet breakfast $12.95 adults, $7.95 children 3–11, free for children 2 and under. Daily 7:30–11:30am.

Artist Point's rustic setting was inspired by the grandeur of Rocky Mountain National Park country. Goofy, Pluto, and Chip 'n' Dale make the scene. The meal is an all-you-can-eat buffet of traditional breakfast fare.

Baskerville's. At the Grosvenor Resort, 1850 Hotel Plaza Blvd. ☎ **407/828-4444.** Reservations not accepted. Character buffet breakfast $8.95 adults, $4.95 children 3–11, free for children 2 and under; character buffet dinner $15.95 adults, $6.95 children 3–11, free for children 2 and under. Tues, Thurs, and Sat 8–10am; Wed 7:30–9:30pm.

Baskerville's hosts character breakfasts Tuesday, Thursday, and Saturday mornings from 8 to 10am and character dinners Wednesday evenings from 7:30 to 9:30pm. At either meal, you can order à la carte. The dinner buffets, always centering on prime rib and themed around a different cuisine nightly, include seafood, chicken, and other meat dishes along with a full salad bar, side dishes, and an extensive choice of desserts. Reservations are not accepted; arrive early to avoid a wait.

Cape May Café. At Disney's Beach Club Resort, 1800 EPCOT Resorts Blvd. ☎ **407/WDW-DINE.** Reservations suggested. Character buffet breakfast $12.95 adults, $7.95 children 3–11, free for children 2 and under. Daily 7:30–11am.

The Cape May Café, a delightful New England–themed dining room, serves lavish buffet character breakfasts daily. Admiral Goofy and his crew—Chip 'n' Dale and Pluto (exact characters may vary)—are hosts.

Chef Mickey's. At Disney's Contemporary Resort, 4600 N. World Dr. ☎ **407/WDW-DINE.** Character buffet breakfast $13.95 adults, $7.95 children 3–11, free for children 2 and under; character prime rib buffet dinner $16.95 adults, $7.95 children 3–11, free for children 2 and under. Daily 7:30–11:30am and 5–9:30pm.

The whimsical Chef Mickey's is the setting for buffet character breakfasts and dinners daily. A 110-foot buffet table is laden with every sort of breakfast dish. On hand to meet, greet, and mingle with guests are Mickey and various pals. Chef Mickey's also hosts character **prime rib buffet dinners** nightly.

✪ **Garden Grill.** In The Land Pavilion at Epcot. ☎ **407/WDW-DINE.** Character breakfast $14.95 adults, $7.95 children 3–9, free for children 2 and under; character lunch/dinner $16.95 adults, $9.95 children, free for children 2 and under. Daily 8:30–11am, 11:15am–4pm, and 4–8pm.

This is a revolving restaurant—as you dine, your table travels past desert, prairie, farmland, and rain-forest environments. There's a "momma's-in-the-kitchen" theme here: You'll be given a straw hat at the entrance, and the just-folks service staff speak in country lingo. Hearty family-style meals are hosted by Mickey, Minnie, and Chip 'n' Dale. Breakfast is extensive and very American. Lunch and dinner include such dishes as rotisserie chicken, deep-fried cornmeal-breaded farm-raised catfish, and hickory-smoked flank steak, all served in a skillet, with salad, homemade mashed potatoes with the skins, fresh vegetables, squaw bread and biscuits, salad, beverage, and dessert.

Garden Grove Café. At the Walt Disney World Swan, 1200 Epcot Resorts Blvd. (☎ **407/934-3000**). Character breakfast buffet $12.50 adults, $6.95 children 3–11, free for children 2 and under; character dinner à la carte. Mon and Thurs–Fri 6–10pm, Wed and Sat 8–11am.

This airy three-story domed greenhouse is the setting for character breakfasts on Wednesday and Saturday and dinners on Monday, Thursday, and Friday. Breakfast offers a choice of à la carte or buffet meals; dinner is à la carte, featuring steak and seafood. Character meals here are hosted by Goofy, Pluto, Pooh, and Tigger.

King Stefan's Banquet Hall. In Cinderella Castle in the Magic Kingdom. ☎ **407/WDW-DINE.** Reservations strongly recommended. Character breakfast $14.95 adults, $7.95 children 3–9, free for children 2 and under. Daily 8–10am.

This Walt Disney World signature castle serves up character breakfast buffets daily. Hosts vary, but Cinderella always puts in an appearance. Fare includes eggs, blintzes, Mickey waffles, fresh fruit, cinnamon rolls, juice, and much more. This is one of the most popular character meals in the park, so reserve far in advance. It's a great way to start your day in the Magic Kingdom.

✪ **Liberty Tree Tavern.** In Liberty Square in the Magic Kingdom. ☎ **407/WDW-DINE.** Character dinner $19.50 adults, $9.95 children 3–11, free for children 2 and under. Daily 4pm to park closing.

This Williamsburg-like 18th-century pub offers character dinners hosted by Mickey, Goofy, Pluto, Chip 'n' Dale, and Tigger (some or all of them). Meals, served family style, consist of salad, roast chicken, marinated flank steak, homemade mashed potatoes, macaroni and cheese, rice pilaf, vegetables, and a dessert of warm apple crisp with vanilla ice cream.

✪ **Luau Cove.** At Disney's Polynesian Resort, 1600 Seven Seas Dr. ☎ **407/WDW-DINE.** Character breakfast (at 'Ohana) $13.50 adults, $8.25 children 3–11, free for children 2 and under; character dinner $30 adults, $14 children 3–11, free for children 2 and under. Daily 7:30–10:30am; dinner at 4:30pm.

Luau Cove, an exotic open-air facility, is the setting for an island-themed character show called Mickey's Tropical Luau daily at 4:30pm. It's an abbreviated version of the Polynesian Luau Dinner Show described below in "Walt Disney World & Orlando After Dark," featuring Polynesian dancers along with Mickey, Minnie, Pluto, and Goofy.

The Polynesian also hosts Minnie's Menehune Character Breakfast daily in the Polynesian-themed 'Ohana (described above). Traditional breakfast foods are prepared on an 18-foot fire pit and served family style. Minnie, Goofy, and Chip 'n' Dale appear, and there are children's parades with Polynesian musical instruments.

✪ **1900 Park Fare.** At Disney's Grand Floridian Beach Resort, 4001 Grand Floridian Way. ☎ **407/WDW-DINE.** Character breakfast $14.95 adults, $9.95 children 3–11, free for children 2 and under; character dinner buffet $19.95 adults, $9.95 children 3–11, free for children 2 and under. Daily 7:30am–noon and 5–9pm.

This exquisitely elegant Disney resort hosts character meals in the festive exposition-themed 1900 Park Fare. Big Bertha—a French band organ that plays pipes, drums, bells, cymbals, castanets, and xylophone—provides music. Mary Poppins, Winnie the Pooh, Goofy, Pluto, Chip 'n' Dale, and Minnie Mouse appear at elaborate buffet breakfasts served daily. And Mickey and Minnie appear at nightly buffets.

Soundstage Restaurant. At Disney–MGM Studios, adjacent to the Magic of Disney Animation. ☎ **407/WDW-DINE.** Character buffet breakfast $12.95 adults, $7.95 children 3–9, free for children 2 and under. Daily 8:30–10:30am.

Selected characters from the movies *Aladdin* and *Pocahontas* sign autographs daily from 8:30 to 10:30am while a vast breakfast buffet meal is set out.

Watercress Café. At the Buena Vista Palace, 1900 Buena Vista Dr. ☎ **407/827-2727.** Reservations not accepted. Character breakfast $11.95 adults, $6.95 children 4–12, free for children 3 and under; à la carte breakfast also available. Sun 8–10:30am.

The tropically festive Watercress Café, with large windows overlooking Lake Buena Vista, is the setting for Sunday-morning character breakfasts featuring Minnie, Goofy, and Pluto. You can order à la carte or buffet meals. Reservations are not accepted; arrive early to avoid a wait.

LAKE BUENA VISTA AREA

There are a number of good choices in this area outside Walt Disney World, but adjacent to the Disney theme parks.

MEALS FOR LESS THAN $10

Chili's. 12172 Apopka-Vineland Rd. (just north of Fla. 535/Palm Pkwy.). ☎ **407/239-6688.** Reservations not accepted. Main courses $5.25–$11. AE, CB, DC, DISC, MC, V. Sun–Thurs 11am–midnight, Fri–Sat 11am–1am. SOUTHWESTERN.

This Texas-based chain has always been a good choice for family dining, especially this branch, where children's books and toys are provided for youngsters. Adults, on the other hand, might appreciate the bar area, where sporting events are aired on four TV monitors and all drinks are priced two-for-one during an extended daily happy hour (11am to 7pm). Its rustic/whimsical interior is appealing, with exposed brick and painted walls and upside-down copper kettles serving as hanging lamps over ceramic-tiled tables.

Chili is, of course, a specialty here. I like it on a half-pound chili cheeseburger served with home-style fries. Other possibilities include battered fried farm-raised catfish with fries and corn on the cob, heaping platters of steak or chicken fajitas, grilled baby back ribs, and salads. Same room for dessert: a chocolate brownie topped with vanilla ice cream and hot fudge. Several low-fat items are specified on the menu.

Romano's Macaroni Grill. 12148 Apopka-Vineland Rd. (just north of Fla. 535/Palm Pkwy.). ☎ **407/239-6676** for priority seating. Main courses $4.95–$8.25 at lunch, $6.95–$15.95 at dinner (most under $10). AE, CB, DC, DISC, MC, V. Sun–Thurs 11am–10pm, Fri–Sat 11am–11pm. NORTHERN ITALIAN.

A Cut Above Fast Food

Personally I hate fast food, and I avoid it at all costs. However, if you move a step up on the fast-food chain, the picture brightens considerably. That brings us into the realm of family restaurants such as Denny's, Perkins, and Shoney's, all of which offer pleasant surroundings and quite good but really inexpensive fare. Menus are vast and varied, and there are rock-bottom rates for seniors and children. All have convenient Lake Buena Vista locations reachable via Exit 27 off I-4; check your phone book for other sites around town.

You'll find a 24-hour **Denny's** at 12375 Apopka-Vineland Rd., between Hotel Plaza Blvd. and Fla. 535 / Palm Pkwy. (☎ **407/239-7900**). It offers specials such as a prime rib dinner with baked potato and Dijon horseradish for $6. You can add soup or salad for $1. And there are full lunch specials for just $3. A wide choice of desserts includes sundaes with homemade ice cream. Wine and beer are available.

A 24-hour **Perkins** can be found in the Crossroads of Lake Buena Vista Shopping Center, 12259 Fla. 535 (☎ **407/827-1060**). Here, from 11am to 11pm, you can enjoy specials such as grilled Cajun chicken ($7) or a 9-ounce charcoal-broiled strip steak ($9) served with two side dishes—perhaps redskin potatoes and sugar snap peas. The same meals in smaller portions are available for even less. Perkins houses an on-premises bakery proffering yummy cinnamon rolls, mammoth muffins, and other breakfast pastries as well as desserts like Heath crunch pie. Beer and wine are available.

A highlight of **Shoney's,** at 12204 Apopka-Vineland Rd., between Lake Ave. and Fla. 535/Palm Pkwy. (☎ **407/239-5416**), is its lavish daily $5 breakfast buffet ($3 for kids 11 and under). For that price, you can help yourself to unlimited quantities of scrambled eggs, breakfast meats, sausage gravy, hash browns, grits, sautéed mushrooms, buttermilk biscuits, muffins, pancakes, Belgian waffles, fresh fruits, cinnamon rolls, doughnuts, dry cereal, and more. Seniors 55 and over enjoy this morning feast for $3 every Tuesday. Shoney's also features a great seafood buffet for $9 every Friday and Saturday night from 4 to 10pm. Other nights there's a country-style buffet ($6.90 for adults, $4 for children), consisting of soups, an array of salads, mashed potatoes, vegetables, fresh fruits, and entrees such as ham, barbecued riblets, fried catfish, and chicken wings. Of course, there's also an extensive à la carte menu. And every Wednesday from 4pm to closing, two kids 11 and under eat free! No alcoholic beverages here. Shoney's is open daily from 6am to midnight.

Note: For those of you who don't share my disdain for fast-food eateries, you'll find Taco Bell, Red Lobster, Pizzeria Uno, and McDonald's at Crossroads.

Though Orlando friends had raved about the Macaroni Grill, I didn't really expect much from a chain restaurant. Upon entering, I was favorably impressed by its cheerful interior and the welcoming glow from the exhibition kitchen, where white-hatted chefs were tending an oak-burning pizza oven, and foodstuffs, chianti, flowers, and desserts were aesthetically arrayed on counters.

But the big surprise was the food. Everything was made from the freshest ingredients, and the quality of cuisine would have been notable at three times the price. The thin-crusted pizzas—such as the Mediterranea, topped with fresh tomato sauce, shrimp, and feta and mozzarella cheeses—were scrumptious, as was a dish of bowtie pasta tossed with grilled chicken, pancetta, and red and green onions in asiago-cream sauce. Equally good: sautéed chicken with mushrooms, artichoke hearts, capers, and pancetta in lemon butter. There were fresh-baked foccacia and ciabatta (a crusty country loaf) for sopping up sauces or dipping in extra-virgin olive oil. And the desserts—especially an apple-custard torte with hazelnut crust and caramel topping—kept to the same lofty standard. There's a full bar, premium wines are sold by the glass, and a children's menu offers an entree and beverage for just $3.25. Bravo Romano!

MEALS FOR LESS THAN $15

Pebbles. In the Crossroads Shopping Center, 12551 Fla. 535, in Lake Buena Vista. ☎ **407/827-1111.** Reservations not accepted. Sandwiches and salads $4.95–$8.50; main courses mostly $7.95–$15.95. AE, CB, DC, DISC, MC, V. Daily 11am–1am. CALIFORNIA-STYLE AMERICAN.

Pebbles is one of Orlando's most popular restaurants, especially with a young yuppie crowd. The multilevel dining room centers on a sunken bar, and wooden shutters and windowed enclosures create a warren of intimate dining areas in the large space with its tropical greenery and garden-party ambience.

The same menu is offered throughout the day, supplemented by specials. Start off with a "lite bite" of creamy baked chèvre served atop chunky tomato sauce with hot garlic bread. Pebbles offers the option of a casual meal—perhaps a Cheddar burger on toasted brioche or a Caesar salad tossed with grilled chicken. More serious entrees are available, but they're pricier. Dessert of choice: the gold brick sundae—a scoop of vanilla ice cream encased in a candylike chocolate/almond shell and served atop caramel sauce with fresh strawberries. There's a full bar, and many premium wines are offered by the glass.

INTERNATIONAL DRIVE & VICINITY

Some of the best area restaurants outside Walt Disney World are along International Drive, within about 10 minutes of WDW parks by car.

MEALS FOR LESS THAN $7

Flipper's. In the Kirkman Shoppes strip mall, 4774 S. Kirkman Rd. (just north of Conroy Rd.). ☎ **407/521-0607.** Reservations not accepted. Main courses $4.25–$6.95; subs $2.95–$5.95; pizzas $6.95–$14.95. No credit cards. Mon–Thurs 11:30am–midnight, Fri 11:30am–1am, Sat 4pm–1am, Sun 4pm–midnight. PIZZERIA.

A casual shopping-center eatery with neon beer signs adorning its walls, Flipper's offers a good variety of fresh-made pizzas. Three people can easily dine on the $9.95 16-inch pizza bianca (my favorite) topped with olive oil, fresh garlic, oregano, and romano, ricotta, and mozzarella cheeses. There's a choice of about 25 toppings. Other options here are calzones, hearty subs, and pastas such as baked ziti tossed with chicken and feta cheese in fresh tomato sauce, and topped with provolone cheese. Beer and wine are available.

✪ **Le Peep.** In the Kirkman Oaks Shopping Center, 4666 Kirkman Rd. (just east of Conroy Rd.). ☎ **407/291-4580.** Reservations accepted only for parties of six or more. Main courses $2–$6.25. AE, DC, DISC, MC, V. Mon–Fri 6:30am–2:30pm, Sat–Sun 7am–2:30pm. AMERICAN.

Le Peep is one of Orlando's best-kept secrets (90% of its devoted clientele is local)—a delightful, inexpensive restaurant serving huge portions of scrumptious food. It has a gardenlike interior, and, weather permitting, you can sit at umbrella tables on the patio.

Le Peep is open for breakfast/brunch and lunch only, and everything on its menu is prepared from scratch—even the orange juice is fresh squeezed. There are all kinds of yummy egg dishes served sizzling in skillets, including southwestern fare such as scrambled eggs, green chiles, onions, and diced chicken wrapped in flour tortillas and topped with chile verde sauce and melted Cheddar. Other choices are eggs Benedict, seafood crêpes, cheese blintzes topped with fresh fruits and sour cream, fabulous French toast, and pancakes. Other options include sandwiches, burgers, salads, and stuffed baked potatoes. There's key lime pie for dessert. No alcoholic beverages are served.

MEALS FOR LESS THAN $10

B-Line Diner. In the Peabody Orlando Hotel, 9801 International Dr. ☎ **407/345-4460.** Reservations not accepted. Main courses $3.25–$8.25 at breakfast, $6.95–$10.95 at lunch, $6.95–$17.95 at dinner. AE, CB, DC, DISC, JCB, MC, OPT, V. Daily 24 hours. INTERNATIONALLY NUANCED AMERICAN.

This popular local eatery is of the nouvelle art deco diner genre, which is to say that it's an idealized version of America's ubiquitous roadside establishments. A jukebox plays oldies tunes. The seasonally varying menu offers sophisticated versions of diner food such as honey-ginger buffalo wings or a ham-and-cheese sandwich on a baguette. Other items have no relation to traditional diner fare. Portions are hearty. A glass display case here is filled with scrumptious fresh-baked desserts: everything from banana-cream pie to white-chocolate/Grand Marnier mousse cake. Ice-cream sundaes are also options. There's a full bar.

PR's. In the Kirkman Shoppes strip mall, 4750 S. Kirkman Rd. (just north of Conroy Rd.). ☎ **407/293-8226.** Reservations accepted only for parties of eight or more. Main courses $5.50–$12.25 (most under $9); lunch specials (served Mon–Sat to 4pm) $3.25–$5.25. AE, DC, MC, V. Mon–Thurs 11am–10pm, Fri–Sat 11am–11pm, Sun noon–10pm. MEXICAN.

In the same shopping center as Flipper's (see above), PR's is a lively local hangout with a funky Margaritaville interior and rock music always playing in the background. It has exposed metal beams, a corrugated-tin warehouse ceiling, and model trains going round and round on an overhead track. A vast terra-cotta–topped horseshoe bar—above which sporting events are aired—is the hub of the action.

People come for good times and humungous portions of freshly made Mexican food. Start off with a platter of jalapeño peppers, breaded, stuffed with cheeses, lightly fried, and served with chili con queso. Main dishes include hearty combination platters, fajitas, and specialties such as green chiles stuffed with blackened chicken, lightly fried, and topped with a spicy cream sauce and Monterey jack cheese, served with rice and beans. The margaritas are made from scratch, and there's a good selection of Mexican beers.

MEALS FOR LESS THAN $15

✪ **Cafe Tu Tu Tango.** 8625 International Dr. (just west of the Mercado). ☎ **407/248-2222.** Reservations not accepted. Tapas (tasting portions) $3.75–$7.95. AE, DISC, MC, V. Daily 11:30am–2am. INTERNATIONAL TAPAS.

Though one might question the need for yet one more themed experience outside the parks, this zany restaurant is a welcome respite from Orlando's predictable "chain gang." For one thing, there's an ongoing performance-art experience taking place while you dine: An elegantly dressed couple might tango past your table, or a magician demonstrate his tricks tableside. In addition, there's a studio area where artists are creating pottery, paintings, and jewelry.

Tu Tu's colorful ambience is a lot of fun, but its food is the real draw. The larger your party, the more dishes you can sample; two full plates will sate most appetites. My favorites include Cajun eggrolls and pepper-crusted seared tuna sashimi with crispy rice noodles and cold spinach in a sesame-soy vinaigrette. International wines can be ordered by the glass or bottle. Great desserts here too—such as creamy almond/amaretto flan and rich guava cheesecake with strawberry sauce.

Enzo's. In the Marketplace Shopping Center, 7600 Dr. Phillips Blvd. (off Sand Lake Rd. just west of I-4). ☎ **407/351-1187.** Reservations not accepted. Panini (sandwiches) $4.75–$5.95; main courses $4.50–$6.95 at lunch, $8.50–$12.75 at dinner. AE, CB, DC, DISC, MC, V. Mon–Thurs 11:30am–10pm, Fri–Sat 11:30am–11pm. ITALIAN.

Upon entering this charming little restaurant and Italian charcuterie, you'll walk past display cases filled with antipasti, deli meats, pâtés, and cheeses and shelves stocked with homemade pastas and other fancy foodstuffs. And if that's not enough to whet your appetite, you'll also glimpse chefs tending a pizza oven in an exhibition kitchen. The dining area is cheerful and inviting. Enzo's is a casual kind of place, very popular locally.

Pretty much the same menu is available throughout the day. Families troop in for pizzas—either the traditional American kind or Napoli pies with more sophisticated toppings and crisp, delicate crusts. Until 4:30pm you can also opt for *panini* (sandwiches on crusty Italian bread) with fillings such as Italian sausage, grilled onions, and peppers. Homemade pastas include fat bucatini tossed with mushrooms, fresh-grated Parmesan, prosciutto, bacon, and peas in a robust sauce. And Enzo's most fabulous entree is pollo alla cecco (roast breast of free-range chicken with rosemary potatoes and an Italian version of ratatouille). Beer and wine are available. For dessert, try zuccotto (Italian sponge cake soaked in Grand Marnier, layered with fresh fruit and crème anglaise, and topped with chocolate shavings). In busy seasons, arrive off-hours to avoid a wait.

✪ Ming Court. 9188 International Dr. (between Sand Lake Rd. and the Beeline Expy.). ☎ **407/351-9988.** Reservations recommended. Dim sum items mostly $1.95–$2.50; main courses $4.50–$7.95 at lunch, $12.50–$19.95 at dinner. AE, CB, DC, DISC, JCB, MC, V. Daily 11am–2:30pm and 4:30pm–midnight. CHINESE REGIONAL.

I was thrilled to find haute-cuisine Chinese fare in Orlando on a par with fine Chinese restaurants in New York and California. The Ming Court is fronted by a serpentine "cloud wall" crowned by engraved sea-green Chinese tiles (it's a celestial symbol; you dine above the clouds here, like the gods). Glass-walled terrace rooms overlook lotus ponds filled with colorful koi, and a plant-filled area under a lofty skylight ceiling evokes a starlit Ming Dynasty courtyard. A musician plays classical Chinese music on a *zheng* (a long zither) at dinner.

The menu offers specialties from diverse regions of China. Begin by ordering a variety of appetizers such as crispy wontons stuffed with vegetables and cream cheese, and wok-smoked shiitake mushrooms topped with sautéed scallions. The entrees will open up new culinary vistas to even the most sophisticated diners. Lightly battered deep-fried chicken breast is served with a delicate lemon-tangerine sauce. And crispy stir-fried jumbo Szechuan shrimp is enhanced by a light fresh tomato sauce nuanced with saké. At lunch, you can order dim sum items in addition to menu offerings. There's an extensive wine list, and, as a concession to Western palates, the Ming Court features sumptuous desserts such as a moist cake layered with Mandarin oranges, key lime, and fresh whipped cream in orange-vanilla sauce.

Wild Jacks. 7364 International Dr. (between Sand Lake Rd. and Carrier Dr.). ☎ **407/ 352-4407.** Reservations not accepted. Main courses $9.45–$17.95. AE, CB, DC, DISC, JCB, MC, V. Daily 4:30–11pm. STEAK/BARBECUE.

This exuberantly western upscale steak and barbecue restaurant whimsically combines honky-tonk and haute elements in its decor. There's an exhibition kitchen with an open-pit grill and a copper bar with an iced beer well. The appetizers here are first-rate: skewers of tangy barbecued shrimp served over Texas rice studded with corn kernels and red and green peppers or miniature tacos filled with smoked chicken and cheeses. The best main choice is the smoked brisket barbecue, served with salad, warm molasses bread and honey, and your choice of two side dishes—take the jalapeño mashed potatoes and grilled corn on the cob. For dessert, there's peach cobbler topped with vanilla ice cream sprinkled with cinnamon.

4 Tips for Visiting Walt Disney World Attractions

Walt Disney World encompasses the Magic Kingdom; Epcot; Disney–MGM Studios; Pleasure Island; the Walt Disney Village Marketplace, a lakeside enclave of shops and restaurants; three water parks (Typhoon Lagoon, River Country, and Blizzard Beach); and Discovery Island, a nature preserve and aviary.

TIPS FOR PLANNING YOUR TRIP

Planning is essential. Unless you're staying for considerably more than a week, you can't possibly experience all the rides, shows, and attractions here, not to mention the vast array of recreational facilities. You'll only wear yourself to a frazzle trying—it's better to follow a relaxed itinerary, including leisurely meals and recreational activities, than to make a demanding job out of trying to see everything.

Read the *Vacations* guide and the detailed descriptions in this book, and plan your visit to include all shows and attractions that interest you. It's a good idea to make a daily itinerary, putting these in some kind of sensible geographical sequence so you're not zigzagging all over the place. Familiarize yourself in advance with the layout of each park. Schedule in sit-down shows, recreational activities (a boat ride or swim late in the afternoon can be wonderfully refreshing), and at least some unhurried meals. My suggested itineraries are given below.

INFORMATION   Call or write the **Walt Disney World Co.,** P.O. Box 10000, Lake Buena Vista, FL 32830-1000 (☎ 407/934-7639), for a copy of the very informative *Walt Disney World Vacations,* an invaluable planning aid. Once you've arrived in town, guest-services and concierge desks in all area hotels—especially Disney properties and "official" hotels—have **up-to-the-minute information** about what's going on in the parks. If your hotel doesn't have this information, call **407/824-4321.**

There are also **information locations** in each park—at City Hall in the Magic Kingdom, at Innoventions East near the World Key terminals in Epcot, and the Guest Services Building in Disney–MGM Studios.

BUY TICKETS IN ADVANCE   You can purchase 4- or 5-day passes (see details below) prior to your trip by calling **Ticket Mail Order** (☎ 407/824-6750). Allow 21 days for processing your request, and include a $2 postage-and-handling charge. Of course, you can always purchase tickets at any of the parks, but why stand in an avoidable line? *Note:* One-day tickets can be purchased only at park entrances.

ARRIVE EARLY   Always arrive at the parks a good 30 to 45 minutes before opening time, thus avoiding a traffic jam entering the park and a long line at the gate. Early arrival also lets you experience one or two major attractions before big lines form. In high season the parking lots sometimes fill up and you may even have to wait to get in. The longest lines in all parks are between 11am and 4pm.

PARKING   Parking—free to guests at WDW resorts—costs $5 per day no matter how many parks you visit. **Be sure to note your parking location before leaving your car.** There are special lots for travelers with disabilities at each park (call

407/824-4321 for details). Don't worry about parking far from the entrance gates; trams constantly ply the route.

WHEN YOU ARRIVE IN THE PARKS　　Upon entering any of the three major Disney parks, you'll be given an **entertainment schedule** and a comprehensive **park guidemap,** which contains a map of the park and lists all attractions, shops, shows, and restaurants. If by some fluke you haven't obtained these, they're available at the information locations mentioned above. If you've formulated an itinerary prior to arrival, you already know the major shows (check show schedules for additional ideas) you want to see during the day and what arrangements you need to make. If you haven't done this, use your early arrival time, while waiting for the park to open, to figure out which shows to attend, and, where necessary, make reservations for them as soon as the gates swing open.

LEAVING THE PARKS　　If you leave any of the parks and plan to return later in the day, be sure to get your hand stamped on exiting.

BEST DAYS TO VISIT　　The busiest days at the Magic Kingdom and Epcot are Monday to Wednesday; at Disney–MGM Studios, Thursday and Friday. Surprisingly, weekends are the least busy at all parks. In peak seasons, especially, arrange your visits accordingly.

THE EASY WAY　　Staying at Disney resorts and "official" hotels simplifies many of the above tasks and procedures. See the full list of perks for Disney and "official" hotel guests under "Where to Stay," earlier in this chapter.

OPERATING HOURS　　Hours of operation vary somewhat throughout the year. The **Magic Kingdom** and **Disney–MGM Studios** are generally open from 9am to 7pm, with extended hours—sometimes as late as midnight—during major holidays and the summer months.

　　Epcot hours are generally from 9am to 9pm, with Future World open from 9am to 7pm and World Showcase from 11am to 9pm—once again with extended holiday hours.

　　Typhoon Lagoon and **Blizzard Beach** are open from 10am to 5pm most of the year (with extended hours during some holidays), 9am to 8pm in summer.

　　River Country and **Discovery Island are** open from 10am to 5pm most of the year (with extended hours during some holidays), 10am to 7pm in summer.

　　Note: Epcot and MGM sometimes open a half hour or more before the posted time. Keep in mind, too, that Disney-resort guests enjoy early admission to all three major parks on designated days.

TICKETS　　There are several ticket options. Most people get the best value from 4- and 5-day passes. All passes offer unlimited use of the WDW transportation system. The prices quoted below include sales tax, and they are, of course, subject to change.

　　Adult prices are paid by anyone over 10 years of age. **Children's rates** are for ages 3 to 9; children 2 and under are admitted free.

　　The **4-Day Value Pass** provides admission for 1 day at the Magic Kingdom, 1 day at Epcot, 1 day at Disney–MGM Studios, and 1 day at your choice of any of those three parks; you can use it on any 4 days following purchase, but you cannot visit more than one park on any given day. Adults pay $129; children, $103.

　　The **4-Day Park-Hopper Pass** provides unlimited admission to the three major parks on any 4 days; in other words, you can hop from park to park on any given day. Adults pay $144; children, $115.

Walt Disney World Parks & Attractions

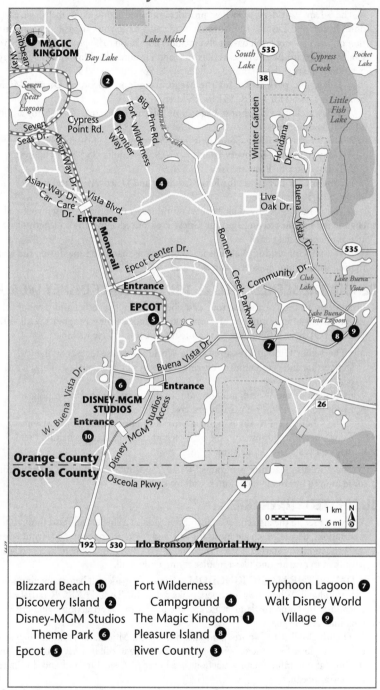

Blizzard Beach ❿

Discovery Island ❷

Disney-MGM Studios
Theme Park ❻

Epcot ❺

Fort Wilderness
Campground ❹

The Magic Kingdom ❶

Pleasure Island ❽

River Country ❸

Typhoon Lagoon ❼

Walt Disney World
Village ❾

The **5-Day World-Hopper Pass** provides unlimited admission to the Magic Kingdom, Epcot, and Disney–MGM Studios on any 5 days; you can visit any combination of parks on any given day. It also includes admission to Typhoon Lagoon, River Country, Blizzard Beach, Discovery Island, and Pleasure Island for a period of 7 days beginning the first date stamped. Adults pay $196; children, $157.

A **1-day, one-park ticket for the Magic Kingdom, Epcot, or Disney–MGM Studios** is $38.50 for adults, $31 for children.

A **1-day ticket to Typhoon Lagoon or Blizzard Beach** is $23.95 for adults, $17.95 for children.

A **1-day ticket to River Country** is $14.75 for adults, $11.50 for children.

A **1-day ticket to Discovery Island** is $10.95 for adults, $5.95 for children.

A **1-day ticket to Pleasure Island** is $16.95.

A **combined 1-day ticket for River Country** and **Discovery Island** is $18.95 for adults, $13.50 for children.

If you're staying at any Walt Disney World resort or "official" hotel, you're also eligible for a money-saving **Be Our Guest Pass** priced according to length of stay. It also offers special perks.

If you plan on visiting Walt Disney World more than one time during the year, inquire about a money-saving **annual pass.**

BEHIND THE SCENES: SPECIAL TOURS IN WALT DISNEY WORLD

In addition to the greenhouse tour described below in Epcot's Land pavilion, the Disney parks offer a number of walking tours and learning programs. Call **407/ WDW-TOUR** (407/939-8687) for more information. These include:

• The 3-hour **Hidden Treasures of the World Showcase** focuses on the architecture and entertainment offerings of Epcot's international pavilions; it's $25 per person.

• **Gardens of the World,** a 3-hour tour of the extraordinary landscaping at Epcot led by a Disney horticulturist, costs $25 per person.

• The 4-hour **Keys to the Kingdom** provides an orientation to the Magic Kingdom and a glimpse into the high-tech operational systems behind the magic; it costs $45 per person.

There are also **learning programs** (☎ **407/363-6000**) on subjects ranging from animation to international cultures. Call for details.

SUGGESTED ITINERARIES

You won't see all the attractions at any of the parks in a single day. Read through the descriptions, decide which are musts for you, and try to get to them. My favorite rides and attractions are starred. I stress once more—it's more enjoyable to keep a relaxed pace than to race around like a maniac trying to do it all.

A DAY IN THE MAGIC KINGDOM   Get to the park well before opening time, tickets in hand. When the gates open, make a dash for Extra"TERROR"estrial Alien Encounter in Tomorrowland, which, as the newest major attraction, will have very long lines later in the day.

Then hightail it to Frontierland and ride Splash Mountain—another biggie— before long lines form there. When you come off, it will still be early enough to beat the lines at one more major attraction; head over to Adventureland and do Pirates of the Caribbean.

Then relax and take it slow. Complete whatever else interests you in Adventureland. Then walk over to Frontierland and enjoy the attractions there until lunchtime. Have lunch while taking in the 12:15 or 1:30pm show at the Diamond Horseshoe Saloon Revue (they don't take reservations, so arrive early).

After lunch, continue visiting Frontierland attractions as desired, or proceed to the Hall of Presidents and the Haunted Mansion in Liberty Square. By 2:30pm (earlier in peak seasons), you should snag a seat on the curb in Liberty Square along the parade route. After the parade, continue around the park taking in Fantasyland and Tomorrowland attractions. If SpectroMagic is on during your stay, don't miss it.

If you have little kids (age 8 and under) in your party, start your day instead by taking the WDW Railroad from Main Street to Mickey's Starland to see the show. Work your way through Fantasyland until lunch, once again at the Diamond Horseshoe. After lunch, visit the Country Bear Jamboree in Frontierland and proceed to Adventureland for the Jungle Cruise, Swiss Family Treehouse, and Tropical Serenade. Once again, stop in good time to get parade seats (in Frontierland). Little kids need to sit right up front to see everything. That's a long enough day for most young children, and your best plan is to go back to your hotel for a nap or swim. If, however, you wish to continue, return to Frontierland and/or Fantasyland for the rides you didn't complete earlier.

IF YOU CAN SPEND ONLY 1 DAY AT EPCOT   Epcot really requires at least 2 days, so this is a highlight tour. As above, arrive early, tickets in hand. If you haven't already made lunch reservations in advance by calling 407/WDW-DINE, make your first stop at the WorldKey terminals in Innoventions East. I suggest a 1pm lunch at the San Angel Inn Restaurant in the Mexico pavilion. If you don't like Mexican food, move up one pavilion to Norway and reserve for the buffet at Akershus. You can make dinner reservations at the same time. Plan dinner for about 7pm, which will allow you time to eat and find a good viewing spot for IllumiNations (usually at 9pm, but check your schedule).

Spend no more than an hour exploring Innoventions East. Then move on to the Universe of Energy show. Continue to the Wonders of Life Pavilion where must-sees include Body Wars, Cranium Command, and The Making of Me.

If time allows—it will depend on line waits at attractions—take in the show at Horizons before heading into World Showcase for lunch in the Mexico pavilion. At lunch, check your show schedule and decide which shows to incorporate into your day.

Then walk around the lagoon, visiting highlight attractions: *Wonders of China, The American Adventure, Impressions de France,* and *O Canada,* allowing yourself some time for browsing and shopping. After dinner, stay on for IllumiNations.

A Word About Epcot Dining: Sit-down meals at World Showcase Pavilions and the Living Seas are a pleasant—but pricey—part of the Epcot experience. There are plenty of less expensive eateries throughout the park, including ethnic ones with café seating in many World Showcase Pavilions. And since these don't require reservations, you're not tied down to specific mealtimes. See your *Epcot Guidemap* for details.

IF YOU CAN SPEND 2 DAYS AT EPCOT   Ignore the 1-day itinerary above, and begin your day by making all necessary restaurant reservations—once again for lunch in Mexico or Norway at about 1pm. Make reservations for Day 2 at the same time.

Skip Innoventions East for now, and work your way thoroughly through the Universe of Energy, Wonders of Life, Horizons, and World of Motion pavilions (it will be closed for renovations through late 1997), keeping your lunch reservation time in mind. After lunch, walk clockwise around the lagoon, visiting each foreign pavilion and taking in as many shows as you like (consult your show schedule and try to keep pace as well as possible). Leave IllumiNations for your second day's visit.

Begin your second day exploring Innoventions East, and proceed counterclockwise, taking in Spaceship Earth, Innoventions West, the Living Seas (its Coral Reef restaurant is a good choice for lunch), and all the other pavilions on the west side of the park. Cap your Epcot visit with IllumiNations.

A DAY AT DISNEY-MGM STUDIOS THEME PARK Since show times change frequently here, it's impossible to really give you a workable itinerary. Upon entering the park, if you haven't already made dining arrangements, stop at the Hollywood Brown Derby and make reservations for lunch. Or you might want to conserve touring time by having a light lunch at a casual eatery and saving the Derby for a relaxing dinner.

Make a beeline for the Twilight Zone Tower of Terror. While you're waiting in line, plan the rest of your schedule, being sure to include these not-to-be-missed attractions: the Magic of Disney Animation, the Great Movie Ride, Jim Henson's Muppet Vision 3-D, and the Monster Sound Show. If you have girls 10 and under in your party, *The Voyage Of The Little Mermaid, The Spirit of Pocahontas,* and *Beauty and the Beast* will probably be major priorities; for the latter, get in line 45 minutes prior to show time at the Theater of the Stars. And all kids love the parade; snag a good seat on the parade route 45 minutes ahead of time as well.

Time for more? Do Superstar Television, the Indiana Jones Epic Stunt Spectacular, Star Tours, Inside the Magic, and the Backstage Studio Tour. In peak seasons stay on for fireworks.

5 The Magic Kingdom

Centered around Cinderella Castle, the Magic Kingdom occupies about 100 acres, with 45 major attractions and numerous restaurants and shops in seven themed sections or "lands." From the parking lot, you have to take a short monorail or ferry ride to the entrance. During peak attendance times, arrive at the Magic Kingdom an hour prior to opening time to avoid long lines at these conveyances.

Upon entering the park, consult your *Magic Kingdom Guidemap* to get your bearings. Also consult your **entertainment schedule** to see what's on for the day.

If you have questions, all park employees are very knowledgeable, and **City Hall,** on your left as you enter, is both an information center and, along with Mickey's Starland, a likely place to meet up with costumed characters. There's a **stroller-rental shop** just after the turnstiles to your right, and the **Kodak Camera Center,** near Town Square, supplies all conceivable photographic needs, including camera and Camcorder rentals and 2-hour film developing.

MAIN STREET, U.S.A.

Designed to replicate a typical turn-of-the-century American street (albeit one that culminates in a 13th-century castle), this is the gateway to the Kingdom. Don't dawdle on Main Street when you enter the park; leave it for the end of the day when you're heading back to your hotel.

WALT DISNEY WORLD RAILROAD & OTHER MAIN STREET VEHICLES You can board an authentic 1928 steam-powered railroad here for a 15-minute journey clockwise around the perimeter of the park. There are stations in Frontierland and Mickey's Starland. There are also horse-drawn trolleys, horseless carriages, jitneys, omnibuses, and fire engines plying the short route along Main Street from Town Square to Cinderella Castle.

MAIN STREET CINEMA   The Main Street Cinema is an air-conditioned hexagonal theater where vintage black-and-white Disney cartoons (including *Steamboat Willie* from 1928, in which Mickey and Minnie debuted) are aired continually on two screens. Viewers have to watch these standing—there are no seats.

CINDERELLA CASTLE   At the end of Main Street, in the center of the park, you'll come to a fairyland castle, 180 feet high and housing a restaurant (King Stefan's Banquet Hall) and shops. Cinderella herself, dressed for the ball, often makes appearances in the lobby area. Don't linger here; save it for the end of the day.

ADVENTURELAND

Cross a bridge to your left and stroll into an exotic jungle of lush tropical foliage, thatch-roofed huts, and carved totems. Amid dense vines and stands of palm and bamboo, drums are beating and swashbuckling adventures are taking place.

SWISS FAMILY TREEHOUSE   This attraction is based on the 1960 Disney movie version of Johann Wyss's *Swiss Family Robinson,* about a shipwrecked family who created an ingenious dwelling in the branches of a sprawling banyan tree. Using materials and furnishings salvaged from their downed ship, the Robinsons created bedrooms, a kitchen, a library, and a living room. Visitors ascend the 50-foot tree for a close-up look into these rooms. Note the Rube Goldberg rope-and-bucket device with bamboo chutes that dips water from a stream and carries it to treetop chambers.

JUNGLE CRUISE   What a cruise! In the course of about 10 minutes, your boat sails through an African veldt in the Congo, an Amazon rain forest, the Mekong River in Southeast Asia, and along the Nile. Lavish scenery, cascading waterfalls, and lush foliage (most of it real), includes dozens of Audio-Animatronic™ birds and animals—elephants, zebras, lions, giraffes, crocodiles, tigers, even fluttering butterflies. On the shore you'll pass an Asian temple cave guarded by snakes and a jungle camp taken over by apes. But the adventures aren't all on shore. Passengers are menaced by everything from water-spouting elephants to fierce warriors who attack with spears.

✪ PIRATES OF THE CARIBBEAN   This is Disney magic at its best. You'll proceed through a long grottolike passageway to board a boat into a pitch-black cave where elaborate scenery and hundreds of Audio-Animatronic™ figures (including lifelike dogs, cats, chickens, and donkeys) depict a pirate raid on a Caribbean town. Passengers view tableaux of fierce-looking pirates swigging rum, looting, and plundering. This might be scary for kids under 5.

TROPICAL SERENADE   In a large hexagonal Polynesian-style dwelling, 250 tropical birds, chanting totem poles, and singing flowers whistle, tweet, and warble songs such as "Let's All Sing Like the Birdies Sing." Highlights include a thunderstorm in the dark (the gods are angry!), a light show over the fountain, and, of course, the famous "in the tiki, tiki, tiki, tiki, tiki room" song. You'll find yourself singing it all day. This is a must for young children.

FRONTIERLAND

From Adventureland, step into the wild and woolly past of the American frontier, where rough-and-tumble architecture runs to log cabins and rustic saloons, and the landscape is southwestern scrubby with mesquite, yucca, and prickly pear. Across the river is Tom Sawyer Island, reachable via log rafts.

The Magic Kingdom

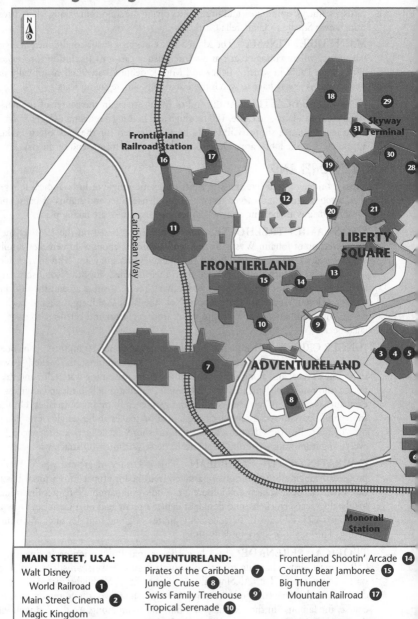

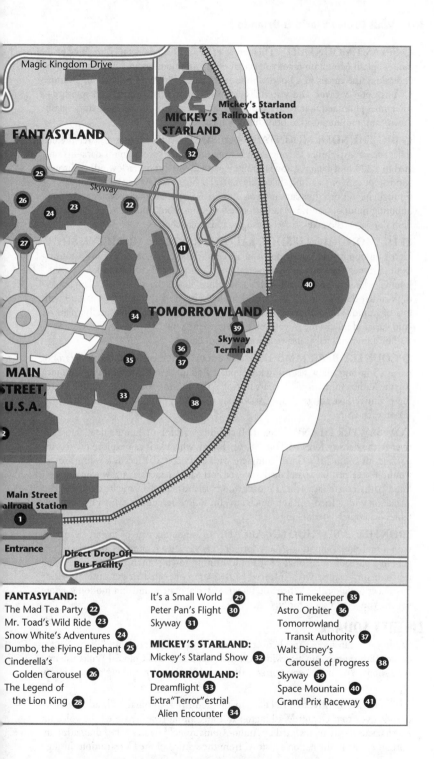

FANTASYLAND:
The Mad Tea Party **22**
Mr. Toad's Wild Ride **23**
Snow White's Adventures **24**
Dumbo, the Flying Elephant **25**
Cinderella's
  Golden Carousel **26**
The Legend of
  the Lion King **28**

It's a Small World **29**
Peter Pan's Flight **30**
Skyway **31**

MICKEY'S STARLAND:
Mickey's Starland Show **32**

TOMORROWLAND:
Dreamflight **33**
Extra"Terror"estrial
  Alien Encounter **34**

The Timekeeper **35**
Astro Orbiter **36**
Tomorrowland
  Transit Authority **37**
Walt Disney's
  Carousel of Progress **38**
Skyway **39**
Space Mountain **40**
Grand Prix Raceway **41**

✪ **SPLASH MOUNTAIN**   Themed after Walt Disney's 1946 film *Song of the South,* Splash Mountain takes you on an enchanting journey in a hollowed-out log craft along the canals of a flooded mountain, past tableaux of backwoods swamps, bayous, spooky caves, and waterfalls. Your log craft twists, turns, and splashes—sometimes plummeting in total darkness—culminating in a thrilling five-story splashdown from mountaintop to briar-filled pond at 40 miles per hour!

✪ **BIG THUNDER MOUNTAIN RAILROAD**   This mining-disaster-themed roller coaster—its thrills deriving from hairpin turns and descents in the dark—is situated in a 200-foot-high redstone mountain with 2,780 feet of track winding through windswept canyons and bat-filled caves. You'll board a runaway train that careens through the ribs of a dinosaur, under a thundering waterfall, past spewing geysers and bubbling mudpots, and over a bottomless volcanic pool. Riders are threatened by flash floods, earthquakes, rickety bridges, and avalanches.

✪ **DIAMOND HORSESHOE SALOON REVUE & MEDICINE SHOW** Here's an opportunity to sit down in air-conditioned comfort and enjoy a rousing western revue. The "theater" is a re-creation of a turn-of-the-century saloon. Marshall John Charles sings and banters with the audience, Jingles the Piano Man plays honky-tonk tunes, there's a magic act, and dancehall girls do a spirited can-can—all with lots of humor and audience participation. There are seven shows daily; plan on going around lunchtime so you can eat during the show. The menu features deli or peanut butter and jelly sandwiches served with chips.

✪ **COUNTRY BEAR JAMBOREE**   I've always loved the Country Bear Jamboree, a 15-minute show featuring a troupe of fiddlin', banjo strummin', harmonica playin' Audio-Animatronic™ bears belting out rollicking country tunes and crooning plaintive love songs. A special holiday show plays throughout the Christmas season each year.

TOM SAWYER ISLAND   Board Huck Finn's raft for a 1-minute float across the river to the densely forested Tom Sawyer Island, where kids can explore the narrow passages of Injun Joe's Cave (complete with scary sound effects), a walk-through windmill, a serpentine abandoned mine, or Fort Sam Clemens. Narrow winding tree-lined paths create an authentic backwoods island feel. You might combine this attraction with a fried-chicken lunch at Aunt Polly's restaurant, which has outdoor tables on a porch overlooking the river.

FRONTIERLAND SHOOTIN' ARCADE   Combining state-of-the-art electronics with a traditional shooting-gallery format, this vast arcade presents an array of targets in a three-dimensional 1850s gold-mining town scenario. Electronic firing mechanisms loaded with infrared bullets are concealed in genuine Hawkins 54-caliber buffalo rifles. When you hit a target, elaborate sound and motion gags are set off. You get 25 shots for 50¢.

LIBERTY SQUARE

Serving as a transitional area between Frontierland and Fantasyland, Liberty Square evokes 18th-century America with Georgian architecture and Colonial Williamsburg–type shops. You might encounter a fife-and-drum corps marching along Liberty Square's cobblestone streets.

THE HALL OF PRESIDENTS   In this red-brick colonial hall, all American presidents—from George Washington to Bill Clinton (who recorded the voice for his character)—are represented by Audio-Animatronic™ figures. They dramatize important events in the nation's history, from the signing of the Constitution through the space age. The show begins with a film, projected on a 180° screen, about the importance of the Constitution. Maya Angelou narrates.

✪ **THE HAUNTED MANSION**   Its eerie ambience enhanced by inky darkness, weird music, and mysterious screams and rappings, this mansion is replete with spooky effects: a ghostly banquet and ball, a graveyard band, a suit of armor that comes alive, luminous spiders, a talking head in a crystal ball, and much more. At the end of the ride, a ghost joins you in your car. The experience is more amusing than terrifying, so you can take most small children inside.

BOAT RIDES   A steam-powered sternwheeler called the *Richard F. Irvine* and two **Mike Fink Keel Boats** (the *Bertha Mae* and the *Gullywhumper*) depart (the latter summers and holidays only) from Liberty Square for scenic cruises along the Rivers of America. Both ply the identical route and make a restful interlude for foot-weary parkgoers.

FANTASYLAND

The attractions in this happy "land"—themed after such Disney film classics as *Snow White* and *Peter Pan*—are especially popular with young visitors. If your kids are 8 or under, you might want to make it your first stop in the Magic Kingdom.

LEGEND OF THE LION KING   This stage spectacular based on Disney's block-buster motion-picture musical combines animation, movie footage, sophisticated puppetry, and high-tech special effects.

SNOW WHITE'S ADVENTURES   This attraction used to focus only on the more sinister elements of Grimm's fairy tale—most notably the evil queen and the cackling toothless witch—leaving small children screaming in terror. It's been toned down now, with Snow White appearing in a number of pleasant scenes—at the castle courtyard wishing well, in the dwarfs' cottage, and riding off with the prince to live "happily ever after." Even so, this could be scary for kids under 7.

MAD TEA PARTY   This is a traditional amusement park ride à la Disney with an *Alice in Wonderland* theme. Riders sit in oversize pink teacups on saucers that careen around a circular platform. Believe it or not, this can be a pretty wild ride or a tame one—it depends on how much you spin, a factor under your control via a wheel in the cup.

MR. TOAD'S WILD RIDE   This ride is based on the 1949 Disney film *The Adventures of Ichabod and Mr. Toad,* which was itself based on the classic children's book *The Wind in the Willows.* Riders navigate a series of dark rooms, hurtling into solid objects (a fireplace, a bookcase, a haystack) and through barn doors into a coop of squawking chickens. They're menaced by snorting bulls and an oncoming locomotive in a pitch-black tunnel, and are sent to jail (for car theft), to hell (complete with pitchfork-wielding demons), and through a fiery volcano.

CINDERELLA'S GOLDEN CAROUSEL   It's a beauty, built by Italian wood carvers in the Victorian tradition in 1917 and refurbished by Disney artists who added scenes from the Cinderella story. The band organ plays such Disney classics as "When You Wish Upon a Star."

DUMBO, THE FLYING ELEPHANT   This is a very tame kiddie ride in which the cars—baby elephants (Dumbos)—go around and around in a circle gently rising and dipping.

IT'S A SMALL WORLD   You know the song—and if you don't, you will. It plays continually as you sail "around the world" through vast rooms designed to represent different countries. They're inhabited by appropriately costumed Audio-Animatronic™ dolls and animals, all singing in tiny voices. This cast of thousands includes Chinese acrobats, Russian kazatski dancers, Indian snake charmers, Arabs on magic carpets, African drummers, a Venetian gondolier, and Australian koalas. Cute. Very cute.

PETER PAN'S FLIGHT   Riding in Captain Hook's ship, passengers careen through dark passages while experiencing the story of *Peter Pan*. The adventure begins in the Darlings' nursery, and includes a flight over nighttime London to Never-Never-Land, where riders encounter mermaids, Indians, a ticking crocodile, the lost boys, Tinkerbell, Hook, Smee, and the rest—all to the movie music "You Can Fly, You Can Fly, You Can Fly." It's fun.

SKYWAY   Its entrance close to Peter Pan's Flight, the Skyway is an aerial tramway to Tomorrowland, which makes continuous round-trips throughout the day.

MICKEY'S STARLAND

This small land, adjacent to Fantasyland, with a topiary maze of Disney characters and a block of "Duckburg" architecture, is accessible from Main Street via the Walt Disney World Railroad. It includes a Walk of Fame à la Hollywood, with Disney character "voiceprints" activated when you step on a star; a hands-on fire station; storefronts that come alive at the push of a button; Grandma Duck's Farm (a petting zoo); funhouse mirrors; a treehouse; and an interactive video area. Mickey's house is here too, complete with living room TV tuned to the Disney Channel and his familiar outfits hanging on a clothesline in the yard.

The main attraction is **Mickey's Starland Show,** which is presented on a stage behind his house. The show, a lively musical, features the Goof Troop, Chip 'n' Dale, a perky hostess named CJ, and a vocal computer-control system called Dude. The cheerful cartoon-inspired scenery, audience participation, and dramatic special effects are all designed to appeal to young viewers. After the show there's an opportunity to meet Mickey backstage.

TOMORROWLAND

This land focuses on the future—most notably, space travel and exploration. In 1994, the Disney people decided that Tomorrowland (originally designed in the 1970s) was beginning to look like "Yesterdayland." It has now been revamped to reflect the future as a galactic, science fiction–inspired community inhabited by humans, aliens, and robots. A vast state-of-the-art video-game arcade has also been added.

✪ **EXTRA"TERROR"ESTRIAL ALIEN ENCOUNTER**   Director George Lucas contributed his space-age vision to this major new Tomorrowland attraction. The action begins at the Interplanetary Convention Center where a mysterious corporation called X-S Tech is marketing an interplanetary "teletransporter" to Earthlings. In order to demonstrate it, X-S technicians try to teleport their sinister corporation head, Chairman Clench, to Earth. But the machine malfunctions, sending him to a distant planet instead and inadvertently teleporting a fearsome man-eating extraterrestrial to Earth. Lots of high-tech special effects here—from the alien's breath on your neck to a mist of alien slime.

THE TIMEKEEPER   This Jules Verne / H. G. Wells–inspired multimedia presentation combines Circle-Vision™ and IMAX footage with Audio-Animatronics™. It's hosted by Timekeeper, a mad scientist robot and his assistant, 9-EYE, a flying female camera-headed droid and time machine test pilot. In an unpredictable jet-speed escapade, the audience visits medieval battlefields in Scotland, watches Leonardo at work, and floats in a hot-air balloon above Moscow's Red Square. There are many other adventures. Timekeeper also throttles his calendar forward—to the 300th anniversary of the French Revolution in 2089.

☼ SPACE MOUNTAIN   Space Mountain entertains visitors on its long lines with space-age music, meteorites, shooting stars, and space debris whizzing about overhead. These "illusioneering" effects, enhanced by appropriate audio, continue during the ride itself, which is a cosmic roller coaster in the inky starlit blackness of outer space. Your rocket climbs high before racing through a serpentine complex of aerial galaxies, making thrilling hairpin turns and rapid plunges. (Though it feels like you're going at breakneck speed, your car actually never goes faster than 28 miles per hour.)

DREAMFLIGHT   The history and wonder of aviation—from barnstorming to space shuttles—is captured in this whimsical fly-through adventure. High-tech special effects and 70mm live-action film footage add dramatic 3-D–style verisimilitude. Guests travel from a futuristic airport up a hillside to witness a flying circus, parachutists, and other stunt flyers; the action moves on to the ocean-hopping age of commercial flight, and finally your vehicle is pulled into a giant jet engine and sent into to outer space at a simulated speed of 300 m.p.h.

WALT DISNEY'S CAROUSEL OF PROGRESS   This 22-minute show in a revolving theater features an Audio-Animatronic™ family in various tableaux demonstrating a century of development (beginning in 1900) in electric gadgetry and contraptions from Victrolas to virtual reality.

SKYWAY   Its Tomorrowland entrance just west of Space Mountain, this aerial tramway to Fantasyland makes continuous round-trips throughout the day.

TOMORROWLAND TRANSIT AUTHORITY   A futuristic means of transportation, these small five-car trains have no engines. They work by electromagnets, emit no pollution, and use little power. Narrated by a computer guide named Horack I, TTA offers an overhead look at Tomorrowland, including a pretty good preview of Space Mountain. If you're only in the Magic Kingdom for 1 day, this can be skipped.

GRAND PRIX RACEWAY   This is a great thrill for kids (including teens still waiting to get their driver's licenses) who get to put the pedal to the metal, steer, and *vroom* down a speedway in an actual gas-powered sports car. Maximum speed on the 4-minute drive around the track is about 7 m.p.h., and kids have to be 4 feet 4 inches tall to drive alone.

ASTRO ORBITER   This is a tame, typical amusement park ride. The "rockets" are on arms attached to "the center of the galaxy," and they move up and down while orbiting spinning planets.

PARADES, FIREWORKS & MORE

You'll get an *Entertainment Show Schedule* when you enter the park, which lists all kinds of special goings-on for the day. These include concerts (everything from steel drums to barbershop quartets), encounters with Disney characters, holiday events, and the three major happenings listed below.

THE 3 O'CLOCK PARADE   You haven't really seen a parade until you've seen one at Walt Disney World. This spectacular daily event kicks off at 3pm year round on Main Street and meanders through Liberty Square and Frontierland. The route is outlined on your *Entertainment Show Schedule*.

The only problem: Even in slow seasons, you have to snag a seat along the curb a good half hour before it begins, and earlier during peak travel times. (That's a long time to sit on a hard curb; consider packing inflatable pillows.)

But the parade is worth a little discomfort. In addition to Mickey and all his Disney pals, there are elaborate floats, stunning costumes, special effects, and a captivating cavalcade of dancers, singers, and other talented performers. Great music, too.

✪ **SPECTROMAGIC**   Along a darkened parade route (the same one as above), 72,000 watts of dazzling high-tech lighting effects (including holography) create a glowing array of pixies and peacocks, seahorses and winged horses, flower gardens and fountains. Roger Rabbit is the eccentric conductor of an orchestra producing a rainbow of musical notes that waft magically into the night air. There are dancing ostriches from *Fantasia,* whirling electric butterflies, bejewelled coaches, luminescent ElectroMen atop spinning whirlyballs, and, of course, Mickey, surrounded by a sparkling confetti of light. And the music and choreography are on a par with the technology.

Once again, very early arrival is essential to get a seat on the curb. SpectroMagic takes place nightly in summer, on selected nights during Christmas and Easter vacation times, and during other special celebrations. Consult your *Entertainment Show Schedule* for details.

✪ **FIREWORKS**   Like SpectroMagic, Fantasy in the Sky Fireworks, immediately preceded by Tinker Bell's magical flight from Cinderella's Castle, take place nightly in summer, on selected nights during Christmas and Easter vacation times, and during other special celebrations. Consult your *Entertainment Show Schedule* for details. Suggested viewing areas are Liberty Square, Frontierland, and Mickey's Starland.

6 Epcot

Ever growing, Epcot today occupies 260 acres so stunningly landscaped as to be worth visiting for botanical beauty alone. There are two major sections, Future World and World Showcase.

Epcot is huge, and walking around it can be exhausting (some say Epcot's acronym stands for "Every Person Comes Out Tired"). Don't try to do it all in one day. Conserve energy by taking launches across the lagoon from the edge of Future World to Germany or Morocco. There are also double-decker buses circling the World Showcase Promenade and making stops at Norway, Italy, France, and Canada.

Unlike the Magic Kingdom, Epcot's parking lot is right at the gate. If you don't get them in the parking lot or at the gate, stop by the Innoventions East information center when you come in to pick up an ***Epcot Guidemap*** and **entertainment schedule,** and, if you so desire, make reservations for lunch or dinner. Many Epcot restaurants are described in "Where to Eat," earlier in this chapter.

Strollers can be rented to your left at the Future World entrance plaza and in World Showcase at the International Gateway between the United Kingdom and France.

FUTURE WORLD

The northern section of Epcot (where you enter the park) comprises Future World, centered on a giant geosphere known as Spaceship Earth. Future World's 10 themed areas, sponsored by major American corporations, focus on discovery, scientific achievements, and tomorrow's technologies in areas running the gamut from energy to underseas exploration.

✪ **SPACESHIP EARTH**   Spaceship Earth, housed in a massive silvery geosphere, is Epcot's most cogent symbol. Inside, a show takes visitors on a 15-minute journey through the history of communications. You board time-machine vehicles to the

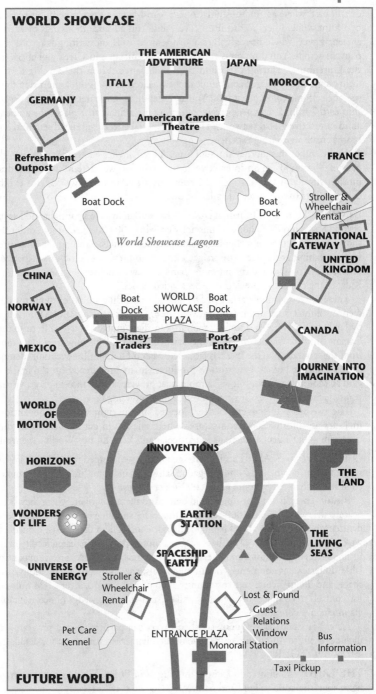

WORLD SHOWCASE

THE AMERICAN ADVENTURE

JAPAN

ITALY

MOROCCO

GERMANY

American Gardens Theatre

Refreshment Outpost

FRANCE

Boat Dock

Boat Dock

Stroller & Wheelchair Rental

World Showcase Lagoon

INTERNATIONAL GATEWAY

UNITED KINGDOM

CHINA

Boat Dock

WORLD SHOWCASE PLAZA

Boat Dock

NORWAY

Disney Traders

Port of Entry

CANADA

MEXICO

JOURNEY INTO IMAGINATION

WORLD OF MOTION

INNOVENTIONS

HORIZONS

THE LAND

WONDERS OF LIFE

EARTH STATION

THE LIVING SEAS

SPACESHIP EARTH

UNIVERSE OF ENERGY

Stroller & Wheelchair Rental

Lost & Found

Guest Relations Window

Pet Care Kennel

ENTRANCE PLAZA

Monorail Station

Bus Information

Taxi Pickup

FUTURE WORLD

distant past, where an Audio-Animatronic™ Cro-Magnon shaman recounts the story of a hunt while others record it on cave walls. You advance thousands of years to ancient Egypt, where hieroglyphics adorn temple walls and writing is recorded on papyrus scrolls. You'll progress through the Phoenician and Greek alphabets, and the Gutenburg printing press and the Renaissance. From the development of technologies that enlarged communications via electricity, it's but a short step to the age of electronic communications. You are catapulted into outer space to see "spaceship earth" from a new perspective, returning for a finale that places the audience amid interactive global networks. High-tech special effects, animated sets, and laser beams create an exciting experience.

At the end of this journey through time, AT&T invites guests to sample its "global neighborhood" in an interactive computer-video wonderland that includes a motion-simulator ride through the company's electronic network. This exhibit complements Innoventions, detailed below.

INNOVENTIONS The pair of crescent-shaped buildings to your right and left just beyond Spaceship Earth house a constantly evolving 100,000-square-foot exhibit that showcases cutting-edge technologies and future products. Leading manufacturers sponsor exhibit areas here. Visitors get a chance to preview electric cars, experience interactive television, and try out more than 200 new computer programs and games. Kids will be thrilled to preview new Sega video games.

There are several show areas: In Dr. Digital's recording studio of tomorrow, audience volunteers lay down four tracks of an original song. You can be interviewed by Jay Leno on TV. Alec Tronic, a robotic comedian, imitates everyone from Johnny Carson to John Wayne. Bill Nye, the Science Guy, explains how new ideas move from the laboratory to the marketplace. The Masco House of Innoventions demonstrates exciting home-of-the-future products (many are already on the market). And at Motorola's "Your Show," a robot host provides the chance to play a virtual-reality game. You can easily spend several hours browsing here.

The two-story **Discovery Center,** located on the right side of Innoventions, includes an information resource area where guests can get answers to all their questions about Epcot attractions in particular and Walt Disney World in general.

✪ THE LIVING SEAS This United Technologies–sponsored pavilion contains the world's sixth "ocean," a 5.7-million-gallon saltwater aquarium (including a complete coral reef) inhabited by more than 4,000 sea creatures.

Visitors enter hydrolators for a rapid descent to the ocean floor, where they board Seacabs that wind around a 400-foot-long tunnel for stunning close-up views of ocean denizens in a natural coral-reef habitat. The ride concludes in the Seabase Concourse, which is the visitor center of Seabase Alpha, a prototype ocean-research facility of the future. Here, informational modules focus on harvestable resources grown in controllable undersea environments, marine mammals, the study of oceanography from space, and life in a coral-reef community. You can step into a diver's JIM Suit and use controls to complete diving tasks, and expand your knowledge of oceanography via interactive computers.

Note: Via **Epcot DiveQuest,** certified divers can participate in a program that includes a 30- to 40-minute scuba dive in the Living Seas aquarium; for details call 407/WDW-TOUR.

THE LAND Sponsored by Nestlé, this largest of Future World's pavilions highlights man's relation to food and nature.

Living with the Land: A 13-minute boatride takes you through three ecological environments (a rain forest, desert, and windswept plain), each populated by appropriate Audio-Animatronic™ denizens. New farming methods and experiments—ranging from hydroponics to plants growing in simulated Martian soil—are showcased in real gardens. If you'd like a more serious overview, take a 45-minute guided walking tour of the growing areas, offered daily. Sign up at the Green Thumb Emporium shop near the entrance to Food Rocks. The cost is $5 for adults, $3 for children 3 to 9, free for children 2 and under. It's not, by the way, really geared to children.

Circle of Life: Combining spectacular live-action footage with animation, this 15-minute, 70mm motion picture based on the *The Lion King* is a cautionary environmental tale.

Food Rocks: Audio-Animatronic™ rock performers deliver an entertaining message about nutrition here.

✪ **JOURNEY INTO IMAGINATION** In this terrific pavilion, presented by Kodak, even the fountains are magical, with arching streams of water that leap into the air like glass rods. Its major attraction is:

Honey I Shrunk the Audience: This 3-D attraction is based on the Disney hit *Honey, I Shrunk the Kids.* The audience, after being menaced by hundreds of mice and a 3-D cat, is shrunk and given a good shaking by a gigantic 5-year-old. Dramatic 3-D action is enhanced by vibrating seats and creepy tactile effects.

Journey into Imagination Ride: Visitors board moving cars for a 14-minute ride. After a simulated flight across the nighttime sky, you enter the "Imaginarium," where whimsical tableaux featuring Audio-Animatronic™ characters explore creativity in the fine arts, performing arts, literature, science, and technology. The ride culminates at Image Works.

Image Works: Here you'll find dozens of hands-on electronic devices and interactive computers. You can activate musical instruments by stepping on hexagons of colored light, participate in a TV drama, draw patterns with laser beams, operate a giant kaleidoscope, and conduct an electronic orchestra.

WORLD OF MOTION Closed at this writing for a total revamp (it may be open by the time you read this), this General Motors–sponsored attraction (which will probably also be renamed) will put guests in the driver's seat to experience the rigors of automobile testing. During a preshow—essentially a GM commercial—guests will learn how the company works to promote automotive safety, reliability, and performance. Then they'll board full-scale six-passenger test cars and travel upon what appears to be an actual roadway. The ride will culminate with a terrifying high-speed outdoor run along the track's steeply banked "speed loop" which extends far beyond the pavilion facility. Cars will go at a top speed of 65 miles per hour.

HORIZONS The theme of this pavilion is the future. You board gondolas for a 15-minute journey into the next millennium. The first tableau honors visionaries of past centuries (like Jules Verne) and looks at outdated visions of the future and classic sci-fi movies. You ascend to an area where an IMAX film projected on two 80-foot-high screens presents a kaleidoscope of brilliant micro and macro images—growing crystals, colonies in space, DNA molecules, and a computer chip. You then travel to 21st-century cityscapes, floating cities under the ocean's surface and outer-space colonies populated by Audio-Animatronic™ denizens. For the return to 20th-century earth, you can select one of three futuristic transportation systems: a personal spacecraft, a desert Hovercraft, or a mini-submarine.

✪ **WONDERS OF LIFE** Housed in a vast geodesic dome fronted by a 75-foot replica of a DNA molecule, this Epcot pavilion offers some of Future World's most engaging shows and attractions.

Find the Hidden Mickeys

Hiding Mickeys in designs began as an inside joke with early Walt Disney World "Imagineers" and became a park tradition. Today dozens of subtle hidden Mickeys (HMs)—the world-famous set of ears, profiles, and full figures—are concealed in attractions and resorts throughout Walt Disney World. No one knows their exact number. See how many you can locate during your visit. A few to look for include:

In the Magic Kingdom: In the Haunted Mansion banquet scene, check out the arrangement of plates and adjoining saucers on the table.

In the Africa scene of It's a Small World, note the purple flowers on a vine on the elephant's left side.

While riding Splash Mountain, look for Mickey lying on his back in the pink clouds to the right of the steamboat.

Hint: There are four HMs in the Timekeeper and five in the Carousel of Progress.

At Epcot: In Journey into Imagination, check out the little girl's dress in the lobby film of "Honey I Shrunk the Audience," one of five HMs in this pavilion.

In The Land pavilion, don't miss the small stones in front of the Native American man on a horse and the baseball cap of the man driving a harvester in the "Circle of Life" film.

As your boat cruises through the Mexico pavilion on the El Rio del Tiempo attraction, notice the arrangement of three clay pots in the marketplace scene.

In Maelstrom, in the Norway pavilion, a Viking wears Mickey ears in the wall mural facing the loading dock.

There are four HMs in Spaceship Earth, one of them in the Renaissance scene, on the page of a book behind the sleeping monk. Try to find the other three.

At Disney–MGM Studios: On the Great Movie Ride, there's an HM on the window above the bank in the gangster scene, and four familiar characters are included in the hieroglyphics wall opposite Indiana Jones.

At Jim Henson's Muppet Vision 3-D, take a good look at the "Top five reasons for turning in your 3-D glasses" sign, and note the balloons in the film's final scene.

At the Monster Sound Show, check out Jimmy Macdonald's bolo tie and ring in the preshow video.

In the Twilight Zone Tower of Terror, note the bell for the elevator behind Rod Serling in the film. There are five other HMs in this attraction.

At Disney Resorts: There are also HMs at many Disney resorts. The best place to look for them is at Wilderness Lodge, which has more than a dozen that I know about.

The Making of Me: Starring Martin Short, this captivating 15-minute motion picture combines live action with animation and spectacular in-utero photography to create the sweetest introduction imaginable to the facts of life. Don't miss it.

Body Wars: You're miniaturized to the size of a single cell for a medical rescue mission inside the immune system of a human body. This motion-simulator ride takes you on a wild journey through gale-force winds (in the lungs) and pounding heart chambers.

Cranium Command: In this hilarious multimedia attraction, Buzzy, an Audio-Animatronic™ brain-pilot-in-training, is charged with the seemingly impossible task of controlling the brain of a typical 12-year-old boy. The boy's body parts are played by Charles Grodin, Jon Lovitz, Bob Goldthwait, Kevin Nealon and Dana Carvey (as

Hans and Franz), and George Wendt. It's another must-see attraction.

Fitness Fairgrounds: This large area is filled with fitness-related shows, exhibits, and participatory activities, including a film called *Goofy About Health* and Coach's Corner, where your tennis, golf, or baseball swing is analyzed by experts. You can also get a computer-generated evaluation of your health habits and take a video voyage to investigate the effects of drugs on your heart. There's much, much more. You could easily spend hours here.

UNIVERSE OF ENERGY   This 35-minute Exxon-sponsored ride-through attraction—with visitors seated in solar-powered "traveling theater" cars—aims to better our understanding of America's energy problems. It's under refurbishment at this writing. Its new storyline will feature Ellen DeGeneres as an energy expert tutored by Bill Nye, the Science Guy, to be a *Jeopardy* contestant. On a massive screen in Theater I, an animated motion picture depicts the earth's molten beginnings, its cooling process, and the formation of fossil fuels. You move from Theater I to travel back 275 million years into an eerie storm-wracked landscape of the Mesozoic Era, a time of violent geological activity. Here, you're menaced by giant Audio-Animatronic™ peryodactyls and dinosaurs before entering a steam-filled tunnel deep through the bowels of the volcano to emerge back in the 20th century in Theater II. In this new setting, which looks like a NASA Mission Control room, a film projected on a massive 210-foot wraparound screen depicts the challenges of the world's increasing energy demands and the emerging technologies that will help meet them. Your moving seats now return to Theater I, where it all ends on an upbeat note with a vision of an energy-abundant future and Ellen as a new *Jeopardy* champion.

WORLD SHOWCASE

Surrounding a 40-acre lagoon at the park's southern end is World Showcase, a permanent community of 11 miniaturized nations, all with authentic landmark architecture, landscaping, background music, restaurants, and shops. The cultural facets of each nation are explored in art exhibits, dance performances, innovative rides, films, and attractions. It's also a shopping mecca for the indigenous goods of every nation. All employees in each pavilion are natives of the country represented.

✪ **CANADA**   Our neighbors to the north are represented by diverse architecture ranging from a mansard-roofed replica of Ottawa's Château Laurier (here called the Hôtel du Canada) to a rustic stone building modeled after a famous landmark near Niagara Falls. A Native American village signifies the culture of the Northwest, while the Canadian wilderness is reflected by a steep mountain (a Canadian Rocky) and a "forest" of evergreens, stately cedars, maples, and birch trees. Don't miss the stunning floral displays inspired by the Butchart Gardens in Victoria, B.C. The pavilion's highlight attraction is *O Canada!*, a dazzling 18-minute, 360° Circle-Vision™ film that reveals Canada's scenic splendor.

UNITED KINGDOM   Centered on Brittania Square—a formal London-style park, complete with a copper-roofed gazebo bandstand and a statue of the Bard—the U.K. pavilion presents a quaint version of England. Four centuries of architecture are represented along quaint cobblestone streets, troubadours and minstrels entertain in front of a traditional British pub, and a formal garden replicates the landscaping of 16th- and 17th-century palaces. High Street and Tudor Lane shops display a broad sampling of British merchandise, and a tea shop occupies a replica of Anne Hathaway's thatch-roofed 16th-century cottage in Stratford-upon-Avon.

✪ **FRANCE**   This pavilion is entered via a replica of the beautiful cast-iron Pont des Arts footbridge over the Seine. It leads to a park inspired by Seurat's painting *A*

Sunday Afternoon on the Island of La Grande Jatte. A one-tenth replica of the Eiffel Tower looms above the *grands boulevards.* The highlight attraction is **Impressions de France.** Shown in a palatial (mercifully sit-down) theater à la Fontainebleau, this 18-minute film is a scenic journey through diverse French landscapes projected on a vast 200° wraparound screen. Emporia in the covered shopping arcade have interiors ranging from a turn-of-the-century bibliothèque to a French château. Another marketplace revives the defunct Les Halles, where Parisians used to sip onion soup in the wee hours. The heavenly aroma of a boulangerie penetrates the atmosphere, and mimes, jugglers, and strolling chanteurs entertain.

MOROCCO   This exotic pavilion is heralded by a replica of the Koutoubia Minaret, the prayer tower of a 12th-century mosque in Marrakesh. The Medina (old city) leads to Fez House, a traditional Moroccan home, and the narrow winding streets of the *souk,* a bustling marketplace where all manner of authentic handcrafted merchandise—pottery, Berber and Rabat carpets, ornate silver boxes, straw baskets, and prayer rugs—is on display. There are weaving demonstrations in the *souk* throughout the day. The Medina's rectangular courtyard centers on a replica of the ornately tiled Najjarine Fountain in Fez, the setting for musical entertainment. The pavilion's Royal Gallery contains an ever-changing exhibit of Moroccan art, and the Center of Tourism offers a continuous three-screen slide show.

JAPAN   Heralded by a flaming red *torii* (gate of honor) on the banks of the lagoon, and the graceful blue-roofed Goju No To pagoda (inspired by a shrine built at Nara in A.D. 700), this pavilion focuses on Japan's ancient culture. In a traditional Japanese garden, trees and flowering shrubs frame a contemplative setting of pebbled footpaths, rustic bridges, waterfalls, and a pond of golden koi. The Yakitori House is based on the renowned 16th-century Katsura Imperial Villa in Kyoto, considered by many to be the crowning achievement of Japanese architecture. Exhibits ranging from 18th-century Bunraki puppets to samurai armor take place in the moated White Heron Castle, a replica of the Shirasagi-Jo, a 17th-century fortress overlooking the city of Himeji. And the Mitsukoshi Department Store (Japan's answer to Macy's) is housed in a replica of the Shishinden (Hall of Ceremonies) of the Gosho Imperial Palace built in Kyoto in A.D. 794. In the courtyard, artisans demonstrate the ancient arts of *anesaiku* (shaping brown rice candy into dragons, unicorns, and dolphins), *sumi-e* (calligraphy), and *origami* (paper folding). Be sure to include a show of traditional Japanese music and dance at this pavilion in your schedule. It's one of the best in the World Showcase.

✪ AMERICAN ADVENTURE   Housed in a vast Georgian-style structure, the American Adventure is a 29-minute dramatization of U.S. history utilizing a 72-foot rear-projection screen, rousing music, and a large cast of lifelike Audio-Animatronic™ figures, including narrators Mark Twain and Ben Franklin. The "adventure" begins with the voyage of the *Mayflower.* You view Jefferson writing the Declaration of Independence, the expansion of the frontier, Mathew Brady photographing a family about to be divided by the Civil War, the stock market crash of 1929, the attack on Pearl Harbor, and the *Eagle* heading toward the moon. While waiting for the show to begin, you'll be entertained by the wonderful Voices of Liberty Singers performing American folk songs in the Main Hall. A shop called Heritage Manor Gifts sells presidential photographs, books on American history, classic political campaign buttons, and souvenirs and folk crafts.

ITALY   One of the prettiest World Showcase pavilions, Italy lures visitors over an arched stone footbridge to a replica of Venice's intricately ornamented Doge's Palace. Other architectural highlights include the 83-foot campanile (bell tower) of St. Mark's Square, Venetian bridges, and a central piazza enclosing a version of Bernini's Neptune Fountain. A garden wall suggests a backdrop of provincial countryside, and Mediterranean citrus, olive trees, cypress, and pine frame a formal garden. Gondolas are moored on the lagoon. A troupe of street actors perform a contemporary version of 16th-century commedia dell'arte in the piazza.

GERMANY   Enclosed by towered castle walls, this festive pavilion is centered on a cobblestone square with pots of colorful flowers girding a fountain statue of St. George and the Dragon. An adjacent clock tower is embellished with whimsical glockenspiel figures that herald each hour with quaint melodies. The pavilion's outdoor biergarten—where it's Oktoberfest all year long—was inspired by medieval Rothenberg. An artisan demonstrates the molding and painting of Hummel figures; another paints exquisite detailed scenes on eggs.

✪ **CHINA**   Bounded by a serpentine wall that snakes around its outer perimeter, the China pavilion is entered via a vast ceremonial gate inspired by the Temple of Heaven in Beijing. Passing through the gate, you'll see a half-size replica of this ornate red-and-gold circular temple, built in 1420 during the Ming Dynasty. Gardens simulate the famous gardens of Suzhou, with miniature waterfalls, fragrant lotus ponds, groves of bamboo, and weeping mulberry trees. The highlight attraction here is *Wonders of China,* a 20-minute, 360° Circle-Vision™ film that explores 6,000 years of dynastic and Communist rule and the breathtaking diversity of the Chinese landscape. Adjacent to the theater, an art gallery houses changing exhibits of Chinese art. A bustling marketplace offers an array of merchandise. Artisans here demonstrate calligraphy.

NORWAY   Centered on a picturesque cobblestone courtyard, this pavilion evokes ancient Norway. A *stavekirke* (stave church), styled after the 13th-century Gol Church of Hallingdal, houses changing exhibits. A replica of Oslo's 14th-century Akershus Castle is the setting for the pavilion's featured restaurant. Other buildings simulate the red-roofed cottages of Bergen and the timber-sided farm buildings of the Nordic woodlands. There's a two-part attraction here. **Maelstrom,** a boatride in a dragon-headed Viking vessel, traverses Norway's fjords and mythical forests to the music of *Peer Gynt*—an exciting journey during which you'll be menaced by polar bears prowling the shore and trolls that cast a spell on the boat. The watercraft crashes through a narrow gorge and spins into the North Sea where a violent storm is in progress. But the storm abates, and passengers disembark safely in a 10th-century Viking village to view the 70mm film *Norway,* which documents a thousand years of history. There's a Lego table where kids can play while you shop for Scandinavian foods, pewterware, and jewelry.

MEXICO   You'll hear the music of marimba and mariachi bands as you approach the festive showcase of Mexico, fronted by a towering Mayan pyramid modeled on the Aztec Temple of Quetzalcoatl (God of Life). Upon entering the pavilion, you'll find yourself in a museum of pre-Columbian art and artifacts. A small lagoon is the setting for **El Rio del Tiempo,** where visitors board boats for 8-minute cruises through Mexico's past and present. Shops are in and around the Plaza de Los Amigos (a "moonlit" Mexican *mercado*). La Casa de Vacaciones, sponsored by the Mexican Tourist Office, provides travel information.

SHOWS & SPECTACULARS

As at the Magic Kingdom, check your show schedule upon entering the park and plan to attend many of the below-listed performances.

WORLD SHOWCASE PAVILION SHOWS   These international entertainments make up an important part of the Epcot experience. There are Chinese lion dancers and acrobats, German oom-pah bands, Caledonian bagpipers, Italian "living statues" and stiltwalkers, colonial fife-and-drum groups, Moroccan belly dancers, and much more. Be sure not to miss the Voices of Liberty Singers at American Adventure and the traditional music and dance displays in Japan.

✪ **ILLUMINATIONS**   A backdrop of classical music by international composers, high-tech lighting effects, darting laser beams, fireworks, strobes, and rainbow-lit dancing fountains combine to create this awesome 16½-minute Epcot spectacular, presented nightly. Each nation is highlighted in turn—colorful kites fly over Japan, the giant Rockies loom over Canada, a gingerbread house rises in Germany, and so on. Don't miss it! Find a seat around the lagoon about a half hour before show time.

RHYTHMS OF THE WORLD   Varied international cultural performances take place at the America Gardens Theater in World Showcase.

7 Disney–MGM Studios

Disney–MGM Studios offers exciting movie and TV-themed shows and behind-the-scenes "reel-life" adventures. Its main streets include Hollywood Boulevard and Sunset Boulevard, with art deco movie sets evocative of Hollywood's glamorous golden age. There's also a New York street lined with Gotham landmarks (the Empire State, Flatiron, and Chrysler buildings) and typical New York characters including peddlers hawking knock-off watches. More important, this is a working movie and TV studio, where shows are in production even as you tour the premises.

Arrive at the park early, tickets in hand. Unlike the Magic Kingdom and Epcot, MGM's 110 acres of attractions can pretty much be seen in 1 day. The parking lot is right at the gate.

If you don't get a *Disney–MGM Studios* **Guidemap** and **entertainment schedule** when you enter the park, you can pick them up at **Guest Services** (MGM's information center). The first thing to do is check show times and work out an entertainment schedule based on highlight attractions and geographical proximity. My favorite MGM restaurants are described in the "Where to Eat" section of this chapter. **Strollers** can be rented at Oscar's Super Service inside the main entrance.

✪ **THE TWILIGHT ZONE TOWER OF TERROR**   A thrilling journey to another dimension! Legend has it that during a violent storm on Halloween night of 1939, lightning struck the Hollywood Tower Hotel, causing an entire wing—along with an elevator full of people—to disappear. And you're about to meet them as you become the star in a special episode of . . . *The Twilight Zone.* After various spooky adventures, the ride ends in a dramatic climax: a terrifying 13-story free-fall plunge into *The Twilight Zone!* Rod Serling is your host.

✪ **THE MAGIC OF DISNEY ANIMATION**   You'll see Disney characters come alive at the stroke of a brush or pencil as you tour actual glass-walled animation studios and watch artists at work. The tour also includes entertaining video talks by animators and a grand finale of magical moments from Disney classics. This popular attraction should be visited early in the morning; long lines form later in the day.

BACKSTAGE STUDIO TOUR   This 25-minute tram tour takes you behind the scenes for a close-up look at the vehicles, props, costumes, sets, and special effects used in your favorite movies and TV shows. You'll see costumers at work in wardrobe, the house facade of *The Golden Girls,* and carpenters building sets. All very interesting

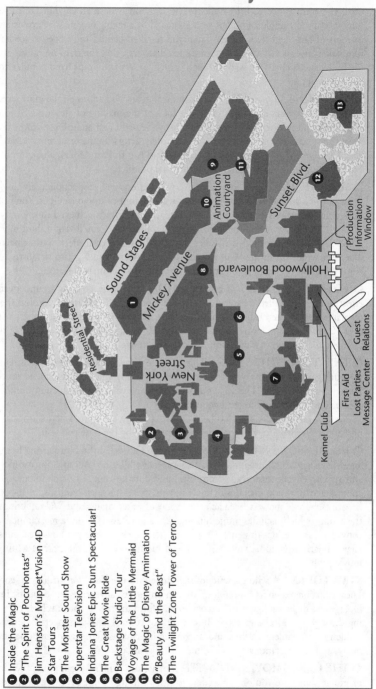

1. Inside the Magic
2. "The Spirit of Pocohontas"
3. Jim Henson's Muppet*Vision 4D
4. Star Tours
5. The Monster Sound Show
6. Superstar Television
7. Indiana Jones Epic Stunt Spectacular!
8. The Great Movie Ride
9. Backstage Studio Tour
10. Voyage of the Little Mermaid
11. The Magic of Disney Animation
12. "Beauty and the Beast"
13. The Twilight Zone Tower of Terror

until the tram ventures into Catastrophe Canyon, where an earthquake causes canyon walls to rumble and riders are threatened by a raging fire, massive explosions, torrents of rain, and flash floods! Then you're taken behind the scenes to see how filmmakers use special effects to create such disasters. After the tram tour, visit Studio Showcase, a changing walk-through display of sets and props from popular and classic movies.

THE MAKING OF...   This attraction, which always focuses on the most recent Disney hit, provides a behind-the-scenes look at the making of an animated film. Intriguing and informative, it takes you into video-edit and audio-post-production rooms and includes interviews with the composers, actors, animators, artists, researchers (*The Lion King,* for instance, involved a field trip to East Africa), and computer experts whose combined efforts create the final product.

INSIDE THE MAGIC   Movie and TV special effects and production facets are the focus of this 40-minute behind-the-scenes walking tour of studio facilities. You'll see how a naval battle is created and how miniaturization was achieved in the movie *Honey, I Shrunk the Kids.* After visiting studio soundstages, you'll view a short movie called *The Lottery* starring Bette Midler and learn how its special effects were achieved. The tour winds up in the Walt Disney Theater, where you'll get to sit down and enjoy a behind-the-scenes look at the company's latest animation feature.

✪ VOYAGE OF THE LITTLE MERMAID   Hazy light, creating an underwater effect in the reef-walled theater, helps set the mood for this charming musical spectacular based on the Disney feature film. The show combines live performers with over 100 puppets and innovative special effects. It has a happy ending, as most of the young audience knows it will—they've seen the movie.

✪ THEATER OF THE STARS   This 1,500-seat covered amphitheater is currently presenting a live Broadway-style production of *Beauty and the Beast,* based on the Disney movie version. The sets and costumes are lavish, the production numbers spectacular. Arrive early to get a good seat.

Note: Beauty and the Beast has been enjoying a long run here; a new show, based on a more recent Disney movie, may be in progress by the time you visit.

✪ JIM HENSON'S MUPPET VISION 3-D   This delightful film starring Kermit and Miss Piggy combines Jim Henson's puppets with Disney Audio-Animatronics™ and special-effects wizardry, 70mm film, and cutting-edge 3-D technology. The coming-at-you action includes flying Muppets, cream pies, cannonballs, fiber-optic fireworks, bubble showers, even an actual spray of water. Statler and Waldorf critique the action (which includes numerous mishaps and disasters) from a mezzanine balcony. Kids in the first row interact with the characters. In the preshow area, guests view a hilarious Muppet video on overhead monitors and see an array of Muppet movie props.

STAR TOURS   A wild galactic journey based on the *Star Wars* trilogy (George Lucas collaborated on its conception), this action-packed adventure uses dramatic film footage and flight-simulator technology to transform the theater into a vehicle careening through space. The spaceship lurches out of control, and passengers experience sudden drops, violent crashes, and oncoming laser blasts. The harrowing ride ends safely, and you exit into a *Star Wars* merchandise shop.

✪ THE GREAT MOVIE RIDE   Film footage and Audio-Animatronic™ replicas of movie stars take you on a nostalgic journey through some of the most famous scenes in movie history. The action is enhanced by dramatic special effects, and your tram is always highjacked en route by outlaws or gangsters. The setting for this

Famous Orlandoans

Mickey Mouse (b. 1928). A prominent Orlando resident since 1971, Mickey also maintains a home in Anaheim, California. Star of more than 120 cartoons and movies, he made his film debut the year of his birth in *Steamboat Willie*. His significant other, Minnie Mouse, also appeared in the film. Mickey's dad almost named him Mortimer, but his mom (Mrs. Disney) persuaded her husband that Mortimer was too pompous a moniker for a mouse and suggested Mickey. Mickey considers the 1940s, when he starred in *Fantasia*, as his "Golden Decade." Having reached the age of retirement, Mickey has no plans to stop working. "Better to wear out than rust out," says the still-teenlike toon.

Donald Duck (b. 1934). Member of a prominent thespian family (which includes nephews Huey, Dewey, and Louie, billionaire Uncle Scrooge, and Grandma Duck), Donald has starred in more than 170 cartoons and movies since his 1930s debut as an extra in *The Wise Little Hen*. As recorded in Disney archives, "he bellowed and strutted his way into that production until, bit part or no, he was practically the star of the piece." Though Disney directors have always liked working with the superbly gifted "mad mallard," his career has been somewhat hindered by his terrible temper. The bellicose duck's most memorable line of dialogue, "Wanna fight?" is said to have inspired Clint Eastwood's "Make my day."

Goofy (b. 1932). Goofy first appeared along with Mickey Mouse in a cartoon called *Mickey's Revue*. Though his original name was Dippy Dawg, which later evolved into Dippy the Goof, and finally, Goofy, there has been, over the years, an ongoing controversy as to exactly what kind of animal he is. The claim of Disney representatives that he is a human being has never been adequately substantiated. And Goofy himself fueled speculation when he answered a reporter's question about his species in 1992 with the words "Gawrsh! I dunno." Tabloid rumors notwithstanding, this dumb but likable toon is the living embodiment of Murphy's Law—whatever can go wrong will go wrong. But he continues to laugh ("hyuk, hyuk") in the face of adversity.

attraction is a full-scale reproduction of Hollywood's famous Mann's Chinese Theatre, complete with hand- and footprints of the stars out front.

✪ **MONSTER SOUND SHOW** Four volunteers are chosen from the audience to create sound effects for a short film starring Chevy Chase and Martin Short that includes thunder, rain, creaking doors, falling chandeliers, footsteps, ringing bells, and explosions. You see the film three times: first with professional sound, then without sound as volunteers frantically scramble to create an appropriate track, and finally with the sound effects they've provided. Errors in timing and volume make it all quite funny, as a knock at the door or crashing glass comes just a few seconds too late. In a postshow area called Soundworks, guests can try their hand at creating sounds via interactive computers.

SUPERSTAR TELEVISION This 30-minute show takes guests through a broadcast day that spans TV history. During the preshow, "casting directors" choose volunteers from the audience to reenact 15 famous television scenes (arrive early if you want to snag a role). The broadcast day begins with a 1955 black-and-white *Today* show featuring Dave Garroway and continues through *Late Night with David Letterman,* including scenes from a classic *I Love Lucy* episode, *General Hospital,*

Gilligan's Island, and *The Golden Girls,* among others. Real footage is mixed with live action, and though occasionally a star is born, there's plenty of fun watching amateur actors freeze up, flub lines, and otherwise deviate from the script.

✪ **INDIANA JONES EPIC STUNT SPECTACULAR**   Visitors get an inside look at the world of movie stunts in this dramatic 30-minute show, which re-creates major scenes from the Indiana Jones series. The show opens on an elaborate Mayan temple backdrop. Indiana Jones crashes dramatically onto the set via a rope, and, as he searches with a torch for the golden idol, he encounters booby traps, fire and steam, and spears popping up from the ground. The set is dismantled to reveal a colorful Cairo marketplace where a swordfight ensues and the action includes jumps from high places, lots of gunfire, and a truck bursting into flame. An explosive finale takes place in a desert scenario. Throughout, guests get to see how elaborate stunts are pulled off. Volunteers are chosen to participate as extras during the preshow.

PARADES, SHOWS, FIREWORKS & MORE   The colorful **Toy Story** parade, based on the movie, features all of its adorable toy-chest characters. Of course, the Green Army Men love a parade (they strew green confetti from a float); "defender of the universe" Buzz Lightyear appears on a float surrounded by a cadre of adoring Martian drones; the Barrel of Monkeys torment Mr. Potato Head®, and the finale float is a wagon overflowing with toys and carrying top toy Cowboy Woody and Rex. The parade takes place daily; check your entertainment schedule for route and times.

The **Sorcery in the Sky** fireworks show is presented nightly during summer and peak seasons. Check your entertainment schedule to see if it's on.

The **Visiting Celebrity** program features frequent appearances by stars such as Betty White, Burt Reynolds, Joan Collins, Leonard Nimoy, and Billy Dee Williams. They visit attractions, record their handprints in front of the Chinese Theatre, and appear at question-and-answer sessions with park guests. Check your entertainment schedule to see if it's on.

A movie set replica serves as a playground in the *Honey, I Shrunk the Kids* **Movie Set Adventure.** Outside props include 30-foot blades of grass, giant Legos, and a sliding pond made from an immense film reel.

Centering on a gleaming $14^1/_2$-foot bronze Emmy, the **Academy of Television Arts & Sciences Hall of Fame Plaza,** adjacent to SuperStar Television, honors TV legends.

8   Other Walt Disney World Attractions

TYPHOON LAGOON

Located off Lake Buena Vista Drive halfway between Walt Disney World Village and Disney–MGM Studios, this is the ultimate in water theme parks. Its fantasy setting is a palm-fringed tropical island village of ramshackle tin-roofed structures, strewn with wreckage left by a legendary "great typhoon." A storm-stranded fishing boat dangles precariously atop the 95-foot-high Mount Mayday, the steep setting for several major park attractions. Every half hour, the boat's smokestack erupts, shooting a 50-foot geyser of water into the air.

In summer, arrive no later than 9am to avoid long lines; the park is often filled to capacity by 10am and closed to later arrivals. Beach towels and lockers can be obtained for a minimal fee, and all beach accessories can be purchased at Singapore Sal's. Light fare is available at two restaurants, and there are picnic tables. Guests are not permitted to bring their own floatation devices into the park.

Major attractions include **Typhoon Lagoon,** a large and lovely blue lagoon, the size of two football fields and surrounded by white sandy beach. It's the park's main swimming area; young children can wade in the lagoon's peaceful bay or cove.

Hop onto a raft or inner tube and meander along the lazy 2,100-foot **Castaway Creek.** Circling the lagoon, Castaway Creek tumbles through a misty rain forest, past caves and secluded grottoes. There are exits along the route where you can leave the creek; the whole thing takes about a half hour. There's also a variety of water slides, and three white-water rides (Keelhaul Falls has the most winding spiral route, Mayday Falls the steepest drops and fastest water, while the slightly tamer Gangplank Falls uses large tubes so the whole family can ride together.) Guests are given free snorkel equipment (and instruction) for a 15-minute swim through **Shark Reef,** a 362,000-gallon simulated coral-reef tank populated by about 4,000 colorful denizens of the deep. If you don't want to get in the water, you can observe the fish via portholes in a walk-through area.

Many of the above-mentioned attractions require that guests be at least 4 feet tall. But the **Ketchakiddie Creek** section of the park is a kiddie area exclusively for those *under* 4 feet. An innovative water playground, it has bubbling fountains to frolic in, mini-water slides, a pint-sized white-water tubing adventure, spouting whales and squirting seals, rubbery crocodiles to climb on, grottoes to explore, and waterfalls to loll under.

BLIZZARD BEACH

✪ **Blizzard Beach** is Disney's newest, and zaniest, water park—a 66-acre "ski resort" in the midst of a tropical lagoon. The park centers on a 90-foot snow-capped mountain (Mt. Gushmore), which swimmers ascend via chair lifts, and the on-premises restaurant resembles a ski lodge.

It's located on World Drive just north of the All-Star Sports and Music resorts. Arrive at—or before—park opening to avoid long lines and to be sure you get in. Beach towels and lockers are available for a small charge, and you can buy beach accessories at the Beach Haus.

Mt. Gushmore attractions include **Summit Plummet,** which starts 120 feet up and makes a 55-m.p.h. plunge straight down to a splash landing at the base of the mountain, and the **Slush Gusher,** another Mt. Gushmore speed slide (a bit tamer than the above) that travels along a snow-banked mountain gully. **Teamboat Springs** is the world's longest white-water raft ride, with six-passenger rafts twisting down a 1,200-foot series of rushing waterfalls, and other water slides, flumes, an inner-tube run, and a chair lift complete the fun.

A nice-size sandy beach below Mt. Gushmore offers **Tike's Peak,** a scaled-down kiddie version of Mt. Gushmore attractions; **Melt-Away-Bay,** a 1-acre free-form wave pool fed by melting-snow waterfalls; **Cross Country Creek,** where inner tubers can float in a lazy circle around the entire park; and **Ski Patrol Training Camp,** which is designed for preteens and features a rope swing, a T-bar drop over water, slides, and a challenging ice-floe walk along slippery floating icebergs.

RIVER COUNTRY

One of the many recreational facilities at the Fort Wilderness Resort campground, this mini-water park is themed after Tom Sawyer's swimming hole. Kids can scramble over man-made boulders that double as diving platforms for a 330,000-gallon clearwater pool. Two 16-foot water slides also provide access to the pool. Attractions on the adjacent Bay Lake, which is equipped with ropes and ships' booms for climbing, include a pair of flumes that corkscrew through Whoop-N-Holler Hollow;

White Water Rapids, which carries inner tubers along a winding 230-foot creek with a series of chutes and pools, and the Ol' Wading Pool, a smaller version of the swimming hole designed for young children. There are poolside and beachside areas for sunning and picnicking, plus a 350-yard boardwalk nature trail. Beach towels and lockers can be obtained for a minimal fee. Light fare is available at Pop's Place.

To get here, take a launch from the dock near the entrance to the Magic Kingdom or a bus from its Transportation and Ticket Center.

DISCOVERY ISLAND

✪ **DISCOVERY ISLAND,** a lushly tropical 11½-acre zoological sanctuary—just a short boat ride away from the Magic Kingdom entrance, the Contemporary Resort, or Fort Wilderness—provides a tranquil counterpoint to Walt Disney World dazzle.

Plan to spend a leisurely afternoon strolling its scenic mile-long nature trail which, shaded by a canopy of trees, winds past gurgling streams, groves of palm and bamboo, ponds and lagoons filled with ducks and trumpeter swans, a bay that's a breeding ground for brown pelicans, and colonies of rose-hued flamingos. Peacocks roam free, and aviaries house close to 100 species of colorful exotic birds. Discovery Island denizens also include Patagonian cavies, alligators and caimans, Galapagos tortoises, small primates, and Muntjac miniature deer from Southeast Asia.

Two different bird shows and a reptile show are scheduled several times throughout the day. Guests can also look through a viewing area to see the nursery complex of the island's animal hospital, where baby birds and mammals are often hand-raised.

9 Universal Studios Florida

Universal Studios Florida, 1000 Universal Studios Plaza (☎ **407/363-8000**), is a working motion-picture and television production studio. As you stroll along "Hollywood Boulevard" and "Rodeo Drive," you'll pass more than 40 full-scale sets and large props from famous movies. On hand to greet visitors are Hanna-Barbera characters (Yogi Bear, Scooby Doo, Fred Flintstone, and others).

A 1-day ticket costs $37 for ages 10 and over, $30 for children 3 to 9; a 2-day ticket is $55 for ages 10 and over, $44 for children 3 to 9; an annual pass (admission for a full year) is $89 for ages 10 and over, $70 for children 3 to 9; ages 2 and under enter free. Parking costs $5 per vehicle, $6 for RVs and trailers.

The park is open 365 days a year from 9am; closing hours vary seasonally (call before you go). To get there, take I-4 East, make a left onto Sand Lake Road, then a right onto Turkey Lake Road, and follow the signs.

MAJOR ATTRACTIONS

Thrilling rides and attractions utilize cutting-edge technology—such as OMNI-MAX™ 70mm film projected on seven-story screens—to create terrific special effects. While waiting in line, you'll be entertained by excellent preshows.

A DAY IN THE PARK WITH BARNEY   Set in in a parklike theater-in-the-round, this musical show—starring the popular purple one, Baby Bop, and BJ—uses song, dance, and interactive play to deliver an environmental message. For young children, this could be the highlight of the day.

TERMINATOR 2: 3-D BATTLE ACROSS TIME   He's back...at least he will be soon—in an attraction billed as "the quintessential sight and sound experience for the 21st century!" Opening shortly after press time, this new Jim Cameron production (which features the *Terminator 2* cast) will combine 70mm 3-D film (utilizing three 23- by 50-foot screens) with live stage action and thrilling technical effects.

JAWS Did you really think it was safe to go back into the water? As your boat heads out to the open seas, an ominous dorsal fin appears on the horizon. What follows is a series of terrifying attacks from a 3-ton, 32-foot-long great white shark that tries to sink its teeth into passengers. And there's more trouble ahead. The boat is surrounded by a 30-foot wall of flame from burning fuel. I won't tell you how it ends, but here's a hint: The pungent stench of charred shark flesh adds verisimilitude!

E.T. ADVENTURE Visitors are given a passport to E.T.'s planet, which needs his healing powers to rejuvenate it. You'll soar with E.T. through the forest and into space, aboard a star-bound bicycle—all to the accompaniment of that familiar movie theme music.

✪ BACK TO THE FUTURE Visitors blast through the space-time continuum, plummeting into volcanic tunnels ablaze with molten lava, colliding with Ice Age glaciers, thundering through caves and canyons, and are briefly swallowed by a dinosaur in a spectacular multisensory adventure.

✪ KONGFRONTATION It's the last thing the Big Apple needed. King Kong is back! As you stand in line in a replica of a grungy, graffiti-scarred New York subway station, CBS newsman Roland Smith reports on Kong's terrifying rampage. Everyone must evacuate to Roosevelt Island, so it's all aboard the tram. Cars collide and hydrants explode below, the tram malfunctions, and, of course, you encounter Kong—32 feet tall and 13,000 pounds. He emits banana breath in your face and menaces passengers, dangling the tram over the East River. A great thrill—or just another day in New York.

✪ EARTHQUAKE, THE BIG ONE You board a BART train in San Francisco for a peaceful subway ride, but just as you pull into the Embarcadero station there's an earthquake—the big one, 8.3 on the Richter Scale! As you sit helplessly trapped, vast slabs of concrete collapse around you, a propane truck bursts into flames, a runaway train comes hurtling at you, and the station floods (60,000 gallons of water cascade down the steps).

GHOSTBUSTERS There are so many ghosts these days, Ghostbusters just has to sell franchises. Lewis Tully delivers a zany high-pressure sales pitch to the audience, and volunteers come up on stage and get slimed. Tully demonstrates flushing ghosts into the Ectoplasmic Container Chamber and discusses starter kits in three price ranges. But the ghosts, of course, break loose from Gozer's Temple and demons lunge at the audience.

NICKELODEON STUDIOS TOUR You'll tour the soundstages where Nick shows are produced, view concept pilots, visit the kitchen where gak and green slime are made, play typical show games, and try out new Sega video games. There's lots of audience participation, and a volunteer will get slimed.

WILD, WILD, WILD WEST SHOW Stunt people demonstrate falls from balconies, gun and whip fights, dynamite explosions, and other oater staples.

THE BEETLEJUICE GRAVEYARD REVUE Dracula, Wolfman, the Phantom of the Opera, Frankenstein and his bride, and Beetlejuice put on a funky—and very funny—rock musical with pyrotechnic special effects and MTV-style choreography.

THE FUNTASTIC WORLD OF HANNA-BARBERA This motion-simulator ride takes guests careening through the universe in a spaceship piloted by Yogi Bear to rescue Elroy Jetson. Prior to this wild ride, you'll learn about how cartoons are created. After it, in an interactive area, you can experiment with animation sound effects—boing! plop! splash!

ADDITIONAL ATTRACTIONS

Other park attractions include the **Gory, Gruesome, & Grotesque Horror Makeup Show** for a behind-the-scenes look at the transformation scenes from movies like *The Fly* and *The Exorcist;* **a tribute to Lucille Ball,** America's queen of comedy; **Fievel's Playland,** an innovative western-themed playground based on the Spielberg movie *An American Tail;* **"Murder She Wrote,"** which puts you on the set with Angela Lansbury and lets you make post-production executive decisions via computer; and **Alfred Hitchcock's 3-D Theatre,** a tribute to the "master of suspense" in which Tony Perkins narrates a reenactment of the famous shower scene from *Psycho,* and *The Birds,* as if it weren't scary enough, becomes an in-your-face 3-D movie.

Descendants of Lassie, Benji, Mr. Ed, and other animal superstars perform their famous pet tricks in the **Animal Actors Show.** During **Screen Test Home Video Adventure,** a director, crew, and team of "cinemagicians" put visitors on the screen in an exciting video production. And **Dynamite Nights Stuntacular,** a nightly show, combines death-defying stunts with a breathtaking display of fireworks.

More than 25 **shops** in the park sell everything from Lucy collectibles to Bates Motel towels, and **restaurants** run the gamut from Mel's Drive-In (of *American Graffiti* fame) to the Hard Rock Café, to Schwab's.

10 Sea World

This popular 200-plus-acre marine-life park, at 7007 Sea World Dr. (☎ **407/351-3600**), explores the mysteries of the deep in a format that combines entertainment with wildlife-conservation awareness. Its beautifully landscaped grounds, centering on a 17-acre lagoon, include flamingo and pelican ponds and a lush tropical rain forest. Shamu, a killer whale, is the star of the park.

A 1-day ticket costs $37.95 for ages 10 and over, $31.80 for children 3 to 9; a 2-day ticket is $42.95 for ages 10 and over, $36.80 for children 3 to 9; children 2 and under enter free. Parking costs $5 per vehicle, $7 for RVs and trailers.

The park is open from 9am to 7pm 365 days a year, later during summer and holidays when there are additional shows at night (call before you go). To get there, take I-4 to the Bee Line Expressway (Fla. 528) and follow the signs.

MAJOR ATTRACTIONS

✪ **WILD ARCTIC**   Enveloping guests in the beauty, exhilaration, and danger of a polar expedition, Wild Arctic combines a high-definition adventure film with flight-simulator technology to evoke breathtaking Arctic panoramas. After a hazardous flight over the frozen north, visitors emerge at a remote research base—home to polar bears (including star residents Klondike and Snow), seals, walruses, and white beluga whales.

✪ **MERMAIDS, MYTHS & MONSTERS**   This nighttime multimedia spectacular is a must-see, featuring fireworks and hologramlike imagery against a towering 60-foot screen of illuminated water. King Neptune rises majestically from the deep, as do terrifying sea serpents, storm-tossed ships, and frolicking mermaids.

BAYWATCH AT SEA WORLD   This Baywatch-themed adventure features watercraft, waterski, and aerial stunts along with musical numbers. Like the television series, the daring rescues are accompanied by messages on safety.

TERRORS OF THE DEEP   This exhibit houses 220 specimens of venomous and otherwise scary sea creatures in a tropical-reef habitat. Immense acrylic tunnels provide close encounters with slithery eels, three dozen sharks, barracudas, lionfish, and poisonous pufferfish. A theatrical presentation focusing on sharks puts across the message that pollution and uncontrolled commercial fishing make humankind the ultimate "terror of the deep."

✪ **MANATEES: THE LAST GENERATION?**   Today the Florida manatee is in danger of extinction, with as few as 2,000 remaining. Underwater viewing stations, innovative cinema techniques, and interactive displays combine to create an exciting format for teaching visitors about the manatee and its fragile ecosystem. Also on display here are hundreds of other native fish as well as alligators, turtles, and shore birds.

✪ **KEY WEST AT SEA WORLD**   This lush 5-acre tropical paradise of palms, hibiscus, and bougainvillea is set in a Caribbean village offering island cuisine, street vendors, and entertainers. The attraction comprises three naturalistic animal habitats: **Stingray Lagoon,** where visitors enjoy hands-on encounters with harmless southern diamond and cownose rays; **Dolphin Cove,** a massive habitat for bottlenose dolphins set up for visitor interaction; and **Sea Turtle Point,** home to threatened and endangered species such as green, loggerhead, and hawksbill sea turtles.

KEY WEST DOLPHIN FEST   At the Whale and Dolphin Stadium, a big partially covered open-air stadium, whales and Atlantic bottlenose dolphins perform flips and high jumps, swim at high speeds, twirl, swim on their backs, and give rides to trainers—all to the accompaniment of calypso music.

THE GOLD RUSH SKI SHOW   This wacky waterski exhibition features a cantankerous prospector and a talented team of cowboy waterskiers performing long-distance jumps, water ballet, flips, and backward and barefoot skiing. Their antics are accompanied by rollicking hoedown music and dance.

SEA WORLD THEATRE: WINDOW TO THE SEA   A multimedia presentation takes visitors behind the scenes at Sea World and explores a variety of marine subjects. These include an ocean dive in search of the rare six-gilled shark, a killer whale giving birth, babies born at Sea World (dolphins, penguins, and walruses), dolphin anatomy, and underwater geology.

SHAMU: WORLD FOCUS   Sea World trainers develop close relationships with killer whales, and in this partly covered open-air stadium they direct performances that are extensions of natural cetacean behaviors—twirling, waving tails and fins, rotating while swimming, and splashing the audience (sit pretty far back if you don't want to get soaked). The evening show here, called "Shamu: Night Magic," utilizes rock music and special lighting effects.

   Shamu: Close Up!, an adjoining exhibit, lets you get close to killer whales and talk to trainers; don't miss the underwater viewing area here.

✪ **PENGUIN ENCOUNTER**   This display of hundreds of penguins and alcids (including adorable babies) native to the Antarctic and Arctic regions also serves as a living laboratory for protecting and preserving polar life. On a moving walkway, you'll view six different penguin species congregating on rocks, nesting, and swimming underwater. There's an additional area for puffins and murres (flying Arctic cousins of penguins).

HOTEL CLYDE & SEAMORE   Two sea lions, along with a cast of otters and walruses, appear in this fishy *Fawlty Towers* comedy with a conservation theme.

ADDITIONAL ATTRACTIONS

The park's other attractions include: **Pacific Point Preserve,** a $2^1/_2$-acre naturalistic setting that duplicates the rocky northern Pacific Coast home of California sea lions and harbor and fur seals; a **Tropical Reef,** a tide pool of touchables, such as sea anemones, starfish, sea cucumbers, and sea urchins, plus a 160,000-galloon man-made **coral-reef aquarium,** home to 1,000 brightly hued tropical fish displayed in 17 vignettes of undersea life; and **Shamu's Happy Harbor,** an innovative 3-acre play area that has a four-story net tower with a 35-foot crow's-nest lookout, water cannons, remote-controlled vehicles, and a water maze.

A **Hawaiian dance troupe** entertains in an outdoor facility at Hawaiian Village; if you care to join in, grass skirts and leis are available. You can ascend 400 feet to the top of the **Sea World Sky Tower** for a revolving 360° panorama of the park and beyond (there's an extra charge of $3 per person for this activity). At the $5^1/_2$-acre **Anheuser-Busch Hospitality Center,** you can try free samples of Anheuser-Busch beers and snacks and stroll through the stables to watch the famous Budweiser Clydesdale horses being groomed (Anheuser-Busch owns Sea World).

The **Aloha! Polynesian Luau Dinner and Show,** a musical revue featuring South Seas food, song, and fire dancing, takes place nightly at 6:30pm. Park admission is not required. The cost is $29.65 for adults, $20.10 for children 8 to 12, $10.55 for kids 3 to 7, and free for kids 2 and under. Reservations are required (☎ **407/363-2559** or 800/227-8048).

There are, of course, numerous **restaurants,** snack bars, and food kiosks through-out the park, offering everything from chicken and biscuits to mesquite-grilled ribs. Dozens of **shops** carry marine-related gifts, as well as wilderness/conservation-oriented items.

And visitors can take 90-minute **behind-the-scenes tours** of the park's breeding, research, and training facilities and/or attend a 45-minute presentation about Sea World's animal behavior and training techniques. The cost for either tour is $5.95 for ages 10 and over, $4.95 for children 3 to 9, and free for children 2 and under.

11 More Area Attractions

KISSIMMEE

Kissimmee's sights are closest to the Walt Disney World area—about a 10- to 15-minute drive.

✪ **Cypress Island.** 1541 Scotty's Rd., Kissimmee. ☎ **407/935-9202.** Admission (all-day pass, including boatride) $24 adults, $17 children 3–12, free for children 2 and under. Call for rates for additional activities. Daily 9am–5pm. Take U.S. 192 East, make a right at Shady Lane, and follow the signs.

About 12 miles from Walt Disney World, you can get a feel for old-time Florida at Cypress Island, a 19th-century Seminole fort site located on Lake Tohopekaliga, the second-largest lake in Central Florida. Visitors reach the island via an excursion boat that offers an eco-tour narrative en route (there are frequent departures throughout the day).

On arrival, you can explore 2 miles of pristine signposted nature trail lined with ancient live oaks and cypress. Wildlife abounds. Emus, peacocks, Sicilian donkeys, Barbados mountain sheep, African pygmy goats, and llamas freely roam grassy savannahs. And avian residents include American bald eagles, osprey, blue herons, white egrets, cranes, ibis, hawks, and owls. Bring your camera and binoculars.

By prior reservation, you can also arrange airboat and swamp-buggy rides, waterskiing, jet skiing, tubing, and horseback riding here. And there are nighttime gator safaris (led by experienced guides) through marshy areas of the lake. On-premises facilities include picnic tables, a country store, and a concession that sells barbecued burgers and other fare.

Gatorland. 14501 S. Orange Blossom Trail (U.S. 441, between Osceola Pkwy. and Hunter's Creek Blvd.). ☎ **407/855-5496.** Admission $11.95 adults, $8.95 children 3–11, free for children 2 and under. Daily 8am–dusk. Free parking.

Founded in 1949 with a handful of alligators living in huts and pens, Gatorworld today features thousands of alligators and crocodiles on a 70-acre spread. Breeding pens, nurseries, and rearing ponds are situated throughout the park, which also displays monkeys, snakes, deer, Florida lake turtles, a Galapagos tortoise, and others. A 2,000-foot boardwalk winds through a cypress swamp and a 10-acre breeding marsh with an observation tower. Or you can take the free Gatorland Express Train around the park. Educational shows are scheduled throughout the day. An open-air restaurant, shop, and picnic facilities are on the premises.

Splendid China. Formosa Gardens Blvd. off W. Irlo Bronson Memorial Hwy. (U.S. 192, between Entry Point Blvd./Sherbeth Rd. and Black Lake Rd.). ☎ **407/396-7111.** Admission $23.55 adults, $13.90 children 5–12, free for children 4 and under. Daily from 9:30am; closing hours vary seasonally (call ahead). Free parking.

This 76-acre outdoor attraction features more than 60 miniaturized replicas of China's most noted man-made and natural wonders, spanning 5,000 years of history and culture. Park highlights include a half-mile-long copy of the 4,200-mile Great Wall, the Forbidden City's Imperial Palace, Tibet's sacred Potala Palace, carved Buddhist grottoes with statuary dating from A.D. 477 to 898, the Stone Forest of Yunan, and the Mongolian mausoleum of Genghis Khan. Live shows (acrobats, martial-arts demonstrations, storytelling, puppetry, and more) take place throughout the day; check your entertainment schedule. More than a dozen shops sell Chinese merchandise, and food concessions, a restaurant, and a Chinese cafeteria are on the premises. There's recorded commentary at each attraction.

Free trams circle the park, stopping at major attractions for pickup and dropoff. The 2-hour guided walking tours, departing several times a day, cost $5 per person (children 11 and under go free), and 1-hour golf-cart tours ($45 per six-person cart) depart every half hour.

INTERNATIONAL DRIVE

Like Kissimmee's attractions, these are about a 10- to 15-minute drive from the Disney area.

Ripley's Believe It or Not! Museum. 8201 International Dr. (1½ blocks south of Sand Lake Rd.). ☎ **407/345-0501.** Admission $9.95 adults, $6.95 children 4–11, free for children 3 and under. Daily 9am–11pm.

It's always fun to peruse a Ripley collection of oddities, curiosities, and fascinating artifacts from faraway places.

Wet 'n Wild. 6200 International Dr. (at Republic Dr.). ☎ **407/351-WILD** or 800/992-WILD. Admission $22.95 adults, $17.95 children 3–9, free for children 2 and under. Open daily; hours vary seasonally (call before you go). Free parking. Take I-4 East to Exit 30A and follow the signs.

When temperatures soar, head for this 25-acre water park and cool off. Among the highlights are **Fuji Flyer** (a six-story toboggan ride along 450 feet of banked curves),

The Surge (one of the longest, fastest multipassenger tube rides in the Southeast), **Bomb Bay** (enter a bomblike casing 76 feet in the air for a speedy vertical flight straight down to a target pool), **Raging Rapids** (a simulated white-water tubing adventure with a waterfall plunge), and **Lazy River** (a leisurely float trip). There are additional flumes, a vast wave pool, a large and innovative children's water playground, a sunbathing area, and a picnic area.

Food concessions are located throughout the park, and lockers and towels can be rented.

ORLANDO

All the following Orlando attractions are in close proximity to one another. Loch Haven Park is about 35 minutes by car from the Disney area. Plan lunch at **Buckets,** 1825 N. Mills Ave., just across the street from Loch Haven Park museums (☎ **407/896-4111**). It has tables overlooking Lake Rowena, some on an open-air deck, and serves American fare. You can probably also incorporate some Winter Park sights in the same day.

✪ **Harry P. Leu Gardens.** 1920 N. Forest Ave. (between Nebraska St. and Corrine Dr.). ☎ **407/246-2620.** Admission $3 adults, $1 children 6–16, free for children 5 and under. Gardens, daily 9am–5pm; Leu House tours, Sun–Mon 1–3:30pm, Tues–Sat 10am–3:30pm. Closed Christmas Day. Take I-4 East to Exit 43 (Princeton Street), follow Princeton Street east, make a right on Mills Avenue, turn left on Virginia Drive, and look for the gardens on your left.

At this delightful 50-acre botanical garden on the shores of Lake Rowena, meandering paths lead through forests of giant camphors, moss-draped oaks, and palms. Exquisite formal rose gardens display 75 varieties. Other highlights include orchids, desert plants, and perennials. Free 20-minute tours of the Leu House, built in 1888, take place on the hour and half hour. The house is a veritable decorative arts museum filled with Victorian, Empire, and Chippendale pieces. It takes about 2 hours to see the house and gardens.

Orange County Historical Museum. 812 E. Rollins St. (between Orange and Mills Aves.), in Loch Haven Park. ☎ **407/897-6350.** Admission $2 adults, $1.50 seniors 65 and over, $1 children 6–12, free for children 6 and under; admission by donation. Mon–Sat 9am–5pm, Sun noon–5pm. Closed New Year's Day, Martin Luther King Day, Memorial Day, July 4, Labor Day, Thanksgiving, and Christmas Day. Take I-4 East to Exit 43 (Princeton Street) and follow the signs to Loch Haven Park.

Sharing a building with the Orlando Science Center (details below), this museum focuses on Central Florida history, beginning with prehistoric cultures that existed here 12,000 years ago and including artifacts through to the early 20th century. Also on the premises is Fire Station No. 3, a restored 1926 firehouse.

Orlando Museum of Art. 2416 N. Mills Ave. (off U.S. 17/92), in Loch Haven Park. ☎ **407/ 896-4231.** Admission $4 adults, $2 children 4–11, free for children 3 and under. Museum, Tues–Sat 9am–5pm, Sun noon–5pm; Art Encounter, Tues–Fri and Sun noon–5pm, Sat 10am–5pm. Closed New Year's Day, Memorial Day, July 4, Labor Day, Thanksgiving, and Christmas Day. Free parking. Take I-4 East to Exit 43 (Princeton Street) and follow the signs to Loch Haven Park.

The museum displays its permanent collection of 19th- and 20th-century American art, pre-Columbian art, and African art on a rotating basis. "Art Encounter" is an interactive hands-on area for children. At this writing, a 31,000-square-foot expansion is under way, which will allow for major exhibitions.

Orlando Science Center. 810 E. Rollins St. (between Orange and Mills Aves.), in Loch Haven Park. ☎ **407/896-7151.** Admission $6.50 adults, $5.50 children 3–11, free for children 2 and under. Mon–Thurs and Sat 9am–5pm, Fri 9am–9pm, Sun noon–5pm. Closed

Thanksgiving and Christmas Day. Take I-4 East to Exit 43 (Princeton Street) and follow the signs to Loch Haven Park.

The Orlando Science Center specializes in hands-on interactive exhibits. Nature Works focuses on four Florida habitats—cypress swamp, sand pine scrub, sinkhole lake, and pine flatwood. There are free planetarium shows and science demonstrations throughout the day. Inquire about nighttime planetarium shows and laser-show rock concerts. *Note:* A vast new facility, which may be open by the time you read this, will quadruple current exhibit space.

WINTER PARK

This lakeside town is a lovely place to spend an afternoon. Visit the Morse Museum, cruise the lakes, and browse in the posh boutiques that line Park Avenue.

Plan to stay for dinner. A good choice is the plant-filled **Park Plaza Gardens,** 319 S. Park Ave., between Lyman and New England avenues (☎ **407/645-2475**). The fare is contemporary American, with Florida seafood specialties, the prices on the upscale side. If you want a less expensive choice, there are plenty of options on the same street.

To get to Winter Park from Orlando (about a 5-mile drive), continue east on I-4 to Fairbanks Avenue (Exit 45), turn right, and proceed about a mile, making a left on Park Avenue.

✪ **Charles Hosmer Morse Museum of American Art.** 445 Park Ave. (between Canton and Cole aves.). ☎ **407/645-5311.** Admission $3 adults, $1 students of any age. Tues–Sat 9:30am–4pm, Sun 1–4pm. Closed New Year's Day, Memorial Day, July 4, Labor Day, Thanksgiving, and Christmas Day.

This gem of a museum was founded by Hugh and Jeannette McKean in 1942 to display their peerless art collection, which includes 40 magnificent windows and 21 paintings by Louis Comfort Tiffany. In addition, there are windows ranging from creations by Frank Lloyd Wright to 15th- and 16th-century German masters; leaded lamps by Tiffany and Emile Gallé; paintings by John Singer Sargent, Maxfield Parrish, and others; and also jewelry, photographic works, and art nouveau furnishings.

Scenic Boat Tour. On the lake at the eastern end of Morse Blvd. ☎ **407/644-4056.** Admission $6 adults, $3 children 2–11, free for children under 2. Weather permitting, tours depart daily, every hour on the hour 10am–4pm. Closed Christmas Day.

Pontoons at this location take you for leisurely hour-long cruises on Winter Park's beautiful chain of natural lakes, winding through canals built by loggers at the turn of the century. You'll view magnificent lakeside mansions, pristine beaches, cypress swamps, and dozens of marsh birds—possibly even an American bald eagle. The captain regales passengers with local lore. It's an utterly delightful trip.

12 Outdoor Activities & Spectator Sports

OUTDOOR ACTIVITIES

In addition to the listings below, check out the Friday "Calendar" section in the *Orlando Sentinel.* It lists numerous outdoor activities in the Orlando area ranging from bass-fishing trips to bungee jumping.

Recreational facilities of every description abound in Walt Disney World and the surrounding area. These are especially accessible to guests at Disney-owned resorts, "official" hotels, and Fort Wilderness Resort and Campground, though many other large resort hotels also offer comprehensive facilities (see details in "Where to Stay," earlier in this chapter). The **Walt Disney World recreational facilities** (☎ **407/ 824-4321**) listed below are all open to the public, no matter where you're staying. Guests at Disney properties can inquire when making hotel reservations or at guest-services/concierge desks.

BIKING   Bike rentals (single- and multispeed bikes for adults, tandems, and children's bikes) are available from the **Bike Barn** (☎ **407/824-2742**) at Fort Wilderness Resort and Campground. Rates are $3 per hour, $10 per day. Both Fort Wilderness and Disney's Village Resort offer good bike trails.

BOATING   At the **Walt Disney World Village Marketplace Marina** (☎ **407/ 828-2204**) you can rent Water Sprites, canopy boats, and 20-foot pontoon boats.

The **Bike Barn** at Fort Wilderness (☎ **407/824-2742**) rents canoes ($4 per hour, $10 per day) and pedalboats ($5 per half hour, $8 per hour).

FISHING   Fishing excursions on **Lake Buena Vista**—mainly for largemouth bass—can be arranged up to 14 days in advance by calling 407/824-2204. No license is required. The fee is $137.50 for up to five people for 2 hours, those rates including gear and guide.

You can also rent cane poles and rods and reels at the **Bike Barn** (☎ **407/ 824-2742**) to fish in Fort Wilderness canals. No license is required.

GOLF   **Walt Disney World Resorts** (☎ **407/824-2270**) operates five championship 18-hole, par-72 golf courses and one 9-hole, par-36 walking course. All are open to the general public and offer pro shops, equipment rentals, and instruction. For tee times and information, call up to 7 days in advance (up to 30 days for Disney resort and "official" hotel guests). Call 407/W-DISNEY for information about golf packages.

HAYRIDES   The hay wagon departs from Pioneer Hall at **Fort Wilderness** nightly at 7 and 9:15pm for hour-long old-fashioned hayrides with singing, jokes, and games. The cost is $6 for adults, $4 for children 3 to 10, free for children 2 and under. Children 11 and under must be accompanied by an adult. No reservations—it's first-come, first-served.

HORSEBACK RIDING   Disney's Fort Wilderness Resort and Campground offers 50-minute scenic **trail rides** (☎ **407/824-2832**) daily, with four to six rides per day. The cost is $17 per person. Children must be at least 9 years old. Call for information and reservations up to 5 days in advance.

TENNIS   There are 17 lighted tennis courts located throughout the Disney properties. Most are free and available on a first-come, first-served basis. If you're willing to pay for court time, courts can be reserved up to several months in advance at the **Contemporary** (☎ **407/824-3578**) or the **Grand Floridian** (☎ **407/824-2433**). Both charge $12 per hour; you can also reserve lesson times with resident pros. There's a large pro shop at the Contemporary where equipment can be rented.

SPECTATOR SPORTS

The Orlando Centroplex administers six public sports and entertainment facilities in the downtown area. These include three major sporting arenas: the Florida Citrus Bowl, the Orlando Arena, and Tinker Field.

The **Florida Citrus Bowl,** 1 Citrus Bowl Place, at West Church and Tampa streets (☎ **407/896-2442** for information, 407/839-3900 to charge tickets), seats 70,000 people for major sporting events including the annual Comp USA Florida Citrus Bowl game, college football games, and NFL preseason games. Parking is $5. Take

I-4 East to the East-West Expressway and head west to U.S. 441, make a left on Church Street, and follow the signs.

The **Orlando Magic** plays at the **Orlando Arena,** 600 W. Amelia St., between I-4 and Parramore Avenue (☎ **407/849-2020** for information, 407/839-3900 to charge tickets). Tickets to Magic games (about $13 to $50) have to be acquired far in advance; they usually sell out by September before the season starts. If money is no object, perhaps a local ticket broker can work a miracle for you. Parking at the arena costs $5 (for up-to-the-minute parking information, tune your car radio to 1620 AM). Take I-4 East to Amelia Avenue, turn left at the traffic light at the bottom of the off-ramp, and follow the signs. Call to find out about other sporting events on here when you're in town.

From April to September, the **Orlando Cubs** (the Chicago Cubs' Class AA Southern League affiliate) play at **Tinker Field,** which adjoins the Citrus Bowl at 287 S. Tampa Ave., between Colonial Drive (Fla. 50) and Gore Street (☎ **407/245-CUBS** for information and to charge tickets). Tickets to Cubs games run $3 to $7. Parking is $2. Take I-4 East to the East-West Expressway, head west to U.S. 441, make a left on Church Street, and follow the signs.

Spring training for the **Houston Astros** begins in late February, with exhibition games through March or early April at the **Osceola County Stadium,** 1000 Bill Beck Blvd., in Kissimmee (☎ **407/933-5400**). Tickets are $5 to $6. Call for details and tickets.

The **Nestlé Invitational Golf Tournament** is held in mid-March at Arnold Palmer's Bay Hill Club, 9000 Bay Hill Blvd. (☎ **407/876-2888** for details). And another stop on the PGA tour is October's **Walt Disney World Oldsmobile Golf Classic** (☎ **407/824-4321**). Daily ticket prices range from $8 to $15. Call for details.

13 Walt Disney World & Orlando After Dark

My hat's off to those of you who, after a long day of traipsing around amusement parks, still have the energy to venture out at night in search of entertainment. You'll find plenty to do. And this being kids' world, many evening shows are geared to families.

Check the "Calendar" section of Friday's *Orlando Sentinel* for up-to-the-minute details on local clubs, visiting performers, concerts, and events. It has hundreds of listings.

Tickets to many performances are handled by **Ticketmaster** (☎ 407/839-3900 to charge tickets).

WALT DISNEY WORLD DINNER SHOWS

Two distinctly different dinner shows are hosted by Walt Disney World. Other nighttime park options include SpectroMagic, fireworks, and IllumiNations (see Sections 4 to 8, earlier in this chapter, for details).

Hoop-Dee-Doo Musical Revue. Disney's Fort Wilderness Resort and Campground. 3520 N. Fort Wilderness Trail. ☎ **407/WDW-DINE.** Reservations required. Admission $36 adults, $18 children 3–11, free for children 2 and under; taxes and gratuities extra. Shows daily at 5, 7:15, and 9:30pm. Free parking.

Fort Wilderness's rustic log-beamed Pioneer Hall is the setting for this 2-hour down-home musical revue. It's a high-energy show, with corny vaudeville jokes, rousing songs, and lots of good-natured audience participation. During the show you'll chow down on an all-you-can-eat barbecue dinner: smoked ribs, country-fried chicken, corn on the cob, fresh-baked bread, and a big slab of strawberry shortcake for dessert, beverages included. If you catch an early show, stick around for the Electrical Water Pageant at 9:45pm, which can be viewed from the Fort Wilderness Beach.

Polynesian Luau Dinner Show. At Disney's Polynesian Resort, 1600 Seven Seas Dr. ☎ **407/ WDW-DINE.** Reservations required. $33 adults, $25 ages 12–20, $17 children 3–11, free for children 2 and under; taxes and gratuities extra. Shows daily at 6:45 and 9:30pm. Free self- and valet parking.

This delightful 2-hour dinner show features a colorfully costumed cast of entertainers from New Zealand, Tahiti, Hawaii, and Samoa performing authentic ceremonial dances on a flower-bedecked stage. There's even a Hawaiian/Polynesian fashion show. It all takes place in a heated open-air theater (dress for the weather). The meal, served family style, includes a big platter of fresh island fruits, half a barbecued chicken, corn on the cob, vegetables, potatoes, cinnamon bread, beverages, and a tropical ice-cream sundae. There's also a 4:30pm version daily (see "Meals with Disney Characters" in Section 3 of this chapter).

ENTERTAINMENT COMPLEXES: PLEASURE ISLAND & CHURCH STREET STATION

Pleasure Island. In Walt Disney World, adjacent to Walt Disney World Village. ☎ **407/ 934-7781.** Free before 7pm, $14.95 after 7pm (admission included in the 5-Day World-Hopper Pass). Clubs, daily 8pm–2am; shops, daily 10am–1am. Valet parking $5, free self-parking.

This Walt Disney World theme park is a 6-acre complex of nightclubs, restaurants, shops, and movie theaters; for a single admission price, you can enjoy a night of club-hopping till the wee hours. The park is designed to suggest an abandoned waterfront industrial district with clubs in "converted" ramshackle lofts, factories, and warehouses, but the streets are festive with brightly colored lights and balloons, and you can feel perfectly secure about teenage kids here for the evening. They must be 18 to get in alone; younger teens must be accompanied by a parent. You'll be given a map and show schedule when you enter the park.

The on-premises clubs come and go. At this writing they include the **Island Jazz Company,** a big barnlike club featuring contemporary and traditional live jazz; **Mannequins Dance Palace,** a high-energy dance club with a large rotating floor and a DJ playing contemporary tunes at an ear-splitting decibel level (you must be 21 to get in); and the **Neon Armadillo Music Saloon,** with country bands nightly (country dance lessons are given on Sunday from 7 to 8pm), and sometimes name stars come in and take the stage. You can order southwestern fare.

The most unusual of Pleasure Island's clubs—and my personal favorite—is the **Adventurers Club,** chock-full of artifacts. In the eerie Mask Room, more than 100 masks move their eyes, jeer, and make odd pronouncements. Improvisational comedy shows take place throughout the evening in the main salon, and diverse 20-minute cabaret shows in the library. You could easily hang out here all night sipping potent tropical drinks in the library and at the bar.

The **Comedy Warehouse**—another of my favorites—has a rustic interior with tiered seating. A very talented troupe performs improvisational comedy based on audience suggestions. There are five shows a night, and bar drinks are available. Arrive early.

Live bands play classic rock at the **Rock & Roll Beach Club,** which has bars on all three floors. The first level contains the dance floor; the second and third offer air hockey, pool tables, pinball, video games, darts, and a pizza and beer stand. There's also **8 Trax,** a 1970s-style club with about 50 TV monitors airing shows and videos over the dance floor. A DJ plays disco music, and guests play Twister.

In addition, live bands—including occasional big-name groups—play the **West End Plaza** outdoor stage and the **Hub Stage;** check your schedule for show times. You can star in your own music video at **SuperStar Studios.** There are carnival games, a video-game arcade, a Velcro wall, and an Orbitron (originally developed for NASA, it lets you experience weightlessness). And every night features a midnight **New Year's Eve celebration** with fireworks and confetti. **Shops and eateries** are found throughout the park. **Planet Hollywood** (see "Where to Eat," earlier in this chapter) is adjacent.

Pleasure Island will soon double in size, adding restaurants and entertainment venues.

Church Street Station. 129 W. Church St. (off I-4 between Garland and Orange aves.), in downtown Orlando. ☎ **407/422-2434.** Free before 5pm, $16.95 after 5pm; always free to restaurants, the Exchange Shopping Emporium, and the Midway game area. Clubs, daily until 2am; shops, daily until 11pm. Valet parking, at Church Street and Garland Avenue, $6; several parking lots are nearby (call for specifics). Take I-4 East to Exit 38 (Anderson Street), stay in the left lane, and follow the blue signs. Most hotels offer transportation to and from Church Street.

Though not part of Walt Disney World, Church Street Station in downtown Orlando operates on a similar principle to Pleasure Island. Occupying a cobblestone city block lined with turn-of-the-century buildings, it, too, is a shopping/dining/nightclub complex offering an evening of diverse entertainment for a single admission price. There are 20 live shows nightly; consult your show schedule on entering.

Highlights include **Rosie O'Grady's Good Time Emporium,** an 1890s saloon, where Dixieland bands and singing waiters entertain nightly. Light fare is available. **Apple Annie's Courtyard** evokes a Victorian tropical garden, where patrons sip potent tropical fresh-fruit and ice-cream drinks while listening to folk and bluegrass music.

The plush interior of **Lili Marlene's Aviator's Pub & Restaurant** is embellished with World War I memorabilia and accoutrements from an 1850 Rothschild Paris town house. The menu features premium aged steaks and fresh seafood. The whimsical **Phineas Phogg's Balloon Works** is a high-energy club playing loud, pulsating music. Every Wednesday from 6:30 to 7:30pm beers cost just 5¢ here. No one under 21 is admitted.

The stunning trilevel **Cheyenne Saloon and Opera House** is constructed of golden oak lumber from a century-old Ohio barn. Genuine western art is displayed throughout, including 11 Remington sculptures. Entertainment ranges from country bands to clogging exhibitions. The menu features steaks, barbecued chicken and ribs, and hickory-smoked brisket, served with buttermilk biscuits and honey-and-bourbon baked beans.

The ornate **Orchid Garden Ballroom** is the setting for an oldies dance club. A DJ plays rock 'n' roll classics interspersed with live bands. As the evening progresses, so do the musical decades. **Crackers Oyster Bar,** a cozy late 1800s–style dining room, features fresh Florida seafood, along with more than 50 imported beers.

You can rent a **horse-drawn carriage** out front for a drive around the downtown area and Lake Eola. And **hot-air balloon flights** can be arranged (☎ 407/841-8787).

MAJOR CONCERT HALLS & AUDITORIUMS

Three large entertainment facilities, administered by the Orlando Centroplex, host most big-name performers playing the Orlando area.

The **Florida Citrus Bowl,** 1610 W. Church St., at Tampa Street (☎ **407/ 849-2020** for information, 407/839-3900 to charge tickets), with 70,000 seats, is the largest. This is the setting for major rock concerts and headliners. To reach the Citrus Bowl, take I-4 East to the East-West Expressway and head west to U.S. 441; make a left on Church Street and follow the signs. Parking is $5.

The 17,500-seat **Orlando Arena,** at 600 W. Amelia St., between I-4 and Parramore Avenue (☎ **407/849-2020** for information, 407/839-3900 to charge tickets), also hosts major performers in addition to an array of family-oriented entertainment: the Ringling Bros. and Barnum & Bailey Circus every January, Tour of World Figure-Skating Champions in April or May, and *Walt Disney's World on Ice* in September. To reach the arena, take I-4 East to Amelia Avenue, turn left at the traffic light at the bottom of the off-ramp, and follow signs. Parking is $5.

The area's major cultural venue is the **Bob Carr Performing Arts Centre,** 401 W. Livingston St., between I-4 and Parramore Avenue (☎ **407/849-2020** for information, 407/839-3900 to charge tickets). Concert prices vary with performers; ballet tickets are $15 to $35; opera tickets, $12 to $45; the Broadway Series, $24.50 to $46.50. This 2,500-seat facility is home to the **Orlando Opera Company** and the **Southern Ballet Theater,** both of which have October-to-May seasons. The **Orlando Broadway Series** (September to May) features original-cast Broadway shows. Also featured at the Bob Carr are concerts and comedy shows. To get here, take I-4 East to Amelia Avenue, turn left at the traffic light at the bottom of the off-ramp, and follow the signs. Parking is $5.

14 A Side Trip to Cypress Gardens

Founded in 1936, **Cypress Gardens** came into being as a 16-acre public garden along the banks of Lake Eloise, with cypress-wood-block pathways and thousands of tropical and subtropical plants. It's located on Fla. 540 at Cypress Gardens Boulevard (40 miles southwest of Walt Disney World), in Winter Haven (☎ **941/324-2111** or 800/282-2123).

Today it has grown to over 200 acres, with ponds and lagoons, waterfalls, classic Italian fountains, topiary, bronze sculptures, manicured lawns, and—most notably—ancient cypress trees shrouded in Spanish moss forming a backdrop to ever-changing floral displays of 8,000 varieties of plants from more than 90 countries. Southern belles in Scarlett O'Hara costumes stroll the grounds or sit on benches under parasols in idyllic tree-shaded nooks.

In the late winter and early spring, more than 20 varieties of bougainvillea, 40 of azalea, and hundreds of kinds of roses burst into bloom. Crape myrtles, magnolias, and gardenias perfume the late-spring air, while brilliant birds of paradise, hibiscus, and jasmine brighten the summer landscape. And in winter, the golden rain trees, floss silk trees, and camellias of autumn give way to millions of colorful chrysanthemums and red, white, and pink poinsettias.

Strolling the grounds is, of course, the main attraction (there are over 2 miles of winding botanical paths, and half the park's acreage is devoted to floral displays), but this being Central Florida, it's not the only one. Several shows are scheduled throughout the day (check your schedule upon entering the park). The world-famous **Greatest American Ski Team** performs on Lake Eloise in a show augmented by an awesome hang-gliding display. The breathtaking **Moscow on Ice Live!** is the Russian answer to America's Ice Capades. **Variété Internationale** features specialty acts from all over the world. An enchanting exhibit called **Wings of Wonder** surrounds visitors with more than 1,000 brightly colored free-flying butterflies in a 5,500-square-foot Victorian-style glass conservatory. **Electric boats** navigate a maze of lushly landscaped canals in the original botanical gardens area. You can ascend 153 feet to the **Island in the Sky** for a panoramic vista of the gardens and a beautiful chain of Central Florida lakes. **Carousel Cove,** with eight kiddie rides and arcade games, centers on an ornate turn-of-the-century–style carousel. It adjoins another kid pleaser, **Cypress Junction,** an elaborately landscaped model railroad that travels over 1,100 feet of track with up to 20 trains moving at one time. **Cypress Roots,** a museum of park memorabilia, displays photographs of famous visitors (Elvis on waterskis, Tiny Tim tiptoeing through the roses) and airs ongoing showings of *Easy to Love* starring Esther Williams (it was filmed here). Wind up your visit with a relaxing 30-minute narrated **pontoon cruise** on scenic Lake Eloise, past virgin forest, bulrushes, and beautiful shoreline homes (there's a $4-per-person charge).

Restaurants are on the premises, as is a picnic area. Admission is $27.95 for ages 10 and over, $17.45 for children 3 to 9; free for children 2 and under; discounts are offered for seniors. It's open daily from 9:30am to 5:30pm, with extended hours during peak seasons. To get there, take I-4 West to U.S. 27 south, and proceed west to Fla. 540 to Cypress Gardens Boulevard in Winter Haven; parking is free.

12

Northeast Florida

by Rena Bulkin

When most people think of Florida, white-sand beaches, snorkling, or deep-sea fishing may come to mind, but few realize that Florida was the place where North American history first began. The first European settlement in America was not Jamestown, Virginia (1607), or Plymouth Plantation (1620), but St. Augustine, Florida. In 1513 Juan Ponce de León discovered and named the Florida coast, and by 1565 the Spanish had settled 1,000 people in St. Augustine and crushed a French attempt to make a similar claim. In Jacksonville you can discover a little-known facet of Florida history at reconstructed Fort Caroline, site of the early brief and failed French colony. In both these popular beach-resort cities, you can visit sites that evoke the earliest European incursions into the New World.

Daytona Beach is famous for a more recent kind of history—automotive speed. It's the "World Center of Racing," and home to the Daytona International Speedway. And, of course, the town is synonymous with the well-known spring-break vacation frenzy.

Sprawling high-rise Jacksonville is one of Florida's major urban areas. And Gainesville is a pretty college town, where football fever rages—the kind of American small town that evokes instant nostalgia.

Throughout the area you'll find nature preserves where you can explore beautiful unspoiled woodlands, tranquil marshes, and ancient Timucuan sites.

SPECIAL EVENTS & FESTIVALS IN NORTHEAST FLORIDA

FEBRUARY   Nineteen days of **Speedweeks** events (taking place the first 3 weeks of February) get under way in Daytona, with a series of races that draw the top names in NASCAR stock-car racing, all culminating in the **Daytona 500**. All events take place at the Daytona International Speedway (☎ **904/253-7223** for ticket information). For the Daytona 500, especially, tickets must be purchased even a year in advance. They go on sale January 1 of the prior year.

MARCH   Bike Week / Camel Motorcycle Week (☎ **904/255-0145**) is an international gathering of motorcycle enthusiasts for 11 days early in March. In addition to major races held at Daytona International Speedway (featuring the world's best road racers,

What's Special About Northeast Florida

Architecture

- Historic houses, constructed of tabby (a kind of primitive concrete made of sand, water, and crushed oyster shells) and a similar but natural shell rock called *coquina*.

Museums

- The Lightner Museum in St. Augustine, a vast collection of Victoriana in a converted turn-of-the-century Spanish Renaissance–style hotel.
- The Cummer Museum of Art in Jacksonville, with a permanent collection comprising works from 2000 B.C. to the present.

Sports

- Daytona International Speedway, the "World Center of Racing."
- Jacksonville Jaguar games at the Gator Bowl and Gator games at the University of Florida in Gainesville.
- Canoeing and kayaking on the Santa Fe River and beyond, from a put-in point at High Springs near Gainesville.

Florida Wilderness & Wildlife

- Dolphins and dozens of sea birds offshore near St. Augustine.
- The Theodore Roosevelt Area at Fort Caroline National Memorial in Jacksonville.

For Kids

- Art Connections at the Cummer Museum of Art in Jacksonville, an innovative art-themed play area with holograms, computer art stations, and other hands-on exhibits
- The Museum of Science & History of Jacksonville, focusing on science and North Florida history, with dozens of hands-on activities for children, plus planetarium shows.
- Jacksonville Zoological Gardens, a lushly landscaped zoo.
- Marineland of Florida in St. Augustine, for close encounters with dolphins and other marine denizens.

motocrossers, and dirt trackers), there are motorcycle shows, beach parties, and the Annual Motorcycle Parade, with thousands of riders.

For 3 weeks in March, college students from all over the United States and Canada flock to Daytona Beach for **spring break**—endless partying, wet T-shirt and bikini contests, free concerts, volleyball tournaments, and more.

During **Gatornationals** (☎ 352/395-3100), a 4-day event taking place during the third week in March, the world's fastest dragsters compete for a $1-million-plus purse at the Gainesville Raceway.

In late March, **The Players Championship,** at the Tournament Players Club in Ponte Vedra Beach (☎ 904/285-7888), is a major golf event, held at the toughest course on the PGA tour.

Also in late March (sometimes in early April), the **Spring Speedway Spectacular,** a car show and swap meet at the Daytona International Speedway (☎ 904/255-7355), features a wide variety of collector vehicles. Admission is charged.

MAY   Riverwalk Arts & Crafts Festival (☎ 904/396-4900), held on Mother's Day, is a local biggie in Jacksonville, with lots of food, crafts booths, and live entertainment. Admission is free.

During the **Greater Daytona Beach Striking Fish Tournament** on Memorial Day weekend (☎ 904/255-0415), some 250 boats from all over the Southeast compete for more than $75,000 in cash and prizes in seven fishing categories.

JUNE   Florida's official state play, ✪ *Cross & Sword,* tells the story of the founding of St. Augustine using drama, dance, music, stage combat, and special effects. Performances run from about mid-June to early September, Tuesday to Sunday at 8:30pm in the outdoor amphitheater of Anastasia State Park, on Fla. A1A South (☎ 904/471-1967). Tickets are $12 for adults, $11 for seniors, $6 for children 4 to 12, free for children 2 and under.

On the third Saturday in June, for the **Spanish Night Watch Ceremony** (☎ 904/ 824-9550) actors in period dress lead a torchlight procession through St. Augustine's Spanish Quarter and reenact the closing of the city gates with music and pageantry.

JULY   The **Pepsi 400** race, marking the halfway point in the NASCAR Winston Cup Series for stock cars, is held the first Saturday in July at 11am at the Daytona International Speedway (☎ 904/253-7223).

The **Florida International Festival** (☎ 904/257-7790), a 17-day musical event taking place in Daytona every other year (in odd-numbered years), features concerts by major classical and pop musicians, as well as preconcert lectures, jazz bands, ballet, and special concerts for children. Events are scheduled at the Peabody Auditorium, Ocean Center, and other local venues in late July, possibly early August. Call for details and ticket information.

OCTOBER   During 4 days in mid-October, road-racing stars compete at the Daytona International Speedway in the **CCS Motorcycle Championship Biketoberfest** (☎ 904/253-7223 for ticket information, 800/854-1235 for additional Biketoberfest activities—parties, parades, concerts, and more).

Mid-October also brings the **Jacksonville Jazz Festival** (☎ 904/353-7770). This free 3-day nonstop music event in Metropolitan Park features major artists.

NOVEMBER   The **Daytona Beach Fall Speedway Spectacular** (☎ 904/ 255-7355), featuring the Annual Turkey Rod Run, is the Southeast's largest combined car show and swap meet, with thousands of street rods and classic vehicles on display and for sale. It takes place at the International Speedway on Thanksgiving weekend. Admission is charged.

Boaters decorate their craft with colored lights and parade down the St. Johns River in the **Jacksonville Light Parade** (☎ 904/396-4900), held November 26. The event also includes fireworks, ice-skating exhibitions, marching bands, and live entertainment.

DECEMBER   On the first Saturday in December, the **Grand Illumination Ceremony** (☎ 904/824-9550) is held in St. Augustine. A torchlight procession from Government House through the Spanish Quarter features reenactments of British colonial customs, encampments, 18th-century music, crafts demonstrations, and cannon firings.

Throughout the month, **Christmas festivities** in St. Augustine include caroling, an 18th-century bazaar, a performance of Handel's *Messiah,* a Christmas parade, and more. The entire city is lit by thousands of lights from mid-November to New Year's.

The **World Karting Association Enduro World Championships,** the biggest karting event in the country, takes place between Christmas and New Year's at the Daytona International Speedway (☎ 904/253-7223).

And between Christmas and New Year's, two of the country's top college football teams battle it out in the **Gator Bowl** (☎ 904/630-3906 for information about the game, 904/353-3309 to charge tickets or 904/353-1188 to find out about postgame festivities at Jacksonville Landing).

1 Cape Canaveral & the Space Center

VISITING THE KENNEDY SPACE CENTER/SPACEPORT USA

NASA's ✪ **John F. Kennedy Space Center** (☎ 407/452-2121) has been the launch site for all U.S. manned space missions since 1968. Astronauts departed earth at this site en route to the most famous "small step" in history—man's first voyage to the moon.

Note: A massive renovation in visitor facilities—under way at this writing and due for completion by the end of 1997—will dramatically alter the experience, making it more of an interactive adventure.

At the **Visitor Center,** the past, present, and future of space exploration are explored on bus tours of the facility and in movie presentations and numerous exhibits. It takes at least a full day to see and do everything. Arrive early and make your first stop at Information Central (it opens at 9am) to pick up a schedule of events and a map and for help in planning your day. Nearby are space-related exhibits and interactive computers.

For now, visitors take the 2-hour **Red Tour,** boarding a double-decker bus to explore the complex. At the first stop—in a simulated launch-control firing room—visitors view a film about the Apollo 11 mission. The countdown, launch, and planting of a flag on the moon are thrilling even at secondhand. The tour continues to the Complex 39 Space Shuttle launch pads (where a stop is made for exploration) and the massive Vehicle Assembly Building where Space Shuttles are assembled. Visitors get a close-up look at an actual Apollo/Saturn V moon rocket, America's largest and most powerful launch vehicle. Also on view are massive six-million-pound Crawler Transporters that carry Space Shuttles to their launch pads. Tours depart at regular intervals beginning at 9:45am, with the last tour leaving late in the afternoon (call for details). Purchase tickets at the Ticket Pavilion as soon as you arrive. *Note:* Itinerary variations may occur subject to launch schedules.

Though most visitors are sated by the Red Tour, a second 2-hour **Blue Tour** (same hours) visits Cape Canaveral Air Station. On this tour, you'll see where America's first satellites and astronauts were launched in the Mercury and Gemini programs, view launch pads currently being used for unmanned launches, visit the original site of Mission Control, and stop at the Air Force Space Museum, which houses a unique collection of missiles and space memorabilia.

Satellites and You is a 45-minute voyage through a simulated future space station. In Disneyesque fashion, the attraction combines animatronic characters with innovative audiovisual techniques to explain satellites and their uses.

In the **Galaxy Center** building, three spectacular IMAX films projected on 5½-story screens are shown continually throughout the day. The Galaxy Center also houses a NASA art exhibit, a walk-through replica of a future Space Station, a manned research laboratory that will be orbiting the earth by 1999, and an exhibit called "Spinoffs from Space," which displays some of the 30,000 spinoffs that have resulted from space program research, including improved consumer products ranging from football helmets to cordless tools.

The **Gallery of Manned Spaceflight,** a large museum, houses hardware and models relating to significant space projects and offers interesting exhibits on lunar exploration and geology.

The **Spaceport Theater** presents films and live demonstrations on a variety of topical space-related subjects. The **Astronauts Memorial,** a $42^1/_2$- by 50-foot black granite "Space Mirror" dedicated on May 9, 1991, honors the 16 American astronauts who have lost their lives in the line of duty. Aboard *Explorer,* a full-size replica of a Space Shuttle orbiter, visitors can experience the working environment of NASA astronauts. And the **Rocket Garden** displays eight actual U.S. rockets.

Admission to the center is free, but tickets for either bus tour described above cost $7 for adults, $4 for children 3 to 11, and free for children 2 and under. IMAX film tickets are $4 for adults, $2 for children 3 to 11, and free for children 2 and under. The center is open daily from 9am to dusk (closed Christmas Day). To get there from Orlando, take the Beeline Expressway (Fla. 528) east, and where the road divides, go left on Fla. 407, make a right on Fla. 405, and follow the signs; parking is free.

If you'd like to see a launch, call 407/452-2121 for current launch information, ext. 260 to make reservations. Tickets for viewing cost $7 for adults, $4 for children 3 to 11, free for children 2 and under. You can reserve tickets up to 7 days before a launch, but they must be picked up at least 2 days before the launch. A special bus takes observers to a site just 6 miles from the launch pad.

CANAVERAL NATIONAL SEASHORE

Adjoining the grounds of the Kennedy Space Center, **Canaveral National Seashore** (☎ 904/428-3384 for information) is a protected stretch of coastline that's a magnet for birdwatchers, who have spotted hundreds of species of shore birds and waterfowl here. There's a visitor center on Fla. A1A, and wooden boardwalks lead from each of the parking areas to the pristine beaches, perfect for swimming and sunbathing. A marked hiking trail leads to an ancient Native American mound, where there are picnic tables. Note that it's forbidden to walk on the dunes or pick the sea grass. The preserve also contains Mosquito Lagoon, where you might spot alligators and sea turtles.

2 Daytona Beach

50 miles NE of Orlando, 260 miles N of Miami, 89 miles S of Jacksonville

The self-proclaimed "World's Most Famous Beach" is even more celebrated as the "Birthplace of Speed" and the "World Center of Racing." It has been a mecca for car-racing enthusiasts since the days when automobiles were called horseless carriages. Early automobile magnates Ransom E. Olds, Henry Ford, the Stanley brothers (of steamer fame), and Louis Chevrolet—along with motor-mad millionaires like the Vanderbilts, Astors, and Rockefellers—wintered in Florida and raced their vehicles on the hard-packed sand beach. The first competition, in 1902, was between Olds and gentleman racer Alexander Winton, who worked up to the then-impressive speed of 57 miles an hour. By 1904 a Daytona Beach event called the Winter Speed Carnival was drawing participants from all over the world. And 3 years later, Fred Marriott wrapped a mile of piano wire around the boiler of his souped-up Stanley Steamer to keep it from blowing up, and raced the course at a spectacular 197 m.p.h. At the end of the stretch he crashed, just as spectacularly, into the pounding surf. He emerged uninjured, but after the accident the Stanley brothers quit racing their steam-driven cars, and gas engines became more prominent.

Many who were to become famous first tested their ideas on the sands of Daytona Beach. Glenn Curtiss, the father of naval aviation, raced motorcycles here. And Sir Malcolm Campbell, a millionaire English sportsman, raced a car powered by an aircraft engine in 1928, reaching a speed of over 206 m.p.h.; in later years he set the

Daytona Beach

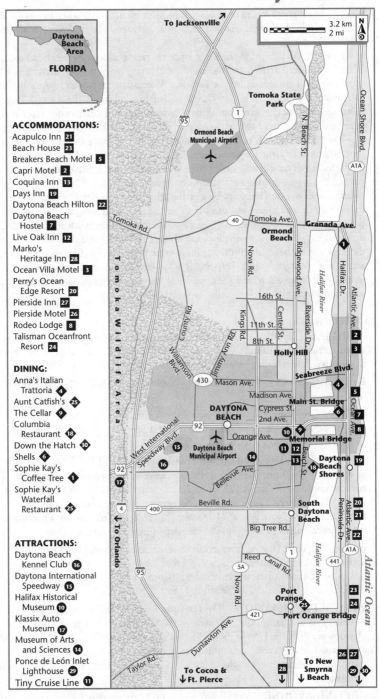

ultimate beach speed record of 276.8 m.p.h. Most of these early beach events, by the way, were individual speed trials rather than actual races. The final speed trials were held in 1935.

The year 1936 ushered in the era of stock-car racing with a new beach racecourse, a host of daredevil drivers, and thousands of cheering fans. In 1947, driver and race promoter Bill France founded the National Association for Stock Car Auto Racing (NASCAR), headquartered at Daytona Beach. Today it's the world's largest motorsports authority, sanctioning the Daytona 500 and other major races at the International Speedway and tracks throughout the United States. The last stockcar race on the beach took place in 1958. A year later, France's dream of a multi-motorsports facility, the Daytona International Speedway, was realized. At press time, the Speedway is completing an $18-million expansion to include **Daytona USA**—a state-of-the-art motorsports entertainment attraction.

Of course, you don't have to be a racing aficionado to enjoy Daytona. It has 23 miles of sandy beach, and you can still drive and park—but not race—on the sand; the maximum speed allowed is 10 m.p.h. The town is filled with college students during spring break—the annual beach blanket Babylon—and during bike events thousands of leather-clad motorcycle buffs make the scene. But barring spring break and major speedway events, Daytona is a laid-back beach resort, offering boating, tennis, golf, water sports, and the opportunity to stroll the sands, swim, and soak up some sunshine.

ESSENTIALS

ARRIVING   By Plane   American, Continental, Delta, and USAir fly into **Daytona Beach International Airport** (☎ 904/248-8030). A taxi from the airport to most beach hotels runs between $8 and $12.

By Train   The closest **Amtrak** station (☎ 800/USA-RAIL) is in DeLand, 23 miles southwest of Daytona Beach.

By Bus   Greyhound buses pull into a very centrally located terminal at 138 S. Ridgewood Ave. (U.S. 1) between International Speedway Boulevard and Magnolia Avenue (☎ 904/255-7076, or 800/231-2222).

From Orlando, **Daytona-Orlando Transit Service (DOTS)** (☎ 904/257-5411, or 800/231-1965) provides van transport between the two cities. They offer 11 round-trips daily. The fare is $26 for adults one-way, $46 round-trip; children 11 and under 12 are charged half price. The service brings passengers to the company's terminal at 1598 N. Nova Rd., at 11th Street (LPGA Boulevard), or, for an additional fee, to beach hotels. In Orlando, the vans depart from the airport.

By Car   If you're coming from north or south, take I-95 and head east on International Speedway Boulevard (U.S. 92). From Tampa or Orlando, take I-4 east and follow the Daytona Beach signs to I-95 North to U.S. 92. From northwestern Florida, take I-10 East to I-95 South to U.S. 92.

VISITOR INFORMATION   The **Daytona Beach Area Convention & Visitors Bureau,** 126 E. Orange Ave., just west of the Silver Beach Bridge (P.O. Box 910), Daytona Beach, FL 32115 (☎ 904/255-0415, or 800/854-1234), can help you with information on attractions, accommodations, dining, and events. Call in advance for maps and brochures, or visit the office when in town. There's also a branch at the Speedway.

GETTING AROUND   VOTRAN, Volusia County's public transit system, runs **buses** throughout major areas of town Monday to Saturday from 6am to 7:30pm and on Sunday from 6:30am to 7pm. Adults pay 75¢, children under 17 and seniors pay 35¢, and children 5 and under accompanied by an adult ride free.

January to September, Votran also operates turn-of-the-century–style **trolleys** between Granada Boulevard and Dunlawton Avenue along Fla. A1A Monday to Saturday from noon to midnight; the fares are the same as bus fares. Call 904/761-7700 for bus or trolley routing information.

You can drive and park directly on the beach. There's a $5 access fee February to November; the rest of the year it's free.

CITY LAYOUT

Daytona Beach is bordered by the Atlantic Ocean on its east coast, and the Halifax River flows north to south through the middle of the city. There are actually four little towns along its beach: **Ormond Beach** to the north, the centrally located **Daytona Beach** and **Daytona Beach Shores,** and **Ponce Inlet** at the southern tip, just above New Smyrna Beach.

Fla. A1A (Atlantic Avenue) runs north-south along the beach. **U.S. 1** runs inland paralleling the west side of the Halifax River, and I-95 vaguely parallels it still farther west. **International Speedway Boulevard (U.S. 92)** is the main east-west artery.

BEACHES

I always look forward to strolling Daytona's 23-mile expanse of beautiful sandy beach and viewing its exceptional number and variety of shore birds. The beach near the Adam's Mark and Main Street Pier, popular with families, is the hub of activity, putting you close to concessions, a boardwalk, and a small amusement park. Couples seeking greater privacy usually prefer the northern or southern extremities of the beach. Surfers congregate at Ponce Inlet and near the Main Street and Sun Glow piers.

You can drive and park directly on the beach here. There's a $5 access fee February to November; the rest of the year it's free.

If Daytona's beaches aren't enough, you can venture south. **New Smyrna Beach** has 7 miles of hard-packed white sand. And farther south still, adjoining the grounds of the Kennedy Space Center, there's **Canaveral National Seashore,** a protected stretch of unspoiled beach. See Section 1, earlier in this chapter, for details.

INTERNATIONAL RACING

✪ **Daytona International Speedway.** 1801 W. International Speedway Blvd. (U.S. 92), at Bill France Blvd. ☎ **904/253-RACE** for tickets, 904/254-2700 for information. Auto events, $30–$150; motorcycle events, $6–$35; go-kart events, under $10. Closed Thanksgiving and Christmas Day. Parking is free for grandstand seating; infield parking charges vary with the event. Daily.

Opened in 1959 with the first Daytona 500, this 480-acre "World Center of Racing" is practically the raison d'être for Daytona Beach—certainly the keynote of the city's fame. It presents about eight weekends of major racing events annually (see "Special Events & Festivals in Northeast Florida," at the beginning of this chapter), and is also used for automobile testing. Big events sell out months in advance (the Daytona 500 at least a year in advance), so plan far ahead and also reserve accommodations well before your trip.

To learn about racing, head for the **World Center of Racing Visitors' Center,** at the east end of the Speedway and NASCAR office complex. Open daily from 9am to 5pm, the center is also the departure site for entertainingly narrated 25-minute guided tram tours of the facility. Admission is $5 for adults, free for children 6 and under. Tours depart daily every 30 minutes between 9:30am and 4pm, except during races and special events. Also at the center are a large gift shop; a snack bar; the Gallery of Legends, where the history of motorsports in the Daytona Beach area is documented through photographs and memorabilia; and the Budweiser Video Wall, tracing the history of racing in the Daytona Beach area. You can "feel the thunder" while listening to a 20-minute Surround-Sound audio presentation called *The Daytona 500: From Dawn to Determination.* The center also stocks information on area accommodations, restaurants, attractions, and nightlife.

Opening on the Speedway grounds shortly after press time is the 50,000-square-foot **Daytona USA**—a state-of-the-art interactive motorsports entertainment attraction that will vividly present the history, color, and excitement of stock-car, go-kart, and motorcycle racing in Daytona. Visitors will be able to "participate" in a pit stop on a NASCAR Winston Cup stock car, design and test their own stock car using computer-aided technology, and play radio or TV announcer by calling the finish of a race. The facility will be open daily except Christmas from 9am to 6pm. Admission for adults will be about $10, with reductions for children and seniors.

OTHER SIGHTS & ACTIVITIES

Daytona Beach Kennel Club. 2201 W. International Speedway Blvd., just west of Fentress Blvd. ☎ **904/252-6484.** Admission $1 adults (seniors 55 and over free at matinees); grandstand seating 50¢–$1.75; restaurant $2. Night races usually Mon–Sat at 7:45pm (call before you go); matinees Mon, Wed, and Sat at 1pm. Doors and restaurant open an hour before post time. Free parking on the premises; preferred parking (closer to the entrance) $1, and valet parking, $2.

This is a fun way to spend a day or evening. There are a variety of ways to bet on the greyhounds; if you've never done it before, pick up a free brochure that explains them all. Each meet includes 14 races. You must be at least 18 years old to enter the betting area.

Halifax Historical Museum. 252 S. Beach St., just north of Orange Ave. ☎ **904/255-6976.** Admission $2 adults, 50¢ children 11 and under; free for everyone on Sat. Tues–Sat 10am–4pm. Closed Thanksgiving and Christmas Day.

This local history museum is housed in a 1912 neoclassical former bank. Its eclectic collection includes Timucuan and other Native American artifacts, historic photographs and artifacts, model cars and other racing-related items, and an extensive collection of scenic Daytona postcards. In a small theater you can watch a 30-minute video/slide show about Daytona history.

Klassix Auto Museum. 2909 W. International Speedway Blvd., at Tomoka Farms Rd., just west of I-95. ☎ **904/252-3800.** Admission $8.50 adults, $4.25 children 7–12, free for children 6 and under. Daily 9am–6pm, with extended hours during special events.

This museum showcases Corvettes—a model from every year since 1953. Also on display are collector cars (including cars from the movie *Days of Thunder*), and historic Daytona vehicles from all motorsports. A 1950s-style soda shop and gift shop are on the premises.

Museum of Arts and Sciences. 1040 Museum Blvd., off Nova Rd. ☎ **904/255-0285.** Admission $4 adults, $1 children and students with ID, free for children 5 and under; planetarium shows, $2. Tues–Fri 9am–4pm, Sat–Sun noon–5pm. Closed New Year's Day, Thanksgiving, and Christmas Day. Take International Speedway Boulevard west, make a left on Nova Road, and look for a sign on your right.

This eclectic museum dates to 1956, when Cuban dictator Fulgencio Batista donated his vacation home and art collection to the city. The collection spans two centuries, from 1759 to 1959. "Masterworks of American Art" includes art and furnishings from the Pilgrim period, Abolitionist paintings, works by Gilbert Stuart and Samuel Morse, Federalist furnishings, and Tiffany silver. In the Karshan Center of Graphic Arts you'll view European prints, posters, and lithographs by artists ranging from William Blake to Degas. A prehistory of Florida section, "Africa: Life and Ritual," and a contemporary sculpture garden complete the collection. A 1-mile nature trail is on the grounds. Planetarium shows take place at 1 and 3pm daily.

Ponce de León Inlet Lighthouse. 4931 S. Peninsula Dr., Ponce Inlet. ☎ **904/761-1821.** Admission $4 adults, $1 children 11 and under. May–Aug, daily 10am–9pm; Sept–Apr, daily 10am–5pm (last admission an hour before closing). Closed Christmas. Follow Atlantic Avenue south, make a right on Beach Street, and follow the signs.

Built in the mid-1880s, this is, at 175 feet, the second-tallest lighthouse in the United States. The present beacon, visible for 16 nautical miles, flashes every 10 seconds. In the 1970s this brick-and-granite coastal sentinel and its original outbuildings were restored and added to the National Register of Historic Places. The head lighthouse keeper's cottage houses a museum, and the first assistant keeper's house is furnished to reflect turn-of-the-century occupancy. Other buildings contain lighthouse-related displays and artifacts and a theater where a 12-minute video on the history of this particular lighthouse is shown (visit it first). In the boatyard you can board the 46-foot oak-and-cypress *F. D. Russell* tugboat, built in 1938. There's an adjoining playground and picnic area with tables and barbecue grills.

CRUISING ON THE RIVER

✪ **Scenic River Boat Tours at the Hontoon Landing Resort & Marina.** 2317 River Ridge Rd., in DeLand. ☎ **904/734-2474** or 800/248-2474. Scenic cruises, $12 adults, $10 seniors and children 5–16, free for children 4 and under. Oct–Apr, cruises daily at 10am and 1pm; May–Sept, daily at 10am (call for reservations). Follow International Speedway Boulevard west until it ends; then turn left on Spring Garden Avenue (Fla. 15A), right on Fla. 44, left on Old New York Avenue, left on Hontoon Road, and left on River Ridge Road.

Just a 35-minute drive from Daytona, this rustic resort on the St. Johns River offers 2-hour narrated nature cruises in open-air pontoon tour boats. Knowledgeable guides point out local flora and fauna. You'll pass an ancient Timucuan shell mound and the remains of stills that once flourished in the dense riverside marshlands. And there's a 15-minute stop at Blue Springs State Park to visit manatee- and alligator-viewing stations. Binoculars can be rented at the resort store. Pack a picnic lunch (or request a deli luncheon when you call). If you want to stay overnight, there are moderately priced riverside accommodations. Hontoon Landing offers a swimming pool, boat rentals (fishing licenses, bait, gear, and tackle can be obtained on the premises), and many other resort activities. In addition, there are camping cabins, nature trails, and a riverside picnic area at the adjacent 1,650-acre **Hontoon Island State Park** (☎ 904/736-5309).

A Tiny Cruise Line River Excursions. 40l S. Beach St., at Halifax Harbor (use the entrance across from the Live Oak Inn). ☎ **904/226-2343.** Cruises, $8.50–$13.50 adults, $6–$8 children 4–12, free for children 3 and under. Weather permitting, Apr–Sept cruises depart Mon–Sat at 11:30am, 1-hour cruises at 2 and 3:30pm. Closed Mon Oct–Mar. Call for reservations, and to inquire about sunset cruises.

Take a leisurely cruise on the Halifax River aboard the 14-passenger, 25-foot *Fancy*, a replica of the old fantail launches used at the turn of the century. Captain Jim regales passengers with river lore and points out dolphins, manatees, and other natural phenomena en route. Morning tours make a 20-minute stop at River Park where there are picnic tables if you bring lunch. If you bring children, be sure they're over 8—old enough not to get bored in a confined space.

SPORTS & OUTDOOR ACTIVITIES

FISHING   If you're interested in deep-sea fishing and/or whale-watching, contact **Critter Fleet,** 4950 S. Peninsula Dr., Ponce Inlet (☎ **904/767-7676**). The **Sea Love Marina,** 4884 Front St., Ponce Inlet (☎ **904/767-3406**), also offers deep-sea fishing.

You can fish from the **Main Street Pier,** near the Adam's Mark (☎ **904/ 253-1212**). Bait and fishing gear are available, and no license is required. A similar— and, I think, a bit nicer—set-up is at the **Sun Glow Fishing Pier,** 3701 S. Atlantic Ave., 4 blocks south of Dunlawton Avenue (☎ **904/756-4219**).

GOLF   There are a dozen golf courses within 25 minutes of the beach, and most hotels can arrange starting times for you. The **Daytona Beach Club,** 600 Wilder Blvd. (☎ **904/258-3119**), is the city's largest, with 36 holes. And the centrally located 18-hole, par-72 **Indigo Lakes Golf Course,** 2620 W. International Speedway Blvd. (☎ **904/254-3607**), designed by Lloyd Clifton with flat fairways and large bunkered Bermuda greens, is recognized as one of the best courses in the state.

HORSEBACK RIDING   **Shenandoah Stables,** 1759 Tomoka Farms Rd., off U.S. 92 (☎ **904/257-1444**), offers daily trail rides and horseback-riding lessons between 10am and 5pm. Call to make riding arrangements.

WATER SPORTS   For jet-ski rentals, contact **Daytona High Performance–MBI,** 925 Sickler Dr., at the Seabreeze Bridge (☎ **904/257-5276**). See also **Hontoon Landing,** in "Cruising on the River" under "Other Sights & Activities," above.

Additional water-sports equipment, as well as bicycles, beach buggies, and mopeds, can be rented along the beach in front of major hotels. A good place to look is in front of the Adam's Mark Hotel at 100 N. Atlantic Ave.

SHOPPING

DAYTONA'S ANTIQUE ROW   Daytona Beach's main riverside drag, **Beach Street,** underwent a face-lift in 1995, transforming it from a rather seedy precinct to a palm-fringed thoroughfare with decorative wrought-iron archways and fancy brickwork. Today Beach Street between Bay Street and Orange Avenue offers more than a dozen antiques shops filled with furnishings, jewelry, glassware and china, Victoriana, and bric-a-brac ranging from kitsch to collector quality. Most notable is **Let's Talk Antiques,** at 140 N. Beach St. (☎ **904/258-5225**), an antiques mall housing 28 dealers under one roof. Also look in at **Dunn Toys & Hobbies,** 166 S. Beach St. (☎ **904/253-3644**), filled with European toys, collector dolls, model trains, and other things delightful. There's a quaintly charming little eatery in the store. Be sure to note Dunn's animated window displays as well. And you might want to stop by the **Angell & Phelps Chocolate Factory,** 154 S. Beach St. (☎ **904/ 252-6531**, to see candies in the making and garner a free sample. There's additional antiquing in Daytona Beach at the 13,500-square-foot **House of Gamble,** 1102 State Ave., at LPGA Boulevard (☎ **904/258-2889**), housing 50 diverse dealers under its roof. Most of the shops, and both malls, are open 7 days a week.

MARKETS   The **Daytona Flea Market,** on Tomoka Farms Road, a mile west of the Speedway at the junction of I-95 and U.S. 92 (☎ **904/252-1999**), is one of the world's largest, with 1,000 covered outdoor booths plus 100 antiques vendors in an air-conditioned building. It's open year round Friday to Sunday from 8am to 5pm (parking is free). There's also a **Farmer's Market** every Saturday from 6am to 2:30pm on City Island; Daytona residents turn out in force to buy fresh farm-grown produce.

WHERE TO STAY

Except for B&Bs, every accommodation listed below is on the beach, and all are within 15 minutes' driving distance of the Speedway. Daytona Beach hotels fill to the bursting point during major races at the Speedway and other special events, and whenever college students are on break. At these times room rates skyrocket and there's often a minimum-stay requirement. If you're planning to be in town at one of these busy times, reserve far in advance. At any time of year, make special note of the Days Inn Super Saver rate (details below).

In addition to the accommodations listed below, you can stay at the **Daytona Beach Hostel,** 1140 S. Atlantic Ave. (☎ 904/258-6937). The hostel has 15 rooms for $20 to $24, and 25 dorms at $15 per person. This typical no-frills hostel, which draws a young European clientele, is conveniently located just a block from the Speedway.

Note that at the budget properties described below, rates will rise to $100 to $125 a night during major events. *Note:* In addition to the 6% state sales tax, Daytona levies a 4% tax on hotel bills.

DOUBLES FOR LESS THAN $40

✪ **Beach House.** 3221 S. Atlantic Ave. (at El Portal Ave., half a mile north of Dunlawton Ave.), Daytona Beach, FL 32118. ☎ **904/788-7107** or 800/647-3448. Fax 904/760-3672. 10 rms, 1 suite. A/C TV TEL. $28–$59 double; $50–$69 ocean-view suite.Extra person $5 extra ($10 extra during special events); children 11 and under stay free in parents' room. Weekly rates available. AE, DISC, MC, V. Free parking.

You'll know as soon as you see its nicely landscaped exterior that owners Pat and Barbara Welsh care about this place. And inside, the furnishings and appointments are excellent for a property in this price range. All accommodations have front lawns with umbrella tables overlooking the ocean, and all but two have full kitchens. There are barbecue grills for guest use, and a swimming pool is in the works at this writing.

Breakers Beach Motel. 27 S. Ocean Ave. (between Harvey and Main sts.), Daytona Beach, FL 32118. ☎ **904/252-0863** or 800/441-8459. Fax 904/238-1247. 21 rms. A/C TV TEL. $37–$80 double. Additional person $5 extra (up to $15 extra during special events); two children 18 and under stay free in parents' room. Weekly and monthly rates available. AE, CB, DC, DISC, MC, V. Free parking.

This is a friendly, just-folks kind of place, where guests (many of them repeat visitors) socialize with each other and affable owners Tom and Virginia Brown. The location is very central—right at the boardwalk and the Main Street Pier (where you can fish without a license; bait and tackle are available). The rooms aren't fancy, but they're clean and well maintained. Especially desirable are the oceanfront efficiencies with full kitchens, though all rooms have small refrigerators. Facilities include a picnic area with barbecue grills, a swimming pool, and coin-op washers and dryers.

Capri Motel. 832 N. Atlantic Ave. (between Riverview and Jessamine blvds.), Daytona Beach, FL 32118. ☎ **904/252-2555** or 800/874-1820. Fax 904/255-7378. 24 rms. A/C TV TEL. $35–$75 double. Additional person $6 extra; two children 18 and under stay free in parents' room. AE, CB, DC, DISC, MC, V. Free parking.

A large pool with a 60-foot water slide, a kiddie pool, barbecue grills, a video games room, a coin-op laundry, and a year-round roster of planned activities for all ages make this a good choice for families, especially since all accommodations here offer full eat-in kitchens or kitchenettes.

Pierside Inn. 3703 S. Atlantic Ave. (4 blocks south of Dunlawton Ave.), Daytona Beach, FL 32127. ☎ **904/767-4650,** or 800/728-4650. Fax 904/756-5532. 35 rms, 2 suites. A/C TV TEL. $35–$85 double; $50–$100 suite. Additional person $5 extra ($10 extra during special events); up to two children 11 and under stay free in parents' room. Weekly and monthly rates available. DISC, MC, V. Free parking.

A beachfront location adjacent to the Sunglow Pier (where bait and tackle are available) makes this a great choice for those who like to fish. And its very large, homey rooms—all with fully equipped kitchens, dining areas, patios or balconies, and cable TV (with HBO and Disney channels)—will also appeal to families. The two-bedroom suites have full living rooms and furnished wooden decks. Services here include a gratis newspaper daily, and free coffee each morning. Among the facilities are a lounge with a pool table, a nice-size swimming pool and kiddie pool, a sundeck, a shuffleboard court, a putting green, and coin-op washers and dryers.

Pierside Motel. 3710 S. Atlantic Ave. (4 blocks south of Dunlawton Ave.), Daytona Beach, FL 32127. ☎ **904/767-4650,** or 800/728-4650. Fax 904/756-5532. 4 rms, 5 efficiencies, 2 two-bedroom apts. A/C TV TEL. $25–$35 double; $28–$45 efficiency; $50–$60 apt. Additional person $5 extra ($10 extra during special events); up to two children 11 and under stay free in parents' room. *Note:* Even during special events here rates are between $50 and $95. Weekly and monthly rates available. DISC, MC, V. Free parking.

This well-run hostelry, under the same ownership as the Pierside Inn (see above), charges considerably lower rates because it's across the street from the beach rather than right on it. Fronted by a neat rock garden with a gazebo, it's rather appealing, and most of its accommodations offer full kitchens. Guests can use all the facilities across the street.

Rodeo Lodge. 301 S. Atlantic Ave. (at International Speedway Blvd.), Daytona Beach, FL 32118. ☎ **904/255-6421,** or 800/76-LODGE. Fax 904/252-6195. 100 rms, 47 suites. A/C TV TEL. $38–$69 double ($110–$135 double during special events); $48–$78 suite ($135–$165 suite during special events). Additional person $5 extra ($10 extra during special events); children 14 and under stay free in parents' room. AE, CB, DC, DISC, MC, V. Free parking.

This very centrally located hostelry occupies a five-story beachfront building, with attractive standard motel rooms, half of them overlooking the ocean. A good deal for families are the reasonably priced suites, offering sizable living room areas with sofas in addition to bedrooms, plus small refrigerators and microwave ovens; some of these have private balconies. Facilities include a very large swimming pool with a sundeck overlooking the beach (there's a pool bar in season, and a concession called the Tiki Hut vends beach accessories), coin-op washers and dryers, and a video-game arcade. A casual hotel coffee shop serves breakfast and lunch. Room service is available during restaurant hours (6am to 2pm daily). And a cozy on-premises pub called the Hole Bar is a popular local hangout featuring music (live or DJ) nightly, pool tables, dart boards, and video games; sporting events—including Monday-night football—are aired on a large-screen TV.

Talisman Oceanfront Resort Lodge. 3411 S. Atlantic Ave. (at Seaway Ave., just north of Dunlawton Ave.), Daytona Beach, FL 32118. ☎ **904/761-0511,** or 800/831-3411. Fax 904/756-2076. 9 rms, 41 efficiencies. A/C TV TEL. $37–$45 double; $42–$72 efficiency. Additional person $10 extra; children 9 and under stay free in parents' room. Weekly and monthly rates available. AE, DISC, MC, V. Free parking.

This beachfront property—many of its accommodations offering balconies or patios and ocean views—isn't a fancy place, but it is homey, clean, and well maintained.

Owners Frank and Monica Vitale are usually on the premises. The accommodations are spacious, especially the pleasant two-room apartments with living rooms and full kitchens; all the efficiencies have kitchenettes, and even the motel rooms feature refrigerators. Facilities include a coffee shop, a video-game room, barbecue grills, and coin-op washers and dryers. The beachfront swimming pool has a large sundeck with expanses of palm-fringed lawn.

DOUBLES FOR LESS THAN $60

Acapulco Inn. 2505 S. Atlantic Ave. (between Dundee Rd. and Seaspray St.), Daytona Beach, FL 32118. ☎ **904/761-2210,** or 800/874-7420. Fax 904/253-9935. 42 rms, 91 efficiencies. A/C TV TEL. $50–$100 double; $54–$124 efficiency. Additional person $6 extra ($10 extra during special events); children 17 and under stay free in parents' room. Monthly rates available. Inquire about golf and honeymoon packages. AE, CB, DC, DISC, MC, V. Free parking.

This Mayan-themed hotel is one of six beachfront properties under the auspices of a company called Oceans Eleven Resorts. All these hotels offer an extensive daily activities program for adults and children, making them a good bet for families. You can reserve at any Oceans Eleven hostelry via the above toll-free number, and the reservations operators can tell you which hostelry will best suit your needs. Rooms at the Mayan, all with ocean-view balconies, are equipped with small refrigerators, safes, and cable TV with Spectravision pay movies and tourist-information channels. The efficiency units have fully equipped eat-in kitchens.

The Fiesta Restaurant here, which overlooks the ocean, serves American fare at breakfast and lunch. Guests get complimentary newspapers each day. On-premises facilities include an oceanfront swimming pool, two whirlpools, a kiddie pool, shuffleboard, a picnic area, a coin-op laundry, a video-game room, and a lobby lounge with TV and card tables. An on-staff PGA pro helps guests plan golf vacations and arranges lessons and tee times.

Days Inn. 1909 S. Atlantic Ave. (at Flamingo Ave.), Daytona Beach, FL 32118. ☎ **904/255-4492,** or 800/224-5056. Fax 904/238-0632. 184 rms, 7 efficiencies. A/C TV TEL. $26–$55 single; $45–$65 double; $65–$85 efficiency for one or two. During special events, $100–$125 single or double; $135–$145 efficiency for one or two. Additional person $10 extra; children 11 and under stay free in parents' room. AE, CB, DC, DISC, MC, V. Free parking.

At this nine-story beachfront hotel, rooms with ocean views offer cable TV with Showtime channels. All have balconies, and some contain small refrigerators and microwave ovens. The large oceanfront efficiencies have fully equipped kitchens. Facilities include a swimming pool/kiddie pool/sundeck overlooking the beach, an on-premises restaurant (serving breakfast only), and a video-game room.

Days Inns nationwide offers a Super Saver rate of just $29 to $49 single or double if you reserve 30 days in advance via the toll-free phone number. This deal is, of course, subject to availability, but it's worth a try. If you can't get in here, there are five other Days Inns in town, all conveniently located beachfront properties. Call 800/329-7466 for details.

✪ Ocean Villa Motel. 828 N. Atlantic Ave. (between Riverview and Jessamine blvds.), Daytona Beach, FL 32118. ☎ **904/252-4644,** or 800/255-3691. Fax 904/255-7378. 17 rms, 15 efficiencies, 6 suites. A/C TV TEL. $41–$79 double; $47–$79 efficiency; $72–$117 suite. Additional person $6 extra; two children 18 and under stay free in parents' room. Rates range reflects view and season; rates may be higher during special events. AE, CB, DC, DISC, MC, V. Free parking.

Like its adjoining sibling hostelry, the Capri (see above), the Ocean Villa offers a year-round recreational program for all ages. The rooms are handsomely decorated, with navy-blue floral-print bedspreads and color-coordinated carpeting, and are equipped with safes and refrigerators; VCRs and movies can be rented in the office. The efficiencies have full kitchens, as do the two-room suites, which accommodate up to six. Many units here have ocean-view patios or balconies. Facilities include a large swimming pool, kiddie pool, shuffleboard court, video-game room, and coin-op washers and dryers. And kids can walk right across the sundeck to the Capri to use its water slide.

Perry's Ocean Edge Resort. 2209 S. Atlantic Ave. (between Moore and Bonner aves.), Daytona Beach, FL 32118. ☎ **904/255-0581** or 800/447-0002. Fax 904/258-7315. 204 rms. A/C TV TEL. $50–$130 for up to four in a room; $108–$242 suite (formed by combining rooms). Rates include continental breakfast. 4- to 5-night minimum stay during special events. Ask about packages and weekly rates. AE, CB, DC, DISC, MC, V. Free parking.

Some people say that the secret of this family-run hostelry's popularity is the fresh-baked doughnuts served with your coffee each morning. They are a treat, but Perry's has more going for it—warm hospitality and lots of activities for adults and children greatly enhance your vacation here. Entered via an attractive lobby, the hotel has a grassy palm-fringed garden beachfront—the prettiest in Daytona. The staff is extremely friendly and helpful. And the spacious rooms (75% of them with ocean views and private balconies or patios) are equipped with coffeemakers and small refrigerators (microwave ovens on request). Many units have full kitchens, as well as living room and dining areas, and most have hair dryers. A supermarket and 7-Eleven are directly across the street. Facilities include a large indoor pool with a retractable roof, two outdoor swimming pools, a kiddie pool, a whirlpool, a nine-hole putting green, a bocci ball court, a video-game room, and more. There are coin-op washers/dryers.

A homey coffee shop is open for breakfast and lunch daily. The above-mentioned doughnuts are served in two comfortable lounges equipped with pianos and large TVs. Guests gather for Monday-night football in the lodgelike South Tower lounge. There are also year-round activities.

WORTH A SPLURGE

✪ **Coquina Inn.** 544 S. Palmetto Ave. (at Cedar St.), Daytona Beach, FL 32114. ☎ **904/254-4969** or 800/805-7533. Fax 904/254-4969. 7 rms. A/C TV. $80–$110 double Fri–Sun, $69–$89 double Mon–Thurs, $150–$175 double during special events. Additional person $10 extra. AE, MC, V. Rates include full breakfast. Free parking.

This charming terra-cotta–roofed coquina and cream-stucco house sits on a tranquil tree-shaded street half a block west of the Halifax River and the Harbor Marina. Guests can relax before a working fireplace in a lovely parlor or in a cheerful wicker-furnished sunroom. The crystal-chandeliered dining room is the setting for breakfasts that include a choice of quiches, homemade muffins and scones, fresh fruit, juice, tea and coffee. Classical music is played in the public areas.

Each room is exquisitely decorated—the Jasmine Room, painted adobe peach, features a working coquina fireplace and a canopied mahogany bed, and in the Hibiscus Room, decorated in soft greens and pinks, French doors lead to a private plant-filled balcony overlooking an ancient live oak draped with Spanish moss. The Jasmine and Hibiscus rooms can be combined to create a two-bedroom/two-bath suite. All rooms have remote-control cable TV and are provided with bubble bath and candles. Portable phones are available on request. Complimentary tea and sherry are served in the parlor throughout the day. Beach cruiser bikes are offered at no cost (the beach is just a mile away), and several restaurants are within easy walking distance. Note that children 11 and under are not accepted.

✪ **Daytona Beach Hilton Oceanfront Resort.** 2637 S. Atlantic Ave. (between Florida Shores Blvd. and Richard's Lane), Daytona Beach, FL 32118. ☎ **904/767-7350**, or 800/525-7350. Fax 904/760-3651. 212 rms, 2 suites. A/C TV TEL. $79–$139 per person standard double;

$89–$149 per person ocean-view double; $99–$164 oceanfront double; $235–$560 suite. Additional person $15 extra; children of any age stay free in parents' room. AE, CB, DC, DISC, JCB, MC, V. Free parking.

This hostelry is one of Daytona's premier hotels, but, outside of special events weeks, its rates are fairly moderate. The Hilton welcomes guests in an elegant terra-cotta–tiled lobby. The large balconied guest rooms are furnished in French provincial oak pieces. All are equipped with safes, coffeemakers, irons and full-size ironing boards, hair dryers, small refrigerators, and satellite TV offering HBO and pay-movie options. All rooms provide ocean and/or river views.

The airy oceanfront Blue Water Grille—one of Daytona's most beautiful restaurants—serves all meals. Seafood, steaks, and pastas are featured, and patio dining is an option. A comfy bar/lounge with game tables adjoins; it's the setting for nightly entertainment—a pianist or jazz combo. In summer reggae bands play poolside and there's a pool bar.

There's a large pool with gorgeous palm-fringed sundeck, a kiddie pool, whirlpool, video-game room with pool table, coin-op washers/dryers, and a fitness room.

✪ **Live Oak Inn.** 444-448 S. Beach St. (at Loomis Ave.), Daytona Beach, FL 32114. ☎ **904/ 252-4667.** 12 rms. A/C TV TEL. $70–90 double. Rates include extended continental breakfast. Additional person $10 extra. AE, MC, V. Free parking.

Occupying two adjoining restored 19th-century houses with a front lawn enclosed by a white picket fence, this charming B&B hostelry is surrounded by centuries-old live oaks. An inviting front porch with white wicker rocking chairs faces the street. The guest rooms—seven with private sun porches or balconies—are delightfully decorated, with area rugs strewn on polished oak floors and wood-bladed fans whirring slowly overhead. Yours might be furnished with an Eastlake bed, or perhaps you'll get a Victorian sleigh bed with a patchwork quilt and a private plant-filled sun porch furnished with Adirondack chairs. The rooms look out on the Halifax Harbor Marina or a garden. All are stocked with books and magazines and equipped with remote-control cable TVs with VCRs; the baths have Victorian soaking tubs or Jacuzzis.

Breakfast is served on an enclosed porch with lace-curtained windows overlooking a yacht basin (or a similar dining area in the other house). The public areas also include a fine steak/seafood/pasta restaurant worth visiting on its own. Other amenities here: fax and copy machines for guest use, complimentary drinks and flowers at check-in, and terry robes. No smoking is permitted in the house, and children 9 and under are not accepted.

WHERE TO EAT

It's easy to stay on your budget in Daytona, especially at places like Aunt Catfish's and Marko's Heritage Inn, where you can eat yourself into oblivion for the price of an entree. Don't forget money-saving early-bird dinners. Enjoy.

MEALS FOR LESS THAN $7

Sophie Kay's Coffee Tree Family Restaurant. 100 S. Atlantic Ave. (at Bosarvey Dr.), Ormond Beach. ☎ **904/677-0300.** Reservations not accepted. Main courses $5–$9; breakfast items mostly under $5. Reduced prices for children and seniors over 55. AE, MC, V. Daily 7am–10pm. AMERICAN.

This casual coffee shop, with sunshine streaming in through numerous windows, is a cheerful spot for inexpensive meals. The same menu—including breakfast fare—is served all day. You might begin the day here with thick slabs of Texas-style French toast, Belgian waffles dusted with powdered sugar, or eggs Benedict. The rest of the day, choices include deli sandwiches, burgers, salads, and main courses ranging from fried shrimp to roast turkey with sage dressing and cranberry sauce. For dessert, try the ultra-rich chocolate midnight ecstasy cake. Everything is fresh and well prepared.

Spring Garden Ranch. 900 Spring Garden Ranch Rd., DeLeon Springs. ☎ **904/985-0526.** Reservations recommended. Breakfast fare $1.95–$6.95; breakfast buffet $4.95 adults, $3.50 children 9 and under; lunch fare $2–$5.50. MC, V. Oct–May, daily 6am–2pm; June–Sept, Tues–Sun 7am–1pm. Closed Easter, Thanksgiving, and Christmas Day. Take International Speedway Boulevard (U.S. 92W), turn right at County Road 1792 (Woodland Boulevard), stay on your left, and take U.S. 17 to Spring Garden Ranch Road; look for the sign on your right and go to Gate 3. AMERICAN.

This is more than a meal, it's an outing. The Spring Garden Ranch is a 148-acre training center for harness-race horses, and from its trackside restaurant you can watch pacers and trotters being schooled. Breakfast choices include a hearty buffet—eggs, biscuits and gravy, pancakes, sausage patties and bacon, citrus fruits, and more. Lunch fare includes sandwiches, salads, burgers, and main dishes like southern fried chicken, with fruit cobbler à la mode for dessert. Ask for a window seat when you reserve. *Note:* February to April you can view qualifying races here on Tuesday at 11am.

MEALS FOR LESS THAN $10

Columbia Restaurant. At the Halifax Harbor Marina, 125 Basin St. ☎ **904/248-1200.** Reservations recommended. Tapas $3.95–$5.95; main courses $4.95–$6.95 at lunch, $7.95–$13.95 at dinner ($7.95 for early-bird dinners); Sun brunch buffet $9.95 adults, $5.95 children 5–12. AE, CB, DC, MC, V. Mon–Thurs 11:30am–9pm, Fri–Sat 11:30am–10pm, Sun 11:30am–2pm (brunch) and 2–9pm. SPANISH.

The most *simpático* spot in Daytona is the boat-filled Halifax Harbor—a complex of water-view restaurants and shops. The Columbia, with windowed walls overlooking the marina, has a lofty skylit interior centering on a tiled fountain. Everything on the menu here is made from scratch. Begin dinner with an assortment of tapas (or compose a meal of them)—perhaps fried calamari, conch fritters, and shrimp sautéed with garlic and red chili pepper. Main courses, served with oven-fresh Cuban bread, include a traditional paella and ropa vieja (shredded beef sautéed with onions, green peppers, and tomatoes, served with plantains and rice). The early-bird dinners are especially economical, and you can watch the sun set over the marina. Lavish Sunday-brunch buffets are also excellent values. For dessert, crema Catalana (a kind of Spanish crème brûlée) is a treat with fresh-roasted coffee. Spanish and California wines are featured. There's free self- and valet parking at the marina.

Down the Hatch. 4894 Front St., Ponce Inlet. ☎ **904/761-4831.** Reservations not accepted; call ahead for priority seating. Main courses mostly $7.95–$12.95; sandwiches $3.25–$5.25; early-bird menu (served ll:30am–5pm) $4.95–$6.95. Reduced prices for children. AE, MC, V. Daily 7am–10pm. Closed Thanksgiving and Christmas Day. Take Fla. A1A south, make a right on Beach Street, and follow the signs. SEAFOOD.

In a half-century-old fish camp on the Halifax River, this restaurant specializes in fresh fish and shrimp—notice their shrimp boat docked outside. During the day, picture windows provide scenic views of a passing parade of boats and shore birds; at night, arrive early to catch the sunset over the river, and also to beat the crowd at this very popular place. Start your meal with an order of piquant buffalo shrimp served with chunky homemade bleu-cheese dressing. Main dishes include fried or broiled fresh fish such as red snapper or grouper, and there's an excellent crab Imperial broiled in tarragon-mayonnaise sauce. If seafood isn't your thing, filet mignon and prime rib are aged on the premises. There's a full bar; desserts include mud pie, key lime pie, and cheesecake. Down the Hatch also offers a full breakfast menu—everything from waffles to three scrambled eggs with fried fish, potatoes, and biscuits.

MEALS FOR LESS THAN $15

Anna's Italian Trattoria. 304 Seabreeze Blvd. (at Peninsula Dr.). ☎ **904/239-9624.** Reservations recommended. Main courses mostly $8.50–$14; early-bird dinners (served 5–6:30pm) $5–$8. AE, DISC, MC, V. Daily 5–10pm. Closed Sun in winter. ITALIAN.

At this friendly little trattoria, the Triani family has created a warm atmosphere enhanced by cheerful Italian music. Everything is homemade—from the creamy Italian dressing on your house salad to the basket of hot crusty bread, the latter ideal for sopping up the tangy dressing of a scungilli salad appetizer. A scrumptious pasta dish is the fettuccine alla campagniola—pasta tossed with strips of sautéed eggplant and chunks of sausage in tomato-cream sauce. Nonpasta recommendables include salmon scampi and risotto alla Anna (the latter is similar to a Spanish paella). Portions are hearty. Main courses come with soup or salad and a side dish of angel-hair pasta or a vegetable. There's a good selection of Italian wines to complement your meal. Both the tiramisù and the homemade ricotta cheesecake are excellent dessert choices. You can park free in a lot on Seabreeze Boulevard across Peninsula Drive.

✪ **Aunt Catfish's.** 4009 Halifax Dr. (at the west end of the Port Orange Bridge). ☎ **904/767-4768.** Reservations not accepted, but you can—and should—call ahead for priority seating. Main courses $4–$8 at lunch, mostly $8–$13.50 at dinner; early-bird dinners (served noon–6:30pm) $7–$10.50. Sun brunch $9 adults, $5.50 for children 4–12, free for children 3 and under. Reduced prices for children and seniors. AE, DC, DISC, MC, V. Mon–Sat 11:30am–9:30pm, Sun 9am–2pm (brunch) and 2–9:30pm. Closed Christmas Day. SOUTHERN/SEAFOOD.

This country-cozy southern restaurant represents one of the best values I've ever encountered. The homey setting is appealing; in daytime, ask for a window seat overlooking the Halifax River. The food is great and there's plenty of it. For one thing, all main courses include hush puppies, a chunk of watermelon, unbelievably yummy hot cinnamon rolls, a side dish, and unlimited helpings from an extensive salad bar. A great main-dish choice is the Florida cracker sampler platter—a spit-roasted quarter chicken with cranberry-orange relish, crab cakes served in hollandaise sauce, fried shrimp, and fried catfish fingerlings. The lightly breaded fried oysters are also highly recommendable. There's a full bar, though you might prefer fresh-squeezed lemonade. For dessert, split a boatsinker fudge pie with Häagen-Dazs coffee ice cream dipped in a coat of hardened chocolate and topped with whipped cream. The lavish Sunday brunch buffet provides an unexampled temptation to overindulgence. Lunch choices include burgers, sandwiches, and a soup-and-salad buffet in addition to ribs, chicken, and seafood dishes.

✪ **The Cellar.** 220 Magnolia Ave. (between Palmetto and Ridgewood aves.). ☎ **904/258-011.** Reservations accepted only for large lunch parties. Main courses $5.50–$6.95 at lunch, $9.95–$15.95 at dinner. AE, CB, DC, DISC, MC, V. Mon–Wed 11am–3pm, Thurs–Fri 11am–3pm and 6–10pm, Sat 6–10pm. AMERICAN.

Housed in a National Historic Register Victorian home built in 1907 for Warren G. Harding, the Cellar couldn't be more charming. Its low-ceilinged interior, with cabbage-rose carpeting, posies of fresh flowers on every table, and backlit stained-glass windows draws a genteel ladies'-fork-luncheon crowd plus a few businessmen. There's also seating in a covered garden patio.

Everything here is homemade, including the soups, fresh-baked breads, and desserts. Cellar crab cakes—available at lunch and dinner—are fluffy and delicious, drizzled with rémoulade sauce and served with seasoned rice and fresh vegetables. Other dinner options range from seafood fettuccine in cream sauce to tenderloin of pork roasted in rosemary and flamed tableside in applejack brandy. At lunch a salad sampler is a good bet; order some banana bread on the side. Wine and beer are available. Flambéed desserts such as cherries jubilee and bananas Foster are featured, though I prefer the luscious cappuccino cake.

Marko's Heritage Inn. 5420 S. Ridgewood Ave. (at Niver St.). ☎ **904/761-9520.** Reservations not accepted, but you can—and should—call ahead for priority seating. Main courses $2.95–$8.95 at lunch, mostly $8–$13 at dinner. Sun breakfast/brunch buffet $5.95 adults, $3.95 children 4–12, free for children 3 and under. Reduced prices for children and seniors. AE, DISC, MC, V. Mon–Sat 11:30am–3:30pm and 4:30–9:30pm, Sun 8am–2pm (breakfast/brunch) and 2–9pm. Closed Christmas Day. SOUTHERN/SEAFOOD.

Like Aunt Catfish's, described above, Marko's gives you a lot of bang for your buck. A honeycomb of cozy dining rooms, it's very southern, complete with a front porch (where overflow crowds wait for tables). One room even has a working fireplace.

This is hearty fare. Your main-course price includes a complimentary bowl of Florida cracker–style fish chowder, salad (go for the fruit with creamy poppyseed dressing), an array of vegetables, potato or broccoli casserole, tangerine sherbet between courses, and a basket of fresh-baked oatmeal and cinnamon rolls. All this bounty precludes the need for appetizers, but there are some great ones nevertheless, such as deep-fried onion petals with creamy peppercorn dip. Main selections range from smoky barbecued back ribs to fried Maryland-style crab cakes. And the desserts—such as a first-rate key lime pie and three-berry shortcake—are not to be missed. There's a full bar. After your meal, browse in the gift shop filled with charming country crafts.

Shells. 200 N. Atlantic Ave. (between 5th Ave. and International Speedway Blvd.). ☎ **904/258-0007.** Reservations not accepted. Main courses $4.95–$6.95 at lunch, $4.95–$14.95 at dinner (most under $10). Reduced prices for children. AE, MC, DISC, V. Sun–Thurs 11:30am–10pm, Fri–Sat 11:30am–11pm. SEAFOOD.

This large and cheerful restaurant—offering delicious, and amazingly low-priced, seafood meals—enjoys great popularity with local families, especially on Wednesday night when kids 11 and under eat free. The ambience is clattery and cluttery—this is not the place for an intimate dinner—with buoys strung overhead, rusty anchors, mounted fish, and neon beer signs.

Start out with a bowl of Shells' superb creamy clam chowder, replete with chunks of potato and smidgens of bacon. Also noteworthy here are the golden-brown crab cakes served with a tangy horseradish-nuanced dipping sauce, available as an appetizer or entree. I also enjoyed the spicy blackened shrimp served atop linguine in cream sauce. Everything is made from scratch; even the breads are fresh baked. And there's a very satisfying apple cobbler topped with vanilla ice cream for dessert. If there's a wait for a table (and there likely will be, unless you come off hours), you can nibble peanuts at the bar, where the floor is appropriately littered with shells.

DAYTONA BEACH AFTER DARK
THE PERFORMING ARTS

At the 2,552-seat **Peabody Auditorium,** 600 Auditorium Blvd., between Noble Street and Wild Olive Avenue (☎ **904/255-1314**), the London Symphony Orchestra has been performing for over 25 years during the semiannual Florida International Festival. The Daytona Beach Symphony Society arranges a series of six classical concerts between December and April. During the same season, Concert Showcase features pop artists such as James Taylor, Henry Mancini, and Steve Lawrence and Eydie Gorme, as well as full Broadway-cast stage shows like *Crazy for You* and *Beauty and the Beast.* Daytona Beach's Civic Ballet performs *The Nutcracker* every Christmas and sponsors another ballet every spring.

Under the same city auspices is the **Oceanfront Bandshell** (☎ **904/258-3169**), on the boardwalk next to the Adam's Mark Hotel. The city hosts a series of free Big Band concerts at the bandshell every Sunday night from early June to Labor Day. It's also the scene of spring-break concerts. Prices at the Peabody vary with the performances. Bandshell concerts are usually free. Parking is $3 in a lot adjacent to the Peabody.

THE CLUB & BAR SCENE

In addition to the following, the piano bar at **Sophie Kay's Waterfall Restaurant** (which offers a special bar menu), the sophisticated **Clocktower Lounge** at the Adam's Mark (for piano and other live music), and the **Chart House** downstairs bar are elegant nighttime settings. For details, see "Where to Eat," above.

Alexander's Blue Note Supper Club. 123 W. Granada Blvd. (between N. Ridgewood Ave. and U.S. 1), in Ormond Beach. ☎ **904/673-5312.**

The cathedral-ceilinged art deco bar/lounge of this upscale restaurant is very popular with local businesspeople and sophisticates. A pianist entertains Wednesday to Saturday night from 7pm on a white baby grand; other nights there's recorded music from the 1930s and 1940s—jazz, big band, and swing. You can order from the extensive wine list, have an appetizer or dessert, try one of the cafe's many single-malt scotches (I recommend the smoky Lagavulin), cognacs, or draft beers—or order up a fine cigar. Open windows supposedly keep the smoke level down, but nonsmokers should take warning. Open Monday to Saturday until somewhere between midnight and 2am, depending on the crowd. At happy hour, Monday to Friday from 4 to 8pm, most drinks are half price.

Cha Cha Coconuts. At the Halifax Harbor Marina, 125 Basin St. ☎ **904/248-8500.** No cover.

Though Cha Cha Coconuts does have a whimsical window-walled interior, it's kind of beside the point. The place to be is on the vast umbrella-tabled deck overlooking the marina, listening—or dancing—to music under the stars. Bands—reggae, rock, Top 40, blues, light jazz—perform here live most nights. Also popular is happy hour, Monday to Friday from 4 to 7pm. A full moderately priced menu of tropical fare is served. There's free valet and self-parking.

Coliseum. 176 N. Beach St. (at Bay St.). ☎ **904/257-9982.** Cover $5–$8 (also includes admission to the Spot; see below).

This upscale Roman-themed dance club occupies a converted movie theater. Inside, a raised dance floor is flanked by Ionic columns, and Roman-style bas-reliefs and sculpture adorn the walls. A DJ plays Top 40 tunes; 16 monitors project music and ambience videos; and nightly laser shows are high-tech, utilizing 3-D and sophisticated graphic-arts effects. The crowd is mostly 20-something with occasional glitterati, rock musicians, and local athletes in attendance. Tom Cruise partied here during the filming of *Days of Thunder*, and *90210*'s Ian Zierling was a recent visitor. During spring break there are special events. The Coliseum is open nightly to 3am. Parking is free behind the club on Bay Street; usually there's ample street parking as well.

Razzles. 611 Seabreeze Blvd. (between Grandview and S. Atlantic aves.). ☎ **904/257-6236.** Cover before 10pm, $6–$8 with free drinks; after 10pm, $5 for 18- to 20-year-olds, $3 for those 21 and over.

At this large and popular dance club, a DJ plays Top 40 tunes and high-energy music till 3am nightly for a largely early-20s crowd. The setting has lots of neon tubing, monitors flashing music videos, and lighting effects over the dance floor. There's plenty to do when you're not dancing—10 pool tables, a blackjack table, air hockey, electronic darts, pinball, and video games. There's free parking behind the club on Grandview between Seabreeze and Oakridge boulevards.

The Spot. 176 N. Beach St. (at Bay St.). ☎ **904/257-9982.** Cover $5–$8 (which includes admission to the Coliseum; see above).

The Spot shares its address, phone, and ownership with the Coliseum (see above). Billing itself as a "premier sports bar," it has large-screen TVs in every corner, which, along with over 30 smaller monitors, air major worldwide sporting events via satellite. This cavernous club centers on a U-shaped bar and also has football, air hockey, video games, pinball machines, a one-on-one basketball court, eight regulation pool tables, and dart boards. Light fare is available. Monday-night football parties raffle tickets to local sporting events. Open nightly till 3am. Parking is free behind the club on Bay Street; usually there's ample street parking as well.

3 St. Augustine

123 miles NE of Orlando, 344 miles N of Miami, 43 miles S of Jacksonville

With its 17th-century fort, horse-drawn carriages clip-clopping along narrow streets, old city gates, and reconstructed 18th-century Spanish Quarter, St. Augustine seems more like a picturesque European village than a modern American city. This is an exceptionally charming town, with its share of palm-fringed ocean beaches—but its primary lure is historic. Here European civilization first took root in the New World.

ST. AUGUSTINE PAST & PRESENT

AMERICA'S EARLIEST CITY   St. Augustine was founded in 1565, 55 years before the Pilgrims landed at Plymouth Rock. Though Juan Ponce de León sighted—and named—the Florida coast as early as 1513, it was Pedro Menéndez de Avilés who established the Spanish supremacy that lasted for two centuries. He arrived with some 1,000 settlers and a priest, and named the town in honor of the saint whose feast day—August 28—coincided with his first sighting of the Florida coast. The newcomers settled in a Timucuan village called Seloy and set about routing the French from nearby Fort Caroline and converting the natives to Christianity. Later, for reasons of military strategy, the colony moved to higher ground about a mile south, near the bayfront. Life was not easy. The fledgling town was beset by famine, fire, hurricanes, plagues, and attacks by Native Americans, pirates, and the rival British Empire. But St. Augustine survived, and its importance grew as it became increasingly vital to Spain's defense of its commercial coastal route. Between 1672 and 1695 the colonists constructed an impregnable fort, the Castillo de San Marcos. Though British troops attacked and burned the town in 1702 and 1740, the populace holed up in the Castillo and survived both onslaughts.

BRIEFLY BRITISH   In 1763 the British finally gained control of St. Augustine when Spain ceded all of Florida to them in exchange for Havana and other territorial possessions after the French and Indian War. Rather than become British subjects, most of the 3,000 Spanish inhabitants sailed to Cuba. During the American Revolution, St. Augustine remained loyal to the Crown. The population increased in 1777 with the arrival of 1,400 Minorcan, Italian, and Greek indentured servants, fleeing the tyranny of harsh servitude in New Smyrna, a town about 80 miles south of St. Augustine.

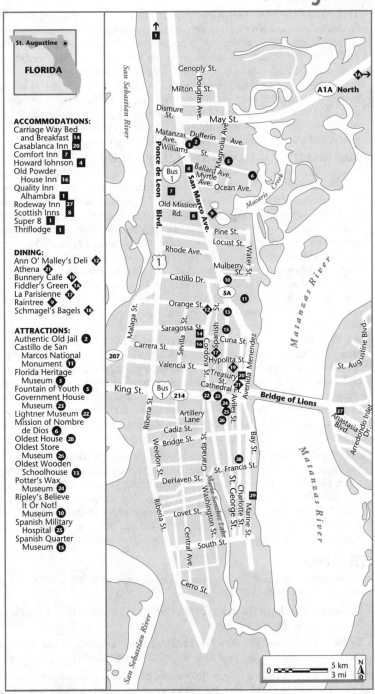

St. Augustine

FLORIDA

St. Augustine

ACCOMMODATIONS:
Carriage Way Bed
and Breakfast **14**
Casablanca Inn **20**
Comfort Inn **7**
Howard Johnson **4**
Old Powder
House Inn **16**
Quality Inn
Alhambra **1**
Rodeway Inn **27**
Scottish Inns **8**
Super 8 **1**
Thriflodge **1**

DINING:
Ann O' Malley's Deli **12**
Athena **21**
Bunnery Café **19**
Fiddler's Green **1A**
La Parisienne **17**
Raintree **9**
Schmagel's Bagels **18**

ATTRACTIONS:
Authentic Old Jail **2**
Castillo de San
Marcos National
Monument **11**
Florida Heritage
Museum **3**
Fountain of Youth **5**
Government House
Museum **23**
Lightner Museum **22**
Mission of Nombre
de Dios **6**
Oldest House **28**
Oldest Store
Museum **26**
Oldest Wooden
Schoolhouse **13**
Potter's Wax
Museum **24**
Ripley's Believe
It Or Not!
Museum **10**
Spanish Military
Hospital **25**
Spanish Quarter
Museum **15**

THE SECOND SPANISH REGIME   In 1784, the Treaty of Paris returned Florida to Spain as a reward for its aid during the American Revolution. Once again the population shifted, as many prior Spanish residents returned and most of the English left. The Minorcans—whose previously British Balearic Island country had come under Spanish rule by this time—stayed on. The British loyalists left the city in a shambles. The inhabitants valiantly tried to rebuild, but by the start of the 19th century the Spanish Empire was already beginning to decline. When it became evident, after numerous incursions, that the Americans would eventually seize Florida anyway, the Spanish sensibly decided to sell it to them. The transfer took place peacefully in 1821, and the Spanish soldiers departed, never to return.

THE TERRITORIAL ERA TO THE GILDED AGE   American rule got off to a shaky start with a massive yellow fever epidemic that decimated the population. Many of St. Augustine's buildings were by this time rundown or in ruins. Nine years after American occupation, there were only 1,700 residents, a third of them slaves. In 1835 the city suffered two major disasters—a freeze that destroyed the orange crop and the onset of a 7-year Seminole War, during which the Seminole struggled to regain control of Florida. But as the focus of hostilities moved away from St. Augustine, the town began to prosper by providing weapons and ships to its embattled neighbors. Roads were built with the profits, and the population grew, as did the pressure for statehood. In 1845 Florida entered the Union as the 27th state.

   During the early days of statehood, seasonal visitors from the chilly north began arriving in Florida to enjoy its warm winters. This growth in tourism was interrupted by the Civil War. But almost immediately after the war was over, the snowbirds began to return. A most important visitor arrived in 1883—Standard Oil magnate Henry M. Flagler. Taken with St. Augustine's Spanish antiquity and mellow charm, he determined to develop the area as a fashionable resort for the wealthy. By the turn of the century Flagler had revolutionized the tourism industry not only in St. Augustine but throughout Florida, building plush hotels and developing rail travel along its eastern coastline. Three of his deluxe hostelries—the Cordova (today the county courthouse), the Alcazar (today the Lightner Museum), and the Ponce de León (now Flagler College)—can still be seen.

THE 20TH CENTURY   It wasn't until well into the 20th century, however, that St. Augustine began to fully appreciate its unique heritage and architectural treasure trove. The Historic St. Augustine Preservation Board, formed in 1959, has been responsible for extensive restoration, preservation, and research into the city's past. Today's visitors can explore fascinating historic sites, relax on beautiful beaches, dine at waterfront fish camps and charming cafés, and stay in quaint antique-furnished bed-and-breakfast lodgings.

ESSENTIALS

ARRIVING   By Plane   St. Augustine is about equidistant (a 1-hour drive) from airports in Jacksonville and Daytona Beach.

By Train   The closest **Amtrak** (☎ **800/USA-RAIL**) station is in Jacksonville (see Section 3 of this chapter for details).

By Bus   Greyhound (☎ **800/231-2222**) buses pull into a very centrally located terminal at 100 Malaga St., near King Street (☎ **904/829-6401**).

By Car   If you're coming from north or south, take I-95 to a St. Augustine exit onto U.S. 1 (Exits 92 to 95; ask when you reserve accommodations which is closest). From points west, take I-10 to I-95 South to U.S. 1.

VISITOR INFORMATION   Before you go, write or call the **St. Johns County Visitors and Convention Bureau,** 88 Riberia St., Suite 250, St. Augustine, FL 32084 (☎ **904/829-1711**), and request its *Visitor's Guide* detailing attractions, events, restaurants, accommodations, shopping, and more. Another source is the **St. Augustine Chamber of Commerce,** 1 Riberia St., St. Augustine, FL 32084 (☎ **904/829-5681**), which will send similar information.

Upon arrival, make your first stop in town the **St. Augustine Visitor Information Center,** 10 Castillo Dr., at San Marco Avenue (☎ **904/825-1000**). Here you can view a free visitor information video; pick up brochures about accommodations, restaurants, sights, and shops; and obtain tickets for sightseeing trains and trolleys (see "Getting Around," below) along with discount tickets to major attractions. While you're here, be sure to see *Dream of Empire,* a 52-minute film about a 16th-century St. Augustine family. There's inexpensive parking. The VIC is open daily from 8:30am: Memorial Day to Labor Day to 7:30pm; April to Memorial Day and the day after Labor Day to the end of October to 6:30pm, and November to March to 5:30pm. Closed Christmas Day.

GETTING AROUND   St. Augustine is a city where a car may not be the best option for sightseeing. Parking can be difficult, and excellent transportation offers an easier option. **Sightseeing trolleys and trains** travel around town along 7-mile loop routes, stopping at or near all major attractions. Entertaining and informative onboard narrations enhance your touring, and for the price of your ticket you can get off at any stop, visit the attractions, and step aboard the next vehicle that comes along; you won't ever have to wait more than 15 to 20 minutes for a trolley to come along. Two companies run trolleys and trains. S**t. Augustine Historical Tours,** 167 San Marco Ave., at Williams Street (☎ **904/829-3800,** or 800/397-4071), operates San Francisco–style green-and-white open-air trolleys between 8:30am and 5pm daily. You can park your car at its headquarters, which is also a stop on the tour and site of two tourist attractions. There are 16 stops on the route; it takes about an hour to complete, barring stops. **St. Augustine Sightseeing Trains,** 170 San Marco Ave., at Fla. A1A (☎ **904/829-6545,** or 800/226-6545), takes a different route and makes 19 stops. Its vehicles are red-and-blue open-air trains.

You can purchase trolley or train tickets at the **Visitor Information Center** (see above) or on board. The price is $12 for adults, $5 for children 6 to 12, free for children 5 and under. Both trolleys and trains depart from the VIC as well. While you're there, inquire about trolley and train tickets that include discount admissions to the attractions. There are numerous plans.

The family-owned **Colee's Carriage Tours** (☎ **904/829-2818**) has been showing people around town in quaint surreys, turn-of-the-century vis-à-vis, and broughams since 1877. The carriages line up at the bayfront, just south of the fort. Slow-paced, entertainingly narrated 45- to 50-minute rides around the major landmarks and attractions are offered from 9am to 9pm daily except Christmas. The cost is $10 for adults, $5 for children 5 to 11, free for children 4 and under, with hotel and restaurant pickup available for an additional charge. Tickets are also available at the VIC.

The Usina family has been running **St. Augustine Scenic Cruises** (☎ **904/ 824-1806,** or 800/542-8316) on Matanzas Bay since the turn of the century. They offer 75-minute narrated tours aboard open-air sightseeing boats, departing from the Municipal Marina just south of the Bridge of Lions. There are often dolphins cavorting on the bay, and you're likely to spot brown pelicans, cormorants, kingfishers, and other water birds. Snacks, soft drinks, beer, and wine are sold on board. Weather permitting, departures are at 11am and 1, 2:45, and 4:30pm daily except Christmas, with an additional tour at 6:15pm Labor Day to October 15 and April 1 to May 14; May 15 to Labor Day there are two additional tours, at 6:45 and 8:30pm. Call ahead—schedules can change. Adults pay $8.50, children 3 to 11 are charged $3, and children 2 and under ride free. If you're driving, allow a little time to find a parking space on the street.

There are a number of inexpensive **parking lots** in the historic district. Drive in on Hypolita Street off Avenida Menendez and look for a lot on your right. If it's full, continue on Hypolita and park in the lot across Cordova Street.

CITY LAYOUT

St. Augustine is quite a small town, and you'll easily find your way around. It's bounded to the west by U.S. 1, to the east (along the coast of the Intracoastal Waterway and Matanzas Bay) by Avenida Menendez. The North Bridge leads to Fla. A1A North and Vilano Beach, the beautiful Bridge of Lions to Fla. A1A South and Anastasia Island. Fla. 16, on the north side of town, provides access to I-95. The heart of town is still the original plaza laid out in the 16th century, bounded east and west by Charlotte and St. George streets, north and south by Cathedral Place and King Street. The old Spanish Quarter is farther north on St. George Street, between Cuna and Orange streets.

EXPLORING HISTORIC ST. AUGUSTINE

St. Augustine's attractions are open 7 days a week. In addition to more than a dozen historic sites and museums, there's almost always some special event going on. It might be anything from a reenactment of Sir Francis Drake's raid on the town in 1586 to a very 20th-century beach festival.

✪ **Authentic Old Jail.** 167 San Marco Ave. (at Williams St.). ☎ **904/829-3800.** Admission $4.25 adults, $3.25 children 6–12, free for children 5 and under. Daily 8:30am–5pm. Closed Easter, Christmas Eve Day, and Christmas Day. Free parking.

This Victorian brick prison was built in 1890, and it served the county through 1953. Fascinating tours are given throughout the day by costumed guides assuming the roles of Sheriff Joe Perry and his wife, Lulu. Perry, 6 feet 6 inches tall and weighing 300 pounds, was sheriff here for 25 years, earning a reputation as a fearless law enforcer. Visitors are shown the Perrys' living quarters and the kitchen where Lulu cooked the inmates gruel for breakfast and one-pot meals (stews) for lunch and dinner. Downstairs are spartan accommodations for women, painted black and provided with straw mattresses (no linens) on bunk beds. On the same floor are a maximum-security cell where murderers, horse thieves, and those convicted of grand theft were confined; a cell housing prisoners condemned to hang (they could see the gallows being constructed from their window); and an especially grim solitary confinement cell— pitch-dark with no windows, bed, or mattress. Minimum-security prisoners—bootleggers, debtors, petty thieves—were kept upstairs in quarters almost as bleak and lightless as those below. Adding to the general level of misery throughout was the fact that the cells were stiflingly hot in summer and freezing in winter, and the bugs were awful.

Additional exhibits include weapons seized from criminals, restraining devices, and an electric chair. A snack bar and picnic tables are on the grounds.

✪ **Castillo de San Marcos National Monument.** 1 S. Castillo Dr. (between Orange and Charlotte sts.). ☎ **904/829-6506.** Admission $2 adults, free for children 15 and under. Daily 8:45am–4:45pm. Closed Christmas Day.

In 1669—a year after English pirates had sacked St. Augustine—Mariana, queen regent of Spain, ordered colonists to construct an impregnable stone fort to stave off future British advances. The Castillo, which took 23 years (1672–95) to build, was stellar in design, with a double drawbridge entrance over a 40-foot moat. Massive coquina (shell rock) walls enclosed a large courtyard lined inside with storage rooms, and diamond-shaped bastions in each corner—which enabled cannons to set up a deadly crossfire—contained domed sentry towers.

The Castillo was never captured in battle, and its coquina walls did not crumble when pounded by enemy artillery. In 1702 the English occupied St. Augustine for 50 days, and though they burned the town, its 1,500 residents holed up in the fort and remained safe. The fort also held up during a 27-day British bombardment in 1740. The Castillo, like the rest of Florida, came under American rule in 1821, and in 1824 its name was changed to Fort Marion in honor of a Revolutionary War general. It was used to house Native American prisoners during the Seminole War of 1835–42 and occupied briefly by Confederate troops during the Civil War. America's oldest—and best-preserved—masonry fortification was decommissioned as an active military base in 1900, designated a National Monument in 1924, and given back its original name in 1942.

Today the old storerooms house museum exhibits documenting the history of the fort, and visitors can also tour the vaulted powder magazine, a dank prison cell, the chapel, and guard rooms. A self-guided tour map and brochure are provided at the ticket booth. In addition, subject to staff availability, interesting 20- to 30-minute ranger talks are given several times a day, and there are occasional living-history presentations and cannon firings (call for times before you go).

Florida Heritage Museum. 167 San Marco Ave. (at Williams St.). ☎ **904/829-3800.** Admission $4.25 adults, $3.25 children 6–12, free for children 5 and under. Daily 8:30am–5pm. Closed Easter, Christmas Eve Day, and Christmas Day. Free parking.

Adjacent to the Authentic Old Jail (see above), this museum documents state and local history in exhibits focusing on the colorful life of Henry Flagler, the Civil War, and the Seminole Wars. Display cases show actual gold, silver, and jewelry recovered from galleons sunk off the Florida coast. A replica of a Spanish galleon, and a typical wattle-and-daub hut of a Timucuan in a forest setting, illustrate the lifestyle of St. Augustine's first residents. There's also an extraordinary collection of toys and dolls, and much more.

Fountain of Youth. 11 Magnolia Ave. (at Williams St.). ☎ **904/829-3168** or 800/356-8222. Admission $4.75 adults, $3.75 seniors, $1.75 children 6–12, free for children 5 and under. Daily 9am–5pm. Closed Christmas Day. Free parking.

This beautifully landscaped 25-acre archeological park, billed as North America's first historic site, is purported to be the Native American village of Seloy visited by Ponce de León upon his arrival in the New World. The famed fountain itself is located in the Springhouse along with a coquina stone cross believed to date from Ponce de León's ostensible visit in 1513. Visitors get to drink a sample of the sulfury spring water—not terrifically delicious…or efficacious.

One of the most fascinating exhibits in the complex is a Timucuan burial ground. More than 100 Native American interments—both Christian and prehistoric—were unearthed by Smithsonian experts. The skeletal remains were once on display, but a reburial was performed in 1991 to pay respect to America's first inhabitants.

Government House Museum. 48 King St. (at St. George St.). ☎ **904/825-5033.** Admission $2 adults, $1 students and children 6–12, free for children 5 and under. Daily 10am–4pm.

On Tour with the Ungrateful Dead

St. Augustine is so charming that some residents refuse to leave, even after death! Wander the city's quaint streets by moonlight and you may encounter some eerie apparitions, not to mention Henry Flagler, who haunts the corridors of Flagler College.

At the Don Pedro Horruytiner House, on St. George Street, a 17th-century Spanish soldier, in uniform, guards the property. His lonely vigil has been observed by a number of people. The spirit of Governor Horruytiner also appeared before the present owner and her grandson, bowing and tipping his hat.

Legend has it that, in the 1780s, Dolores Martí's husband discovered that his wife was having an affair with Capt. Manuel Abela. He chained the adulterous couple to a dungeon wall in the Castillo and built a new wall in front of it, entombing them. Their skeletons, still in chains, were discovered half a century later by an engineer who broke through the hollow section. At this spot, modern-day passersby have sometimes seen an eerie glow, accompanied by the aroma of a lady's perfume.

The Casablanca Inn on the Bay (see "Where to Stay," below) has always been an inn or boarding house, and during Prohibition, rumrunners were among its clientele. When G-men were in town, the owner would go up to the widow's walk and wave her lantern back and forth as a warning. But why do fishermen and shrimpers out on the bay at night still report seeing her swinging beacon? Residents of another bayfront house have been startled by a distressed female figure attired in a long skirt, jacket, and hat, standing at the top of the stairs carrying a carpet bag. In the 19th century a woman visiting at this address got sick and died. Her friends returned home, but she can never leave, and remains eternally in limbo.

If you're interested in trying for a sighting, call **Tour St. Augustine** (☎ **904/471-9010,** or 800/797-3778), which provides licensed guides for 1½-hour entertainingly narrated ghost tours, nightly at 8pm. The price is $5 per person. Call for reservations.

Closed Christmas Day. Park in the lot at the Visitor Information Center at San Marco Avenue and Castillo Drive.

Government House—on the site of the 16th-century Spanish colonial governor's office—houses an exhibit entitled "The Dream, the Challenge, the City" that focuses on St. Augustine's rich heritage. Many artifacts are on display and visitors can listen to a recording about the early days while looking at a scale model of the town.

✪ **Lightner Museum.** 75 King St. (at Granada St.). ☎ **904/824-2874.** Admission $5 adults, $1 college students with ID and children 12–18, free for children 11 and under. Daily 9am–5pm. Closed Christmas Day. Free parking.

Henry Flagler's opulent Spanish Renaissance–style Alcazar Hotel, built in 1889, closed during the Depression and stayed vacant until Chicago publishing magnate Otto C. Lightner bought the building in 1948 to house his vast collection of Victoriana. The former hotel makes a gorgeous museum, centering on an open palm courtyard with an arched stone bridge spanning a fish pond. The first floor houses a Victorian village, with shopfronts representing emporia selling period wares. Other exhibits include a Victorian Science and Industry Room, steam engine models, amazing examples of Victorian glassblowing, Victorian furnishings, and 18th- and

19th-century decorative arts, including Tiffany glass. A room of automated musical instruments is best seen during the daily concerts of period music at 11am and 2pm.

Take some time to look at the building itself, designed by Thomas Hastings and John Carrère; it's listed on the National Register of Historic Places.

Mission of Nombre de Dios. San Marco Ave. and Old Mission Rd. ☎ **904/824-2809.** Free admission; donations appreciated. Daily 7am–6pm. Free parking.

This serene setting overlooking the Intracoastal Waterway is believed to be the site of the first permanent mission in the United States, founded in 1565. Recent archeological digs have indicated the early fortifications of the colony; these may be marked by the time you visit. The mission is a popular destination of religious pilgrimages. A towering 208-foot gleaming stainless-steel cross marks the spot where Christianity was first preached in a permanent settlement in the New World. Whatever your beliefs, it's a beautiful tree-shaded spot, ideal for quiet meditation.

✪ **The Oldest House.** 14 St. Francis St. (at Charlotte St.). ☎ **904/824-2872.** Admission $5 adults, $4.50 seniors 55 and over, $3 students, free for children 6 and under; $12 families. Daily 9am–5pm; tours depart on the hour and half hour, with the last tour leaving at 4:30pm. Closed Christmas Day. Free parking.

Archeological surveys indicate that a dwelling stood on this site as early as the beginning of the 17th century. Like the rest of the town, it was probably burned by the British in 1702. What you see today, called the Gonzáles-Alvarez House, evolved from a two-room coquina dwelling built between 1702 and 1727. Tomás Gonzáles, a colonist from the Canary Islands, lived here with his fourth-generation St. Augustine wife, Francisca, from about 1727 to 1763. Tomás worked as an artilleryman at the Castillo, supplementing his meager salary by fishing, hunting, and tending fruit trees and a vegetable garden out back. The Gonzáleses had 10 children, 6 of whom survived infancy. One of the original two rooms is simply furnished to represent this period.

After the Gonzáleses' departure for Havana, Mary and Joseph Peavett took possession. They added a second story, a front door, a fireplace, and glass window panes. The ambitious Mary operated a tavern on the premises. In 1783, when Florida became Spanish once again, the British were forced to leave unless they publicly professed conversion to Catholicism. Joseph Peavett was already a Catholic, and Mary converted at the age of 56, shortly after Joseph's death in 1786. That same year she remarried, this time to 28-year-old John Hudson. Deemed a "profligate wastrel," Hudson ran up outrageous debts and got himself arrested for tearing down a government edict and making "the indecent gesture of wiping his backside" with it. After serving time in the Castillo, he was banished from St. Augustine and died in exile at the age of 33. A room upstairs with a tea-tray ceiling re-creates the era of Mary's tenancy.

In 1790 the house was auctioned to pay the Hudsons' debts, and it became the property of Gerónimo Alvarez, a Spanish immigrant who owned a bakery close by. Alvarez and his son Antonio went on to become important figures in local politics, and the family's descendants lived in the house for almost a century. A dining room suggestive of their period is upstairs.

Admission also entitles you to explore the adjacent **Museum of Florida's Army** and the **Manucy Museum of St. Augustine History,** where artifacts, maps, and photographs document the town's history from its origins through the Flagler era.

The Oldest Store Museum. 4 Artillery Lane (between St. George and Aviles sts.). ☎ **904/ 829-9729.** Admission $4 adults, $1.50 children 6–12, free for children 5 and under. Mon–Sat 9am–5pm, Sun noon–5pm (in summer, Sun 10am–5pm). Closed Christmas Day.

The C&F Hamblen General Store was St. Augustine's one-stop shopping center from 1835 to 1960, and the museum on its premises today replicates the emporium at the turn of the century. A harness maker's shop, blacksmith, gunmaker, cobbler, and ship's chandlery were on the premises, and vehicles sold here included Model-T Fords. Itinerant dentists and doctors treated patients at the store as well. It all makes for fascinating browsing.

The Oldest Wooden Schoolhouse in the U.S.A.. 14 St. George St. (between Orange and Cuna sts.). ☎ **904/824-0192,** or 800/428-0222. Admission $2 adults, $1.50 for seniors 55 and over, $1 children 6–12, free for children 5 and under. Daily 9am–5pm. Closed Christmas Day. You can park in the pay lot on the corner of Orange Street and Avenida Menéndez.

This red cedar and cypress structure, with hand-wrought beams, that's held together by wooden pegs and handmade nails, is more than two centuries old. Greek immigrant Juan Genoply acquired the house in 1788. He lived upstairs with his wife and three children and ran a school downstairs. His classroom is re-created today using animated pupils and teacher, complete with a dunce and a below-stairs "dungeon" for unruly children. The last class was held here in 1864.

Spanish Military Hospital. 3 Aviles St. (at King St.). ☎ **904/825-6808.** Free admission; donations appreciated. Generally daily 10am–4pm (it's run by volunteers, so days and hours vary).

What you see today is a reconstruction of the Royal Hospital of Our Lady of Guadalupe, which occupied this site from 1791 to 1821. A docent in period dress explains exhibits, which include grisly tools of 18th-century medicine, an apothecary's office where medicines were made, a herb garden with plants marked for medicinal uses, a typical ward, and a display on the history of medicine.

✪ **Spanish Quarter Museum.** Entrance at 33 St. George St. (between Cuna and Orange sts.). ☎ **904/825-6830.** Admission (to all exhibit buildings) $5 adults, $3.75 seniors, $2.50 students 6–18, free for children 5 and under; $10 per family. Daily 9am–5pm. Closed Christmas Day. You can park in the lot at the Visitor Information Center at San Marco Avenue and Castillo Drive.

This 2-block area south of the City Gate is St. Augustine's most comprehensive historic section, where the city's colonial architecture and landscape have been re-created. Interpreters in 18th-century attire are on hand to help you envision the life of early inhabitants. About 90% of the buildings in the area are reconstructions, with houses named for prominent occupants. The Spanish Colonial–style **Florencia House** serves as the museum entrance and store. Unless otherwise indicated, the buildings described below evoke the mid-18th century. Highlights include:

The **Gómez House** was the home of Lorenzo Gómez, a foot soldier, and his Native American wife, Catalina. They lived in this sparsely furnished one-room cypress A-frame with three children, operating a store on the premises. There's a loft upstairs where the children slept in cold weather on straw-filled mattresses. Generally, whole families slept in the same room (privacy was not an issue for them). Cooking was done in the yard outdoors, where you'll also see a square coquina well (the family's water source) and a typical vegetable garden.

The **Gallegos House** is a reconstruction of the 1740s home of Martín Martínez Gallegos and his wife, Victoria, who lived here with three children and Juan Garcia, a retired infantryman in his 60s. The Gallegos family was more affluent than the Gómez family. Martín was an officer—an artillery sergeant stationed at the Castillo. Their two-room tabby (oyster-shell concrete) home has a built-in interior masonry stove. An outdoor wooden trough served the Gallegos family as a sink, washing machine, and bathtub, with whelk shells used for dippers. In addition to fruit trees, vegetables, and herbs, there's aloe growing in the walled garden; it was used for healing purposes. Note the swinging shelf used to store food over the table; its motion scared rats away. Outside is a *metate* made of volcanic rock as well as a mortar and pestle—all used for grinding corn. It may interest you to know that hand-grinding corn for 3 hours produces enough for just one loaf of bread!

Nearby, a **woodworker** demonstrates how items such as furniture, kitchen implements, and religious artifacts were made in the 18th century. And farther along is a **blacksmith shop** where a craftsman turns out hand-wrought hardware using 18th-century methods.

The rectangular **Gonzáles House** is set up to represent a tavern run by a widow. The architecture is typical of the first Spanish Period, with a flat roof constructed of hand-hewn boards laid across hand-hewn rafters.

The tabby **Geronimo de Hita y Salazar House** was home to a cavalry soldier with a large family. Today it shows the lifestyle of a soldier and his wife. The wife takes in mending in exchange for goods the family needs. An outdoor coquina hearth was reconstructed at this site based on archeological evidence.

The **DeMesa-Sánchez House** exemplifies two periods. Two rooms date to the residence of shore guard Antonio de Mesa in the late 1700s, while a second story was added in the 19th century. Furnishings reflect the comfortable lifestyle of Charles and Mary Jane Loring, who lived here during the American Territorial Period (1821–45). They even had a bathtub in the kitchen, the practice of bathing having recently come into vogue. The Lorings had servants and slaves to do rough work, and, unlike earlier residents, enjoyed some leisure. The house is made of coquina, which has been plastered over and painted pink. There are quilting demonstrations on Thursday morning.

The **José Peso de Burgo and Francisco Pellicer House,** a wooden structure dating from the British Period (1763–83), was shared by two families. Peso de Burgo, a Corsican, was a merchant and shopkeeper, and Francisco Pellicer was a Minorcan carpenter. The families had separate kitchens. Today the house is used for an exhibition on Minorcan culture.

After you've left the Spanish Quarter, explore the quaint narrow streets nearby. They also contain many reconstructed and original historic buildings (indicated by markers), as well as charming boutiques and antiques shops.

BEACHES, GOLF & OTHER OUTDOOR ACTIVITIES

BEACHES   There are several places to go to the beach, but **Anastasia State Recreation Area,** 1340A Fla. A1A South (Anastasia Boulevard), on your left just past the Alligator Farm (☎ 904/461-2033), has the most extensive facilities; call for details about camping and fishing. This 1,800-acre state-run recreation area has 4 miles of sandy beach bordered by picturesque dunes and a lagoon flanked by tidal marshes. It offers shaded picnic areas with grills, rest rooms, windsurfing, sailing and canoeing (on a saltwater lagoon), a nature trail, and saltwater fishing (for bluefish, pompano, and whiting from the surf; sea trout, redfish, and flounder; a license is required for out-of-state residents). In summer you can rent chairs, beach umbrellas, and surfboards. There's good birdwatching here too, especially in spring and fall; pick up a brochure at the entrance. The site also has 139 secluded **campsites** in a wooded area—all with picnic tables and grills—which rent for $12 to $15 a night. Admission is $3.25 per vehicle, and the day-use area is open daily from 8am to sunset.

To reach **St. Augustine Beach,** take the Bridge of Lions to Fla. A1A and proceed south to Dondanville Road, where you can park right on the beach. Or head over to **Vilano Beach,** taking the Vilano Bridge and making a left on Fla. A1A; there's a parking lot at Surfside Ramp (on your right shortly after your turn onto Fla. A1A). You can park on the beach at Vilano too, but beware of soft sand. A few miles farther along Fla. A1A you'll come to a parking area with covered picnic tables and grills. This is a popular beach for fishing, but the surf is too rough for swimming.

All St. Augustine beaches charge a fee of $3 per car at official access points Memorial Day to Labor Day; the rest of the year you can park free, but there are no lifeguards on duty and no portable toilet facilities on the beach.

FISHING   For full-, half-day, and overnight deep-sea fishing excursions (for snapper, grouper, porgy, amberjack, and sea bass, among other fish), contact the **Sea Love Marina** (☎ **904/767-3406,** or 800/940-FISH). No license is required, and rod, reel, bait, and tackle are supplied. For additional options, call the St. Johns County Visitors and Convention Bureau (details above) and ask them to send you *A Guide to Fishing & Boating.*

GOLF   There are several golf courses open to the public—including those at the **Ponce de León Golf & Conference Resort,** 4000 U.S. 1 North (☎ **904/824-2821,** or 800/228-2821), and the **St. Augustine Shores Country Club,** 707 Shores Blvd., off U.S. 1 (☎ **904/794-4653**).

TENNIS   There are 24 **municipal tennis courts,** that are open to the public at no charge, including two behind the Visitor Information Center. You don't need reservations; play is on a first-come, first-served basis. Call 904/471-6616 for details.

WATER SPORTS   Jet skis and surfing and windsurfing equipment can be rented at **Surf Station,** 1020 Anastasia Blvd., a block south of the Alligator Farm (☎ **904/471-9463**); the staff here can also tell you the best surfing locations and provide lessons.

OTHER ATTRACTIONS

Marineland of Florida. 9507 Ocean Shore Blvd. (Fla. A1A), Marineland. ☎ **904/471-1111.** Admission $14.95 adults, $9.95 for children 13–18, $7.95 children 3–12, free for children 2 and under. Daily 9am–5:30pm. Free parking.

This beachfront marinelife park on the Atlantic Ocean was the first establishment to successfully maintain dolphins in an oceanarium. Today Marineland features dolphin shows in a vast saltwater oceanarium as well as displays of other marine animals. A second oceanarium is home to marine specimens representing more than 125 species; native Florida species can be viewed in the 35,000-gallon Wonders of the Spring aquarium. Marineland is 18 miles south of St. Augustine.

Potter's Wax Museum. 17 King St. (between Aviles and St. George sts.). ☎ **904/829-9056.** Admission $5.50 adults, $4.50 seniors 55 and over, $3 children 6–12, free for children 5 and under. Daily 9am–5pm (to 9pm June 15–Labor Day). Closed Christmas Day.

Over 150 wax figures are on display at Potter's, not only key players in local Florida history but figures of international renown, along with the requisite torture section, here focusing on the Spanish Inquisition. Every effort was spent on authenticity; Francis Drake and de Soto are clad in actual armor from their eras. A craftsperson can be seen at work on wax figures.

Ripley's Believe It or Not! Museum. 19 San Marco Ave. (at Castillo Dr.). ☎ **904/824-1606.** Admission $7.50 adults, $4.25 children 5–12, free for children 4 and under. Daily 9am–10pm. Free parking.

Housed in a converted 1887 Moorish Revival residence known as Warden Castle, this immense display comprises hundreds of oddities and fascinating artifacts from faraway places collected by Robert Ripley. Exhibits run a wide gamut, from a Haitian voodoo doll that was owned by "Papa Doc" Duvalier to letters carved on a pencil with a chain saw by Ray "Wild Mountain Man" Murphy.

✪ **St. Augustine Alligator Farm.** 999 Anastasia Blvd. (Fla. A1A; at Old Quarry Rd.). ☎ **904/ 824-3337.** Admission $9.95 adults, $8.95 seniors 65 and over, $5.95 children 3–10, free for children 2 and under. Daily 9am–5pm (to 6pm June–Labor Day). Free parking.

The world's most complete collection of crocodilians—a category that includes alligators, crocodiles, caiman, and gharial—is here, encompassing all 23 species and arranged zoogeographically by continent. Gomek, at 1,800 pounds and almost 18 feet in length, is the largest crocodile in captivity in the Western Hemisphere. Many other species are also on exhibit, and there's a petting zoo with pygmy goats, pot-bellied pigs, miniature horses, and other animals.

Entertaining (and educational) 20-minute alligator and reptile shows take place hourly throughout the day, and spring through fall you can often see narrated feedings.

WHERE TO STAY

St. Augustine is famous for its lovely bed-and-breakfast lodgings, most of them in beautifully restored historic homes—and most expensive for a traveler on a budget. Nevertheless, I've included a few that are reasonably priced. If you visit during the week, rates are lower. Generally, the B&Bs don't take young children, so if you're traveling with the family consider a beach hotel or one of St. Augustine's very acceptable inexpensive motels. There are nice **campsites at the Anastasia State Recreation Area** (see "Beaches, Golf & Other Outdoor Activities," above). All but beach accommodations are just a few minutes from the historic district, and even those are within a 15-minute drive.

Note: In addition to the 6% state sales tax, St. Augustine levies an additional 3% tax on hotel bills.

IN TOWN

Doubles for Less than $40

Scottish Inns. 110 San Marco Ave. (at Old Mission Ave.), St. Augustine, FL 32084. ☎ **904/ 824-2871,** or 800/251-1962. Fax 904/826-4149. 27 rms. A/C TV TEL. $26–$45 double Sun–Thurs, $55–$75 Fri–Sat. Rates may be higher during special events. Additional person $5 extra; children 12 and under stay free in parents' room. AE, DISC, MC, V. Free parking.

I like the original look of this hostelry. It's housed in a yellow-brick building embellished with lacy green wrought-iron pillars and balconies with large potted plants. The courtyard centers on a 400-year-old live oak draped in Spanish moss (long ago, it was a hanging tree!). The recently renovated rooms have patios or balconies furnished with Adirondack chairs. Coffee is served in the lobby each morning. Pets are allowed.

Super 8. 3552 N. Ponce de Leon Blvd. (between Rambla and Fairbanks sts.), St. Augustine, FL 32084. ☎ **904/824-6399,** or 800/800-8000. 49 rms. A/C TV TEL. $35–$38 room for one person Sun–Thurs, $40–$43 Fri–Sat. Additional person $3–$5 extra; children 18 and under stay free in parents' room. AE, CB, DC, DISC, MC, V. Free parking.

Just a few minutes' drive from the Historic District, this spiffy Super 8 was completely renovated in 1995. Its attractively landscaped grounds include a palm-fringed lawn with a swimming pool and shuffleboard and volleyball courts. The large rooms have balconies or patios; especially appealing are the upstairs accommodations with peaked beamed ceilings. A seafood restaurant is next door, and conveniently across the street is a large shopping center with a 24-hour supermarket. Pets are permitted.

Thriftlodge. 2500 N. Ponce de Leon Blvd. (at Pacific St., just south of Fla. 16), St. Augustine, FL 32084. ☎ **904/824-1341,** or 800/525-9055. Fax 904/823-9850. 31 rms. A/C TV TEL. $28–$60 double. Rates may be higher during special events. Rates include continental breakfast. Additional person $5 extra; children 9 and under stay free in parents' room. AE, CB, DC, DISC, MC, V. Free parking.

This well-maintained family-run property is housed in a U-shaped peach building with turquoise doors and trim. The attractive rooms offer extensive cable TV selections plus movie stations. Coffee and doughnuts are served gratis in the lobby each morning. A small swimming pool is on the premises, an IHOP is adjacent, and Nacho Mamas (see below) is right across the street.

Doubles for Less than $60

Comfort Inn. 1111 Ponce de Leon Blvd. (U.S. 1 North, at Old Mission Rd.), St. Augustine, FL 32084. ☎ **904/824-5554,** or 800/575-5288. Fax 904/829-2948. 78 rms, 6 suites. A/C TV TEL. $42–$79.95 double Sun–Fri, $89 Sat; $52–$89.95 suite Sun–Fri, $99 Sat. During special events and holidays, $99.95 double; $109.95 suite. Rates include continental breakfast. Additional person $5 extra; children 17 and under stay free in parents' room. AE, CB, DC, DISC, JCB, MC, V. Free parking.

The Comfort Inn is just 2 minutes from the historic district, in a two-story stucco building with a terra-cotta roof and mission-style facade. Ideal for families are the large suites containing dressing rooms with double sinks and parlor areas with extra TVs and pull-out sofas. A continental breakfast is served in a pleasant room with windows overlooking the pool. There's no on-premises restaurant, but several fast-food eateries are close by. Facilities include a nice-size swimming pool/whirlpool and coin-op washers and dryers.

Howard Johnson. 137 San Marco Ave. (between Sebastian/Myrtle aves. and Sanchez Ave.), St. Augustine, FL 32084. ☎ **904/824-6181,** or 800/575-5290. Fax 904/825-2775. 70 rms, 7 suites. A/C TV TEL. $49–$79 room for up to four Sun–Thurs, $59–$89 Fri–Sat, $99.95 during special events and holidays; $99–$129 Jacuzzi room; $129–$199 Jacuzzi suite. Rates include continental breakfast. AE, CB, DC, DISC, JCB, MC, V. Free parking.

Under the same ownership as the Comfort Inn—and very similar to it—Hojo also has rooms in a mission-style building evocative of the Spanish Colonial period. The hostelry's garden courtyard, planted with palms and hibiscus, centers on a massive 500-year-old live oak draped in Spanish moss. The standard motel rooms here offer remote-control cable TV with visitor-information channels. On-premises facilities include a medium-size swimming pool, a whirlpool, and a coin-op washer/dryer. Hojo is just a few minutes from the historic district.

✪ Quality Inn Alhambra. 2700 Ponce de Leon Blvd. (U.S. 1, at Fla. 16), St. Augustine, FL 32084. ☎ **904/824-2883,** or 800/223-4153. 72 rms, 5 Jacuzzi suites. $42–$75 double; $125–$175 Jacuzzi suite. Additional person $5 extra; children 17 and under stay free in parents' room. Rates higher during major events. AE, CB, DC, DISC, JCB, MC, V. Free parking.

This well-run family-owned property offers large, attractively decorated rooms with porches or balconies. Most luxurious are the Jacuzzi suites with living room areas; guests in these accommodations get hair dryers, terry robes, and complimentary champagne on arrival. VCRs and rental movies are available in the lobby gift shop, and an IHOP on the premises provides room service. Additional facilities include a gift shop, a large swimming pool, and a whirlpool.

AT THE BEACH
Doubles for Less than $60

La Fiesta Oceanside Inn. 810 Beach Blvd. (Fla. A1A, at F St.), St. Augustine Beach, FL 32084. ☎ **904/471-2220,** or 800/852-6390. Fax 904/471-0186. 34 rms, 2 bridal suites. A/C TV TEL.

Labor Day to early Feb, $49–$59 double; $69 ocean-view double or bridal suite. Early Feb to Labor Day, $89–$109 double; $109–$129 ocean-view double or bridal suite. Additional person $5 extra. CB, DC, DISC, MC, V. Free parking.

La Fiesta's cheerful beachfront accommodations are housed in two-story tan stucco buildings with Spanish-style terra-cotta roofs and fragrant Confederate jasmine climbing the columns. Eight units offer ocean views, and two are ocean-view bridal suites equipped with extra-large tubs, wet bars, small refrigerators, and king-size beds. The sunny NASCAR-themed Beachhouse Cafe serves breakfast daily. Other on-premises facilities include coin-op washers and dryers, a boardwalk over the dunes, a children's playground, a swimming pool, an 18-hole beachfront miniature golf course, and a picnic area with a barbecue grill.

BETWEEN THE BEACH AND TOWN

Doubles for Less than $60

Rodeway Inn. 107 Anastasia Blvd. (directly across the Bridge of Lions, between Gerado St. and Zorayda Ave.), St. Augustine, FL 32084. ☎ **904/826-1700** or 800/228-2000. Fax 904/823-8811. 21 rms. A/C TV TEL. Sun–Thurs, $29–$79.95 double; $79.95 double with Jacuzzi. Fri–Sat $59.95–$109 double; $139 double with Jacuzzi. Rates may be higher during special events. Rates include continental breakfast. Additional person $6 extra; children 18 and under stay free in parents' room. AE, CB, DC, DISC, MC, V. Free parking.

This gleaming new hostelry, close to the beach and the historic district, has immaculate, cheerful rooms equipped with hair dryers, coffeemakers, small refrigerators, and microwave ovens. One unit has a Jacuzzi tub. Complimentary coffee, juices, danish, and doughnuts are served in the lobby each morning. There's a very small swimming pool on the premises. A supermarket and several good restaurants are within easy walking distance.

WORTH A SPLURGE

Generally bed-and-breakfasts, because they're in historic homes and filled with antiques, do not accept children or permit smoking on the premises. Most innkeepers will happily arrange romantic extras on request, such as roses or champagne in your room, a gourmet picnic lunch, a moonlit carriage ride—even a wedding or renewal of your vows. All the below-listed are within walking distance of (or right in) the historic district.

Carriage Way Bed and Breakfast. 70 Cuna St. (between Cordova and Spanish sts.), St. Augustine, FL 32084. ☎ **904/829-2467**, or 800/908-9832. Fax 904/826-1461. 9 rms. A/C TEL. $59–$99 double Sun–Thurs; $69–$125 Fri–Sat. Rates include full breakfast. DISC, MC, V. Free parking.

Occupying an 1883 Victorian wood-frame house fronted by roses and hibiscus, the Carriage Way has furnished its rooms with quality antiques. One unit has an oak four-poster bed with carved pineapple posts; others have brass, wicker, or even canopy beds. The accommodations are enhanced by dried-flower arrangements and lovely window treatments, and one room has a working fireplace.

A console TV, books, magazines, and games are provided in a comfortable parlor. And a second-story veranda offers a view of the picturesque historic area. Breakfast, served in the dining room or alfresco on the front porch, includes eggs, breakfast meats, and homemade fruit breads and muffins. Hospitable owner/hosts Bill and Diane Johnson offer many complimentary extras: bicycles for touring the area; decanters of crème de menthe, red wine, and sherry available on a buffet table in the entrance hallway; and a refrigerator stocked with iced glasses, beer, and soft drinks. Guests can also use the Johnsons' washer and dryer.

✪ **Casablanca Inn on the Bay.** 24 Avenida Menendez (between Hypolita and Treasury sts.), St. Augustine, FL 32084. ☎ **904/829-0928,** or 800/826-2626. Fax 904/826-1892. 2 rms, 10 suites. A/C. Mon–Thurs, $79–$99 double; $99–$139 suite. Fri–Sun, $119–$139 double; $139–$179 suite. Rates include full breakfast. AE, DISC, MC, V. Free parking.

This 1914 Mediterranean-style white stucco house faces directly on the bay. Guests enjoy stunning water views from rocking chairs on the colonnaded portico. And though over half the rooms and suites offer full marine vistas—and all have private balconies or porches—most divinely decadent are the two second-floor suites whose bayfront balconies are equipped with hammocks.

Delightful owners Brenda and Tony Bushell have done a great job decorating here. The white-walled, carpeted rooms are furnished with turn-of-the-century American oak pieces (some have four-poster beds), and the windows are framed by pretty floral-chintz curtains. Homey touches might include a Victorian birdcage or a grouping of antique dolls on your mantel. All offer a selection of books, fan chandeliers, cassette players, and alarm-clock radios. The suites have sitting room areas, and, in some cases, Jacuzzis. Guests can use the microwave and refrigerator in the kitchen and help themselves to complimentary beer, wine, soft drinks, chocolates, and cookies at all times; hors d'oeuvres are served every afternoon; and weekend visitors get gratis champagne. A scrumptious breakfast—enjoyed alfresco on the porch or in a glass-enclosed conservatory—includes thick slabs of French toast or a Minorcan baked eggs and sausage soufflé. Bicycles are available free of charge.

The Old Powder House Inn. 38 Cordova St. (between Carrera and Cuna sts.), St. Augustine, FL 32084. ☎ **904/824-4149,** or 800/447-4149. 8 rms, 1 suite. $59–$125 double Mon–Thurs, $69–$150 Fri–Sun. Rates include full breakfast. Additional person $10 extra. AE, DISC, MC, V. Free parking in a lot behind the house.

This turn-of-the-century classic Victorian house occupies the site of an 18th-century powder house that supplied gunpowder to Spanish soldiers at the Castillo. Today it serves a more peaceful function as a delightful and well-run B&B. Guests can relax in the cozy parlor where a grandfather clock chimes the hours or on four verandas furnished with wicker rockers and Adirondack chairs. The immaculate rooms are charming. Your bed might be brass, a four-poster mahogany, a high Victorian half-canopy, or a Jenny Lind (spindlebed) made up with a patchwork quilt. One room, called Memories, contains antique toys and a little rocking horse. All rooms are equipped with alarm-clock radios and fan chandeliers; a TV is available on request. Hostess Eunice Howes goes all-out to please her guests, cosseting them with hearty breakfasts that include daily-changing entrees such as apple-pecan pancakes or egg-cheese soufflés. Afternoon teas feature homemade cakes and pastries, and late-afternoon wine is served with hors d'oeuvres. You'll scarcely have to go out for a meal.

SHORT- & LONG-TERM STAYS

Ocean Gallery. 4600 Fla. A1A South (between Dondonville Rd. and Trade Winds Lane), St. Augustine, FL 32084. ☎ **904/471-6663** or 800/940-6665. 200 condo apts. A/C TV TEL. Mar–Apr and June–Aug, $470 one-bedroom/one-bath apt; $495 two-bedroom/one-bath apt; $520–$755 two-bedroom/two-bath apt; $600–$935 three-bedroom/two-bath apt. Jan–Feb, $355 one-bedroom/one-bath apt; $380 two-bedroom/one-bath apt; $405–$570 two-bedroom/two-bath apt; $480–$700 three-bedroom/two-bath apt. May and Sept–Dec, $330 one-bedroom/one-bath apt; $350 two-bedroom/one-bath apt; $370–$530 two-bedroom/two-bath apt; $430–$635 three-bedroom/two-bath apt. Rates are per week, with a 1-week minimum. Maid service $40–$45 extra for length of stay. Reduced monthly rates. DISC, MC, V. Parking $10 for length of stay.

The Ocean Gallery may represent one of the country's top vacation bargains. Set on 44 attractively landscaped acres with gardens, lakes, and lagoons, it comprises beautiful vacation homes with access to 17 miles of palm-fringed, white-sand beach. Its spacious condos are decorated in upscale resort style; some have VCRs and/or CD and cassette players. All offer fully equipped kitchens, full living and dining areas, and furnished balconies or patios. About half have beach views, but keep in mind that the more stunning your ocean view, the higher the price. There are many restaurants nearby, but none on the premises. There are, however, five swimming pools, five whirlpools, four tennis courts, two racquetball courts, two shuffleboard courts, an exercise room, two saunas, a video-game arcade, a clubhouse/library, picnic tables, and barbecue grills. Daily activities are offered January to March. Book as far in advance as possible—the Ocean Gallery is very popular.

✪ **Villas on the Bay.** 105 Marine St. (between San Salvador and St. Francis sts.), St. Augustine, FL 32084. ☎ **904/823-8885,** or 800/826-2626. Fax 904/826-1892. 9 one-bedroom suites. A/C TV TEL. $350–$750 suite per week, $1,200–$2,500 suite per month. AE, DISC, MC, V. Free parking.

You couldn't find a more idyllic spot than this for a romantic getaway. Tony and Brenda Bushell, owners of the Casablanca Inn (see above), bought this beautiful bayfront property in 1995. The building dates to 1864, when it was a Civil War military hospital. The Bushells have totally revamped its interior space, creating three luxurious levels of spacious one-bedroom suites, most with double Jacuzzi tubs. All have full kitchens and dining areas. Best of all, private balconies, furnished with rocking chairs and/or hammocks, provide spectacular bay views. Each suite is furnished with antiques and Victoriana. All are equipped with cable TV, irons and ironing boards, phones, alarm-clock radios, ceiling fans, cassette players (with an assortment of tapes), and books and magazines. On-premises amenities/facilities include complimentary bicycles, a small swimming pool and sundeck, a comfortable library with wicker rocking chairs on an enclosed porch, a workout room, washers/dryers for guest use, and once-a-week maid service. Your refrigerator is stocked with soft drinks, and a decanter of sherry is provided. Hostess Marie Register provides warm hospitality and conciergelike service.

WHERE TO EAT

For a small town, St. Augustine has a lot of excellent restaurants, including many budget choices. Local specialties include red-hot datil peppers, Minorcan clam chowder, alligator, and oysters.

MEALS FOR LESS THAN $7

Ann O'Malley's Deli. 23 Orange St. (between Spanish and Cordova sts.). ☎ **904/825-4040.** Reservations not accepted. Main courses $3.50–$4.25. No credit cards. Daily 11:30am–11pm. IRISH DELI.

Conveniently located in the heart of the historic district, this popular local hangout abounds in Irish pub ambience. There's a dart board, and a picture of Elvis over the bar; "he's by way of being a patron saint in Ireland," says Ann. The menu is very limited, but everything on it is made from scratch. There's a good choice of sandwiches (perhaps freshly prepared chicken salad on whole-wheat toast). Ann's homemade soups and chili are noteworthy, as are her daily specials which range from chicken Florentine to meatball subs. There are no desserts, but beverage choices include a good variety of Irish beers and ales. You'll find inexpensive paid parking in adjacent lots.

Athena Restaurant. 14 Cathedral Place (between Charlotte and St. George sts.). ☎ **904/ 823-9076.** Reservations not accepted. Main courses $2.30–$10.95. MC, V. Sun–Thurs 7am– 9:30pm, Fri–Sat 7am–11pm. GREEK/AMERICAN.

This pleasant Greek coffee shop, a local standby, is the domain of owner/chef Costa Roussopoulos and his wife, Maria, who came to St. Augustine on their honeymoon and fell in love with the town. They've created a friendly homelike setting, with seating in comfortable booths, and walls embellished with colorful murals of historic St. Augustine and the Parthenon.

Everything is fresh, authentic (expecting big portions of so-so food, I was pleasantly surprised), and made from scratch. Costa's hefty combination dinners—such as a platter of Greek salad, spinach pie, pastitsio, moussaka, grape leaves, and meatballs (plus soup) for $10.95—are an incredible value. If you have room after all that, order Maria's delicious cheesecake for dessert. A full breakfast menu lists everything from fresh-baked bagels to Greek omelets. A wide selection of sandwiches are priced under $5. And an inexpensive children's menu makes this an appealing choice for families.

Bono's Pit Bar-B-Q and Sports Pub. In the Anastasia Publix Plaza, 100l Beach Blvd. (take the Bridge of Lions and go about 6 miles along Fla. A1A). ☎ **904/46l-0157.** Reservations not accepted. Main courses $3.50–$6.50 at lunch, $3.50–$10 at dinner. AE, MC, V. Sun–Thurs 11am–9pm, Fri–Sat llam–10pm. BARBECUE.

At this rambunctious restaurant and pub, sporting events are always on the TV at full volume and the purple walls are hung with sports paraphernalia. Many people love the action, which also includes video poker and other bar games, electronic darts, and a video-game room in the back. If, however, cacophony drives you crazy, order your meal to go and enjoy a picnic at the beach.

Two or three people can eat their fill on Bono's Feast ($18)—oak-barbecued spareribs, beef, chicken, turkey, or smoked sausage, served family style with garlic toast, french fries, homemade cole slaw, and baked beans. Recommended side dishes include a baked sweet potato and deep-fried corn on the cob rolled in garlic butter.

The Bunnery Café. 35 Hypolita St. (at St. George St.). ☎ **904/829-6166.** Reservations not accepted. Everything is under $4. No credit cards. Daily 9am–5:30pm. BAKERY.

Alluring aromas waft from this bakery/cafe in the heart of the historic district. Come here for breakfast or after a hard day's sightseeing, plop yourself into a chair on the arcaded terra-cotta patio, and indulge in a fresh-baked cinnamon roll or strawberry and cream cheese croissant accompanied by a big cup of cappuccino.

Schmagel's Bagels. 69 Hypolita St. (at Cordova St.). ☎ **904/824-4444.** Reservations not accepted. Sandwiches $3.95–$4.75. No credit cards. Mon–Sat 7:30am–3pm, Sun 8:30am–2pm. BAGEL SANDWICHES.

On sunny mornings my favorite thing is to sit outdoors at one of Schmagel's umbrella-shaded patio tables and read the morning paper over coffee and Schmagel's authentically New York–style oven-fresh bagels. They come in 12 varieties, with all kinds of cream-cheese spreads. There are traditional sandwiches, and the menu lists breakfast bacon and eggs, fresh soups du jour, soft drinks, and fresh-baked fruit muffins. There's metered parking in a lot across Cordova Street.

MEALS FOR LESS THAN $10

La Parisienne. 60 Hypolita St. (between Spanish and Cordova sts.). ☎ **904/829-0055.** Reservations recommended. Main courses $4.95–$6.50 at lunch, $13–$18 at dinner. AE, DISC, MC, V. Tues–Sat 11am–3pm and 5:30–9pm (afternoon tea 3–4pm), Sun llam–3pm. FRENCH.

Though it's above our budget at dinner, consider La Parisienne for lunch. Both its ambience and its authentic cuisine will indeed remind you of Paris. And its location in the heart of the picturesque historic district further enhances the illusion. The lunch menu offers traditional bistro fare, such as quiche Lorraine, croque monsieur, croissant sandwiches, and salade niçoise. An extensive international wine list is available. At afternoon tea, or for dessert, there are oven-fresh chocolate eclairs, praline ganaches, or fruit tarts.

Nacho Mamas. 2601 Ponce de Leon Blvd. (between Fla. 16 and Center St.). ☎ **904/826-4114.** Reservations not accepted. Main courses $3.95–$7.95. No credit cards. Tues–Thurs 11:30am–9pm, Fri 11:30am–10pm, Sat 4:30–10pm, Sun 4:30–9pm. MEXICAN.

A mom-and-pop operation run by Mike and Ernie Hill (he cooks, she serves; sometimes the baby's here as well), this popular local hangout is your classic Jimmy Buffet–song roadhouse. Neon beer signs announce its exterior; seating is at picnic-style tables, and the background music is southern rock and blues.

Start off with yummy fresh-made nachos topped with seasoned ground beef. Good main-course choices include enchildas, sizzling platters of beef, and chicken fajitas. If you have room, there's flan or margarita cheesecake for dessert. Free parking.

✪ **Oscar's Old Florida Grill.** 614 Euclid Ave. (off Fla. A1A on the Intracoastal Waterway). ☎ **904/829-3794.** Reservations not accepted; call ahead for priority seating. Main courses $5.50–$14.95. MC, V. Wed–Thurs 5–9pm, Fri 5–10pm, Sat noon–10pm, Sun noon–9pm. Go over the Vilano Bridge, veer left on Fla. A1A North, drive about 2¹/₂ miles, and turn left at Compton's. OLD FLORIDA/SEAFOOD.

Boats have been docking here for grub since the late 19th century when Frank and Catherine Usina served up oyster roasts to Henry Flagler and his Vanderbilt pals. The Usinas' old fish camp today is Oscar's, a rustic eatery housed in a 1909 roadhouse with pine-plank floors and a steeply pitched tin ceiling. In this very casual setting the mood ranges from convivial to rollicking—especially on Wednesday and Thursday night from 6 to 9pm when live bluegrass and country music groups perform. That's definitely the time to visit, though I also love weekend lunches here, when you can sit outside at riverside picnic tables shaded by a grove of live oaks. A bait shop adjoins, and people frequently fish from the dock after lunch. Parking is free.

Order up a large bucket of steamed oysters or a platter of fried shrimp, fresh fish, or oysters, all accompanied by french fries *and* hush puppies. Try the piquant pink sauce composed of mayonnaise and datil peppers. These fried items can also be enjoyed as sandwiches. Wine and beer are available, and there's rich sweet-potato pie for dessert.

MEALS FOR LESS THAN $15

✪ **Creekside Dinery.** 160 Nix Boat Yard Rd. (off U.S. 1; turn at Long John Silver). ☎ **904/829-6113.** Reservations not accepted. Main courses $4.50–$6 at lunch, $8–$14 at dinner. AE, DISC, MC, V. Mon–Thurs 11:30am–2:30pm and 5–9pm, Fri 11:30am–2:30pm and 5–10pm, Sat 5–10pm, Sun noon–8pm. TRADITIONAL FLORIDIAN.

This cozy restaurant occupies a dormer-windowed white frame house fronted by live oak, pecan, and magnolia trees. Guests wait for tables on a rose vine–covered porch furnished with wicker rocking chairs; the rough-hewn cedar interior has seating at candlelit tables under a peaked cathedral ceiling. There's additional seating on a screened patio overlooking a creek and boatyard.

A good beginning here is a dish of garlicky, buttery oysters Creekside topped with oven-browned provolone cheese and herbed breadcrumbs (six for just $4!). And there are several entrees under $10, among them roast chicken glazed with rosemary-plum sauce and lightly battered pan-broiled shrimp. The all-American wine list highlights selections from Florida vineyards. Leave room for a dessert called "the chocolate thing," basically an old-fashioned icebox cake made of chocolate cookie and whipped cream layers. Arrive early to avoid a wait. A complimentary courtesy car can provide transportation from/to local hotels.

✪ Fiddler's Green. 2750 Anahma Dr. (at Ferrell Rd., on Vilane Beach). ☎ **904/824-8897.** Reservations recommended Sun–Fri, not accepted Sat. Main courses $9–$17. AE, CB, DC, DISC, MC, V. Sun–Thurs 5–9pm, Fri–Sat 5–10pm. Head north on San Marco Avenue, cross the Vilano Bridge (Fla. A1A North), and bear right to Vilano Beach. FLORIDIAN/SEAFOOD.

This shiplike restaurant is right on the Atlantic Ocean, and is appropriately entered via a kind of gangplank. Rustic elegance is the keynote here, with pecky cypress and cedar paneling and two blazing coquina stone fireplaces. Though it's a bit high for our budget, you can enjoy Fiddler's delightful ambience without going bust if you order carefully. For instance, several sautéed pasta dishes—such as angel hair tossed with aspargus tips, sun-dried tomatoes, and roasted garlic in tomato-basil butter—are just $9, including a Caesar salad. And for $11 you can order Jamaican jerk chicken with sour-orange and green-onion chutney, black beans, and rice. A low-priced children's menu makes family dining affordable. You might want to adjourn for dessert and after-dinner drinks to the cozy upstairs lounge—try the chocolate mousse laced with Kahlúa and crowned with fresh whipped cream. There's a carefully chosen and fairly extensive wine list. A complimentary courtesy car can provide transportation from/to local hotels.

Raintree. 102 San Marco Ave. (at Bernard St.). ☎ **904/824-7211.** Reservations recommended. Early dinner selections (served 5–6pm) $8.95–$10.95; full children's dinners $6.95. AE, DC, MC, V. Sun–Fri 5–9:30pm, Sat 5–10pm. CONTINENTAL.

Occupying an 1879 Victorian house, this is one of St. Augustine's most romantic upscale restaurants, with some dishes as high as $19.95. But if you're willing to dine early, it's very affordable. Bamboo furnishings, ficus trees, and a striped canvas awning create a cozy indoor-garden setting, and cut-crystal lamps cast a soft glow. Weather permitting, there's seating on an open-air porch, balcony, or lushly planted brick patio.

From 5 to 6pm daily, you can feast on such fancy fare as filet mignon tips sautéed with artichokes in red-wine/mushroom sauce, or boneless pork loin sautéed in Grand Marnier (selections change monthly) for under $11. After early-bird hours, you can still eat inexpensively by ordering a pasta dish such as linguine tossed with sun-dried tomatoes, artichoke hearts, and black olives in sherry-cream sauce ($11.95). There's a full bar and an extensive wine list. After your early meal, you can linger at the elegant dessert bar over crêpes Suzette, bananas Foster, and/or after-dinner drinks. A complimentary courtesy car provides transportation from/to local hotels.

✪ Salt Water Cowboy's. 299 Dondanville Rd. (off Fla. A1A). ☎ **904/471-2332.** Reservations not accepted, so arrive early to avoid a wait. Main courses $8–$15. AE, DISC, MC, V. Sun–Thurs 5–9pm, Fri–Sat 5–10pm. Go over the Bridge of Lions and follow Fla. A1A South for about 10 minutes; look for the restaurant's billboard, and make a right onto Dondanville Road just before you see a 7-Eleven store. OLD FLORIDA/SEAFOOD/BARBECUE.

Arrive early for dinner—not only to beat the crowd but to enjoy a spectacular view of the sun setting over a saltwater marsh. Designed to resemble a turn-of-the-century fish camp, this rambling Intracoastal Waterway restaurant has a rustic candlelit interior paneled with cedar lapwood and shingles. A mix of dining areas ranges from intimate booths to an outdoor plant-filled deck shaded by live oaks and illumined by tiki torches. The background music is great—ragtime, Dixieland, and banjo tunes played at a low decibel level.

Like its ambience, Cowboy's cuisine harks back to Old Florida. For openers, there's a very rich and creamy chowder with big chunks of clam, potato, and celery. A main course of fork-tender baby back ribs ($12) is a great choice. Another winner for just $10: oysters, scallops, or shrimp fried in light cornmeal batter and served with salad or cole slaw, hot bread, a baked potato, and a vegetable. Plan on dessert—creamy chocolate-almond pie on a chocolate cookie crust.

ST. AUGUSTINE AFTER DARK
BARS & CLUBS

A1A Ale House. 1 King St. (at Avenida Menendez). ☎ **904/829-2977**. No cover.

The *simpático* two-story Ale House—with its own microbrewery on the premises—is a popular local hangout. On weekend nights, light rock and R&B tunes are performed downstairs by a singer and acoustic guitarist. An extensive menu features "Floribbean" cuisine items such as mojito-grilled chicken breast with papaya-banana chutney. The food here is excellent, and you can wash it down with any of seven home-brewed beers. Weather permitting, you can dine on a New Orleans–style balcony.

Bobby D's. At the Monson Bayfront Resort, 32 Avenida Menendez (between Treasury and Hypolita sts.). ☎ **904/829-2277**. No cover.

The comfortable bar/lounge at this bayfront resort is the setting for talented pianist and singer Bobby Dubik, Thursday to Saturday night from about 8:30pm to midnight. Sometimes accompanied by brother Teddy on bongos, Bobby plays standards and show tunes (he takes requests), and does humorous imitations of Maurice Chevalier and Carmen Miranda. This piano bar has a loyal local following, and there's a dance floor. Parking is free.

Mill Top Tavern. 19^1/$_2$ St. George St. (at Fort Alley). ☎ **904/829-2329.** Cover varies Mon, Wed, and Sat, depending on the performer.

There's live entertainment nightly from 1pm to closing in this rustic tavern, housed in a 19th-century mill building (the water wheel is still outside). The music varies from classical guitar to bluegrass, rock, blues, and country rock offered on Friday and Saturday and featuring local and nationally known artists. Weather permitting, the stage is an open-air space, and there's also actual outdoor seating. A full menu is served till 10 p.m. and there's a large selection of specialty drinks with names like "Beam Me Up Scotty." Most of the crowd is 30-something (you must be 21 to get in after 9pm). Free parking is available.

Panama Hattie's Saloon. 361 Fla. A1A (Beach Blvd.). ☎ **904/471-2255**. No cover. Take the Bridge of Lions to Anastasia Boulevard, continue to Fla. 312, turn left, and follow Fla. A1A.

This funky beach bar has a rustic interior with bars and dance floors on two levels. During the week Hattie's functions as a popular local bar; on Friday and Saturday night there are oldies bands, and a DJ plays Top 40 tunes. Light fare is available. You must be 21 to get in. Open nightly till 1am.

Scarlett O'Hara's. 70 Hypolita St. (at Cordova St.). ☎ **904/824-6535**. Usually no cover; sometimes $1 Fri–Sat.

In the heart of St. Augustine's historic district, Scarlett O'Hara's offers a catacomb of cozy rooms with working fireplaces in a rambling 19th-century wood-frame house. Rock, jazz, and R&B bands play Tuesday to Saturday from 9pm to 12:30am, and though there's no dance floor, people get up and dance wherever. Sunday and Monday are karaoke nights. Sporting events are aired on a large-screen TV. Sandwiches, seafood, Florida specialties like fried gator, and munchies are served until midnight. You must be 21 to get in after 9pm. You can park in a lot across Cordova Street.

Trade Winds Tropical Lounge. 124 Charlotte St. (between Cathedral Place and Treasury St.). ☎ **904/829-9336.** No cover Sun–Thurs, $1–$2 Fri–Sat.

Toni Leonard and her daughters, Janet and Julie, have been operating this funky-friendly local hangout for four decades. The music is a mix of southern rock, oldies, folk, country, and blues. Toni gets a kick out of telling how she fired Jimmy Buffett before he was famous because she didn't think he had any talent (they're still friends). Most of the groups playing Trade Winds are local, but well-known oldies groups like the Platters, the Coasters, the Drifters, and the Byrds do occasional gigs here. And on Palm Sunday every year, many of the musicians who've played the club come back for a music marathon. Light fare is available. You must be 21 to get in after 9pm. A weekday happy hour from 5 to 8pm also offers live entertainment. Street parking only.

White Lion. 20 Cuna St. (between Charlotte and St. George sts.) ☎ **904/829-2388.** No cover.

This comfortable British-style pub is a great place to hang out. Friday to Sunday night an acoustic guitarist or duo play Top 40 tunes here; March to November, there's also afternoon entertainment daily on a large patio overlooking the Castillo. A full menu featuring steak and fish and chips is offered through 9pm nightly; frozen daiquiris and margaritas, imported draft beers, and potent tropical drinks are specialties. The White Lion is open Sunday to Thursday till about 11pm, on Friday and Saturday to 1am. Use the parking lot on Charlotte Street, less than half a block away.

4 Jacksonville

36 miles S of Georgia, 160 miles NE of Orlando, 400 miles N of Miami

This sprawling metropolis is an important Atlantic seaport, the insurance and banking capital of the South, and corporate headquarters to many Fortune 500 companies. Economic growth is bringing cosmopolitan trappings to town—fancy hotels, fine restaurants, and first-rate entertainment. Jacksonville has a downtown of gleaming glass skyscrapers stunningly mirrored on the waterfront. The St. Johns River bisects the city, creating breathtaking marine views against a landscape of pine wilderness and parkland. A downtown riverside "festival marketplace" called Jacksonville Landing is just one of many places where you can enjoy a passing parade of seagulls, sandpipers, pelicans, and boats over a leisurely lunch.

In this modern city, you'll also encounter America's earliest history. In search of wealth and religious freedom, the French founded a short-lived settlement, Fort Caroline, here in 1564; it was destroyed by the Spanish a year later and the entire colony was massacred. When Florida became a territory of the United States in 1821, the sleepy town here, with about two dozen residents, served as a cattle crossing. By the 1840s Jacksonville—named in 1822 for Florida's first territorial governor, Gen. Andrew Jackson—had established itself as a viable port town exporting cotton and timber. After the Civil War it emerged as a winter resort, and by the end of the 19th century, with the arrival of a railway system, it was drawing 75,000 tourists each year to its beaches. World War I brought a boom in shipbuilding and saw the beginnings of development along the downtown skyline. After World War II, Jacksonville took its place as a leading southern financial center.

More recent developments include the creation of the riverfront recreational areas, Jacksonville Landing and the Riverwalk, in the 1980s. And football fever hit the city big time in 1993 with the acquisition of a new NFL team, the Jacksonville Jaguars, sparking a $121-million renovation of the Gator Bowl.

Downtown Jacksonville

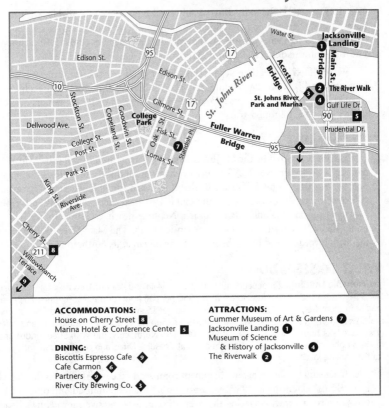

ACCOMMODATIONS:
House on Cherry Street **8**
Marina Hotel & Conference Center **5**

DINING:
Biscottis Espresso Cafe **9**
Cafe Carmon **6**
Partners **9**
River City Brewing Co. **3**

ATTRACTIONS:
Cummer Museum of Art & Gardens **7**
Jacksonville Landing **1**
Museum of Science
   & History of Jacksonville **4**
The Riverwalk **2**

ESSENTIALS

ARRIVING **By Plane** Air South, American, Continental, Delta, Gulf Stream International, Lufthansa, Northwest, Midway, TWA, United, USAir, and ValuJet fly into the spiffy-looking **Jacksonville International Airport,** on the city's north side, about 12 miles from downtown. The First Coast Information Booth, on the lower level (☎ 904/741-4902), is open daily from 8am to 10pm. A taxi from the airport will cost about $20 to downtown, $40 to $50 to beach hotels.

By Train There's an **Amtrak** station in Jacksonville at 3570 Clifford Lane, off U.S. 1, just north of 45th Street (☎ **800/USA-RAIL**).

By Bus Greyhound (☎ **800/231-2222**) buses connect Jacksonville with most of the country. They pull into a terminal at 10 N. Pearl St., between Bay and Forsyth streets in the heart of downtown (☎ **904/356-9976**).

By Car If you're coming from north or south, take I-95. From points west, take I-10.

VISITOR INFORMATION Write, call, or visit the **Jacksonville and the Beaches Convention & Visitors Bureau,** 3 Independent Dr. (just north of Water Street, at Main Street), Jacksonville, FL 32202 (☎ **904/798-9148**), for informative literature, maps, brochures, events calendars, and suggestions on accommodations, restaurants, and shopping. It's open Monday to Friday from 8am to 5pm.

GETTING AROUND   By Bus   Daily local bus service is available, with most buses running between 6am and 8pm. The fare is 60¢ for adults, free for seniors and children under 42 inches accompanied by an adult. A beach bus costs $1.10 each way. For route information, call 904/630-3100.

By Water Taxi   Weather permitting, water taxis ply the route between the Riverwalk and Jacksonville Landing from about 11am to 10pm (hours vary a bit seasonally). The fare is $2 one-way, $3 round-trip; children 3 to 10 and seniors over 60 pay $1 one-way, $2 round-trip.

CITY LAYOUT

Jacksonville is bisected by the **St. Johns River,** so getting around will usually involve crossing a bridge or two. **I-295** forms a beltway around the city, **I-95** is the major north-south artery, and **J. Turner Butler Boulevard** (providing access to Jacksonville and Ponte Vedra Beaches) is the major west-east artery. **Fla. A1A** runs from Amelia Island south along Atlantic Beach, Neptune Beach, Jacksonville Beach, and Ponte Vedra Beach, all bordering the Atlantic Ocean. The Main Street bridge spans the St. Johns River leading to the heart of downtown at its northern end.

WHAT TO SEE & DO

Jacksonville Landing. 2 Independent Dr. (between Main and Pearl sts.), on the St. Johns River. ☎ **904/353-1188.** Free admission. Parking 35¢ per half hour for the first 3 hours, 70¢ each half hour thereafter, to a $7.50 maximum daily charge ($5 evenings after 6pm and Sat–Sun and holidays). Mon–Thurs 10am–8pm, Sat 10am–9pm, Sun noon–5:30pm; restaurants and cafés may have later hours. Closed Christmas Day. Take I-95 North, cross the Main Street bridge and make a right on Newnan Street, turn right again at Coastline Drive, and continue straight ahead to the parking lot.

This 6-acre dining/shopping/entertainment complex on the waterfront was developed by the Rouse Company in 1987. Its vast two-story Main Building adjoins other structures to form a semicircle facing the river; the entrance takes you into King's Road Market, where open-air stalls display an array of produce. Upstairs is a vast video-game arcade, and Dawson & Buckles Market, with pushcart vendors. There are over 65 shops in the complex, including all the mall regulars as well as specialty emporia. Diners have a choice of about half a dozen full-service restaurants, including a sunny second-floor fast-food court. Also on the premises are such nighttime haunts as Fat Tuesdays and Hooters, and a small maritime museum. The Landing is the scene of numerous special events, and from March through the end of December there are free outdoor rock, blues, country, and jazz concerts every Friday and Saturday night.

The Riverwalk. On the south bank of the St. Johns River between Crawdaddy's Restaurant and the Friendship Fountain. ☎ **904/396-4900.** Take I-95 North to the Prudential Drive exit, make a right, and follow the signs; look for Crawdaddy's Restaurant on your left.

The Riverwalk is a 1.2-mile wooden zigzag boardwalk bordering the river, a popular recreational area. Throughout the day it's filled with joggers, tourists, and folks sitting on benches watching the passing parade of river boats and shore birds. The downtown skyline across the river is reflected on the water. The spectacular **Friendship Fountain,** at the west end, is, at 200 feet in diameter, the nation's largest self-contained fountain. Farther along, you'll pass military memorials, the Maritime Museum (admission is free) and the Jacksonville Historical Society (a small history museum; admission is free). A local biggie, the Riverwalk Arts & Crafts Festival, is held here in May on Mother's Day. And for the picturesque Jacksonville Light

Parade, on November 26, boaters decorate their craft with colored lights and parade down the St. Johns River.

MUSEUMS

✪ **Cummer Museum of Art & Gardens.** 829 Riverside Ave. (between Post and Fisk sts.). ☎ **904/356-6857.** Admission $3 adults, $2 seniors over 62, $1 students and children 5–18, free for children 4 and under, free for everyone Tues after 4pm. Tues 10am–9:30pm, Wed–Fri 10am–4pm, Sat noon–5pm, Sun 2–5pm. Closed New Year's Day, Easter, July 4, Labor Day, Thanksgiving, and Christmas Day. Free parking in lot across the street.

This stunning museum houses a permanent collection that encompasses works from Greek and Egyptian antiquities to the present. It's especially rich in American impressionist paintings, and has an outstanding collection of 18th-century Meissen porcelain and 18th- and early 19th-century Japanese Netsuke ivory carvings. Take a stroll outside to view the Cummer's riverside English, azalea, and Italian gardens. Bring the kids—an extensive facility called Art Connections features child-size hands-on exhibits and computer art stations.

Jacksonville Art Museum. 4160 Boulevard Center Dr. (between Beach and Atlantic blvds.). ☎ **904/398-8336.** Admission $3 adults, $2 seniors over 60 and students, free for children 6 and under; there may be an extra charge for special shows. Tues–Wed and Fri 10am–4pm, Thurs 10am–10pm, Sat–Sun 1–5pm. Closed New Year's Day, July 4, Thanksgiving, and Christmas Day. Free parking.

Founded in 1924, this is Jacksonville's oldest museum, and displays two unrelated collections. The museum has a notable pre-Columbian collection which spans a geographical range from northern Mexico to southern Peru and a time range from 3000 B.C. to A.D. 1500. Three Mayan stelae (monumental stones) from A.D. 849–870 grace the museum's outdoor sculpture garden. There's also a modern collection of art from 1945 to the present, including works by Picasso. Inquire about tours, lectures, films, and other museum programs.

Museum of Science & History of Jacksonville. 1025 Museum Circle (on the Riverwalk between Main St. and San Marco Blvd.). ☎ **904/396-7062.** Admission $5 adults, $4 seniors, $3 children 3–12, free for children 2 and under. Mon–Fri 10am–5pm, Sat 10am–6pm, Sun 1–6pm. Closed New Year's Day, Thanksgiving, and Christmas Day. Free parking.

This children's museum focuses on science and northeastern Florida history. Permanent exhibits include a 1,200-gallon aquarium of Florida fish (which is also home to a 25-pound alligator snapping turtle) and Great Marine Mammals of Northeast Florida, where exhibits are complemented by high-tech interactive stations. A sinuous pathway called "The Ribbon of Life" explores the history and ecology of the St. Johns River area.

In Kidspace, activities include face painting, a puppet theater, miniature cars and gas pumps, and a water-play table. And on the second floor kids utilize interactive stations to test their knowledge of nutrition and exercise, learn about electricity and motion, and construct bridges. A vast exhibit called "Currents of Time" traces Jacksonville/Northeast Florida history from 10,000 B.C. to the present.

Planetarium shows for adults and children (included in the price of museum admission) are scheduled daily (call ahead for show times, and to inquire about science demonstrations, "creature feature" shows, workshops, and lectures).

HISTORIC SITES

✪ **Fort Caroline National Memorial.** 12713 Fort Caroline Rd. (off Monument Rd.). ☎ **904/641-7155.** Free admission. Daily 9am–5pm; 30-minute ranger-guided tours of Fort Caroline given weekends, followed by 1¹/₂-hour guided nature walks through the Theodore Roosevelt Area (call ahead for tour times). Closed Christmas Day. Free parking at both sites. Take

Atlantic Boulevard east, make a left on Monument Road, and turn right on Fort Caroline Road. The Theodore Roosevelt Area is entered from Mt. Pleasant Road, about a mile southeast of the fort; look for an inconspicuous sign on your left that says TRAILHEAD PARKING and follow the narrow dirt road to the parking lot.

This 16th-century colony on the St. Johns River was a French outpost in the European struggle for ascendancy in the New World. The French admiral and Huguenot leader Gaspard de Coligny hoped to discover gold and silver as well as establish a haven for persecuted French Huguenots. Jean Ribault was sent on an exploratory expedition to the area in 1562; he claimed the land for France and then sailed home to gather colonists and supplies. He found France in the midst of a civil war, and, unable to secure support there, turned to Queen Elizabeth of England, who threw him in jail. In 1564, while Ribault was still imprisoned, de Coligny sent René de Laudonnière to Florida with 300 soldiers, sailors, and colonists. They founded a settlement here named La Caroline in honor of Charles IX. The native Timucuan initially welcomed the colonists, but the relationship soon soured. The settlers were on the brink of starvation, ready to abandon the colony, when Ribault sailed into the harbor in August 1565 with seven ships loaded with food, supplies, and 600 more settlers.

But the French colony's relief was short-lived. Ribault's arrival was viewed with alarm by the Spanish king, Philip II, who sent Admiral Pedro Menéndez de Avilés to rout the French. When Menéndez established a base of operations in nearby St. Augustine, Ribault sailed down the coast to attack and destroy it. However, a hurricane devastated his fleet. Menéndez rushed to take advantage of the situation, storming the poorly guarded fort and massacring 140 settlers. Returning south with booty from La Caroline, Menéndez's troops encountered Ribault and the shipwrecked Frenchmen and slaughtered 350 of them. Ribault's head was cut into quarters which were displayed on lances at each corner of a Spanish fort in St. Augustine. The French avenged their defeat in 1568, when Dominque de Gourge's force routed the Spanish at La Caroline. But shortly thereafter the French abandoned the colony, leaving Florida to Spain.

Today an almost full-size model of Fort Caroline near the original site is under the auspices of the National Park Service, as is the nearby 600-acre **Theodore Roosevelt Area.** This beautiful woodland, rich in history and undisturbed since the Civil War, contains natural salt- and freshwater marsh and dune scrub. On a 2-mile hike along a centuries-old park trail, you'll see a wide variety of birds, wildflowers, and maritime hammock forest. After the trail crosses Hammock Creek, you're in ancient Timucuan country, inhabited as far back as 500 B.C. Farther along is the site of a cabin in the wilderness that belonged to reclusive brothers Willie and Saxon Browne, who lived without electricity or running water and supported their needs by hunting and fishing. Saxon died in 1953 and Willie stayed on alone. In 1969 he dedicated his property to the Nature Conservancy for safekeeping, so that people could come here and "learn about God." The land became part of the National Park System in 1988.

I strongly suggest that you take the guided tours of the fort and Theodore Roosevelt Area; park rangers provide a wealth of fascinating information about history, flora, and fauna. If you can't fit a guided tour into your schedule, pick up trail maps and information at the Fort Caroline Visitor Center. Bring binoculars if you have them; hiking boots are recommended but not mandatory. There are picnic areas at both the fort and the Theodore Roosevelt Area.

✪ **Zephaniah Kingsley Plantation.** 11676 Palmetto Ave. (just off Fla. A1A). ☎ **904/ 251-3537.** Free admission; donations appreciated. Daily 9am–5pm; park ranger programs

Jacksonville's Glamorous Movie Past

Hollywood hasn't always been the hub of filmdom. Originally based in New York, the fledgling industry soon sought warmer weather for winter shoots. Mayor J. E. T. Bowden led a campaign to make his city a year-round movie colony, and by 1916 more than 30 studios had set up shop in Jacksonville. Oliver Hardy's first movie (before he linked up with Stan Laurel), and dozens of later ones, were shot here under the auspices of the Vim Comedy Company. Also Jacksonville-based was Metro Pictures, which would later evolve into Metro-Goldwyn-Mayer; its early stable of actors included Ethel Barrymore and Francis X. Bushman. But the industry's Florida honeymoon was a brief one, and soon erupted in friction between the companies and the locals. Residents lost money when independent companies sold them stock in risky film ventures, and locals, on their part, began to jack up prices on goods and services to their glamorous visitors. Further friction was generated by film directors, who, lacking the technological panache that would come later, would turn in a false alarm in order to shoot scenes of firetrucks racing to a blaze. Insensitive to Bible Belt mores, one studio staged a bank robbery on a Sunday, disrupting a nearby church service. And during a mob scene for a film called *The Clarion* in 1916, the mob actually did get out of control, all but destroying a saloon and a two-story building. Such creative methods made the industry less than popular with local citizenry, who voted Bowden out of office in 1917. His defeat caused a halt on construction of a vast studio complex in the works, and by 1920 most of the studios had moved on to the friendlier climate of Los Angeles.

available (call ahead for times). Closed Christmas. Take I-95 North to Heckscher Drive and follow the signs.

A winding 3-mile road under a canopy of trees, with dense tropical foliage on either side, is what remains of an elegant palmetto drive that led to the 19th-century plantation of Zephaniah Kingsley. Here, on the banks of the Fort George River, Kingsley lived from 1813 to 1839 with his Senegalese wife, Anna Madgigaine Jai, whom he had originally purchased as a slave in Havana. A man of contradictions, he was a Quaker who believed that "the coloured race were superior to us, physically and morally," yet made a fortune in the slave trade and utilized over 200 slaves to tend his 30,000 acres of Sea Island cotton, sugar cane, and citrus orchards. To motivate his work force he assigned his slaves to daily tasks; on completion of their tasks, they could spend any remaining daylight hours growing their own crops, hunting, or improving their dwellings. Kingsley's will contained provisions to enable them to buy their freedom after his death. When Florida changed from a Spanish colony to an American territory in 1821, Kingsley was appointed to the Legislative Council by President Monroe. In 1838, alarmed by rising sentiment against free blacks, he sent Anna and their four children to Haiti to live.

Visitors can tour the two-story residence, kitchen house, barn/carriage house, and the remains of 23 slave cabins. The site is under the auspices of the National Park Service.

OTHER ATTRACTIONS

Anheuser-Busch Brewery. 111 Busch Dr. ☎ **904/751-8118.** Free admission. Mon–Sat 9am–4pm, with tours departing on the hour. Free parking on premises. Take I-95 North to the Busch Drive exit.

On free guided or self-guided Anheuser-Busch tours, you'll view the entire beer-making process, from grain mashing through bottling, labeling, and packaging. You'll also learn about the history of beer and the famed Budweiser Clydesdales. And at the end, there's a brewski for you (two gratis 10-ounce cups actually) served in a comfortable lounge.

✪ Jacksonville Zoological Gardens. 8605 Zoo Rd. (off Heckscher Dr.). ☎ **904/757-4462** or 904/757-4463. Admission (including all shows) $6.50 adults, $4.50 seniors 65 and over, $4 children 3–12, free for children 2 and under. Daily 9am–5pm. Closed New Year's Day, Thanksgiving, and Christmas Day. Take I-95 North to Hecksher Drive (Exit 124) and follow the signs.

This lushly landscaped zoo, bordering the Trout River, exhibits over 700 mammals, birds, and reptiles—many in large, natural enclosures that simulate native habitats. At the entrance is Main Camp Safari Lodge; Zulus were brought over from South Africa to construct its authentic thatched roof. Walk through the Birds of the Rift Valley Aviary en route to the Plains of the Serengeti, an 18-acre African-veldt habitat housing over 100 animal species. Here lions reside with ostriches, rhinos, elephants, and antelopes as neighbors. A walk-through aviary of exotic birds on the St. Johns River adjoins the junglelike Okavango Village, home to Nile crocodiles, blue duikers, Kirk's dik-diks, and South African crested porcupines; it also contains a petting zoo offering close encounters with domestic African animals such as pygmy goats and dwarf zebus. You can see cute newborns at the baby animal nursery. Chilean flamingos grace a marshy lagoon, and a boardwalk traverses naturally occurring Florida wetlands. Two on-premises eateries offer light fare. Visitors can take a miniature train ride around the zoo. And there are often animal shows and special events (storytelling, lectures, workshops); inquire when you come in. Strollers and wheelchairs can be rented.

SPORTS & OUTDOOR ACTIVITIES
ENJOYING THE OUTDOORS

BEACHES   Fish, swim, snorkel, sail, sunbathe, or stroll on the sand dunes along Jacksonville's ocean beaches—they're just 12 to 15 miles from downtown via Atlantic, Beach, or J. Turner Butler Boulevard. At 4th Avenue North you'll find free beach parking and rest rooms.

FISHING   You can go fishing for whiting, mackerel, flounder, bluefish, catfish, and more off the **Jacksonville Beach Fishing Pier,** just south of Beach Boulevard at 6th Avenue (☎ **904/246-6001**). No license is required, and rods, reels, and bait can be rented on the premises. The pier is open daily from 6am: to 11pm Memorial Day to Labor Day, until 8pm the rest of the year. It costs $3.50 for adults to fish the pier, $1.75 for children 8 and under and seniors over 60. The pier is also the site of Jacksonville's most popular surfing beach.

Another option is to fish—for red snapper, grouper, sea bass, small sharks, amberjack, and more—15 to 25 miles offshore in the Atlantic Ocean aboard the *King Neptune* (☎ **904/246-0104**), a 65-foot air-conditioned deep-sea fishing boat. It departs at 8am daily from 4378 Ocean St., half a mile south of the Mayport Ferry. The price is $35 per person, including all bait and tackle. Light fare can be purchased on board. You don't need a license, but reservations are required.

GOLF   As home to the PGA Tour's world headquarters, the city has over a dozen major public golf courses, some of them top-rated. Most notable are those on Amelia Island and in Ponte Vedra, but unless you stay at those resorts, they're not open to the public. Call **Tee Times USA** (☎ **800/374-8633**) for free information on the

Jacksonville golf scene; they can tell you which local courses meet your needs and budget, create golf packages, and book advanced tee times for you—all at no charge.

HORSEBACK RIDING   **Sawgrass Stables,** 23900 Marsh Landing Pkwy., off Fla. A1A in Ponte Vedra Beach (☎ **904/285-3791**), has trail rides, supervised riding, and riding lessons. Call for details.

NATURE WALKS   Take the kids for self-guided nature walks along marked paths at **Tree Hill,** a 40-acre urban wilderness at 7152 Lone Star Rd., off Arlington Road (☎ **904/724-4646**). Signs indicate woodpecker holes, aspects of wetland vegetation, types of lichen, species of trees and shrubs, and other interesting natural phenomena. A small natural-history museum, gardens, and a picnic area are on the premises. It's open Monday to Saturday from 8:30am to 5pm. Admission is $1 for adults, 50¢ for children 17 and under. Free naturalist-guided tours are given the first and third Saturday of every month at 10am.

TENNIS   As home to the international Association of Tennis Professionals, Jacksonville also abounds in high-quality tennis courts, including notable facilities at Ponte Vedra and Amelia Island resorts (once again open only to guests). **Southside Park,** 1541 Hendricks Ave., off Atlantic Avenue (☎ **904/399-1761**), has six city-run Har-Tru courts, all lit for night play. There's no charge to play. There are additional city courts (14 clay, two Har-Tru, and a practice wall, all lit for night play) at **Boone Park,** 3730 Park St., just east of Roosevelt Boulevard (☎ **904/384-8687**). There's a charge here of $1 per person per 1 1/2 hours of play. Both locations are open daily year round and offer lessons from resident tennis pros. Call for hours, and make reservations a day or two in advance.

WILDERNESS TOURS & OTHER TRIPS   An organization called **Outdoor and Balloon Adventures** (☎ **904/739-1960**) offers wilderness tours, kayaking and canoeing, ballooning, bicycle trips, and other outdoor adventures, both day trips and longer camping trips.

SPECTATOR SPORTS

The colossal 73,000-seat **Jacksonville Municipal Stadium,** 1 Stadium Place, at East Duval and Haines streets (☎ **904/630-3900** for information, 904/353-3309 to charge tickets), one of the nation's largest stadiums, is the site of the annual Florida/ Georgia football game every October and the Gator Bowl every New Year's Eve. It hosts additional college football games September to December, NFL pre-season football games, and motorsports events. And it's the home of the Jacksonville Jaguars (NFL), who play 10 games here between August and December. Call 904/633-6000 for ticket information.

Adjacent to it, and under the same auspices, is the 10,600-seat **Jacksonville Veterans Memorial Coliseum,** 1145 E. Adams St. (☎ **904/630-3900** for information, 904/353-3309 to charge tickets), home of East Coast Hockey (the Jacksonville Lizards) and a venue for NHL exhibition games, Division I college basketball games, ice-skating exhibitions, and wrestling matches.

Gator Bowl tickets run $30 to $40 and should be purchased as far in advance as possible. Tickets to the Florida/Georgia game are also in the $30 to $40 range. There's paid parking for ticketed events. (*Note:* During Gator Bowl and NFL games, water taxis ply the route between Jacksonville Landing and the stadium; the fare is $5 round-trip.)

The 10,500-seat **Wolfson Park,** 1201 E. Duval St. (☎ **904/358-2846** for information, 904/353-3309 to charge tickets), is home to the minor-league Class AA

Jacksonville Suns baseball team, whose season runs from April to September. There's paid parking for ticketed events.

WHERE TO STAY

Jacksonville, much like Los Angeles, is a sprawling mass of freeways, with no location convenient to everything. If you're here on business you'll probably want to stay downtown, while tourists might prefer a beach location. If you have a car, the Baymeadows area (about 10 minutes south of downtown and west of the beach) is also a good choice with many excellent budget properties.

Note: Sales tax in Jacksonville is 6.5%, and an additional 6% is levied on hotel bills.

AT THE BEACH

Doubles for Less than $60

✪ **Sea Horse Oceanfront Inn.** 120 Atlantic Blvd. (between Ocean Blvd. and the beach), Jacksonville, FL 32266. ☎ **904/246-2175,** or 800/881-2330. 37 rms, 1 penthouse. A/C TV TEL. $49–$99 double; $69–$109 double with a kitchenette; $175–$225 penthouse for up to six. Additional person $10 extra; children 21 and under stay free in parents' room. AE, CB, DC, DISC, JCB, MC, V. Free parking.

All the rooms at this well-run beachfront property offer ocean views from balconies or patios. Families will appreciate the six units here with fully equipped kitchenettes, not to mention a nice-size oceanfront pool, volleyball, shuffleboard, picnic tables, and a barbecue grill. And young couples will enjoy proximity to some of Jacksonville's top nightspots. If you have a large family or group, consider the vast and lovely third-floor penthouse—it has a big living room and dining area, a full kitchen, a separate bedroom as well as sofa beds, and a huge balcony furnished with a dining table and chaises longues. A coffee shop adjoins the motel, and many other restaurants are within easy walking distance, as is a launderette.

Doubles for Less than $80

Comfort Inn Oceanfront. 1515 N. 1st St. (off Fla. A1A), Jacksonville Beach, FL 32250. ☎ **904/241-2311,** or 800/654-8776. Fax 904/249-3830. 177 rms, 3 suites. A/C TV TEL. $59–$79 standard double; $79–$99 pool- or ocean-view double; $89–$ll9 oceanfront double; $125–$175 suite. Rates include continental breakfast. Additional person $10 extra; children 17 and under stay free in parents' room. AE, CB, DC, DISC, JCB, MC, V. Free parking.

The Comfort Inn offers a lot of facilities: 3,000 feet of pristine white-sand beach, a large pool with rock waterfalls and a palm-fringed sundeck, a secluded grotto whirlpool, a small fitness room, a video-game room, and a multicourt sand volleyball park (scene of major tournaments). The attractive rooms have balconies or screened patios and are equipped with cable TV with pay-movie options. Microwave/refrigerator units are available for $6 a night. An especially good deal here is a honeymoon suite with Jacuzzi tub and living room area. Continental breakfast and light fare are served in a small poolside eatery, and Kokomo's, a beautiful lounge overlooking the ocean, features live music for dancing on weekend nights April to Labor Day.

IN BAYMEADOWS

This pleasant (and very safe) area offers proximity to lots of good restaurants and easy freeway access so you can zoom to the beach or downtown.

In addition to the places listed below, there's a centrally located **Motel 6** at 8285 Dix Ellis Trail, off I-95 at the Baymeadows exit (☎ **904/731-8400,** or 800/4-MOTEL6; fax 904/730-0781). It has the usual standard rooms and amenities, and costs $32 for a double. It's set far back from the highway so there's no traffic noise. Small pets are allowed.

Jacksonville Accommodations & Dining

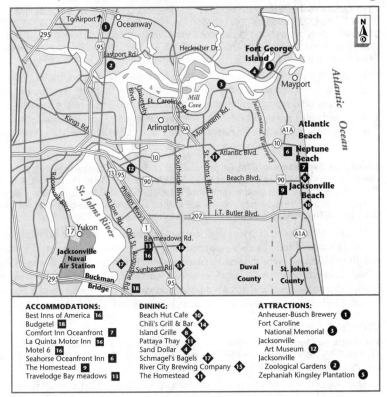

ACCOMMODATIONS:
Best Inns of America 16
Budgetel 18
Comfort Inn Oceanfront 7
La Quinta Motor Inn 16
Motel 6 16
Seahorse Oceanfront Inn 6
The Homestead 9
Travelodge Bay meadows 13

DINING:
Beach Hut Cafe 10
Chili's Grill & Bar 14
Island Grille 8
Pattaya Thay 11
Sand Dollar 4
Schmagel's Bagels 17
River City Brewing Company 15
The Homestead 11

ATTRACTIONS:
Anheuser-Busch Brewery 1
Fort Caroline
   National Memorial 3
Jacksonville
   Art Museum 12
Jacksonville
   Zoological Gardens 2
Zephaniah Kingsley Plantation 5

Doubles for Less than $40

✪ **Best Inns of America.** 8220 Dix Ellis Trail (at Freedom Commerce Pkwy.), Jacksonville, FL 32256. ☎ **904/739-3323,** or 800/BEST-INN. Fax 904/739-3323. 109 rms. A/C TV TEL. $38–$43.90 room for one person. Rates include continental breakfast. Additional person $6 extra; children 17 and under stay free in parents' room. Discounts for seniors 50 and over. AE, CB, DC, DISC, MC, V. Free parking. Take the Baymeadows exit off I-95.

Though its rooms are already immaculate, Best Inns will be even better by the time you read this—a total overhaul is nearing completion at this writing. This is a nicely landscaped property, with a pool and sundeck in a wooded area. Guests enjoy complimentary breakfast in a breakfast nook off the lobby. Small pets are allowed.

Doubles for Less than $60

Budgetel. 3199 Hartley Rd. (just off San Jose Blvd.), Jacksonville, FL 32257. ☎ **904/268-9999,** or 800/428-3438. Fax 904/268-9611. 103 rms. A/C TV TEL. $39.95–$45.95 single, $46.95–$51.95 room for up to four. Rates include continental breakfast. AE, CB, DC, DISC, MC, V. Free parking.

A few minutes away from the other properties listed in this section, the Budgetel is set sedately back from the highway, its swimming pool and sundeck enclosed by shrubbery and backed by lofty pines. Its standard motel rooms, attractively decorated in tropical motif, have coffeemakers and satellite TV offering pay-per-view and Showtime movies. On-premises facilties include coin-op washers and dryers. Local calls are free. Small pets are allowed.

✪ **La Quinta Motor Inn.** 8255 Dix Ellis Trail (at Freedom Commerce Pkwy.), Jacksonville, FL 32256. ☎ **904/731-9940**, or 800/531-5900. Fax 904/731-3854. 106 rms. A/C TV TEL. $59–$68 room for one person. Rates include continental breakfast. Additional person $7 extra; children 17 and under stay free in parents' room. AE, CB, DC, DISC, MC, V. Free parking. Take the Baymeadows exit off I-95.

Housed in a two-story terra-cotta–roofed Mission-style stucco building, the La Quinta welcomes guests in a cheerful plant-filled lobby. Its newly renovated rooms look brand new; they're equipped with satellite TV offering HBO, pay-movie options, and video games. There's a secluded swimming pool and sundeck, as well as a courtyard area with tree-shaded tables. A Steak & Ale restaurant is adjacent. And guests can use a nearby gym at no cost. Small pets are allowed.

Travelodge Baymeadows. 8765 Baymeadows Rd. (at Freedom Commerce Pkwy.), Jacksonville, FL 32256. ☎ **904/731-7317**, or 800/578-7878. Fax 904/737-8836. 119 rms. A/C TV TEL. $49–$59 double. Rates include continental breakfast. Additional person $5 extra; children 11 and under stay free in parents' room. Rates may be higher during special events. AE, DC, DISC, MC, V. Free parking. Take the Baymeadows exit off I-95.

Offering quite a lot in its price range, this well-maintained Travelodge has nicely furnished standard motel rooms equipped with coffeemakers and satellite TV with HBO; microwave ovens and small refrigerators are available on request. Those rooms with king-size beds have sofas. A secluded swimming pool amid lush greenery is backed by woodlands and adjoins a pond, and guests enjoy gratis use of a nearby health club. Also complimentary are local phone calls and *USA Today* weekdays.

WORTH A SPLURGE

The House on Cherry Street. 1844 Cherry St. (on the St. Johns River), Jacksonville, FL 32205. ☎ **904/384-1999.** Fax 904/384-5013. 4 rms. A/C TV. $79–$99 double. Rates include full breakfast. Additional person $15 extra. MC, V. Free parking.

This colonial-style wood-frame house, nestled in a tree-shaded cul-de-sac on the St. Johns River, is ideal for a romantic vacation (no small children are accepted). You might select the exquisite river-view Rose Room, with a canopied four-poster bed and floral-print wallpaper. A four-poster also graces the Duck Room, which has shelves of books and a bath with a Victorian tub. It, too, offers river views. Ducks are rather a theme here; hundreds of antique decoys are displayed in the rooms and public areas. All accommodations offer adjacent sitting rooms, ceiling fans, and remote-control color TVs. They're supplied with fresh flowers, books, and magazines.

A full breakfast—including an entree (perhaps Gouda soufflé or eggs Benedict) and fresh-baked muffins, croissants, or breads—is served daily. And French doors open to a delightful screened-in back porch furnished with rocking chairs; it overlooks an expanse of tree-shaded lawn (where guests play croquet) leading to the river. Complimentary wine and hot and cold hors d'oeuvres are served daily at 6pm on the patio or in the dining room, and an upstairs refrigerator is stocked with free soft drinks and beer. There are bicycles for guest use. Genial owner/hosts Carol and Merrill Anderson keep a gentle pet greyhound—formerly a racing dog—named Streak. No smoking is permitted.

Radisson Riverwalk Hotel. 1515 Prudentioal Dr. (on the Riverwalk), Jacksonville, FL 32207. ☎ **904/396-5100** or 800/333-3333. Fax 904/396-8007. 322 rms, 13 suites. A/C TV TEL. Sun–Thurs $98–$149 single, $99–$159 double; Fri–Sat $79. Suites $159–$259. Extra person $10. Children under 18 stay free in parent's room. Highpend raters are for river views. Inquire about packages. AE, CB, DC, DISC, MC, V. Free parking.

Proximity to the Riverwalk, Jacksonville Landing, and the Jacksonville Municipal Stadium make the Marina a great choice for tourists. Right on the St. Johns River, it was newly renovated in 1996. Rooms—half with river views—are cheerfully decorated and equipped with cable TVs offering HBO and Spectravision movies, irons and ironing board, coffeemakers, and dataport phones.

Dining/Entertainment: The pretty Café St. John, serving all meals, highlights steaks and seafood. A pleasant lobby lounge adjoins.

Services: Room service, complimentary *USA Today* delivered to your room daily, complimentary morning coffee, airport shuttle ($21 round trip), business services.

Facilities: Two tennis courts, swimming pool, gift/sundries shop, exercise room, extensive business center.

WHERE TO EAT

Jacksonville has plenty of low-priced restaurants, many of them pleasingly upscale in decor and ambience. If the weather is good, pick up reasonably priced gourmet fixings at **Biscottis** (see below) adjacent take-out operation, and enjoy a riverside picnic on the grass at Stinson Park (at the end of San Juan Avenue), or if you prefer picnic tables, at Metropolitan Park (just south of the Gator Bowl on Adams Street). Biscottis take-out features roasted sesame-honey chicken, rosemary-roasted potatoes, pasta salads, fresh-baked breads, superb desserts, and much, much more.

A marvelous beach restaurant—above our price range at dinner, but affordable at lunch when main dishes are $4.95 to $7.95—is the **Island Grille,** 981 N. 1st St. (☎ 904/241-1881). Come by to graze on such gourmet appetizers as Bahamian conch fritters with spicy rémoulade or blackened quail stuffed with shiitake mushrooms and andouille sausage topped with crayfish/chive cream sauce. There are excellent desserts here too, not to mention a *simpático* bar with an extensive happy hour (Monday to Friday from 11:30am to 7pm).

MEALS FOR LESS THAN $7

Beach Hut Cafe. In the South Beaches Plaza strip mall, 1281 S. 3rd St. (Fla. A1A, at 13th Ave. South). ☎ **904/249-3516.** Reservations not accepted. Main courses $1.75–$5.75. DC, MC, V. Daily 6am–3pm. AMERICAN.

You're at the beach. Where do you go that's cheap and good? This casual mom-and-pop operation run by locals Richard and Desiree Downing is the place, and it's not just locals who are onto it. When Ladybird Johnson was in town she was a regular, and tennis great Andre Agassi drops in when he's playing tournaments nearby. The Beach Hut is sunny and pleasant; the walls are hung with children's art from the Downings' son's third-grade class.

Everything here is prepared from scratch. Stop by anytime for hearty home-cooked breakfast fare such as country ham with redeye gravy, eggs, home-fries or grits, and oven-fresh biscuits. Fresh-baked muffins are a lighter option. Lunch fare includes good chili, sandwiches stuffed with fresh-cooked deli meats or homemade chicken or tuna salad, burgers, omelets, and salads. Save room for Desiree's delicious apple pie à la mode. No alcoholic beverages are served.

Chili's Grill & Bar. In the Baymeadows Commons Shopping Center, 9500 Baymeadows Rd. (just west of Southside Blvd.). ☎ **904/739-2476.** Reservations not accepted. Main courses $4.95–$10.95. AE, CB, DC, DISC, MC, V. Mon–Thurs 11am–11pm, Fri–Sat 11am–midnight, Sun 11am–10:30pm. SOUTHWESTERN.

Chili's is a national chain, based in Texas, offering superior "bowls of red" and other southwestern specialties. It's a great choice for inexpensive family dining, with a children's menu listing full meals for under $3. This branch is sunny and plant-filled, with seating in comfortable upholstered booths. You can also eat in the lively bar area where the TV is always tuned to sporting events.

The same menu is offered all day. Chili is, of course, a specialty, available with or without beans. Fabulous half-pound burgers, perhaps topped with cheese and chili, are served with home-style fries. Another big item here: chicken or steak fajitas served with guacamole, sour cream, pico de gallo, Cheddar cheese, rice, beans, and flour tortillas. Save room for dessert—perhaps a brownie topped with vanilla ice cream, hot fudge, chopped walnuts, and whipped cream.

Schmagel's Bagels. 9850-51 San Jose Blvd. (at Pall Mall Rd.). ☎ **904/268-5273.** No reservations. Bagel sandwiches and salad platters $1.30–$4.60. No credit cards. Mon–Fri 6:30am–3pm, Sat–Sun 6:30am–2pm.

I love to start my day at Schmagel's with the *New York Times* (which can be purchased just outside, even on Sunday), a fresh-baked bagel, and a steaming cup of coffee. Later in the day, come by for bagel sandwiches filled with whitefish salad, pastrami, lox and cream cheese, or chicken salad. There are also soups, and side dishes include knishes and potato salad. Just about everything is homemade. Schmagel's has a sunny interior as well as outdoor tables.

MEALS FOR LESS THAN $10

Biscottis Espresso Cafe. 3556 St. Johns Ave. (between Talbot and Ingleside aves.). ☎ **904/387-2060.** Reservations accepted only for large parties. Soups, salads, sandwiches, and pizzas $5.75–$7.95; main courses (dinner only) $8.95–$11.95. AE,CB, DC, DISC, MC, V. Tues–Thurs 7am–10pm, Fri 7am–midnight, Sat 8am–midnight, Sun 8am–3pm. CONTEMPORARY CALIFORNIAN.

This schmoozy neighborhood hangout is conducive to leisurely meals and conversation. Everything here is fresh and homemade, and owners Karin Tucker and Barbara Sutton are engaged in a constant search for superior wines (they visit Napa Valley each year to update their list). California-style pizzas with foccacia-like crusts come with yummy combinations of toppings such as sun-dried tomatoes, pesto, goat cheese, and mozzarella. Other choices include sandwiches, such as grilled portobello mushroom, bleu cheese, spinach, and pancetta bacon, drizzled with thyme vinaigrette on fresh-baked bread; and nightly specials (perhaps grilled sea bass topped with fried spinach and served atop a polenta cake in garlic-tomato broth). There's a choice of 15 or 20 superb desserts daily, which you can enjoy with fresh-ground gourmet coffees and fancy espresso and cappuccino concoctions. The bar features beers and wines only, the latter category including many by-the-glass selections.

Cafe Carmon. 1986 San Marco Blvd. (between Carlo St. and Naldo Ave.). ☎ **904/399-4488.** Reservations not accepted. Main courses $6.95–$8.95 at lunch, $6.95–$15.95 at dinner. AE, DC, DISC, MC, V. Mon–Thurs 11am–11pm, Fri 11am–midnight, Sat 8am–midnight, Sun 9am–3pm. AMERICAN.

This casual restaurant is located in the heart of the San Marco shopping district. During the week it's a mecca for foot-weary shoppers, while on Friday and Saturday nights the place is jammed with post-movie and theatergoers who come in for cappuccino and dessert. The sunny interior is decorated in pristine black and white, with stark gallery-white walls hung with paintings. There's also café seating out front on a brick patio. At lunch or dinner you can order delicious sandwiches (including a classic Reuben) or salads, or pastas. Dinner options additionally include a grilled, sautéed, or blackened fresh catch (often grouper) prepared provençal, in beurre blanc sauce, or with pineapple salsa. Portions are huge, everything is made from scratch, and it's all first-rate. Leave room for dessert. The rich, moist carrot cake is the *ne plus ultra* of its genre. Premium wines are available by the glass. Great breakfast/brunch fare here, too.

The Homestead. 1712 Beach Blvd. (between 15th and 19th sts. North). ☎ **904/249-5240.** Reservations accepted only for large parties. Main courses $6.75–$12.95 (most under $10); kids' meals half price. AE, DISC, MC, V. Mon–Sat 5pm–midnight (sometimes later), Sun noon–midnight or later. SOUTHERN.

The Homestead's tree-shaded front porch, enclosed by a white picket fence, has a little house for the resident cat, DC (for doorcat) at the entrance. Inside, the snuggest-ever log cabin interior centers on a massive stone fireplace. On Sunday this warmly welcoming eatery attracts a big after-church and family crowd; at night the clientele is more eclectic.

The big draw (and it only costs $6.75!) is southern fried chicken served in a skillet with homemade buttermilk biscuits (as many as you like) and fresh-from-the-hives honey, cole slaw, black-eyed peas, rice and gravy, creamed peas, and another vegetable. Of course, you can order your chicken grilled or broiled as well, and the menu also lists steak and seafood items. If you haven't totally pigged out on biscuits, you may have some room for homemade pie or strawberry shortcake. The narrow 50-foot-long copper-topped bar is a popular hangout for the local beach crowd and the major nighttime haunt of celebrity golfers during Tournament Players Club championship games.

Pattaya Thai. In the Justin Plaza shopping center, 10916 Atlantic Blvd. (between St. John's Bluff Rd. and Mindanao Dr.). ☎ **904/649-9506.** Reservations accepted only for large parties. Main courses $5.95–$10.95; lunch specials (Tues–Fri) $5.75 for a full meal. AE, DC, DISC, MC, V. Tues–Fri 11am–2pm and 5–10pm, Sat 5–10pm, Sun 5–9pm. THAI.

Locals are always telling me about some "great Asian restaurant" that, upon investigation, turns out to be stunningly mediocre. So I approached Pattaya Thai, an un-assuming-looking establishment in a strip mall, with some skepticism. Happy surprise: Charming owner/chef Lek Clayton's fare was both delicious and totally authentic, and prepared from scratch using the freshest ingredients.

I'll warn you right off that authentic Thai food means that menu items described as hot are near radioactive. I love red-peppery fare; if you don't, ignore the starred entrees and select something like mee krob—crisp-fried rice noodles tossed with shrimp, scallions, and bean sprouts and garnished with coriander in sweet-and-sour sauce. Spicier items include fiery curries and big platters of beef, chicken, or pork sautéed with hot basil. Portions are large. Cool your palate afterward with yummy homemade ice cream redolent of fresh fruits and topped with crushed peanuts. There's a full bar.

MEALS FOR LESS THAN $15

Partners. 3585 St. Johns Ave. (at Ingleside Ave.). ☎ **904/387-3585.** Reservations not accepted; but call ahead for priority seating. Main courses $6.50–$9.95 at lunch/interim menu, $6.95–$15.95 at dinner. AE, MC, V. Mon–Thurs 11am–10:30pm, Fri 11am–11:30pm, Sat 5–11:30pm, Sun 5–10:30pm. INNOVATIVE AMERICAN.

A mellow ambience and great food combine to make Partners a big favorite locally. The main dining room's porcelain tile floor bespeaks a former drugstore at this location; brass ceiling fans are suspended from a lofty rough-hewn beamed ceiling. There's live jazz Wednesday to Saturday night, recorded light jazz other nights. The menu changes every few months to reflect market specialties, but it always includes signature appetizers of crisp-fried shrimp- and cream cheese–filled wontons served with fruity sweet-and-sour sauce. Home-style favorites might include meatloaf served with roasted garlic mashed potatoes, gravy, and a vegetable. Or select pan-seared sea scallops tossed with angel-hair pasta in lemon beurre blanc and chive dijonnaise topped with fried spinach. A dessert standout is brown-sugary, walnut-studded deep-dish apple pie served warm with vanilla Häagen-Dazs. Most of the above is available at lunch or dinner, or you can opt for a lighter sandwich meal. There's a full bar.

○ **River City Brewing Company.** 9810–13 Baymeadows Rd. (at Southside Blvd.). ☎ **904/ 642-6310.** Reservations accepted only for large parties. Main courses, sandwiches, and pizzas mostly $5.95–$7.95 at lunch, $7.95–$14.95 at dinner; kids' meals $4.95. AE, CB, DC, DISC, MC, V. Sun–Thurs 11am–midnight, Fri–Sat 11am–1:30am. URBAN FUSION.

This is the second venue for one of Jacksonville's most talented culinary teams, Wolfgang Puck disciples Tim and Barbar Felver. Like their downtown Riverwalk restaurant, this lower-priced Baymeadows branch attracts a sophisticated crowd and houses an on-premises brewery. The owners have created a distressed/whimsical warehouselike interior with a corrugated tin ceiling. Dividers and multilevel dining areas create intimate alcoves, and the overall effect is chic and appealing.

Menu standouts include crispy-crunchy shrimp and vegetable spring rolls with orange Thai sauce and chutney; superb pizzas baked in an oak-burning oven (try the spicy Cajun); and tender herbed rotisserie chicken served au jus with heavenly mashed potatoes and thin crisp-fried onion rings. Pastas are also noteworthy, and, for dessert, the crème brûlée topped with seasonal fruit is not to be missed. The lunch menu includes great sandwiches on foccacia bread. There's a full bar.

This is also a wonderful place to come for a leisurely brunch, where you can sit outdoors and read your newspaper and enjoy the Lucullan brunch buffet from 11am to 3pm. The price is $15.95 for adults, $12.95 for seniors, $7.95 for children 11 and under.

Sand Dollar. 9716 Heckscher Dr. (just north of the Mayport Ferry). ☎ **904/251-2449.** Reservations accepted only for large parties. Burgers and sandwiches $3.95–$5.50; main courses $7.25–$9.25 at lunch, $11.95–$20.95 at dinner. Sun–Thurs 11am–10pm, Fri–Sat 11am–11pm (closes an hour earlier in winter). SEAFOOD.

This is the perfect place to stop for lunch en route to or from the Kingsley Plantation, the Jacksonville Zoo, or the Anheuser-Busch Brewery. All tables offer great water views, and in summer you can dine on a riverside wooden deck. Many boats dock here for meals. Fried, broiled, or steamed seafood is the specialty. Order a combination plate with a baked potato and cole slaw. Another good choice is the Fort George roaster—grilled shrimp, served with new potatoes, fresh corn on the cob, and steamed cabbage. Or you might select a fried shrimp po-boy sandwich. Chicken, steaks, and burgers are available and a children's menu offers $3.95 meals. The bar is a popular hangout for locals. Homemade desserts include mud and key lime pies.

JACKSONVILLE AFTER DARK

There's lots to do at night in this lively beach town. Check the papers for concerts and events at Jacksonville Landing and other entertainment venues.

THE PERFORMING ARTS

Jacksonville's 3,200-seat **Florida Times Union Center for the Performing Arts,** 300 Water St., between Hogan and Pearl streets (☎ **904/630-3900** for information, 904/353-3309 to charge tickets), is home to the Jacksonville Symphony Orchestra. Visiting soloists with the orchestra have included flautist James Galway and violinist Itzhak Perlman. The auditorium also hosts ballet performances, headliner concerts (Julio Iglesias, Barry Manilow), and theatrical productions, including Broadway shows. The auditorium is located on the St. Johns River, and the waterfront setting provides a beautiful backdrop for the lobby.

The huge **Jacksonville Municipal Stadium,** 1 Stadium Place, at East Duval and Haines streets (☎ **904/630-3900** for information, 904/353-3309 to charge tickets), is the setting for major superstar rock concerts. Adjacent to it, and under the same auspices, is the 10,600-seat **Jacksonville Veterans Memorial Coliseum,** 1145 E. Adams St. (☎ **904/630-3900** for information, 904/353-3309 to charge tickets). This is another venue for major headliners (ZZ Top, Arrowsmith, Michael Bolton), as well as for such family shows as the circus and *Disney on Ice.*

The **Alhambra Dinner Theatre,** 12000 Beach Blvd., between Hodges and St. Johns Bluff roads (☎ **904/641-1212,** or 800/688-SHOW), presents entertaining professional productions of Broadway shows. Recent shows have included *The Odd Couple, The Sound of Music, Guys and Dolls,* and *South Pacific.* There are five to seven productions each year, always including *A Christmas Carol* at holiday time. The price of admission includes a full buffet dinner. A full bar and wine list are available. Tuesday to Sunday the buffet dinner begins at 6:30pm, the show at 8:15pm; for the Saturday matinee, the buffet begins at 11:30am, the show at 1:15pm; and for the Sunday matinee, the buffet begins at 12:15pm, the show at 2pm. Admission is $29.50 Sunday to Thursday, $31.50 on Friday and Saturday, and $26.50 for the Saturday and Sunday matinees; seniors 55 and older, active military, and children 16 and under pay $2 less except on Friday and Saturday nights. Reservations are recommended.

THE CLUB & BAR SCENE

Champs. At the Marriott at Sawgrass Resort, 1000 TPC Blvd. (off Fla. A1A), Ponte Vedra Beach. ☎ **904/285-7777.** No cover.

This handsome mahogany-paneled club is popular with locals and visitors alike. It has a wall of windows overlooking a lagoon and offers outdoor seating on a flagstone patio. There's a nice-size dance floor, and a live band plays Top 40 tunes Tuesday to Saturday night. A menu offers light fare and a wide range of specialty drinks. Open nightly until 12:30am. Parking is free on the premises.

Club Carousel. 8550 Arlington Expy. (Fla. 115/U.S. 90 Alt.), on the service road just south of Mill Creek Rd. ☎ **904/725-2582.** Cover usually $5, higher for some concerts.

A 30,000-square-foot facility, with a 4,000-square-foot dance floor enhanced by high-tech laser/lighting effects and a revolving stage, the Club Carousel offers an eclectic mix of entertainment. Call ahead for hours and to find out what's on—hip-hop night, country high-energy techno, international recording stars, Top 40, or a mix of several of the above. It's open Monday and Thursday to Sunday night. There are also bars—and pool tables—at either end of the club, and a quieter bar is up front. You must be 18 to get in. There's free on-premises parking.

The Comedy Zone. In the Ramada Inn Conference Center, 3130 Hartley Rd. (just above the junction of I-295 and San Jose Blvd.) in Mandarin. ☎ **904/292-4242.** Cover $5 Tues–Thurs, $8 Fri–Sat, $2 amateur night—plus a one-drink minimum (average drink is $3.50).

The Comedy Zone presents nationally known comics—acts you may have seen on comedy channels or the Leno and Letterman shows. Show times are Tuesday to Thursday at 8:30pm, on Friday at 9pm, and on Saturday at 8 and 10pm. The first Monday of every month is amateur night. Light fare is available. You must be 18 to get in.

Crazy Horse Saloon/Masquerade. 5800 Phillips Hwy. (a block south of University Blvd.). ☎ **904/731-8892.** Cover $3 good for both clubs; on Wed women are admitted free and enjoy free drinks 9pm–midnight.

This large facility has two clubs on its premises. At the Crazy Horse—a mini Gilley's-style urban-cowboy club—a DJ plays country-western music. Neon beer signs adorn the walls; the crowd wears boots, jeans, and cowboy hats; and there are half a dozen pool tables off the dance floor. Free dance lessons are offered Monday to Friday night from 7 to 9pm. At Masquerade, a DJ plays Top 40 tunes and progressive rock. There are good lighting effects on the dance floor, and a large video monitor backs the stage. The club is the scene of frequent contests—hot buns, wet T-shirts, hot legs, and the like—most offering $100 prizes. Dress is casual. You must be 21 to get into either part of the club. Crazy Horse is open Monday to Saturday till 2am; Masquerade, Wednesday to Saturday till 2am. Parking is free on the premises.

Ragtime Tavern and Taproom. 207 Atlantic Blvd. (off Fla. A1A). ☎ **904/241-7877.** No cover.

This popular beach bar and restaurant features local groups playing jazz and blues Thursday to Sunday night. On weekends, especially, the place is really jumping and the crowd is young and lively. Ragtime brews its own beer—lager, stout, red ale, and wheat beer—on the premises. A fairly extensive menu highlights fresh Florida seafood and New Orleans specialties. You must be 21 to get in on Friday or Saturday after 11pm. There are other clubs on this corner, so you can begin an evening at Ragtime and go bar-hopping. It's open Sunday to Thursday till 12:30am, on Friday and Saturday till 1am.

T-Birds. 9039 Southside Blvd. (between Baymeadows Rd. and Phillips Hwy.; look for a shopping center fronted by a Target and Home Depot). ☎ **904/363-3399.** No cover Tues–Wed, $2 (for men) Thurs, $3 Fri–Sat.

This snazzy dance club fronted by a 1955 red T-Bird has a DJ spinning "dance music and good time rock 'n' roll" Tuesday to Saturday night until 2am. Several times nightly the staff does crowd-participatory exhibition dances (like "Hand Jive"), and there are frequent humorous lip-synch skits. Occasionally, headliner acts, such as the Little River Band, Starship, Kansas, and ELO, appear. Also big here is happy hour, featuring a lavish complimentary buffet and drink specials from 5 to 7:30pm Monday to Friday. You must be 21 to get in. Adjoining the club are a liquor store (specializing in imported and microbrewery beers) and the Pasta Café (☎ 904/363-8319) for Italian fare.

5 Gainesville

109 miles NW of Orlando, 335 miles NW of Miami, 70 miles SW of Jacksonville

In its most recent best-places-to-live-in-America survey, *Money* magazine awarded Gainesville the no. 1 spot! This archetypical American town offers a nostalgic respite from urban woes. Here you can linger over a malted at the local drugstore soda fountain, go to a football game, or stroll through a 63-block historic district whose notable buildings include Greek Revival, Colonial Revival, Queen Anne, and Victorian homes that range from cottages to mansions. Of course, Gainesville is primarily a college town (it has been the home of the University of Florida since 1906), and Gator football fever is epidemic. Surrounding areas abound in "real Florida" natural attractions; drive a few miles out of downtown and the scenery changes to rolling hills and verdant woodlands dotted with lakes, creeks, springs, and rivers.

ESSENTIALS

ARRIVING   By Plane   ASA, ComAir, Delta, Gulfstream, and USAir Express fly into the **Gainesville Regional Airport,** about 12 miles from downtown. Many hotels offer transport to and from the airport; a cab will cost you about $12 each way.

Gainesville

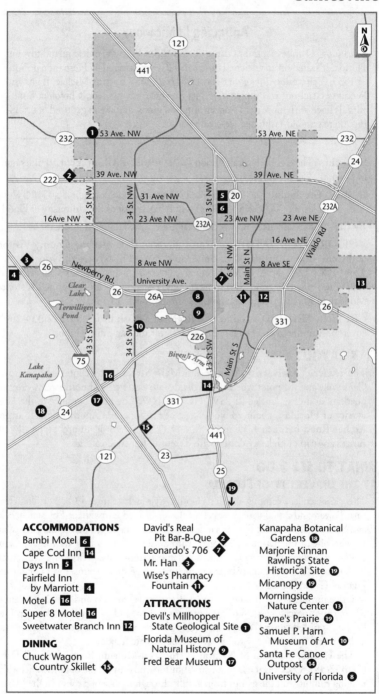

ACCOMMODATIONS
Bambi Motel **6**
Cape Cod Inn **14**
Days Inn **5**
Fairfield Inn
  by Marriott **4**
Motel 6 **16**
Super 8 Motel **16**
Sweetwater Branch Inn **12**

DINING
Chuck Wagon
  Country Skillet **15**

David's Real
  Pit Bar-B-Que **2**
Leonardo's 706 **7**
Mr. Han **3**
Wise's Pharmacy
  Fountain **11**

ATTRACTIONS
Devil's Millhopper
  State Geological Site **1**
Florida Museum of
  Natural History **9**
Fred Bear Museum **17**

Kanapaha Botanical
  Gardens **18**
Marjorie Kinnan
  Rawlings State
  Historical Site **19**
Micanopy **19**
Morningside
  Nature Center **13**
Payne's Prairie **19**
Samuel P. Harn
  Museum of Art **10**
Santa Fe Canoe
  Outpost **14**
University of Florida **8**

Antiquing in Micanopy

Micanopy, 11 miles south of Gainesville on U.S. 441, is the oldest inland town in Florida. It's sited on an ancient Timucuan village discovered by Hernando de Soto in 1539. A charming tiny town today (*Doc Hollywood,* starring Michael J. Fox and Woody Harrelson, was filmed here), its tree-lined main street, Cholokka Boulevard, is lined with more than a dozen antiques shops, and if you get tired of browsing, there's an old-fashioned ice-cream parlor.

By Train   The closest **Amtrak** station (☎ **800/USA-RAIL**) is about 10 miles north of town in Waldo, Florida.

By Bus   Greyhound (☎ **800/231-2222**) buses pull into a terminal at 516 SW 4th Ave., at 5th Street (☎ **352/376-5252**), just 8 blocks east of the University of Florida.

By Car   The main arteries into Gainesville are I-75, U.S. 301, and U.S. 441.

VISITOR INFORMATION   Write, call, or visit the **Alachua County Visitors and Convention Bureau,** 30 E. University Ave. (at NE 1st Street), Gainesville, FL 32601 (☎ **352/374-5231**), for informative literature, maps, brochures, an events calendar, and suggestions on accommodations, restaurants, and shopping. It's open Monday to Friday (except legal holidays) from 8:30am to 5pm.

GETTING AROUND   Gainesville Regional Transit buses (☎ **352/334-2600**) cover most of the town. The fare is 75¢. Call for routing information.

CITY LAYOUT

The corner of **University Avenue** and **Main Street** is the center of downtown Gainesville and the point where streets divide into east/west and north/south, creating quadrant addresses labeled SE, SW, NE, and NW. The main entrance to the **University of Florida** is about 13 blocks west of that junction. Another notable artery, **Archer Road** between I-75 and U.S. 441 (13th Street) is an archetypically all-American strip of highway dotted with dozens of fast-food eateries.

WHAT TO SEE & DO
AT THE UNIVERSITY OF FLORIDA

This classic college campus—with its Gothic-style architecture, 49-bell carillon Century Tower, and 2,000-acre greenbelt of flower-bedded lawns shaded by stately oaks and blossoming trees—is Florida's oldest university, established before the Civil War. It's also one of the nation's 10 largest, with a student body of about 40,000. Campus facilities include several fine museums and an impressive performing-arts center. And, of course, the university boasts numerous college sports teams, most notably the Fightin' Gators football team.

Drive into its main entrance at SW 13th Street (U.S. 441) and SW 2nd Avenue, where you can get a pass to tour the campus, a map, and parking information. Free 1½-hour **guided tours** (☎ **352/392-1365** for reservations) depart from Criser Hall at 10am and 2pm Monday to Friday (except on state holidays).

The **Florida Museum of Natural History,** on Museum Road at Newell Drive (☎ **352/392-1721**), is the largest natural-history museum in the Southeast. Its wide-ranging exhibits run the gamut from a walk-through replica of a room in the Mayan Bonampak Palace (built in A.D. 800) to a meandering Florida "cave" populated by barn owls, woodrats, raccoons, rattlesnakes, opossum, crickets, and bats. A fossil study center provides data via computer as well as exhibits, including the skeleton of a giant sloth that roamed Florida nine million years ago. Florida Environments explores the dazzling biodiversity of the state's ecosystems, there's a Florida History Hall and a Florida Indian Peoples Room, and a hands-on Object Gallery. Admission is free, and the museum is open Monday to Saturday from 10am to 5pm and on Sunday and holidays from 1 to 5pm.

Also on the campus is the ✪ **Samuel P. Harn Museum of Art,** on Hull Road at SW 34th Street (☎ **352/392-9826**). This architecturally notable museum is entered via a bridge crossing tiered pools of cascading water; its interior centers on a skylit rotunda. The museum owns impressive collections of art from West Africa, pre-Columbian America, New Guinea, Asia, and contemporary America. Works are displayed on a rotating basis. The Harn also sponsors a comprehensive schedule of traveling exhibits, lectures, films, concerts, and gallery talks. Admission is free, and it's open Tuesday to Friday from 11am to 5pm and on Saturday from 10am to 5pm. Docent-guided tours are given on Wednesday at 12:30pm and on Saturday and Sunday at 2pm.

MORE ATTRACTIONS

Devil's Millhopper State Geological Site. 4732 Millhopper Rd. (off 53rd Ave. NW, Fla. 232). ☎ **352/462-7905.** Admission $2 per car. Mar–Sept, Mon–Fri 9am–5pm, Sat–Sun 9am–sunset; Oct–Feb, daily 9am–5pm. Guided walks depart Sat at 10am.

It's *de rigueur* for Florida tourists to explore a sinkhole, and this state-run site is a big one—120 feet deep and 500 feet across, with a nature trail around its rim, cascading waterfalls along its slopes, and 232 steps leading to its foundation (getting *down* is effortless). Its colorful name derives from the funnel-shaped containers (hoppers) that fed grain into grist mill grinders in the 1800s. Since fossilized teeth and bones from ancient life forms were found at the bottom of this sinkhole, it was said to be the millhopper that fed bodies to the devil. Slopes of the sinkhole provide a cut-away view of Central Florida's geological past and a fossil record of the events and animals particular to each period. Interestingly, present flora and fauna here include life forms that grow only in sinkholes. You can view an informational video at the entrance. There's a shaded picnic grove on the premises.

Fred Bear Museum. Archer Rd. (Fla. 24) at I-75 (Exit 75). ☎ **352/376-2411.** Admission $3.50 adults, $3 for seniors, $2 children 6–12; $8.50 families. Wed–Sun 10am–6pm. Closed Christmas Day. Free parking.

Fred Bear (1902–88) was the founder of the Bear Archery Company, to this day the world's largest manufacturer of archery equipment. He pioneered its use as a hunting weapon, and during his lifetime "took down" a variety of animals, including such endangered species as African elephants and Bengal tigers. The factory doubles as a museum exhibiting mounted trophies, tributes to famous bow-hunting pioneers, and Bear's personal hunting memorabilia.

✪ **Kanapaha Botanical Gardens.** 4625 SW 63rd Blvd. (off SW Archer Rd./Fla. 24), at Exit 75 off I-75. ☎ **352/372-4981.** Admission $2 adults, $1 children 6–13. Free parking. Mon–Tues and Fri 9am–5pm, Wed and Sat–Sun 9am–dusk.

No gardener should miss this 62-acre botanical garden, viewed along a 1½-mile paved loop path shaded by ancient live oaks and lush woodlands. Its array of gardens include the largest herb garden in the Southeast, containing a Renaissance-design knot garden; Florida's largest bamboo grove; and many others. Particularly interesting is the cycad garden of predinosaur-era plants. The gardens, which also include a 250-acre lake, several sinkholes, and stretches of rolling meadow, provide a home for many birds and animals. A 29-acre arboretum is under development. A shaded picnic area, gift shop, and plant nursery are on the premises. Free guided tours are offered the first Saturday of every month at 10am.

Marjorie Kinnan Rawlings State Historic Site. County Rd. 325, 21 miles southeast of Gainesville in Cross Creek. ☎ **352/466-3672.** Admission $2 adults, $1 children 6–12, free for children 5 and under. Tours Oct–July, Thurs–Sun on the hour (except at noon) 10am–4pm. Closed Thanksgiving and Christmas Day. Free parking. Take U.S. 441 to SE County Road 346 to County Road 325.

Here you can tour the turn-of-the-century Florida cracker–style home, reconstructed barn, and citrus farm (12 acres of an original 74-acre grove remain) of Marjorie Kinnan Rawlings, author of the Pulitzer Prize–winning *The Yearling*. Rawlings came here in 1928 with her sportswriter husband, Charles, to what she described as "this half-wild backwoods country." Gregory Peck and Robert Frost were among her prominent guests. On a 40-minute tour, you'll see the dining room (where Rawlings served the sumptuous southern meals she described in *Cross Creek* and *Cross Creek Cookery;* she once said that she didn't mind anyone questioning her literary ability, but indifference to her cooking put her into a rage), the veranda where she did most of her writing, and much more. Rawlings found writing a painful process; sometimes, working a 10-hour day, she produced only a single acceptable sentence!

Look for a sign in the parking lot which leads to a tour sign-in book near the barn. Since only 10 people are permitted per tour, and admission is first-come, first-served, there may be a wait. A playground, picnic tables, and a three-quarter-mile hammock trail are on the grounds, and there are scrapbooks of clippings about Rawlings to peruse while you wait.

Way Down Upon the Suwanee River

One of my most lazily delightful Florida experiences was paddling a canoe along the beautiful Santa Fe River (a tributary of the Suwanee), its banks lined with cypress, Spanish moss–draped live oaks, palmetto, dogwood, magnolias, and holly. A variety of wildlife can also be observed along this tranquil waterway—great blue herons, egrets, ibis, turtles, deer, wild boar, fox, raccoons, possums, and more. Canoes and kayaks can be obtained from outfitter Jim Wood at the **Santa Fe Canoe Outpost,** on U.S. 441 (Santa Fe Boulevard) at the Santa Fe River Bridge, 23 miles north of town in High Springs (☎ **904/454-2050**). Wood offers day trips of 3 to 15 miles (you paddle downstream with the current and he picks you up in a van at your destination and brings you back); 2- to 7-night camping trips (all necessary gear can be rented here) which might take you as far as 90 miles to the Gulf of Mexico; and customized trips (often led by a naturalist/historian; Native Americans inhabited this area 10,000 years ago, and arrowheads are still found along the riverbanks).

There are picnic tables and grills at the input and at Poe Spring Park, 5 miles downriver. About 4 miles farther along, you can enjoy tubing, diving, and snorkeling in crystal-clear **Ginnie Springs** (☎ **904/454-2202,** or 800/874-8571), where lessons and equipment rental are available; there are also playgrounds, campsites, and picnic tables/grills there.

If you're in town on the right date, Wood's romantic full-moon tours are a must. Call for rates and details.

The Morningside Nature Center. 3540 E. University Ave. (Fla. 26, between 34th and 36th sts. NE). ☎ **352/334-2170.** Free admission. Daily 9am–5pm. Closed New Year's Day, Thanksgiving, and Christmas Day.

This city-operated 278-acre "living history" farm provides a glimpse into the lifestyle of a late 19th-century Florida farm family. Visitors can hike along signposted nature trails/boardwalks through habitats that provide sanctuary for a diverse population of birds (over 130 resident species), animals, and wildflowers. Also on the grounds are a turn-of-the-century one-room schoolhouse, a period Florida homestead garden, and Hogan's Cabin, a farmhouse built in 1840 from hand-hewn pine. Afternoon visitors can often assist in feeding the resident farm animals, or milk a goat. A picnic area is on the premises.

✪ **Payne's Prairie State Preserve.** U.S. 441, 10 miles south of Gainesville. ☎ **352/466-3397,** 352/466-4100 for ranger-tour reservations. Admission $3.25 per vehicle. Daily 8am–sundown (visitor center, daily 9am–5pm); ranger-guided tours Sat–Sun from early Nov to late Mar. Take U.S. 441 south to Savannah Boulevard and the entrance is on your left; it's a 3-mile drive to the visitor center.

Named for a Seminole chief, this pristine 21,000-acre nature preserve of freshwater marsh, lakes, pine flatwoods, hammock, scrub, and grasslands is home to 350 kinds of mammals, reptiles (including alligators), fish, and amphibians. Native Americans lived on this land 12,000 years ago, and during the late 1600s it was the site of the largest cattle ranch in Spanish Florida. You can hike nature trails (varying in length from half a mile to 8 miles), and view exhibits and a film about the preserve at the visitor center. A viewing tower houses a telescope—visitors can scan a panoramic expanse of prairie for wild horses, bison, cattle, and other fauna. Visitors can also fish (a license is required), bike, or go birding (this is a wintering area for migratory cranes, hawks, and waterfowl). RV and tent sites are available, as well as a picnic area with barbecue grills.

SPORTS & OUTDOOR ACTIVITIES

OUTDOOR ACTIVITIES The **Gainesville-to-Hawthorne State Trail,** off SE 15th Street, just south of the junction of East University Avenue and Hawthorne Road, is a 17-mile trail for walking and cycling that takes you past prairie, lake, and lush forest vistas; it also offers **horseback riding** (call 352/466-3397 for details). See "More Attractions," above, for nature trail **hiking** at the Morningside Nature Center and Payne's Prairie State Preserve. Bicycles can be rented at **Bikes & More, Inc.,** 2133 NW 6th St., at 21st Avenue (☎ **352/373-6574**), open Monday to Saturday from 9am to 6pm and on Sunday from noon to 5pm. Call 904/344-2107 to obtain a free map of bicycle trails.

Gainesville's **golf courses** include the 18-hole, par-72 **Meadowbrook,** a fifth of a mile west of I-75 on NW 98th Street, south of NW 39th Avenue (☎ **352/332-0577**); and the lighted 18-hole, par-60 **West End,** 3¹/₂ miles west of I-75 on Newberry Road (☎ **352/332-2721**).

For additional options, contact the **Alachua County Visitors and Convention Bureau** (☎ **352/374-5260**).

SPECTATOR SPORTS The athletic program at the **University of Florida** has numbered among the nation's top 10 for 12 consecutive years. The **Florida Gators football team** plays six home games each year between September and December at the 85,000-seat Ben Hill Griffin Stadium on North South Drive. Tickets (which aren't easy to come by, but it's worth a try) cost $20 to $22. The **Florida Gators basketball team** plays about 15 home games between October and March at the

12,000-seat Stephen C. O'Connell Center; tickets are $9. For ticket information on all University of Florida athletic events call 352/375-4683, or 800/344-2867 in Florida.

The **Gainesville Raceway,** 11211 N. County Rd. 225 (☎ **352/377-0046**), hosts a year-round calendar of professional and amateur drag racing, auto shows, and motorcycle racing. The biggest event here is Gatornationals in March (see "Special Events & Festivals in Northeast Florida," at the beginning of this chapter).

WHERE TO STAY

Accommodations aren't generally pricey in this town, but if there's some major event at the university it can be hard to find a room. Especially if you're looking for low prices, book far in advance.

In addition to the accommodations listed below, there's a **Motel 6** at 4000 SW 40th Blvd. (☎ **352/373-1604**, or 800/4-MOTEL6), nicely located in a wooded enclave of hotels and restaurants. In the same location is a **Super 8** motel at 4202 SW 40th Blvd (☎ **352/378-3888**, or 800/800-8000). Both are off Archer Road, and there's a large shopping center with restaurants directly across the street.

Note: In addition to the 6% state sales tax, Gainesville levies an additional 3% tax on hotel bills.

DOUBLES FOR LESS THAN $40

Bambi Motel. 2119 SW 13th St. (between SW 21st and SW 25th aves.), Gainesville, FL 32608. ☎ **352/376-2622**, or 800/34-BAMBI. Fax 352/372-5562. 29 rms, 5 two-bedroom suites. A/C TV TEL. $22–$25 single; $28–$32 double; $36 suite for four. Rates may be higher during special events. Additional person $4 extra; children 11 and under stay free in parents' room. Weekly rates available. AE, DISC, MC, V. Free parking.

This family-run budget motel, housed in a freshly painted one-story building, offers clean and spacious rooms, each individually decorated. All accommodations have patios and are equipped with cable TV with HBO. Some rooms offer microwave ovens and small refrigerators; others, with large fully equipped eat-in kitchens, are a good choice for families. A Waffle House is right across the street, and numerous other restaurants are close by.

Days Inn. 2820 NW 13th St. (between Mall and NW 29th Rd.), Gainesville, FL 32609. ☎ **352/376-1211**, or 800/325-2525. Fax 352/376-1211. 64 rms. A/C TV TEL. $32–$49 double. Rates may be higher during special events. Rates include continental breakfast. Additional person $5 extra; children 15 and under stay free in parents' room. AE, DC, DISC, MC, V. Free parking. Take Exit 77 off I-75 to U.S. 441 South.

Stands of palm, oak, and maple trees provide a sylvan setting here, and your room will overlook lush woodlands or a tree-shaded lawn with picnic tables and barbecue grills (a nice feature for families). The accommodations—all with furnished balconies or patios—are nicely decorated in mauve and teal with oak furnishings; they offer satellite TV with HBO and phones with computer jacks. Guests enjoy a free newspaper along with coffee, juice, and doughnuts each morning. An immense shopping center adjoins, and at least a dozen restaurants are within easy walking distance. On-premises facilities include a large swimming pool and coin-op washers and dryers. Room service is available from local eateries.

DOUBLES FOR LESS THAN $60

Cape Cod Inn. 3820 SW 13th St. (U.S. 441 North, just north of Fla. 331), Gainesville, FL 32608. ☎ **352/371-2500**. Fax 352/373-5829. 40 rms. A/C TV TEL. $41.95 double; $46.95 double with whirlpool tub. Rates may be higher during special events. Rates include continental breakfast. Additional person $5 extra; children 11 and under stay free in parents' room. AE, CB, DC, DISC, MC, V. Free parking.

This friendly family-run facility is housed in a pale-gray clapboard building with white trim and planters of geraniums hanging from the balconies. The immaculate rooms, with traditional mahogany furnishings, offer remote-control cable TV with HBO; eight are equipped with whirlpool tubs. A gratis newspaper comes with your continental breakfast, served in the lobby each morning. And though there's no restaurant, several are within easy walking distance. On the premises is a small secluded swimming pool. Pets are allowed (there's a fee). Local calls are free.

Fairfield Inn by Marriott. 6901 NW 4th Blvd. (off NW 75th St.), Gainesville, FL 32608. ☎ **352/332-8292**, or 800/228-2800. Fax 352/332-2800, ext. 709. 135 rms. A/C TV TEL. $46.95–$53.95 single; $53.95–$61.95 double. Rates may be higher during special events. Rates include continental breakfast. Additional person $4 extra; children 18 and under stay free in parents' room. AE, CB, DC, DISC, MC, V. Free parking. Take Exit 76 off I-75.

A pleasant and conveniently located hostelry, the Fairfield offers immaculate and attractively decorated rooms furnished in sturdy oak pieces. They're equipped with remote-control cable TV and phones with computer and fax ports. An extended continental breakfast is served in a breakfast room/lounge where gratis daily newspapers are supplied; a TV airs morning news shows; and there's a microwave oven for guest use. Amenities include a heated outdoor swimming pool and sundeck. Local calls are free, and small pets are permitted.

WORTH A SPLURGE

✪ **Sweetwater Branch Inn.** 625 E. University Ave. (between 3rd and 7th sts. SE), Gainesville, FL 32601. ☎ **352/373-6760**, or 800/451-7111. Fax 352/371-3771. 7 rms, 1 carriage-house apt. A/C TEL. Sun–Thurs, $62–$75 double; $75 apt. Fri–Sat, $67–$95 double; $105 apt. Weekly rates available. AE, MC, V. Free parking.

This romantic hideaway could, in itself, lure you to Gainesville for a weekend stay. Genial owner/hostess Cornelia Holbrook has transformed her restored 1885 Victorian house into a delightful bed-and-breakfast, complete with a wicker-furnished front porch and lovely fountained flower gardens front and back. Downstairs, a cozy Victorian parlor with a working fireplace connects, via French doors, to an elegant crystal-chandeliered dining room. There's an additional parlor upstairs as well as a writing room stocked with books and magazines. The exquisite guest rooms (named for varieties of roses) have cedar paneling and glossy pine floors strewn with Kilim and Karastan rugs. You might stay in the Picadilly, which has pale-yellow walls hung with botanical prints, swagged floral-print curtains, a cherrywood sleigh bed made up with a patchwork quilt, and an antique oak dresser; its adjacent plant-filled sunroom has small multipaned windows and antique wicker furnishings. Most luxurious is the carriage house, which offers a full kitchen and a cathedral-ceilinged living room. Some accommodations have working fireplaces. Breakfast includes fresh fruit, a choice of three entrees (perhaps crabmeat crêpes, stuffed French toast, and pumpkin pancakes), juice, and tea or coffee. A guest refrigerator is stocked with complimentary wine and iced tea, guests have free use of washers and dryers, TVs are available on request, and local calls are free. No smoking is permitted in the house.

WHERE TO EAT

As in any university town, it's easy to find restaurants serving up hearty portions of inexpensive fare to ravenous students. Parents should note that Wednesday is magic night for kids at Leonardo's (see below).

MEALS FOR LESS THAN $7

The Chuck Wagon Country Skillet. 3483 SW Williston Rd. (Fla. 331, at Exit 74 off I-75). ☎ **352/336-5677**. Reservations accepted. Main courses $4.50–$6.50 at lunch, $4.50–$11 at dinner (all-you-can-eat dinner specials $6–$9); children's menu, all items under $3. AE, DISC, MC, V. Sun–Thurs 6am–9pm, Fri–Sat, 6am–10pm. SOUTHERN.

With its children's menu and all-you-can-eat dinner specials, the Chuck Wagon is a great choice for hungry families. It's fronted by a porch with rocking chairs, and inside is a homey ambience; the knotty-pine-paneled walls are hung with a cozy clutter of copper pots and antique tools. You might start out with an order of crispy onion rings or fried green tomatoes served with ranch dressing. Main dishes, such as golden-fried farm-raised catfish battered in cracker meal, pot roast, and southern fried chicken, are served with homemade cornbread and a choice of vegetables or soup. Burgers and sandwiches are accompanied by similar fixings. For dessert, dig into a hot homemade blackberry cobbler à la mode. The Chuck Wagon also serves up hearty country breakfasts—from buttermilk pancakes to pork chops and eggs with fresh-baked biscuits and grits, hash browns, or fried cinnamon apples.

David's Real Pit Bar-B-Que. In the Timber Village Shoppes mall, 5121 NW 39th Ave. (between 51st and 52nd sts.). ☎ **352/373-2002.** Reservations not accepted. Sandwiches $2.90–$3.90; platters $5–$8; breakfast items all under $4. AE, DC, DISC, MC, V. Mon–Sat 7am–9pm, Sun 8am–9pm. BARBECUE.

This funky eatery is a good choice any time you have a hankerin' for authentic southern barbecue. Its no-frills fluorescent-lit interior is minimalist, with seating at plastic-covered picnic tables. If you're only moderately hungry, order up a shredded-pork sandwich on a bun or a less traditional barbecued-chicken sandwich on garlic bread. For heartier appetites I recommend a platter of piquant pork ribs served with Texas toast, barbecued beans, and cole slaw. Fried onion rings are the recommended side dish (skip the macaroni and potato salads, which are not homemade). There's also breakfast fare. Desserts are an afterthought here, but they're very inexpensive; banana puddin' is your best bet.

Wise's Pharmacy Fountain. 239 W. University Ave. (between W. 2nd and 3rd sts.). ☎ **352/372-4371.** Reservations not accepted. Almost everything under $3. MC, V. Mon–Fri 8:30am–4pm. SMALL-TOWN LUNCHEONETTE.

This downtown drugstore has been run by the Wise family for over 50 years, and its sandwich/soda-fountain counter has always been popular with locals. It is, in fact, a power-lunch locale for Gainesville judges and attorneys. For tourists like us, however, Wise's offers a nostalgic glimpse of a simpler era, and the freshly made sandwiches and sundaes are delicious to boot. You can sit at the counter or at tables covered with green-and-white-checkered plastic cloths. Order up a steaming bowl of homemade soup and a sandwich (my favorite is barbecued pork on a toasted sesame bun). A thick, creamy milkshake is the beverage of choice, though you might want to forgo it to save room for a hot-fudge sundae or banana split. A full breakfast menu is offered through 10:30am.

Meals for Less than $15

✪ **Leonardo's 706.** In the Colonial Plaza strip mall, 706 W. University Ave. (at 7th St. NW). ☎ **352/378-2001.** Main courses $11.95–$18.95; pizzas $4.95–$12.95; pastas $7.95–$13.95. MC, V. Mon–Thurs 5–10pm, Fri–Sat 5pm–midnight, Sun 4–10pm. CALIFORNIA STYLE/PASTAS/PIZZAS.

Leonardo's attracts a hip New York–style crowd open to more sophisticated culinary concepts than are usually found in Gainesville. Though some of its dishes are upscale for this book, a wide selection of pizzas and pastas are affordable. The rustic/funky pine-paneled interior, candlelit at night, features walls hung with works of local artists and seating in wooden church pews. A magician entertains tableside on Tuesday night, and on Wednesday from 6 to 9pm he does a special show for kids in a separate room (mom and dad dine in peace). On Monday, Thursday, and Saturday night a classical guitarist plays. On balmy evenings, I like to dine alfresco on the candlelit patio.

Portions here are vast. A very good shared Caesar salad followed by a shared pizzette (small pizza) makes an inexpensive meal for two people. A notable pasta dish is angel hair tossed with grilled chicken, peppers, mushrooms, and onions in tequila-cream sauce, accompanied by jalapeño salsa. Everything here is fresh and homemade, including the garlic rolls (a must) and desserts; peruse the display case at the entrance (the chocolate espresso torte was heaven). Wine and beer are available.

Mr. Han. 6944 NW 10th Place (at Newberry Rd., Fla. 26). ☎ **352/331-6400.** Reservations suggested. Main courses $3–$4.75 at lunch, mostly $6–$12 at dinner. AE, DC, MC, V. Sun–Thurs 11:30am–10pm, Fri–Sat 11:30am–10:30pm. MANDARIN/SZECHUAN.

Watching your pennies doesn't mean that you can't enjoy a little elegance. Mr. Han's upscale setting utilizes black walls hung with Chinese art, white-linened tables adorned with sprays of orchids, and 5-foot Chinese vases flanking a moon gate that separates dining areas. Yet you can dine lavishly here for about $15 per person. Order an appetizer of steamed four-star dumplings and an entree of flavorful mu-shi pork served with pancakes. Finish up with a dramatic dessert—a sesame seed–coated toffee apple that arrives sizzling hot at your table and is immediately plunged into ice water. It's a yummy, chewy treat. The bar specializes in exotic Polynesian rum drinks.

GAINESVILLE AFTER DARK

With its stunning performing-arts center, college stadiums, and other entertainment facilities, Gainesville offers a surprising abundance of nighttime activities. And as the hub of a lively college town, its historic downtown section is a pub crawler's paradise.

THE PERFORMING ARTS

The impressive **Center for the Performing Arts,** 315 Hull Rd., at 34th Street, on the campus of the University of Florida (☎ **352/392-ARTS,** or 800/905-ARTS), offers a varied schedule of headliner performances, ballet, classical and pop concerts, and touring Broadway plays in a 1,725-seat state-of-the-art theater. It also stages small productions and experimental works in its 220-seat Black Box Theatre. Recent seasons have featured such diverse headliners as Bill Cosby, Itzhak Perlman, Johnny Cash, and Dave Brubeck; theatrical productions like *42nd Street* and *The Will Rogers Follies;* and classical concerts featuring the New York City Opera Company and the Moscow Radio Symphony Orchestra. Call to find out what will be on during your stay. Parking is free.

Housed in a 1911 neoclassic former post office that's on the National Register of Historic Places, the **Hippodrome State Theatre,** 25 SE 2nd Place, at SE 1st Street (☎ **352/375-4477**), stages six contemporary plays during its annual September-to-May season in the 266-seat Mainstage theater. Recent productions have ranged from Wendy Wasserstein's *The Sisters Rosensweig* to Steven Dietz's off-Broadway comedy *Lonely Planet.* Additionally, the Hippodrome offers a number of family/children's productions. The theater's Second Stage facility presents an avant-garde/foreign-film series, and an on-premises gallery showcases works of local artists.

The 12,000-seat **Stephen C. O'Connell Center,** on the University of Florida campus (☎ **352/392-5500**), is worth a call to find out if any big-name concerts will be on during your stay. The Allman Brothers, Boyz II Men, Rod Stewart, Reba McEntire, and Sting are among those who've performed here.

THE CLUB & BAR SCENE

Harry's. 110 SE 1st St. (at 1st Ave.). ☎ **352/372-1555.**

Housed in an 1886 building that's on the National Register of Historic Places, Harry's centers on a big U-shaped bar that's a popular watering hole for Gainesville professionals. The convivial crowd comes partly for the Cajun fare, which can be enjoyed at the bar (where sporting events are aired on two TVs), indoor restaurant tables, or sidewalk cafe tables. Drinks are half price from 2 to 7pm daily. Open Sunday to Thursday to 10:30pm, on Friday and Saturday to 11:30pm.

Lillian's Music Store. 112 SE 1st St. (between 1st and 2nd aves.). ☎ **352/372-1010.**

Drawing a 30-something-and-up professional crowd, Lillian's has a flamboyant, turn-of-the-century interior including stained-glass panels from a New Orleans church and a beautiful carved backbar from a Mississippi riverboat. The club offers live music for dancing—Top 40 rock bands—supplemented during breaks by a jukebox stocked with oldies. On Monday night locals come in and jam with the band, Wednesday is karaoke night, and during happy hour (3 to 8pm daily) everyone gets a dollar discount on drinks. Sporting events—especially Gator games—are aired. A sidewalk cafe is a plus. Open Monday to Saturday till 2am; closed Sunday.

Rickenbacher's. At Main St. and 1st Ave. SW. ☎ **352/375-5363.** Cover usually $3.

Big, dark, and funky Rickenbacher's attracts a high-energy college-age crowd. It features live music—southern rock, jazz rock, and funk rock bands—and offers a pool table and a large-screen TV airing MTV videos and sporting events. You must be 18 to get in. On Wednesday night local bands often play and on Thursday night women drink free until midnight. Open Wednesday to Saturday to 2am.

Northwest Florida: The Panhandle

13

by Bill Goodwin

Often called the Panhandle, since it reaches westward like a handle attached to the state's main peninsula, Northwest Florida is justly famous for more than 100 miles of incomparably white beaches, the product of quartz washed down from the Appalachian Mountains. So finely ground is this brilliant, talcumlike sand that it actually squeaks when you walk across it. Although the busy resorts of Pensacola Beach, Fort Walton Beach, Destin, and Panama City Beach are lined with cottages and condominiums, many miles have been preserved in state parks and in the gorgeous Gulf Islands National Seashore, one of our nation's natural treasures.

These great beaches have long been a favorite summertime vacation retreat for working- and middle-class families, couples, and singles from the adjoining states of Georgia and Alabama, whose demands for inexpensive lodging and meals have helped to keep Northwest Florida's prices among the most reasonable in the state.

The beaches aren't all Northwest Florida offers to lovers of the outdoors. Offshore, abundant marine life grows over the gulf's natural sand-bar system, which makes for good snorkeling and scuba diving and great fishing both in the gulf and the region's beautiful bays and brackish bayous. In the interior near Pensacola, the Blackwater, Shoal, and Yellow rivers teem with bass, bream, catfish, and large-mouth bass, and also offer some of Florida's best canoeing and kayaking adventures.

With humid summers sandwiched between long, pleasant springs and autumns, Northwest Florida is also a mecca for golfers, with more than 30 top-quality courses gracing the entire length of its shores. And tennis players can find ample courts on which to score a few aces.

The close proximity of Georgia and Alabama also lends this area the languid charm of the Deep South. On the other hand, immigrants from many states and nations have been drawn to the Panhandle's mild climate and relaxed atmosphere. Some came originally to serve at huge military installations along the coast; others, to take advantage of the growing sunbelt economy. These new residents have added cultural diversity and sophistication to a region blessed not only with beaches but with fragrant pine forests, beautiful bays, crystal-clear rivers, and spring-fed lakes and streams.

This is also a good place to sample some of Old Florida. The picturesque waterfront town of Pensacola carefully preserves a heritage

What's Special About Northwest Florida

Best Experiences for Free
- Strolls along more than 100 miles of dazzling white sand and rolling dunes.
- Walks, trolley rides, museums, and art galleries in historic downtown Tallahassee—plus a 20-mile clear-day view from atop the New Capitol to the Gulf of Mexico.
- Examining historic aircraft at the U.S. Museum of Naval Aviation in Pensacola and the U.S. Air Force Armament Museum in Fort Walton Beach, two of America's finest military depositories.
- Watching birds and other creatures in St. Vincent National Wildlife Refuge near Apalachicola and in St. Marks National Wildlife Refuge and Apalachicola National Forest, both near Tallahassee.
- Seeing the Blue Angels soar skyward off Pensacola Beach.

Beaches
- Gulf Islands National Seashore, preserving beaches in their natural states from Perdido Key to Fort Walton Beach.
- Grayton Beach State Recreation Area near Destin, rated among America's top 10 beaches.
- St. George Island and St. Joseph Peninsula state parks, both near Apalachicola, also ranked among the top 10 beaches.

Attractions
- Fort Pickens, a spectacular setting in Gulf Islands National Seashore, where Apache medicine man Geronimo was imprisoned.
- Lake Jackson Mounds in Tallahassee, an 81-acre Native American settlement dating to A.D. 1200.
- Historic Pensacola Village, with 10 preserved buildings and museums, plus a lively dining and entertainment complex.

Parks & Gardens
- Edward Ball Wakulla Springs State Park, near Tallahassee, one of the world's deepest freshwater springs, where the old Tarzan movies were filmed.
- Alfred B. Maclay State Gardens in Tallahassee, with more than 300 acres of gorgeous magnolias, camellias, and azaleas, plus the restored Maclay House.

Architecture
- Seaside, east of Grayton Beach, a unique resort community built in the early 1980s and acclaimed as one of the top U.S. architectural achievements.
- Eden State Gardens and Mansion, north of Grayton Beach, a restored 1898 Greek Revival mansion.
- Old State Capitol in Tallahassee, an 1845 white-columned American Renaissance building.

derived from Spanish, French, English, and American conquest dating to the 1500s. Famous for its oysters, Apalachicola saw the invention of the air conditioner, a moment of great historical note in Florida. And Tallahassee, seat of state government since 1824, has a host of 19th-century buildings and homes, including the Old State Capitol.

Note: The third-most-destructive storm ever to hit the United States, Hurricane Opal destroyed many homes and businesses in Northwest Florida's beach

The Panhandle

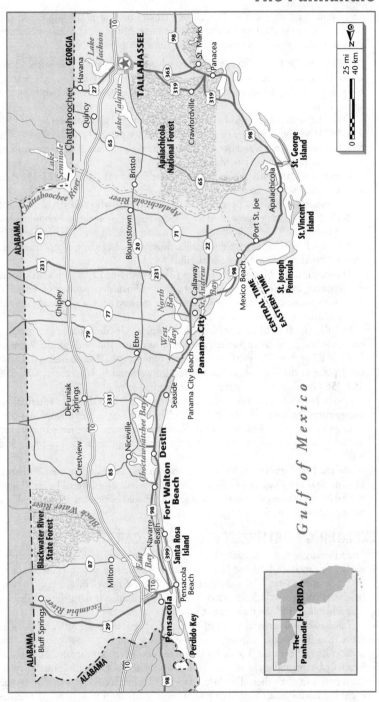

communities during October 1995. The establishments mentioned in this chapter will be fully operational by the time you get there, but some may have raised their rates and prices slightly in order to help pay for the repairs.

SPECIAL EVENTS & FESTIVALS Northwest Florida almost hibernates during its cool-to-cold winter months, but the area roars back to life in March, with the blooming of daffodils and azalea—and an invasion of college students suffering from spring fever.

One of the South's largest celebrations, **Springtime Tallahassee** (☎ 904/224-1373) welcomes in the new season with parades, arts and crafts, balloon rallies, food festivals, road races, and live music from bluegrass to blues. The celebrations run for 4 weeks, beginning in late March.

In mid-April, the **Fort Walton Beach Seafood Festival** (☎ 800/322-3319) sees a eating frenzy at this beach resort.

In June, Fort Walton Beach throws the **Billy Bowlegs Festival** (☎ 800/322-3319), a weeklong bash named for William Augustus Bowles, the notorious buccaneer known as "Capt. Billy Bowlegs," who once proclaimed himself to be "King of Florida." Events include a pirate flotilla, treasure hunts, fishing competitions, and contests for kids. Call for dates and details.

Also in June, the **Fiesta of Five Flags** (☎ 904/433-6512) is Pensacola's annual extravaganza, commemorating the 1559 arrival of Spanish conquistador Tristan de Luna with parades, a Spanish fiesta, a children's treasure hunt, a sand-sculpture contest, a billfish tournament, and much, much more.

In July, the first of two annual **Blue Angels Air Shows** sees the thrilling, world-famous flight crews do their aerial acrobatics just 100 yards off the Pensacola Beach Fishing Pier. The even more exciting **Blue Angels Homecoming Air Show** takes place at the same locale on the second weekend in November. Call **904/452-2583** for dates and information about both shows.

Also in November, the Pensacola area sees the annual **Frank Brown International Songwriters' Festival** (☎ 904/492-4660). The main host is the famous Flora-Bama Lounge, on Perdido Key at the Florida-Alabama line, but composers gather at various other beach venues on both sides of the border to perform their country-music hits.

On the first Saturday in November, Apalachicola is literally packed during the **Florida Seafood Festival** (☎ 904/653-9419), one of Northwest Florida's biggest annual events. Rooms at the town's Gibson Inn should be booked 5 *years* in advance for this all-you-can-eat extravaganza.

EXPLORING NORTHWEST FLORIDA BY CAR

Only Pensacola and Tallahassee have public bus systems, so the Panhandle is best visited by car. Both I-10 and U.S. 98 link the Tallahassee area to Pensacola, some 200 miles to the west. I-10 is the fastest route, but it runs well inland away from the beaches. Plan to take U.S. 98, a scenic excursion in itself as it skirts the gulf through Apalachicola and all the major resort beaches.

Tallahassee will demand a stop of its own. The resorts, on the other hand, are no more than 90 minutes' driving time apart, so one can be an easy excursion from another if you have a car. For example, you can stay in centrally located Fort Walton Beach or Destin and make an easy day trip to Pensacola in one direction or Panama City Beach in the other. The lovely town of DeFuniak Springs can be an easy excursion from Pensacola or from Fort Walton Beach and Destin, where I've placed it in this chapter.

Keep this in mind when you plan your trip: Just because an attraction or excursion is included in one section of this chapter doesn't mean that it can't be easily seen or done from another nearby destination.

1 Pensacola

200 miles W of Tallahassee, 375 miles W of Jacksonville

More than any other destination in Northwest Florida, Pensacola offers a blend of history, beautiful inland bays, and miles of white-sand beach, many of them preserved in their natural state by the Gulf Islands National Seashore.

Native Americans left pottery shards and artifacts in the coastal dunes here centuries before Tristan de Luna arrived with a band of Spanish colonists in 1559. Although his settlement lasted only 2 years, modern Pensacolans claim that de Luna made their town the oldest in North America. St. Augustine wins this friendly feud, having been permanently settled in 1564. Pensacola dates its permanence to a Spanish colony established here in 1698.

France, Great Britain, the United States, and the Confederacy subsequently captured this strategically important deep-water port, leaving Pensacola with a charming blend of Old Spanish brickwork, colonial French balconies reminiscent of New Orleans, and magnificent Victorian mansions built by British and American lumber barons.

West of town, the National Museum of Naval Aviation at the U.S. Naval Air Station celebrates the storied past of naval pilots who trained at Pensacola. Based here, the Blue Angels demonstrate the high-tech present with thrilling exhibitions of precision flying in the navy's fastest fighters.

Also on the Naval Station, historic Fort Barrancas looks across the bay to Perdido Key and Santa Rosa Island, which reach out like narrow pinchers to form the harbor. Out there, powdery white-sand beaches beckon sun-and-surf lovers to their spectacular gulf shores, which include Pensacola Beach, a small family-oriented resort, and most of Florida's share of the Gulf Islands National Seashore, home of historic Fort Pickens.

ESSENTIALS

ARRIVING   By Plane   American, America Southeast, Continental, Delta, Northwest, and USAir serve **Pensacola Regional Airport,** on 12th Avenue at Airport Road (☎ **904/435-1746**). Taxis wait outside the modern terminal. Fares are approximately $11 to downtown, $15 to Gulf Breeze, and $19 to Pensacola Beach. For local bus connections, see "Getting Around," below.

By Train   The **Amtrak** transcontinental *Sunset Limited* stops in Pensacola at 940 E. Heinberg St., near the bayfront (☎ **800/USA-RAIL** for information and reservations).

By Bus   The **Greyhound** terminal is at 505 W. Burgess Rd., at Pensacola Blvd. (U.S. 29), in Pensacola (☎ **904/476-4800,** or 800/231-2222).

By Car   From the east or west take I-10, U.S. 90, or U.S. 98. From I-10, Exit 4 puts you on I-110, which terminates in downtown Pensacola. From I-65 in Alabama, take Exit 69 and follow Ala. 113 south to Flomaton near the Alabama-Florida line, then U.S. 29 south to Pensacola.

VISITOR INFORMATION   The **Pensacola Visitor Information Center,** 1401 E. Gregory St., Pensacola, FL 32501 (☎ **904/434-1234,** or 800/874-1234;

fax 904/432-8211), gives away helpful information about the Greater Pensacola area, including maps of self-guided tours of the historic districts, and sells a detailed street map of the area. The office is located at the mainland end of Pensacola Bay Bridge.

Near the Santa Rosa Island end of the Bob Sikes Bridge is the **Pensacola Beach Visitors Center,** 735 Pensacola Beach Blvd. (P.O. Box 1174), Pensacola Beach, FL 32561 (☎ **904/932-1500,** or 800/635-4803), open daily from 9am to 5pm.

TIME   Pensacola is in the central time zone, 1 hour behind Miami, Orlando, and the rest of the U.S. East Coast.

GETTING AROUND   By Bus   Along with Tallahassee, Pensacola is the only community in Northwest Florida with a public bus system, but unfortunately it doesn't go to the beaches. The Escambia County Area Transit System (ECAT) runs the buses around town Monday to Saturday from 6am to 6pm. The base fare is $1. The ECAT transfer center is on Fairfield Drive at North L Street. Route no. 2 connects the airport and bus transfer center via 9th Avenue and Fairfield Drive. Routes no. 10A and 10B link the Greyhound bus terminal to the transfer center via Pensacola Boulevard and Palafox Street. From the transfer center, take Route no. 4, 6, or 13 to downtown, or Route no. 9 to the University Mall and its motels. For schedules call 904/463-9383, ext. 611. If you anticipate using the bus, contact ECAT in advance and ask for a copy of its "Ride Guide."

By Trolley   Out at Pensacola Beach, a free **Island Trolley** operates from May to September on Friday, Saturday, and Sunday from 10am to 3am. One route runs parallel to the beach on Via de Luna and Fort Pickens Road. A second runs along Pensacola Beach Boulevard from the Bob Sikes Bridge to Casino Beach, the heart of the action at the Via de Luna / Fort Pickens Road intersection.

By Taxi   Call **Airport Express Taxi** (☎ 904/572-5555), **Yellow Cab** (☎ 904/433-3333), **Green Cab** (☎ 904/456-TAXI), or **Pensacola Red & Gold Taxi** (☎ 904/478-7811 or 904/484-9482). Fares are $1.50 for the first sixth of a mile, 20¢ for each additional sixth of a mile.

By Bike   You can rent bicycles at Pensacola Beach from **Paradise Scooter & Bicycle Rental,** 715 Pensacola Beach Blvd. (☎ **904/934-0014**), near the beach end of Bob Sikes Bridge.

BEACHES & OUTDOOR ACTIVITIES

BEACHES   Stretching eastward 47 miles from the entrance to Pensacola Bay to Fort Walton Beach, skinny **Santa Rosa Island** is home to the resorts, condominiums, cottages, restaurants, and shops of **Pensacola Beach,** the area's prime vacation spot. This small and low-key resort began life a century ago as the site of a beach pavilion, or "casino" as such facilities were called back then, and the heart of town is still known as Casino Beach.

The highlight for beach lovers here, however, is the local branch of ✪ **Gulf Islands National Seashore,** 1801 Gulf Breeze Pkwy., Gulf Breeze, FL 32561 (☎ **904/934-2600**). Jumping from island to island from Mississippi to Florida, this magnificent preserve includes mile after mile of undeveloped white-sand beach and rolling dunes covered with sea grass and sea oats. Established in 1971, the national seashore is a protected environment for over 280 species of birds. Visitors enjoy swimming, boating, fishing, scuba diving, camping, and ranger-guided fort tours and nature hikes.

Fort Pickens, built in the 1830s to team with Fort Barrancas in guarding Pensacola's harbor entrance, stands silent guard in the dunes at the western end of

Pensacola

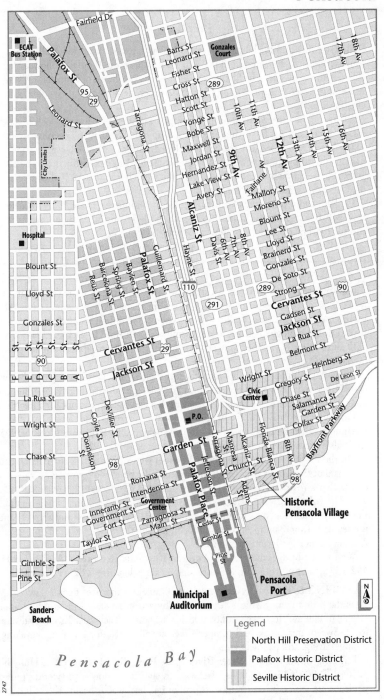

Legend

North Hill Preservation District

Palafox Historic District

Seville Historic District

Dog Gone

Rufus Godwin's hunting hound Flojo was wearing an electronic tracking collar when it mysteriously disappeared not long ago. To find his mutt, Godwin followed the collar's radio signals into the Blackwater River Swamp northeast of Pensacola. When the strongest signals kept coming from underwater, he went to state wildlife officials for help.

Searching the site, two state-licensed trappers captured a 10-foot 11-inch alligator. During the struggle, the huge reptile spit up Flojo's collar, still beeping away.

Declared a nuisance gator, the beast was killed. Inside its stomach were five brass nameplates from other dogs, one of them missing for 14 years. Estimated to be 50 years old, the gator apparently would lie in wait when it heard barking, then snatch the dogs as they ran along a game trail.

Godwin had several offers for Flojo's collar, including one from *Ripley's Believe It or Not*, but he loaned it instead to the Pensacola Historical Museum, where it and the five brass nametags are now on display.

Said Godwin: "That was the best dog I ever owned."

Santa Rosa Island. This huge brick structure saw combat during the Civil War, but it's famous today as the prison home of Apache medicine man Geronimo from 1886 to 1888. A small museum features displays about Geronimo, coastal defenses, and the seashore's ecology. The fort and museum are open April to October, daily from 9:30am to 5pm; November to March, daily from 8:30am to 4pm. Both are closed Christmas Day.

Seven-day admission permits to both Fort Pickens and Perdido Key (see below) cost $4 per vehicle, $2 per pedestrian or bicyclist. Seniors can purchase a lifetime Golden Age Pass for a one-time $10 fee, and disabled persons can ask for a free pass.

East of Pensacola Beach, the pristine national seashore resumes for 11 miles until reaching Navarre Beach. This area was heavily damaged by Hurricane Opal in 1995. Officials hope to have its free day-use facilities reopened in 1997.

On the Florida-Alabama line about 15 miles west of Pensacola, the narrow barrier island of **Perdido Key** has such wide, spectacular beaches of powdery, pure-white quartz that a road sign warns newcomers: RED CLAY IS PROHIBITED ON PERDIDO KEY. The **Johnson Beach Area** of Gulf Islands National Seashore, which occupies the totally undeveloped eastern third of the island, has rest rooms and showers and is open daily from 8am to sunset. Admission fees are the same as to the Fort Pickens Area on Santa Rosa Island (see above).

West of the bridge, the beach at **Perdido Key State Recreation Area** (☎ **904/ 492-1575**) is open from 8am to sunset daily. Admission here is $2 per vehicle.

CANOEING & KAYAKING   Less than 20 miles northeast of Pensacola via U.S. 90 is the little town of Milton, the official (by act of the state legislature) "Canoe Capital of Florida." It's a well-earned title, for the nearby Blackwater River, Coldwater River, Sweetwater Creek, and Juniper Creek are all perfect for canoeing, kayaking, tubing, rafting, and paddleboating.

Running through **Blackwater River State Park,** Rte. 1, Box 57-C, Holt, FL 32564 (☎ **904/623-2363**), the Blackwater is considered one of the world's purest sand-bottom rivers. It has retained its primordial, backwoods beauty. Plant life and wildlife can be closely observed along the park's nature trails. The park also contains

Florida's largest state forest, with about 183,000 acres of oak, pine, and juniper. Blackwater has facilities for fishing, picnicking, camping, and cabin stays.

Adventures Unlimited, Rte. 6, Box 283, Milton, FL 32570 (☎ **904/623-9197,** or 800/239-6864), is a year-round resort with canoeing, kayaking, rafting, camping, and paddleboating expeditions in the state park and surrounding rivers. Special arrangements are made for novices. The company also rents 14 cottages on the Coldwater River ranging from $29 to $89 a night. Campsites cost $15 a night.

Blackwater Canoe Rental, 10274 Pond Rd., Milton, FL 32570 (☎ **904/ 623-0235,** or 800/967-6789), also rents canoes, kayaks, floats, tubes, and camping equipment. It has day trips by canoe, kayak, or inner tubes ranging from $8 to $19 per person, and overnight excursions ranging from $19 to $28 per person. Tents, sleeping bags, and coolers are available for rent.

FISHING   Red snapper, grouper, mackerel, tuna, and billfish are abundant in these waters. Admission is free to the Pensacola Bay Bridge Fishing Pier (it's on the old bridge and claims to be the world's longest fishing pier) and to the Bob Sikes Bridge Fishing Pier (also on the old bridge). The Fort Pickens Fishing Pier, the Pensacola Beach Fishing Pier (☎ 904/932-0444), and Navarre Beach Pier, 20 miles east of Pensacola Beach (☎ 904/939-5658), were all damaged by Hurricane Opal; check to see if they've reopened.

Fishing here is primarily by charter boat, which is a costly $300 to $750 a day for one to four passengers, depending on length of trip. A more affordable option is offered in Destin or Panama City. Charter services are offered by **Scuba Shack/ Charter Boat** *Wet Dream,* 719 S. Palafox St., in Pensacola (☎ 904/433-4319); *Hooligan* **Charters** (☎ 904/968-1898) and *Rocky Top* **Charters** (☎ 904/ 432-7536), both at Pitt Slip Marina off East Main Street in Pensacola; and *Lo-Baby* **Charters,** 38 Highpoint Dr., in Gulf Breeze (☎ 904/934-5285). At Pensacola Beach, choose from *Chulamar* (☎ 904/434-6977), *Lively One* (☎ 904/932-5071), *Boss Lady* ☎ 904/932-0305 or 904/477-4033), *Entertainer* (☎ 904/932-0305), *Exodus* (☎ 904/626-2545 or 904/932-0305), and *Lady Kady* (☎ 904/932-2065 or 904/932-0305). Sightseeing and evening cruises on these vessels go for about $50 per person.

GOLF   Reasonably priced golf packages can be arranged through many local hotels and motels.

The Pensacola area has its share of Northwest Florida's numerous championship golf courses. Among them are the **Creekside Golf Course,** 2355 W. Michigan Ave. (☎ **904/944-7969**); the **Marcus Pointe Golf Course** (site of the Ben Hogan PGA Tour, Pensacola Open, and American Amateur Classic), Marcus Pointe Boulevard off North W Street (☎ **904/484-9770**); the **Osceola Municipal Golf Course,** 300 Tonawanda, off Mobile Highway (☎ **904/456-2761**); the **Tiger Point Golf Course and Country Club,** 1255 Country Club Rd., overlooking Santa Rosa Sound east of Gulf Breeze (☎ **904/932-1330**); **The Moors,** on Avalon Boulevard north of I-10 (☎ **904/995-GOLF**); and the **Hidden Creek Golf Course,** 3070 PGA Blvd., in Navarre (☎ **904/939-4604**).

In addition, the **Perdido Bay Golf Resort,** 1 Doug Ford Dr., near Perdido Key (☎ **904/492-1223,** or 800/874-5355), has accommodations available for visiting golfers. Its 7,154-yard course was home of the PGA Pensacola Open from 1978 to 1987.

SAILING & SURFBOARDING   Kirk Newkirk's **Key Sailing Center,** 500 Quietwater Beach Rd., on the Quietwater Beach Boardwalk (☎ **904/**

932-5550), rents Hobie Cats, pontoon boats, Waverunners, jet skis, and windsurfing boards. So does **Radical Rides,** 444 Pensacola Beach Blvd., near the Bob Sikes Bridge (☎ **904/934-9743**). Rates range from $15 a hour for a Sunfish to $50 a hour for jet skis.

SCUBA DIVING & SNORKELING Visibility in the waters around Pensacola can range from 30 to 50 feet inshore to 100 feet 25 miles offshore. Although the bottom is sandy and it's too far north for coral, the battleship USS *Massachusetts,* submerged in 30 feet of water 3 miles offshore, is one of some 35 artificial reefs where you can sight loggerhead turtles and other creatures.

   Gulf Coast Pro Dive, 7203 U.S. 98 West (☎ **904/456-8845**), is the area's largest scuba specialist, offering rentals, all levels of instruction, and diving excursions. There's another branch in Gulf Breeze (☎ 904/934-8845). **Scuba Shack / Charter Boat** *Wet Dream,* 719 S. Palafox St. (☎ **904/433-4319**), located at the waterfront, is Pensacola's oldest dive shop, offering rentals and NASDS classes. The *Chulamar,* at Pensacola Beach (☎ **904/434-6977**), and the *Lo-Baby,* in Gulf Breeze (☎ **904/ 934-5285**), both make arrangements for diving excursions.

SPECTATOR SPORTS The **Pensacola Greyhound Track,** 951 Dog Track Rd. (Fla. 297) (☎ **904/455-8595**), features races year round Tuesday to Saturday at 7pm and on Saturday and Sunday at 1pm. Admission is $1. **Five Flags Speedway,** 7450 Pine Forest Rd. (☎ **904/944-0466**), offers speed racing Friday night on one of the fastest half-mile tracks in the country. Top race-car drivers varoom around the course for the prize money. Call for the schedule and prices.

TENNIS Beautifully situated beside Bayou Texar in Pensacola, the **Bayview Community Center,** 20th Avenue and Lloyd Street (☎ **904/435-1788**), has six hard courts free to the public daily from 8am to 5pm. Pensacola also has the area's largest facility, the **Roger Scott Tennis Center,** Summit Boulevard at Piedmont (☎ **904/432-2939**), offering 18 lighted hard courts at $3 per adult, $2.50 for children. It's open Monday to Friday from 8am to 9:30pm and on Saturday, Sunday, and holidays from 9am to 5pm. Over in Gulf Breeze, the **South Santa Rosa Recreation Center,** Sunset and Shoreline Drive (☎ **904/934-5140** or 904/934-5141), has six lighted hard courts available free to the public on a first-come basis anytime. See "Where to Stay," below, for hotels and motels with tennis courts.

EXPLORING HISTORIC PENSACOLA

In addition to Historic Pensacola Village in the Seville Historic District, the city has two other preservation areas worth a stroll. The Pensacola Visitor Information Center provides free walking-tour maps.

✪ **Historic Pensacola Village.** 205 E. Zaragossa St. (just east of Tarragona St.). Admission $5.50 adults, $4.50 seniors and military, $2.25 children 4–16, free for children 3 and under; $13 families; $10.50 couples. Memorial Day–Labor Day, daily 10am–4pm; off-season, Mon–Sat 10am–4pm.

Nowhere is the town's past better preserved than in Historic Pensacola Village, in the Seville Historic District. Bounded by Government, Zaragossa, Adams, and Alcanz streets near the waterfront, the village resembles a shady English colonial town— albeit with Spanish-named streets. It has some of Florida's oldest homes (now owned and preserved by the state), along with charming boutiques and interesting restaurants. Costumed characters go about their daily chores and demonstrate old crafts, and University of Florida archeologists unearth the old Spanish commanding officer's compound at Zaragossa and Tarragona streets. Among the landmarks to visit are the

Museum of Industry, the Museum of Commerce, the French Créole-style Charles Lavalle House, the elegant Victorian Dorr House, the French colonial-Créole Quina House, and St. Michael's Cemetery (land was deeded by the king of Spain).

A highlight here is the **Pensacola Historical Museum,** 405 S. Adams St., at Zaragossa St. (☎ 904/433-1559), in the old Christ Church, built in 1823 and reminiscent of Bruton Parish in Colonial Williamsburg. The museum covers just about everything pertaining to the city's history, including Native American artifacts. Its **library** of more than 2,000 volumes, many pertaining to Northwest Florida, is at 117 E. Government St. (☎ 904/434-5455). Admission to both the museum and library is $2 for adults, $1 for children 4 to 16, free for children 3 and under. The museum is open May to October, Monday to Saturday from 9am to 4:30pm; November to April, Monday to Saturday from 10am to 4:30pm. Admission to the museum includes the library, which is open year round, Tuesday to Thursday and on Saturday from 10am to noon and 1 to 3pm. Both are closed holidays.

Another fascinating site is the **Julee Cottage Black History Museum,** 204 Zaragossa St. Built around 1790, this small house was owned by Julee Panton, a freed slave who ran her own business, invested in real estate, and loaned money to slaves so they could buy their freedom. Today the museum recalls her life and deeds, as well as the achievements of other African-Americans with Pensacola associations.

Admission to the village includes the T. T. Wentworth, Jr., Florida State Museum (see "Historic Districts," below). Good for 2 days, tickets may be purchased at the T. T. Wentworth museum and at Tivoli House, 205 E. Zaragossa St., just east of Tarragona Street.

Adjacent to the village, Pensacola's **Vietnam Memorial,** on Bayfront Parkway at 9th Avenue, is known as the "Wall South," since it is a three-quarters-size replica of the touching national Vietnam Veterans Memorial at Washington, D.C. Carved on the wall are the names of every American killed during the Vietnam conflict. Look for the Huey helicopter sitting atop the wall.

Palafox Historic District. Palafox St. from the waterfront to Wright St. ☎ **904/444-8905** for information.

This was Old Pensacola's harborfront and commercial center, and it still is the downtown business district. Beautiful Spanish Renaissance– and Mediterranean-style buildings stand from the early days, when more than a dozen foreign consulates were located here. The ornate Saenger Theatre and other structures have been restored to their original beauty, including their New Orleans–style wrought-iron balconies. In 1821, Gen. Andrew Jackson formally accepted Florida into the United States during a ceremony in Plaza Ferdinand VII, now a National Historic Landmark. His statue commemorates the event.

The Palafox district is home to the **Pensacola Museum of Art,** 407 S. Jefferson St., at Main Street (☎ 904/432-6247). Located in what was the city jail from 1906 to 1954, the museum showcases permanent art and sculpture collections as well as art on loan. Shows range from tribal art to classic European masterpieces to avant-garde modern works. Admission is $2 for adults, $1 for active-duty military and children 15 and under 16; free for everyone on Tuesday. The museum is open Tuesday to Friday from 10am to 5pm, on Saturday from 10am to 4pm, and on Sunday from 1 to 4pm.

A block north stands the **T. T. Wentworth, Jr., Florida State Museum,** 330 S. Jefferson St., at Church Street (☎ 904/444-8586), which houses exhibits of western Florida's history, and has a special hands-on Discovery Museum for children on the third floor. Admission is $5.50 for adults, $4.50 for senior citizens and military,

$2.25 for children 4 to 16, free for children 3 and under, $13 for families, and $10.50 for couples. Admission includes Historic Pensacola Village. The museum is open from Memorial Day to Labor Day, daily from 10am to 4pm; the rest of the year, Monday to Saturday from 10am to 4pm.

The **Civil War Soldiers Museum,** 108 S. Palafox St., south of Romana Street (☎ 904/469-1900), was founded by Dr. Norman Haines, Jr., a local physician who grew up discovering Civil War relics in Sharpsburg, Maryland. This storefront museum emphasizes how ordinary soldiers lived during that bloody conflict. The doctor's collection of military medical equipment and treatment methods is especially informative. A 23-minute video tells of Pensacola's role during the Civil War. The museum's bookstore carries more than 600 titles about the war. Admission is $4 for adults, $2 for children 6 to 12, and free for children 5 and under. It's open Monday to Saturday from 10am to 4:30pm.

North Hill Preservation District. ☎ **904/444-8905** for information.

Another entry in the National Register of Historic Places, this area covers the 50 square blocks north of the Palafox Historic District bounded by Wright, Blount, Palafox, and Reus streets. Descendants of early settlers still live in some of the more than 500 homes, and family backgrounds include Spanish nobility, timber barons, British merchants, French Créoles, buccaneers, and Civil War soldiers. The private homes here are not open to the public but are a bonanza for anyone interested in Mediterranean Revival, Queen Anne, neoclassical, art moderne, Victorian, Craftsman Bungalow, and other architectural styles. In 1863 Union troops erected a fort in Lee Square, at Palafox and Gadsden streets. It later was dedicated to the Confederacy, complete with a 50-foot-high obelisk and sculpture based on John Elder's painting *After Appomattox.*

While touring North Hill, plan to have an inexpensive breakfast, lunch, or dinner at Hopkins' Boarding House (see "Where to Eat," below).

✪ **National Museum of Naval Aviation.** Radford Blvd. on the U.S. Naval Air Station. ☎ **904/452-3604.** Free admission. Daily 9am–5pm. Guided tours daily at 9:30am, 11am, 1pm, and 2:30pm. Closed New Year's Day, Thanksgiving, and Christmas Day. The Naval Station is southwest of downtown Pensacola; enter either at the Main Gate at the south end of Navy Boulevard (Fla. 295) or at the Back Gate on Blue Angel Parkway (Fla. 173). No passes are required.

Members of the U.S. Navy and Marine Corps have trained at the sprawling U.S. Naval Air Station since they began flying airplanes early this century. Celebrating their heroics, this truly remarkable museum has more than 100 aircraft dating from the 1920s to the space age. There's even a torpedo bomber flown by former President George Bush during World War II action in the South Pacific. Both children and adults can sit at the controls of a jet trainer. Due to be open by 1997, a breathtaking IMAX film will make you feel as if you're flying high with the Blue Angels (there will be a charge for the film).

Fort Barrancas (☎ 904/934-2600) also is definitely worth a visit while you're at the naval station. On Hovey Road near the museum, this imposing brick structure overlooks the deep-water pass into Pensacola Bay. The Spanish built the water battery in 1797. Linked to the battery by a tunnel, the incredibly intricate brickwork of the upper section was constructed by American troops between 1839 and 1844. Entry is by a drawbridge across a dry moat, and an interior scarp gallery goes all the way around the inside of the fort. Meticulously restored by the National Park Service as part of Gulf Islands National Seashore, it's open from April to October, daily from 9:30am to 5pm; November to March, Wednesday to Sunday from 10:30am to 4pm. Guided tour schedules change from season to season, so call for the latest information. Admission is free.

Pensacola Lighthouse, opposite the museum entrance on Radford Boulevard, has guided ships to the harbor entrance since 1825. The lighthouse is not open to the public, but you can drive right up to it. The nearby **Lighthouse Point Restaurant** (☎ 904/452-3251) offers bountiful, all-you-can-eat luncheon buffets and magnificent bay views for just $4.50 per person; it's open Monday to Friday from 10:30am to 2pm, and reservations are not required.

PARKS & NATURE PRESERVES

The major nature preserve here is Gulf Islands National Seashore (see "Beaches & Outdoor Activities," above), but there are smaller parks offering a variety of terrain and wildlife.

The **Naval Live Oaks Area** is a picturesque, 1,378-acre section of Gulf Islands National Seashore on U.S. 98 a few miles east of Gulf Breeze (☎ 904/934-2600). Ideal for shipbuilding, these super-strong oak trees have been protected from logging interests since the early 1800s. Artifacts discovered in the area indicate that prehistoric tribes lived here 10,000 years ago. Today this former federal tree plantation is a place of primitive beauty. Nature trails lead through the oaks and pines to picnic areas and a beach; pick up a map at the headquarters building, which has a small museum and a gorgeous view through the pines to Santa Rosa Sound. Picnic areas and trails are open from 8am to sunset all year except Christmas. The visitor center is open April to October, daily from 8:30am to 5pm; November to March, daily from 8:30am to 4:30pm. Admission is free.

The **Edward Ball Nature Trail,** located on the northwest side of the 1,000-acre University of West Florida campus, features a mile of boardwalk around a shaded bayou, where the Escambia River wetlands and woodlands have been left in their natural states. Abundant wildlife here include alligators, turtles, opossum, and many birds. The nature trail is free and open daily. The university's information center on University Drive (☎ 904/474-3000) has maps of the campus, including the nature walk. The information center is open Monday to Friday from 7:30am to 4:30pm. The trail was named in honor of Edward Ball, a Florida millionaire who donated much of his fortune to preserving Florida's wildlife.

Bay Bluffs Park, at the corner of Scenic Highway (U.S. 90) and Summit Boulevard, offers rustic boardwalks and 20 acres of nature trails. One boardwalk descends Florida's only scenic bluffs, a prehistoric formation dating back 20,000 years. The park is open daily from sunrise to 11pm. Admission is free.

Big Lagoon State Recreation Area, on County Road 292A about 10 miles west of Pensacola on the way to Perdido Key (☎ 904/492-1595), offers a bay beach for swimming, boating, picnicking, fishing, and camping (see "Where to Stay," below). An observation tower provides panoramic views over the Big Lagoon and nearby bays and islands. The salt marshes attract great blue herons, brown thrashers, cardinals, and many other species of birds. The area is open daily from 8am to sunset. Admission is $3.25 for up to eight people in a vehicle, $1 for pedestrians and bicyclists.

Although it's not an official nature preserve or wildlife refuge, more than 700 exotic animals—including white tigers, rhinos, and gorillas—live on 50 acres of landscaped habitats at **The Zoo,** on U.S. 98 about 10 miles east of Gulf Breeze and 15 miles east of Pensacola (☎ 904/932-2229). Japanese gardens, elephant shows, a giraffe feeding tower, and a petting farm make for a fun visit. A Safari Line train chugs through a 30-acre wildlife preserve with free-ranging herds. There's a lakeside restaurant and gift shop. Admission is $9.25 for adults, $8.25 for seniors, $5.25 for

416 Northwest Florida: The Panhandle

children 3 to 11, free for children 2 and under. Open daily: from 9am to 5pm during the summer months, from 9am to 4pm off-season.

SHOPPING

Sightseeing and shopping can be combined in Pensacola's Palafox and Seville Historic districts, where many shops are housed in renovated centuries-old buildings.

Among the many unusual shops is the **Quayside Art Gallery,** on Plaza Ferdinand at the corner of Zaragossa and Jefferson streets (☎ **904/438-2363**), the largest cooperative gallery in the Southeast. More than 100 artists display their works here, and the friendly staff will direct you to other nearby galleries.

A fun way to shop for fine art is on a **Gallery Night tour,** sponsored every month or so by the Downtown Arts District Association (☎ **904/432-9906**) and the Arts Council of Northwest Florida. They provide free bus transportation to more than a dozen galleries, with musical entertainment and refreshments along the way.

Some of the best buys here are antiques, and Pensacola has plenty of places to hunt for them. North T Street between West Cervantes Street and West Fairfield Drive has so many antiques dealers and small flea markets that it's known as **Antique Alley.** Other dealers have booths in the **Ninth Avenue Antique Mall,** 380 N. 9th Ave. between Gregory and Strong streets (☎ **904/438-3961**). Get a complete list of local antiques dealers from the Pensacola Visitor Information Center (see "Essentials," above).

Bargain-hunters will enjoy poking through the 400 dealer spaces covering 45 acres at the **Flea Market,** on U.S. 98 opposite the Zoo about 10 miles east of Gulf Breeze (☎ **904/934-1971**). It's open on Saturday and Sunday from 9am to 5pm. Admission is free.

Pecans grow in abundance in these parts, and the **J. W. Renfroe Pecan Co.,** 2400 W. Fairfield Dr., at North S Street (☎ **904/432-2083**), prepares them just about every way describable, from chocolate covered to barbecued.

WHERE TO STAY

The busy season here and all along Northwest Florida's gulf coast runs from mid-May to Labor Day, when hotel or motel reservations are essential. Room rates are highest from mid-May to mid-August, with premiums charged at Easter, Memorial Day, July 4th, and Labor Day. There's another high-priced peak in March, when thousands of raucous college students invade Northwest Florida during spring break. The most economical times to visit, therefore, are from April (except Easter) to mid-May and in September and October. The weather's pleasantly warm during these "shoulder seasons," most establishments are open, and room rates are significantly lower than during summer. The price categories in this chapter are based on the least expensive double room available during these shoulder seasons: less than $40, less than $60, and less than $80.

Escambia County adds 1% to the statewide 6% sales tax, making the local sales tax 7%, and it adds a 3% tax on all accommodations bills, including campgrounds.

The accommodations and restaurants listed below are arranged by geographic area: Pensacola, Pensacola Beach, and Gulf Breeze. Needless to say, you'll pay more for a room at the beach during summer than you will in Pensacola and Gulf Breeze. More convenient to the beach than downtown, Gulf Breeze is south of Pensacola via the 3-mile-long Pensacola Bay Bridge (locals call it the "Three-Mile Bridge"). The 1-mile-long Bob Sikes Bridge runs from Gulf Breeze to the beach; there's a $1 toll going to the beach, free coming back. There is no public bus service between Pensacola and the beach.

In addition to the establishments recommended below, several well-known chains have motels on Plantation Road in the University Mall complex at I-10 and Davis Highway, about 5 miles north of downtown Pensacola and 15 miles from the beach. There is public bus service between the mall and downtown, but not to the beaches. There's an ample supply of inexpensive restaurants on Plantation Road and in the adjacent mall.

The least expensive rooms in town are at the **Motel 6–East,** 7226 Plantation Rd. (☎ **904/474-1060,** or 800/466-8356), and at the recently renovated **Motel 6– North,** just across I-10 at 7827 N. Davis Hwy. (☎ **904/476-5386,** or 800/ 466-8356). Both charge just under $40 for a double year round. Also here are the inexpensive **Super 8 Motel,** 7220 Plantation Rd. (☎ **904/476-8038,** or 800/ 800-8000), and the **Red Roof Inn,** 7340 Plantation Rd. (☎ **904/476-7960,** or 800/ 843-7663). More expensive are the **Residence Inn by Marriott,** 7230 Plantation Rd. (☎ **904/479-1000,** or 800/331-3131), in which all rooms and apartments have kitchens and fireplaces; the **Hampton Inn–University Mall,** 7330 Plantation Rd. (☎ **904/477-3333,** or 800/426-7866); the **Marriott Fairfield Inn,** 7325 N. Davis Hwy. (☎ **800/228-2800**); and the **Holiday Inn–University Mall,** 7200 Plantation Rd. (☎ **904/474-0100,** or 800/465-4329).

Long-term stays can represent savings, especially if you want to be on the gulf. In fact, Pensacola Beach has at least as many **beach condominiums and cottages** as it does hotel and motel rooms. Contact the Pensacola Visitor Information Center for its list of rental town homes, condos, and vacation cottages (see "Essentials," above).

PENSACOLA
Doubles for Less than $40

Seville Inn. 223 E. Garden St., Pensacola, FL 32501. ☎ **904/433-8331,** or 800/277-7275. Fax 904/432-6849. 120 rms. A/C TV TEL. Summer, $65–$79 double. Winter, $39–$44 double. Rates include continental breakfast. AE, DC, MC, V.

This dated but clean two-story motel is conveniently located at the edge of the Seville Historic District, across the street from the Civic Center and about 4 blocks from the Saenger Theatre. Two outdoor swimming pools are open during the warm months. Guests receive complimentary airport transfers, local phone calls, and passes to the Pensacola Greyhound track.

PENSACOLA BEACH
Doubles for Less than $60

Five Flags Inn. 299 Fort Pickens Rd., Pensacola Beach, FL 32561. ☎ **904/932-3586.** Fax 904/ 934-0257. 49 rms. A/C TV TEL. Summer, $75 double. Off-season, $45–$65 double. Packages available. MC, V.

This friendly motel looks like a jail from the road, but don't be fooled. Big picture windows look out to the swimming pool and gorgeous white-sand beach, which comes right up to the property (there's new decking around the pool, thanks to Hurricane Opal). Although the accommodations are small, the rates are a bargain for well-furnished gulf-front rooms.

Doubles for Less than $80

Best Western Pensacola Beach. 16 Via de Luna Dr., Pensacola Beach, FL 32561. ☎ **904/ 934-3300,** or 800/934-3301. Fax 904/934-4366. 122 rms. A/C TV TEL. Summer, $105–$115 double. Off-season, $63–$73 double. Rates include continental breakfast. Packages available. AE, DC, DISC, MC, V.

On the gulf-front, this casual hotel is notable for bright, clean, and extra-spacious accommodations, complete with refrigerators, coffeemakers, microwaves, and wet bars. Outside corridors lead to all rooms. Although no room has its own balcony or patio, those facing the beach have great views; some others don't. The two swimming pools, Cabana Bar, and children's playground are on the beach. Chan's Market Café (see "Where to Eat," below) sits in the parking lot.

Comfort Inn–Pensacola Beach. 40 Fort Pickens Rd., Pensacola Beach, FL 32561. ☎ **904/ 934-5400,** or 800/934-5470. Fax 904/932-7210. 98 rms, 1 suite. A/C TV TEL. Summer, $89– $99 double. Off-season, $49–$79 double. Rates include continental breakfast. AE, DC, DISC, MC, V.

On the bay side of Fort Pickens Road opposite Casino Beach and the Quietwater Boardwalk, this four-story motel was built and opened in 1995. The medium-size rooms with bright furniture, spreads, and drapes all open to external walkways, thereby eliminating balconies and reducing views and privacy. Armoires hide the TVs and provide closets. There's a pool and exercise room here. Breakfast is served in a room off the lobby.

The Dunes. 333 Fort Pickens Rd., Pensacola Beach, FL 32561. ☎ **904/932-3536,** or 800/ 83-DUNES. Fax 904/932-7088. 76 units. A/C TV TEL. Summer, $109–$135 double; $220–$255 suite. Off-season, $69–$79 double; $195–$220 suite. Packages available. AE, DISC, MC, V.

Local owners built this eight-story tower to replace a low-slung, beachside motel partially destroyed by Hurricane Elena in 1985. The spacious rooms have balconies with gorgeous gulf or bay vistas. The small but pleasant Gulf Front Cafe serves breakfast, lunch, and dinner. The kids can participate in the supervised children's program from May to Labor Day. The hotel will even take care of the kids so mom and dad can take Saturday night off. The facilities also include a heated swimming pool, a jogging trail, a bike path, and a volleyball area. There's an undeveloped dune preserve next door.

Hampton Inn–Pensacola Beach. 2 Via de Luna, Pensacola Beach, FL 32561. ☎ **904/ 932-6800,** or 800/HAMPTON. Fax 904/932-6833. 180 rms, 1 suite. A/C TV TEL. Summer, $101–$140 double. Off-season, $65–$111. Rates include continental breakfast. AE, DC, DISC, MC, V.

Another 1995-vintage establishment, this pastel, four-story hotel sits right by the gulf next to Casino Beach. The bright lobby opens to a wooden sundeck with beachside swimming pools on either side (one is heated). In an unusual but attractive touch, purple splashed with bright tropical floral prints provides the color scheme for the carpets, spreads, and drapes here. Half the oversize rooms have balconies overlooking the gulf. These are more expensive than those on the bay side, which have nice views but no outside sitting areas. Each room is equipped with a refrigerator, microwave oven, and wet bar. There's no restaurant on the premises, but Chan's Gulfside Café and Surfside Saloon is next door. Guests have their own coin laundry.

GULF BREEZE
Doubles for Less than $40

Gulf Coast Inn Motel. 843 Gulf Breeze Pkwy. (U.S. 98), Gulf Breeze, FL 32561. ☎ **904/ 932-2222.** 32 rms. A/C TV TEL. Summer, $38–$48 double. Winter, $30–$40 double. Weekly rates available. AE, DISC, MC, V.

This unpretentious brick motel is convenient to the Bob Sikes Bridge leading to Pensacola Beach. Situated in one- and two-story blocks, some rooms have kitchenettes, and there's a small swimming pool open March to October. The Chinese family who operate this establishment also have a Cantonese-style restaurant across the street. A Waffle House is next door, and a host of fast-food restaurants are nearby.

Doubles for Less than $80

Holiday Inn–Bay Beach. 51 Gulf Breeze Pkwy. (U.S. 98), Gulf Breeze, FL 32561. ☎ **904/ 932-2214,** or 800/HOLIDAY. Fax 904/932-2214. 168 rms. A/C TV TEL. Summer, $70–$100 double. Off-season, $60–$80 double. AE, DC, DISC, MC, V.

On a small beach with a grand view of Pensacola across the bay, this two-story, coral-colored motel offers complimentary coffee, newspapers, and drinks served Monday to Thursday evening in a special cocktail suite. Enjoying the view, the best rooms here face a courtyard with a swimming pool plus a wading pool for the kids. These units have refrigerators and better furnishings than the less expensive rooms, which face the parking lot. All units have coffeemakers. Several large bay-view rooms also have microwaves. Also feasting on the view, the Bon Appetit Cafe and Bakery serves breakfast (fresh croissants and bagels), lunch, and dinner. Pensacola Beach is a short drive to the south via the Bob Sikes toll bridge.

CAMPING

The **Fort Pickens Area** of Gulf Islands National Seashore (☎ **904/934-2621** for recorded information) has 200 campsites (135 with electricity) in a pine forest about 7 miles west of Pensacola Beach on the bay side of Santa Rosa Island. Nature trails lead from the camp through Blackbird Marsh and to the beach. A small store sells provisions. It's first-come, first-served, but you must register at the ranger station east of the campground. Sites cost $12 a night without power, $16 a night with it.

Big Lagoon State Recreation Area, Fla. 292A, Pensacola, FL 32507 (☎ **904/ 492-1595**), near Perdido Key, offers 75 campsites for $10 with electricity, $8 without. Reservations may be made up to 60 days in advance. Gasoline, groceries, and a laundry are within a quarter mile of the park, which has modern rest rooms and hot showers. Cabins may be added here in 1997. See "Parks & Nature Preserves," above, for details about what's here.

Timberlake, 2600 W. Michigan Ave., Pensacola, FL 32505 (☎ **904/944-5487**), east of Memphis Avenue, is a permanent mobile-home park which offers RV camping for $15 per day or $200 per month. Facilities include a swimming pool and tennis, basketball, and volleyball courts. There's also a lake for fishing and an adjoining golf course.

WHERE TO EAT

Like the hotels listed above, the restaurants are arranged below by geographic location: Pensacola and Pensacola Beach. Plantation Road, off North Davis Highway behind the University Mall at I-10 in Pensacola, has a host of moderately priced national-chain family restaurants. Although Pensacola Beach lacks national fast-food outlets, the strip of U.S. 98 in Gulf Breeze has them all—plus a Delchamps supermarket with a huge deli section carrying a wide array of picnic fare (it even has tables in a dining area).

PENSACOLA

Meals for Less than $7

Barnhill's Country Buffet. N. Davis Hwy. (at Olive Rd.). ☎ **904/477-5465.** Reservations not accepted. Lunch $5.30 adults, $4.90 seniors, 40¢ times age for children 12 and under; dinner $6.80 adults, $6.20 seniors, 45¢ times age for children 12 and under. MC, V. Sun–Thurs 10:45am–8:30pm, Fri–Sat 10:45am–9pm. AMERICAN.

Local families line up at the door to pay the one price here, then eat all they can hold from seven buffet tables laden with a cornucopia of fried chicken and fish, boiled cabbage and collard greens, baked ham, roast beef, an extraordinarily tasty pot roast, a wide range of fresh salads, and a dessert table stocked with old-fashioned 'nilla wafer banana pudding. No one goes away from this popular, friendly establishment hungry—or broke.

There's another Barnhill's Country Buffet on U.S. 98 at Oriole Drive, 3 miles east of Gulf Breeze (☎ 904/932-0403). Hours and prices are the same.

✪ Hopkins' Boarding House. 900 N. Spring St. (at Strong St.). ☎ **904/438-3979.** Reservations not accepted. Full meals $6.50. No credit cards. Tues–Sat 7–9:30am, 11:15am–2pm, and 5:15–7:30pm; Sun noon–2pm. SOUTHERN.

There's a delicious peek into the past when you dine at this Victorian boarding house in the heart of the North Hill Preservation District. Outside, ancient trees shade a wraparound porch with old-fashioned rocking chairs in which to await the next available place at the large dining tables inside. You could be seated next to the mayor or a mechanic, for everyone in town dines here, and everyone eats family style. Platters are piled high with seasonal southern-style vegetables from nearby farms. Tuesday is famous as Fried Chicken Day, and you're likely to be served fried fish on Friday. Every Yankee should sample the piping-hot grits accompanying each bountiful breakfast. In true boarding-house fashion, guests bus their own dishes and pay the one price when they're finished eating.

Marina Oyster Barn. 505 Bayou Blvd., on Bayou Texar. ☎ **904/433-0511.** Reservations not accepted. Main courses $5.50–$11.50; lunch specials (served 11am–2pm) $3.75–$5.50. AE, DISC, MC, V. Tues–Sat 11am–9pm. Go east on Cervantes Street across the Bayou Texar Bridge, turn left on Perry Avenue, and left again to the end of Strong Street. SEAFOOD.

This plain but clean restaurant at the Johnson-Rooks Marina has been a favorite with seafood lovers since 1969, for both its view and its down-home–style seafood. Freshly shucked oysters are the main feature, but locals also are fond of the fried mullet and the seafood salad. The daily luncheon specials are a bargain.

Mr. P's Sandwich Shop. In Historic Pensacola Village, 221 E. Zaragossa St. ☎ **904/433-0294.** Reservations not accepted. Lunch items $3–$6. MC, V. Mon–Fri 11am–2:30pm. SANDWICHES.

Located opposite Old Christ Church in the 1879-vintage Moreno Cottage, Will and Sandy Noble's little sandwich emporium is an excellent choice for an inexpensive lunch while touring Historic Pensacola Village. The clapboard house has high tropical windows to let plenty of light onto simple stack chairs and tables covered with oilcloth. Daily specials such as red beans and rice, jambalaya, or shrimp Créole augment a regular menu of soups, salads, quiches, and made-to-order sandwiches.

Meals for Less than $10

Cock of the Walk. 550 Scenic Hwy. (U.S. 90, at E. Cervantes St.). ☎ **904/432-6766.** Reservations not accepted. Main courses $8–$13. AE, DISC, MC, V. Mon 5–8:30pm, Tues–Thurs and Sun 11am–2pm and 5–8:30pm, Fri–Sat 11am–2pm and 5–10pm. SEAFOOD.

A Dogpatch ambience pervades this barnlike building. Cast-iron buckets hold each table's silverware and paper napkins, and meals are served on china of the purest tin. Dressed in Pappy Yokum–style hats, the service staff tosses and catches the skillet-baked rounds of cornbread that accompany each meal. Tried-and-true southern favorites are offered here, such as fried dill pickles (thinly sliced and breaded in a sweet batter to balance the piquant pickle, they're the regional version of fried calamari). A pot of greens cooked to smithereens is another popular appetizer. Don't come here to keep the waistline under control, for the budget-priced meals of catfish, shrimp, oysters, and chicken are all breaded with cornmeal and deep-fried in true southern country fashion and served with the obligatory hush puppies, slaw, and potatoes.

Short weekend waits can be whiled away with a drink on the outside deck with a view of the bay through sprawling oak trees.

Landry's Seafood House. 905 E. Gregory St. (at Bayfront Pkwy. near the Pensacola Bay Bridge). ☎ **904/434-3600.** Reservations not accepted. Main courses $9–$20. AE, DC, DISC, MC, V. Sun–Thurs 11am–10pm, Fri–Sat 11am–11pm. SEAFOOD.

In keeping with other members of the Landry chain, a neon entry makes this lively restaurant look more like a cinema, but its double-hung windows provide beautiful water views to enjoy while eating the main attractions: fried, broiled, grilled, or Cajun-style seafood. In keeping with Landry's Louisiana roots, the house specialty is blackened snapper. The menu also offers gumbo and crayfish étouffée. Wait for a table at the bar, where seats face the bay.

McGuire's Irish Pub & Brewery. 600 E. Gregory St. (between 11th and 12th aves.). ☎ **904/433-6789.** Reservations not accepted. Snacks, burgers, and sandwiches $5.50–$7; meals $8–$18. AE, DC, DISC, MC, V. Mon–Sat 11am–2am, Sun 11am–3pm (brunch) and 3pm–1am. AMERICAN/IRISH.

Every day is a lively St. Patrick's Day here, with corned beef and cabbage, Irish stew, and such hybrids as Seafood O'Fettuccine. Super-size hamburgers, grilled fish, beer-batter shrimp, barbecued and prime ribs, nachos, pizzas, and other treats are also on the menu. Guests can watch the house beer being brewed in copper kettles. You can buy a personalized beer mug, thus joining the Family Mug Club. If your mother comes from Ireland, you can leave an autographed dollar bill; more than 100,000 such signed bucks already line the bar's walls and ceiling. Live music is offered most nights (see "Pensacola After Dark," below).

PENSACOLA BEACH
Meals for Less than $7
Chan's Market Café. 16 Via de Luna. ☎ **904/932-8454.** Reservations not accepted. Breakfast/lunch/snacks $4–$7; dinner $7–$10. AE, DISC, MC, V. Mon–Fri 7–10:45am and 11am–9pm, Sat–Sun 7–11:45am and noon–9pm. AMERICAN.

The aroma of cappuccino and pastries in the oven permeates this pleasant little cafe and bakery, which shares quarters with a liquor store in the parking lot of the Best Western Pensacola Beach. It's the best place on the beach for a breakfast of freshly baked croissants or bagels. Lunches and dinners feature economical ($4 to $7) Blue Plate Specials of such favorites as meatloaf, turkey and dressing, and grilled fish, all served with a choice of southern-style veggies. Or you can order a heaping sandwich made with one of Chan's large, flaky croissants.

Meals for Less than $15
Chan's Gulfside Cafe & Surfside Saloon. 2½ Via de Luna (at Fort Pickens Rd.). ☎ **904/932-3525.** Reservations recommended upstairs, not accepted downstairs. Upstairs, main courses $12–$18. Downstairs, main courses $12–$17; sandwiches, burgers, baskets $5–$8. AE, DC, DISC, MC, V. Upstairs, Sun–Thurs 5:30–10pm, Fri–Sat 5:30–11pm; downstairs, Mon–Sat 11am–2am, Sun 10am–noon (brunch) and noon–2am. SEAFOOD.

Offering Pensacola Beach's only gulf-front dining, this modern complex on Casino Beach offers two lively dining choices. Upstairs is somewhat more formal yet still relaxed, with widely spaced tables enjoying terrific views of the beach and gulf. The cuisine here features pecan wood-fired tuna, grouper, and shrimp, served separately or as a mixed grill. The downstairs pub is completely informal, with a long bar where fans can sample an extensive collection of beers from microbreweries while watching their favorite teams on several TVs. Many of the same wood-grilled items are offered down there, along with pub-style fare such as burgers and baskets full of fried seafood or chicken. The pub opens to a beachside patio which has outdoor dining and live entertainment during summer.

Flounder's Chowder and Ale House. Via de Luna at Fort Pickens Rd. ☎ **904/932-2003.** Reservations not accepted. Main courses $14–$18; burgers and sandwiches $6–$7. AE, DC, DISC, MC, V. Mon–Sat 11am–2am, Sun 11am–2pm (brunch) and 2pm–2am. SEAFOOD.

Baked flounder stuffed with crabmeat is but one seafood specialty at this publike establishment whose fern-bar decor features stained-glass windows from an old New York convent and confessional booth walls from a New Orleans church. Bookshelves give a cozy, studious feel to one dining room, but Flounder's lively atmosphere is more accurately captured by the glass walls of another dining area facing a popular beachside bar where patrons boogie to live reggae bands during the summer season (see "Pensacola After Dark," below). Meals include a loaf of freshly baked bread and a large salad or cup of chowder. Burgers and sandwiches are offered all day, and there's a children's menu. On Sunday, a "bottomless" glass of champagne accompanies a sumptuous bayside brunch.

✪ **Jubilee Restaurant & Entertainment Complex.** 400 Quietwater Beach Rd. (Via de Luna at Fort Pickens Rd.), on Quietwater Beach Boardwalk. ☎ **904/934-3108.** Reservations not required. Beachside Café, main courses $7.50–$12. Topside, main courses $13–$25. AE, DC, DISC, MC, V. Beachside Café, Mon–Thurs 11:30am–10pm, Fri–Sat 11:30am–11pm, Sun 9am–3pm (champagne brunch); Topside, daily 6–10pm. SEAFOOD/STEAK/POULTRY.

At this beachside restaurant complex, complete with Island Bar and cocktail lounge, most dining is very casual, even in the elegant, gourmet Topside Restaurant, where the chef excels in the preparation of local fish and shellfish. Chicken de Luna, topped by sautéed fresh chunks of crabmeat, is deliciously different. The juicy steaks are mesquite-grilled. Lunch and dinner are served in the pub-style Beachside Café, offering a varied menu of fish and deli sandwiches, seafood combinations, oysters, pastas, and more. The J-Sweet Coffee & Dessert Room has homemade sweets and gourmet coffees. On summer evenings there are live bands for dancing under the stars, and indoor entertainment year round.

WORTH A SPLURGE

✪ **Jamie's.** 424 E. Zaragossa St. (between Alcanz and Florida Blanca), in Historic Pensacola Village. ☎ **904/434-2911.** Reservations recommended. Main courses $8–$9 at lunch, $17.50–$23 at dinner. AE, DC, MC, V. Mon 6–10pm, Tues–Sat 11:30am–2:30pm and 6–10pm. FRENCH.

In a restored Victorian home, Pensacola's classiest and most romantic restaurant enhances the dining experience with glowing fireplaces, soft candlelight, gleaming antiques, and subdued background music. Among Jamie's gourmet offerings are grilled lamb chops coated with rosemary and mustard seed and topped with a stock of mint glacé, and sautéed snapper lightly topped by a piquant herb-butter sauce and garnished with lump crabmeat. For a luscious dessert, try the chocolate-walnut torte del ray. The menu includes Jamie's recommended wines for each course. This a fine place for a classy but reasonably priced lunch while touring Historic Pensacola Village, since Jamie drops his prices by half at midday.

PENSACOLA AFTER DARK

Pensacola has a surprisingly sophisticated array of entertainment choices for such a relatively small city. For a schedule of upcoming events, get a copy of *Vision,* a bimonthly newsletter published by the Arts Council of Northwest Florida, P.O. Box 731, Pensacola, FL 32594 (☎ **904/432-9906**). Also pick up *Sneak Preview,* a calendar of events at the Pensacola Civic Center and the Saenger Theatre. Both publications are available at the Pensacola Visitor Information Center (see "Essentials," above). Tickets for all major performances can be purchased by phone from **Ticketmaster** (☎ 904/433-6311, or 800/488-5252).

THE PERFORMING ARTS

A masterpiece of Spanish baroque architecture, Pensacola's ornate **Saenger Theatre,** 118 S. Palafox St., near Romano Street (☎ 904/444-7686), has been painstakingly restored, including the original bricks salvaged from the old Pensacola Opera House. The variety of presentations include the Pensacola Opera Company, Broadway musicals, and touring performers. The **Pensacola Symphony Orchestra** (☎ 904/435-2533), considered the oldest continuous symphonic organization on the Gulf Coast, also performs at the Saenger and other venues. Once a year there's a performance with the city's Choral Society. Call ahead to find out where the orchestra is performing.

The **Pensacola Little Theater,** 400 S. Jefferson St., at Zaragossa Street (☎ 904/432-2042), is the Southeast's oldest continuing community theater.

The 10,000-seat **Pensacola Civic Center,** 201 E. Gregory St., at Alcanz Street (☎ 904/433-6311), hosts a variety of entertainment: touring productions of Broadway plays and musicals, famous bands, family shows, equestrian events, sports, and more. Call ahead for the current schedule.

The **Pensacola Jazz Society** (☎ 904/433-8382) invites jazz musicians to perform at local venues and is the primary supporter of the annual Jazz Fest.

THE CLUB & BAR SCENE

PENSACOLA The town's entertainment center is at ✪ **Seville Quarter,** 130 E. Government St., at Jefferson Street (☎ 904/434-6211), in the Seville Historic District. This restored antique brick complex with New Orleans–style wrought-iron balconies is actually a collection of pubs and restaurants whose names capture the ambience: Rosie O'Grady's Goodtime Emporium, Lili Marlene's Aviator's Pub, Apple Annie's Courtyard, End o' the Alley Bar, Phineas Phogg's Balloon Works (a dance hall, not a balloon shop), and Fast Eddie's Billiard Parlor (which has electronic games for kids, too). The pubs all serve food, but you can take in live entertainment from Dixieland jazz to country and western for the price of a drink. Get a monthly calendar at the information booth next to Rosie O'Grady's. Open daily from 11am to 2am.

Every night is party time at **McGuire's Irish Pub & Brewery,** 600 E. Gregory St. (☎ 904/433-6789), the city's popular Irish pub, brewery, and eatery (see "Where to Eat," above). Irish bands appear nightly during summer, on Saturday and Sunday the rest of the year. McGuire's is open Monday to Saturday from 11am to 2am and on Sunday from 4pm to 1am.

For live laughs, the **Coconuts Comedy Club,** in the Holiday Inn–University Mall, 7200 Plantation Rd. (☎ 904/484-NUTS), features comedians Thursday to Saturday night. Doors open at 7:30pm, with the first performance usually at 8:30pm. Cover charge is $4 on Thursday, $6 on Friday and Saturday.

PENSACOLA BEACH Nightlife at the beach centers around **Quietwater Boardwalk,** Via de Luna at Fort Pickens Road, a shopping/dining complex on Santa Rosa Sound. During summer you can stroll along the boardwalk and listen to the music without having to go into the establishments. Jubilee's Beachside Café and Entertainment Complex heads the list. The Sun Ray Taco Shop offers live bands nightly during the summer, on weekends off-season, and a no-name sports bar keeps the TVs going. With the lively Flounder's Chowder and Alehouse just a few steps away, it's easy to bar-hop until you find a band and crowd to your liking. (See "Where to Eat," above, for details about Jubilee's and Flounder's.)

PERDIDO KEY Almost a shrine to country music, the **Flora-Bama Lounge,** on Fla. 292 at the Florida-Alabama line (☎ 904/492-0611), is a slapped-together gulfside pub that's famous for its special jam sessions from noon until way past midnight on Saturday and Sunday. Flora-Bama is the prime sponsor and a key venue for the Frank Brown International Songwriters' Festival during the first week of November. If you've never attended an Interstate Mullet Toss, catch the fun here during the last weekend of April. The raw oyster bar is popular all the time. Take in the great gulf views from the Deck Bar. It's open daily from 8:30am to 2:30am.

2 Fort Walton Beach & Destin

40 miles E of Pensacola, 160 miles W of Tallahassee

At the outbreak of the Civil War in 1861, a small Confederate contingent arrived in front of a large Native American mound on the banks of narrow Santa Rosa Sound and set up camp to guard the eastern approaches to Pensacola. The Rebels beat a hasty retreat when Yankee troops shelled their position from Okaloosa Island, but the name they gave their little outpost has remained to this day: Fort Walton.

Back then the only settlement in these parts was Destin, a tiny fishing village east of Fort Walton and separated from it by East Pass, which lets broad, beautiful Choctawhatchee Bay flow into the Gulf of Mexico. And even though the U.S. government established sprawling Eglin Air Force Base here in the 1930s, Fort Walton had just 90 residents as late as 1940. But then came World War II, when Eglin grew into a major army air corps training base. When Okaloosa Island became popular with Alabamians and Georgians after the war, Fort Walton officially added "Beach" to its name. Although summertime tourism dominates Okaloosa Island, mainland Fort Walton Beach still relies on the U.S. Air Force for its year-round living.

Destin stands in contrast to its friendly, down-to-earth neighbor. On a picturesque harbor 6 miles to the east, Destin is a major and quickly growing vacation destination which attracts a generally more affluent crowd than does Fort Walton Beach. It has multitudes of high-rise condominiums, several excellent golf courses, and some of Northwest Florida's best restaurants and lively nightspots.

Development to the east of Destin in southern Walton County has been slower and more controlled, with mostly cottages nestled among sand dunes and sea oats. Walton County is home both to charming DeFuniak Springs and to the award-winning village of Seaside. While DeFuniak Springs is a genuine Victorian town nestled around an inland lake, Seaside was built on a lovely stretch of beach in the 1980s—but its Victorian architecture makes it look a century older. Even local residents consider a honeymoon cottage in Seaside to be the perfect romantic retreat. The village has interesting shops and art galleries, delightful restaurants, and a postcard-size post office. Seaside has a resident population of artists, writers, and other creative folks, who permit no cars in their pleasant little enclave. Although relatively expensive, Seaside is worth an excursion just to see its architecture and to enjoy its beautiful beach, both of which you can do for free.

ESSENTIALS

ARRIVING   By Plane   Flights arriving at and departing from **Okaloosa County Air Terminal** (☎ 904/651-0822) actually use the runways at Eglin Air Force Base. The terminal is on Fla. 85 north of Fort Walton Beach and is served by Atlantic Southeast, Delta Connection, Northwest, and USAir Express. There's no public bus service here, but taxis and limousines wait outside the modern terminal. Fares are based on a zone system: to Fort Walton Beach, $10 to $14; to Destin, $20 to $22; and to Sandestin, $28 to $30.

By Train The **Amtrak** (☎ **800/USA-RAIL**) transcontinental *Sunset Limited* stops at Crestview, 26 miles north of Fort Walton Beach.

By Bus The **Greyhound** station is at 105 Chestnut Ave., in downtown Fort Walton Beach (☎ **904/243-1940,** or 800/231-2222).

By Car From east or west, take I-10 or U.S. 98. For Fort Walton Beach, exit I-10 at Crestview and follow Fla. 85 south for 24 miles. For Destin and the beaches of southern Walton County, exit I-10 at DeFuniak Springs and follow U.S. 331 south to Santa Rosa Beach. You can avoid the beach traffic between there and Destin by leaving U.S. 331 at Freeport and taking Fla. 20 west to Villa Tasso, then Fla. 293 across the Mid Bay Bridge ($2 toll). From the north, take U.S. 331 south through Alabama.

VISITOR INFORMATION Contact the **Emerald Coast Convention and Visitors Bureau,** P.O. Box 609, Fort Walton Beach, FL 32549 (☎ **904/651-7131,** or 800/322-3319; fax 904/651-7149), for information about both Fort Walton Beach and Destin. The bureau shares quarters with the **Okaloosa County Visitors Welcome Center,** a tin-roofed, beachside building on Miracle Strip Parkway (U.S. 98) on Okaloosa Island at the eastern edge of Fort Walton Beach. Stop there for brochures, maps, and other information.

The **Destin Chamber of Commerce,** 1021 U.S. 98E, Suite A (P.O. Box 8), Destin, FL 32541 (☎ **904/837-6241**), opposite the Holiday Inn in Destin, also gives away brochures and sells maps pertaining to the area.

For information about what have been called the "Beaches of South Walton," contact the **South Walton Tourist Development Council,** P.O. Box 1248, Santa Rosa Beach, FL 32459 (☎ **904/267-1216,** or 800/822-6877). Its **visitor center** is at the intersection of U.S. 98 and U.S. 331 in Santa Rosa Beach (☎ **904/267-3511**).

TIME The area is in the central time zone, an hour behind Miami and Orlando.

GETTING AROUND **By Taxi** In **Fort Walton Beach,** call Charter Taxis (☎ 904/863-5466), JC's Cab (☎ 904/865-0578), Veterans Cab Co. (☎ 904/243-1403), Yellow Cab (☎ 904/244-3600), or Checker Cab (☎ 904/244-4491). In **Destin,** call Destin Taxi (☎ 904/654-5700). Fares are based on a zone system rather than meters, with a $3 minimum. Trips within Fort Walton Beach or Destin should range from $3 to $5.

BEACHES & BEACH PARKS

Despite extensive damages to the dunes inflicted by Hurricane Opal in 1995, this area still has some of the nation's top-rated beaches. The undeveloped stretches at Henderson Beach State Recreation Area in Destin, and at Grayton Beach State Recreation Area in southern Walton County, are among the world's finest. Here's where to soak up the sun:

FORT WALTON BEACH Do your beaching here on the white sands of **Okaloosa Island,** joined to the mainland by the high-rise Brooks Bridge over Santa Rosa Sound. Most resort hotels and amusement parks are grouped around the Gulfarium on U.S. 98 east of the bridge. **The Boardwalk,** a collection of tin-roofed beachside buildings between the Gulfarium and the Ramada Inn, has a games arcade for the kids, the Soggy Dollar Saloon for adults, and covered picnic areas, a summertime snack bar, and Harpoon Hanna's restaurant (see "Where to Eat," below).

If you're not staying on the island, you can do your beaching there or use the free facilities at **Beasley Park** (home of the Okaloosa County Visitor Welcome Center), whose dunes and shelter escaped serious damage from Hurricane Opal. Across U.S. 98, the **Okaloosa Area, Gulf Islands National Seashore** has picnic areas and sailboats for rent on Choctawhatchee Bay, plus access to the gulf. Admission to this part of the national seashore is free.

DESTIN   The 208-acre **Henderson Beach State Recreation Area,** just east of Destin on U.S. 98E (☎ **904/837-7550**), allows easy access to swimming, sunning, surf fishing, picnicking, and seabird-watching. The area is open daily from 8am to sunset. Admission is $2 per vehicle, $1 for pedestrians and cyclists. Several good restaurants are just outside the park's western boundary. The **James W. Lee Park,** east of Destin on Old U.S. 98, has a fine beach overlooked by covered picnic tables, a restaurant, and an ice-cream parlor. See "Where to Eat," below, for information about restaurants at or near the parks.

SOUTHERN WALTON COUNTY   On County Road 30A, ✪ **Grayton Beach State Recreation Area** (☎ **904/231-4210**) has one of the finest stretches of gulf beach and 356 acres of pine forests surrounding scenic Western Lake. There's a boat ramp and campground with electric hookups on the lake. Get a self-guided-tour leaflet for the nature trail at the main gate. It's open daily from 8am to sunset. Admission is $3.25 per vehicle with up to eight occupants, $2 per pedestrian or bicyclist. **Seaside** has public parking along County Road 30A and is a good spot for a day at the beach, a stroll or bike ride around the quaint village, and a tasty meal at one of its restaurants.

OTHER OUTDOOR ACTIVITIES

BOATING & BOAT RENTALS   A wide variety of waterborne activities await in this area blessed with both gulf and bays to be explored.

The *Glass Bottom Boat II* (☎ **904/654-7787**) offers underwater viewing, dolphin encounters, sightseeing, crab trapping, bird feeding, and nature cruises from Capt. Dave's Marina, 304 U.S. 98E, Destin. The *Southern Star* (☎ **904/244-4536**) has daily dolphin and sunset cruises all year. It's based in Destin at the Harbor Walk Marina at the foot of the Destin Bridge. Expect to pay between $12 and $20 per person, depending on the cruise.

For a nature cruise, the *Osprey* (☎ **904/837-7245**) goes on 3¹/₂-hour Cypress Wilderness Treks in search of bald eagles, osprey, alligators, and other wildlife in the swamps and bayous on the eastern end of Choctawhatchee Bay. It's based at the Sandestin Resort's Baytowne Marina and charges $38 for adults, $29 for children 9 and under.

Powerboat lovers can get their thrills on the **Sea Blaster** (☎ **904/837-1136** or 904/664-7872), one of the world's largest speedboats. It roars out every 2 hours from 10am to 6pm from Boogie's Water Sports, at the eastern end of the Destin Bridge. Rides cost $12 for adults, $6 for children 12 and under. For another noisy experience, **Wind Blown Air Boat Tours** (☎ **904/654-7878** or 904/585-5559) uses a boat driven by an airplane engine, like those in the Everglades. It's based at Capt. Dave's Marina on Destin Harbor.

Sailing enthusiasts can go quietly cruising on the 65-foot *Flying Eagle* (☎ **904/837-4986** or 904/837-3700) or the 54-foot *Blackbeard* (☎ **904/837-2793**), both of which have afternoon and sunset trips for $25 per person. They're gaff-rigged schooners. **Sailing South Charters** (☎ **904/837-7245**) has sailing cruises on a modern sloop-rigged yacht. Its prices start at $35 per person. The 41-foot ketch *Harbor Star* (☎ **904/837-2506**) has half- and full-day charters, including food and beverages, for $45 and $85 per person, respectively. All these boats are based at Destin Harbor. On Okaloosa Island, **Leeside Bareboat Sailing,** at the Leeside Motel, 1352 U.S. 98E (☎ **904/244-5454**), rents bareboats (you do the skippering) for $75 per half day, $140 per day.

Pontoon boats are highly popular for use on the back bays and on Sunday-afternoon floating parties in East Pass. Several companies rent them, including **Adventure Pontoon Rentals** (☎ **904/837-3041**) and **Premier Powerboat Rentals** (☎ **904/837-7755**), both on Destin Harbor. Expect to pay about $70 for a half day, $120 for all day, per boat. Some can hold up to a dozen passengers, so splitting the cost can make them a bargain. Premier Powerboat Rentals also has Four Winns and Chaparral speedboats for rent, at $120 a half day, $170 all day.

Hobie Cats, Waverunners, jet boats, jet skis, and fishing craft rentals are available from many marinas, as well as from several beachfront resorts. **Paradise Water Sports** (☎ **904/664-7872**) rents equipment and offers parasailing rides at seven locations along U.S. 98.

FISHING   Destin bills itself as the "World's Luckiest Fishing Village," and almost every month a different fishing competition pays off big money for the big ones. (Comedian Bob Hope won first prize with a big white marlin when he first visited the area.)

Destin also claims Florida's largest charter-boat fleet, with more than 140 vessels, many of them based at the marinas along the north shore of Destin Harbor, on U.S. 98 east of the Destin Bridge. The **Okaloosa County Visitor Welcome Center** distributes copies of the Destin Charter Boat Association's helpful *Charter Boat Guide,* and the **Destin Chamber of Commerce** provides a list of its member boats and captains (see "Essentials," above). You can call the skippers directly or visit several agents—such as **Pelican Charters** (☎ 904/837-2343), **Harbor Cove Charters** (☎ 904/837-2222), and **Fishermen's Charter Service** (☎ 904/654-4665)—who have booths on the boardwalks along Destin Harbor. Rates for the smaller vessels range from $300 to $800 per boat, depending on length of voyage.

The least expensive way to try your luck is on a larger group-oriented party boat, such as those operated by **Moody's,** at 194 U.S. 98E on Destin Harbor (☎ **904/ 837-1293**). Moody's charges $30 per person for its morning runs (the best fishing) and $25 for afternoon trips. Children 8 to 12 and nonfishing sightseers pay half price. Other party boats are the *Emmanuel* (☎ **904/837-6313**), the *Lady Eventhia* (☎ **904/837-6212**), and three craft operated by **Capt. Duke's Boat Service** (☎ **904/837-6152**), all based at Destin Harbor.

You don't have to pay or go to sea to fish from the catwalk of the 3,000-foot **Destin Bridge** over East Pass. Although damaged by Hurricane Opal, the **Okaloosa Island Fishing Pier,** on U.S. 98 next to the Boardwalk and Gulfarium in Fort Walton Beach, should be repaired and open by 1997.

GOLF   The area takes great pride in its 14 courses—more than 200 holes of golf altogether. For advance information on all area courses, contact the **Emerald Coast Golf Association,** P.O. Box 304, Destin, FL 32540 (☎ **904/654-7086**).

The public **Fort Walton Beach Golf Course,** on Lewis Turner Boulevard (County Road 189), north of town (☎ **904/862-3314**), is an 18-hole, par-72 course, complete with pro shop. Other privately owned, more expensive courses here are open to the public, including the **Santa Rosa Golf & Beach Club,** off U.S. 98E (turn right on County Road 30A to Dune Allen Beach; ☎ **904/267-2229**), which offers a challenging 18-hole course through tall pines looking out to vistas of the gulf. The club has a pro shop, Beach Club restaurant and lounge, and also tennis courts.

The **Sandestin Golf & Tennis Resort,** on U.S. 98E (☎ **904/267-8000**), offers 63 holes on two outstanding championship golf courses open to the public (see "Where to Stay," below). The **Seascape Resort & Conference Center,** 100 Seascape Dr. (☎ **904/837-9181**), off County Road 30A in southern Walton County, features an 18-hole course that the public is invited to play. Another beautiful 18-hole public golf course is at the **Emerald Bay Golf Club,** 40001 Emerald Coast Pkwy. (☎ **904/837-4455**). Nonguests may play golf (36 holes) or tennis (21 courts) at the **Bluewater Bay Resort** in Niceville (☎ **904/897-3613**), a 20-minute drive via the Mid Bay Bridge. Call ahead for reservations and fees.

HORSEBACK RIDING   The **Brand'n Iron Corral,** on U.S. 98 in Santa Rosa Beach (☎ **904/267-2433**), features guided tours on horseback on trails winding through Santa Rosa's forests and around Choctawhatchee Bay.

Area stables include **Sleepy Oaks,** 1344 Blueberry Lane (☎ **904/863-2919**); the **Equestrian Center,** 268 Vicki Leigh Rd. (☎ **904/863-3295**); and the **Southern Cross Equestrian Center,** on Tropic Trail in Destin (☎ **904/654-9309**).

SCUBA DIVING & SNORKELING   At least a dozen dive shops are located along the beaches. Considered one of the best, **Scuba Tech Diving Charters** has two locations in Destin: on the harbor at Capt. Dave's Marina, 312 U.S. 98E (☎ **904/ 837-2822**), and at 10004 U.S. 98E (☎ **904/837-1933**), about half a mile west of the Sandestin Golf & Tennis Resort. Two-tank reef or wreck dives cost $40 to $65, depending on length. Open-water courses cost $225; resort courses, $75. **Fantasea,** at 1 U.S. 98E (☎ **904/837-6943,** or 800/326-2732), and the **Aquanaut Scuba Center,** 24 U.S. 98E (☎ **904/837-0359**), are other local operators.

These three diving operators and *Kokomo* **Snorkeling Adventures,** 500 U.S. 98E in Destin (☎ **904/837-9029**), all take snorkelers on excursions into the Gulf of Mexico and Choctawhatchee Bay for $20 per person, including gear.

TENNIS   On the mainland, the **Fort Walton Beach Municipal Tennis Center,** 45 W. Audrey Dr., at Rogers Street (☎ **904/243-8789**), features 12 lighted courts, a clubhouse, lounge, lockers, and showers. Rates are $2.75 per person for daylight play, $3.75 at night. Open Monday to Thursday from 8am to 9pm, on Friday from 8am to 5pm, and on Saturday and Sunday from 9am to 5pm.

The **Destin Racquet & Fitness Center,** at 995 Airport Rd. (☎ **904/837-7300**), provides six Rubico tennis courts. It's open Monday to Thursday from 6am to 8pm, on Friday from 6am to 7pm, on Saturday from 8am to 6pm, and on Sunday from 9am to 6pm, but phone ahead for reservations. Rates are $10 per person per day to play tennis or racquetball, or participate in the activities here.

The **Sandestin Golf & Tennis Resort,** U.S. 98E (☎ **904/837-2121**), offers 16 courts open to the public, including hard, clay, and grass. *Tennis* magazine rated Sandestin one of the nation's top 50 tennis resorts and the only ranked resort with natural grass courts. The **Seascape Resort & Conference Center,** 100 Seascape Dr. in southern Walton County (☎ **904/837-9181**), has eight courts open to the public.

OTHER ATTRACTIONS
IN FORT WALTON BEACH

Gulfarium. Miracle Strip Pkwy. (U.S. 98) on Okaloosa Island. ☎ **904/244-5169.** Admission $12 adults, $10 seniors, $8 children 4–11, free for children 3 and under. Daily 9am through last show; shows at 10am, noon, 2pm, and 4pm all year, with additional shows at 6 and 8pm in summer.

One of the nation's original marine parks features on-going shows with dolphins, California sea lions, Peruvian penguins, and Ridley turtles. There are at least 14 fascinating exhibits, including the Living Sea, with special windows that provide viewing of undersea life. A gift shop offers an extensive collection of marine-oriented souvenirs. Although the Gulfarium experienced no loss of its animal and sea life, the beachside facility was damaged by Hurricane Opal; it has been repaired, but admission charges and hours may have changed by 1997.

Indian Temple Mound and Museum. 139 Miracle Strip Pkwy., on the mainland. ☎ **904/243-6521.** Park, free; museum, $2 adults, $1 children 6–17, free for children 5 and under. Park, daily dawn–dusk. Museum, Oct–May, Mon–Fri 11am–4pm, Sat 9am–4pm; June–Sept, Mon–Sat 9am–5pm (summer hours may vary, so call ahead).

This ceremonial mound, one of the largest ever discovered, dates back to A.D. 1200. The museum, located next to it, showcases ceramic artifacts from southeastern Native American tribes. The largest such collection, it contains more than 6,000 items. Exhibits depict the lifestyles of the four tribes that lived in the Choctawhatchee Bay region for 10,000 years.

✪ U.S. Air Force Armament Museum. At Eglin Air Force Base, Eglin Blvd. (Fla. 85), 5 miles north of downtown. ☎ **904/882-4062.** Free admission. Daily 9:30am–4:30pm. Closed New Year's Day, Thanksgiving, and Christmas Day.

Located on the world's largest air force base (more than 700 square miles), this fascinating museum has 28 reconnaissance planes, fighters, and bombers, including the SR-71 Blackbird Spy Plane, spanning developments from World War II to the Persian Gulf. Also exhibited are war films, photographs, rockets, bombs, missiles, and more. The base itself is home to the world's largest environmental test chamber, in the McKinley Climatic Laboratory, and to the 33rd Tactical Fighter Wing, the "Top Guns" of Desert Storm. World War II's historic Doolittle's Tokyo Raiders trained here.

In Southern Walton County

✪ Eden State Gardens and Mansion. County Rd. 395, Point Washington. ☎ **904/231-4214.** Grounds and gardens, free; mansion tours, $1.50 adults, 50¢ children 12 and under. Gardens and grounds, daily 8am–5pm; mansion, Thurs–Mon 9am–4pm (tours on the hour).

Evoking images from *Gone With the Wind,* the magnificent 1895 Greek Revival–style Wesley Mansion has been lovingly restored and richly furnished. It stands overlooking scenic Choctawhatchee Bay and is surrounded by immense moss-draped oak trees and resplendent gardens. The gardens and mansion are north of Seagrove Beach.

SHOPPING

The major shopping attractions here are two manufacturers' outlet malls whose shops usually are as well stocked as any I've seen. On the Fort Walton Beach mainland, a free tram runs between the two branches of the **Manufacturer's Outlet Center,** at 127 and 255 Miracle Strip Pkwy. (U.S. 98), which has Levi's, Jerzees, Polly Flinders, Bass, and other shops. On U.S. 98 between Destin and Sandestin, shops in the **Silver Sands Factory Stores** offer substantial discounts on upmarket designer fashions. There's excellent window-shopping at the Sandestin Golf & Tennis Resort on U.S. 98, where 28 shops in the **Market at Sandestin** purvey expensive clothing, gifts, and Godiva chocolates.

WHERE TO STAY

Condominiums offer good value, especially for stays of a week or more. The tourist information offices (see "Essentials," above) will provide lists of other condos and cottages for rent. The largest agent, **Abbott Realty Services** (☎ 904/837-4853 or

800/336-4853), will send a brochure describing its many accommodations throughout the area.

If you decide on a splurge in the quaint village of Seaside, contact the **Seaside Cottage Rental Agency,** P.O. Box 4730, Seaside, FL 32459 (☎ **904/231-1320** or 800/277-8696; fax 904/231-2219), or **Monarch Realty,** P.O. Box 4767, Seaside, FL 32459 (☎ **904/231-1940** or 800/848-1840; fax 904/561-8596). The beachside honeymoon cottages are a favorite getaway for newlyweds or anyone else looking for a romantic escape.

For a relatively inexpensive Old Florida cottage experience, **Seaview Cottages,** 385 U.S. 98E, Suite 360, Destin, FL 32541 (☎ **904/837-6211**), has 10 small, pastel-painted houses sitting in two rows between the highway and a shady yard with a wooden stairway that leads down an embankment to the docks on Destin Harbor. All are air-conditioned and have phones, TVs, and screened porches. They range from $89 to $115 a night during summer, from $59 to $85 off-season, with a 2-night minimum stay required.

In addition to those mentioned below, the area has a number of chain motels. In Fort Walton Beach, the moderately priced **Rodeway Inn,** 866 Santa Rosa Blvd. (☎ **904/243-3114** or 800/458-8552), and the **Days Inn & Suites Gulfside R esort,** 573 Santa Rosa Blvd. (☎ **904/244-8686** or 800/DAYS-INN), both are right on Okaloosa Island's beach. The least expensive place to stay on Okaloosa Island is a branch of **Econo Lodge,** 1284 Marler Dr. (☎ **904/243-7123** or 800/564-0137), on the bay side in the noisy and congested Shanty Town area near the Brooks Bridge.

None of Destin's chain motels is directly on the beach. The **Best Rest Inn,** 402 U.S. 98E (☎ **904/837-7326** or 800/847-0470), is on the Destin Harbor boardwalk, giving quick access to nearby restaurants and charter fishing boats. Just outside Henderson Beach State Recreation Area, the **Hampton Inn,** 1625 U.S. 98E (☎ **904/654-2677** or 800/426-7866), is near the sands and several restaurants. A **Days Inn,** 1029 U.S. 98E (☎ **904/837-2599** or 800/325-2525), sits across the road from the beachside Holiday Inn (see below). A **Comfort Inn,** 405 U.S. 98E (☎ **904/ 837-0007** or 800/336-8903), also is near the harbor. A modern **Sleep Inn,** 5000 U.S. 98E (☎ **904/654-7022** or 800/627-5337), is near the Sandestin Golf & Tennis Resort.

See "Where to Stay" in the Pensacola section, above, for information about rate seasons and categories, which are for the lowest priced double room during the shoulder seasons of April to mid-May and in September and October. State and local governments add 9% to all hotel bills.

Accommodations are listed below by geographic location: Fort Walton Beach, Destin, and southern Walton County. In making your choice, remember that there is no public transportation here—only taxis.

FORT WALTON BEACH
Doubles for Less than $60

Howard Johnson Lodge. 314 Miracle Strip Pkwy. SW (U.S. 98), Fort Walton Beach, FL 32548. ☎ **904/243-6162** or 800/654-2000. Fax 904/664-2735. 140 rms. A/C TV TEL. Summer, $60–$75 double. Winter, $42–$58 double. Weekly rates available. AE, DC, DISC, MC, V.

A lovely courtyard with majestic oaks, magnolias, and a swimming pool distinguishes this establishment from other inexpensive chain motels here. Although it's located on Santa Rosa Sound on the mainland, the best rooms enjoy this pleasant vista rather than the water, since the soundside units face a parking lot. A Waffle House on the premises is open 24 hours.

Marina Bay Resort. 80 Miracle Strip Pkwy. (U.S. 98), Fort Walton Beach, FL 32548. ☎ **904/ 244-5132.** Fax 904/244-0491. 120 rms. A/C TV TEL. Summer, $50–$150 double. Off-season, $40–$91 double. AE, DC, DISC, MC, V.

This pleasant resort is built around a lushly landscaped courtyard on Santa Rosa Sound in town. It sports its own dock, fishing pier, and small beach, plus a volleyball court, swimming pool, whirlpool, putting green, shuffleboard, and exercise room and sauna. More than half the guest rooms are equipped with kitchenettes (request one, if that's your preference). The big bargain here is the special off-season $40 rate for accommodations with sleeper sofas. The best rooms face the sound. A restaurant is open daily from 11am to 9pm.

Marina Motel. 1345 U.S. 98E, Fort Walton Beach, FL 32548. ☎ **904/244-1129** or 800/ 237-7021. Fax 904/243-6063. 38 rms, 2 one-bedroom apts. A/C TV TEL. Summer, $53–$90 double; $92 apt. Off-season, $32–$68 double; $55–$70 apt. AE, DC, DISC, MC, V.

This rather pedestrian-looking motel makes up for a lack of charm with clean, comfortable rooms and a location directly across U.S. 98 from the magnificent public beach at Beasley Park. A low-slung, brick-fronted motel block holds most of the rooms, which cost $43 a night double during spring and autumn. Others units are in two-story stucco structures near a marina whose 560-foot pier is home to charter fishing boats. Two one-bedroom apartments at the end of the complex overlook the marina and bay. All units here have at least a refrigerator; 16 have full kitchens. If traffic is too busy to cross U.S. 98 to the beach, you can sun at the motel's little bayside beach or take a dip in its roadside pool. There's also a guest laundry.

Venus Condos. 885 Santa Rosa Blvd., Fort Walton Beach, FL 32548. ☎ **904/243-0885** or 800/476-1885. 45 apts. A/C TV TEL. Summer, $90–$135 apt for two. Off-season, $55–$100 apt for two. DISC, MC, V.

Offering considerably more space than hotels at these rates, this pleasant, three-story enclave on western Okaloosa Island has been immaculately maintained since opening in the early 1970s. Each of the one-, two-, and three-bedroom condo apartments has a long living/dining/kitchen room, with a rear door leading to a balcony or patio. Facilities include a guest laundry and a grassy courtyard with palm trees, a swimming pool, and a large barbecue pit. A lighted tennis court destroyed by Hurricane Opal should be rebuilt by the time you arrive. The beach is a short walk across the dunes.

Doubles for Less than $80

Ramada Plaza Beach Resort. 1500 Miracle Strip Pkwy. (U.S. 98), Fort Walton Beach, FL 32548. ☎ **904/243-9161** or 800/447-0010. Fax 904/243-2391. 458 rms and suites. A/C TV TEL. Summer, $95–$150 double; $210–$260 suite. Off-season, $60–$100 double; $130–$190 suite. AE, DC, DISC, MC, V.

Considered Fort Walton Beach's prime hotel, this big resort with a gaudy, Las Vegas–like gold facade boasts one of the most beautiful swimming pool–patio areas anywhere, with waterfalls cascading over lofty rocks and a romantic grotto bar. It would be even more delightful if this courtyard opened to the beach. The tastefully furnished rooms have gulf or courtyard views from a six-story building, but the less expensive units overlook a parking lot from an older two-story structure next door.

On-site dining options include the casual Pelican's Roost, which features seafood favorites year round, and a barbecue shack near the pool. The family-oriented Lobster House serves moderately priced seafood during summer. The Boardwalk beach pavilion and restaurants are next door (see "Where to Eat," below). For entertainment, there's dancing in Bubble's Lounge. Facilities here include three swimming pools (one indoors), a children's pool, and three whirlpools. Two lighted tennis courts and a health spa, destroyed by Hurricane Opal, should be replaced by 1997.

Sheraton Inn. 1325 Miracle Strip Pkwy. (U.S. 98), Fort Walton Beach, FL 32548. ☎ **904/ 243-8116,** or 800/874-8104. Fax 904/244-3064. 154 rms. A/C TV TEL. Summer, $90–$135 double. Off-season, $70–$105 double. AE, DC, DISC, MC, V.

This beachfront motel-style resort sports spacious rooms enhanced by beautiful views of the gulf or of a lush courtyard and heated swimming pool. Many rooms here have refrigerators and kitchenettes. A few choice units open directly to the beach. Dining here is limited to the Plantation Grill dining room, which specializes in local seafood. Dempsey's Lounge and the beach bar have entertainment during summer. There's an exercise room and coin laundry.

DESTIN

Doubles for Less than $40

Village Inn. 215 U.S. 98E, Destin, FL 32541. ☎ **904/837-7413** or 800/821-9342. Fax 904/ 654-3394. 100 rms. A/C TV TEL. Summer, $50–$70 double. Off-season, $30 double. Children 17 and under stay free in parents' room. Weekly rates available. AE, CB, DC, DISC, MC, V.

Directly across the street from the charter fishing fleet docked in Destin Harbor, this friendly, two-story motel features oversize rooms, some with refrigerators. A swimming pool is on the premises. The drive to the gulf beaches is 5 minutes; restaurants, shopping, golf, and some attractions are within a 2-mile radius. A 24-hour Waffle House is next door.

Doubles for Less than $80

Holiday Inn of Destin. 1020 U.S. 98E, Destin, FL 32541. ☎ **904/837-6181** or 800/ HOLIDAY. Fax 904/837-1523. 233 rms. A/C TV TEL. Summer, $115–$155 double. Off-season, $65–$95 double. Packages and senior discounts available. AE, DC, DISC, MC, V.

Most of the nicely furnished rooms in this gulf-front resort are in a round high-rise building; get one facing south or east because a tall condo next door blocks southwest-facing units from enjoying the spectacular gulf views. The rooms in an older, four-story building are more spacious than those in the tower. Some of these older units open to an enclosed, fountained lobby sporting a comfortable mezzanine lounge with indoor pool and billiards, Ping-Pong, and foosball tables. The Destin Cafe in the lobby serves breakfast, lunch, and dinner. Children can play in their own pool or in a video-game arcade (there's a summertime activities program for them). Adults can use a whirlpool, sauna, and exercise room, or spend money at the gift shop.

SOUTH WALTON COUNTY

Doubles for Less than $80

✪ **Sandestin Golf & Tennis Resort.** 9300 U.S. 98W, Destin, FL 32541. ☎ **904/267-8000,** or 800/277-0800 in the U.S., 800/933-7846 in Canada. Fax 904/267-8222. 175 rms, 400 condo apts. Spring and summer, $125–$175 double; $175–$540 condo apt. Off-season, $55–$135 double; $82–$450 condo apt. Packages available. AE, DC, DISC, MC, V.

One of Florida's best sports-oriented resorts, this luxurious establishment sprawls over 2,300 acres complete with a spectacular beach 5 miles west of Destin. An array of handsomely decorated accommodations overlook the gulf or Choctawhatchee Bay, the golf fairways, lagoons, or a nature preserve. The least expensive lodgings here are in the hotel rooms of the Inn at Sandestin, on the bay side of the complex, where double rooms cost $75 to $85 a night from mid-August to October, $55 to $65 during winter. More expensive, and out of our budget are the junior suites, condominium apartments, villas, and three-bedroom penthouses. Most amenities are a short walk or bike or tram ride away, and a tunnel runs under U.S. 98 to connect Sandestin's gulf and bay areas.

The Sunset Bay Café offers breakfast, lunch, and dinner by the bay, but the dining delight here is the romantic Elephant Walk (☎ 904/267-4800), located on the gulf. There's a story behind the name of this fine eatery, for in 1890 in Ceylon (now Sri Lanka) a tea planter named John Whiley tried to prevent damage to his trees by building a huge home across an elephant herd's path to the river. When their thirsty stampede reduced his house to ruins, Whiley vowed never to return. He roamed for 30 years, buying treasures in all four corners of the world. Then he discovered Northwest Florida and settled here. His purchases are displayed in this lovely building designed to evoke his Ceylon mansion. The candlelit dining room features entirely different, gourmet-quality choices for dinner each evening.

Services include a free shuttle tram around the resort, arrangements for deep-sea fishing and other outside activities, a tennis clinic, a summer children's program for ages 3 to 13, and a juniors' tennis and golf academy. Facilities include rental bikes, boats, and water-sports equipment; fishing and charter boats based at the Baytowne Marina; tennis courts with hard, Rubico, and grass surfaces at both beach and bayside tennis centers; 63 holes of championship golf; a fully equipped sports spa and health center; nine swimming pools; three wading pools; a children's playground; a conference center; and the Market at Sandestin with 30 upscale shops.

CAMPING

Grayton Beach State Recreation Area, on Grayton Beach (Rte. 2, Box 6600), Santa Rosa Beach, FL 32459 (☎ **904/231-4210**), offers hookups for camping vehicles as well as primitive campsites in this beautiful 356-acre park. Campfire interpretive programs are available to campers (call for the current schedule). Camping fees are $14 from March to September, $8 from October to February. See "Beaches & Beach Parks," above, for details about the park and its other facilities.

The **Emerald Coast RV Resort,** 7525 W. County Rd. 30A, Santa Rosa Beach, FL 32459 (☎ **904/267-2808**, or 800/232-2478; fax 904/267-3500), offers more than 140 RV-only sites on 90 acres, shaded by beautiful trees on County Road 30A about a quarter mile south of U.S. 98, east of the Sandestin Golf & Tennis Resort. Although about a mile from Dune Allen Beach, the resort offers a shuttle to the sands plus an on-site heated swimming pool, putting green, fishing lake, hiking and nature trails, tennis court, and more. Sites cost $28 a day in summer, $26 a day in winter.

Camping on the Gulf Holiday Travel Park, 5380 U.S. 98E, Destin, FL 32541 (☎ **904/837-6334**), just west of the Sandestin Golf & Tennis Resort, is the area's largest and oldest campground and the only one with sites directly on the beach. It offers 235 campsites, about half next to the sands. Facilities include three bath houses, picnic tables, a fishing pond, a grocery store, and a gift shop. During summer, campsites cost $40 on the beach, $30 inland. Off-season, they go for $25 and $20, respectively.

The **Crystal Beach RV Park,** 2825 Scenic Hwy. 98, Destin, FL 32541 (☎ **904/ 837-6447**), has 77 sites for RVs in a quickly developing area east of Destin. The grounds are sandy, lack shade, and are somewhat crowded, but the beach is just across the road. Facilities include a bathhouse, games room, store, and swimming pool. Sites cost $25 a day in summer, $19 off-season.

WHERE TO EAT

A plethora of national fast-food and family chain restaurants line Eglin Parkway and U.S. 98 (except for the strip on Okaloosa Island). There are more than 110 restaurants in Fort Walton Beach, Destin, and southern Walton County, so you won't have trouble finding a meal in these parts. The restaurants below are organized by geographic area.

FORT WALTON BEACH

Meals for Less than $7

Barnhill's Country Buffet. 431 Mary Ester Cutoff (opposite the Santa Rosa Mall). ☎ **904/243-1103.** Reservations not accepted. Lunch $5.30 adults, $4.90 seniors, 40¢ times age for children 12 and under 13; dinner $6.80 adults, $6.20 seniors, 45¢ times age for children 12 and under. MC, V. Sun–Thurs 10:45am–8:30pm, Fri–Sat 10:45am–9pm. AMERICAN.

Just as they do in Pensacola, local families flock to the seven buffet tables here, all of them laden with fried chicken and fish, boiled cabbage and collard greens, baked ham, roast beef, an extraordinarily tasty pot roast, a wide range of fresh salads, and a dessert table stocked with old-fashioned 'nilla wafer banana pudding.

✪ **Caffè Italia.** 234 SE Miracle Strip Pkwy. (near the north end of Brooks Bridge). ☎ **904/664-0035.** Reservations recommended in winter. Main courses $5.50–$12. AE, DC, DISC, MC, V. Tues–Sun 11am–10pm. NORTHERN ITALIAN.

Nada Eckhardt is from Croatia, but she met her American husband, Jim, while working at a restaurant named Caffè Italia in northern Italy. The Eckhardts duplicated that establishment here, and her former Italian boss has since bought this building, which from the highway looks like the scuba shack it once was. Inside, Nada has brightened things considerably with floral tablecloths, hanging plants, and photos from the old country. Her menu is limited to excellent pizzas, a few pasta dishes, northern Italian risotto (rice) with either asparagus or smoked salmon, and meat and seafood dishes to fit the season. Don't expect to make a full meal by ordering only a pasta here, for courses are served in the authentic Italian fashion, with a small portion of pasta preceding the seafood or meat selections. On the other hand, you can quickly fill up on the soft, pizza-dough breadsticks accompanied by seasoned olive oil for dipping. The cappuccino is absolutely first-rate, as are Nada's genuine Italian desserts. There's outside courtyard seating in good weather.

Rick's Crab Trap. 104 SW Miracle Strip Pkwy. (U.S. 98), on the mainland. ☎ **904/664-0110.** Reservations not accepted. Main courses $7–$14; sandwiches and burgers $3–$5.50. AE, DISC, MC, V. Mon–Sat 11am–10pm, Sun noon–10pm. SEAFOOD.

Looking every bit like an Old Florida crab shack, Rick's cozy main dining room looks out on the real star here: a split-level, soundside dining deck. This extraordinary setting and Rick's very reasonable prices bring locals as well as visitors here for traditional fried, grilled, or steamed oysters, shrimp, amberjack, snapper, and crab cakes (for more spice than I could stand, opt for a cup of red-hot gumbo). Daily specials such as all-you-can-eat steamed crabs or fried catfish are excellent value.

Mary's Kitchen. 575-D N. Beal Pkwy. (County Rd. 189, at Mary Esther Cutoff). ☎ **904/863-1141.** Reservations not accepted. Sandwiches and salads $2–$5; barbecue plates $5–$7. No credit cards. Mon–Fri 11am–8pm. BARBECUE.

Mary Jones's storefront eatery is famous in these parts for husband Ray's barbecue. Cuts of beef and pork are slowly smoked in a brick pit that sits in the middle of the dining room. Ray's beef can be a bit on the dry side, but his pork butts and ribs are absolutely first-rate. Ask for the spicy sauce on the side, then apply as little or as much as your taste buds can tolerate. Daily specials feature a meat served with a host of country-style vegetables. Mary's homemade pies are both huge and delicious.

Meals for Less than $15

Harpoon Hanna's at the Boardwalk. 1450 E. Miracle Strip Pkwy. ☎ **904/243-5500.** Reservations not accepted. Main courses $9–$17; sandwiches and burgers $5.50–$9. AE, DISC, MC, V. Summer, daily 11am–11pm; off-season, Mon–Sat 11am–9pm, Sun noon–9pm. SEAFOOD.

Part of the Boardwalk complex built to look like an old-fashioned beach pavilion, this high-ceilinged restaurant has a deck for alfresco dining in good weather, and the outdoor Ship's Deck Bar is a great spot to catch a sunset. The menu features such items as Caribbean-style blackened chicken mako shark fajitas, and dinners of shellfish and soft-shell crabs. There's a children's menu. The restaurant's snack menu is available at the Boardwalk's Soggy Dollar Saloon, which has live entertainment during the summer months.

✪ **Pandora's Restaurant & Lounge.** 1120 Santa Rosa Blvd., Okaloosa Island. ☎ **904/244-8669.** Reservations recommended. Main courses $11–$29. AE, DC, DISC, MC, V. Sun–Thurs 5–10pm, Fri–Sat 5–10:30pm. STEAKS/PRIME RIB/SEAFOOD.

The front part of this unusual restaurant is a beached yacht now housing the main-deck lounge. Freshly caught local fish are among the seafood choices here, but steaks and prime rib keep the locals coming back for more. The tender beef is cut on the premises and grilled to perfection. The delicious breads and pies are homemade. Live entertainment and dancing are an added attraction in the lounge.

✪ **Staff's Seafood Restaurant.** 24 SW Miracle Strip Pkwy. (U.S. 98), on the mainland. ☎ **904/243-3526.** Reservations not necessary. Main courses $12–$27. AE, DISC, MC, V. Summer, daily 5–11pm; off-season, Mon–Thurs 5–9:30pm, Fri–Sat 5–10pm. SEAFOOD.

Considered the first Emerald Coast restaurant, Staff's started as a hotel in 1913 and moved to this barnlike building in 1931. Among the display of memorabilia are an old-fashioned phonograph lamp and a 1914 cash register. All main courses are served with heaping baskets of hot, home-baked wheat bread from a secret 70-year-old recipe. One of the most popular main dishes is the Seafood Skillet, sizzling with broiled grouper, shrimp, scallops, and crabmeat drenched in butter and sprinkled with cheese. Tangy seafood gumbo also has gained fame for this casual, historic restaurant. Main courses are accompanied by salad and dessert.

DESTIN

Meals for Less than $7

Callahan's Island Restaurant & Deli. 950 Gulf Shore Dr. ☎ **904/837-6328.** Reservations not accepted. Main courses $5.50–$7; sandwiches and burgers $3.50–$6. DISC, MC, V. Mon–Thurs 10am–8pm, Fri 10am–9pm, Sat 8am–9pm. STEAKS/DELI.

The best place in the area for picnic fare, this family-operated deli offers burgers, made-to-order sandwiches, and nightly specials such as charcoal-grilled chicken and teriyaki-style stir-fry. A refrigerator case across the rear holds steaks and chops (choose your own cut, pay by the ounce, and the chef with charcoal-grill it to order). Tables and booths are set up garden fashion, adding an outdoorsy ambience to this pleasant storefront establishment. Locals like to do lunch here. Breakfast is served only on Saturday morning.

✪ **The Donut Hole.** 635 U.S. 98E. ☎ **904/837-8824.** Reservations not accepted. Breakfast $3–$7; sandwiches, salads, burgers $3.50–$5.50; meals $6. No credit cards. Daily 24 hours (daily specials 11am–8pm). SOUTHERN/AMERICAN.

Having spent his early career as a traveling salesman, owner Bill Chandler designed this very popular establishment to be "the restaurant I couldn't find when I was on the road." Available around the clock, his breakfasts highlight freshly baked doughnuts and other pastries. Daily-special meals feature southern favorites such as meatloaf, country-style steak, and chicken and dumplings, all cooked on the premises using fresh vegetables and top-quality ingredients. His deliciously sweet cole slaw comes from an old Appalachian Mountain recipe.

There's a Donut Hole II Café and Bakery (☎ 904/267-3239) on U.S. 98E in southern Walton County, 2½ miles east of the Sandestin Golf & Tennis Resort; it's open daily from 6am to 7pm.

June's Dunes. 1780 Old U.S. 98E. ☎ **904/837-9938.** Reservations not accepted. Breakfasts $2–$4; sandwiches and burgers $2–$3. No credit cards. Daily 5:30am–3pm. AMERICAN.

Locals love to eat at the rustic picnic tables of this red wooden structure, where June Decker has served beachside breakfasts and lunches since 1951. June's menu is chalked on a board over the counter of her screened-in kitchen. Give her your order and pick up your food when she calls your name. Breakfasts include waffles, French toast, fruit plates, and biscuits with sausage gravy. Lunches feature sandwiches, burgers (for $2, believe it or not), and German and Polish sausages with sauerkraut. June's little establishment is just west of Henderson Beach State Recreation Area (see the Back Porch, below, for directions). Windows along three walls let in gulf breezes and lovely beach views.

Meals for Less than $10

✪ **Harry T's Boat House.** 320 U.S. 98E, Destin Harbor. ☎ **904/654-6555.** Reservations not accepted. Main courses $6.50–$15.50; sandwiches and burgers $6.50–$9. AE, DC, MC, V. Summer, Mon–Sat 11am–2am, Sun 10am–2pm (brunch) and 2pm–2am; off-season, Mon–Sat 11am–11pm, Sun 10am–2pm (brunch) and 2–11pm. AMERICAN.

The family of trapeze artist "Flying Harry T" Baben opened this fun restaurant on the ground floor of Destin Harbor's tallest building to honor his memory. Standing guard is a stuffed Stretch, Harry's beloved giraffe. The tabloid-style menu offers a wide range of such taste-tempters as chimichangas, Cajun-style burgers, and buffalo wings. Both the dining room and downstairs lounge (with billiard tables and live entertainment several nights a week) enjoy harbor views.

Scampi's. 1741 County Rd. 2378 (Old U.S. 98E). ☎ **904/837-7686.** Reservations not accepted. Seafood buffet $8–$10 adults, $7 children 8–12, $4 for children 7 and under; main courses $8–$14. AE, DC, DISC, MC, V. Daily 4:30–9:30pm. SEAFOOD.

Constructed from the historic pilings of the old Destin Bridge, this two-level restaurant is especially popular for the bountiful bargain seafood buffet. An entire baked fish is the star of this veritable groaning board. For starters, the regular menu has just-shucked oysters, and a steaming hot bowl of piquant seafood gumbo that's almost a meal in itself. Just about any piscine preference will be satisfied in this casual, friendly restaurant. The lengthy bar and cocktail lounge are a local rendezvous. For directions, see the Back Porch, below.

Meals for Less than $15

✪ **The Back Porch.** 1740 County Rd. 2378 (Old U.S. 98E). ☎ **904/837-2022.** Reservations not accepted. Main courses $9–$15; sandwiches and burgers $6. AE, DC, DISC, MC, V. Summer, daily 11am–11pm; off-season, daily 11am–9pm. SEAFOOD.

A cedar-shingled seafood shack whose long porch offers glorious beach and gulf views, this popular, casual restaurant originated charcoal-grilled amberjack (a favorite local fish). Other fish and seafood as well as chicken and juicy hamburgers also come from the coals. Two daily specials are good value at $9 to $11. Come early, order a rum-laden Key Lime Freeze, and enjoy the sunset. The Back Porch sits with a number of other restaurants (see above for Scampi's and June's Dunes) near the western boundary of Henderson Beach State Recreation Area. From U.S. 98, turn toward the beach at the Hampton Inn.

SOUTH WALTON COUNTY
Meals for Less than $7
Chan's Market Cafe. In the Market at Sandestin Resort, 5494 U.S. 98E. ☎ **904/837-1334.** Reservations not accepted. Sandwiches and salads $3–$6; meals $5–$8. DISC, MC, V. Mar–Labor Day, daily 7am–9pm; Labor Day–Feb, daily 7am–6pm. AMERICAN.

The low prices and good food at this red- and black-accented café draw scores of families vacationing at the Sandestin Golf & Tennis Resort. A wide array of offerings include freshly baked croissants and bagels at breakfast or deli sandwiches at lunch, charcoal-grilled chicken and meals featuring amberjack or yellowfin tuna grilled over coals. Featuring the likes of meatloaf and roast turkey with dressing, the "White Plate" specials are good value at $4 to $6. Seating is both indoors and, in good weather, outside on a shaded veranda beside a pond filled with lilypads. An outdoor bar is open from March to Labor Day.

Meals for Less than $10
Bayou Bill's Crab House. U.S. 98 (near Mussett Bayou Rd.), Santa Rosa Beach. ☎ **904/267-3849.** Reservations not accepted. Main courses $10.50–$16. MC, V. Summer, daily 5–10pm; off-season, Tues–Sun 5–9pm. SEAFOOD.

Notable for rustic, nautical decor plus dining in the outdoorlike Garden Room, Bayou Bill's features nightly chalkboard specials in addition to a variety of chowders, salads, buckets of steamed garlic crabs and steamed shrimp, and charcoal-grilled and fried fish. Sometimes offered as a main course, the sautéed alligator appetizer is an interesting choice.

Buster's Oyster Bar and Seafood Restaurant. In Delchamps Plaza, U.S. 98E at Scenic Hwy. 98 (1 mile west of the Sandestin Golf & Tennis Resort). ☎ **904/837-4399.** Reservations not required. Main courses $7–$13; sandwiches and burgers $3.50–$6. AE, DC, DISC, MC, V. Daily 11am–9:30pm. SEAFOOD.

Buster claims that more than five million oysters have been shucked here, and with good reason, since they go for 99¢ a dozen during his daily 5 to 6pm happy hour. Buster also likes to add something outrageous to his tabloid-style menu, such as "a toasted sea spider sandwich" (actually made with soft-shell crab). Fried, broiled, steamed, or blackened fish and seafood dinners are prepared to order. Kids have their own menu.

WORTH A SPLURGE
✪ The Lake Place Restaurant. 5960 County Rd. 30A, Dune Allen Beach. ☎ **904/267-2871.** Reservations required in summer, recommended off-season. Main courses $15–$22. No credit cards. Summer, Tues–Sat 5:30–9:30pm; off-season, Wed–Sat 5:30–9:30pm. Closed Dec–Jan. SEAFOOD.

Chef Peter Mulcahy scours the markets each morning for fresh fish which he and wife Susan use for daily specials at their rustic plank building on the shores of picturesque Lake Allen. Inscribed on a chalkboard, Peter's preparations vary—the Mulcahys usually offer oysters in winter and local crab in summer, plus filet mignon and lamb all year. In addition to seasonal fruit specials, Susan's delicious desserts always include key lime and silky chocolate pies.

✪ **Marina Café.** 320 U.S. 98E, Destin Harbor. ☎ **904/837-7960.** Reservations recommended. Main courses $14–$25; pizza and pasta $9–$17. AE, DC, DISC, MC, V. Daily 5–10pm. ITALIAN/NEW AMERICAN.

One of the town's finest restaurants, Jim Altamura's establishment provides a classy atmosphere with soft candlelight, subdued music, and formally attired waiters. The creative chef prepares pizza and pastas with a special flair, with an emphasis on light, spicy fare. Menu highlights include a fettuccine combined with andouille sausage, shrimp, crayfish tails, and a piquant tomato-cream sauce.

FORT WALTON BEACH & DESTIN AFTER DARK

Most resorts spotlight live entertainment during the summer season, including the Holiday Inn and Ramada Beach Resort in Fort Walton Beach, and the Sandestin Hilton and Sandestin Golf & Tennis Resort in Destin (see "Where to Stay," above). Several of the restaurants listed above also have live entertainment, especially during the summer season. It's a good idea to inquire ahead to make sure entertainment is scheduled at a particular lounge or restaurant, especially during the off-season months when things slow down at the beaches.

FORT WALTON BEACH Country music and dancing fans will find a home at the **High Tide Oyster Bar,** at the Okaloosa Island of the Brooks Bridge (☎ **904/ 244-2624**). The tunes start at 10pm daily. Over at the Boardwalk on U.S. 98E, the **Soggy Dollar Saloon** (☎ **904/243-5500**) has live music on weekends.

The young beach set is attracted to rock and reggae at the lively pubs of Shanty Town, on the east side of Brooks Bridge. The **Hog's Breath Saloon,** 1230 Seibert St. (☎ **904/244-2199**), and the neighboring **Hoser's,** 1225 Santa Rosa Blvd. (☎ **904/664-6113**), are both lively pubs. Whichever has the band draws the crowd. **Thunderbirds** nightclub (☎ **904/244-1320**) is right across Santa Rosa Boulevard.

DESTIN Twentysomethings are attracted to the dance club, rowdy saloon, Jimmy Buffet–style reggae bar, and sports TV–and–billiards parlor at the acclaimed **Nightown,** 140 Palmetto St. (☎ **904/837-6448**), near the harbor on the inland side of U.S. 98E. One admission of $5 covers it all. Not far away, the **Fish Heads** pub, at 414 U.S. 98E (☎ **904/837-4848**), features the "Big Red Snapper," a lethal mixture of rum, vodka, and more.

Several Destin restaurants offer entertainment in their lounges. The dockside **AJ's Club Bimini,** 116 U.S. 98E (☎ **904/837-1913**), offers live reggae under a big thatch-roofed deck every night during summer. A somewhat older, if not more sober, crowd gathers for entertainment at **The Deck,** on U.S. 98E at the Harbor Docks restaurant (☎ **904/837-2506**), and at **Harry T's Boat House** (☎ **904/654-6555**).

Out toward Sandestin, **Fudrucker's Beachside Bar & Grill,** 20001 U.S. 98E (☎ **904/654-4200**), opposite Henderson Beach State Recreation Area, offers double the fun with two summertime stages, one on the bayside deck, the other in the Down Under Bar. There's another Fudrucker's at 108 Santa Rosa Blvd. on Okaloosa Island in Fort Walton Beach (☎ **904/243-3833**).

You can wager on blackjack, craps, and slots with *ExtaSea* **Casino Cruises** (☎ **904/837-3031**), which has day and evening cruises into the gulf from its dock at the east end of Destin Bridge. Lunch or dinner is included for a reasonable $35 a person and there's no charge for dancing and entertainment on board. Reservations are recommended.

AN EASY EXCURSION TO DEFUNIAK SPRINGS

Noted for its well-preserved Victorian homes encircling a round, 60-foot-deep lake, DeFuniak Springs makes for an interesting sightseeing excursion. Founded in 1882 when the L&N Railroad built a station at the lake, the little town (pop. 5,100) came to prominence a few years later when the Chautauqua Society of New York decided to make its winter home here. Built of clapboard in 1909, the impressively domed and columned **Chautauqua Auditorium** still overlooks the lake, as does the tiny 1886 building that houses **Florida's oldest library.**

The town is still a hotbed of cultural activities, highlighted by the annual **Chautauqua Festival,** usually in late April, featuring sports activities and arts and crafts. The first weekend in December, townsfolk are joined by visitors from all over for the annual costume **Victorian Ball** and homes tour.

Chautauqua Vineyards, at I-10 and U.S. 331 (☎ **904/892-5887**), has free tours and tastings Monday to Saturday from 9am to 5pm and on Sunday from noon to 5pm. The office is behind the Econo Lodge.

To get there, take U.S. 331 north to I-10. Look for the HISTORIC DISTRICT sign about 2 miles north of the Interstate and turn right on Live Oak Avenue to Circle Drive, which circles the lake. Main Street, the old train station, and the town's business district lie on the lake's north shore.

The **Walton County Chamber of Commerce,** in the Chautauqua Auditorium on the lakeshore (P.O. Box 29), DeFuniak Springs, FL 32433 (☎ **904/892-3191**), has maps and booklets for self-guided tours and a list of local shops and antiques dealers. The staff will know when special events are scheduled. The office is open Monday to Friday from 8am to 5pm.

Dressed in Victorian finery, **Dianne Pickett** (☎ **904/892-4300**) leads guided tours of the town. Book at least a day in advance.

3 Panama City & Panama City Beach

100 miles E of Pensacola, 100 miles SW of Tallahassee

Ask O. J. Simpson what the Panhandle's main attraction is and he probably will tell you Panama City Beach. This was, after all, the first place outside southern California he visited after his 1995 acquittal. Simpson came here to see his then-girlfriend's family and to play a little golf. He was one of an increasing number of upper-scale visitors who are changing the image of this 22-mile stretch of gorgeous white sand. Panama City Beach has long been known as the "Redneck Riviera," since it's a summertime mecca for millions of low- and moderate-income vacationers from nearby southern states. It still has a seemingly unending strip of bars, amusement parks, and old-fashioned motels. But this lively and crowded destination also has luxury resorts and condominiums to go along with its great beaching, golfing, fishing, boating, and fresh seafood.

The British founded the first European settlement at Panama City in 1765, impressed by the beautiful and strategic harbor of St. Andrew Bay. Now what was once a sleepy fishing village is one of the state's leading ports and an industrial center whose downtown harbor is fringed by a civic center and a 400-slip marina at the foot of Harrison Avenue.

Panama City Beach is a seasonal resort—many restaurants, attractions, and even some hotels close between October and spring break in March.

ESSENTIALS

ARRIVING By Plane Atlantic Southeast, Delta Connection, Northwest Airlink, and USAir Express fly into **Panama City / Bay County International Airport,** on Airport Road, north of St. Andrews Boulevard in Panama City (☎ **904/ 763-6751**). Once there, you can rent a car or take a taxi to your hotel, motel, or condo (see "Getting Around," below). Taxi fares from the airport to the beach range from $11.50 to $25.

By Train The **Amtrak** (☎ 800/USA-RAIL) transcontinental *Sunset Limited* stops at Chipley, 45 miles north of Panama City.

By Bus The **Greyhound** depot is at 917 Harrison Ave. in Panama City (☎ 904/785-7861, or 800/231-2222).

By Car Interstate 10 runs east-west, 45 miles to the north. From I-10, head south on U.S. 231 for Panama City, Fla. 77 for the beach. U.S. 98, the gulf-hugging east-west artery, runs through both cities.

VISITOR INFORMATION For advance information, contact the **Panama City Beach Convention & Visitors Bureau,** P.O. Box 9473, Panama City Beach, FL 32407 (☎ 904/233-6503, or 800/PC-BEACH). The bureau shares quarters with the **James I. Lark, Sr., Visitors Information Center,** on the beach at 12015 Front Beach Rd., opposite the Miracle Strip Amusement Park. The information center provides information about accommodations, restaurants, and attractions in Panama City Beach.

MAPS Detailed maps are available at **Alvin's Island Tropical Department Store,** 12010 Front Beach Rd., opposite the visitors center.

TIME The Panama City area is in the central time zone, 1 hour behind Miami and Orlando.

GETTING AROUND **By Taxi** Call **AAA Taxi** (☎ 904/785-0533), **Yellow Cab** (☎ 904/763-4691), or **Deluxe Coach Service** (☎ 904/763-0211, or 800/763-0211). Fares are on a zone system rather than meters. Local fares in Panama City Beach will range from $4.50 to $9.

BEACHES & OUTDOOR ACTIVITIES

BEACHES & BEACH PARKS A nearly unbroken strand of fine white sand fronts the 22 miles of Panama City Beach, but the highlight for many here is **St. Andrews State Recreation Area,** 4607 State Park Lane, at the east end of the beach (☎ 904/233-5140). With more than 1,000 acres of dazzling white sand and dunes, this preserved wilderness demonstrates what this area looked like before motels and condominiums lined the beach. Lacy, golden sea oats sway in the refreshing gulf breezes, and fragrant rosemary grows wild. Picnic areas, rest rooms, and open-air showers are available for beachgoers. For anglers, there are jetties and a boat ramp. A nature trail reveals wading birds and perhaps an alligator or two. And drive carefully here, for the area is home to a herd of deer. Overnight camping is permitted. On display is a historic turpentine still formerly utilized by lumbermen to make turpentine and rosin, important for caulking the old wooden ships. Admission is $3.25 per car (maximum of eight people), $1 for pedestrians and cyclists. The area is open daily from 8am to sunset.

A few hundred yards across an inlet from St. Andrews State Recreation Area sits pristine **Shell Island,** a 7¹/₂-mile-long, 1-mile-wide barrier island. This uninhabited natural preserve is great for shelling and also fun for swimming or just relaxing. The island is accessible only by boat. A **ferry shuttle** (☎ 904/233-5140) runs from St. Andrews State Recreation Area to the island daily: every 30 minutes between 9am and 5pm during the summer, from 10am to 3pm off-season. Fares are $7 for adults, $5 for children 11 and under 12, plus admission fees to the state recreation area (see above).

Several cruise boats go to Shell Island. The *Lady Anderson* and the glass-bottom *Capt. Anderson III* both cruise there from **Capt. Anderson's Marina,** 5500 N. Lagoon Dr. at Thomas Drive (☎ **904/234-3435**). The *Island Queen* paddlewheeler departs from the pier at Marriott's Bay Point Resort, 4200 Marriott Dr., off Jan Cooley Road (☎ **904/234-3307,** ext. 1816). The *Island Star* and *Island Runner* (☎ **904/235-2809**) both leave from Hathaway Marina, on U.S. 98 at the west end of Hathaway Bridge. All five of these boats charge $10 for adults, $5 for children. More expensive are 2¹/₂-hour tours offered by **Shell Island Wave Runner Tours** (☎ **904/785-4878**), at the east end of Hathaway Bridge. Times vary by season and reservations are required, so call ahead.

BOATING & BOAT RENTALS   A variety of rental boats are available at the marinas near the Thomas Drive bridge over Grand Lagoon. These include the **Capt. Davis Queen Fleet,** based at Capt. Anderson's Marina, 5500 N. Lagoon Dr. (☎ 904/234-3435, or 800/874-2415 from nearby states); the **Panama City Boat Yard,** 5323 N. Lagoon Dr. (☎ 904/234-3386); the **Passport Marina,** 5325 N. Lagoon Dr. (☎ 904/234-5609); the **Port Lagoon Yacht Basin,** 5201 N. Lagoon Dr. (☎ 904/234-0142); the **Pirates Cove Marina,** 3901 Thomas Dr. (☎ 904/234-3839); and the **Treasure Island Marina,** 3605 Thomas Dr. (☎ 904/234-6533).

Days under sail can be spent on the *Jolly Mon* (☎ 904/234-7794), the *Glory Days* (☎ 904/233-5499, or 904/832-1454 on board), and the *Grrr* (☎ 904/230-2814, or 904/832-7184 on board). **Port to Port Sailing Charters** (☎ 904/230-0830) rents Sunfish and regular sailboats, with or without a captain.

Many resorts and hotels provide beach toys for their guests' use. Waverunners, jet boats, inflatables, and other equipment can be rented from **Panama City Beach Sports** (☎ 904/234-0067), **Raging Rentals** (☎ 904/234-6775), and **Lagoon Rentals** (☎ 904/234-7245).

CRUISES   The **Capt. Davis Queen Fleet,** based at Capt. Anderson's Marina, 5500 N. Lagoon Dr. (☎ **904/234-3435,** or 800/874-2415 from neighboring states), has daily sightseeing trips, nature cruises, dolphin-watching and bird-feeding excursions, and dinner-dance cruises during the summer season. So do the *Island Star* and *Island Runner* (☎ **904/235-2809**), both at the Hathaway Marina on U.S. 98 at the west end of Hathaway Bridge. The *Glass Bottom Boat* (☎ **904/234-8944**) offers underwater viewing cruises from the Treasure Island Marina, 3605 Thomas Dr., at Grand Lagoon. The 32-foot *AquaStar* (☎ **904/230-2800**) has dolphin-watching cruises to the shallow waters off Shell Island, where larger boats can't go.

FISHING   Close to 250,000 visitors come just to fish in these bountiful waters. Panama City Beach boasts three fishing piers, two of which were partially destroyed by Hurricane Opal. The concrete Dan Russell Municipal Pier, the city's longest at 1,642 feet, escaped serious damage.

The least expensive way for novices to cast their lines—or watch others cast theirs—is with **Capt. Anderson's Deep Sea Fishing,** at Capt. Anderson's Marina on Thomas Drive at Grand Lagoon (☎ **904/234-5940,** or 800/874-2415). The Captain's party-boat trips last from 5 to 12 hours, with prices ranging from $27 to $46 per person, including bait and tackle. Observers can go along for $12 to $20 each.

Much more expensive are the charter-fishing boats which depart daily March to November from **Hathaway's Landing Marina,** 6424 W. U.S. 98 (☎ 904/234-0609), at the west end of the Hathaway Bridge; and from **Capt. Anderson's Marina** (☎ 904/234-3435), the **Treasure Island Marina** (☎ 904/234-6533), the

Panama City Boat Yard (☎ 904/234-3386), the **Passport Marina** (☎ 904/234-5609), the **Port Lagoon Yacht Basin** (☎ 904/234-0142), and the **Pirates Cove Marina** (☎ 904/234-3839), all on Thomas Drive at Grand Lagoon.

GOLF If you want to splurge, **Marriott's Bay Point Resort,** 4200 Marriott Dr., off Jan Cooley Road, in Panama City Beach (☎ **904/234-3307**), offers 36 holes of championship golf. The Lagoon Legends course is one of the country's most difficult. Greens fees range from $40 to $55, depending on the season and day of the week. O. J. Simpson played the 18 holes of **The Hombre,** 120 Coyote Pass, Panama City Beach (☎ **904/234-3573**), a venue for golf tournaments. You can also tee off at **Holiday Golf & Tennis,** 100 Fairway Blvd., Panama City Beach (☎ **904/234-1800**); the very flat **Signal Hill,** 9516 N. Thomas Dr., Panama City Beach (☎ **904/234-3218**); or at the **Edgewater Beach Resort,** 11212 U.S. 98A (☎ **904/235-4044**). Reservations for tee times are highly recommended.

SCUBA DIVING & SNORKELING Although the area is too far north for coral formations, more than 50 artificial reefs and shipwrecks in the gulf waters off Panama City attract a wide variety of sealife. Local operators include the **Hydrospace Dive Shop,** with two bases: at 3605 Thomas Dr., at Treasure Island Marina on Grand Lagoon, and at Hathaway Landing Marina next to the bridge (☎ **904/234-3036**); the **Panama City Dive Center,** 4823 Thomas Dr. (☎ **904/235-3390**); and **Emerald Coast Divers,** 5121 Thomas Dr. (☎ **904/233-3355,** or 800/945-DIVE). These companies lead dives, teach courses, and take snorkelers to the grass flats off Shell Island. They charge $75 for resort courses; $45 to $78 for dives, depending on length; and $20 for snorkeling trips.

TENNIS & RACQUETBALL **Sports Park,** 15238 Front Beach Rd., at Hill Avenue (☎ **904/235-1081**), features tennis and racquetball courts, an indoor pool, Nautilus workout equipment, aerobics classes, whirlpool, sauna, tanning bed, and massages. Daily and weekly passes cost $8 and $35, respectively. Open Monday to Friday from 7am to 9pm, on Saturday from 9am to 5pm, and on Sunday from 8am to 1pm.

Call the **Panama City Recreation Department** (☎ **904/872-3005**) for information about the municipal courts.

WHAT TO SEE & DO
MUSEUMS & ZOOLOGICAL PARKS

Gulf World. 15412 Front Beach Rd. (at Hill Ave.), Panama City Beach. ☎ **904/234-5271.** Admission $14 adults, $8 children 5–12, free for children 4 and under. Summer, daily 9am–7pm; off-season, daily 9am–3pm.

This landscaped tropical garden and marine showcase features shows with talented dolphins, sea lions, penguins, and more. Sea turtles, alligators, and other critters also call Gulf World home. Scuba demonstrations, shark feedings, and underwater shows keep the crowds entertained.

Museum of Man in the Sea. 17314 Back Beach Rd. (at Heather Dr., west of Fla. 79), Panama City Beach. ☎ **904/235-4101.** Admission $4 adults, $2 children 6–16, free for children 5 and under. Daily 9am–5pm. Closed New Year's Day, Thanksgiving, and Christmas Day.

Owned by the Institute of Diving, this unusual museum exhibits historical displays of the underwater world dating back to 1500, and treasures recovered from sunken ships, including Spanish treasure galleons. Hands-on exhibits include experiments on water and air pressure, light refraction, and why diving bells work. Both kids and adults can climb through a submarine, pet live sea animals in a pool, and look out of a diving helmet. Videos and aquariums explain the sealife found in St. Andrew Bay.

ZooWorld Zoological & Botanical Park. 9008 Front Beach Rd. (near Moylan Dr.), Panama City Beach. ☎ **904/230-0096.** Admission $9 adults, $8 seniors, $7 children 3–11, free for children 2 and under. Daily 9am–sunset. Closed Christmas Day.

The largest captive alligator in Florida ("Mr. Bubba") lives in a re-created pine forest habitat at this educational and entertaining zoo, an active participant in the Species Survival Plan, which helps protect endangered species with specific breeding and housing programs. Other guests here include rare and endangered animals as well as orangutans and other primates, big cats, more reptiles, and other creatures. Also included are a walk-through aviary, a bat exhibit, and a petting zoo.

AMUSEMENT PARKS

Marvelous at night when everything is gaudily illuminated, the **Miracle Strip Amusement Park,** 12000 Front Beach Rd., at Alf Coleman Road (☎ **904/234-5810**), has been rated one of Florida's top 10 attractions. An exciting, 105-foot-high roller coaster is just one of the 30 rides in this fun park. Little ones will love the traditional carousel. The 9 acres of fun include nonstop live entertainment and snackeries with junk food. Admission (including all rides) is less than $20 for adults, less than $15 for children under 50 inches tall. You may pay a gate admission and buy tickets for individual rides and activities, but not that much is saved. The park is open June to mid-August, Monday to Friday from 5 to 11:30pm, on Saturday from 1 to 11:30pm, and on Sunday from 5 to 11:30pm; mid-March to May and mid-August to Labor Day, on Friday from 6 to 11pm and on Saturday from 1 to 11:30pm. It's closed from Labor Day to mid-March.

Adjoining the amusement park, the **Shipwreck Island Water Park** (☎ **904/234-0368**) offers a variety of water-related fun, including the 1,600-foot winding Lazy River for tubing and a daring 35-m.p.h. Speed Slide. The Rapid River Cascades and the White Water Tube Trip offer further adventures. Lounge chairs, umbrellas, and inner tubes are free, and lifeguards are on duty. Admission charges and hours are the same as at the Miracle Strip Amusement Park.

SHOPPING

An attraction in itself, the main branch of **Alvin's Island Tropical Department Store,** 12010 Front Beach Rd. (☎ **904/234-3048**), opposite the Visitors Information Center, not only sells a wide range of beach gear and apparel, it has cages containing colorful parrots, tanks with small sharks, and an enclosure with alligators. The sharks are fed at 11am daily; the gators get theirs at 4pm in summer (they're too lethargic to eat during the cool winter months).

More than 100 dealers have booths at **Barron's Antique Mall,** a blue metal warehouse at 8010 Front Beach Rd. near Wilkinson Avenue (☎ **904/230-0612**). Some of the dealers have larger shops elsewhere in the area. Barron's summer hours are Monday to Saturday from 10am to 6pm and on Sunday from 1 to 6pm; off-season, Monday to Saturday from 9am to 5pm and on Sunday from 1 to 5pm.

WHERE TO STAY

Among the many agencies offering fully furnished condominium apartments for long-term stays are **St. Andrew Bay Resort Management,** 726 Thomas Dr., Panama City Beach, FL 32408 (☎ **904/235-4075,** or 800/621-2462); and **Condo World,** 8815-A Thomas Dr. (P.O. Box 9456), Panama City Beach, FL 32408 (☎ **904/234-5564,** or 800/232-6636).

One good choice is **Horizon South,** 17462 Front Beach Rd., Panama City Beach, FL 32413 (☎ **904/234-6663,** or 800/476-6458), a group of 75 town houses just across the road from the beach. The resort community features three swimming pools (one heated), a wading pool for kids, a whirlpool, lighted tennis courts, an 18-hole miniature golf course, and games and exercise rooms. Summer rates range from $60 to $125 per town house for two people; off-season, they go for $45 to $72. Weekly and monthly rates are available.

You'll have to contend with heavy traffic getting to the beach during summer months, but staying in Panama City is less expensive than at the beach. One good choice, overlooking the bay at St. Andrews Marina, is the **Ramada Harbor View,** 3001 W. 10th St. (☎ **904/785-0561** or 800/228-3344). Several other chain motels are located along U.S. 98 east of the Hathaway Bridge. These include the **Howard Johnson on the Bay** (☎ **904/785-0222** or 800/654-2000), which backs up to St. Andrew Bay; the **Days Inn Central** (☎ **904/784-1777** or 800/329-7466); and an **Econo Lodge** (☎ **904/785-2700** or 800/424-4777). Every room has a kitchenette at the **Admiral Benbow Inn,** on U.S. 98 at the west end of Hathaway Bridge (☎ **904/234-2114** or 800/451-1986).

Beachside on Front Beach Road, you'll find the **Best Western Casa Loma** (☎ **904/234-1100** or 800/528-1234); the **Days Inn Beach** (☎ **904/233-3333** or 800/329-7466); and the **Ramada Inn Beach & Convention Center** (☎ **904/ 234-1700** or 800/228-3344). The somewhat less expensive **Best Western Del Coronado** (☎ **904/234-1600** or 800/528-1234) is open from March to September.

Bay County adds 3$^1/_2$% tax to all hotel and campground bills, bringing the total add-on tax to 9$^1/_2$%. See "Where to Stay" in the Pensacola section, above, for information about the seasons and how the rate categories are organized.

DOUBLES FOR LESS THAN $40

La Brisa Inn. 9424 Front Beach Rd., Panama City Beach, FL 32404. ☎ **904/235-1122** or 800/ 523-4369. Fax 904/235-1122. 60 rms. A/C TV TEL. Spring and summer, $54–$63 double. Fall and winter, $28–$30 double. AE, DC, DISC, MC, V.

Although a 20-minute walk from the beach on the inland stretch of Front Beach Road, this simple but clean two-story motel is one of the better bargains here. All rooms have one king-size bed or two double beds. Eight rooms also sport money-saving kitchenettes, but everyone can partake of complimentary coffee and doughnuts in the lobby every morning. Local telephone calls are free, and cribs are supplied for the little ones. There's a coin laundry for guests' use.

DOUBLES FOR LESS THAN $60

Flamingo Motel. 15525 Front Beach Rd., Panama City Beach, FL 32413. ☎ **904/234-2232** or 800/828-0400. 67 units. A/C TV TEL. Summer, $66–$129 unit. Off-season, $32–$70 unit. Children 15 and under stay free in parents' room. AE, DISC, MC, V.

This well-maintained, family-owned motel takes great pride in its gorgeous tropical garden under a peaked roof with skylights. Bordering the garden, a heated swimming pool and large sundeck overlook the gulf. The brightly decorated rooms with kitchenettes sleep two to six people, some in separate bedrooms. The kitchenette rooms across the road are less appealing but will accommodate six to eight. Budget-conscious families can opt for the low-priced rooms with small refrigerators, accommodating two to four. Some units have shower-only baths. The Dan Russell fishing pier is only half a mile away, and Shuckums Oyster Pub and Seafood Grill is within walking distance (see "Where to Dine," below).

Georgian Terrace. 14415 Front Beach Rd., Panama City Beach, FL 32413. ☎ **904/ 234-2144** or 904/234-8413. 28 apts. A/C TV TEL. Mid-May to mid-Sept, $70 apt for two. Off-season, $39–$59 apt for two. AE, DISC, MC, V.

A two-level motel right on the beach, this locally owned establishment offers clean, quiet, and cozy apartments. Opening to the beach, they all have full kitchens separated by room dividers. The homey decor is extended to each unit's private enclosed sunporches. A greenhouse-enclosed heated pool area with lush tropical plantings and attractive lounge chairs makes this establishment a good pick off-season. There's a rare stretch of undeveloped beach almost next door.

Sunset Inn. 8109 Surf Dr., Panama City Beach, FL 32408 ☎ and fax **904/234-7370.** 50 units. A/C TV TEL. Summer, $50–$95 unit. Off-season, $30–$70 unit. Weekly, monthly, and family rates available. AE, DISC, MC, V.

This very well maintained, two-level motel off Thomas Drive near the east end of the beach is right on the gulf but away from the crowds. It accommodates families in one- and two-bedroom units with kitchens or in efficiencies across the street. The inn sports a large heated swimming pool and a spacious sun deck with steps leading down to the beach.

DOUBLES FOR LESS THAN $80

Holiday Inn SunSpree Resort. 11127 Front Beach Rd., Panama City Beach, FL 32407. ☎ **904/234-1111** or 800/633-0266. Fax 904/235-1907. 342 rms. A/C TV TEL. Summer, $140–$180 double. Off-season, $70–$90 double. Weekly and monthly rates available; discount for seniors. AE, DC, DISC, MC, V.

This 15-story hotel is designed in an arch, so that all rooms have balconies that look directly down on a foot-shaped swimming pool and wooden sundeck beside the beach. Named as one of the top 20 Holiday Inns, the hotel has won architectural awards for its dramatic lobby with waterfall, tropical decor, and Fountain of Wishes (coins go to charity). The attractive, spacious guest rooms feature full-size icemaking refrigerators, microwave ovens, and two spacious vanity areas with their own lavatory sinks.

Charlie's Grill serves poolside lunches, while in the lobby the Blue Marlin restaurant, with seating under a skylight dome, features good breakfasts, lunches, and dinners at moderate prices. There's a Pizza Hut outlet for carryout pies. The lively Starlight Lounge serves drinks until late and usually offers entertainment during the peak summer season. The lobby bar has sports TVs, and there's poolside entertainment during summer evenings.

Other facilities include a whirlpool, exercise and games rooms, a gift shop, and a children's playground.

CAMPING

✪ **St. Andrews State Recreation Area,** 4607 State Park Lane, Panama City Beach, FL 32407 (☎ **904/233-5140**), is one of this area's major attractions and offers some of the best camping sites anywhere, some of them right on the shores of Grand Lagoon. From March to September, rates are $17 to $19 for waterfront sites, $15 to $17 for others; October to February they drop to $8 to $12; $2 extra for electrical hookup. The park is open daily all year from 8am to sunset.

The **Magnolia Beach RV Park,** 7800 Magnolia Beach Rd., Panama City Beach, FL 32408 (☎ **904/235-1581**), is one of the best private campgrounds around, with great views of Panama City from an idyllic setting under magnolias and moss-draped oaks on the shores of St. Andrew Bay. Some of the 94 sites are right on the water. The park has a boat ramp, fishing pier, pool, laundry, and recreation room, and all sites have cable TV hookups. There are no tent sites. Rates are $20 to $24 a night in summer, $15 to $18 off-season. The park is 2 miles from Marriott's Bay Point Resort. Take Magnolia Beach Road off Thomas Drive and go straight to the camp.

WHERE TO EAT

In most restaurants, local fish and shellfish predominate on the reasonably priced menus. Most places are very casual, and just about every restaurant features a children's menu. Pay attention to the hours, for some are closed from October to March; call ahead if you're here during this period.

MEALS FOR LESS THAN $10

Billy's Steamed Seafood Restaurant. 3000 Thomas Dr. (between Grand Lagoon and Magnolia Beach Rd.). ☎ **904/235-2349.** Reservations not accepted. Sandwiches $2.50–$5; seafood $6–$14. AE, MC, V. Summer, Sun–Thurs 11am–9:30pm, Fri–Sat 11am–10pm; off-season, daily 11am–9pm. SEAFOOD.

More a lively raw bar than a restaurant, Billy and Eloise Poole's casual establishment is famous for "the best crabs in town." These are hard-shell blue crabs prepared Maryland style: steamed with lots of spicy Old Bay Seasoning. Unlike the crab houses in Baltimore, however, Billy and Eloise remove the top shell, clean out the "mustard" (intestines), and cut the crabs in two for you: All you have to do is "pick" the meat. Other steamed morsels include shrimp (also with spicy seasoning), oysters, crabs, and lobster served with corn on the cob and garlic bread. Order anything from the briny deep here, but pass over other items. If you're in town during the off-season, check to see if the Pooles have an all-you-can-eat crab feast scheduled.

Cajun Inn. In the Shoppes at Edgewater, 477 Beckrich Rd. (at Front Beach Rd.). ☎ **904/235-9987.** Reservations not accepted. Main courses $8–$14; sandwiches $4–$6. AE, DC, DISC, MC, V. Daily 11am–10pm. LOUISIANA CAJUN.

Almost hidden away in the "elbow" of the Shoppes at Edgewater, next to a multiscreen cinema, this cozy, family-owned restaurant brings the Big Easy to the gulf. Offerings include jambalaya, seafood étouffée, peppered shrimp or crayfish, and Cajun-style blackened fish. Po-boys (overstuffed hoagie sandwiches of fried oysters or fried shrimp) are a lunchtime specialty. You won't get gourmet New Orleans cuisine at these prices, but your tongue will have plenty of spice to savor. Dine inside, or outside on the shopping center walkway.

Shuckums Oyster Pub & Seafood Grill. 15614 Front Beach Rd. (at Powell Adams Dr.). ☎ **904/235-3214.** Reservations not accepted. Main courses $8–$12; burgers and sandwiches $5–$7. DISC, MC, V. Summer, daily 11am–2am; off-season, daily 11am–9:30pm. SEAFOOD.

"We shuck 'em, you suck 'em" is the motto of this extremely informal pub which became famous when comedian Martin Short tried unsuccessfully to shuck oysters here during the making of an MTV special about spring-break fun. The original bar is virtually papered over with dollar bills signed by patrons who've been flocking here since 1967. The obvious specialty is fresh Apalachicola oysters served either raw, steamed, or baked with a variety of toppings. Pub fare and seafood main courses are also offered.

MEALS FOR LESS THAN $15

Capt. Anderson's Restaurant. 5551 N. Lagoon Dr. (at Thomas Dr.). ☎ **904/234-2225.** Reservations not accepted. Main courses $10–$35. AE, DC, DISC, MC, V. Feb–Oct, Mon–Sat 4–10pm (or later depending on crowds). Closed Nov–Jan. SEAFOOD.

Overlooking the Grand Lagoon, this famous restaurant attracts early diners who come to watch the fishing fleet unload the catch-of-the-day at the busy marina. Capt. Anderson's is so popular that sometimes there's almost a 2-hour backup for a table during the peak summer months. The Captain's menu is noted for grilled local fish, crabmeat-stuffed jumbo shrimp, and a heaped-high seafood platter. A Greek salad accompanies dinner. For the first-time visitor, Capt. Anderson's is a highly recommendable place to sample the local atmosphere.

✪ **Hamilton's Seafood Restaurant & Lounge.** 5711 N. Lagoon Dr. (at Thomas Dr.). ☎ **904/234-1255.** Reservations not accepted. Main courses $10–$19. AE, DISC, MC, V. Summer, daily 4:30–10pm; winter, daily 5–9pm. SEAFOOD.

Proprietor Steve Stevens continues in the tradition of his noted Biloxi, Mississippi, restaurateur father at this attractive establishment on Grand Lagoon. His baked oysters Hamilton appetizer—a rich combination of oysters, shrimp, and crabmeat—filled me up before I got to my main course. Several other dishes are unique to Hamilton's, such as spicy snapper étouffée and a Greek-accented shrimp Cristo. Mesquite-grilled fish and steaks are also house specialties, and vegetarians can order a coal-fired vegetable kebab served over angel-hair pasta. A Lagoon Saloon makes the wait for a table go by quickly.

WORTH A SPLURGE

○ **Canopies.** 4423 W. 18th St. (1 mile east of Hathaway Bridge), in Panama City. ☎ **904/872-8444.** Reservations recommended. Main courses $12–$23. AE, DISC, MC, V. Daily 5–10pm. Closed Thanksgiving and Christmas Day. SEAFOOD.

Easily this area's most elegant restaurant and purveyor of its finest cuisine, Canopies occupies a 1910-vintage gray clapboard house with a magnificent view of St. Andrews Bay. Dining is on an enclosed veranda, but the dark, cozy bar in the old living room invites before- or after-dinner drinks. The menu changes every week or two, but consistent favorites are a creamy she-crab soup under a flaky croissant dome; grilled tuna, salmon, or grouper with a trio of sauces; sautéed grouper with lump crabmeat in a sherry-butter sauce; and sushi-quality yellowfin tuna in a sherry-soy sauce and served over a haystack of leeks. Landlubbers can partake of award-winning beef, lamb, and game dishes. Several gourmet dessert and coffee creations top off these delicious meals.

DINING ON LAND & SEA

The Treasure Ship, at the Treasure Island Marina, 3605 S. Thomas Dr., at Grand Lagoon (☎ **904/234-8881**), must be seen to be believed, for this amazing 2 acres of ship space claims to be the world's largest land-based Spanish galleon, a replica of the three-masted sailing ships that carried loot from the New World to Spain in the 16th and 17th centuries. You can get anything from an ice-cream cone to peel-it-yourself shrimp to a sophisticated dinner in the various dining rooms and eateries. The Dockside Galley serves lunch and sandwiches at reasonable prices from 11am to 5pm. Seafood specialties are highlighted in the Treasure Ship Dining Room, open daily from 4:30 to 10pm and for Sunday brunch from 10am to 2pm; dinner prices range from about $12 to $20. Live entertainment and dancing continue until the wee hours in the Brig. Two other cocktail lounges as well as games rooms and boutiques are on board. Admission is free to the Treasure Ship. It's a good idea to call ahead for current dining hours in the various restaurants, most of which close from October to December.

Lady Anderson **dinner-dance cruises** are a romantic evening escape from Memorial Day to Labor Day. Boarding is at Capt. Anderson's Marina, 5550 N. Lagoon Dr. (☎ **904/234-5940,** or 800/874-2415), at 6:30pm Monday to Saturday. Buffet dinners are featured, followed by live music for dancing. Tickets cost about $25 per adult, about $20 for children 11 and under. Tips are included, which helps make this good value for a night out. This triple-decker fun boat is so popular that reservations must be made well in advance.

PANAMA CITY & PANAMA CITY BEACH AFTER DARK

THE PERFORMING ARTS   The Rader family and a cast of 20 perform year round in the **Ocean Opry Show,** 8400 Front Beach Rd., Panama City Beach (☎ 904/234-5464), the area's answer to the Grand Ole Opry. Nationally known country-music stars are spotlighted October to March. There's a show every night at 8pm during the summer, less frequently off-season. Admission is $15 for adults, $7.50 for children (prices vary when the big stars are in town). The box office opens daily at 9am on show days, and reservations are recommended.

The **Marina Civic Center,** 8 Harrison Ave. (☎ 904/763-4696), is Panama City's waterfront showplace, providing a venue for a variety of performances by nationally known troupes and artists throughout the year.

THE CLUB & BAR SCENE   **The Breakers,** 12627 Front Beach Rd. (☎ 904/234-6060), is the area's long-standing supper club, a large establishment with unsurpassed gulf views and music for dining and dancing. Open daily at 5pm during summer; call for information on special shows during the season. The beachfront **Harpoon Harry's Waterfront Cafe** is part of the same complex.

Romantic lounges with both live entertainment and dancing are at **The Treasure Ship,** 3605 S. Thomas Dr. (☎ 904/234-8881). See "Where to Eat," above, for more information.

Hathaway's Landing, on U.S. 98 at the west end of the Hathaway Bridge (☎ 904/230-0409), has live entertainment nightly and on Saturday and Sunday afternoons from March to September. The emphasis is on Jimmy Buffet–style music, reggae, and some country and western. Away from the beach, it draws lots of customers over 30.

The young crowd likes to boogie all night at "beach clubs" such as **Schooners,** 5121 Gulf Dr. (☎ 904/235-9074), where every table has a gulf view, and **Spinnaker's,** on the beach at 8795 Thomas Dr. (☎ 904/234-7882). They often stay open until 4am in summer while their bands play on and on for dancing and listening. **Pineapple Willie's Lounge,** beachside at 9900 S. Thomas Dr. (☎ 904/235-0928), is open from 11am until 2am, serving pub food and spotlighting live entertainment in summer and a host of sports TVs all year.

4 Apalachicola

60 miles E of Panama City, 80 miles SW of Tallahassee

Sometimes called Florida's Last Frontier, the relatively undeveloped Gulf Coast between Panama City and Tallahassee is a fascinating day trip for many visitors, a destination in itself for others. Reminiscent of North Carolina's Outer Banks, the beaches here are long and gorgeous, the bays and estuaries are great for fishing and boating, and the seafood is as fresh and succulent as it can be.

The area also is rich in history, which makes a visit to the little town of Apalachicola (pop. 2,600) a highlight of any venture into this beautiful area. Strategically located at the mouth of the Apalachicola River, this charming community was a major seaport during autumns from 1827 to 1861, when plantations in Alabama and Georgia shipped tons of cotton down the river to the gulf. The town had a racetrack, an opera house, and a civic center which hosted balls, socials, and gambling. The area's population shrank during the mosquito-infested summer months, however, when yellow fever and malaria epidemics struck. It was during one of these outbreaks that Dr. John Gorrie of Apalachicola tried to develop a method of cooling his patients' rooms. In doing so, he invented the forerunner of the air conditioner that made Florida tourism possible.

The Civil War put an end to Apalachicola's cotton boom, and although lumbering became important in the late 1800s, that industry eventually found a home at Port St. Joe's deep-water harbor 30 miles to the west. From that time on, Apalachicola has made its living primarily from the gulf and the lagoonlike bay behind a chain of offshore barrier islands. Today Apalachicola produces the bulk of Florida's oyster crop, and shrimping and fishing are major industries. It also has been "discovered" by a number of expatriates from large cities, who have moved here, restored many old homes, and opened interesting antique and gift shops.

The area also is rich in wildlife preserves, and two of its barrier-island beaches are considered to be among the nation's finest.

ESSENTIALS

ARRIVING   You'll have to drive to get to Apalachicola, which is about 65 miles east of Panama City via U.S. 98 and about 80 miles west of Tallahassee via U.S. 319 and U.S. 98. From I-10, take Exit 21 at Marianna, then follow Fla. 71 south to Port St. Joe, then U.S. 98 east to Apalachicola.

VISITOR INFORMATION   The **Apalachicola Bay Chamber of Commerce,** 84 Market St., Apalachicola, FL 32320 (☎ **904/653-9419**), supplies information about the area from its office on Market Street (U.S. 98) between Avenues D and E.

TIME   The town is in the eastern time zone, like Orlando and Miami. Many shops are closed on Wednesday afternoon, when Apalachicolans go fishing.

WHAT TO SEE & DO

HISTORIC DISTRICT   Start your visit by picking up a map and a self-guided tour brochure from the chamber of commerce and then stroll around Apalachicola's waterfront, business district, and Victorian-era homes. Along Water Street, several tin warehouses evoke the town's seafaring days of the late 1800s, as does the 1840s-era **Sponge Exchange** at Commerce Street and Avenue E. A highlight of the residential area, centered around Gorrie Square at Avenue D and 6th Street, is the Greek Revival–style **Trinity Episcopal Church,** built in New York and shipped here in 1837. At the water end of 6th Street, Battery Park has a children's playground. A number of excellent **art galleries** and gift shops are grouped on Market Street, Avenue D, and Commerce Street. You won't miss them on the 3 blocks of these streets.

MUSEUMS   Showpiece at the **John Gorrie State Museum,** Avenue D at 6th Street (☎ **904/653-9347**), is a display replica of Doctor Gorrie's cooling machine, a prototype of today's air conditioner. Open Thursday to Monday from 10am to noon and 1 to 5pm; closed New Year's Day, Thanksgiving, and Christmas Day. Admission is $1.

There's a small **Maritime Museum** at 57 Market St., open Monday to Saturday from 10am to 4pm. Admission is free.

The **Estuarine Walk,** at the north end of Market Street on the grounds of the Apalachicola National Estuarine Research Reserve (☎ **904/653-8063**), contains aquariums full of fish and alligators, cages with snakes and tortoises, and displays of various other estuarine life. It's open Monday to Friday from 8am to 5pm. Admission is free.

BEACHES, PARKS & WILDLIFE REFUGES   Countless terns, snowy plover, black skimmers, and other birds nest along the dunes and 9 miles of beaches (which some experts consider to be among America's best) at **St. George Island State Park,** on the island's eastern end (☎ **904/927-2111**). The wildlife can be viewed from a hiking trail and observation platform. The park has picnic areas, rest rooms, showers, a boat launch, and a campground with electricity hookups. Entry fees are $3.25 per vehicle with up to eight occupants, $1 for pedestrians and bicyclists. Camping fees are $10 per night with electricity, $8 without. Primitive camping (take everything with you, including water) costs $3 a night for adults, $2 for children.

The beaches are even longer at **St. Joseph Peninsula State Park,** at the end of County Road 30, about 35 miles west of Apalachicola (☎ **904/227-1327**). The peninsula is populated by cottages and a few shops around Cape San Blas, but beyond the park entrance it's totally preserved. Facilities include picnic areas, a marina with a boat ramp, campgrounds with electricity, and eight remote cabins. Admission and camping fees are the same as at St. George Island State Park (see above), except add $2 for electricity at the campsites. The cabins rent for $70 a night in summer, $55 a night off-season, with minimum stays of 5 nights in summer and 2 nights off-season.

There are no facilities whatsoever at the **St. Vincent National Wildlife Refuge** (☎ **904/653-8808**), southwest of Apalachicola. This 12,358-acre barrier island is being left in its natural state by the U.S. Fish and Wildlife Service, but visitors are welcome to walk through its pine forests, marshlands, ponds, dunes, and beaches. In addition to native species like the bald eagle and alligators, the island is home to a small herd of sambar deer from Southeast Asia. Red wolves are bred here for reintroduction to other wildlife areas. Access is by boat only, usually from Indian Pass, 21 miles west of Apalachicola via U.S. 98 and County Roads 30A and 30B. The chamber of commerce (see "Essentials," above) will arrange to have a boat captain take you over. The refuge headquarters, at the north end of Market Street in town, has exhibits of wetland flora and fauna. It's open Monday to Friday from 8am to 4:30pm. The rangers conduct managed hunts for deer and wild hogs from November to January.

CRUISES　The *Governor Stone,* an 1877-vintage Gulf Coast schooner, makes cruises on Apalachicola Bay each day during the summer months, less frequently off-season. This fine old craft has seen duty as a cargo freighter, oyster buyer, sponge boat, and U.S. Merchant Marine training vessel. It departs from the Rainbow Inn dock on Water Street, but book in advance at the Maritime Museum at 57 Market St. (☎ **904/653-8708**); call for schedule and reservations, which are recommended. The cruises cost $20 for adults, $10 for children 12 and under.

Jeanni McMillan of **Jeanni's Journeys** (☎ **904/927-3259** or 904/927-3297) takes guests on narrated nature cruises out to the barrier islands and on canoe trips in the creeks and streams of the Apalachicola River basin. One of her trips is by boat and mountain bike to St. Vincent National Wildlife Refuge. Prices range from $15 to $70.

FISHING　Fishing is excellent in these waters, where trout, redfish, flounder, tarpon, shark, drum, and other species abound. The chamber of commerce (see "Essentials," above) can help arrange charters on the local boats, many of which dock at the Rainbow Inn on Water Street. For guides, contact **Professional Guide Service** (☎ 904/670-8834) or **Boss Guide Services** (☎ 904/653-8139).

WHERE TO STAY

Outside the state park, the dunes of St. George Island are virtually lined with beach cottages and a few condominiums. Most are available on a weekly or monthly basis for less than you'd pay nightly at a hotel. Among the rental agents are **Anchor Realty,** HCR Box 222, St. George Island, FL 32328 (☎ **904/927-2735** or 800/824-0416); **Gulf Coast Realty,** HCR Box 90, St. George Island, FL 32328 (☎ **904/**

927-2596, or 800/367-1680); and **Sun Coast Realty,** HCR Box 2, St. George Island, FL 32328 (☎ **904/927-2282,** or 800/341-2021).

✪ **Coombs House Inn.** 80 6th St., Apalachicola, FL 32320. ☎ **904/653-9199.** 10 rms. A/C TV TEL. $60–$105 double. Rates include continental breakfast. AE, MC, V.

This large house in the historic district was built in 1905 by a lumber baron. The house had gone to seed by the early 1990s, when noted interior designer Lynn Wilson bought it and completely restored it, furnishing it throughout with Victorian reproductions. Each room is tastefully decorated; outstanding is the Coombs Suite, with bay windows, sofa, four-poster bed, and its own Jacuzzi. One room is equipped for disabled guests. A major truck route, U.S. 98, runs along the north side of the property; request a south room to escape the periodic road noise. Guests can use the house bikes for free.

✪ **Gibson Inn.** 51 Ave. C, Apalachicola, FL 32320. ☎ **904/653-2191.** 29 rms, 1 suite. A/C TV TEL. $65–$85 double; $110 suite. AE, MC, V.

Built in 1907 as a seaman's hotel and gorgeously restored in 1985, this cupola-topped inn is such a brilliant example of Victorian architecture that it's listed on the National Register of Historic Inns. No two guest rooms are alike (some still have the original sinks in the sleeping area), but all are richly furnished with antiques. Nonguests are welcome to wander upstairs and peek into unoccupied rooms (whose doors are left open) or partake of a sumptuous seafood meal in the comfortable dining room. Room and dining reservations are advised, especially on weekends, and rooms should be booked well in advance in summer—and as much as 5 years ahead for the seafood festival in November. Grab a drink from the bar and relax in one of the high-back rockers on the old-fashioned veranda.

Rainbow Inn. 123 Water St., Apalachicola, FL 32320. ☎ **904/653-8139.** 27 rms. A/C TV TEL. Summer, $54–$69 double. Off-season, $44–$59 double. AE, DC, DISC, MC, V.

This two-story inn's rough-hewn exterior timbers make it look like one of the neighboring waterfront warehouses, and there's absolutely nothing fancy here except the rooms' views of Apalachicola Bay. Units on the second floor are newer and better appointed and have better views than those at dockside. Caroline's Restaurant serves breakfast, lunch, and seafood dinners, and the Spoonbill Cocktail Lounge over the restaurant is a popular local watering hole.

WHERE TO EAT

Townsfolk still plop down on the round stools at the marble-topped counter to order ham sandwiches and Coca-Colas at the **Old Time Soda Fountain & Luncheonette,** 93 Market St. (☎ **904/653-2000**). This relic of the 1950s was once the town drugstore. It's open Monday to Saturday from 10am to 5pm. Inexpensive, tasty pies and submarine sandwiches are available at **Risa's Pizza,** 80 Market St. (☎ **904/653-8578**), open Tuesday to Friday from 11:30am to 9:30pm and on Saturday from 4 to 9:30pm.

Apalachicola Seafood Grill & Steakhouse. 100 Market St. (at Ave. E/U.S. 98). ☎ **904/653-9510.** Reservations recommended in summer. Main courses $7–$17. AE, DISC, MC, V. Mon–Thurs 11am–3pm and 4:30–9pm, Fri–Sat 11am–3pm and 6–10pm. SEAFOOD/STEAKS.

With cafe curtains bedecking its storefront windows, this establishment looks like a typical small-town diner. It once was, but don't be mistaken by outward appearances. Today's menu features southern-style fried oysters, fish, and shrimp, but the daily specials feature such delicious selections as mixed seafood combined with a light garlic-cream sauce and linguine. Charcoal-broiled steaks run up to a full pound of sirloin.

Boss Oyster. 125 Water St. ☎ **904/653-9364.** Reservations not accepted. Main courses $9–$17; sandwiches $6–$8. AE, DC, DISC, MC, V. Mon–Thurs 11:30am–9pm, Fri–Sun 11am–10pm. SEAFOOD.

You've probably heard about the famous Apalachicola oysters and their reputedly aphrodisiac properties. Well, this simple, dockside eatery is a good place to see if they work. The bivalves are served raw, steamed, or under a choice of 10 toppings ranging from capers to crabmeat. They'll even steam three dozen of them and let you do the shucking. Steamed crabs and shrimp and fried seafood platters are also offered, as are delicious po-boy sandwiches with fried oysters or shrimp. Dine inside or at picnic tables on a screened dockside porch. Everyone in town eats here, from bankers to watermen.

✪ **Magnolia Grill.** Ave. E (U.S. 98, at 11th St.). ☎ **904/653-8000.** Reservations recommended. Main courses $9–$20. No credit cards (personal checks accepted). Mon–Sat 6–10pm. SEAFOOD/LOUISIANA.

Known locally as "Chef Eddie's Cafe" in honor of Boston-bred owner/chef Ed Cass, this pleasant restaurant occupies a small bungalow built in the 1880s and still in possession of original black cypress paneling in its central hallway. Ed has turned the old living room into the dining quarters, where he offers nightly specials emphasizing fresh local seafood and New Orleans–style sauces. He received more that 2,000 orders for his spicy seafood gumbo at a recent Florida Seafood Festival. His snapper Pontchartrain, with cream and artichoke hearts, is a delightful main course. Ed permits no smoking inside the house.

AN EXCURSION TO APALACHICOLA NATIONAL FOREST

The huge Apalachicola National Forest begins a few miles northeast of town. The largest of Florida's three national forests, this preserve encompasses 600,000 acres, stretching from Tallahassee's outskirts southward to the Gulf Coast and westward some 70 miles to the Apalachicola River. Included are a variety of woodlands, rivers, streams, lakes, and caves populated by a host of wildlife.

There are campgrounds with tent and RV sites and a number of other facilities, some especially designed for the physically disabled. There are canoeing and mountain bike trails, and picnic facilities with sheltered tables and grills. Hunting is permitted; this is one of two areas in the state where the American black bear can be hunted.

A necessary stop before heading into this wilderness is the **Wakulla Area Ranger Station,** Rte. 6, Box 7860, Crawfordville, FL 32327 (☎ **904/926-3561**), which provides information about the forest and its facilities and sells topographical and canoe trail maps. The station is on U.S. 319 about TK miles north of Apalachicola, 20 miles south of Tallahassee and 5 miles north of Crawfordville. It's open Monday to Thursday from 7:30am to 5pm and on Friday from 7:30am to 4pm.

5 Tallahassee

200 miles W of Jacksonville, 200 miles E of Pensacola, 250 miles NW of Orlando

Tallahassee has been Florida's capital since 1824, selected for its midpoint location between St. Augustine and Pensacola, then the state's major cities. An Old South atmosphere prevails in this slow-paced area dotted with lovingly restored antebellum mansions, plantations, beautiful lakes and streams, towering pine and cypress trees,

Tallahassee

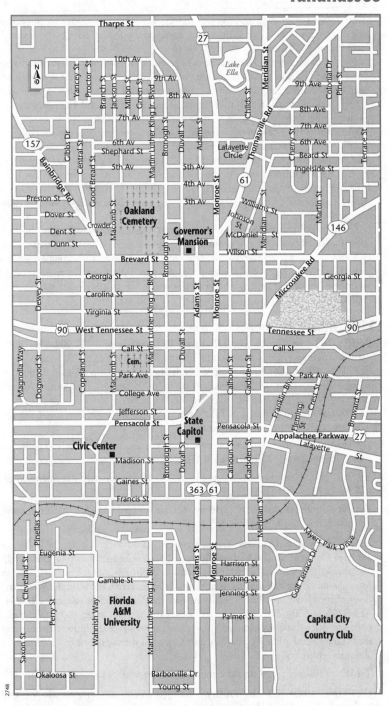

richly scented magnolias, and colorful azaleas. Tradition and history are important here, and many of the city's 19th-century homes and buildings have been preserved, including the 1845 Old Capitol.

Nestled in what seems like an enormous forest (local residents need permits to cut down trees), Tallahassee offers picturesque drives along five official Canopy Roads over which majestic, moss-draped live oaks form virtual tunnels. They're lined with historic plantations, ancient Native American settlement sites and mounds, gorgeous gardens, quiet parks with picnic areas, and lakes for bass fishing.

Combining the elegance of its bygone era with a modern state capitol complex, usually sleepy Tallahassee takes on an entirely different persona when the legislature is in session and when the powerful football teams of Florida State University and Florida A&M University take to the gridiron. With so many students in town, it's little wonder that Tallahassee enjoys lively entertainment. And with the state government and a sophisticated populace present, it has good museums along with its many historic buildings.

Given its mild climate and nearby state parks and federal forests and wildlife refuges, the Tallahassee area also abounds in outdoor activities: boating and canoeing, golf and tennis, biking and hiking. The nearby Apalachicola National Forest is a virtual gold mine of outdoor recreational pursuits. And for those more inclined to browse and spend money, the nearby town of Havana is Florida's antiqueing capital.

ESSENTIALS

ARRIVING   By Plane   The **Tallahassee Regional Airport** (☎ 904/891-7800), 10 miles southwest of downtown on SE Capital Circle, is served by Air South, American Eagle, Atlantic Southeast, ComAir, Gulf Stream International, Continental Express, Delta, and USAir. Local buses don't go to the airport, but **Annett Airport Shuttle** (☎ 904/878-3261 or 800/328-6033) operates vans from both the airport and Amtrak station to hotels in Tallahassee and other points in Northwest Florida. The fare is $10 per person to any destination in Tallahassee.

By Train   The **Amtrak** transcontinental *Sunset Limited* stops in Tallahassee at 918½ Railroad Ave. (☎ 800/USA-RAIL).

By Bus   The **Greyhound** bus depot is at 112 W. Tennessee St., at Adams Street (☎ 904/222-4240 or 800/231-2222).

By Car   From east and west, highway access is via I-10 and U.S. 90. From north and south, it's U.S. 27 and U.S. 319.

VISITOR INFORMATION   For information in advance, contact the **Tallahassee Area Convention and Visitors Bureau,** 200 W. College Ave. (P.O. Box 1369), Tallahassee, FL 32302 (☎ 904/413-9200 or 800/628-2866). Your first stop in town should be the **Tallahassee Area Visitor Information Center,** in the West Plaza foyer of the New Capitol Building, just inside the Duvall Street entrance (☎ 904/413-9200 or 800/628-2866). The staff here dispenses free street and public transportation maps, brochures, and pamphlets outlining tours of the historic districts and the Canopy Roads. The Florida Welcome Center in the same foyer has information about the entire state.

TIME   Tallahassee is in the eastern time zone, the same as Orlando and Miami.

GETTING AROUND   By Trolley   Built like an old-time streetcar, the free **Old Town Trolley** (☎ 904/891-5200) is the best way to see the sights of historic downtown Tallahassee. You can get on or off at any point between Adams Street

Commons, at the corner of Jefferson and Adams streets, and the Governor's Mansion. The trolley runs every 10 minutes between 7am and 6pm Monday to Friday.

By Bus TALTRAN provides city **bus** service from its downtown terminal at Tennessee and Adams streets (☎ **904/891-5200**). The fare is 75¢. Both the ticket booth there and the Tallahassee Area Visitors Information Center in the New Capitol Building have route maps and schedules for the Old Town Trolley and TALTRAN buses.

By Taxi & Limo For taxi service call **Red Cab** (☎ 904/425-4606), **Yellow Cab** (☎ 904/222-3070), or **City Taxi** (☎ 904/562-4222).

WHAT TO SEE & DO
THE CAPITOL COMPLEX

Florida's Capitol Complex, on South Monroe Street at Apalachee Parkway, dominates the downtown area and should be the start of your sightseeing here.

The **New Capitol Building,** a $43-million skyscraper, was built in 1977 to replace the 1845-vintage Old Capitol. State legislators meet here from March to May. The chambers of the House and the Senate have public viewing galleries. For a spectacular view, take the elevators to the 22nd-floor **observatory,** where on a clear day you can see all the way to the Gulf of Mexico. The New Capitol is open Monday to Friday from 8am to 5pm (closed major holidays). **Guided tours** (☎ 904/413-9200) are scheduled on the hour, Monday to Friday from 9 to 11am and 1 to 3pm and on Saturday and Sunday from 9am to 3pm. Weekend visitors can go up to the observatory and take a guided tour.

Directly in front of the skyscraper is the strikingly white **Old Capitol** (☎ 904/487-1902). With its majestic dome, this "Pearl of Capitol Hill" has been restored to its original beauty. An eight-room exhibit portrays Florida's political history. The Old Capitol is open Monday to Friday from 9am to 4:30pm, on Saturday from 10am to 4:30pm, and on Sunday and holidays from noon to 4:30pm. Admission is free to both capitols.

Facing the Old Capitol across Monroe Street are the twin granite towers of the **Vietnam Veterans Memorial,** honoring Florida's Vietnam vets.

The Old Town Trolley will take you to the lovely Georgian-style **Governor's Mansion,** north of the capitol at Adams and Brevard streets (☎ 904/488-4661). Enhanced by a portico patterned after Andrew Jackson's columned antebellum home, the Hermitage, and surrounded by giant magnolia trees and landscaped lawns, the mansion is furnished with 18th- and 19th-century antiques. The public rooms display such collectibles as the hollowware from the battleship USS *Florida.* Tours of the mansion are given at Christmas and when the legislature is in session. Call for a schedule and reservations.

Adjacent to the Governor's Mansion, **The Grove** was home to Ellen Call Long, known as "The Tallahassee Girl," the first child born after Tallahassee was settled.

HISTORIC DISTRICTS

While modern buildings have made inroads in downtown, Tallahassee has an on-going effort to preserve many of its historic homes and buildings, led by the **Historical Preservation Board** (☎ 904/488-3901), whose offices are in the Brokaw-McDougall House (see "Calhoun Street Historic District," below). The board arranges guided tours for groups. The three historic districts are an easy walk north of the capitol complex. The information center in the New Capitol (see "Essentials," above) distributes free walking-tour brochures. Taken together, the three areas are about 4 miles long and should take half a day. Most interesting is the Park Avenue District, 3 blocks north of the capitol.

ADAMS STREET COMMONS This 1-block winding brick and landscaped area along Adams Street begins on the north side of the Capitol Complex. It retains an old-fashioned town-square atmosphere. Restored buildings include the Governor's Club, a 1900s Masonic Lodge, and Gallie's Hall, where Florida's first five African-American college students received their Florida A&M University diplomas in 1892. Adams Street crosses Park Avenue 3 blocks north of the capitol.

PARK AVENUE HISTORIC DISTRICT The 7 blocks of Park Avenue between Martin Luther King, Jr., Boulevard and North Meridien Street is a lovely promenade of beautiful trees, gardens, and outstanding old mansions. This broad avenue with a shady median strip was once known as McCarthy Street, but was renamed Park Avenue to satisfy a snobbish Anglophile society matron who wanted no Irish name imprinted on her son's wedding invitations.

Several Park Avenue historic buildings are open to the public, including the **Knott House Museum,** at Calhoun Street (see "Museums," below). **The Columns,** at Duvall Street, was built in the 1830s and is the city's oldest surviving building (it's home of the Tallahassee Chamber of Commerce). The **First Presbyterian Church,** at Adams Street, built in 1838, is the city's oldest church, and is an important African-American historic site since slaves were welcome to worship here without their masters' consent. The **Walker Library,** between Monroe and Calhoun streets, was one of Florida's first libraries, dating back to 1903. Just north of Park Avenue on Gadsden Street, the **Meginnis-Monroe House** contains the Lemoyne Art Gallery.

At Martin Luther King, Jr., Boulevard, the adjacent **Old City Cemetery** and **Episcopal Cemetery** contain the graves of Prince Achille Murat, Napoleon's nephew, and Princess Catherine Murat, his wife and George Washington's grand-niece. Also buried here are two governors and soldiers who died at the Battle of Natural Bridge during the Civil War. The cemeteries are also important to African-American history since a number of slaves and the first African-American Florida A&M graduates are among those interred here. The visitor information center in the New Capitol has a cemetery walking-tour brochure.

CALHOUN STREET HISTORIC DISTRICT Affectionately called "Gold Dust Street" in the old days, the 3 blocks of Calhoun Street between Tennessee and Georgia streets and east on Virginia Street, sports elaborate homes built by prominent citizens between 1830 and 1880. A highlight here is the **Brokaw-McDougall House,** in front of Leon High School at the eastern end of Virginia Street; built in 1856, it's now home to the Historic Tallahassee Preservation Board.

MUSEUMS & ART GALLERIES

✪ **Black Archives Research Center and Museum.** On the Florida A&M University campus, at Martin Luther King, Jr., Blvd. and Gamble St. ☎ **904/599-3020.** Free admission. Mon–Fri 9am–4pm. Closed major holidays. Visitor parking permits available at the security office.

Housed in the columned library built by Andrew Carnegie, this fascinating research center and museum displays one of the nation's most extensive collections of African-American artifacts as well as such treasures as the 500-piece Ethiopian cross collection. The archives contain one of the world's largest collections on African-American history. Visitors here can listen to tapes of gospel music and of elderly people reminiscing about the past. Florida Agricultural and Mechanical University (FAMU) was founded in 1887, primarily as a black institution. Today it's acclaimed for its business, engineering, and pharmacy schools.

✪ **Knott House Museum ("The House That Rhymes").** 301 E. Park Ave. (at Calhoun St.). ☎ **904/488-3901.** Admission (including a 1-hour tour) $3 adults, $1.50 children 17 and under. Wed–Fri 1–4pm, Sat 10am–4pm.

Adorned by a columned portico, this stately 1843 mansion is furnished with Victorian elegance and boasts the nation's largest collection of 19th-century gilt-framed mirrors. The curiousity here is the rhymes written by Mrs. Knott and attached by satin ribbons to tables, chairs, and lamps. Her verses comment on 19th-century women's issues, plus the social, economic, and political events of the era. The house is in the Park Avenue Historic District, and is listed in the National Register of Historic Places. It's preserved as it looked in 1928, when the Knott Family left it and all its contents to the city.

Florida State University Museum of Fine Arts. 250 Fine Arts Building, at Copeland and Call sts. on the FSU Campus. ☎ **904/644-6836.** Free admission. Mon–Fri 10am–4pm, Sat–Sun 1–4pm.

A permanent art collection here features 16th-century Dutch paintings, 20th-century American paintings, Japanese prints, pre-Columbian artifacts, and much more. Touring exhibits are displayed every few weeks.

Foster Tanner Fine Arts Gallery. Florida A&M University, off Martin Luther King, Jr., Blvd. (between Osceola and Gamble sts.). ☎ **904/599-3161.** Free admission. Mon–Fri 9am–5pm.

The focus in this gallery is on works by African-American artists, with a wide variety of paintings, sculptures, and more. Exhibits change monthly, with local, national, and international artists in the limelight.

Lemoyne Art Gallery. 125 N. Gadsden St. (between Park Ave. and Call St.). ☎ **904/222-8800.** Free admission. Tues–Sat 10am–5pm, Sun 1–5pm.

This restored 1852 antebellum home is listed on the National Register of Historic Places and is a lovely setting for fine art. Known as the Meginnis-Monroe House, the gallery itself is named in honor of Jacques LeMoyne, a member of a French expedition to Florida in 1564 and the first artist known to have visited North America. He was commissioned to depict the natives' dwellings and map the seacoast. Exhibits include local artists, sculpture, pottery, and photography. The gardens are spectacular during the Christmas holiday season. Check for the current schedule of concerts and art exhibits.

Museum of Florida History. In the R. A. Gray Building, 500 S. Bronough St. (at Pensacola St.). ☎ **904/488-1484.** Free admission. Mon–Fri 9am–4:30pm, Sat 10am–4:30pm, Sun and holidays noon–4:30pm. Closed Thanksgiving and Christmas Day.

The official state history museum, this institution takes visitors back 12,000 years, beginning with the first Native Americans to live in Florida. You're greeted by an 11-foot-tall mastodon, once hunted by those first inhabitants. Ancient artifacts are exhibited, plus such relics from Florida's past as 16th- and 17th-century sunken Spanish galleon treasures and a reconstructed steamboat. Inquire about guided tours and special exhibits. There's an interesting museum gift shop.

Tallahassee Museum of History and Natural Science. 3945 Museum Dr. (off Lake Bradford Rd.). ☎ **904/576-1636.** Admission $6 adults, $5.50 senior citizens, $4 children 4–15, free for children 3 and under. Mon–Sat 9am–5pm, Sun 12:30–5pm.

There's something of interest here for all ages. Along a winding trail through a 55-acre natural woodland habitat, the wildlife includes alligators, red wolves, Florida panthers, and a variety of other animals. Farm animals roam around the re-creation of an 1880s farm where special programs demonstrate butter churning, blacksmithing, sheep shearing, spinning, weaving, and quilt making. Other exhibits feature science and history displays, a restored one-room schoolhouse, and an old church. Bellevue, the restored plantation home of Princess Murat, was moved here in 1967, a century after her death, and is on the National Register of Historic Places. Special events are always scheduled, from arts-and-crafts shows to wildflower walks. Picnic facilities, a snack bar, and a gift shop are on the premises.

ARCHEOLOGICAL SITES

De Soto Archeological and Historical Site. 1022 DeSoto Park Dr. (off Lafayette St.). ☎ **904/922-6007.** Free admission. Grounds, daily 8am–5pm. Mansion closed to public.

During the winter of 1539 Spanish conquistador Hernando de Soto, his troops and friars, set up an encampment here before continuing their ill-fated search for gold. It's believed that these friars celebrated the first Christmas mass in North America. An archeologist searching for Spanish mission ruins discovered the de Soto encampment site in 1986. Rare copper coins and armor fragments have been unearthed. Former Gov. John Martin had no idea de Soto had camped here when he built his English hunting lodge–style mansion at the site in the 1930s. A colorful living-history time trail with exhibits and speakers is presented in January. Call for dates and program schedules.

Lake Jackson Mounds State Archeological Site. 3600 Indian Mounds Rd. (off N. Monroe St. north of I-10). ☎ **904/922-6007.** Free admission. Daily 8am–sundown.

Artifacts discovered on this 18-acre excavation have revealed that native tribes settled on the shores of Lake Jackson (still one of the nation's best bass-fishing spots) centuries ago. A ceremonial complex flourished here around A.D. 1200, which includes six earth temple mounds and a burial mound. Part of the village and plaza area and two of the largest mounds are within the state site. The largest mound is 36 feet high with a base that measures 278 by 312 feet.

San Luis Archeological and Historic Site. 2020 Mission Rd. (between W. Tennessee St. and Tharpe St.). ☎ **904/487-3711.** Free admission. Mon–Fri 9am–4:30pm, Sat 10am–4:30pm, Sun noon–4:30pm. Public tours Mon–Fri at noon, Sat at 11am and 3pm. Closed Thanksgiving and Christmas Day. From downtown, take Tennessee Street (U.S. 90) west, turn right on White Drive, and right again on Misson Road to the entrance.

A Spanish Franciscan mission was set up in 1656 on this hilltop, a principal village of the Apalachee tribes. From then until 1704 it served as the capital of a chain of Spanish missions in Northwest Florida. The mission complex included a tribal council house, a Franciscan church, a Spanish fort, and residential areas. Although there are no visible remains from this period, the first of two 17th-century reconstructions was completed in 1996. Interpretive displays are located across the 60-acre site and inside the visitor center. Call for information about archeological excavations and living-history programs.

THE CANOPY ROADS

Graced by canopies of Spanish moss–draped live oaks and colorful flowers, the St. Augustine, Miccousukee, Meridian, Old Bainbridge, and Centerville roads are the five official Canopy Roads leading out of Tallahassee. Driving is slow on these winding, two-lane country roads, some canopied for as much as 20 miles. Take along a picnic lunch, since there are few places to eat along these tranquil byways.

The visitor information center in the New Capitol (see "Essentials," above) provides a useful driving guide map of the Canopy Roads and Leon County's country lanes. Here are highlights of each Canopy Road:

Old Bainbridge Road is considered the most scenic Canopy Road. It leads to the Lake Jackson Mounds State Archeological Site in the northwest suburbs. About 15 miles north of Tallahassee stands Havana, an old-fashioned typical southern town known for a plethora of quality antiques shops (see "Easy Excursions from Tallahassee," below).

Centerville Road was used by six-mule-team wagons to transport cotton to St. Marks near the gulf, where it was loaded onto schooners. Plantation owners planted the majestic live oaks around 1800 to shade the mules. Bradley's Country Store is on Centerville Road (see "Shopping," below).

Meridian Road was built in 1825 according to a federal survey and is the only straight Canopy Road. The mule-drawn wagons made deep ruts, however, and the packed clay on both sides created walls, now covered by lichen.

Miccousukee Road was an early Native American trail leading 30 miles northeast to the plantation town of Thomasville, Georgia, which has many beautiful antebellum homes as well as the All American Rose Test Gardens, where 2,000 roses bloom April to November.

St. Augustine Road dates back to early Native American tribes and the subsequent Spanish friars, who established missions here in the mid-16th century. All the area's 20 missions were destroyed by the end of the 17th century, victims of battles between Spain and England.

PARKS & NATURE PRESERVES

In 1923 New York financier Alfred B. Maclay and his wife, Louise, began planting the floral wonderland of **Maclay State Gardens,** around their winter home on Lake Hall, 3540 Thomasville Rd. (U.S. 319), north of I-10 (☎ **904/487-4556**). After her husband's death in 1944, Louise Maclay continued his dream of an ornamental garden to delight the public. In 1953 the land was bequeathed to the state of Florida. The more than 300 acres of flowers feature at least 200 varieties. The beautifully restored home contains a camellia information center, and the surrounding park offers nature trails, canoe rentals, boating, picnicking, swimming, and fishing. The high blooming season is January to April, with the peak about mid-March. Admission to the park is $3.25 per vehicle with up to eight passengers, $1 for pedestrians and cyclists. Admission to the gardens during the blooming season, from January to April, is $3 for adults, $1.50 for children 11 and under. The gardens are free from May to December. The park is open daily from 8am to sunset. The gardens are open daily from 9am to 5pm. The Maclay House is open from January to April, daily from 9am to 5pm.

OUTDOOR ACTIVITIES & SPECTATOR SPORTS

BICYCLING & IN-LINE SKATING The 16-mile **Tallahassee–St. Marks Historic Railroad State Trail** is the city's most popular bike route. Constructed with the financial assistance of wealthy Panhandle cotton-plantation owners and merchants, this was Florida's oldest railroad, functioning from 1837 to 1984. In recent years the tracks were removed and 16 miles of the historic trail were improved for joggers, hikers, bicyclists, and horseback riders. A paved parking lot is at the north entrance, on Woodville Highway (Fla. 363) just south of SE Capital Circle. Use of the trail is free.

Rental bikes and in-line skates are available at the north entrance from **St. Marks Trail Bikes & Blades** (☎ **904/656-0001**). Bike-rental rates are $9 for 2 hours, $16 for 4 hours, and various rates for three to five bikes' rental for families and groups. Guide maps and refreshments are also on hand. The shop is open Monday to Friday from noon to dark and on Saturday and Sunday from 9am to 5pm.

BOATING & CANOEING The **FSU Seminole Reservation** on Lake Bradford (☎ **904/644-5730**), one of the countless lakes in this area, rents boats and canoes.

Among the nearby river recreation areas with boat and canoe rentals are **Three Rivers State Recreation Area** (☎ 904/482-9006), the **Ochlockonee River** in Ochlockonee River State Park (☎ 904/962-2771), and the **St. Marks River** in the St. Marks National Wildlife Refuge (☎ 904/925-6121). All are within a 20- to 50-mile drive from Tallahassee. The nearby **Apalachicola National Forest** has an extensive system of canoe trails. Stop at the Wakulla Area Ranger Station, on U.S. 319 in Crawford-ville (☎ 904/926-3561), for maps of the trails.

FISHING   Bass abound in Tallahassee-area lakes, with record-size catches having been made in Lake Jackson and Lake Talquin. For guides, contact **Lake Talquin Tours** (☎ 904/877-3198) or **Paul Tyre's Guide Service** (☎ 904/599-5826). Lake Talquin Tours also provides pontoon cruises on this lovely lake west of Tallahassee.

In the nearby gulf, deep-sea fishing excursions are available for grouper, snapper, and king mackerel. Check with the marinas at **Shell Point, Alligator Point,** and **Panacea** (also known as "The Blue Crab Capital of the World").

GOLF & TENNIS   Play golf at outstanding Hilaman Park, 2731 Blair Stone Dr., where the **Hilaman Park Municipal Golf Course** (☎ 904/891-3935 for informa-tion and fees) features a par-72 18 holes, a driving range, racquetball and squash courts, and a swimming pool. Rental equipment is at the club, and there's a restau-rant, too. The park also includes the **Jake Gaither Municipal Golf Course,** at Bragg and Pasco streets, with a 9-hole, par-35 fairway and a pro shop (☎ 904/891-3942). The leading golf course is at the **Killearn Country Club and Inn** (☎ 904/893-2186, or 800/476-4101), home of the Sprint Classic. Moss-draped oaks enhance the beautiful 27-hole championship course, which is for members and hotel guests only (see "Where to Stay," below).

Local residents are such avid tennis players that the **Tallahassee Parks & Recre-ation Department,** 4750 N. Meridien Rd., Tallahassee, FL 32312 (☎ 904/891-3920), has a host of courts and programs all over town, including Hilaman Park, mentioned above. Get a complete list from the Visitor Information Center in the New Capitol, or contact the department.

HIKING & NATURE WALKS   In addition to the 16-mile **Tallahassee–St. Marks Historic Railroad State Trail,** there are numerous trails in state parks—the **Florida National Scenic Trail** (☎ 904/488-7326) meanders 110 miles through St. Marks National Wildlife Refuge and the Apalachicola National Forest. On the trail you'll encounter sink holes, the Bradwell Bay Wilderness Area, Confederate salt evaporation ponds, and more. Eventually the trail will be extended to span 1,300 miles across Florida. The Leon Sinks Area of the **Apalachicola National Forest,** on U.S. 319 near the Leon-Wakulla county line, has nature trails and boardwalks that lead from one sink hole (a lake formed when water erodes the underlying limestone) to another. The trails are open daily from 8am to 8pm.

For a pleasant stroll in town, a paved walkway follows the shores of **Lake Ella** on North Monroe Street at Lake Ella Drive.

HUNTING   Hunting is permitted in the **St. Marks National Wildlife Refuge** only with such primitive weapons as cross-bows and muzzle-loading guns, and in the **Apalachicola National Forest** (see Section 4 of this chapter for information).

SPECTATOR SPORTS   Tallahassee succumbs to football frenzy whenever the perennially powerful Seminoles of **Florida State University** take to the gridiron. Hollywood star Burt Reynolds, who played halfback for the 'Noles in 1957, can easily get tickets; the rest of us should call 904/644-1830 well in advance. Even when the Seminoles play on the road, everything except Tallahassee's many sport bars comes to a stop while fans watch the games on TV. The **Florida A&M University** Rattlers are cheered on by the school's high-stepping, world-famous Marching 100 Band. Call 904/599-3230 for FAMU schedules and tickets. Both FSU and FAMU have seasonal basketball, baseball, tennis, and track schedules. Call the numbers above for information.

Ice hockey fans can watch the **Tallahassee Tiger Sharks** compete in the East Coast Hockey League from October to March. Games are played in the Tallahassee–Leon County Civic Center, 505 W. Pensacola St. (☎ **904/222-0400** or 800/322-3602, for schedules and ticket information).

SHOPPING

Bradley's Country Store, about 8 miles north of I-10 on Centerville Road (☎ **904/893-1647**), sells more than 80,000 pounds of homemade sausage per year, both over the counter and from mail orders. Other country-style southern specialties produced and sold at Bradley's are coarse-ground grits, country-milled cornmeal, and specially cured hams. On the National Register of Historic Places, the store is also a sightseeing attraction and everyone is welcome to stop in for a taste of the old-fashioned, friendly atmosphere. Open Monday to Friday from 9am to 6pm and on Saturday from 9am to 5pm.

If you like antiquing, some of Florida's best shopping is in **Havana,** 17 miles north on U.S. 27 (see "Easy Excursions from Tallahassee," below).

WHERE TO STAY

There is no high or low season here, but every hotel and motel for miles around is completely booked during FSU and FAMU football weekends from September to November. Reserve well in advance or you may have to stay 60 miles or more from the city. Rates go up on football weekends as well. For the schedules, call FSU or FAMU (see "Spectator Sports" under "Outdoor Activities & Spectator Sports," above).

Leon County adds 1% to the 6% statewide sales tax, making the local tax 7%, and adds an extra 3% to all hotel and campground bills. (See "Where to Stay," in Section 1 of this chapter for what the price categories mean.)

Except for special weekends, rates at Tallahassee's hotels and motels are less than you'll pay at the beaches. Accordingly, the inexpensive establishments here offer much better quality accommodation than you'll find for the same price at the resort areas.

Most hotels are concentrated in three areas: downtown Tallahassee, north of downtown along North Monroe Street at Exit 29 off I-10, and along Apalachee Parkway east of downtown. I have organized them below in this fashion.

The area along North Monroe Street at I-10 has several chain motels. At $36 a night, the least expensive double rooms are at **Motel 6,** 2738 N. Monroe St. (☎ **904/386-7878,** or 800/466-8356), a four-story building with 101 rooms and a pool. Also here are a **Comfort Inn,** 2720 Graves Rd. (☎ **904/562-7200** or 800/228-5150); a **Days Inn,** 2800 N. Monroe St. (☎ **904/385-0136** or 800/325-2525); an **Econo Lodge,** 2681 N. Monroe St. (☎ **904/385-6155** or 800/553-2666); a **Hampton Inn,** 3210 N. Monroe St. (☎ **904/562-4300** or 800/HAMPTON); a **Holiday Inn,** 2714 Graves Rd. (☎ **904/562-2000** or 800/465-4329); a **La Quinta Inn,** 2905 N. Monroe St. (☎ **904/385-7172** or 800/531-5900); and a **Super 8,** 2702 N. Monroe St. (☎ **904/386-8818** or 800/800-8000).

Apalachee Parkway also has a number of chain establishments. The least expensive choice is **Motel 6,** 1027 Apalachee Pkwy. (☎ **904/877-6171** or 800/466-8356), at $34 a night for a double. This two-story, glass-and-steel motel sports a small pool in an attractive courtyard. Others along the parkway are the **Best Western Pride Inn & Suites,** 2016 Apalachee Pkwy. (☎ **904/656-6312** or 800/827-7390); a **Days Inn,** 722 Apalachee Pkwy. (☎ **904/224-2181** or 800/235-2525); a **La Quinta Inn,** 2850 Apalachee Pkwy. (☎ **904/878-5099** or 800/531-5900); and a **Ramada Inn,** 1355 Apalachee Pkwy. (☎ **904/877-3171** or 800/721-9890).

DOWNTOWN
Doubles for Less than $60
Holiday Inn University Center Downtown. 316 W. Tennessee St., Tallahassee, FL 32301. ☎ **904/222-8000,** or 800/465-4329. Fax 904/222-8113. 174 rms. A/C TV TEL. $49–$79 double. AE, DC, DISC, MC, V.

Distinguished by its cylindrical 12-story design, this hotel is convenient to FSU, the State Capitol, and the Governor's Mansion. All guest rooms overlook the city panorama or the rolling hills. There's a private lounge for guests of the higher-priced concierge level. An International House of Pancakes sits at street level, and the lobby lounge is especially lively during football season. There's an outdoor pool, and guests get golfing privileges.

Doubles for Less than $80
Holiday Inn Capitol Plaza. 101 S. Adams St., Tallahassee, FL 32301. ☎ **904/224-5000** or 800/465-4329. Fax 904/222-9216. 244 rms, 8 suites. A/C TV TEL. $70–$130 double; $175–$300 suite. AE, DC, DISC, MC, V.

This 16-story hotel—one of the tallest buildings in town—is such a favorite with politicians and lobbyists that it's usually booked solid during legislative sessions from March to May. A block from the Capitol Building at Park Avenue, it's notable for spacious, attractive guest rooms and beautiful public rooms. The Cafe in the Court is a favorite rendezvous for power breakfasts, lunches, and dinners. When the political celebrities aren't here, they're in Fat Tuesday's Sports Bar. Services here include room service, Gold's Gym and golf privileges, same-day laundry service, and complimentary airport transportation. There's an outdoor swimming pool, a gift shop, a parking garage, and convention facilities.

Riedel House Bed & Breakfast. 1412 Fairway Dr., Tallahassee, FL 32301. ☎ **904/222-8569.** 3 rms, 2 with bath. A/C. $75 double with or without bath. Rates include continental breakfast. No credit cards.

Surrounded by majestic live oaks, pines, and magnolias, this white-brick, Federal-style, two-story home was built in 1937 for the Cary D. Landis family (he was a former Florida attorney general). The innkeeper is talented artist and art teacher Carolyn Riedel. A spiral staircase leads from the beautiful foyer to the upstairs art gallery and spacious the guest rooms, each adorned with period furniture and antiques. Located in the prestigious Capitol Country Club area, the Riedel House is just minutes away from Florida State University and the Capitol, and within walking distance of public tennis courts and the club's golf course.

NORTH OF DOWNTOWN
Doubles for Less than $60
Shoney's Inn. 2801 N. Monroe St., Tallahassee, FL 32303. ☎ **904/386-8286** or 800/222-2222. Fax 904/422-1074. 112 rms, 26 suites. A/C TV TEL. $58–$73 double; $80–$90 townhouse suite; $120 Jacuzzi suite. Rates include continental breakfast. AE, DC, DISC, MC, V.

This Mediterranean-style hotel is built around a courtyard with moss-draped trees and a pool. A variety of accommodations are available here, including standard guest rooms, town house suites, and bilevel suites with Jacuzzis. A Shoney's Restaurant is next door, and shopping and theaters are within walking distance. Restaurants are close by.

Doubles for Less than $80

Cabot Lodge North. 2735 N. Monroe St., Tallahassee, FL 32303. ☎ **904/386-8880** or 800/223-1964. Fax 904/386-4254. 160 rms. A/C TV TEL. $65–$71 double. Rates include continental breakfast. AE, DC, DISC, MC, V.

A clapboard plantation-style house with a tin roof and a wraparound porch provides country charm to distinguish this friendly motel from its nearby competitors. Guests can sit and relax in southern fashion on either straight-back rockers on the screened part of the porch or on comfy sofas and easy chairs by the living room fireplace. Although the guest rooms in the two-story motel buildings out back don't hold up their end of the atmosphere factor, they're still quite satisfactory at these rates, and they give quick access to the outdoor swimming pool. Guests can graze at a continental breakfast buffet, drink coffee all day, and partake of free cocktails between 5:30 and 7:30pm daily.

Killearn Country Club and Inn. 100 Tyron Circle, Tallahassee, FL 32308. ☎ **904/893-2186.** Fax 904/668-7637. 39 rms and suites. A/C TV TEL. $78 double; $110 suite. Golf packages available. AE, DISC, MC, V.

Located in upscale Killearn Estates between Thomasville and Centerville roads north of I-10, this country club is home to Tallahassee's leading links. Visiting golfers can rent attractive rooms and suites with sitting areas and dressing rooms. Some have a wet bar. Each unit is individually decorated and has a balcony overlooking the woodland-bordered golf course. The club also offers four lighted hard and four soft tennis courts, plus racquetball and handball courts. The swimming pool is Olympic size, and there's an exercise facility and miles of surrounding roads for jogging. Moderate prices prevail in the classy, beamed-ceiling Oak View restaurant. This is one of the region's best golf resort bargains, but since its location is isolated, you'll need a car to do your sightseeing.

Ramada Inn Tallahassee. 2900 N. Monroe St., Tallahassee, FL 32303. ☎ **904/386-1027** or 800/228-2828. Fax 904/422-1025. 198 rms. A/C TV TEL. $75–$85 double. Two children 17 and under stay free with existing bed space in parents' room. Packages available. AE, DC, DISC, MC, V.

On 13 landscaped acres just south of I-10, this brick structure has the appearance of a modern suburban office park. A courtyard swimming pool and a jogging trail help keep guests fit. The Monroe Street Grill, off a tropically decorated lobby bar with a waterfall, serves breakfast, lunch, and dinner. Dooley's Down Under becomes the Comedy Zone on weekends (see "Tallahassee After Dark," below). For the executive, there's a business center and conference rooms. The rooms here are either in a tower building or in motel blocks; the choice quarters in the motel buildings face the courtyard, not the parking lot.

ON APALACHEE PARKWAY

Doubles for Less than $80

✪ **Courtyard by Marriott.** 1018 Apalachee Pkwy., Tallahassee, FL 32301. ☎ **904/222-8822** or 800/321-2211. Fax 904/561-0354. 154 rms. A/C TV TEL. $89 double Sun–Thurs, $59 Fri–Sat. AE, DC, DISC, MC, V.

If you'll be in a town over Friday and Saturday nights, the weekend rates are very good value at this comfortable modern hotel just a mile east of the capital. About half the rooms here face a landscaped courtyard with a swimming pool and gazebo; the others face parking lots. All have sofas or easy chairs, plus features like long telephone cords, voice mail, and hand-basin faucets dispensing piping-hot water for tea and instant coffee (which are supplied). Other facilities include an exercise room and indoor spa pool. The marble-floored lobby features a lounge with fireplace and a dining area open for breakfast only (the extensive breakfast buffet ranges from $4 to $6). An Olive Garden Italian and Bennigan's restaurants are across Apalachee Parkway, and other restaurants are nearby. The Parkway Shopping Center is also across the parkway.

Quality Inn. 2020 Apalachee Pkwy., Tallahassee, FL 32301. ☎ **904/877-4437** or 800/253-4787. Fax 904/878-9964. 100 rms, 13 suites. A/C TV TEL. $62–$67 double; $67–$72 suite. Rates include continental breakfast. AE, DC, DISC, MC, V.

Although the exterior is thoroughly contemporary, there's an English country atmosphere inside this establishment's classy, marble-lined lobby and spacious guest rooms. Guests can partake of a free wine bar from 5 to 7pm Monday to Thursday. There's a pool on the premises, and guests receive passes to the nearby YMCA. Several fast-food and family-style restaurants are within a short walk.

Camping

The **Tallahassee RV Park,** 6504 Mahan Dr. (☎ **904/878-7641**), features 66 RV campsites with full hookups in a scenic setting of rolling hills and a fishing lake. It's on U.S. 90 some 7 miles east of the capitol. Sites cost $21 a night.

WHERE TO EAT

Numerous budget-priced fast-food and family chain restaurants lie along Apalachee Parkway and North Monroe Street. For the biggest steaks around, Tallahasseeans love to dine at the charming Nicholson Farmhouse near Havana (see "Easy Excursions from Tallahassee," below).

Downtown

Meals for Less than $7

Andrew's Adams Street Cafe. In Adams Street Commons, 228 S. Adams St. ☎ **904/222-3444.** Reservations not accepted. Sandwiches and salads $3–$5. MC, V. Mon–Fri 11:30am–2pm. DELI.

Enjoy dining on bentwood cafe chairs amid a decor of brass and wood-paneled walls at this cafeteria-style establishment. An array of soups, salads, made-to-order sandwiches, barbecued chicken, and thick, juicy charcoal-grilled hamburgers are offered. Delightful in warm weather is an outdoor dining area directly on the Adams Street Commons.

Bahn Thai. 1319 S. Monroe St. (near Oakland Ave.). ☎ **904/224-4765.** Reservations accepted. Main courses $5–$15. DISC, MC, V. Mon–Thurs 11am–2:30pm and 5–10pm, Fri 11am–2:30pm and 5–10:30pm, Sat 5–10:30pm, Sun 5–9:30pm. THAI/CANTONESE.

Lamoi (Sue) Snyder and progeny have been serving the spicy cuisine of her native Thailand at this storefront since 1979. In deference to local Floridians, who may never have sampled anything spicier than cheese grits, much of her menu is devoted to mild Cantonese-style Chinese dishes. More sophisticated diners flock here to order such authentic tongue-burners as yon voon-sen, a combination of shrimp, chicken, bean threads, onions, lemongrass, ground peanuts, and the obligatory chili peppers. Sue's specialty, however, is her deliciously sweet, ginger-hinted version of Penang curry; you can ask her to turn down the heat in her other Thai dishes.

Meals for Less than $15

۞ Chez Pierre. 115 N. Adams St. (between Park Ave. and Call St.). ☎ **904/222-0936.** Reservations recommended. Main courses $11–$18. MC, V. Mon 11am–2:30pm, Tues–Sat 11am–2:30pm and 6–9:30pm. FRENCH.

You become an instant Francophile at this chic restaurant featuring traditional French specialties such as garlic-buttered escargots, salade niçoise, and crusty French bread. Seafood lovers recommend crêpes St-Jacques. Roast duck and veal dishes are also featured. French table wines are moderately priced, and California house wines are also served. Cheese and pastry trays brought to your table present irresistible delights which can be purchased separately at the deli case. Live music accompanies dining on Friday and Saturday night. Chez Pierre is a no-smoking establishment.

NORTH OF DOWNTOWN

Meals for Less than $7

Food Glorious Food. In the Betton Place Shops, Bradford Rd. at Thomasville Rd. ☎ **904/224-9974.** Reservations not required. $3.50–$9.50. AE, MC, V. Mon–Sat 11am–8pm. AMERICAN/INTERNATIONAL.

Very unusual and very healthy sandwiches, salads, and pastas have made this deli/café the talk of the town. Items displayed in a cold case change daily and could include such mouth-waterers as Tijuana lasagne, a tasty dish of layered baked polenta with piquantly spiced chicken, tomato-chili sauce, and a topping of Monterey Jack cheese. There's always a daily quiche and plenty of desserts featuring tempting pastries and cookies. Take-out food can also be ordered. Dine at a few tables inside or, in good weather, on the outside courtyard.

Meals for Less than $10

Barnacle Bill's Seafood Restaurant. 1830 N. Monroe St. (north of Tharpe St.). ☎ **904/385-8734.** Reservations recommended. Main courses $8–$18 (most $8–$10). AE, MC, V. Sun–Thurs 11am–11pm, Fri–Sat 11am–midnight. SEAFOOD.

There's always plenty of action at this noisy, very casual establishment with sports TVs over an enormous tile-topped raw bar in the middle of the room. Freshly shucked Apalachicola oysters are the feature at the bar, but the menu offers a variety of seafood to please the palates of the singles, couples, and families who flock to the tables here. A winner is a broiled combination of a dozen oysters, a dozen shrimp, a dozen scallops, and 6 ounces of fresh fish. Skillet dishes offer shrimp, oysters, or scallops sautéed with keilbasa, which gives everything a smoked flavor, or you can order the real thing: mahi mahi or amberjack smoked on the premises. The cooking here is simple, but the ingredients are the freshest available. During summer, guests can sit at outdoor tables under a lean-to tent. Bands play in the Half Shell Lounge every weekend.

Meals for Less than $15

۞ Anthony's. In the Betton Place Shops, Bradford Rd. at Thomasville Rd. ☎ **904/224-1447.** Reservations recommended. Main courses $10–$16. AE, MC, V. Mon–Thurs 5:30–10pm, Fri–Sat 5:30–10pm, Sun 5:30–9pm. ITALIAN.

Locals come to see and be seen at Dick Anthony's friendly and comfortable trattoria. Among his specialties are pesce Venezia—spinach fettuccine tossed in a cream sauce with scallops, crabmeat, and fish. Chicken piccata and chicken San Marino are also favorites, as are Dick's thick, juicy steaks. A wall-size wine cupboard features choices from Italy and the United States by the bottle or glass. Espresso pie leads the dessert menu.

The Melting Pot. 1832 N. Monroe St. (north of Tharpe St. behind Barnacle Bill's Seafood Emporium). ☎ **904/386-7440.** Reservations recommended. Main courses $9–$16.50. AE, DISC, MC, V. Sun–Thurs 6–10:30pm, Fri–Sat 6–11:30pm. SWISS.

A romantic atmosphere prevails in this dimly lit basement, especially popular with couples enjoying the beef or seafood fondue for two: House rules require anyone who inadvertently drops food into the pot to kiss the person sitting next to him or her. The bubbling hot cheese fondue with chunks of French bread for dipping is always a favorite. Chocoholics can get their fix by dipping fresh strawberries into a rich chocolate fondue.

✪ **Silver Slipper.** 531 Scotty's Lane (1 block south of the Tallahassee Mall, behind Scotty's Hardware). ☎ **904/386-9366.** Reservations recommended. Main courses $10–$30. AE, DC, DISC, MC, V. Mon–Sat 5–11pm. STEAK/SEAFOOD.

The oldest family-operated restaurant in Florida, the Silver Slipper has served thick, tender, juicy Black Angus steaks to Presidents John F. Kennedy, Lyndon Johnson, Jimmy Carter, Ronald Reagan, and George Bush. From the award-winning menu you can also select seafood, lamb, veal, and quail dishes. A dozen bacon-wrapped big shrimp or bits of Black Angus beef are meal-size appetizers. Featuring live entertainment Tuesday to Saturday, the cocktail lounge is a favorite haunt of politicians and lobbyists; it's open until midnight Monday to Thursday, until 2am on Friday and Saturday. Private, curtained booths are available in the dining room.

ON APALACHEE PARKWAY
Meals for Less than $10

Lucy Ho's Bamboo Garden and Furusato Japanese Cuisine. 2814 Apalachee Pkwy. ☎ **904/878-3366.** Reservations accepted. Main courses $7–$18. AE, DC, MC, V. Mon–Thurs 11:30am–10pm, Fri 11:30am–11pm, Sat 5–11pm, Sun noon–10pm. CHINESE/JAPANESE.

A popular rendezvous for years, this establishment actually is two restaurants in one. You enter through an authentic sushi bar and pass a Japanese-style hibachi room next door (that's the Furusato part). The rear Bamboo Garden is traditional Chinese, with gilt dragons and carved mahogany screens. Although there are separate Japanese and Chinese menus, you can order from either regardless of where you sit. Choosing from the extensive Chinese card, I opted for garlic shrimp and Cantonese beef and broccoli. The shrimp proved to be marvelously spicy, and the exceptionally tender beef strips were surrounded by a surprisingly good brown sauce laced with crushed fresh ginger. The luncheon buffet here is a great Chinese-style smörgåsbord of Cantonese and Szechuan choices. There's karaoke in the cocktail lounge on Thursday, Friday, and Saturday night.

Mom and Dad's Italian Restaurant. 4175 Apalachee Pkwy. (2 miles east of Capital Circle). ☎ **904/877-4518.** Reservations not accepted. Main courses $7–$15.50. AE, DC, DISC, MC, V. Tues–Thurs 5–10pm, Fri–Sat 5–11pm. ITALIAN.

Diane Violante, a native of Abruzzo, Italy, and Gary McLean have been making their own pastas and baking Italian breads at this popular, aroma-filled trattoria since 1963. Diane's specialty is spaghetti a la Bruzzi—a casserole of vermicelli, sautéed mushrooms, and tomato meat sauce topped with mozzarella and parmesan cheeses. Diane, Gary, and their son, Gene, ensure that all plates are piled high, making the drive out here well worth the time.

✪ **The Wharf.** 4141 Apalachee Pkwy. (2 miles east of Capital Circle). ☎ **904/656-2332.** Reservations not accepted. Main courses $8–$23 (most $10–$13). AE, DC, DISC, MC, V. Sun–Thurs 4–9pm, Fri–Sat 4–10pm. SEAFOOD.

With or without children, local residents drive out in droves to this rough-hewn establishment evoking the ambience of an Old Florida fish camp. The basic fried, broiled, or blackened dinners here are in the old-time tradition too, with flounder or the day's fresh catch served with their heads off but their bones left very much intact. Accompanied by a salad or cole slaw, potatoes or cheese grits, these filling main courses are a bargain at $8. If you don't feel up to dissecting your catch, you can choose shrimp or scallops for a few dollars more. Several dining rooms—most divided by skinny aquariums built into the walls—make the Wharf seem smaller and more intimate than a 400-seat restaurant. Sweet tooths are satisfied by homemade desserts such as an anything-but-ordinary bread pudding. There's also a kids' menu.

TALLAHASSEE AFTER DARK

THE PERFORMING ARTS With two universities and a sophisticated populace, it's not surprising to find a broad variety of entertainment choices in Tallahassee. Check the "Limelight" section of Friday's *Tallahassee Democrat* for what's playing.

The major venue is the **Tallahassee–Leon County Civic Center,** 505 W. Pensacola St. (☎ **904/222-0400** or 800/322-3602), which features a Broadway play series, a concert series, performances by celebrity pop singers, and much more. Special concerts are presented by the **Tallahassee Symphony Orchestra** at FSU Ruby Diamond Auditorium, College Avenue and Copeland Street (☎ **904/224-0462**). The **FSU Mainstage / School of Theatre,** in the Fine Arts Building, Call and Copeland streets (☎ **904/644-6500**), presents excellent productions from classic dramas to comedies. The **Tallahassee Little Theatre,** 1861 Thomasville Rd. (☎ **904/224-8474**), is noted for exceptional presentations.

THE CLUB & BAR SCENE As a college town, Tallahassee has numerous pubs and nightclubs with live dance music, not to mention a multitude of sports bars. Barnacle Bill's Seafood Emporium is a good place to pick up copies of the *Break* and other entertainment tabloids with news about what's going on. **Barnacle Bill's** is one of several restaurants featuring entertainment. Others include the **Silver Slipper,** and **Lucy Ho's Bamboo Garden** (see "Where to Eat," above).

For laughs, Dooley's Down Under pub becomes the **Comedy Zone,** a weekend comedy club in the Ramada Inn, 2900 N. Monroe St., at I-10 (☎ **904/386-1027**).

EASY EXCURSIONS FROM TALLAHASSEE
WAKULLA SPRINGS

Located 15 miles south of Tallahassee, the 2,860-acre **Edward Ball Wakulla Springs State Park,** entered just east of the junction of Fla. 61 and Fla. 267 (☎ **904/ 922-3632**), is the location of the world's largest and deepest freshwater spring. Edward Ball, a financier who administered the DuPont estate, turned the springs into a preservation area. Divers have mapped an underwater cave system extending more than 6,000 feet back from the spring's mouth. Wakulla has been known to dispense an amazing 14,325 gallons of water per second at certain times. Mastodon bones, including those of Herman, in Tallahassee's Museum of Florida History, were found in the caves. The 1930s Tarzan movies starring Johnny Weissmuller were filmed here.

A free orientation movie is offered at the park's theater. You can hike or bike along the nature trails, and swimming is allowed, but only in designated areas. It's important to observe swimming rules since alligators are present. Glass-bottom-boat sightseeing and wildlife-observation tours are offered daily, from 9:45am to 5pm during daylight saving time, 9:15am to 4:30pm the rest of the year. They cost $4.50 for adults, half price for children.

Entrance fees to the park are $3.25 per vehicle with up to eight passengers, $1 for pedestrians and bicyclists. The park is open daily from 8am to dusk.

Where to Stay & Eat

Wakulla Springs Lodge. 1 Springs Dr., Wakulla Springs, FL 32305. ☎ **904/224-5950.** Fax 904/561-7251. 27 rms, 1 suite. A/C TV TEL. $55–$85 double; from $250 suite. MC, V.

On the grounds of Edward Ball Wakulla Springs State Park, the lodge is distinctive for its magnificent Spanish architecture and furnishings, featuring rare Spanish tiles, black-granite tables, marble floors, and ceiling beams painted with Florida scenes by a German artist (supposedly Kaiser Wilhelm's court painter). The high-ceilinged guest rooms are simple by today's standards but are beautifully furnished and have marble bathrooms.

You don't have to be a lodge guest to dine in the lovely Ball Room, enhanced by an immense fireplace and arched windows looking onto the springs. Very reasonably priced meals feature southern cuisine. Dining hours are 7:30 to 10am for breakfast, 11:30am to 2pm for lunch, and 6 to 8:30pm for dinner. For snacks and light meals, the coffee shop is open Monday to Friday from 8am to 5pm and on Saturday, Sunday, and holidays from 9am to 5pm (there's a 60-foot-long marble drugstore-style counter for old-fashioned ice-cream sodas).

ST. MARKS AREA

Rich history lives in the area around the little village of **St. Marks,** 18 miles south of the capital at the end of both Fla. 363 and the Tallahassee–St. Marks Historic Railroad State Trail. After marching overland from Tampa Bay in 1528, the Spanish conquistador Panfilo de Narvaez and 300 men arrived at this strategic point at the confluence of the St. Marks and Wakulla rivers near the Gulf of Mexico. Since their only avenue back to Spain was by sea, they built and launched the first ships made by Europeans in the New World. Some 11 years later Hernando de Soto and his 600 men arrived here after following Narvaez's route from Tampa. They marked the harbor entrance by hanging banners in the trees, then moved inland. Two wooden forts were built here, one in 1679 and one in 1718, and a stone version was begun in 1739. The fort shifted among Spanish, British, and Native Americans until Gen. Andrew Jackson took it from the Spanish in 1819.

Parts of the old Spanish bastion wall and Confederate earthworks built during the Civil War are in the **San Marcos de Apalache State Historic Site** (☎ **904/925-6216**), reached by turning right at the end of Fla. 363 in St. Marks and following the paved road. A museum built on the foundation of the old marine hospital holds exhibits and artifacts covering the area's history. The site is open Thursday to Monday from 9am to 5pm; closed New Year's Day, Thanksgiving, and Christmas Day. Admission to the site is free; admission to the museum costs $1, free for children 5 and under.

DeSoto's men marked the harbor entrance in what is now the **St. Marks Lighthouse and National Wildlife Refuge,** P.O. Box 68, St. Marks, FL 32355 (☎ **904/925-6121**). Operated by the U.S. Fish and Wildlife Service, this 65,000-acre preserve occupies much of the coast from the Aucilla River east of St. Marks to the Ochlockonee River west of Panacea, and is home to more species of birds than anyplace else in Florida except the Everglades. The visitor center is off U.S. 98 about 2 miles east of St. Marks (turn south at Newport on Lighthouse Road (County Road 59). Stop there for self-guided-tour maps of the roads and hiking trails through the preserve. Built of limestone blocks 4 feet thick at the base, the 80-foot-tall St. Marks Lighthouse has marked the harbor entrance since 1842. The nearby beach is a popular crabbing spot.

Admission to the refuge is $4 per vehicle. The refuge is open daily from sunrise to sunset; the visitor center, Monday to Friday from 8am to 4:15pm and on Saturday and Sunday from 10am to 5pm (closed all federal holidays). Call or write for information about seasonal tours and hunting.

In 1865, during the final weeks of the Civil War, Federal troops landed at the lighthouse and launched a surprise attack on Tallahassee. An impromptu army of wounded soldiers, old men, and boys as young as 14 was quickly assembled, and this rag-tag bunch fought the Federal regulars for 5 days at what is now the **Natural Bridge State Historic Site.** Surprisingly, they won, and as a result, Tallahassee remained the only Confederate state capital east of the Mississippi never to fall into Yankee hands. The historic site is on County Road 2192 about 6 miles east of Woodville on the St. Marks River halfway between Tallahassee and St. Marks (follow the signs from Fla. 363 and go to the end of the pavement). It's open daily from 8am to sunset, and admission is free. For more information, contact the San Marcos de Apalache State Historic Site (see above).

HAVANA

A trip to Havana, 12 miles northwest of I-10 on U.S. 27, must be considered a shopping expedition, for this little village truly is the antique-ing capital of Florida. Havana used to make its living from shade tobacco, and when that industry went into decline in the 1960s the town went with it. Things turned around about 20 years later, however, when Havana began opening art galleries and antiques, handcraft, and collectible shops. Today these interesting establishments are housed in lovingly restored turn-of-the-century brick buildings along Havana's commercial streets. Just drive into town on Main Street (U.S. 27), turn left on 7th Avenue, find a parking place, and start browsing. You'll have plenty of company on weekends, when Tallahasseeans flock here to add to their collections.

Where to Eat

✪ **Nicholson Farmhouse.** Fla. 12 (3¹/₂ miles west of Havana). ☎ **904/539-5931.** Reservations recommended. Main courses $9–$30. AE, DISC, MC, V. Tues–Sat 4–10pm. STEAKS.

Talk to anyone in Tallahassee about where to dine and you'll invariably be told "Nicholson Farmhouse." This quaint cottage was built in 1828 by Dr. Malcolm Nicholson and is now on the National Register of Historic Places. Longing for a place where he could order a 32-ounce steak, the doctor's great-great-grandson, Paul Nicholson, turned the old house into a restaurant in 1988. His casual, very informal operation has been so successful that he has added two turn-of-the-century farmhouses and made extra dining space of the smokehouse and other outbuildings.

At least 1-inch thick and aged on the premises, Paul's tender steaks are charcoal-grilled to perfection. Grilled chicken breasts, boneless pork chops, shrimp, and fish are also offered. Every meal comes with hearty portions of salad, baked potato, and freshly baked bread, and each table gets a bowl of boiled peanuts as munchies. There's a children's menu.

No alcoholic beverages are served, but you may bring your own wine or spirits. Guests can take mule-drawn-wagon rides around the farm Thursday to Saturday. This is the most popular weekend dining spot in the area, so make reservations well in advance for FSU football and graduation weekends.

14 | The Tampa Bay Area

by Cindy Dupre

The miles of wide, sandy beaches extending throughout Pinellas, Manatee, and Sarasota counties put the Tampa Bay area on the tourist map. They extend the length of the Gulf of Mexico shoreline and include offshore barrier islands, some of which remain pristine and untouched by development. Today the revival of the European travel market and increased air service to the newly renovated Tampa and St. Petersburg–Clearwater international airports have brought new energy to the area.

Though united by a common history and a stretch of beaches, the Tampa Bay area cities and towns are very different from one another. Tampa, the business hub of the Bay Area, is home to Ybor City, an ethnic enclave rich in Spanish and Cuban architecture and tradition, and the 2-year-old Florida Aquarium. Ybor City is fast becoming the next South Beach or Key West with an abundance of affordable nightclubs and cafés lining trendy 7th Avenue. Sports fans can enjoy everything from New York Yankees spring training to a hockey game in the brand-new, state-of-the-art Ice Palace.

The St. Petersburg/Clearwater area offers 28 miles of beaches speckled with small towns just waiting to be explored. Clearwater Beach has the best selection of hotels, especially for active families and couples. North of Clearwater, the off-the-beaten-path Greek village of Tarpon Springs has funky antiques shops, tiny cafés, and a few charming B&Bs. In St. Petersburg you can stroll down the shop-filled Pier, then visit the world's largest collection of works by the Spanish surrealist Salvador Dalí.

Sarasota's upscale Longboat Key is the playground for the very wealthy in the area, while the nearby town of Bradenton offers an alternative to Sarasota's high-rise luxury hotels and pricy cafés. These less expensive motels (especially around Anna Maria Island) are certainly less glamorous, but great on a budget.

Peak season, with its high room rates, lasts from January to April. The busiest time, especially around the beaches from Clearwater to St. Petersburg, is in March when the snowbirds up north get fed up with the cold and flock down to sunny Tampa Bay.

The average room rate is high, but visiting in the off-season (after May 1) is one way to get around steep prices. Sure, Florida can be hot and rainy in the summer, but the tropical downpours are brief, and the many great discount hotel packages often include admission to various Tampa Bay attractions. And, of course, what

What's Special About the Tampa Bay Area

Beaches
- Miles of them, from the fun water-sports activities in the St. Petersburg / Clearwater area to isolated Caladesi Island.
- The Sarasota Keys, 20 miles of barrier-island beaches, running from Longboat and Lido to St. Armands and Siesta keys.
- Anna Maria Island at Bradenton, a $7^{1}/_{2}$-mile stretch of tree-shaded and sandy beaches.

Museums
- Salvador Dalí Museum in St. Petersburg, housing the world's largest collection of works by the Spanish surrealist.
- Ringling Museum Complex in Sarasota, one-time home of circus master John Ringling and now Florida's official state art museum.
- Museum of Science and Industry in Tampa, for a look at a simulated space shuttle operation, ham radio center, or weather station.

Attractions
- Busch Gardens, for thrilling rides and up-close views of 3,000 animals in natural settings.
- The new $84-million Florida Aquarium.
- Lowry Park Zoo, for a glimpse of the endangered manatees.

Activities
- Swimming, sunning, shelling, or shore walking along the strip of sandy white beaches stretching from Tarpon Springs to Sarasota.
- Sailing aboard a ketch, sloop, yacht, or windjammer from St. Petersburg Beach or Clearwater Harbor.
- Jogging, in-line skating, biking, or walking along the Pinellas Trail from St. Petersburg to Tarpon Springs.

could be better on a hot summer's day than your pick of miles of sandy beaches and gulf surf?

SPECIAL EVENTS & FESTIVALS IN THE TAMPA BAY AREA

JANUARY   Lots of Greek food, music, singing and dancing fill the Greek town of Tarpon Springs during the **Epiphany** celebrations in January (☎ 813/937-3540). The day-long Greek Orthodox celebration attracts 40,000 visitors. After a morning service at St. Nicholas Cathedral, crowds roar as the youth of the town dive for the Epiphany cross in Spring Bayou.

FEBRUARY   Tampa's ✪ **Gasparilla Pirate Festival** (☎ 813/272-1939) attracts 400,000 people each February as hundreds of boats fill Hillsborough Bay and up to 700 rowdy "pirates" descend on the city. After the invasion, the pirates parade along Bayshore Boulevard, showering crowds with beads and coins. Musical groups perform at various locations throughout downtown.

Major-league baseball heats up in February, as several teams arrive for **spring training.** The **New York Yankees** just opened a new complex in Tampa in 1996, so they're sure to be around for years to come. Though the locations of other teams are subject to change, in 1996 they were as follows: the **Cincinnati Reds** in Plant City (☎ 813/752-7337 for ticket information), the **Detroit Tigers** in Lakeland

(☎ 941/499-8229), the **Philadelphia Phillies** in Clearwater (☎ 813/442-8496), the **Pittsburgh Pirates** in Bradenton (☎ 941/748-4610), the **St. Louis Cardinals** in St. Petersburg (☎ 314/421-3060 or 813/894-4773), and the **Toronto Blue Jays** in Dunedin (☎ 813/733-0429). With so many teams concentrated in the Greater Tampa Bay area, this is perhaps the best destination for catching training and exhibition games, which extend through March.

MARCH The **Florida Strawberry Festival** (☎ 813/876-1747), held in Plant City the first weekend in March, attracts people from all over the Bay Area and includes daily entertainment by country music's biggest stars. You'll overdose on lots of strawberry shortcake, since Plant City is the "Winter Strawberry Capital of the World."

March also finds Tampa hosting the nation's best riders as they compete in the **Winter Equestrian Festival** at the Bob Thomas Equestrian Center, Florida Expo Park (☎ **813/623-5801**). This event is part of the hunter-jumper horse-show circuit—Princess Anne joined the horsey set one year.

Sarasota's most spectacular and colorful annual event, the **Medieval Fair** (☎ **941/355-5101**), includes knights in shining armor and jesters and jugglers and mimes. Fair maidens in flowing gowns and jesters perform on the grounds of the Ringling Museum. Locals audition to play historically correct parts for Largo's **Renaissance Festival** (☎ 813/586-5423). Enjoy knights jousting for honor, arts and crafts, entertainment, rides, plus medieval food and drink. Both events are held in March.

In late March, Brandenton holds its **Manatee Heritage Week** (☎ **941/749-7162**), a celebration of Manatee County's rich history, including tours of the Gamble Mansion, Cortez Fishing Village, and the Manatee Village Historical park. Enjoy craft demonstrations of weaving, woodworking, and quilting.

APRIL In April, Bradenton residents try to break into the *Guinness Book of World Records* by burying 200,000 eggs in the sand of Coquina Beach in the **World's Largest Easter Egg Hunt** (☎ 941/746-7117). Everybody's welcome to join in.

The entire community of Dunedin celebrates its Scottish heritage each April at the **Highlands Games and Festival** (☎ **813/733-6240**). Since 1966, competitors from throughout the United States and Canada have taken part in Scottish band contests and Highland dancing, piping, and drumming.

JUNE Sample many of the area's finest restaurants when they set up shop in St. Petersburg's Straub Park for the **Taste of Pinellas** (☎ **813/898-7451**). The weekend event, with entertainment, takes place each June.

JULY All of the Tampa Bay cities try to outdo each other with fireworks and celebrations on the **Fourth of July.** St. Petersburg has a day-long gala of entertainment and food, and a giant fireworks display over the waterfront. Clearwater has concerts, arts and crafts shows, food festivals, and a gigantic fireworks display.

OCTOBER The exclusive Colony Beach & Tennis Resort on Sarasota's Longboat Key features some of the culinary world's brightest stars in its **Annual Stone Crab & Seafood Festival** (☎ 941/383-6464). Not to be outdone, the funky little seaside town of Madeira Beach invites more than 100,000 people to town to consume tons of fish, shrimp, crab, and other seafood specialties at the **John's Pass Seafood Festival** (☎ 813/391-7373)—one of the state's largest.

Since 1981 the **Clearwater Jazz Holiday** (☎ 813/461-0011) has featured top-name jazz musicians. Hundreds of visitors sit outside at Coachman Park and enjoy the sounds for free over the course of 4 days and nights in October.

October also sees the **Mailou Art Festival** (☎ **813/272-2466**) in downtown Tampa, where leading American artists are celebrated with special exhibitions, workshops, entertainment, and an outdoor juried art show at the Museum of African-American Art.

Crowds throng Tampa's Ybor City every October 31 for the outrageous **Guavawwen** (☎ 813/248-3712). The Latin-style Halloween celebration begins with the wacky costume parade called the "Mama Guava Stumble." Later, concerts from rock to reggae keep the revelers entertained all night.

NOVEMBER   In November, the **Sarasota French Film Festival** (☎ 941/351-9010) attracts acclaimed French films, directors, and celebrities for premier screenings over the course of a month.

DECEMBER   Artists and craftsmen from all over Florida set up shop on Holmes Beach on Anna Maria Island for the island's annual **Festival** (☎ 941/778-3577) the first weekend in December.

Tampa closes the year out on New Year's Eve with its downtown **First Night** celebration (☎ 813/240-1734) of the arts as hundreds of entertainers perform throughout a 10-square-block area.

1 Tampa

200 miles SW of Jacksonville, 254 miles NW of Miami, 63 miles N of Sarasota

Tampa is a great place to use as a home base when exploring Florida's west coast. Travel 20 miles west and you're walking along the wide sandy beaches of Pinellas County on the Gulf of Mexico. Heading south brings you to beautiful upscale Sarasota. Travel 80 miles east and you're in the heart of Orlando's tourist attractions.

Not that Tampa itself doesn't have plenty to keep you busy. Busch Gardens continues to be the number one tourist attraction. It's expensive, but you really do get your money's worth. Call ahead about special promotions and reduced admissions—sometimes just presenting a can of Coke or a local coupon will land you up to $10 off the admission charge.

The biggest new attraction, opened in the spring of 1996, is the New York Yankees' spring-training complex on a 31-acre site across from Tampa Stadium. The $30-million project will help Tampa Bay become the baseball capital of the country, since 10 teams already play in the West Central Florida area.

In October 1996 the Tampa Bay Lightning National Hockey League franchise was slated to unveil its new $153-million home in downtown. The Ice Palace Arena is a 660,000-square-foot palace of glass that will seat visitors for hockey, basketball, and center-stage events like the circus, ice shows, and major concerts.

At press time, football fans were still waiting to hear the fate of the Buccaneers. Businessman Malcom Glazer bought the team for a record $192 million, but was threatening to move it out of Tampa if the city didn't build the Bucs a new stadium. Locals feel they can't afford the new stadium, but a recent study suggests that the franchise brings $84 million to the area annually, so losing the team might be even harder to afford.

Tampa isn't just for sports fans, though. The Florida Aquarium has been a definite "wow" and much applauded since it opened in March 1995. You can see over 5,300 animals and plants representing 600 species native to Florida at the Garrison Seaport Center. Attendence has not been as high as hoped, a problem not helped by the fact that the admission prices are some of the highest in the country, and that there's little else in the downtown waterfront location to attract visitors. The Aquarium is a sight to see, however, so watch for special holiday and anniversary promotions (in March) when the rates come down.

Tampa & St. Petersburg

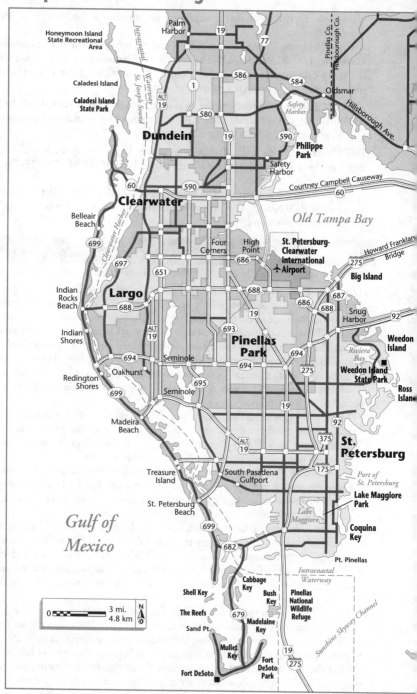

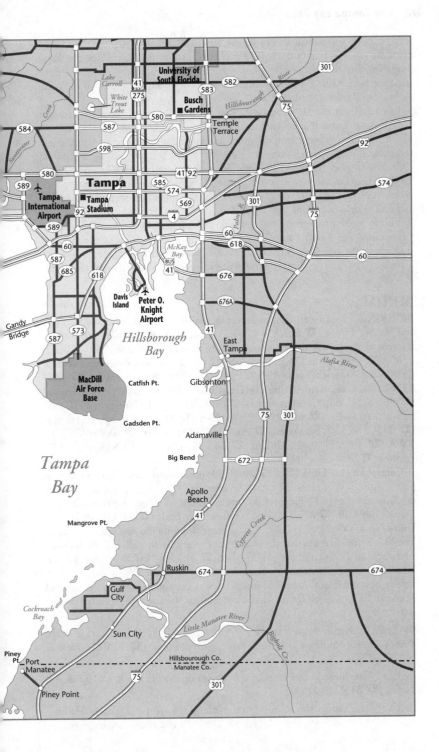

Visitors to Tampa will also enjoy the Tampa Museum of Art, which recently opened a vast new beautiful sculpture garden facing downtown. Strolling the shopping district of the upscale Hyde Park residential neighborhood makes for a relaxing afternoon, while the more active can skate or jog along the bay on the wide sidewalk of Bayshore Boulevard.

Just outside the downtown area is the historic Latin Quarter of Ybor City, a former cigar-making district that has been totally rejuvenated and now pulses with Tampa's nightlife scene. Wrought-iron balconies, brick buildings, a string of art galleries, secondhand shops, coffeehouses, and dozens of restaurants and late-night bars and clubs give this neighborhood a unique Bourbon Street– or Key West–type atmosphere. There's music at every corner and anything goes, from dueling pianos to jazz clubs. At press time there were plans to build the district's first country-western bar and grill to be called Spurs.

Visitors looking for entertainment should pick up the local free alternative newspaper called the *Weekly Planet,* distributed at hundreds of restaurants and shops throughout the Bay Area. Also check out the Friday entertainment sections of the *Tampa Tribune* and *St. Petersburg Times* newspapers for additional listings of affordable events.

ESSENTIALS

ARRIVING   By Plane   Tampa International Airport, off Memorial Highway and Fla. 60, Tampa (☎ **813/870-8700**), 5 miles northwest of downtown Tampa, is served by most major airlines, including **Air Canada** (☎ 800/268-7240 in Canada or 800/776-3000 in the U.S.), **Air South** (☎ 800/247-7688), **American** (☎ 800/433-7300), **America Trans Air** (☎ 800/225-2995), **America West** (☎ 800/235-9292), **Canadian Airlines International** (☎ 800/426-7000), **Carnival** (☎ 800/824-7386), **Cayman Airways** (☎ 800/422-9626), **Continental** (☎ 800/525-0280), **Delta** (☎ 800/221-1212), **Kiwi** (☎ 800/538-5494), **Northwest** (☎ 800/225-2525), **Southwest** (☎ 800/435-9792), **SunJet** (☎ 800/4-SUNJET), **TWA** (☎ 800/221-2000), **United** (☎ 800/241-6522), and **USAir** and **USAir Express** (☎ 800/428-4322).

Central Florida Limo (☎ **813/396-3730**) operates van service between the airport and hotels. The fare is $7 to $15 for one or two passengers, depending on the destination (about $11 for most downtown hotels). Taxi service is provided by **Tampa Bay Cab** (☎ 813/251-5555), **Yellow Cab Taxis** (☎ 813/253-0121), and **United Cabs** (☎ 813/253-2424). The average fare from the airport to downtown Tampa is $10 to $12 and the ride takes about 15 minutes. In addition, Hillsborough Area Regional Transit Authority / HARTline (☎ 813/254-HART) operates **bus service** between the airport and downtown on its no. 31 bus. This is not an airport express bus, but a local route that makes stops at the airport between the hours of 6am and 8:15pm. Look for the HARTline bus sign outside each terminal; the fare is $1.

By Train   Amtrak trains from New York and Washington, D.C., arrive at the Tampa Amtrak Station, 601 Nebraska Ave. North, Tampa (☎ **813/221-7600** or 800/872-7245).

By Bus   Greyhound buses arrive at the carrier's downtown depot at 610 Polk St., Tampa (☎ **813/229-2174**).

**By Car   The Tampa area is linked to the Interstate system and is accessible from I-275, I-75, I-4, U.S. 19, U.S. 41, U.S. 92, U.S. 301, and many state highways.

VISITOR INFORMATION   For brochures and helpful advice about Tampa, as well as hotel reservations, contact the **Tampa / Hillsborough Convention and Visitors Association, Inc. (THCVA),** 111 Madison St., Tampa, FL 33602-4706 (☎ **813/223-2752**, or 800/44-TAMPA). The THCVA also maintains unstaffed information/brochure centers at the Convention Center and at the Shops on Harbour Island.

A good source of on-the-spot information north of downtown in the Busch Gardens area is the **Tampa Bay Visitor Information Center,** 3601 E. Busch Blvd., Tampa, FL 33612 (☎ **813/985-3601**). It offers free brochures about attractions in Tampa and other parts of Florida as well as a sightseeing tour-booking service.

GETTING AROUND   By Car   Although downtown Tampa's Franklin Street area was designed as a pedestrian mall with no cars, it's virtually impossible to see the major sights and enjoy the best restaurants without a car. Most visitors step off a plane and pick up a car right at the airport for use throughout their stay. Five major firms are represented at Tampa International Airport: **Avis** (☎ 813/396-3500), **Budget** (☎ 813/877-6051), **Dollar** (☎ 813/396-3640), **Hertz** (☎ 813/874-3232), and **National** (☎ 813/396-3782). Most of these companies also maintain offices downtown and in other parts of Tampa, such as the Busch Gardens area.

In addition, many smaller firms and local companies have premises just outside the airport. These firms, which provide van pickups to/from the airport and often post the most competitive rates, include **Alamo** (☎ 813/289-4323), **A-Plus** (☎ 813/289-4301), **Enterprise Payless** (☎ 813/289-6554), **Thrifty** (☎ 813/289-4006), and **Value** (☎ 813/289-8870).

By Bus   You really need a car in Tampa Bay, but the **Hillsborough Area Regional Transit / HARTline** (☎ **813/254-HART**) does provide regularly scheduled bus service between downtown Tampa and the suburbs. The service is geared mainly to commuters, although visitors can use it to get downtown from the airport or out to major shopping centers. The fare is $1 for local service, $1.50 for express routes; correct change is required. Many buses start or finish their routes downtown at the Marion Street Transit Parkway, between Tyler and Whiting streets.

By the People Mover   This motorized tram on elevated tracks connects downtown Tampa with Harbour Island. It operates from the third level of the Fort Brooke Parking Garage, on Whiting Street between Franklin Avenue and Florida Street. Travel time is 90 seconds, and service is continuous, Monday to Saturday from 7am to 2am and on Sunday from 8am to 11pm. The fare is 25¢ each way.

By Taxi   Taxis in Tampa don't normally cruise the streets for fares, but they do line up at public loading places, such as hotels, the performing arts center, and bus and train depots. If you need a taxi, call **Tampa Bay Cab** (☎ 813/251-5555), **Yellow Cab** (☎ 813/253-0121), or **United Cab** (☎ 813/253-2424).

By Trolley   The City of Tampa provides a **trolley service** (☎ **813/223-2752** for information) from downtown. It makes frequent stops at the Florida Aquarium and Garrison Seaport Center. Trolleys operate daily (including holidays) from 7:30am to 5:30pm, with a fare of 25¢ per person.

By Water Taxi   The **Tampa Town Water Taxi** (☎ **813/253-3076**) plies the Hillsborough River connecting downtown locations including Harbour Island, the Tampa Convention Center, the Tampa Performing Arts Center, and the University of Tampa / Henry B. Plant Museum. This shuttle ferry operates at half-hour intervals, Monday to Thursday from 2 to 11pm, on Friday from 2pm to 1am, on

Saturday from noon to 1am, and on Sunday from noon to 11pm. Daytime round-trips cost $5, going up to $6 after 8pm.

CITY LAYOUT

Tampa's downtown district is laid out on a grid pattern. **John F. Kennedy Boulevard (Fla. 60)** cuts across the city in an east-west direction. The two major arteries bringing traffic into the downtown area are **I-275,** which skirts the northern edge of the city, and the **Crosstown Expressway,** which extends along the southern rim.

All the streets in the central core of the city are one-way, with the exception of pedestrians-only Franklin Street. From the southern tip of Franklin, you can also board the People Mover, an elevated tram to Harbour Island.

The core of Tampa, the compact **downtown** area, is primarily a business and financial hub, where John F. Kennedy Boulevard (Fla. 60) and Florida Avenue intersect.

While downtown Tampa is virtually dead after 5pm, **Ybor City,** east of downtown, comes alive after dark. This is Tampa's Latin Quarter, settled for more than 100 years by Cuban immigrants. Today it's home to dozens of cool new restaurants, clubs, and shops run by local artists and craftspeople.

South of downtown, small **Harbour Island** is linked by the elevated People Mover to the mainland. It has an elegant hotel and busy marina. Many of the struggling restaurants and shops have closed, but there are plans to revive this little island.

West of downtown, **Hyde Park** is the city's classiest residential neighborhood, the place to see and be seen. Many of its homes are part of a National Register Historic District. The upscale shops and trendy restaurants make this Tampa's "in" spot.

West of Hyde Park, from Tampa International Airport southward, particularly along Westshore Boulevard, lies **West Shore**, a commercial and financial hub with office buildings, business-oriented hotels, and a popular shopping mall.

The **Courtney Campbell Causeway** runs west of the airport, as Kennedy Boulevard (Fla. 60) crosses Old Tampa Bay. It's a small beach strip with several hotels and restaurants. You don't want to be near here at rush hour when commuters turn this area into a parking lot of cars.

North of downtown is a huge area centered on the **Busch Gardens** theme park. Busch Boulevard, which runs east-west, is a busy commercial tourist strip just south of the park entrance where you'll find dozens of restaurants and hotels and lots of inexpensive fast-food joints.

WHAT TO SEE & DO
THEME PARKS & ANIMAL PARKS

Adventure Island. 4545 Bougainvillea Ave. ☎ **813/987-5660,** or 813/987-5000 for information on special discounts. Admission $22.30 adults, $20.15 children 3–9, free for children 2 and under; $2 for lockers (you pay $4, but get $2 back when you leave). Mar–Oct, Mon–Fri 10am–5pm, Sat–Sun 9:30am–6pm; extended hours in summer. Closed Nov–Feb. Take I-275 to Busch Boulevard (Exit 33), go east for 2 miles to 40th Street (McKinley Drive), make a left, and follow the signs.

The prices keep rising, but it's so much fun the kids will talk about this place for years. Before you go, call ahead and ask about special promotions and discount coupons. Bring bathing suits, a towel, and lots of suntan lotion. It can get a little crowded, but the 36-acre outdoor water theme park is perfect for really hot days. Kids and teens especially love the three swimming pools, water slides, and play areas. There's an outdoor café, picnic and sunbathing areas, a games arcade, and a volleyball complex. Returning patrons note: For safety reasons, inner tubes are no longer for sale.

☼ Busch Gardens. 3000 E. Busch Blvd. ☎ **813/987-5171,** or 813/987-5000 for informtion on special discounts. Admission $36.15 adults, $29.75 children 3–9, free for children 2 and under. Daily 9:30am–6pm, with extended hours in summer and holiday periods. Parking $4. Take I-275 northeast of downtown to Busch Boulevard (Exit 33) and go east 2 miles to the entrance on 40th Street (McKinley Drive).

Yes, admission prices are extremely high, but it's worth the splurge for an entire day's entertainment at Tampa Bay's most popular attraction.

Note: You'll always get a discount if you mention that you're an AAA member or a senior citizen. And sometimes you can find coupons at local fast-food restaurants like Wendy's for $6 off admission or at local supermarkets like Winn Dixie for $5 off. A special Coke promotion sometimes offers $10 off and is worth investigating. Call before you arrive and find out what the specials are.

The 335-acre family entertainment park features a unique combination of thrill rides, live entertainment, animal habitats in naturalistic environments, shops, restaurants, and games. Capturing the spirit of turn-of-the-century Africa, the park ranks among the top zoos in the country with nearly 3,400 animals.

Busch Gardens was slated to open Montu, the tallest and largest inverted steel roller coaster in the world, in May 1996 as part of **Egypt,** the park's new, ninth theme area. The area will mirror the country's culture, history, and claims to fame, including a replica of King Tut's tomb. There'll be a sand dig area for kids to discover their own treasures.

Timbuktu is an ancient desert trading center with African craftspeople at work, plus a sandstorm-style ride, boat-swing ride, roller coaster, and electronic games arcade.

Morocco, a walled city with exotic architecture, has Moroccan craft demonstrations, a sultan's tent with snake charmers, and the Marrakesh Theaters.

The **Serengeti Plain** is an open area with more than 500 african animals roaming freely in herds. This 80-acre natural grassy veldt can be viewed from the monorail, Trans-Veldt Railway, or skyride.

Nairobi is home to the Myombe Reserve: The Great Ape Domain, a natural habitat for various types of gorillas and chimpanzees, and a baby animal nursery, as well as a petting zoo, reptile displays, and Nocturnal Mountain, where a simulated environment allows visitors to observe animals that are active in the dark.

Stanleyville, a prototype African village, has a shopping bazaar and live entertainment, as well as two water rides, the Tanganyika Tidal Wave and Stanley Falls.

The Congo features Kumba, the largest steel roller coaster in the southeastern United States, and Claw Island, a display of rare white Bengal tigers in a natural setting, plus white-water-raft rides.

Bird Gardens, the original core of Busch Gardens, offers rich foliage, lagoons, and a free-flight aviary for hundreds of exotic birds including golden and American bald eagles, hawks, owls, and falcons. This area also features **Land of the Dragons,** a new children's adventure area with a variety of play elements in a fairytale setting as well as just-for-kids rides such as a small ferris wheel, dragon carousel, slides, and a miniflume ride. The area is dominated by Dumphrey, a whimsical dragon who interacts with visitors and guides children around a three-story tree house with winding stairways, tall towers, stepping stones, illuminated water geysers, and an echo chamber.

Crown Colony is the home of a team of Clydesdale horses, the Anheuser-Busch hospitality center, and Questor, a flight-simulator adventure ride.

To get the most from your visit, arrive early and wear comfortable shoes. Many visitors pack a bathing suit because some of the rides get you totally soaked. Don't forget to bring extra money for snacks. Best bet: Brown-bag your lunch—the restaurant prices are outrageous.

Tampa Area Attractions

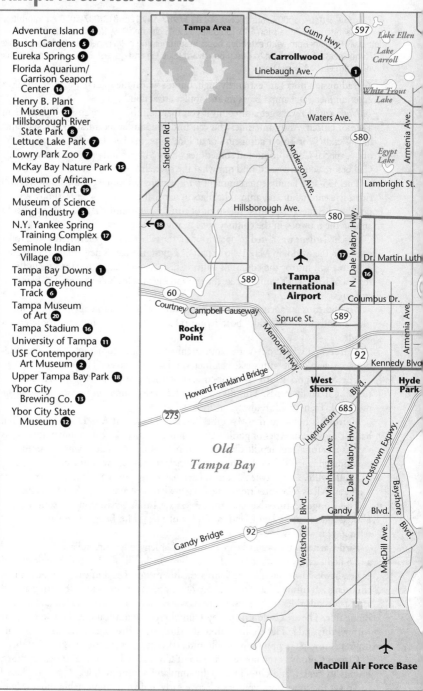

Tampa Area

Gunn Hwy. 597 Lake Ellen
Lake Carroll
Carrollwood
Linebaugh Ave. 1
White Trout Lake
Waters Ave.
Armenia Ave.
580
Egypt Lake
Lambright St.
Sheldon Rd
Anderson Ave.
Hillsborough Ave.
580
←18
N. Dale Mabry Hwy.
Dr. Martin Luth
17
16
Tampa International Airport
589
Columbus Dr.
60
Courtney Campbell Causeway
Spruce St.
589
Armenia Ave.
Rocky Point
Memorial Hwy.
92
Kennedy Blvd
West Shore
Blvd.
Hyde Park
Howard Frankland Bridge
275
Henderson Ave.
685
Manhattan Ave.
S. Dale Mabry Hwy.
Crosstown Expwy.
Bayshore Blvd.
Old Tampa Bay
Westshore Blvd.
Gandy
Blvd.
MacDill Ave.
Gandy Bridge
92
MacDill Air Force Base

Tyler St.
Cass St.
Polk St.
Zack St.
Twiggs St.
Madison St.
Kennedy Blvd.
Jackson St.
Washington St.
Whiting St.
Ashley St.

Downtown

Florida Ave.
Marion St.
Morgan St.
Tampa St.
Franklin St.

Hillsborough River

Crosstown Expwy.

University
of South Florida
Fowler Ave.

582

Busch Gardens

Busch Blvd.

Temple Terrace

580

301

75

41

Sligh Ave.

Sligh Ave.

275

Hillsborough Ave.

92

4

Bellows Lake

Tampa

Dr. Martin Luther King Jr. Blvd.

574

BUS 41

ng Jr. Blvd.

Nebraska Ave.

22nd St.

585

Columbus Dr.

50th St.

7th Ave.

Downtown Ybor City   Adamo Dr.

Area of Inset

60

Crosstown Expwy.

60

BUS 41

Harbour Island

McKay Bay

Davis Blvd.

Causeway Blvd.

676

Davis Islands

Peter O. Knight Airport

Bayshore Rd.

676A

Ballast Point

41

Hillsborough Bay

Nebraska Ave.

Florida Ave.

56th St.

Malcolm McKinley Dr.

0   2 mi
        3.4 km

N

481

✪ **The Florida Aquarium.** 701 Channelside Dr. ☎ **813/273-4000.** Admission $13.95 adults, $12.55 seniors and children 13–18, $6.95 children 3–12, free for children 2 and under. Daily 9am–6pm.

Tampa's newest tourist attraction, the Florida Aquarium is educational but fun, while introducing guests to more than 5,300 aquatic animals and plants that call Florida home. It's located along downtown Tampa's waterfront in the Channel District and easy to find thanks to dozens of well-placed green signs. Once inside, follow the pristine springs of the Florida Wetlands Gallery, go through a mangrove forest in the Bays and Beaches Gallery, and stand amazed at the Coral Reefs. The most awesome view is a 43-foot-wide, 14-foot-tall panoramic window with schools of fish and lots of sharks and stingrays. You can watch a diver twice a day. The half-million-dollar "Explore A Shore" playground was slated to open in the summer of 1996 as an outdoor playground adventure for kids. Watch for special reduced rates around March during its anniversary celebrations.

Lowry Park Zoo. 7530 North Blvd. ☎ **813/932-0245.** Admission $6.50 adults, $5.50 seniors, $4.50 children 3–11, free for children 2 and under. Daily 9:30am–5pm. Take I-275 to Sligh Avenue (Exit 31) and follow the signs.

Watching the 2,000-pound manatees (also known as sea cows) is the awesome highlight of this zoo experience. With lots of greenery, bubbling brooks, and cascading waterfalls, this 24-acre zoo displays animals in settings that closely resemble their natural habitats. The major attractions include the manatees, a Florida wildlife display, Asian Domain, Primate World, and the children's petting zoo. You can pack a picnic and eat at one of the picnic tables outside the zoo.

MUSEUMS

✪ **Museum of African-American Art.** 1308 N. Marion St. (between Scott and Laurel sts.), downtown. ☎ **813/272-2466.** Admission $2 adults, $1 seniors and children grades K–12. Daily Tues–Sat 10am–4:30pm. Take Exit 26 off I-275.

Recently renovated, this museum is touted as the first of its kind in Florida and one of only four in the United States. It's the home of the Barnett-Aden collection, with more than 80 artists represented, including sculpture and paintings that depict the history, culture, and lifestyle of African-Americans from the 1800s to the present. Special emphasis is on the works of artists active during the Harlem Renaissance.

Museum of Science and Industry (MOSI). 4801 E. Fowler Ave. ☎ **813/987-6300.** Admission $8 adults, $7 seniors, $5 children 2–12, free for children 2 and under. Daily 9am–5pm or later. Head north of downtown on I-275 and exit on East Fowler Avenue (Fla. 582).

Since adding MOSIMAX, Florida's first IMAX dome theater, this is a "must see" attraction for all ages. MOSI is the largest science center in the Southeast and has over 450 hands-on interactive activities with a Florida touch. Guests can step into the Gulf Hurricane and experience gale-force winds, defy the laws of gravity in the unique Challenger space experience, or cruise the mysterious world of microbes in LifeLab. Three major exhibitions in MOSI's new West Wing include "The Amazing You," exploring the body; "Our Florida," focusing on environmental factors; and "Our Place in the Universe," which introduces guests to space, flight, and beyond.

✪ **Tampa Museum of Art.** 600 N. Ashley St. ☎ **813/274-8130.** Admission $5 adults, $4 seniors and college students, $3 children 6–18, free for children 5 and under; free for everyone Wed 5–9pm and Sun 1–5pm. Mon–Tues and Thurs–Sat 10am–5pm, Wed 10am–9pm, Sun 1–5pm. Tours Wed and Sat at 1pm, Sun at 2pm. Take I-275 to Exit 25 (Ashley Street).

It's so pretty here at the new 7-acre riverfront park and sculpture garden that you won't believe you're in a city. Located on the east bank of the Hillsborough River, just south of the Tampa Bay Performing Arts Center, this fine-arts complex offers eight galleries with changing exhibits ranging from classical antiquities to contemporary Florida art.

✪ Henry B. Plant Museum. 401 W. Kennedy Blvd. (Fla. 60). ☎ **813/254-1891.** Free admission; suggested donation, $3 adults, $1 children 12 and under. Tues–Sat 10am–4pm, Sun noon–4pm. Take Fla. 60 west of downtown.

History buffs will love this place, and the kids will think they're visiting a castle. Journey back to turn-of-the-century Florida in downtown Tampa. A Victorian palace featuring Moorish Revival architecture, its 13 dramatic minarets are the focal point of the Tampa skyline. Originally built in 1891 as the 511-room Tampa Bay Hotel by railroad tycoon Henry B. Plant, it's now a National Historic Landmark, filled with art and furnishings from Europe and the Orient.

YBOR CITY

A few short years ago this part of Tampa was known simply as the Latin Quarter, a historic district famous for cigars and the Columbia, the largest Spanish restaurant in the world. Ybor is still home to the famous Columbia, but cigar factories have given way to art galleries, shops, nightclubs, and cool new restaurants and cafes—the main drag, 7th Avenue, suddenly became the "happening" side of Tampa. By day, stroll by the shops, cafes, and galleries. At night, good food and great music dominate the scene. It's a cross between New Orleans' Bourbon Street, crazy Key West, and eclectic New York's SoHo. Hundreds of people throng the streets every night from 9pm to 4am. Unique shops offer a wide assortment of goodies from silk boxer shorts to unique tatoos. Dozens of outstanding nightclubs and dance clubs have waiting lines out the door. Piano bars are popular, as well as clubs offering jazz, blues, reggae, and rock. There are lots of police around in the wee hours, but be as cautious here as you would exploring any big-city nightlife area.

✪ Ybor City Walking Tours are an ideal way to check out the the highlights of this historic district. Free 1¹/₂-hour tours are sponsored by the Ybor City State Museum (☎ 813/247-6323) and are led by enthusiastic local volunteers. They start at the information desk in Ybor Square, between 8th and 9th avenues, and cover over three dozen points of interest. January to April the tours depart at 10:30am on Tuesday, Thursday, and Saturday; May to December, only on Thursday and Saturday. Reservations are suggested.

Ybor City Brewing Company. 2205 N. 20th St., Ybor City. ☎ **813/242-9222.** Admission $2 per person. Tues–Sat 11am–3pm or by appointment. Take I-4 to Exit 1 (Ybor City); the brewery is just off the exit between 11th and 12th avenues.

Housed in a 100-year-old former cigar factory, this newly established microbrewery produces 15,000 barrels a year of Ybor Gold, Calusa Wheat, and Ybor Brown Ale. Visitors are welcome to tour the brewery and watch the process, topping it off with a tasting of the brew. Check out the gift shop for funky cigars. Half the admission charge is donated to the restoration of other historic Ybor City buildings.

PARKS & NATURE PRESERVES

Hillsborough River State Park, 15402 U.S. 301 North, 6 miles southwest of Zephyrhills (☎ 813/987-6771), is a 2,994-acre state park offering 118 campsites year round. Picnic facilities, swimming, freshwater fishing, nature and hiking trails, plus a ramp for boats and canoes, are available. Visitors can rent canoes and there's a fee for swimming in a half-acre pool. The park is open daily from 8am to sunset; admission is $3.25 per car.

Eureka Springs, on Eureka Springs Road north of I-4, near the junction of I-4 and U.S. 301 (☎ 813/744-5536), is the only botanical garden in the local park system. It features 31 acres with a greenhouse, trellised walks, trails, boardwalks, and a picnic area. It's open daily from 8am to 6pm.

Lettuce Lake, 6920 E. Fletcher Ave., just west of I-75 at the Hillsborough River (☎ 813/985-7845), is one of the area's newest parks. It consists of 240 acres with an interpretive center featuring exhibits where visitors can observe a cypress swamp inhabited by birds and other wildlife. Other facilities include picnic areas and a playground. The park is open daily from 8am to 8pm. A $1 donation is requested.

McCay Bay Nature Park, at the Crosstown Expressway and 34th Street, is a 150-acre nature habitat and refuge for more than 180 species of birds and rabbits, snakes, turtles and other wildlife. Boardwalk plans are in the future.

Upper Tampa Bay, at 8001 Double Branch Rd., off Fla. 580 on Old Tampa Bay (☎ 813/855-1765), is a 595-acre peninsula filled with freshwater ponds, pine flatwoods, salt marshes, oyster beds, salt barrens, and a mangrove forest. Picnic facilities are available. Open daily (except Christmas) from 8am to sunset.

ORGANIZED TOURS

Sea Wings Aviation, Inc., 2047 Los Lomas Dr., Clearwater (☎ 813/445-9464), offers sightseeing tours of the Tampa Bay area via a three-seat float plane. Flights depart from various points, including Rocky Point Drive off the Courtney Campbell Causeway. The 15-minute trips cost $54 per person; longer trips can be arranged. They've even been known to fly couples over to nearby islands to become formally engaged. Flights are available throughout the day, and advance reservations are required.

Located opposite Busch Gardens, **Swiss Chalet Tours,** 3601 E. Busch Blvd. (☎ 813/985-3601), operates guided bus tours of Tampa, Ybor City, and environs. Half-day 4-hour tours are given on Monday and Thursday and cost $35 for adults and $20 for children. Full-day 8-hour tours are offered on Tuesday and Friday at $45 for adults and $35 for children. Reservations are required at least 24 hours in advance; passengers are picked up at major hotels and various other points in the Tampa / St. Petersburg area. Tours can also be booked to Sarasota, Bradenton, and other regional destinations.

OUTDOOR ACTIVITIES & SPECTATOR SPORTS

Tampa Outdoor Adventures (☎ 813/223-2752, or 800/44-TAMPA, ext. 6), is a one-stop source of information and reservations for a variety of recreational activities in the Tampa area, from fishing to yachting and other sports. In addition, try these contacts directly:

BOAT RENTALS Paddle downstream in a two- to four-person canoe along a 20-mile stretch of the Hillsborough River amid 16,000 acres of rural lands in Wilderness Park, the largest regional park in Hillsborough County. The trips take 2 to 4 hours, covering approximately 2 to 3 miles per hour. **Canoe Escape,** 9335 E. Fowler Ave. (☎ 813/986-2067), charges $26 for 2-hour trips, $30 for 4-hour trips, and is open Monday to Friday from 9am to 5pm and on Saturday and Sunday from 8am to 6pm.

FISHING Tampa's opportunities for casting a line are confined primarily to lakes, rivers, and bays. There's good freshwater fishing for trout in **Lake Thonotosassa,** east of the city, or for bass along the **Hillsborough River.** Pier fishing on Hillsborough Bay is also available from **Ballast Point Park,** 5300 Interbay Blvd. (☎ 813/831-9585).

Light Tackle Fishing Expeditions (☎ **813/963-1930**) offers sportfishing trips for tarpon, redfish, cobia, trout, and snook. Chartering the boat for a half-day trip costs $250; a full-day trip is $350.

GOLF The **Arnold Palmer Golf Academy World Headquarters** is located 12 miles north of Tampa at the world-renowned Saddlebrook Resort, 5700 Saddlebrook Way, Wesley Chapel (☎ **813/973-1111**). Programs are available for adults and juniors of all skill levels. The 2-, 3-, and 5-day programs begin at $235 per person per night. You'll receive accommodations, breakfast, daily instruction, 18 holes of golf daily, cart and greens fees, and nightly club cleaning and storage.

The **University of South Florida Golf Course,** Fletcher Avenue and 46th Street (☎ **813/974-2071**), is just north of the USF campus. This 18-hole, par-72 course is nicknamed "The Claw" because of its challenging layout. It offers lessons and club rentals. The charge is $18, $30 with a cart. It's open daily from 7am to dusk.

Other area 18-hole courses include the **Babe Zaharias Municipal Golf Course** (☎ 813/932-8932), the **Hall of Fame Golf Club** (☎ 813/876-4913), the **Rocky Point Municipal Golf Course** (☎ 813/884-5141), and the **Rogers Park Municipal Golf Course** (☎ 813/234-1911).

IN-LINE SKATING Rent in-line skates at **Blades & Bikes,** the authority in the area. Look for the pink-and-blue shop at 201-A W. Platt St. (☎ **813/251-1780**), near Bayshore Boulevard. Ask about the free in-line skating classes every Saturday.

JOGGING **Bayshore Boulevard,** stretching for 7 miles along Hillsborough Bay, is famous for its 6.3-mile sidewalk. Reputed to be the world's longest continuous sidewalk, it's a favorite for runners, joggers, walkers, and in-line skaters. The route goes from the western edge of downtown in a southward direction, passing stately old homes, condos, retirement communities, and houses of worship, ending at Gandy Boulevard.

For more information on other recommended running areas, contact the **Parks and Recreation Department,** 7225 North Blvd. (☎ **813/223-8230**).

TENNIS The **City of Tampa Tennis Complex,** Hillsborough Community College, 4001 Tampa Bay Blvd. (☎ **813/870-2383**), across from Tampa Stadium, is the largest public complex in Tampa, with 16 hard courts and 12 clay courts. It also has four racquetball courts, a pro shop, locker rooms, and showers, and offers lessons. Reservations are recommended. Prices range from $1.75 (non–prime-time) to $4.50 per person per hour. It's open Monday to Friday from 8am to 9pm and on Saturday and Sunday from 8am to 6pm.

On the water overlooking Harbour Island, **Marjorie Park,** 59 Columbia Dr., Davis Islands (☎ **813/253-3997**), has eight clay courts. Reservations are required. The charge is $4.50 per person per hour and it's open Monday to Friday from 8am to 9pm and on Saturday and Sunday from 8am to 6pm.

The **Harry Hopman Tennis Academy,** 5700 Saddlebrook Way, Wesley Chapel (☎ **813/973-1111**, or 800/729-8383), with its 45 tennis courts, is a well-equipped school that caters to beginners as well as skilled players of all ages. A basic 5-day/6-night package includes 25 hours (minimum) of tennis instruction, unlimited playing time, match play with instructors, audiovisual analysis, agility exercises, and accommodations at the Saddlebrook Resort. Prices range from $678 to $1,092 per person, double occupancy. You must be a member or a guest to play here.

SPECTATOR SPORTS

BASEBALL The **New York Yankees** made their spring-training Tampa debut in 1996 at the brand-new Legends Field, a 31-acre site opposite Tampa Stadium at the southwest corner of Dale Mabry Highway and Dr. Martin Luther King, Jr., Boulevard (☎ **813/875-7753**). The new Yankee complex is the largest spring-training facility in Florida, with a 10,000-seat capacity, and many fans claim there's not a bad seat in the house. You can catch the Bronx Bombers in action every February and March.

About a half-hour drive from downtown Tampa, the **Plant City Stadium,** Park Road in Plant City (☎ **813/757-9221**), is the spring-training turf of the **Cincinnati Reds.** The season is from mid-February to April and admission is $4 to $7.

DOG RACING   The **Tampa Greyhound Track,** 8300 N. Nebraska Ave. (☎ **813/932-4313**), features 13 races daily, with eight dogs competing in each. Live races are offered July to December, Monday to Saturday at 7:30pm, with matinees on Monday, Wednesday, and Saturday at 12:30pm. From January to June there's simulcasting for horse and dog racing. Admission is $1 to the grandstand, $2 to $3 to the clubhouse. Valet parking is $3; self-parking is free.

FOOTBALL   Home field to the **Tampa Bay Buccaneers** football team is **Tampa Stadium,** 4201 N. Dale Mabry Hwy. (☎ **813/872-7977** or 813/879-BUCS). At press time, Tampa Bay residents were fighting to keep the Bucs in town and the coach had just been fired. What happens next is anybody's guess. Stay tuned to the local sports pages for updates to see if Tampa still even has a football team.

HOCKEY   Starting with the 1996 season the NHL's **Tampa Bay Lightning** were slated to be based at a new $153-million, 20,000-seat arena, the Ice Palace, located between the Tampa Convention Center and the new Florida Aquarium. For complete details at the time of your visit, contact the Tampa Bay Lightning, 501 Kennedy Blvd., Tampa (☎ **813/229-8800**). Ticket prices range from $8 to $50.

HORSE RACING   The only oval thoroughbred race course on Florida's west coast, ✪ **Tampa Bay Downs,** 11225 Racetrack Rd., Oldsmar (☎ **813/855-4401**), is the home of the Tampa Bay Derby. The program features 10 races a day. Admission is $1.50 to the grandstand, $3 to the clubhouse; there's free grandstand admission for seniors on Wednesday and for women on Friday. Parking costs $1. From December to May, post time on Monday, Tuesday, Thursday, and Friday is 12:30pm; on Saturday and Sunday, 1pm. The track presents simulcasts June to November.

JAI-ALAI   This Spanish game, somewhat reminiscent of indoor lacrosse, is considered the world's fastest ball game (the ball can go over 180 m.p.h.). At **Tampa Jai-Alai Fronton,** 5125 S. Dale Mabry Hwy. (☎ **813/831-1411**), professional players volley the lethal *pelota* with a long, curved glove called a *cesta*. Spectators, protected by a wall of glass, place bets on the players. Admission is $1 to $3 and parking is $1 or free. It's open year round: Monday to Saturday at 7pm, with matinees on Monday, Wednesday, and Saturday at noon.

POLO   Mallets swing at the **Tampa Bay Polo Club,** Walden Lake Polo and Country Club, 2001 Clubhouse Dr., Plant City (☎ **813/754-2234**). Admission is $3; play begins on Sunday at 2pm, mid-January to May.

SHOPPING
SHOPPING CENTERS
✪ **Old Hyde Park Village.** 1509 W. Swann Ave., Hyde Park. ☎ **813/251-3500.**

Tampa's answer to Rodeo Drive and Madison Avenue is a terrific alternative to the same old boring suburban malls. Walk around little shops outside in the sunshine and check out one of the city's oldest and most historic neighborhoods at the same time. A cluster of 50 upscale shops and boutiques is set in a village layout. Even if you can't afford to buy, it's fun to browse around William Sonoma, Pottery Barn, Banana Republic, Brooks Brothers, Crabtree & Evelyn, and Godiva Chocolatier. Open Monday to Wednesday and Saturday from 10am to 6pm, on Thursday and Friday from 10am to 9pm, and on Sunday from noon to 5pm.

Ybor Square. 1901 13th St., Ybor City. ☎ **813/247-4497.**

Listed on the National Register of Historic Places, this complex consists of three brick buildings (dating to 1886) that once comprised the largest cigar factory in the world, employing over 4,000 workers. Today it's a specialty mall, with over three dozen shops selling everything from clothing, crafts, and jewelry to (of course) cigars. Open Monday to Saturday from 10am to 6pm and on Sunday from noon to 5:30pm.

SPECIALTY STORES

Adams City Hatters. 1621 E. 7th Ave., Ybor City. ☎ **813/229-2850.**

Established over 75 years ago and reputed to be Florida's largest hat store (with a mind-boggling inventory of more than 18,000 hats), this shop offers all types of headgear, from Stetsons and Panamas to top hats, sombreros, and caps. Open Monday to Friday from 9:30am to 5:30pm.

Heads Flags. 4109 Henderson. ☎ **813/248-5019.**

Here you'll find colorful flags from all nations and all states, as well as banners, ethnic items, T-shirts, and hats. Open Monday to Friday from 9:30am to 5:30pm and on Saturday from 9:30am to 3pm.

La France. 1612 E. 7th Ave., Ybor City. ☎ **813/248-1381.**

Racks upon racks of vintage clothing await in this funky store filled to the brim with costumes and period pieces. Open Sunday to Friday from 11am to 6pm and on Saturday from 11am to 10:30pm.

✪ One World Gift Shop. 412 Zack St. ☎ **813/229-0679.**

Tucked into a garden entrance of the First Presbyterian Church, this downtown shop sells handcrafted jewelry and gifts made by artisans from Central and South America, Asia, India, and Mexico. Open Monday to Friday from 11am to 2pm and (October to December only) on Sunday from 11:30am to 1:30pm.

St. Fiacre's Herb Shop. 1709 N. 16th St., Ybor City. ☎ **813/248-1234.**

Named after the Irish monk who became the patron saint of gardeners, this unique shop stocks a wide array of fresh herbs, herbal products, fragrances, exotic teas, herbal T-shirts, herbal gift baskets, and books. Open Monday to Thursday from 10am to 6pm, on Friday and Saturday from 10am to 8pm, and on Sunday from noon to 5pm.

Tampa Rico Cigar Co. 1901 13th St. North. ☎ **813/247-6738.**

You can't leave Tampa without buying at least one cigar for that special occasion. Check out these hand-rolled stogies, brought to you by the same family for the past 50 years. Open daily from 11am to 5pm.

Whaley's Markets. 533 S. Howard Ave. ☎ **813/254-2904.**

This store is a favorite source for Florida Indian River citrus fruit, marmalades, and other local foods, including gourmet picnic items. Open Monday to Saturday from 7am to 9pm and on Sunday from 7am to 8pm.

WHERE TO STAY

The average room rate in Tampa is $78, but it's possible to call ahead and get a better deal on prices—through packages, promotions, or membership in the AAA or AARP. Always ask if the hotel has a special rate with breakfast thrown in or a "Super Saver" rate.

Business travelers usually concentrate near the Westshore area and downtown, but they pay more for the location. In high season (January to April), many of the hotels in these areas will often be booked solid by conventions.

The budget and family-oriented hotels tend to be north of downtown, near Busch Gardens and around the University of South Florida. Most hotels have pools and, with the exception of a few downtown hotels, parking is free. You'd have to head over to the St. Petersburg / Clearwater area to find most of the region's inexpensive mom-and-pop–run motels (see Section 2 of this chapter).

In summer, hotels often combine tickets to major attractions like Busch Gardens and Adventure Island in their package deals. Call the **Tampa / Hillsborough Convention and Visitors Association** (☎ 813/223-2752) to get the latest updates on hotel and special value packages.

There are some excellent publications that offer up to a 50% reduction in prices on hotels, restaurants, and attractions in the area. *Entertainment '97* (☎ 800/374-4464) is one book with lots of Florida listings. A free guide listing inexpensive hotels is called the *Exit Information Guide* (☎ 352/371-3948). But be warned: While hotels may honor these special discount publications, you're at the mercy of their discounted room availability. For a cheap place minutes away from Busch Gardens, there's always the **Motel 6** at 333 E. Fowler Ave. (☎ 813/932-4948). In high season, singles are $29 and doubles run $34.

The local hotel-occupancy tax is 11%, added to your hotel room.

DOUBLES FOR LESS THAN $45

Masters Economy Inn. 27807 Fla. 54, Wesley Chapel, FL 33608. ☎ **813/973-0155.** 120 rms. High season, $43 double. Low season, $40.95 double. MC, V.

Way off the beaten path but very affordable, this two-story motel is a 20-minute ride north of Busch Gardens in Pasco County. The rooms are standard, with two double beds and your typical shower/bath with ample closet space. There's no dining room, but Denny's is just next door.

DOUBLES FOR LESS THAN $60

Behind the Fence Bed and Breakfast. 1400 Viola St. (off U.S. 301), Brandon, FL 33617. ☎ 813/685-8201. 8 rms, 1 cottage. High season, $49 double without bath, $69 double with bath; $69 cottage. Off-season, $59 double without bath, $62.10 double with bath. Rates include full breakfast. No credit cards.

This out-of-the-way but popular B&B is located just a few miles west of Tampa next to a pretty park in the quiet suburb of Brandon. The house itself is made from salvaged turn-of-the-century materials and filled with antiques, reminding one of a country farmhouse in Connecticut. A separate cottage is also available for only $69 in the high season—great for families. It has a duplex with two bedrooms and a private bath with pool.

Days Inn Busch Gardens/Maingate. 2901 E. Busch Blvd., Tampa, FL 33612. ☎ 813/933-6471 or 800/DAYS INN. Fax 813/931-0261. 170 rms. High season, $59 double. Off-season, $34 double. AE, DC, DISC, MC, V.

This place is great for families on a budget—you can walk to Busch Gardens from this two-story motel just off the main drag. The rooms are in the quiet back section with an outdoor swimming pool. There's no restaurant, but a Denny's and a Taco Bell are both nearby.

Red Roof Inn. 2307 E. Busch Blvd., Tampa, FL 33612. ☎ **813/932-0073** or 800/THE-ROOF. Fax 813/933-5689. 108 rms. A/C TV TEL. High season, $58 double. Off-season, $31 double. AE, DC, DISC, MC, V.

This two-story property is less than a mile from Busch Gardens. Set back from the road in a well-landscaped grassy setting, the rooms are done up in bright colors. An outdoor pool and whirlpool are in the center of the complex.

DOUBLES FOR LESS THAN $80

✪ **Days Inn Rocky Point.** 7627 Courtney Campbell Causeway, Tampa, FL 33607. ☎ **813/281-0000** or 800/DAYS-INN. Fax 813/281-1067. 152 rms. A/C TV TEL. High season, $67.50 double. Off-season, $54. AE, DC, DISC, MC, V.

No, it's not on the Gulf of Mexico, but it does have a small strip of beach near the causeway overlooking Old Tampa Bay 2 miles west of the airport. Cars whiz by, but it's set back from the main road. This motel-style property encompasses four two-story wings surrounding an outdoor swimming pool with a landscaped courtyard, so the bedrooms offer either bay or pool views. The rooms have a cheery decor with cherry-wood furniture. For dining or imbibing, try the Waterfront Cafe and Sports Bar. Facilities include an outdoor swimming pool, two tennis courts, a shuffleboard court, a horseshoe pit, badminton, two volleyball courts, a children's playground, rentals for jet skis and waterskis, and a coin-operated guest laundry.

DOUBLES FOR LESS THAN $100

Best Western Resort Tampa at Busch Gardens. 820 E. Busch Blvd., Tampa, FL 33612. ☎ **813/933-4011** or 800/288-4011. Fax 813/932-1784. 255 rms. A/C TV TEL. High season, $89–$99 double. Off-season, $59–$69 double. AE, CB, DC, DISC, MC, V.

This property used to be called the Colony Hotel and sits off the Busch Boulevard exit from I-275 a few miles from Tampa's best-known attractions. It's great for families. The lobby leads to a skylit, atrium-style courtyard with fountains, streetlights, benches, a pool, and tropical foliage. The guest rooms have outside doors opening into the courtyard and standard furnishings enlivened by colorful, eye-catching fabrics. The Palm Grill Restaurant, off the lobby, features a variety of dishes. Charades Nite Club offers themed happy hours. On the premises are indoor and outdoor heated swimming pools, two Jacuzzis, a sauna, four lighted tennis courts, an exercise room, a games room, a coin-operated laundry, and a gift shop. There's courtesy transport to Busch Gardens.

✪ **Doubletree Guest Suites.** 4400 W. Cypress St., Tampa, FL 33607. ☎ **813/873-8675** or 800/222-TREE. Fax 813/879-7196. 260 suites. A/C TV TEL. High season, $99–$149 suite for two. Off-season, $89 suite for two. AE, CB, DC, MC, V.

With an exterior of salmon-toned, Spanish-style architecture, this eight-story building adds an old-world charm to the busy corridor beside the airport and Westshore Boulevard. The interior includes a plant-filled atrium with cascading waterfalls and a tropical garden courtyard. Regional dishes and local seafoods are the specialties at the St. James Bar & Grill. Facilities include an indoor swimming pool, a sauna, a steam room, and a gift shop.

   The guest units are suites with separate bedrooms and living areas, contemporary furniture, muted color schemes, and wet bars, and most have sofa beds, microwave ovens, coffeemakers, and private patios or balconies—a roominess perfect for families. Ask about affordable "Suite Romance" weekend packages in the off-season that include a champagne breakfast and late check-out.

Tampa Area Accommodations & Dining

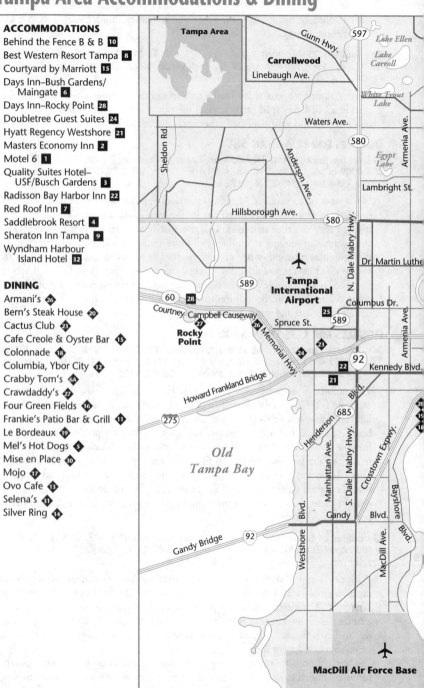

ACCOMMODATIONS

Behind the Fence B & B **10**
Best Western Resort Tampa **8**
Courtyard by Marriott **15**
Days Inn–Bush Gardens/
   Maingate **6**
Days Inn–Rocky Point **28**
Doubletree Guest Suites **24**
Hyatt Regency Westshore **21**
Masters Economy Inn **2**
Motel 6 **1**
Quality Suites Hotel–
   USF/Busch Gardens **3**
Radisson Bay Harbor Inn **22**
Red Roof Inn **7**
Saddlebrook Resort **4**
Sheraton Inn Tampa **9**
Wyndham Harbour
   Island Hotel **32**

DINING

Armani's **26**
Bern's Steak House **20**
Cactus Club **23**
Cafe Creole & Oyster Bar **15**
Colonnade **18**
Columbia, Ybor City **12**
Crabby Tom's **6A**
Crawdaddy's **27**
Four Green Fields **16**
Frankie's Patio Bar & Grill **11**
Le Bordeaux **19**
Mel's Hot Dogs **5**
Mise en Place **30**
Mojo **17**
Ovo Cafe **13**
Selena's **31**
Silver Ring **14**

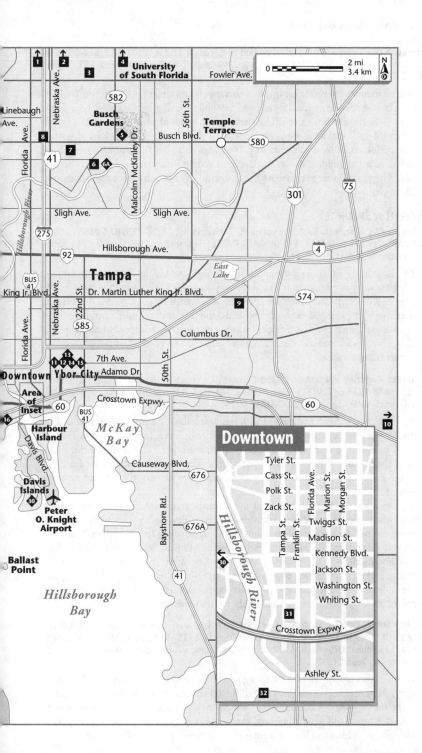

Sheraton Inn Tampa. 7401 E. Hillsborough Ave., Tampa, FL 33610. ☎ **813/626-0999** or 800/325-3535. Fax 813/622-7893, ext. 246. 276 rms. A/C TV TEL. Year round, $85 double. AE, CB, DC, MC, V.

Just 10 minutes from downtown, this Sheraton is conveniently situated off I-4 in a palm tree–shaded setting, adjacent to the Seminole Gaming Palace and an hour away from Orlando-area attractions. The guest rooms, many of which surround a central courtyard and pool area, are contemporary in decor, with dark woods and restful tones. Most units have balconies or patios. The lobby has an informal lounge bar, and an adjacent building houses the Cypress Landing Restaurant and Sky Box Sports Bar. They have great summer packages, including a Busch Gardens / Adventure Island deal.

WORTH A SPLURGE

Courtyard by Marriott. 3805 W. Cypress St., Tampa, FL 33607. ☎ **813/874-0555** or 800/321-2211. Fax 813/870-0685. 145 rms. A/C TV TEL. High season, $109 double. Off-season, $89 double. AE, CB, DC, DISC, MC, V.

You wouldn't want to walk around this part of town at night, but this contemporary four-story hotel is a clean "find" if you want to be 3 miles from the airport. It's a typical Marriott: The central courtyard is surrounded by guest rooms that offer a choice of a king-size bed or two double beds, and feature dark-wood furnishings and in-room coffeemakers. The facilities include a café/lounge, outdoor swimming pool, indoor whirlpool, exercise room, and guest laundry. The hotel offers complimentary airport transportation.

✪ **Hyatt Regency Westshore.** 6200 Courtney Campbell Causeway, Tampa, FL 33607. ☎ **813/874-1234** or 800/233-1234. Fax 813/870-9168. 445 rms. A/C TV TEL. $204 double Sun–Thurs, $165 Fri–Sat. AE, CB, DC, DISC, MC, V.

Very elegant, civilized, and packed with business folks—the ambience is subdued at this 14-story property nestled on a 35-acre nature preserve. It overlooks Old Tampa Bay 1 mile west of Tampa International Airport, and is just a 20-minute car ride away from the beaches of Pinellas County. Subtle shades of peach and gray are featured in the guest rooms, most of which provide expansive views of the bay and evening sunsets.

Armani's is the most sophisticated and romantic restaurant in town, with candles everywhere and an incredible night view of Tampa Bay. Locals flock to this rooftop restaurant to celebrate special occasions and enjoy northern Italian cuisine. The "create your own" antipasto bar is the best-kept secret in town. Behind the hotel is a 250-foot boardwalk leading to Oystercatchers, a Key West–style seafood eatery with indoor and outdoor seating overlooking the bay. Room service and baby-sitting are available. On the premises are two outdoor swimming pools, two lighted tennis courts, a whirlpool, saunas, a health club, nature walks, and jogging trails.

Quality Suites Hotel–USF/Busch Gardens. 3001 University Center Dr., Tampa, FL 33612. ☎ **813/971-8930** or 800/228-5151. Fax 813/971-8935. 150 suites. A/C TV TEL. High season, $159 suite. Off-season, $109 suite. Rates include full breakfast and evening cocktail reception. AE, DC, DISC, MC, V.

This is a great family place for exploring nearby attractions. The hacienda-style, three-story, all-suite hotel sits directly behind Busch Gardens, although the actual entrance to the theme park is 4 blocks away. Each guest suite has a separate bedroom with a built-in armoire and well-lit mirrored vanity area, a living/dining room with a queen-size sofa bed, plus a wet bar, coffeemaker, microwave, and stereo/VCR unit.

Radisson Bay Harbor Inn. 7700 Courtney Campbell Causeway, Tampa, FL 33607. ☎ **813/ 281-8900** or 800/333-3333. Fax 813/281-0189. 257 rms. A/C TV TEL. High season, $115–$140. Off-season, $85–$110 double. Rates include full breakfast. AE, CB, DC, MC, V.

This six-story hostelry with great water views of Old Tampa Bay is in a good location for exploring the Bay Area: It's 20 minutes east of the Pinellas County beaches, 15 minutes south of the tourist attractions in Tampa, and only 2 miles east of the airport. The guest rooms all have a balcony or patio. The decor, in mostly sea-toned fabrics, reflects an art deco influence. Water views are the prime attraction in the popular lobby-level Damon's Restaurant and Lounge.

✪ **Wyndham Harbour Island Hotel.** 725 S. Harbour Island Blvd., Harbour Island, Tampa, FL 33602. ☎ **813/229-5000** or 800/WYNDHAM. Fax 813/229-5322. 300 rms. A/C MINIBAR TV TEL. High season, $199–$239 double. Off-season, $165–$185 double. AE, CB, DC, MC, V.

There's not much action on the little island, but you'll enjoy quiet elegance at this upscale 12-story luxury hotel. It's perfect for a romantic getaway with great views of the water, surrounded by the channels linking the Hillsborough River and the bay. Guests enjoy privileges at the Harbour Island Athletic Club. The bedrooms, all with views of the water, are furnished in dark woods and floral fabrics, and each has a well-lit marble-trimmed bathroom, executive desk, and work area, plus such in-room conveniences as coffeemakers, irons, and ironing boards. Special touches like the makeup mirrors, in-room honor bar, and terrycloth robes add to the elegance.

You can watch the yachts drift by as you dine at the Harbourview Room, or enjoy your favorite drink in the Bar, a clubby room with equally good views. Snacks and drinks are available during the day at the Pool Bar. Room service is available, and on the premises are an outdoor heated swimming pool and deck, 50 boat slips, and a newsstand/gift shop.

WHERE TO EAT

Tampa is brimming with restaurant options and becoming more eclectic in its menu offerings. Romantic French bistros and upscale Italian restaurants will please your palate when you want to splurge. Those on a more frugal budget will enjoy exploring the ethnic diversity around town, especially Ybor City's restaurants, where you can always find reasonably priced food. The chain restaurants and fast-food joints congregate north of downtown on Fowler Avenue near Busch Gardens and south of downtown on Dale Mabry Highway.

You can't go wrong at any restaurant if you order seafood, a favorite with everybody in this area. Try the local amberjack, grouper, pompano, snapper, stone crabs (in season), mahi mahi, swordfish, wahoo, or Florida lobster.

MEALS FOR LESS THAN $7

Crabby Tom's Old Time Oyster Bar and Seafood Restaurant. 3120 W. Hillsborough Ave. ☎ **813/870-1652.** Reservations accepted only for parties of 10 or more. Main courses $4.95–$11.95. AE, DISC, MC, V. Mon–Thurs 11am–10pm, Fri–Sat 11am–11pm, Sun 4–9pm. SEAFOOD.

Although this spot lacks waterside views and an impressive decor, seafood lovers don't care. Sit back at a picnic table, relax, and crack open a pile of stone crab claws (only in season) or a huge lobster. Other favorites? Alaska snow crab claws or king crab legs.

Four Green Fields. 205 W. Platt St. ☎ **813/254-4444.** Reservations not required. Main courses $3.95–$8.95. AE, MC, V. Mon–Sat 11am–midnight, Sun 1pm–midnight. IRISH/AMERICAN.

Set in the style of a traditional Irish cottage complete with thatched roof, this pub offers authentic Irish cooking near the heart of downtown Tampa. It smells of beer but attracts all the youngish people in town who gather nightly to meet and greet after hours. It's ideal for salads and sandwiches with Irish music Tuesday to Saturday night.

✪ **Mel's Hot Dogs.** 4136 E. Busch Blvd. ☎ **813/985-8000.** Reservations not accepted. Main courses $3–$6. No credit cards. Mon–Sat 10am–10pm, Sun 11am–9pm. AMERICAN.

"The big daddy" of hot-dog eateries has been a favorite with locals for years and caters to area college students and hungry families. This informal place offers everything from bagel-dogs to bacon-, Cheddar-Reuben-, and corndogs. All are served on a poppyseed bun and most come with french fries and a choice of cole slaw or baked beans. The decor is weiner-centered, but the menu does offer a few alternatives (sausages, chicken breast, and beef and veggie burgers).

Silver Ring. 1831 E. 7th Ave., Ybor City. ☎ **813/248-2549.** Reservations not required. Main courses $2.25–$4.95. No credit cards. Mon–Sat 6:30am–5pm. SPANISH/AMERICAN.

At this Ybor City tradition since 1947, the walls are lined with old pictures, vintage radios, a 1950s jukebox, fishing rods, and deer heads. It's *the* place to get a genuine Cuban sandwich—smoked ham, roast pork, Genoa salami, Swiss cheese, pickles, salad dressing, mustard, lettuce, and tomato on Cuban bread. Other menu items include Spanish bean soup, deviled crab, and other types of sandwiches.

MEALS FOR LESS THAN $10

Cactus Club. 1601 Snow Ave. ☎ **813/251-4089** or 813/251-6897. Reservations not required. Main courses $5.95–$12.95. AE, MC, V. Mon–Thurs 11am–midnight, Fri–Sat 11am–1am, Sun 11am–11pm. AMERICAN SOUTHWEST.

Watch all the shoppers go by at Old Hyde Park from this fun and casual cafe with a southwestern accent. It's the place to be if you're in the mood for fajitas, tacos, enchiladas, chili, hickory-smoked baby back ribs, Texas-style pizzas, blackened chicken, or guacamole/green-chili burgers. It's packed at lunchtime, so get there early.

✪ **Cafe Creole and Oyster Bar.** 1330 9th Ave., Ybor City. ☎ **813/247-6283.** Reservations recommended. Main courses $8.95–$14.95. AE, CB, DC, MC, V. Mon–Thurs 11:30am–10pm, Fri–Sat 11:30am–11pm, Sun noon–4pm. CREOLE/CAJUN.

Enjoy Tampa's great weather at this Ybor City indoor/outdoor hot spot and breathe in the history. The building, dating back to 1896, was originally known as El Pasaje, the home of the Cherokee Club, a gentlemen's hotel and private club with a casino and a decor rich in stained-glass windows, wrought-iron balconies, Spanish murals, and marble bathrooms. Locals crowd the place, where seasonably priced specialties include Louisiana crab cakes for $6.95 and a blackened grouper special is $12.95. Bourbon Street–style jazz livens the night Thursday to Saturday.

The Colonnade. 3401 Bayshore Blvd. ☎ **813/839-7558.** Reservations accepted only for large parties. Main courses $7.95–$16.95. AE, DC, MC, V. Sun–Thurs 11am–10pm, Fri–Sat 11am–11pm. AMERICAN/SEAFOOD.

Locals have thronged this place since the 1930s, and you'll often see big groups of families. The view is pretty, overlooking Hillsborough Bay and nestled in Hyde Park's palm-shaded residential neighborhood. Fresh seafood is the specialty, from crab-stuffed flounder or grouper in lemon butter to Cajun catfish or broiled lobster—even wild Florida alligator. Prime rib, steaks, and chicken are also available.

Frankie's Patio Bar & Grill. 1905 E. 7th Ave., Ybor City. ☎ **813/248-3337.** Reservations accepted only for large parties. All items $3.95–$12.95. AE, MC, V. Mon 11am–3pm, Tues 11am–10pm, Wed–Thurs 11am–1am, Fri–Sat 11am–3am. INTERNATIONAL.

The exposed industrial pipes of this large three-story restaurant known for its outstanding musical acts stand out amid the usual Spanish-themed 19th-century architecture of Ybor. You can sit indoors, on a large outdoor patio, or on an open-air balcony overlooking the street action. The food blends Cuban, American, Jamaican, Créole, and Italian cuisines. House specials include Frankie's Fancy meatloaf of veal and mushrooms on a bed of mashed potatoes, peppers, and onions or the southwestern pot pie of chicken chili topped with Cheddar. Live jazz, blues, reggae, and rock add to the atmosphere Wednesday to Saturday.

Ovo Cafe. 1901 E. 7th Ave., Ybor City. ☎ **813/248-6979.** Reservations not necessary. Dinner main courses $8.95–$12.95. Open Mon–Tues 11am–4pm, Wed–Sat 11am–2am, Sun 11am–10pm.

This very popular café—with businesspeople by day and the clubby crowd by night—is Tampa's answer to a funky New York City SoHo café, with the art on the walls as eclectic as the menu. Locals love their "menage à trois" omelets at breakfast. The fresh Ovo's chicken feta salad is to die for at lunch. Other menu offerings include pierogies, smoked-tuna sandwiches, and shrimp bisque soup. The big surprise is finding Dom Perignon alongside root beer floats made with Absolut vodka.

Selena's. In the Old Hyde Park shopping complex, 1623 Snow Ave. ☎ **813/251-2116.** Reservations recommended. Main courses $7.95–$17.95. AE, CB, DC, MC, V. Sun–Wed 11am–10pm, Thurs 11am–11pm, Fri–Sat 11am–midnight. CREOLE/SICILIAN.

This charming restaurant suggests the heart of New Orleans. Sit in the plant-filled Patio Room, the eclectic Queen Anne Room, or watch the world go by at the outdoor café. Local seafoods, especially grouper and shrimp, top the menu at dinner, with many of the dishes served Créole style or blackened. Choices also include pastas, chicken, steak, and veal. The jambalaya under "family entree" is a great value at just $6.95. At night musical groups perform in the upstairs lounge.

MEALS FOR LESS THAN $15

✪ **The Columbia.** 2117 E. 7th Ave., Ybor City. ☎ **813/248-4961.** Reservations recommended. Main courses $10.95–$21.95. AE, CB, DC, DISC, MC, V. Daily 11am–11pm. SPANISH.

This famous restaurant dates back to 1905 and occupies a full city block in the heart of Ybor City. Tourists may flock here to soak up the ambience, but so do the locals because it's so much fun. You can't help coming back time after time for the famous Spanish bean soup and original "1905" salad. The paella a la valenciana is outstanding, with more than a dozen ingredients from gulf grouper and gulf pink shrimp to calamares, mussels, clams, chicken, and pork. The decor throughout is graced with hand-painted tiles, wrought-iron chandeliers, dark woods, rich red fabrics, and stained-glass windows. New this year is the Cigar Room.

Crawdaddy's. 2500 Rocky Point Dr. ☎ **813/281-0407.** Reservations recommended. Main courses $3.95–$7.95 at lunch, $10.95–$17.95 at dinner. AE, CB, DC, MC, V. Mon–Thurs 11am–2pm and 5–10pm, Fri 11am–2pm and 5–11pm, Sat 5–11pm, Sun 5–10pm. REGIONAL/SEAFOOD.

Overlooking Old Tampa Bay near the airport off the Courtney Campbell Causeway, this informal spot is named after Beauregard "Crawdaddy" Belvedere, a Roaring Twenties tycoon. He owned a fish camp on this site and the decor hasn't changed much since his day—seven dining rooms bedecked with Victorian furnishings, books, pictures, and collectibles. The down-home–style menu ranges from beer-battered shrimp and fish camp fry (shrimp, scallops, and fresh fish, deep-fried in corn crisp-and-almond coating, with jalape of hush puppies) to shrimp and chicken jambalaya, prime rib, and steak.

Le Bordeaux. 1502 S. Howard Ave. ☎ **813/254-4387.** Reservations accepted only for parties of six or more. Main courses $12–$18. AE, DC, MC, V. Mon–Thurs 5:30–10pm, Fri–Sat 5:30–11pm, Sun 5:30–9:30pm. FRENCH.

This bistro is a real find—authentic French food at affordable prices in a romantic atmosphere. The domain of French-born chef/owner Gordon Davis, it offers seating in a living room–style main dining area or a plant-filled conservatory. The menu changes daily, but you can count on homemade pâtés and pasteries, and the specials often include salmon en croûte, pot au feu, veal with wild mushrooms, and filet of beef au roquefort.

✪ **Mise en Place.** 442 W. Kennedy Blvd. (opposite the University of Tampa). ☎ **813/254-5373.** Reservations accepted only for parties of six or more. Main courses $4.95–$7.95 at lunch, $9.95–$17.50 at dinner. AE, CB, DC, DISC, MC, V. Mon 11am–3pm, Tues–Thurs 11am–3pm and 5:30–10pm, Fri 11am–3pm and 5:30–11pm, Sat 5:30–11pm. NEW AMERICAN.

Look around at all the happy, stylish patrons and you'll know why chef Marty Blitz and wife Marianne are the culinary darlings of Tampa. They present a constantly changing and creative "Floribbean" menu made from the freshest ingredients. The ambience is trendy and main courses include such choices as roast duck with Jamaica wild-strawberry sauce, grilled swordfish with tri-melon/mint salsa. They've recently added "442," an upscale bar with live jazz and blues that features champagne by the glass on weekends.

MoJo. 238 E. Davis Blvd., Davis Island. ☎ **813/259-9949.** Reservations not necessary. Main courses $9.95–$12.95. AE, DC, DISC, MC, V. Daily 11am–11pm. NEW AMERICAN.

The creators of Tampa's popular Mise en Place restaurant opened this hot new restaurant on sleepy Davis Island to show off their love of tropical cuisine. The atmosphere is casual with bright-yellow colors shouting "have fun" and paper tablecloths saying "relax." The dishes are hot and spicy, so be prepared to give your mouth a taste treat. The roast pork loin with plaintains is perfection.

WORTH A SPLURGE

Armani's. On the 14th floor of the Hyatt Regency Westshore, 6200 Courtney Campbell Causeway. ☎ **813/281-9165** Reservations required. Jackets required for men. Main courses $14–$26.75. AE, CB, DC, DISC, MC, V. Mon–Sat 6–11pm. NORTHERN ITALIAN.

At the most elegant dining room in town the ambience is romantic and subdued. The candlelit lounge is perfect for intimate gatherings for before-dinner cocktails, appetizers, desserts, or just coffee. The outstanding cuisine includes scaloppine Armani's and the lamb and marinated salmon filet stuffed with spinach and fennel.

✪ **Bern's Steak House.** 1208 S. Howard Ave. ☎ **813/251-2421.** Reservations required. Main courses $18.50–$35. AE, CB, DC, DISC, MC, V. Daily 5–11pm. AMERICAN.

You really must make reservations at this two-story, seven-room Tampa institution known for its steak—ordered to your own weight and thickness specifications—and a 200,000-bottle wine collection. If beef's not your fancy, there are dozens of other menu options. Most vegetables served at Bern's are grown in the restaurant's own organic garden, which is tended by aspiring waiters-to-be serving out the first part of their 3-year internship; this rigorous training translates into excellent service. All main dishes come with onion soup, salad, baked potato, garlic toast, and onion rings.

Many guests skip the main meal and head straight upstairs to the dessert room. The atmosphere is a little too dark for some, but the plush, private and semi-enclosed booths—converted from old wine casks—are equipped with TVs and phones for placing requests to the live pianist. You can order more than 40 desserts, or sip some port or special after-dinner drink. You can reserve a booth for dessert only, but preference is given to those who dine.

TAMPA AFTER DARK

Tampa never used to have much nightlife, but the rebirth of Ybor has changed all that. The new hot spot doesn't even get started until after midnight, with an ecclectic offering of nightlife activities that extend into the wee hours.

To assist visitors, the Tampa/Hillsborough Arts Council maintains an **Artsline** (☎ **813/229-ARTS**), a 24-hour information service providing the latest on current and upcoming cultural events.

THE PERFORMING ARTS

With a prime downtown location on 9 acres along the east bank of the Hillsborough River, the huge **Tampa Bay Performing Arts Center,** 1010 N. MacInnes Place (☎ **813/229-STAR,** or 800/955-1045), is a four-theater complex and the focal point of Tampa's performing-arts scene. It presents a wide range of Broadway plays, classical and pop concerts, operas, cabarets, improv, and special events.

The 74,296-seat **Tampa Stadium,** 4201 N. Dale Mabry Hwy. (☎ **813/ 872-7977**), is frequently the site of headliner concerts. The **USF Sun Dome,** 4202 E. Fowler Ave. (☎ **813/974-3111**), on the University of South Florida campus, hosts major concerts by touring pop stars, rock bands, jazz groups, and other contemporary artists.

Theaters

Off Center Theater. Tampa Bay Performing Arts Center, 1010 N. MacInnes Place. ☎ **813/ 221-1001,** or 813/222-1021. Tickets $3–$12.

The Off Center Theater has recently been recognized for its excellence and innovation. It's dedicated to local artists who present dance, comedy, music, film, and poetry. The resident theater company, The Loft, presents a six-show season. Open every weekend.

✪ **Tampa Theatre.** 711 Franklin St. ☎ **813/223-8981.** Tickets $5.25 adults, $4 seniors, $2.25 children 2–12; $3.25 adults and seniors on Tues and at weekend matinees. Some special events cost $15–$20 or more.

On the National Register of Historic Places, this restored 1926 theater is the jewel of the Franklin Street Mall and presents a varied program of classic, foreign, and alternative films, as well as concerts and special events. The setting is a believable replica of the outdoor courtyard in a Spanish *hacienda*, complete with terra-cotta roof tiles, trailing ivy, and a dark blue domed ceiling pinpricked with lights for stars. An organist often plays on the stage before the movie starts.

THE CLUB & MUSIC SCENE

A Comedy Club

Sidesplitters Comedy Club. 12938 N. Dale Mabry Hwy. ☎ **813/960-1197.** Cover $6–$8.

Located northwest of downtown, Sidesplitters features professional stand-up comedians on most nights. Shows begin Tuesday to Thursday at 8:30pm and on Friday and Saturday at 8 and 10:30pm.

Jazz/Blues/Reggae

Blues Ship. 1910 E. 7th Ave., Ybor City. ☎ **813/248-6097.** Cover $2–$5.

With a mural of a ship adorning the wall, this club presents live blues, jazz, and reggae in an informal meeting-house atmosphere. Most gigs start at 8:30pm, Tuesday to Sunday.

Brothers Lounge. 5401 W. Kennedy Blvd. ☎ **813/286-8882.** No cover.

A jazz haven for 20 years, this lounge sticks to its great jazz 6 nights a week. Open Monday to Saturday from 8:30pm to 2:30am.

Jazz Cellar. 1916 N. 14th St., Ybor City. ☎ **813/248-1862.** Cover $2–$3.

In the heart of the city's Latin Quarter, the Jazz Cellar Underground Orchestra draws fans from near and far. Performances are Thursday to Saturday from 9pm to 2am.

Skipper's Smokehouse Restaurant & Oyster Bar. 910 Skipper Rd. ☎ **813/971-0666** or 813/977-6474. Cover $3–$8, $10 and up for special events.

Because its great for dinner as well as concerts, music lovers from all over Tampa Bay keep this place in north Tampa constantly sold out. It's a prime spot for live reggae or blues outside "under the stars" with a sandy beach and wooden dance floor in front of the stage. It's always popular with University of South Florida students, but visitors of all ages come here from all over the area.

Rock & Top 40 Music

Brass Mug Pub. 1441 E. Fletcher Ave. ☎ **813/972-8152.** Cover $3.

This pub near the University of South Florida features nightly music from heavy metal to rock 'n' roll. There's a jam session on Monday, and pool, darts, and video games are always available.

2 The St. Petersburg / Clearwater Area

20 miles SW of Tampa, 289 miles NW of Miami, 84 miles SW of Orlando

Almost four million visitors come each year to this spit of land that separates Tampa Bay from the Gulf of Mexico in search of sunshine and outdoor activities. According to a study from the world's foremost beach experts, three of the area's beaches are among the absolute finest in the country: Caladesi Island State Park in Dunedin, Ft. Desoto Park in St. Petersburg, and Sand Key Park in Clearwater attract sun worshippers year round.

St. Petersburg blends sleek high-rise office and condominium towers with historic Spanish-style haciendas and palm-lined parks. The bayfront section of the city is a hot spot for visitors—the pyramid-shaped pier offers a great water view with shops, restaurants, and a mini-aquarium.

St. Petersburg is still a relaxing haven for retirees, but a younger, more lively side of the city has been growing lately, with eclectic cafés and shops clustered around Central Avenue.

For the first time in more than a decade, the city of Clearwater has a redevelopment plan to help create more activity in sleepy downtown. City officials hope to attract more shops and restaurants with their "Clearwater—the Traditional Town Center" plan, which calls for $150 million in public and private financial investments over a 20-year period. Four nightclubs, to be themed by different decades, were slated to open at press time.

ESSENTIALS

ARRIVING   By Plane   Tampa International Airport, off Memorial Highway and Fla. 60 in Tampa (☎ 813/870-8700), approximately 16 miles northeast of St. Petersburg, is the prime gateway for all scheduled domestic and international flights serving the area (see the Tampa section for a list of airlines).

St. Petersburg–Clearwater International Airport, Roosevelt Boulevard / Fla. 686, Clearwater (☎ 813/535-7600), is approximately 10 miles north of St. Petersburg. It's primarily a charter facility.

The Limo, Inc., 11901 30th Court North, St. Petersburg (☎ **813/572-1111,** or 800/282-6817), offers 24-hour door-to-door van service between Tampa International or St. Petersburg–Clearwater airport and any St. Petersburg area destination. No reservations are required; on arrival just head to any of the Limo desks outside the baggage-claim area. The flat-rate one-way fare is $13 from the Tampa airport or $10.50 from the St. Petersburg–Clearwater airport to any St. Pete or gulf beach destination. **Red Line Limo, Inc.** (☎ **813/535-3391**), also provides a daily 24-hour van service from Tampa International or St. Petersburg–Clearwater airport to St. Petersburg or any other destination in Pinellas County. The cost is $10.75 from the Tampa airport and $10 from St. Petersburg–Clearwater. Reservations are required 24 hours in advance.

Yellow Cab Taxis (☎ **813/821-7777**) line up outside the baggage-claim areas. The average fare from the Tampa airport to St. Petersburg or any of the gulf beaches is approximately $25 to $35 per taxi (one or more passengers). The fare from the St. Petersburg–Clearwater airport is approximately $15 to $20.

For car rentals, see "Getting Around" below.

By Train   Passengers heading for St. Petersburg arrive first at the Tampa **Amtrak** Station at 601 Nebraska Ave. North in Tampa (☎ **813/221-7600**) and are then transferred by bus to the St. Petersburg Amtrak Station, 33rd Street North and 37th Avenue North, St. Petersburg (☎ **813/522-9475**).

By Bus   **Greyhound** buses arrive at 180 9th St. North, St. Petersburg (☎ **800/231-2222**).

By Car   The St. Petersburg area is linked to the Interstate system and is accessible from I-75, I-275, I-4, U.S. 19, and Fla. 60.

VISITOR INFORMATION   For information on the area, contact the **St. Petersburg/Clearwater Area Convention & Visitors Bureau,** in the ThunderDome, 1 Stadium Dr., Suite A, St. Petersburg, FL 33705-1706 (☎ **813/582-7892,** or 800/354-6710 for advance hotel reservations).

Specific information about downtown St. Petersburg is also available from the **St. Petersburg Area Chamber of Commerce,** 100 2nd Ave. North, St. Petersburg, FL 33701 (☎ **813/821-4069**). There are also walk-in **visitor information centers** at the Pier in downtown St. Petersburg, and at St. Petersburg Beach, Treasure Island, Madeira Beach, Indian Rocks Beach, Clearwater, and Clearwater Beach.

GETTING AROUND   **By Bus**   The **Pinellas Suncoast Transit Authority/ PSTA** (☎ **813/530-9911**) operates regular bus service. **BATS City Transit,** 5201 Gulf Blvd., St. Petersburg Beach (☎ **813/367-3086**), offers bus service along the St. Petersburg Beach strip. The **Treasure Island Transit System,** c/o City Hall, 120 108th Ave. (☎ **813/360-0811**), runs along the Treasure Island strip. Fares for all of the above are $1.

By Car   All major car-rental firms are represented at the airports and in the St. Pete/ Clearwater area, including **Avis** (☎ 813/867-6662), **Dollar** (☎ 813/367-3779), **Hertz** (☎ 813/360-1631), and **National** (☎ 813/530-5491). Local car-rental companies include **Pinellas** (☎ 813/535-9891) and **Suncoast** (☎ 813/393-3133).

By Trolley   The **Jolley Trolley** (☎ **813/445-1200**), operated in conjunction with the City of Clearwater, provides service in the Clearwater Beach area. A ride costs 25¢.

By Taxi   Call either **Yellow Cab** (☎ 813/821-7777) or **Independent Cab** (☎ 813/327-3444). Along the beach, the major cab company is **BATS Taxi,** 5201 Gulf Blvd., St. Petersburg Beach (☎ 813/367-3702).

CITY LAYOUT

St. Petersburg is laid out according to a grid system, with streets running north-south and avenues running east-west. **Central Avenue** is the dividing line for north and south addresses.

With the exception of Central Avenue, most streets and avenues downtown are one-way. Two-way traffic is also permitted on boulevards, usually diagonal thoroughfares west or north of downtown, including Tyrone Boulevard, Gandy Boulevard, and Roosevelt Boulevard.

St. Petersburg's **downtown** district sits between two bays—Tampa and Boca Ciega. The major focus is on the section lining Tampa Bay, known as the Bayfront. Here you'll find the Pier, major museums, and most downtown hotels.

Fanning out from the Bayfront, the city is composed of various residential neighborhoods.

St. Petersburg Beach, west of downtown and between Boca Ciega Bay and the Gulf of Mexico, is a 7¹/₂-mile stretch of beach. **Gulf Boulevard** is the main two-way north-south thoroughfare, and most avenues, which cross in an east-west direction, have two-way traffic.

The **Clearwater** area is located north of St. Petersburg Beach and west of downtown, and includes Treasure Island (3¹/₂ miles in length), Sand Key Island (a 12-mile island composed of Madeira Beach, Redington Beach, North Redington Beach, Redington Shores, Indian Shores, Indian Rocks Beach, and Belleair Beach), Clearwater Beach, Dunedin, and Tarpon Springs.

BEACHES

According to one of the word's foremost beach experts, Dr. Stephen Leatherman of the University of Maryland—who annually rates 650 beaches in the country from Hawaii to Maine using a rating system that includes cleanliness, natural beauty, and water and sand quality—three of the area's beaches are among the finest in the United States:

CALADESI ISLAND STATE PARK   This 3¹/₂-mile beach at 3 Causeway Blvd. in Dunedin (☎ 813/469-5918) was voted the second-finest beach in the country. Its no-cars policy means no noise and no pollution. The island is accessible only by a **ferry** ($4 for adults and $2.50 for kids) that leaves from Honeymoon Island hourly every day year round (☎ 813/734-1501). There's another ferry service operating less frequently from downtown Clearwater (☎ 813/442-7433 for a recording with details).

The lovely, relatively secluded beach has fine soft sand and is edged in sea grass and palmettos. Dolphins cavort in the calm waters offshore. In the park itself, there's a nature trail. Rattlesnakes, black racers, raccoons, armadillos, and rabbits live on the island. A concession stand, a ranger station, and bathhouses (with rest rooms and showers) are available at no charge.

FORT DESOTO PARK   This group of five connected barrier islands has been set aside as a bird, animal, and plant sanctuary. Besides a glorious white-sugar sand beach where you can watch the manatees and dolphins play, this 900-acre Pinellas County park has a Spanish-American War–era fort, fishing piers, and a campground that's almost always sold out. Not surprising—this was ranked the 10th-finest beach in the country. It has over 230 camping sites that go for $17.75 a night, which includes electric hookup and water. Reservations must be made in person and paid in cash within 30 days of your stay. The fishing is great, there's a large playgroud for kids, and 4 miles of trails wind through the park for in-line skaters, bicyclists, and joggers. The park is located off I-275 South at Exit 4, on the Pinellas Byway (☎ **813/ 866-2662**).

SAND KEY PARK   This county park south of Clearwater Beach consistently ranks up there around the 15th finest in the country. It's nice because it's off the beaten path from the more commercial Clearwater Beach, and visitors love the wide beach and gentle surf. For information, call 813/464-3347.

SPORTS & OUTDOOR ACTIVITIES

With year-round sunshine and 28 miles of coastline along the Gulf of Mexico, the St. Petersburg area offers a wealth of recreational activities.

When visiting St. Petersburg, you can get up-to-the-minute recorded information about the city's sports and recreational activities by calling the **Leisure Line** (☎ **813/ 893-7500**).

BICYCLING   With miles of flat terrain, St. Petersburg is ideal for bikers. Among the prime biking routes are Straub Park and along the bayfront, Fort DeSoto Park, Pass-a-Grille, and the Pinellas Trail (see the accompanying box).

Beach Cyclist, 7517 Blind Pass Rd. (☎ **813/367-5001**), on the northern tip of St. Petersburg Beach, offers several types of bikes, from a beach cruiser (allowed on the beaches at Treasure Island and Madeira Beach) to a selection of standard racing bikes. Prices begin at $10 for 4 hours, $12 for 24 hours, or $39 for the week. It's open Monday to Saturday from 10am to 6pm.

The **Transportation Station,** 652 Bayway Blvd. (☎ **813/443-3188**), on Clearwater Beach, rents all types of bikes, from single-speed to racers, tandems, and mountain bikes, as well as in-line skates and one- and two-passenger scooters. Helmets and baby seats are also available. Prices for bicycles start at $5 to $8 an hour, $14.95 to $21.95 for the overnight special, $44 to $66 per week; scooters are $13 to $18 an hour, $39.95 to $54.95 for the overnight special, $109 to $169 per week. It's open daily from 9am to 7pm.

BOAT RENTALS   Captain Dave's Watersports, 9540 Blind Pass Rd., St. Petersburg Beach (☎ **813/367-4336**), offers Waverunner and powerboat rentals, parasail rides, snorkeling trips, sailing, and shelling trips. Waverunner rentals begin at $35 per half hour, $60 per hour; powerboat rentals are $50 and up for 1 hour, $70 and up for 2 hours, $135 and up per day; parasail rides are $30 to $35; snorkeling trips are $35. Captain Dave is open daily from 9am to 5pm or later.

A downtown facility, **Waterworks Rentals,** on the Pier (☎ **813/363-0000**), rents Waverunners and jet boats. Waverunner rentals begin at $25 for a half hour; for jet boats, from $45 per hour. Open daily from 9am to 6pm or later.

FISHING   One of the largest party-boat fishing fleets in the area, Capt. Dave Spaulding's **Queen Fleet,** Slip 52, Clearwater Beach Marina, 25 Causeway Blvd. (☎ **813/446-7666**), offers trips of varying duration. Bait is furnished, but rod rental is extra. Prices are $22 for a half day, $35 for three-quarters of a day, $5 extra for rods.

Capt. Kidd, in the Dolphin Village Shopping Center, 4737 Gulf Blvd., St. Petersburg Beach (☎ **813/360-2263**), in the heart of the downtown St. Pete beach strip, takes passengers on half- and full-day fishing trips in the gulf. Rates, including rod, reel, and bait, are $25 for adults and $22 for children and seniors on a half-day trip, $37.25 for adults and $34.25 for seniors on a full-day outing.

If you want a change from the usual fishing boat, try **Double Eagle's Deep Sea Fishing Boats,** Slip 50, Clearwater Beach Marina, 25 Causeway Blvd., Clearwater Beach (☎ 813/446-1653). It offers two catamarans, 88 feet and 65 feet in length, that go 20 to 25 miles offshore into the gulf on 4- or 8-hour trips, with bait provided. Prices are $22 to $35 for adults, $18 to $30 for children, and $4 to $5 for tackle. The 4-hour trip departs daily at 8am and 1pm, and the 8-hour trip leaves daily at 9am and returns at 5pm.

Miss Pass-A-Grille, Dolphin Landings Charter Boat Center, 4737 Gulf Blvd., St. Petersburg Beach (☎ 813/367-4488 or 813/367-7411), is conveniently docked in the heart of the St. Petersburg Beach hotel strip. This fishing boat offers daily trips into Tampa Bay and the gulf. Prices are $24.95 for 4 hours, $37.95 for 7 hours; for both trips, children 11 and under are charge $5 less and seniors are charged $3 less. Sailings are scheduled on Tuesday, Wednesday, and Friday at 8am and 1pm, and on Thursday, Saturday, and Sunday at 9am.

GOLF One of the top 50 municipal golf courses in the United States, the **Mangrove Bay Golf Course,** 875 62nd Ave. NE (☎ 813/893-7797), hugs the inlets of Old Tampa Bay and offers 18-hole, par-72 play. Facilities include a driving range; lessons and golf-club rental are also available. Greens fees are $19, $29 including a cart. It's open daily from 6:30am to 6pm.

Adjacent to the St. Petersburg–Clearwater airport, the **Airco Flite Golf Course,** 3650 Roosevelt Blvd., Clearwater (☎ 813/573-4653), is a championship 18-hole, par-72 course with a driving range. Golf-club rentals are available. The price per person, including a cart, is $28. It's open daily from 7am to 6pm.

SAILING The **Annapolis Sailing School,** 6800 34th St. South (☎ 813/867-8102, or 800/638-9192), can teach you to sail or perfect your sailing skills. Various courses are offered at this branch of the famous Maryland-based school, lasting 2, 5, or 8 days. Prices, depending on season and length of course, are $225 to $1,920 per person.

If you prefer to be part of the crew, or just want to relax for 2¹/₂ hours enjoy ing the views of the gulf waters, sail aboard the 40-foot racing yacht *Southern Romance,* Slip 16, Clearwater Beach Marina, Clearwater Beach (☎ 813/446-5503). Reservations are required. Prices are $18 per person. The boat departs daily at 11am, 1:30pm, 4:30pm, and sunset.

TENNIS **Hurley Park,** 1600 Pass-a-Grille Way, Pass-a-Grille, St. Petersburg Beach, sports just one court and it's available on a first-come, first-served basis. It's free, but there's a 1-hour limit. The park is open daily from 8am to 10pm.

On a larger scale, with 15 Har-Tru courts, the **St. Petersburg Tennis Center,** 650 18th Ave. South (☎ 813/893-7301), provides lessons, clinics, and open play. Prices are $6 per person per day, or $4.50 after 1pm. It's open Monday to Friday from 8am to 9pm and on Saturday and Sunday from 8am to 6pm.

WATERSKIING **Captain Dave's Watersports,** 9540 Blind Pass Rd., St. Petersburg Beach (☎ 813/367-4336), offers waterskiing lessons for $45 per half hour or $70 per hour.

WHAT TO SEE & DO

✪ **The Pier.** 800 2nd Ave. NE. ☎ **813/821-6164.** Free admission to all the public areas and decks; donations welcome at the aquarium; parking $1. Shops, Mon–Sat 10am–9pm, Sun 11am–7pm; restaurants, daily 11am–11pm; bars, daily 10am–midnight or 1am; aquarium, Mon–Sat 10am–8pm, Sun 11am–6pm.

Biking & Skating Along the Pinellas Trail to Dunedin

The Pinellas Trail, a 15-foot-wide, paved 47-mile trail built along an abandoned railroad bed, passes right through the heart of picturesque downtown Dunedin. Cars are forbidden on the trail, making it popular with joggers, in-line skaters, bikers, and walkers exploring nature. It's packed on the weekends.

Founded in 1870, the Scottish town of Dunedin is located less than 10 miles north of Clearwater off Alt. U.S. 19 and is filled with kooky antiques shops and cafés. It's worth visiting this sibling city of Stirling, Scotland, for its atmospheric waterfront, revitalized downtown, and villagelike atmosphere.

Fishermen, swimmers, and boaters know this area well. Honeymoon State Park is a 5-minute drive from the mainland, and Caladesi State Park is here also, though accessible only by private boat or public ferry. The islands are refuges to many endangered species of birds and are a nesting site for the osprey.

Forget your in-line skates? You can rent them at **Skate 2000** (☎ 813/734-7849), located right off Main Street in a converted old box car, where you can get free lessons on Sunday from 10am to noon.

Downtown, you can skate right into the pink, European-style **Cafe Alfresco** at 344 Main St. (☎ 813/736-4299). It features a light lunch and dinner menu with salads and sandwiches, offers a famous weekend brunch, and is great for people-watching. Also very casual and people-friendly is a coffee shop–type place called **Kelly's for Just About Anything,** at 319 Main St. (☎ 813/736-5284), which has great breakfast items like blueberry flapjacks. **Bon Appetit,** at 148 Marina Plaza (☎ 813/733-2151), caters to the upscale crowd; open daily, it serves up continental cuisine with a waterfront view. The tiny, chic, romantic **Sabel's** offes an eclectic menu at 315 Main St. (☎ 813/734-DINE).

Within walking distance of Main Street is the **Jamaica Inn,** at 150 Marine Plaza (☎ 813/733-4121), which overlooks St. Joseph's Sound. Every room faces the water and, though they're tiny, all have microwaves, minibars, and refrigerators.

A touch of Scotland comes to Dunedin every spring with the **Highland Games and Festival.** Bands and dancers from around the world compete in games. For further information about Dunedin, contact the **Dunedin Chamber of Commerce,** 301 Main St., Dunedin, FL 34698 (☎ 813/733-3197).

Walk out on the Pier and enjoy this festive waterfront complex overlooking Tampa Bay. Originally built as a railroad pier in 1889, over the years it was redesigned in various formats until taking its present shape of an inverted pyramid in 1988. Today it's the city's gathering spot, with five levels of shops and restaurants, plus an aquarium, tourist information desk, observation deck, catwalks for fishing, boat docks, a small bayside beach, miniature golf, water-sports rentals, and sightseeing boats. A free trolley service operates between the Pier and nearby parking lots.

St. Petersburg ThunderDome. 1 Stadium Dr. ☎ **813/825-3100.** Admission $4–$30, depending on the event. Tours available when events are not scheduled.

This place is huge and offers year-round sporting events, concerts, and conventions. The skyline of St. Petersburg was dramatically changed when "the dome" was built on a 66-acre downtown site. The translucent roof is the first cable-supported dome of its kind in the United States and the largest of its type in the world.

MUSEUMS

Florida International Museum. 100 2nd St. North. ☎ **813/822-3693**, or 800/777-9882. Admission $14.50 adults, $13.25 seniors, $5 children 5–16. Daily 9am–6pm. From I-275, take Exit 10 to I-375, then go east to 2nd Street North and make a right; it's between 1st and 2nd avenues North.

This awesome museum made a big media splash in 1995 with its first exhibit, Treasures of the Czars, and aims to be a cultural mecca for downtown St. Petersburg with major international rotating exhibits January to June. It's housed in the former Maas Brothers Department Store, long an area landmark. A 1997 exhibit will include a salute to Greece. Call in advance of your visit to check what show will be up when you're in town. Tickets must be reserved and purchased in advance for a specific day and entry time.

Great Explorations. 1120 4th St. South. ☎ **813/821-8885.** Admission $5 adults, $4.50 seniors, $4 children 4–17, free for children 3 and under. Mon–Sat 10am–5pm, Sun noon–5pm.

With a variety of hands-on exhibits, this museum is great for kids who've overdosed on the sun and need to cool off inside. They can explore a long, dark touch-tunnel; measure their strength, flexibility, and fitness; paint a work of art with sunlight; and play a melody with a sweep of the hand.

✪ Museum of Fine Arts. 255 Beach Dr. NE. ☎ **813/896-2667.** Admission $5 adults, $3 seniors, $2 students. Tues–Sat 10am–5pm, Sun 1–5pm; plus the third Thurs of each month 10am–9pm.

Resembling a Mediterranean villa on the waterfront, this museum houses a permanent collection of European, American, pre-Columbian, and Far Eastern art, with works by such artists as Fragonard, Monet, Renoir, Cézanne, and Gauguin. Other highlights include period rooms with antiques and historical furnishings, plus a gallery of Steuben crystal, a new decorative-arts gallery, and major rotating exhibits.

✪ Salvador Dalí Museum. 1000 3rd St. South. ☎ **813/823-3767.** Admission $6 adults, $5 seniors, $4 students, free for children 9 and under. Mon–Sat 9:30am–5:30pm, Sun noon–5pm. Closed Thanksgiving and Christmas Day.

Nestled on Tampa Bay south of the Pier, this starkly modern museum houses the world's largest collection of works by the renowned Spanish surrealist. The museum was created in 1982, thanks to a donation of Dalí works owned by Cleveland industrialist A. Reynolds Morse and his wife, Eleanor R. Morse, who were friends of Dalí and his wife, Gala. Valued at over $150 million, the collection includes 94 oil paintings, over 100 watercolors and drawings, and 1,300 graphics, plus posters, photos, sculptures, and objets d'art, and a 5,000-volume library on Dalí and surrealism.

✪ St. Petersburg Museum of History. 335 2nd Ave. NE. ☎ **813/894-1052.** Admission $4.50 adults, $3.50 seniors, $1.50 children 7–17, free for children 6 and under. Mon–Sat 10am–5pm, Sun 1–5pm.

Located on the approach to the Pier, this museum features a permanent interactive exhibit chronicling St. Petersburg's history. The thousands of items on display range from prehistoric artifacts to documents, clothing, and photographs. There are also computer stations enabling visitors to flip through the past. Walk-through exhibits include a prototype general store and post office (ca. 1880) and a replica of the Benoist airboat, suspended in mock flight from a 25-foot ceiling and commemorating the first scheduled commercial flight in the world, which took off from St. Petersburg in 1914.

NATURE & WILDLIFE EXPERIENCES

Clearwater Marine Science Center Aquarium. 249 Windward Passage, Clearwater. ☎ **813/447-0980.** Admission $5.25 adults, $3.50 children 3–11, free for children 2 and under. Mon–Fri 9am–5pm, Sat 9am–4pm, Sun 11am–4pm. From the mainland, turn right at Island Way; the center is 1 mile east of Clearwater Beach on Island Estates.

This little jewel of an aquarium on Clearwater Harbor is very low key and friendly. It's dedicated to the rescue and rehabilitation of marine mammals and sea turtles. Exhibits include dolphins, otters, sea turtles, sharks, stingrays, mangroves, and sea grass.

✪ **Suncoast Seabird Sanctuary.** 18328 Gulf Blvd., Indian Shores. ☎ **813/391-6211.** Free admission, but donations welcome. Daily 9am–dusk. Take I-275 North to Fla. 694 West (Exit 15), cross the Intracoastal Waterway, turn left on Gulf Boulevard, and the sanctuary is a quarter mile south.

Visit the largest wild-bird hospital in the nation, dedicated to the rescue, repair, recuperation, and release of sick and injured wild birds. At any one time there are usually more than 500 sea and land birds living at the sanctuary, from cormorants, white herons, and birds of prey to the ubiquitous brown pelican.

Sunken Gardens. 1825 4th St. North. ☎ **813/896-3186.** Admission $14 adults, $8 children 3–11, free for children 2 and under. Daily 10am–5pm.

One of the city's oldest attractions, this 7-acre tropical garden park dates back to 1935. It contains a vast array of 5,000 plants, flowers, and trees. In addition, there are a walk-through aviary, bird and alligator shows, and a wax museum depicting biblical figures.

✪ **John's Pass Village and Boardwalk.** 12901 Gulf Blvd., Madeira Beach. ☎ **813/391-7373.** Free admission. Shops and activities, daily 9am–6pm or later; most restaurants, daily 7am–11pm. From downtown, take Central Avenue west via the Treasure Island Causeway to Gulf Boulevard; turn right, go for 20 blocks, cross over the bridge, and the entrance is on the right.

Casual and charming, this rustic Florida fishing village lies on the southern edge of Madeira Beach. A string of simple wooden structures topped by tin roofs rest on pilings 12 feet above sea level, all connected by a 1,000-foot boardwalk. Most of the buildings have been converted into shops, art galleries, and restaurants. The focal point is the large fishing pier and marina, where many water sports are available for visitors.

Bay Cruises

Shell Key Shuttle, Merry Pier, 801 Pass-a-Grille Way, St. Petersburg Beach (☎ **813/360-1348**), offers shuttle service to nearby Shell Island, south of St. Petersburg, via a 57-passenger catamaran. The ride takes 15 minutes, and you can return on any shuttle you wish. Boats leave daily at 10am, noon, 2pm, and (summer only) 4pm, and prices are $10 for adults, $5 for children 12 and under.

Cruises around Boca Ciega Bay are offered on *The Lady Anderson,* St. Petersburg Beach Causeway, 3400 Pasadena Ave. South (☎ **813/367-7804**). The three-deck boat offers luncheon, dinner/dance, and gospel-music cruises. Cruises take place from October to mid-May. The lunch cruises operate Tuesday to Friday and cost $19.50 for adults and $13.50 for children 9 and under. Dinner cruises are offered on Friday and Saturday from 6:30 to 10pm and cost $29.50 for adults, $19.50 for children; cocktails extra. Gospel-music cruises operate on Tuesday and Thursday, boarding at 6:30pm, for $24.50 for adults and $17.50 for children. Reservations are required.

The *Caribbean Queen* (☎ **813/895-BOAT**) departs from the Pier and offers 1-hour sightseeing and dolphin-watching cruises around Tampa Bay. Sailings are daily at 11:30am and 1, 3, and 5pm; they cost $10 for adults, $8 for juniors 12 to 17, $5 for children 3 to 11, free for children 2 and under.

Captain Memo's Pirate Cruise, Clearwater Beach Marina, Slip 3 (☎ 813/446-2587), sails on the *Pirate's Ransom,* an authentic reproduction of a pirate ship. Swashbuckling 2-hour daytime pirate cruises and evening champagne cruises are offered, under the direction of fearless Captain Memo and his crew. Cruises operate year round daily at 10am and 2, 4:30, and 7pm. For adults, daytime cruises cost $25; evening cruises, $28; both daytime and evening cruises cost $18 for seniors and juniors 13 to 17, $15 for children 2 to 12, free for children under 2. Sunset cruises and weddings and birthday party cruises are also offered.

The *Sea Screamer,* Clearwater Beach Marina, Slip 10, Clearwater Beach (☎ 813/447-7200), claims to be the world's largest speedboat. This 73-foot turbo-charged twin-engine vessel provides an exhilarating spin in Gulf of Mexico waters with opportunities to view birds and marine life along the way. Prices are $9.35 for adults, $6.55 for children 6 to 12. Sailings are September to May, daily at noon, 2pm, and 4pm; and June to September, daily at noon and 2, 4, and 6pm.

SPECTATOR SPORTS

BASEBALL   The **St. Petersburg ThunderDome,** 1 Stadium Dr. (☎ 813/825-3100), is St. Petersburg's sporting centerpiece. This $110-million domed stadium has a seating capacity of 43,000. The locals are going wild getting ready for their major-league baseball team, the **Tampa Bay Devil Rays,** who will start playing here in April 1998. Exact details of schedule and prices were not available at press time.

The St. Petersburg area is also the winter home of several major-league and a couple of minor-league teams. **Spring training** for all major-league teams runs from mid-February to April. The **Baltimore Orioles** and the **St. Louis Cardinals** play at Al Lang Stadium, 180 2nd Ave. SE (☎ 813/822-3384). The **St. Petersburg Cardinals**, a Class A minor-league team, plays there April to September. Admission is $3 to $7. The **Philadelphia Phillies** play their spring-training season at the Jack Russell Stadium, 800 Phillies Dr., Clearwater (☎ 813/442-8496). Admission is $7 to $8. The **Clearwater Phillies,** a Class A minor-league Team, play April to September. Admission is $2 to $4. The recently expanded winter home of the **Toronto Blue Jays** is Grant Field, 373 Douglas Ave., Dunedin (☎ 813/733-0429). Admission is $7 to $9.

DOG RACING   Founded in 1925, **Derby Lane,** 10490 Gandy Blvd. (☎ 813/576-1361), is the world's oldest continually operating greyhound track, with indoor and outdoor seating and standing areas. Admission is $1, $2.50 for the Derby Club. There's racing January to June, Monday to Saturday at 7:30pm, with matinees on Monday, Wednesday, and Saturday at 12:30pm.

SHOPPING
SHOPPING COMPLEXES

Gas Plant Antique Arcade. 1246 Central Ave., St. Petersburg. ☎ 813/895-0368.

This four-story complex is the largest antiques mall on Florida's west coast—over 100 dealers display their wares. You'll find unusual items ranging from hat pins to armoires with prices from $1 to $1,000. They'll ship anywhere in the world. Open Monday to Saturday from 10am to 5pm and on Sunday from noon to 5pm.

John's Pass Village and Boardwalk. 12901 Gulf Blvd., Madeira Beach. ☎ 813/391-7373.

This converted fisherman's village houses over 60 shops, selling everything from antiques and arts and crafts to beachwear, right on the water. There are also several art galleries, including the Bronze Lady, which is the largest single dealer in the world of works by Red Skelton, the comedian-artist. Open daily from 9am to 6pm or later.

✪ **The Pier.** 800 2nd Ave. NE, St. Petersburg. ☎ **813/821-6164.**

The hub of shopping for the downtown area, this five-story pyramid-shaped complex houses more than a dozen boutiques and craft shops. The Pier also leads to Beach Drive, one of the most fashionable downtown strolling and shopping streets. Open Monday to Saturday from 10am to 9pm and on Sunday from 11am to 7pm.

SPECIALTY SHOPS

Evander Preston Contemporary Jewelry. 106 8th Ave., St. Petersburg Beach. ☎ **813/367-7894.**

If you're in the market for some one-of-a-kind hand-hammered jewelry, this unique gallery/workshop, housed in a 75-year-old building on Pass-a-Grille, is well worth visiting. Open Monday to Saturday from 10am to 5:30pm.

Florida Craftsmen Gallery. 237 2nd Ave. South, St. Petersburg. ☎ **813/821-7391.**

This is a showcase for the works of over 150 Florida artisans and craftspeople, offering jewelry, ceramics, woodwork, fiberworks, glassware, paper creations, and metal works. Open Tuesday to Saturday from 10am to 4pm.

Glass Canvas Gallery. 233 4th Ave. NE (off Beach Dr.), St. Petersburg. ☎ **813/821-6767.**

This modern gallery features a dazzling array of glass sculpture, tableware, art, and craft items, many of which have a sea, shell, or piscine theme. Open Monday to Friday from 10am to 6pm and on Saturday and Sunday from 10am to 5pm.

✪ **Haslams Book Store.** 2025 Central Ave., St. Petersburg. ☎ **813/822-8616.**

Although the St. Pete area has lots of bookshops, this huge emporium, established in 1933, claims to be Florida's largest, with over 300,000 new and used books, in hardcover, paperback, and electronic editions. Open Monday to Thursday and Saturday from 9am to 5:30pm, on Friday from 9am to 9pm.

P. Buckley Moss. 190 4th Ave. NE, St. Petersburg. ☎ **813/894-2899.**

This gallery/studio features the works of one of Florida's most individualistic artists, best known for her portrayal of Amish and Mennonite people. The works include paintings, graphics, figurines, and collector dolls. Open Monday to Saturday from 10am to 5pm (September to April, also on Sunday from noon to 5pm).

✪ **Red Cloud.** 208 Beach Dr. NE, St. Petersburg. ☎ **813/821-5824.**

This is an oasis for Native American works, from jewelry and headdresses to sculpture and art. Open Tuesday to Saturday from 10am to 6pm and on Sunday from 10am to 4pm.

✪ **Senior Citizen Craft Center Gift Shop.** 940 Court St., Clearwater. ☎ **813/442-4266.**

Opened about 30 years ago, this most unique gift shop is an outlet for the work of about 400 local senior citizens. The items for sale include knitwear, crochetwork, woodwork, stained glass, clocks, scrimshaw, jewelry, pottery, tilework, ceramics, and hand-painted clothing. It's well worth a visit, even though it's a little off the usual tourist track. Open June to August, Monday to Friday from 10am to 4pm; September to May, Monday to Saturday from 10am to 4pm.

The Shell Store. 440 75th Ave., St. Petersburg Beach. ☎ **813/360-0586.**

This shop specializes in corals and shells and an on-premises mini-museum illustrates how they both live and grow. You'll find a good selection of shell home decorations, shell hobbyist supplies, shell art, planters, and jewelry. Open Monday to Saturday from 9:30am to 5pm.

WHERE TO STAY

The St. Petersburg/Clearwater area offers a great variety of accommodations, from posh resorts on the beach and inland to small family-run motels and efficiencies—almost always with a pool.

While most resorts tend to be pricy, there are alternatives. Quiet Pass-a-Grille, at the southern tip of St. Petersburg Beach, is a mostly residential enclave with eclectic shops and smaller motels. North of St. Petersburg Beach stretch a cluster of beaches from Treasure Island northward to Clearwater Beach, scattered with small, family-oriented motels—especially along Indian Rocks and Madeira Beach.

For visitors looking for alternative accommodations, the St. Petersburg / Clearwater Area Convention & Visitors Bureau recently introduced a **Superior Small Lodgings** program showcasing smaller hostelries that offer 50 units or fewer (☎ **800/345-6710** for a brochure). While there's no guarantee you'll find low rates (especially along the beaches in high season), these can be an alternative to the larger more expensive beach resorts.

The high season, with high prices, is from January to April. Inquire about special hotel packages in the summer, when great discounts can be found for the asking. Also, consider renting an apartment, with a kitchen, by the week. You may save over a daily hotel rate, as well as cut down on meal expenses.

It's wise to make reservations early around here, especially in the high season between January and April when the more popular beach resorts along St. Petersburg Beach, Sand Key, and Clearwater Beach are booked.

The local hotel tax is 10%.

DOUBLES FOR LESS THAN $40

Pelican East & West. 108 21st Ave., Indian Rocks Beach, FL 34635. ☎ **813/595-9741.** 8 apts. A/C TV. $35–$55 apt for two at Pelican East; $55–$70 apt for two at Pelican West. MC, V.

P.D.I.P. (Perfect Day in Paradise) is the motto at this well-kept motel complex offering a choice of two settings, depending on your budget. The lowest rates are at Pelican East, 500 feet from the beach, with four units, each with bedroom and separate kitchen. Pelican West sits on the beachfront, offering four apartments, each with living room, bedroom, kitchen, patio, and unbeatable views of the gulf.

DOUBLES FOR LESS THAN $60

✪ **Sun West Beach Motel.** 409 Hamden Dr. South, Clearwater Beach, FL 34630. ☎ **813/442-5008.** 4 rms, 10 efficiencies. A/C TV TEL. High season, $59 double; $79 efficiency. Off-season, $40–42 double; $56 efficiency. DISC, MC, V.

Overlooking the bay and only a 2-block walk from the beach, this well-maintained one-story motel has a heated pool, fishing/boating dock, sundeck, shuffleboard court, and guest laundry. All units, which face either the bay, the pool, or the sundeck, have contemporary resort-style furnishings. The four motel rooms have small refrigerators and the 10 efficiencies have kitchens.

DOUBLES FOR LESS THAN $80

Alpaugh's Gulf Beach Motel Apartments. 68 Gulf Blvd., Indian Rocks Beach, FL 34635. ☎ **813/595-2589.** 16 rms. A/C TV TEL. High season, $80–$85 double. Off-season, $56–$60 double. MC, V.

This long-popular family-oriented motel sits beside the beach with a grassy central courtyard. The rooms offer modern furnishings with a kitchenette and dining area. Facilities include a coin-operated laundry, lawn games, picnic tables, and shuffleboard at each location.

There's a second Alpaugh's motel at 1912 Gulf Blvd., Indian Rocks Beach, FL 34635 (☎ 813/595-9421), with similar facilities and room rates, plus a one-bedroom cottage for $68 to $91 and some two-bedroom suites for $74 to $103.

Captain's Quarters Inn. 10035 Gulf Blvd., Treasure Island, FL 33706. ☎ **813/360-1659** or 800/526-9547. 6 efficiencies, 3 suites. A/C TV TEL. $70 efficiency; $65-$95 suite. Minimum stay 3 nights. MC, V.

This nautically themed property is a real find, offering well-kept accommodations on the gulf at inland rates. Six rooms are efficiencies with new mini-kitchens (including microwave oven, coffeemaker, and wet bar or sink), and three units have a separate bedroom and a full kitchen. The complex sits on 100 yards of beach, an ideal vantage point for sunset watching. Facilities include an outdoor solar-heated freshwater swimming pool, a sundeck, guest barbecues, and a library.

Palm Pavilion Inn. 18 Bay Esplanade, Clearwater Beach, FL 34630. ☎ **813/446-6777** or 800/433-PALM. 24 rms, 4 efficiencies. A/C TV TEL. High season, $82-$102 double; $102 efficiency. Off-season, $49-$64 double; $64 efficiency. AE, MC, V.

A real find, this quiet spot is away from the noise of Clearwater Beach yet within walking distance of all the action. The three-story art deco building is trimmed in pink and blue. The lobby area and guest rooms are equally art deco, with rounded light-wood and rattan furnishings, bright sea-toned fabrics, photographs from the 1920 to 1950s, and vertical blinds. Rooms in the front of the house face the gulf and those in the back face the bay; four units have kitchenettes. Also available are a rooftop sundeck, beach access, a heated swimming pool, and complimentary coffee.

DOUBLES FOR LESS THAN $100

✪ **Bayboro House Bed and Breakfast.** 1719 Beach Dr. SE, St. Petersburg, FL 33701. ☎ **813/823-4955.** Fax 813/823-4955. 4 rms. A/C TV. High season, $100-$120 double. Off-season, $85-$105 double. Rates include breakfast. MC, V.

Situated in a residential area a few minutes south of Bayboro Harbor, this three-story Victorian historic landmark overlooks Tampa Bay opposite a small beach. An Old South ambience prevails here, with a wide veranda bedecked with rockers and cozy upstairs bedrooms filled with antique beds and armoires, lace, and quilts. There's a VCR in each room along with the morning paper. Splurge on the romantic suite that includes roses and champagne.

Bay Gables Bed & Breakfast. 136 4th Ave. NE, St. Petersburg, FL 33701. ☎ **813/822-8855** or 800-822-8803. Fax 813/822-8855. 9 rms. A/C. $85-$135 double year-round. Rates include continental breakfast. AE, MC, V.

You can walk to the Pier from this charming B&B that overlooks a flower-filled garden with a gazebo and faces a fanciful Victorian-style tea room/restaurant. The rooms in this 1930s building have been furnished with ceiling fans and period-style pieces, including some canopy beds. All units have bathrooms outfitted with clawfoot tubs and modern showers; half the rooms have a porch, while the rest have a separate sitting room and kitchenette. Each morning a champagne continental breakfast is served in the common room, on the garden deck, or in the gazebo.

Colonial Gateway Inn. 6300 Gulf Blvd., St. Petersburg Beach, FL 33706. ☎ **813/267-2711** or 800/237-8918. Fax 813/367-7068. 200 rms. A/C TV TEL. High season, $93-$121 double. Off-season, $69-$111 double. AE, CB, DC, DISC, MC, V.

Spread over a quarter mile of beachfront, this U-shaped complex of one- and two-story units is a favorite with families. The rooms, most of which face the pool and a

St. Petersburg Accommodations & Attractions

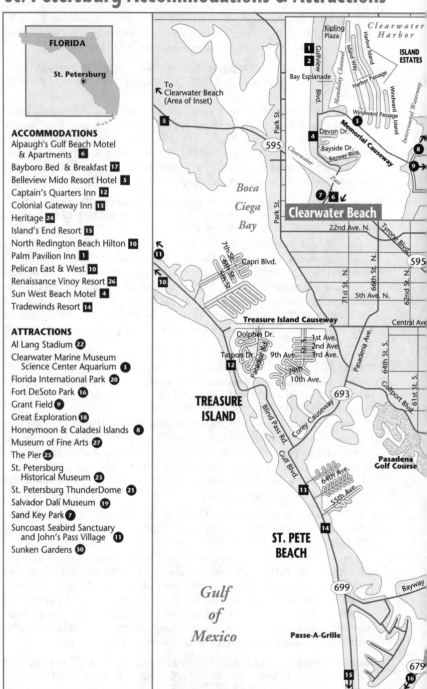

FLORIDA

St. Petersburg

ACCOMMODATIONS

Alpaugh's Gulf Beach Motel
& Apartments **6**
Bayboro Bed & Breakfast **17**
Belleview Mido Resort Hotel **5**
Captain's Quarters Inn **12**
Colonial Gateway Inn **13**
Heritage **24**
Island's End Resort **15**
North Redington Beach Hilton **10**
Palm Pavilion Inn **1**
Pelican East & West **10**
Renaissance Vinoy Resort **26**
Sun West Beach Motel **4**
Tradewinds Resort **14**

ATTRACTIONS

Al Lang Stadium **22**
Clearwater Marine Museum
Science Center Aquarium **3**
Florida International Park **20**
Fort DeSoto Park **16**
Grant Field **9**
Great Exploration **18**
Honeymoon & Caladesi Islands **8**
Museum of Fine Arts **27**
The Pier **25**
St. Petersburg
Historical Museum **23**
St. Petersburg ThunderDome **21**
Salvador Dalí Museum **19**
Sand Key Park **7**
Suncoast Seabird Sanctuary
and John's Pass Village **11**
Sunken Gardens **30**

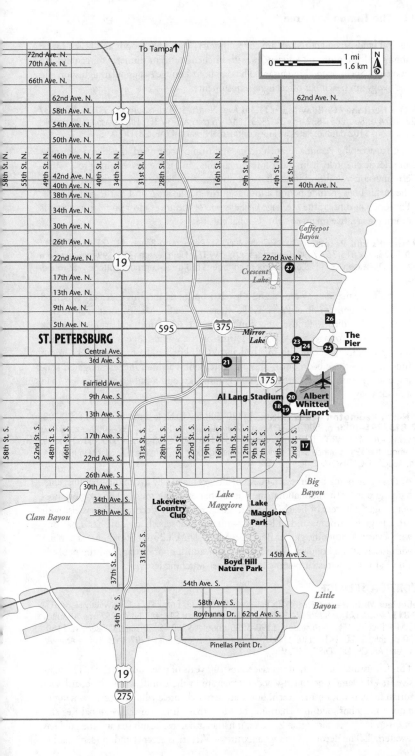

central landscaped courtyard, are contemporary, with light woods and beach tones; about half the units are efficiencies with kitchenettes. For dinner, you can enjoy a branch of Shells seafood restaurant. The Bambooz Lounge is a popular nightspot, and the Swigwam beach bar offers light refreshments.

✪ **The Heritage / Holiday Inn.** 234 3rd Ave. North, St. Petersburg, FL 33701. ☎ **813/ 822-4814** or 800/283-7829. Fax 813/823-1644. 75 rms. A/C TV TEL. High season, $86 double. Low season, $102 double. Rates include continental breakfast. AE, CB, DC, MC, V.

With a sweeping veranda, French doors, and tropical courtyard, the Heritage attracts an eclectic clientele, from older folks to families, and is the nearest thing to a southern mansion you'll find in the heart of downtown. Dating back to the early 1920s, the furnishings include period antiques in the public areas and in the guest rooms. For lunch or dinner, the Heritage Grille is one of the area's most popular restaurants offering a creative menu of light regional cuisine.

✪ **Island's End Resort.** 1 Pass-a-Grille Way, St. Petersburg Beach, FL 33706. ☎ **813/ 360-5023.** Fax 813/367-7890. 6 cottages. A/C, TV, TEL. High season, $75–$99 one-bedroom cottage. Off-season $61–$78,one bedroom cottage. $160 three-bedroom cottage year-round. MC, V.

Far from the maddening crowd and a lovely tropical escape, this hideaway is nestled in the quiet southern tip of Pass-a-Grille where the Gulf of Mexico meets Tampa Bay. It's a good choice for those who don't want the standard hotel atmosphere. Six contemporary cottages enjoy a shady setting on the water's edge. Each cottage has a dining area, living room with sofa bed and VCR, kitchen, bathroom, and bedroom (one unit has three bedrooms), plus a private pool. Facilities include a lighted fishing dock, patios, decks, barbecues, and hammocks; and a public beach is less than a block away.

✪ **North Redington Beach Hilton.** 17120 Gulf Blvd., N. Redington Beach, FL 33708. ☎ **813/391-4000** or 800/HILTONS or 800/447-SAND. Fax 813/391-4000, ext. 7777. 125 rms. A/C MINIBAR TV TEL. High season, $125–$190 double. Off-season, $100–$160 double. Ask about the $99 "Bounce Back" package, including room and breakfast, available in high season. AE, CB, DC, DISC, MC, V.

At this outstanding beach resort, guests of all ages practically live in their bathing suits, hanging out by the pool and at the outside bar enjoying music. The six-story hostelry edges 250 feet of beachfront, and guest rooms are decorated in pastels, with extra-large bathrooms and full-length–mirrored closets. Each unit has a balcony with a view of either the gulf or Boca Ciega Bay. The Gulffront Steakhouse is popular with locals at the holidays and offers outdoor and indoor dining, and the poolside Tiki Bar is popular each evening for its sunset-watching festivities.

WORTH A SPLURGE

Belleview Mido Resort Hotel. 25 Belleview Blvd. (P.O. Box 2317), Clearwater, FL 34617. ☎ 813/442-6171 or 800/237-8947. Fax 813/441-4173 or 813/443-6361. 252 rms, 40 suites. A/C MINIBAR TV TEL. High season, $190–$260 double; $260 –$450 suite. Off-season, $150– $190 double; $220–$410 suite. Special discount packages during 1997, their 100th Anniversary year. AE, CB, DC, DISC, MC, V.

This Clearwater landmark hotel celebrates 100 years of operation in 1997. The massive (it's the largest occupied wooden structure in the world) white clapboard Victorian hotel is not on the beach, but it attracts a clientele who appreciate staying in a quiet neighborhood in a charming building that's listed on the National Register of Historic Places. Sitting on 21 acres, it has an attractive health spa and the pool has a waterfall. The decor is a strange mixture of Victorian accents and modern marble and glass. The high-ceilinged guest rooms are very large and decorated in Queen Anne style, with dark-wood period furniture. The new 3,400-square-foot Presidential Suite is awesome, with a huge dining room.

The main restaurants are the informal indoor/outdoor Terrace Cafe for breakfast, lunch, or dinner; and the elegant, upscale Madame Ma's for gourmet Chinese cuisine. There's also a pub in the basement, a lounge, and a poolside bar. Room service is available; other services include dry cleaning and valet laundry, nightly turndown, a currency-exchange desk, and baby-sitting.

On the property are an 18-hole, par-72 championship golf course, four red-clay tennis courts, indoor and outdoor heated swimming pools, a Jacuzzi, a sauna, Swiss showers, a workout gym, jogging and walking trails, bicycle rentals, yacht charters, gift shops, an art gallery, and a newsstand. Guests have access to a private Cabana Club on the Gulf of Mexico.

✪ **Renaissance Vinoy Resort.** 501 5th Ave. NE, St. Petersburg, FL 33701. ☎ **813/ 894-1000,** or 800/HOTELS-1. Fax 813/822-2785. 360 rms. A/C MINIBAR TV TEL. High season, $189–$279 double. Off-season, $129–$169 double. AE, CB, DC, DISC, MC, V.

This place exudes elegance with its seven-story, peach-toned Mediterranean-style facade. It overlooks Tampa Bay and is within walking distance of the Pier, Central Avenue, museums, and other attractions. Dating back to 1925, in its early years it saw some of the country's most influential people: Calvin Coolidge, Herbert Hoover, Babe Ruth, and F. Scott Fitzgerald. The hotel reopened in 1992 after a meticulous $93-million restoration and refurbishment.

All the guest rooms, many of which enjoy lovely views of the bayfront, are designed to offer the utmost comfort and include three phones, an additional TV in the bathroom, hair dryer, and more; some units in the new wing have individual Jacuzzis and private patios/balconies.

For fine dining, Marchand's Grille, an elegant room overlooking the bay, specializes in steaks, seafood, and chops. The Terrace Room is the main dining room for breakfast, lunch, and dinner. Casual lunches and dinners are at the indoor-outdoor Alfresco near the pool deck or the Clubhouse at the golf course on Snell Isle. There are also two bar/lounges. There's 24-hour room service, plus the services of a concierge, laundry service, tour desk, and child care facility.

On the premises are two swimming pools, a 14-court tennis complex (9 lighted), a private 74-slip marina, two croquet courts, a fitness center (with sauna, steam room, spa, massage, and exercise equipment), a hair salon, and a gift shop. Guests have access to two bayside beaches (there's shuttle service to gulf beaches) and a private 18-hole championship golf course on nearby Snell Isle.

TradeWinds Resort. 5500 Gulf Blvd., St. Petersburg Beach, FL 33706. ☎ **813/367-6461** or 800/237-0707. Fax 813/360-3848. 377 units. A/C TV TEL. High season, $195–$259 double. Off-season, $165–$319 double. Discount packages available in the summer. AE, CB, DC, DISC, MC, V.

Enjoy the beach, swim, play, and hop into a paddleboat with your kids on one of the private lagoons to watch the swans and ducks. This six- and seven-story resort sits amid 18 acres of beachfront property, sand dunes, and tropical gardens. The guest units, which look out on the gulf or the extensive grounds, have modern kitchens or kitchenettes, contemporary furnishings, and private balconies. The children's program is a big hit with families from all around the world.

The top spot for lunch or dinner is the Palm Court, with an Italian-bistro atmosphere. For dinner, there's also Bermudas, a casual family spot. Other food outlets include the Flying Bridge, a beachside floating restaurant in Florida cracker house style, the Fountain Square Deli, a Pizza Hut, and Tropic Treats. Drinking spots include the Reflections piano lounge, B. R. Cuda's, with live entertainment and dancing, and the poolside Salty's Beach Bar. Room service and a valet laundry are available.

On the grounds are four heated swimming pools, whirlpools, a sauna, a fitness center, four tennis courts, a racquetball court, croquet, water-sports rentals, gas grills, a guest laundry, a video-game room, gift shops, and a hair salon.

WHERE TO EAT

Seafood lovers will really enjoy this area. Madeira Beach (near St. Petersburg Beach) is the grouper capital of the United States. Ten million pounds of domestic grouper are pulled each year from the Gulf of Mexico and 80% of that total comes from Florida's west coast.

The four busy "main drags" in the area, full of fast-food and chain restaurants, are Ulmerton Road, Gulf to Bay Boulevard, East Bay Drive (which turns into West Bay Drive as you head toward the gulf), and U.S. 19.

Meals for Less Than $7

Apple Cobbler Restaurant. 2923 W. Bay Dr., Belleair Bluffs. ☎ **813/584-1213**. Main courses $3.95–$6.95. Mon–Sat 7am–8pm, Sun 7am–2pm. AE, DC, DISC, MC, V. AMERICAN.

Locals love this place in the upscale town of Bellair near Clearwater because of the weekly $5.95 dinner specials, such as pot roast or turkey breast, that come with soup or salad. The ambience is country friendly. It's in a little strip mall just a few miles east of the beach.

Stavros's. In Kenne Plaza, 2200 E. Bay Dr., Largo. ☎ **813/587-9558**. Main courses $3.95–$4.95. No credit cards. Mon–Thurs 11am–8pm, Fri 11am–9pm, Sat noon–9pm. GREEK/AMERICAN.

Because it's located in a tiny little strip mall off busy East Bay Drive, most of the customers crowding the few little tables are locals. The Greek owner takes pride in always using fresh and low-fat ingredients. He serves inexpensive authentic Greek salads, along with beef, lamb, and chicken gyros. Philly cheese steaks are also popular.

Whistle Stop. 915 Main St., Safety Harbor. ☎ **813/726-1956**. Main courses $1.30–$3.95. No credit cards. Mon–Sat 11am–9pm. AMERICAN.

Stroll down Main Street in the sleepy little town of Safety Harbor, order at the Whistle Stop's window, and relax at an outdoor picnic table with the hamburgers, hot dogs, and ice-cream sundaes you remember as a kid. This place is also known for its homemade soups and salads and the New Jersey cheese steak—a seasoned, grilled steak sandwich stuffed with onions, peppers, and melted provolone.

Meals for Less Than $10

Bay Gables Tea Room. 136 4th Ave. NE, St. Petersburg. ☎ **813/822-0044**. Reservations recommended for lunch, required for afternoon tea. Main courses $6–$12, plus 18% service charge. MC, V. Tues–Sat 11am–2pm, plus afternoon tea at 3pm. AMERICAN.

Set in a beautifully restored 1910 Victorian house replete with Old Florida antiques and frilly trimmings, this spot located on a residential street less than 2 blocks from the bayfront caters mostly to the "ladies who lunch" crowd. Meals are served on heirloom china and silver in the cozy atmosphere of three small rooms and a tiny porch upstairs or on a wraparound ground-floor veranda. The menu is simple but freshly prepared, featuring salads, quiches, soups, and finger sandwiches.

Fourth Street Shrimp Store. 1006 4th St. North, St. Petersburg. ☎ **813/822-0325.** Reservations not accepted. Main courses $4–$12. No credit cards. Mon–Thurs and Sat 11:30am–8:30pm, Fri 11am–9pm, Sun noon–8pm. SEAFOOD.

Come to this busy street north of downtown for great no-frills seafood at rock-bottom prices. The tablecloths, utensils, and glasses are plastic and the plates are made of paper, but the seafood is the real thing, with heaping servings of fresh grouper, smelts, frogs' legs, shrimp of all sizes, oysters, and clams. Paper towels are on the tables—the place is very family-friendly.

Frenchy's Cafe. 41 Baymont St., Clearwater Beach. ☎ **813/446-3607.** Reservations not accepted. Main courses $3.95–$15.00. AE, MC. V. Daily 11:30am–midnight. SEAFOOD.

Always popular with locals, this casual restaurant makes the best grouper sandwiches in the area and has all the awards to prove it. They're fresh, thick and juicy and delicious. The atmosphere is pure Florida casual hangin' out, and there's always a wait—but it's well worth it.

Owner Michael "Frenchy" Preston also runs the casual restaurant directly on the beach, Frenchy's Rockaway Grill, at 7 Rockaway St. (☎ 813/446-4844), voted "best outdoor dining."

Guppy's. 1701 Gulf Blvd., Indian Rocks Beach. ☎ **813/593-2032.** Reservations not accepted. Main courses $5.25–$19.95. MC, V. Daily 11am–10:30pm. SEAFOOD.

Constantly voted "Best Seafood" by the local folks, this small grill and bar across from the beach serves up amberjack, mahi mahi, swordfish, black grouper, tuna, snapper, and wahoo—all native to these waters and always fresh. The atmosphere is casual beach-friendly. The bar is fun, and you can dine alfresco. For dessert, try Scotty's famous upside-down apple-walnut pie with ice cream.

Nick's on the Water. On the Pier, 800 2nd Ave. NE, St. Petersburg ☎ **813/898-5800.** Reservations recommended for dinner. Main courses $7.95–$29.95. AE, DC, MC, V. Sun–Thurs 11:30am–10pm, Fri–Sat 11:30am–11pm. ITALIAN/SEAFOOD.

This informal restaurant offers expansive views of downtown St. Petersburg and the bayfront marina from the ground level of the Pier. The menu features a variety of Italian specialties. Stick with traditional pasta and tomato sauce for less than $10, or splurge on the surf and turf for $29.95. All the veal dishes are a big hit, especially the veal française with sautéed medallions.

Seafood & Sunsets at Julie's. 351 S. Gulfview Blvd., Clearwater Beach. ☎ **813/441-2548.** Reservations recommended. Main courses $8.95–$13.95. AE, MC, V. Daily 11am–10pm. SEAFOOD.

A Key West–style tradition takes place here every night as both locals and visitors gather to toast the sunset over the beach across the street. The best seats are in the tiny upstairs dining room. Check out the seafood menu featuring mahi mahi charcoal-broiled with sour cream, fresh Florida grouper, and Mike Macy's stuffed flounder.

Ted Peter's Famous Smoked Fish. 1350 Pasadena Ave. South, St. Petersburg. ☎ **813/381-7931.** Reservations not accepted. Main courses $3.95–$13.95. No credit cards. Wed–Mon 11:30am–7:30pm. SMOKED SEAFOOD.

Seafood lovers looking for a very casual restaurant should head southwest of downtown toward the aroma of smoked fish. The menu is limited, focusing primarily on smoked salmon, mackerel, or mullet, served with German potato salad.

MEALS FOR LESS THAN $15

Apropos. 300 2nd Ave. NE, St. Petersburg. ☎ **813/823-8934.** Reservations accepted for dinner only. Main courses $8–$15. CB, DC, MC, V. Tues–Wed 7:30–10:30am and 11am–3pm;

Thurs–Sat 7:30–10:30am, 11am–3pm, and 6pm–midnight; Sun 8:30am–2pm (brunch) and 6pm–midnight. AMERICAN/SEAFOOD.

The view is spectacular over the marina and the Pier at this trendy art deco–style restaurant. In warm weather you can dine on an outdoor deck. The menu, which features small portions of light nouvelle cuisine, specializes in fresh seafood.

China Moon. 4399 Gulf Blvd., St. Petersburg Beach. ☎ **813/367-3008.** Reservations accepted. Main courses $8–$14.50. MC, V. Mon–Thurs 11am–9pm, Fri 11am–10pm, Sat 5–10:30pm, Sun 5–9pm. CREATIVE CHINESE.

You'll never think of St. Petersburg Beach the same way again when you dine on the gourmet Oriental cuisine here surrounded by a youngish, cool crowd. Chef Edward Chang creates outstanding dishes from his varied background in New York, Dallas, and Taiwan. Leave the kids behind—the tables are black and the candles are glowing. It's a romantic spot for trying grilled duck in ginger port wine or citrus scallops with vegetables and raspberry vinegar.

The Garden Bistro. 217 Central Ave., St. Petersburg. ☎ **813/896-3800.** Reservations recommended for dinner. Main courses $5.95–$12.95. AE, MC, V. Daily noon–2pm and 5–10pm. MEDITERRANEAN.

A popular weekend spot with locals, this lively downtown restaurant has a European feel. The decor blends a 19th-century tiled floor with modern local art and lots of flowers and plants. The creative menu offers fresh seafood selections such as salmon and shrimp. On Friday and Saturday night live jazz adds to the ambience, starting at 8:30pm.

Hurricane. 807 Gulf Way, St. Petersburg Beach. ☎ **813/360-9558.** Reservations not accepted. Main courses $6.95–$17.95. MC, V. Daily 8am–1am. SEAFOOD.

Join locals and visitors from all over to toast the sunset at the beach with a grouper sandwich. All the seafood selections here are tasty. Overlooking quiet Pass-a-Grille Beach, this informal, three-level indoor/outdoor restaurant is extra-special at night when you can choose between dancing (beginning at 10pm) on one level or dining on another.

Keystone Club. 320 4th St. North, St. Petersburg. ☎ **813/822-6600.** Reservations recommended. Main courses $8.95–$17.95. MC, V. Mon–Thurs 11am–2:30pm and 5–10pm, Fri 11am–2:30pm and 5–11pm, Sat 5–11pm. AMERICAN.

Beef is king here, served in the clubby atmosphere of a male-dominated Manhattan-style chophouse. Specialties include roast prime rib of beef, New York strip steak, and filet mignon. Seafood also makes an appearance on the nightly special menu.

Silas Dent's. 5501 Gulf Blvd., St. Petersburg Beach. ☎ **813/360-6961.** Reservations recommended. Main courses $7.95–$18.95. AE, CB, DC, DISC, MC, V. Sun–Thurs 5–10pm, Fri–Sat 5–11pm. STEAK/SEAFOOD.

With a rustic facade of driftwood and an interior of palm fronds and cedar poles, this restaurant seeks to replicate the home of popular local folk hero Silas Dent, who lived on a nearby island for many years early in this century. The menu aims to reflect Silas's diet—including alligator, amberjack, grouper, squid, and other local seafood—along with such modern favorites as mahi mahi, lobster tails, and scallops, as well as charcoal-broiled steaks, barbecued ribs, and chicken Silas (with red bell-pepper sauce).

WORTH A SPLURGE

✪ **Bob Heilman's Beachcomber.** 447 Mandalay Ave., Clearwater Beach. ☎ **813/442-4144.** Reservations recommended. Main courses $10.95–$25.95. AE, DC, MC, V. Mon–Sat 11:30am–11pm, Sun noon–10pm. AMERICAN.

This huge white restaurant across from Clearwater Beach has been popular for over 45 years. The menu presents a variety of fresh seafood and beef, veal, and lamb selections. Fresh filet of Florida black grouper is one of the most popular items on the menu, and the back-to-the-farm fried chicken from an original 1910 Heilman family recipe is incredible. The crowd here tends to be older; the younger set prefers the owner's newest dining spot, Bobby's Bistro, next door.

Heritage Grill. 256 2nd St. North, St. Petersburg. ☎ **813/823-6382**. Reservations recommended. Main courses $14.25–$21.95. AE, CB, DC, MC, V. Mon–Fri 11:30am–2:30pm and 5:30–9:30pm, Sat 5:30–9:30pm. AMERICAN.

Folks from all over Tampa Bay drive to downtown St. Petersburg to enjoy this popular restaurant. Chef Angus Donaldson presents "casual American cuisine" in a dining room lined with modern art. Waiters in tuxedo shirts serve dishes like sautéed macadamia nut–crusted chicken breast stuffed with prosciutto and sun-dried tomatoes, or roasted walnut Dijon rack of lamb.

✪ **Lobster Pot.** 17814 Gulf Blvd., Redington Shores. ☎ **813/391-8592**. Reservations recommended. Main courses $12.95–$36.95. AE, CB, DC, MC, V. Mon–Sat 4:30–10pm, Sun 4–10pm. SEAFOOD.

Step into this weathered-looking restaurant near the beach on a Saturday night and you'll feel the party atmosphere, hosted by owner Eugen Fuhrmann. The prices are high but the variety of lobster dishes is amazing and worth the splurge. The lobster américaine is flambéed in brandy with garlic, and the bouillabaisse is as authentic as you'd find in the south of France. In addition to lobster, there's a wide selection of seafood—grouper, snapper, salmon, swordfish, shrimp, scallops, crab, Dover sole—prepared simply or in elaborate sauces.

✪ **The Wine Cellar.** 17307 Gulf Blvd., North Redington Beach. ☎ **813/393-3491**. Reservations recommended. Main courses $11.75–$28.75. AE, CB, DC, MC, V. Tues–Sun 4:30–11pm. CONTINENTAL.

In the high season, the cars pack the parking lot at this restaurant popular with locals and visitors alike. You'll find several divided dining rooms (often with private birthday parties going on) and cuisine offering the best of Europe and the States. Start off with caviar, move on to a fresh North Carolina rainbow trout or chateaubriand, and top it all off with chocolate velvet torte. There's jazz in the lounge in the evening.

ST. PETERSBURG AFTER DARK
THE PERFORMING ARTS

The **St. Petersburg ThunderDome,** 1 Stadium Dr. (☎ **813/825-3100**), has a capacity of 50,000 for major concerts, but also hosts a variety of smaller events.

The **Bayfront Center,** 400 1st St. South (☎ **813/892-5767**, or 813/892-5700 for recorded information), houses the 8,100-seat Bayfront Arena and the 2,000-seat Mahaffey Theater. The schedule includes a variety of concerts, Broadway shows, big bands, ice shows, and circus performances.

The 2,200-seat **Ruth Eckerd Hall,** 1111 McMullen-Booth Rd., Clearwater (☎ **813/791-7400**), hosts a varied program of Broadway shows, ballet, drama, symphonic works, popular music, jazz, and country music.

St. Petersburg's resident professional theater, the **American Stage Company,** 211 3rd St. South (☎ **813/822-8814**), presents contemporary dramas and comedies. Tickets are $14 to $24.

THE CLUB & MUSIC SCENE

Beach Nutts. 9600 W. Gulf Blvd., Treasure Island. ☎ **813/367-7427.** No cover.

This is a quintessential beach bar, perched atop a stilt foundation like a wooden beach cottage on the Gulf of Mexico. The music ranges from Top 40 to reggae and rock. Open daily from 5pm to 1am.

Big Catch. 91st St. NE, St. Petersburg. ☎ **813/821-6444.** Cover $3.

This casual downtown club features live and danceable rock and Top 40 hits, as well as darts, pool, and hoops. Open Thursday and Saturday from 9pm to 2am, on Friday from 5pm to 2am.

Club Detroit. 16 2nd St. North, St. Petersburg. ☎ **813/896-1244.** Cover $2 and up indoors, $10–$18 for outdoor concerts.

Housed in the landmark Hotel Detroit, this lively spot includes a lounge, Channel Zero, and an outdoor courtyard, Jannus Landing. Look for blues, reggae, and progressive DJ dance music indoors and live rock concerts outdoors. Open daily from 9pm to 2am.

Coconuts Comedy Club. 5300 Gulf Blvd., St. Petersburg Beach. ☎ **813/360-5653.** Cover $7–$10.

One of the oldest and best-known comedy spots on the beach strip, this club features an ever-changing program of live stand-up comedy acts. Shows are Wednesday to Sunday at 9:30pm.

Coliseum Ballroom. 535 4th Ave. North, St. Petersburg. ☎ **813/892-5202.** Cover $4–$15.

Dating back to 1924, this landmark Moorish-style building is the place to go in downtown St. Petersburg when an evening is scheduled of dancing to big-band, country, ballroom, and other kinds of show music. There is also a tea dance, offered most days from 1–3:30pm with live music.

Gators on the Pass. 12754 Kingfish Dr., Treasure Island. ☎ **813/367-8951.** Cover $2 for most acts.

Located at Kingfish Wharf, on the northern tip of Treasure Island, this place claims to have the world's longest waterfront bar, with a huge deck overlooking the waters of John's Pass. The complex also includes a no-smoking sports bar and a three-story tower with a top-level observation deck for panoramic views of the Gulf of Mexico. There's live music, from acoustic and blues to rock, most nights from 8 or 9pm to 1am.

The Hurricane Lounge. 807 Gulf Way, St. Petersburg Beach. ☎ **813/260-4875.** No cover.

Long recognized as one of the best places for jazz, this beachside spot has a varied program of jazz on Sunday, Wednesday, and Thursday from 9pm to 1am and on Friday and Saturday from 9:30pm to 1:30am. Drinks run $2 to $4.

Jammin'z Dance Shack. 470 Mandalay Ave., Clearwater Beach. ☎ **813/441-2005,** or 813/442-5754 for recorded information. Cover $3–$5.

This nightclub offers a beachy atmosphere and a dance floor with state-of-the-art sound, light, video, and laser effects. A DJ spins Top 40 tunes from 8pm to 2am daily.

Joyland. 11225 U.S. 19, Clearwater. ☎ **813/573-1919.** Cover $3–$10.

This is the area's only country-western ballroom, featuring live bands and well-known performers Wednesday to Sunday. Hours TK.

Manhattans. 11595 Gulf Blvd., Treasure Island. ☎ **813/363-1500.** No cover.

Nestled on the beach strip, this club offers a variety of live music, from country to contemporary and classic rock, 7 nights a week from 8pm until 2am.

Ringside Cafe. 2742 4th St. North, St. Petersburg. ☎ **813/894-8465.** Cover $2 or more.

Housed in a renovated boxing gymnasium, this informal neighborhood café has a decided sports motif, but the music focuses on jazz and blues (and sometimes reggae), on Friday and Saturday night from 10pm to 2am.

3 Tarpon Springs

30 miles N of St. Petersburg, 23 miles W of Tampa International Airport

Historic and picturesque, this area is known as the "sponge capital of the world" and makes for an interesting side trip while visiting Tampa Bay. While boatloads of natural sponges still arrive at the Sponge Docks weekly, Tarpon Springs' heyday was during the 1930s, when the sponge industry brought in $3 million yearly. Divers from Greece brought their families over from Europe, and Tarpon Springs became known as a Greek fishing village. Today an estimated one-third of the 20,000 residents are of Greek descent.

ESSENTIALS

ARRIVING   In Pinellas County, take U.S. 19 North to Tarpon Avenue and make a left. Follow Tarpon Avenue west and you'll bump into downtown Tarpon Springs. The Downtown Tarpon Springs National Historic District is located near the intersection of County Road 582 (Tarpon Avenue) and Alt. U.S. 19 (Pinellas Avenue).

WHAT TO SEE & DO

From the Sponge Docks, take a leisurely sightseeing cruise down the Anclote River or a dinner cruise on the gulf. Exhibition boats take visitors daily to the mouth of the river to watch a diver harvest sponges and to learn about the history of the industry. The Sponge Docks also house Tarpon Springs' 120,000-gallon saltwater aquarium.

At the heart of Tarpon Springs is the historic district, the business area developed back in the 1880s. Stroll the brick streets, gaze at the Victorian houses with gables, and wander around the "other Tarpon Springs."

Fred Howard Park and Beach and **Sunset Beach** attract many sun lovers to the gulf side of Tarpon Springs. Both have picnic shelters and barbecue grills. **A. L. Anderson Park** on Lake Tarpon offers picnicking, fishing, boat ramps, and nature trails.

SHOPPING

Frilly Flamingo. 204 E. Tarpon Ave. ☎ **813/943-8550.**

Celebrate Christmas year round at this unique shop of ornaments, angels, and collectibles like Cherish Teddy and Mary Engles.

Oxford House. 118 E. Orange St. ☎ **813/937-0133.**

Visit the gift shop of this well-known English Tea Room (so popular that reservations are required 24 hours in advance for afternoon tea) for a large assortment of English/Chinese specialty teas, flowers, copper, and gift items. The shop is in a restored Victorian home in the midst of the historical district.

Vintage Department Store. 167 E. Tarpon Ave. ☎ **813/942-4675.**

Would you belive that signed art from Renoir, Cézanne, Dalí, Picasso, and Manet is sitting in the heart of the Tarpon Springs historic district? This shop also sells antiques from local estates at very reasonable prices.

Swimming with the Manatees at Crystal River

Fill up your gas tank and head about 2 hours north of Clearwater on busy U.S. 19 to watch the endangered manatees play.

Along the way, you'll pass the tacky but entertaining tourist attraction of **Weeki Wachee Spring** (☎ **904/596-2062**), where "mermaids" put on a show from 9:30am to 5:30pm daily in an underwater theater. Admission is $14.95 for adults $10.95 for children.

Then travel about 20 minutes north to Homosassa Springs and check out the **Homosassa State Wildlife Park** (☎ **904/628-2311**), 1 mile west of U.S. 19. The highlight of this place is the floating observatory where visitors can "walk" underwater and watch manatees (in the winter) as well as thousands of fresh- and saltwater fish. You'll also see deer, bear, bobcats, otters, egrets, and flamingos along unspoiled nature trails. Admission is $6.95 for adults and $3.95 for children. The park is open from 9am to 5:30pm every day.

From roughly mid-October to March you can swim, snorkel, or scuba with the 10-foot-long, 1,200-pound "sea cows" that gather at warm-water sources like the natural spring of Kings Bay in Crystal River, about 7 miles north of Homosassa Springs. Call the **Nature Coast Chamber of Crystal River** (☎ **904/795-3149**) for names of dive shops that will take you out to swim with the manatees.

The **American Pro Diving Center,** located on U.S. 19 (☎ **800/291-DIVE**), is the area's only five-star PADI dive store offering daily dive and snorkel tours of Kings Bay. Its boat leaves at 7:30am and returns about 11:30am. The dive trip is $27.50 per person (same price for kids and adults) but the equipment is extra. You'll get a mask, snorkel, fins, and wetsuit for an additional $18 each.

It's not uncommon in the warm 72° water to be surrounded by 30 to 40 manatees which nudge and caress you as you swim with them. About 300 manatees spend the winter in Crystal River.

In Crystal River, a few hotels have their own dive shops and marinas, among them the 142-room **Plantation Inn and Golf Resort,** at 9301 W. Fort Island Trail (☎ **904/795-5797**), with doubles for $69 to $89; and the 100-room **Best Western Crystal River Resort,** at 614 NW U.S. 19 (☎ **904/795-3171**), charging $67 to $76 double. They will take you out to see the manatees for an extra fee of about $25 per hour.

All the islands in Kings Bay are part of the National Wildlife Refuge Chassahowitzka which encompasses about 3,000 acres of estuarian habitat accessible only by boat.

During the third week in February, you can enjoy the Crystal River's **Florida Manatee Festival,** with a seafood festival, golf tournament, art show, concerts, and manatee displays.

WHERE TO STAY

In addition to my recommendations below, there's also the **Holiday Inn Hotel and Suites,** 38724 U.S. 19 North, Tarpon Springs (☎ **813/934-5781**), charging $75 for a double in the high season. Yes, it's right on busy U.S. 19, but it's an okay alternative to the expensive resort and tiny B&B in town. It has a heated swimming pool and it's only a 5-minute drive to downtown.

Innisbrook Hilton Resort. 36750 U.S. 19, Tarpon Springs, FL 34688. ☎ **813/942-2000** or 800/456-2000. 1,000 units. High season, $192 double; $228 one-bedroom suite; $368 two-bedroom suite. Off-season, $91 double; $126 one-bedroom suite; $183 two-bedroom suite. AE, DISC, DC, MC, V.

This sprawling golf-oriented resort draws visitors from around the world. The spacious condos and suites have fully equipped kitchens with lots of space for families on vacation. Their children's program is called "Zoo Crew" and charges $26 a day to take care of the kids. The sports-minded visitor will find great tennis and golf packages available. There are 63 holes of golf on three championship courses. The Nick Bollitieri Tennis Academy is famous, with 11 clay and four Laykold courts. The Toscana dining room offers fine Italian dining.

Spring Bayou Inn. 32 W. Tarpon Ave., Tarpon Springs. FL 34689. ☎ **813/938-9333.** 5 rms. $60–$110 double year-round. Rates include breakfast. 10% discount for stays of more than a night. No credit cards.

This bed-and-breakfast built around the turn of the century is within walking distance of the historic district. It's a large comfortable home that reflects an elegance of the past along with modern-day conveniences. Enjoy a complimentary cup of tea or glass of wine in the afternoon and complimentary breakfast in the morning. The best room in the house has a king-size bed, a balcony, a sitting area, and a private bath, all for $110.

WHERE TO EAT

La Brasserie. 200 E. Tarpon Ave. ☎ **813/942-3011.** Reservations required for dinner. Main courses $4.95–$17.45. AE, DISC, MC, V. Tues–Thurs 4–10pm, Fri–Sat 11am–4pm and Sun noon–10pm. FRENCH.

White lace curtains, cozy warm wood, and soothing French music create a charming bistro atmosphere. The owners, a couple from France, serve authentic French cuisine: the onion soup, thick with cheese, is their signature. This place is known for its crêpes; the crêpe végétarienne is filled with ratatouille. There's live jazz every Friday and Saturday night after dinner until midnight.

Pappas Restaurant. 10 Dodecanese Blvd. ☎ **813/937-5101.** Main courses $8.95–$22. AE, MC, V. Daily 11:30am–10pm. GREEK/SEAFOOD.

Bustling with happy chatter from enthusastic diners, Pappas is famous statewide for "fresh from the dock" seafood. This family-run restaurant has been operating on the banks of the Anclote River since 1925 when it was founded by Louis Pappamichaelopoulus of Sparta, Greece. Try any seafood offering: shrimp, grouper, red snapper, or even stone crab claws in season.

Yours Truly Gourmet. 150 Tarpon Ave. ☎ **813/934-1770.** Main courses $9.95–$19.95 (most under $12.95). AE, DISC, MC, V. Daily 11:30am–10pm. NEW AMERICAN.

This place is a favorite with locals. The winding wrought-iron staircase leads to a second-floor balcony, lending a quaint Bourbon Street–café feel. Fresh seafood is the specialty (check out the french-fried shrimp with cherry sauce), but other items, like a rack of lamb, are also available.

4 Sarasota

52 miles S of Tampa, 150 miles SW of Orlando, 225 miles NW of Miami.

Sarasota is a lovely, refined city on the Gulf of Mexico known for its cultural events and fine sugary-white sandy beaches. For a relatively small city, (pop. 55,000) there's an amazing amount to do. There are tons of outdoor activities, from sailing and windsurfing to playing top golf courses.

Spend the day wandering around sophisticated St. Armands Circle, which is *the* place to shop, dine, and people-watch. You'll need big bucks around this uptown side of Sarasota, but there are affordable alternatives for the traveler on a shoestring budget.

Sarasota also has its off-the-beaten-path getaways. Siesta Key, a quiet and mostly residential enclave, attracts artisans and writers. Lido Key, flanked by a string of popularly priced hotels, is a favorite with family vacationers. North Lido Beach was known as the "topless beach" a few years ago, but things have changed.

Legend has it that Sarasota was named after Hernándo de Soto's daughter, Sara—hence, Sara-sota. The town is also connected to circus legend John Ringling, who moved here in the 1920s, built a palatial home, and brought his excellent collection of baroque paintings to the city.

Sarasota is known as the cultural capital of Florida's west coast. It's home to Florida's official state art museum and state theater, as well as the Florida West Coast Symphony, the Asolo Performing Arts Center, and the Van Wezel Performing Arts Hall, plus a host of theaters, jazz clubs, art galleries, and many other artistic venues.

ESSENTIALS

ARRIVING   By Plane   Sarasota-Bradenton International Airport, 6000 Airport Circle (☎ **941/359-2770**), is located north of downtown between U.S. 41 and U.S. 301. Airlines serving the airport include **American Eagle** (☎ 800/433-7300), **Continental** (☎ 800/525-0280), **Delta** (☎ 800/221-1212), **Northwest** (☎ 800/225-2525), **TWA** (☎ 800/221-2000), **United** (☎ 800/241-6522), and **USAir** (☎ 800/428-4322).

Rental-car companies with desks at the airport include **Avis** (☎ 941/359-5240), **Budget** (☎ 941/359-5353), **Dollar** (☎ 941/355-2996), **Hertz** (☎ 941/355-8848), and **Payless** (☎ 941/359-1238).

West Coast Airport Limousine (☎ **941/355-9645**) provides van transfers from the airport to hotels in the Sarasota area. The price averages $6 to $10 per person. Taxi services include **Diplomat Taxi** (☎ 941/355-5155), **Green Cab Taxi** (☎ 941/922-6666), and **Yellow Cab of Sarasota** (☎ 941/955-3341).

By Train   Amtrak (☎ **800/342-2520**) trains arrive at Tampa station, with bus connections to Sarasota.

By Bus   Greyhound buses arrive at the Sarasota depot at 575 N. Washington Blvd. (☎ **941/955-5735**).

By Car   From points north and south, Sarasota can be reached via I-75, U.S. 41, U.S. 301, and U.S. 19. From the east coast of Florida, use Fla. 70 or Fla. 72.

VISITOR INFORMATION   Contact the **Sarasota Convention & Visitors Bureau,** 655 N. Tamiami Trail (U.S. 41), Sarasota, FL 34236 (☎ **941/957-1877** or 800/522-9799).

GETTING AROUND   By Bus   The **Sarasota County Area Transit/SCAT** (☎ **941/951-5851**) provides regularly scheduled bus service for the area. The standard fare is 25¢; exact change is required.

By Taxi   Taxi companies serving the Sarasota area include **Diplomat Taxi** (☎ 941/355-5155), **Green Cab Taxi** (☎ 941/922-6666), and **Yellow Cab of Sarasota** (☎ 941/955-3341). Taxis are metered, but you can often get a flat rate.

By Trolley   For public transport between the mainland and the beach strip, the **Siesta Key Trolley,** 615 Beach Rd., Suite 3B, Siesta Key (☎ **941/346-3115**), provides regular service Tuesday to Saturday from November to May. The South Trolley

Bradenton & Sarasota

Tampa Bay

679

Fort DeSoto

Fort DeSoto Park

Edgemont Channel

Edgemont Key National Wildlife Refuge

Southwest Channel

Passage Key National Wildlife Refuge

Ana Maria

Holmes Beach

Ana Maria Island

Bradenton Beach

Cortez

Palma Sola

Madira Bickel Mound Historic Site

Terra Ceia

Potavant Indian Mound

Memphis

Terra Ceia Bay

Rubonia

Gillette

Parrish

Manatee River

Palmetto

Ellenton

Bradenton

Samoset

Oneco

Bayshore Gardens

Tallevast

Whitfield Estates

Sarasota-Bradenton Airport

University Parkway

Longboat Key

Sarasota Bay

Mote Marine Aquarium

Sarasota

Fruitville

Lido Key

Siesta Key

Bee Ridge Road

Bee Ridge

Gulf Gate

Gulf of Mexico

Crescent

Vamo

Osprey

Historic Spanish Point

Casey Key

Oscar Scherer State Park

Laurel

Nokomis

Venice

Arcadia Rd.

Braden River

0   3 mi.
     4.8 km

N

41, 683, 75, 301, 70, 64, 684, 789, 780, 773, 758, 72, 681, 19, 275, 791

goes to major shopping areas, restaurants, and beaches from 10am to 6pm; the North Trolley goes to downtown Sarasota, St. Armands Circle, Lido Beach, and major hotels and attractions, from 9:30am to 5:30pm. Both trolleys start and finish at the Best Western Siesta Beach Resort in Siesta Village. The fare is $1.

CITY LAYOUT

Sarasota is divided into two sections. The **downtown** area, on the mainland, hugs the bayfront with a modern urban skyline edged by picturesque marinas, landscaped drives, and historic Spanish-style buildings. U.S. 41 runs north-south through downtown.

The adjacent beach strip to the west, on the Gulf of Mexico, is composed of four islands, or keys, separated from downtown by Sarasota Bay. With white-sand beaches, lagoons, and lush vegetation, **Siesta Key** exudes a tropical ambience. The streets are narrow and shaded by overhanging branches draped with Spanish moss. The **Siesta Drive Causeway** and the **Stickney Point Road Causeway** link Sarasota with Siesta Key.

Lido Key is a lively and well-developed island with a string of motels, restaurants, and nightclubs. At the entrance to Lido Key is **St. Armands Key,** a tiny enclave named after Charles St. Amand (early spelling), a 19th-century French homesteader. It owes its development to circus-master John Ringling, who built the four-lane **John Ringling Causeway** that provides access to Lido, St. Armands, and **Longboat Key,** a narrow, 12-mile-long island that's one of Florida's wealthiest areas.

BEACHES

Sarasota has 35 miles of powdery white sand, 150 miles of waterfront, and six barrier islands. All 10 public beaches are unique.

After you've driven the length of Longboat Key and admired the luxurious homes, take a right off St. Armands Circle to **North Lido Beach,** graced by Australian pines and great for long walks and soul searching. Farther south is **Lido Beach,** with changing rooms and a pool and pavilion. **South Lido Beach Park** is a good spot for picnics and walks.

Sarasota's most popular beach, **Siesta Key Public Beach,** is wide and long, with beautiful white sand, a picnic area, a 700-car parking lot, and crowds of families.

More secluded and quiet is **Turtle Beach,** at the key's south end, with shelters, boat ramps, picnic tables, and volleyball nets. **Nokomis Beach** is a quiet spot for walking and **North Jetty Beach,** at the south end of Casey Key, is one of the best surfing beaches, and it also attracts fishermen.

Venice Municipal Beach is heaven for collectors of shark's teeth and divers alike. **Caspersen Beach,** south of Venice, is more remote and offers a nature trail winding through marshes, mangroves, and tidal flats.

Manasota Beach, on Manasota Key at the west end of the Manasota Bridge, has a scenic boardwalk through the mangroves.

SPORTS & OUTDOOR ACTIVITIES

With an average temperature of 71°, this is a happy haven for outdoor buffs and companies offer everything for rent from bikes to in-line skates to kayaks.

BICYCLING   Fun Rentals of Siesta Key, 6551 Midnight Pass Rd. (☎ **941/ 346-1797**), rents everything from standard models to 10-speeds, 18- and 21-speed mountain bikes, tandems, two- and four-passenger surreys, and duo cycles. Prices begin at $3 per hour, $18 a day, and $35 per week. It also rents Moped/scooters for $12 per hour, $35 a day, and $110 per week. It's open daily from 8:30am to 5:30pm.

Just east of downtown, the **Sarasota Bicycle Center,** 4084 Bee Ridge Rd. (☎ **941/377-4505**), rents in-line skates and bikes of various types, from 3- to 10-speed, for $15 a day, $30 per week, or $50 for 2 weeks. It will even deliver to your door. It's open Monday to Friday from 9am to 6pm and on Saturday from 9am to 4pm.

BOAT RENTALS   All Watersports, in the Boatyard Shopping Village, 1504 Stickney Point Rd. (☎ **941/921-2754**), rents personal watercraft (Waverunners, jet boats, jet skis) for $45 to $65 per hour, as well as speedboats, runabouts, and bowriders beginning at $50 per day. Parasail rides can also be arranged; a 10-minute ride is $45. Located on the approach to Siesta Key, it's open daily from 10am to 5pm.

Cannons Marina, 6040 Gulf of Mexico Dr. (☎ **941/383-1311**), on the north end of Longboat Key, rents 14- to 24-foot runabout speedboats that cost $65 to $195 for a half day and $100 to $290 for a full day. Open skiffs are $50 for a half day and $65 for a full day. Waterskis are $30 for a full day. It's open daily from 8am to 6pm.

Mr. C. B.'s, 1249 Stickney Point Rd. (☎ **941/349-4400**), is located beside the Stickney Point Bridge. Here you can rent 16- to 18-foot runabouts, 24-foot pontoons, and other craft for bay fishing and cruising. Runabouts cost $75 to $95 for 4 hours, $110 to $140 for a full day; pontoons are $100 for 4 hours, $160 for a full day. Bicycles rent for $10 a day, and bait and tackle are available. It's open daily from 7am to 6pm.

FISHING   Locals say the **Flying Fish Fleet,** located at Marina Jack's Marina, U.S. 41 at Island Park Circle (☎ **941/366-3373**), has the best charter fishing boats in the area. Docked along the bayfront of downtown, it offers half-day, full-day, and 6-hour deep-sea fishing excursions, with bait and tackle furnished. Half-day trips cost $24 for adults, $19 for seniors, and $15 for children; 6-hour trips are $30 for adults, $25 for seniors, and $20 for children; all-day trips go for $35 for adults, $30 for seniors, and $25 for children. Monday to Saturday, half-day trips are 8am to 12:30pm and 1 to 5:30pm; on Sunday, from 1 to 5:30pm. The 6-hour trip is offered Sunday to Tuesday and on Thursday and Friday from 9am to 3pm. The all-day trip takes place on Wednesday and Saturday from 9am to 5pm, and the sunset trip (in June, July, and August only) is on Tuesday and Friday from 4 to 8:30pm. A new addition to the fleet, the *Big Catch,* is a 39-foot custom sportfishing boat; 4-hour trips start at $295.

Capt. Joe Bonaro, Midnight Pass Marina, Siesta Key (☎ **941/349-3119**), takes small groups of up to six passengers deep-sea fishing aboard the *Rumrunner,* a 36-foot custom-built fishing boat, docked across from Turtle Beach. Prices are $50 per person for a half day and $85 for a full day. It departs daily, by reservation only.

GOLF   The **Bobby Jones Golf Complex,** 1000 Azinger Way, off Circus Boulevard (☎ **941/365-GOLF**), is Sarasota's only municipal facility, with two 18-hole championship layouts (par 72 and par 71) and a 9-hole, par-30 executive course. Tee time reservations are accepted 3 days in advance. Prices are $28 from November to April and $18 from May to October, including cart rental. It's open daily from 7am to dusk.

The **Rolling Green Golf Club,** 4501 Tuttle Ave. (☎ **941/355-6620**), is an 18-hole, par-72 course. A driving range, rental clubs, and lessons are available. Tee times are assigned 2 days in advance. Prices, including cart, are $32 before noon, $24 after noon. Open daily from 7am to dusk.

The **Sarasota Golf Club,** 7820 N. Leewynn Dr. (☎ **941/371-2431**), is an 18-hole, par-72 course. Facilities include a driving range, lessons, and club rentals. Prices, including carts, are $36 if you arrive before noon and $28 after noon. It's open daily from 7am to dusk.

SPECTATOR SPORTS **Ed Smith Stadium,** 2700 12th St., at Tuttle Avenue (☎ 941/954-7699), is the winter home of the **Chicago White Sox,** who hold spring training in February and March. East of downtown, this stadium seats 7,500 fans. Admission is $5 to $10.

At the **Sarasota Kennel Club,** 5400 Bradenton Rd. (☎ 941/355-7744), you can watch sleek greyhounds in action. The club is located 2 blocks east of the Ringling Museum Complex, off De Soto Road. Admission is $1 per person; races are held from December to June, Monday to Saturday at 7:30pm, with matinees on Monday, Wednesday, and Saturday at 1pm.

TENNIS The **Payne Park Tennis Center,** 2050 Adams Lane (☎ 941/364-4605), is a downtown public facility with nine Har-Tru tennis courts, available for play on a first-come, first-served basis. The price is $4.30 per person per hour. It's open daily from 8am to 9pm.

Four hard courts are located east of downtown at the **Forest Lakes Tennis Club,** 2401 Beneva Rd. (☎ 941/922-0660). A pro shop and lessons are available. The price is $4 per person for 1¹/₂ hours of play. It's open Monday to Saturday from 9am to 6pm.

WATER SPORTS Situated on the bayfront downtown, **O'Leary's,** Island Park Marina, Island Park Circle (☎ 941/953-7505), rents jet skis and offers sailing lessons and other water-sports activities by appointment. Jet skis rent for $35 per half hour, $50 per hour. Sailing lessons are $40 for 2 hours, $80 for 4 hours, $150 for a full day. It's open daily from 8am to 8pm.

Sweet Water Kayaks, 5263 Ocean Blvd., Suite 7 (☎ 941/346-1179), rents fully equipped single and double sea kayaks for use in the gulf, bays, and Intracoastal Waterway. Prices range from $20 per hour for one person or $25 per hour for two people to $50 and $60 per day, respectively. It's open daily from 9am to 6pm.

WHAT TO SEE & DO

Bellm's Cars & Music of Yesterday. 5500 N. Tamiami Trail. ☎ **941/355-6228.** Admission $8 adults, $4 children 6–12, free for children 5 and under. Daily 9:30am–5:30pm. Take U.S. 41 north from downtown and it's 1 mile south of the airport.

Here you can view more than 50 classic and antique autos, from Rolls-Royces and Pierce Arrows to four of circus czar John Ringling's personal cars. In addition, there are over 1,200 antique music boxes, from tiny boxes to a 30-foot Belgian organ. Check out the Penny Arcade with antique games.

✪ **Marie Selby Botanical Gardens.** S. Palm Ave. (off U.S. 41). ☎ **941/366-5731.** Admission $6 adults, $3 children 6–11, free for children 5 and under accompanied by an adult. Daily 10am–5pm.

This peaceful getaway is said to be the only botanical garden in the world to specialize in the preservation, study, and research of epiphytic plants, such as orchids, pineapples, and ferns. Its 9 acres are home to more than 20,000 exotic plants, including over 6,000 orchids, as well as a bamboo pavilion, butterfly and hummingbird garden, medicinal plant garden, waterfall garden, cactus and succulent garden, fernery, hibiscus garden, palm grove, two tropical food gardens, and a native shore-plant community.

✪ **Mote Marine Aquarium.** 1600 Thompson Pkwy. ☎ **941/388-4441,** or 800/691-MOTE. Admission $8 adults, $6 children 4–17, free for children 3 and under. Daily 10am–5pm.

Take St. Armands Circle north to City Island; it's at the foot of the bridge between Lido and Longboat keys.

Kids love this place because it's so small and they get to touch cool stuff like a stingray (minus the stinger, of course) and watch sharks in the shark tank. Part of the noted Mote Marine Laboratory complex, this facility focuses on the marine life of the Sarasota area and nearby gulf waters. The kids won't believe all the seahorse babies that come from the *dad's* pouch (one of Mother Nature's strange-but-true surprises). There are also many research-in-progress exhibits.

Myakka River State Park. 13207 Fla. 72. ☎ **941/361-6511.** Admission $3.25 per car (up to eight passengers); airboat or tram tours, $6 adults, $3 children 6–12, free for children 5 and under. Daily 8am–sunset. Take U.S. 41 south to Stickney Point Road and go 15 miles east on Fla. 72.

Check out the alligators at Florida's largest state park covering more than 35,000-acres of wetlands, prairies, and dense woodlands along the Myakka River. It's an outstanding wildlife sanctuary and breeding ground, home to hundreds of species of plants and animals. There are two ways to get an overview of the entire park, either via a 1-hour tram tour (seasonal) or a 1-hour airboat ride (year-round).

Pelican Man's Bird Sanctuary. 1708 Thompson Pkwy., Ken Thompson Park. ☎ **941/388-4444.** Free admission; donations encouraged. Daily 10am–5pm. Take St. Armands Circle north to Ken Thompson Park.

The whole family will enjoy meeting "Pelican Man" Dale Shields, who will guide you through this rehabilitation center for up to 7,000 injured birds and other wildlife a year. Nearly 300 different species of birds are cared for in the public viewing area.

✪ Ringling Museum Complex. 5401 Bayshore Rd. ☎ **941/359-5700** or 941/351-1660 for recorded information. Admission $8.50 adults, $7.50 seniors, free for children 12 and under. Daily 10am–5:30pm. From downtown, take U.S. 41 north to De Soto Road and turn left onto Ringling Plaza.

Showman John Ringling collected art on a grand scale. Wander around his ultimate achievement: the pink Italian Renaissance villa of the **John and Mabel Ringling Museum of Art.** Its 22 galleries are filled with significant European and American art from the past five centuries, including one of the world's most important collections of grand 17th-century baroque paintings. The old masters collection also includes five world-renowned tapestry cartoons by Peter Paul Rubens and his studio.

The Ringling's 30-room winter residence, **Ca' d'Zan** (House of John), built in 1925 and modeled after a Venetian palace, is also open to the public, filled with personal mementos. The **Circus Galleries** are devoted to circus memorabilia, including parade wagons, calliopes, costumes, and colorful posters. The grounds also include the historic **Asolo Theater,** a 19th-century Italian court playhouse, plus a classical courtyard, rose garden, restaurant, and shops.

Sarasota Jungle Gardens. 37–01 Bayshore Rd. ☎ **941/355-5305.** Admission $9 adults, $5 children 3–12, free for children 2 and under. Daily 9am–5pm. From downtown, take U.S. 41 north to Myrtle Street, turn left, and go 2 blocks.

This 10-acre preserve of lush tropical vegetation features cool jungle trails, tropical plants, exotic waterfowl, and reptiles, all in their natural habitats. In addition, there's a petting zoo, bird shows and reptile shows, and a shell and butterfly museum. Kids will love their own jungle with a petting zoo.

Sarasota Visual Art Center. 707 N. Tamiami Trail. ☎ **941/365-2032.** Free admission. Mon–Fri 10am–4pm, Sat–Sun 1–4pm.

Located next to the Sarasota Convention and Visitors Bureau information office, this newly renovated center contains three galleries, presenting the area's largest display of art by national and local artists, from paintings and pottery to sculpture, cartoons, jewelry, and enamelware. There are also art demonstrations and special events.

BAY CRUISES

Head over to **Marina Jack's Marina,** U.S. 41 at Island Park Circle (☎ **941/ 366-6116**), for 2-hour cruises around Sarasota's waterways aboard the 65-foot, two-deck *Le Barge* from October to May. The hours for the sunset cruise change with the time of sunset, but leave Tuesday to Sunday between 5 and 7pm. The early-afternoon cruise departs daily at 2pm. Both cruises cost $8.50 for adults and $4.50 for children 12 and under.

The 41-foot, 12-passenger sailboat *Enterprise,* at Marina Jack's Marina, U.S. 41 at Island Park Circle (☎ **941/951-1833**), cruises the waters of both Sarasota Bay and the Gulf of Mexico. The 3-hour cruise costs $35; the 2-hour sunset cruise costs $20. Departure times vary; reservations are required.

SHOPPING

Yes, it's very upscale, but visitors on budgets big and small still come from all over to wander around **St. Armands Circle** on St. Armands Key. Shoppers in the know get their Worth Avenue fix here on Florida's west coast. You, too, can wander around this outdoor circle of more than 150 international boutiques, gift shops, galleries, restaurants, and nightspots, all surrounded by lush landscaping, patios, and antiques.

Downtown's main shopping focus is on **Sarasota Quay,** a peach-toned multilevel mixed-use facility housing shops and galleries amid a bayfront layout of piazzas and fountains.

Favorite shopping streets include historic **Palm Avenue** and **Main Street** downtown and **Avenue of the Flowers** off Gulf of Mexico Drive on Longboat Key. The area's largest enclosed mall, the **Sarasota Square Mall,** is south of downtown at 8201 S. Tamiami Trail, at Beneva Road (☎ **941/922-9600**). The city's largest and most interesting bookstore for browsers and shoppers alike is the **Main Bookshop,** 1962 Main St. (☎ **941/366-7653**), open daily from 9am to 11pm.

WHERE TO STAY

Staying in Sarasota can definitely put a strain on the budget—there aren't many doubles below $100 in high season. Rates are going to be higher along the beaches at all times, so bargain hunters will have to stick to the downtown area and Tamiami Trail (U.S. 41). The **Sarasota Convention & Visitors Bureau** (☎ **800/522-9799**) can be a good place to start when looking for affordable places to stay.

There is one main alternative to the very pricy hotel rooms in this jewel of a city—you can stay overnight in the nearby town of Bradenton (see Section 5 of this chapter) and still be close enough to enjoy all the attractions of Sarasota. There are plenty of mom-and-pop motels along the beaches that offer the same views as Sarasota, but with less luxurious accommodations and with no nearby gourmet restaurants.

Price-wise, the high season is from January to April. You can always ask about package deals, but be warned: Not many hotels offer them in this area. You'll pay a 7% Florida sales tax plus a 2% resort tax no matter what the season.

DOUBLES FOR LESS THAN $60

Southland Motel. 2229 N. Tamiami Trail, Sarasota, FL 34230. ☎ **941/954-5775**. 31 rms. High season, $54 double. Off-season, $40 double. MC, V.

Just 7 minutes from the beaches of Sarasota, this small motel is next to busy U.S. 41 but a bargain for this part of town. Summer rates can be lower based on availability, but call ahead to get the best prices. Rooms are adequate and what you'd expect from a mom-and-pop motel.

Sunnyside Motel. 2601 S. Tamiami Trail, Sarasota, FL 34239. ☎ **941/953-4363**. 28 rms. High season, $45 double. Off-season, $35 double. MC, V.

Located on the safe, south side of town, this small motel is just 5 minutes from Siesta Key and the beaches. All the rooms are on the ground floor level with bath and/or shower.

DOUBLES FOR LESS THAN $80

Flamenco Colony Motel. 4703 N. Tamiami Trail, Sarasota, FL. 34260. ☎ **941/355-5135**. 26 rms. Year-round, $50 single; $79 double. Credit cards TK.

Just 3 miles from Lido Beach, here all rooms are in a one-story building. Each guest room has two double beds and ample closet space. The new owners were in the process of refurbishing at press time.

Book early as this off-the-beaten-path place is always full. About 10 miles east of Sarasota and only a few miles from the beach, here you'll enjoy breakfast on the back porch of an old farmhouse overlooking a lake (stocked with fish) and a waterfall. All rooms have a private bath and the house is tastefully decorated and situated on a 5-acre estate.

DOUBLES FOR LESS THAN $100

Best Western Midtown. 1425 S. Tamiami Trail, Sarasota, FL 34239. ☎ **941/955-9841** or 800/528-1234 or 800/722-8227. Fax 941/349-7915. 100 rms. A/C TV TEL. High season, $99 double. Off-season, $60 double. Rates include continental breakfast. AE, DC, DISC, MC, V.

Location and convenience are the buzzwords that draw families to this modern, recently refurbished L-shaped hotel. It's less than 2 miles south of downtown, and 2 miles from the main causeways leading to the offshore islands. Although next to the Midtown Plaza shopping center, it's set back from the busy main road in a world of its own, with lots of tropical plants and palms surrounding a central courtyard, a heated outdoor swimming pool, and a sundeck. Other facilities include a buffet-style breakfast room, a fitness room, and a guest laundry. The rooms are modern and cheery, with light woods and Florida pastel tones.

Hampton Inn. 5000 N. Tamiami Trail, Sarasota, FL 34234. ☎ **941/351-7734** or 800/HAMPTON. Fax 941/351-7734. 97 rms. A/C TV TEL. High season, $99 double. Off-season, $67 double. Rates include buffet breakfast. AE, CB, DC, DISC, MC, V.

An elaborate breakfast buffet awaits you at this completely renovated property. It's one of the closest downtown hotels to the airport (a quarter mile away) in a quiet garden setting. The bedrooms, offering a choice of one king-size bed or two double beds, are decorated in pastel tones, with light-wood furnishings. Facilities include a heated swimming pool, an exercise room, and a guest laundry.

Wellesley Inn. 1803 N. Tamiami Trail, Sarasota, FL 34234. ☎ **941/366-5128** or 800/444-8888. Fax 941/953-4322. 106 rms. A/C TV. High season, $99 double. Off-season, $49 double. Rates include continental breakfast. AE, DISC, MC, V.

Just north of the downtown district on the main thoroughfare, this imposing four-story hotel overlooks a marina and boatyard. The fourth floor has recently been refurbished. A welcoming ambience prevails in the elegant, plant-filled lobby. The bedrooms are spacious, with standard furnishings of light woods and pastel tones, and many have views of the marina. Valet service is available, and there's an outdoor heated swimming pool and a complimentary airport shuttle.

WORTH A SPLURGE

The Colony Beach & Tennis Resort. 1620 Gulf of Mexico Dr., Longboat Key, FL 34228. ☎ **941/383-6464** or 800/4-COLONY. Fax 941/383-7549. 235 suites. High season, $280–$375 suite for two. Off-season, $160–$250 suite for two. AE, DISC, MC, V.

This is a terrific, tasteful beach and tennis resort. The luxurious one- or two-bedroom villa suites, complete with living rooms, dining areas, fully equipped kitchenettes, and sun balconies, overlook 18 gulf-front acres on Longboat Key. The tennis programs for adults and children are highly acclaimed. If you're ready for a real splurge, treat the family to one of three private beachhouses. Check out the Stone Crab Festival every October.

The award-winning Colony Restaurant offers continental cuisine for lunch and dinner. Windows Patio is for casual poolside dining. The lavish Sunday brunch is also popular with locals. And room service is available.

There's an outstanding year-round supervised children's program for 3- to 5- and 5- to 12-year-olds. On the premises are a health spa, complimentary tennis, a beachfront swimming pool, a fitness center, golf, deep-sea fishing, water sports, and aerobic classes.

The Resort at Longboat Key Club. 301 Gulf of Mexico Dr., Longboat Key, FL 34228. ☎ **941/383-8821** or 800/237-8821. Fax 941/383-0359. 232 suites. High season, $230–$295 suite for two. Off-season, $135–$105 suite for two. Ask about $99 midweek specials. Tennis and golf packages available May–Dec 20. AE, DISC, MC, V.

Located on 410 acres at the southern tip of Longboat Key, this award-winning resort pampers guests with upscale restaurants and a variety of recreational activities in a lush tropical setting. The suites are luxurious, with private balconies overlooking the Gulf of Mexico, a lagoon, or the golf course fairways. The rooms have custom-designed furnishings and fabrics with contemporary, tropical themes. A complimentary supervised Kid's club is available Monday to Saturday in the summer.

For fine dining, Orchid's Restaurant has the feel of an elegant supper club (jackets are required for men), with continental cuisine in a romantic setting. Barefoots Bar & Grille offers casual poolside dining, and the Island House Restaurant, famous for its champagne brunch, overlooks the golf course. Room service and a valet laundry are available.

For the physically active, there are two golf courses, two tennis centers, 500 feet of beach, an exercise track, sailing, boating, jogging paths, a swimming pool, and a Jacuzzi. A new fitness center is slated to open in May 1997.

WHERE TO EAT

You'll have to get away from the beaches for more affordable dining spots, but for a night to remember, head to St. Armands Key and enjoy dining alfresco at one of the romantic and elegant restaurants/cafés located around St. Armands Circle.

MEALS FOR LESS THAN $7

Emphasis. 1301 1st St., Sarasota. ☎ **941/954-4085.** Reservations recommended for dinner. Main courses $6.95–$12.95. MC, V. Daily 11am–midnight or later. INTERNATIONAL.

This combination café/coffeehouse/gallery in Sarasota's theater-arts district highlights local artworks against a contemporary black-and-white decor. It's a favorite after-show spot for theatergoers and performers. The menu features pizzas, pastas, salads,

Jack's Chophouse and Downunder Jazz Bar. 214 Sarasota Quay, Sarasota. ☎ **941/951-2467.** Reservations recommended. Main courses $14.95–$19.95. AE, MC, V. Mon–Thurs 11:30am–2pm and 5–10pm, Fri 11:30am–2pm and 5–11pm, Sat 5–11pm, Sun 11:30am–2:30pm (brunch) and 5–10pm. AMERICAN.

Enjoy expansive water views in a clubby, bilevel art deco setting. The award-winning cuisine offers regional and international favorites. Fresh seafood and locally farmed produce is presented daily. The menu offers such culinary classics as chateaubriand and rack of lamb, as well as such innovative choices as potato-crusted red snapper and pan-seared Atlantic salmon. On a budget? Go and hang out at the downstairs bar, known for its jazz sessions and bistro menu. Jazz Bar Happy Hours are famous with locals. The sunset menus offer low-priced entrees from 5 to 7pm.

Ristorante Bellini. 1551 Main St., Sarasota. ☎ **941/365-7380.** Reservations recommended. Main courses $10.95–$23. DISC, MC, V. Mon–Fri 11:30am–2pm and 6–10pm, Sat 6–10pm. NORTHERN ITALIAN.

This midtown restaurant produces homemade cooked-to-order pastas and northern Italian cuisine produced nightly. The menu includes such creative choices as scaloppine Bellini (veal topped with asparagus and mozzarella) and grouper zuppa di pesce, a huge seafood presentation with snapper, lobster, scallops, calamari, clams, and mussels. It's a wow for big appetites. Follow up with espresso or cappuccino or traditional Italian *dolce vita* desserts.

Turtles. 8875 Midnight Pass Rd., Siesta Key. ☎ **941/346-2207.** Reservations preferred. Main courses $10.95–$17.95. AE, DISC, MC, V. Daily 11:30am–midnight. AMERICAN.

With tropical overtones and breathtaking vistas across from Turtle Beach, this informal restaurant sits on Little Sarasota Bay, offering views of the water from tables both indoors and on an outside deck. The menu features dishes such as nut-crusted chicken breast and baked pink snapper.

WORTH A SPLURGE

✪ **Cafe l'Europe.** 431 St. Armands Circle, St. Armands Key. ☎ **941/388-4415.** Reservations recommended. Main courses $13.95–$25. AE, CB, DC, MC, V. Mon–Sat 11am–3pm and 5–11pm, Sun 5–10pm. CONTINENTAL.

This award-winning, favorite upscale dining spot on St. Armands Key continues to impress no matter how many times you visit. A European atmosphere prevails with a decor of brick walls and arches, dark woods, brass fixtures, pink linens, and hanging plants. The menu offers selections ranging from bouillabaisse Marseilles (with lobster, snapper, shrimp, and clams) to veal and portobello Napoléon (with fresh tomato, garlic, and herb sauce over bow-tie pasta).

Charley's Crab. 420 St. Armands Circle, St. Armands Key. ☎ **941/388-3964.** Reservations recommended. Main courses $8.95–$24.95. AE, MC, V. Mon–Thurs 11:30am–10pm, Fri–Sat 11:30am–10:30pm, Sun noon–2:30pm and 5–10pm. SEAFOOD.

This popular place is dedicated to delicate and savory crab. Crab claws, crab cakes, and crab salad are specialties. Alfresco diners fill tables early at lunch and dinner just a few feet from strolling shoppers. A pianist adds to the lively atmosphere, and large windows in the comfortable indoor dining room give a great view of the passing parade.

Michael's On East. 1212 East Ave. South, Sarasota. ☎ **941/366-0007.** Reservations recommended. Main courses $13.95–$26.95. AE, DC, MC, V. Lunch Mon–Sat 11:30am–2pm; dinner Mon–Thurs 5–9pm, Fri–Sat 5pm–midnight. Closed Sun. AMERICAN/SEAFOOD.

This is one of the best restaurants in town. In what feels like a contemporary American bistro, you'll find a friendly bar, bright pastel colors, and interesting artwork in the large open room. The constantly changing menu—specializing in Florida seafood like swordfish, grouper, stone crabs in season (October to May)—is made with the freshest ingredients.

SARASOTA AFTER DARK

To get the latest update on what's happening during your visit, call the city's 24-hour **Artsline** (☎ 941/365-ARTS).

THE PERFORMING ARTS

Designated as the State Theater of Florida in 1965, the **Asolo Center for the Performing Arts,** 5555 N. Tamiami Trail (☎ 941/351-8000), is home to the professional **Asolo Theatre Company** and the Conservatory for Professional Actor Training, the Sarasota French Film Festival, and the Florida State University's Master of Fine Arts program in motion picture, television, and recording arts. The main stage, the Harold E. and Ethel M. Mertz Theatre, with seating for 487, is an attraction in itself—the former Dumfermline Opera House, originally constructed in Scotland in 1900 and transferred piece by piece to Sarasota in 1987. In 1994–95 the 161-seat Asolo Conservatory Theatre was added as a smaller venue for experimental and alternative offerings. The season runs from November to mid-June for the main stage and from October to May for the smaller theater. Ticket prices range from $5 to $39.

Free guided tours of the center are offered Monday to Saturday at 10, 10:30, 11, and 11:30am except from June to August and during technical rehearsals between plays; call in advance to check.

The lavender seashell-shaped **Van Wezel Performing Arts Hall,** 777 N. Tamiami Trail (☎ 941/953-3366), is visible for miles on the Sarasota skyline. It offers excellent visual and acoustic conditions, with year-round programs ranging from symphony and jazz concerts, opera, musical comedy, and choral productions to ballet and international performers. It's the home of the Florida West Coast Symphony, the Jazz Club of Sarasota, the Sarasota Ballet of Florida, and the Sarasota Concert Band.

The Opera House, 61 N. Pineapple Ave. (☎ 941/953-7030), presents performances by the Sarasota Opera in February and March; tickets cost $15 to $48. Other companies, including the Sarasota Ballet, present their works during the rest of the year at this downtown venue.

THEATERS

Florida Studio Theatre. 1241 N. Palm Ave. (at Coconut Ave.), downtown. ☎ 941/366-9796. Tickets $12–$20.

The Florida Studio Theatre is Sarasota's theater for contemporary works. The season runs from December to August with presentations Tuesday to Sunday. It hosts a New Play Festival each May.

The Players of Sarasota. 838 N. Tamiami Trail, Sarasota. ☎ 941/365-2494. Tickets $14–$16.

Founded in 1930, this is Sarasota's longest-established theater, a community group presenting plays all year—a mix of musicals and dramas and a concert series featuring jazz, blues, and country music. Evening performances are Tuesday to Saturday, with a matinee on Sunday.

Theatre Works. 1247 1st St. (at Coconut Ave.), Sarasota. ☎ 941/952-9170. Tickets $7.50–$15.

This professional non-Equity company presents musical revues and other works Tuesday to Saturday in the evening with a matinee on Sunday, year round.

Dinner Theater

Golden Apple Dinner Theatre. 25 N. Pineapple Ave., Sarasota. ☎ **941/366-5454.** Tickets $27.50 evening, $20.50 matinees.

This downtown theater presents cocktails, dinner, and a professional Broadway-style show, Tuesday to Sunday year round.

THE CLUB & MUSIC SCENE

Bumpers Nightclub. 1927 John Ringling Blvd., Sarasota. ☎ **941/951-0335.** Cover $3–$15.

This club presents a variety of danceable pop dance music, with DJs spinning the tunes starting at 8:30pm Tuesday to Thursday. Live groups begin performing at 9pm on Friday and Saturday.

Coconuts Comedy Club. 8440 N. Tamiami Trail, Sarasota. ☎ **941/351-8225.** Cover $7.

Well-known national and local comics perform at this club, north of downtown, at 9pm Thursday to Saturday.

Downunder Jazz Bar. 214 Sarasota Quay (at U.S. 41 and 3rd St.), Sarasota. ☎ **941/951-2467.** No cover.

Part of the innovative Sarasota Quay shopping and entertainment complex, this club offers contemporary jazz Sunday to Thursday from 9pm to 12:30am and on Friday and Saturday from 9pm to 1:30am. Drinks run $2 to $4.

In Extremis. 204 Sarasota Quay, Sarasota. ☎ **941/954-2008.** Cover $3–$7.

Located downtown in the waterfront Sarasota Quay shopping complex, this trendy new club is known for its laser sound-and-light video shows, accompanied by high energy Top 40 music played by DJs. It's open from 8pm to 2am: nightly from January to April, and on Tuesday and Saturday the rest of the year.

Limerick Junction. 1296 1st St., Sarasota. ☎ **941/366-6366.** Cover $2–$3.

Around the corner from the Sarasota Opera House, this Irish-themed indoor/outdoor pub presents a variety of music (jazz, blues, rock, bluegrass, and more), including authentic Irish music, Wednesday to Sunday. Times vary, but performances usually run from 9pm to midnight or later.

Paradise Cafe. 1311 1st St., Sarasota. ☎ **941/955-8500.** Cover $8 for cabaret, none for piano music.

This popular downtown spot presents musical cabarets on Thursday, Friday, and Saturday at 8:30pm, and live piano music Tuesday to Saturday from 6pm.

Patio Lounge. St. Armands Circle, St. Armands Key. ☎ **941/388-3987.** Cover $2 Tues–Thurs, $3 Fri–Sat.

One of the liveliest spots along the beach strip, the Patio Lounge features live entertainment performing high-energy dance music Tuesday to Saturday from 9:30pm to 2am.

5 Bradenton

26 miles S of St. Petersburg, 41 miles SW of Tampa, 15 miles N of Sarasota

Visitors to Florida's Tampa Bay area often overlook Bradenton and the Gulf Island beaches on their way from Tampa to Sarasota. But outdoor enthusiasts in search of a casual getaway will thoroughly enjoy this area, home to over 27 miles of public and private beaches. There are no glitzy resorts—just lots of affordable waterfront getaways.

Although it has been touched by urban sprawl in recent years, especially along the U.S. 41, Fla. 64, and Fla. 684 corridors, Bradenton still maintains some links with the past such as its historic Old Main Street, a pristine riverfront, and many Spanish-style buildings. Bradenton's star attraction, however, is Anna Maria Island, west of downtown, a 7^1/$_2$-mile stretch of sandy and tree-shaded beaches that rim the Gulf of Mexico. The island is popular with family vacationers and seniors, offering a variety of public beaches, fishing piers, bungalows, and low-rise motels.

Bradenton is also synonymous with the sweet aroma of fresh oranges. As the home of Tropicana, this city of 40,000 people is a major producer of orange juice and citrus products, as well as other agricultural products such as tomatoes and ornamental plants.

ESSENTIALS

ARRIVING   By Plane   Bradenton shares an airport with Sarasota. For full details on the Sarasota-Bradenton International Airport, see "Essentials" in Section 4 of this chapter. Van transport from the airport to hotels in Bradenton is provided by **West Coast Airport Limousine** (☎ **941/355-9645**). The price depends on the destination, but averages $10 to $15.

By Train   Amtrak (☎ **800/USA-RAIL**) trains arrive at the Tampa Amtrak Station (see "Essentials" in Section 1 of this chapter) and bus connections are provided to Bradenton.

By Bus   Greyhound buses arrive at the carrier's depot at 501 17th Ave. West, Bradenton (☎ **941/747-2984**).

By Car   Bradenton is accessible from points north via the Sunshine Skyway Bridge (U.S. 19/I-275). Other north-south routes leading into Bradenton include I-75, U.S. 41, and U.S. 301. From the east, take Fla. 64 and Fla. 70.

VISITOR INFORMATION   For travel information about Bradenton, Anna Maria Island, and the surrounding Manatee County area, contact the **Greater Bradenton Convention & Visitors Bureau,** P.O. Box 1000, Bradenton, FL 34206 (☎ **941/729-9177**, or 800/4-MANATEE). The county also maintains walk-in **visitor centers** at the Civic Center, 1 Haben Blvd., off U.S. 301, Palmetto (☎ **941/729-9177**), and at 5030 U.S. 301, Ellenton (☎ **941/729-7040**).

GETTING AROUND   By Bus   Manatee County Area Transit, known locally as **Manatee CAT** (☎ **941/749-7116**), operates scheduled bus service throughout the area. The basic fare is $1 Monday to Friday and 50¢ on Saturday.

By Taxi   Taxi companies serving the Bradenton area include **Bruce's Taxi** (☎ 941/755-6070), **Dependable Cab** (☎ 941/749-0993), and **Yellow Cab** (☎ 941/748-4800).

By Car   Major car-rental companies maintain desks at the Sarasota-Bradenton Airport (see "Essentials" in Section 4 of this chapter).

CITY LAYOUT

Bradenton is a rectangle, with U.S. 41 running north-south through the center. **Streets** are numbered and run parallel to U.S. 41 in a north-south direction, and they are designated as east or west of that route. **Avenues,** which run east-west across U.S. 41, start at the Braden River and continue southward in ascending numerical order. Addresses on avenues are also labeled as east or west of U.S. 41.

The basic core of **downtown** hugs the Manatee River near 12th Street (Old Main Street). 12th Street contains a row of historic old buildings leading to the Manatee River and a waterfront pier.

West of downtown is the **Intracoastal Waterway** and **Anna Maria Island.** The city is traversed in an east-west direction by two state highways: **Fla. 64** (also known as Manatee Avenue), crossing the north side of the city, and **Fla. 684** (Cortez Road), crossing the southern sector. Two bridges, the **Anna Maria Island Bridge** (on Fla. 64) and the **Cortez Bridge** (on Fla. 684) connect Anna Maria Island to the mainland. Situated 7 miles west of downtown between the Intracoastal Waterway and the Gulf of Mexico, this subtropical barrier island is 7^1/$_2$ miles long and varies from a quarter of a mile to nearly 2 miles wide. It's composed of three island cities: Anna Maria to the north, Holmes Beach in the center, and Bradenton Beach to the south.

Cortez Island is on the east side of the Cortez Bridge, on the approach from the mainland to Bradenton Beach on Anna Maria Island.

BEACHES & OUTDOOR ACTIVITIES

BEACHES   Swimming along safe and sandy beaches is a prime reason to visit the Bradenton area. There are four public beaches on Anna Maria Island: **Anna Maria Bayfront Park,** on Bay Boulevard at the northwest end of the island, fronting both the Intracoastal Waterway and the Gulf of Mexico; **Coquina Beach,** at the southwest end of Gulf Drive on Anna Maria Island, with a gulf and a bay side, sheltered by towering pines and palm trees; **Cortez Beach,** on Gulf Drive in Bradenton Beach, just north of Coquina Beach; and **Manatee County Public Beach,** at Gulf Drive, Holmes Beach, at the west end of Fla. 64.

BOAT RENTALS   On the east side of the Cortez Bridge, **Cortez Watercraft Rentals,** 4328 127th St. West (☎ **941/792-5263**), rents fishing, ski and pontoon boats, Waverunners, and other equipment. Prices are $85 to $125 for fishing boats, $95 to $135 for ski boats, $105 to $155 for pontoon boats, and $45 per hour for Waverunners. It's open daily from 8am to 6pm.

Captain's Marina, 5501 Marina Dr., Holmes Beach (☎ **941/778-1977**), rents six-passenger 18-foot fishing boats, 10-passenger 21-foot pontoons, waterskis, and other watercraft. Fishing boats begin at $90 for a half day and $135 for a full day; pontoons, at $115 for a half day and $155 for a full day. Waterskis are $20 per half day and $25 for a full day. It's open daily from 8am to 5pm.

Five O'Clock Marine, 412 Pine Ave., Anna Maria Island (☎ **941/778-5577**), rents fishing and speed boats of various sizes, accommodating two to seven passengers, for $75 to $125 per half day and $75 to $175 for a full day. As well, 10-passenger 28-foot pontoons begin at $80 per half day and $150 per day. It's open daily from 8am to 5pm.

FISHING   Whether off a pier or from a boat, Bradenton offers many angling opportunities. There's pier fishing at **Anna Maria City Pier** on the north end of Anna Maria Island, and at the **Bradenton Beach City Pier** at Cortez Road. Both are free of charge.

For deep-sea fishing, the **Cortez Fleet,** 12507 Cortez Rd., Cortez (☎ **941/794-1223**), offers 4-, 6-, and 9-hour trips, departing from the east side of the Cortez Bridge. The boats are equipped with the latest in electronic fish finders, and rod, bait, and tackle are provided. Prices for a 4-hour trip are $22.50 for adults, $20.50 for seniors, and $12 for children 14 and under; a 6-hour trip costs $31.50 for adults, $28.50 for seniors, and $16.50 for children 14 and under; and a 9-hour trip is $38.50 for adults, $34.50 for seniors, and $20 for children 14 and under.

The 4-hour trips depart on Monday and Friday at 8am and 1pm; the 6-hour trips, on Tuesday, Thursday, and Sunday at 9am; and the 9-hour trips, on Wednesday and Saturday at 8am.

GOLF The **Bradenton Area Convention & Visitors Bureau,** P.O. Box 1000, Bradenton, FL 34206 (☎ **941/729-9177** or 800/4-MANATEE), publishes a free **"Golf Passport"** booklet about area courses and valuable coupons and discounts, valid from May to October, good for reduced rates or equipment discounts.

Just off U.S. 41, the **Heather Hills Golf Club,** 101 Cortez Rd. West (☎ **941/755-8888**), operates an 18-hole, par-61 course on a first-come, first-served basis. There's a driving range and clubs can be rented. The price, including a cart, is $19 per person until 3pm and $12.75 after 3pm. It's open daily from 6:30am until dark.

The **Manatee County Golf Course,** 5290 66th St. West (☎ **941/792-6773**), sports an 18-hole, par-72 course on the southern rim of the city and requires that tee times be set up at least 2 days in advance. There's also a driving range and golf clubs for rent. The price, including a cart, is $31 per person. It's open daily from 7am to dusk.

Located just north of Fla. 684 and east of Palma Sola Bay, the **Palma Sola Golf Club,** 3807 75th St. West (☎ **941/792-7476**), has an 18-hole, par-72 course that requires 2-day advance booking for tee times. The charge is $34 per person, including a cart. It's open daily from 7am to dusk.

The **River Run Golf Links,** 1801 27th St. East (☎ **941/747-6331**), set beside the Braden River, is an 18-hole, par-70 course with lots of water in its layout. A 2-day advance notice is required for tee times. Golf clubs can be rented. The price, including a cart, is $20 to $25 per person and it's open daily from 7am to dusk.

To improve your game, you might want to enroll in the **David Leadbetter Golf Academy,** 1414 69th Ave. (at U.S. 41), Bradenton, FL 34210 (☎ **941/739-2483**), located on the grounds of the Nick Bollitieri Sports Academy. Presided over by one of golf's leading instructors, this facility offers practice tee instruction, video analysis, and scoring strategy as well as general tuition, priced from $160 per day or $235 for a 1-day course with overnight accommodations.

TENNIS The **Walton Racquet Center,** 5502 33rd Ave. West (☎ **941/742-5973**), is a part of the county park system. The center has eight clay and eight hard courts. It's open Monday to Thursday from 7:30am to 9:45pm, on Friday from 7:30am to 5:30pm, and on Saturday and Sunday from 7:30am to 2:45pm. Prices are $2.40 per person for 1½ hours on hard courts, $4.45 on clay courts.

WHAT TO SEE & DO

DeSoto National Memorial Park. DeSoto Memorial Hwy., 75th Street West. ☎ **941/792-0458.** Free admission. Daily 9am–5pm. Take Manatee Avenue (Fla. 64) west to 75th Street West and turn right; the park entrance is at the end of the road.

Nestled on the Manatee River northwest of downtown, this park commemorates the Spanish explorer Hernándo de Soto's 1539 Florida landing. Aiming to reflect the look and atmosphere you might have found here 400 years ago, it includes a restoration of de Soto's original campsite, and a scenic half-mile nature trail that circles a mangrove jungle and leads to the ruins of one of the first European settlements in the area. December to March, park employees dress in 16th-century costumes and portray the way the early settlers lived, including demonstrations of cooking and musket firing.

Gamble Plantation. 3708 Patten Ave., Ellenton. ☎ **941/723-4536.** Admission (including tour) $3 adults, $1.50 children 6–12, free for children 5 and under. Thurs–Mon 9am–5pm; guided tours given at 9:30am, 10:30am, and hourly 1–4pm. Take U.S. 301 north from downtown to Ellenton; the site is on the left at the junction of U.S. 301 and Fla. 683 (Ellenton-Gillette Road).

This fine example of an antebellum plantation home is the oldest structure on Florida's southwest coast and is maintained as a state historic site. Built in the late

1840s by Maj. Robert Gamble, and constructed primarily of a primitive material known as tabby (a mixture of oyster shells, sand, molasses, and water), it comprises 10 rooms, verandas on three sides, 18 exterior columns, and eight fireplaces. Inside is a fine collection of 19th-century furnishings. Entrance into the house is by tour only, although the grounds may be explored independently.

Manatee Village Historical Park. 6th Ave. East and 15th St. East. ☎ **941/749-7165.** Free admission; donations welcome. Mon–Fri 9am–4:30pm, Sun 1:30–4:30pm. Closed Sat; closed Sun in July–Aug. From U.S. 41, take 6th Avenue East east to 15th Street East at the junction of Manatee Avenue East.

A tree-shaded park with a courtyard of hand-laid bricks, this national historic site features restored buildings from the city of Bradenton and the surrounding county. It contains the Manatee County Court House from 1860—the oldest structure of its kind still standing on the South Florida mainland—a Methodist church built in 1887, a typical Cracker Gothic house built in 1912, and the Wiggins General Store, dating to 1903 and full of local memorabilia from swamp root and grub dust to louse powder, as well as antique furnishings and an art gallery.

✪ **South Florida Museum and Bishop Planetarium.** 201 10th St. West. ☎ **941/746-4131.** Admission $5.50 adults, $3.50 children 5–12, free for children 4 and under. Tues–Sat 10am–5pm, Sun noon–6pm. From U.S. 41, take Manatee Avenue west to 9th Street West and turn right.

The museum tells the story of Florida's history from prehistoric times to the present. It includes a Native American collection with life-size dioramas, a Spanish courtyard with replicas of 16th-century buildings, and an indoor aquarium. The adjacent Bishop Planetarium features a 50-foot hemispherical dome arcing above a seating area for laser light shows and star-gazing activities.

CRUISES & OTHER TOURS

AIRBOAT TOURS   The latest recreational craze sweeping Bradenton is sightseeing via airboat. Eight-passenger open-air craft are operated by **Manatee Airboat Tours, Inc.,** Perico Harbour Marina, Manatee Avenue (U.S. 64), Bradenton (☎ **941/730-1011**). The ride lasts 55 minutes, with departures slated on the hour daily from 9am to 5pm, year round. The price is $10 per person.

CRUISES   The two-deck *Miss Cortez XI,* part of the Cortez Fleet, 12507 Cortez Rd., Cortez (☎ **941/794-1223**), offers a 1½-hour narrated sightseeing cruise around Anna Maria Bay. It costs $6 for adults and $3 for children 14 and under, and departs Monday to Thursday at 3pm. There's also a 4-hour cruise along the Intracoastal Waterway to Egmont Key, a nearby tropical island where there's an opportunity to disembark for snorkeling and shelling. This cruise costs $14 for adults and $8 for children 14 and under, and departs Monday to Thursday at 10:30am.

Departing from Port Manatee, near the southern end of the Skyway Bridge north of Bradenton, **Regal Cruises,** Port Manatee, 13231 Eastern Ave., Palmetto (☎ **813/867-1300** or 800/270-SAIL), offers 6-hour cruises on the Gulf of Mexico aboard the eight-deck, 1,180-passenger *Regal Empress;* the cost begins at $29 per person. There are also overnight cruises (from $59 per person) and 4-night trips to Mexico (from $299 per person).

A TRAIN TOUR   See the sights of rural Manatee County northwest of Bradenton on a 1¼-hour narrated sightseeing tour on a 1950s diesel-engine train operated by the **Florida Gulf Coast Railroad,** 83rd Street East, off U.S. 301 in Parrish (☎ **941/776-3266**). There's a choice of seating: in open-window coaches, air-conditioned lounge cars, or the caboose. Tickets—priced at $6 to $9 for adults, $4 to $5 for children 2 to 11, and free for children under 2—are sold on a first-come, first-served basis. Departures are on Saturday at 11am, 1pm, and 3pm, and on Sunday at 1 and 3pm.

SPECTATOR SPORTS

East of downtown, the 6,562-seat **McKechnie Field,** 9th Street and 17th Avenue West (☎ **941/748-4610**), is the home of the **Pittsburgh Pirates** during its March-to-April spring-training season. Admission to games is $5.50 to $8.50.

The **Sarasota Polo Club,** 8201 Polo Club Lane, Sarasota (☎ **941/359-0000**), midway between Sarasota and Bradenton, is the site of weekly polo matches November to April on Sunday at 1pm. They're open to the public for an admission charge of $4.

SHOPPING

For discount shopping, the focal point of the Bradenton area is the **Gulf Coast Factory Shops** complex at 60th Avenue East, Ellenton (☎ **941/723-1150**), about a 10-minute drive northeast of Bradenton, off I-75 at Exit 43. There are over 100 factory and outlet stores, including such names as Bass Shoes, Corning Revere, Danskin, Jockey, Levi's, Nike, Aileen, Ann Taylor, Chaus, Donna Karan, Geoffrey Beene, Jones New York, Maidenform, Royal Doulton, Sony, and Van Heusen. Shops are open Monday to Saturday from 10am to 9pm and on Sunday from noon to 6pm.

WHERE TO STAY

DOUBLES FOR LESS THAN $80

Catalina Beach Resort. 1325 Gulf Dr. North, Bradenton Beach, FL 34217. ☎ **941/778-6611.** Fax 941/778-6748. 35 rms. A/C TV TEL. High-season, $77 double. Off-season, $47 double. Ask about weekly rentals. AE, DC, DISC, MC, V.

Nestled in a shady spot across the street from the beach, this two-story Spanish-style motel offers well-kept rooms with modern furnishings and bright Florida colors, some with kitchenettes. Facilities include Tia Lena's restaurant, an outdoor solar-heated swimming pool, barbecue grills, shuffleboard courts, a guest laundry, a fishing and boating dock, and water-sports rentals.

Five Oaks Bed and Breakfast Inn. 1102 Riverside Dr., Palmetto, FL 34221. ☎ **941/723-1236.** 4 rms. A/C TEL. $65–$100 double. Rates include full breakfast. AE, MC, V.

Those in search of total quiet will enjoy it here because potentially noisy kids are not welcome (children under a certain age—at the discretion of the owner—are not permitted). Known for its full breakfast served southern style, this inn is across the Manatee River directly north of downtown, surrounded by palm trees, oaks, and gardens overlooking the water. Guests enjoy use of a parlor with fireplace, and an enclosed wraparound solarium/sunporch or formal dining room filled with wicker and rattan furnishings.

DOUBLES FOR LESS THAN $100

✪ **Harrington House.** 5626 Gulf Dr., Holmes Beach, FL 34217. ☎ **941/778-5444.** 12 rms. A/C TV. Year-round, $89–$169 double, depending on the view. MC, V.

This is a true beach lover's getaway. Flowers are everywhere, there's a private beach, and the innkeepers are charming. In a tree-shaded setting on the beach overlooking the Gulf of Mexico, this three-story bed-and-breakfast built in 1925 exudes an Old Florida ambience. The eight bedrooms are individually decorated with antiques, wicker, or rattan furnishings. Some units have four-poster or brass beds, and the higher-priced rooms have French doors leading to balconies overlooking the gulf. In addition to the bedrooms in the main house, four rooms are available in the adjacent Beach House, a 1920s captain's home recently remodeled and updated.

All guests enjoy use of the high-ceilinged living room with fireplace, an outdoor pool and patio, and complimentary use of bicycles, kayaks, and other sports equipment.

Park Inn Club and Breakfast. 4450 47th St. West, Bradenton, FL 34210. ☎ **941/795-4633,** or 800/437-PARK. Fax 941/795-0808. 120 rms, 8 suites. A/C TV TEL. High season, $97–$127 double; $TK suite. Off-season, $64–$94 double; $TK suite. Rates include continental breakfast. AE, DC, DISC, MC, V.

Families will enjoy this place nestled on its own well-landscaped grounds and set back from the busy Fla. 684 (Cortez Road) corridor. It's not near a beach, but the three-story contemporary building is wrapped around a central courtyard with a patio and swimming pool. The spacious guest rooms are furnished in pastel tones with light woods; the suites have Jacuzzis. The Pub in the Park Lounge is where guests are served breakfast and complimentary cocktails each evening.

Sand & Sea Motel. 2412 Gulf Dr., Bradenton Beach, FL 34217. ☎ **941/778-2231.** 30 rms. A/C TV TEL. High-season, $95 double. Off-season, $45–$95 double. MC, V. Free parking.

This family-oriented motel is directly on the beach overlooking the Gulf of Mexico, a modern two-story building surrounded by palm trees. The bedrooms, which look out on the beach or the garden, are spacious, with standard furnishings and tiled bathrooms. The gulf-front rooms have balconies. Facilities include an outdoor heated swimming pool, beach umbrellas, lounge chairs, shuffleboard courts, and a guest laundry. Efficiency apartments are also available.

WHERE TO EAT
MEALS FOR LESS THAN $10

The Beachhouse. 200 Gulf Dr. North, Bradenton Beach. ☎ **941/779-2222.** Reservations not accepted; preferred seating system. Main courses $9.95–$15.95. AE, MC, V. Daily 11:30am–10pm. AMERICAN.

This place sits right on the beach with a huge open deck and a covered pavilion facing out to the gulf. On most afternoons and evenings local musicians play steel drums to enhance the tropical atmosphere. It's known as a front seat for extraordinary sunsets and an "in" spot for beachgoers seeking good food in a casual atmosphere. The menu offers daily fresh fish specials prepared in various styles, as well as the signature dish: Beachhouse grouper, with a nutty crust in citrus-butter sauce. There's also a good variety of prime ribs, steaks, and pastas.

Miller's Dutch Kitchen. 3401 14th St. West. ☎ **941/746-8253.** Reservations not accepted. Main courses $5.25–$11.95. MC, V. Mon–Sat 11am–8pm. AMERICAN.

With a sprinkling of Pennsylvania Dutch recipes, this restaurant is an oasis of home-style cooking nestled along a busy road known more for fast food. The menu includes Dutch casserole (noodles, peas, cheese, potatoes, beef, mushrooms, and chicken soup with croutons), pan-fried chicken, and cabbage rolls, as well as prime rib, stuffed flounder, veal parmesan, barbecued pork ribs, and lasagne. To top it off, there are over 20 freshly baked pies.

MEALS FOR LESS THAN $15

The Pier. 1200 1st Ave. West. ☎ **941/748-8087.** Reservations recommended. Main courses $9.95–$21.95. AE, DC, DISC, MC, V. Sun–Thurs 11:30am–9pm, Fri–Sat 11:30am–10pm. AMERICAN.

With commanding views of the Manatee River, this restaurant is *the* place to dine downtown. It sits at the foot of 12th Street on Memorial Pier, housed in a stately Spanish-style landmark building. The menu offers such local favorites as red snapper meunière, crab-stuffed shrimp, baked oysters imperial, and Florida crab cakes, as well as steaks and prime rib. Lighter fare is available on the outdoor River Deck.

Rotten Ralph's. 902 S. Bay Blvd., Anna Maria, Anna Maria Island. ☎ **941/778-3953.** Reservations not accepted. Main courses $6.95–$15.95. MC, V. Daily 11am–10pm. INTERNATIONAL.

On the north end of the island overlooking the Anna Maria Yacht Basin, this casual Old Florida–style restaurant offers indoor and outdoor seating. The menu provides many seafood choices (from scallops and shrimp to crab cakes, snow crab, oysters, and grouper), as well as such British favorites as fish and chips and steak-and-kidney pie. Other choices include Danish baby back ribs, chicken pot pie, and Anna Maria chicken (marinated and grilled with a honey-mustard sauce).

The Sandbar. 100 Spring Ave. (off Gulf Dr.), Anna Maria, Anna Maria Island. ☎ **941/778-0444.** Reservations not accepted on deck; preferred seating policy in main restaurant. Main courses $10.95–$19.95. CB, DC, MC, V. Daily 11:30am–3pm and 4–10pm. SEAFOOD.

"We are seafood" is the motto of this popular restaurant, perched on the beach overlooking the Gulf of Mexico. Established in 1979, it offers air-conditioned seating indoors and deck-style seating outside. The seafood choices change daily, depending on the local catch, but often include soft-shell crab and crab cakes, sautéed scallops, shrimp scampi, and stuffed grouper or flounder. Steaks, surf and turf, pastas, and chicken round out the menu.

The Seafood Shack. 4110 127th St. West, Cortez. ☎ **941/794-1235.** Reservations not accepted. Main courses $8.95–$23.95. AE, MC, V. Sun–Thurs 11:30am–9pm, Fri–Sat 11:30am–10pm. SEAFOOD.

A tradition in the area for over 20 years, this informal spot sits on the marina along the edge of the mainland beside the Fla. 684 bridge (Cortez Bridge) leading to Bradenton Beach. The menu offers many different seafood combinations and at least six different shrimp dishes (from scampi to stuffed), as well as freshly caught Florida lobster, stone crabs, grouper, and snapper. The Shack specialty is sautéed frogs' legs, and beef and chicken are also available.

The ***Seafood Shack Showboat*** (☎ 941/794-5048), docked beside the restaurant, offers sightseeing cruises, priced at $10 to $14, which entitle participants to discounts off dinner dishes in the restaurant.

WORTH A SPLURGE

The Beach Bistro. 6600 Gulf Blvd., Holmes Beach. ☎ **941/778-6444.** Reservations recommended. Main courses $17.95–$29.95. MC, V. Daily 5:30–9:30pm. INTERNATIONAL.

This small, 12-table culinary oasis sits right beside the beach, offering wide-windowed views of the gulf waters. The decor is bright and modern, with an overall elegance enhanced by crisp linens, sparkling crystal, and fresh flowers on every table. Check out the salmon Benjamin with lime-dill butter in potato parchment, prime medallions of veal smothered in eggplant and provolone with a plum-tomato and marsala-wine sauce.

BRADENTON AFTER DARK

THE PERFORMING ARTS

A community hub for meetings, conventions, and sports events, the huge circular **Manatee Convention & Civic Center,** 1 Haben Blvd., Palmetto (☎ 941/722-6626), is also a popular venue for plays, concerts, and other types of entertainment. The box office is open Monday to Friday from noon to 6pm.

The **Riverfront Theatre,** 102 Old Main St. / 12th St. West (☎ 941/748-5875), across from the pier on the Manatee River, is a community theater featuring the Manatee Players. Established in 1948, the Players present musicals and dramas throughout the year as well as a summer musical revue, band concerts, and a series of nontraditional works. Tickets are $13 to $15.

THE CLUB & BAR SCENE

Aces Lounge. 4343 Palma Sola Blvd. ☎ **941/795-3896.** No cover.

West of downtown on Palma Sola Bay, this lounge features a variety of live music, including karaoke on Wednesday, from 9pm to 1am.

Cafe Robar. 204 Pine Ave. (at Gulf Dr.), Anna Maria, Anna Maria Island. ☎ **941/778-6969.** No cover.

This elegant place offers piano music and a sing-along bar Tuesday to Sunday from 8pm until midnight.

D. Coy Ducks. In the Island Shopping Center, 5410 Marina Dr., Holmes Beach, Anna Maria Island. ☎ **941/778-5888.** No cover.

This bar is known for its varied program of live Dixieland bands, jazz pianists, and guitarists/vocalists. Music starts at various times (from 5 to 8pm) and usually continues until midnight or 1am nightly.

The Pewter Mug. 108 44th Ave. East (1 block east of U.S. 41). ☎ **941/756-7577.** No cover.

Situated downtown, this lively place offers a blend of jazz bands or contemporary tunes from 9pm until midnight on Friday and Saturday.

Scoreboard Sports Pub. 7004 Cortez Rd. West. ☎ **941/792-6768.** No cover.

Bradenton's only original sports pub is an ideal place to watch football games and other sports. Open from 8pm until midnight, depending on what's scheduled.

15 Southwest Florida

by Bill Goodwin

Residents of Sanibel keep McDonald's from putting a fast-food franchise on their remarkably beautiful island. Members of the Naples zoning board reject a bed-and-breakfast inn proposed for their historic district. The Nature Conservancy moves to buy and preserve more wilderness land. And the federal government kicks airboats out of the pristine Everglades National Park.

If these victories make you think the environmentalists and preservationists are holding their own in Southwest Florida, you're right.

Granted, the areas around Fort Myers and Naples sport their share of development, but the number of high-rise condos and hotels here pales in comparison to many other parts of South Florida, especially Miami to the east and Tampa Bay to the north. Indeed, Southwest Florida is one of the best parts of the state both to enjoy the great outdoors and to discover many remnants of Old Florida.

The region traces its nature-loving roots to inventor Thomas A. Edison, who was so enamored of this beautiful corner of Florida that he spent his winters in Fort Myers from 1885 until 1931. His friend Henry Ford built his own winter home next to the Edisons'. The world's best tarpon fishing lured President Teddy Roosevelt and his buddies to Useppa, one of literally 10,000 islands along this coast. Some of the planet's best shelling helped entice the du Ponts of Delaware to Gasparilla Island, where they built the Nantucket-like village of Boca Grande. The unspoiled beauty of Sanibel and Captiva so entranced *New York Times* Pulitzer Prize–winning political cartoonist J. N. (Ding) Darling that he campaigned to preserve much of those islands in their natural states. The then-remote islands also gave inspiration to novelists Anne Morrow Lindbergh and Mary Roberts Rhinehart. And lovely Naples came to have its own Millionaires Row along its beautiful beach.

Many well-heeled individuals still are attracted to Southwest Florida, making it one of the more expensive parts of the state to visit during the winter from mid-December to April. This is especially true of favorite enclaves of the rich and famous such as Naples and Sanibel, Captiva, and Marco islands. During the off-season, however, even the most expensive resorts drop their room rates drastically. Consider visiting here during the "shoulder seasons" of November to mid-December and during May. The weather is warm and pleasant, and most establishments that close during the slow summer season are open.

SPECIAL EVENTS & FESTIVALS IN SOUTHWEST FLORIDA

Southwest Florida has several fun-filled special events that will add luster to any visit here.

Stan Gober's Idle Hour Seafood Restaurant in Goodland is mobbed on the third weekend in January for the **Goodland Mullet Festival** (☎ **941/394-3041**), a massive party featuring the Buzzard Lope dance and the Best Men's Legs Contest.

The area's top festival is the **Edison Pageant of Light** (☎ **941/334-2550** or 800/237-6444), in Fort Myers the first two weeks in February, topped off by the spectacular Parade of Lights.

Beginning the first Thursday in March, the 4-day **Sanibel Shell Fair** (☎ **941/472-2155**) draws collectors to Sanibel and Captiva islands.

The second Wednesday and Thursday of July see some $175,000 at stake in the **World's Richest Tarpon Tournament,** in the great tarpon waters off Boca Grande. Call the event hotline (☎ **941/964-2995** or 800/237-6444).

In Fort Myers Beach the first weekend in November, some 50,000 participants and spectators gather for the **Fort Myers Beach Sand Sculpting Contest** (☎ **941/463-6451** or 800/782-9283). The masters compete among themselves; everyone can join in.

During the first week of December, lights and music hail the holiday season at the **Edison/Ford Winter Homes Holiday House** (☎ **941/334-3614**) in Fort Myers. At the same time, candles in bags create a spectacular **Luminary Trail** along the full length of Sanibel Island's Periwinkle Way.

EXPLORING SOUTHWEST FLORIDA BY CAR

Most visitors who arrive by air land at Southwest Florida International Airport on the outskirts of Fort Myers. From here it's only 35 miles to Naples, 46 miles to Marco Island. Both I-75 and U.S. 41 run north-south through the region, making for easy travel by car. This means that you can see the sights and participate in most activities easily from one base of operations. For example, you can stay in centrally located Fort Myers Beach and make easy excursions into Fort Myers on one day, over to Sanibel and Captiva Islands on another, and south to Naples, Marco Island, or Everglades City on a third. Fort Myers, Fort Myers Beach, and Sanibel and Captiva islands are so close together—no more than 14 miles apart—that you can stay in one and pop over to the other for dinner. The same is true of Naples and nearby Marco Island.

THE GREAT OUTDOORS

Few areas of the state have the variety of outdoor activities as does Southwest Florida. In close proximity, the Gulf of Mexico laps nearly 50 miles of great white-sand beaches, no fewer than 10,000 uninhabited islands wait to be explored, and the western side of the wild and exciting Everglades is just a few miles away.

The successes of conservationists and preservationists have made the region a heaven for lovers of unspoiled nature. Bird and wildlife watchers, canoeists, and kayakers can all indulge their passions at several nature preserves here. Almost a third of Sanibel is protected by the wonderful J. N. "Ding" Darling National Wildlife Refuge. East of Naples, the National Audubon Society's 11,000-acre Corkscrew Swamp Sanctuary is the home of wood storks and countless other birds. The Conservancy's Naples Nature Center and its Briggs Nature Center near Marco Island both have canoe and kayak trails through their wildernesses, as do Collier Seminole State Park near Marco Island and the Darling wildlife refuge on Sanibel. Near Fort Myers, Babcock Wilderness Adventures offers "swamp buggy" rides through the

What's Special About Southwest Florida

Best Experiences for Free
- Hunting for seashells on Sanibel Island, or building sandcastles on Fort Myers Beach.
- Sunset on Naples Pier, with a view of Millionaires Row glowing in the golden light.
- If you have your own canoe or kayak, paddling to Mound Key State Archeological Site, one of the largest Calusa-made shell islands.
- Window-shopping along 3rd Avenue, Naples's answer to Rodeo Drive.
- Friday-night block parties in downtown Fort Myers.

Beaches
- Sanibel, Captiva, North Captiva, Cayo Costa, and Keewaydin islands beaches—some of the world's best for collecting seashells.
- Lover's Key, whose pristine sands are accessible only by tram or footpath from an adjoining state park.

Wildlife Sanctuaries
- J. N. (Ding) Darling National Wildlife Refuge, encompassing more than 5,000 acres on Sanibel, with biking, hiking, canoeing, kayaking, and driving trails for observing alligators, hundreds of species of birds, and luxuriant Florida flora.
- Briggs Nature Center, in the Rookery Bay National Estuarine Research Reserve, with boat excursions, canoe trails, and a mile-long boardwalk.
- Corkscrew Swamp Sanctuary, owned and preserved by the National Audubon Society, where wood storks migrate to 11,000 acres of America's largest virgin bald cypress forest.
- Babcock Wilderness Adventures, with excursions led by trained naturalists to observe alligators, bison, exotic birds, wild turkey, snakes, cougars, and wild hogs in Telegraph Swamp.

Regional Food & Drink
- Outstanding locally caught fish, two-thirds of Florida's stone crab catch.

Outdoor Activities
- Abundant golf courses, some rated among the top in the nation.
- Canoeing and kayaking through a maze of inland waterways.

Historic Buildings
- Seminole Lodge, winter home of inventor Thomas Alva Edison from 1885 to 1931, showing his talent for horticulture, with exotic plants from around the world.
- Mangoes, Henry Ford's winter home next door to the Edisons', designed in the style of the late Victorian era.

alligator-infested Telegraph Swamp. And Everglades City, of course, is the "backdoor" to Everglades National Park and the western terminus of its 99-mile Wilderness Waterway.

Beachgoers have a problem deciding where to go here, for the entire southwestern coast is lined by gorgeous white sands. Although Sanibel Island is famous for the shells that wash up there, the entire coast is a collector's dream. Much of the beaches are lined with high-rise hotels and condominiums, but many miles are protected by state parks. The best for shelling, swimming, and birdlife are Cayo Costa State

Park, north of Captiva Island, and Carl E. Johnson–Lover's Key State Recreation Area, just south of Fort Myers Beach, both of which occupy entire barrier islands. Delnor-Wiggins State Park and Clam Pass County Park in Naples also have their in-city charms. And Tigertail Public Beach is a refreshing respite from Marco Island's line of high-rise buildings.

Fishing here is among Florida's best, especially the tarpon grounds in Boca Grande Pass and Pine Island Sound, which are as productive today as they were in Teddy Roosevelt's time. Every destination covered in this chapter has its own deep-sea fishing fleet. Fort Myers Beach and Naples are the best places to go on less expensive "party boats."

Although free public facilities are scarce here, the region definitely is friendly to bicyclists on a budget. Even though they charge for parking cars, residents of Sanibel have crisscrossed their island with free paved bike paths. The governments in Fort Myers and Naples also have laid out extensive networks of bike trails in their cities. The bikers have to dodge in-line skaters on all of these smooth pathways.

1 Fort Myers

148 miles NW of Miami, 142 miles S of Tampa, 42 miles N of Naples

It's difficult to picture this pleasant city with broad avenues along the Caloosahatchee River as a raucous cowtown, but that's exactly what Fort Myers once was. Thanks to cattle brought by the Spaniards in the 1500s, native Seminole tribes amassed huge herds, and vast ranches sprang up after the Seminole Wars, with cowpokes driving steers by the thousands down McGregor Boulevard.

Settlers began coming in 1866, attracted by the warm climate, good fishing, and land for farming and ranching. The city's most famous part-time resident arrived in 1885 when inventor Thomas Alva Edison came here to regain his health after years of incessant toil and the recent death of his wife. Edison built a home, Seminole Lodge, and laboratory on the banks of the Caloosahatchee. His pal, Henry Ford, built next door. Edison planted lush tropical gardens around Seminole Lodge and royal palms along McGregor Boulevard in front of his property. The trees now extend for 15 miles, leading to Fort Myers's nickname: "The City of Palms."

Inland from the town, incredible numbers of wildlife wait to be observed in their river and swamp habitats, including those at the Babcock Ranch, largest of the surviving cattle producers and a major game preserve.

ESSENTIALS

GETTING THERE   By Plane   The **Southwest Florida International Airport,** on Daniels Parkway east of I-75, is served by Air Canada, American, America West, British, Canadian International, Continental, Delta, JetSouth, KLM, Midway, Northwest, TWA, United, and USAir. Flights into Fort Myers increase markedly during winter, as some carriers don't fly here at all during the off-season.

The baggage-claim area has an information booth (with maps) and a board with advertisements and free phones to various hotels in the region. There's no public bus service to the airport, but **limousines** (actually multipassenger vans) are available at a booth across the street from the baggage claim. **Yellow Cab** (☎ 941/352-1055) or **Aaron Limo & Taxi** (☎ 941/768-1898 or 800/998-1898), which charge 10% to 15% less than the maximum legal fares, have free phones at the information board. The maximum fares for one to three passengers are $20 to downtown Fort Myers, $26 to Fort Myers Beach, $30 to $36 to Sanibel Island, $46 to Captiva Island, $28 to Bonita Beach, $84 to Boca Grande, $38 to $46 to Naples, $60 to Marco Island, and $68 to Everglades City. Each additional passenger (above three) pays $8.

By Train   Amtrak (☎ 800/USA-RAIL) provides bus connections between Fort Myers and its nearest station, in Tampa.

By Bus   The **Greyhound** bus station is at 2275 Cleveland Ave. (☎ **941/334-1011** or 800/231-2222).

By Car   To reach downtown from Tampa, take Exit 25 off I-75 and follow Palm Beach Boulevard (Fla. 80). From Naples or Miami, take Exit 23 off I-75 and follow Dr. Martin Luther King Jr. Boulevard (Fla. 82).

VISITOR INFORMATION   For advance information about Fort Myers, Fort Myers Beach, and Sanibel and Captiva islands, contact the **Lee County Visitor and Convention Bureau,** P.O. Box 2445, Fort Myers, FL 33902 (☎ **941/ 338-3500** or 800/237-6444; fax 941/334-1106). Once in town, drop by the **Greater Fort Myers Chamber of Commerce Visitor Center,** at the corner of Edwards Drive and Lee Street on the downtown waterfront (☎ **941/332-3624** or 800/366-3622). The chamber gives away brochures and other information and sells a detailed street map of the area. The **North Fort Myers Chamber of Commerce** (☎ **941/ 997-9111**) has an information office at the Shell Factory, 2787 N. Tamiami Trail (U.S. 41).

GETTING AROUND   **By Bus**   Fort Myers is the only city in Southwest Florida with public bus service (it links to the trolley serving Fort Myers Beach). **LeeTran** (☎ **941/275-8726**) operates the buses Monday to Saturday from 6:30am to 8pm. One-ride fares are $1 (exact change is required). Orange route no. 50 runs hourly between downtown and the McGregor Point Shopping Center, at McGregor Boulevard and Gladiolus Drive, where you can catch the Beach Connection Trolley to Fort Myers Beach during the winter months (see "Essentials" in the Fort Myers section, later in this chapter). This route runs along U.S. 41 past the Greyhound bus station and the Edison and Bell Tower malls. There's no public bus service to Sanibel and Captiva islands. System maps are available from the Greater Fort Myers Chamber of Commerce (see "Visitor Information," above).

By Taxi   Call **Yellow Cab** (☎ 941/332-1055), **Bluebird Taxi** (☎ 941/275-8294), or **Admiralty Taxi** (☎ 941/275-7000). Metered fares are $1.35 at flag fall plus $1.35 for each mile.

By Rental Car   Agencies at the airport are **Alamo** (☎ 800/327-9633), **Avis** (☎ 800/831-2847), **Budget** (☎ 800/527-0700), **Dollar** (☎ 800/800-4000), **Enterprise** (☎ 800/325-8007), **Hertz** (☎ 800/654-3131), **National** (☎ 800/ 227-7368), and **Value** (☎ 800/468-2583).

By Bicycle   Rent from **Trikes, Bikes & Mowers,** 3451 Fowler St. (☎ **941/ 936-4301**), or **Bike Route,** 14530 U.S. 41 South (☎ **941/481-3376**).

OUTDOOR ACTIVITIES

CANOEING & KAYAKING   The area's slow-moving rivers and quiet, island-speckled inland waters offer fine canoe and kayak ventures, with birds and manatees to be visited along the way. Two popular local venues are the winding waterways around Pine Island west of town and the Estero River south of Fort Myers. The Estero River is an official Florida canoe trail which leads 3 1/2 miles from U.S. 41 to Estero Bay, which is itself a state aquatic preserve. Near the mouth of the river lies the **Mound Key State Archeological Site,** one of the largest Calusa shell middens.

Fort Myers/Naples Area

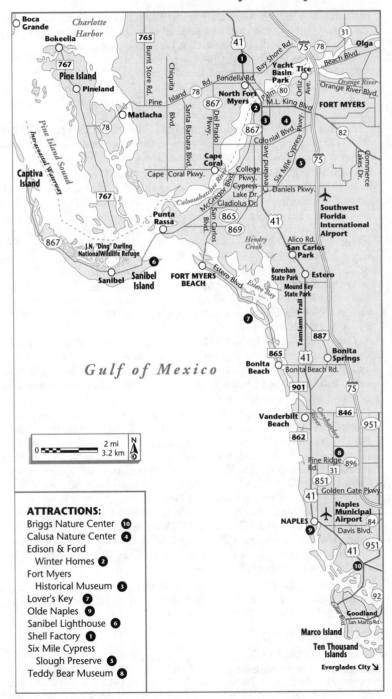

ATTRACTIONS:
Briggs Nature Center ❿
Calusa Nature Center ❹
Edison & Ford
  Winter Homes ❷
Fort Myers
  Historical Museum ❸
Lover's Key ❼
Olde Naples ❾
Sanibel Lighthouse ❻
Shell Factory ❶
Six Mile Cypress
  Slough Preserve ❺
Teddy Bear Museum ❽

Scholars believe that this mostly artificial island dates back some 2,000 years and was the capital of the Calusa chief who ruled all of South Florida when the Spanish arrived. There's no park ranger on the key, but signs explain its history.

Estero River Outfitters, at the Estero River bridge on U.S. 41 (☎ **941/ 992-4050**), rents both canoes and kayaks. Canoes cost $17.50 to $22.50 a day, depending on size; kayaks range from $12.50 to $17.50. **Koreshan State Historic Park,** a half mile south of the bridge on U.S. 41 (☎ **941/922-0311**), rents canoes for $3 an hour, $15 per day.

Based in Matlacha on Pine Island, the **Gulf Coast Kayak Company** (☎ **941/ 283-1125**) has daily nature, manatee-watching, and sunset trips, plus overnight and longer expeditions out to North Captiva and Cayo Costa.

CRUISES   J. C. Boat Cruises, at the downtown Fort Myers City Yacht Basin, Edwards Drive at Lee Street, opposite the chamber of commerce (☎ **941/ 334-7474**), presents a variety of year-round cruises on the Caloosahatchee River and its tributaries, including lunch and dinner voyages on the sternwheeler *Captain J.P.* The 3-hour Everglades Jungle Cruise is a good way to observe the area's wildlife, with lots of manatees to be seen from November to April. A full-day cruise goes all the way up the Caloosahatchee to Lake Okeechobee and back. Prices range from $12 to $74. Schedules change and advance reservations are strongly recommended.

The **Sanibel Harbour Resort & Spa,** 17260 Harbour Pointe Rd., near the Sanibel Causeway (☎ **941/466-4000**), welcomes nonguests on its champagne sunset cruises on San Carlos Bay between the mainland and Sanibel Island. They cost $18 for adults, $10 for children.

The *Tropic Star* (☎ **941/283-0015**) leaves Four Winds Marina on Pine Island every morning for Boca Grande, Cayo Costa, Cabbage Key, and North Captiva. Fares are $17 for adults, $10 for children 3 to 12. See "An Easy Excursion to Boca Grande," below, and "Easy Island Excursions" in the Sanibel and Captiva islands section for information about these offshore destinations.

GOLF & TENNIS   Public courses **in Fort Myers** are at the Fort Myers Country Club (☎ 941/936-2457), the Eastwood Golf Club (☎ 941/275-4848), the River's Edge Country Club (☎ 941/433-4211), and the Gateway Golf & Country Club (☎ 941/561-1010); **in North Fort Myers,** at El Rio Golf Club (☎ 941/995-2204) and the Riverbend Golf Club (☎ 941/543-2200); **in Cape Coral,** at the Coral Oaks Country Club (☎ 941/283-4100) and the Cape Coral Golf and Tennis Resort (☎ 941/542-3191); **on Pine Island,** at the Alden Pines Country Club (☎ 941/ 283-2179); **in South Fort Myers,** at the San Carlos Country Club (☎ 941/ 267-3131) and Terraverde (☎ 941/433-7733); and **in Bonita Springs,** at the Bonita Springs Golf & Country Club (☎ 941/992-2800). Call for tee times and greens fees.

Tennis buffs can play at the **Fort Myers Racquet Club,** 4900 Deleon St. (☎ **941/ 278-7277**), which has eight lighted courts.

HORSEBACK RIDING   Two stables in North Fort Myers offer riding: **D.J.'s Ranch,** 17840 Shelby Lane (☎ **941/543-4050**), and the **Hancock Creek Riding Stables,** 865 Moody Rd. (☎ **941/997-3322**).

WHAT TO SEE & DO
THE MAIN ATTRACTIONS

✪ **Edison and Ford Winter Estates.** 2350 McGregor Blvd. ☎ **941/334-3614** for a recording, or 941/334-7419. Edison home, $8 adults, $4 children 6–12, free for children 5 and under; Both homes, $10 adults, $5 children 6–12, free for children 5 and under. Homes, Mon–Sat 9am–3:30pm, Sun 12:30–3:30pm; grounds, daily until 5:30pm. Closed Thanksgiving and Christmas Day.

Thomas Edison and his second wife, Mina, brought their family to this porch-surrounded Victorian retreat, known as Seminole Lodge, in 1886 and wintered here until the inventor's death in 1931. Mrs. Edison gave the 14-acre estate to the City of Fort Myers in 1947, but it stands exactly as it did during Edison's lifetime. Some of his lightbulbs dating from the 1920s still burn in the laboratory where he and his staff worked on some 1,093 inventions. An avid amateur botanist, Edison experimented with the exotic foliage he planted in the lush tropical gardens surrounding the mansion (he used bamboo for lightbulb filaments and turned goldenrod into rubber). A museum displays some of his inventions, as well as his unique Model-T Ford, a gift from friend Henry Ford. In 1916 Ford and his wife, Clara, built Mangoes, their bungalow-style house next door, so they could winter with the Edisons. Like Seminole Lodge, Mangoes is furnished as it appeared in the 1920s.

Koreshan State Historic Site. U.S. 41, Estero (15 miles south of downtown). ☎ **941/992-0311.** Admission $3.25 per vehicle, $1 pedestrians or bikers. Park, daily 8am–sunset; settlement buildings, daily 8am–5pm.

This 300-acre landmark along the narrow Estero River was the site of the Koreshan Unity Movement (pronounced Kor-*esh*-en), a now-extinct 19th-century religious sect. The Koreshans believed that humans lived *inside* the earth, and—ahead of their time—that women should have equal rights. Cyrus Reed Teed and his followers from Chicago established a self-sufficient settlement here in 1894. Several of their buildings and gardens have been restored. Nature and canoe trails wind through the settlement and downriver to Mound Key, an islet made of the Calusas' discarded shells. There's a picnic and camping area.

OTHER ATTRACTIONS

All dressed up in 1918-vintage finery, sisters Mona and Jetta Burroughs lead "living history" tours through riverside gardens at the **Burroughs Home,** 2505 1st St., at Fowler Street (☎ 941/332-6125). This Georgian Revival mansion was built in 1901 by cattleman John Murphy and later sold to the Burroughs family. You must take a tour in order to visit the premises. Admission is $3 for adults, $1 for children 6 to 12, free for children 5 and under 6. Open from Thanksgiving to April, Tuesday to Friday from 10am to 4pm. Tours every are given 45 minutes. Park free in the Sheraton Harbor Place garage.

Housed in the restored Spanish-style depot served by the Atlantic Coast Line from 1924 to 1971, the **Fort Myers Historical Museum,** 2300 Peck St., at Jackson Street (☎ 941/332-5955), features exhibits depicting Fort Myers' history from the ancient Calusas and the Spanish conquistadors to the first settlers. A replica of an 1800s "Cracker" home stands outside, as does the Esperanza—the longest and one of the last of the plush Pullman private cars. Including the remains of a P-39 Aircobra which crashed off Fort Myers Beach in 1943, one exhibit explains Page Field's role as a base for training fighter pilots during World War II. Admission is $2.50 for adults, $1 for children 11 and under. Open Tuesday to Friday from 9am to 4pm and on Saturday from 10am to 4pm.

Rather than have the kids go stir crazy on a rainy day, head for the **Imaginarium,** 2000 Cranford Ave., at Martin Luther King, Jr., Boulevard (☎ 941/337-3332), an entertaining, hands-on museum in the old city water plant. A host of toylike exhibits explain such basic scientific principles as gravity and the weather. There are nature shows in the theater every 30 minutes, and both children and adults can examine living creatures in a touch tank. Plans call for shark and reef tanks and a walk through a re-created Everglades environment. Admission is $6 for adults, $3 for children3 to 12. In winter it's open daily from 10am to 5pm; off-season, Tuesday to Sunday from 10am to 5pm. Closed Thanksgiving and Christmas Day.

PARKS & NATURE PRESERVES

One of the most informative ways to see Southwest Florida's abundant wildlife is on a "swamp buggy" ride with ✪ **Babcock Wilderness Adventures,** on Fla. 31 about 11 miles northeast of Fort Myers (☎ **941/338-6367** for information, 800/500-5583 for reservations). Experienced naturalists lead 90-minute tours through the Babcock Ranch, the largest contiguous cattle operation east of the Mississippi River and home to countless birds and wildlife as well as domesticated bison and quarter horses. Alligators scurry from a bridge or lie motionless in the dark-brown waters of the mysterious Telegraph Swamp when the buggies pass overhead. Visitors dismount to visit an enclosure where southern cougars stand in for their close cousins, the rare Florida panthers (which are tan, not black). Unlike most wildlife tours here, this one covers five different ecosystems, from open prairie to cypress swamp. The crew making the Sean Connery movie *Just Cause* built a replica of an old Florida courthouse here; the ranch uses it as a small museum. Admission is $18 for adults, $10 for children 3 to 12. Reservations are required, so call for tour times.

Closer to town, visitors can observe Florida's inland flora and fauna on three nature trails winding through 105-acres at the **Calusa Nature Center & Planetarium,** on Ortiz Avenue just north of Colonial Boulevard (☎ **941/ 275-3435**), where there's also an aviary, a children's natural-history museum, a live-reptile exhibit, a 400-gallon freshwater aquarium, and a museum store. The planetarium features star and laser-light shows. Admission to the nature center is $3 for adults, $1.50 for children 3 to 12. The planetarium shows range from $2 to $3.50. The center is open Monday to Saturday from 9am to 5pm and on Sunday from 11am to 5pm. The office will tell of guided walks and special programs.

A mile-long boardwalk leads through a 2,000-acre wetland ecosystem at **Six Mile Cypress Slough Preserve,** on Six Mile Cypress Parkway, at Penzance Boulevard between Colonial Boulevard and Daniels Parkway (☎ **941/338-3300**). Admission is $3 per vehicle. The boardwalk is open daily from 8am to 5pm. A ranger leads guided walks on Wednesday and Saturday at 9:30am. Call for a schedule of other programs.

ORGANIZED TOURS

One economical and informative way to see the sights of downtown is on a narrated **trolley tour,** which makes a circuit of the Edison and Ford Winter Estates, the Burroughs Home, the Fort Myers Historical Museum, and the Imaginarium. During the winter the trolley leaves the parking lot at the Edison home Tuesday to Saturday every hour on the hour from 10am to 4pm. The fare is $5 for adults, $2 for children, with free reboarding. Tickets include admission discounts of $1 at the Burroughs Home and the Imaginarium, and 50¢ at the Fort Myers Historical Museum. Check with the Edison and Ford Winter Estates (☎ **941/334-7419**) to find out if the trolley is operating during the off-season.

The old-fashioned **Seminole Gulf Railway** (☎ **941/275-8487**), the original railroad between Fort Myers and Naples, chugs as far south as Bonita Springs. Dinner trains usually depart at 6:30pm on Friday. Sightseeing excursions usually leave twice a day at least 3 days a week, and there's an occasional Sunday-brunch run. Call for the schedules. Reservations are required for the dinner trip. The trains depart Fort Myers from the Metro Mall Station, a small blue building on the western edge of the Metro Mall parking lot on Colonial Boulevard at Metro Parkway. The Bonita Springs station is on Old U.S. 41 at Pennsylvania Avenue.

Spectator Sports

The locals start counting balls and strikes in February when the Boston Red Sox and the Minnesota Twins arrive for **spring training.** The **Boston Red Sox** play at the 6,500-seat City of Palms Park, at Edison Avenue and Broadway (☎ **941/334-4700**). The **Minnesota Twins** work out at the 7,500-seat Lee County Sports Complex, on Six Mile Cypress Parkway between Daniels and Metro parkways (☎ **941/768-4270,** or 800/338-9467).

The hounds race at the **Naples–Fort Myers Kennel Club,** at Old U.S. 41 and Bonita Beach Road in Bonita Springs (☎ **941/922-2411**). The club has both matinee and evening races on a seasonal schedule (call for the latest). It's closed August and September.

Shopping

An institution for more than 50 years, ✪ **The Shell Factory,** 5 miles north of the Caloosahatchee River bridge on U.S. 41 (☎ **941/995-2141**), carries one of the world's largest collections of shells, corals, sponges, and fossils. Entire sections are devoted to shell jewelry and shell lamps. Many items here cost under $10, some under $1. Open daily from 10am to 6pm.

Bargain hunters can browse more than 800 booths carrying antiques, crafts, fashions, and produce at **Fleamasters,** on Dr. Martin Luther King, Jr., Boulevard (Fla. 82), 1¹/₂ miles west of I-75. There are snack bars and entertainment, too. Open on Friday, Saturday, and Sunday from 8am to 4pm.

Outlet shoppers will find most of the major brand names discounted at **Sanibel Factory Stores,** on the way to the beaches at the junction of Summerlin Road and McGregor Boulevard.

WHERE TO STAY

The most expensive time to visit Southwest Florida is during the winter months from mid-December to April, when even many of the usually inexpensive chain motels along U.S. 41 charge more than $100 a night for a double room. And even if you can find an inexpensive room in winter, you may have to reserve months advance. On the other hand, hotel rates drop dramatically between May and the middle of December. The most economical time to visit is during June, July, and August, but the summertime weather can be brutally hot and humid. From both a climate and a cost standpoint, the best times to visit are May and November to mid-December, when the weather is warm and pleasant and most rooms are priced well below their peak winter rates.

The categories in this chapter are determined by the price of the least expensive double room during the fall and spring shoulder seasons: doubles for less than $40, doubles for less than $60, and doubles for less than $80.

Regardless of the season, all hotel bills in Southwest Florida are subject to both the state's 6% sales tax and a 3% county add-on, resulting in 9% total tax.

In addition to the hostelries mentioned below, Fort Myers has several standard chain motels offering clean, comfortable accommodations.

Along Cleveland Avenue (U.S. 41) south of downtown are an **Econo Lodge** (☎ 941/995-0571 or 800/553-2666); a **La Quinta Inn,** 4850 S. Cleveland Ave. (☎ 941/275-3300 or 800/531-5900); a **Ramada Limited** (☎ 941/275-1111 or 800/272-6232); and a **Red Carpet Inn** (☎ 941/9366-3229 or 800/251-1962). On Daniels Parkway, near the airport at Exit 22 off I-75, are three new, completely modern establishments: a **Hampton Inn** (☎ 941/768-2525 or 800/426-7866), a **Comfort Suites** (☎ 941/768-0005 or 800/435-8234), and a **Sleep Inn** (☎ 941/561-1117 or 800/358-3170).

Among the least expensive places here is the local **Motel 6** (☎ 941/656-5544 or 800/466-8356), a converted older property on U.S. 41 just across the river in North Fort Myers. It's basic by today's standards, but double rooms cost just $51 in winter, $33 off-season.

DOUBLES FOR LESS THAN $40

Budgetel Inn. 2717 Colonial Blvd., Fort Myers, FL 33907. ☎ **941/275-3500**, or 800/428-3438. Fax 941/275-5426. 102 rms, 20 suites. Winter, $79 double; $89.95 suite. Off-season, $39 double; $46.95 suite. Rates include continental breakfast. AE, DC, DISC, MC, V.

The small but growing Budgetel Inn chain offers exceptional value for its large, well-equipped rooms, and this modern, four-story version is no different. It's centrally situated on Colonial Boulevard near Metro Mall and the Courtyard by Marriott and offers an outdoor swimming pool. Entered from exterior walkways, the spacious, comfortably furnished rooms have extras like desks and long cords on the telephones from which to make free local calls. Sweetening the deal here are in-room coffeemakers and complimentary juice and a Danish left on your doorknob before dawn.

DOUBLES FOR LESS THAN $60

Holiday Inn Central. 2431 Cleveland Ave. (U.S. 41, at Edison Ave.), Fort Myers, FL 33901. ☎ **941/332-3232**, or toll free 800/998-0466. Fax 941/332-0590. 126 rms. A/C TV TEL. Winter, $139–$149 double. Off-season, $59–$79 double. AE, DC, DISC, MC, V.

It's not an exaggeration to describe the bubbling fountain in the tiled lobby of this coral-and-aqua art deco hotel as an oasis along busy Cleveland Avenue. The present owners completely renovated the four-story structure in 1991 and had the good sense to leave the shady live oaks standing in the parking lot. The coral-and-green theme is carried throughout, with bright furniture and spreads lending a tropical ambience to match the lobby and palm-bordered outdoor swimming pool. The baths are a bit small but have adequate counter space and several nooks in the tub-showers for toiletries. The location is a 2-block walk to the Boston Red Sox training facility (minor-league hopefuls stay here during spring training) and a short drive to the Edison and Ford homes.

DOUBLES FOR LESS THAN $80

○ **Courtyard by Marriott.** 4450 Metro Pkwy. (at Colonial Blvd.), Fort Myers, FL 33901. ☎ **941/275-8600**, or 800/321-2211. Fax 941/275-7087. 149 rms. A/C TV TEL. Winter, $130 double. Off-season, $64 double. Weekend packages available. AE, DC, DISC, MC, V.

Like most members of this exceptional chain designed for business travelers, this comfortable modern hotel encloses a landscaped courtyard with a swimming pool. About half the sizable rooms face the courtyard; the others face the surrounding parking lots. All have sofas or easy chairs and rich mahogany writing tables and chests of drawers, plus extra little features like long telephone cords and hand-basin faucets dispensing piping-hot water for tea and instant coffee. The comfortable lobby features a fireplace and dining area that's open for breakfast. Other facilities include an exercise room, an indoor spa pool, and a guest laundry.

CAMPING

About 15 miles south of downtown on U.S. 41, the **Koreshan State Historic Site,** P.O. Box 7, Estero, FL 33928 (☎ **941/992-0311**), has the only true campground here, with 60 wooded sites for tents or RVs at $16 per night in winter, $10 a night off-season (see "What to See & Do," above, for information about the historic site). Reservations are accepted up to 60 days in advance year round.

All other camping facilities in or near Fort Myers are really long-term RV parks which may or may not have sites available during the winter months. The most convenient to the beaches is **Groves Campground,** 19175 John Morris Rd., Fort Myers, FL 33908 (☎ **941/466-5909**). It's just north of McGregor Boulevard and a 10-minute drive to both Fort Myers Beach and Sanibel Island. Monthly rentals are required in winter at $445 a month. They cost $18 a day off-season.

Three other campgrounds are on U.S. 41 in Estero, about 13 miles south of downtown. Preferable is the **Shady Acres Travel Park,** 19370 Tamiami Trail South, Fort Myers, FL 33908 (☎ **941/267-8448**), and **Woodsmoke Camping,** 19251 Tamiami Trail South, Fort Myers, FL 33908 (☎ **941/267-3456**). Both are built around lakes and have wooded sites. The Shady Acres Travel Park is slightly less expensive, with sites going for $24 a day in winter, $20 off-season. The third of these is the **Fort Myers Campground,** 16800 Tamiami Trail South, Fort Myers, FL 33908 (☎ **941/ 267-2141**), which doesn't have as many shady sites.

WHERE TO EAT

Unlike the region's hotels, its restaurants have no seasons for prices—they're the same year-round. Some adjust their hours from season to season and even year to year, however, so you may want to call ahead to make sure of an establishment's business hours. The categories used in this chapter are based on the price of an average main course and tea, coffee, or a soft drink: less than $7, less than $10, and less than $15.

Fort Myers's main commercial strip, Cleveland Avenue (U.S. 41), has most national fast-food and family chain restaurants, especially near College Parkway, where you'll find an Olive Garden, a Bennigans, and an Outback Steakhouse. A Lone Star Steakhouse and a Bob Evans Family Restaurant are near the junction of U.S. 41 and Cypress Lake Drive/Daniels Parkway.

MEALS FOR LESS THAN $7

Farmers Market Restaurant. 2736 Edison Ave. (at Cranford Ave.). ☎ **941/334-1687.** Reservations not accepted. Breakfast $3–$5; sandwiches $2–$6; meals $4–$8. No credit cards. Mon–Sat 6am–8pm, Sun 6am–7pm. SOUTHERN.

The retail Farmers Market next door may be tiny, but the best of the cabbage, okra, green beans, and tomatoes end up here at this plain and simple eatery frequented by everyone from business executives to truck drivers. The specialties of the house are smoked beef, pork barbecue, and other southern favorites like country-fried steak, fried chicken livers and gizzards, and smoked hamhocks with a bowl of black-eyed peas. Yankees can order fried chicken, roast beef, or pork chops, and they can have hash browns instead of grits with their big breakfast.

Hickory Bar-B-Que. 15400 McGregor Blvd. (at Gladiolus Dr.). ☎ **941/481-2626.** Reservations not accepted. Main courses $5–$9; sandwiches $4. No credit cards. Mon–Thurs 11am–8pm, Fri–Sat 11am–8:30pm. BARBECUE.

More convenient to the beaches than the downtown restaurants, this now-modern establishment still displays its original 1957 menu, which offered plates of barbecued pork ribs for $1.55 and sandwiches for 60¢. Relatively speaking, you won't pay much more today for fine products from the pit: down-home–style ribs, pork, beef, or chicken platters served with french fries, slaw, and bread. A special attraction for dinner is lightly breaded and fried shrimp fresh from the boats at Fort Myers Beach. Draft beer is the only alcoholic beverage sold here. The yummy homemade pies and cheesecakes are famous around town.

Melanie's Family Restaurant. In Edison-Ford Square, 2158 McGregor Blvd. (at Clifford St.). ☎ **941/334-3139.** Reservations not accepted. Main courses $5–$12; sandwiches and salads $2–$6; breakfast $2.50–$5. No credit cards. Mon–Fri 6am–3pm, Sat–Sun 8am–2pm. AMERICAN.

Usually packed at lunch, Melanie McMahan's storefront establishment near the Edison and Ford homes features a plain dining room with dark-wood tables, captain's chairs, and a few booths at which to have big breakfasts or daily specials such as fried mullet, baked grouper, or meatloaf, all served with country-style vegetables. The sandwich menu includes shrimp and Greek salads.

MEALS FOR LESS THAN $10

Basile's. In the Edison Park Shopping Center, 2215-C Winkler Ave. (opposite the Edison Mall). ☎ **941/278-4600.** Reservations recommended in winter. Main courses $7–$13; early-bird specials $6.50. MC, V. Mon–Fri 11am–10pm, Sat noon–10pm, Sun noon–9:30pm; early-bird specials Mon–Sat 4–6pm, Sun noon–4pm. ITALIAN.

Operated by transplanted New Yorkers, this small dining room has a wall-size mural of an Italian scene to set the stage for food worthy of Little Italy. A wide range of pastas come in huge portions and are accompanied by soup, salad, and very garlicky homemade rolls. These same monstrous meals are offered for lunch at greatly reduced prices, and complete dinners are served on Friday, Saturday, and Sunday for $12. Early birds get a choice of pastas. A Taste of New York, an excellent pizza carryout, is next door.

MEALS FOR LESS THAN $15

The Chart House. 2024 W. 1st St. (at Henley Place). ☎ **941/332-1881.** Reservations recommended. Main courses $13–$29. AE, DC, DISC, MC, V. Mon–Thurs 5–9:30pm, Fri–Sat 5–10:30pm, Sun 4–9pm. SEAFOOD.

Great views are a prime draw at this friendly riverside restaurant with appropriately nautical decor. Early birds get fine sunsets and a specially priced menu between 5 and 6pm. The lengthy salad bar is one of the area's best. Seafood includes charcoal-broiled fresh fish. The mud pie is a dessert not to be soon worked off.

The Prawnbroker Restaurant and Fish Market. In the Cypress Point Shopping Center, McGregor Blvd. and Cypress Lake Dr. ☎ **941/489-2226.** Reservations recommended. Main courses $12–$25. AE, MC, V. Mon–Sat 4:30–10pm, Sun 4:30–9pm. (Fish market, Mon–Sat noon–10pm, Sun 3–9pm.) SEAFOOD.

Really fresh fish and moderate prices provide enough bait for a drive to this very friendly establishment, one of a small family of popular area restaurants. From peel-it-yourself shrimp to spicy Jamaican jerk grouper, it seems that everything from the briny deep is served here. Steaks are cooked to order for beef lovers. This restaurant and its popular sports bar are very casual and often crowded.

✪ **Sasse's.** 3651 Evans Ave. (between Carrell Rd. and Winkler Ave.). ☎ **941/278-5544.** Reservations not accepted. Main courses $8–$15. No credit cards. Tues 11:30am–2pm, Wed–Fri 11:30am–2pm and 5:30–8:45pm, Sat 5:30–8:45pm. CONTINENTAL/ITALIAN.

In a small shopping strip near the Fort Myers Recreation Center north of the Edison Mall, this little establishment offers one of the area's most unusual and reasonably priced dining experiences, which makes it very popular with young professionals. Delightful aromas waft from the open kitchen with a wood-fired oven, from which come log-roasted lemon chicken and other specialties of a quality rarely found at these prices. A recent menu offered oxtails with sun-dried tomatoes, braised lamb shank served over steamed vegetables, and cavatappi pasta with tomato, basil, and four cheeses. The selections change daily. There's open seating here, which means that patrons grab the first available table, whether they smoke or not.

WORTH A SPLURGE

✪ **Peter's La Cuisine.** 2224 Bay St. (at Bayview Court). ☎ **941/332-2228.** Reservations recommended. Main courses $24–$25; snacks in upstairs bar $8–$12. AE, DC, MC, V. Mon–Fri 11:30am–2pm and 5:30–9:30pm, Sat–Sun 5:30–9:30pm. (Upstairs Bar & Bistro, daily 4:30pm–2am.) CONTINENTAL.

Bavarian-born chef Peter Schmid masterfully blends European cuisine with local seafood, fruits, and vegetables at his elegant downtown restaurant, which most locals consider to be the city's best. Even other restaurateurs say that it's their favorite place to dine. In addition to seafood, Peter offers pheasant, veal, and steaks with continental sauces. His quarters have a refined ambience, while his lively Upstairs Bar & Bistro is more casual, with a light-fare menu (best bets are the same appetizers served downstairs) and nightly entertainment.

FORT MYERS AFTER DARK

For entertainment ideas and schedules, consult the daily *News-Press,* especially Friday's "Gulf Coasting" section.

THE PERFORMING ARTS

The city's showcase venue is the $7-million **Barbara B. Mann Performing Arts Hall,** 8099 College Pkwy., at Summerlin Road (☎ 941/489-3033), on the campus of Edison Community College. It features performances by world-famous performers, Broadway plays, and regular concerts by the **Southwest Florida Symphony.**

Originally a downtown vaudeville playhouse, the 1908-vintage **Arcade Theater,** 2267 1st St. (☎ 941/332-6688), has been completely renovated and now presents a variety of performances. Nearby, the 3,000-seat **Harborside Convention Complex,** 1375 Monroe St. (☎ 941/334-7637 for information, 941/334-4958 for the box office), spotlights national entertainers and is host to conventions and trade exhibits such as the Fort Myers Boat Show in early November.

Broadway musicals and comedy hits are the attractions at the **Broadway Palm Dinner Theatre,** in Royal Palm Square, on Colonial Boulevard between Summerlin Road and McGregor Boulevard (☎ 941/278-4422). Patrons can opt for the buffet or order à la carte in the Café Cabaret and pay separately for the show.

THE CLUB & BAR SCENE

Previously plagued by sporadic street crime and fleeing businesses, downtown Fort Myers has been undergoing somewhat of a renaissance lately, as free **block parties** at 1st and Hendry streets keep the crowds around after work on Friday from 6 to 10pm. Call 941/332-6813 to find out if one's planned while you're in town.

Shooters Waterfront Café USA, at the Holiday Inn SunSpree Resort, 2220 W. 1st St. (☎ 941/334-2727), was the city's most popular hangout during my recent visit, with bands playing at the riverside chickee hut bar almost every night. Jazz and blues are highlighted 7 nights a week in the casual **Upstairs Bar & Bistro** above Peter's La Cuisine, 2224 Bay St. (☎ 941/332-2228). The Marina Lounge in the **Sheraton Harbor Place,** 2500 Edwards Dr. (☎ 941/337-0300), has karaoke during the winter months.

AN EASY EXCURSION TO BOCA GRANDE

After he lost to Bill Clinton in 1992, George Bush and First Lady Barbara went on vacation to Boca Grande (pronounced *Grand*). They chose well, for this charming village on Gasparilla Island is a president's kind of place. Legend says that the infamous pirate José Gaspar lived in style on this 7-mile-long barrier island. So did the du Pont family, who founded Boca Grande in the 1880s. They were followed by the Astors, Morgans, Vanderbilts, and other rich clans, who still turn the island into a Florida version of Nantucket during their winter "social season."

In addition to the warm weather, the lure was some of the world's best tarpon fishing. Descendants of the watermen who were here first—and who guided the rich and famous—still work their 1920s-vintage marinas and live on streets named Dam-If-I-Know, Dam-If-I-Care, and Dam-If-I-Will. Their modest homes with backyards full of boats and fish nets you can see, but high hedges hide the "beachfronter" mansions around 29th Street.

GETTING THERE   Take I-75 to Exit 32, then go west to the end of Toledo Blade Boulevard. Turn right there onto Fla. 776, then left on Fla. 771 to Placida and the Boca Grande Causeway ($3.20 toll to the island, free coming back). It's about 1 1/2 hours from Fort Myers. Or you can go on a fascinating excursion via the *Tropic Star* (☎ 941/283-0015), which has cruises daily from Pine Island (see "Cruises" under "Outdoor Activities," above). **Captiva Cruises** (☎ 941/472-5300) has day trips from Captiva Island.

GETTING AROUND   The best way to see the town is on foot or by bicycle or golf cart, rented from **Island Bike 'n' Beach,** 333 Park Ave. (☎ 941/964-0711). The company also rents baby strollers, beach chairs and umbrellas, snorkeling gear, and other items.

WHAT TO SEE & DO

In the center of town, the pink-brick **Railroad Depot,** at the corner of Park Avenue and 4th Street, has been restored to its turn-of-the-century grandeur when it was Boca Grande's lifeline to the world. It now houses a cluster of classy boutiques and the Loose Caboose Restaurant and Ice Cream Parlor, where Katherine Hepburn once satiated her sweet tooth. It also offers rolls and coffee daily from 9:30 to 11:30am and reasonably priced sandwiches, salads, and burgers daily from 11am to 6pm. Across the street, **Fugate's** has been selling everything from rain slickers to wedding gowns since 1916. Now a paved **bike path,** the bed of the old Charlotte Harbor and Northern Railroad runs by the depot on its way from the island's south end all the way north to the causeway.

At the corner of Palm Avenue and 5th Street stands the **Gasparilla Inn & Cottages,** an Old Florida architectural beauty that opened in 1912 and still hosts a regular coterie of rich and famous guests during the winter social season. The inn takes no credit cards but gladly accepts personal checks from those who can afford its $340 to $480 winter rates. It's closed from mid-July to October.

Banyan Street (actually 2nd Street) is canopied with tangled banyan trees and is one of the prettiest places for a stroll. Nearby, **St. Andrew's Episcopal Church** and the **First Baptist Church,** both at Gilchrist and 4th streets, and the **United Methodist Church,** at Gilchrist and 3rd streets, all date from the town's early years.

To the north of town, the **Johann Fust Community Library,** at Gasparilla Road and 10th Street (☎ 941/964-2488), contains 12,000 volumes and the extraordinary ✪ **Du Pont Shell Collection,** all gathered by Henry Francis du Pont during nearly 50 years of combing the island's beaches. The library has a lovely interior garden and outdoor reading room. Open December to April, Monday to Friday from 10am to noon and 4 to 6pm; the rest of the year, Monday to Friday from 4 to 6pm.

At the south end of the island, the **Boca Grande Lighthouse** began marking the pass into Charlotte Harbor in 1890 (the steel tower on Gulf Boulevard served as the light from 1966 to 1986, when the old building was restored). Around the lighthouse, the beach at **Gasparilla Island State Recreation Area** is open daily from 8am to sunset. Admission is $2 per vehicle, free for pedestrians and bikers.

By far the biggest event here is the chamber of commerce–sponsored **World's Richest Tarpon Tournament,** usually the second week in July, when anglers try to reel in $100,000. Charter fishing and rental boats are available at **Miller's Marina** (☎ 941/964-2283) and **Whidden's Marina** (☎ 941/964-2878), both on Harbor Drive. **Boca Grande Pass Marina** (☎ 941/964-0607), on the south end of the island at the old phosphate port (now an oil transshipment facility), also is a base for charter fishing boats. Miller's Marina is also the base for backwater nature tours and parasailing during the winter season.

Beach access is limited by the expensive homes along the gulf, but there's a free **public beach** just south of town on Gulf Boulevard. **Gasparilla Island State Recreation Area** has a lovely strip of sand (see above).

From December to July, the **Boca Grande Ferry Service** (☎ **941/964-1100**) takes passengers out to Cayo Costa, Cabbage Key, and other islands. It departs at 10:30am daily from the Boca Grande Pass Marina on the island's south end. Fares are $17 to $21, depending on destination. See "Easy Island Excursions" in the Sanibel and Captiva islands section, later in this chapter, for information about Cayo Costa and Cabbage Key.

WHERE TO STAY

Boca Grande is a relatively expensive place to stay. The only way to stay on the beach here is to rent a condo or a house, but the lowest rates range from $770 a week. If you're interested, contact **Boca Grande Real Estate,** P.O. Box 686, Boca Grande, FL 33921 (☎ **941/964-0338,** or 800/881-2622; fax 941/964-2301).

Innlet on the Waterfront. 11th St. (at Boca Grande Bayou), Boca Grande, FL 33921. ☎ **941/964-2294.** Fax 941/964-0382. 32 rms and efficiencies. A/C TV TEL. Winter, $100 double; $125 efficiency. Off-season, $75 double; $85 efficiency. MC, V.

This motel has a large veranda across the back, from which guests can view Boca Grande Bayou, the creeklike waterway forming the town's eastern boundary. Rooms opening to the veranda and equipped with kitchens are more expensive than the standard motel units. There's a swimming pool and marina on the premises, but no restaurant.

WHERE TO EAT

For picnic fixings, go to the village's sole grocery, **Hudson's,** on Park Avenue between 4th and 5th streets opposite the Railroad Depot (☎ **941/964-2570**). It's open Monday to Saturday from 8am to 5:30pm.

Jam's Italian Restaurant. Railroad Ave. (at 5th St.). ☎ **941/964-2002.** Reservations accepted. Pizzas $5–$16.50; pastas $5.50–$12; subs $5–$7. AE, MC, V. Mon–Thurs 11am–9pm, Fri–Sat 11am–10pm, Sun noon–9pm. ITALIAN.

Although President Bush usually hobnobbed at the Gasparilla Inn, he did join his White House staffers once at their hangout in this pleasant Italian restaurant, whose motto is "More food for less lira." Neither the food nor the value has changed since they scarfed down tons of excellent pizza, pasta, and charcoal-grilled steaks and chicken while watching ball games on three TVs. Jam's even has a White House plaque to prove the staffers were here.

Lighthouse Hole Restaurant. At Miller's Marina, Harbor Dr. ☎ **941/964-0511.** Reservations accepted. Main courses $15–$20; sandwiches and burgers $5–$8. DISC, MC, V. Daily 11am–2am. SEAFOOD.

This very casual seafood emporium over Miller's Marina has a large screened porch overlooking the marina, Boca Grande Bayou, and the mangroves along the opposite shore. The menu leans heavily on shrimp and grouper, but daily specials feature seasonal items like stone crab claws and Florida lobsters. Wednesday usually is all-you-can-eat shrimp night, while Friday offers a stuffing of fish. Sandwiches and burgers are available during the day, and the house special grouper sandwich is also offered at night.

Loons on a Limb. 3rd St. (at Railway Ave.). ☎ **941/964-0155.** Reservations recommended for dinner. Main courses $11–$20; breakfast $4–$8. No credit cards. Winter, daily 7:30–11:30am and 6–9pm; off-season, daily 7:30–11:30am. Closed Aug, Thanksgiving, and Christmas Day. SEAFOOD/THAI/CREOLE.

Owned and operated by Boca Grande natives, "The Loon" is famous for both eggs Benedict and grits, which speaks reams about this town's split personality. It's also one of the few places on the island serving breakfast. From October to May, talented chef Michael Perlov prepares a chalkboard dinner menu featuring seafood prepared in Créole and Thai fashions. Photos and paintings of wild birds share the tongue-in-groove walls with a stuffed deer's head.

Temptation Restaurant. Park Ave. (between 3rd and 4th sts.). ☎ **941/964-2610.** Reservations recommended. Main courses $17.50–$24; lunch $5.50–$10. MC, V. Mon–Sat 11:30am–2pm and 6–9:30pm. SEAFOOD/STEAK.

This storefront looks very much the same as when it opened in 1947. The regular menu offers fried grouper and shrimp and charcoal-grilled steaks, but the chef's nightly specials, such as mahi mahi with yellow pepper and artichoke-heart compôte, are fit for a president. The Caribbean Room to the rear offers lighter fare and smaller portions from the regular menu.

❖ **Theater Restaurant.** Park Ave. and 4th St. ☎ **941/964-0806.** Reservations recommended. Main courses $15–$21; lunch $5–$9. MC, V. Mon–Sat 11:30am–2:30pm and 5:30–10pm. Closed Aug–Sept. CONTINENTAL.

Among the dining room stars at this 1928 movie theater turned into a mini-mall and fine restaurant is a large bubbling saltwater aquarium. Nightly specials on the playbill include a variety of fresh-off-the-boat seafoods and steaks grilled over an open flame. Daily lunch specials such as smoked salmon pasta are good value at $5. Dine inside or on a screened porch.

2 Fort Myers Beach

13 miles S of Fort Myers, 28 miles N of Naples, 12 miles E of Sanibel Island

Often overshadowed by trendy Sanibel and Captiva islands to the north and ritzy Naples to the south, Fort Myers Beach on Estero Island offers just as much sun and sand—and at more moderate prices—than its affluent neighbors.

It's also much more of a typical beach resort, with droves of young people flocking to the busy intersection of San Carlos and Estero boulevards, an area so packed with bars, beach apparel shops, restaurants, and motels that the locals call it "Times Square." But that Coney Island–like image doesn't apply to the rest of Estero Island, where old-fashioned beach cottages, manicured condos, and quiet motels beckon couples and families in search of more sedate vacations. In fact, local promoters say that they're on Estero Island, not in Fort Myers Beach; it's their way of distinguishing their part of the island from noisy Times Square.

Fort Myers Beach has more than the usual beach vacation attractions, however, for Estero Island is separated from the mainland by narrow Matanzas Pass and broad

Estero Bay. While the pass is the area's largest commercial fishing port, the bay is an official state aquatic preserve inhabited by a host of birds as well as manatees and other sealife. Nature cruises go forth onto this lovely protected bay dotted with islands.

A few miles south of Fort Myers Beach, a chain of pristine barrier islands includes Lover's Key, now a state park. A tractor-pulled tram runs through a mangrove forest to a lovely beach on this totally undeveloped islet.

ESSENTIALS

GETTING THERE By Plane & Train See Section 1 on Fort Myers, earlier in this chapter, for information about Southwest Florida International Airport and Amtrak's bus/train service.

By Car From Fort Myers, take either McGregor Boulevard or Summerlin Road and turn left on San Carlos Boulevard (County Road 865). From I-75 and the airport, follow Daniels Parkway (which becomes Cypress Lake Drive) due west. Turn left on Summerlin Road, then left again on San Carlos Boulevard. From Naples, take either I-75 or U.S. 41 north to Bonita Springs, then go west on Bonita Beach Road (County Road 865), which turns north into Estero Boulevard through Fort Myers Beach.

VISITOR INFORMATION The **Fort Myers Beach Chamber of Commerce,** 17200 San Carlos Blvd., Fort Myers Beach, FL 33931 (☎ **941/454-7500,** or 800/ 782-9283; fax 941/454-7910), provides free information, sells a detailed street map, and operates a **visitor information center** on the mainland portion of San Carlos Boulevard just south of Summerlin Road.

GETTING AROUND By Trolley An alternative to the heavy wintertime traffic and limited parking is the **Beach Connection Trolley,** which during winter operates daily from 8am to 8pm between the Summerlin Square Shopping Center, at Summerlin Road and San Carlos Boulevard on the mainland, and Bonita Beach. The route takes it along the full length of Estero Boulevard, including Lover's Key. During the off-season, it runs from Bowditch Regional Park at the north end of Estero Boulevard south to Lover's Key. It costs 25¢ a ride. Ask your hotel staff or call LeeTran (☎ **941/275-8726**) for schedules.

During the winter, LeeTran also operates a Monday-to-Saturday **Beach Shuttle** from the parking lots at the Summerlin Square Shopping Center, Summerlin Road at San Carlos Boulevard; the Sanibel Factory Outlets, Summerlin Road at McGregor Boulevard; the McGregor Point Shopping Center, Gladiolus Drive at McGregor Boulevard; and the Main Street Park 'n' Ride Lot on San Carlos Island. The Main Street–Bowditch Park section also runs on Sunday. It also costs 25¢ a ride.

By Taxi Call **Local Motion Taxi** (☎ 941/463-4111).

By Bicycle & Scooter A variety of rental bikes, scooters, and in-line skates are available at **Fun Rentals,** 1901 Estero Blvd. (☎ 941/463-8844), and **Scooters, Inc.,** 1698 Estero Blvd. (☎ 941/463-1007).

BEACHES & OUTDOOR ACTIVITIES

BEACHES A prime attraction for beachgoers is the gorgeous ✪ **Carl E. Johnson– Lover's Key State Recreation Area** (☎ **941/463-4259**), on the totally preserved Lover's Key, south of Estero. Although the main road runs down the center of the island, access to this unspoiled beach is restricted to foot paths or a tractor-pulled tram through a forest of mangroves and Australian pines replete with birdlife. The beach itself is known for its multitude of shells. The park is open daily from 8am to 5pm. Admission is $3 per vehicle. No pets or alcohol are allowed.

On Estero Island, **Lynn Hall Memorial Park** features a fishing pier and beach right in the middle of "Times Square." It has one of the few public parking lots in the area; meters charge 75¢ per hour. At the island's north end, **Bowditch Regional Park** has picnic tables, cold-water showers, and changing rooms. It has parking only for drivers with disabled permits, but it's the turn-around point for the Beach Connection Trolley.

Several beach locations are hotbeds of parasailing, Waverunners, sailboats, and other beach activities. **Times Square,** at the intersection of San Carlos and Estero boulevards, and the **Best Western Beach Resort,** about a quarter mile north, are popular spots on Estero's busy north end. Another hotbed is on the beach in front of the Skipper's Galley and Anthony's on the Gulf restaurants in the middle beach area (see "Where to Eat," below). Down south, activities are centered around the **Holiday Inn** and the **Outrigger Beach Resort** (see "Where to Stay," below).

BOATING & BOAT RENTALS Powerboats are available from the **Mid Island Marina** (☎ 941/765-4371), the **Fort Myers Beach Marina** (☎ 941/463-9552), the **Fish Tail Marina** (☎ 941/463-4448), the **Palm Grove Marina** (☎ 941/463-7333), and the **Summer Winds Marina** (☎ 941/454-6333).

FISHING Anglers can surf-cast, throw their lines off the pier at Times Square, or venture offshore on a number of charter fishing boats that dock at marinas under both ends of the Skyway Bridge. Agents have booths there to take reservations even when the boats are out.

The least expensive way to fish offshore is on the *Black Whale III* (☎ 941/765-5550), the *Miss Barnegat Light* (☎ 941/463-5665), and the *Island Lady* (☎ 941/936-7470), three large "party boats" that take groups out from December to April daily from Fisherman's Wharf, virtually under the San Carlos Island end of the Skyway Bridge. In addition, the *Great Getaway* and *Great Getaway II* (☎ 941/466-3600) dock at Getaway Marina on San Carlos Boulevard about half a mile north of the bridge. They all depart about 8am, charge between $25 and $40 per person, and have air-conditioned lounges with bars. No reservations are required on these boats.

GOLF In addition to the plethora of nearby mainland courses, duffers can play at the **Bay Beach Golf Club,** 7401 Estero Blvd. (☎ **941/463-2064**). It's open to the public daily from 7:30am to 5pm.

SCUBA DIVING & SNORKELING Scuba diving is available at **Seahorse Scuba,** 17849 San Carlos Blvd. (☎ **941/454-3111**). Two-tank dives cost $50. Groups of four snorkelers can go on their own excursions for $50 each.

CRUISES

The pontoon boats *Pelican Queen* (☎ 941/765-4354), *Miss Daisy* (☎ 941/463-4448), *Sand Dollar* (☎ 941/466-3600), and *Virginia Gentleman* (☎ 941/472-0982) all go on nature cruises in search of porpoises, manatees, and a multitude of birds in Matanzas Pass and out on the Estero Bay state aquatic preserve. Prices range from $12.50 to $18 for adults, $6 to $8 for children. They also have fishing, sightseeing, and sunset cruises. Reservations are recommended.

For sailing enthusiasts, the 72-foot topsail schooner *Island Rover* (☎ 941/765-7447) has morning, afternoon, sunset, and moonlight cruises on the gulf from its base under the Sky Bridge on Estero Island. Soft drinks, beer, wine, and champagne are available on board. At least two smaller sailboats go cruising on the gulf: the 36-foot *Quest* (☎ 941/334-0670) and the 42-foot *Sundance* (☎ 941/463-7333). Their schedules and rates change by season, so call ahead for information and reservations.

Gamblers can do some serious wagering on the *SeaKruz* (☎ **941/463-5000,** or 800/688-7529), a floating casino that makes morning and evening cruises several days a week. Daytime trips start at $27 per person. See "Fort Myers Beach After Dark," below, for more information.

WHERE TO STAY

The hostelries recommended below are removed from the crowds of Times Square, but two chain motels offer comfortable accommodations right in the center of the action: a **Ramada Inn** (☎ 941/463-6158, or 800/544-4592) and a **Days Inn** (☎ 941/463-9759, or 800/544-4592). The **Best Western Beach Resort** (☎ 941/463-6000, or 800/336-4045) is just far enough north to escape the noise but still has a lively beach.

The **Holiday Inn,** 6890 Estero Blvd., Fort Myers Beach, FL 33931 (☎ **941/463-5711,** or 800/465-4329; fax 941/463-7038), is the center of beach activity on the south end of the island. Winter rates range from $110 to $170 for double rooms; $190 to $360 for suites. Off-season, they drop to $80 to $90 for a double, $100 to $210 for a suite.

Fort Myers Beach has a number of condominiums and cottages which offer good value, especially for families or groups. The chamber of commerce publishes a complete list of condos and time-shares (see "Essentials," above).

See "Where to Stay" in Section 1 on Fort Myers, earlier in this chapter, for information about rate seasons.

DOUBLES FOR LESS THAN $40

Island House Motel. 701 Estero Blvd., Fort Myers Beach, FL 33931. ☎ **941/463-9282.** Fax 941/463-2080. 5 efficiencies. A/C TV TEL. Winter, $89 efficiency. Off-season, $39 efficiency. Weekly rates available. MC, V.

Sitting on stilts in the Old Florida fashion, but with modern furnishings, Ken and Slyvia Lachapelle's clapboard-sided establishment enjoys a quiet location within walking distance of busy Times Square. Four of their units have screened porches, while all have kitchens and ceiling fans. Ken and Slyvia maintain an open-air lounge with a small library beneath one of the units, and they provide free local calls and beach chairs (access to the gulf is across Estero Boulevard). They also have a small pool and sundeck area. They stay heavily booked during February and March.

DOUBLES FOR LESS THAN $60

Palm Terrace Apartments. 3333 Estero Blvd., Fort Myers Beach, FL 33931. ☎ **941/765-5783,** or 800/320-5783. Fax 941/765-5783. 9 apts. Winter, $79–$120 apt. Off-season, $46–$79 apt. Weekly rates available. MC, V.

Hosts Walter and Barbara Kudla draw many guests from their native Germany during the winter months, attracted to their comfortable, well-maintained apartments about midway down the beach. The Kudlas' smaller, less-expensive units are on the ground level, with sliding glass doors opening to a grassy yard, but even these have cooking facilities including microwave ovens. Most units here are upstairs, with screened porches or decks overlooking a courtyard with swimming pool. There's beach access across Estero Boulevard.

DOUBLES FOR LESS THAN $80

Outrigger Beach Resort. 6200 Estero Blvd. (P.O. Box 271), Fort Myers Beach, FL 33931. ☎ **941/463-3131,** or 800/749-3131. Fax 941/463-6577. 76 rms, 68 efficiencies. A/C TV TEL. High season, $105–$120 double; $110–$180 efficiency. Off-season, $75–$85 double; $85–$125 efficiency. DISC, MC, V.

The same friendly owners have maintained this clean, pleasant gulfside motel since 1965. Their "ranch efficiencies" in the original building aren't fancy—cinderblock walls, shower-only baths, and kitchenettes—but they have the feel of small cottages, with excellent ventilation through both front- and rear-louvered windows. They're also Fort Myers Beach's best bargain during the winter season. Other buildings here are two-story blocks containing motel-style rooms and efficiencies. The latter have window-style air-conditioning units but also sport front and rear jalousie windows to let in natural breezes. Most face a courtyard with a swimming pool, a large wooden deck for sunning, and one of Florida's best beachside tiki bars, which dispenses libations all day. The Deckside Café serves inexpensive breakfasts and is open for sandwiches and snacks until 8pm. There's a coin laundry on the premises.

Sandpiper Gulf Resort. 5550 Estero Blvd., Fort Myers Beach, FL 33931. ☎ **941/463-5721.** Fax 941/463-5721, ext. 299. 63 suites. A/C TV TEL. Winter, $99–$125 suite for two. Off-season, $60–$80 suite for two. DISC, MC, V.

The units at this clean gulfside motel all have living and sleeping areas, full kitchens, convertible sofas, and sundecks overlooking either the gulf or a courtyard with a heated swimming pool and hot tub. Steps lead from the bedecked pool directly to the beach. Some units are in two- or three-story buildings arranged in a U with flattened ends right on the beach; others are in the Sandpiper II, a palm-fronted highrise with its own heated pool next door. All units are identical, but those facing directly on the beach are more expensive. Facilities include a coin laundry and gift shop. Restaurants are nearby.

CAMPING

Although a bit crowded, the **Red Coconut RV Resort,** 3001 Estero Blvd., Fort Myers Beach, FL 33931 (☎ **941/463-7200;** fax 941/463-2609), has sites for RVs and tents both on the gulf side of the road and right on the beach. They aren't cheap: $43 to $53 a night in winter, $30 to $48 off-season. Less expensive are the **Gulf Air Travel Park,** 17279 San Carlos Blvd., Fort Myers Beach, FL 33931 (☎ **941/ 466-8100;** fax 941/466-4044), and the **San Carlos RV Park & Islands,** 18071 San Carlos Blvd., Fort Myers Beach, FL 33931 (☎ **941/466-3133**), both on San Carlos Island.

WHERE TO EAT

Lively pubs, such as **The Beached Whale** at 1249 Estero Blvd. (☎ 941/463-5505), offer burgers, sandwiches, salads, and meals at very reasonable prices (the Beached Whale even has a rooftop dining area). A row of national chain family restaurants, including a Shoney's and a Perkins, is at the Summerlin Square shopping center, on the mainland at San Carlos Boulevard and Summerlin Road. The beach trolley runs to Summerlin Square during the winter.

One way to save is to take advantage of early-bird specials offered to diners who arrive before 6pm. These three-course meals are good value.

See "Where to Eat" in Section 1 on Fort Myers, earlier in this chapter, for an explanation of the price categories used below.

MEALS FOR LESS THAN $15

Anthony's on the Gulf. 3040 Estero Blvd. (on the beach). ☎ **941/463-2600.** Reservations not accepted. Main courses $9–16; early-bird specials (served daily 4:30–6pm) $9–$10; burgers and sandwiches $5–$7. AE, DISC, MC, V. Daily 11:30am–4pm and 4:30–11pm. ITALIAN.

Right on the beach, this lively establishment has large windows with gulf views unmatched except by the Skipper's Galley next door (see below). The appropriately named Sunset Terrace is one of the best places on the island for a day-ending cocktail or an alfresco lunch or dinner. Inside, a casual, unpretentious tropical ambience is enhanced by an old-fashioned, pole-driven ceiling fan reaching the full length of the dining room. This setting more than makes up for an uninspired menu offering traditional Italian pizzas and pastas, and main courses of veal, chicken, and seafood.

✪ **Channel Mark.** 19001 San Carlos Blvd. (at the north end of San Carlos Island). ☎ **941/463-9127.** Reservations not accepted. Main courses $14–$18; pastas $8.50–$13; sandwiches $6–$8. AE, DC, DISC, MC, V. Sun–Thurs 11am–10pm, Fri–Sat 11am–11pm. ITALIAN/SEAFOOD.

This place is nestled by the "Little Bridge" leading onto San Carlos Island's northern end—every table here looks out on a maze of channel markers on Hurricane Bay. A dock with palms growing through it makes this a relaxing place for a waterside lunch. The atmosphere changes dramatically at night, with ceiling fans, potted plants, rattan chairs, well-spaced tables, and soft, indirect lighting creating a relaxed tropical ambience ideal for kindling romance. Congenial owners Mike McGuigan and Andy Welsh greet each guest and put a creative spin on their seafood dishes, such as a rich concoction of snapper smothered in a roasted macadamia-nut sauce and topped with fresh strawberry butter. Even their fried items are innovative, such as delicately seasoned crab cakes lightly breaded with corn flakes and almonds (available as a sandwich at lunch). Calorie-counters can opt for shrimp or mahi mahi perfectly grilled over mesquite.

Gulf Shore Restaurant. 1270 Estero Blvd. (on the beach). ☎ **941/463-9951.** Reservations recommended. Main courses $11–$22; early-bird specials (served daily 4:30–6pm) $10. AE, MC, V. Daily 7am–3pm and 4:30–10pm. SEAFOOD.

Home of the Crescent Beach Casino back in the 1920s, this old clapboard building offers splendid views of the gulf and beach, especially of young folk frolicking at the lively Lani Kai Resort next door. Breakfast is served until 3pm; if a little hair-of-the-dog will help after a hard night at the Lani Kai, "red beer"—tomato juice and suds—will wash down spicy eggs caliente or any of 16 different omelets. Lunch offers heaped-high sandwiches, salads, and seafood plates, while dinners provide a variety of seafood, prime rib, baby back ribs, and chicken teriyaki. Lunches and light fare are also served in the Cottage Bar, perhaps the most infamous drinking establishment on the beach.

Matanzas Seafare Company. 416 Crescent St. (under the Skyway Bridge on Estero Island). ☎ **941/463-3838.** Reservations not accepted. Main courses $13–$17; sandwiches and light fare $6–$8. AE, DISC, MC, V. Daily 11am–10pm. Closed Thanksgiving and Christmas Day. SEAFOOD.

Although it's in the busy Times Square tourist district, this casual and friendly restaurant is popular with local residents who appreciate seafood fresh off the boats docking at Matanzas Marina. Dining is on a dock next to the marina or inside a dark-paneled dining room hung with ceiling fans. The menu highlights fried, broiled, blackened, or charcoal-grilled seafood, with some Italian-accented selections such as grouper scampi and seafood fettuccine. A light-fare menu offers shrimp salad, fish sandwiches, and hamburgers.

CAFES

✪ **Greco's Italian Deli.** In Villa Santini Plaza, 7205 Estero Blvd. ☎ **941/463-5634.** Reservations not accepted. Subs and sandwiches $4–$5; pizzas $12–$15; ready-to-cook meals $6–$8. No credit cards. Daily 8am–6pm. ITALIAN.

Wonderful aromas of baking pizzas, calzones, cannolis, breads, and cookies have been wafting from Greco's since 1958. Order at the counter over a chiller packed with fresh deli meats, Italian sausage, and cheeses, then devour your goodies at tables inside or out on the covered walkway, or take them to the beach for a picnic. You can also take "heat-and-eat" meals of spaghetti, lasagne, eggplant parmigiana, manicotti, and ravioli back to your hotel or condo oven. Shelves are loaded with Italian wines, pastas, butter cookies, and anisette toast.

Strawberrie Corner Café & Ice Cream Parlor. 6035 Estero Blvd. ☎ **941/463-1155.** Reservations not accepted. Light fare $3.50–$5.50. No credit cards. Daily 11am–9:30pm. DELI.

YOUR WILLPOWER ENDS HERE says a sign on the front door of this bright ice-cream parlor and deli on Estero Boulevard's only sharp curve, known as Strawberry Corner. Strawberry-print wallpaper, strawberry dolls, and photos of strawberries provide the decor, and strawberry shortcake is the house specialty. In addition, the menu offers soups, seafood salads, and made-to-order deli sandwiches. Each white table here is adorned with colorful fresh flowers.

WORTH A SPLURGE

✪ The Skipper's Galley. 3040 Estero Blvd. (on the beach). ☎ **941/463-6139.** Reservations not accepted. Main courses $14–$22; early-bird specials (served daily 4–5:30pm) $9–$13. AE, DISC, MC, V. Daily 4–10pm. SEAFOOD/STEAK.

Estero Island's finest restaurant features casual but elegant dining with excellent views of the beach and gulf. Most selections here are breaded and fried or broiled, but the pick are the chef's tempting specials such as pompano baked in parchment. Landlubbers can feast on prime rib, steaks, and chicken dishes. Early birds get great sunsets over the gulf to enhance their good values.

FORT MYERS BEACH AFTER DARK

THE CLUB & BAR SCENE   The area around Times Square always seems active, but the real night owls and the 20-something crowd hang out at the **Lani Kai Resort,** 1400 Estero Blvd. (☎ **941/765-6500**), where live rock and reggae bands roar virtually all night at the beachside tiki bar. A good vantage point to watch the action is from the **Cottage Bar,** at the Gulf Shore Restaurant next door (☎ **941/ 463-9951**). Both establishments can become raucous late at night. Across the street, **The Beached Whale** (☎ **941/463-5505**) draws a more diverse crowd age-wise and is a bit tamer. Nearby, live bands and DJs liven up the nights at the **Top O'Mast Restaurant & Lounge,** 1028 Estero Blvd. (☎ **941/463-9424**). Facing due west, **Jimmy's Beach Bar,** in the Days Inn at 1130 Estero Blvd. (☎ **941/463-9759**), has live music nightly for the "best sunsets on the island."

Farther south, in the more couples- and family-oriented part of the beach, the **Holiday Inn,** 6890 Estero Blvd. (☎ **941/463-5711**), has live music for dancing Thursday to Saturday from 9pm to 1am.

Gambling Cruises   The floating casino *SeaKruz* (☎ **941/463-5000,** or 800/ 688-7529) sails 9 miles out into the gulf, where gambling is legal. In addition to craps and other tables, there's dining and dancing. These night voyages cost $27 per person Sunday to Friday, $32 on Saturday. Reservations are required. See "What to See & Do," above, for daytime cruise information.

3 Sanibel & Captiva Islands

18 miles W of Fort Myers, 40 miles N of Naples

Sanibel and Captiva seem a world removed from the neon signs, amusement parks, and high-rise condos that clutter many other beach resorts. Sanibel's main drag, Periwinkle Way, runs under a canopy of whispery pines, gnarled oaks, and twisted banyans so thick they almost obscure the signs for chic shops and restaurants. This wooded ambience is the work of local voters, who have saved their trees, limited the size and appearance of signs, and enacted tough zoning laws that keep all buildings lower than the tallest palm and prohibit Waverunners and other noisy beach toys within 300 yards of their shores. Furthermore, nearly 40% of the islands are preserved in its natural state as wildlife refuges. All this makes Sanibel and Captiva a relatively expensive destination, but one that's extraordinarily appealing to both eyes and ears. They certainly are worth a day's outing, even if you don't stay here.

Legend says that Ponce de León named the larger of these two barrier islands "San Ybel," after his queen, Santa Isabella of Spain. Another legend claims that Captiva's name is derived from infamous pirate José Gaspar's practice of keeping kidnapped women prisoners there. Nothing much happened on Sanibel and Captiva from Gaspar's time until 1892, when a few farmers settled here, and in 1899 the Bailey family opened what is still Bailey's General Store. An early settler named Clarence Chadwick started an unsuccessful key lime and copra plantation on Captiva; many of his towering coconut palms still stand at the exclusive South Seas Plantation Resort & Yacht Harbour, which takes up the northern third of this skinny island.

Concluding that their terrific fishing grounds could be more profitable than their sandy soil, local residents soon switched from farming to fishing camps. Affluent anglers flocked to sleepy Captiva, first by private boat and then by ferry. When the Sanibel Causeway connected the islands to the mainland in 1963, the public at large began discovering Sanibel's world-famous shelling beaches. But thanks to zoning laws—and to wealthy settlers who built their luxury retreats back in the bush—both Sanibel and Captiva still have that hideaway feel the fishermen found here a century ago.

ESSENTIALS

GETTING THERE   By Plane & Train   See Section 1 on Fort Myers, earlier in this chapter, for information about Southwest Florida International Airport and Amtrak's bus/train service.

By Car   From Fort Myers, take McGregor Boulevard or Summerlin Road, which merges with McGregor, to the Sanibel Causeway ($3-per-car toll going over, free coming back). From I-75 and the airport, follow Daniels Parkway due west, turn left on Summerlin Road (County Road 869), and proceed to the Sanibel Causeway.

VISITOR INFORMATION   The **Sanibel-Captiva Islands Chamber of Commerce,** 1159 Causeway Rd., Sanibel Island, FL 33957 (☎ **941/472-1080;** fax 941/472-1070), maintains a visitor center on Causeway Boulevard as you drive onto Sanibel from Fort Myers. The chamber gives away an "Island Guide" and sells a detailed street map for $2 ($3 by mail). Other books are for sale, including comprehensive shelling guides and a helpful collection of menus from the islands' restaurants. There's a board for making hotel and condo reservations.

GETTING AROUND   By Taxi   Call **Sanibel Taxi** (☎ 941/472-4160).

By Car   No parking is permitted on the main roads on Sanibel, and parking on residential streets marked as Areas A and B is prohibited. Free beach parking is available at the end of the Sanibel Causeway. Other municipal lots are either reserved for local residents or have a 75¢ hourly fee payable at machines designated by a large "P."

By Bicycle   Sanibel is a bicyclist's paradise, since paved paths follow alongside most major roads, including the entire length of Periwinkle Way and along Sanibel-Captiva Road to Blind Pass (there are no bike paths on Captiva). Walkers, joggers, and in-line skaters also use the Sanibel paths. The chamber of commerce visitor center has bike maps (see "Essentials," above), as do Sanibel's rental firms: **Fennimore's Cycle Shop,** 2353 Periwinkle Way (☎ 941/472-5577); **The Bike Rental, Inc.,** 2330 Palm Ridge Rd. (☎ 941/472-2241); **Island Moped,** 1470 Periwinkle Way (☎ 941/472-5248); and **Tarpon Bay Recreation,** at the north end of Tarpon Bay Road (☎ 941/472-8900). On Captiva, **Jim's Bike & Skate Rentals** on Andy Rosse Lane (☎ 941/472-1296) rents bikes and beach equipment, and **Wheel Happy South** at McCarthy's Marina (☎ 941/395-0662) will deliver bikes to your hotel and provide them for island excursions. Bike rates range from $3 per hour to $12 a day for basic models. Both Fennimore's and Jim's rent in-line skates.

BEACHES & OUTDOOR ACTIVITIES

BEACHES Sanibel has four public beach-access areas with metered parking: the eastern point around **Sanibel Lighthouse,** which has a fishing pier; **Gulfside City Park,** at the end of Algiers Lane, off Casa Ybel Road; **Tarpon Bay Road Beach,** at the south end of Tarpon Bay Road; and **Bowman's Beach,** off Sanibel-Captiva Road. **Turner Beach,** at Blind Pass between Sanibel and Captiva, is highly popular at sunset since it faces due west, but parking on the Sanibel side is limited to holders of local permits. All except Tarpon Bay Road Beach have rest rooms. Be forewarned: Although nude bathing is illegal, the end of Bowman's Beach near Blind Pass often sees more than its share of bare bodies.

On Captiva, the most popular beaches are the long stretch north of **Blind Pass,** where the houses are on the bay side of the road, and at the end of Andy Rosse Lane in front of the Mucky Duck Restaurant. Although free, parking along these stretches is scarce during the winter season.

BOATING & FISHING On Sanibel, rental boats and charter-fishing excursions are available from **The Boat House** at Sanibel Marina (☎ 941/472-2531), on North Yachtsman Drive, off Periwinkle Way east of Causeway Boulevard. **Tarpon Bay Recreation,** at the north end of Tarpon Bay Road (☎ 941/472-8900), rents boats with electric trolling motors and light tackle for fly casting.

On Captiva, check with **Sweet Water Rentals** at 'Tween Waters Inn Marina (☎ 941/472-6376), **Jenson's Twin Palms Marina** (☎ 941/472-5800), and **McCarthy's Marina** (☎ 941/472-5200), all on Captiva Road. Rental boats cost about $125 for half a day, $200 for a full day (that's about twice the price you'll pay elsewhere in Southwest Florida, including Naples).

Many **charter-fishing captains** are docked at these marinas. Half-day rates are about $200 for up to four people. The skippers leave free brochures at the chamber of commerce visitor center (see "Essentials," above), and they're listed in the free tourist publications found there.

CANOE & KAYAK TRIPS **Tarpon Bay Recreation** (☎ 941/472-8900) has guided canoe and kayak trips in the J. N. (Ding) Darling National Wildlife Refuge (see below). A local resident for many years, naturalist **Mark "Bird" Westphal** (☎ 941/472-5218) leaves at dawn on guided canoe trips through the wildlife refuge and on the Sanibel River. The trips cost about $20 for adults, $10 for children 11 and under. On Captiva, naturalist **Brian Houston** leads kayaking trips from the 'Tween Waters Marina (☎ 941/472-5161). He charges $35 per person. Reservations are essential with both Bird and Brian.

Do-it-yourselfers can rent canoes and kayaks from **Tarpon Bay Recreation** (☎ 941/472-8900), at the north end of Tarpon Bay Road on Sanibel; and at the **'Tween Waters Inn Marina** (☎ 941/472-5161) on Captiva. The boats cost about $7 an hour, $12 for half a day.

GOLF & TENNIS   Golfers can tee off on the 6,000-yard, par-70, 18-hole course—and hackers can play tennis—at the **Dunes Golf and Tennis Club,** 949 Sandcastle Rd., Sanibel (☎ **941/472-2535**). The **Beachview Golf Club,** 1100 Par View Dr., Sanibel (☎ **941/472-2626**), has a 6,200-yard, par-71 course. Call a day in advance for a tee time. The **South Seas Plantation Resort & Yacht Harbour** has tennis courts and a 9-hole golf course, but for its guests only.

SAILING   Based on Captiva, two sailboats take guests out on the waters of Pine Island Sound: Mike McMillan's *Adventure* (☎ **941/472-7532**) and Mic Gurley's *New Moon* (☎ **941/395-1782**). Noted yachties Steve and Doris Colgate have a branch of their **Offshore Sailing School** at the South Seas Plantation Resort & Yacht Harbour (☎ **941/472-5111**, ext. 7141).

Water Sports   Both scuba divers and snorkelers can go along with the **Redfish Dive Center** (☎ **941/472-3483**) and the **Pieces of Eight Dive Center** (☎ **941/472-9424**), both of which also rent equipment and teach diving. Sanibel may prohibit motorized water-sports equipment on its beaches, but **Yolo Watersports** (☎ **941/472-9656**) offers parasailing and Waverunner rentals on the beach in front of the Mucky Duck Restaurant, at the gulf end of Andy Rosse Lane on Captiva.

WHAT TO SEE & DO
J. N. (DING) DARLING NATIONAL WILDLIFE REFUGE

Named for the *New York Times* cartoonist who was a frequent visitor here and who helped create 330 other wildlife sanctuaries, the 5,000-acre preserve on Sanibel-Captiva Road (☎ **941/472-1100**) occupies nearly a third of Sanibel Island. Alligators, raccoons, otters, and hundreds of species of birds make their homes in its mangrove swamps, winding waterways, and uplands. A boardwalk and a 5-mile, one-way Wildlife Drive begin at the visitor center, which shows brief videos about the refuge's inhabitants every half hour. The best times for viewing the refuge are early morning, late afternoon, and at low tide (tables are posted at the visitor center). Mosquitoes and "no-see-ums" (tiny, biting sandflies) are especially prevalent at dawn and dusk, so bring repellent.

Admission to the visitor center is free. The Wildlife Drive costs $4 per vehicle, $1 for hikers and bicyclists (free to holders of current Federal Duck Stamps and Golden Age, Golden Access, and Golden Eagle passports). The visitor center is open from November to April, Saturday to Thursday from 9am to 5pm; off-season, Saturday to Thursday from 9am to 4pm. The Wildlife Drive is open all year, Saturday to Thursday from an hour after sunrise to an hour before sunset. Both are closed on federal holidays.

A highly informative alternative to doing the Wildlife Drive yourself is to take a 2-hour **tram tour** narrated by a naturalist. These are given by Tarpon Bay Recreation, at the north end of Tarpon Bay Road (☎ **941/472-8900**), and cost $8 for adults, $4 for children 12 and under. Schedules are seasonal, so call ahead.

As the refuge's concessionaire, Tarpon Bay Recreation also offers a variety of guided **canoe and kayak tours** in season, with an emphasis on the historical, cultural, and environmental aspects of the refuge. It also rents canoes, kayaks, and small boats with electric trolling motors.

Almost across the road from the refuge visitor center, the nonprofit **Sanibel/Captiva Conservation Foundation** ☎ **941/472-2329**) maintains a nature center, native plant nursery, and 4¹/₂ miles of nature trails on a 247-acre wetlands tract along the Sanibel River. Environmental workshops, guided trail walks, beach walks, and a natural-history boat cruise help guests learn more about the islands' unusual ecosystems. Various items are for sale, including native plants, and the Nature Shop carries publications about the islands' birds and other wildlife. Admission is $2, free for children 11 and under. The nature center is open Monday to Saturday from 8:30am to 4pm. Call for a schedule of walks and cruises.

SHELLING & SEALIFE

Sanibel is famous for its seashells, and local residents and visitors alike can been seen hunched over in the "Sanibel stoop" in search of some 200 species found on its shores. February to April—or after any storm—are the best times to look for whelks, olives, scallops, sand dollars, conch, and many other varieties. Low tide is the best time of day.

To learn all about the world's mollusks before you start stooping, visit the ✪ **Baily-Mathews Shell Museum,** on Sanibel-Captiva Road near the Ding Darling wildlife refuge (☎ **941/395-2233**). Opened in 1995, this impressive institution is the only museum in the United States devoted solely to saltwater, freshwater, and land shells (yes, snails are included). Shells surround a 6-foot globe in the middle of the main exhibit hall, thus showing their geographic origins. A spinning-wheel case identifies shells likely to wash up on Sanibel. Other exhibits are devoted to shells in tribal art, fossil shells found in Florida, medicinal qualities of various mollusks, the endangered Florida tree snail, and "sailor's Valentines"—works created by old-time sailors to kill time at sea. Upstairs is an extensive library and a huge collection of color slides of shells. The museum is open Tuesday to Sunday from 10am to 4pm. Admission is $4 for adults, $2 for children 8 to 16, free for children 7 and under.

With so many residents and visitors scouring Sanibel, you may have better luck on the adjacent shoals and nearby islands, such as Upper Captiva and Cayo Costa (see "Easy Island Excursions," below). At least 15 charter-boat skippers offer to take guests on shelling expeditions to these less-explored areas. A half-day excursion will cost about $180 for up to six people—in other words, get up a group to make it affordable. Several guides operate from the **'Tween Waters Inn Marina** (☎ **941/ 472-5161**) on Captiva, including **Capt. Mike Fuery** (☎ **941/472-1015,** or 941/994-7195 on his boat). Others are based at **Jenson's Twin Palms Marina,** on Captiva (☎ **941/472-5800**), and at the **Sanibel Marina,** on North Yachtsman Drive, off Periwinkle Way east of Causeway Boulevard, on Sanibel (☎ **941/ 472-2723**). They all distribute brochures at the chamber of commerce visitor center and are listed in the free tourist publications found there.

Note: It's against the law to take live shells from Sanibel's beaches or in the J. N. (Ding) Darling National Wildlife Refuge, and Florida law permits just two live shells to be taken each day elsewhere.

HISTORIC ATTRACTIONS

The **Sanibel Historical Village & Museum,** 950 Dunlop Rd., Periwinkle Way (☎ **941/472-4648**), includes the pioneer-vintage Rutland home and the 1926 versions of Bailey's General Store (complete with Red Crown gasoline pumps), the post office, and Miss Charlotta's Tea Room. Displays highlight the islands' prehistoric Calusa tribal era, and have a variety of memorabilia from pioneer days. Special exhibits feature quilts in January, Valentines and old lace in February, and antique toys, doll houses, and 200 teddy bears in December. Open Wednesday to Saturday from 10am to 4pm; closed mid-August to mid-October. Admission is by $1 donation.

At the east end of Periwinkle Way, the **Sanibel Lighthouse** has marked the entrance to San Carlos Bay since 1884. It's now operated by remote control and electricity, but the lightkeepers used to live in the cottages at the base of the 94-foot tower and climb the steps inside the cylinder every day to fill the giant lantern with oil and turn it on and off. The lighthouse itself isn't open to visitors, but the grounds are.

ORGANIZED TOURS

Loaded with history and local insights, a narrated **Trolley Tour** (☎ **941/472-6374**) operates from November to August, starting at the chamber of commerce visitor center (see "Essentials," above). It departs at 10am and 1pm Monday to Friday from January to April, and at 10am and 1pm on Monday, Wednesday, and Friday from May to mid-August and in October. Fares are $10 for adults, $5 for children 4 and under.

CRUISES

In addition to its island trips (see "Easy Island Excursions," below), **Captiva Cruises** (☎ **941/472-5300**) goes out daily on informative and fun nature and sunset cruises from the South Seas Plantation Resort & Yacht Harbour on Captiva. These cost $17.50 per person. Reservations are required.

SHOPPING

If you have no luck scouring the beaches for shells, several Sanibel shops sell thousands of them. **Sanibel Sea Shell Industries,** 905 Fitzhugh St. (☎ 941/472-1063), has one of the largest collections, with more than 10,000 shells in stock. **She Sells Sea Shells** has two locations: 1157 Periwinkle Way (☎ 941/472-6991) and 2422 Periwinkle Way (☎ 941/472-8080). Others include **Neptune's Treasures Shell Shop,** in the Tree Tops Center, 1101 Periwinkle Way (☎ 941/472-3132); and **Tuttle's Seahorse Shell Shop,** 342 Periwinkle Way, near the lighthouse (☎ 941/472-0707).

Sanibel has scores of upscale boutiques carrying expensive jewelry and apparel. Many are in **Periwinkle Place, Tahitian Gardens,** and **The Village,** the main shopping centers along Periwinkle Way. The **Audubon Nature Store,** in Tahitian Gardens (☎ 941/395-2020), carries gifts and books with a wildlife theme.

Bailey's General Store is still going strong at the corner of Periwinkle Way and Tarpon Bay Road (☎ **941/472-1516**), with a supermarket, deli, salad bar, hardware store, beach shop, shoe repair, and Western Union all under one roof.

WHERE TO STAY

While modern resorts may try to re-create a South Seas island setting, there still are many Old Florida–style cottages on the two islands which really do look like they belong on Bora Bora. Some also represent good value if you can do without modern luxuries, or for off-season stays. The 32 pink clapboard structures at **Beachview Cottages,** 3325 W. Gulf Dr., Sanibel Island, FL 33957 (☎ **941/ 472-1202,** or 800/860-0532; fax 941/472-4720), flank a narrow, unpaved lane running from the road to the beach and lined with coconut palms and colorful hibiscus. Winter rates here are $120 to $180 a day, but book well in advance, so popular is this clean, well-managed property. Off-season, they go for $85 to $155 a day. Also strongly reminiscent of the genuine South Pacific is **McCarthy's Marina & Cottages,** 15041 Captiva Dr., Captiva Island, FL 33924 (☎ **941/472-5200;** fax 941/472-6405), where four simple houses sit in a bayside palm and orange grove. The popular beach at the end of Andy Rosse Lane is just a block away. McCarthy's cottages range from $115 to $150 a day in winter, $70 to $105 a day off-season.

Sanibel has many condominium resorts; in fact, some of the expensive accommodations here are condo complexes operated as hotels. The largest rental agents are **Priscilla Murphy Realty,** 1177 Causeway Blvd. (P.O. Box 5), Sanibel Island, FL

33957 (☎ **941/472-4883,** or 800/237-6008; fax 941/472-8995), and **VIP Vacation Rentals,** 1509 Periwinkle Way, Sanibel Island, FL 33957 (☎ **941/ 472-1613,** or 800/237-7526; fax 941/481-8477). The chamber of commerce's **"Island Guide"** lists others (see "Essentials," above).

In general, Sanibel and Captiva room and condo rates are highest during the shelling season, February to April. January is usually somewhat less expensive. See "Where to Stay" in Section 1 on Fort Myers section, earlier in this chapter, for an explanation of the price categories.

SANIBEL ISLAND
Doubles for Less than $60
✪ **Palm View Motel.** 706 Donax St., Sanibel Island, FL 33957. ☎ **941/472-1606.** Fax 941/ 472-6733. 2 rms, 6 apts. A/C TV. High season, $75 double; $55–$90 apt. Off-season, $45 double; $95–$150 apt. MC, V.

In a quiet residential area less than a block from the Holiday Inn Beach Resort, Werner and Edelgard Papke's little motel is the jewel of Sanibel's few inexpensive accommodations. Originally from Germany, the Papkes have lived here since 1979, keeping their grounds groomed and their units clean and very well maintained. The traditional furnishings are from the 1970s but are nonetheless comfortable. The choices here are spacious, well-ventilated one- and two-bedroom apartments. All units except two motel rooms have kitchens; these two rooms interconnect and are often rented together.

Doubles for Less than $80
Anchorage Inn of Sanibel. 1245 Periwinkle Way, Sanibel Island, FL 33957. ☎ **941/ 395-9688.** 9 rms, 3 cottages. A/C TV. High season, $110 double; $165 cottage. Off-season, $89 double; $150 cottage. AE, DC, DISC, MC, V.

Formerly the Isle of Capri Motel, this modest establishment recently got a thorough face-lift from the owners of the Holiday Inn Beach Resort (guests here can use the beach and play tennis there). Standard rooms, efficiencies, and two-bedroom apartments are in low-slung buildings with broad porches facing a central courtyard with small pool. Although these units would rent for half these rates elsewhere, they're clean and good value for Sanibel. The three cottages are A-frame contraptions with spiral staircases to a second-story sleeping loft.

CAPTIVA ISLAND
Doubles for Less than $80
✪ **'Tween Waters Inn.** 15951 Captiva Rd., Captiva Island, FL 33924. ☎ **941/472-5161,** or 800/223-5865. Fax 941/472-0249. 40 rms, 22 efficiencies, 22 suites, 20 apts, 49 cottages. A/C TV TEL. Winter, $140–$275. Off-season, $70–$205. DISC, MC, V.

Wedged between the gulf beach and the bay on one of narrowest parts of the island, this venerable establishment was the regular haunt of cartoonist J. N. (Ding) Darling, and Anne Morrow Lindbergh spent a winter here writing *A Gift from the Sea.* Just as Darling preserved the islands' wildlife, the 'Tween Waters has saved the cottages he stayed in. These pink shiplap buildings capture Old Florida with simple white furniture and terrazzo floors. Although some face the gulf, most open to a parking lot, not gardens. The hotel rooms and apartments are in a two modern buildings on stilts with screened balconies facing the gulf or bay.

On the bay side, charter captains dock at the full-service marina and are available for fishing, shelling, and sightseeing excursions, and canoes and bikes can be rented. There's a very large swimming pool complex, complete with the Oasis Bar & Grill. Tennis courts are lighted for night play.

Dining here is a bargain on Captiva, with inexpensive salads, sandwiches, burgers, and pizzas offered by the Canoe Club, which has a bayside deck for lunches. The Old Captiva House restaurant appears very much as it did in Ding Darling's days (his cartoons adorn the walls) and offers reasonably priced breakfasts, lunches, and seafood dinners in winter (off-season, breakfast and dinner only). The popular Crow's Nest Lounge has live entertainment and provides snacks and light evening meals from 9pm to 1am.

CAMPING

The islands' sole campground, the **Periwinkle Trailer Park,** 1119 Periwinkle Way, Sanibel Island, FL 33957 (☎ **941/472-1433**), is so popular that it doesn't even advertise. Most of its wintertime clientele stay for months; if you can get a vacant site, it will cost $27 a day regardless of the time of year. No other camping is permitted on either Sanibel or Captiva.

WHERE TO EAT

Sanibel and Captiva have far too many restaurants to mention them all here. The chamber of commerce visitor center (see "Essentials," above) and some bookstores sell the very helpful *Menu & Dining Guide to Sanibel & Captiva Islands.* It lists them all, and reproduces the menus of many. Some restaurants close or take long vacations during the off-season, so it's wise to call ahead.

Only two fast-food chains have outlets on the islands: a **Dairy Queen,** 1048 Periwinkle Way (☎ **941/472-1170**), and a **Subway,** 2496 Palm Ridge Rd. (☎ **941/ 472-1155**).

The lively **Cheeburger Cheeburger,** 2413 Periwinkle Way, at Palm Ridge Road (☎ **941/472-6111**), has the island's biggest and best burgers, ranging from $3 to $9.

The "help" on this affluent island dines at **Jerry's Family Restaurant,** in Jerry's Center, 1700 Periwinkle Way at Casa Ybel Road (☎ **941/472-9300**). A sterile (in both appearance and cleanliness) appendage to Jerry's Supermarket, it offers inexpensive diner fare. Both the supermarket and the restaurant are open daily from 6am to 11pm.

Another way to save on meals is to take advantage of early-bird specials before 6pm. Also, Sanibel's sports bars dispense very reasonably priced pub fare such as conch chowder, salads, burgers, and fried seafood and chicken finger baskets—plus raw-bar items such as steamed shrimp. The best are the **Lazy Flamingo I,** 1036 Periwinkle Way, near Causeway Road (☎ **941/472-6939**), and its sibling, the **Lazy Flamingo II,** 6530 Pine Ave., just off Sanibel-Captiva Road near Blind Pass (☎ **941/ 472-5353**). The **Sanibel Grill,** 703 Tarpon Bay Rd., near Palm Ridge Road (☎ **941/472-3128**), actually serves as the bar for the Timbers, a fine seafood restaurant next door (see below). You'll find the bars open daily from 11am to 1am.

SANIBEL ISLAND

Meals for Less than $10

✪ **Hungry Heron.** In Palm Ridge Place, 2330 Palm Ridge Rd. (at Periwinkle Way). ☎ **941/ 395-2300.** Reservations recommended. Main courses $8–$15; sandwiches, burgers, snacks $4.50–$9; weekend breakfast buffet $6. AE, DISC, MC, V. Winter, Mon–Fri 10:30am–9:30pm, Sat–Sun 7:30–11:30am (buffet) and 7:30–9:30pm; off-season, daily 11:30am–9:30pm. AMERICAN.

TVs, cartoons, and a magician make Rob DeGennaro's tropically decorated eatery Sanibel's most popular family restaurant. There's something for everyone on Rob's huge, tabloid-size menu—from hot and cold "appeteezers" and overstuffed "seawiches" to "pasta bilities" and "stews for you." And if his 208 regular items aren't enough, there's a list of nightly specials. Seafood, steaks, and stir-fries from a sizzling skillet are popular with local residents, who bring the kids here for fun and a $5 children's menu. Cartoons run all the time and the magician circulates among the tables from 5 to 9pm every day except Tuesday. An all-you-can-eat breakfast buffet is good value on Saturday and Sunday from 7:30 to 11:30am during winter.

Lighthouse Café. In the Seahorse Shops, 362 Periwinkle Way (east of Causeway Blvd.). ☎ **941/472-0303.** Reservations not accepted. Main courses $8–$12; breakfast $3.50–$6; lunch $5–$6. MC, V. Daily 7am–3pm and 5–9pm. Closed for dinner mid-April to mid-Dec. AMERICAN.

This casual storefront establishment near the Sanibel Lighthouse dishes up breakfast omelets that are meals in themselves, especially the ocean frittata containing delicately seasoned scallops, crabmeat, shrimp, broccoli, and fresh mushrooms and crowned by an artichoke heart and creamy Alfredo sauce. Seafood Benedict is another unusual offering. There's also an interesting sandwich menu, and reasonably priced dinners are served in winter.

✪ Sanibel Café. In the Tahitian Gardens Shops, 2007 Periwinkle Way. ☎ **941/472-5323.** Reservations not accepted. Breakfast $3–$6; lunch salads and burgers $2.50–$7. No credit cards. Daily 7am–8pm. AMERICAN.

Seashells are the theme at this pleasant café whose tables are museumlike glass cases containing delicate fossilized specimens from the Miocene and Pliocene epochs. Fresh-squeezed orange and grapefruit juices, Danish Havarti omelets, eggs Benedict, and homemade muffins and biscuits highlight the breakfast menu (eggs Benedict and fruit-filled waffles are served until closing), while lunch features specialty sandwiches and shrimp, Greek, and chicken-and-grape salads made with a very light, fat-free mayonnaise dressing. Proprietors Lynda and Ken Boyce even serve a sugar-free pancake syrup.

Meals for Less than $15

Harbor House. 1244 Periwinkle Way (near Donax St.). ☎ **941/472-1242.** Reservations not required. Main courses $10–$19; early-bird specials (served daily 5–6pm) $9. AE, MC, V. Winter, daily 11:30am–2pm and 5–9:30pm; off-season, daily 5–9:30pm. AMERICAN.

Dating back to 1948, this family-owned establishment is Sanibel's oldest seafood restaurant, and a warm, Old Florida atmosphere prevails under the beamed ceilings of its paneled dining room. The seafood selections are down-home as well, with shrimp, scallops, and freshly caught fish either broiled, fried, blackened, or "bronzed" (not quite blackened, in order to preserve the seafood's natural flavor). Stone crab claws and Florida lobster are offered during their seasons. The early-bird specials are a bargain. Made with limes from the family's own trees, the key lime pie here is an award-winner.

The Jacaranda. 1223 Periwinkle Way (near Donax St.). ☎ **941/472-1771.** Reservations recommended. Main courses $13–$22. AE, DC, DISC, MC, V. Daily 5–10pm. SEAFOOD/PASTA.

Named for the purple-flowered jacaranda tree, this friendly and casual restaurant features a raw bar and lounge in a screened patio. Recipient of several dining awards, the Jacaranda is best known for expertly prepared fish and seafood, which the chef will bake, sauté, or blacken. A favorite pasta dish is linguine and a dozen littleneck clams tossed in a piquant red or white clam sauce. For dessert, the gooey turtle pie—

with ice cream crowned by caramel, fudge sauce, chopped nuts, and whipped cream—will send you away stuffed. The Patio Lounge has live music nightly.

McT's Shrimp House & Tavern. 1523 Periwinkle Way (at Fitzhugh St.). ☎ **941/472-3161.** Reservations not accepted. Main courses $12–$17; early-bird specials (served daily 4:45–6pm) $8. AE, DC, DISC, MC, V. Shrimp House, daily 4:45–10pm. McT's Tavern, daily 4:45pm–12:30am. SEAFOOD.

An Old Florida atmosphere prevails in the casual Shrimp House, where diners line up for the $8 early-bird specials that are served to the first 100 people who show up before 6pm. The selections include prime rib, steamed shrimp platters, seafood Créole or pasta, fish and chips, or barbecued ribs. The regular menu features all-you-can-eat shrimp and crab platters, and there's a kids' menu. With a pinball machine and huge sports TV in the rear of the building, McT's Tavern offers an extensive choice of appetizers and light dinners from 4:45 to 10pm and burgers and pizza from 10pm until closing.

The Timbers. 703 Tarpon Bay Rd. (at Palm Ridge Rd.). ☎ **941/472-3128.** Reservations recommended. Main courses $12–$20; early-bird specials (served daily 4:30–6pm in winter, 5–6pm off-season) $5–$6. AE, DISC, MC, V. Winter, daily 4:30–10pm; off-season, daily 5–10pm. SEAFOOD/STEAK.

A sibling of the Prawnbroker Restaurant and Fish Market in Fort Myers, this casual, upstairs restaurant is justly proud of consistently winning the Taste of the Islands award for its seafood and steaks. A new menu of specials is printed every day and always features the freshest fish available, which the chef will charcoal-grill or blacken to order. The steaks are aged and cut on the premises. The adjoining Sanibel Grill sports bar serves as the Timbers' lounge and shares its kitchen.

Worth a Splurge

✪ **The Mad Hatter.** 6467 Sanibel-Captiva Rd. (at Blind Pass). ☎ **941/472-0033.** Reservations required. Main courses $18–$28. AE, MC, V. Daily 5–9:30pm. Closed Sun off-season. NEW AMERICAN.

Brian and Jayne Baker's popular gulf-front restaurant has only 12 tables, but each has a glorious water view that's perfect at sunset. A fantasy of New American cuisine, based on California, the Southwest, and the South, with some exotic accents, the Bakers' food is worthy of the view. A frequent favorite on their otherwise changing menu (so as not to bore their loyal local following) is a delicious mixture of angel-hair pasta, grilled marinated shrimp, tomatoes, capers, wild mushrooms, and green olives accompanied by fresh avocado and a vegetable crêpe topped with a tomato-mole sauce.

CAPTIVA ISLAND
Meals for Less than $10

✪ **Sunshine Cafe.** In Captiva Village Square, Captiva Rd. and Laika Lane. ☎ **941/472-6200.** Reservations recommended. Small platters $6–$9; large platters $19–$22; sandwiches $7–$7.50. AE, DISC, MC, V. Daily 11:30am–9:30pm. ECLECTIC.

This friendly café has only 10 tables—five inside, five on the shopping center's porch—but the food is worth the wait. Specialties are charcoal-grilled steak and shrimp, tandoori chicken breast, po-boy sandwiches, and Italian-style pastas. The delicious daily specials feature fresh seafood (especially good over linguine with fresh herbs, roasted garlic, and imported cheese). Or you can order light dishes such as a plate of black beans and rice or a Caesar salad. Various desserts are offered daily, with the white-chocolate cheesecake in an Oreo-cookie crust a constant favorite. Anything on the menu can be ordered to carry out.

Meals for Less than $15

☻ Bellini's of Captiva. Andy Rosse Lane. ☎ **941/472-6866.** Reservations suggested. Main courses $10.50–$25. AE, MC, V. Daily 5:30–10pm. (Cocktail lounge, daily 7pm–late.) NORTHERN ITALIAN.

"Bella, bella!" describes both the beautiful indoor dining room and the garden courtyard of this large, casual Italian restaurant. The house specialty frozen peach Bellini cocktail is a version of the world-famous Bellini served at Harry's Bar in Venice, Italy. Crabmeat manicotti with basil-cream sauce provides a rich opener, while excellent pasta, fish, chicken, veal, and beef dishes comprise the main courses. Desserts include homemade pastries and Italian ice cream. Bellini's cocktail lounge provides live evening entertainment.

The Mucky Duck. Andy Rosse Lane (on the gulf). ☎ **941/472-3434.** Reservations not accepted. Main courses $12–$18; lunch $4–$10. AE, DISC, MC, V. Mon–Sat 11:30am–2:30pm and 5–9:30pm. SEAFOOD/PUB FARE.

This lively, British-style pub is the one place on Captiva with dining right by the beach—and it's the island's most popular. If you don't get a seat with this great view, the staff will gladly roll a fake window over to appease you. The menu offers a selection of fresh seafood items, plus English fish and chips, steak-and-sausage pie, and a ploughman's lunch. There's a children's menu and a vegetarian platter. No smoking is allowed inside.

Worth a Splurge

☻ The Bubble Room. 15001 Captiva Rd. (at Andy Rosse Lane). ☎ **941/472-5558.** Reservations not accepted. Main courses $19–$27; lunch $6–$12. AE, DC, DISC, MC, V. Daily 11:30am–2:30pm and 5:30–10pm. STEAK/SEAFOOD.

The gaudy bubble-gum pink, yellow, purple, and green exterior of this amusing restaurant is only a prelude to the 1930s, 1940s, and 1950s Hollywood motif inside. The dining rooms are adorned with a collection of puppets, statues of great movie stars, toy trains, thousands of movie stills, and antique jukeboxes that play big band–era tunes. The menu carries on the cinematic theme: prime ribs Weismuller, Eddie Fisherman filet of fresh grouper, and Henny Young-One boneless breast of young chicken. Both adults and children (who can dine for $7 at dinner, $5 at lunch) are attracted to this fun establishment.

GREAT PICNIC FARE

For inexpensive picnics at Sanibel's beaches or on a canoe, **Isabella's Italian Food & Deli,** 1523 Periwinkle Way (☎ **941/472-0044**), has subs, pastas, and the island's best pizza, all by carryout or delivery only. The deli and bakery in **Bailey's General Store,** at the intersection of Periwinkle Way and Tarpon Bay Road (☎ **941/ 472-1516**), carries a gourmet selection of breads, cheeses, and meats. **Huxter's Deli and Market,** 1203 Periwinkle Way (☎ **941/472-6988**), has sandwich fixings and "beach box" lunches to go.

On Captiva, big deli sandwiches and picnic fare are available at the **Captiva Island Store,** Captiva Road at Andy Rosse Lane (☎ **941/472-2374**), and at **C. W.'s Market and Deli,** at the entrance to the South Seas Plantation Resort & Yacht Harbour (☎ **941/472-5111**). The beach is a block from these stores.

SANIBEL & CAPTIVA ISLANDS AFTER DARK

THE PERFORMING ARTS   From December to April, professional actors per-form Broadway dramas and comedies in Sanibel's state-of-the-art, 150-seat **Pirate Playhouse,** 2200 Periwinkle Way (☎ **941/472-0006**). Recent productions have included *Don't Dress for Dinner, The Hasty Heart,* and *Bus Stop.* Shows are held Monday to Saturday at 8pm; matinees are usually on Wednesday and Saturday. Call for schedule and ticket prices.

Originally a one-room school built in 1896, and later housing the Pirate Playhouse before its new facility was constructed across the road, the **Old Schoolhouse Theater,** 1905 Periwinkle Way (☎ **941/472-6862**), compliments its neighbor by offering Broadway musicals and revues from December to April. During the sum-mer, the local Off Beach Players take over. Call for the current schedule and prices.

For laughs, **Sanibel Island Comedy Club,** 975 Rabbit Rd., at Sanibel-Captiva Road (☎ **941/472-8833**), features national touring comedians (call for schedule).

THE CLUB & BAR SCENE   You won't find glitzy lounges or nightclubs on these family-oriented islands, but night owls will enjoy fun places to roost at some of the resorts and restaurants mentioned above. Here's a brief recap:

On Sanibel, the Sundial Beach and Tennis Resort's **Lobby Lounge,** 1451 Middle Gulf Dr. (☎ **941/472-4151**), features entertainers during dinner, then live bands for dancing from 9pm on. The **Patio Lounge,** in the Jacaranda, 1223 Periwinkle Way (☎ **941/472-1771**), has live music every evening. **McT's Tavern,** 1523 Periwinkle Way (☎ **941/472-3161**), has darts, video games, and a large-screen TV for sports fans. **Tarwinkle's,** 2447 Periwinkle Way, at Tarpon Bay Road (☎ **941/ 472-1366**), the **Sanibel Grill,** 703 Tarpon Bay Rd. (☎ **941/472-4453**), and the two **Lazy Flamingo** branches (see "Where to Eat," above) are popular sports bars.

On Captiva, nightly entertainment is spotlighted at **Bellini's of Captiva,** 11521 Andy Rosse Lane (☎ **941/472-6866**). **Chadwick's Lounge,** at the entrance to the South Seas Plantation Resort & Yacht Harbour (☎ **941/472-5111**), has a large dance floor and music from 8:30pm on. Captiva's no. 1 nightspot for dancing is the **Crow's Nest Lounge,** in the 'Tween Waters Inn, on Captiva Road (☎ **941/472-5161**).

EASY ISLAND EXCURSIONS

Sanibel and Captiva are jumping-off points for island-hopping boat trips to barrier islands and keys imbued with ancient legends and Robinson Crusoe–style beaches. You don't have to get completely lost out there, however, for several islets have com-fortable inns and restaurants. The trip across shallow Pine Island Sound is itself a sightseeing adventure, with playful dolphins surfing on the boat's wake and a plethora of cormorants, egrets, frigate birds, and (in winter) rare white pelicans flying above or lounging on sandbars between meals.

Captiva Cruises (☎ **941/472-5300**) has daily trips from the South Seas Plantation Resort & Yacht Harbour on Captiva. The *Lady Chadwick* goes to Cabbage Key and Useppa Island, where passengers disembark for lunch. The *Andy Rosse* goes to Boca Grande by way of Cayo Costa State Park. These day trips cost $27.50 per person to Cabbage Key or Useppa, $35 to Boca Grande or Cayo Costa. They usually leave at 10:30am. Reservations are required. For information about Boca Grande, see "An Easy Excursion to Boca Grande," in Section 1 on Fort Myers, earlier in this chapter.

The **Cabbage Key Inn** (see below) operates its own launch twice a day Mon-day to Friday, once daily on weekends, from the Pineland Marina on Pine Island. Transportation from Captiva is via Captiva Cruises.

CABBAGE KEY

You never know who's going to get off a boat at 100-acre Cabbage Key and walk unannounced into the funky **Cabbage Key Inn,** P.O. Box 200, Pineland, FL 33945 (☎ **941/283-2278;** fax 941/283-1384), a rustic house built in 1938 by the son and daughter-in-law of mystery novelist Mary Roberts Rinehart. Ernest Hemingway liked to hang out here in the early days, and novelist John D. MacDonald was a frequent guest 30 years later. Today you could find yourself rubbing elbows at the bar with the likes of Walter Cronkite, Ted Koppel, Sean Connery, or Julia Roberts. Singer and avid yachtie Jimmy Buffett likes Cabbage Key so much that it inspired his hit song "Cheeseburger in Paradise."

A path leads from the tiny marina across a lawn dotted with coconut palms to this white clapboard house that sits atop an ancient Calusa shell mound. Guests dine in the comfort of two screened porches and seek libations in Mrs. Rinehart's library-turned-bar, its pine-paneled walls now plastered with dollar bills left by visitors. The straight-back chairs and painted wooden tables are showing their age, but that's part of Cabbage Key's laid-back, don't-give-a-hoot charm.

In addition to the famous thick, juicy cheeseburgers so loved by Jimmy Buffett, the house specialties are fresh broiled fish and shrimp steamed in beer. Lunches range from $4 to $9; dinners are $16 to $20.

For overnight or longer, Cabbage Key Inn has six rooms and six cottages, all with original 1920s furnishings, private baths, and air conditioners. Four of the cottages have kitchens, and one room reputedly has its own ghost. Year-round rates are $65 single or double for rooms, $145 to $200 for cottages. Reserve well in advance for major holidays and during the tarpon season from February to May, when rates are highest.

CAYO COSTA STATE PARK

You can't get any closer to a deserted tropical island than 2,132-acre Cayo Costa (pronounced *Key*-oh *Cos*-tah), an unspoiled barrier island with miles of white-sand beaches, pine forests, mangrove swamps, oak-palm hammocks, and grasslands. Other than the island's natural wildlife, the only permanent residents here are three park rangers.

Daytrippers can bring their own supplies and use a picnic area with pavilions. A tram carries visitors from the soundside dock to the gulf beach (50¢ round-trip fare). The state maintains 12 very basic cabins and a primitive campground on the northern end of the island near Johnson Shoals, where the shelling is spectacular. Cabins cost $20 a day and campsites are $13 a day all year. There's running water on the island but no electricity.

The park is open daily from 8am to sundown. There's a $2-per-person honor-system admission fee for day visitors. Overnight slips at the dock cost $13 a day. For more information or cabin reservations, contact **Cayo Costa State Park,** P.O. Box 1150, Boca Grande, FL 33921 (☎ **941/964-0375**). Office hours are Monday to Friday from 8am to 5pm.

USEPPA ISLAND

Lying near Cabbage Key, Useppa was a refuge of President Theodore Roosevelt and his tarpon-loving industrialist friends at the turn of the century. New York advertising magnate Barron G. Collier bought the island in 1906 and built a lovely wooden home overlooking Pine Island Sound. Collier's mansion is now the **Collier Inn,** where daytrippers and overnight guests can partake of lunches and seafood dinners in a country-club ambience (at prices to match the upmarket clientele here).

They also can visit the **Useppa Museum,** which explains the island's history and displays 4,000-year-old Calusa artifacts. The museum is open Tuesday to Sunday from 12:15 to 2pm. Admission is by $2 donation.

The Collier Inn is the centerpiece of the **Useppa Island Club,** an exclusive development with more than 100 luxury homes. Although of recent vintage, all are of the clapboard-sided, tin-roofed style of Old Florida. Paved walkways connect the houses to the mansion and to Collier's original service buildings down by the marina, but there are no roads and few motorized vehicles other than golf carts on the island.

The club rents some of the houses and rooms in the old buildings near the wharf. The air-conditioned rooms have Old Florida–style furniture plus telephones and cable TVs. Facilities include a heated swimming pool and whirlpool, tennis and croquet courts, a small fitness center, a general store, and a lounge with billiards. For information, rates (all on the Modified American Plan), and reservations, contact **Collier Inn & Cottages,** P.O. Box 640, Bokeelia, FL 33922 (☎ **941/283-1061;** fax 941/283-0290).

4 Naples

42 miles S of Fort Myers, 106 miles W of Miami, 185 miles S of Tampa

Because its wealthy residents are accustomed to the very best, Naples is easily Southwest Florida's most sophisticated city. Many of its boutiques and galleries would upstage those in Palm Beach or Beverly Hills, and two of its resorts are consistently rated among America's best. And yet Naples has an easy-going friendliness to all comers, who can find some surprisingly affordable places to stay within easy reach of its long, magnificent beach.

Naples began in 1886 when a group of 12 Kentuckians and Ohioans bought 8,700 acres, laid out a town, and started selling lots. They built a pier and the 16-room Naples Hotel, whose first guest was President Grover Cleveland's sister Rose. She and other notables soon built a line of beach homes known as "Millionaires' Row." Known today as Olde Naples and carefully protected by its modern residents, their original settlement still retains the air of that time a century ago.

Even the newer sections of Naples have their beautiful charm, thanks to Ohio manufacturer Henry B. Watkins Sr. In 1946 Watkins and his partners bought the Naples Hotel and all the town's undeveloped land and laid out the Naples Plan, which created the environmentally conscious city you see today. While strict zoning laws preserve the old part of town, the Naples Plan blends development with the natural environment along the town's 10 miles of beachfront.

ESSENTIALS

GETTING THERE   By Plane   Most visitors arrive at the Southwest Florida International Airport, 35 miles north of Naples (see "Getting There," in the Fort Myers section, above). **Naples Municipal Airport,** on North Road off Airport-Pulling Road (☎ **941/643-6875**), is served by American Eagle, Delta Connection, and USAir Express. Taxis await all flights outside the small terminal building.

By Bus   The **Greyhound** bus terminal is at 2669 Davis Blvd. (☎ **941/774-5660,** or 800/231-2222).

By Car   From Miami, U.S. 41 (the Tamiami Trail) leads through the Everglades to Naples. A faster route is via I-75 ("Alligator Alley") from Miami and Fort Lauderdale. From Tampa and Fort Myers, take either I-75 or U.S. 41 due south. From I-75, take Immokalee Road (Exit 17) for Vanderbilt Beach, Pine Ridge Road

(Exit 16) for the Pelican Bay area north of downtown, or Davis Boulevard (Exit 15) for downtown.

VISITOR INFORMATION   For free advance information, contact the **Naples Area Tourism Bureau,** P.O. Box 10129, Naples, FL 33942 (☎ **941/598-3202,** or 800/605-7878). The Naples Area Chamber of Commerce maintains a **visitor center** at 895 5th Avenue South, Naples, FL 33940 (☎ **941/262-6141;** fax 941/ 262-8374), which has a host of free brochures and other information and sells a detailed street map for $2. By mail, they will send a complete Naples vacation packet for $7 ($12 to Canada, $25 outside North America) and the street map for $3. Drivers arriving on I-75 can stop at the **Golden Gate Visitors Center,** 8801 Davis Blvd., which is near Exit 15.

GETTING AROUND   By Taxi   Call **Yellow Cab** (☎ 941/262-1312), **Maxi Taxi** (☎ 941/262-8977), or **Naples Taxi** (☎ 941/775-0505). Fares are $1.75 for the first tenth of a mile, 30¢ for each two-tenths of a mile thereafter.

By Trolley   The **Naples Trolley** (☎ **941/262-7300**) clangs around 25 stops between the Marketplace at Tin City in Olde Naples and Vanderbilt Beach Monday to Saturday from 8:30am to 5:15pm and on Sunday from 10:15am to 5:15pm. Daily fares are $10 for adults, $5 for children 5 to 12, free for children 4 and under, with free reboarding. The main office is at 179 Commerce St., Vanderbilt Beach. Pick up a schedule and tickets there, at the information booth in Tin City (see "What to See & Do," below), at the chamber of commerce visitor center (see "Essentials," above), or in brochure racks in the lobbies of most hotels and motels.

By Bicycle   The Naples Area Chamber of Commerce distributes an area bicycle route map. Rent a bike from **The Bike Route,** 655 N. Tamiami Trail (☎ **941/262-8373**). For scooters, call **Good Times Rental,** 1947 Davis Blvd. (☎ **941/775-7529**).

BEACHES & OUTDOOR ACTIVITIES

BEACHES   Access to Olde Naples's gorgeous white-sand beach is at the gulf end of each avenue, although parking in the neighborhood can be precious (try the metered lots near the Naples Pier on 12th Avenue South). **Lowdermilk Park** (☎ 904/263-6078) is on the beach at Gulf Shore Boulevard North Banyan Boulevard. It has a pavilion, rest rooms, showers, a refreshment counter, volleyball nets, and picnic tables. A few blocks farther north is a metered parking lot with beach access beside the Naples Beach Hotel & Golf Resort, 851 Gulf Shore Blvd. North, at Golf Drive.

At Pelican Bay north of the historic district, the popular ✪ **Clam Pass County Park** (☎ **941/353-0404**) has a 3,000-foot boardwalk winding through mangrove swamps and across a back bay to a beach of fine white sand. Some 6 miles of canoe and kayak trails—with multitudes of birds and an occasional alligator—run from Clam Pass into the backwaters. The beach pavilion here has a snack bar, rest rooms (foot showers only), picnic tables, and beach equipment rentals, including one- and two-person kayaks and 12-foot canoes ($10 to $20 per hour). Entry is from a metered parking lot beside the Registry Resort at the end of Seagate Drive. There's a $3-per-vehicle parking fee, but a free tram runs from the parking lot to the beach daily from 8am to sunset. Bicycles cannot be ridden on the boardwalk.

At Vanderbilt Beach north of town, **Delnor-Wiggins State Recreation Area,** at the west end of Bluebill Avenue–111th Avenue North (☎ **941/597-6196**), has bath houses, picnic areas, and a boat ramp. Fishing from the beach is excellent here. The area is open daily from 8am to sunset. Admission is $3.25 for vehicles with up to eight occupants, $1 for pedestrians and bikers.

BOAT RENTALS   Powerboat rentals are available from **Club Nautico,** at the Boat Haven Marina, 1484 Tamiami Trail East (☎ 941/774-0100), on the east bank of the Gordon River behind Kelly's Fish House; the **Port-O-Call Marina,** 550 Port of Call Way (☎ 941/774-0479); the **Parkshore Marina,** 4310 Gulf Shore Blvd. North (☎ 941/434-6964), in the Village Shops at Venetian Bay; the **Brookside Marina,** 2023 Davis Blvd. (☎ 941/774-9100); and the **Cove Marina,** 860 12th Ave. South (☎ 941/263-7250), at the City Docks.

Sailing enthusiasts can line up a charter with **Sailboats Unlimited,** at the City Docks on 12th Avenue South (☎ **941/262-0139**).

DIVING   The **Under Seas Dive Academy,** 998 6th Ave. South, in Olde Naples (☎ **941/262-0707**), takes divers into the gulf, teaches diver-certification courses, and rents water-sports equipment. So does Kevin Sweeney's **SCUBAdventures,** 971 Creech Rd., at the Tamiami Trail (☎ **941/434-7477**).

FISHING   The least expensive way for singles, couples, and small families to fish without paying for an entire boat is on the 34-foot *Lady Brett* (☎ **941/263-4949**), which makes scheduled daily trips from Tin City for $40 per adult, $35 per child. A number of charter boats are based at the marinas mentioned under "Boat Rentals," above; call or visit them for booking information and prices.

GOLF   Nearby public courses include the **Lely Flamingo Island Club** (☎ 941/793-2223), **Boyne USA South** (☎ 941/732-5108), the **Ironwood Golf Club of Naples** (☎ 941/775-2584), the **Hibiscus Golf Club** (☎ 941/774-3559), and the **Riviera Golf Club** (☎ 941/774-1081).

The **Naples Beach Hotel & Golf Club** (☎ 941/261-2222) has an interesting 18-hole course for its guests. The Ritz-Carlton Naples, the Registry Resort, and LaPlaya Beach Resort send their guests to the private **Pelican's Nest Golf Club.** In Golden Gate, west of I-75, the **Quality Inn Golf & Country Club,** 4100 Golden Gate Pkwy. (☎ 941/455-1010, or 800/228-5151), has an 18-hole course and 153 rooms, suites, and efficiencies.

TENNIS   In Olde Naples, the city's **Cambier Park Tennis Courts,** 755 8th Ave. South, at 9th Street South (☎ **941/434-4694**), offers 12 lighted courts. It's one of the few public tennis facilities anywhere to match those found at luxury resorts. Play costs $6 for 90 minutes. They're open in winter, Monday to Friday from 8am to 10pm, on Saturday to 5pm, and on Sunday to 4pm; off-season, Monday to Friday from 8am to 10pm, on Saturday to 5pm, and on Sunday to 1pm. Book with the pro in the middle of the courts. There's a children's playground next to the courts.

Nonguests can arrange to play at the **Naples Beach Hotel & Golf Club,** 851 Gulf Shore Blvd. North (☎ **941/261-2222**), but call ahead.

WATER SPORTS   **Good Times Rental,** 1947 Davis Blvd. (☎ **941/775-7529**), rents Waverunners, windboards, skim boards, canoes, snorkeling gear, rafts, and other beach equipment. Hobie Cats and windsurfers can also be rented on the beach at the **Naples Beach Hotel & Golf Club,** 851 Gulf Shore Blvd. North (☎ 941/261-2222).

WHAT TO SEE & DO
OLDE NAPLES

Its history may only go back to 1886, but Olde Naples still has the charm of that Victorian era when it was founded as a real-estate development. It's the part of town lying below 5th Avenue South. The city docks are on the bay side, the glorious beach along the gulf. Laid out on a grid, the tree-lined streets run between many houses—some dating from the beginning—and along Millionaires' Row between Gulf Shore Boulevard and the beach. With these gorgeous homes virtually hidden in the palms and casuarinas, the Olde Naples beach seems a century removed from the high-rise condos found farther north.

The **Naples Pier,** at the gulf end of 12th Avenue South, is a focal point of the neighborhood. Built in 1888 to let steamers land potential real-estate customers, the original 600-foot-long, T-shaped structure was destroyed by hurricanes and damaged by fire. Local residents have rebuilt it because they like strolling its length to catch fantastic gulf sunsets—and to get a gulfside glimpse of Millionaire's Row. The pier is now a state historic site and admission is free. It's open 24 hours a day, but parking in the nearby lots is restricted between 11pm and 7am.

Nearby, **Palm Cottage,** 137 12th Ave. South, between 1st Street and Gordon Drive (☎ 941/261-8164), was built in 1885 by one of Naples's founders, *Louisville Courier-Journal* publisher Walter Haldeman, as a winter retreat for his chief editorial writer. After World War II its socialite owners hosted many galas attended by the likes of Hollywood stars Hedy Lamarr, Gary Cooper, and Robert Montgomery. One of the few remaining Southwest Florida houses built of tabbie mortar (a mixture made by burning shells), Palm Cottage today is the home of the Naples Historical Society, which maintains it as a museum filled with authentic furniture, paintings, photographs, and other memorabilia. It's open in winter only, Monday to Friday from 2 to 4pm. Adult admission is by $3 donation; free for children.

Just 3 blocks from the pier, there's great window-shopping along **3rd Street South,** at Broad Avenue, where chic shops and fine restaurants equal those on Rodeo Drive in Beverly Hills (see "Shopping," below). Businesses and more shops line **5th Avenue South.**

Near the Gordon River Bridge on 5th Avenue South, the old corrugated waterfront warehouses are now a shopping-and-dining complex known as the **Marketplace at Tin City,** which is thronged by tourists and assiduously avoided by local residents during the winter months.

MUSEUMS & ZOOS

Caribbean Gardens. 1590 Goodlette-Frank Rd. (at Fleischmann Blvd.). ☎ **941/262-5409.** Admission $12 adults, $8 children 4–15, free for children 3 and under. Daily 9:30am–5:30pm (last entry at 4:30pm). Closed Thanksgiving and Christmas Day.

A family favorite formerly known as "Jungle Larry's," for noted animal trainer and owner Larry Tetzlaff, this zoo features a variety of animals and birds, including a fascinating community of primates living free on their own island. A safari through the premises includes spectacular tropical gardens and a boat tour, from which the primates can be observed. Many visitors are captivated by the Big Cat Show, in which lions and tigers are put through their paces by Larry's son, David Tetzlaff, himself a talented trainer. Big Cat Show times vary, so call for the schedule. For kids, there's a petting farm, elephant rides, and a playground. Picnic facilities are on the premises.

✪ **Teddy Bear Museum.** 2511 Pine Ridge Rd. (at Airport-Pulling Rd.). ☎ **941/598-2711.** Admission $6 adults, $4 senior citizens and children 13–19, $2 children 4–12, free for children 3 and under. Winter, Mon and Wed–Sat 10am–5pm, Sun 1–5pm; off-season, Wed–Sat 10am–5pm, Sun 1–5pm. Closed New Year's Day, Thanksgiving, and Christmas Day.

Another family favorite, this entertaining museum contains 3,000-plus examples of stuffed teddy bears from around the world. They're cleverly displayed descending from the rafters in hot-air balloons, attending board meetings, sipping afternoon tea, celebrating a wedding, even doing bear things like hibernating. There's a gift shop where you can buy your own bears.

PARKS & NATURE PRESERVES

You don't have to go far east of Naples to reach the magnificent Everglades, much of it protected by Everglades National Park and Big Cypress National Preserve. See Chapter 8 for information about activities in and near the national park. Other nearby nature preserves are described in Section 5 on Marco Island, later in this chapter.

One of the largest private preserves is the ✪ **Corkscrew Swamp Sanctuary** (☎ 941/657-3771), 16 miles northeast of Naples off Immokalee Road (County Road 846). Maintained by the National Audubon Society, this 11,000-acre wilderness is home to countless wood storks, which nest high in the cypress trees from November to April. Wading birds also are best seen in winter, when the swamp is likely to be dry (they don't nest when water levels are high). The birds congregate around pools near a boardwalk that leads 2 miles through the largest bald cypress forest with some of the oldest trees in the country. Ferns and orchids also flourish. Admission is $6.50 for adults, $5 for full-time college students, $3 for children 6 to 18, and free for children 5 and under. The sanctuary is open December to April, daily from 7am to 5pm; May to November, daily from 8am to 5pm. To reach the sanctuary, take Exit 17 off I-75 and go east on Immokalee Road (County Road 846).

Nearby, the **Corkscrew Marsh Trail System,** on Corkscrew Road south of Fla. 82, consists of a 5-mile loop through mostly pine forests managed jointly by the Corkscrew Regional Ecosystem Watershed Trust and the South Florida Water Management District. Only hikers are allowed to use these trails, which are free but have no drinking water or rest rooms.

You can also experience Southwest Florida's abundant natural life without leaving Naples. The **Conservancy Naples Nature Center,** 14th Avenue North, east of Goodlette-Frank Road (☎ 941/262-0304), is one of two preserves operated by The Conservancy (the other is the Briggs Nature Center; see Section 5 on Marco Island, later in this chapter). The Naples Nature Center includes a well-stocked serpentarium and an aquarium inhabited by stingrays, turtles, and all sorts of crustaceans. Outdoors, there are nature trails, a butterfly garden, an aviary with bald eagles and other birds, and boat rides through a mangrove forest to observe wildlife (you can also rent canoes and kayaks and see it by yourself). A nature store carries interesting gift items. The trails and boat ride are free. Admission to the wildlife exhibits is $4 for adults, $2 for children 7 to 17, and free for children 6 and under. Canoe and kayak rentals are $13 for 2 hours. The center is open in winter, Monday to Saturday from 9am to 4:30pm and on Sunday from 1 to 5pm; call for off-season hours.

CRUISES

The Gordon River and Naples Bay from the U.S. 41 bridge on 5th Avenue South to the gulf are prime territory for sightseeing and sunset cruises. The double-decked *Double Sunshine* (☎ 941/263-4949) sallies forth onto the river and bay from Tin City, where it has a ticket office. The 1½-hour cruises usually leave at noon, 2:30pm, and an hour before sunset. They cost $15 per person.

The *Sweet Liberty* (☎ 941/793-3525), a 53-foot sailing catamaran, makes morning shelling cruises to Keewaydin Island, a private wildlife sanctuary south of Olde Naples. The vessel then spends the afternoon sightseeing and the evening on sunset cruises on Naples Bay before docking at Boat Haven Marina on the east side of the

Gordon River Bridge. Shelling cruises cost $25 per person; sightseeing and sunset cruises cost $20 a head.

For a good deal more luxury, the 83-foot *Naples Princess* (☎ 941/649-2275) has lunch and sunset dinner cruises from Olde Naples Seaport, 10th Avenue South at 10th Street South. These usually leave at noon, 1:30pm, and 5pm. With an extensive sandwich buffet, the lunch cruise is excellent value at $20 per person. The sunset dinner cruises cost $35 per person. Sightseers can pay $15 each to go on any of the cruises and not dine.

The back bays of Vanderbilt Beach 10 miles north of Naples are the home of **Nautilus Boat Tours** (☎ 941/597-4408). It has narrated nature and sunset cruises daily through the Vanderbilt Lagoon to the Delnor-Wiggins State Recreation Area and the nearby Barefoot Beach Preserve. Nature cruises depart daily at 11am; sunset cruises go forth daily at 1 hour before sundown. Both cost $15 for adults, $5 for children 2 to 12. Call for reservations. The company also has a full-day excursion from Vanderbilt Beach to Captiva Island for $45 per person.

SHOPPING

Two blocks of **3rd Street South,** at Broad Avenue, are the Rodeo Drive of Naples. Its glitzy collection of jewelers, clothiers, and art galleries may be too rich for many wallets, but the window-shopping here is unmatched. The **5th Avenue South** shopping area, between 3rd and 9th streets South, is longer and a bit less chic, with stockbrokerages and real-estate offices thrown into the mix of boutiques and antiques dealers. Both areas have several bistros and other dining spots. Also in Olde Naples, the **Old Marine Marketplace at Tin City,** 1200 5th Ave. South, at the Gordon River (☎ 941/262-4600), has 50 boutiques selling everything from souvenirs to avant-garde resortwear and imported statuary.

Even the malls in Naples have their charms. The **Village at Venetian Bay,** 4200 Gulf Shore Blvd., at Park Shore Drive, evokes images of its Italian namesake, with 50 canalside shops featuring high-fashion men's and women's clothiers and fine-art galleries. Ornate Mediterranean architecture and a tropical waterfall highlight the **Waterside Shops at Pelican Bay,** Seagate Drive at Tamiami Trail North, where the anchor stores are Saks Fifth Avenue and Jacobsen's.

WHERE TO STAY

While Naples has some of the most expensive resorts in the region, it also has some surprisingly reasonable rates, particularly at several older but very well maintained "apartment hotels" within a few blocks of the beach (see the Olde Naples Inn, below). The problem is getting a reservation, so popular are they during the high season from mid-December to mid-April. February and March are especially busy, when many guests stay a month or more. Rates here drop dramatically during the off-season, when even the very expensive resorts suddenly fall into the moderate range. See "Where to Stay" in Section 1 on Fort Myers, earlier in this chapter, for an explanation of the rate seasons and categories.

Most Naples establishments offer weekly and monthly rates during winter, especially the town's many condominium complexes. One is the **Cove Inn,** 1191 8th St. South, Naples, FL 33940 (☎ 941/262-7161, or 800/225-4365; fax 941/261-6905). It was originally built as a motel right on the City Docks at the south end of 9th Street, but its rooms are now privately owned so they have a variety of decors and arrangements. All look out over the Naples River, and the waterfront Dock at Crayton Cove (see "Where to Eat," below) and a chain seafood restaurant virtually flank the property. Daily rates are $108 to $120 during winter, but weekly and monthly rates are less. Off-season rates are $49 to $69. One of the biggest condo-rental agents here is **Bluebill Properties,** 26201 Hickory Blvd., Bonita Springs, FL 33923 (☎ 941/597-1102, or 800/237-2010; fax 941/597-7175).

Even the national chain motels in Naples tend to be of higher quality and better value than their counterparts elsewhere in Southwest Florida. Near Olde Naples, the **Comfort Inn on the Bay,** 1221 5th Ave. South, Naples, FL 34102 (☎ 941/ 649-5800, or 800/228-5150), enjoys a picturesque setting on Naples Bay. Known for its poolside tiki bar, the **Howard Johnson Resort Lodge,** 221 9th St. South, Naples, FL 34102 (☎ 941/262-6181, or 800/654-2000), is within walking distance of the historic district. Several chain establishments are on or near U.S. 41, including the **Best Western Naples Inn,** 2329 9th St. North, Naples, FL 34102 (☎ 941/261-1148, or 800/243-1148); the **Days Inn Naples,** 1925 Davis Blvd., Naples, FL 34102 (☎ 941/774-3117, or 800/272-0106); the **Hampton Inn,** 3210 Tamiami Trail North, Naples, FL 34102 (☎ 941/261-8000, or 800/732-4667); the **Holiday Inn Naples,** 1100 9th St. North, Naples, FL 34102 (☎ 941/262-7146, or 800/465-6329); and the **Quality Inn Gulf Coast,** 2555 Tamiami Trail North, Naples, FL 34102 (☎ 941/261-6046, or 800/330-0046). Out near Exit 15 off I-75 are a **Budgetel Inn,** 185 Bedzel Circle, Naples, FL 34102 (☎ 941/352-8400, or 800/428-3438); and a **Super 8,** 3880 Tollgate Blvd., Naples, FL 34102 (☎ 941/ 455-0808, or 800/800-8000).

DOUBLES FOR LESS THAN $40

Stoney's Courtyard Inn. 2630 N. Tamiami Trial (U.S. 41), Naples, FL 33940. ☎ 941/ 261-3870, or 800/432-3870. Fax 941/261-4932. 72 rms, 4 suites. A/C TV TEL. Winter, $85–$90 double; $120 suite. Off-season, $35–$40 double; $55–$90 suite. Rates include continental breakfast. AE, DISC, MC, V.

This pleasant, locally owned motel does indeed have a courtyard, with tropical foliage and a genuine thatch pavilion next to a heated swimming pool. The rooms facing this scene are worth an additional $5 per night over those on the parking lot side. All open to external walkways, and most are of standard motel configuration, with two double beds, a spacious dressing area with an open closet, armoires for the cable TVs, and combination baths. Restaurants are nearby on U.S. 41.

DOUBLES FOR LESS THAN $60

Lighthouse Inn. 9140 Gulf Shore Dr., Naples, FL 33963. ☎ 941/597-3345. Fax 941/ 592-1518. 1 rm, 3 efficiencies, 11 apts. A/C TV. High season, $75 double, $85 efficiency; $95 apt. Off-season, $40 double; $49 efficiency; $59 apt. MC, V.

A relic from decades gone by, this spotlessly clean, two-story motel sits across the street from other more expensive properties on Vanderbilt Beach and within walking distance of the Ritz-Carlton Naples. The efficiencies and apartments are simple, with freshly painted cinderblock walls and small kitchens. The least expensive unit here is a kitchenless room which has a small fridge and coffeemaker. Most guests take advantage of weekly and monthly rates in winter, when it's heavily booked. Buzz's Lighthouse Café next door is a pleasant place for an inexpensive, dockside lunch or dinner.

Olde Naples Inn. 801 3rd St. South, Naples, FL 33940. ☎ 941/262-5194, or 800/637-6036. Fax 941/262-4876. 60 units. A/C TV TEL. High season, $75 double; $85 efficiency; $95apt. $40 double; $49 efficiency; $59 apt. Off-season, $49–$82 double. Rates include continental breakfast. AE, DISC, MC, V.

In the heart of Olde Naples, this dated but extraordinarily well maintained apartment hotel is just 2 blocks from the beach and 4 blocks from the 3rd Street South shopping area (which more than makes up for the lack of an on-site restaurant). Its eclectic combination of rooms, efficiencies, and one- and two-bedroom suites are in three buildings occupying about 60% of a city block, but the tropical landscaping makes it seem smaller. Some of the bath and kitchen fixtures apparently date from the 1950s, but otherwise the units are comfortably furnished, are immaculately maintained, and have excellent ventilation through louvered windows front and back. There are two heated swimming pools, laundry facilities, and off-street parking.

If you can't get a unit here during winter, other comparable Olde Naples apartment hotels include the **Beachcomber Club,** 290 5th Ave. South, Naples, FL 33940 (☎ 941/262-8112); the **Mahalo Apartment Motel,** 441 8th Ave. South, Naples, FL 33940 (☎ 941/261-6332; fax 941/263-0182); and the **Neptune Apartment Hotel,** 651 3rd Ave. South, Naples, FL 33940 (☎ 941/262-6126; fax 941/263-6126).

✪ **The Tides Inn of Naples.** 1801 Gulf Shore Blvd. North, Naples, FL 33940. ☎ **941/262-6196,** or 800/438-8763. Fax 941/262-3055. 35 units. A/C TV TEL. Winter, $90–$205 double. Off-season, $59–$125 double. AE, MC, V.

There's a very good reason why this immaculate two-story motel stays heavily booked during the winter months: It's right on the beach, just one door removed from the Edgewater Beach Hotel, and on the edge of Millionaires' Row and Olde Naples. The comfortable motel rooms, suites, and efficiencies are all tropically furnished and decorated. Each has a screened balcony or patio angled to face the beach across a courtyard with coconut palms and heated swimming pool. The suites and efficiencies must be reserved during winter for at least a month; otherwise, ask for a room and pray for a cancellation. It's certainly worth a try, for you can't stay anywhere else on a Naples beach for these rates.

DOUBLES FOR LESS THAN $80

Inn at Naples. 4055 Tamiami Trail (U.S. 41), Naples, FL 33940. ☎ and fax **941/649-5500,** or 800/237-8858. 63 rms, 1 suite. A/C MINIBAR TV TEL. Winter, $130–$156 double; $250 suite. Off-season, $65–$115 double; $125–$175 suite. Rates include continental breakfast. AE, DC, DISC, MC, V.

Near Park Shore Drive and Pelican Bay, this five-story Spanish-style building with red-tile roof and arches contains guest rooms furnished with oak and pine furniture. All are equipped with easy chairs or love seats, writing desks, two telephones, TVs and VCRs, refrigerators as well as minibars, and spacious baths with separate dressing areas. Each room also has a balcony, although some are postage-stamp size and close to noise from external air-conditioning units. The inn's one suite is a 1,200-square-foot apartment called the Grand Mizner. An Italian restaurant serves lunch and dinner, either indoors or in a screened patio next to a heated, terra-cotta–lined swimming pool and whirlpool, both surrounded by colorful bougainvillea and other tropical foliage. Many business travelers who can't afford the Ritz-Carlton like to stay at this comfortable, semi-elegant establishment.

Park Shore Resort. 600 Neapolitan Way, Naples, FL 33940. ☎ **941/263-2222,** or 800/548-2077. Fax 941/262-0946. 156 suites. A/C TV TEL. Winter, $185–$210 suite. Off-season, $78–$162 suite. AE, MC, V.

Surrounding a man-made lagoon with waterfalls cascading on its own island, these attractive one- and two-bedroom condos offer much more space than hotel rooms. Guests can walk across a bridge to an artificial island, where they can swim, order from the bar, and barbecue. The Island Club restaurant serves lunch, dinner, and Sunday brunch, and there are plenty of other restaurants nearby. The resort also has tennis, racquetball, volleyball, basketball, and shuffleboard courts, plus a whirlpool, laundry room, and a children's activities program. A complimentary shuttle runs to the beach daily at 11am and 2:30pm. Although the address is on Neapolitan Way, the resort is actually at the south end of West Boulevard North.

WORTH A SPLURGE

Inn by the Sea. 287 11th Ave. South, Naples, FL 33940. ☎ **941/649-4124.** 5 rms. A/C. Winter, $130–$165 double. Off-season, $80–$95 double. Rates include continental breakfast. AE, MC, V.

Listed in the National Register of Historic Places, this home 2 blocks from the beach in the heart of Olde Naples was built in 1937 as a boarding house by Alice Bowling, one of Naples's first schoolteachers and a grocer and entrepreneur to boot. Now owned and operated by Peggy Cormier, the Federal-style house still has much of its original pine floors, matching pine or cypress woodwork, and exterior pinkish galvanized shingles. Comfy wicker furniture and ceiling fans add to the Old Florida ambience. Two of the five rooms have separate sitting areas. Guests are provided bicycles, continental breakfast, and oranges from the backyard tree. Guests must be at least 14 years old.

CAMPING

Since Naples's campgrounds are primarily long-term RV parks, you have to go 16 miles east on U.S. 41 to **Collier Seminole State Park** for a traditional camping environment (see "Parks & Nature Preserves" in Section 5 on Marco Island, later in this chapter). Of the RV parks, **Rock Creek Campgrounds,** 3100 North Rd., Naples, FL 33942 (☎ **941/643-3100**), at the corner of North and Airport-Pulling roads, is the closest to Olde Naples and the beaches. It has 200 RV-only sites for adults only. The others are about equidistant between Olde Naples and Marco Island. For RVs only, the **Kountree Kampinn R.V. Resort,** 5200 Fla. 951, Naples, FL 33961(☎ **941/775-4340**) is between I-75 and U.S. 41. Both tents and RV sites are available at both the **Naples R.V. Resort,** 10000 Alligator Alley, Naples, FL 33962 (☎ **941/455-7275**), at I-75 and Fla. 951 (Exit 15), and the **Naples/Marco Island KOA Kampground,** 1700 Barefoot Williams Rd., Naples, FL 33962 (☎ **941/774-5455**), off Fla. 951 about 1½ miles south of U.S. 41.

WHERE TO EAT

Many first-time visitors opt to have a lunch or dinner at the Marketplace at Tin City, on the Gordon River at 5th Avenue South, where the **Riverwalk Fish & Ale House** (☎ 941/262-2734) and **Merriman's Wharf** (☎ 941/261-1811) specialize in moderately priced seafood and have live entertainment during the season.

You'll find budget-priced fast-food and family-style restaurants along U.S. 41.

MEALS FOR LESS THAN $7

The English Pub. 2408 Linwood Ave. (off Commercial Dr.). ☎ **941/774-2408.** Reservations not accepted. Main courses $6.50–$15; burgers and sandwiches $5–$7. MC, V. Mon–Fri 11am–9:30pm, Sat noon–9:30pm. (Bar stays open to midnight.) ENGLISH.

Since 1982 hospitable Brits Viv and Brian Stuart have been offering darts, English draft beers, and authentic pub meals like fish and chips, Yorkshire pudding, and steak-and-kidney pie at this establishment in a warehouse district east of the Gordon River. The chow isn't spicy or great—it's English, after all—but the fish and chips are worthy of London. The Stuarts have karaoke entertainment on Friday after 9:30pm.

✪ **First Watch.** In Gulf Shore Square, 1400 Gulf Shore Blvd. (at Banyon Rd.). ☎ **941/ 434-0005.** Reservations not accepted. Breakfast, lunch salads, sandwiches $3.50–$6.50. AE, DISC, MC, V. Daily 7am–2:30pm. AMERICAN.

This corner shop with big louvered shutters to temper the morning sun is one of Naples' favorite spots for breakfast, late brunch, or a midday meal. The First Watch is far from being a diner, however, for classical music sets the tone, the tables are widely spaced and topped with pitchers of lemon-tinged ice water, and a young service staff provides quick and friendly service. While bacon and eggs are served, the morning specialties here are omelets, made-from-scratch pancakes, and crêpes. Some dishes are creative, such as a sizzling skillet with layers of potatoes, vegetables, melted cheese, and fried eggs. Lunch features large salads, sandwiches, and quesadillas. In addition to the dining room, there's additional seating in the shopping center's courtyard.

MEALS FOR LESS THAN $10

Bayside, A Seafood Grill and Bar. In the Village on Venetian Bay, 4270 Gulf Shore Blvd. North. ☎ **941/649-5552.** Reservations required upstairs only. Downstairs, sandwiches, pasta, and light meals $6.50–$11.50. Upstairs, main courses $15.50–$25. AE, DC, DISC, MC, V. Winter, downstairs, daily 2–11pm; upstairs, daily 11am–2pm and 5:30–10pm. Off-season, downstairs, daily 2–10pm; upstairs, daily 11:30am–2pm and 5:30–9pm. SEAFOOD.

This restaurant in the southern half of the Village on Venetian Bay shops is a two-level eatery. Upstairs is more expensive and formal, with gorgeous water views enhancing continental gourmet cuisine featuring seafood with an appropriate Mediterranean flair. The casual downstairs dining area specializes in inexpensive pastas, sandwiches, and salads. Both have sinfully delicious desserts. Entertainment is featured in the downstairs bar, nightly during the winter season and on weekends the rest of the year. There's valet parking after 6pm in winter.

Silver Spoon Café. In the Waterside Shops at Pelican Bay, 5395 Tamiami Trail North (at Seagate Dr.). ☎ **941/591-2123.** Reservations not accepted, but call ahead for preferred seating. Main courses $7–$14; pizza and pasta $6.50–$8.50; soups, salads, sandwiches $6–$8.50. AE, DC, DISC, MC, V. Sun–Thurs 11am–10pm, Fri–Sat 11am–11pm. AMERICAN/ ITALIAN.

Befitting the swanky Waterside Shops complex, this chic cafe flaunts sophisticated black-and-white high-tech decor and sports large window walls looking out to the mall action. Thick sandwiches are served either with french fries, spicy pecan rice, or black beans. The tomato-dill soup and the gourmet pizzas and pasta dishes are popular, especially with the after-theater crowds from the nearby Philharmonic Center for the Arts. The Silver Spoon doesn't accept reservations, but call ahead to get on the waiting list.

MEALS FOR LESS THAN $15

✪ **Bistro 821.** 821 5th Ave. South (between 8th and 9th sts. South). ☎ **941/261-5821.** Reservations recommended. Main courses $9–$16. AE, MC, V. Daily 5–10:30pm. MEDITERRANEAN.

At the eastern end of the chic 5th Avenue South shopping strip, this casual, noisy bistro is very popular with local professionals of every age. A tapestry-covered bench runs down one side of this storefront to an open kitchen in the rear. Small spotlights hanging from the ceiling illuminate each table. Although the house specialty is rotisserie chicken, a daily risotto leads a menu featuring Mediterranean flavors, such as penne pasta in a vodka sauce, bouillabaisse, and a seasonal vegetable plate with herb couscous. There's sidewalk dining here, too.

✪ **Chef's Garden/Truffles.** 1300 3rd St. South (actually faces 13th Ave. South between 2nd and 3rd sts. South), in Olde Naples. ☎ **941/262-5500.** Reservations recommended in the

Chef's Garden. Chef's Garden, main courses $18.50–$27. Truffles, main courses $11.50–$18; sandwiches and salads $7–$11. AE, DC, DISC, MC, V. Chef's Garden, Mon–Sat 11:30am–2:30pm and 6–9:30pm, Sun 6–9:30pm. Truffles, Mon–Thurs 11am–10pm, Fri–Sat 11am–11pm, Sun 11am–2pm (brunch). Closed lunch at the Chef's Garden June–Sept. CREATIVE/CLASSICAL.

These two casual eateries are located in the heart of the 3rd Avenue South shopping district. Rated one of Naples's finest, the expensive Chef's Garden downstairs looks out on a screened tropical garden patio. Soft lighting and tropical foliage lend it a romantic air. Its intriguing dinner selections such as Dijon honey-glazed Chilean salmon served on a bed of dill mashed potatoes with a roasted-shallot/port-wine vinaigrette are worth a splurge. Frugal travelers will head upstairs to the lively bistro known as Truffles, which offers moderately priced pastas, a grand variety of sandwiches, interesting salads, and light main dishes.

The Dock at Crayton Cove. 12th Ave. South (at the City Dock), in Olde Naples. ☎ **941/263-9940.** Reservations not accepted. Main courses $11–$14; sandwiches $4.50–$9. AE, DISC, MC, V. Mon–Sat 11:30am–1am, Sun noon–midnight. SEAFOOD.

Right on the City Dock, brothers Phil and Vin De Pasquale's restaurant is a lively place for an open-air meal or a libation while watching the action out on Naples Bay. Their chow emphasizes local seafood, from hearty chowders by the mug to grilled swordfish, with Jamaican-style jerk shrimp thrown in for spice. On the light side, there's grilled seafood Caesar salad, and the Dock offers a good selection of sandwiches, hot dogs, and other pub-style fare. Unlike the De Pasquales' other establishment, the tourist-frequented Riverwalk Fish House at Tin City, this one is highly popular with local residents.

Michelbob's Rib Capital of Florida. 371 Airport-Pulling Rd. (at Progress Ave.). ☎ **941/643-7427.** Reservations not accepted. Sandwiches $3.50–$6.50; platters $8–$19. AE, DC, MC, V. Winter, Mon–Thurs 11am–9pm, Fri–Sat 11am–10pm, Sun 8am–1:30pm (brunch) and 1:30–9pm; off-season, Mon–Sat 11am–9pm, Sun 8:30am–1:30pm (brunch) and 1:30–9pm. BARBECUE.

The name says it all about this barnlike establishment, winner of national and international cook-offs for the best ribs and barbecue sauces. The big specialty is baby back ribs, imported from Denmark (where the hogs are reputedly tulip-fed). Sliced pork or beef are the least expensive items here, but they can be dry and don't come close to matching the quality of the ribs. There's a children's menu, and an extensive Sunday brunch buffet. The smoke aroma comes from the barbecue pit, not cigarettes, since no smoking is permitted.

St. George and the Dragon. 936 5th Ave. South (at 10th St. South). ☎ **941/262-6546.** Reservations not accepted. Main courses $10.50–$30. AE, DC, MC, V. Winter, Mon–Sat 11am–10pm, Sun 5–9pm; off-season, Mon–Sat 11am–10pm. Closed Sun Apr–Dec and Christmas Day. STEAK/SEAFOOD.

A local favorite since 1969, this establishment definitely is a respite from the subtropical sun, since it looks like the dark below-decks of a Spanish galleon. Exposed beams, a collection of marine antiques, and ships' lanterns providing dim lighting all create a cozy, romantic atmosphere in which to enjoy the famous conch chowder, succulent prime rib, juicy steaks, and grilled fresh fish. The lunch menu offers soups, salads, burgers, and smaller portions of the dinner selections—the latter are excellent value. Jackets are required for men in the dining room after 4pm, but not in the cocktail lounge where a round bar is surrounded by cozy tables. Valet parking is provided after 5pm, or enter the lot directly from 6th Avenue South.

Villa Pescatore / Plum's Café. 8920 Tamiami Trail North (at Vanderbilt Beach and Hickory rds.). ☎ **941/597-8119.** Reservations recommended for Villa Pescatore, not accepted at Plum's Café. Villa Pescatore, main courses $20–$25. Plum's Café, main courses $9–$17; salads and sandwiches $6–$8.50. AE, DC, DISC, MC, V. Villa Pescatore, daily 6–10pm. Plum's Café, Mon–Sat 11am–11pm, Sun 5–11pm. From the Tamiami Trail (U.S. 41), turn east on Hickory Road, then make an immediate left onto the service road running beside the Tamiami Trail. ITALIAN.

Another of Naples's two-in-one eateries, these highly acclaimed restaurants offer a choice of dining elegantly in Villa Pescatore or lightly and casually in Plum's Café. Plum's scrumptious and reasonably priced sandwiches, salads, and pastas are especially popular with local families. The recipient of numerous dining and wine selection awards, Villa Pescatore is noted for its regional Italian specialties. Sturdy wicker chairs help create a tropical elegance in Villa Pescatore, and windowed walls present a view of tropical foliage outside the building.

WORTH A SPLURGE

✪ **Sign of the Vine.** 980 Solana Rd. (off Tamiami Trail North, behind DeVoe Cadillac). ☎ **941/261-6745.** Reservations required. Main courses $25–$48. AE. Oct–May, Mon–Sat 6–10pm; Aug–Sept, Fri–Sat 6–10pm. Closed June–July. INTERNATIONAL.

Ever since owners/chefs Nancy and John Christiansen converted this gracious, old-fashioned house in 1985, their gourmet restaurant has been the kind of place Neapolitans go for special celebrations when price comes second to fine cuisine and romantic ambience. Flickering candlelight, a fireplace, fresh flowers, antique dinnerware, and hand-lettered menus presented in a silver picture frame are perfect for such occasions. The Christiansens offer a creative international menu, including Jack's lobster hash with mushrooms and artichokes in a sassy Pernod-cream sauce accompanied by vegetable baklava. All dinners come with homemade country cheese, relish cart, salad with Nancy's own dressing, home-baked French bread, Ohio tomato pudding, corn soufflé with sweet-onion cream, hot popovers with tangerine-and-lime butter, and fresh orange-and-ginger sorbet. Nancy specializes in grandmother-style desserts like warm bread pudding with a whiskey-and-brown-sugar sauce.

GREAT PICNIC FARE

Naples's beaches are ideal for picnics. In Olde Naples, you can get freshly baked breads and pastries, prepacked gourmet sandwiches, and fruit plates at **Tony's Off Third,** 1300 3rd St. South (☎ **941/262-7999**). Although inexpensive, it shares the quality kitchen of the excellent Chef's Garden and Truffles restaurants next door (see above). It's also a fine place for coffee while window-shopping on 3rd Avenue South. The **Pelicatessen,** in the Waterside Shops at Pelican Bay, Seagate Drive at Tamiami Trail North (☎ **941/597-3003**), offers imported cheeses, freshly sliced meats, unusual salads, and shelves of gourmet items. Buy there and take it to Clam Pass County Park, at the end of Seagate Drive.

NAPLES AFTER DARK

For entertainment ideas, check the *Naples Daily News,* especially the "Neapolitan" section in Friday's edition.

THE PERFORMING ARTS   The impressive ✪ **Philharmonic Center for the Arts,** 5833 Pelican Bay Blvd., at West Boulevard (☎ **941/597-1900**), is the home of the **Naples Philharmonic,** but its year-round schedule is filled with cultural events like the Bolshoi Ballet, concerts by celebrated artists and internationally known orchestras, as well as Broadway plays and shows aimed at children and families. Call ahead or pick up a copy of its seasonal calendar at the chamber of commerce (see "Essentials," above).

The ornately decorated, turn-of-the-century–style **Naples Dinner Theater,** 1025 Piper Blvd., off Immokalee Road near Airport-Pulling Road (☎ **941/ 597-6031,** or 800/741-3108 in Florida), features a "Music Mania" format—high-energy revues drawn from Broadway and Hollywood musicals of the 1950s and other memorable eras. The entertainers bring the fun to your table by delivering the meals. Cocktails and dinner begin Tuesday to Saturday at 5:30pm, with show time at 8:15pm. Thursday, Saturday, and Sunday matinees begin at 11:15am, with curtain at 1:15pm. Tickets cost $20 and are credited toward the entree of your choice.

THE CLUB & BAR SCENE Much of Naples's nightlife centers on the local hotels and restaurants. The beachside "Chickee Hut" bar and Brassie's at the **Naples Beach Hotel & Golf Club,** 851 Gulf Shore Blvd. (☎ 941/261-2222), are always popular and have live entertainment many nights. So is the beachside bar at the **Vanderbilt Inn on the Gulf,** 11000 Gulf Shore Dr. (☎ 941/597-3151), starting at sunset. Revels nightclub in the **Registry Resort,** 475 Seagate Dr. (☎ 941/ 597-3232), has live music for listening nightly during winter, on weekends off-season. Among the restaurants, both **Bayside, a Seafood Grille & Bar,** 4270 Gulf Shore Blvd. North, in the Village on Venetian Bay (☎ 941/649-5552), and the **Chef's Garden,** 1300 3rd St. South (☎ 941/262-5500), have pianists or jazz musicians. Since their schedules vary by season, it's always best to call ahead.

The **Olde Naples Pub,** 255 13th Ave. South (☎ 941/649-8200), in the 3rd Street South shopping area, has a pianist Monday to Saturday evening and jazz in the courtyard on Sunday from 5 to 8pm. This American-style pub serves soups, sandwiches, salads, burgers, and pizza. Open Monday to Saturday from 11am to midnight and on Sunday from noon to 11pm.

The **Old Marine Marketplace at Tin City,** the restored waterfront warehouses on 5th Avenue South on the west side of the Gordon River, comes alive during the winter when visitors flock to its shops and two lively restaurants, the **Riverwalk Fish & Ale House** (☎ 941/262-2734) and **Merriman's Wharf** (☎ 941/261-1811), both of which have live entertainment during the season.

5 Marco Island

15 miles SE of Naples, 53 miles S of Fort Myers, 100 miles W of Miami

Captain William Collier would hardly recognize Marco Island if he were to come back from the grave today. No relation to Collier County founder Barron Collier, the captain settled his family on the north end of this largest of Florida's Ten Thousand Islands back in 1871. He traded pelts with the Native Americans, caught and smoked fish to sell to Key West and Cuba, and charged fishermen and other guests $2 a day for a room in his home. By 1896 he was doing such a roaring tourist business that he built a proper inn.

His Old Marco Inn still stands (it's now a fine restaurant), along with a few other turn-of-the-century buildings. But Captain Collier would be shocked to find the western half of Marco Island now sliced by man-made canals and virtually covered by resorts, condos, shops, restaurants, and vacation homes, all products of an extensive real-estate development begun in 1965. Indeed, Collier's little outpost has become a modern beach retreat for a broad spectrum of visitors, from the famous on down.

Marco's year-round population of 10,000 swells to more than 30,000 during the winter season. What makes it attractive to so many visitors is a long, crescent-shaped beach along its western gulf shore, nearby waterways running through a multitude of small islands, excellent boating and fishing on both the gulf and those waterways, and proximity to thousands of acres of wildlife preserves.

ESSENTIALS

GETTING THERE By Plane See "Essentials" in both Section 1 on Fort Myers and Section 2 on Naples, earlier in this chapter, for information about the Southwest Florida International Airport and the Naples Municipal Airport, respectively.

By Car From either I-75 or U.S. 41, take Fla. 951 south directly to Marco Island.

VISITOR INFORMATION The **Marco Island Area Chamber of Commerce,** 1102 N. Collier Blvd., Marco Island, FL 33937 (☎ **941/394-7549** or 800/ 788-6272; fax 941/394-3061), provides free information about the island. There's a board and phone outside for making hotel reservations even when the office is closed.

GETTING AROUND By Taxi & Limo Call **A-Action Taxi** (☎ 941/ 394-4400), **Classic Taxi** (☎ 941/394-1888), or **Kay's Executive Limo** (☎ 941/ 394-1033).

By Trolley Starting and ending at the Marriott resort, **Marco Island Trolley Tours** (☎ **941/394-1600**) makes four complete loops around the island Monday to Saturday from 10am to 3:15pm. The conductors sell tickets and render an informative narration about the island's history. Daily fare is $10 for adults, $4 for children 11 and under, with free reboarding.

By Bicycle Depending on the type, rental bicycles cost $10 to $20 a day at **Beach Sports,** 571 S. Collier Blvd. (☎ **941/642-4282**), opposite the Hilton, and at **Scootertown,** 842 Bald Eagle Dr. (☎ **941/394-8400**), north of North Collier Boulevard near Old Marco. Scooters cost $45 a day.

BEACHES & OUTDOOR ACTIVITIES

BEACHES A 3¹/₂-mile-long sugar-white beach curves down the entire western shore of Marco Island. The southern 2 miles are fronted by an unending row of high-rise condos and hotels, but the northern 1¹/₂ miles is preserved in ✪ **Tigertail Public Beach** (☎ **941/642-8414**). A sandbar offshore here creates a shallow lagoon safe for swimming and perfect for learning to windsurf. There are rest rooms, cold-water outdoor showers, a children's playground, and volleyball nets. Tigertail Beach Rentals gives windsurfing lessons, conducts pontoon-boat nature and shelling tours, and rents cabanas, chairs, umbrellas, sailboats, windsurfers, kayaks, water tricycles, and other toys. A display illustrates the shells you'll find lying on the beach. **Todd's at Tigertail** (☎ **941/394-8828**) has a fully screened patio where it serves inexpensive hot dogs, sandwiches, salads, and other snacks daily from 10am to 4pm. The park is at the end of Hernando Drive. It's open daily from dawn to dusk. There's no admission charge for the beach, but parking in the lot costs $3 per vehicle.

Collier County also maintains a free parking lot and access to the developed beach on the southern end of the island, on Swallow Avenue at South Collier Boulevard.

BOATING & FISHING Sailing enthusiasts can slice the waters on **Captain Quinn's Catamaran Tours,** at Marriott's Marco Island Resort and Golf Club, 400 S. Collier Blvd. (☎ **941/642-2740**).

Powerboats can be rented for $65 half a day, $100 all day, at the **Marco Island Marina** (☎ 941/394-2502), **Pier 81 Marina Power Boat Rental** at the Pier 81 Marina (☎ 941/642-7881), the **Factory Bay Marina** (☎ 941/642-6717), and **Marco Island Power Boats** (☎ 941/394-1006). All are on Bald Eagle Drive north of Collier Boulevard.

Those same marinas are home to a number of **charter-fishing captains** and will help make arrangements for half- or full-day excursions. Call at least a day in advance.

CANOEING   Both Collier Seminole State Park and Briggs Nature Center have canoe trails and rent canoes. See "Parks & Nature Preserves" under "What to See & Do," below.

GOLF & TENNIS   The closest golf courses are at the **Marco Shores Golf Club,** 1450 Mainsail Dr. (☎ **941/394-2581**), and **Marriott's Golf Club at Marco** (☎ **941/353-7061**), both in the marshlands off Fla. 951 north of the island (a sign at the Marriott's course ominously warns: PLEASE DON'T DISTURB THE ALLIGATORS).

Tennis courts are at the **Marco Island YMCA** (☎ 941/394-3144) and the **Collier County Racquet Club** (☎ 941/394-5454), both on San Marco Road, and at the **Tommie Barfield Elementary School,** at Trinidad Avenue and Kirkwood Street (☎ 941/394-2611).

WATER SPORTS   **Marco Island Jet Ski & Watersports,** at the Marriott's Marco Island Resort and Golf Club, 400 S. Collier Blvd. (☎ **941/394-6589**); and **Day Sports,** at the Marco Island Hilton Beach Resort, 560 S. Collier Blvd. (☎ **941/ 394-5000,** ext. 659), both rent jet skis, Waverunners, bumper tubes, aqua-trikes, and windsurfers, and take guests parasailing and waterskiing. **Beach Sports,** 571 S. Collier Blvd. (☎ **941/642-4282**), opposite the Marco Island Hilton Beach Resort, rents jet skis, windsurfers, snorkeling gear, skim boards, fishing gear, tennis racquets, and a wide range of other equipment, including beach baby strollers.

WHAT TO SEE & DO
PARKS & NATURE PRESERVES

Many species of birds inhabit ✪ **Collier Seminole State Park,** 20200 Tamiami Trail East (U.S. 41), just east of Fla. 92 (☎ **941/394-3397**), an inviting, 6,423-acre preserve on the edge of Big Cypress Swamp 12 miles east of Marco Island. Given to the state by Barron Collier, it offers fishing, boating, picnicking, canoeing over a 13-mile loop with a primitive campsite, observing nature along 6 miles of hiking trails (open during dry periods) and a 1-mile nature walk, and regular tent and RV camping (see "Where to Stay," below). A "walking" dredge used to build the Tamiami Trail in the 1920s sits just inside the park entrance. Housed in a replica of a Seminole Wars–era log fort, an interpretive center has information about the park. Narrated boat tours wander through the winding waterways daily from 9am to 5pm. Canoes can be rented, but the park has room for only four people to camp along the canoe trails. Admission to the park is $3.25 per vehicle, $1 for pedestrians and bikers. The boat tours cost $8.50 for adults, $5.50 for children 6 to 12, and free for children 5 and under. Canoes rent for $3 per hour, $15 a day. The park is open daily from 8am to sundown.

Operated by the Conservancy and part of the Rookery Bay National Estuarine Research Reserve, the ✪ **Briggs Nature Center,** on Shell Island Road, off Fla. 951 between U.S. 41 and Marco Island (☎ **941/775-8569**), has a half-mile boardwalk from which visitors can observe a great variety of birds in their natural habitat (binoculars and a guidebook are provided). Narrated pontoon-boat trips take place Tuesday to Saturday from December to April. Another trip goes shelling on Keewaydin Island. The park also has narrated canoe excursions twice a week, including sunset trips when the birds are nesting, as well as a self-guided canoe trail and canoes for rent. The center is open October to June, Monday to Saturday from 9am to 4:30pm (plus Sunday from 1 to 5pm January to March); July to September, Monday to Friday from 9am to 4:30pm. The nature center is free. Admission to the boardwalk is $2 for adults, $1 for children 6 to 17, free for children 5 and under. Canoe trips cost $20. Canoe rentals are $12 for the first 2 hours, $2 for each additional hour.

CRUISES

In addition to the boat and canoe excursions at Collier Seminole State Park and the Briggs Nature Center (see above), several Marco Island boats offer backcountry fishing, shelling, sightseeing, and sunset excursions through these beautiful inland waterways. The best source of information, and the easiest way to book any of them, is through **Sea Excursions, Inc.** (☎ **941/642-6400**). Per-person prices are all the same: $20 for sightseeing, $25 for shelling, $35 for fishing, and $25 for sunset cruises. Reservations are required.

Two airboats, the *Everglades Flyer* and the *Marco Eagle,* make two or more Ten Thousand Islands voyages a day during the winter, one during the off-season, from Factory Bay Marina on Bald Eagle Drive (☎ **941/642-6717**). Fares are $20 per person.

The *Rosie* (☎ **941/394-7673**), an old-fashioned, 105-foot-long paddlewheeler, has year-round sightseeing cruises for $15 per person and lunch buffet and dinner cruises for $27. You can take either the lunch or sunset cruise without the meal for $20. The *Rosie* docks at Pier 81 Marina on Bald Eagle Drive north of Collier Boulevard.

Royal Princess **Casino Cruises** (☎ **941/642-1001,** or 800/310-5665) has two daylight gambling cruises on the *Royal Princess* daily during the winter, less often off-season (see "Marco Island After Dark," below).

WHERE TO STAY

There are no chain hotels on Marco Island other than the expensive Marriott's Marco Island Resort and Golf Club, the Marco Island Hilton Beach Resort, and the Radisson Suite Beach Resort, which stand in a row along the beach on the island's southwestern corner and are the center of beach activities. On the other hand, Marco is loaded with condominium-style resorts. Ask the **Marco Island Area Chamber of Commerce** (see "Essentials," above) for its list of condos and rental agents.

As elsewhere in South Florida, the high season here is from mid-December to mid-April. See "Where to Stay" in Section 1 on Fort Myers, earlier in this chapter, for how the price categories were determined.

DOUBLES FOR LESS THAN $60

Boat House Motel. 1180 Edington Place, Marco Island, FL 33937. ☎ **941/642-2400.** Fax 941/642-2435. 20 rms, 3 condos, 1 cottage. A/C TV TEL. Winter, $75–$149 double; $125–$200 condo or cottage. Off-season, $50–$70 double; $75–$125 condo or cottage. MC, V.

One of the best bargains in these parts, this comfortable little motel sits beside the Marco River in Old Marco, on the island's northern end. The rooms are in a two-story, lime-green-and-white building ending at a wooden dock. Here there's a small heated swimming pool with lounge furniture, picnic tables, and barbecue grills. Two rooms on the end have their own decks, and all open to tiny courtyards. Bright paint, ceiling fans, and louvered doors add a tropical ambience throughout. The one-bedroom condos next door open to a riverside dock, upon which is built a two-bedroom cottage named "The Gazebo," whose peaked roof is supported by umbrellalike spokes from a central pole. Facilities include a guest laundry, a small library, and bicycle rentals. Olde Marco restaurants are a short stroll away.

CAMPING

There's no campground in the developed part of Marco Island. **Collier Seminole State Park,** 20200 Tamiami Trail East, Naples, FL 33961 (☎ **941/394-3397;** fax 941/394-5113), 12 miles east via Fla. 92, has 130 tent and RV sites laid out in circles and shaded by palms and live oaks. It has hot showers and a screened, open-air lounge. In winter, sites cost $16 with electricity, $14 without. Off-season rates are $10.75 with electricity, $8.50 without. Reservations are accepted 2 to 6 weeks in advance.

WHERE TO EAT

You won't go hungry here. Every shopping center has at least two eateries, and most pubs offer light fare. The *Marco Islander* weekly newspaper and the free *Marco Review* tourist publication, available from the chamber of commerce (see "Essentials," above) contain lists with descriptions of restaurants.

For inexpensive fare, head for the Town Center Mall, at the corner of North Collier Boulevard and Bald Eagle Drive, where you'll find three good choices. **Breakfast Plus** (☎ **941/642-6900**) has terrific eye-openers ranging from bacon and eggs to kippers to latkes. It's open daily from 7am to 2:30pm. **Susie's Diner** (☎ **941/ 642-6633**) is popular with the locals for breakfasts and especially for Susie's $5 full-meal lunch specials. She's open Monday to Saturday from 6:30am to 2:30pm and on Sunday from 6:30am to 1pm (for breakfast only). The **Kahuna Restaurant** (☎ **941/394-4300**) provides inexpensive family fare, including some of Marco's best burgers, daily from 11am to 9pm.

The island's popular sports bars also offer inexpensive pub fare to go with their multitudinous TVs. Most popular is **Rookie's Bar & Grill,** in Mission de San Marco Plaza, at the corner of South Collier Boulevard and Winterberry Drive (☎ **941/ 394-6400**). Others are the **Crazy Flamingo,** in the Town Center Mall, at North Collier Boulevard at Bald Eagle Drive (☎ **941/642-9600**); and the **Sand Bar,** on Bald Eagle Drive north of North Collier Boulevard (☎ **941/642-3625**).

MEALS FOR LESS THAN $15

Bavarian Inn. 960 Winterberry Dr. (at S. Collier Blvd.). ☎ **941/394-7233.** Reservations recommended in winter. Main courses $13–$17; early-bird specials (served daily 4:30–6pm) $9–$11. AE, DC, DISC, MC, V. Daily 4:30–10:30pm (with a late-night menu 10:30pm–1:30am). GERMAN/STEAKS.

This cozy establishment with exposed beams and dark-wood furniture has a suitably Bavarian-inn atmosphere in which to serve German cuisine. The house specialty is sauerbraten in rotwein (pork marinated for 3 days in a red-wine sauce and then slowly roasted). Prime rib, aged in-house, and steaks are also featured. German wines and draft beers are offered from a casual lounge.

✪ **Kretch's.** 527 Bald Eagle Dr. (south of N. Collier Blvd.). ☎ **941/394-3433.** Reservations recommended in winter. Main courses $11.50–$23. DC, MC, V. Mon–Sat 11am–9pm, Sun 5–9pm. Closed Sun Easter–Thanksgiving, and major holidays. SEAFOOD/MEXICAN.

Noted pastry chef Bruce Kretschmer has created a sinfully rich seafood strudel by combining shrimp, crab, scallops, cheeses, cream, and broccoli in a flaky Bavarian pastry and serving it all under a lobster sauce. Cholesterol counters can choose from broiled or charcoal-grilled fish, shrimp, Florida lobster tail, steaks, or lamb chops. Bruce's popular "Mexican Friday" lunches feature delicious tacos and other inexpensive south-of-the-border selections. Sunday is home-cooking night in winter, with chicken and dumplings, Yankee pot roast, and braised lamb shanks.

Little Bar & Restaurant. Harbor Place (County Rd. 892), Goodland. ☎ **941/394-5663.** Reservations recommended for dinner. Main courses $13–$21. DISC, MC, V. Daily 11:30am–10pm. (Bar stays open until 2am.) Closed Aug. SEAFOOD.

This very casual waterfront establishment is located in the heart of Goodland, an Old Florida fishing village on the eastern edge of Marco Island, some 7 miles—and at least 30 years—removed from the heavily developed western end of the island. One dining room here actually was the interior of the *Star of the Everglades,* a boat which took Presidents Truman and Eisenhower around and appeared in the Burl Ives movie *Winds Across the Everglades.* Other rooms possess antique bits and pieces from various buildings in the Chicago area, including an old pipe organ. A screened porch beside Goodland's fishing boat harbor is this area's most popular spot for lunches featuring seafood and other sandwiches. Daily specials from a nightly chalkboard might include Everglades frogs' legs.

✪ **Olde Marco Inn.** 100 Palm St., Old Marco. ☎ **941/394-3131.** Reservations recommended. Main courses $13–$25. AE, DC, DISC, MC, V. Mon–Fri 11:30am–2:30pm and 5:30–10pm, Sat–Sun 5:30–10pm. INTERNATIONAL.

Built by Capt. William Collier in 1883 and fully restored to Victorian elegance by its present-day owner, Marion Blomeier, this large clapboard building has several dining rooms and a pleasant veranda, all richly furnished (the huge crystal chandelier dominating the ballroom belonged to the late band leader Guy Lombardo). Seafood, beef, chops, and poultry are prepared with an international flair appropriate to Mrs. Blomeier's continental birth. Relax before or after dinner in the popular piano bar.

Snook Inn. 1215 Bald Eagle Dr. (at Palm St.), Old Marco. ☎ **941/394-3313.** Reservations not accepted. Main courses $10–$18; sandwiches $7.50–$9. AE, DC, DISC, MC, V. Daily 11am–10pm. SEAFOOD.

On the scenic Marco River, this Old Florida establishment offers indoor and outdoor seating at lunch and dinner. Although seafood is the specialty, tasty steaks, chicken, burgers, and sandwiches are among the choices. The dockside Chickee Bar is a fun place, especially during sunset happy hour Monday to Friday from 4 to 6pm. Live entertainment is featured during the winter season. Call for free shuttle service from anywhere on Marco Island.

MARCO ISLAND AFTER DARK

The **Olde Marco Inn,** the **Snook Inn,** and **Konrad's** all have live entertainment nightly during the winter season. The schedules vary by season, so call ahead.

One of the most lively local spots is **La Casita Mexican Restaurant,** in the Shops of Marco, San Marco Road at Barfield Drive (☎ **941/642-7600**), where owners Frankie Ray and Maryellen play a variety of Mexican, Irish, popular, and traditional music Monday to Saturday. On Sunday, 1950s and 1960s dance music is highlighted.

Other establishments with entertainment include **Alan's Hideaway Piano Bar,** 23 Front St. (☎ **941/642-0770**), where owner Alan Bogdan plays.

Royal Princess **Casino Cruises** (☎ **941/642-1001,** or 800/310-5665) sends the 157-foot-long *Royal Princess* 9 miles offshore so patrons can legally wager at the blackjack, roulette, and craps tables and play stud poker and slots. There's also dining and live music for dancing on board. Call for seasonal schedules and prices. No one under 18 is allowed on board. The ship departs from Pier 81 Marina on Bald Eagle Drive near Old Marco.

Index

FOR RESERVATIONS CALL:

Sleep	1-800-62-SLEEP
Comfort	1-800-228-5150
Quality	1-800-228-5151
Clarion	1-800-CLARION
Econo Lodge	1-800-55-ECONO
Rodeway	1-800-228-2000

Advance reservations are required through 1-800-4-CHOICE. Discounts are based on availability at participating hotels and cannot be used in conjunction with other discounts or promotions.

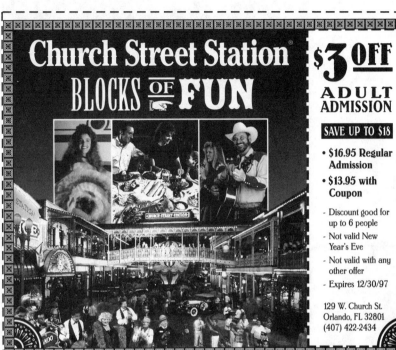

DAYS INN
Follow the Sun™

- **Available at participating properties.**
- **This coupon cannot be combined with any other special discount offer.**
- **Limit one coupon per room, per stay.**
- **Not valid during blackout periods or special events.**
- **Void where prohibited.**
- **No reproductions accepted.**
- **Expires December 31, 1997.**

1-800-DAYS INN

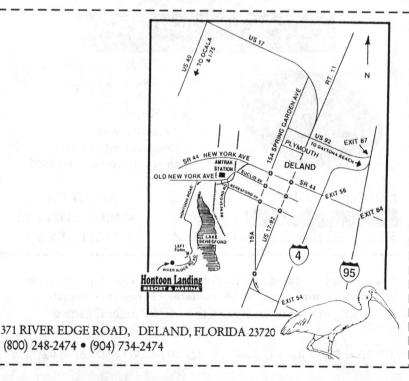

371 RIVER EDGE ROAD, DELAND, FLORIDA 23720
(800) 248-2474 • (904) 734-2474

Limit six guests per certificate. Not valid with other discounts or on purchase of multi-park/multi-visit passes or tickets. Present certificate at Front Gate before bill is totaled. Redeemable only at time of ticket purchase. Photocopies not accepted. Operating hours and general admission price subject to change without notice.

Valid through 12/30/97 only.

Orlando, Florida
Let the Adventure Begin.

4858/4857

$3.00 OFF ADULT ADMISSION
ONE-DAY STUDIO PASS

Regular adult admission price $38.50 (plus tax) Valid for up to 6 people through 12/31/97.
See back of coupon for details.

**Thrill to over 400 acres of incredible ride, shows and attractions!
Face the all out attack of JAWS®!
Meet Barney® and friends, Baby Bop™ and BJ™
in their live sing-along new show.
Face the fury of King Kong. Rocket Back To The Future®
on the greatest ride in history! All of this and more!
Universal Studios Florida® — the only place on earth
where you can Ride the Movies®!
New for 1997: Terminator 2: 3-D℠ The World's First and Only
3-D Virtual Adventure!**

Save $2 on
admission to

Wet'n Wild®
INTERNATIONAL DRIVE, ORLANDO

Good for up to six people.
Not to be used in conjunction with
any other offer or afternoon pricing.
Expires 12/31/97
Macmillan Travel PLU 6A 7C

**Discount valid for up to 6 people
through 12/31/97. Coupon has no cash value
and is not valid with any other offers.
Offer subject to change without notice.
Parking fee not included.
©1996 Universal Studios Florida
All Rights Reserved.**

Gatorland
Orlando

Located on Hwy 441 in South Orlando. From I-4 take exit 26A to 417 north - take exit 11 to Hwy 441 south one mile and Gatorland is on the left.

Call: 800-393-JAWS or 407-855-5496

$1.00 OFF   **$1.00 OFF**

TWO GREAT LOCATIONS!

5390 W. Irlo Bronson Hwy.192
KISSIMMEE, FL

8815 International Drive
ORLANDO, FL

407-345-0501

$1.50 OFF ADULT   **$1.00 OFF CHILD**

Ripley's
Believe It or Not!®
ORLANDO MUSEUM

8201 International Drive, Orlando, FL
407-345-0501

Green Meadows Farm, Ltd.
P.O. Box 420787
Kissimmee, FL 34742-0787

Call: 407/846-0770

FROMMER'S COMPLETE TRAVEL GUIDES
*(Comprehensive guides to destinations around the world, with
selections in all price ranges—from deluxe to budget)*

FROMMER'S FRUGAL TRAVELER'S GUIDES
*(The grown-up guides to budget travel, offering dream vacations
at down-to-earth prices)*

Australia from $45 a Day	India from $40 a Day
Berlin from $50 a Day	Ireland from $45 a Day
California from $60 a Day	Italy from $50 a Day
Caribbean from $60 a Day	Israel from $45 a Day
Costa Rica & Belize from $35 a Day	London from $60 a Day
Eastern Europe from $30 a Day	Mexico from $35 a Day
England from $50 a Day	New York from $70 a Day
Europe from $50 a Day	New Zealand from $45 a Day
Florida from $50 a Day	Paris from $65 a Day
Greece from $45 a Day	Washington, D.C. from $50 a Day
Hawaii from $60 a Day	

FROMMER'S PORTABLE GUIDES
(Pocket-size guides for travelers who want everything in a nutshell)

Charleston & Savannah	New Orleans
Las Vegas	San Francisco

FROMMER'S IRREVERENT GUIDES
(Wickedly honest guides for sophisticated travelers)

Amsterdam	Miami	Santa Fe
Chicago	New Orleans	U.S. Virgin Islands
London	Paris	Walt Disney World
Manhattan	San Francisco	Washington, D.C.

FROMMER'S AMERICA ON WHEELS
*(Everything you need for a successful road trip, including full-color
road maps and ratings for every hotel)*

California & Nevada	Northwest & Great Plains
Florida	South Central & Texas
Mid-Atlantic	Southeast
Midwest & the Great Lakes	Southwest
New England & New York	

FROMMER'S BY NIGHT GUIDES
(The series for those who know that life begins after dark)

Amsterdam	Los Angeles	New York
Chicago	Miami	Paris
Las Vegas	New Orleans	San Francisco
London		